HOUGHTON MIFFLIN LITERATURE SERIES

MOMENTS IN LITERATURE

EXPLORATIONS IN LITERATURE

REFLECTIONS IN LITERATURE

PERCEPTIONS IN LITERATURE

FORMS IN ENGLISH LITERATURE

THEMES IN WORLD LITERATURE

THEMES IN WORLD LITERATURE

with
A Guide for Writing About Literature

George P. Elliott
Philip McFarland
Harvey Granite
Morse Peckham

THEMES IN WORLD LITERATURE

with
A Guide for Writing About Literature

HOUGHTON MIFFLIN COMPANY · BOSTON

Atlanta · Dallas · Geneva, Illinois · Palo Alto · Princeton · Toronto

ABOUT THE TITLE PAGES: *The art on the title page is a series of drawings by Piet Mondrian in which a realistic sketch of a tree evolves into an abstract form.*

PRINTED IN THE U.S.A.

ISBN. 0–395–48991–1

HIJ–RM–95

George P. Elliott, author of four novels and numerous volumes of short stories, essays, and poems, was the recipient of various literary honors, including an award from the National Institute of Arts and Letters. Mr. Elliott taught in secondary schools in Berkeley and at St. Mary's College, Cornell, Barnard, the Universities of Iowa and California, and Syracuse University.

Philip McFarland is a writer and head of the English department at Concord (Mass.) Academy. A graduate of Oberlin, he holds a master's degree from Cambridge University, where he received First Honors in English Literature. He is the author of two works of fiction and three works of nonfiction, including *Sojourners,* an account of the life and times of Washington Irving.

Harvey Granite, formerly with the Rochester (New York) Public Schools, teaches Shakespeare and poetry in the Athenaeum of the Rochester Institute of Technology. With degrees from Cornell, the University of Rochester, and the University of Pittsburgh, he also studied Humanities at Columbia as a John Hay Fellow. A teacher at the secondary and college level, he has published fiction as well as professional articles.

Morse Peckham has spent many years studying the relationship among the arts of literature, painting, and music, and evolving a new theory of art. The result can be seen in two volumes — *Beyond the Tragic Vision* and *Man's Rage for Chaos.* Dr. Peckham has taught at the Citadel, Rutgers, the University of Pennsylvania, and the University of South Carolina, where he has been Emeritus Professor of English and Comparative Literature since 1980.

Mary Ellen Chase taught high school English in Wisconsin, Illinois, and Montana before going to Smith College where she became a widely known professor. Among her writings are *The Bible and the Common Reader* and many novels.

David Daiches is Dean of the School of English and American Studies at the University of Sussex in England. He has taught at the University of Chicago, Cornell, and Indiana.

Walter Havighurst is Professor of English at Miami University in Ohio. A native of Wisconsin, he has written distinguished fiction and nonfiction about the Middle West.

Elizabeth Janeway is well known as a novelist, essayist, and critic. A frequent lecturer and conference speaker, she actively supports the humanities.

Mark Schorer was professor of English at the University of California at Berkeley. Besides writing novels, stories, and reviews of modern fiction, he wrote a noted critical work on William Blake, *William Blake: The Politics of Vision,* and a major biography of Sinclair Lewis.

Mark Van Doren taught at Columbia for years. He wrote scholarly works on a wide range of subjects in English and American literature, as well as prize-winning poems, plays, and short stories.

Contents

THEMES AND VOICES

George P. Elliott   xvi

The Question of Truth

The Nature
of Justice

The Meaning of Greatness

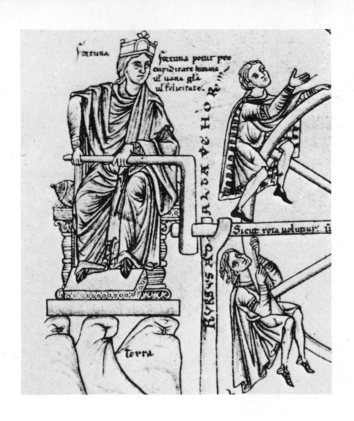

Fate and Free Will

Man and Nature

Good and Evil

Love and Hate

The Question of Identity

Themes and Voices

GEORGE P. ELLIOTT

There are a great many things to say about what good literature is, but they must all include two essential points. It is a special way of talking, and it is about humanly important themes.

You may find it odd to consider literature a way of talking. Literature as we commonly think of it comes in books; we do not listen to sounds but look at black marks on white pages. But consider this. When Robert Frost, one of the great poets America has produced, used to appear for what would be advertised as a "poetry reading," he would tell the audience that he was going to "say" some poems. Frost reminds us that the important thing about the marks on the page is that they are signs standing for motions in the air made by a human voice. These signs (which we call words) perform two functions, both important. As we ordinarily think of words, they stand for ideas, emotions, things, and grammatical connections that mean something to those who speak the language. However, to a good writer, as to a good reader, it is equally important that words strike the physical ear pleasantly or unpleasantly, as does the whistle of a robin or the screech of chalk on blackboard.

One of the finest kinds of praise a poet can receive is to be told that he has a "good ear," that is, that the rhythms and sound patterns which his words make are pleasing in themselves and are satisfyingly connected with what the words mean. Good prose is like good poetry in that it too needs to be heard, and in the same way, in order to be fully appreciated. In fact, the difference between prose and poetry is a matter of which element is more emphasized, the sound or the sense, and there is an area of good writing in which it does not matter much whether you call it poetry or prose.

Unless you hear a work of literature either in your physical ear or in your mind's ear, you have missed an essential part of it. Obviously, the *Hamlet* (page 726) printed in this volume is only partly there, for a play exists completely only when it is being spoken by actors to an audience. Poems also are only partly there on the page. Anyone who has had the good fortune to hear Dylan Thomas recite, almost chant, "The Force That Through the Green Fuse Drives the Flower" (page 412) knows how much more there is to this poem than meets the eye. To a lesser extent but still importantly, even the essay is not all there on the page. Behind the words of Montaigne (page 19), even though we have them in translation, is the voice of a wise and learned man talking with friends.

A primary question to ask of any work of literature is this: who is speaking to whom and in what tone of voice? Usually the question is answered before it needs to be asked. In stories like "Haircut" (page 146), by Ring Lardner, it does not take long to figure out who is speaking and in what circumstances. But this is by no means always the case. Take the last speech in Sophocles' play *Oedipus the King* (page 349). Literally, it is uttered by some actors to an audience. It is also some old men of the city of Thebes addressing the other Thebans present. Finally, at the very end of the speech, it is also the poet-playwright speaking to whoever is listening; to all men; to himself; to you. To hear all three voices simultaneously, you must listen with three minds at once. This is not the easiest thing in the world to learn to do, but, once learned, it seems natural and is enormously satisfying.

The other primary question to be asked of a work of literature matters just as much: what is the author talking about?

All serious literature is concerned with universal themes — that is, subjects which touch all normal men's lives. Yet we do not use the term "universal theme" to cover everything which touches all men. For example, though we all need shelter, it is not thought of as a universal theme in art. A universal theme is one which primarily concerns man's spiritual life rather than his material life: justice rather than food distribution, love rather than sex. Great themes touch our strongest emotions, the deepest needs of our spirits as well as of our bodies, and the ways we are related to one another both socially and personally. In addition, they cause us to think as well and as hard as we can about the truth of these matters which concern us so much.

It is hard to make me care what John had for breakfast. I am much more likely to care about what happens to survivors of a shipwreck in an open boat on the high seas, and if I also find in the telling of that adventure something of importance about many men, about the world we live in, perhaps about myself, then I will call that story splendid and read it more than once. It is interesting to compare Stephen Crane's classic story "The Open Boat" (page 456), which he wrote a few weeks after the shipwreck he had been in, with the newspaper account of the episode which he wrote as soon as he was able after the rescue. The identical adventure is, in the journalistic version, just what happened to this man at this time — somewhat exciting but thoroughly forgettable. Crane had not yet developed a theme large enough to make the experience significant, to make the story penetrate to something that matters to any man at any time. When a writer arranges the circumstances of experience to figure forth large themes, then what he says, if he says it well, has a chance of leaping the barriers of custom and language, and even the barriers of time, to be heard by men of many countries and many ages. Such literature is of and for the world, not just for one people, one era, or one class.

In our own time, literature (like architecture) has become more international than at any time since the Middle Ages in Europe. Then, just as the Gothic style of church architecture knew no national boundaries, so all educated men knew Latin and moved freely from country to country. Now, just as there is an "international modern" style of architecture for office buildings, airports, factories, hotels, and the like, so there is a real sense of the mingling of cultures in literature.

Take some the twentieth-century writers included in this book. Julio Cortázar is an Argentine who was born in Belgium, and now lives in Paris where he writes in Spanish. James Baldwin, a native of the United States, is descended from African forebears and lives most of the time in Turkey. James Joyce left his native Ireland and lived, famously, for the rest of his life in various European countries, in "silence, exile, and cunning." Our century provides many more examples than these of writers who seem to belong to the world rather than to one country.

Not only is our age in many ways more international than most ages have been, but also it is amazingly hospitable to the art and literature of previous ages. Perhaps the main reason for this is that scholarship has made the past more available to us in many ways. For example, because scholars have taught us so much about the Elizabethan stage and language, we are able to perform and to read *Hamlet* better than we could have done a century ago — or at least in a way closer to the way Shakespeare's audience saw and heard the play. Of course, reading literature of the past is something like going to a museum of past art, and there is a danger in spending too much time in museums. But surely that danger is a risk worth running for the enormous pleasure which the experience of great art offers us. Long after the death of the artist, his art can live in us again.

Nothing is known of the writer of *Job*, (page 175) not even his century. Yet, in dozens of languages and over dozens of generations, millions of people have listened to the voices of his dramatic poem speak to them. Those words have moved them more than the words of most men they have heard in real life. Indeed, only under unusual circumstances are your own words likely to move you as much as can these words of a scattered handful of dust, of a nameless, disembodied voice. How strange that a man who isn't there, and who didn't know you would be there, can say more to you than some flesh-and-blood neighbor has ever said or will ever say.

I am not alone. There are, have been, will be others like me as I am in my inmost being, and I can talk with them. To experience this is one of life's greatest goods.

Of course, the themes listed in this book do not pretend to exhaust all the great themes of literature. Death, the nature of God, war and peace, society and the individual — these and others are as important as those included here. Nor is it inevitable that a piece of writing should be in one section rather than another. *Don Quixote* (page 56), for instance, raises questions of "identity" as well as questions of "truth." This book is a mere introduction to vast treasures, and the groupings are made mostly for convenience. If you are stimulated to make other groupings of your own, go ahead! Just don't let yourself be diverted from the main thing, really reading these stories, poems, plays, and essays. It is infinitely more important to hear a great poem than to find the right pigeonhole for it.

Truth is often judged by appearances. Relativity, a wood engraving by the Dutch artist Maurits Escher, illustrates how complex and deceptive appearances can be.

4

The Question of Truth

What is truth?" said jesting Pilate; and would not stay for an answer.* So wrote the great philosopher Francis Bacon; and Rembrandt, in a famous painting, portrays Pilate as a cultivated, thoughtful administrator, washing his hands as though disavowing responsibility for the sentencing of Jesus. Pilate is condemned not because he said "what is truth?" but because he jested about it. He did not care enough. Socrates claimed to know only one thing: that he did not know. But, though he knew he could not know the truth absolutely, there was nothing else whatever that he cared about so much as truth. He was willing to die for it, and did.

Not all literature is greatly concerned with the question of truth. A lot of the loveliest writing is evocative and magical — "In Xanadu did Kubla Khan / A stately pleasure dome decree." Some is playful nonsense — " 'Twas brillig, and the slithy toves / Did gyre and gimble in the wabe." Some fine comedy is so fantastically grotesque that you give up wondering how much truth there may be to it and ask only that it keep you laughing. But most serious literature raises the question of truth, at least indirectly.

What does the word *truth* mean? It is used in dozens of ways, from something as frivolous as the name of a game ("truth or consequences") to an ideal so sublime that it soars almost out of sight ("Beauty is truth, truth beauty — that is all / Ye know on earth, and all ye need to know"). Without getting wound up in the subtleties of philosophy, one can use the following definition at least as a point of departure. *"Truth" signifies a statement which corresponds to what is actually the case.* So, the "truth" means that an idea in my mind corresponds accurately to what exists *out there* in the world whether I think so or not. That seems simple and straightforward enough, and for ordinary purposes it will do quite well.

Of course, any statement can be quibbled to bits, even one as innocent-looking as this: "George Washington never set foot on another planet." Did he ever say he hadn't? How can we be positive he did not live on some

5

other planet in a previous incarnation? But, if you will forego the pleasures of quibbling, you will have no trouble accepting this statement as true. Unfortunately, like most obviously true statements, it is not very interesting. Who cares, really, that Washington never went to another planet? The more interesting and important an idea is, the more likely it is to raise profound issues concerned with truth. As these issues appear in literature, they can be grouped into those touching the nature of reality and those having to do with sincerity.

Other things being equal, the more important the truth which a work of literature reveals, the more highly we value it. For we want to and are pleased to understand something about the realities of human existence. A great play, such as Ibsen's *An Enemy of the People,* can be seen as a pack of lies and trivialities. Actors are pretending to be people they are not. (The Greek word for actor was *hypocrite,* though of course an actor need not be a hypocrite in the English sense of the word.) Moreover, the personal concerns of this man or that are their business, not ours, whether there ever were such people as the playwright puts in his play or he just invented them. But behind and above all these superficial deceptions and particular matters, a great play like this one obliges us to think about social and moral issues which apply to many nations and peoples. In the case of *An Enemy of the People,* these questions apply to us in our present condition directly. The play was written nearly a century ago by a Norwegian. Yet it can make us see some of the realities of America now more profoundly and more truly than most of the movies and TV shows currently being made by our fellow Americans.

A story, to be great, must reveal or lead us to important truths. Yet the characters in such a story may very well be liars or in error about reality, since it is true to life that there are many such people. Perhaps the noblest quality for a character who is concerned with the truth is sincerity. When Don Quixote says a windmill is a giant, he is not lying, even though the statement is untrue; he is mistaken. For statements go two ways, out and in. Don Quixote's statement is untrue to external reality but true to what he believes. He is confused about reality but sincere in his devotion to finding the truth, just as his creator, Cervantes, is sincere in his endeavor to reveal the truth in the story. Reading this novel, like reading the story of Socrates, we are set off on a quest for the truth a good deal like Don Quixote's quest, and we are obliged to ask ourselves questions of ultimate importance sincerely. "Am I as dedicated to finding the truth as he? Do I believe in any truth deeply enough to be willing to die for it, even knowing that I may be mistaken?"

George P. Elliott

6

The Night Face Up

JULIO CORTÁZAR

The capital city of our neighbor to the south was built on the ruins of another capital, Tenochtitlán, which had been built by the Aztec Indians about 1325. The Aztecs had arrived in the Valley of Mexico during the twelfth century, and formed an impressive and complex civilization based on the heritage of other Indian groups. Indian pyramids still brood over the outskirts of modern Mexico City, reminding the twentieth century of a culture that was flourishing there six centuries earlier, an awesome culture that indulged in religious rites involving human sacrifices by the thousands to nourish its gods. Many unfortunate souls were hunted down and taken prisoner during a ritual war, the Xochiyaóyotl, or War of the Blossom, so called because the Aztecs believed that the blood spilt in the holy war became a flower. Prisoners were sacrificed to Huitzilopochtli, the god who represented the sun and the ever youthful warrior, and who had to be nourished with the magic substance in the blood of man, "the precious liquid," the terrible nectar with which the gods are fed.

But all that was long ago. The following story was written about a nameless young man in a modern, sophisticated city who sets out one fine morning on a motorcycle ride.

Halfway down the long hotel vestibule, he thought that probably he was going to be late, and hurried on into the street to get out his motorcycle from the corner where the next-door superintendent let him keep it. On the jewelry store at the corner he read that it was ten to nine; he had time to spare. The sun filtered through the tall downtown buildings, and he — because for himself, for just going along thinking, he did not have a name — he swung onto the machine, savoring the idea of the ride. The motor whirred between his legs, and a cool wind whipped his pantslegs.

He let the ministries[1] zip past (the pink, the white), and a series of stores on the main street, their windows flashing. Now he was beginning the most pleasant part of the run, the real ride: a long street bordered with trees, very little traffic, with spacious villas[2] whose gardens rambled all the way down to the sidewalks, which were barely indicated by low hedges. A bit inattentive perhaps, but tooling along on the right side of the street, he allowed himself to be carried away by the freshness, by the weightless contraction of this hardly begun day. This involuntary relaxation, possibly, kept him from preventing the accident. When he saw that the woman standing on the corner had rushed into the crosswalk while he still had the green light, it was already somewhat too late for a simple solution. He braked hard with foot and hand, wrenching himself to the left; he heard the woman scream, and at

Julio Cortázar: pronounced hü′lyō kōr·tä′zär.

[1] ministries: government buildings.

[2] villas: country houses.

"The Night Face Up," reprinted by permission of Pantheon Books, Inc., from *End of the Game and Other Stories* by Julio Cortázar. Copyright 1967 by Random House, Inc.

the collision his vision went. It was like falling asleep all at once.

He came to abruptly. Four or five young men were getting him out from under the cycle. He felt the taste of salt and blood, one knee hurt, and when they hoisted him up he yelped, he couldn't bear the pressure on his right arm. Voices which did not seem to belong to the faces hanging above him encouraged him cheerfully with jokes and assurances. His single solace was to hear someone else confirm that the lights indeed had been in his favor. He asked about the woman, trying to keep down the nausea which was edging up into his throat. While they carried him face up to a nearby pharmacy, he learned that the cause of the accident had gotten only a few scrapes on the legs. "Nah, you barely got her at all, but when ya hit, the impact made the machine jump and flop on its side. . . ." Opinions, recollections of other smashups, take it easy, work him in shoulders first, there, that's fine, and someone in a dustcoat giving him a swallow of something soothing in the shadowy interior of the small local pharmacy.

Within five minutes the police ambulance arrived, and they lifted him onto a cushioned stretcher. It was a relief for him to be able to lie out flat. Completely lucid, but realizing that he was suffering the effects of a terrible shock, he gave his information to the officer riding in the ambulance with him. The arm almost didn't hurt; blood dripped down from a cut over the eyebrow all over his face. He licked his lips once or twice to drink it. He felt pretty good, it had been an accident, tough luck; stay quiet a few weeks, nothing worse. The guard said that the motorcycle didn't seem badly racked up. "Why should it," he replied. "It all landed on top of me." They both laughed, and when they got to the hospital, the guard shook his hand and wished him luck. Now the nausea was coming back little by little; meanwhile they were pushing him on a wheeled stretcher toward a pavilion further back, rolling along under trees full of birds; he shut his eyes and wished he were asleep or chloroformed. But they kept him for a good while in a room with that hospital smell, filling out a form, getting his clothes off, and dressing him in a stiff, grayish smock. They moved his arm carefully, it didn't hurt him. The nurses were constantly making wisecracks, and if it hadn't been for

ABOUT THE AUTHOR • Born in Belgium, the son of an Argentinian diplomat, first recognized by Mexico, and now living on the Left Bank in Paris, **Julio Cortázar** (1914–   ) carries on the tradition of South American fanciful literature in his *Bestiary* (1949) and later tales. He has broken many rules in his lifetime. He once taught French literature at a university without possessing an academic degree, he writes stories without drawing up outlines, and he refuses to do much correcting of what he writes. But like the jazz artists who figure in much of his fiction, he is a master of improvising. "I have never adhered to the precept," he says, "that a story should never be begun unless it has been thought through." Cortázar uses subjects from mythology, dreams, and animal stories, spinning out tales with magical inventiveness. But at the same time, he is a realist, intelligent, poetic, and often humorous. We see these qualities in his admirable short novel *The Pursuer* (1959), a story about a Negro musician in Paris, inspired supposedly by the famous jazz artist Louis Armstrong.

the stomach contractions he would have felt fine, almost happy.

They got him over to X-ray, and twenty minutes later, with the still-damp negative lying on his chest like a black tombstone, they pushed him into surgery. Someone tall and thin in white came over and began to look at the X-rays. A woman's hands were arranging his head, he felt that they were moving him from one stretcher to another. The man in white came over to him again, smiling, something gleamed in his right hand. He patted his cheek and made a sign to someone stationed behind.

It was unusual as a dream because it was full of smells, and he never dreamt smells. First a marshy smell, there to the left of the trail the swamps began already, the quaking bogs from which no one ever returned. But the reek lifted, and instead there came a dark, fresh composite fragrance, like the night under which he moved, in flight from the Aztecs. And it was all so natural, he had to run from the Aztecs who had set out on their manhunt, and his sole chance was to find a place to hide in the deepest part of the forest, taking care not to lose the narrow trail which only they, the Motecas, knew.

What tormented him the most was the odor, as though, notwithstanding the absolute acceptance of the dream, there was something which resisted that which was not habitual, which until that point had not participated in the game. "It smells of war," he thought, his hand going instinctively to the stone knife which was tucked at an angle into his girdle[1] of woven wool. An unexpected sound made him crouch suddenly stock-still and shaking. To be afraid was nothing strange, there was plenty of fear in his dreams. He waited, covered by the branches of a shrub and the starless

[1] **girdle**: sashlike belt.

night. Far off, probably on the other side of the big lake, they'd be lighting the bivouac[2] fires; that part of the sky had a reddish glare. The sound was not repeated. It had been like a broken limb. Maybe an animal that, like himself, was escaping from the smell of war. He stood erect slowly, sniffing the air. Not a sound could be heard, but the fear was still following, as was the smell, that cloying incense of the war of the blossom. He had to press forward, to stay out of the bogs and get to the heart of the forest. Groping uncertainly through the dark, stooping every other moment to touch the packed earth of the trail, he took a few steps. He would have liked to have broken into a run, but the gurgling fens[3] lapped on either side of him. On the path and in darkness, he took his bearings. Then he caught a horrible blast of that foul smell he was most afraid of, and leaped forward desperately.

"You're going to fall off the bed," said the patient next to him. "Stop bouncing around, old buddy."

He opened his eyes and it was afternoon, the sun already low in the oversized windows of the long ward. While trying to smile at his neighbor, he detached himself almost physically from the final scene of the nightmare. His arm, in a plaster cast, hung suspended from an apparatus with weights and pulleys. He felt thirsty, as though he'd been running for miles, but they didn't want to give him much water, barely enough to moisten his lips and make a mouthful. The fever was winning slowly and he would have been able to sleep again, but he was enjoying the pleasure of keeping awake,

[2] **bivouac**: camp.
[3] **fens**: marshy swamps.

eyes half-closed, listening to the other patients' conversation, answering a question from time to time. He saw a little white pushcart come up beside the bed, a blond nurse rubbed the front of his thigh with alcohol and stuck him with a fat needle connected to a tube which ran up to a bottle filled with a milky, opalescent liquid. A young intern arrived with some metal and leather apparatus which he adjusted to fit onto the good arm to check something or other. Night fell, and the fever went along dragging him down softly to a state in which things seemed embossed as through opera glasses, they were real and soft and, at the same time, vaguely distasteful; like sitting in a boring movie and thinking that, well, still, it'd be worse out in the street, and staying.

A cup of a marvelous golden broth came, smelling of leeks, celery, and parsley. A small hunk of bread, more precious than a whole banquet, found itself crumbling little by little. His arm hardly hurt him at all, and only in the eyebrow where they'd taken stitches a quick, hot pain sizzled occasionally. When the big windows across the way turned to smudges of dark blue, he thought it would not be difficult for him to sleep. Still on his back so a little uncomfortable, running his tongue out over his hot, too-dry lips, he tasted the broth still, and with a sigh of bliss, he let himself drift off.

First there was a confusion, as of one drawing all his sensations, for that moment blunted or muddled, into himself. He realized that he was running in pitch darkness, although, above, the sky criss-crossed with treetops was less black than the rest. "The trail," he thought, "I've gotten off the trail." His feet sank into a bed of leaves and mud, and then he couldn't take a step that the branches of shrubs did not whiplash against his ribs and legs. Out of breath, knowing despite the darkness and silence that he was surrounded, he crouched down to listen.

Maybe the trail was very near, with the first daylight he would be able to see it again. Nothing now could help him to find it. The hand that had unconsciously gripped the haft[1] of the dagger climbed like a fen scorpion up to his neck where the protecting amulet[2] hung. Barely moving his lips, he mumbled the supplication of the corn which brings about the beneficent moons, and the prayer to Her Very Highness, to the distributor of all Motecan possessions. At the same time he felt his ankles sinking deeper into the mud, and the waiting in the darkness of the obscure grove of live oak grew intolerable to him. The war of the blossom had started at the beginning of the moon and had been going on for three days and three nights now. If he managed to hide in the depths of the forest, getting off the trail further up past the marsh country, perhaps the warriors wouldn't follow his track. He thought of the many prisoners they'd already taken. But the number didn't count, only the consecrated period. The hunt would continue until the priests gave the sign to return. Everything had its number and its limit, and it was within the sacred period, and he on the other side from the hunters.

He heard the cries and leaped up, knife in hand. As if the sky were aflame on the horizon, he saw torches moving among the branches, very near him. The smell of war was unbearable, and when the first enemy jumped him, leaped at his throat, he felt an almost-pleasure in sinking the stone blade flat to the haft into his chest. The lights were already around him, the happy cries. He managed to cut the air once or twice, then a rope snared him from behind.

"It's the fever," the man in the next bed said. "The same thing happened to me when they operated on my duodenum.[3] Take

---

[1] **haft**: handle.
[2] **amulet**: charm.
[3] **duodenum**: section of the small intestine.

some water, you'll see, you'll sleep all right."

Laid next to the night from which he came back, the tepid shadow of the ward seemed delicious to him. A violet lamp kept watch high on the far wall like a guardian eye. You could hear coughing, deep breathing, once in a while a conversation in whispers. Everything was pleasant and secure, without the chase, no. . . . But he didn't want to go on thinking about the nightmare. There were lots of things to amuse himself with. He began to look at the cast on his arm, and the pulleys that held it so comfortably in the air. They'd left a bottle of mineral water on the night table beside him. He put the neck of the bottle to his mouth and drank it like a precious liqueur. He could now make out the different shapes in the ward, the thirty beds, the closets with glass doors. He guessed that his fever was down, his face felt cool. The cut over the eyebrow barely hurt at all, like a recollection. He saw himself leaving the hotel again, wheeling out the cycle. Who'd have thought that it would end like this? He tried to fix the moment of the accident exactly, and it got him very angry to notice that there was a void there, an emptiness he could not manage to fill. Between the impact and the moment that they picked him up off the pavement, the passing out or what went on, there was nothing he could see. And at the same time he had the feeling that this void, this nothingness, had lasted an eternity. No, not even time, more as if, in this void, he had passed across something, or had run back immense distances. The shock, the brutal dashing against the pavement. Anyway, he had felt an immense relief in coming out of the black pit while the people were lifting him off the ground. With pain in the broken arm, blood from the split eyebrow, contusion[1] on the knee; with all that, a relief in returning to daylight, to the day, and to feel sustained and attended. That was weird. Someday he'd ask the doctor at the office about that. Now sleep began to take over again, to pull him slowly down. The pillow was so soft, and the coolness of the mineral water in his fevered throat. The violet light of the lamp up there was beginning to get dimmer and dimmer.

As he was sleeping on his back, the position in which he came to did not surprise him, but on the other hand the damp smell, the smell of oozing rock, blocked his throat and forced him to understand. Open the eyes and look in all directions, hopeless. He

[1] **contusion**: bruise.

11

was surrounded by an absolute darkness. Tried to get up and felt ropes pinning his wrists and ankles. He was staked to the ground on a floor of dank, icy stone slabs. The cold bit into his naked back, his legs. Dully, he tried to touch the amulet with his chin and found they had stripped him of it. Now he was lost, no prayer could save him from the final. . . . From afar off, as though filtering through the rock of the dungeon, he heard the great kettledrums of the feast. They had carried him to the temple, he was in the underground cells of Teocalli[1] itself, awaiting his turn.

He heard a yell, a hoarse yell that rocked off the walls. Another yell, ending in a moan. It was he who was screaming in the darkness, he was screaming because he was alive, his whole body with that cry fended off what was coming, the inevitable end. He thought of his friends filling up the other dungeons, and of those already walking up the stairs of the sacrifice. He uttered another choked cry, he could barely open his mouth, his jaws were twisted back as if with a rope and a stick, and once in a while they would open slowly with an endless exertion, as if they were made of rubber. The creaking of the wooden latches jolted him like a whip. Rent, writhing, he fought to rid himself of the cords sinking into his flesh. His right arm, the strongest, strained until the pain became unbearable and he had to give up. He watched the double door open, and the smell of the torches reached him before the light did. Barely girdled by the ceremonial loincloths, the priests' acolytes[2] moved in his direction, looking at him with contempt. Lights reflected off the sweaty torsos and off the black hair dressed with feathers. The cords went slack, and in their place the grappling of hot hands, hard as bronze; he felt himself lifted, still face up, and jerked along by the four acolytes who

carried him down the passageway. The torchbearers went ahead, indistinctly lighting up the corridor with its dripping walls and a ceiling so low that the acolytes had to duck their heads. Now they were taking him out, taking him out, it was the end. Face up, under a mile of living rock which, for a succession of moments, was lit up by a glimmer of torchlight. When the stars came out up there instead of the roof and the great terraced steps rose before him, on fire with cries and dances, it would be the end. The passage was never going to end, but now it was beginning to end, he would see suddenly the open sky full of stars, but not yet, they trundled him along endlessly in the reddish shadow, hauling him roughly along and he did not want that, but how to stop it if they had torn off the amulet, his real heart, the life-center.

In a single jump he came out into the hospital night, to the high, gentle, bare ceiling, to the soft shadow wrapping him round. He thought he must have cried out, but his neighbors were peacefully snoring. The water in the bottle on the night table was somewhat bubbly, a translucent shape against the dark azure shadow of the windows. He panted, looking for some relief for his lungs, oblivion for those images still glued to his eyelids. Each time he shut his eyes he saw them take shape instantly, and he sat up, completely wrung out, but savoring at the same time the surety that now he was awake, that the night nurse would answer if he rang, that soon it would be daybreak, with the good, deep sleep he usually had at that hour, no images, no nothing. . . . It was difficult to keep his eyes open, the drowsiness was more powerful than he. He made one last effort, he sketched a gesture toward the bottle of water with his good hand and did not manage to reach it, his fingers closed again on a black emptiness, and the passageway went on endlessly, rock after rock, with momentary ruddy flares, and face up he choked out a dull moan

---

[1] **Teocalli** (tā·ō·kä′yē) : from *Teo*, meaning "god," and *calli*, meaning "house"; thus, temple.

[2] **acolytes**: ceremonial attendants.

An ancient depiction of human sacrifice at the shrine of Huitzilopochtli, the Aztec god of the sun and war.

because the roof was about to end, it rose, was opening like a mouth of shadow, and the acolytes straightened up, and from on high a waning moon fell on a face whose eyes wanted not to see it, were closing and opening desperately, trying to pass to the other side, to find again the bare, protecting ceiling of the ward. And every time they opened, it was night and the moon, while they climbed the great terraced steps, his head hanging down backward now, and up at the top were the bonfires, red columns of perfumed smoke, and suddenly he saw the red stone, shiny with the blood dripping off it, and the spinning arcs cut by the feet of the victim whom they pulled off to throw him rolling down the north steps. With a last hope he shut his lids tightly, moaning to wake up. For a second he thought he had gotten there, because once more he was immobile in the bed, except that his head was hanging down off it, swinging. But he smelled death, and when he opened his eyes he saw the blood-soaked figure of the executioner-priest coming toward him with the stone knife in his hand. He managed to close his eyelids again, although he knew now he was not going to wake up, that he was awake, that the marvelous dream had been

the other, absurd as all dreams are — a dream in which he was going through the strange avenues of an astonishing city, with green and red lights that burned without fire or smoke, on an enormous metal insect that whirred away between his legs. In the infinite lie of the dream, they had also picked him up off the ground, someone had approached him also with a knife in his hand, approached him who was lying face up, face up with his eyes closed between the bonfires on the steps.

For Discussion

1. At night in the hospital bed, after a long day and evening, the motorcyclist ponders: "Who'd have thought that it would end like this? He tried to fix the moment of the accident exactly, and it got him very angry to notice that there was a void there, an emptiness he could not manage to fill" (page 11). What had caused the accident? Whose fault had it been? In the shock that followed the accident, the cyclist at times found himself lying in a hospital being attended to, at other times taking part in a weird game. Describe the game. When would it end?

2. Where does the truth lie in this story? That is, which part is dream and which is reality? No doubt various interpretations are possible. The young man might be an Aztec contemporary, living back in the fifteenth century, and all the rest — the motorcycle, and the accident, and the hospital — all the rest that takes place in the modern world is only "a dream in which he was going through the strange avenues of an astonishing city, with green and red lights that burned without fire or smoke." But what rather obvious difficulties do you see in that interpretation?

3. Consider other possibilities. Is the cyclist really in the hospital after all, and will he wake from his nightmare yet again? What reasons can you offer for and against that interpretation? Or perhaps the entire story — Aztec and modern — was imagined in the instant of shock and semi-consciousness immediately after the accident; after all, an entire lifetime is supposed to flash instantaneously through the mind of a drowning man. Do you find objections to this interpretation? What other interpretations would you suggest?

4. The author of "The Night Face Up" works a trick on the reader, so that at first what seemed to be an awful dream — dark and fear-filled and unreal and comfortless — turns out to be the truth, and what first seemed to be the truth — attentive, well-lit, and comforting — turns out to be a dream. Examine how the trick is made to work. For example, the cyclist's two worlds after the accident alternate with each other. Which comes first? Is that first episode after the accident longer or shorter than the one that follows it? Which world is described at the end?

For Composition

Writing about literature will help you understand your responses to it, just as writing in general will clarify your thoughts about any subject. Most of what you write — here and elsewhere throughout your life — will be either exposition or argument. *Exposition* deals with facts; *argument* deals with opinions. The one informs; the other persuades. If, for example, you write a letter reporting to a friend on a trip you took, you will inform him of where you went, and that part of your letter will be exposition. You may also try to persuade him that he should go there too, and that part will be argument. (As used here, *argument* refers to giving reasons in support of opinions, not, as in its common use, to disagreements.) Again, if you apply for a job, what your qualifications are will be presented as exposition; why you should be given the job will be contained in your argument.

1. **Exposition.** Limiting yourself to the hospital scenes and what precedes them, explain precisely what is said to take place after the accident in "The Night Face Up." Your explanation should clarify the time sequence. Approximately when does the accident occur? At what times of day do the successive hospital scenes occur? Stick to the facts given in the story.

2. **Argument.** Which interpretation of this story is the true one? Reconsider "The Night Face Up" carefully, then persuasively present your interpretation of what is reality and what is hallucination in it, quoting from the story where necessary to support your argument.

Words and Allusions

SYNONYMS. The word *synonym* refers to a word that has the same meaning as another. But words never have exactly the same meanings. Even when they denote, or refer to, the same thing, they seldom have exactly the same connotations.

The following words relate to events in "The Night Face Up": *hallucination, mirage, vision, illusion, delusion.* The words are related in meaning, and yet their meanings differ. Using a good dictionary, explain how they are alike and how they differ. Then write a sentence for each to illustrate its usage.

WORD ROOTS. The root of a word is the basis on which the word is built. *Sacrifice* contains a root that is shared by other words. What is that root, and what is its meaning? List five other words built on that root, together with their meanings.

The Wayfarer

STEPHEN CRANE

The truth presents problems. For one thing, it is not always easy to discover, as the preceding story demonstrates. Nor, once discovered, is it always easy to follow.

The wayfarer,
Perceiving the pathway to truth,
Was struck with astonishment.
It was thickly grown with weeds.
"Ha," he said,   5
"I see that no one has passed here
In a long time."
Later he saw that each weed
Was a singular knife.
"Well," he mumbled at last,   10
"Doubtless there are other roads."

For Discussion

1. What is a wayfarer? This wayfarer makes a discovery that astonishes him. What does he discover? Why is he astonished by it?

2. What characteristics of truth are suggested in this poem?

3. **Subject, Theme.** A *theme* is a general meaning that emerges from the specific *subject* of a literary work. The subject of "The Wayfarer" is a discovery, made by a specific individual, of a specific pathway covered with knifelike weeds. What general meaning emerges from the specific detail that "no one has passed here / In a long time" (lines 6–7)? That is, what thematic meaning about truth in general does that specific detail convey?

For Composition

• **Exposition.** The wayfarer finds the path to truth "thickly grown with weeds," and later he discovers "that each weed / Was a singular knife." Explain how each of these observations can be related to truth or to the search for truth. Support your explanation with examples from your own experience or from other sources.

About the Poet. Although **Stephen Crane** (1871–1900) was born years after the end of the Civil War, his experience as a correspondent and his understanding of the psychology of combat enabled him to produce a realistic portrayal of that war in *The Red Badge of Courage.* The reputation based on this work and his own continuing interest in men at war brought him assignments as a war correspondent in the Graeco-Turkish and Spanish-American Wars. Crane is best known for his realistic fiction, in which he attempts to take the glamor out of heroism and the glory out of war, but in recent years his naturalistic poetry has commanded wide attention. His free-verse poems, collected in *The Black Riders* and *War Is Kind,* show Crane as a pathfinder for later poets in their revolt against sentimentality. One critic has described these poems as "the ungarnished utterances of primitive man."

The Persian Version

R O B E R T   G R A V E S

The truth is difficult to recognize and hard to follow. It can appear to be relative, too; in a quarrel, for example, what looks like truth to one side may not look the same to the other. Consider Marathon — that battle in 490 B.C. where the Athenians defeated the Persians and, according to Athenian poets and historians, saved all Greece from foreign conquest. What is the truth about Marathon?

Truth-loving Persians do not dwell upon
The trivial skirmish fought near Marathon.
As for the Greek theatrical tradition
Which represents that summer's expedition
Not as a mere reconnaissance* in force   5
By three brigades of foot and one of horse
(Their left flank covered by some obsolete
Light craft detached from the main Persian fleet)
But as a grandiose, ill-starred attempt
To conquer Greece — they treat it with contempt; 10
And only incidentally refute
Major Greek claims, by stressing what repute
The Persian monarch and the Persian nation
Won by this salutary* demonstration:
Despite a strong defense and adverse weather   15
All arms combined magnificently together.

5. **reconnaissance**: survey of an enemy area.   14. **salutary**: beneficial.

For Discussion

1. Contrast the two views of the battle stated and implied in this poem. How does the "Greek theatrical tradition" present Marathon? In line 10, who are "they"? What is "it"? How do the truth-loving Persians refute major Greek claims about the battle?

2. "In wartime, truth is the first casualty." Is this the theme of "The Persian Version"?

3. Apply the insight the poem expresses to other differences of opinion in ancient or modern times, in peace or war. Consider, for example, the race to the moon, or the battles of the American Revolution as a modern Englishman and a modern American might regard them, or, say, the arguments for and against vigorous exercise.

For Composition

Literature frequently makes use of *allusions* — references to people and places that the reader may be assumed to know. Marathon is such an allusion. The poet here compliments the reader by assuming a familiarity with that important battle; otherwise he would laboriously have had to explain the allusion, thereby weakening the force of his poem and offending those readers who in fact do know about the battle.

1. **For Research.** Consult an encyclopedia and at least one other source for information about the Battle of Marathon and its significance to the western world. Take notes; then, in a logical way, organize what you have discovered. You might, for example, organize your facts and evaluations under three headings: Background, Battle, Significance.

2. **Exposition.** Write a paper conveying the facts about Marathon that you have discovered in your research and explaining how those facts agree or disagree with Graves' poem. Be sure to acknowledge your sources in footnotes or within the paper itself; for example, "The battle, according to *Encyclopedia Americana*, Volume 18, page 263, was. . . ."

About the Poet. From his youth independence has marked the career of **Robert Graves** (1895–). The son of Alfred Percival Graves, himself a poet and scholar, Robert was born into a large family and seemed in his youth to be more interested in boxing and mountain-climbing than in studies. Although he attended six different preparatory schools, he joined the British army to fight in France in 1914 rather than enter Oxford. While in the army he published three volumes of poetry, and he continued to write for the rest of his life. In his early career he lived in poverty while struggling to support an ailing wife, their four children, and his own belated Oxford education. By 1929 Graves was famous as author of a first novel, *I, Claudius*, a best-seller that in 1934 won two literary prizes. Graves has won a number of other literary prizes and continues to be a vigorous and youthful writer, a man "who does not choose to lose himself in crowds, one whose particular genius is impatient of mediocrity."

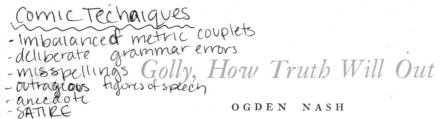

Golly, How Truth Will Out

OGDEN NASH

One more trouble with truth: it isn't always rewarding. In fact, a man who can lie with a straight face sometimes seems to have quite an advantage over the rest of us.

How does a person get to be a capable liar?
That is something that I respectfully inquiar,
Because I don't believe a person will ever set the world on fire
Unless they are a capable lire.
Some wise man said that words were given to us to conceal our thoughts,   5
But if a person has nothing but truthful words why their thoughts haven't even the
    protection of a pair of panties or shoughts,
And a naked thought is ineffectual as well as improper,
And hasn't a chance in the presence of a glib chinchillaclad whopper.
One of the greatest abilities a person can have, I guess,

"Golly, How Truth Will Out" from *Verses From 1929 On* by Ogden Nash. Copyright 1939, 1940 by Ogden Nash. First appeared in *American Magazine*.

Is the ability to say Yes when they mean No and No when they mean Yes.   10
Oh to be Machiavellian,* oh to be unscrupulous, oh, to be glib!
Oh to be ever prepared with a plausible fib!
Because then a dinner engagement or a contract or a treaty is no longer a fetter,
Because liars can just logically lie their way out of it if they don't like it or if one
    comes along that they like better;
And do you think their conscience prickles?   15
No, it tickles.
And please believe that I mean every one of these lines as I am writing them
Because once there was a small boy who was sent to the drugstore to buy some
    bitter stuff to put on his nails to keep him from biting them,
And in his humiliation he tried to lie to the clerk
And it didn't work,   20
Because he said My mother sent me to buy some bitter stuff for a friend of mine's
    nails that bites them, and the clerk smiled wisely and said I wonder who that
    friend could be,
And the small boy broke down and said Me,
And it was me, or at least I was him,
And all my subsequent attempts at subterfuge have been equally grim,   *[lying]*
And that is why I admire a suave prevarication because I prevaricate so awkwardly
    and gauchely,   25
And that is why I can never amount to anything politically or socially.   *[SATIRE]*

[Anecdote — handwritten annotation brace spanning lines 17–24]

    11. **Machiavellian**: crafty and deceitful.

For Discussion

1. "Some wise man said that words were given to us to conceal our thoughts" (line 5). Discuss the meaning of the remark, and what it implies about human nature. Do you agree with it? In what two areas of human activity does the poem suggest that a gift for the plausible fib is especially useful?

2. **Rhyme.** Rhyming words have final accented syllables that sound alike. Vowels and consonants after the accented syllable should be identical, although preceding consonants should differ: *dove, love, locket, pocket.* Ogden Nash is noted for his ingenious, unexpected rhyming. What is the effect of these unexpected rhymes? How does Nash create them? How do the lines here rhyme: alternately, in pairs, or in some other way?

3. What allusion do you find in Nash's poem? Can you explain it?

For Composition

• **Exposition.** What makes Nash's poem humorous? Point out the devices he uses for humorous effect, and explain as best you can how they work.

About the Poet. Born in Rye, New York, and later a resident of Baltimore, **Ogden Nash** (1902–1971) was for many years America's most widely read composer of light verse. Early in his career Nash decided that it would be better to be "a good bad poet than a bad good poet," and his success at combining humor with a touch of social satire was attested to by the longtime popularity of his innovative writing. In the last years of his life, Nash was said to regard himself as "a dear old gentleman . . . baffled by the younger generation," but even so, as critic Ben Ray Redman commented, there was "still a sharp sting in the tail of the smiling scorpion."

On Liars

MICHEL DE MONTAIGNE

Is it true that one of the greatest abilities people can have "is the ability to say Yes when they mean No and No when they mean Yes"? With tongue in cheek, Ogden Nash in the preceding selection suggests that it is. But a celebrated sixteenth-century French essayist thought otherwise. We are justified in punishing lying more severely than any other crime, Montaigne asserts emphatically in the course of the following portion of a somewhat longer essay that examines lying and liars in detail.

Not without reason is it said that no one who is not conscious of having a sound memory should set up to be a liar. I know quite well that grammarians make a distinction between telling an untruth and lying. They say that to tell an untruth is to say something that is false, but that we suppose to be true, and that the meaning of the Latin *mentiri*, from which our French word for lying derives, is to go against one's conscience, and that consequently it applies only to those who say the opposite of what they know; and it is of them I am speaking.

Now liars either invent the whole thing, or they disguise and alter an actual fact. If they disguise and alter, it is hard for them not to get mixed up when they refer to the same story again and again because, the real facts having been the first to lodge in the memory and impress themselves upon it by way of consciousness and knowledge, they will hardly fail to spring into the mind and dislodge the false version, which cannot have as firm or assured a foothold. The circumstances, as they were first learned, will always rush back into the thoughts, driving out the memory of the false or modified details that have been added.

If liars make a complete invention, they apparently have much less reason to be afraid of tripping up, inasmuch as there is no contrary impression to clash with their fiction. But even this, being an empty thing that offers no hold, readily escapes from the memory unless it is a very reliable one. I have often had amusing proof of this, at the expense of those who profess to suit their speech only to the advantage of the business in hand, and to please the great men to whom they are speaking. The circumstances to which it is their wish to subordinate their faith and their conscience being subject to various changes, their language has also to change from time to time; and so they call the same thing gray one moment and yellow the next, say one thing to one man, and another to another. Then, if these listeners happen to bring all this contrary information together as a common booty, what becomes of all their fine art? Besides they trip up so often when they are off their guard. For what memory could be strong enough to retain all the different shapes they have invented for the same

Michel de Montaigne: pronounced mē′shel′ də mōⁿ′ten′y′ (in French); mon·tän′ (in English).

subject? I have seen many in my time who have desired a reputation for this subtle kind of discretion, not seeing that the reputation and the end in view are incompatible.

Lying is indeed an accursed vice. We are men, and we have relations with one another only by speech. If we recognized the horror and gravity of an untruth, we should more justifiably punish it with fire than any other crime. I commonly find people taking the most ill-advised pains to correct their children for their harmless faults, and worrying them about heedless acts which leave no trace and have no consequences. Lying — and in a lesser degree obstinacy — are, in my opinion, the only faults whose birth and progress we should consistently oppose. They grow with a child's growth, and once the tongue has got the knack of lying, it is difficult to imagine how impossible it is to correct it. Whence it happens that we find some otherwise excellent men subject to this fault and enslaved by it. I have a decent lad as my tailor, whom I have never heard to utter a single truth, even when it would have been to his advantage.

If, like the truth, falsehood had only one face, we should know better where we are, for we should then take the opposite of what a liar said to be the truth. But the opposite of a truth has a hundred thousand shapes and a limitless field.

The Pythagoreans[1] regard good as certain and finite, and evil as boundless and uncertain. There are a thousand ways of missing the bull's-eye, only one of hitting it. I am by no means sure that I could induce myself to tell a brazen and deliberate lie even to protect myself from the most obvious and extreme danger. An ancient father[2] says that we are better off in the company of a dog we know than in that of a man whose language we do not understand. Therefore those of different nations do not regard one another as men, and how much less friendly is false speech than silence!

King Francis the First boasted of having by this means drawn circles round Francesco Taverna, ambassador of Francesco Sforza, Duke of Milan — a man of great reputation in the art of speechmaking. Taverna had been sent to make his master's excuses to His Majesty in a matter of great importance, which was this: the king wished

[1] **Pythagoreans** (pi·thag′ə·rē′ənz): followers of the teachings of Pythagoras, sixth-century B. C. Greek philosopher and mathematician.
[2] **an ancient father:** St. Augustine.

ABOUT THE AUTHOR • A modest, truthful, humorous man, the French aristocrat **Michel de Montaigne** (1533–1592) invented what we call the essay (from the French word *essai* meaning a trial, or attempt). At the age of thirty-eight, he built a library in a tower of his country chateau near Bordeaux, France, and began writing "to keep from going mad from the contradictions he found among mankind — and to work some of those contradictions out for himself." But he was soon called away by public service, acted as mayor of Bordeaux for a while, traveled, took notes, and observed mankind beyond his tower and himself. His essays reflect a wide range of reading, a lively mind capable of finding meaning everywhere, and the sharp eye of the journalist.

to have constant channels of information in Italy, from which he had recently been expelled, and especially in the Duchy of Milan. He had decided, therefore, to keep a gentleman of his own at the Duke's court, an ambassador in effect, but in appearance a private individual ostensibly there on his own personal business. For the Duke very much depended on the Emperor — especially at that moment when he was negotiating a marriage with his niece, the King of Denmark's daughter, now the Dowager Duchess of Lorraine — and he could not establish open relations or intercourse with us without great prejudice to himself. A Milanese gentleman named Merveille, one of the King's equerries,[1] was chosen for this office, and was despatched with secret credentials and instructions as ambassador, also with letters of recommendation to the Duke in the matter of his own private affairs as a mask and a show. However, he was at Court so long that the Emperor began to grow suspicious; and it was this, we believe, that gave rise to the subsequent events, which were that one fine night the Duke had Merveille's head cut off on a false charge of murder, his whole trial having been hurried through in a couple of days!

Francesco Taverna had come with a long falsified account of the affair — for the King had addressed himself to all the princes in Christendom, as well as to the Duke, demanding satisfaction — and he was received in audience one morning. In support of his case he advanced several plausible justifications of the deed, carefully prepared for the purpose. He pleaded that his master had never taken our man for anything but a private gentleman and a subject of his own, who had come to Milan on his own business and resided there in no other character. He denied all knowledge that Merveille was a

---

member of the King's household or was even known to the King, much less that he was his ambassador. King Francis, in his turn, pressed objections and questions upon him, attacking him from all sides and cornering him at last on the point of the execution, carried out at night and apparently in secret. To which the poor embarrassed man replied, as if to put an honest face on the matter, that out of respect for His Majesty, the Duke would have been sorry to let the execution take place in daylight. You can guess how quickly he was caught out in this clumsy self-contradiction, made in the presence of such a nose[2] as King Francis had.

Pope Julius the Second having sent an ambassador to the King of England, to incite him against King Francis,[3] and having stated his case, the English King, in his reply, dwelt on the difficulties he would find in making the necessary preparations for attacking so powerful a king, and put forward certain reasons for them. The ambassador then, ill-advisedly, answered that he had himself considered these difficulties, and had put them before the Pope. From this statement, so foreign[4] to his purpose, which was to urge him to immediate war, the King of England at once inferred what he afterwards found to be the case, that this ambassador was privately inclined to the French side. When he informed the Pope of this, the ambassador's property was confiscated, and he barely escaped with his life.

---

[1] equerries: officers in charge of the horses of the nobility.

[2] nose: King Francis' nose was very large.

[3] King Francis: This incident may actually have involved Louis XII, rather than Francis I, since Pope Julius II died before the latter became king.

[4] foreign: i.e., inappropriate.

For Discussion

1. Lying, according to Montaigne, is "an accursed vice." Why? He notes approvingly the observation that false speech is really much less friendly than silence. What is meant by that statement? Do you agree with the thought it expresses?

2. Why is a good memory essential to a liar? A lie that is a "complete invention" is particularly hard to maintain. For what reason? Why is even a lie that only disguises or alters the truth hard to sustain over a long period?

3. Preceding selections have touched on some of the difficulties that truth presents us with. In the course of this essay Montaigne suggests yet another difficulty. "There are a thousand ways of missing the bull's eye, only one of hitting it." What further difficulty about truth do that statement and its context suggest?

4. The essay ends with two anecdotes that are not altogether easy to understand. You will probably find that you have to reread them both, and carefully, in order to follow what is going on. Francis I (1494–1547), king of France, sent a man to spy on the Duke of Milan. The man, Merveille, was subsequently put to death. Why was Francis offended? What excuse did the Duke offer for having had the man murdered? What did the answer of the "poor embarrassed man" who reported the death to the King reveal? After having reread it two or three times, explain as clearly as you can the point of the second anecdote, about Pope Julius and the King of England.

For Composition

There are several ways to conduct an exposition or an argument, one of which is through *analysis* — the process of dividing something into its parts and examining each part in order to understand the whole. You may analyze a person's character, or the content of an idea, or the functioning of a machine, and in doing so you will explain the character or the idea or the machine — and at the same time perhaps support an argument about each one: that the character is weak, say, or the idea faulty, or the machine efficient. The argument of "On Liars" analyzes lying first by distinguishing between lying and untruth.

1. **Analysis.** Describe the manner in which Montaigne analyzes lying. You will no doubt begin with his distinction between lying and untruth. Where next does he distinguish between two similar but different qualities? Note where his analysis of lying concludes (clearly somewhere before the two illustrative anecdotes at the end).

2. **Argument.** "Lying — and in a lesser degree obstinacy — are, in my opinion, the only faults whose birth and progress we should consistently oppose." How does Montaigne relate obstinacy to lying? Support or refute his assertion that obstinacy is also a serious defect of character that those responsible for rearing children should work to correct.

Words and Allusions

COGNATES. Words in different languages derived from the same source are called *cognates*. For Montaigne *essai* meant a trial or a test, and in English it retains its meaning of an attempt or an endeavor.

1. The word *essay* is sometimes used in English as a verb. Look up its meaning and use it in a sentence.
2. The word *sally*, which appears in the translation of *Don Quixote* (page 56), is related to *essay*. Explain the relationship.
3. Another related word is *assay*. What does it mean, and how is it related to *essay?*

SYNONYMS. The following synonyms (page 14) all refer to ways of misstating truth: *prevaricate, equivocate, falsify, misstate, lie.* Describe a situation in which you would use each word, and write a sentence for each to illustrate its usage.

Dover Beach

MATTHEW ARNOLD

What kind of world do we live in? If we were musing on a quiet evening in a room that faces the sea — lights on the water, the moon making the land glow white — we might feel one way about the universe, just as we might feel quite differently if we were exposed to winter's cold or the lashings of a hurricane. But which of our many shifting attitudes toward this world of ours contains the ultimate truth about it?

The sea is calm tonight.
The tide is full, the moon lies fair
Upon the straits; — on the French coast the light
Gleams and is gone; the cliffs of England stand,
Glimmering and vast, out in the tranquil bay.   5
Come to the window, sweet is the night air!
Only, from the long line of spray
Where the sea meets the moon-blanched* land,
Listen! you hear the grating roar   9
Of pebbles which the waves draw back, and fling,
At their return, up the high strand,
Begin, and cease, and then again begin,
With tremulous cadence slow, and bring
The eternal note of sadness in.

Sophocles* long ago   15
Heard it on the Aegean, and it brought
Into his mind the turbid ebb and flow
Of human misery; we
Find also in the sound a thought,
Hearing it by this distant northern sea.   20

The Sea of Faith
Was once, too, at the full, and round earth's shore
Lay like the folds of a bright girdle furled
But now I only hear
Its melancholy, long, withdrawing roar,   25
Retreating, to the breath
Of the night wind, down the vast edges drear
And naked shingles* of the world.

---

8. **moon-blanched:** whitened by moonlight. 15. **Sophocles** (sof'ə·klēz): fifth-century B.C. Greek dramatist. 28. **shingles:** beaches covered with pebbles.

Ah, love, let us be true
To one another! for the world, which seems   30
To lie before us like a land of dreams,
So various, so beautiful, so new,
Hath really neither joy, nor love, nor light,
Nor certitude, nor peace, nor help for pain;
And we are here as on a darkling* plain   35
Swept with confused alarms of struggle and flight,
Where ignorant armies clash by night.

35. **darkling**: in the dark.

For Discussion

1. With what kind of scene — tempestuous, serene, ugly, beautiful, or what — does the poem open? Which words in the first stanza do most to convey the mood of that scene? Considering what has gone before, a rather unexpected aspect of the opening mood is expressed at line 14. What aspect does the line introduce?

2. What do you suppose the poet means by "Sea of Faith" (line 21)? Arnold, like many of his sensitive contemporaries, was profoundly troubled by what science in the middle of the nineteenth century was revealing about the world we live in. Biology, geology, astronomy — all seemed to be disclosing a vast, indifferent universe in which man's history was no more than an instant, man's ancestry by no means noble, man's position in the universe far from central. Where does the poem most clearly reflect the poet's dismay?

3. "Come to the window," the speaker says in line 6. By the end of the poem we know to whom he is speaking. Who is it? Line 34 suggests that nothing is certain in this world. Does the speaker accordingly conclude that no values — whether of honesty or loyalty or decency or whatever — have meaning? Explain. The mood of the scene pictured in the last three lines of the poem contrasts sharply with how the poem begins. One scene, the speaker suggests, is only appearance; the other is reality. Which is which?

4. **Imagery.** Poets — and prose writers, too — frequently use imagery to help convey their meaning concretely. An image is commonly a word picture, but it may appeal to any other of the four senses as well as to the sense of sight. And it may be figurative as well as literal. For example, "The Sea of Faith" is not a literal sea, but a figurative image of faith. What specific images do you find in the last stanza of the poem?

5. **Free Verse.** "Dover Beach" is written in *free verse*, a verse form in which no set pattern is followed from stanza to stanza, or even from line to line. That is, stanza and line lengths vary widely. (Here the poet uses the liberties of free verse to imitate the irregular ebb and flow of waves on a beach, as in lines 21–28.) Moreover, free verse often abandons such devices as rhyme. "Dover Beach" uses rhyme, but does it follow a regular pattern of rhyme from stanza to stanza? With what — if anything — is "breath" in line 26 made to rhyme?

For Composition

• **Analysis.** Analyze the scene presented in the last three lines of the poem. Consider each detail carefully, and explain what the scene says about human existence.

About the Poet. **Matthew Arnold** (1822–1888) began his literary career as a poet. He turned to literary criticism with his appointment at the age of thirty-five as professor of poetry at Oxford and later to essays on cultural, social, political, and religious questions. Strongly influenced by Goethe, Wordsworth, and especially by ancient Greek authors, Arnold developed his own standards for poetry and wrote poems to exemplify those standards. His ideas about poetry have remained extremely influential, but ironically, the poems by which he is best known, such as "Dover Beach," "The Scholar-Gipsy," "Thyrsis," and "Stanzas from the Grande Chartreuse," are poems that do not adhere to his own critical standards.

Young Goodman Brown

NATHANIEL HAWTHORNE

In the seventeenth century, New England was a part of the American frontier. Villages like Salem that faced the sea to the east confronted to the west a forest wilderness that spread back farther than anyone in the village knew. Those Puritan days were days of strict morality — of soberness of dress, hourlong prayers, and stern punishment of the slightest wrongdoing. Yet always at the edge of the lives of even the most pious and devout — indeed all around that little bit of humanity on the fringe of a continent — loomed temptations darker than the forest itself, forbidden but often irresistible.

Young Goodman Brown came forth at sunset into the street of Salem village; but put his head back, after crossing the threshold, to exchange a parting kiss with his young wife. And Faith, as the wife was aptly named, thrust her own pretty head into the street, letting the wind play with the pink ribbons of her cap while she called to Goodman Brown.

"Dearest heart," whispered she, softly and rather sadly, when her lips were close to his ear, "prithee put off your journey until sunrise and sleep in your own bed tonight. A lone woman is troubled with such dreams and such thoughts that she's afeard of herself sometimes. Pray tarry with me this night, dear husband, of all nights in the year."

"My love and my Faith," replied young Goodman Brown, "of all nights in the year, this one night must I tarry away from thee. My journey, as thou callest it, forth and back again, must needs be done 'twixt now and sunrise. What, my sweet, pretty wife, dost thou doubt me already, and we but three months married?"

"Then God bless you!" said Faith, with the pink ribbons; "and may you find all well when you come back."

"Amen!" cried Goodman Brown. "Say thy prayers, dear Faith, and go to bed at dusk, and no harm will come to thee."

So they parted; and the young man pursued his way until, being about to turn the corner by the meeting house, he looked back and saw the head of Faith still peeping after him with a melancholy air, in spite of her pink ribbons.

"Poor little Faith!" thought he, for his heart smote him. "What a wretch am I to leave her on such an errand! She talks of dreams, too. Methought as she spoke there was trouble in her face, as if a dream had warned her what work is to be done tonight. But no, no; 'twould kill her to think it. Well, she's a blessed angel on earth; and after this one night I'll cling to her skirts and follow her to heaven."

With this excellent resolve for the future, Goodman Brown felt himself justified in making more haste on his present evil purpose. He had taken a dreary road, darkened by all the gloomiest trees of the forest, which barely stood aside to let the narrow path creep through, and closed immediately behind. It was all as lonely as could be; and there is this peculiarity in such a solitude, that the traveler knows not who may be concealed by the innumerable trunks and thick boughs overhead; so that with lonely footsteps he may yet be passing through an unseen multitude.

"There may be a devilish Indian behind every tree," said Goodman Brown to himself; and he glanced fearfully behind him as he added, "What if the devil himself should be at my very elbow!"

His head being turned back, he passed a crook of the road, and, looking forward again, beheld the figure of a man, in grave and decent attire, seated at the foot of an old tree. He arose at Goodman Brown's approach and walked onward side by side with him.

"You are late, Goodman Brown," said he. "The clock of the Old South[1] was striking as I came through Boston; and that is full fifteen minutes agone." In SALEM

"Faith kept me back awhile," replied the young man, with a tremor in his voice, caused by the sudden appearance of his companion, though not wholly unexpected.

It was now deep dusk in the forest, and deepest in that part of it where these two were journeying. As nearly as could be discerned, the second traveler was about fifty years old, apparently in the same rank of life as Goodman Brown, and bearing a considerable resemblance to him, though perhaps more in expression than features. Still they might have been taken for father and son. And yet, though the elder person was as simply clad as the younger and as simple in manner too, he had an indescribable air of one who knew the world, and who would not have felt abashed at the governor's dinner table or in King William's[2] court, were it possible that his affairs should call him thither. But the only thing about him that could be fixed upon as remarkable was his staff, which bore the like-

ness of a great black snake, so curiously wrought that it might almost be seen to twist and wriggle itself like a living serpent. This, of course, must have been an ocular deception,[3] assisted by the uncertain light.

"Come, Goodman Brown," cried his fellow traveler, "this is a dull pace for the beginning of a journey. Take my staff, if you are so soon weary."

"Friend," said the other, exchanging his slow pace for a full stop, "having kept covenant[4] by meeting thee here, it is my purpose now to return whence I came. I have scruples touching the matter thou wot'st of." [5]

"Sayest thou so?" replied he of the serpent, smiling apart. "Let us walk on, nevertheless, reasoning as we go; and if I convince thee not, thou shalt turn back. We are but a little way in the forest yet."

"Too far! too far!" exclaimed the goodman, unconsciously resuming his walk. "My father never went into the woods on such an errand, nor his father before him. We have been a race of honest men and good Christians since the days of the martyrs; and shall I be the first of the name of Brown that ever took this path and kept —"

"Such company, thou wouldst say," observed the elder person, interpreting his pause. "Well said, Goodman Brown! I have been as well acquainted with your family as with ever a one among the Puritans; and that's no trifle to say. I helped your grandfather, the constable, when he lashed the Quaker woman so smartly through the streets of Salem; and it was I that brought your father a pitch-pine knot, kindled at my own hearth, to set fire to an Indian village, in King Philip's war.[6] They were my good friends, both; and many a

---

[1] **Old South:** Old South Church.
[2] **King William:** William III, king of England 1689–1702.

[3] **ocular deception:** optical illusion.
[4] **kept covenant:** fulfilled agreement.
[5] **thou wot'st of:** you know of.
[6] **King Philip's war:** war between English settlers and Wampanoag Indians, 1675–1676.

pleasant walk have we had along this path, and returned merrily after midnight. I would fain[1] be friends with you for their sake."

"If it be as thou sayest," replied Goodman Brown, "I marvel they never spoke of these matters; or, verily, I marvel not, seeing that the least rumor of the sort would have driven them from New England. We are a people of prayer, and good works to boot, and abide no such wickedness."

"Wickedness or not," said the traveler with the twisted staff, "I have a very general acquaintance here in New England. The deacons of many a church have drunk the communion wine with me; the selectmen of divers[2] towns make me their chairman; and a majority of the Great and General Court[3] are firm supporters of my interest. The governor and I, too — But these are state secrets."

"Can this be so?" cried Goodman Brown, with a stare of amazement at his undisturbed companion. "Howbeit,[4] I have nothing to do with the governor and council; they have their own ways, and are no rule for a simple husbandman[5] like me. But, were I to go on with thee, how should I meet the eye of that good old man, our minister, at Salem village? O, his voice would make me tremble both Sabbath day and lecture day." [6]

Thus far the elder traveler had listened with due gravity; but now burst into a fit of irrepressible mirth, shaking himself so violently that his snakelike staff actually seemed to wriggle in sympathy.

"Ha! ha! ha!" shouted he again and again; then composing himself. "Well, go on, Goodman Brown, go on; but, prithee, don't kill me with laughing."

"Well, then, to end the matter at once," said Goodman Brown, considerably nettled, "there is my wife, Faith. It would break her dear little heart; and I'd rather break my own."

"Nay, if that be the case," answered the other, "e'en go thy ways, Goodman Brown. I would not for twenty old women like the

---

[1] **fain**: gladly.
[2] **divers** (dī′vẽrz): several.
[3] **Great and General Court**: Massachusetts legislature.
[4] **Howbeit**: nevertheless.

[5] **husbandman**: farmer.
[6] **lecture day**: day on which sermons were delivered in church outside the regular services.

ABOUT THE AUTHOR • Born in Salem, Massachusetts, **Nathaniel Hawthorne** (1804–1864) is the author of what many critics consider America's greatest novel, *The Scarlet Letter.* Two of his other novels are *The House of the Seven Gables,* which recalls the sin of an ancestor who sentenced innocent colonists to die in the Salem witch hunt of the 1690's, and *The Marble Faun,* a story of sin and tormented conscience with a setting in Rome. Together with his many short stories, the novels reflect Hawthorne's preoccupation with sin and its effects upon one's heart and personality, and the power of conscience. He was, according to Stanley T. Williams, "completely integrated . . . with the soil and spirit of a New England which had bred his introspective forebears." Although Hawthorne was a recluse as a youth, after his marriage to Sophia Peabody he entered public life, worked in the Boston and Salem custom houses, and for four years served the American consulate in Liverpool.

one hobbling before us that Faith should come to any harm."

As he spoke, he pointed his staff at a female figure on the path, in whom Goodman Brown recognized a very pious and exemplary dame, who had taught him his catechism in youth, and was still his moral and spiritual adviser, jointly with the minister and Deacon Gookin.

"A marvel, truly, that Goody Cloyse should be so far in the wilderness at nightfall," said he. " But, with your leave, friend, I shall take a cut through the woods until we have left this Christian woman behind. Being a stranger to you, she might ask whom I was consorting with and whither I was going."

"Be it so," said his fellow traveler. "Betake you to the woods, and let me keep the path."

Accordingly the young man turned aside, but took care to watch his companion, who advanced softly along the road until he had come within a staff's length of the old dame. She, meanwhile, was making the best of her way, with singular speed for so aged a woman, and mumbling some indistinct words — a prayer, doubtless — as she went. The traveler put forth his staff and touched her withered neck with what seemed the serpent's tail.

"The devil!" screamed the pious old lady.

"Then Goody Cloyse knows her old friend?" observed the traveler, confronting her and leaning on his writhing stick.

"Ah, forsooth, and is it your worship indeed?" cried the good dame. "Yea, truly is it, and in the very image of my old gossip,[1] Goodman Brown, the grandfather of the silly fellow that now is. But — would your worship believe it? — my broomstick hath strangely disappeared, stolen, as I suspect, by that unhanged witch, Goody Cory, and that, too, when I was all anointed with the juice

of smallage[2] and cinquefoil,[3] and wolf's banc[4] — "

"Mingled with fine wheat and the fat of a newborn babe," said the shape of old Goodman Brown. *disguised*

"Ah, your worship knows the recipe," cried the old lady, cackling aloud. "So, as I was saying, being all ready for the meeting, and no horse to ride on, I made up my mind to foot it; for they tell me there is a nice young man to be taken into communion tonight. But now your good worship will lend me your arm, and we shall be there in a twinkling."

"That can hardly be," answered her friend. "I may not spare you my arm, Goody Cloyse; but here is my staff, if you will."

So saying, he threw it down at her feet, where, perhaps, it assumed life, being one of the rods which its owner had formerly lent to the Egyptian magi.[5] Of this fact, however, Goodman Brown could not take cognizance. He had cast up his eyes in astonishment, and, looking down again, beheld neither Goody Cloyse nor the serpentine staff, but his fellow traveler alone, who waited for him as calmly as if nothing had happened.

"That old woman taught me my catechism," said the young man; and there was a world of meaning in this simple comment.

They continued to walk onward, while the elder traveler exhorted his companion to make good speed and persevere in the path, discoursing so aptly that his arguments seemed rather to spring up in the bosom of his auditor than to be suggested by himself. As they went, he plucked a branch of maple to serve for a walking stick, and began to strip it of the twigs and little boughs, which were wet with evening

---

[1] **gossip**: close friend.

[2] **smallage**: kind of wild celery.
[3] **cinquefoil**: plant of the rose family.
[4] **wolf's bane**: poisonous flower.
[5] **Egyptian magi**: priestly caste of sorcerers and astrologers.

dew. The moment his fingers touched them they became strangely withered and dried up as with a week's sunshine. Thus the pair proceeded, at a good free pace, until suddenly, in a gloomy hollow of the road, Goodman Brown sat himself down on the stump of a tree and refused to go any farther.

"Friend," said he, stubbornly, "my mind is made up. Not another step will I budge on this errand. What if a wretched old woman do choose to go to the devil when I thought she was going to heaven: is that any reason why I should quit my dear Faith and go after her?"

"You will think better of this by and by," said his acquaintance, composedly. "Sit here and rest yourself a while; and when you feel like moving again, there is my staff to help you along."

Without more words, he threw his companion the maple stick, and was as speedily out of sight as if he had vanished into the deepening gloom. The young man sat a few moments by the roadside, applauding himself greatly, and thinking with how clear a conscience he should meet the minister in his morning walk, nor shrink from the eye of good old Deacon Gookin. And what calm sleep would be his that very night, which was to have been spent so wickedly, but so purely and sweetly now, in the arms of Faith! Amidst these pleasant and praiseworthy meditations, Goodman Brown heard the tramp of horses along the road, and deemed it advisable to conceal himself within the verge of the forest, conscious of the guilty purpose that had brought him thither, though now so happily turned from it.

On came the hoof tramps and the voices of the riders, two grave old voices, conversing soberly as they drew near. These mingled sounds appeared to pass along the road, within a few yards of the young man's hiding place; but, owing doubtless to the depth of the gloom at that particular spot, neither the travelers nor their steeds were visible. Though their figures brushed the small boughs by the wayside, it could not be seen that they intercepted, even for a moment, the faint gleam from the strip of bright sky athwart which they must have passed. Goodman Brown alternately crouched and stood on tiptoe, pulling aside the branches and thrusting forth his head as far as he durst[1] without discerning so much as a shadow. It vexed him the more, because he could have sworn, were such a thing possible, that he recognized the voices of the minister and Deacon Gookin, jogging along quietly, as they were wont[2] to do, when bound to some ordination[3] or ecclesiastical council.[4] While yet within hearing, one of the riders stopped to pluck a switch.

"Of the two, reverend sir," said the voice like the deacon's, "I had rather miss an ordination dinner than tonight's meeting. They tell me that some of our community are to be here from Falmouth and beyond, and others from Connecticut and Rhode Island, besides several of the Indian powwows, who, after their fashion, know almost as much deviltry as the best of us. Moreover, there is a goodly young woman to be taken into communion."

"Mighty well, Deacon Gookin!" replied the solemn old tones of the minister. "Spur up, or we shall be late. Nothing can be done, you know, until I get on the ground."

The hoofs clattered again; and the voices, talking so strangely in the empty air, passed on through the forest, where no church had ever been gathered or solitary Christian prayed. Whither, then, could these holy men be journeying so deep into the heathen wilderness? Young Goodman Brown caught

---

[1] **durst**: dared.

[2] **wont**: accustomed.

[3] **ordination**: ceremony of admission to the Christian ministry.

[4] **ecclesiastical council**: gathering of church officials.

hold of a tree for support, being ready to sink down on the ground, faint and over-burdened with the heavy sickness of his heart. He looked up to the sky, doubting whether there really was a heaven above him. Yet there was the blue arch, and the stars brightening in it.

"With heaven above and Faith below, I will yet stand firm against the devil!" cried Goodman Brown.

While he still gazed upward into the deep arch of the firmament[1] and had lifted his hands to pray, a cloud, though no wind was stirring, hurried across the zenith[2] and hid the brightening stars. The blue sky was still visible except directly overhead, where this black mass of cloud was sweeping swiftly northward. Aloft in the air, as if from the depths of the cloud, came a confused and doubtful sound of voices. Once the listener fancied that he could distinguish the accents of townspeople of his own, men and women, both pious and ungodly, many of whom he had met at the communion table, and had seen others rioting[3] at the tavern. The next moment, so indistinct were the sounds, he doubted whether he had heard aught but the murmur of the old forest, whispering without a wind. Then came a stronger swell of those familiar tones, heard daily in the sunshine at Salem village, but never until now from a cloud of night. There was one voice, of a young woman, uttering lamentations, yet with an uncertain sorrow, and entreating for some favor, which, perhaps, it would grieve her to obtain; and all the unseen multitude, both saints and sinners, seemed to encourage her onward.

"Faith!" shouted Goodman Brown, in a voice of agony and desperation; and the echoes of the forest mocked him, crying, "Faith! Faith!" as if bewildered wretches were seeking her all through the wilderness.

[1] **firmament**: sky.
[2] **zenith**: point in the sky directly overhead.
[3] **rioting**: acting in a noisy and reckless manner.

What loneliness is more lonely than distrust?

— George Eliot

The cry of grief, rage, and terror was yet piercing the night, when the unhappy husband held his breath for a response. There was a scream, drowned immediately in a louder murmur of voices, fading into far-off laughter, as the dark cloud swept away, leaving the clear and silent sky above Goodman Brown. But something fluttered lightly down through the air and caught on the branch of a tree. The young man seized it, and beheld a pink ribbon.

"My Faith is gone!" cried he, after one stupefied moment. "There is no good on earth; and sin is but a name. Come, devil; for to thee is this world given."

And, maddened with despair, so that he laughed loud and long, did Goodman Brown grasp his staff and set forth again, at such a rate that he seemed to fly along the forest path rather than to walk or run. The road grew wilder and drearier and more faintly traced, and vanished at length, leaving him in the heart of the dark wilderness, still rushing onward with the instinct that guides mortal man to evil. The whole forest was peopled with frightful sounds — the creaking of the trees, the howling of wild beasts, and the yell of Indians; while sometimes the wind tolled like a distant church bell, and sometimes gave a broad roar around the traveler, as if all Nature were laughing him to scorn. But he was himself the chief horror of the scene, and shrank not from its other horrors.

"Ha! ha! ha!" roared Goodman Brown when the wind laughed at him. "Let us hear which will laugh loudest. Think not to frighten me with your deviltry. Come witch, come wizard, come Indian pow-wow, come devil himself, and here comes

Goodman Brown. You may as well fear him as he fear you."

In truth, all through the haunted forest there could be nothing more frightful than the figure of Goodman Brown. On he flew among the black pines, brandishing his staff with frenzied gestures, now giving vent to an inspiration of horrid blasphemy, and now shouting forth such laughter as set all the echoes of the forest laughing like demons around him. The fiend in his own shape is less hideous than when he rages in the breast of man. Thus sped the demoniac[1] on his course, until, quivering among the trees, he saw a red light before him, as when the felled trunks and branches of a clearing have been set on fire, and throw up their lurid blaze against the sky, at the hour of midnight. He paused, in a lull of the tempest that had driven him onward, and heard the swell of what seemed a hymn, rolling solemnly from a distance with the weight of many voices. He knew the tune; it was a familiar one in the choir of the village meeting house. The verse died heavily away, and was lengthened by a chorus, not of human voices, but of all the sounds of the benighted wilderness pealing in awful harmony together. Goodman Brown cried out; and his cry was lost to his own ear by its unison with the cry of the desert.

In the interval of silence he stole forward until the light glared full upon his eyes. At one extremity of an open space, hemmed in by the dark wall of the forest, arose a rock, bearing some rude, natural resemblance either to an altar or a pulpit, and surrounded by four blazing pines, their tops aflame, their stems untouched, like candles at an evening meeting. The mass of foliage that had overgrown the summit of the rock was all on fire, blazing high into the night and fitfully illuminating the whole field. Each pendent twig and leafy festoon was in a blaze. As

the red light arose and fell, a numerous congregation alternately shone forth, then disappeared in shadow, and again grew, as it were, out of the darkness, peopling the heart of the solitary woods at once.

"A grave and dark-clad company," quoth Goodman Brown.

In truth they were such. Among them, quivering to and fro between gloom and splendor, appeared faces that would be seen next day at the council board of the province, and others which, Sabbath after Sabbath, looked devoutly heavenward, and benignantly over the crowded pews, from the holiest pulpits in the land. Some affirm that the lady of the governor was there. At least there were high dames well known to her, and wives of honored husbands, and widows, a great multitude, and ancient maidens, all of excellent repute, and fair young girls, who trembled lest their mothers should espy[2] them. Either the sudden gleams of light flashing over the obscure[3] field bedazzled Goodman Brown, or he recognized a score of the church members of Salem village famous for their especial sanctity. Good old Deacon Gookin had arrived, and waited at the skirts of that venerable saint, his revered pastor. But, irreverently consorting with these grave, reputable, and pious people, these elders of the church, these chaste dames and dewy virgins, there were men of dissolute lives and women of spotted fame, wretches given over to all mean and filthy vice, and suspected even of horrid crimes. It was strange to see that the good shrank not from the wicked, nor were the sinners abashed by the saints. Scattered also among their palefaced enemies were the Indian priests, or powwows, who had often scared their native forest with more hideous incantations than any known to English witchcraft.

---

[1] **demoniac:** person possessed by a demon.

[2] **espy:** catch sight of.
[3] **obscure:** *here,* dark.

"But, were I to go on with thee, how should I meet the eye of that good old man, our minister, at Salem village? O, his voice would make me tremble both Sabbath day and lecture day."

"But where is Faith?" thought Goodman Brown, and, as hope came into his heart, he trembled.

Another verse of the hymn arose, a slow and mournful strain, such as the pious love, but joined to words which expressed all that our nature can conceive of sin, and darkly hinted at far more. Unfathomable to mere mortals is the lore of fiends. Verse after verse was sung; and still the chorus of the desert swelled between like the deepest tone of a mighty organ; and with the final peal of that dreadful anthem there came a sound, as if the roaring wind, the rushing streams, the howling beasts, and every other voice of the unconverted wilderness were mingling and according[1] with the voice of guilty man in homage to the prince of all.[2] The four blazing pines threw up a loftier flame, and obscurely discovered shapes and visages of horror on the smoke wreaths above the impious assembly. At the same moment the fire on the rock shot redly forth and formed a glowing arch above its base, where now appeared a figure. With reverence be it spoken, the figure bore no slight similitude,

[1] **according**: harmonizing.
[2] **the prince of all**: *i. e.,* the devil.

both in garb and manner, to some grave divine[1] of the New England churches.

"Bring forth the converts!" cried a voice that echoed through the field and rolled into the forest.

At the word, Goodman Brown stepped forth from the shadow of the trees and approached the congregation, with whom he felt a loathful brotherhood by the sympathy of all that was wicked in his heart. He could have well nigh sworn that the shape of his own dead father beckoned him to advance, looking downward from a smoke wreath, while a woman, with dim features of despair, threw out her hand to warn him back. Was it his mother? But he had no power to retreat one step, nor to resist, even in thought, when the minister and good old Deacon Gookin seized his arms and led him to the blazing rock. Thither came also the slender form of a veiled female, led between Goody Cloyse, that pious teacher of the catechism, and Martha Carrier, who had received the devil's promise to be queen of hell. A rampant[2] hag was she. And there stood the proselytes[3] beneath the canopy of fire.

"Welcome, my children," said the dark figure, "to the communion of your race. Ye have found thus young your nature and your destiny. My children, look behind you!"

They turned; and flashing forth, as it were, in a sheet of flame, the fiend worshipers were seen; the smile of welcome gleamed darkly on every visage.

"There," resumed the sable form,[4] "are all whom ye have reverenced from youth. Ye deemed them holier than yourselves, and shrank from your own sin, contrasting it with their lives of righteousness and prayerful aspirations heavenward. Yet here are they all in my worshiping assembly. This night it shall be granted you to know their secret deeds; how hoary-bearded[5] elders of the church have whispered wanton[6] words to the young maids of their household; how many a woman, eager for widows' weeds, has given her husband a drink at bedtime and let him sleep his last in her bosom; how beardless youths have made haste to inherit their fathers' wealth; and how fair damsels — blush not, sweet ones — have dug little graves in the garden, and bidden me, the sole guest, to an infant's funeral. By the sympathy of your human hearts for sin ye shall scent out all the places — whether in church, bed chamber, street, field, or forest — where crime has been committed, and shall exult to behold the whole earth one stain of guilt, one mighty blood spot. Far more than this. It shall be yours to penetrate, in every bosom, the deep mystery of sin, the fountain of all wicked arts, and which inexhaustibly supplies more evil impulses than human power — than my power at its utmost — can make manifest in deeds. And now, my children, look upon each other."

They did so; and, by the blaze of the hell-kindled torches, the wretched man beheld his Faith, and the wife her husband, trembling before that unhallowed[7] altar.

"Lo, there ye stand, my children," said the figure, in a deep and solemn tone, almost sad with its despairing awfulness, as if his once angelic nature[8] could yet mourn for our miserable race. "Depending upon one another's hearts, ye had still hoped that virtue were not all a dream. Now are ye undeceived. Evil is the nature of mankind. Evil must be your only happiness. Welcome again, my children, to the communion of your race."

---

[1] **divine**: clergyman.
[2] **rampant**: fierce.
[3] **proselytes**: converts.
[4] **sable form**: dark figure; that is, the devil.

[5] **hoary-bearded**: having white or gray beards.
[6] **wanton**: improper.
[7] **unhallowed**: unholy.
[8] **once angelic nature**: Satan was originally a heavenly angel, later cast down to hell as punishment for his rebellion against God's rule.

"They turned; and flashing forth, as it were, in a sheet of flame, the fiend worshipers were seen. . . ." The Witches' Sabbath, *by the Dutch painter, Bartholomeus Spranger.*

"Welcome," repeated the fiend worshipers, in one cry of despair and triumph.

And there they stood, the only pair, as it seemed, who were yet hesitating on the verge of wickedness in this dark world. A basin was hollowed, naturally, in the rock. Did it contain water, reddened by the lurid light? or was it blood? or, perchance, a liquid flame? Herein did the shape of evil dip his hand and prepare to lay the mark of baptism upon their foreheads, that they might be partakers of the mystery of sin, more conscious of the secret guilt of others, both in deed and thought, than they could now be of their own. The husband cast one look at his pale wife, and Faith at him. What polluted wretches would the next glance show them to each other, shuddering alike at what they disclosed and what they saw!

"Faith! Faith!" cried the husband, "look up to heaven, and resist the wicked one."

Whether Faith obeyed, he knew not. Hardly had he spoken when he found himself amid calm night and solitude, listening to a roar of the wind which died heavily away through the forest. He staggered against the rock, and felt it chill and damp; while a hanging twig, that had been all on fire, besprinkled his cheek with the coldest dew.

The next morning young Goodman Brown came slowly into the street of Salem village, staring around him like a bewildered man. The good old minister was taking a walk along the graveyard to get an appetite for breakfast and meditate his sermon, and bestowed a blessing, as he passed, on Goodman Brown. He shrank from the venerable saint as if to avoid an anathema. Old Deacon Gookin was at domestic worship,[1] and the holy words of his prayer were heard through the open window. "What God doth the wizard pray to?" quoth Goodman Brown. Goody Cloyse, that excellent old Christian, stood in the early sunshine at her own lattice,[2] catechizing[3] a little girl who had brought her a pint of morning's milk. Goodman Brown snatched away the child as from the grasp of the fiend himself. Turning the corner by the meeting house, he spied the head of Faith, with the pink ribbons, gazing anxiously forth, and bursting into such joy at sight of him that she skipped along the street and almost kissed her husband before the whole village. But Goodman Brown looked sternly and sadly into her face, and passed on without a greeting.

Had Goodman Brown fallen asleep in the forest and only dreamed a wild dream of a witch meeting?

Be it so, if you will; but, alas; it was a dream of evil omen for young Goodman Brown. A stern, a sad, a darkly meditative, a distrustful, if not a desperate, man did he become from the night of that fearful dream. On the Sabbath day, when the congregation were singing a holy psalm, he could not listen, because an anthem of sin rushed loudly upon his ear and drowned all the blessed strain. When the minister spoke from the pulpit, with power and fervid

[1] **domestic worship:** *i.e.,* praying at home.
[2] **lattice:** gate.
[3] **catechizing:** teaching the catechism to.

eloquence and with his hand on the open Bible, of the sacred truths of our religion, and of saintlike lives and triumphant deaths, and of future bliss or misery unutterable, then did Goodman Brown turn pale, dreading lest the roof should thunder down upon the gray blasphemer and his hearers. Often, awaking suddenly at midnight, he shrank from the bosom of Faith; and at morning or eventide, when the family knelt down at prayer, he scowled, and muttered to himself, and gazed sternly at his wife, and turned away. And when he had lived long, and was borne to his grave, a hoary corpse, followed by Faith, an aged woman, and children and grandchildren, a goodly procession, besides neighbors not a few, they carved no hopeful verse upon his tombstone; for his dying hour was gloom.

For Discussion

1. A single story may explore many themes — about the nature of man, say, or about good and evil, or about faith versus reason, or about any number of other insights with which literature and life abound. "Young Goodman Brown" explores those three themes mentioned, and might profitably be examined in the light of each of them. But what does the story have to say about the theme of truth? "Had Goodman Brown fallen asleep in the forest and only dreamed a wild dream of a witch meeting?" Which was dream and which reality, which false and which true? What are the consequences of Goodman Brown's experience in the forest? Are those consequences real, or does he only imagine them?

2. The story concerns a journey that "must needs be done 'twixt now and sunrise." At what time of day does the journey begin? How long have Goodman Brown and his wife been married when he makes the journey? Why does she particularly want him to stay at home?

3. Goodman Brown keeps covenant by meeting the devil in the forest. What is a covenant? Notice that — although he is obliged only to meet the devil, not accompany him to the witches' sabbath — he does, however reluctantly, follow the devil to the end of the journey. Briefly indicate the influences that successively overcome Goodman Brown's reluctance. What is the significance of the pink ribbon caught on the branch of a tree in the forest (page 31)?

4. The character of the devil is carefully thought out and presented. What attributes are his? That is, is he ill-tempered or congenial, young or middle-aged, handsome or ugly, cosmopolitan or provincial, reasonable or unreasonable? What do these and his other attributes tell you about Hawthorne's feelings regarding the nature of sin? Does evil, for example, always appear in a form that is instantly recognizable?

5. **Irony.** *Irony* is the effect gained by implying a meaning quite different from the apparent or literal meaning. An old witch of a woman flies through the woods "mumbling some indistinct words — a prayer, doubtless" (page 29). The remark is ironical; such an old woman would be mumbling hexes or curses, but not, assuredly, prayers — though indeed many old women do mumble prayers. Goodman Brown's title itself is ironical. That title, which corresponds to our *mister,* was a standard form of address in Salem in the seventeenth century. But why in this instance is it ironical? What other examples of irony do you discover in the story?

For Composition

Description is often a useful device for developing a composition. If you are explaining about that trip you took last summer, you will probably want to describe what you saw. If you are arguing that your friend should make the same trip, you may find vivid description a persuasive way to urge your point. As with analysis and with comparison and contrast, description should be used in your writing when it will add to the effectiveness of what you want to say.

1. **Analysis.** Consider Hawthorne's description of the witches' sabbath in the forest. To how many senses — sight, taste, touch, smell, and hearing — does the description appeal? Write a brief paper mentioning and illustrating the senses appealed to.

2. **Description.** Describe the devil as he appears in Hawthorne's story. Be sure to consider all relevant details of appearance and behavior.

3. **Argument.** "Evil is the nature of mankind." Refer to historical or personal insights to support or refute that statement in a well-organized composition of two or three paragraphs.

Words and Allusions

CONNOTATION. The denotation of a word is what the word specifically refers to. Its connotation consists of related meanings the word suggests or implies. Thus *home* denotes simply the place where one lives, but it also connotes various states of feeling depending on one's experience.

Images, too, carry connotations. From the earliest days of man, before the discovery of fire when the sun was the only source of light and warmth, images of darkness and light have possessed strong connotations. Hawthorne makes use of these ancient connotations by having Goodman Brown make his journey into the forest at night, not in the light of day. Consider the persistence of these connotations. What is the difference between a white lie and a black lie? Why do brides wear white? What clothes are worn at funerals? What connection have these connotations today with their ancient origins? What other examples can you think of?

De Chirico

The Mystery and Melancholy of a Street

One of man's oldest ideas is that life is a dream — that is, that dreams possess reality. It seems strange to say that a dream is real and that waking life is unreal, but it is less strange than it appears if we understand these statements as exaggerated ways of saying that the real meaning of life is to be found in dreams.

That dreams foretell the future is one of man's oldest convictions; a modern theory is that dreams reveal the past. There is something to be said for both views. Consider a man who is unable to express emotion and is aware of his inhibition. He dreams, let us say, of a beautiful fountain sparkling in the sunlight — a vision of the way he would like to live, with emotional freedom. His dream reveals the past by revealing his desire to free his emotions, but it can also affect the future by revealing the possibility of emotional freedom. As it enters his understanding, the dream becomes a way of telling him how to live and consequently suggests ways of directing and controlling his emotional life. Thus in dreams patterns are worked out that can help us to organize our relationship to the world. In art and literature similar patterns appear that can affect us in the same way.

In each part of "The Night Face Up" (page 7), the hero is at the center of a violent event. But which part is the dream? In the painting by de Chirico similar problems appear. All the details are taken from towns in the Po valley in northern Italy where de Chirico lived and grew up — the solid blocks of buildings, the long empty arcades, the wide squares, the trolley line, the statue that casts a shadow, the sharp contrast between sunlight and shadow, the flood-line on the building at the left, a result of the Po overflowing its banks.

Yet the scene is transformed into something dreamlike, magical, visionary. The artist has achieved this effect by altering and distorting ordinary appearances. The picture has at least two vanishing points; the perspective system for each of the two buildings is quite different. Thus they seem to belong to two different worlds, and the picture seems to lose visual meaning. The van appears too small for the size of the little girl and seems to have a third perspective, or none. Is that the shadow of a statue, and is that a spear beside it? The girl is as real as the van, yet she is painted as if she were a shadow. Her reality is at once affirmed and denied. What other such dreamlike distortions do you find?

Every object in the picture is recognizable, but the relations among the objects are not. Hence the picture is at once understandable and not understandable, meaningful and meaningless. Which do you prefer? Why? If you prefer to make it meaningful, what meanings can you construct? Do these meanings tell as much about the picture as they tell about you?

MORSE PECKHAM

Giorgio de Chirico (1888–) *The Mystery and Melancholy of a Street.* Collection of Mr. and Mrs. Stanley Resor, Washington, D.C.

Harmen van Steenwijck (1612-c.1656) *Vanitas.* Museum De Lakenhal, Leiden.

Van Steenwijck

Vanitas

This painting is an allegory, a way of thinking that can be used in all forms of writing and the various arts. An allegory presents abstract ideas in pictures or word-pictures. It can help us understand a difficult or complex idea in the same way an example does. It can also help us to express complex ideas or emotions by giving them concrete form. In his "Allegory of the Cave" (page 49), Plato was striving to understand and express a complex conception of reality. In *Vanitas,* the painter wishes to present in a novel and attractive way a very common idea.

Vanitas is a technical term for a particular kind of *still-life,* that is, a painting which presents things of ordinary life, such as flowers, fruit, food, dishes, musical instruments, organized to make them as attractive as possible. Three hundred years ago, when this picture was painted, such pictures were very popular. In Holland, the home of Van Steenwijck, many people were enjoying ease and prosperity for the first time in their history. Yet they still lived in an economy in which goods were scarce — as do most people today, including most Americans until recently. In this situation still-life paintings of food, mostly characterized by rich profusion, were widely painted and sold. And to this day European grocery stores display their food in a rich profusion that is puzzling to eyes used to the cool efficiency of supermarkets in which the aim is convenience for the shopper, not emotional pleasure at seeing a profusion of goods.

In this context, *Vanitas* does not mean *vanity* as the word is commonly used today. It refers instead to the relative worthlessness of all human pleasures when contrasted to the briefness of life, the certainty of death, and the eternal existence of God.

This painting is divided into two halves. On the right is a basket of fruit suggesting the pleasures of taste and sight. Below is a flutelike instrument indicating the pleasures of sound, and a feather—probably a quill pen—indicating the pleasures of poetry. To the left is a skull, the certainty of death. It sits on a legal document with an official seal — probably a will — and a very large book, no doubt the Bible, then and still the largest book people are likely to be familiar with. In front are two other books, no doubt of a serious nature. Why are the objects of pleasure set on a velvetlike cloth, while the objects to the left are set on a bare table? Which of the senses has not yet been mentioned? Can you explain why the background to the right is dark and that to the left is light?

A final detail is worth noting. On the right the leaves of the peaches are still crisp and green, but the stalks of the grapes are brown and dead. Where are these stalks placed, and what does their writhing form suggest? Why?

MORSE PECKHAM

Daumier

Don Quixote and Sancho Panza

There is a difference between an illustration of a literary work and an interpretation. If the artist aims at presenting the details of a scene as the author has done, adding only what is necessary for completion, we call his work an illustration. But if he selects some aspect of the literary work and emphasizes certain details in order to express his understanding, we call his work an interpretation. Daumier's painting is an interpretation of *Don Quixote.*

In his lifetime Daumier was famous as a caricaturist and political cartoonist. Only long after his death was he recognized as a fascinating painter. In his time the ideal was still a picture finished in every detail, but Daumier anticipated later developments by painting only enough to establish the scene and situation and to imply his comment on it (for a comparative technique see Munch, *The Scream,* page 691). He was ahead of other painters because his political cartooning had already taught him how simplification and distortion could be used to imply an attitude about subject matter.

Fascinated by the theme of *Don Quixote,* Daumier painted the Don a number of times, both with and without Sancho Panza. In the Don and Sancho, Daumier saw conflicting demands in human nature. On the one hand there is man's sensuous attachment to the earth, and on the other hand there are ideas, feelings, and beliefs, by which man makes sense out of reality. The two impulses are independent, but they are also interdependent because man cannot live without both.

In this painting Daumier gives the greatest weight and importance to the earth by allowing it to occupy roughly two thirds of the picture. Sancho Panza is completely enclosed in the earth. He is fat, sleepy, earthbound, and his mount is plodding along. Notice that the outline of the hill is repeated in the front line of Sancho's figure. What does this repetition stress? Notice also the spot of red on the bridle and the spot of blue on the saddle blanket.

In placing Don Quixote against the sky, Daumier makes use of very ancient symbolism for the division between the senses and the mind. Poor old Rocinante looks lively, and the Don carries his spear without effort. But why do they appear ghostly? What does this ghostly quality contribute to Daumier's interpretation? Don Quixote has just enough substance to embody mind and spirit separate from the earth.

However, Daumier does not wish to identify mind and spirit with good, and earth or flesh with bad. The yellow light in the sky suggests a *setting,* not a rising sun. And the blue is a greenish blue, a dark color hinting at storm clouds, difficulties, and trouble. Where do colors of sun and sky appear in Sancho's part of the picture? What qualities do those colors have here? What contrast do they suggest between the Don and Sancho?

MORSE PECKHAM

42

Honoré Daumier (1808-1879) *Don Quixote and Sancho Panza.* Glasgow Art Gallery and Museum, Scotland.

43

William Gropper (1897–   ) *The Senate*. Museum of Modern Art, New York.

Gropper

The Senate

This painting comes from the 1930's, the period of the Great Depression when many people felt that the Congress was not carrying out its responsibilities effectively. In Ibsen's *An Enemy of the People* (page 75) the mayor and his followers avoid an unpleasant social problem and substitute words for significant action. Although their settings differ, Gropper's point is much the same as that of Ibsen.

Gropper's immediate subject is political oratory and its lack of meaning. To understand what is going on, observe first the curving step at the lower right-hand corner of the picture. It indicates one of the rising curved platforms that form the amphitheater on which the Senatorial desks are placed. In reality all of these desks are identical, and the Senate chamber is in fact arranged in a carefully symmetrical way, the universal way for arranging space and furniture in places of public importance and dignity. But Gropper has given the desks different colors and different shapes, and he has turned the chairs of the Senators every which way. By the way he presents a random section of the Chamber from an odd angle and by what he has done to the furniture, Gropper has reduced order and dignity to confusion.

Why are there only four senators in the chamber? Is the senator speaking engaged in a filibuster? Whatever his purpose, he is using the most forceful and exaggerated oratorical gestures possible. He has a low brow, a flat head, and a big stomach, indicating a life of self-indulgence. What impression does his appearance make on you? One very old senator is listening. Do you think he is impressed? What does his posture suggest about his interest? Another, younger, senator is present. How much attention is he giving the speaker? Is he more or less intelligent than the speaker? What clues does Gropper give you?

The overall impression is that the orating senator is engaging in some kind of pointless and meaningless activity. Is the purpose of such activity to deceive? Is he only deceiving the public, or is he also deceiving himself? Which is worse? The general effect of the color is a dreary drabness; even the blues are grayish and washed out. Thus Gropper suggests that the real life of the nation, whatever it is, is not here.

We see the tops of the desks and the seats of the chairs because we are viewing the scene from the public gallery. Gropper's picture suggests that the public has arrived at a different view of the Senate from what it had in the past or from what it is supposed to have. Or is Gropper suggesting that this is the way a certain kind of oratory should be viewed?

MORSE PECKHAM

Ode on a Grecian Urn

JOHN KEATS

Whatever truth is — and however difficult it may be to discover — it is clearly of the most profound importance in man's life and attitudes. But how is truth to be defined? One celebrated definition occurs at the end of the following ode by the English poet John Keats. (An ode, incidentally, is a lyric poem that deals with a serious subject in dignified language and with nobility of feeling.) Keats' "Ode on a Grecian Urn" was inspired by his study of Greek sculpture and artifacts in the British Museum, among which might have been such a pictorial urn, or vase, as the one he addresses here.

Thou still unravished bride of quietness,
   Thou foster child of silence and slow time,
Sylvan historian, who canst thus express
   A flowery tale more sweetly than our rhyme:
What leaf-fringed legend haunts about thy shape   5
   Of deities or mortals, or of both,
      In Tempe* or the dales of Arcady?*
   What men or gods are these? What maidens loath?*
What mad pursuit? What struggle to escape?
      What pipes and timbrels?* What wild ecstasy? 10

Heard melodies are sweet, but those unheard
   Are sweeter; therefore, ye soft pipes, play on;
Not to the sensual ear, but, more endeared,
   Pipe to the spirit ditties of no tone.
Fair youth, beneath the trees, thou canst not leave   15
   Thy song, nor ever can those trees be bare;
      Bold lover, never, never canst thou kiss,
Though winning near the goal — yet, do not grieve;
      She cannot fade, though thou hast not thy bliss,
Forever wilt thou love, and she be fair!   20

Ah, happy, happy boughs; that cannot shed
   Your leaves, nor ever bid the spring adieu;
And, happy melodist, unwearièd,
   Forever piping songs forever new;
More happy love! more happy, happy love!   25
   Forever warm and still to be enjoyed,
      Forever panting, and forever young;

7. **Tempe:** valley near Mount Olympus. **Arcady:** Arcadia, renowned for its simple, happy way of life. 8. **loath:** unwilling. 10. **timbrels:** tambourines.

"What leaf-fringed legend haunts about thy shape . . . ?" An ancient Grecian urn like the ones Keats would have seen in the British Museum.

All breathing human passion far above,
    That leaves a heart high-sorrowful and cloyed,*
        A burning forehead, and a parching tongue.   30

Who are these coming to the sacrifice?
    To what green altar, O mysterious priest,
Lead'st thou that heifer* lowing at the skies,
    And all her silken flanks with garlands dressed?
What little town by river or sea shore,   35
    Or mountain-built with peaceful citadel,
    Is emptied of this folk, this pious morn?
And, little town, thy streets for evermore
    Will silent be; and not a soul to tell
        Why thou art desolate, can e'er return.   40

O Attic* shape! Fair attitude! with brede*
    Of marble men and maidens overwrought,

29. **cloyed:** oversatisfied and repulsed with too much sweetness. 33. **heifer:** young cow. 41. **Attic:** characteristic of Athens. **brede:** design.

With forest branches and the trodden weed;
  Thou, silent form, dost tease us out of thought
As doth eternity. Cold pastoral!*   45
  When old age shall this generation waste,*
    Thou shalt remain, in midst of other woe
  Than ours, a friend to man, to whom thou say'st,
"Beauty is truth, truth beauty — that is all
    Ye know on earth, and all ye need to know."   50

45. **Cold pastoral:** refers to the scene on the urn of shepherds or country life (pastoral) where existence is perfect, frozen, not alive, and thus cold. 46. **waste:** lay waste.

For Discussion

1. Before appreciating a poem adequately, it is necessary to comprehend it, and comprehension is first of all a matter of knowing what the words mean. In Keats' poem what does "loath" (line 8) mean? What is a "heifer" (line 33)? A "garland" (line 34)? A "citadel" (line 36)? Line 28 rendered in prose would put the preposition *above* before its object. What, specifically, is above all human passion?

2. Describe the scenes that are presented on the vase. Be precise; for example, is the "little town" (line 35) pictured there? How do you know?

3. Lines 13–14 imply a contrast between two worlds — the world of the senses on the one hand, and the world of the spirit on the other. Notice that the two scenes depicted on the vase correspond to those two worlds — the religious sacrifice, and the "wild ecstasy" of the pursuit of maidens by their lovers. Even though the lover will never reach his goal of kissing the maiden, why should he not grieve (line 18)? In what sense are the boughs, the melodist, and the lovers of stanza 3 happy?

4. In understanding the final lines of the poem, it is important to notice who is speaking to whom and in what context. In the first eight lines of the last stanza, the speaker in the poem addresses the urn, and the final two lines are presented as if they were spoken by the urn. It is also important to remember the contrast that has been drawn in the poem between human life and life as depicted on the urn. What part of that contrast is stressed in lines 46–48? The urn is a work of art, and when it speaks, it speaks of life as depicted in a work of art. What qualities does that life possess? In what sense can it be called true as well as beautiful? In what sense can the urn be called "a friend to man" (line 48)?

5. **Diction.** *Diction* refers to the choice of individual words by means of which thought is expressed. In line 2, Keats refers to the urn as a *"foster* child of silence and slow time." The word is carefully chosen to convey a subtle distinction accurately. Silence and time might together produce, say, Mount Everest, and looking at such a feat, the poet might well address the mountain as "Thou child of silence and slow time." But the urn is only a foster child of those two. Who is its true parent? Select one other distinctive use of diction in the poem and discuss its effectiveness; you might find it helpful to consider alternatives that the poet might have chosen instead of the word he did select.

For Composition

● **Exposition.** In the second and third stanzas of the poem, the speaker contrasts actual human existence with life as it appears on the urn. What are the differences between those two forms of existence — their advantages and disadvantages? Explain the contrast that is expressed in those two stanzas.

About the Poet. The son of a livery-stable keeper, **John Keats** (1795–1821) trained for a career in surgery but at an early age was diverted from it by his love of poetry. Before he was twenty he had written "On First Looking into Chapman's Homer," generally regarded as one of the finest sonnets in English. Many of his poems reflect his concern with what one critic has called "the tension between the ideal and the actual." Although he found much joy in life, he was constantly threatened by poverty and incurable illness. Before his death at the age of twenty-five, Keats despaired of his ambition to be a great poet, and he requested that on his gravestone be inscribed these words: "Here lies one whose name was writ in water." But in his despair Keats was mistaken. Although he had barely begun his poetic career when he died, he is regarded as one of the greatest English poets.

The Allegory of the Cave

PLATO

One of the most influential discussions concerning the nature of truth occurs in Plato's *Republic*, a dialogue — or conversation — between the Greek philosopher Socrates and a small group of Athenian citizens, including one named Glaucon, sometime in the fourth century B.C. Plato presents the dialogue as having taken place at a house near Athens, and Socrates himself tells others the following day about what was said there. The conversation had ranged over many subjects, beginning with a discussion of old age, moving on to a definition of justice, evolving a concept of the ideal state — a republic — under which citizens could live most advantageously, and delving into a consideration of the best sort of education for the individual in that state. During the course of the dialogue, at the beginning of Book VII in this work of ten books, or chapters, occurs the following allegory or parable.

Next, said I, here is a parable to illustrate the degrees in which our nature may be enlightened or unenlightened. Imagine the condition of men living in a sort of cavernous chamber underground, with an entrance open to the light and a long passage all down the cave. Here they have been from childhood, chained by the leg and also

"The Allegory of the Cave," from *The Republic of Plato*, translated by F. M. Cornford. Oxford University Press, 1945. Reprinted by permission.

by the neck, so that they cannot move and can see only what is in front of them, because the chains will not let them turn their heads. At some distance higher up is the light of a fire burning behind them; and between the prisoners and the fire is a track with a parapet[1] built along it, like the screen at a puppet show, which hides the performers while they show their puppets over the top.

I see, said he.

Now behind this parapet imagine persons carrying along various artificial objects, including figures of men and animals in wood or stone or other materials, which project above the parapet. Naturally, some of these persons will be talking, others silent.

It is a strange picture, he said, and a strange sort of prisoners.

Like ourselves, I replied; for in the first place prisoners so confined would have seen nothing of themselves or of one another, except the shadows thrown by the firelight

[1] **parapet**: wall.

on the wall of the Cave facing them, would they?

Not if all their lives they had been prevented from moving their heads.

And they would have seen as little of the objects carried past.

Of course.

Now, if they could talk to one another, would they not suppose that their words referred only to those passing shadows which they saw?

Necessarily.

And suppose their prison had an echo from the wall facing them? When one of the people crossing behind them spoke, they could only suppose that the sound came from the shadow passing before their eyes.

No doubt.

In every way, then, such prisoners would recognize as reality nothing but the shadows of those artificial objects.

Inevitably.

Now consider what would happen if their release from the chains and the healing of

ABOUT THE AUTHOR • Living his first twenty-three years in an atmosphere of war only to see his native Athens conquered by the Peloponnesians, **Plato** (427–347? B.C.) had great faith in the new democracy that followed the truce. But when his friend and teacher, Socrates, called "the wisest man in Greece" by the Delphic oracle, was put on trial on the charge of impiety and condemned to die, the disillusioned Plato declared, "The only hope of finding justice for society or for the individual lies in true philosophy; mankind will have no respite from trouble until either real philosophers gain political power or politicians become by some miracle true philosophers." The Republic presents Plato's conception of the ideal state. Like most of his philosophical works, it is in the form of a dialogue. Plato believed that truths about the nature of justice, honor, wisdom, and the good life could best be learned through the interaction of men reasoning together. So successful was he in exploring these truths that all philosophy since his time has been called "a footnote to Plato."

their unwisdom should come about in this way. Suppose one of them set free and forced suddenly to stand up, turn his head, and walk with eyes lifted to the light; all these movements would be painful, and he would be too dazzled to make out the objects whose shadows he had been used to see. What do you think he would say, if someone told him that what he had formerly seen was meaningless illusion, but now, being somewhat nearer to reality and turned towards more real objects, he was getting a truer view? Suppose further that he were shown the various objects being carried by and were made to say, in reply to questions, what each of them was. Would he not be perplexed and believe the objects now shown him to be not so real as what he formerly saw?

Yes, not nearly so real.

And if he were forced to look at the firelight itself, would not his eyes ache, so that he would try to escape and turn back to the things which he could see distinctly, convinced that they really were clearer than these other objects now being shown to him?

Yes.

And suppose someone were to drag him away forcibly up the steep and rugged ascent and not let him go until he had hauled him out into the sunlight, would he not suffer pain and vexation at such treatment, and, when he had come out into the light, find his eyes so full of its radiance that he could not see a single one of the things that he was now told were real?

Certainly he would not see them all at once.

He would need, then, to grow accustomed before he could see things in that upper world. At first it would be easiest to make out shadows, and then the images of men and things reflected in water, and later on the things themselves. After that,

One of the greatest pains to human nature is the pain of a new idea.
— Walter Bagehot

it would be easier to watch the heavenly bodies and the sky itself by night, looking at the light of the moon and stars rather than the Sun and the Sun's light in the daytime.

Yes, surely.

Last of all, he would be able to look at the Sun and contemplate its nature, not as it appears when reflected in water or any alien medium, but as it is in itself in its own domain.

No doubt.

And now he would begin to draw the conclusion that it is the Sun that produces the seasons and the course of the year and controls everything in the visible world, and moreover is in a way the cause of all that he and his companions used to see.

Clearly he would come at last to that conclusion.

Then if he called to mind his fellow prisoners and what passed for wisdom in his former dwelling place, he would surely think himself happy in the change and be sorry for them. They may have had a practice of honoring and commending one another, with prizes for the man who had the keenest eye for the passing shadows and the best memory for the order in which they followed or accompanied one another, so that he could make a good guess as to which was going to come next. Would our released prisoner be likely to covet those prizes or to envy the men exalted to honor and power in the Cave? Would he not feel like Homer's Achilles, that he would far sooner "be on earth as a hired servant in the house of a landless man" or endure anything rather than go back to his old beliefs and live in the old way?

Yes, he would prefer any fate to such a life.

Now imagine what would happen if he went down again to take his former seat in the Cave. Coming suddenly out of the sunlight, his eyes would be filled with darkness. He might be required once more to deliver his opinion on those shadows, in competition with the prisoners who had never been released, while his eyesight was still dim and unsteady; and it might take some time to become used to the darkness. They would laugh at him and say that he had gone up only to come back with his sight ruined; it was worth no one's while even to attempt the ascent. If they could lay hands on the man who was trying to set them free and lead them up, they would kill him.

Yes, they would.

Every feature in this parable, my dear Glaucon, is meant to fit our earlier analysis. The prison dwelling corresponds to the region revealed to us through the sense of sight, and the firelight within it to the power of the Sun. The ascent to see the things in the upper world you may take as standing for the upward journey of the soul into the region of the intelligible; then you will be in possession of what I surmise, since that is what you wish to be told. Heaven knows whether it is true; but this, at any rate, is how it appears to me. In the world of knowledge, the last thing to be perceived and only with great difficulty is the essential[1] Form of Goodness. Once it is perceived, the conclusion must follow that, for all things, this is the cause of whatever is

[1] essential: *here*, basic.

right and good; in the visible world it gives birth to light and to the lord of light, while it is itself sovereign in the intelligible world and the parent of intelligence and truth. Without having had a vision of this Form no one can act with wisdom, either in his own life or in matters of state.

So far as I can understand, I share your belief.

Then you may also agree that it is no wonder if those who have reached this height are reluctant to manage the affairs of men. Their souls long to spend all their time in that upper world — naturally enough, if here once more our parable holds true. Nor, again, is it at all strange that one who comes from the contemplation of divine things to the miseries of human life should appear awkward and ridiculous when, with eyes still dazed and not yet accustomed to the darkness, he is compelled, in a law court or elsewhere, to dispute about the shadows of justice or the images that cast those shadows, and to wrangle over the notions of what is right in the minds of men who have never beheld Justice itself.

It is not at all strange.

No; a sensible man will remember that the eyes may be confused in two ways — by a change from light to darkness or from darkness to light; and he will recognize that the same thing happens to the soul. When he sees it troubled and unable to discern anything clearly, instead of laughing thoughtlessly, he will ask whether, coming from a brighter existence, its unaccustomed vision is obscured by the darkness, in which case he will think its condition enviable and its life a happy one; or whether, emerging from the depths of ignorance, it is dazzled by excess of light. If so, he will rather feel sorry for it; or, if he were inclined to laugh, that would be less ridiculous than to laugh at the soul which has come down from the light.

That is a fair statement.

For Discussion

1. "It is a strange picture," says Glaucon to Socrates, "and a strange sort of prisoners." How long have the prisoners been in the cave? They are chained. About what parts of the body? For what purpose? There is a fire in the cave. Where is it in relation to the prisoners? What stands between the fire and the prisoners? Which way are the prisoners facing? What do they see before them? What do they imagine they see?

2. What would happen if the prisoners in the cave were released? Suppose one cave dweller escaped and adjusted his eyes so that he could see the outside world. What would be his attitude toward prisoners still in the cave? What would be the consequences of his returning to the cave after having accustomed himself to the light outside?

3. To such people as those prisoners in the cave — and they are, Socrates says, "like ourselves" — truth is nothing but the shadows of the images, or puppets, being held up behind the wall. The entire cave allegory is, in fact, a kind of extended metaphor, in which comparisons are made between dissimilar things. All of us are compared to prisoners. To what is the cave being compared in the metaphor? What do the shadows on the cave represent? Later in the parable, what does the ascent to the mouth of the cave and sunlight correspond to? What does the sun itself stand for?

For Composition

In describing a place, you will find it helpful to station yourself mentally at some vantage point in relation to that place, then proceed with your description in a logical manner — building up to the most important of the objects being described, for example, or moving systematically from left to right or from foreground to background. A logical movement will help your reader visualize what you are describing (and after all, the purpose of your composition is in large part to communicate with a reader). You will help him further if you keep in mind and make use of relevant transitional expressions — *behind, before, above, below, in the foreground, beside,* and the like.

1. **Description.** Carefully reread the description of the cave and the prisoners within it. Picture the details in your mind, and continue rereading until the details are firmly established and the picture is in sharp focus. Then, without referring back to Plato's description, undertake to describe the scene as you visualize it. See if you can make your description as comprehensive as his — and perhaps even clearer.

2. **Analysis.** In a paragraph or two, indicate ways in which the allegory of the cave corresponds to the world all of us live in. Examine the allegory as thoroughly as possible within reasonable limits.

Words and Allusions

ALLUSIONS. An allusion is a brief reference to a specific person, place, thing, or event that a writer or speaker assumes will be recognized by his audience. Our use of language can be greatly enlarged by the use of allusions because they enable us in a brief space to call to mind a large body of material. To be effective, the allusion must be recognized by the reader or listener, and what it refers to must be understood.

Allusions appear in many parts of speech. For example, the noun *Platonist* refers to someone who views the world as Plato did. On the basis of what you have read, what would *Platonist* mean? The adjective *platonic* also contains an allusion. You have probably heard of *platonic love.* What kind of relationship does this term describe? What other characteristics would you associate with the adjective *platonic?*

WORD ROOTS. Plato wrote in the form of the dialogue. What are the roots (page 14) of the word *dialogue?* The following words are derived from the same roots: *monologue, loquacious, colloquial, interlocutor.* What do these words mean? Write a sentence for each to illustrate its meaning.

Appearance and Reality

There are concepts so vast that in Keats' memorable words they "tease us out of thought." The mind cannot actually grasp them. Eternity, as "Ode on a Grecian Urn" suggests, is one such concept. How long is eternity? Imagine, with a character in one of James Joyce's novels, a mountain of sand a million miles high and a million miles wide. Once every million years a little bird comes and takes away one single grain of sand. How long would it take to remove the whole mountain? And yet, Joyce writes, "at the end of that immense stretch of time not even one instant of eternity could be said to have ended."

Infinity is another such concept. How far is infinity? The telescope at Palomar Observatory in California has photographed objects that are two billion light-years away. But before one can absorb that piece of information, he must realize that a light-year is about six trillion miles. And that is not the end. The mind moves out beyond our own huge galaxy, past millions of other galaxies, each with its billions of stars, on into dark space, toward the edge of the universe — and yet there is no edge, no end, no end at all.

Whereas eternity and infinity stagger the mind by the extent of time and space, reality teases us by its complexity. What is reality? (Or, much the same thing: what is truth?) At first the question seems easy enough. Reality is what we can see and touch and taste and hear and smell. Hit a desk top hard with your fist if you doubt that the desk is real. A particular desk feels real enough, and so does a book, a cup, a wheel.

Yet, according to Plato (In Book IV of the *Republic*, just before "The Allegory of the Cave") such objects are not real at all. Why, you might ask, is a desk not real? Because once that desk was a tree, then it was pieces of lumber, and in time it will rot and disintegrate and be nothing at all. How can such a changing, perishing quantity be real? So with a cup that will break, and a wheel that will crumble, and a book that will yellow and mildew. So with all the multitudes of objects that surround us.

What, then, is real? Only the *idea* of a cup is real, said Plato, whereas all the cups that have ever been actually shaped on the potter's wheel are only imperfect copies of that reality. At one time they did not exist at all, and at some time in the future they will once more cease to be. But the *idea* of a cup exists forever.

So with a desk. There are big desks and little desks, rolltops and flattops, Chippendales and Hepplewhites, but all of them are only transient approximations of the eternal idea of a desk. So with wheels — little wheels in watches, big wheels on tractors, wagon wheels, bicycle wheels, wheels in pulleys — all pass away, but the idea of a wheel remains. The idea is eternal. Thus only the idea is real.

Plato's view of reality draws a sharp distinction between what is real and what is unreal, and this view has had an enormous influence in western culture, especially in religious thought. Why should we concern ourselves with the aches and pains of this transient life, the traditional Christian asks, when reality is to be found elsewhere — in a life hereafter? Plato's view is also seen in a slightly different form in Keats' "Ode on a Grecian Urn," where human passion, the burning forehead, the parching tongue, are presented as less real than the enduring beauty of life as depicted on the urn.

But in our own experience we do not usually observe such sharp distinctions. We cannot deny the evidence of our senses, and indeed it can be dangerous to do so. For instance, we might get burned or frostbitten. Yet we must go beyond evidence of the senses if we are to see the complexity of reality. Experience reveals at least two levels of reality. The world of physical objects we regard as real because we perceive it through our senses. Yet behind the surface of that changing world lies an imperceptible world of ideas that often contradict what our senses tell us.

Appearances can deceive. When Arnold looked toward the coast of France across calm waters that lapped the beach at Dover (page 23), his senses revealed to him a world of peace and beauty. But underneath that dreamlike surface he discovered another reality — a world without joy or love or light, "Where ignorant armies clash by night." And Goodman Brown (page 26), after his fateful night in the forest, saw a reality quite different from what he saw on the surface, and heard words different from those holy ones the congregation sang on the Sabbath day. Both were looking — so they thought — at naked truth, and in neither case did it correspond to the surface appearance of things.

It was those surface appearances that Plato saw as merely shadows of puppets cast by firelight upon the walls of a dark cave. Through that image he indicates that man's vision is faulty, that he sees only the external appearances of things and not their true nature. Although we might not accept every detail of Plato's vision, we can recognize the deceptiveness of appearances and the unseen reality that often lurks beneath. As we do so, we become aware of the complexity of the question "What is reality?" And we are better able to appreciate the efforts of poets, painters, and other artists to answer that question.

1. Examine your own concept of reality. To what extent is it based on your own experience? How is "reality" affected by personal experience?

2. What do we usually mean by the terms *idealist* and *realist*? How does the idealist's concept of reality differ from that of the realist? Do ideas have any effect on reality?

FROM

Don Quixote

MIGUEL DE CERVANTES

Chivalry is dead. It had already been dead a long while when the Spaniard Miguel de Cervantes, an impoverished ex-soldier in his late fifties, published his novel *Don Quixote* early in the seventeenth century. That novel was destined to become the most celebrated work in Spanish literature and — with the exception of the Bible — the most widely translated book in all the world.

Don Quixote is a long book that deals with the values of chivalry while rambling genially and endearingly over much of the Spanish countryside, through a world full of incident and adventure that is amply populated by unforgettable people from Dukes and Duchesses down to the humblest swineherds. Humor and wisdom fill its pages, and hardly a dull passage is to be encountered from beginning to end.

The novel starts this way.

In a village of La Mancha the name of which I have no desire to recall, there lived not so long ago one of those gentlemen who always have a lance in the rack, an ancient buckler,[1] a skinny nag, and a greyhound for the chase. A stew with more beef than mutton in it, chopped meat for his evening meal, scraps for a Saturday, lentils[2] on Friday, and a young pigeon as a special delicacy for Sunday, went to account for three-quarters of his income. The rest of it he laid out on a broadcloth greatcoat and velvet stockings for feast days, with slippers to match, while the other days of the week he cut a figure in a suit of the finest homespun. Living with him were a housekeeper in her forties, a niece who was not yet twenty, and a lad of the field and market place who saddled his horse for him and wielded the pruning knife.

Don Quixote: pronounced dōn kē·hō′tä (in Spanish); don kwik′sət (in English).

[1] **buckler:** small, round shield.
[2] **lentils:** edible pealike seeds.

This gentleman of ours was close on to fifty, of a robust constitution but with little flesh on his bones and a face that was lean and gaunt. He was noted for his early rising, being very fond of the hunt. They will try to tell you that his surname was Quijada or Quesada — there is some difference of opinion among those who have written on the subject — but according to the most likely conjectures we are to understand that it was really Quejana. But all this means very little so far as our story is concerned, providing that in the telling of it we do not depart one iota from the truth.

You may know, then, that the aforesaid gentleman, on those occasions when he was at leisure, which was most of the year around, was in the habit of reading books of chivalry with such pleasure and devotion as to lead him almost wholly to forget the life of a hunter and even the administration of his estate. So great was his curiosity and infatuation in this regard that he even sold many acres of tillable land in order to be able to buy and read the books that he loved, and he would carry home with him as many of them as he could obtain. . . .

In short, our gentleman became so immersed in his reading that he spent whole nights from sundown to sunup and his days from dawn to dusk in poring over his books, until, finally, from so little sleeping and so much reading, his brain dried up and he went completely out of his mind. He had filled his imagination with everything that he had read, with enchantments, knightly encounters, battles, challenges, wounds, with tales of love and its torments, and all sorts of impossible things, and as a result had come to believe that all these fictitious happenings were true; they were more real to him than anything else in the world. He would remark that the Cid Ruy Diaz had been a very good knight, but there was no comparison between him and the Knight of the Flaming Sword, who with a single backward stroke had cut in half two fierce and monstrous giants. He preferred Bernardo del Carpio, who at Roncesvalles had slain Roland despite the charm the latter bore, availing himself of the stratagem which Hercules employed when he strangled Antaeus, the son of Earth, in his arms.

He had much good to say for Morgante who, though he belonged to the haughty, overbearing race of giants, was of an affable disposition and well brought up. But, above all, he cherished an admiration for Rinaldo of Montalbán,[1] especially as he beheld him sallying forth from his castle to rob all those that crossed his path, or when he thought of him overseas stealing the image of Mohammed which, so the story has it, was all of gold. And he would have liked very well to have had his fill of kicking that traitor Galalón,[2] a privilege for which he would have given his housekeeper with his niece thrown into the bargain.

[1] **Rinaldo of Montalbán:** a character from Matteo Maria Boiardo's *Orlando Innamorato.*
[2] **Galalón:** more commonly, Ganelon; traitor of the Charlemagne legend.

At last, when his wits were gone beyond repair, he came to conceive the strangest idea that ever occurred to any madman in this world. It now appeared to him fitting and necessary, in order to win a greater amount of honor for himself and serve his country at the same time, to become a knight-errant and roam the world on horseback, in a suit of armor; he would go in quest of adventures by way of putting into practice all that he had read in his books; he would right every manner of wrong, placing himself in situations of the greatest peril such as would redound to the eternal glory of his name. As a reward for his valor and the might of his arm, the poor fellow could already see himself crowned Emperor of

". . . our gentleman became so immersed in his reading. . . ." Don Quixote, *by Francisco Goya.*

Trebizond[1] at the very least; and so, carried away by the strange pleasure that he found in such thoughts as these, he at once set about putting his plan into effect.

The first thing he did was to burnish up some old pieces of armor, left him by his great-grandfather, which for ages had lain in a corner, moldering and forgotten. He polished and adjusted them as best he could, and then he noticed that one very important thing was lacking: there was no closed helmet, but only a morion, or visorless headpiece, with turned up brim of the kind foot soldiers wore. His ingenuity, however, enabled him to remedy this, and he proceeded to fashion out of cardboard a kind of half-helmet, which, when attached to the morion, gave the appearance of a whole one. True, when he went to see if it was strong enough to withstand a good slashing blow, he was somewhat disappointed; for when he drew his sword and gave it a couple of thrusts, he succeeded only in undoing a whole week's labor. The ease with which he had hewed it

to bits disturbed him no little, and he decided to make it over. This time he placed a few strips of iron on the inside, and then, convinced that it was strong enough, refrained from putting it to any further test; instead, he adopted it then and there as the finest helmet ever made.

After this, he went out to have a look at his nag; and although the animal had more *cuartos*, or cracks, in its hoof than there are quarters in a real,[2] and more blemishes than Gonela's[3] steed which *tantum pellis et ossa fuit*,[4] it nonetheless looked to its master like a far better horse than Alexander's Bucephalus or the Babieca of the Cid. He spent all of four days in trying to think up a name for his mount; for — so he told himself — seeing that it belonged to so famous and worthy a knight, there was no reason why it should not have a name of equal renown. The kind of name he wanted was one that would at once indicate what the nag had been before it came to belong to a knight-

---

[1] **Trebizond:** prosperous Byzantine port, taken by the Crusaders in 1204.

[2] **than . . . real:** (rā·äl′; *pl.*, rā·äl′ās) Spanish coins; the real is worth eight quarters.
[3] **Gonela:** famous Italian court jester.
[4] *tantum . . . fuit:* was all skin and bones.

ABOUT THE AUTHOR • **Miguel de Cervantes** (1547–1616), a contemporary of Shakespeare and Montaigne, was Spain's greatest author. As a young soldier he fought at Lepanto, Tunis, Naples, and Palermo. Captured by Barbary pirates in 1575, he was sold into slavery, which he endured until his escape five years later. For the next twenty-five years Cervantes sank deeper and deeper into poverty while he tried to make a living as a writer, tax collector, and businessman. During those years he was often in trouble with the civil authorities or with the Inquisition. It was while serving jail sentences in 1597 and 1602 that he is said to have conceived of the famous Don Quixote, who often resembles his creator. Cervantes was nearly sixty when he published *The Adventures of Don Quixote*, the novel that made him famous.

errant and what its present status was; for it stood to reason that, when the master's worldly condition changed, his horse also ought to have a famous, high-sounding appellation, one suited to the new order of things and the new profession that it was to follow.

After he in his memory and imagination had made up, struck out, and discarded many names, now adding to and now subtracting from the list, he finally hit upon "Rocinante,"[1] a name that impressed him as being sonorous and at the same time indicative of what the steed had been when it was but a hack, whereas now it was nothing other than the first and foremost of all the hacks in the world.

Having found a name for his horse that pleased his fancy, he then desired to do as much for himself, and this required another week, and by the end of that period he had made up his mind that he was henceforth to be known as Don Quixote, which, as has been stated, has led the authors of this veracious history to asume that his real name must undoubtedly have been Quijada, and not Quesada as others would have it. But remembering that the valiant Amadis was not content to call himself that and nothing more, but added the name of his kingdom and fatherland that he might make it famous also, and thus came to take the name Amadis of Gaul, so our good knight chose to add his place of origin and become "Don Quixote de la Mancha"; for by this means, as he saw it, he was making very plain his lineage and was conferring honor upon his country by taking its name as his own.

And so, having polished up his armor and made the morion over into a closed helmet, and having given himself and his horse a

name, he naturally found but one thing lacking still: he must seek out a lady of whom he could become enamored; for a knight-errant without a ladylove was like a tree without leaves or fruit, a body without a soul.

"If," he said to himself, "as a punishment for my sins or by a stroke of fortune I should come upon some giant hereabouts, a thing that very commonly happens to knights-errant, and if I should slay him in a hand-to-hand encounter or perhaps cut him in two, or finally, if I should vanquish and subdue him, would it not be well to have someone to whom I may send him as a present, in order that he, if he is living, may come in, fall upon his knees in front of my sweet lady, and say in a humble and submissive tone of voice, 'I, lady, am the giant Caraculiambro, lord of the island Malindrania, who has been overcome in single combat by that knight who never can be praised enough, Don Quixote de la Mancha, the same who sent me to present myself before your Grace that your Highness may dispose of me as you see fit'?"

Oh, how our good knight reveled in this speech, and more than ever when he came to think of the name that he should give his lady! As the story goes, there was a very good-looking farm girl who lived near by, with whom he had once been smitten, although it is generally believed that she never knew or suspected it. Her name was Aldonza Lorenzo, and it seemed to him that she was the one upon whom he should bestow the title of mistress of his thoughts. For her he wished a name that should not be incongruous with his own and that would convey the suggestion of a princess or a great lady; and, accordingly, he resolved to

[1] **Rocinante** (rōth·ē·nän′tā; ròs′ə·nan′tē): from the Spanish *rocin* meaning "hack" and *ante* meaning "before"; thus, literally, "once a hack (old, worn-out horse)."

call her "Dulcinea[1] del Toboso," she being a native of that place. A musical name to his ears, out of the ordinary and significant, like the others he had chosen for himself and his appurtenances.[2]

Having, then, made all these preparations, he did not wish to lose any time in putting his plan into effect, for he could not but blame himself for what the world was losing by his delay, so many were the wrongs that were to be righted, the grievances to be redressed,[3] the abuses to be done away with, and the duties to be performed. Accordingly, without informing anyone of his intention and without letting anyone see him, he set out one morning before daybreak on one of those very hot days in July. Donning all his armor, mounting Rocinante, adjusting his ill-contrived helmet, bracing his shield on his arm, and taking up his lance, he sallied forth by the back gate of his stable yard into the open countryside. It was with great contentment and joy that he saw how easily he had made a beginning toward the fulfillment of his desire.

No sooner was he out on the plain, however, than a terrible thought assailed him, one that all but caused him to abandon the enterprise he had undertaken. This occurred when he suddenly remembered that he had never formally been dubbed a knight, and so, in accordance with the law of knighthood, was not permitted to bear arms against one who had a right to that title. And even if he had been, as a novice knight he would have had to wear white armor, without any device on his shield, until he should have earned one by his exploits. These thoughts led him to waver in his purpose, but, madness prevailing over reason, he resolved to have himself knighted by the first person he met, as many others had done if what he had read in those books that he had at home was true. And so far as white armor was concerned, he would scour his own the first chance that offered until it shone whiter than any ermine. With this he became more tranquil and continued on his way, letting his horse take whatever path it chose, for he believed that therein lay the very essence of adventures. . . .

He rode slowly, and the sun came up so swiftly and with so much heat that it would have been sufficient to melt his brains if he had had any. He had been on the road almost the entire day without anything happening that is worthy of being set down here; and he was on the verge of despair, for he wished to meet someone at once with whom he might try the valor of his good right arm. Certain authors say that his first adventure was that of Puerto Lápice, while others state that it was that of the windmills; but in this particular instance I am in a position to affirm what I have read in the annals[4] of La Mancha; and that is to the effect that he went all that day until nightfall, when he and his hack found themselves tired to death and famished. Gazing all around him to see if he could discover some castle or shepherd's hut where he might take shelter and attend to his pressing needs, he caught sight of an inn not far off the road along which they were traveling, and this to him was like a star guiding him not merely to the gates, but rather, let us say, to the palace of redemption. Quickening his pace, he came up to it just as night was falling.

By chance there stood in the doorway two lasses of the sort known as "of the district"; they were on their way to Seville in the company of some mule drivers who were spending the night in the inn. Now, everything that this adventurer of ours thought, saw, or imagined seemed to him to

---

[1] **Dulcinea** (dŭl·thē·nā′ä; dŭl·sin′ē·ä): from *dulce* meaning "sweet."

[2] **appurtenances**: gear.

[3] **redressed**: corrected and compensated for.

[4] **annals**: historical records.

be directly out of one of the storybooks he had read, and so, when he caught sight of the inn, it at once became a castle with its four turrets[1] and its pinnacles[2] of gleaming silver, not to speak of the drawbridge and moat and all the other things that are commonly supposed to go with a castle. As he rode up to it, he accordingly reined in Rocinante and sat there waiting for a dwarf to appear upon the battlements and blow his trumpet by way of announcing the arrival of a knight. The dwarf, however, was slow in coming, and as Rocinante was anxious to reach the stable, Don Quixote drew up to the door of the hostelry[3] and surveyed the two merry maidens, who to him were a pair of beauteous damsels or gracious ladies taking their ease at the castle gate.

And then a swineherd came along, engaged in rounding up his drove of hogs — for, without any apology, that is what they were. He gave a blast on his horn to bring them together, and this at once became for Don Quixote just what he wished it to be: some dwarf who was heralding his coming; and so it was with a vast deal of satisfaction that he presented himself before the ladies in question, who, upon beholding a man in full armor like this, with lance and buckler, were filled with fright and made as if to flee indoors. Realizing that they were afraid, Don Quixote raised his pasteboard visor and revealed his withered, dust-covered face.

"Do not flee, your Ladyships," he said to them in a courteous manner and gentle voice. "You need not fear that any wrong will be done you, for it is not in accordance with the order of knighthood which I profess to wrong anyone, much less such highborn damsels as your appearance shows you to be."

The girls looked at him, endeavoring to scan his face, which was half hidden by his ill-made visor. Never having heard women of their profession called damsels before, they were unable to restrain their laughter, at which Don Quixote took offense.

"Modesty," he observed, "well becomes those with the dower of beauty, and, moreover, laughter that has not good cause is a very foolish thing. But I do not say this to be discourteous or to hurt your feelings; my only desire is to serve you."

The ladies did not understand what he was talking about, but felt more than ever like laughing at our knight's unprepossessing figure. This increased his annoyance, and there is no telling what would have happened if at that moment the innkeeper had not come out. He was very fat and very peaceably inclined; but upon sighting this grotesque personage clad in bits of armor that were quite oddly matched as were his bridle, lance, buckler, and corselet,[4] mine host was not at all indisposed to join the lasses in their merriment. He was suspicious, however, of all this paraphernalia and decided that it would be better to keep a civil tongue in his head.

"If, Sir Knight," he said, "your Grace desires a lodging, aside from a bed — for there is none to be had in this inn — you will find all else that you may want in great abundance."

When Don Quixote saw how humble the governor of the castle was — for he took the innkeeper and his inn to be no less than that — he replied, "For me, Sir Castellan,[5] anything will do, since

Arms are my only ornament,
My only rest the fight, etc."

The landlord thought that the knight had called him a castellan because he took him for one of those worthies of Castile,[6]

---

[1] **turrets**: towers.
[2] **pinnacles**: spires.
[3] **hostelry**: inn.

[4] **corselet**: armor for the body.
[5] **Sir Castellan**: "Castellan" means keeper of a castle.
[6] **Castile**: former kingdom of central Spain.

whereas the truth was, he was an Andalusian from the beach of Sanlúcar, no less a thief than Cacus[1] himself, and as full of tricks as a student or a page boy.

"In that case," he said,

"Your bed will be the solid rock,
Your sleep: to watch all night.

This being so, you may be assured of finding beneath this roof enough to keep you awake for a whole year, to say nothing of a single night."

With this, he went up to hold the stirrup for Don Quixote, who encountered much difficulty in dismounting, not having broken his fast all day long. The knight then directed his host to take good care of the steed, as it was the best piece of horseflesh in all the world. The innkeeper looked it over, and it did not impress him as being half as good as Don Quixote had said it was. Having stabled the animal, he came back to see what his guest would have and found the latter being relieved of his armor by the damsels, who by now had made their peace with the new arrival. They had already removed his breastplate and backpiece but had no idea how they were going to open his gorget[2] or get his improvised helmet off. That piece of armor had been tied on with green ribbons which it would be necessary to cut, since the knots could not be undone, but he would not hear of this, and so spent all the rest of that night with his headpiece in place, which gave him the weirdest, most laughable appearance that could be imagined.

Don Quixote fancied that these wenches who were assisting him must surely be the chatelaine[3] and other ladies of the castle, and so proceeded to address them very gracefully and with much wit:

---

[1] **Cacus**: famous robber in Roman mythology.
[2] **gorget**: piece of armor that protects the throat.
[3] **chatelaine**: mistress of a castle.

"Never was knight so served
By any noble dame
As was Don Quixote
When from his village he came,
With damsels to wait on his every need
While princesses cared for his hack. . . ."

"By hack," he explained, "is meant my steed Rocinante, for that is his name, and mine is Don Quixote de la Mancha. I had no intention of revealing my identity until my exploits done in your service should have made me known to you; but the necessity of adapting to present circumstances that old ballad of Lancelot has led to your becoming acquainted with it prematurely. However, the time will come when your Ladyships shall command and I will obey and with the valor of my good right arm show you how eager I am to serve you."

The young women were not used to listening to speeches like this and had not a word to say, but merely asked him if he desired to eat anything.

"I could eat a bite of something, yes," replied Don Quixote. "Indeed, I feel that a little food would go very nicely just now."

He thereupon learned that, since it was Friday, there was nothing to be had in all the inn except a few portions of codfish, which in Castile is called *abadejo*, in Andalusia *bacalao*, in some places *curadillo*, and elsewhere *truchuella* or small trout. Would his Grace, then, have some small trout, seeing that was all there was that they could offer him?

"If there are enough of them," said Don Quixote, "they will take the place of a trout, for it is all one to me whether I am given in change eight reales or one piece of eight. What is more, those small trout may be like veal, which is better than beef, or like kid, which is better than goat. But however that may be, bring them on at once, for the weight and burden of arms is not to be borne without inner sustenance."

Placing the table at the door of the hostelry, in the open air, they brought the guest a portion of badly soaked and worse cooked codfish and a piece of bread as black and moldy as the suit of armor that he wore. It was a mirth-provoking sight to see him eat, for he still had his helmet on with his visor fastened, which made it impossible for him to put anything into his mouth with his hands, and so it was necessary for one of the girls to feed him. As for giving him anything to drink, that would have been out of the question if the innkeeper had not hollowed out a reed, placing one end in Don Quixote's mouth while through the other end he poured the wine. All this the knight bore very patiently rather than have them cut the ribbons of his helmet.

At this point a gelder[1] of pigs approached the inn, announcing his arrival with four or five blasts on his horn, all of which confirmed Don Quixote in the belief that this was indeed a famous castle, for what was this if not music that they were playing for him? The fish was trout, the bread was of the finest, the wenches were ladies, and the innkeeper was the castellan. He was convinced that he had been right in his resolve to sally forth and roam the world at large, but there was one thing that still distressed him greatly, and that was the fact that he had not as yet been dubbed a knight; as he saw it, he could not legitimately engage in any adventure until he had received the order of knighthood.

Wearied of his thoughts, Don Quixote lost no time over the scanty repast which the inn afforded him. When he had finished, he summoned the landlord and, taking him out to the stable, closed the doors and fell on his knees in front of him.

"Never, valiant knight," he said, "shall I arise from here until you have courteously

[1] **gelder:** one who makes animals sexually neuter.

granted me the boon I seek, one which will redound to your praise and to the good of the human race."

Seeing his guest at his feet and hearing him utter such words as these, the innkeeper could only stare at him in bewilderment, not knowing what to say or do. It was in vain that he entreated him to rise, for Don Quixote refused to do so until his request had been granted.

"I expected nothing less of your great magnificence, my lord," the latter then continued, "and so I may tell you that the boon I asked and which you have so generously conceded me is that tomorrow morning you dub me a knight. Until that time in the chapel of this your castle, I will watch over my armor, and when morning comes, as I have said, that which I so desire shall then be done, in order that I may lawfully go to the four corners of the earth in quest of adventures and to succor the needy, which is the chivalrous duty of all knights-errant such as I who long to engage in deeds of high emprise."[2]

The innkeeper, as we have said, was a sharp fellow. He already had a suspicion that his guest was not quite right in the head, and he was now convinced of it as he listened to such remarks as these. However, just for the sport of it, he determined to humor him; and so he went on to assure Don Quixote that he was fully justified in his request and that such a desire and purpose was only natural on the part of so distinguished a knight as his gallant bearing plainly showed him to be.

He himself, the landlord added, when he was a young man, had followed the same honorable calling. He had gone through various parts of the world seeking adventures, among the places he had visited being the Percheles of Málaga, the Isles of Riarán, the District of Seville, the Little Market Place of Segovia, the Olivera of Valencia,

[2] **emprise:** adventure.

the Rondilla of Granada, the beach of San-lúcar, the Horse Fountain of Cordova, the Small Taverns of Toledo, and numerous other localities[1] where his nimble feet and light fingers had found much exercise. He had done many wrongs, cheated many widows, ruined many maidens, and swindled not a few minors until he had finally come to be known in almost all the courts and tribunals that are to be found in the whole of Spain.

At last he had retired to his castle here, where he lived upon his own income and the property of others; and here it was that he received all knights-errant of whatever quality and condition, simply out of the great affection that he bore them and that they might share with him their possessions in payment of his good will. Unfortunately, in this castle there was no chapel where Don Quixote might keep watch over his arms, for the old chapel had been torn down to make way for a new one; but in case of necessity, he felt quite sure that such a vigil could be maintained anywhere, and for the present occasion the courtyard of the castle would do; and then in the morning, please God, the requisite ceremony could be performed and his guest be duly dubbed a knight, as much a knight as anyone ever was.

He then inquired if Don Quixote had any money on his person, and the latter replied that he had not a cent, for in all the story-books he had never read of knights-errant carrying any. But the innkeeper told him he was mistaken on this point: supposing the authors of those stories had not set down the fact in black and white, that was because they did not deem it necessary to speak of things as indispensable as money and a clean shirt, and one was not to assume for that reason that those knights-errant of whom the books were so full did not have any. He looked upon it as an absolute certainty that they all had well-stuffed purses, that they might be prepared for any emergency; and they also carried shirts and a little box of ointment for healing the wounds that they received.

For when they had been wounded in combat on the plains and in desert places, there was not always someone at hand to treat them, unless they had some skilled enchanter for a friend who then would succor them, bringing to them through the air, upon a cloud, some damsel or dwarf bearing a vial of water of such virtue that one had but to taste a drop of it and at once his wounds were healed and he was as sound as if he had never received any.

But even if this was not the case, knights in times past saw to it that their squires were well provided with money and other necessities, such as lint and ointment for healing purposes; and if they had no squires — which happened very rarely — they themselves carried these objects in a pair of saddlebags very cleverly attached to their horses' croups[2] in such a manner as to be scarcely noticeable, as if they held something of greater importance than that, for among the knights-errant saddlebags as a rule were not favored. Accordingly, he would advise the novice before him, and inasmuch as the latter was soon to be his godson, he might even command him, that henceforth he should not go without money and a supply of those things that have been mentioned, as he would find that they came in useful at a time when he least expected it.

Don Quixote promised to follow his host's advice punctiliously; and so it was arranged that he should watch his armor in a large barnyard at one side of the inn. He gathered up all the pieces, placed them in a horse

---

[1] **Percheles ... localities:** All these places are said to have been the haunts of rogues and thieves.

[2] **croups:** rumps of four-legged animals.

trough that stood near the well, and, bracing his shield on his arm, took up his lance and with stately demeanor began pacing up and down in front of the trough even as night was closing in.

The innkeeper informed his other guests of what was going on, of Don Quixote's vigil and his expectation of being dubbed a knight; and, marveling greatly at so extraordinary a variety of madness, they all went out to see for themselves and stood there watching from a distance. For a while the knight-to-be, with tranquil mien,[1] would merely walk up and down; then, leaning on his lance, he would pause to survey his armor, gazing fixedly at it for a considerable length of time. As has been said, it was night now, but the brightness of the moon, which well might rival that of Him who lent it, was such that everything the novice knight did was plainly visible to all.

At this point one of the mule drivers who were stopping at the inn came out to water his drove, and in order to do this it was necessary to remove the armor from the trough.

As he saw the man approaching, Don Quixote cried out to him, "O bold knight, whoever you may be, who thus would dare to lay hands upon the accouterments[2] of the most valiant man of arms that ever girded on a sword, look well what you do and desist if you do not wish to pay with your life for your insolence!"

The muleteer gave no heed to these words — it would have been better for his own sake had he done so — but, taking it up by the straps, tossed the armor some distance from him. When he beheld this, Don Quixote rolled his eyes heavenward and with his thoughts apparently upon his Dulcinea exclaimed, "Succor, O lady mine, this vassal[3] heart in this my first encounter; let not

your favor and protection fail me in the peril in which for the first time I now find myself."

With these and other similar words, he loosed his buckler, grasped his lance in both his hands, and let the mule driver have such a blow on the head that the man fell to the ground stunned; and had it been followed by another one, he would have had no need of a surgeon to treat him. Having done this, Don Quixote gathered up his armor and resumed his pacing up and down with the same calm manner as before. Not long afterward, without knowing what had happened — for the first muleteer was still lying there unconscious — another came out with the same intention of watering his mules, and he too was about to remove the armor from the trough when the knight, without saying a word or asking favor of anyone, once more adjusted his buckler and raised his lance, and if he did not break the second mule driver's head to bits, he made more than three pieces of it by dividing it into quarters. At the sound of the fracas everybody in the inn came running out, among them the innkeeper; whereupon Don Quixote again lifted his buckler and laid his hand on his sword.

"O lady of beauty," he said, "strength and vigor of this fainting heart of mine! Now is the time to turn the eyes of your greatness upon this captive knight of yours who must face so formidable an adventure."

By this time he had worked himself up to such a pitch of anger that if all the mule drivers in the world had attacked him he would not have taken one step backward. The comrades of the wounded men, seeing the plight those two were in, now began showering stones on Don Quixote, who shielded himself as best he could with his buckler, although he did not dare stir from the trough for fear of leaving his armor unprotected. The landlord, meanwhile, kept calling to them to stop, for he had told them

[1] mien: air.
[2] accouterments: equipment.
[3] vassal: subject.

that this was a madman who would be sure to go free even though he killed them all. The knight was shouting louder than ever, calling them knaves and traitors. As for the lord of the castle, who allowed knights-errant to be treated in this fashion, he was a lowborn villain, and if he, Don Quixote, had but received the order of knighthood, he would make him pay for his treachery.

"As for you others, vile and filthy rabble, I take no account of you; you may stone me or come forward and attack me all you like; you shall see what the reward of your folly and insolence will be."

He spoke so vigorously and was so undaunted in bearing as to strike terror in those who would assail him; and for this reason, and owing also to the persuasions of the innkeeper, they ceased stoning him. He then permitted them to carry away the wounded, and went back to watching his armor with the same tranquil, unconcerned air that he had previously displayed.

The landlord was none too well pleased with these mad pranks on the part of his guest and determined to confer upon him that accursed order of knighthood before something else happened. Going up to him, he begged Don Quixote's pardon for the insolence which, without his knowledge, had been shown the knight by those of low degree. They, however, had been well punished for their impudence. As he had said, there was no chapel in this castle, but for that which remained to be done there was no need of any. According to what he had read of the ceremonial of the order, there was nothing to this business of being dubbed a knight except a slap on the neck and one across the shoulder, and that could be performed in the middle of a field as well as anywhere else. All that was required was for the knight-to-be to keep watch over his armor for a couple of hours, and Don Quixote had been at it more than four. The latter believed all this and announced that he was ready to obey and get the matter over with

as speedily as possible. Once dubbed a knight, if he were attacked one more time, he did not think that he would leave a single person in the castle alive, save such as he might command be spared, at the bidding of his host and out of respect to him.

Thus warned, and fearful that it might occur, the castellan brought out the book in which he had jotted down the hay and barley for which the mule drivers owed him, and, accompanied by a lad bearing the butt of a candle and the two aforesaid damsels, he came up to where Don Quixote stood and commanded him to kneel. Reading from the account book — as if he had been saying a prayer — he raised his hand and, with the knight's own sword, gave him a good thwack upon the neck and another lusty one upon the shoulder, muttering all the while between his teeth. He then directed one of the ladies to gird on Don Quixote's sword, which she did with much gravity and composure; for it was all they could do to keep from laughing at every point of the ceremony, but the thought of the knight's prowess which they had already witnessed was sufficient to restrain their mirth.

"May God give your Grace much good fortune," said the worthy lady as she attached the blade, "and prosper you in battle."

Don Quixote thereupon inquired her name, for he desired to know to whom it was he was indebted for the favor he had just received, that he might share with her some of the honor which his strong right arm was sure to bring him. She replied very humbly that her name was Tolosa and that she was the daughter of a shoemaker, a native of Toledo who lived in the stalls of Sancho Bienaya. To this the knight replied that she would do him a very great favor if from then on she would call herself Doña[1] Tolosa, and she promised to do so. The

---

[1] **Doña** (dōn′yä; dōn′ä): feminine of *Don;* a title of courtesy and respect.

other girl then helped him on with his spurs, and practically the same conversation was repeated. When asked her name, she stated that it was La Molinera and added that she was the daughter of a respectable miller of Antequera. Don Quixote likewise requested her to assume the "don" and become Doña Molinera and offered to render her further services and favors.

These unheard-of ceremonies having been dispatched in great haste, Don Quixote could scarcely wait to be astride his horse and sally forth on his quest for adventures. Saddling and mounting Rocinante, he embraced his host, thanking him for the favor of having dubbed him a knight and saying such strange things that it would be quite impossible to record them here. The innkeeper, who was only too glad to be rid of him, answered with a speech that was no less flowery, though somewhat shorter, and he did not so much as ask him for the price of a lodging, so glad was he to see him go.

D ay was dawning when Don Quixote left the inn, so well satisfied with himself, so gay, so exhilarated, that the very girths[1] of his steed all but burst with joy. But remembering the advice which his host had given him concerning the stock of necessary provisions that he should carry with him, especially money and shirts, he decided to turn back home and supply himself with whatever he needed, and with a squire as well; he had in mind a farmer who was a neighbor of his, a poor man and the father of a family but very well suited to fulfill the duties of squire to a man of arms. With this thought in mind he guided Rocinante toward the village once more, and that animal, realizing that he was homeward bound, began stepping out at so lively a gait that it seemed as if his feet barely touched the ground.

[1] girths: bands put around a horse's belly for holding the saddle.

The knight had not gone far when from a hedge on his right hand he heard the sound of faint moans as of someone in distress.

"Thanks be to Heaven," he at once exclaimed, "for the favor it has shown me by providing me so soon with an opportunity to fulfill the obligations that I owe to my profession, a chance to pluck the fruit of my worthy desires. Those, undoubtedly, are the cries of someone in distress, who stands in need of my favor and assistance."

Turning Rocinante's head, he rode back to the place from which the cries appeared to be coming. Entering the wood, he had gone but a few paces when he saw a mare attached to an oak, while bound to another tree was a lad of fifteen or thereabouts, naked from the waist up. It was he who was uttering the cries, and not without reason, for there in front of him was a lusty farmer with a girdle who was giving him many lashes, each one accompanied by a reproof and a command, "Hold your tongue and keep your eyes open"; and the lad was saying, "I won't do it again, sir; by God's Passion, I won't do it again. I promise you that after this I'll take better care of the flock."

When he saw what was going on, Don Quixote was very angry. "Discourteous knight," he said, "it ill becomes you to strike one who is powerless to defend himself. Mount your steed and take your lance in hand" — for there was a lance leaning against the oak to which the mare was tied — "and I will show you what a coward you are."

The farmer, seeing before him this figure all clad in armor and brandishing a lance, decided he was as good as done for. "Sir Knight," he said, speaking very mildly, "this lad that I am punishing here is my servant; he tends a flock of sheep which I have in these parts and he is so careless that every day one of them shows up missing. And when I punish him for his carelessness or his roguery, he says it is just because I am a miser and do not want to pay him the wages that I owe him, but I swear to God and upon my soul that he lies."

"It is you who lie, base lout,"[1] said Don Quixote, "and in my presence; and by the sun that gives us light, I am minded to run you through with this lance. Pay him and say no more about it, or else, by the God who rules us, I will make an end of you and annihilate you here and now. Release him at once."

The farmer hung his head and without a word untied his servant. Don Quixote then asked the boy how much his master owed him. For nine months' work, the lad told him, at seven reales the month. The knight did a little reckoning and found that this came to sixty-three reales; whereupon he ordered the farmer to pay over the money immediately, as he valued his life. The cowardly bumpkin replied that, facing death as he was and by the oath that he had sworn — he had not sworn any oath as yet — it did not amount to as much as that; for there were three pairs of shoes which he had given the lad that were to be deducted and taken into account, and a real for two blood-lettings[2] when his servant was ill.

"That," said Don Quixote, "is all very well; but let the shoes and the blood-lettings go for the undeserved lashes which you have given him; if he has worn out the leather of the shoes that you paid for, you have taken the hide off his body, and if the barber let a little blood for him when he was sick, you have done the same when he was well; and so far as that goes, he owes you nothing."

"But the trouble is, Sir Knight, that I have no money with me. Come along home with me, Andrés, and I will pay you real for real."

"I go home with him!" cried the lad.

"Never in the world! No, sir, I would not even think of it; for once he has me alone he'll flay me like a St. Bartholomew."[3]

"He will do nothing of the sort," said Don Quixote. "It is sufficient for me to command, and he out of respect will obey. Since he has sworn to me by the order of knighthood which he has received, I shall let him go free and I will guarantee that you will be paid."

"But look, your Grace," the lad remonstrated, "my master is no knight; he has never received any order of knighthood whatsoever. He is Juan Haldudo, a rich man and a resident of Quintanar."

"That makes little difference," declared Don Quixote, "for there may well be knights among the Haldudos, all the more so in view of the fact that every man is the son of his works."

"That is true enough," said Andrés, "but this master of mine — of what works is he the son, seeing that he refuses me the pay for my sweat and labor?"

"I do not refuse you, brother Andrés," said the farmer. "Do me the favor of coming with me, and I swear to you by all the orders of knighthood that there are in this world to pay you, as I have said, real for real, and perfumed at that."

"You can dispense with the perfume," said Don Quixote; "just give him the reales and I shall be satisfied. And see to it that you keep your oath, or by the one that I myself have sworn I shall return to seek you out and chastise you, and I shall find you though you be as well hidden as a lizard. In case you would like to know who it is that is giving you this command in order that you may feel the more obliged to comply with it, I may tell you that I am the valorous Don Quixote de la Mancha, righter of wrongs and injustices; and so, God be with you, and do not fail to do as you have

---

[1] **base lout**: coarse, stupid fellow.
[2] **blood-lettings**: opening the vein to remove blood.

[3] **St. Bartholomew**: martyred in Armenia, A. D. 44, by being flayed alive with a knife.

promised, under that penalty that I have pronounced."

As he said this, he put spurs to Rocinante and was off. The farmer watched him go, and when he saw that Don Quixote was out of the wood and out of sight, he turned to his servant, Andrés.

"Come here, my son," he said. "I want to pay you what I owe you as that righter of wrongs has commanded me."

"Take my word for it," replied Andrés, "your Grace would do well to observe the command of that good knight — may he live a thousand years; for as he is valorous and a righteous judge, if you don't pay me then, by Roque,[1] he will come back and do just what he said!"

"And I will give you my word as well," said the farmer; "but seeing that I am so fond of you, I wish to increase the debt, that I may owe you all the more." And with this he seized the lad's arm and bound him to the tree again and flogged him within an inch of his life. "There, Master Andrés, you may call on that righter of wrongs if you like and you will see whether or not he rights this one. I do not think I have quite finished with you yet, for I have a good mind to flay you alive as you feared."

Finally, however, he unbound him and told him he might go look for that judge of his to carry out the sentence that had been pronounced. Andrés left, rather down in the mouth, swearing that he would indeed go look for the brave Don Quixote de la Mancha; he would relate to him everything that had happened, point by point, and the farmer would have to pay for it seven times over. But for all that, he went away weeping, and his master stood laughing at him.

Such was the manner in which the valorous knight righted this wrong. Don Quixote was quite content with the way everything had turned out; it seemed to him that he had made a very fortunate and noble beginning

with his deeds of chivalry, and he was very well satisfied with himself as he jogged along in the direction of his native village, talking to himself in a low voice all the while.

"Well may'st thou call thyself fortunate today, above all other women on earth, O fairest of the fair, Dulcinea del Toboso! Seeing that it has fallen to thy lot to hold subject and submissive to thine every wish and pleasure so valiant and renowned a knight as Don Quixote de la Mancha is and shall be, who, as everyone knows, yesterday received the order of knighthood and this day has righted the greatest wrong and grievance that injustice ever conceived or cruelty ever perpetrated, by snatching the lash from the hand of the merciless foreman who was so unreasonably flogging that tender child...."

After that he remained at home very tranquilly for a couple of weeks, without giving sign of any desire to repeat his former madness. During that time he had the most pleasant conversations with his two old friends, the curate and the barber, on the point he had raised to the effect that what the world needed most was knights-errant and a revival of chivalry. The curate would occasionally contradict him and again would give in, for it was only by means of this artifice[2] that he could carry on a conversation with him at all.

In the meanwhile Don Quixote was bringing his powers of persuasion to bear upon a farmer who lived near by, a good man — if this title may be applied to one who is poor — but with very few wits in his head. The short of it is, by pleas and promises, he got the hapless rustic to agree to ride forth with him and serve him as his squire. Among other things, Don Quixote told him that he ought to be more than willing to go, because no telling what adventure might occur

---

[1] **by Roque:** an obscure oath.

[2] **artifice:** trick.

Pablo Picasso interprets Don Quixote and Sancho in this lithograph of the knight-errant and his squire.

which would win them an island, and then he (the farmer) would be left to be the governor of it. As a result of these and other similar assurances, Sancho Panza forsook his wife and children and consented to take upon himself the duties of squire to his neighbor.

Next, Don Quixote set out to raise some money, and by selling this thing and pawning that and getting the worst of the bargain always, he finally scraped together a reasonable amount. He also asked a friend of his for the loan of a buckler and patched up his broken helmet as well as he could. He advised his squire, Sancho, of the day and hour when they were to take the road and told him to see to laying in a supply of those things that were most necessary, and, above all, not to forget the saddlebags.

Sancho replied that he would see to all this and added that he was also thinking of taking along with him a very good ass that he had, as he was not much used to going on foot.

With regard to the ass, Don Quixote had to do a little thinking, trying to recall if any knight-errant had ever had a squire thus asininely[1] mounted. He could not think of any, but nevertheless he decided to take Sancho with the intention of providing him with a nobler steed as soon as occasion offered; he had but to appropriate the horse of the first discourteous knight he met. Having furnished himself with shirts and all the other things that the innkeeper had recommended, he and Panza rode forth one night unseen by anyone and without taking leave of wife and children, housekeeper or niece. They went so far that by the time morning came they were safe from discovery had a hunt been started for them.

Mounted on his ass, Sancho Panza rode along like a patriarch,[2] with saddlebags and flask, his mind set upon becoming governor of that island that his master had promised him. Don Quixote determined to take the same route and road over the Campo de Montiel that he had followed on his first journey; but he was not so uncomfortable this time, for it was early morning and the sun's rays fell upon them slantingly and accordingly did not tire them too much.

"Look, Sir Knight-errant," said Sancho, "your Grace should not forget that island you promised me; for no matter how big it is, I'll be able to govern it right enough."

"I would have you know, friend Sancho Panza," replied Don Quixote, "that among the knights-errant of old it was a very common custom to make their squires governors of the islands or the kingdoms that they won, and I am resolved that in my case so pleasing a usage shall not fall into desue-

---

[1] **asininely:** stupidly; here, a pun on "ass."
[2] **patriarch:** man of great age and dignity.

tude.[1] I even mean to go them one better; for they very often, perhaps most of the time, waited until their squires were old men who had had their fill of serving their masters during bad days and worse nights, whereupon they would give them the title of count, or marquis at most, of some valley or province more or less. But if you live and I live, it well may be that within a week I shall win some kingdom with others dependent upon it, and it will be the easiest thing in the world to crown you king of one of them. You need not marvel at this, for all sorts of unforeseen things happen to knights like me, and I may readily be able to give you even more than I have promised."

"In that case," said Sancho Panza, "if by one of those miracles of which your Grace was speaking I should become king, I would certainly send for Juana Gutiérrez, my old lady, to come and be my queen, and the young ones could be infantes."[2]

"There is no doubt about it," Don Quixote assured him.

"Well, I doubt it," said Sancho, "for I think that even if God were to rain kingdoms upon the earth, no crown would sit well on the head of Mari Gutiérrez,[3] for I am telling you, sir, as a queen she is not worth two maravedis.[4] She would do better as a countess, God help her."

"Leave everything to God, Sancho," said Don Quixote, "and he will give you whatever is most fitting; but I trust you will not be so pusillanimous[5] as to be content with anything less than the title of viceroy."

"That I will not," said Sancho Panza, "especially seeing that I have in your Grace so illustrious a master who can give me all that is suitable to me and all that I can manage."

---

[1] **desuetude**: disuse.
[2] **infantes**: children of royal blood.
[3] **Mari Gutiérrez**: Sancho's wife.
[4] **maravedis**: old Spanish coins, worth less than a fraction of a cent.
[5] **pusillanimous**: fainthearted.

Don't part with your illusions. When they are gone, you may still exist, but you have ceased to live.

— Mark Twain

At this point they caught sight of thirty or forty windmills which were standing on the plain there, and no sooner had Don Quixote laid eyes upon them than he turned to his squire and said, "Fortune is guiding our affairs better than we could have wished; for you see there before you, friend Sancho Panza, some thirty or more lawless giants with whom I mean to do battle. I shall deprive them of their lives, and with the spoils from this encounter we shall begin to enrich ourselves; for this is righteous warfare, and it is a great service to God to remove so accursed a breed from the face of the earth."

"What giants?" said Sancho Panza.

"Those that you see there," replied his master, "those with the long arms some of which are as much as two leagues in length."

"But look, your Grace, those are not giants but windmills, and what appear to be arms are their wings which, when whirled in the breeze, cause the millstone to go."

"It is plain to be seen," said Don Quixote, "that you have had little experience in this matter of adventures. If you are afraid, go off to one side and say your prayers while I am engaging them in fierce, unequal combat."

Saying this, he gave spurs to his steed Rocinante, without paying any heed to Sancho's warning that these were truly windmills and not giants that he was riding forth to attack. Nor even when he was close upon them did he perceive what they really were, but shouted at the top of his lungs, "Do not seek to flee, cowards and vile creatures that you are, for it is but a single knight with whom you have to deal!"

Windmills like the one confronted by Don Quixote dot the horizon in this town in the modern La Mancha area and contrast with television antennas and telephone lines in the foreground.

At that moment a little wind came up and the big wings began turning.

"Though you flourish as many arms as did the giant Briareus,"[1] said Don Quixote when he perceived this, "you still shall have to answer to me."

He thereupon commended himself with all his heart to his lady Dulcinea, beseeching her to succor him in this peril; and, being well covered with his shield and with his lance at rest, he bore down upon them at a full gallop and fell upon the first mill that stood in his way, giving a thrust at the wing, which was whirling at such a speed that his lance was broken into bits and both horse and horseman went rolling over the plain, very much battered indeed. Sancho upon his donkey came hurrying to his master's assistance as fast as he could, but when he reached the spot, the knight was unable to move, so great was the shock with which he and Rocinante had hit the ground.

"God help us!" exclaimed Sancho, "did I not tell your Grace to look well, that those were nothing but windmills, a fact which no one could fail to see unless he had other mills of the same sort in his head?"

"Be quiet, friend Sancho," said Don Quixote. "Such are the fortunes of war, which more than any other are subject to constant change. What is more, when I come to think of it, I am sure that this must be the work of that magician Frestón, . . . who has thus changed the giants into windmills in order to deprive me of the glory of overcoming them, so great is the enmity that he bears me; but in the end his evil arts shall not prevail against this trusty sword of mine."

"May God's will be done," was Sancho Panza's response. And with the aid of his squire the knight was once more mounted

[1] **Briareus:** giant with fifty heads and a hundred arms.

on Rocinante, who stood there with one shoulder half out of joint. And so, speaking of the adventure that had just befallen them, they continued along the Puerto Lápice highway; for there, Don Quixote said, they could not fail to find many and varied adventures, this being a much traveled thoroughfare. The only thing was, the knight was exceedingly downcast over the loss of his lance.

"I remember," he said to his squire, "having read of a Spanish knight by the name of Diego Pérez de Vargas, who, having broken his sword in battle, tore from an oak a heavy bough or branch and with it did such feats of valor that day, and pounded so many Moors, that he came to be known as Machuca,[1] and he and his descendants from that day forth have been called Vargas y Machuca. I tell you this because I too intend to provide myself with just such a bough as the one he wielded, and with it I propose to do such exploits that you shall deem yourself fortunate to have been found worthy to come with me and behold and witness things that are almost beyond belief."

"God's will be done," said Sancho. "I believe everything that your Grace says; but straighten yourself up in the saddle a little, for you seem to be slipping down on one side, owing, no doubt, to the shaking-up that you received in your fall."

"Ah, that is the truth," replied Don Quixote, "and if I do not speak of my sufferings, it is for the reason that it is not permitted knights-errant to complain of any wound whatsoever, even though their bowels may be dropping out."

"If that is the way it is," said Sancho, "I have nothing more to say; but, God knows, it would suit me better if your Grace did complain when something hurts him. I can assure you that I mean to do so, over the

[1] **Machuca**: from *machucar* meaning "to pound."

least little thing that ails me — that is, unless the same rule applies to squires as well."

Don Quixote laughed long and heartily over Sancho's simplicity, telling him that he might complain as much as he liked and where and when he liked, whether he had good cause or not; for he had read nothing to the contrary in the ordinances of chivalry. Sancho then called his master's attention to the fact that it was time to eat. The knight replied that he himself had no need of food at the moment, but his squire might eat whenever he chose. Having been granted this permission, Sancho seated himself as best he could upon his beast, and, taking out from his saddlebags the provisions that he had stored there, he rode along leisurely behind his master, munching his victuals and taking a good, hearty swig now and then at the leather flask in a manner that might well have caused the biggest-bellied tavernkeeper of Málaga to envy him. Between draughts he gave not so much as a thought to any promise that his master might have made him, nor did he look upon it as any hardship, but rather as good sport, to go in quest of adventures however hazardous they might be.

For Discussion

1. *Don Quixote* opens with an introduction to a gentleman who, when "close on to fifty," had the misfortune of going out of his mind. (*Don*, incidentally, is a Spanish title for a nobleman or gentleman.) What caused his brain to "dry up" (page 57)? In such a state he conceived "the strangest idea that ever occurred to any madman in this world." What was that idea? For what purposes did he intend to carry out the idea? What steps did he take to put the idea into practice? Why was it essential to the plan that the Don have a lady-love?

2. Much of the appeal and complexity of *Don Quixote* arises from the contrast it presents between reality and illusion. Sallying forth for the first time, the Don passes a frustrating day devoid of adventures before finally encountering an inn. How does the inn look to him? Two girls of easy virtue are standing before the inn. What does Quixote take them for? The innkeeper, like so many of the people in this rich novel, is characterized quite fully during the course of Quixote's encounter with him. What kind of person is the innkeeper? Point to specific details in the story to support your evaluation. Why, finally, is he eager to go through with dubbing Quixote a knight? In what manner does he perform the ritual of dubbing?

3. The Don is a type of person met with throughout the ages, a man of high ideals who sets out to right the world's wrongs. But along the way, alas, he is guilty of committing a number of evils. Consider the plight of Andrés. Is Quixote's interference well-intentioned? Does he, in other words, mean well? What is the ultimate consequence of that interference? Is Andrés better or worse off after the Don comes along? And yet, and yet. . . . Consider the situation even more closely: in the best of all worlds — which is what Don Quixote aspires to create, after all — should Andrés, "powerless to defend himself," have been beaten at all? Who is "right," and who is "wrong"? Discuss.

4. How mad is Quixote? His squire Sancho points out that the so-called giants are really windmills — an observation that Quixote does not contradict. How does the Don account for their being windmills? He is a man possessed, no doubt, but is he mad? Discuss the question of his madness as thoroughly as this brief portion of the novel will permit.

For Composition

Narration, the telling of a story, is a major technique both in fiction and (though to a lesser extent) in exposition and argument. Usually narration relates events in the order in which they occur in time — that is, in chronological order — although in a complicated narrative it may be necessary to move backward and forward in time in order to keep track of all the events that occur. Transitional expressions such as *meanwhile, later, simultaneously, after a time, first, next,* and *finally* help keep the order of events clear.

1. **Narrative.** Reconsider that portion of the narrative of *Don Quixote* that is given here. In a brief paper clarify the chronological order of events in your own words.

2. **Description.** Throughout this section of *Don Quixote* you form an ever clearer impression of what the Don looks like. The withered bough stuck in his lance head and the dusty face behind his visor are only two of the several sharp details of Quixote's appearance that are provided in the course of the passage. Reread the selection, noting all the details about Quixote's physical appearance and accouterments that are given; then write as vivid a description of the knight as you can. You might choose to imagine him mounted on his horse at the outset of another adventure.

3. **Exposition.** To what extent can Don Quixote be thought of as a Platonist (see In Perspective, pages 54–55), that is, one who finds reality apart from the surface appearance of things?

Words and Allusions

ALLUSIONS. From Cervantes' *Don Quixote* has come the adjective *quixotic* (kwik·sot'ik). It is an allusion (page 53) to the characteristics of the Don. From what you know of Don Quixote, what do you think *quixotic* means? Check your own answer with a dictionary. Then write a sentence using the word to illustrate its meaning.

Other common phrases in English allude directly to *Don Quixote*. One of these, from the selection you have read, is "tilting at windmills." What does the phrase mean? Use it in three separate sentences that illustrate its meaning.

An Enemy of the People

HENRIK IBSEN

A certain seaside town in southern Norway in the second half of the nineteenth century was a little world unto itself. All walks of life were represented there, and every interest. Officialdom — the Establishment — was represented by the mayor. He spoke for a wealthy class intent on growing wealthier as the town became a popular health resort. Then there were the small shopkeepers — quite a few of these — and a liberal-minded newspaper editor and his staff, and the old folks no longer consulted on matters of importance, and the children too young to be consulted or even to understand what was going on.

As the citizens of that Norwegian town looked forward eagerly to the promised influx of tourists and prosperity, their medical officer — brother of the mayor — was on the verge of a great discovery, a truth about the town that would change the lives of almost everyone who lived there. That truth, and how the town received it, form the basis of Ibsen's celebrated play *An Enemy of the People*. But from that basis the meaning of the play rises beyond the little world of a single seaside town into the larger world in which all of us live — and beyond the nineteenth century when it was written into this troubled century of our own.

CHARACTERS

DOCTOR THOMAS STOCKMANN, *medical officer of the Baths.*
MRS. KATHERINE STOCKMANN, *his wife.*
PETRA, *their daughter, a teacher.*
EILIF } *their sons, thirteen and*
MORTEN } *ten years old respectively.*
PETER STOCKMANN, *the doctor's elder brother, Mayor, Chief of Police, Chairman of the Board of the Baths.*
MORTEN KIIL,[1] *owner of a tannery, Mrs. Stockmann's foster father.*
HOVSTAD, *editor of the* People's Messenger.
BILLING, *on the staff of the paper.*
HORSTER, *a ship's captain.*
ASLAKSEN, *a printer.*
Participants in a public meeting: all classes of men, some women, and some schoolboys.

[1] KIIL: pronounced kēl.

The action takes place in a town on the south coast of Norway.

Act I

Evening. DR. STOCKMANN'S *living room, simply decorated and furnished. In the wall to the right are two doors, the further one leading to the hall, the nearer one to the* DOCTOR'S *study. In the opposite wall, facing the hall door, a door leading to the other rooms of the house. In the middle of this wall stands the stove; further forward a sofa with a mirror above it, and in front of it an oval table. On the table is a lighted lamp, with a shade. In the back wall an open door leading to the dining room, in which is seen a supper table, with a lamp on it.*

BILLING *is seated at the supper table, with a napkin under his chin.* MRS. STOCKMANN *is standing by the table and placing before him a dish of roast beef. The other chairs round the table are empty; the table is in disorder, as after a meal.*

MRS. STOCKMANN. If you come an hour late, Mr. Billing, you must put up with a cold supper.

BILLING (*eating*). It is excellent — really first rate.

MRS. STOCKMANN. You know how Stockmann insists on regular mealtimes —

BILLING. Oh, I don't mind at all. I almost think I enjoy my supper more when I can sit down to it like this, alone and undisturbed.

MRS. STOCKMANN. Oh, well, if you enjoy it — (*Listening toward the direction of the hall*) That may be Mr. Hovstad.

BILLING. Very likely.

[MAYOR STOCKMANN *enters, wearing an overcoat and his official gold-braided cap, and carrying a stick.*]

MAYOR. Good evening, sister-in-law.

MRS. STOCKMANN (*coming forward into the living room*). Oh, good evening. It is good of you to look in.

MAYOR. I was just passing, and so — (*Looks towards the dining room.*) Oh, I see you have company.

MRS. STOCKMANN (*rather embarrassed*). Oh no, not at all. He just dropped in. (*Hurriedly*) Won't you sit down and have a little supper?

MAYOR. I? No, thank you. A full meal in the evening! Not with my digestion.

MRS. STOCKMANN. Oh, for once —

MAYOR. No, no — much obliged to you. I stick to tea and bread and butter. It's more wholesome — and rather more economical, too.

MRS. STOCKMANN (*smiling*). You mustn't think Thomas and I are extravagant.

MAYOR. Not you, sister-in-law: far be it from me to say that. (*Pointing to the Doctor's study*) Is he at home?

MRS. STOCKMANN. No, he has gone for a walk after supper — with the boys.

MAYOR. I wonder if that is a good thing to do? (*Listening*) There he is, no doubt.

MRS. STOCKMANN. No, that is not he. (*A knock*) Come in!

[HOVSTAD *enters from the hall.*]

MRS. STOCKMANN. Oh, it's Mr. Hovstad —

HOVSTAD. You must excuse me; I was detained at the printer's. Good evening, Mr. Mayor.

MAYOR (*bowing rather stiffly*). Mr. Hov-

ABOUT THE AUTHOR • "My deepest craving is the moral honesty of man towards himself," said **Henrik Ibsen** (1828–1906), the Norwegian who has come to be considered one of the world's greatest dramatists. His plays, which stress the theme of truth in conflict with society, exerted far-reaching moral effects upon British and European drama of his day.

In early life Ibsen was attracted by drama when he played with a toy theater that he devised. Later he became the manager and official playwright of various theaters in his native land. His major dramas include *The Doll's House, The Wild Duck,* and *Hedda Gabler.* His poetic drama *Peer Gynt* was set to music by Edvard Grieg.

stad? You come on business, I presume?

HOVSTAD. Partly. About an article for the paper.

MAYOR. So I supposed. I hear my brother is an extremely prolific[1] contributor to the *People's Messenger*.

HOVSTAD. Yes, when he wants to unburden his mind on one thing or another, he gives the *Messenger* the benefit.

MRS. STOCKMANN (*to* HOVSTAD). But will you not — ? (*Points to the dining room.*)

MAYOR. Well, well, I don't blame him for writing for the class of readers he finds most in sympathy with him. And, personally, I have no reason to bear your paper any ill will, Mr. Hovstad.

HOVSTAD. No, I should think not.

MAYOR. One may say, on the whole, that a fine spirit of tolerance prevails in our town — an excellent public spirit. And that is because we have a great common interest to hold us together — an interest in which all right-minded citizens are equally concerned —

HOVSTAD. Yes — the Baths.

MAYOR. Just so. We have our magnificent new Baths. Mark my words! The whole life of the town will center around the Baths, Mr. Hovstad. There can be no doubt of it!

MRS. STOCKMANN. That is just what Thomas says.

MAYOR. How marvelously the place has developed, even in this couple of years! Money has come into circulation, and brought life and movement with it. Houses and land rise in value every day.

HOVSTAD. And there are fewer people out of work.

MAYOR. That is true. There is a gratifying reduction in the burden imposed on the well-to-do classes by the taxes; and they will be still further lightened if we have a really good summer this year — a rush of visitors — plenty of invalids, to give the Baths a reputation.

HOVSTAD. I hear there is every prospect of that.

MAYOR. Things look most promising. Inquiries about apartments and so forth keep pouring in.

HOVSTAD. Then the Doctor's paper will come at the right time.

MAYOR. Has he been writing again?

HOVSTAD. This is a thing he wrote during the winter, enlarging on the virtues of the Baths, and on the excellent sanitary conditions of the town. But at that time I held it over.

MAYOR. Ah — I suppose there was something not quite judicious[2] about it?

HOVSTAD. Not at all. But I thought it better to keep it till the spring, when people are beginning to look about them, and think of their summer plans —

MAYOR. You were right, quite right, Mr. Hovstad.

MRS. STOCKMANN. Yes, Thomas is really indefatigable[3] where the Baths are concerned.

MAYOR. It is his duty as one of the staff.

HOVSTAD. And of course he was really their creator.

MAYOR. Was he? Indeed! I gather that certain persons are of that opinion. But I should have thought that I, too, had a modest share in that undertaking.

MRS. STOCKMANN. Yes, that is what Thomas is always saying.

HOVSTAD. No one dreams of denying it, Mr. Mayor. You set the thing going, and put it on a practical basis; everybody knows that. I only meant that the original idea was the Doctor's.

MAYOR. Yes, my brother has certainly had ideas enough in his time — worse luck! But when it comes to realizing them, Mr. Hovstad, we want men of another stamp.[4] I should have thought that in this house at any rate —

---

[1] **prolific**: producing a great volume.

[2] **judicious**: wise, discreet.
[3] **indefatigable**: tireless.
[4] **stamp**: *here,* sort.

This well-ordered village at Tvedestrand on the southern coast of Norway is typical of the seaside town in which Ibsen set An Enemy of the People.

MRS. STOCKMANN. Why, my dear brother-in-law —

HOVSTAD. Mr. Mayor, how can you — ?

MRS. STOCKMANN. Do go in and have some supper, Mr. Hovstad; my husband is sure to be home soon.

HOVSTAD. Thanks; just a bite, perhaps. (*He goes into the dining room.*)

MAYOR (*lowering his voice*). It is extraordinary how people who spring direct from the peasant class never can get over their want[1] of tact.

MRS. STOCKMANN. But why should you care? Surely you and Thomas can share the honor, like brothers.

MAYOR. Yes, one would suppose so; but it seems a share of the honor is not enough for some persons.

MRS. STOCKMANN. What nonsense! You and Thomas always get on so well together. (*Listening*) There, I think I hear him. (*Goes and opens the door to the hall.*)

DR. STOCKMANN (*laughing and talking loudly*). Here's another visitor for you, Katherine. Isn't this splendid? Come in, Captain Horster. Hang your coat on that peg. What! you don't wear an over-

[1] **want:** lack.

coat? Imagine, Katherine, I caught him in the street, and I could hardly get him to come in.

[CAPTAIN HORSTER *enters and bows to* MRS. STOCKMANN.]

DR. STOCKMANN (*in the doorway*). In with you, boys. They're starving again! Come along, Captain Horster; you must try our roast beef —

[*He forces* HORSTER *into the dining room.* EILIF *and* MORTEN *follow them.*]

MRS. STOCKMANN. But, Thomas, don't you see —

DR. STOCKMANN (*turning round in the doorway*). Oh, it's you, Peter! (*Goes up to him and holds out his hand.*) Now this is really splendid.

MAYOR. Unfortunately, I have only a moment to spare —

DR. STOCKMANN. Nonsense! We shall have some toddy[2] in a minute. You're not forgetting the toddy, Katherine?

MRS. STOCKMANN. Of course not; the water's boiling.

[*She goes into the dining room.*]

MAYOR. Toddy too — !

DR. STOCKMANN. Yes; sit down, and let's make ourselves comfortable.

[2] **toddy:** sweetened liquor and hot water.

MAYOR. Thanks; I never join in drinking parties.

DR. STOCKMANN. But this isn't a party.

MAYOR. I don't know what else — (*Looks towards the dining room.*) It's extraordinary how they can get through all that food.

DR. STOCKMANN (*rubbing his hands*). Yes, doesn't it do one good to see young people eat? Always hungry! That's as it should be. They need good, solid food to put stamina into them! They're the ones who will stir things up in the future, Peter.

MAYOR. May I ask what there is to be "stirred up," as you call it?

DR. STOCKMANN. You'll have to ask the young people that — when the time comes. We shan't see it, of course. Two old fogies like you and me —

MAYOR. Come, come! Surely that is a very extraordinary expression to use —

DR. STOCKMANN. Oh, you mustn't mind my nonsense, Peter. I'm in such glorious spirits, you see. I feel so unspeakably happy in the midst of all this growing, vigorous life. Isn't it a marvelous time we live in! It seems as though a whole new world was springing up around us.

MAYOR. Do you really think so?

DR. STOCKMANN. Of course, you can't see it as clearly as I do. You have passed your life in the midst of it all, and that deadens the impression. But I who had to vegetate all those years in that little hole in the north, hardly ever seeing a soul who could speak a stimulating word to me — all this affects me as if I had suddenly dropped into the heart of some teeming metropolis.

MAYOR. Well, metropolis —

DR. STOCKMANN. Oh, I know well enough that things are on a small scale here, compared with many other places. But there's life here — there's promise — there's an infinity of things to work and strive for; and that is the main point. (*Calling*) Katherine, isn't there any mail?

MRS. STOCKMANN (*in the dining room*). No, none at all.

DR. STOCKMANN. And a good income, Peter! That's a thing one learns to appreciate when one has lived on starvation wages —

MAYOR. But surely — !

DR. STOCKMANN. Oh, yes, I can tell you we often had hard times of it up there. And now we can live like princes! Today, for example, we had roast beef for dinner; and we've had some of it for supper too. Won't you have some? Come along — just look at it, at any rate —

MAYOR. No, no; certainly not —

DR. STOCKMANN. Well then, look here. We've bought a table-cover.

MAYOR. Yes, so I observed.

DR. STOCKMANN. And a lampshade, too. Do you see? Katherine has been saving up for them. They make the room look comfortable, don't they? Come over here. No, no, no, not there. Here! Now you see how it concentrates the light — . I really think it has quite an artistic effect. Eh?

MAYOR. Yes, when one can afford such luxuries —

DR. STOCKMANN. Oh, I can afford it now. Katherine says I make almost as much as we spend.

MAYOR. Almost!

DR. STOCKMANN. Besides, a man of science should live in some style. Why, I believe a mere sheriff spends much more a year than I do.

MAYOR. Yes, I should think so! A government official.

DR. STOCKMANN. Well then, even a common shipowner! A man of that sort will get through many times as much —

MAYOR. That is natural, in your relative positions.

DR. STOCKMANN. And after all, Peter, I really don't squander any money. But I can't deny myself the delight of having people about me. I must have them. After living so long out of the world, I find it a necessity of life to have bright, cheerful, freedom-loving, hard-working young fellows around me — and that's what they are, all of those sitting there eating so heartily. I wish you knew Hovstad better.

MAYOR. Oh, that reminds me — Hovstad was telling me that he is going to publish another article of yours.

DR. STOCKMANN. An article of mine?

MAYOR. Yes, about the Baths. An article you wrote last winter.

DR. STOCKMANN. Oh, that one! But I don't want that to appear just now.

MAYOR. Why not? It seems to me this is the very time for it.

DR. STOCKMANN. Very likely — under ordinary circumstances —(*Crosses the room.*)

MAYOR (*following him with his eyes*). And what is unusual in the circumstances now?

DR. STOCKMANN (*standing still*). The fact is, Peter, I really cannot tell you just now; not this evening, anyway. There may prove to be a great deal that is unusual in the circumstances. On the other hand, there may be nothing at all. Very likely it's only my imagination.

MAYOR. Upon my word, you are very mysterious. Is anything unusual going on? Anything I do not know about? I should think, as Chairman of the Baths —

DR. STOCKMANN. And I should think that I — Well, well, don't let us get our backs up, Peter.

MAYOR. God forbid! I am not in the habit of "getting my back up," as you express it. But I must absolutely insist that all arrangements be made and carried out in a businesslike manner, and through the properly constituted authorities. I cannot be a party to crooked or underhand courses.

DR. STOCKMANN. Have *I* ever been given to crooked or underhand courses?

MAYOR. At any rate you have a bad habit of taking your own course. And that, in a well-ordered community is almost as bad. The individual must subordinate himself to society, or, more precisely, to the authorities whose business it is to watch over the welfare of society.

DR. STOCKMANN. Maybe. But what the devil has that to do with me?

MAYOR. Why this is the very thing, my dear Thomas, that it seems you will never learn. But take care; you will have to pay for it — sooner or later. Now I have warned you. Good-by.

DR. STOCKMANN. Are you stark mad? You're on a totally wrong track —

MAYOR. I am not often on the wrong track. Moreover, I must protest against — (*Bowing towards dining room*) Good-by, sister-in-law; good-day to you, gentlemen. (*He goes.*)

MRS. STOCKMANN (*entering the living room*). Has he gone?

DR. STOCKMANN. Yes, and in a fine temper, too.

MRS. STOCKMANN. Why, my dear Thomas, what have you been doing to him now?

DR. STOCKMANN. Nothing at all. He can't possibly expect me to account to him for everything — before the time comes.

MRS. STOCKMANN. What have you to account to him for?

DR. STOCKMANN. H'm; — never mind about that, Katherine. — It's very odd the mailman doesn't come.

[HOVSTAD, BILLING, *and* HORSTER *have risen from the table and come forward into the living room.* EILIF *and* MORTEN *follow.*]

BILLING (*stretching himself*). Ah! Strike me dead if one doesn't feel a new man after such a meal.

HOVSTAD. The Mayor didn't seem in the best of tempers this evening.

DR. STOCKMANN. That's his stomach. He has a very poor digestion.

HOVSTAD. I suspect it's the staff of the

Messenger he finds it hardest to stomach.

MRS. STOCKMANN. I thought you got on well with him.

HOVSTAD. Oh, yes; but it's only a sort of armistice[1] between us.

BILLING. That's it. That sums up the situation.

DR. STOCKMANN. We must remember that Peter is a lonely bachelor, poor devil! He has no home to be happy in; only business, business. And then all that cursed weak tea he pours down his throat! Now then, chairs round the table, boys! Katherine, can we have the toddy now?

MRS. STOCKMANN (*going towards the dining room*). I am getting it.

DR. STOCKMANN. And you, Captain Horster, sit beside me on the sofa. So rare a guest as you — Sit down, gentlemen, sit down. [*The men sit round the table;* MRS. STOCKMANN *brings in a tray with kettle, glasses, decanters, etc.*]

MRS. STOCKMANN. Here you have it: here's arrak,[2] and this is rum, and this cognac. Now, help yourselves.

DR. STOCKMANN (*taking a glass*). So we will. (*While the toddy is being mixed*) And now let's have cigars. Eilif, I think you know where the box is. And Morten, you may fetch my pipe. (*The boys go into the room on the right.*) I have a suspicion that Eilif sneaks a cigar now and then, but I pretend not to notice. (*Calls.*) And my smoking cap, Morten! Katherine, can't you tell him where I left it? Ah, he's got it. (*The boys bring in the things.*) Now, friends, help yourselves. I stick to my pipe, you know; this one has been on many a stormy journey with me, up there in the north. (*They clink glasses.*) Your health! Ah, I can tell you it's more fun to sit cosily here, safe from wind and weather.

MRS. STOCKMANN (*who sits knitting*). Do you sail soon, Captain Horster?

HORSTER. I hope to be ready by next week.

MRS. STOCKMANN. And you're going to America?

HORSTER. Yes, that's the intention.

BILLING. But then you'll miss the election of the new Town Council.

HORSTER. Is there to be an election again?

BILLING. Didn't you know?

HORSTER. No, I don't trouble myself about those things.

BILLING. But I suppose you take an interest in public affairs?

HORSTER. No. I don't understand anything about them.

BILLING. All the same, one should at least vote.

HORSTER. Even those who don't understand anything about it?

BILLING. Understand? Why, what do you mean by that? Society is like a ship: every man must put his hand to the helm.

HORSTER. That may be all right on shore; but at sea it wouldn't do at all.

HOVSTAD. It's remarkable how little sailors care about public affairs.

BILLING. Most extraordinary.

DR. STOCKMANN. Sailors are like birds of passage; they are at home both in the south and in the north. So it is up to the rest of us to be all the more energetic, Mr. Hovstad. Will there be anything of public interest in the *People's Messenger* tomorrow?

HOVSTAD. Nothing of local interest. But the day after tomorrow I thought of printing your article —

DR. STOCKMANN. Oh, yes, that article! No, you'll have to hold it over.

HOVSTAD. Really? We happen to have plenty of space, and I would say this was the very time for it —

DR. STOCKMANN. Yes, yes, you may be right; but you must hold it over all the same. I shall explain to you later.

---

[1] **armistice**: pause in a war.
[2] **arrak**: an Oriental alcoholic beverage.

[PETRA, *wearing a hat and cloak, and with a number of books under her arm, enters from the hall.*]

PETRA. Good evening.

DR. STOCKMANN. Good evening, Petra.
[*General greetings.* PETRA *puts her cloak, hat, and books on a chair by the door.*]

PETRA. Here you all are, enjoying yourselves, while I've been out slaving.

DR. STOCKMANN. Well then, you come and enjoy yourself too.

BILLING. May I mix you a little — ?

PETRA (*coming towards the table*). Thank you, I'd rather help myself — you always make it too strong. By the way, father, I have a letter for you. (*Goes to the chair where her things are lying.*)

DR. STOCKMANN. A letter! From whom?

PETRA (*searching in the pocket of her cloak*). I got it from the mailman just as I was going out —

DR. STOCKMANN (*rising and going towards her*). And you give it to me only now?

PETRA. I really hadn't time to run back with it. Here it is.

DR. STOCKMANN (*seizing the letter*). Let me see, let me see, child. (*Reads the address.*) Yes; this is it — !

MRS. STOCKMANN. Is it the one you have been so anxious about, Thomas?

DR. STOCKMANN. Yes, it is. I must go at once. Where shall I find a light, Katherine? Is there no lamp in my study again!

MRS. STOCKMANN. Yes — the lamp is lighted. It's on the desk.

DR. STOCKMANN. Good, good. Excuse me one moment — (*He goes into the room on the right.*)

PETRA. What can it be, mother?

MRS. STOCKMANN. I don't know. For the last few days he has been continually on the lookout for the mailman.

BILLING. Probably a patient out in the country —

PETRA. Poor father! He'll soon have far too much to do. (*Mixes her toddy.*) Ah, this will taste good!

HOVSTAD. Have you been teaching in the night school as well today?

PETRA (*sipping from her glass*). Two hours.

BILLING. And four hours in the morning at the institute —

PETRA (*sitting down by the table*). Five hours.

MRS. STOCKMANN. And I see you have exercises to correct this evening.

PETRA. Yes, a heap of them.

HORSTER. It seems to me you have plenty to do, too.

PETRA. Yes; but I like it. You feel so delightfully tired after it.

BILLING. Do you like that?

PETRA. Yes, for then you sleep so well.

MORTEN. I say, Petra, you must be a great sinner.

PETRA. A sinner?

MORTEN. Yes, if you work so hard. Mr. Rörlund says work is a punishment for our sins.

EILIF. How silly you are, to believe such stuff as that.

MRS. STOCKMANN. Come come, Eilif.

BILLING (*laughing*). Oh, that's good!

HOVSTAD. Don't you like to work hard, Morten?

MORTEN. No, I don't.

HOVSTAD. Then what will you do when you grow up?

MORTEN. I want to be a Viking.

EILIF. But then you'd have to be a heathen.

MORTEN. Well, so I would.

BILLING. There I agree with you, Morten! I say just the same thing.

MRS. STOCKMANN (*making a sign to him*). No, no, Mr. Billing, I'm sure you don't.

BILLING. Strike me dead but I do, though. I am a heathen, and I'm proud of it. You'll see we shall all be heathens soon.

MORTEN. And we can do anything we like then?

BILLING. Well, you see, Morten —

MRS. STOCKMANN. Now run along boys; I'm sure you have homework to do.

EILIF. Can't I stay just a little longer —

MRS. STOCKMANN. No, you must go too. Be off, both of you.

[*The boys say good night and go into the room on the left.*]

HOVSTAD. Do you really think it can hurt the boys to hear these things?

MRS. STOCKMANN. Well, I don't know; I don't like it.

PETRA. Really, mother, I think you are quite wrong there.

MRS. STOCKMANN. Perhaps. But I don't like it — not here, at home.

PETRA. There's no end of hypocrisy both at home and at school. At home you must hold your tongue, and at school you have to stand up and tell lies to the children.

HORSTER. Do you have to tell lies?

PETRA. Yes; we have to tell them many things we don't believe ourselves.

BILLING. Ah, that's too true.

PETRA. If I could afford it, I would start a school myself, and things would be very different there.

BILLING. Oh, money — !

HORSTER. If you really think of doing that, Miss Stockmann, I would be delighted to let you have a room at my place. You know my father's old house is nearly empty; there's a great big dining room on the ground floor —

PETRA (*laughing*).Oh, thank you very much — but I'm afraid it won't come to anything.

HOVSTAD. No, I fancy Miss Petra is more likely to go into journalism. By the way, have you had time to look into the English novel you promised to translate for us?

PETRA. Not yet. But you shall have it in good time.

[DR. STOCKMANN *enters from his room, with the letter open in his hand.*]

DR. STOCKMANN (*flourishing the letter*). Here's news, I can tell you, that will wake up the town!

BILLING. News?

MRS. STOCKMANN. What news?

DR. STOCKMANN. A great discovery, Katherine!

HOVSTAD. Indeed?

MRS. STOCKMANN. Made by you?

DR. STOCKMANN. Precisely — by me! (*Walks up and down.*) Now let them accuse me of crack-brained notions. But they won't dare to! Ha-ha! I tell you they won't dare!

PETRA. Do tell us what it is, father.

DR. STOCKMANN. Well, well, give me time, and you shall hear all about it. If only I had Peter here now! This just shows how we men can go about forming judgments like the blindest moles —

HOVSTAD. What do you mean, doctor?

DR. STOCKMANN (*stopping beside the table*). Isn't it generally believed that our town is a healthy place?

HOVSTAD. Of course.

DR. STOCKMANN. A quite exceptionally healthy place, indeed — a place to be warmly recommended, both to invalids and people in health —

MRS. STOCKMANN. My dear Thomas —

DR. STOCKMANN. And we haven't failed to recommend and praise it. I've sung its praises again and again, both in the *Messenger* and in pamphlets —

HOVSTAD. Well, what then?

DR. STOCKMANN. These Baths, that we have called the pulse of the town, its vital nerve, and — and the devil knows what else —

BILLING. Its "palpitating heart," I once ventured to call them in a festive moment —

DR. STOCKMANN. Yes, I dare say. Well — do you know what they really are, these mighty, magnificent Baths, that have cost so much money — do you know what they are?

HOVSTAD. No, what are they?

MRS. STOCKMANN. Do tell us.

DR. STOCKMANN. Simply a cesspool.[1]

PETRA. The Baths, father?

MRS. STOCKMANN (*at the same time*). Our Baths!

HOVSTAD (*also at the same time*). But, Doctor — !

BILLING. That's incredible!

DR. STOCKMANN. I tell you the whole place is a poisonous whited sepulcher;[2] noxious[3] in the highest degree! All that filth up there in the Mill Dale — the stuff that smells so horribly — taints the water in the feed pipes of the pump-room; and the same accursed poisonous refuse oozes out by the beach —

HOVSTAD. Where the sea baths are?

DR. STOCKMANN. Exactly.

HOVSTAD. But what makes you so sure of all this, Doctor?

DR. STOCKMANN. I've investigated the whole thing as thoroughly as possible. I've long had my suspicions about it. Last year we had some extraordinary cases of illness among the patients — typhoid and gastric[4] attacks —

MRS. STOCKMANN. Yes, I remember.

DR. STOCKMANN. We thought at the time that the visitors had brought the infection with them; but afterwards — last winter — I began to question that. So I set about testing the water as well as I could.

MRS. STOCKMANN. So that's what you were working so hard at!

DR. STOCKMANN. Yes, you may well say I've worked, Katherine. But here, you know, I didn't have the necessary scientific equipment; so I sent samples both of our drinking water and of our sea water to the University, for exact analysis by a chemist.

HOVSTAD. And you have received his report?

DR. STOCKMANN (*showing letter*). Here it is! And it proves beyond doubt the presence of putrified[5] organic matter in the water — millions of microorganisms.[6] It's absolutely pernicious[7] to health, whether used internally or externally.

MRS. STOCKMANN. What a blessing you found it out in time.

DR. STOCKMANN. Yes, you may well say that.

HOVSTAD. And what do you intend to do now, Doctor?

DR. STOCKMANN. Why, to set things right, of course.

HOVSTAD. You think it can be done, then?

DR. STOCKMANN. It must be done. Otherwise the whole Baths are useless, ruined. But there's no fear. I am quite clear as to what is required.

MRS. STOCKMANN. But, my dear Thomas, why should you have made such a secret of all this?

DR. STOCKMANN. Would you want me to rush all over town and chatter about it, before I was quite certain? No, thank you; I'm not so mad as that.

PETRA. But to us at home —

DR. STOCKMANN. I couldn't say a word to a living soul. But tomorrow you may look in at the Badger's —

MRS. STOCKMANN. Oh, Thomas!

DR. STOCKMANN. Well, then, at your grandfather's. The old fellow will be astonished! He thinks I'm not quite right in my head — yes, and plenty of others think the same, I've noticed. But now these good people shall see — yes, they shall see now! (*Walks up and down rubbing his hands.*) What a stir there will

---

[1] **cesspool**: sewer tank which collects waste matter.

[2] **whited sepulcher**: something outwardly clean but inwardly corrupt and filthy.

[3] **noxious**: harmful to health.

[4] **gastric**: relating to the stomach.

[5] **putrified**: decomposed, rotten.

[6] **microorganisms**: germs.

[7] **pernicious**: extremely destructive.

be in the town, Katherine! Just think of it! All the water pipes will have to be relaid.

HOVSTAD (*rising*). All the water pipes — ?

DR. STOCKMANN. Why, of course. The intake is too low down; it must be moved much higher up.

PETRA. So you were right after all.

DR. STOCKMANN. Yes, do you remember, Petra? I wrote against it when they were beginning the works. But no one would listen to me then. Now, you may be sure, I shall give them a full broadside[1] — for of course I've prepared a statement for the Directors. It has been lying ready a whole week; I've only been waiting for this report. (*Points to letter.*) But now they shall have it at once. (*Goes into his room and returns with a manuscript in his hand.*) See! Four closely written pages! And I'll enclose the report. A newspaper, Katherine! Get me something to wrap them up in. There — that's it. Give it to — to — (*Stamps.*) — what the devil's her name? Give it to the girl, I mean, and tell her to take it at once to the Mayor.

[MRS. STOCKMANN *goes out with the packet through the dining room.*]

PETRA. What do you think Uncle Peter will say, father?

DR. STOCKMANN. What can he say? He can't fail to be pleased that so important a fact has been brought to light.

HOVSTAD. I suppose you will let me put a short announcement of your discovery in the *Messenger.*

DR. STOCKMANN. Yes, I shall be much obliged if you will.

HOVSTAD. It is highly desirable that the public should know about it as soon as possible.

DR. STOCKMANN. Yes, certainly.

MRS. STOCKMANN (*returning*). She's gone with it.

BILLING. Strike me dead if you won't be

[1] **broadside**: attack.

the most important man in town, Doctor!

DR. STOCKMANN (*walks up and down in high glee*). Oh, nonsense! After all, I have only done my duty. I've been lucky, that's all. But all the same —

BILLING. Hovstad, don't you think the town ought to get up a parade in honor of Dr. Stockmann?

HOVSTAD. I shall certainly propose it.

BILLING. And I'll talk it over with Aslaksen.

DR. STOCKMANN. No, my dear friends; let all such claptrap alone. I won't hear of anything of the sort. And if the Directors should want to raise my salary, I won't accept it. I tell you, Katherine, I will not accept it.

MRS. STOCKMANN. You are quite right, Thomas.

PETRA (*raising her glass*). Your health, father!

HOVSTAD *and* BILLING. Your health, your health, Doctor!

HORSTER (*clinking glasses with the* DOCTOR). I hope you may have nothing but joy from your discovery.

DR. STOCKMANN. Thanks, thanks, my dear friends! I can't tell you how happy I am — ! Oh, what a blessing it is to feel that you have deserved well of your native town and your fellow citizens. Hurrah, Katherine!

[*He puts both his arms round her neck, and whirls her round with him.* MRS. STOCKMANN *screams and struggles. A burst of laughter, applause, and cheers for the* DOCTOR. *The boys thrust their heads in at the door.*]

For Discussion

1. How would you describe the opening mood of the play? Go beyond simply "happy"

or "sad"; with what earlier period in the life of Thomas Stockmann is this mood contrasted? How does the doctor feel about the life he is leading now? How would you characterize that way of life? What is the first sound you hear from him?

2. In a play we must learn everything we know about a character from what he says and does, and from what others say about him. Unlike the novelist with his novel, the dramatist usually stays out of the play entirely. What impression does Peter Stockmann make on you at first meeting? Notice what he says and how he acts before his sister-in-law. Does he seem to be relaxed, jovial, generous, retiring, meddlesome, pompous, or what? Point to specific things that he says and does to justify your answer.

3. Toward the end of the act Dr. Stockmann receives a letter. From what source? What does the letter tell him? Why has he kept secret until now the suspicions that the letter confirms? Although the act ends on a note of triumph, a question has been raised before the curtain descends. "What do you think Uncle Peter will say, Father?" Petra wants to know. What do *you* suppose he will say?

4. **Exposition, Complication.** Through dialogue alone, a play must identify the characters on stage, explain their relationships to one another, and clarify at what point in their lives we are meeting them. All of this is called *exposition* — explaining the initial situation. But if from that starting point the action of the play should move straight forward without a surprise to its conclusion, it would hardly hold the interest of the audience. There must be *complication* in the action; instead of moving ahead as anticipated, the action must get sidetracked and start off in an unexpected direction. The first complication in this play is introduced when Dr. Stockmann tells the mayor that he would rather his article recommending the baths not appear just now. How does his brother react to that news? How do Hovstad and Billing react to the news that an article quite different from the one they had expected will be given them to print?

Act II

The DOCTOR's *living room. The dining room door is closed. Morning.*

MRS. STOCKMANN (*enters from the dining room with a sealed letter in her hand, goes to the door of the Doctor's study, and peeps in*). Are you there, Thomas?

DR. STOCKMANN (*within*). Yes, I have just come in. (*Enters.*) What is it?

MRS. STOCKMANN. A letter from your brother. (*Hands it to him.*)

DR. STOCKMANN. Aha, let us see. (*Opens the envelope and reads.*) "The manuscript sent me is returned herewith — " (*Reads on, mumbling to himself.*) H'm.

MRS. STOCKMANN. Well, what does he say?

DR. STOCKMANN (*putting the paper in his pocket*). Nothing; only that he'll come by himself about noon.

MRS. STOCKMANN. Then be sure you remember to stay at home.

DR. STOCKMANN. Oh, I can easily manage that; I've finished my morning's calls.

MRS. STOCKMANN. I am very curious to know how he takes it.

DR. STOCKMANN. He won't be over-pleased that I was the one who made the discovery, and not he himself.

MRS. STOCKMANN. That's just what I'm afraid of.

DR. STOCKMANN. Actually he'll be glad, of course. But still — Peter is damnably unwilling that anyone but himself should do anything for the good of the town.

MRS. STOCKMANN. Do you know, Thomas, I think you might stretch a point, and share the honor with him. Couldn't it appear that it was he who put you on the track — ?

DR. STOCKMANN. By all means, for all I care. If only I can get things put straight —
[*Old* MORTEN KIIL *puts his head in at the hall door, and questions slyly.*]

MORTEN KIIL. Is it — is it true?

MRS. STOCKMANN (*going towards him*). Why, it's Father!

DR. STOCKMANN. Hello, father-in-law! Good morning, good morning.

MRS. STOCKMANN. Do come in.

MORTEN KIIL. Yes, if it's true; if not, I'm off again.

DR. STOCKMANN. If what is true?

MORTEN KIIL. This crazy business about the waterworks. Now, is it true?

DR. STOCKMANN. Why, of course it is. But how did you hear of it?

MORTEN KIIL (*coming in*). Petra looked in on her way to school —

DR. STOCKMANN. Oh, did she?

MORTEN KIIL. Yes — and she told me — I thought she was only making fun of me; but that's not like Petra.

DR. STOCKMANN. No, indeed; how could you think so?

MORTEN KIIL. Oh, you can never be sure of anybody. You may be made a fool of before you know where you are. So it is true, after all?

DR. STOCKMANN. Most certainly it is. Do sit down, father-in-law. (*Forces him down on the sofa.*) Now isn't it a real blessing for the town — ?

MORTEN KIIL (*suppressing his laughter*). A blessing for the town?

DR. STOCKMANN. Yes, that I made this discovery in time —

MORTEN KIIL (*as before*). Oh, yes! — Well, I could never have believed that you would play monkey tricks on your very own brother.

DR. STOCKMANN. Monkey tricks!

MRS. STOCKMANN. Why, father dear —

MORTEN KIIL (*resting his hands and chin on the top of his stick and blinking slyly at the* DOCTOR). What was it again? Wasn't it that some animals had got into the water pipes?

DR. STOCKMANN. Yes; microorganisms.

MORTEN KIIL. And any number of these animals had got in, Petra said — whole swarms of them.

DR. STOCKMANN. Certainly, hundreds of thousands.

MORTEN KIIL. But no one can see them — isn't that it?

DR. STOCKMANN. Quite right; no one can see them.

MORTEN KIIL (*with a quiet, chuckling laugh*). I'll be damned if that isn't the best thing I've heard of yet.

DR. STOCKMANN. What do you mean?

MORTEN KIIL. But you'll never in this world make the Mayor believe anything of the sort.

DR. STOCKMANN. Well, we shall see.

MORTEN KIIL. Do you really think he'll be so crazy?

DR. STOCKMANN. I hope the whole town will be so crazy.

MORTEN KIIL. The whole town! Well, maybe it will be. It'll serve them right; it'll teach them a lesson. They think they're so much cleverer than we old fellows. They hounded me out of the Town Council. Yes; I tell you they hounded me out like dogs, they did. But now it's their turn. Just you keep up the game with them, Stockmann.

DR. STOCKMANN. Yes, but, father-in-law —

MORTEN KIIL. Keep it up, I say. (*Rising*) If you can make the Mayor and his gang eat humble pie, I'll give a hundred crowns straight away to the poor.

DR. STOCKMANN. That's good of you.

MORTEN KIIL. Of course I've little enough to throw away; but if you can manage that, I shall certainly remember the poor at Christmas time, to the tune of fifty crowns.

[HOVSTAD *enters from hall.*]

HOVSTAD. Good morning! (*Pausing*) Oh! I beg your pardon —

DR. STOCKMANN. Not at all. Come in, come in.

MORTEN KIIL (*chuckling again*). Him! Is he in it too?

HOVSTAD. What do you mean?

DR. STOCKMANN. Yes, of course he is.

MORTEN KIIL. I might have known it! It's to go into the papers. Ah, you're a good one, Stockmann! You two put your heads together; I'm off.

DR. STOCKMANN. Oh no; don't go yet, father-in-law.

MORTEN KIIL. No, I'm off now. Play them all the monkey tricks you can think of. I'm damned sure you won't lose by it.

[*He goes,* MRS. STOCKMANN *accompanying him.*]

DR. STOCKMANN (*laughing*). Can you imagine it? The old man doesn't believe a word of all this about the waterworks.

HOVSTAD. Was that what he — ?

DR. STOCKMANN. Yes; that was what we were talking about. And I dare say you have come on the same business?

HOVSTAD. Yes. Have you a moment to spare, Doctor?

DR. STOCKMANN. As many as you like, my dear fellow.

HOVSTAD. Have you heard anything from the Mayor?

DR. STOCKMANN. Not yet. He'll be here later.

HOVSTAD. I have been thinking the matter over since last evening.

DR. STOCKMANN. Well?

HOVSTAD. To you, as a doctor and a man of science, this business of the waterworks appears an isolated affair. I dare say it hasn't occurred to you that a good many other things are bound up with it?

DR. STOCKMANN. Indeed! In what way? Let us sit down, my dear fellow. — No; there, on the sofa.

[HOVSTAD *sits on sofa, the* DOCTOR *in an easy chair on the other side of the table.*]

DR. STOCKMANN. Well, so you think — ?

HOVSTAD. You said yesterday that the water is polluted by impurities in the soil.

DR. STOCKMANN. Yes, undoubtedly; the mischief comes from that poisonous swamp up in the Mill Dale.

HOVSTAD. Excuse me, Doctor, but I think it comes from a very different swamp.

DR. STOCKMANN. What swamp is that?

HOVSTAD. The swamp in which our whole community life is rotting.

DR. STOCKMANN. The devil, Mr. Hovstad! What notion is this you've got hold of?

HOVSTAD. All the affairs of the town have gradually drifted into the hands of a pack of bureaucrats —

DR. STOCKMANN. Come now, they're not all bureaucrats.

HOVSTAD. No; but those who are not are the friends and supporters of those who are. We are entirely under the thumb of a ring of wealthy men, men of old family and position in the town.

DR. STOCKMANN. Yes, but they are also men of ability and insight.

HOVSTAD. Did they show ability and insight when they laid the water pipes where they are?

DR. STOCKMANN. No; that, of course, was a piece of stupidity. But that will be set right now.

HOVSTAD. Do you think it will go so smoothly?

DR. STOCKMANN. Well, smoothly or not, it will have to be done.

HOVSTAD. Yes, if the press exerts its influence.

DR. STOCKMANN. Not at all necessary, my dear fellow; I am sure my brother —

HOVSTAD. Excuse me, Doctor, but I must tell you that I intend to take the matter up.

DR. STOCKMANN. In the paper?

HOVSTAD. Yes. When I took over the *People's Messenger*, I was determined to break up the ring of obstinate old blockheads who held everything in their hands.

DR. STOCKMANN. But you told me yourself what came of it. You nearly ruined the paper.

HOVSTAD. Yes, at that time we had to draw in our horns, that's true. The whole Bath scheme might have fallen through if these men had been turned out then. But now the Baths are an accomplished fact, and we can get on without these gentlemen.

DR. STOCKMANN. Get on without them, yes; but still we owe them a great deal.

HOVSTAD. The debt shall be duly acknowledged. But a journalist of my democratic tendencies cannot let such an opportunity slip through his fingers. We must explode the belief in official infallibility. That rubbish must be got rid of, like every other superstition.

DR. STOCKMANN. There I am with you with all my heart, Mr. Hovstad. If it's a superstition, away with it!

HOVSTAD. I should be sorry to attack the Mayor, as he is your brother. But I know you agree with me — the truth before all other considerations.

DR. STOCKMANN. Why, of course. (Vehemently) But still — ! but still — !

HOVSTAD. You mustn't think ill of me. I am no more egotistical or ambitious than other men.

DR. STOCKMANN. Why, my dear fellow — who says you are?

HOVSTAD. I come from a poor family, as you know; and I have had ample opportunity to see what the lower classes really require. And that is to have a share in the direction of public affairs, Doctor. That is what develops ability and knowledge and self-respect —

DR. STOCKMANN. I understand that perfectly.

HOVSTAD. Yes; and I think a journalist incurs a heavy responsibility if he neglects a chance to help free the downtrodden masses. I know very well that the people in power will denounce me as an agitator, and so forth; but what do I care? If only my conscience is clear, I —

DR. STOCKMANN. Just so, just so, my dear Mr. Hovstad. But still — damn it all — ! (A knock at the door) Come in!

[ASLAKSEN, the printer, appears at the door leading to the hall. He is humbly but respectably dressed in black, wears a white necktie, slightly crumpled, and has a silk hat and gloves in his hand.]

ASLAKSEN (bowing). I beg pardon, Doctor, intruding —

DR. STOCKMANN (rising). Well! If it isn't Mr. Aslaksen!

ASLAKSEN. Yes, it's me, Doctor.

HOVSTAD (rising). Were you looking for me, Aslaksen?

ASLAKSEN. No, not at all. I didn't know you were here. No, it's the Doctor himself —

DR. STOCKMANN. Well, what can I do for you?

ASLAKSEN. Is it true, what Mr. Billing tells me, that you plan to improve the water supply?

DR. STOCKMANN. Yes, for the Baths.

ASLAKSEN. Of course, of course. Then I just looked in to say that I'll back up the movement with all my might.

HOVSTAD (to the DOCTOR). You see!

DR. STOCKMANN. I'm sure I thank you heartily; but —

ASLAKSEN. You may find it useful to have us small middle-class men at your back. We form what you may call a solid majority in the town — when we really make up our minds, that is. And it's always well to have the majority with you, Doctor.

DR. STOCKMANN. No doubt, no doubt; but I can't conceive that any special measures will be necessary in this case. I should think in so clear and straightforward a matter —

ASLAKSEN. Yes, but all the same, it can do no harm. I know the local authorities very well — the powers that be are not eager to adopt suggestions from outsiders. So I think it might be a good idea if we made some sort of demonstration.

HOVSTAD. Precisely my opinion.

DR. STOCKMANN. A demonstration, you say? But in what way would you demonstrate?

ASLAKSEN. With great moderation, of course,

Doctor. I always insist upon moderation; for moderation is a citizen's first virtue — at least that's what I think.

DR. STOCKMANN. We all know of your moderation, Mr. Aslaksen.

ASLAKSEN. Yes, I think my moderation is generally recognized. And this affair of the waterworks is very important for us small middle-class men. The Baths promise to become, you might say, a little gold mine for the town. We shall all have to depend on the Baths for our living, especially we home owners. So we want to support the Baths all we can; and as I am Chairman of the Home Owners' Association —

DR. STOCKMANN. Well — ?

ASLAKSEN. And as I'm an active worker for the Temperance Society[1] — of course you know, Doctor, that I'm a temperance man?

DR. STOCKMANN. To be sure, to be sure.

ASLAKSEN. Well, you'll understand that I come in contact with a great many people. And as I'm known to be a prudent and law-abiding citizen, as you yourself remarked, Doctor, I have a certain influence in the town, and hold some power in my hands — though I do say so myself.

DR. STOCKMANN. I know that very well, Mr. Aslaksen.

ASLAKSEN. Well then, you see — it would be easy for me to get up a petition, if necessary.

DR. STOCKMANN. A petition?

ASLAKSEN. Yes, a kind of vote of thanks to you, from the citizens of the town, for your action in a matter of such general concern. Of course it will have to be drawn up with all fitting moderation, so as to give no offence to the authorities and parties in power. But so long as we're careful about that, no one can object, I should think.

---

[1] **Temperance Society**: group which is opposed to the use of alcoholic beverages.

HOVSTAD. Well, even if they didn't particularly like it —

ASLAKSEN. No, no, no; no offense to the powers that be, Mr. Hovstad. Nothing to antagonize people in power. I've had enough of that in my time; no good ever comes of it. But no one can object to the free but temperate expression of a citizen's opinion.

DR. STOCKMANN (*shaking his hand*). I can't tell you, my dear Mr. Aslaksen, how heartily it delights me to find so much support among my fellow townsmen. I'm so happy — so happy! Come, you'll have a glass of sherry? Eh?

ASLAKSEN. No, thank you; I never touch spirituous[2] liquors.

DR. STOCKMANN. Well, then, a glass of beer — what do you say to that?

ASLAKSEN. No, thanks, Doctor. I never take anything so early in the day. And now I'll be off round the town, and talk to some of the home owners, and prepare public opinion.

DR. STOCKMANN. It's extremely kind of you, Mr. Aslaksen; but I really cannot see that all these preparations are necessary. The affair seems to me so simple and self-evident.

ASLAKSEN. The authorities always move slowly, Doctor — God forbid I should blame them for it —

HOVSTAD. We'll stir them up in the paper tomorrow, Aslaksen.

ASLAKSEN. No violence, Mr. Hovstad. Proceed with moderation, or you'll get nowhere. Take my advice; I've picked up experience in the school of life. — And now I'll say good morning, Doctor. You know now that at least you have us small middle-class men behind you, solid as a wall. You have the solid majority on your side, Doctor.

DR. STOCKMANN. Many thanks, my dear Mr.

---

[2] **spirituous**: alcoholic.

Aslaksen. (*Holds out his hand.*) Good-by, good-by.

ASLAKSEN. Are you coming to the office, Mr. Hovstad?

HOVSTAD. I shall be along presently. I have still one or two things to arrange.

ASLAKSEN. Very well.

[*Bows and goes.* DR. STOCKMANN *accompanies him into the hall.*]

HOVSTAD (*as the* DOCTOR *re-enters*). Well, what do you say to that, Doctor? Don't you think it is high time we gave all this weak-kneed, half-hearted cowardice a good shaking up?

DR. STOCKMANN. Are you speaking of Aslaksen?

HOVSTAD. Yes, I am. He's a decent enough fellow, but he's one of those who are sunk in the swamp. And most people here are just like him. They are forever wavering and wobbling from side to side; what with scruples and misgivings, they never dare advance a step.

DR. STOCKMANN. Yes, but Aslaksen seems to me thoroughly well-intentioned.

HOVSTAD. There is one thing I value more than good intentions, and that is an attitude of firm self-confidence.

DR. STOCKMANN. There I quite agree with you.

HOVSTAD. So I am going to seize this opportunity, and try whether I can't for once put a little backbone into their good intentions. The worship of authority must be rooted up in this town. This gross, inexcusable blunder of the waterworks must be brought home clearly to every voter.

DR. STOCKMANN. Very well. If you think it's for the good of the community, do so, but not till I have spoken to my brother.

HOVSTAD. I shall be drafting an editorial in the meantime. And if the Mayor won't take the matter up —

DR. STOCKMANN. But how can you think he will refuse?

HOVSTAD. Oh, it's not inconceivable. And then —

DR. STOCKMANN. Well then, I promise you —; look here — in that case you may print my article — put it in just as it is.

HOVSTAD. May I? Is that a promise?

DR. STOCKMANN (*handing him the manuscript*). There it is; take it with you. You may as well read it in any case; you can return it to me afterwards.

HOVSTAD. Very good; I shall do so. And now, good-by, Doctor.

DR. STOCKMANN. Good-by, good-by. You'll see it will all go smoothly, Mr. Hovstad — quite smoothly.

HOVSTAD. H'm — we shall see. (*Bows and goes out through the hall.*)

DR. STOCKMANN (*going to the dining room door and looking in*). Katherine! Oh! are you back, Petra?

PETRA (*entering*). Yes, I've just got back from school.

MRS. STOCKMANN (*entering*). Hasn't he been here yet?

DR. STOCKMANN. Peter? No; but I've had a long talk with Hovstad. He's quite enthusiastic about my discovery. It turns out to have wider implications than I thought at first. So he has placed his paper at my disposal, if I should require it.

MRS. STOCKMANN. Do you think you will?

DR. STOCKMANN. No! But at the same time, it makes one proud to know that the enlightened, independent press is on one's side. And what do you think? I have had a visit from the Chairman of the Home Owners' Association too.

MRS. STOCKMANN. Really? What did he want?

DR. STOCKMANN. To assure me of his support. They will all stand by me if needed. Katherine, do you know what I have behind me?

MRS. STOCKMANN. Behind you? No. What do you have behind you?

DR. STOCKMANN. The solid majority!

MRS. STOCKMANN. Oh! Is that good for you, Thomas?

DR. STOCKMANN. Yes, indeed; I think it is. (*Rubbing his hands as he walks up and down*) What a delight it is to feel in such harmony with one's fellow townsmen.

PETRA. And to do so much that's good and useful, father!

DR. STOCKMANN. And all for one's native town, too!

MRS. STOCKMANN. There's the bell.

DR. STOCKMANN. That must be Peter. (*Knock at the door*) Come in!

[*Enter the* MAYOR *from the hall.*]

MAYOR. Good morning.

DR. STOCKMANN. I'm glad to see you, Peter.

MRS. STOCKMANN. Good morning, brother-in-law. How are you?

MAYOR. Oh, thanks, so-so. (*To the* DOCTOR) Yesterday evening, after office hours, I received from you a dissertation[1] upon the state of the water at the Baths.

DR. STOCKMANN. Yes. Have you read it?

MAYOR. I have.

DR. STOCKMANN. And what do you think of the affair?

MAYOR. H'm — (*With a sidelong glance*)

MRS. STOCKMANN. Come, Petra.

[*She and* PETRA *go into the room on the left.*]

MAYOR (*after a pause*). Was it necessary to make all these investigations behind my back?

DR. STOCKMANN. Yes, till I was absolutely certain, I —

MAYOR. And are you absolutely certain now?

DR. STOCKMANN. My paper must surely have convinced you of that.

MAYOR. Is it your intention to submit this statement to the Board of Directors, as a sort of official document?

DR. STOCKMANN. Of course. Something must be done in the matter, and quickly.

MAYOR. As usual, you use very strong expressions in your statement. Among other things, you say that what we offer our visitors is sheer poison.

DR. STOCKMANN. Why, Peter, what else can it be called? Only think — poisoned water both internally and externally! And to poor invalids who come to us in all confidence, and pay us handsomely to cure them!

MAYOR. And then you announce as your conclusion that we must build a sewer to carry off the alleged impurities from the Mill Dale, and must re-lay all the water pipes.

DR. STOCKMANN. Yes. Can you suggest any other plan? — I know of none.

MAYOR. I found an excuse to look in at the town engineer's this morning, and — in a half-joking way — I mentioned these alterations as things we might possibly have to consider, at some future time.

DR. STOCKMANN. At some future time!

MAYOR. Of course he smiled at what he thought my extravagance. Have you taken the trouble to think what your proposed alterations would cost? From what the engineers said, I gathered that the expenses would probably mount up to several hundred thousand crowns.

DR. STOCKMANN. So much as that?

MAYOR. Yes. But that is not the worst. The work would take at least two years.

DR. STOCKMANN. Two years! Two whole years?

MAYOR. At least. And what are we to do with the Baths in the meantime? Are we to close them? We should have no alternative. Do you think anyone would come here, if it got abroad that the water was polluted?

DR. STOCKMANN. But, Peter, that's precisely what it is.

MAYOR. And all this now, just now, when the Baths are doing so well! Neighboring towns, too, could develop into health

[1] dissertation: long, written treatment of a subject.

resorts. Do you think they would not at once set to work to divert our visitors to themselves? Undoubtedly they would; and we should be left stranded. We should probably have to give up the whole costly undertaking; and so you would have ruined your native town.

DR. STOCKMANN. I — ruined — !

MAYOR. It is only through the Baths that the town has any future worth speaking of. You surely know that as well as I do.

DR. STOCKMANN. Then what do you think should be done?

MAYOR. I have not succeeded in convincing myself that the condition of the water at the Baths is as serious as your statement indicates.

DR. STOCKMANN. I tell you if anything it's worse — or will be in the summer, when the hot weather sets in.

MAYOR. I repeat that I believe you exaggerate greatly. A competent physician should know what measures to take — he should be able to remove any dangerous influences, and to counteract any effects they might have.

DR. STOCKMANN. Indeed — ? And then — ?

MAYOR. The existing waterworks are, once for all, a fact, and must be treated as such. But when the time comes, the Directors will probably not be unwilling to consider whether it may not be possible, without unreasonable financial sacrifices, to introduce certain improvements.

DR. STOCKMANN. And do you imagine I could ever be a party to such dishonesty?

MAYOR. Dishonesty?

DR. STOCKMANN. Yes, it would be dishonesty — a fraud, a lie, an absolute crime against the public, against society as a whole!

MAYOR. I have not, as I before remarked, been able to convince myself that there is really any such imminent danger.

DR. STOCKMANN. Oh yes, you have! You must have! I know that my report is absolutely clear and convincing. And you understand it perfectly, Peter, only you won't admit it. It was you who insisted that both the Bath buildings and the waterworks should be placed where they now are; and it's that — it's that damned blunder that you won't confess. Do you think I don't see through you?

MAYOR. And even if it were so? If I do watch over my reputation with a certain anxiety, I do it for the good of the town. Without moral authority I cannot guide and direct affairs in the way I consider best for the general welfare. Therefore — and on various other grounds — it is imperative that your statement should not be submitted to the Board of Directors. It must be kept back, for the good of the community. Later on I will bring up the matter for discussion, and we will do the best we can, quietly; but not a word, not a whisper, of this unfortunate business must be made public.

DR. STOCKMANN. But it can't be prevented now, my dear Peter.

MAYOR. It must and shall be prevented.

DR. STOCKMANN. It can't be, I tell you; far too many people know about it already.

MAYOR. Know about it! Who? Surely not those fellows who are on the *People's Messenger* — ?

DR. STOCKMANN. Oh, yes; they know. The liberal, independent press will take good care that you do your duty.

MAYOR (*after a short pause*). You are an amazingly reckless man, Thomas. Have you considered what the consequences of this may be to yourself?

DR. STOCKMANN. Consequences? — Consequences to me?

MAYOR. Yes — to you and yours.

DR. STOCKMANN. What the devil do you mean?

MAYOR. I believe I have always shown myself ready and willing to lend you a helping hand.

DR. STOCKMANN. Yes, you have, and I thank you for it.

MAYOR. I ask for no thanks. Indeed, I was in some measure forced to act as I did — for my own sake. I always hoped I should be able to keep you a little in check, if I helped to improve your financial position.

DR. STOCKMANN. What! So it was only for your own sake — !

MAYOR. In a measure, I say. It is painful for a man in an official position, when his nearest relative is always compromising himself.

DR. STOCKMANN. And you think I do that?

MAYOR. Yes, unfortunately, you do, without knowing it. You have a turbulent, unruly, rebellious spirit. And you have an unfortunate habit of rushing into print upon every possible and impossible occasion. You no sooner hit upon an idea than you must write a newspaper article or a whole pamphlet about it.

DR. STOCKMANN. Isn't it a citizen's duty, when he has conceived a new idea, to communicate it to the public!

MAYOR. Oh, the public has no need for new ideas. The public gets on best with the good old recognized ideas it has already.

DR. STOCKMANN. That puts it bluntly.

MAYOR. Yes, I must speak frankly to you for once. I have tried to avoid it, for I know how irritable you are; but now I must tell you the truth, Thomas. You have no idea how much you injure yourself by your constant criticism. You complain of the authorities, yes, of the Government itself — you do nothing but find fault and then maintain that you have been slighted, persecuted. But what else can you expect, with your impossible disposition?

DR. STOCKMANN. Oh, indeed! So I am impossible, am I?

MAYOR. Yes, Thomas, you are an impossible man to work with. I know that from experience. You have no consideration for anyone or anything; and you seem to forget that you have me to thank for your position as medical officer of the Baths —

DR. STOCKMANN. It was mine by right! Mine, and no one else's! I was the first to discover the possibility of a health resort; I saw it, and I was the only one who did. For years I fought single-handed for this idea of mine; I wrote and wrote —

MAYOR. No doubt; but then the right time had not come. Of course, in that out-of-the-world corner, you could not judge of that. As soon as the appropriate moment arrived, I — and others — took the matter in hand —

DR. STOCKMANN. Yes, and you went and bungled the whole of my glorious plan. Oh, we see now how clever you were!

MAYOR. All *I* can see is that you are trying to start an argument. You want an excuse to attack your superiors — that is an old habit of yours. You cannot endure any authority over you; you regard anyone who holds a post higher than your own as a personal enemy — and you do not care what kind of weapon you use against him. But now I have shown you how much is at stake for the town, and consequently for me too. And therefore I warn you, Thomas, that I am inflexible in the demand I am about to make of you!

DR. STOCKMANN. What demand?

MAYOR. As you have not had the sense to refrain from chattering to outsiders about this delicate business, which should have been kept an official secret, of course it cannot now be hushed up. All sorts of rumors will get abroad, and spiteful persons will invent all sorts of additions to them. It will therefore be necessary for you publicly to contradict these rumors.

DR. STOCKMANN. I! How? I don't understand you.

MAYOR. We expect that after further investigation you will come to the conclusion that the situation is not nearly so serious or pressing as you had at first imagined.

DR. STOCKMANN. Aha! So you expect that?

MAYOR. Furthermore, we expect you to express your confidence that the Board of Directors will thoroughly and conscientiously carry out all measures to remedy any possible defects.

DR. STOCKMANN. Yes, but you'll never be able to do that, so long as you go on tinkering and patching. I tell you that, Peter, and it's my deepest, sincerest conviction —

MAYOR. As an official, you have no right to hold any individual conviction.

DR. STOCKMANN (starting). No right to — ?

MAYOR. As an official, I say. As a private citizen, of course, it is another matter. But as a subordinate official of the Baths, you have no right to express any conviction opposed to that of your superiors.

DR. STOCKMANN. This is too much! I, a doctor, a man of science, have no right to — !

MAYOR. The matter in question is not a purely scientific one. It is a complex affair; it has both a technical and an economic side.

DR. STOCKMANN. What the devil do I care what it is! I will be free to speak my mind upon any subject under the sun!

MAYOR. As you please — so long as it does not concern the Baths. About them we forbid you to speak.

DR. STOCKMANN (shouts). You forbid — ! You! A set of —

MAYOR. I forbid it — I, your chief; and when I give an order, you must obey.

DR. STOCKMANN (controlling himself). Peter, if you weren't my brother —

PETRA (tears open the door). Father, you must not submit to this!

MRS. STOCKMANN (following her). Petra, Petra!

MAYOR. Ah! So we have been listening!

MRS. STOCKMANN. You were talking so loud, we couldn't help —

PETRA. I stood and listened on purpose.

MAYOR. Well, actually, I am not sorry —

DR. STOCKMANN (coming nearer to him). You spoke to me of forbidding and obeying —

MAYOR. You forced me to speak like that.

DR. STOCKMANN. And I am to deny my own words, in a public statement?

MAYOR. We consider it absolutely necessary that you should issue a statement along the lines I have indicated.

DR. STOCKMANN. And if I do not obey?

MAYOR. Then we shall ourselves put forth a statement to reassure the public.

DR. STOCKMANN. Well and good; then I shall write against you. I shall stick to my point and prove that I am right, and you wrong. And what will you do then?

MAYOR. Then I shall be unable to prevent your dismissal.

DR. STOCKMANN. What — !

PETRA. Father! Dismissal!

MRS. STOCKMANN. Dismissal!

MAYOR. Your dismissal from the Baths. I shall be compelled to move that notice be given you at once, and that you have henceforth no connection whatever with the Baths.

DR. STOCKMANN. You would dare to do that!

MAYOR. It is you who are playing the daring game.

PETRA. Uncle, this is a shameful way to treat a man like father!

MRS. STOCKMANN. Do be quiet, Petra!

MAYOR (looking at PETRA). Aha! We have opinions of our own already, eh? To be sure, to be sure! (To MRS. STOCKMANN) Sister-in-law, you are presumably the most rational member of this household. Use all your influence with your husband; try to make him realize what all this will mean both for his family —

DR. STOCKMANN. My family is my concern!

MAYOR. — both for his family, I say, and for the town he lives in.

DR. STOCKMANN. I'm the one who has the real good of the town at heart! I want to lay bare the evils that sooner or later must come to light. Oh! You shall see whether I love my native town or not.

MAYOR. You in your blind obstinacy would cut off the town's chief source of prosperity!

DR. STOCKMANN. That source is poisoned, man! Are you mad? We live by selling filth and corruption! The whole of our prosperity is rooted in a lie!

MAYOR. Idle fancies — or worse. The man who makes such charges against his own birthplace must be an enemy of society.

DR. STOCKMANN (*going towards him*). You dare to — !

MRS. STOCKMANN (*throwing herself between them*). Thomas!

PETRA (*seizing her father's arm*). Keep calm, father!

MAYOR. I will not expose myself to violence. You have had your warning. Consider what you owe to yourself and to your family. Good-by. (*He goes.*)

DR. STOCKMANN (*walking up and down*). And I must put up with such treatment! In my own house, Katherine! What do you say to that!

MRS. STOCKMANN. Indeed, it's a shame and a disgrace, Thomas —

PETRA. Oh, if I could get my hands on uncle — !

DR. STOCKMANN. It's my own fault. I should have stood up to them long ago — shown my teeth — and used them too! — And to be called an enemy of society! Me! I won't bear it; by Heaven, I won't!

MRS. STOCKMANN. But my dear Thomas, after all, your brother has the power —

DR. STOCKMANN. Yes, but I have the right.

MRS. STOCKMANN. Ah, yes, right, right! But what good is the right, if you don't have the might?

PETRA. Oh, mother — how can you talk so?

DR. STOCKMANN. What! No good, in a free community, to have right on your side? What an absurd idea, Katherine! And besides — don't I have the free and independent press before me — and the solid majority at my back? That is might enough, I should think!

MRS. STOCKMANN. Why, good heavens, Thomas! surely you are not thinking of — ?

DR. STOCKMANN. What am I not thinking of?

MRS. STOCKMANN. — of setting yourself up against your brother, I mean.

DR. STOCKMANN. What the devil would you have me do, if not stick to what is right and true?

PETRA. Yes, that's what I would like to know.

MRS. STOCKMANN. But it will be of no earthly use. If they won't, they won't.

DR. STOCKMANN. Aha, Katherine! just wait a while, and you shall see whether I can fight my battles to the end.

MRS. STOCKMANN. Yes, to the end of getting your dismissal; that is what will happen.

DR. STOCKMANN. Well then, at least I shall have done my duty towards the public, towards society — I who am called an enemy of society!

MRS. STOCKMANN. But what about your family, Thomas? What about us at home? Will you be doing your duty towards those who are dependent on you?

PETRA. Oh, mother, don't always think first of us.

MRS. STOCKMANN. Yes, it's easy for you to talk; you can stand alone if necessary. — But remember the boys, Thomas; and think a little of yourself too, and of me —

DR. STOCKMANN. You must be out of your mind, Katherine! If I was such a coward as to knuckle under to this Peter and his confounded crew — would I ever have another happy hour in all my life?

MRS. STOCKMANN. I don't know about that; but God preserve us from the happiness we will all have if you persist in defying them. There you will be again, with nothing to live on, with no regular income. I thought we had enough of that in the old days. Remember them, Thomas; think of what it all means.

DR. STOCKMANN (*struggling with himself and clenching his hands*). It's disgraceful what these damned bureaucrats can do to a free and honest man! Isn't it revolting, Katherine!

MRS. STOCKMANN. Yes, no doubt they are treating you shamefully. But God knows there's plenty of injustice one must submit to in this world. — Here are the boys, Thomas. Look at them! What is to become of them? Oh, no, no! you cannot have the heart —

[EILIF *and* MORTEN *enter, carrying schoolbooks.*]

DR. STOCKMANN. The boys — ! (*With sudden firmness and decision*) Never, though the whole earth should crumble, will I bow my neck beneath the yoke. (*Goes towards his room.*)

MRS. STOCKMANN (*following him*). Thomas — what are you going to do?

DR. STOCKMANN (*at the door*). I must have the right to look my boys in the face when they have grown into free men. (*Goes into his room.*)

MRS. STOCKMANN (*bursts into tears*). Oh, God help us all!

PETRA. Father is wonderful! He will never give in!

[*The boys ask wonderingly what it all means;* PETRA *signs to them to be quiet.*]

For Discussion

1. An additional complication in the action is introduced early in Act II. Kiil's unexpected response to the discovery about the baths suggests that Dr. Stockmann's truth may encounter some difficulty before the community will accept it. How does Kiil respond to the discovery? Why is the old man hostile to the mayor and the mayor's party?

2. Thomas and Peter represent strikingly different points of view. "The matter in question," the mayor tells his brother, "is not a purely scientific one; it is a complex affair; it has both a technical and an economic side" (page 95). What makes the question of the baths particularly complex? According to the mayor, what course must the doctor follow as a public servant? How does Dr. Stockmann respond to his brother's arguments?

3. Toward the end of the act, Mrs. Stockmann puts forth another argument to discourage the doctor from following the course he has set for himself. She reminds him of his responsibilities. To whom? What does she feel will be the outcome if he persists in challenging the authorities? What finally determines the doctor to go ahead with his plans?

Act III

The editorial office of the People's Messenger. *In the background, to the left, an entrance door; to the right another door, with glass panes, through which can be seen the composing room. A door in the right-hand wall. In the middle of the room a large table covered with papers, newspapers, and books. In front, on the left, a window, and by it a desk with a high stool. A couple of armchairs beside the table; some other chairs along the walls. The room is dismal and cheerless, the furniture shabby, the armchairs dirty and torn. In the composing room are seen a few compositors at work; further back, a hand press in operation.*

HOVSTAD *is seated at the desk, writing. Presently* BILLING *enters from the right, with the* DOCTOR'S *manuscript in his hand.*

BILLING. Well, I must say — !

HOVSTAD (*writing*). Have you read it through?

BILLING (*laying the manuscript on the desk*). Yes, indeed I have.

HOVSTAD. Don't you think the Doctor comes out strong?

BILLING. Strong! Why, strike me dead if he isn't crushing! Every word falls like a — well, like a sledgehammer.

HOVSTAD. Yes, but these fellows won't collapse at the first blow.

BILLING. True enough; but we'll keep on hammering away, blow after blow, till the whole setup comes crashing down. As I sat in there reading that article, I seemed to hear the revolution thundering in the distance.

HOVSTAD (*turning round*). Hush! Don't let Aslaksen hear that.

BILLING (*in a lower voice*). Aslaksen's a white-livered coward, without a spark of manhood in him. But this time you'll insist, won't you? You'll print the Doctor's article?

HOVSTAD. Yes, if only the Mayor doesn't give in —

BILLING. That would be damned annoying.

HOVSTAD. Well, whatever happens, we can gain from the situation. If the Mayor won't agree to the Doctor's proposal, he'll have all the small middle-class down upon him — all the Home Owners' Association, and the rest of them. And if he does agree to it, he'll make enemies of the big shareholders in the Baths, who have been his main support —

BILLING. Yes, of course. They'd have to fork out a lot of money —

HOVSTAD. No doubt of that. And then, don't you see, when the ring is broken up, we'll din it into[1] the public day after day that the Mayor is totally incompetent and that all responsible positions in the town must be entrusted to men of liberal ideas.

[1] **din it into**: impress by constant repetition.

BILLING. Strike me dead if that isn't the truth! I see it — I see it: we are on the eve of a revolution! (*A knock at the door*)

HOVSTAD. Hush! (*Calls.*) Come in!

[DR. STOCKMANN *enters from the back, left.*]

HOVSTAD (*going towards him*). Ah, here is the Doctor. Well?

DR. STOCKMANN. Print away, Mr. Hovstad!

HOVSTAD. So it has come to that?

BILLING. Hurrah!

DR. STOCKMANN. Print away, I tell you. Yes, it has come to that. Now they'll get what they ask for. War is declared, Mr. Billing!

BILLING. War to the knife, I say! War to the death, Doctor!

DR. STOCKMANN. This article is only the beginning. I have four or five others sketched out in my head already. But where do you keep Aslaksen?

BILLING (*calling into the printing room*). Aslaksen! come here a moment.

HOVSTAD. Four or five more articles, eh? On the same subject?

DR. STOCKMANN. Oh, no — not at all, my dear fellow. No; they will deal with quite different matters. But they're all related to the waterworks and sewer question. One thing leads to another. It's just like trying to fix up an old house, don't you know?

BILLING. Strike me dead, but that's true! You feel you can't stop till you've pulled the whole thing to pieces.

ASLAKSEN (*enters from the printing room*). Pulled to pieces! Surely the Doctor isn't thinking of pulling the Baths to pieces?

HOVSTAD. Not at all. Don't be alarmed.

DR. STOCKMANN. No, we were talking of something quite different. Well, what do you think of my article, Mr. Hovstad?

HOVSTAD. I think it's simply a masterpiece —

DR. STOCKMANN. Yes, isn't it? I'm glad you think so — very glad.

HOVSTAD. It's so clear and to the point. You

don't need to be a specialist to understand it. I am certain every intelligent man will be on your side.

ASLAKSEN. And all the prudent ones too, I hope?

BILLING. Both the prudent and imprudent — in fact, almost the whole town.

ASLAKSEN. Then I suppose we may venture to print it.

DR. STOCKMANN. I should think so!

HOVSTAD. It will go in tomorrow.

DR. STOCKMANN. Yes, not a day must be lost. Look here, Mr. Aslaksen, this is what I wanted to ask you: Will you take personal charge of the article?

ASLAKSEN. Certainly I will.

DR. STOCKMANN. Be as careful as if it were gold. No printers' errors; every word is important. I shall look in again later; perhaps you'll be able to let me see a proof. — Oh! I can't tell you how I long to have the thing in print — to see it launched —

BILLING. Yes, like a thunderbolt!

DR. STOCKMANN. — and submitted to the judgment of every intelligent citizen. Oh, you have no idea what I have had to put up with today. I've been threatened with all sorts of things. I was to be robbed of my basic rights as a human being —

BILLING. What! Your rights as a human being!

DR. STOCKMANN. — I was to humble myself, and eat the dust; I was to set my personal interests above my deepest, holiest convictions —

BILLING. Strike me dead, that's outrageous.

HOVSTAD. Oh, what can you expect from that crowd?

DR. STOCKMANN. But they won't get away with it. They'll learn that in black and white, I promise them! I'll blast them every day in the *Messenger*, bombard them with one explosive article after another —

ASLAKSEN. Yes, but look here —

BILLING. Hurrah! It's war! War!

DR. STOCKMANN. I'll batter them to the ground, I'll crush them, I'll blast their defenses open in the eyes of all right-thinking men! That's what I'll do!

ASLAKSEN. But above all things be temperate, Doctor; bombard with moderation —

BILLING. No! No! Don't spare the dynamite!

DR. STOCKMANN (*going on imperturbably*). For now it's not just a question of waterworks and of sewers, you see. No, the whole community must be purged, disinfected —

BILLING. That's the word of salvation!

DR. STOCKMANN. All the old bunglers must be thrown out, you understand. No matter who they are! Such endless vistas have opened out before me today. I am not quite clear about everything yet, but I'll see my way presently. It's young and vigorous standard-bearers we must look for, my friends; we must have new captains at all the outposts.

BILLING. Hear, hear!

DR. STOCKMANN. And if only we hold together, it will go so smoothly, so smoothly! The whole revolution will glide down the ways just like a ship. Don't you think so?

HOVSTAD. For my part, I believe we have now every prospect of placing our municipal affairs in the right hands.

ASLAKSEN. As long as we proceed with moderation, I really don't think there can be any danger.

DR. STOCKMANN. Who the devil cares whether there's danger or not! What I do, I do in the name of truth and for conscience' sake.

HOVSTAD. You deserve support, Doctor.

ASLAKSEN. Yes, there's no doubt the Doctor is a true friend to the town; he's what I call a friend of society.

BILLING. Strike me dead, he's a Friend of the People, Aslaksen!

ASLAKSEN. I'm sure the Home Owners' Association will soon adopt that expression.

DR. STOCKMANN (*shaking their hands, deeply*

moved). Thanks, thanks, my dear, faithful friends; it does me good to hear you. My respected brother called me something very different. Never mind! I'll pay him back with interest! But I must be off now to see a poor devil of a patient. I shall look in again though. Be sure you look after the article, Mr. Aslaksen; and don't leave out any exclamation points! If anything, put in a few more! Well, good-by for now, good-by, good-by.

[*General good-bys as they accompany him to the door. He goes out.*]

HOVSTAD. He will be invaluable to us.

ASLAKSEN. Yes, as long as he confines himself to this matter of the Baths. But if he goes further, it might not be wise to follow him.

HOVSTAD. H'm — that depends on —

BILLING. You're always so damned timid, Aslaksen.

ASLAKSEN. Timid? Yes, when it's a question of attacking local authorities, I am timid, Mr. Billing; I have learnt caution in the school of experience, let me tell you. But turn me to higher politics, confront me with the government itself, and then see if I'm timid.

BILLING. No, not there; but you're so inconsistent.

ASLAKSEN. The fact is, I am keenly alive to my responsibilities. If you attack the government, you at least do society no harm; for the men attacked don't care, you see — they stay where they are. But local authorities can be turned out; and then we might get inexperienced men in power who would harm the interests both of home owners and other people.

HOVSTAD. But how can citizens gain experience except by self-government — do you never think of that?

ASLAKSEN. When a man has vested[1] interests to protect, he can't think of everything, Mr. Hovstad.

[1] **vested**: personal.

HOVSTAD. Then I hope I never have vested interests to protect.

BILLING. Hear, hear!

ASLAKSEN (*smiling*). H'm! (*Points to the desk.*) Governor Stensgård sat in that editorial chair before you.

BILLING (*spitting*). Pooh! That turncoat!

HOVSTAD. I am no weathercock[2] — and never will be.

ASLAKSEN. A politician should never be too sure of anything on earth, Mr. Hovstad. And as for you, Mr. Billing, you ought to be a bit cautious, I should say, now that you are applying for the job of secretary to the Town Council.

BILLING. I — !

HOVSTAD. Is that so, Billing?

BILLING. Well, yes — but, damn it, you understand, I'm only doing it to spite the bigwigs.

ASLAKSEN. Well, that has nothing to do with me. But if I am to be accused of cowardice and inconsistency, I would just like to point out this: My political record is open to everyone. I have not changed at all, except in becoming more moderate. My heart still belongs to the people; but I don't deny that my reason inclines somewhat towards the authorities — the local ones, I mean. (*Goes into the printing room.*)

BILLING. Don't you think we should try to get rid of him, Hovstad?

HOVSTAD. Do you know of anyone else who will pay for our paper and printing?

BILLING. What a nuisance it is to have no capital!

HOVSTAD (*sitting down by the desk*). Yes, if we only had that —

BILLING. Suppose you approached Dr. Stockmann?

HOVSTAD (*turning over his papers*). What good would that do? He has no money.

[2] **weathercock**: literally, weather vane; here, one who turns in the direction of the prevailing wind of opinion.

BILLING. No; but he has a good man behind him — old Morten Kiil — "The Badger," as they call him.

HOVSTAD (*writing*). Are you so sure he has money?

BILLING. Yes, strike me dead if he hasn't. And part of it must certainly go to Stockmann's family. He's bound to provide for — for the children at any rate.

HOVSTAD (*half turning*). Are you counting on that?

BILLING. Counting? Why should I be counting on it?

HOVSTAD. Better not! And you shouldn't count on that job as secretary either; for I can assure you you won't get it.

BILLING. Do you think I don't know that? A refusal is the very thing I want. To be rejected fires the spirit of opposition in you, gives you a fresh supply of gall,[1] as it were; and that's just what you need in a god-forsaken hole like this, where nothing really stimulating ever happens.

HOVSTAD (*writing*). Yes, yes.

BILLING. Well — they shall soon hear from me! — Now I'll go and write the appeal to the Home Owners' Association. (*Goes into the room on the right.*)

HOVSTAD (*sits at his desk, biting his penholder, and says slowly*): H'm — so that's the way it is. — (*A knock at the door*) Come in.

[PETRA *enters from the back, left.*]

HOVSTAD (*rising*). Well! What are you doing here?

PETRA. Please excuse me —

HOVSTAD (*offering her an armchair*). Won't you sit down?

PETRA. No, thanks; I can't stay.

HOVSTAD. Perhaps you bring a message from your father — ?

PETRA. No, I have come on my own account. (*Takes a book from the pocket of her cloak.*) Here is that English story.

HOVSTAD. Why have you brought it back?

¹ **gall**: anger, bitterness.

PETRA. Because I won't translate it.

HOVSTAD. But you promised —

PETRA. Yes; but then I hadn't read it. I suppose you have not read it either?

HOVSTAD. No; you know I can't read English; but —

PETRA. Exactly; and that's why I wanted to tell you that you must find something else. (*Putting the book on the table*) This will never do for the *Messenger*.

HOVSTAD. Why not?

PETRA. Because it's against everything you stand for.

HOVSTAD. Well, what of that?

PETRA. You don't understand me. It's all about a supernatural power that looks after the so-called good people in this world, and turns everything to their advantage; while all the so-called bad people are punished.

HOVSTAD. Yes, but that's all right. That's the very thing the public likes.

PETRA. And would you supply the public with such stuff? You don't believe a word of it yourself. You know well enough that things do not really happen like that.

HOVSTAD. Of course not; but an editor can't always do as he likes. He often has to humor people's fancies in minor matters. After all, politics is the chief thing in life — at any rate for a newspaper; and if I want the people to follow me along the path of freedom and progress, I mustn't scare them away. If they find a moral story like this on the back pages, they are all the more ready to accept what we tell them on the front page — they feel themselves safer.

PETRA. Yes, but you're not a hypocrite who would set traps like that for your readers. You're not a spider.

HOVSTAD (*smiling*). Thanks for your good opinion. In fact the idea is Billing's, not mine.

PETRA. Mr. Billing's!

HOVSTAD. Yes, at least he was talking about it the other day. It was Billing who was so anxious to get the story into the paper; I don't even know the book.

PETRA. But how can Mr. Billing, with his modern point of view —

HOVSTAD. Well, Billing is many-sided. He's applying for the job of secretary to the Town Council, I hear.

PETRA. I don't believe that, Mr. Hovstad. How could he stoop to such a thing?

HOVSTAD. You'd better ask him.

PETRA. I would never have thought it of Mr. Billing!

HOVSTAD (*looking more closely at her*). No? Is it such a surprise to you?

PETRA. Yes. And yet — perhaps not. Oh, I don't know —

HOVSTAD. We journalists are not worth much, Miss Petra.

PETRA. Do you really mean that?

HOVSTAD. I think so, now and then.

PETRA. In daily routine matters — that I can understand. But now that you have taken up a great cause —

HOVSTAD. You mean this affair of your father's?

PETRA. Of course. I should think you must feel yourself worth more than the general run of people now.

HOVSTAD. Yes, today I do feel something of the sort.

PETRA. Yes, surely you must. Oh, it's a glorious career you have chosen! To be the pioneer of unrecognized truths and new and daring ways of thought! — even, if that were all, to stand forth fearlessly in support of an injured man —

HOVSTAD. Especially when the injured man is — I hardly know how to put it —

PETRA. You mean when he is so upright and true?

HOVSTAD (*in a low voice*). I mean — especially when he is your father.

PETRA (*suddenly taken aback*). What!

HOVSTAD. Yes, Petra — Miss Petra.

PETRA. So that is your first thought, is it?

Not the cause itself? Not the truth? Not father's great, warm heart?

HOVSTAD. Oh, that too, of course.

PETRA. No, thank you; you said too much that time, Mr. Hovstad. Now I can never trust you again, in anything.

HOVSTAD. Can you be so hard on me because it's mainly for your sake — ?

PETRA. What I blame you for is that you have not been honest with father. You have talked to him as if you cared only for the truth and the good of the community. You have deceived both father and me. You are not the man you pretended to be. And that I will never forgive you — never.

HOVSTAD. You shouldn't speak so bitterly, Miss Petra — least of all now.

PETRA. Why not now?

HOVSTAD. Because your father cannot do without my help.

PETRA (*measuring him from head to foot*). So you are capable of that, too?

HOVSTAD. No, no. I spoke without thinking. You must believe me.

PETRA. I know what to believe. Good-by.

[ASLAKSEN *enters from printing room hurriedly, with an air of mystery.*]

ASLAKSEN. What do you think, Mr. Hovstad — (*Seeing* PETRA) Oh, excuse me —

PETRA. There is the book. You must give it to someone else. (*Going towards the main door*)

HOVSTAD (*following her*). But, Miss Petra —

PETRA. Good-by. (*She goes.*)

ASLAKSEN. I say, Mr. Hovstad!

HOVSTAD. Well, well; what is it?

ASLAKSEN. The Mayor's out there, in the print shop.

HOVSTAD. The Mayor?

ASLAKSEN. Yes. He wants to speak to you; he came in by the back way — he didn't want to be seen, you understand.

HOVSTAD. What does this mean? Wait, I'll go myself — (*Goes towards the print shop, opens the door, bows, and invites the* MAYOR *to enter.*)

HOVSTAD. Keep an eye open, Aslaksen, that no one —

ASLAKSEN. I understand. (*Goes into the print shop*)

MAYOR. You didn't expect to see me here, Mr. Hovstad.

HOVSTAD. No, I cannot say that I did.

MAYOR (*looking about him*). You are very well settled here — comfortable quarters.

HOVSTAD. Oh —

MAYOR. And here I have come, without an appointment, to take up your time —

HOVSTAD. You are very welcome, Mr. Mayor; I am at your service. Let me take your cap and stick. (*He does so, and puts them on a chair.*) And won't you sit down?

MAYOR (*sitting down by the table*). Thanks. (HOVSTAD *also sits by the table.*) I have been much — very much worried today, Mr. Hovstad.

HOVSTAD. Really? Well, I suppose with all your various duties —

MAYOR. It is the Doctor who has been causing me annoyance today.

HOVSTAD. Indeed! The Doctor?

MAYOR. He has written a sort of report to the Directors about some alleged shortcomings in the Baths.

HOVSTAD. Has he really?

MAYOR. Yes; hasn't he told you? I thought he said —

HOVSTAD. Oh, yes, he did mention something —

ASLAKSEN (*from the print shop*). I'll need the manuscript —

HOVSTAD (*in a tone of annoyance*). Oh! — there it is on the desk.

ASLAKSEN (*finding it*). All right.

MAYOR. Why, surely that's the —

ASLAKSEN. It's the Doctor's article, Mr. Mayor.

HOVSTAD. Oh, is that what you were speaking of?

MAYOR. Precisely. What do you think of it?

HOVSTAD. I have no technical knowledge of the matter, and I've only glanced through it.

MAYOR. And yet you are going to print it!

HOVSTAD. I can't very well refuse an article signed by —

ASLAKSEN. I have nothing to do with the editing of the paper, Mr. Mayor —

MAYOR. Of course not.

ASLAKSEN. I merely print what is placed in my hands.

MAYOR. Quite right, quite right.

ASLAKSEN. So I must — (*Goes towards the printing room.*)

MAYOR. No, just a moment, Mr. Aslaksen. With your permission, Mr. Hovstad —

HOVSTAD. By all means, Mr. Mayor.

MAYOR. You are a discreet and thoughtful man, Mr. Aslaksen.

ASLAKSEN. I am glad you think so, Mr. Mayor.

MAYOR. And a man of very wide influence.

ASLAKSEN. Well — chiefly among the lower middle-class.

MAYOR. The small taxpayers form the majority — here as everywhere.

ASLAKSEN. That's very true.

MAYOR. And I have no doubt that you know the general feeling among them. Am I right?

ASLAKSEN. Yes, I think I may say that I do, Mr. Mayor.

MAYOR. Well — since the poorer classes appear to be so heroically eager to make sacrifices —

ASLAKSEN. What do you mean?

HOVSTAD. Sacrifices?

MAYOR. It shows an admirable sense of public spirit — a most admirable sense. I admit it is more than I expected. But, of course, you know public feeling better than I do.

ASLAKSEN. Yes, but, Mr. Mayor —

MAYOR. And indeed it is no small sacrifice the town will have to make.

HOVSTAD. The town?

ASLAKSEN. But I don't understand —. It's the Baths —

MAYOR. At a rough estimate, the alterations the Doctor thinks desirable will come to two or three hundred thousand crowns.

ASLAKSEN. That's a lot of money; but —

MAYOR. Of course we shall be obliged to ask for a municipal loan.

HOVSTAD (*rising*). You surely can't mean that the town — ?

ASLAKSEN. It cannot come from taxes! From the scanty savings of the lower middle-class!

MAYOR. Why, my dear Mr. Aslaksen, where else is the money to come from?

ASLAKSEN. The owners of the Baths must take care of that.

MAYOR. The owners are not in a position to go to any further expense.

ASLAKSEN. Are you quite sure of that, Mr. Mayor?

MAYOR. I have positive information. So if these extensive alterations are to be made, the town itself will have to bear the cost.

ASLAKSEN. But damn it all — I beg your pardon! — but this is quite another matter, Mr. Hovstad.

HOVSTAD. Yes, it certainly is.

MAYOR. The worst of it is we would be forced to close the Baths for a couple of years.

HOVSTAD. To close them? Completely?

ASLAKSEN. For two years!

MAYOR. Yes, the work will require that time — at least.

ASLAKSEN. But, damn it all! We can't stand that, Mr. Mayor. What are we home owners to live on in the meantime?

MAYOR. It's extremely difficult to say, Mr. Aslaksen. But what do you expect us to do? Do you think a single visitor will come here if we go about telling stories that the water is poisoned, that the place is polluted, that the whole town —

ASLAKSEN. And it's all nothing but a fantasy?

MAYOR. With the best will in the world, I cannot convince myself that it is anything else.

ASLAKSEN. In that case it's simply inexcus-able of Dr. Stockmann — I beg your pardon, Mr. Mayor, but —

MAYOR. I'm sorry to say you are speaking only the truth, Mr. Aslaksen. Unfortunately, my brother has always been noted for his rashness.

ASLAKSEN. And yet you want to support him, Mr. Hovstad!

HOVSTAD. But who would have thought — ?

MAYOR. I have drawn up a short statement of the facts, as they appear from a sober-minded standpoint; and I have indicated that any defects that may possibly exist can no doubt be remedied by measures within the financial resources of the Baths.

HOVSTAD. Do you have the article with you, Mr. Mayor?

MAYOR (*feeling in his pockets*). Yes; I brought it with me, in case you —

ASLAKSEN (*quickly*). Good heavens! there he is!

MAYOR. Who? My brother?

HOVSTAD. Where? Where?

ASLAKSEN. He's coming through the composing room.

MAYOR. This is unfortunate! I don't want to meet him here, and there are several things I want to talk to you about.

HOVSTAD (*pointing to the door on the right*). Go in there for a moment.

MAYOR. But — ?

HOVSTAD. There's nobody there but Billing.

ASLAKSEN. Quick, quick, Mr. Mayor, he's coming.

MAYOR. Very well, then. But try to get rid of him quickly.

[*He goes out by the door on the right, which* ASLAKSEN *opens, and closes behind him.*]

HOVSTAD. Pretend to be busy, Aslaksen.

[*He sits down and writes.* ASLAKSEN *turns over a heap of newspapers on a chair, right.*]

DR. STOCKMANN (*entering from the composing room*). Here I am, back again. (*Puts down his hat and stick.*)

HOVSTAD (*writing*). Already, Doctor?

Hurry up with what you were doing, Aslaksen. We've no time to lose today.

DR. STOCKMANN (*to* ASLAKSEN). No proof yet, I hear.

ASLAKSEN (*without turning round*). You could hardly expect it yet.

DR. STOCKMANN. Of course not; but you understand my impatience. I can have no rest or peace until I see the thing in print.

HOVSTAD. H'm; it will take a good while yet. Don't you think so, Aslaksen?

ASLAKSEN. I'm afraid it will.

DR. STOCKMANN. All right, all right, my good friend; then I shall look in again. I'll look in twice if necessary. With so much at stake — the welfare of the whole town — one mustn't mind a little trouble. (*Is on the point of going but stops and comes back.*) Oh, by the way — there's one other thing I must speak to you about.

HOVSTAD. Excuse me; wouldn't some other time — ?

DR. STOCKMANN. I can tell you quickly. You see it's this: when people read my article in the paper tomorrow, and find I have spent the whole winter working quietly for the good of the town —

HOVSTAD. Yes, but, Doctor —

DR. STOCKMANN. I know what you're going to say. You don't think it was a bit more than my duty — my simple duty as a citizen. Of course I know that, as well as you do. But you see, my fellow townsmen — good Lord! The poor souls think so much of me —

ASLAKSEN. Yes, the townspeople have thought very highly of you up to now, Doctor.

DR. STOCKMANN. That's exactly why I'm afraid that — . What I wanted to say was this: when all this comes to them — especially to the poorer classes — as a summons to take the affairs of the town into their own hands for the future —

HOVSTAD (*rising*). H'm, Doctor, I won't conceal from you —

DR. STOCKMANN. Aha! I thought there was something brewing! But I won't hear of it. If they are getting up anything of that sort —

HOVSTAD. Of what sort?

DR. STOCKMANN. Well, anything of any sort — a parade, or a banquet, or a testimonial dinner, or whatever it may be — you must give me your solemn promise to put a stop to it. And you too, Mr. Aslaksen; do you hear?

HOVSTAD. Excuse me, Doctor; we may as well tell you the whole truth now as later.

[MRS. STOCKMANN *enters from the back, left.*]

MRS. STOCKMANN (*seeing the* DOCTOR). Just as I thought.

HOVSTAD (*going towards her*). Mrs. Stockmann, too?

DR. STOCKMANN. What the devil do you want here, Katherine?

MRS. STOCKMANN. You know very well what I want.

HOVSTAD. Won't you sit down? Or perhaps —

MRS. STOCKMANN. Thanks, please don't bother. And you must forgive my following my husband here; remember, I am the mother of three children.

DR. STOCKMANN. What's this nonsense! We all know that well enough.

MRS. STOCKMANN. Well, it doesn't look as if you thought very much about your wife and children today, or you wouldn't be so ready to plunge us all into ruin.

DR. STOCKMANN. Are you quite mad, Katherine! Does a man with a wife and children have no right to proclaim the truth? Has he no right to be an active and useful citizen? Has he no right to do his duty by the town he lives in?

MRS. STOCKMANN. Everything in moderation, Thomas!

ASLAKSEN. That's just what I say. Moderation in everything.

MRS. STOCKMANN. You are doing us a great

wrong, Mr. Hovstad, in luring my husband away from house and home, and fooling him in this way.

HOVSTAD. I am not fooling anyone —

DR. STOCKMANN. Fool me! Do you think I would let myself be fooled?

MRS. STOCKMANN. Yes, that's just what you do. I know you are the cleverest man in town; but you're very easily made a fool of, Thomas. (*To* HOVSTAD.) Remember that he loses his job at the Baths if you print what he has written —

ASLAKSEN. What!

HOVSTAD. Well now, really, Doctor —

DR. STOCKMANN (*laughing*). Ha, ha! just let them try — ! No, no, my dear, they'll think twice about that. I have the solid majority behind me, you see!

MRS. STOCKMANN. That's just the trouble, that you have such a horrid thing behind you.

DR. STOCKMANN. Nonsense, Katherine; — you go home and look after your house, and let me take care of society. How can you be so afraid when you see me so confident and happy? (*Rubbing his hands and walking up and down*) Truth and the People will win the day; you may be sure of that. Oh! I can see all our free citizens standing shoulder to shoulder like a conquering army — ! (*Stopping by a chair*) What the devil is that?

ASLAKSEN (*looking at it*). Oh, Lord!

HOVSTAD (*the same*). H'm —

DR. STOCKMANN. Why, here's the crown of authority!

[*He takes the* MAYOR's *official cap carefully between the tips of his fingers and holds it up.*]

MRS. STOCKMANN. The Mayor's cap!

DR. STOCKMANN. And here's the staff of office, too! But how in the devil's name did they — ?

HOVSTAD. Well then —

DR. STOCKMANN. Ah, I see! He has been here to win you over. Ha, ha! He picked the wrong man that time! And when he saw me in the print room — (*Bursts out laughing*) — he took to his heels, eh, Mr. Aslaksen?

ASLAKSEN (*hurriedly*). Yes, he took to his heels, Doctor.

DR. STOCKMANN. Went off without his stick and —. No, that won't do! Peter never leaves anything behind him. But where the devil have you hidden him? Ah — in here, of course. Now you'll see, Katherine!

MRS. STOCKMANN. Thomas — please — !

ASLAKSEN. Be careful, Doctor!

[DR. STOCKMANN *has put on the* MAYOR's *cap and grasped his stick; he now goes up to the door, throws it open, and makes a military salute.*]

[*The* MAYOR *enters; red with anger. Behind him comes* BILLING.]

MAYOR. What is the meaning of this?

DR. STOCKMANN. Show some respect, Peter! Now, I am in power in this town. (*He struts up and down.*)

MRS. STOCKMANN (*almost in tears*). Oh, Thomas!

MAYOR (*following him*). Give me my cap and stick!

DR. STOCKMANN (*as before*). You may be Chief of Police, but I am the Mayor. I am master of the whole town I tell you!

MAYOR. Put down my cap, I tell you. Remember it's an official badge of office.

DR. STOCKMANN. Pooh! Do you think the awakening lion of democracy will let itself be scared by a gold-braided cap? There'll be a revolution in the town tomorrow, let me tell you. You threatened me with dismissal; but now *I* dismiss you — dismiss you from all your offices. You think I can't do it? — Oh, yes, I can! I have the irresistible forces of society on my side. Hovstad and Billing will thunder in the *People's Messenger*, and Aslaksen will take the field at the head of the Home Owners' Association —

ASLAKSEN. No, Doctor, I shall not.

DR. STOCKMANN. Why, of course you will.

MAYOR. Aha! Perhaps Mr. Hovstad would like to join the agitation after all?

HOVSTAD. No, Mr. Mayor.

ASLAKSEN. No, Mr. Hovstad's not such a fool. He won't ruin both himself and the paper for the sake of a delusion.

DR. STOCKMANN (*looking about him*). What does all this mean?

HOVSTAD. You have presented your case in a false light, Doctor; therefore I am unable to give you my support.

BILLING. And after what the Mayor was kind enough to explain to me, I —

DR. STOCKMANN. In a false light! You leave that to me. You just print my article, and I promise you I'll prove the truth of every word.

HOVSTAD. I shall not print it. I cannot, and will not, and dare not print it.

DR. STOCKMANN. You dare not? What nonsense is this? You are editor; and I suppose the editor controls a paper.

ASLAKSEN. No, it's the subscribers, Doctor.

MAYOR. Fortunately.

ASLAKSEN. It's public opinion, the enlightened majority, the home owners and all the rest. It's they who control a paper.

DR. STOCKMANN (*calmly*). And all these powers are against me?

ASLAKSEN Yes, they are. It would mean absolute ruin for the town if your article were printed.

DR. STOCKMANN. So that's the way it is.

MAYOR. My cap and stick!

[DR. STOCKMANN *takes off the cap and lays it on the table along with the stick.*]

MAYOR (*taking them both*). Your term of office has come to an abrupt end.

DR. STOCKMANN. This is not the end. (*To* HOVSTAD) So you are quite determined not to print my article in the *Messenger*?

HOVSTAD. Quite; for the sake of your family, if for no other reason.

MRS. STOCKMANN. Oh, please leave his family out of it, Mr. Hovstad.

MAYOR (*takes a manuscript from his pocket*). When this appears, the public will have all the necessary information; it is an official statement. I place it in your hands.

HOVSTAD (*taking the manuscript*). Good. It will appear without delay.

DR. STOCKMANN. But not mine! You think you can silence me and suppress the truth! But it won't be that easy. Mr. Aslaksen, will you be good enough to print my article at once, as a pamphlet? I'll pay for it myself, and be my own publisher. I'll have four hundred copies — no, five — six hundred.

ASLAKSEN. No. If you offered me its weight in gold, I dare not lend my press to such a purpose, Doctor. I don't dare fly in the face of public opinion. You won't get it printed anywhere in the whole town.

DR. STOCKMANN. Then give it back to me.

HOVSTAD (*handing him the manuscript*). By all means.

DR. STOCKMANN (*taking up his hat and cane*). It shall be made public all the same. I shall read it at a great mass meeting; all my fellow citizens shall hear the voice of truth!

MAYOR. No one in the town will give you a hall for such a purpose.

ASLAKSEN. No one, I'm quite certain.

BILLING. No, strike me dead if they would!

MRS. STOCKMANN. That's disgraceful! Why do they turn against you like this, every one of them?

DR. STOCKMANN (*irritated*). I'll tell you why. It's because in this town all the men are old women — like you. They all think of nothing but their families, not of the general good.

MRS. STOCKMANN (*taking his arm*). Then I'll show them that an — an old woman can be a man for once. I'll stand by you, Thomas.

DR. STOCKMANN. Bravely said, Katherine! I swear by my soul and conscience the truth shall out! If they won't give me a hall, I'll hire a drum and march through the town with it; and I'll read my paper at every street corner.

MAYOR. You can scarcely be such a raving lunatic as that?

DR. STOCKMANN. Oh yes, I am.

ASLAKSEN. You won't get a single man in the whole town to go with you.

BILLING. No, strike me dead if you will!

MRS. STOCKMANN. Don't give in, Thomas. I'll ask the boys to go with you.

DR. STOCKMANN. That's a splendid idea!

MRS. STOCKMANN. Morten will be delighted; and Eilif will go too, I am sure.

DR. STOCKMANN. Yes, and so will Petra! And you yourself, Katherine!

MRS. STOCKMANN. No, no, not I. But I'll stand at the window and watch you — that's what I'll do.

DR. STOCKMANN (*throwing his arms about her and kissing her*). Thank you for that! Now, gentlemen, we're ready for the fight! Now we shall see whether your shabby tricks can stop an honest citizen from cleaning up his town!

[*He and his wife go out together by the door in the back, left.*]

MAYOR (*shaking his head dubiously*). Now he has made her mad too!

For Discussion

1. At the start of Act III, Hovstad and Billing are in high spirits. Why? What finally causes them to join the mayor in opposing Dr. Stockmann?

2. Opposed now by the town authorities, by the shopkeepers, and by the liberals Dr. Stockmann, still confident, determines to embark on a more daring course. "You think you can silence me and suppress the truth!" he exclaims. What does he plan to do? How does his wife respond to these latest plans?

3. **Motivation.** To make characters believable, authors must *motivate* them convincingly — that is, must show why they move, or behave, as they do. Petra discovers in the course of this act what motivates Hovstad to support her father. What is it? Although Hovstad and Billing feel contempt for Aslaksen's timidity, they nevertheless ally themselves with him. What motivates them to do so?

Act IV

A large old-fashioned room in CAPTAIN HORSTER'S *house. An open folding-door in the background leads to an anteroom. In the wall on the left are three windows. About the middle of the opposite wall is a platform, and on it a small table, two candles, a water bottle and glass, and a bell. For the rest, the room is lighted by wall lamps between the windows. In front, on the left, is a table with a candle on it, and by it a chair. In front, to the right, a door, and near it a few chairs.*

A large crowd of all classes of townspeople including some women and schoolboys. More people gradually stream in from the back until the room is full.

FIRST CITIZEN (*to another standing near him*). You here too, Lamstad?

SECOND CITIZEN. I never miss a public meeting.

A BYSTANDER. I suppose you brought your whistle?

SECOND CITIZEN. Of course, didn't you?

THIRD CITIZEN. I sure did. And Skipper Evensen said he'd bring a thumping big horn.

SECOND CITIZEN. He's a good 'un, Evensen is! (*Laughter in the group.*)

A FOURTH CITIZEN (*joining them*). Tell me, what's it all about? What's going on here tonight?

SECOND CITIZEN. Dr. Stockmann's going to debate the Mayor.

FOURTH CITIZEN. But the Mayor's his brother.

FIRST CITIZEN. That makes no difference. Dr. Stockmann's not afraid of him.

THIRD CITIZEN. But he's all wrong; the *People's Messenger* says so.

SECOND CITIZEN. Yes, he must be wrong this time. Neither the Home Owners' Association nor the Citizens' Club would let him have a hall.

FIRST CITIZEN. They wouldn't even lend him the hall at the Baths.

SECOND CITIZEN. No, of course they wouldn't.

A MAN (*in another group*). Who should we support in this business, eh?

ANOTHER MAN (*in the same group*). Just watch Aslaksen, and do as he does.

BILLING (*with a briefcase under his arm, makes his way through the crowd*). Excuse me, gentlemen. May I get through? I'm here to report for the *People's Messenger*. Many thanks. (*Sits by the table on the left.*)

A WORKING-MAN. Who's he?

ANOTHER WORKING-MAN. Don't you know him? It's that fellow Billing, that writes for Aslaksen's paper.

[CAPTAIN HORSTER *enters by the door in front on the right, escorting* MRS. STOCKMANN *and* PETRA. EILIF *and* MORTEN *follow them.*]

HORSTER. This is where I thought you might sit; you can easily slip out if anything happens.

MRS. STOCKMANN. Do you think there will be any trouble?

HORSTER. You can never tell — with such a crowd. But there's no need to worry.

MRS. STOCKMANN (*sitting down*). It was kind of you to offer Stockmann this room.

HORSTER. Since no one else would, I —

PETRA (*who has also seated herself*). And it was brave too, Captain Horster.

HORSTER. Oh, I don't see where the bravery comes in.

[HOVSTAD *and* ASLAKSEN *enter at the same moment, but make their way through the crowd separately.*]

ASLAKSEN (*going up to* HORSTER). Has the Doctor come yet?

HORSTER. He's waiting in there.

[*A movement at the door in the background.*]

HOVSTAD (*to* BILLING). There's the Mayor! Look!

BILLING. Yes, strike me dead if he hasn't turned up after all!

[MAYOR STOCKMANN *makes his way blandly through the meeting, bowing politely to both sides, and sits by the wall on the left. Soon afterwards,* DR. STOCKMANN *enters by the door on the right. He wears a black frock coat and white necktie. Faint applause and some hissing. Then silence.*]

DR. STOCKMANN (*in a low tone*). How do you feel, Katherine?

MRS. STOCKMANN. Quite comfortable, thank you. (*In a low voice.*) Now don't lose your temper, Thomas.

DR. STOCKMANN. Oh, I shall keep myself well in hand. (*Looks at his watch, ascends the platform, and bows.*) It's a quarter past the hour, so I shall begin — (*Takes out his manuscript.*)

ASLAKSEN. But surely we must first elect a chairman.

DR. STOCKMANN. No, that's not at all necessary.

SEVERAL GENTLEMEN (*shouting*). Yes, yes, it is!

MAYOR. Certainly we should elect a chairman.

DR. STOCKMANN. But I've called this meeting to give a lecture, Peter!

MAYOR. Dr. Stockmann's lecture may possibly lead to differences of opinion.

SEVERAL VOICES IN THE CROWD. A chairman! A chairman!

HOVSTAD. The general voice of the meeting seems to be for a chairman!

DR. STOCKMANN (*controlling himself*). Very well then; let the meeting have its way.

ASLAKSEN. Will the Mayor take the chair?

THREE GENTLEMEN (*clapping*). Bravo! Bravo!

MAYOR. For reasons you will easily understand, I must decline. But, fortunately, we have among us someone I think we can all accept. I refer to the president of the Home Owners' Association, Mr. Aslaksen.

MANY VOICES. Yes, yes! Good old Aslaksen! Hurrah for Aslaksen!

[DR. STOCKMANN *takes his manuscript and descends from the platform.*]

ASLAKSEN. Since my fellow citizens request me, I cannot refuse — (*Applause and cheers.* ASLAKSEN *ascends the platform.*)

BILLING (*writing*). So — "Mr. Aslaksen was elected by acclamation — "[1]

ASLAKSEN. And now, as I have been called to the chair, I take the liberty of saying a few brief words. I am a quiet, peace-loving man; I am in favor of discreet moderation, and of — and of moderate discretion. Everyone who knows me, knows that.

MANY VOICES. Yes, yes, Aslaksen!

ASLAKSEN. I have learnt in the school of life and of experience that moderation is the virtue that most benefits the individual citizen —

MAYOR. Hear, hear!

ASLAKSEN. — and it is discretion and moderation, too, that best serve the community. I would therefore suggest to our respected fellow citizen, who has called this meeting, that he should try to keep within the bounds of moderation.

A MAN (*by the door*). Three cheers for the Temperance Society!

A VOICE. Shut up there!

VOICES. Sh! Sh!

ASLAKSEN. No interruptions, gentlemen! — Does anyone wish to offer any observations?

MAYOR. Mr. Chairman!

ASLAKSEN. Mayor Stockmann will address the meeting.

MAYOR. Because of my close relationship — of which you are probably aware — to the present medical officer of the Baths, I would have preferred not to speak here this evening. But my position as chairman of the Baths, and my care for the vital interests of this town, force me to offer a resolution. I assume that not a single citizen here thinks it desirable that untrustworthy and exaggerated statements should get abroad as to the sanitary condition of the Baths and of our town.

MANY VOICES. No, no, no! Certainly not! We protest.

MAYOR. I therefore beg to move, "That this meeting declines to hear the proposed lecture or speech on the subject by the medical officer of the Baths."

DR. STOCKMANN (*flaring up*). Declines to hear — ! What do you mean?

MRS. STOCKMANN (*coughing*). H'm! h'm!

DR. STOCKMANN (*controlling himself*). So I am not to be heard?

MAYOR. In my statement in the *People's Messenger* I have made the public acquainted with the essential facts, so that all right-thinking citizens can easily form their own judgment. From that statement it will be seen that the medical officer's proposal — aside from being a vote of censure[2] against the leading men of the town — only means saddling the taxpayers with an unnecessary outlay of at least a hundred thousand crowns. (*Sounds of protest and some hissing*)

ASLAKSEN (*ringing the bell*). Order, gentlemen! I support the Mayor's resolution. I quite agree with him that there is something beneath the surface of the Doctor's agitation. In all his talk about the Baths, it is really a revolution he is aiming at; he wants to overthrow the people in power.

---

[1] **acclamation:** unanimous vote, indicated by cheers rather than ballots.

[2] **censure:** criticism, reproach.

No one doubts the excellence of Dr. Stockmann's intentions — of course there cannot be two opinions about that. I, too, am in favor of self-government by the people, as long as it doesn't cost the taxpayers too much. But in this case it would do so; and therefore I'll be damned if — excuse me — in short, I cannot support Dr. Stockmann on this occasion. You can buy even gold too dear; that's my opinion. (*Loud applause on all sides*)

HOVSTAD. I also feel I should explain my position. Dr. Stockmann's agitation seemed at first to find favor in several quarters, and I supported it as impartially as I could. But it soon appeared that we had been misled by a false presentation of the facts —

DR. STOCKMANN. False — !

HOVSTAD. Well, then, an untrustworthy presentation. This the Mayor's report has proved. I trust no one here doubts my liberal principles; the attitude of the *Messenger* on all great political questions is well known to you all. But I have learned from men of judgment and experience that in purely local matters a paper must observe a certain amount of caution.

ASLAKSEN. I entirely agree with the speaker.

HOVSTAD. And in the matter under discussion it is quite evident that Dr. Stockmann has public opinion against him. But, gentlemen, what is an editor's clearest and most imperative duty? Is it not to work in harmony with his readers? Has he not received a sort of tacit mandate[1] to serve loyally and unweariedly the interests of his constituents? Or am I mistaken in this?

MANY VOICES. No, no, no! Hovstad is right!

HOVSTAD. It has cost me a bitter struggle to break with a man in whose house I have of late been a frequent guest — with a man who, up to this day, has enjoyed the

---

[1] tacit mandate: command that is unspoken but understood.

unqualified goodwill of his fellow citizens — with a man whose only, or, at any rate, whose chief fault is that he consults his heart rather than his head.

A FEW SCATTERED VOICES. That's true! Hurrah for Dr. Stockmann!

HOVSTAD. But my duty towards the community has forced me to break with him. Then, too, there is another consideration that impels me to oppose him, and, if possible, to stop him on the rash course that he is taking: consideration for his family —

DR. STOCKMANN. Keep to the waterworks and sewers!

HOVSTAD. — consideration for his wife and his helpless children.

MORTEN. Is that us, mother?

MRS. STOCKMANN. Hush!

ASLAKSEN. I will now put the Mayor's motion to a vote.

DR. STOCKMANN. You need not. I have no intention of saying anything this evening about all the filth at the Baths. No! You shall hear something quite different.

MAYOR (*half aloud*). Now what?

A DRUNKEN MAN (*at the main entrance*). I'm a taxpayer, so I've a right to my opinion! And it's my full, firm, incomprehensible opinion that —

SEVERAL VOICES. Silence out there!

OTHERS. He's drunk! Throw him out!

[*The drunken man is put out.*]

DR. STOCKMANN. Can I speak?

ASLAKSEN (*ringing the bell*). Dr. Stockmann will address the meeting.

DR. STOCKMANN. A few days ago, I should like to have seen anyone try to gag me as they have here tonight! I would have fought like a lion for my sacred rights! But that doesn't matter now; for now I have more important things to speak of.

[*The people crowd closer round him.* MORTEN KIIL *can be seen among them.*]

DR. STOCKMANN (*continuing*). I have been pondering a great many things during these last days — thinking such a multitude of thoughts, that at last my head was positively in a whirl —

MAYOR (*coughing*). H'm — !

DR. STOCKMANN. But gradually things seemed to straighten themselves out, and I saw them clearly in all their bearings. That is why I stand here this evening. I am about to reveal a great truth, my fellow citizens! I am going to announce to you a far-reaching discovery, beside which the trifling fact that our waterworks are poisoned, and that our health resort is built on polluted ground, is insignificant.

MANY VOICES (*shouting*). Don't speak about the Baths! We don't want to hear it! No more of that!

DR. STOCKMANN. I have said I would speak of the great discovery I have made within the last few days — the discovery that all our sources of spiritual life are poisoned, and that our whole society rests upon a pernicious lie.

SEVERAL VOICES (*in astonishment and half aloud*). What's he saying?

MAYOR. Such an insinuation — !

ASLAKSEN (*with his hand on the bell*). I call upon the speaker to moderate his expressions.

DR. STOCKMANN. I have loved my native town as dearly as any man can love the home of his childhood. I was young when I left our town, and distance, homesickness and memory threw, as it were, a glamor over the place and its people. (*Some applause and cries of approval*) Then I spent many years in a horrible hole, far away in the north. As I went about among the people scattered here and there over the stony wilderness, it seemed to me, many a time, that it would have been better for these poor famishing creatures to have had a cattle doctor to attend them, instead of a man like me. (*Murmurs in the room*)

BILLING (*laying down his pen*). Strike me dead if I've ever heard — !

HOVSTAD. What an insult to respectable people!

DR. STOCKMANN. Wait a moment! — I don't think anyone can reproach me with forgetting my native town up there. I sat brooding like an eider duck, and what I hatched was — the plan for the Baths. [*Applause and expressions of dissent*] And when, at last, fate ordered things so happily that I could come home again — then, fellow citizens, it seemed to me that I had no other desire in the world. Yes, one desire I had: an eager, constant, burning desire to be of service to my birthplace, and to its people.

MAYOR (*gazing into vacancy*). A strange method to select — !

DR. STOCKMANN. So I went about reveling in my happy illusions. But yesterday morning — no, it was really two nights ago — my mind's eyes were opened wide, and the first thing I saw was the colossal stupidity of the authorities —

[*Noise, cries, and laughter.* MRS. STOCKMANN *coughs repeatedly.*]

MAYOR. Mr. Chairman!

ASLAKSEN (*ringing his bell*). By virtue of my position — !

DR. STOCKMANN. It's petty to fuss about a word, Mr. Aslaksen! I only mean that I became aware of the extraordinary muddle our leading men had been guilty of, down at the Baths. I cannot for the life of me stand leading men — I've seen enough of them in my time. They are like goats let loose in a young orchard: they do damage everywhere; they block the path of a free man wherever he turns — and I should be glad if we could exterminate them like other noxious animals —

[*Uproar in the room.*]

MAYOR. Mr. Chairman, are such expressions permissible?

ASLAKSEN (*with his hand on the bell*). Dr. Stockmann —

DR. STOCKMANN. I can't understand why it has taken me so long to see through these gentlemen; for I've had a magnificent example before my eyes here every day — my brother Peter — empty of ideas, full of prejudice.

[*Laughter, noise, and whistling.* MRS. STOCKMANN *coughs.* ASLAKSEN *rings violently.*]

THE DRUNKEN MAN (*who has come in again*). Is it me you're talking about? Sure enough, my name's Petersen; but devil take me if —

ANGRY VOICES. Out with that drunken man! Put him out!

[*The man is again put out.*]

MAYOR. Who is that person?

A BYSTANDER. I don't know him, Mr. Mayor.

ANOTHER. He doesn't belong here.

A THIRD. He's a lumber dealer from —

[*The rest is inaudible.*]

ASLAKSEN. The man was evidently intoxicated. — Continue, Dr. Stockmann; but please try to be moderate.

DR. STOCKMANN. Well, fellow citizens, I shall say no more about our leading men. If anyone imagines, from what I have just said, that it's these gentlemen I'm here to attack tonight, he is mistaken — altogether mistaken. For I cherish the comfortable conviction that these reactionaries, these relics of a decaying order of thought, are busily engaged in cutting their own throats. They need no doctor to hasten their end. And besides, they are not the real danger to society. They are not the ones most active in poisoning the sources of our spiritual life and polluting the ground beneath our feet. They are not the most dangerous enemies of truth and freedom in our society.

CRIES FROM ALL SIDES. Who, then? Who is it? Name them!

DR. STOCKMANN. Oh, I shall name them! For this is the great discovery I made yesterday: (*In a louder tone*) The most dangerous foe to truth and freedom in our midst is the solid majority. Yes, it's the damned, solid, liberal majority — that, and nothing else! There, I've told you.

[*Great commotion in the room. Most of the audience are shouting, stamping, and whistling. Several elderly gentlemen exchange furtive glances and seem to be enjoying the scene.* MRS. STOCKMANN *rises in alarm.* EILIF *and* MORTEN *advance threateningly towards some schoolboys who are jeering at them.* ASLAKSEN *rings the bell and calls for order.* HOVSTAD *and* BILLING *both speak, but nothing can be heard. At last quiet is restored.*]

ASLAKSEN. I request the speaker to withdraw his outrageous statement.

DR. STOCKMANN. Never, Mr. Aslaksen! It's this very majority that robs me of my freedom, and wants to forbid me to speak the truth.

HOVSTAD. The majority is always right.

BILLING. Yes, and it has truth on its side too.

DR. STOCKMANN. The majority is never right. Never, I say! That is one of the social lies that a free, thinking man is bound to rebel against. Who make up the majority in any given country? Is it the wise men or the fools? I think we must agree that the fools are in a terrible, overwhelming majority, all the wide world over. But how in the devil's name can it ever be right for fools to rule over wise men? (*Uproar and yells*) Yes, yes, you can shout me down, but you cannot prove me wrong. The majority has might — unhappily — but right it does not have. It is I, and the few, the individuals, who are in the right. The minority is always right. (*Renewed uproar*)

HOVSTAD. Ha, ha! Dr. Stockmann has turned aristocrat since the day before yesterday!

DR. STOCKMANN. I have said that I will waste no words on the little crew of narrow-chested, short-winded has-beens. The stream of life has nothing more to do with them. I am speaking of the few, the individuals among us with new, vigorous ideas. These men stand at the outposts, so far in front that the solid majority has not begun to reach them — and there they fight for truths that are too new and daring to be accepted by the majority.

HOVSTAD. So the Doctor's a revolutionist now!

DR. STOCKMANN. Yes, by Heaven, I am, Mr. Hovstad! I am in revolt against the lie that truth belongs exclusively to the majority. What sort of truths do the majority accept? Truths so old they are practically senile. When a truth is as old as that, gentlemen, you can hardly tell it from a lie. (*Laughter and jeers*) You can believe me or not, as you like; but truths are not the tough old Methuselahs some people think them. A normal, ordinary truth lives — let us say — as a rule, seventeen or eighteen years; at the outside twenty; very seldom more. And truths as venerable as that are always worn terribly thin; yet it's not till then that the majority takes them up and recommends them to society as wholesome food. I can assure you there's not much nourishment in that sort of diet; you may take my word as a doctor for that. All these majority-truths are like last year's salt pork; they're like rancid, moldy ham, producing all the moral scurvy[1] that plagues society.

ASLAKSEN. It seems to me that the honorable speaker is wandering rather far from the subject.

MAYOR. I endorse the Chairman's remark.

DR. STOCKMANN. You must be mad, Peter! I'm keeping as closely to my subject as I possibly can; for my subject is precisely this — that the masses, the majority, this devil's own solid majority — it's that, I say, that's poisoning the sources of our spiritual life, and polluting the ground beneath our feet.

HOVSTAD. And you make this charge against the great, independent majority, just because they have the sense to accept only well-founded and acknowledged truths?

DR. STOCKMANN. My dear Mr. Hovstad, don't talk about well-founded truths! The truths acknowledged by the masses, the multitude, were well-founded truths to the vanguard[2] in our grandfathers' days. We, the vanguard of today, don't acknowledge them any longer; and I don't believe there exists any other well-founded truths but this — that no society can live a healthy life upon truths so old and marrowless.[3]

HOVSTAD. But instead of all this vague talk, why don't you give us some example of these old marrowless truths that we are living upon. (*Approval from several quarters*)

DR. STOCKMANN. Oh, I could give you no end of samples from the rubbish-heap; but, for the present, I shall point to one acknowledged truth, which is actually a hideous lie, but which Mr. Hovstad, and the *Messenger*, and all supporters of the *Messenger*, live by.

HOVSTAD. And that is — ?

DR. STOCKMANN. That is the doctrine you have inherited from your forefathers, and go on thoughtlessly proclaiming far and wide — the doctrine that the multitude, the common herd, the masses, are the heart of the people — that they are the people — that the common man, the ignorant, undeveloped member of society, has the same right to approve and to con-

---

[1] **scurvy:** disease caused by lack of fresh food.

[2] **vanguard:** leaders of thought, taste, and opinion.

[3] **marrowless:** *i.e.*, brittle and weak.

demn, to counsel and to govern, as the intellectually distinguished few.

BILLING. Well, now, strike me dead — !

HOVSTAD (*shouting at the same time*). Citizens, please note this!

ANGRY VOICES. Aren't we the people? Are only a few folks to govern?

A WORKING MAN. Out with anyone who talks like that!

OTHERS. Throw him out!

A CITIZEN (*shouting*). Blow your horn, Evensen.

[*The deep notes of a horn are heard; whistling, and terrific noise in the room.*]

DR. STOCKMANN (*when the noise has somewhat subsided*). Be reasonable! Can't you bear to hear the truth for once? I don't expect you all to agree with me. But I certainly expected Mr. Hovstad to back me up, as soon as he had pulled himself together. Mr. Hovstad claims to be a freethinker[1] —

SEVERAL VOICES (*subdued and wondering*). Freethinker, did he say? What? Mr. Hovstad a freethinker?

HOVSTAD (*shouting*). Prove it, Dr. Stockmann. When have I said so in print?

DR. STOCKMANN (*reflecting*). No, damn it, you're right there; you've never had the courage to do that. Well, I won't put you on the rack, Mr. Hovstad. Let me be the freethinker then. And now I'll make it clear to you all, and on scientific grounds too, that the *Messenger* is leading you shamefully by the nose, when it tells you that you, the masses, the crowd, are the true heart of the people. I tell you that's only a newspaper lie. The masses are nothing but the raw material that must be fashioned into a People. (*Murmurs, laughter, and commotion in the room*) Isn't it the same with all other living creatures? What a difference be-

[1] **freethinker**: one who forms opinions independently, especially in matters of religion.

tween a cultivated and an uncultivated breed of animals! Just look at a common barnyard hen. What meat do you get from such a skinny creature? Not much, I can tell you! And what sort of eggs does she lay? A decent crow or raven can lay nearly as good. Then take a cultivated Spanish or Japanese hen, or take a fine pheasant or turkey — ah! then you'll see the difference! And now look at the dog, our near relation. Think first of an ordinary vulgar cur — I mean one of those wretched, ragged, common mongrels that haunt the gutters and dirty the sidewalks. Compare such a mongrel with a pedigreed poodle bred through many generations from aristocratic stock, who has lived on good food, and heard harmonious voices and music. Don't you think the brain of the poodle is very differently developed from that of the mongrel? Yes, you can be sure it is! It's well-bred poodle pups like this that jugglers train to perform the most marvelous tricks. A common mongrel could never learn anything of the sort — not if he tried till doomsday. (*Noise and laughter are heard all round.*)

A CITIZEN (*shouting*). Do you want to make dogs of us now?

ANOTHER MAN. We're not animals, Doctor!

DR. STOCKMANN. Of course we are, my good sir! We're one and all of us animals, whether we like it or not. But there are few aristocratic animals among us. Oh, there's a terrible difference between poodle-men and mongrel-men! And the ridiculous part of it is, that Mr. Hovstad quite agrees with me so long as it's four-legged animals we're talking of —

HOVSTAD. Animals are animals.

DR. STOCKMANN. Perhaps — but as soon as I apply the principle to two-legged animals, Mr. Hovstad rebels. He no longer has the courage of his convictions. He refuses to think things through. Then he turns the whole principle upside down, and proclaims in the *People's Messenger* that the ordinary hen and the common mongrel are the finest specimens in the menagerie. And that's the way it will be as long as commonness still dominates your system, and you haven't worked your way up to any spiritual or intellectual distinction.

HOVSTAD. I make no claim to any sort of distinction. I come from simple peasant stock and I am proud that my roots lie deep down among the common people, who are here being insulted.

WORKMEN. Hurrah for Hovstad. Hurrah! hurrah!

DR. STOCKMANN. The sort of common people I am speaking of are not found only among the lower classes; they crawl and swarm all around us — up to the highest level of society. Just look at your own smug, respectable Mayor! Why, my brother Peter is as common as any man that walks on two legs — (*Laughter and hisses*)

MAYOR. I protest against such personal remarks.

DR. STOCKMANN. — and that's not because, like me, he's descended from a good-for-nothing old pirate from Pomerania, or thereabouts — for that's our ancestry —

MAYOR. An absurd story! Utterly groundless.

DR. STOCKMANN. — it's because he thinks the thoughts and holds the opinions of his official superiors. Men who do that are common in spirit; and that is why my distinguished brother Peter is really so undistinguished, — and consequently so illiberal.

MAYOR. Mr. Chairman — !

HOVSTAD. So the distinguished people in this country are the liberals? That's a new idea. (*Laughter.*)

DR. STOCKMANN. Yes, that is part of my new discovery. And this, too: that liberality of thought is almost exactly the same thing as morality. That's why I say it's absolutely unpardonable of the *Messenger* to proclaim, day out, day in, the false doctrine that the masses, the multitude, the solid majority has a monopoly on morality and liberal thought — and that vice and corruption and all sorts of spiritual uncleanness ooze out of culture, just as all that filth oozes down to the Baths from the Mill Dale tanneries. (*Noise and interruptions. The* DOCTOR *goes on imperturbably, smiling in his eagerness.*) And yet this same *Messenger* can preach about elevating the masses to a higher level of being! Why, if the *Messenger's* own doctrine is true, the elevation of the masses would simply mean hurling them straight to damnation! But, happily, the notion that culture corrupts is nothing but an old traditional lie. No, it's stupidity, poverty, the ugliness of life, that do the devil's work! In a house that isn't aired and swept every day — my wife maintains that the floors ought to be scrubbed too, but perhaps that is going too far; — well, — in such a house, I say, within two or three years, people lose the power of thinking or acting morally. Lack of oxygen weakens the conscience. And there seems to be precious little oxygen in many houses in this town, since the whole solid majority is unscrupulous enough to want to build its prosperity on a quagmire of lies and fraud.

ASLAKSEN. I cannot allow such an insult to be leveled against a whole community.

A GENTLEMAN. I move that the Chairman order the speaker to sit down.

EAGER VOICES. Yes, yes! That's right! Sit down! Sit down!

DR. STOCKMANN (*flaring up*). Then I'll shout the truth at every street corner! I'll write to newspapers in other towns! The whole country will know what's going on here!

HOVSTAD. It almost seems that the Doctor wants to ruin the town.

DR. STOCKMANN. I love my native town so much that I would rather ruin it than see it prosper on a lie.

ASLAKSEN. That's plain speaking.

[*Noise and whistling.* MRS. STOCKMANN *coughs in vain; the* DOCTOR *no longer hears her.*]

HOVSTAD (*shouting above the noise*). A man who would ruin a community is an enemy to his fellow citizens!

DR. STOCKMANN (*with growing excitement*). What does it matter if a lying community is ruined! Let it be leveled to the ground! All men who live on lies ought to be exterminated like vermin! You'll end by poisoning the whole country, so that the whole country will deserve to perish. And if ever it comes to that, I shall say, from the bottom of my heart: Let the country perish! Let all its people perish!

A MAN (*in the crowd*). Why, he talks like an enemy of the people!

BILLING. Strike me dead, there's the voice of the people!

THE WHOLE ASSEMBLY (*shouting*). Yes! yes! yes! He's an enemy of the people! He hates his country! He hates his people!

ASLAKSEN. Both as a citizen of this town and as a human being, I am deeply shocked at what I have heard tonight. Dr. Stockmann has unmasked himself in a way I should never have dreamt of. I must reluctantly agree with the opinion just expressed by my fellow citizens; and I think we ought to formulate this opinion in a resolution. I therefore beg to move "That this meeting declares the medical officer of the Baths, Dr. Thomas Stockmann, to be an enemy of the people."

[*Thunders of applause and cheers. Many form a circle round the* DOCTOR *and jeer at him.* MRS. STOCKMANN *and* PETRA *have risen.* MORTEN *and* EILIF *fight other schoolboys, who also have been jeering. Some adults separate them.*]

DR. STOCKMANN (*to the people jeering*). Oh, you fools! I tell you that —

ASLAKSEN (*ringing*). The Doctor is out of order. A formal vote must be taken; but out of consideration for personal feelings, it will be taken by secret ballot. Do you have any blank paper, Mr. Billing?

BILLING. Here are both blue and white paper —

ASLAKSEN. Good. That will save time. Tear it into strips. That's it. (*To the meeting*) Blue means no, white means yes. I'll collect the votes myself.

[*The* MAYOR *leaves the room.* ASLAKSEN *and a few others go round with pieces of paper in hats.*]

A GENTLEMAN (*to* HOVSTAD). What's the matter with the Doctor? What does it all mean?

HOVSTAD. Why, you know how impetuous he is.

ANOTHER GENTLEMAN (*to* BILLING). Tell me, you've been at his house. Have you noticed if the fellow drinks?

BILLING. Strike me dead if I know what to say. The toddy's always on the table when anyone looks in.

A THIRD GENTLEMAN. No, I would say he's out of his mind.

FIRST GENTLEMAN. I wonder if there's madness in the family?

BILLING. I wouldn't be surprised.

A FOURTH GENTLEMAN. No, it's just spite. He wants revenge for something or other.

BILLING. He did talk about a raise in his salary the other day; but he didn't get it.

ALL THE GENTLEMEN (*together*). Aha! That explains it.

THE DRUNKEN MAN (*in the crowd*). I want a blue one! And I'll have a white one too.

SEVERAL PEOPLE. There's that drunk again! Throw him out.

MORTEN KIIL (*approaching the* DOCTOR). Well, Stockmann, you see now what such monkey tricks lead to?

DR. STOCKMANN. I have done my duty.

MORTEN KIIL. What was that you said

about the Mill Dale tanneries?

DR. STOCKMANN. You heard what I said — that all the filth comes from them.

MORTEN KIIL. From my tannery as well?

DR. STOCKMANN. I'm sorry to say yours is the worst of all.

MORTEN KIIL. Are you going to put that in the papers, too?

DR. STOCKMANN. I shall hide nothing.

MORTEN KIIL. This may be costly to you, Stockmann! (*He goes out.*)

A FAT GENTLEMAN (*goes up to* HORSTER, *ignoring the ladies*). Well, Captain, so you lend your house to enemies of the people.

HORSTER. I suppose I can do as I please with my own property, Sir.

THE GENTLEMAN. Then of course you can have no objection if I follow your example?

HORSTER. What do you mean, Sir?

THE GENTLEMAN. You shall hear from me tomorrow. (*Turns away and goes out.*)

PETRA. Isn't that the owner of your ship, Captain Horster?

HORSTER. Yes, that is Mr. Vik.

ASLAKSEN (*with the ballots in his hands, ascends the platform and rings*). Gentlemen! I shall now announce the result of the vote. All the voters, with one exception —

A YOUNG GENTLEMAN. That's the drunk!

ASLAKSEN. With the exception of one intoxicated person, this meeting of citizens unanimously declares the medical officer of the Baths, Dr. Thomas Stockmann, to be an enemy of the people. (*Cheers and applause*) Three cheers for our fine community! (*Cheers*) Three cheers for our

able and energetic Mayor, who so loyally set family prejudice aside! (*Cheers*) The meeting is adjourned. (*He descends.*)

BILLING. Three cheers for the Chairman!

ALL. Hurrah for Aslaksen.

DR. STOCKMANN. My hat and coat, Petra. Captain, have you room for passengers to the new world?

HORSTER. For you and yours, Doctor, we'll make room.

DR. STOCKMANN (*while* PETRA *helps him on with his coat*). Good! Come, Katherine, come, boys! (*He gives his wife his arm.*)

MRS. STOCKMANN (*in a low voice*). Thomas, dear, let us go out by the back way.

DR. STOCKMANN. No back ways, Katherine! (*In a loud voice*) You'll hear more from the enemy of the people, before he shakes the dust from his feet! I am not so forbearing as a certain person; I don't say: I forgive you, for you know not what you do.

ASLAKSEN (*shouts*). That is a blasphemous comparison, Dr. Stockmann!

BILLING. Strike me — ! This is more than a decent man can stand!

A COARSE VOICE. And now he threatens us!

ANGRY CRIES. Let's smash his windows! Duck him in the fjord![1]

A MAN (*in the crowd*). Blow your horn, Evensen! Blow, man, blow!

[*Horn-blowing, whistling, and wild shouting. The* DOCTOR, *with his family, goes towards the door.* HORSTER *clears the way for them.*]

ALL (*yelling after them as they go out*). Enemy of the people! Enemy of the people! Enemy of the people!

BILLING. Strike me dead! I wouldn't want to drink toddy at Stockmann's tonight!

[*The people move towards the door; the shouting is continued outside; from the street are heard cries of "Enemy of the people! Enemy of the people!"*]

[1] fjord (fyôrd): narrow inlet of the sea between high banks or cliffs.

For Discussion

1. At the town meeting Dr. Stockmann is really beaten before he starts. What tactic is used right at the beginning to make sure those in power will control what goes on? Why do you suppose the doctor allows them to get away with it?

2. Closely consider Dr. Stockmann's argument in his speech before the townspeople. How does he regard truth — as static or dynamic, that is, as something fixed and absolute, or as something constantly changing? "The majority is always right," Hovstad cries. What is the doctor's answer to that? How does he justify his answer?

3. Notice on page 117 how the townspeople try to understand Dr. Stockmann's motivations for speaking to them publicly as he does. His real motivation, of course, is simply a desire to tell them the truth. But in what different ways do they account for his saying what he says?

4. **Rising Action, Climax, Falling Action.** The *climax* is the point of no return in a narrative or drama. Here the climax, which you may be able to see more clearly after finishing the play, occurs where the doctor identifies the solid majority as the most dangerous enemy of truth and freedom (page 113). Before that point, he still might solve the dilemma in which he finds himself in a number of ways (apologize to the mayor, leave town, agree to tinker with the baths, woo the solid majority more subtly to gain their support, etc.). After that point, however, the outcome is inevitable. The climax is the crest of a wave; all before it is *rising action*, and all that follows is *falling action*. Accordingly, in reading Act V, notice how the playwright maintains your interest in the drama even though the climax is past.

Act V

DR. STOCKMANN's *Study. Bookshelves and medicine cabinets along the walls. In the back, a door leading to the hall; in front, on the left, a door to the living room. In the wall to the right are two windows, with all the panes smashed. In the middle of the room is the* DOCTOR's *desk, covered with books and papers. The room is in disorder. It is morning.*

DR. STOCKMANN, *in dressing gown, slippers, and skullcap, is bending down and raking with an umbrella under one of the cabinets; at last he rakes out a stone.*

DR. STOCKMANN (*speaking through the living room doorway*). Katherine, I've found another!

MRS. STOCKMANN (*in the living room*). Oh, I'm sure you'll find plenty more.

DR. STOCKMANN (*placing the stone on a pile of others on the table*). I'm going to keep these stones as sacred relics. Eilif and Morten must see them every day, and they will inherit them. (*Raking under the bookcase*) Hasn't — what the devil is her name? — the girl — hasn't she gone for the glazier yet?

MRS. STOCKMANN (*coming in*). Yes, but he said he didn't know if he would be able to come today.

DR. STOCKMANN. He probably doesn't dare to come.

MRS. STOCKMANN. Well, Randina also thought he was afraid to come, because of the neighbors. (*Speaks through the living room doorway.*) What is it, Randina? — Very well. (*Goes out, and returns immediately.*) Here is a letter for you, Thomas.

DR. STOCKMANN. Let me see. (*Opens the letter and reads.*) Aha!

MRS. STOCKMANN. Who is it from?

DR. STOCKMANN. From the landlord. He gives us notice.

MRS. STOCKMANN. Really? He is such a nice man —

DR. STOCKMANN (*looking at the letter*). He doesn't dare do otherwise, he says. He is very unwilling to do it; but he doesn't dare do otherwise — on account of his fellow citizens — out of respect for public opinion — is in a dependent position — doesn't dare to offend certain influential men —

MRS. STOCKMANN. There, you see, Thomas.

DR. STOCKMANN. Yes, yes, I see well enough; they are all cowards in this town, every one of them. No one dares do anything for fear of all the rest. (*Throws the letter on the table.*) But it's all the same to us, Katherine. We're leaving for the new world, and then —

MRS. STOCKMANN. But are you sure this idea of leaving is altogether wise, Thomas?

DR. STOCKMANN. Do you want me to stay here, where they have branded me as an enemy of the people and smashed my windows! And look here, Katherine, they've torn a hole in my black trousers, too.

MRS. STOCKMANN. Oh, dear; and those are your best ones, too!

DR. STOCKMANN. A man should never put on his best trousers when he goes out to battle for freedom and truth. Well, I don't care so much about the trousers; you can always patch them up for me. What I can't stomach is that that mob, that rabble, should dare to attack me as if they were my equals!

MRS. STOCKMANN. Yes, they have behaved abominably to you here, Thomas; but is that any reason for leaving the country altogether?

DR. STOCKMANN. Do you think the masses are less insolent in other towns? Of course not, my dear; they're all the same. Well, never mind; let the curs yelp. That's not the worst; the worst is that everyone, all over the country, has to toe the party line. Not that it's likely to be better in the free West either. The solid majority, and enlightened public opinion, and all the other devil's trash are rampant there too. But at least it's on a bigger scale there than here. They may kill you, but they don't put you to slow torture; they don't clamp a free soul in a vise, as they do at home here. And then, if necessary, you can get away from it all. (*Walks up and down.*) If I only knew of a primeval forest, or a little South Sea island that was for sale cheap —

MRS. STOCKMANN. Yes, but the boys, Thomas.

DR. STOCKMANN (*comes to a standstill*). What an extraordinary woman, you are, Katherine! Would you rather have the boys grow up in a society like ours? Why, you could see for yourself yesterday evening that one half of the population is absolutely mad, and if the other half hasn't lost its wits, that's only because they are such blockheads they haven't any wits to lose.

MRS. STOCKMANN. But really, my dear Thomas, you do say such imprudent things.

DR. STOCKMANN. What! Isn't it the truth? Don't they turn all ideas upside down? Don't they make a hodge-podge of right and wrong? Don't they call lies everything that I know to be the truth? But the maddest thing of all is to see crowds of grown men, calling themselves liberals, go about persuading themselves and others that they are friends of freedom! Did you ever hear anything like it, Katherine?

MRS. STOCKMANN. Yes, yes, no doubt. But —

[PETRA *enters from the living room.*]

MRS. STOCKMANN. Back from school already?

PETRA. Yes; I have been dismissed.

MRS. STOCKMANN. Dismissed?

DR. STOCKMANN. You too!

PETRA. Mrs. Busk gave me notice, and so I thought it best to leave at once.

DR. STOCKMANN. You did perfectly right!

MRS. STOCKMANN. Who could have thought Mrs. Busk was such a bad woman!

PETRA. Oh, mother, Mrs. Busk isn't bad at all; I saw clearly how sorry she was. But she didn't dare do otherwise, she said; and so I am dismissed.

DR. STOCKMANN (*laughing and rubbing his hands*). She didn't dare do otherwise — just like the rest! Oh, that's great!

MRS. STOCKMANN. Oh, well, after that frightful scene last night —

PETRA. It wasn't only that. Listen to this, father.

DR. STOCKMANN. Well?

PETRA. Mrs. Busk showed me no fewer than three letters she had received this morning —

DR. STOCKMANN. Anonymous, of course?

PETRA. Yes.

DR. STOCKMANN. They never dare give their names, Katherine!

PETRA. And two of them stated that a gentleman who is often at our house said at the club last night that I held extremely advanced opinions upon various things —

DR. STOCKMANN. I hope you didn't deny it.

PETRA. Of course not. You know Mrs. Busk herself is pretty advanced in her opinions when we're alone together; but now that this has been said about me, she dared not keep me on.

MRS. STOCKMANN. Someone who is often at our house, too. There, you see, Thomas, what comes of all your hospitality.

DR. STOCKMANN. We won't live in this pigsty any longer! Pack up as quickly as you can, Katherine; let's get away — the sooner the better.

MRS. STOCKMANN. Hush! I think there is someone in the hall. See who it is, Petra.

PETRA (*opening the door*). Oh, it's you, Captain Horster. Please come in.

HORSTER (*from the hall*). Good morning. I thought I'd look in and ask how you are.

DR. STOCKMANN (*shaking his hand*). Thanks; that's very good of you.

MRS. STOCKMANN. And thank you for helping us through the crowd last night, Captain Horster.

PETRA. How did you ever get home again?

HORSTER. Oh, it wasn't bad. I'm pretty tough, you know; and those fellows' bark is worse than their bite.

DR. STOCKMANN. Yes, isn't it extraordinary what cowards they are? Come here, and let me show you something! Look, here are all the stones they threw in at us. Just look at them! There aren't more than two real stones in the whole heap; the rest are nothing but pebbles — mere gravel. They stood down there, and yelled, and swore they'd kill me —; but as for really doing it— no, there's mighty little fear of that in this town!

HORSTER. You may thank your stars for that this time, Doctor.

DR. STOCKMANN. I do, of course. But it's depressing all the same; for if it ever came to the point of a serious national struggle, you may be sure public opinion would be for taking to its heels, and the liberal majority would scamper for their lives like a flock of sheep, Captain Horster. That's what's so depressing about it; that's what really upsets me. But damn it — it's foolish of me to feel anything of the sort! They have called me an enemy of the people; so then, I'll be an enemy of the people!

MRS. STOCKMANN. You'll never be that, Thomas.

DR. STOCKMANN. You'd better not bet on it, Katherine. A bad name may act like a pinprick in the lung. And that damned name — I can't get rid of it; it has sunk deep into my heart; and there it lies gnawing like an acid. And no magnesia can cure me.

PETRA. Pooh; you should just laugh at them, father.

HORSTER. People will change their minds, Doctor.

MRS. STOCKMANN. Yes, Thomas, they will, as sure as you are standing here.

DR. STOCKMANN. Yes, perhaps, when it is too late. Well, it will serve them right! Let them go on wallowing here in their pigsty. They'll wish they hadn't driven a patriot into exile. When do you sail, Captain Horster?

HORSTER. Well — that's really what I came to speak to you about —

DR. STOCKMANN. What? Anything wrong with the ship?

HORSTER. No; just that I won't be sailing with her.

PETRA. Surely you have not been dismissed?

HORSTER (*smiling*). Yes, I have.

PETRA. You too!

MRS. STOCKMANN. There, you see, Thomas.

DR. STOCKMANN. And for the cause of truth! Oh, if I had imagined such a thing was possible —

HORSTER. Don't be upset. I shall soon find a job with some other company, elsewhere.

DR. STOCKMANN. To think that a man like Vik — ! A wealthy man, independent of everyone! Faugh!

HORSTER. Oh, for that matter, he's a very well-meaning man. He said himself he would gladly have kept me on if only he dared —

DR. STOCKMANN. But he didn't dare? Of course not!

HORSTER. It's not so easy, he said, when you belong to a party —

DR. STOCKMANN. Our fine friend has hit the nail on the head there! A party is like a sausage machine; it grinds all the brains together into hash, and that's why we see nothing but porridge-heads and pulp-heads all around!

MRS. STOCKMANN. Now really, Thomas!

PETRA (*to* HORSTER). If you hadn't seen us home, perhaps it would not have come to this.

HORSTER. I don't regret it.

PETRA (*gives him her hand*). Thank you for that!

HORSTER (*to* DR. STOCKMANN). And I wanted to tell you this: if you are really determined to go abroad, I've thought of another way —

DR. STOCKMANN. That's good — as long as we can get away quickly —

MRS. STOCKMANN. Hush! Isn't that a knock?

PETRA. I believe it is uncle.

DR. STOCKMANN. Aha! (*calls.*) Come in!

MRS. STOCKMANN. My dear Thomas, now do promise me —

[*The* MAYOR *enters from the hall.*]

MAYOR (*in the doorway*). Oh, you are engaged. Then I'd better —

DR. STOCKMANN. No, no; come in.

MAYOR. But I want to speak to you alone.

MRS. STOCKMANN. We can go into the living room.

HORSTER. And I shall look in again later.

DR. STOCKMANN. No, no; go with the ladies, Captain Horster; I want to hear more about —

HORSTER. All right, then I'll wait.

[*He follows* MRS. STOCKMANN *and* PETRA *into the living room. The* MAYOR *says nothing, but glances at the windows.*]

DR. STOCKMANN. I dare say you find it rather drafty here today? Put on your cap.

MAYOR. Thanks, if I may. (*Does so.*) I must have caught cold yesterday evening. I stood there shivering —

DR. STOCKMANN. Really. I found it quite warm enough.

MAYOR. I regret that it was not in my power to prevent that unfortunate incident.

DR. STOCKMANN. Do you have anything else in particular to say to me?

MAYOR (*producing a large letter*). I have this document for you from the Directors of the Baths.

DR. STOCKMANN. My dismissal?

MAYOR. Yes; dated today. (*Places the letter on the table.*) We are very sorry — but frankly, we didn't dare do otherwise, because of public opinion.

DR. STOCKMANN (*smiling*). Didn't dare? I've heard that phrase already today.

MAYOR. I want you to realize your position clearly. In the future, you cannot count on any sort of practice in the town.

DR. STOCKMANN. To hell with the practice! But how can you be so sure of that?

MAYOR. The Home Owners' Association is sending round a petition from house to house, urging all respectable citizens not to employ you; and I am confident that not a single head of a family will refuse to sign it; he simply would not dare.

DR. STOCKMANN. I don't doubt that. But what then?

MAYOR. If I might advise you, I would suggest that you leave the town for a time —

DR. STOCKMANN. Yes, I've thought of that already.

MAYOR. Good. And when you have had six months or so to think things over, you might be ready to acknowledge your error, with a few words of apology —

DR. STOCKMANN. Then perhaps I might be reinstated, you think?

MAYOR. Perhaps it's not quite out of the question.

DR. STOCKMANN. Yes, but what about public opinion? You won't dare because of public opinion.

MAYOR. Opinion is extremely changeable. And to speak candidly, it is very important for us to have a signed statement from you to that effect.

DR. STOCKMANN. Yes, I guess it would be most convenient for you! But remember what I've said to you before about such dishonesty!

MAYOR. At that time your position was quite different. At that time you thought you had the whole town at your back —

DR. STOCKMANN. Yes, and now I have the whole town *on* my back — (*Flaring up*) But no — not if I had the devil and his dam on my back —! Never — never, I tell you!

MAYOR. The father of a family has no right to act as you are doing. You have no right to do it, Thomas.

DR. STOCKMANN. I have no right! There's only one thing in the world that a free man has no right to do; and do you know what that is?

MAYOR. No.

DR. STOCKMANN. Of course not; but *I* will tell you. A free man has no right to wallow in filth; he has no right to act so that he ought to spit in his own face!

MAYOR. That might sound extremely convincing if there were not another explanation for your obstinacy — but we all know there is —

DR. STOCKMANN. What do you mean by that?

MAYOR. You know very well what I mean. But as your brother, and as a man who knows the world, I warn you not to build too confidently upon prospects and expectations that may very likely come to nothing.

DR. STOCKMANN. Why, what on earth are you driving at?

MAYOR. Do you really expect me to believe that you are ignorant of the terms of old Morten Kiil's will?

DR. STOCKMANN. I know that what little he has is to go to a home for old and needy workmen. But what has that got to do with me?

MAYOR. To begin with, "what little he has" is no trifle. Morten Kiil is a pretty wealthy man.

DR. STOCKMANN. I have never had the least notion of that!

MAYOR. H'm — really? Then I suppose you have no notion that a large part of his fortune is to go to your children, and that you and your wife are to have the income from the money during your lifetime. Has he not told you that?

DR. STOCKMANN. No, I'll be hanged if he has! On the contrary, he has done nothing but grumble about the taxes he has to pay. But are you really sure of this, Peter?

MAYOR. I have it from a thoroughly reliable source.

DR. STOCKMANN. Why, good heavens, then Katherine's provided for — and the children too! Oh, I must tell her — (*Calls.*) Katherine, Katherine!

MAYOR (*holding him back*). Hush! don't say anything about it yet.

MRS. STOCKMANN (*opening the door*). What is it?

DR. STOCKMANN. Nothing, my dear; go back again.

[MRS. STOCKMANN *closes the door.*]

DR. STOCKMANN (*pacing up and down*). Provided for! Only think — all of them provided for! And for life! It's a grand thing to feel yourself secure!

MAYOR. Yes, but that is just what you are not. Morten Kiil can change his will any day or hour he chooses.

DR. STOCKMANN. But he won't, my good Peter. The Badger is delighted to see me expose you and your precious friends.

MAYOR (*starts and looks searchingly at him*). Aha! That throws a new light on a good many things.

DR. STOCKMANN. What things?

MAYOR. So the whole affair was a carefully planned intrigue. Your recklessly violent onslaught — in the name of truth — upon the leading men of the town —

DR. STOCKMANN. Well, what of it?

MAYOR. It was nothing but part of a bargain for being included in vindictive old Morten Kiil's will.

DR. STOCKMANN (*almost speechless*). Peter — you are the most abominable person I have ever known in all my born days.

MAYOR. All is over between us. Your dismissal is irrevocable — for now we have a weapon against you. (*He goes out.*)

DR. STOCKMANN. Of all the filthy — ! (*Calls.*) Katherine! The floor must be scrubbed after him! Tell her to come here with a pail — what's her name? damn it — the girl with the smudge on her nose —

MRS. STOCKMANN (*in the living room doorway*). Hush, Thomas, please!

PETRA (*also in the doorway*). Father, here's grandfather; he wants to know if he can speak to you alone.

DR. STOCKMANN. Yes, of course he can. (*By the door*) Come in, father-in-law.

[MORTEN KIIL *enters.* DR. STOCKMANN *closes the door behind him.*]

DR. STOCKMANN. What is it? Do sit down.

MORTEN KIIL. I won't sit down. (*Looking about him*) It looks cheerful here today, Stockmann.

DR. STOCKMANN. Yes, doesn't it?

MORTEN KIIL. Yes indeed. And you've got plenty of fresh air too; you've got your fill of that oxygen you were talking about yesterday. You must have a rare good conscience today, I should think.

DR. STOCKMANN. Yes, I have.

MORTEN KIIL. So I should suppose. (*Tapping himself on the breast*) But do you know what *I* have got here?

DR. STOCKMANN. A good conscience, too, I hope.

MORTEN KIIL. Pooh! No; something far better than that.

[*Takes out a large wallet, opens it, and shows* STOCKMANN *a bundle of papers.*]

DR. STOCKMANN (*looking at him in astonishment*). Shares in the Baths!

MORTEN KIIL. They weren't difficult to get today.

DR. STOCKMANN. And you've gone and bought these up — ?

MORTEN KIIL. All I had the money to pay for.

DR. STOCKMANN. Why, my dear sir, — just when things at the Baths are in such a mess!

MORTEN KIIL. If you behave like a reasonable man, you can soon make the Baths all right again.

DR. STOCKMANN. Well, you can see for yourself I'm doing all I can. But the people of this town are mad!

MORTEN KIIL. You said yesterday that the worst filth came from my tannery. Now, if that's true, then my grandfather, and my father before me, and I myself have been poisoning the town all these years with filth, like demons of destruction. Do you think I'm going to accept such a reproach?

DR. STOCKMANN. Unfortunately, you can't help it.

MORTEN KIIL. No, thank you. I care too much for my good name. I hear that people call me "the Badger." A badger's a sort of a pig, they tell me, but I intend to prove them wrong. I will live and die a clean man.

DR. STOCKMANN. And how will you manage that?

MORTEN KIIL. You will make me clean, Stockmann.

DR. STOCKMANN. I!

MORTEN KIIL. Do you know what money I used to buy these shares? No, you can't know; but now I'll tell you. It's the money Katherine and Petra and the boys are to have after my death. For, you see, I've managed to save quite a bit.

DR. STOCKMANN (*flaring up*). And you've used Katherine's money for this!

MORTEN KIIL. Yes; it is all invested in the Baths now. And now I want to see if you're really stark, staring mad, after all, Stockmann. If you go on saying that these beasts and other filthy animals dribble down from my tannery, it'll be just as if you were to flay broad stripes of Katherine's skin — and Petra's too, and the boys'. No decent father would do that — unless he was a madman.

DR. STOCKMANN (*walking up and down*). But I am a madman; I am a madman!

MORTEN KIIL. Surely you can't be so raving mad where your wife and children are concerned.

DR. STOCKMANN (*stopping in front of him*). Why couldn't you have spoken to me before you went and bought all that rubbish?

MORTEN KIIL. What's done can't be undone.

DR. STOCKMANN (*walking restlessly about*). If only I wasn't so certain! But I am absolutely convinced that I'm right.

MORTEN KIIL (*weighing the wallet in his hand*). If you stick to this lunacy, these won't be worth much. (*Puts the wallet into his pocket.*)

DR. STOCKMANN. Damn it! Surely science can find some antidote, some sort of preventive —

MORTEN KIIL. You mean something to kill the beasts?

DR. STOCKMANN. Yes, or at least to make them harmless.

MORTEN KIIL. Why not try rat poison?

DR. STOCKMANN. Oh, don't talk nonsense! — But since everyone declares it's nothing but my imagination, why let it be that! Let them have it their own way! These ignorant mongrels, calling me an enemy of the people and tearing the clothes off my back!

MORTEN KIIL. And smashing all your windows too!

DR. STOCKMANN. Yes, and one does have a duty to one's family! I must talk this over with Katherine. She's better at such things than I am.

MORTEN KIIL. That's right! You just follow the advice of a sensible woman.

DR. STOCKMANN (*turning upon him angrily*). How could you do this! Risking Katherine's money, and torturing me this way! When I look at you, I seem to see the devil himself — !

MORTEN KIIL. Then I'd better be off. But I must hear from you, yes or no, by two o'clock. If it's no, all the shares go to charity this very day.

DR. STOCKMANN. And what will Katherine get?

MORTEN KIIL. Not a cent.

[*The hall door opens.* HOVSTAD *and* ASLAKSEN *are seen outside it.*]

MORTEN KIIL. Well! look who's here.

DR. STOCKMANN (*staring at them*). What! Do you actually dare to come here?

HOVSTAD. We do indeed.

ASLAKSEN. You see, we've something to discuss with you.

MORTEN KIIL (*whispers*). Yes or no — by two o'clock.

ASLAKSEN (*with a glance at* HOVSTAD). Aha!

[MORTEN KIIL *goes out.*]

DR. STOCKMANN. Well, what do you want with me? Be quick about it.

HOVSTAD. I can well understand that you might resent our attitude at the meeting yesterday —

DR. STOCKMANN. Your attitude? Yes, it was a pretty attitude! I call it the attitude of cowards — of old women — !

HOVSTAD. Call it what you will; but we could not act otherwise.

DR. STOCKMANN. You didn't dare, I suppose? Isn't that so?

HOVSTAD. Yes, if you like to put it that way.

ASLAKSEN. But why didn't you drop a hint to us beforehand? Just a word to Mr. Hovstad or to me —

DR. STOCKMANN. A hint? What about?

ASLAKSEN. About what was really behind it all.

DR. STOCKMANN. I don't understand you at all.

ASLAKSEN (*nods confidentially*). Oh, yes, you do, Dr. Stockmann.

HOVSTAD. There's no use making a mystery of it now.

DR. STOCKMANN (*looking from one to the other*). What the devil is this all about?

ASLAKSEN. May I ask — isn't your father-in-law going about town buying up shares in the Baths?

DR. STOCKMANN. Yes, he has been buying Bath stock today but —

ASLAKSEN. It would have been more prudent to let somebody else do that — someone not so closely connected with you.

HOVSTAD. And you should not have acted in your own name either. No one needed to know that the attack on the Baths came from you. You should have taken me into your confidence, Dr. Stockmann.

DR. STOCKMANN (*stares straight in front of him; a light seems to break in upon him, and he says as though thunderstruck*). This is incredible! Are such things possible?

ASLAKSEN (*smiling*). Obviously they are. But they should be managed more subtly, you understand.

HOVSTAD. And there ought to be more people in it. It's always easier to avoid responsibility when there are several to share it.

DR. STOCKMANN (*calmly*). Come to the point, gentlemen — what is it you want?

ASLAKSEN. Mr. Hovstad can best —

HOVSTAD. No, you explain, Aslaksen.

ASLAKSEN. Well, it's like this: now that we know how the matter really stands, we believe we can venture to place the *People's Messenger* at your disposal.

DR. STOCKMANN. You can venture to now, eh? But what about public opinion? Aren't you afraid of raising a storm of protest?

HOVSTAD. We must be prepared to ride out the storm.

ASLAKSEN. And you must be ready to change your tactics quickly, Doctor. As soon as your attack has done its work —

DR. STOCKMANN. As soon as my father-in-law and I have bought up the shares cheaply, you mean?

HOVSTAD. I assume it is mainly for scientific purposes that you want to gain control of the Baths.

DR. STOCKMANN. Of course; it was for scientific purposes that I got the old Badger to go in with me. And then we'll patch up the pipes a little, and putter about a bit down at the beach. And it won't cost the town a penny. That ought to do it, don't you think?

HOVSTAD. I think so — if you have the *Messenger* to back you up.

ASLAKSEN. In a free community the press has great power, Doctor.

DR. STOCKMANN. Yes, indeed; and so does public opinion. And you, Mr. Aslaksen — I suppose you will answer for the Home Owners' Association?

ASLAKSEN. Both for the Home Owners' Association and the Temperance Society. You may count on that.

DR. STOCKMANN. But, gentlemen — I'm quite ashamed to mention such a thing — but — what do you get out of this?

HOVSTAD. Actually we'd prefer to give you our support for nothing. But the *Messenger* is not very firmly established. It doesn't have the funds that it should have; and I'd be very sorry to have to stop the paper just now, when there's so much political work to be done.

DR. STOCKMANN. Naturally; that would be very hard for a friend of the people like you. (*Flaring up*) But I — I am an enemy of the people! (*Striding about the room*) Where's my stick? Where the devil is my stick?

HOVSTAD. What do you mean?

ASLAKSEN. Surely you wouldn't —

Tension is revealed in the lines of this lithograph, titled Anxiety *by the Norwegian painter Edvard Munch.*

DR. STOCKMANN (*standing still*). And suppose I don't give you a single penny out of all my shares? You must remember we rich people don't like to part with our money.

HOVSTAD. And you must remember that this business of the shares can be presented in two very different ways.

DR. STOCKMANN. Yes, and you are just the man to do it. If I don't come to the rescue of the *Messenger*, you'll manage to make the affair look pretty ugly. You'll hunt me down, I suppose — bait me — throttle me as a dog throttles a hare!

HOVSTAD. That's a law of nature — every animal fights for its own survival.

127

ASLAKSEN. And must take its food where it can find it, you know.

DR. STOCKMANN. Then see if you can find some out in the gutter; (*Striding about the room*) for now, by heaven! we shall see which is the strongest animal of us three. (*Finds his umbrella and brandishes it.*) Now, get out!

HOVSTAD. You wouldn't dare attack us!

ASLAKSEN. Be careful with that umbrella.

DR. STOCKMANN. Out at the window with you, Mr. Hovstad!

HOVSTAD (*by the hall door*). Are you out of your mind?

DR. STOCKMANN. Out the window, Mr. Aslaksen! Jump, I tell you! Be quick about it!

ASLAKSEN (*running round the desk*). Moderation, Doctor; I'm not at all strong; I can't stand much — (*Screams.*) Help! help!

[MRS. STOCKMANN, PETRA, *and* HORSTER *enter from living room.*]

MRS. STOCKMANN. Good heavens, Thomas! What is the matter?

DR. STOCKMANN (*brandishing the umbrella*). Jump, I tell you! Out into the gutter!

HOVSTAD. An unprovoked assault! You're a witness, Captain Horster. (*Rushes off through the hall.*)

ASLAKSEN (*bewildered*). If I only knew the law in this matter! (*He slinks out by the living room door.*)

MRS. STOCKMANN (*holding back the* DOCTOR). Now, control yourself, Thomas!

DR. STOCKMANN (*throwing down the umbrella*). Damn them! They got away after all.

MRS. STOCKMANN. What did they want with you?

DR. STOCKMANN. I'll tell you later; I have other things to think of now. (*Goes to the desk and writes on a visiting card.*) Look, Katherine, look what's written here.

MRS. STOCKMANN. Three big "No's." What does that mean?

DR. STOCKMANN. I'll tell you about that later, too. (*Handing the card*) Here, Petra; let smudgy-face run to the Badger's with this as fast as she can. Be quick! (PETRA *goes out through the hall with the card.*) Well, I've had visits today from all the agents of the devil! But now I'll sharpen my pen against them till it becomes a goad; I'll dip it in gall and venom; I'll hurl my inkwell straight at their heads.

MRS. STOCKMANN. But aren't we going away, Thomas?

[PETRA *returns.*]

DR. STOCKMANN. Well?

PETRA. She has gone.

DR. STOCKMANN. Good. Going away? No, I'll be damned if we are. We're staying right here, Katherine.

PETRA. We're staying?

MRS. STOCKMANN. Here in the town?

DR. STOCKMANN. Yes, here; the battlefield is here. Here the fight must be fought; here I will conquer! As soon as my trousers are mended, I shall go out into the town and look for a house; we must have a roof over our heads for the winter.

HORSTER. You can have my house.

DR. STOCKMANN. Can I?

HORSTER. Yes, there's no difficulty about that. I have lots of room, and I'm hardly ever at home.

MRS. STOCKMANN. Oh, how kind of you, Captain Horster.

PETRA. Thank you!

DR. STOCKMANN (*shaking his hand*). Thank you! That's a load off my mind. Now I can go to work in earnest. Oh, there's no end of work to be done here, Katherine! It's a good thing I have all my time at my disposal now; for you must know I've been dismissed from the Baths —

MRS. STOCKMANN (*sighing*). Oh, yes, I was expecting that.

DR. STOCKMANN. — And now they want to take away my practice too. Well let them! The poor will stay with me — those who can't pay; and they're the ones who need me most. But by heaven! I'll make them listen to me; I'll preach to them in season and out of season, as the saying goes.

MRS. STOCKMANN. My dear Thomas, I thought you had learned how much good preaching does.

DR. STOCKMANN. Don't be absurd, Katherine. Do you think I would let myself be driven from the field by public opinion, and the solid majority, and all that sort of devilry? No, thank you! Besides, my point is so simple, so clear and straightforward. I only want to drive it into the heads of these mongrels that these so-called liberals are the enemies of freedom; that party programs wring the necks of all young and living truths; that policies of expediency[1] turn justice and morality upside down, until life here becomes not worth living. Captain Horster, don't you think I can make the people understand that?

HORSTER. Maybe; I don't know much about these things myself.

DR. STOCKMANN. Well, you see — it's like this. First the party bosses must be exterminated. Because a party boss is just like a wolf, you see — a ravening[2] wolf; he must devour a certain number of smaller animals a year, if he's to exist at all. Just look at Hovstad and Aslaksen! How many small animals they destroy — or at least debase and corrupt, so that they're fit for nothing else but to be home owners and subscribers to the *People's Messenger!* (*Sits on the edge of the table*). Come here, Katherine — see how brightly the sun shines today! And feel the glorious fresh spring air.

MRS. STOCKMANN. Yes, if we could live only on sunshine and spring air, Thomas.

DR. STOCKMANN. Well, you'll have to pinch and save, but we shall get on all right. That doesn't trouble me. No, what does trouble me is that I don't see any man free enough and high-minded enough to dare take up my work after me.

PETRA. Oh, don't think about that, father; you have time enough before you. — Why, here are the boys already.

[EILIF *and* MORTEN *enter from the living room.*]

MRS. STOCKMANN. Is today a holiday?

MORTEN. No; we had a fight with some other boys.

EILIF. That's not true; it was the other boys who fought us.

MORTEN. And then Mr. Rörlund said we'd better stay home for a few days.

DR. STOCKMANN (*snapping his fingers and springing down from the table*). Now I have it! That's it! You shall never set foot in that school again!

THE BOYS. Never go to school!

MRS. STOCKMANN. Really, Thomas —

DR. STOCKMANN. Never, I say! I'll teach you myself. That is, I won't teach you a blessed thing —

MORTEN. Hurrah!

DR. STOCKMANN. — but I shall help you to grow into free, high-minded men. — And you must help me, Petra.

PETRA. Yes, father, I certainly will.

DR. STOCKMANN. And we'll have our school in the very room where they branded me an enemy of the people. But we must have more pupils. I must have at least a dozen boys to begin with.

MRS. STOCKMANN. You'll never get them in this town.

DR. STOCKMANN. We shall see. (*To the*

---

[1] **policies of expediency**: doing what is most convenient or advantageous without regard to fairness or rightness.

[2] **ravening**: prowling for food.

boys) Do you know any street urchins — any regular ragamuffins — ?

MORTEN. Yes, father, I know lots!

DR. STOCKMANN. Then bring me a few of them. I shall experiment with mongrels for once. Sometimes there are excellent heads among them.

MORTEN. But what do we do when we're grown into free and high-minded men?

DR. STOCKMANN. Drive all the wolves out to the far west, boys!

[EILIF *looks rather doubtful;* MORTEN *jumps about shouting "Hurrah!"*]

MRS. STOCKMANN. But suppose the wolves drive you out, Thomas.

DR. STOCKMANN. Are you mad, Katherine! Drive me out! Now that I am the strongest man in the town?

MRS. STOCKMANN. The strongest — now?

DR. STOCKMANN. Yes, I would even say that now I am one of the strongest men in the whole world.

MORTEN. Are you really?

DR. STOCKMANN (*in a subdued voice*). Hush; you mustn't speak about it yet; but I have made a great discovery.

MRS. STOCKMANN. What, another?

DR. STOCKMANN. Yes, of course! (*Gathers them about him, and speaks confidentially.*) This is what I have discovered: the strongest man in the world is the man who stands alone.

MRS. STOCKMANN (*shakes her head, smiling*). Oh, Thomas dear — !

PETRA (*grasping his hands*). Father!

For Discussion

1. Dr. Stockmann's public accusation has serious consequences to those around him. How does it affect Petra? Morten and Eilif? Horster? Thomas himself? Notice the kinds of people directly responsible for these consequences. What sort of people are Mrs. Busk and Mr. Vik, for instance?

2. Near the end of the play the doctor sends a message to Morten Kiil. What does the message say? Explain what Morten Kiil had proposed to Dr. Stockmann. What will be the consequences of the doctor's answer to that proposal?

3. The play ends with a final discovery that the doctor makes. What is that discovery? What are his plans henceforth? (Here is one way the dramatist maintains your interest in the play even after the climax is past; he introduces further complications that create questions left unanswered and suspense left unresolved until the very end. For instance, will the Stockmanns leave their native town? The question is not answered until just before the final curtain.)

The Play as a Whole

1. "One may say, on the whole," the mayor announces very early in the play, "that a fine spirit of tolerance prevails in our town" (page 77). How does he account for that spirit? Evaluate the accuracy of the remark in the light of what happens during the play. If the town is in fact intolerant, of what is it intolerant? Discuss.

2. "You have a turbulent, unruly, rebellious spirit," Peter Stockmann tells his brother (page 94). And later (page 104) we hear him telling Aslaksen, "Unfortunately, my brother has always been noted for his rashness." How accurate are these evaluations? At the start, is the doctor a misfit, hostile to his fellow citizens? Is he rash, or impulsive? Consider his course of conduct when he first suspects that the baths may be polluted and his response to Hovstad's attack on "bureaucrats" (page 88). Are these the actions and responses of an unreasonable revolutionary? How, then, do you account for the change in his attitude? Is it clearly motivated? Is he at all responsible for what happens to him? In short, what kind of man is Thomas Stockmann?

3. In one sense *An Enemy of the People* may be thought of as a demonstration of the ways different people seek to exploit the truth to serve their own ends. Why do Billing and

Hovstad at first find the truth that Dr. Stock-mann presents them with so useful? From what background does Hovstad come (a background, incidentally, bound to make him envious of the wealthy owners of the baths)? For what purposes does Morten Kiil want to exploit what he learns from the doctor?

4. **Structure, Denouement, Resolution.** Every work of literature has a *structure*, or shape, that holds the work together. A conventionally structured play, as we have noticed, is shaped rather like a wave, rising from exposition through complications to crest at the climax, then falling away through what is called the *denouement*, or unknotting of the strands of the plot, to the *resolution*, which resolves (by death perhaps, or departure, or triumph) the issues raised earlier. How would you describe the mood at the resolution of this play? Be as specific as you can.

For Composition

A curtain goes up to disclose characters on a stage. Who are they? What are their names and relationships to each other? Is that lady the wife of the man to whom she is speaking? Who is that other man who enters? At what point in the lives of these people are we meeting them? All of this information, which emerges during the exposition, must be conveyed through dialogue. For example, the first speech in *An Enemy of the People* tells us Billing's name and clarifies that he is not married to Mrs. Stockmann, with whom he is speaking.

1. **Analysis.** Write a composition explaining the situation when *An Enemy of the People* begins. Include nothing that happens after the action starts; rather, limit your remarks to clarifying the relationships and past history of the participants as revealed in the opening scenes of the play.

2. **Comparison and Contrast.** Contrast is the essence of drama. There is nothing dramatic about your and your best friend's discussion of someone both of you dislike. It becomes dramatic only if your friend likes the person you are discussing, and you don't — or if perhaps you and the person you dislike are confronting each other.

Compare and contrast Peter and Thomas Stockmann in as many ways as you can. For instance, the former is a public figure, whereas the latter has lived most of his life away from the public. One is practical, the other is idealistic. Organize the terms of your contrast in some logical way, and include a consideration of contrasting attitudes toward duty and responsibility.

3. **Argument.** "Oh, the public has no need for new ideas. The public gets on best with the good old recognized ideas it has already" (page 94). Support or refute that position in a well-organized composition. Illustrate your general remarks with specific examples from your reading or personal experience.

4. **Analysis.** Reconsider the doctor's long speech in Act IV, then write a composition analyzing his remarks. If the majority is always wrong, does it follow that the minority is always right? Is what may be true for dogs necessarily true for people? Your analysis should first of all follow the doctor's arguments carefully, but you may want to evaluate the logic of those arguments as well.

Words and Allusions

WORDS IN CONTEXT. Usually the meaning of a word cannot be exactly determined until we know how it is being used. That information is provided by the context — that is, from the other words in the passage in which the word appears and from the situation in which the word is used.

1. A number of words that are common in everyday life are applicable to the characters and situations in *An Enemy of the People*. Consider the words *liberal* and *conservative*. During most of the play, Doctor Stockmann regards himself as a liberal. Hovstad and Billing also regard themselves as liberals. Yet during the town meeting in Act IV, Doctor Stockmann denounces the views of Hovstad. What does the term *liberal* appear to mean in this context? What is your understanding of the

term *liberal?* In your opinion, who, if anyone, in this play should be called a *liberal?* Whom would you label *conservative?* Why?

2. At other times during the play, Doctor Stockmann is called an *aristocrat* and a *revolutionary*. From what you understand of these terms, to what extent do they apply to Doctor Stockmann?

3. Two other common terms are *idealist* and *realist.* Can Doctor Stockmann be called an *idealist?* If so, why? Who in the play can be called a *realist?* Why?

4. Two commonly confused terms are *uninterested* and *disinterested.* What is the difference between them? Is Captain Horster uninterested or disinterested? Why? Is there anyone else in the play you would label *disinterested?* Why, or why not?

In Summary

1. "I search after truth," wrote the Roman statesman and philosopher Marcus Aurelius. "I search after truth, by which man never yet was harmed." This first section of *Themes in World Literature* has searched after truth, too, and disclosed some of the aspects it assumes and some of the difficulties it offers. What light do the selections throw on the remark of Marcus Aurelius? Has truth ever harmed anyone? Why is a search after truth a considerable undertaking? Refer to specific selections in answering, and in suggesting some of the difficulties with which truth presents us.

2. Plato's "Allegory of the Cave" makes a distinction between what appears to be true and what is actually true. Explain the distinction. Which of the selections in this section develop a contrast between how things seem on the surface, and how they really are? Do any of the selections accept the surface appearance of things as embodying reality and the truth?

3. Don Quixote's name has come to designate any man of lofty ideals intent upon righting the wrongs of the world, but with little practical sense of how to deal with his fellow men. To what extent does Dr. Thomas Stockmann in *An Enemy of the People* qualify as a quixotic figure? Is he naive and innocent about the world around him? Is he at all mad? Does he "tilt at windmills"? Is he motivated solely by a desire to right wrongs?

4. Distinguish between allegory and parable. Irony involves a contrast between appearance and actuality. What irony do you find in "The Night Face Up"? What is an image? An ode? An allusion? Describe the structure of a conventional play.

5. **Creative Writing.** Although "Young Goodman Brown" is a short story, it contains a number of dramatic scenes. Demonstrate your understanding of the problems of playwriting, as revealed in earlier discussions of *An Enemy of the People*, by casting a portion of "Young Goodman Brown" into play form. First decide which part you want to dramatize. The story takes place in Salem Village, in the forest, at the altar, and back in the village. Of those locales, which scene will allow you to disclose most about the story? Which scene is most dramatic? Set your scene in stage directions like those at the beginning of each act in Ibsen's play. (Hint: Don't begin the play at the beginning of the story or you will have to change scenes almost immediately, from the street before Goodman Brown's house to the forest.) Now, how will you reveal who the people on stage at the start are and what they have been doing just before the curtain rises? As you proceed, try to make dialogue appropriate to those speaking it. You need not complete the play, or even a scene, but write enough — say, two or three pages — to demonstrate that you understand the difficulties and advantages of the drama as a literary form.

Samuel Beckett, *Waiting for Godot.*

Two tragicomic tramps, Gogo and Didi, wait endlessly — they are not sure why — to keep an appointment that was never made. "Nothing happens, nobody comes, nobody goes, it is terrible," said one critic of this fascinating play.

Lewis Carroll, *Alice in Wonderland* and *Through the Looking-Glass.*

In two famous journeys Alice visits a world in which nothing is as it seems and another world in which everything is its opposite.

William Faulkner, *Absalom, Absalom!*

Two young men, Shreve and Quentin, piece together the truth about Thomas Sutpen, whose design for greatness and ultimate downfall mirror the rise and collapse of the Southern plantation aristocracy.

E. M. Forster, *A Passage to India.*

An English woman, Miss Quested, imagines an assault by the Indian Dr. Aziz, thereby exposing British prejudice toward colonials.

Hermann Hesse, *Siddhartha.*

In a story subtly resembling the life of the Buddha, a young man makes a spiritual journey through sin into perfect awareness.

Arthur Koestler, *Darkness at Noon.*

Rubashov, once a powerful leader of a Communist country, now a political prisoner, is forced to confess himself a traitor to a government he has faithfully served.

Sinclair Lewis, *Arrowsmith.*

A young doctor, seeking for scientific truth, learns that society often shapes truths to fit its needs, even when human lives are at stake.

Bernard Malamud, *The Fixer.*

In a novel based on an actual event, Yakov Bok, a Russian Jew, is tortured by his Czarist captors to swear falsely that he murdered a Christian child and used his blood in a Passover rite.

Herman Melville, *Moby-Dick.*

Ishmael narrates a vast tale in which Captain Ahab relentlessly pursues the elusive white whale and the truth he believes it represents, with ship, crew, and damnation in the balance.

George Orwell, *1984.*

In a society in which history is constantly rewritten and facts reinterpreted to fit the needs of the state, Big Brother watches everyone for signs of subversion.

Luigi Pirandello, *Six Characters in Search of an Author.*

Six characters born from a playwright's imagination enter an empty theater in which a group of actors are about to rehearse, and insist that the drama for which they were created be performed.

William Shakespeare, *The Tempest.*

A powerful magician exiled on a desert island conjures up a storm that washes his terrified enemies ashore. In the end Prospero, the magician, is restored to his true place in society, and his daughter, Miranda, is happily married, in a tale of spirits, terrors, and delight.

Natsume Soseki, *Kokoro.*

In this subtle psychological novel from Japan, a young man gradually learns the truth about the tortured life of his older friend Sensei.

Good clearly outweighs evil in this Spanish altar panel from the thirteenth century. But is justice always that easy to arrive at?

The Nature of Justice

Suppose you live in an American city in this last third of the twentieth century. Why should you want to read a story about a well-to-do Bedouin named Job (page 175), written a good twenty-five centuries ago in a language so difficult that not even the scholars understand every word of it now? Particularly, why should you put out the energy to read it — and reading great literature, like anything else worth doing, demands a certain effort — when there are so many books, and comic books, which you can read without even trying? Why indeed?

But wait a minute. Job was a man terribly afflicted, and even if you personally have not suffered affliction of any important kind, you should hear the voice of affliction pure just because you are human. "Man was born to sorrow as the sparks fly upwards." Affliction is one of the profoundest of human experiences. Besides, probably some of your family or ancestors have endured terrible affliction. If you are a Negro, your ancestors were dragged here in chains as slaves. If you are an Indian, they were killed and humiliated and cheated just for being in the Europeans' way. If you are an Oriental or Mexican or Puerto Rican, they were in all likelihood fleeing dreadful poverty. Even if you are a white European by descent, they were probably escaping persecution for their religious or political beliefs. But suppose your ancestors came over on the *Mayflower* and have been conquering and ruling ever since; there is a suite on the thirty-third floor waiting for you with your name on the door; you believe in God, but you don't believe He makes deals with Satan to torment innocent men, as He does in this story. Why should you read *Job?* Plenty of reason. Job had it made too, yet he lost all he had and for no reason he could understand. If you have even an ounce of imagination, you know that like him you could suddenly lose everything and that, if this happened to you, you would have feelings like his.

Even if you do not believe that a man can converse directly with God, Job can still speak for you and to you. *Why? What have I done to deserve this?*

135

Is it just that I am as I am? The answer to this last question, whatever your station in life, is usually *No, it is not just.* What are you going to do about it? You may not have thought about that question yet, though sooner or later you doubtless will. What Job did about it is worth your finding out, for, according to the story, his acceptance of God's incomprehensible authority so pleased the Lord that He rewarded Job in a way we can understand as just and reasonable.

In Dante's *Inferno* (page 194), we see justice in its pure state. Here you will find sinners who have broken God's law and not repented of their transgressions. They are being punished according to God's law, even though they do not fully understand that law. What Dante believes and wants us to believe is that God's authority is absolute, reasonable, and infallible. Once you accept that authority, you can accept afflictions as punishments for sins.

But what about man-made laws, passed by legislatures, enforced by the police, and administered by law courts — all of them staffed by men, all far from infallible? Justice requires us to obey the laws of the land. But what shall we do about those laws which we believe to be unjust? Most acute dilemma of all, what shall I do when the duly constituted authority of my government convicts me of a crime of which I am not guilty?

Then there is a more general kind of social injustice, the kind which Sarah Cleghorn threw this pretty little bomb at:

> The golf links lie so near the mill
> That almost every day
> The laboring children can look out
> And see the men at play.

It is to remedy such injustices that many of our laws have been passed and will continue to be passed.

When poverty and exploitation were believed to be in the nature of things, like disease and death, then they were blamed on the gods. But we now believe them to be evils which society can and should get rid of. More and more of our lives are coming under our control, are coming to be the responsibility of society. More and more, we are to blame rather than nature or the divine order. Never before has social justice mattered so much as now.

The Romans, who were great law-makers, commonly portrayed the goddess Justitia as a woman blindfolded and holding scales. Why blindfolded? To suggest that she distributes rewards and punishments according to principles entirely different from those we see when we look at our world. It is perhaps not a very jolly notion, but it is worth thinking about. See how Karl Shapiro expressed such meditation in his poem "Auto Wreck" (page 155).

George P. Elliott

The Jar

LUIGI PIRANDELLO

"Justice," said the English statesman Disraeli, "is truth in action." Accordingly, one task of justice — working through lawyers' briefs, courtroom interrogations, jury deliberations — is to arrive at what is the truth in a given instance. How? Well, look dispassionately at both sides of an argument, and the truth will frequently come clear. Then you can administer justice. Or sometimes you can. In the case of Don Lollo and his wine jar, even though the truth was known and agreed on, justice presented some problems.

The olive crop was a bumper[1] one that year: the trees had flowered luxuriantly the year before, and, though there had been a long spell of misty weather at the time, the fruit had set well. Lollo Zirafa had a fine plantation on his farm at Primosole. Reckoning that the five old jars of glazed earthenware which he had in his wine cellar would not suffice to hold all the oil of that harvest, he had placed an order well beforehand at Santo Stefano di Camastra, where they are made. His new jar was to be of greater capacity — breast-high and pot-bellied; it would be the mother superior to the little community of five other jars.

I need scarcely say that Don Lollo Zirafa had had a dispute with the potter concerning this jar. It would indeed be hard to name anyone with whom he had not picked a quarrel; for every trifle — be it merely a stone that had fallen from his boundary wall, or a handful of straw — he would shout out to the servants to saddle his mule, so that he could hurry to the town and file

a suit. He had half-ruined himself, because of the large sums he had had to spend on court fees and lawyers' bills, bringing actions against one person after another, which always ended in his having to pay the costs of both sides. People said that his legal adviser grew so tired of seeing him appear two or three times a week that he tried to reduce the frequency of his visits by making him a present of a volume which looked like a prayer book; it contained the judicial code — the idea being that he should take the trouble to see for himself what the rights and wrongs of the case were before hurrying to bring a suit.

Previously, when anyone had a difference with him, they would try to make him lose his temper by shouting out: "Saddle the mule!" but now they changed it to: "Go and look up your pocket code!" Don Lollo would reply: "That I will and I'll break the lot of you, you swine!"

In course of time, the new jar, for which he had paid the goodly sum of four florins, duly arrived; until room could be found for it in the wine cellar, it was lodged in the crushing shed[2] for a few days. Never had

---

Luigi Pirandello: pronounced lwē′jē pē·rän-del′lō.

[1] **bumper:** unusually large.

[2] **crushing shed:** where grapes are crushed into juice.

A Sicilian olive tree. To some ancients, olive oil symbolized peace and goodwill.

not only the men who were beating down the fruit from the trees, but also a number of others who had come with mule loads of manure to be deposited in heaps on the hillside, where he had a field in which he was going to sow beans for the next crop. He felt that it was really more than one man could manage. He was at his wits' ends whom to attend to. Cursing like a trooper, he vowed he would exterminate, first this man and then that, if an olive — one single olive — was missing. He almost talked as if he had counted them, one by one, on his trees. Then he would turn to the muleteers and utter the direst threats as to what would happen, if any one heap of manure were not exactly the same size as the others. A little white cap on his head, his sleeves rolled up and his shirt open at the front, he rushed here, there, and everywhere; his face was a bright red and poured with sweat, his eyes glared about him wolfishly, while his hands rubbed angrily at his shaven chin, where a fresh growth of beard always sprouted the moment the razor had left it.

At the close of the third day's work, three of the farm hands — rough fellows with

there been a finer jar. It was quite distressing to see it lodged in that foul den, which reeked of stale grape juice and had that musty smell of places deprived of light and air.

It was now two days since the harvesting of the olives had begun, and Don Lollo was almost beside himself, having to supervise

ABOUT THE AUTHOR • The genius of **Luigi Pirandello** (1867–1936) went unrecognized by his Italian countrymen until he was well into middle age. It was after World War I that Pirandello's successes abroad awoke the Italian reading public to his talents. By that time, despite two decades spent with a hopelessly mad wife in a household deserted by their children, Luigi Pirandello had already written his greatest novels and hundreds of short stories. He had begun a new career as a playwright, for which he is best known in the United States. Ironically with his recognition in Italy came rejection by Mussolini's fascist regime, so that when he received the Nobel Prize in 1934, he was an exile in his own country.

Pirandello's short stories are based upon life in his native Sicily, the characters drawn from the peasantry and lower middle class. His plays, although still retaining the local flavor of his stories, move away from regionalism into a thoroughly unconventional exploration of reality and illusion.

dirty, brutish faces — went to the crushing shed; they had been beating the olive trees and went to replace their ladders and poles in the shed. They stood aghast at the sight of the fine new jar in two pieces, looking for all the world as if someone had caught hold of the bulging front and cut it off with a sharp sweep of the knife.

"Oh, my God! look! look!"

"How on earth has that happened?"

"My holy aunt! When Don Lollo hears of it! The new jar! What a pity, though!"

The first of the three, more frightened than his companions, proposed to shut the door again at once and to sneak away very quietly, leaving their ladders and poles outside leaning up against the wall; but the second took him up sharply.

"That's a stupid idea! You can't try that on Don Lollo. As like as not he'd believe we broke it ourselves. No, we will stay here!"

He went out of the shed and, using his hands as a trumpet, called out:

"Don Lollo! Oh! Don LOLLOOOOO!"

When the farmer came up and saw the damage, he fell into a towering passion. First he vented his fury on the three men. He seized one of them by the throat, pinned him against the wall, and shouted:

"By the Virgin's blood, you'll pay for that!"

The other two sprang forward in wild excitement, fell upon Don Lollo and pulled him away. Then his mad rage turned against himself; he stamped his feet, flung his cap on the ground, and slapped his cheeks, bewailing his loss with screams suited only for the death of a relation.

"The new jar! A four-florin jar! Brand new!"

Who could have broken it? Could it possibly have broken of itself? Certainly someone must have broken it, out of malice or from envy at his possession of such a beauty. But when? How? There was no sign of violence. Could it conceivably have come in a broken condition from the pottery? No, it rang like a bell on its arrival.

As soon as the farm hands saw that their master's first outburst of rage was spent, they began to console him, saying that he should not take it so to heart, as the jar could be mended. After all, the break was not a bad one, for the front had come away all in one piece; a clever riveter[1] could repair it and make it as good as new. Zi'[2] Dima Licasi was just the man for the job: he had invented a marvelous cement made of some composition which he kept a strict secret — miraculous stuff! Once it had set, you couldn't loosen it, even with a hammer. So they suggested that, if Don Lollo agreed, Zi' Dima Licasi should turn up at daybreak and — as sure as eggs were eggs — the jar would be repaired and be even better than a new one.

For a long time Don Lollo turned a deaf ear to their advice — it was quite useless, there was no making good the damage — but in the end he allowed himself to be persuaded, and punctually at daybreak Zi' Dima Licasi arrived at Primosole, with his outfit in a basket slung on his back. He turned out to be a misshapen old man with swollen, crooked joints, like the stem of an ancient Saracen olive tree. To extract a word from him, it looked as if you would have to use a pair of forceps[3] on his mouth. His ungraceful figure seemed to radiate discontent or gloom, due perhaps to his disappointment that no one had so far been found willing to do justice to his merits as an inventor. For Zi' Dima Licasi had not yet patented his discovery; he wanted to make a name for it first by its successful application. Meanwhile he felt it necessary to keep a sharp lookout, for fear someone steal the secret of his process.

---

[1] **riveter:** one who fastens with rivets.

[2] **Zi':** from *zio,* meaning "uncle."

[3] **forceps:** instrument for grasping and pulling.

"Let me see that cement of yours," began Don Lollo in a distrustful tone, after examining him from head to foot for several minutes.

Zi' Dima declined, with a dignified shake of the head.

"You'll see its results."

"But, will it hold?"

Zi' Dima put his basket on the ground and took out from it a red bundle composed of a large cotton handkerchief, much the worse for wear, wrapped round and round something. He began to unroll it very carefully, while they all stood round watching him with close attention. When at last, however, nothing came to light save a pair of spectacles with bridge and sides broken and tied up with string, there was a general laugh. Zi' Dima took no notice, but wiped his fingers before handling the spectacles, then put them on and, with much solemnity, began his examination of the jar, which had been brought outside onto the threshing floor. Finally he said:

"It'll hold."

"But I can't trust cement alone," Don Lollo stipulated. "I must have rivets as well."

"I'm off," Zi' Dima promptly replied, standing up and replacing his basket on his back.

Don Lollo caught hold of his arm:

"Off? Where to? You've got no more manners than a pig! . . . Just look at this pauper putting on an air of royalty! . . . Why! you wretched fool, I've got to put oil in that jar, and don't you know that oil oozes? Yards and yards to join together, and you talk of using cement alone! I want rivets — cement and rivets. It's for me to decide."

Zi' Dima shut his eyes, closed his lips tightly and shook his head. People were all like that — they refused to give him the satisfaction of turning out a neat bit of work, performed with artistic thoroughness and proving the wonderful virtues of his cement.

"If," he said, "the jar doesn't ring as true as a bell once more. . . ."

"I won't listen to a word," Don Lollo broke in. "I want rivets! I'll pay you for cement and rivets. How much will it come to?"

"If I use cement only. . . ."

"My God! what an obstinate fellow! What did I say? I told you I wanted rivets. We'll settle the terms after the work is done. I've no more time to waste on you."

And he went off to look after his men.

In a state of great indignation Zi' Dima started on the job, and his temper continued to rise as he bored hole after hole in the jar and in its broken section — holes for his iron rivets. Along with the squeaking of his tool went a running accompaniment of grunts which grew steadily louder and more frequent; his fury made his eyes more piercing and bloodshot and his face became green with bile. When he had finished that first operation, he flung his borer angrily into the basket and held the detached portion up against the jar to satisfy himself that the holes were at equal distances and fitted one another; next he took his pliers and cut a length of iron wire into as many pieces as he needed rivets, and then called to one of the men who were beating the olive trees to come and help him.

"Cheer up, Zi' Dima!" said the laborer, seeing how upset the old man looked.

Zi' Dima raised his hand with a savage gesture. He opened the tin which contained the cement and held it up towards heaven, as if offering it to God, seeing that men refused to recognize its value. Then he began to spread it with his finger all round the detached portion and along the broken edge of the jar. Taking his pliers and the iron rivets he had prepared, he crept inside the open belly of the jar and instructed the farm hand to hold the piece up, fitting it closely to the jar as he had himself done a short time previously. Before starting to put in the rivets, he spoke from inside the jar:

"Pull! Pull! Tug at it with all your might! . . . You see it doesn't come loose. Curses on people who won't believe me! Knock it! Yes, knock it! . . . Doesn't it ring like a bell, even with me inside it? Go and tell your master that!"

"It's for the top dog to give orders, Zi' Dima," said the man with a sigh, "and it's for the underdog to carry them out. Put the rivets in. Put 'em in."

Zi' Dima began to pass the bits of iron through adjacent holes, one on each side of the crack, twisting up the ends with his pliers. It took him an hour to put them all in, and he poured with sweat inside the jar. As he worked, he complained of his misfortune, and the farm hand stayed near, trying to console him.

"Now help me to get out," said Zi' Dima, when all was finished.

But large though its belly was, the jar had a distinctly narrow neck — a fact which Zi' Dima had overlooked, being so absorbed in his grievance. Now, try as he would, he could not manage to squeeze his way out. Instead of helping him, the farm hand stood idly by, convulsed with laughter. So there was poor Zi' Dima, imprisoned in the jar which he had mended and — there was no use in blinking at the fact — in a jar which would have to be broken to let him out, and this time broken for good.

Hearing the laughter and shouts, Don Lollo came rushing up. Inside the jar Zi' Dima was spitting like an angry cat.

"Let me out," he screamed, "for God's sake! I want to get out! Be quick! Help!"

Don Lollo was quite taken aback and unable to believe his own ears.

"What? Inside there? He's riveted himself up inside?"

Then he went up to the jar and shouted out to Zi' Dima:

"Help you? What help do you think I can give you? You stupid old dodderer, what d'you mean by it? Why couldn't you measure it first? Come, have a try! Put an arm out . . . that's it! Now the head! Up you come! . . . No, no, gently! . . . Down again. . . . Wait a bit! . . . Not that way. . . . Down, get down. . . . How on earth could you do such a thing? . . . What about my jar now? . . .

"Keep calm! Keep calm!" he recommended to all the onlookers, as if it was they who were becoming excited and not himself. . . . "My head's going round! Keep calm! This is quite a new point! Get me my mule!"

He rapped the jar with his knuckles. Yes, it really rang like a bell once again.

"Fine! Repaired as good as new. . . . You wait a bit!" he said to the prisoner; then instructed his man to be off and saddle the mule. He rubbed his forehead vigorously with his fingers, and continued:

"I wonder what's the best course. That's not a jar, it's a contrivance of the devil himself. . . . Keep still! Keep still!" he exclaimed, rushing up to steady the jar, in which Zi' Dima, now in a towering passion, was struggling like a wild animal in a trap.

"It's a new point, my good man, which the lawyer must settle. I can't rely on my own judgment. . . . Where's that mule? Hurry up with the mule! . . . I'll go straight there and back. You must wait patiently; it's in your own interest. . . . Meanwhile, keep quiet, be calm! I must look after my own rights. And, first of all, to put myself in the right, I fulfill my obligation. Here you are! I am paying you for your work, for a whole day's work. Here are your five lire. Is that enough?"

"I don't want anything," shouted Zi' Dima. "I want to get out!"

"You shall get out, but meanwhile I, for my part, am paying you. There they are — five lire."

He took the money out of his waistcoat pocket and tossed it into the jar, then enquired in a tone of great concern:

"Have you had any lunch? . . . Bread and something to eat with it, at once! . . . What! You don't want it? Well, then, throw it to the dogs! I shall have done my duty when I've given it to you."

Having ordered the food, he mounted and set out for the town. His wild gesticulations made those who saw him galloping past think that he might well be hastening to shut himself up in a lunatic asylum.

As luck would have it, he did not have to spend much time in the anteroom before being admitted to the lawyer's study; he had, however, to wait a long while before the lawyer could finish laughing, after the matter had been related to him. Annoyed at the amusement he caused, Don Lollo said irritably:

"Excuse me, but I don't see anything to laugh at. It's all very well for your Honor, who is not the sufferer, but the jar is my property."

The lawyer, however, continued to laugh and then made him tell the story all over again, just as it had happened, so that he could raise another laugh out of it.

"Inside, eh? So he's riveted himself inside?" And what did Don Lollo want to do? . . . "To ke . . . to ke . . . keep him there inside — ha! ha! ha! . . . keep him there inside, so as not to lose the jar?"

"Why should I lose it?" cried Don Lollo, clenching his fists. "Why should I put up with the loss of my money, and have people laughing at me?"

"But don't you know what that's called?" said the lawyer at last. "It's called 'wrongful confinement.'"

"Confinement? Well, who's confined him? He's confined himself! What fault is that of mine?"

The lawyer then explained to him that the matter gave rise to two cases: on the one hand he, Don Lollo, must straightway liberate the prisoner, if he wished to escape from being prosecuted for wrongful confinement; while, on the other hand, the riveter would be responsible for making good the loss resulting from his lack of skill or his stupidity.

"Ah!" said Don Lollo, with a sigh of relief. "So he'll have to pay me for my jar?"

"Wait a bit," remarked the lawyer. "Not as if it were a new jar, remember!"

"Why not?"

"Because it was a broken one, badly broken, too."

"Broken! No, Sir. Not broken. It's perfectly sound now and better than ever it was — he says so himself. And if I have to break it again, I shall not be able to have it mended. The jar will be ruined, Sir!"

The lawyer assured him that that point would be taken into account and that the riveter would have to pay the value which the jar had in its present condition.

"Therefore," he counseled, "get the man himself to give you an estimate of its value first."

"I kiss your hands," Don Lollo murmured, and hurried away.

On his return home towards evening, he found all his laborers engaged in a celebration around the inhabited jar. The watch dogs joined in the festivities with joyous barks and capers. Zi' Dima had not only calmed down, but had even come to enjoy his curious adventure and was able to laugh at it, with the melancholy humor of the unfortunate.

Don Lollo drove them all aside and bent down to look into the jar.

"Hallo! Getting along well?"

"Splendid! An open-air life for me!" replied the man. "It's better than in my own house."

"I'm glad to hear it. Meanwhile I'd just like you to know that that jar cost me four florins when it was new. How much do you think it is worth now?"

"With me inside it?" asked Zi' Dima.

The rustics laughed.

"Silence!" shouted Don Lollo. "Either your cement is of some use or it is of no use. There is no third possibility. If it is of no use you are a fraud. If it is of some use, the jar, in its present condition, must have a value. What is that value? I ask for your estimate."

After a space of reflection, Zi' Dima said:

"Here is my answer: if you had let me mend it with cement only — as I wanted to do — first of all I should not have been shut up inside it and the jar would have had its original value, without any doubt. But spoilt by these rivets, which had to be done from inside, it has lost most of its value. It's worth a third of its former price, more or less."

"One-third? That's one florin, thirty-three cents."

"Maybe less, but not more than that."

"Well," said Don Lollo. "Promise me that you'll pay me one florin, thirty-three cents."

"What?" asked Zi' Dima, as if he did not grasp the point.

"I will break the jar to let you out," replied Don Lollo. "And — the lawyer tells me — you are to pay me its value according to your own estimate — one florin thirty-three."

"I? Pay?" laughed Zi' Dima, "I'd sooner stay here till I rot!"

With some difficulty he managed to extract from his pocket a short and peculiarly foul pipe and lighted it, puffing out the smoke through the neck of the jar.

Don Lollo stood there scowling. The possibility that Zi' Dima would no longer be willing to leave the jar had not been foreseen either by himself or by the lawyer. What step should he take now? He was on the point of ordering them to saddle the mule, but reflected that it was already evening.

"Oh ho!" he said. "So you want to take up your abode in my jar! I call upon all you men as witnesses to his statement. He refuses to come out, in order to escape from paying. I am quite prepared to break it. Well, as you insist on staying there, I shall take proceedings against you tomorrow for unlawful occupancy of the jar and for preventing me from my rightful use of it."

Zi' Dima blew out another puff of smoke and answered calmly:

"No, your Honor. I don't want to prevent you at all. Do you think I am here because I like it? Let me out and I'll go away gladly enough. But as for paying, I wouldn't dream of it, your Honor."

In a sudden access of fury Don Lollo made to give a kick at the jar but stopped in time. Instead he seized it with both hands and shook it violently, uttering a hoarse growl.

"You see what fine cement it is," Zi' Dima remarked from inside.

"You rascal!" roared Don Lollo. "Whose fault is it, yours or mine? You expect me to pay for it, do you? You can starve to death inside first. We'll see who'll win."

He went away, forgetting all about the five lire which he had tossed into the jar that morning. But the first thing Zi' Dima thought of doing was to spend that money in having a festive evening, in company with the farm hands, who had been delayed in their work by that strange accident, and had decided to spend the night at the farm, in the open air, sleeping on the threshing floor. One of them went to a neighboring tavern to make the necessary purchases. The moon was so bright that it seemed almost day — a splendid night for their carousal.

Many hours later Don Lollo was awakened by an infernal din. Looking out from the farmhouse balcony, he could see in the moonlight what looked like a gang of devils on his threshing floor; his men, all roaring drunk, were holding hands and performing a dance round the jar, while Zi' Dima, inside it, was singing at the top of his voice.

This time Don Lollo could not restrain himself, but rushed down like a mad bull and, before they could stop him, gave the jar a push which started it rolling down the slope. It continued on its course, to the delight of the intoxicated company, until it hit an olive tree and cracked in pieces, leaving Zi' Dima the winner in the dispute.

For Discussion

1. In the end, Zi' Dima wins the dispute. Is there justice in his victory? What reasons can you give to support a claim that Zi' Dima was not to be blamed for what happened to Don Lollo's jar? If you were arguing on Don Lollo's behalf, on what would you rest your case?

2. "I wonder what's the best course," Don Lollo cried out while Zi' Dima was struggling inside the jar like a wild animal in a trap. Unable to decide for himself, he hurried off to a lawyer. How did the lawyer first react to Don Lollo's case? On what grounds might Don Lollo have been prosecuted? For what, specifically, would Zi' Dima be responsible?

3. What was Zi' Dima doing inside the jar in the first place? It may seem a bit incredible that a man could get himself into Zi' Dima's fix. Look back through the story to the fateful moment when the riveter steps inside. Why is he unaware just then of the consequences of what he is doing? How does he finally get back out of the jar?

4. As with a play, the plot of a short story usually comes to a climax at some point during the action. Often it is difficult to recognize the climax until you have read the story completely through; then with the conclusion in mind, you can go back and locate that point in the action after which the outcome is inevitable. Identify the climax of "The Jar." Does it come when Don Lollo seeks a lawyer's advice? When Zi' Dima takes out his pipe and settles down for a long stay? When Don Lollo kicks at the jar "in a sudden access of fury"? Or at some point in the story earlier or later than any of those? Explain.

For Composition

In literature, as in life, we get to know the people we meet by what they do, by how they talk, and by what other people say and do about them. "The Jar" introduces us to Don Lollo Zirafa, and by the end of the story, we have come to know him pretty well.

1. **Character Sketch.** Write a brief character sketch of Don Lollo. First determine what are his three or four outstanding traits, and which of his actions or remarks in the story best illustrate those traits. That is, organize what you are going to say before beginning to write. The trait that strikes you as most significant or revealing should be put either first or — probably more effectively — last in your essay.

2. **Comparison and Contrast.** Compare and contrast Don Lollo's character with that of Zi' Dima. Your contrast might well indicate to what extent their different temperaments and attitudes contribute to the humor of the story.

Words and Allusions

SYNONYMS. Each of the following words can be applied to the central situation in "The Jar": *dilemma, impasse, plight, predicament, quandary.* Which do you regard as synonyms (page 14)? Which carry slightly different meanings? Invent a situation for each word in which that word would be appropriate. Then use each word in a sentence that will illustrate its meaning.

The Isle of Portland

A. E. HOUSMAN

Off the south coast of England protrudes the Isle of Portland, actually a peninsula now, from whose wild, rocky coast convicts have for centuries been made to quarry great quantities of building stone.

The star-filled seas are smooth tonight
   From France to England strown;*
Black towers above the Portland light
   The felon-quarried stone.

On yonder island, not to rise,   5
   Never to stir forth free,
Far from his folk a dead lad lies
   That once was friends with me.

Lie you easy, dream you light,
   And sleep you fast for aye;   10
And luckier may you find the night
   Than ever you found the day.

2. **strown:** spread out.

For Discussion

1. In what sense might seas be "star-filled"? Is *towers* (line 3) a verb or noun? How is *aye* (line 10) pronounced? What does it mean?

2. To whom does the speaker of the poem address the last stanza? His friend is "Never to stir forth free." Why not? Why is the friend on the Isle of Portland now? Why was he there earlier? What details and diction in the poem let you make an intelligent inference about the man's life and fate?

3. The poem suggests an attitude toward the laws of man, and toward the guilty and innocent as well. Has the friend of the speaker, in the latter's estimation, been guilty of a grievous crime? One word in line 11 should help you arrive at an answer. What is that word, and what does it suggest?

4. **Alliteration, Assonance.** Like rhyme, both assonance and alliteration involve repetition of sound. *Alliteration* is the repetition of initial consonant sounds: "Never to stir forth free, / Far from his folk . . . " (lines 6–7). *Assonance* is the repetition of vowel sounds close together: in line 1 the vowel sound $\overline{oo}$ of *smooth* is repeated in *tonight*. What vowel sounds are repeated in line 4? Identify the assonance in line 9. In line 11. Where else in the poem, besides in lines 6 and 7, do you encounter alliteration?

For Composition

The opening of "The Isle of Portland" bears certain striking similarities, both in geography and in mood or atmosphere, to that of "Dover Beach" (page 23).

● **Comparison and Contrast.** Compare and contrast the initial situations of Housman's poem and Arnold's. Your composition should indicate briefly how the two poets differ in the ways they exploit the *calmness* of their respective scenes.

About the Poet. **A. E. Housman** (1859–1936) was a classical scholar at Cambridge University whose chief work was the editing and trans-lating of Greek and Latin texts. Austere and aloof in his dealings with his colleagues, in his poetry he was the spokesman of youth, often of embittered youth — "I, a stranger and afraid / In a world I never made." He once explained that poetry was a sort of fever, which he had the strength to endure only during a few brief periods. Insisting that only his best work be published, he destroyed many more poems than he allowed to be printed. Thus within his lifetime he published only two slim volumes — *A Shropshire Lad* and *Last Poems.* A third collection, *More Poems,* was brought out posthumously by his brother. "Of all the poets of modern times," as one critic observed, "none has won so great a reputation from so small a body of work."

[Handwritten annotations: "Subjective narraration — something untrustworthy about what we're being told — mimics life" and "trustworthiness based on: intelligence & integrity / Whitey — poor grammar — repetition — explains obvious — idea association thinking — doesn't see signif of facts ie MURDER! — provincial, naive"]

Haircut

RING LARDNER

According to the testimony of one man who knew him, Jim Kendall was "all right at heart, but just bubblin' over with mischief." By contrast, another acquaintance thought he "ought not to be let live." See how you feel about the life and death of a man who was able to keep a whole town in an uproar.

I got another barber that comes over from Carterville and helps me out Saturdays, but the rest of the time I can get along all right alone. You can see for yourself that this ain't no New York City and besides that, the most of the boys works all day and don't have no leisure to drop in here and get themselves prettied up.

You're a newcomer, ain't you? I thought I hadn't seen you round before. I hope you like it good enough to stay. As I say, we ain't no New York City or Chicago, but we have pretty good times. Not as good, though, since Jim Kendall got killed. When he was alive, him and Hod Meyers used to keep this town in an uproar. I bet they was more laughin' done here than any town its size in America.

Jim was comical, and Hod was pretty near a match for him. Since Jim's gone, Hod tries to hold his end up just the same as ever, but it's tough goin' when you ain't got nobody to kind of work with.

They used to be plenty fun in here Saturdays. This place is jam-packed Saturdays, from four o'clock on. Jim and Hod would show up right after their supper, round six o'clock. Jim would set himself down in that big chair, nearest the blue spittoon. Whoever had been settin' in that chair, why they'd get up when Jim come in and give it to him.

You'd of thought it was a reserved seat like they have sometimes in a theayter. Hod would generally always stand or walk up and down, or some Saturdays, of course, he'd be settin' in this chair part of the time, gettin' a haircut.

Well, Jim would set there a w'ile without openin' his mouth only to spit, and then finally he'd say to me, "Whitey," — my right name, that is, my right first name, is Dick, but everybody round here calls me Whitey — Jim would say, "Whitey, your nose looks like a rosebud tonight. You must of been drinkin' some of your aw[1] de cologne."

So I'd say, "No, Jim, but you look like you'd been drinkin' somethin' of that kind or somethin' worse."

Jim would have to laugh at that, but then he'd speak up and say, "No, I ain't had nothin' to drink, but that ain't sayin' I wouldn't like somethin'. I wouldn't even mind if it was wood alcohol."

Then Hod Meyers would say, "Neither would your wife." That would set everybody to laughin' because Jim and his wife wasn't on very good terms. She'd of divorced him only they wasn't no chance to get alimony and she didn't have no way to take care of herself and the kids. She couldn't never understand Jim. He *was* kind of rough, but a good fella at heart.

Him and Hod had all kinds of sport with Milt Sheppard. I don't suppose you've seen Milt. Well, he's got an Adam's apple that looks more like a mushmelon. So I'd be shavin' Milt and when I'd start to shave down here on his neck, Hod would holler, "Hey, Whitey, wait a minute! Before you

[1] **aw**: French *eau* (ō), meaning "water."

The barber shop was — and still is — more than just a place to get a haircut. Tattoo and Haircut, *by Reginald Marsh.*

cut into it, let's make up a pool and see who can guess closest to the number of seeds."

And Jim would say, "If Milt hadn't of been so hoggish, he'd of ordered a half a cantaloupe instead of a whole one and it might not of stuck in his throat."

All the boys would roar at this and Milt himself would force a smile, though the joke was on him. Jim certainly was a card!

There's his shavin' mug, settin' on the shelf, right next to Charley Vail's. "Charles M. Vail." That's the druggist. He comes in regular for his shave, three times a week. And Jim's is the cup next to Charley's. "James H. Kendall." Jim won't need no shavin' mug no more, but I'll leave it there just the same for old time's sake. Jim certainly was a character!

Years ago, Jim used to travel for a canned goods concern over in Carterville. They sold canned goods. Jim had the whole northern half of the State and was on the road five days out of every week. He'd drop in here Saturdays and tell his experiences for that week. It was rich.

I guess he paid more attention to playin' jokes than makin' sales. Finally the concern let him out and he come right home here and told everybody he'd been fired instead of sayin' he'd resigned like most fellas would of.

It was a Saturday and the shop was full and Jim got up out of that chair and says, "Gentlemen, I got an important announcement to make. I been fired from my job."

Well, they asked him if he was in earnest and he said he was and nobody could think of nothin' to say till Jim finally broke the ice himself. He says, "I been sellin' canned goods and now I'm canned goods myself."

You see, the concern he'd been workin' for was a factory that made canned goods. Over in Carterville. And now Jim said he was canned himself. He was certainly a card!

Jim had a great trick that he used to play w'ile he was travelin'. For instance, he'd be ridin' on a train and they'd come to some little town like, well, like, we'll say, like Benton. Jim would look out the train window and read the signs on the stores.

For instance, they'd be a sign, "Henry Smith, Dry Goods." Well, Jim would write

down the name and the name of the town and when he got to wherever he was goin' he'd mail back a postal card to Henry Smith at Benton and not sign no name to it, but he'd write on the card, well, somethin' like "Ask your wife about that book agent that spent the afternoon last week," or "Ask your Missus who kept her from gettin' lonesome the last time you was in Carterville." And he'd sign the card, "A Friend."

Of course, he never knew what really come of none of these jokes, but he could picture what *probably* happened and that was enough.

Jim didn't work very steady after he lost his position with the Carterville people. What he did earn, doin' odd jobs round town, why he spent pretty near all of it on gin and his family might of starved if the stores hadn't of carried them along. Jim's wife tried her hand at dressmakin', but they ain't nobody goin' to get rich makin' dresses in this town.

As I say, she'd of divorced Jim, only she seen that she couldn't support herself and the kids and she was always hopin' that some day Jim would cut out his habits and give her more than two or three dollars a week.

They was a time when she would go to whoever he was workin' for and ask them

explains obvious Duh!

ABOUT THE AUTHOR • **Ring Lardner**'s reputation as a serious writer rests almost exclusively on his short stories. Lardner (1885–1933) began his literary career, after flunking out of engineering school and failing as a freight agent, by helping his brother write news stories. As a reporter Ring Lardner's specialty was sports news, particularly baseball, which took him to small towns and one-barbershop hamlets and gave him that intimate knowledge of the American language that he captures in such stories as "Haircut."

In most of his early stories Lardner wrote about baseball players, but soon he began to deal with characters drawn from other walks of life. Today he is remembered as a humorist, a satirist, and a relentless exposer of the phony.

to give her his wages, but after she done this once or twice, he beat her to it by borrowin' most of his pay in advance. He told it all round town how he had outfoxed his Missus. He certainly was a caution!

But he wasn't satisfied with just out-wittin' her. He was sore the way she had acted, tryin' to grab off his pay. And he made up his mind he'd get even. Well, he waited till Evans's Circus was advertised to come to town. Then he told his wife and two kiddies that he was goin' to take them to the circus. The day of the circus, he told them he would get the tickets and meet them outside the entrance to the tent.

Well, he didn't have no intentions of bein' there or buyin' tickets or nothin'. He got full of gin and laid round Wright's pool-room all day. His wife and the kids waited and waited and of course he didn't show up. His wife didn't have a dime with her, or nowhere else, I guess. So she finally had to tell the kids it was all off and they cried like they wasn't never goin' to stop.

Well, it seems, while they was cryin', Doc Stair came along and he asked what was the matter, but Mrs. Kendall was stubborn and wouldn't tell him, but the kids told him and he insisted on takin' them and their mother in the show. Jim found this out afterwards and it was one reason why he had it in for Doc Stair.

Doc Stair come here about a year and a half ago. He's a mighty handsome young fella and his clothes always look like he has them made to order. He goes to Detroit two or three times a year and w'ile he's there he must have a tailor take his measure and then make him a suit to order. They cost pretty near twice as much, but they fit a whole lot better than if you just bought them in a store.

For a w'ile everybody was wonderin' why a young doctor like Doc Stair should come to a town like this where we already got old Doc Gamble and Doc Foote that's both been here for years and all the practice in town was always divided between the two of them.

Then they was a story got round that Doc Stair's gal had throwed him over, a gal up in the Northern Peninsula somewheres, and the reason he come here was to hide himself away and forget it. He said himself that he thought they wasn't nothin' like general practice in a place like ours to fit a man to be a good all-round doctor. And that's why he'd came.

Anyways, it wasn't long before he was makin' enough to live on, though they tell me that he never dunned[1] nobody for what they owed him, and the folks here certainly has got the owin' habit, even in my business. If I had all that was comin' to me for just shaves alone, I could go to Carterville and put up at the Mercer for a week and see a different picture every night. For instance, they's old George Purdy — but I guess I shouldn't ought to be gossipin'.

Well, last year, our coroner died, died of the flu. Ken Beatty, that was his name. He was the coroner. So they had to choose another man to be coroner in his place and they picked Doc Stair. He laughed at first and said he didn't want it, but they made him take it. It ain't no job that anybody would fight for and what a man makes out of it in a year would just about buy seeds for their garden. Doc's the kind, though, that can't say no to nothin' if you keep at him long enough.

But I was goin' to tell you about a poor boy we got here in town — Paul Dickson. He fell out of a tree when he was about ten years old. Lit on his head and it done somethin' to him and he ain't never been right. No harm in him, but just silly. Jim Kendall used to call him cuckoo; that's a name Jim had for anybody that was off their head, only he called people's head their bean. That was another of his gags, callin' head

---

[1] **dunned**: demanded payment of debt.

bcan and callin' crazy people cuckoo. Only poor Paul ain't crazy, but just silly.

You can imagine that Jim used to have all kinds of fun with Paul. He'd send him to the White Front Garage for a left-handed monkey wrench. Of course they ain't no such thing as a left-handed monkey wrench.

And once we had a kind of a fair here and they was a baseball game between the fats and the leans and before the game started Jim called Paul over and sent him way down to Schrader's hardware store to get a key for the pitcher's box.

They wasn't nothin' in the way of gags that Jim couldn't think up, when he put his mind to it.

Poor Paul was always kind of suspicious of people, maybe on account of how Jim had kept foolin' him. Paul wouldn't have much to do with anybody only his own mother and Doc Stair and a girl here in town named Julie Gregg. That is, she ain't a girl no more, but pretty near thirty or over.

When Doc first come to town, Paul seemed to feel like here was a real friend and he hung round Doc's office most of the w'ile; the only time he wasn't there was when he'd go home to eat or sleep or when he seen Julie Gregg doin' her shoppin'.

When he looked out Doc's window and seen her, he'd run downstairs and join her and tag along with her to the different stores. The poor boy was crazy about Julie and she always treated him mighty nice and made him feel like he was welcome, though of course it wasn't nothin' but pity on her side.

Doc done all he could to improve Paul's mind and he told me once that he really thought the boy was gettin' better, that they was times when he was as bright and sensible as anybody else.

But I was going' to tell you about Julie Gregg. Old Man Gregg was in the lumber business, but got to drinkin' and lost the most of his money and when he died, he didn't leave nothin' but the house and just enough insurance for the girl to skimp along on.

Her mother was a kind of a half invalid and didn't hardly ever leave the house. Julie wanted to sell the place and move somewheres else after the old man died, but the mother said she was born here and would die here. It was tough on Julie, as the young people round this town — well, she's too good for them.

She's been away to school and Chicago and New York and different places and they ain't no subject she can't talk on, where you take the rest of the young folks here and you mention anything to them outside of Gloria Swanson or Tommy Meighan[1] and they think you're delirious. Did you see Gloria in *Wages of Virtue?* You missed somethin'!

Well, Doc Stair hadn't been here more than a week when he come in one day to get shaved and I recognized who he was as he had been pointed out to me, so I told him about my old lady. She's been ailin' for a couple years and either Doc Gamble or Doc Foote, neither one, seemed to be helpin' her. So he said he would come out and see her, but if she was able to get out herself, it would be better to bring her to his office where he could make a completer examination.

So I took her to his office and w'ile I was waitin' for her in the reception room, in come Julie Gregg. When somebody comes in Doc Stair's office, they's a bell that rings in his inside office so as he can tell they's somebody to see him.

So he left my old lady inside and come out to the front office and that's the first time him and Julie met and I guess it was what they call love at first sight. But it wasn't fifty-fifty. This young fella was the

[1] **Gloria Swanson ... Tommy Meighan:** movie stars of the 1920's.

slickest lookin' fella she'd ever seen in this town and she went wild over him. To him she was just a young lady that wanted to see the doctor.

She'd come on about the same business I had. Her mother had been doctorin' for years with Doc Gamble and Doc Foote and without no results. So she'd heard they was a new doc in town and decided to give him a try. He promised to call and see her mother that same day.

I said a minute ago that it was love at first sight on her part. I'm not only judgin' by how she acted afterwards but how she looked at him that first day in his office. I ain't no mind reader, but it was wrote all over her face that she was gone.

Now Jim Kendall, besides bein' a joke-smith and a pretty good drinker, well, Jim was quite a lady-killer. I guess he run pretty wild durin' the time he was on the road for them Carterville people, and besides that, he'd had a couple little affairs of the heart right here in town. As I say, his wife could of divorced him, only she couldn't.

But Jim was like the majority of men, and women, too, I guess. He wanted what he couldn't get. He wanted Julie Gregg and worked his head off tryin' to land her. Only he'd of said bean instead of head.

Well, Jim's habits and his jokes didn't appeal to Julie and of course he was a married man, so he didn't have no more chance than, well, than a rabbit. That's an expression of Jim's himself. When somebody didn't have no chance to get elected or somethin', Jim would always say they didn't have no more chance than a rabbit.

He didn't make no bones about how he felt. Right in here, more than once, in front of the whole crowd, he said he was stuck on Julie and anybody that could get her for him was welcome to his house and his wife and kids included. But she wouldn't have nothin' to do with him; wouldn't even speak to him on the street. He finally seen he

wasn't gettin' nowheres with his usual line so he decided to try the rough stuff. He went right up to her house one evenin' and when she opened the door he forced his way in and grabbed her. But she broke loose and before he could stop her, she run in the next room and locked the door and phoned to Joe Barnes. Joe's the marshal. Jim could hear who she was phonin' to and he beat it before Joe got there.

Joe was an old friend of Julie's pa. Joe went to Jim the next day and told him what would happen if he ever done it again.

I don't know how the news of this little affair leaked out. Chances is that Joe Barnes told his wife and she told somebody else's wife and they told their husband. Anyways, it did leak out and Hod Meyers had the nerve to kid Jim about it, right here in this shop. Jim didn't deny nothin' and kind of laughed it off and said for us all to wait; that lots of people had tried to make a monkey out of him, but he always got even.

Meanw'ile everybody in town was wise to Julie's bein' wild mad over the Doc. I don't suppose she had any idear how her face changed when him and her was together; of course she couldn't of, or she'd of kept away from him. And she didn't know that we was all noticin' how many times she made excuses to go up to his office or pass it on the other side of the street and look up in his window to see if he was there. I felt sorry for her and so did most other people.

Hod Meyers kept rubbin' it into Jim about how the Doc had cut him out. Jim didn't pay no attention to the kiddin' and you could see he was plannin' one of his jokes.

One trick Jim had was the knack of changin' his voice. He could make you think he was a girl talkin' and he could mimic any man's voice. To show you how good he was along this line, I'll tell you the joke he played on me once.

You know, in most towns of any size, when a man is dead and needs a shave, why the barber that shaves him soaks him five dollars for the job; that is, he don't soak *him*, but whoever ordered the shave. I just charge three dollars because personally I don't mind much shavin' a dead person. They lay a whole lot stiller than live customers. The only thing is that you don't feel like talkin' to them and you get kind of lonesome.

Well, about the coldest day we ever had here, two years ago last winter, the phone rung at the house w'ile I was home to dinner and I answered the phone and it was a woman's voice and she said she was Mrs. John Scott and her husband was dead and would I come out and shave him.

Old John had always been a good customer of mine. But they live seven miles out in the country, on the Streeter road. Still I didn't see how I could say no.

So I said I would be there, but would have to come in a jitney[1] and it might cost three or four dollars besides the price of the shave. So she, or the voice, it said that was all right, so I got Frank Abbott to drive me out to the place and when I got there, who should open the door but old John himself! He wasn't no more dead than, well, than a rabbit.

It didn't take no private detective to figure out who had played me this little joke. Nobody could of thought it up but Jim Kendall. He certainly was a card!

I tell you this incident just to show you how he could disguise his voice and make you believe it was somebody else talkin'. I'd of swore it was Mrs. Scott had called me. Anyways, some woman.

Well, Jim waited till he had Doc Stair's voice down pat; then he went after revenge.

He called Julie up on a night when he knew Doc was over in Carterville. She never questioned but what it was Doc's

voice. Jim said he must see her that night; he couldn't wait no longer to tell her somethin'. She was all excited and told him to come to the house. But he said he was expectin' an important long distance call and wouldn't she please forget her manners for once and come to his office. He said they couldn't nothin' hurt her and nobody would see her and he just *must* talk to her a little w'ile. Well, poor Julie fell for it.

Doc always keeps a night light in his office, so it looked to Julie like they was somebody there.

Meanw'ile Jim Kendall had went to Wright's poolroom, where they was a whole gang amusin' themselves. The most of them had drank plenty of gin, and they was a rough bunch even when sober. They was always strong for Jim's jokes and when he told them to come with him and see some fun they give up their card games and pool games and followed along.

Doc's office is on the second floor. Right outside his door they's a flight of stairs leadin' to the floor above. Jim and his gang hid in the dark behind these stairs.

Well, Julie come up to Doc's door and rung the bell and they was nothin' doin'. She rung it again and she rung it seven or eight times. Then she tried the door and found it locked. Then Jim made some kind of a noise and she heard it and waited a minute, and then she says, "Is that you, Ralph?" Ralph is Doc's first name.

They was no answer and it must of come to her all of a sudden that she'd been bunked. She pretty near fell downstairs and the whole gang after her. They chased her all the way home, hollerin', "Is that you, Ralph?" and "Oh, Ralphie, dear, is that you?" Jim says he couldn't holler it himself, as he was laughin' too hard.

Poor Julie! She didn't show up here on Main Street for a long, long time afterward.

And of course Jim and his gang told everybody in town, everybody but Doc

[1] jitney: small bus.

Stair. They was scared to tell him, and he might of never knowed only for Paul Dickson. The poor cuckoo, as Jim called him, he was here in the shop one night when Jim was still gloatin' yet over what he'd done to Julie. And Paul took in as much of it as he could understand and he run to Doc with the story.

It's a cinch Doc went up in the air and swore he'd make Jim suffer. But it was a kind of a delicate thing, because if it got out that he had beat Jim up, Julie was bound to hear of it and then she'd know that Doc knew and of course knowin' that he knew would make it worse for her than ever. He was goin' to do somethin', but it took a lot of figurin'.

Well, it was a couple days later when Jim was here in the shop again, and so was the cuckoo. Jim was goin' duck-shootin' the next day and had come in lookin' for Hod Meyers to go with him. I happened to know that Hod had went over to Carterville and wouldn't be home till the end of the week. So Jim said he hated to go alone and he guessed he would call it off. Then poor Paul spoke up and said if Jim would take him he would go along. Jim thought a w'ile and then he said, well, he guessed a half-wit was better than nothin'.

I suppose he was plottin' to get Paul out in the boat and play some joke on him, like pushin' him in the water. Anyways, he said Paul could go. He asked him had he ever shot a duck and Paul said no, he'd never even had a gun in his hands. So Jim said he could set in the boat and watch him and if he behaved himself, he might lend him his gun for a couple of shots. They made a date to meet in the mornin' and that's the last I seen of Jim alive.

Next mornin', I hadn't been open more than ten minutes when Doc Stair come in. He looked kind of nervous. He asked me had I seen Paul Dickson. I said no, but I knew where he was, out duck-shootin' with

Jim Kendall. So Doc says that's what he had heard, and he couldn't understand it because Paul had told him he wouldn't never have no more to do with Jim as long as he lived.

He said Paul had told him about the joke Jim had played on Julie. He said Paul had asked him what he thought of the joke and the Doc had told him that anybody that would do a thing like that ought not to be let live.

I said it had been a kind of a raw thing, but Jim just couldn't resist no kind of a joke, no matter how raw. I said I thought he was all right at heart, but just bubblin' over with mischief. Doc turned and walked out.

At noon he got a phone call from old John Scott. The lake where Jim and Paul had went shootin' is on John's place. Paul had came runnin' up to the house a few minutes before and said they'd been an accident. Jim had shot a few ducks and then give the gun to Paul and told him to try his luck. Paul hadn't never handled a gun and he was nervous. He was shakin' so hard that he couldn't control the gun. He let fire and Jim sunk back in the boat, dead.

Doc Stair, bein' the coroner, jumped in Frank Abbott's flivver and rushed out to Scott's farm. Paul and old John was down on the shore of the lake. Paul had rowed the boat to shore, but they'd left the body in it, waitin' for Doc to come.

Doc examined the body and said they might as well fetch it back to town. They was no use leavin' it there or callin' a jury, as it was a plain case of accidental shootin'.

Personally I wouldn't never leave a person shoot a gun in the same boat I was in unless I was sure they knew somethin' about guns. Jim was a sucker to leave a new beginner have his gun, let alone a half-wit. It probably served Jim right, what he got. But still we miss him round here. He certainly was a card!

Comb it wet or dry?

For Discussion

1. Imagine yourself charged with preparing a lawyer's brief on behalf of Paul Dickson; an eyewitness has come forward who claims to have seen the boy in the boat accepting the gun from Kendall and tremblingly aiming it at him, then firing. What case can you make in Paul's behalf? Where does justice lie in this mischance?

2. "I hope you like it good enough to stay," the barber remarks to the newcomer early in the story (page 146). Would you like to stay in the town he describes? Why, or why not? "I bet they was more laughin' done here than any town its size in America." How about that? What provoked the laughter? How genuine and heartfelt was it?

3. The barber insists that Kendall was "a card," "a caution" — the life of the town. But look closely at what he does. How would you describe him? Where in the story did you first suspect that he was hardly the "good fella at heart" (page 147) that the barber imagined him to be?

4. The character of Doc Stair comes through less flamboyantly than — but just as clearly as — that of Kendall. What does Doc's refusal to dun people for their bills tell you about him? What do you learn from his attitude toward Kendall's wife and children at the circus? What do you infer from Kendall's fear of him?

5. Lardner has taken care to motivate his characters adequately. You might wonder why Mrs. Kendall doesn't leave the man to whom she finds herself married. What is the reason? Why has a man as accomplished as Doc Stair moved to this little town near Carterville? Why doesn't a lovely and intelligent girl like Julie Gregg move away? Why is she still unmarried?

6. The story contains a great deal of irony. "I guess I shouldn't ought to be gossipin'," the barber tells his customer at one point (page 149). Explain the irony. Where else in the story did you notice irony?

For Composition

Just about every time we open our mouths, we betray the sort of person we are. Throughout the barber's *monologue*, or uninterrupted speech, in "Haircut," he reveals his own inability to see things as they really are.

1. **Analysis.** What evidence do you find in "Haircut" to support the assertion that the barber never sees beyond the surface of things? Analyze his remarks to demonstrate his literalism and lack of imagination.

2. **Analysis.** In a good story, each sentence adds to the effect of the whole, and the opening sentences communicate perhaps the most information of all. Look again at the first two sentences of "Haircut"; together they make up the opening paragraph of the story. In a brief composition indicate how much information those two sentences alone convey.

Words and Allusions

SLANG. The informal language of a particular group of people is called *slang*. In his story "Haircut," Ring Lardner uses many expressions of American slang that were common in the 1920's. Among them are *prettied up* (page 146), *travel for a concern* (147), *bean* (149), *cuckoo* (149), *skimp along* (150), *jitney* (152), *flivver* (153). What do these slang expressions mean? How many of them do you still hear today? What other expressions do you know that express the same meanings?

Is the use of slang appropriate in Lardner's story? Why, or why not? Why does Lardner deliberately misspell the word *theayter?* What are the advantages and disadvantages of using slang in literature?

Auto Wreck

KARL SHAPIRO

What justice can there be in that sudden, terrifying shriek of brakes, that skid, that metal crunching, that ghastly burst of flames, and the silence afterwards?

Its quick soft silver bell beating, beating
And down the dark one ruby flare
Pulsing out red light like an artery,
The ambulance at top speed floating down
Past beacons and illuminated clocks   5
Wings in a heavy curve, dips down,
And brakes speed, entering the crowd.
The doors leap open, emptying light;
Stretchers are laid out, the mangled lifted
And stowed into the little hospital.   10
Then the bell, breaking the hush, tolls once,
And the ambulance with its terrible cargo
Rocking, slightly rocking, moves away,
As the doors, an afterthought, are closed.

We are deranged, walking among the cops 15
Who sweep glass and are large and composed.
One is still making notes under the light.
One with a bucket douches* ponds of blood
Into the street and gutter.   19
One hangs lanterns on the wrecks that cling,
Empty husks of locusts, to iron poles.

Our throats were tight as tourniquets,
Our feet were bound with splints, but now,
Like convalescents intimate and gauche,
We speak through sickly smiles and warn 25
With the stubborn saw* of common sense,
The grim joke and the banal resolution.
The traffic moves around with care,
But we remain, touching a wound
That opens to our richest horror.   30

18. **douches**: cleans with water. 26. **saw**: common saying or general truth expressed in a few words.

Already old, the question Who shall die?
Becomes unspoken Who is innocent?
For death in war is done by hands;
Suicide has cause and stillbirth, logic.
But this invites the occult mind,   35
Cancels our physics with a sneer,
And spatters all we knew of dénouement
Across the expedient* and wicked stones.

38. **expedient**: appropriate for the purpose they serve.

For Discussion

1. The helpless spectators of an accident find themselves "touching a wound" in their lives; that is, the awful knowledge that such a thing could occur has wounded their own fancied security. Why not me, they wonder. After all, "Who is innocent?" How does death in war differ from death by auto wreck? How is suicide different? How is an incurable disease different?

2. All we know of dénouement (line 37) suggests that a good life should develop to a climax somewhere in its prime, then fall gently off to a satisfying resolution. Any ending different from that seems unjust, inviting "the occult mind" of man to speculate on the nature of the universe we live in. How do you interpret line 36?

3. Much of the effectiveness of this powerful poem grows out of the vividness with which it creates a gruesome scene. Diction and imagery work together: "The doors *leap* open, *emptying* light" from within the ambulance to the dark roadway, where "*ponds* of blood" are visible (consider the unexpected, innocent suggestions of *ponds*). The wrecks "*cling* . . . to iron poles." What other diction in the poem struck you as unexpected and yet forcefully effective?

4. **Metaphor, Simile.** A *metaphor* is an implied comparison between two objects that are generally regarded as unlike. When the comparison is stated directly, by means of *like, as,* or *than,* it is called a *simile.* Notice the metaphors and similes that contribute to the precision of the scene in "Auto Wreck." The red light on the ambulance pulses "like an artery." What similarities exist between the ambulance light and an artery? Why is the simile particularly appropriate here? In the same way, discuss the simile in line 22. What metaphors do you find in lines 21 and 23? Are they accurate? Are they appropriate? Explain.

For Composition

Structure is the term that designates the arrangement of details that make up a literary work. Without a structure the work collapses, like a body without a skeleton.

• **Analysis.** In a well-reasoned composition, analyze the structure of "Auto Wreck." Why is the poem divided into four stanzas? That is, what does each stanza accomplish, and in what ways does each differ from the other three? Interested students will include some indication of the structure within stanzas as well; for instance, what structural element holds the first stanza together, so that the first stanza properly begins where it begins and ends where it ends?

About the Poet. **Karl Shapiro** (1913–   ) was born in Baltimore and began to write poetry while still in high school. It was not until he was serving in the army during World War II that he received any notice as a writer, but when notice came, it came swiftly. While Shapiro was overseas, his fiancée served as his agent and editor and succeeded in having three volumes of his poetry published. One of the volumes, *V-Letter*, won the Pulitzer prize for poetry in 1945.

Since then Shapiro's life has been that of a man of letters. In recent years, in addition to writing poetry and criticism, he has been editor of *Poetry* magazine and a teacher of both writing and literature in several major universities.

Counterparts

JAMES JOYCE

Farrington was employed as a clerk in the Dublin office of Crosbie & Alleyne early in the twentieth century. Not that it was much of a job he had, being at the boss's call all day long. No, it didn't seem right that a man of Farrington's caliber should be made to put up with indignities, and the fact that he had to enraged him sometimes. More than that, it had a way of making him thirsty.

The bell rang furiously and, when Miss Parker went to the tube,[1] a furious voice called out in a piercing North of Ireland accent:

"Send Farrington here!"

Miss Parker returned to her machine, saying to a man who was writing at a desk:

"Mr. Alleyne wants you upstairs."

The man muttered "*Blast* him!" under his breath and pushed back his chair to stand up. When he stood up he was tall and of great bulk. He had a hanging face, dark wine-colored, with fair eyebrows and moustache: his eyes bulged forward slightly and the whites of them were dirty. He lifted up the counter and, passing by the clients, went out of the office with a heavy step.

[1] tube : office intercommunication system.

He went heavily upstairs until he came to the second landing, where a door bore a brass plate with the inscription *Mr. Alleyne*. Here he halted, puffing with labor and vexation, and knocked. The shrill voice cried:

"Come in!"

The man entered Mr. Alleyne's room. Simultaneously Mr. Alleyne, a little man wearing gold-rimmed glasses on a clean-shaven face, shot his head up over a pile of documents. The head itself was so pink and hairless it seemed like a large egg reposing on the papers. Mr. Alleyne did not lose a moment:

"Farrington? What is the meaning of this? Why have I always to complain of you? May I ask you why you haven't made a copy of that contract between Bodley and Kirwan? I told you it must be ready by four o'clock."

"But Mr. Shelley said, sir — "

"*Mr. Shelley said, sir.* . . . Kindly attend to what I say and not to what *Mr. Shelley says, sir.* You have always some excuse or another for shirking work. Let me tell you that if the contract is not copied before this evening I'll lay the matter before Mr. Crosbie. . . . Do you hear me now?"

"Yes, sir."

"Do you hear me now? . . . Ay and another little matter! I might as well be talking to the wall as talking to you. Understand once for all that you get a half an hour for your lunch and not an hour and a half. How many courses do you want, I'd like to know. . . . Do you mind me now?"

"Yes, sir."

Mr. Alleyne bent his head again upon his pile of papers. The man stared fixedly at the polished skull which directed the affairs of Crosbie & Alleyne, gauging its fragility. A spasm of rage gripped his throat for a few moments and then passed, leaving after it a sharp sensation of thirst. The man recognized the sensation and felt that he must have a good night's drinking. The middle of the month was passed and, if he could get the copy done in time, Mr. Alleyne might give him an order on the cashier. He stood still, gazing fixedly at the head upon the pile of papers. Suddenly Mr. Alleyne began to upset all the papers, searching for something. Then, as if he had been unaware of the man's presence till that moment, he shot up his head again, saying:

"Eh? Are you going to stand there all day? Upon my word, Farrington, you take things easy!"

"I was waiting to see. . . ."

"Very good, you needn't wait to see. Go downstairs and do your work."

The man walked heavily towards the door and, as he went out of the room, he heard Mr. Alleyne cry after him that if the contract was not copied by evening Mr. Crosbie would hear of the matter.

He returned to his desk in the lower office and counted the sheets which remained to be copied. He took up his pen and dipped it in the ink but he continued to stare stupidly at the last words he had written: *In no case shall the said Bernard Bodley be.* . . . The evening was falling and in a few

ABOUT THE AUTHOR • James Joyce (1882–1941) is the literary genius who created great literature out of the conscious and unconscious minds of his characters. In so doing he transformed the English language as a medium of art, bringing to it a mastery of some twenty languages and an astounding knowledge of history, science, philosophy, and literature. *Dubliners* (1914) — which includes "Counterparts" — is a collection of sketches and short stories dealing with Dublin life and character. Joyce said that his intention here was to write a chapter of the moral history of his country, and particularly of its capital city — to him "the center of paralysis." Some of his sketches are simply deft pictures of Dublin types. Others are richer, complex with irony and symbolism.

Most of Joyce's greatest works were written while he was nearly blind, an exile from his native Ireland, a widely recognized genius who nevertheless lived in virtual poverty. He died penniless in Switzerland after fleeing with his wife from German-occupied France in World War II.

minutes they would be lighting the gas: then he could write. He felt that he must slake the thirst in his throat. He stood up from his desk and, lifting the counter as before, passed out of the office. As he was passing out the chief clerk looked at him inquiringly.

"It's all right, Mr. Shelley," said the man, pointing with his finger to indicate the objective of his journey.

The chief clerk glanced at the hatrack, but, seeing the row complete, offered no remark. As soon as he was on the landing the man pulled a shepherd's plaid cap out of his pocket, put it on his head, and ran quickly down the rickety stairs. From the street door he walked on furtively on the inner side of the path towards the corner and all at once dived into a doorway. He was now safe in the dark snug of O'Neill's shop, and filling up the little window that looked into the bar with his inflamed face, the color of dark wine or dark meat, he called out:

"Here, Pat, give us a g.p.,[1] like a good fellow."

The curate[2] brought him a glass of plain porter. The man drank it at a gulp and asked for a caraway seed. He put his penny on the counter and, leaving the curate to grope for it in the gloom, retreated out of the snug as furtively as he had entered it.

Darkness, accompanied by a thick fog, was gaining upon the dusk of February and the lamps in Eustace Street had been lit. The man went up by the houses until he reached the door of the office, wondering whether he could finish his copy in time. On the stairs a moist pungent odor of perfumes saluted his nose: evidently Miss Delacour had come while he was out in O'Neill's. He crammed his cap back again into his pocket and re-entered the office, assuming an air of absentmindedness.

[1] g.p.: glass of porter.
[2] curate: bartender.

"Mr. Alleyne has been calling for you," said the chief clerk severely. "Where were you?"

The man glanced at the two clients who were standing at the counter as if to intimate that their presence prevented him from answering. As the clients were both male the chief clerk allowed himself a laugh.

"I know that game," he said. "Five times in one day is a little bit.... Well, you better look sharp and get a copy of our correspondence in the Delacour case for Mr. Alleyne."

This address in the presence of the public, his run upstairs, and the porter he had gulped down so hastily confused the man and, as he sat down at his desk to get what was required, he realized how hopeless was the task of finishing his copy of the contract before half past five. The dark damp night was coming and he longed to spend it in the bars, drinking with his friends amid the glare of gas and the clatter of glasses. He got out the Delacour correspondence and passed out of the office. He hoped Mr. Alleyne would not discover that the last two letters were missing.

The moist pungent perfume lay all the way up to Mr. Alleyne's room. Miss Delacour was a middle-aged woman of Jewish appearance. Mr. Alleyne was said to be sweet on her or on her money. She came to the office often and stayed a long time when she came. She was sitting beside his desk now in an aroma of perfumes, smoothing the handle of her umbrella and nodding the great black feather in her hat. Mr. Alleyne had swiveled his chair round to face her and thrown his right foot jauntily upon his left knee. The man put the correspondence on the desk and bowed respectfully but neither Mr. Alleyne nor Miss Delacour took any notice of his bow. Mr. Alleyne tapped a finger on the correspondence and then flicked it towards him as if to say: *That's all right: you can go.*

The man returned to the lower office and sat down again at his desk. He stared intently at the incomplete phrase: *In no case shall the said Bernard Bodley be . . .* and thought how strange it was that the last three words began with the same letter. The chief clerk began to hurry Miss Parker, saying she would never have the letters typed in time for post. The man listened to the clicking of the machine for a few minutes and then set to work to finish his copy. But his head was not clear and his mind wandered away to the glare and rattle of the public house.[1] It was a night for hot punches. He struggled on with his copy, but when the clock struck five he had still fourteen pages to write. Blast it! He couldn't finish it in time. He longed to execrate aloud, to bring his fist down on something violently. He was so enraged that he wrote *Bernard Bernard* instead of *Bernard Bodley* and had to begin again on a clean sheet.

He felt strong enough to clear out the whole office singlehanded. His body ached to do something, to rush out and revel in violence. All the indignities of his life enraged him. . . . Could he ask the cashier privately for an advance? No, the cashier was no good, no damn good; he wouldn't give an advance. . . . He knew where he would meet the boys: Leonard and O'Halloran and Nosey Flynn. The barometer of his emotional nature was set for a spell of riot.

His imagination had so abstracted him that his name was called twice before he answered. Mr. Alleyne and Miss Delacour were standing outside the counter and all the clerks had turned round in anticipation of something. The man got up from his desk. Mr. Alleyne began a tirade of abuse, saying that two letters were missing. The man answered that he knew nothing about them, that he had made a faithful copy. The tirade continued: it was so bitter and violent

[1] **public house**: bar.

that the man could hardly restrain his fist from descending upon the head of the manikin[2] before him:

"I know nothing about any other two letters," he said stupidly.

"*You — know — nothing.* Of course you know nothing," said Mr. Alleyne. "Tell me," he added, glancing first for approval to the lady beside him, "do you take me for a fool? Do you think me an utter fool?"

The man glanced from the lady's face to the little egg-shaped head and back again; and, almost before he was aware of it, his tongue had found a felicitous moment:

"I don't think, sir," he said, "that that's a fair question to put to me."

There was a pause in the very breathing of the clerks. Everyone was astounded (the author of the witticism no less than his neighbors) and Miss Delacour, who was a stout amiable person, began to smile broadly. Mr. Alleyne flushed to the hue of a wild rose and his mouth twitched with a dwarf's passion. He shook his fist in the man's face till it seemed to vibrate like the knob of some electric machine:

"You impertinent ruffian! You impertinent ruffian! I'll make short work of you! Wait till you see! You'll apologize to me for your impertinence or you'll quit the office instanter![3] You'll quit this, I'm telling you, or you'll apologize to me!"

He stood in a doorway opposite the office watching to see if the cashier would come out alone. All the clerks passed out and finally the cashier came out with the chief clerk. It was no use trying to say a word to him when he was with the chief clerk. The man felt that his position was bad enough. He had been obliged to offer an abject apology to Mr. Alleyne for his impertinence but he knew what a hornet's nest the office would be for him. He could remember the way in which Mr. Alleyne had hounded

[2] **manikin**: little man.
[3] **instanter**: instantly.

little Peake out of the office in order to make room for his own nephew. He felt savage and thirsty and revengeful, annoyed with himself and with everyone else. Mr. Alleyne would never give him an hour's rest; his life would be a hell to him. He had made a proper fool of himself this time. Could he not keep his tongue in his cheek? But they had never pulled together from the first, he and Mr. Alleyne, ever since the day Mr. Alleyne had overheard him mimicking his North of Ireland accent to amuse Higgins and Miss Parker: that had been the beginning of it. He might have tried Higgins for the money, but sure Higgins never had anything for himself. A man with two establishments to keep up, of course he couldn't. . . .

He felt his great body again aching for the comfort of the public house. The fog had begun to chill him and he wondered could he touch Pat in O'Neill's. He could not touch him for more than a bob[1] — and a bob was no use. Yet he must get money somewhere or other: he had spent his last penny for the g.p. and soon it would be too late for getting money anywhere. Suddenly, as he was fingering his watch chain, he thought of Terry Kelly's pawn-office in Fleet Street. That was the dart![2] Why didn't he think of it sooner?

He went through the narrow alley of Temple Bar quickly, muttering to himself that they could all go to hell because he was

[1] **bob**: slang for British shilling.
[2] **That . . . dart**: that was it.

going to have a good night of it. The clerk in Terry Kelly's said *A crown!*[1] but the consignor[2] held out for six shillings; and in the end the six shillings was allowed him literally. He came out of the pawn-office joyfully, making a little cylinder of the coins between his thumb and fingers. In Westmoreland Street the footpaths were crowded with young men and women returning from business and ragged urchins ran here and there yelling out the names of the evening editions. The man passed through the crowd, looking on the spectacle generally with proud satisfaction and staring masterfully at the office girls. His head was full of the noises of tram[3] gongs and swishing trolleys and his nose already sniffed the curling fumes of punch. As he walked on he preconsidered the terms in which he would narrate the incident to the boys:

"So, I just looked at him — coolly, you know, and looked at her. Then I looked back at him again — taking my time, you know. 'I don't think that that's a fair question to put to me,' says I."

Nosey Flynn was sitting up in his usual corner of Davy Byrne's, and when he heard the story, he stood Farrington a half-one, saying it was as smart a thing as ever he heard. Farrington stood a drink in his turn. After a while O'Halloran and Paddy Leonard came in and the story was repeated to them. O'Halloran stood tailors of malt, hot, all round[4] and told the story of the retort he had made to the chief clerk when he was in Callan's of Fownes's Street; but, as the retort was after the manner of the liberal shepherds in the eclogues,[5] he had to admit that it was not as clever as Farrington's retort. At this Farrington told the

boys to polish off that and have another.

Just as they were naming their poisons who should come in but Higgins! Of course he had to join in with the others. The men asked him to give his version of it, and he did so with great vivacity for the sight of five small hot whiskies was very exhilarating. Everyone roared laughing when he showed the way in which Mr. Alleyne shook his fist in Farrington's face. Then he imitated Farrington, saying, *"And here was my nabs, as cool as you please,"* while Farrington looked at the company out of his heavy dirty eyes, smiling and at times drawing forth stray drops of liquor from his moustache with the aid of his lower lip.

When that round was over there was a pause. O'Halloran had money but neither of the other two seemed to have any; so the whole party left the shop somewhat regretfully. At the corner of Duke Street Higgins and Nosey Flynn beveled off to the left while the other three turned back towards the city. Rain was drizzling down on the cold streets and, when they reached the Ballast Office, Farrington suggested the Scotch House. The bar was full of men and loud with the noise of tongues and glasses. The three men pushed past the whining match sellers at the door and formed a little party at the corner of the counter. They began to exchange stories. Leonard introduced them to a young fellow named Weathers who was performing at the Tivoli as an acrobat and knockabout *artiste*. Farrington stood a drink all round. Weathers said he would take a small Irish and Apollinaris. Farrington, who had definite notions of what was what, asked the boys would they have an Apollinaris too; but the boys told Tim to make theirs hot. The talk became theatrical. O'Halloran stood a round and then Farrington stood another round, Weathers protesting that the hospitality was too Irish. He promised to get them in behind the scenes and introduce them to some nice girls. O'Halloran said

---

[1] *crown:* British silver coin, worth about sixty cents in American money.

[2] **consignor:** one who dispatches goods.

[3] **tram:** streetcar.

[4] **stood . . . round:** bought drinks for everyone.

[5] **after . . . eclogues:** abusive personal remarks, as in the Eclogues of Theocritus and Virgil.

that he and Leonard would go, but that Farrington wouldn't go because he was a married man; and Farrington's heavy dirty eyes leered at the company in token that he understood he was being chaffed. Weathers made them all have just one little tincture[1] at his expense and promised to meet them later on at Mulligan's in Poolbeg Street.

When the Scotch House closed they went round to Mulligan's. They went into the parlor at the back and O'Halloran ordered small hot specials all round. They were all beginning to feel mellow. Farrington was just standing another round when Weathers came back. Much to Farrington's relief he drank a glass of bitter this time. Funds were getting low but they had enough to keep them going. Presently two young women with big hats and a young man in a check suit came in and sat at a table close by. Weathers saluted them and told the company that they were out of the Tivoli. Farrington's eyes wandered at every moment in the direction of one of the young women. There was something striking in her appearance. An immense scarf of peacock-blue muslin was wound round her hat and knotted in a great bow under her chin; and she wore bright yellow gloves, reaching to the elbow. Farrington gazed admiringly at the plump arm which she moved very often and with much grace; and when, after a little time, she answered his gaze he admired still more her large dark brown eyes. The oblique staring expression in them fascinated him. She glanced at him once or twice and, when the party was leaving the room, she brushed against his chair and said "O, *pardon!*" in a London accent. He watched her leave the room in the hope that she would look back at him, but he was disappointed. He cursed his want of money and cursed all the rounds he had stood, particularly to all the whiskies and Apollinaris which he had stood to

Weathers. If there was one thing that he hated it was a sponge. He was so angry that he lost count of the conversation of his friends.

When Paddy Leonard called him he found that they were talking about feats of strength. Weathers was showing his biceps muscle to the company and boasting so much that the other two had called on Farrington to uphold the national honor. Farrington pulled up his sleeve accordingly and showed his biceps muscle to the company. The two arms were examined and compared and finally it was agreed to have a trial of strength. The table was cleared and the two men rested their elbows on it, clasping hands. When Paddy Leonard said "*Go!*" each was to try to bring down the other's hand on to the table. Farrington looked very serious and determined.

The trial began. After about thirty seconds Weathers brought his opponent's hand slowly down on to the table. Farrington's dark wine-colored face flushed darker still with anger and humiliation at having been defeated by such a stripling.

"You're not to put the weight of your body behind it. Play fair," he said.

"Who's not playing fair?" said the other.

"Come on again. The two best out of three."

The trial began again. The veins stood out on Farrington's forehead, and the pallor of Weathers' complexion changed to peony. Their hands and arms trembled under the stress. After a long struggle Weathers again brought his opponent's hand slowly onto the table. There was a murmur of applause from the spectators. The curate, who was standing beside the table, nodded his red head towards the victor and said with loutish familiarity:

"Ah! that's the knack!"

"What the hell do you know about it?" said Farrington fiercely, turning on the man. "What do you put in your gab for?"

"Sh, sh!" said O'Halloran, observing the

[1] tincture : alcoholic mixture.

violent expression of Farrington's face.
"Pony up,[1] boys. We'll have just one little
smahan[2] more and then we'll be off."

A very sullen-faced man stood at the
corner of O'Connell Bridge waiting for the
little Sandymount tram to take him home.
He was full of smoldering anger and re-
vengefulness. He felt humiliated and dis-
contented; he did not even feel drunk; and
he had only twopence in his pocket. He
cursed everything. He had done for himself
in the office, pawned his watch, spent all his
money; and he had not even got drunk.
He began to feel thirsty again and he longed
to be back again in the hot reeking public
house. He had lost his reputation as a strong
man, having been defeated twice by a mere
boy. His heart swelled with fury, and when
he thought of the woman in the big hat who
had brushed against him and said *Pardon!*
his fury nearly choked him.

His tram let him down at Shelbourne
Road and he steered his great body along in
the shadow of the wall of the barracks. He
loathed returning to his home. When he
went in by the side door he found the kitchen empty and the kitchen fire nearly out.
He bawled upstairs:

"Ada! Ada!"

His wife was a little sharp-faced woman
who bullied her husband when he was
sober and was bullied by him when he was
drunk. They had five children. A little boy

[1] **Pony up:** pay the bill.
[2] **smahan:** drink.

came running down the stairs.

"Who is that?" said the man, peering
through the darkness.

"Me, pa."

"Who are you? Charlie?"

"No, pa. Tom."

"Where's your mother?"

"She's out at the chapel."

"That's right. . . . Did she think of leaving any dinner for me?"

"Yes, pa. I — "

"Light the lamp. What do you mean by
having the place in darkness? Are the other
children in bed?"

The man sat down heavily on one of the
chairs while the little boy lit the lamp. He
began to mimic his son's flat accent, saying
half to himself: "*At the chapel. At the
chapel, if you please!*" When the lamp was
lit he banged his fist on the table and
shouted:

"What's for my dinner?"

"I'm going . . . to cook it, pa," said the
little boy.

The man jumped up furiously and pointed
to the fire.

"On that fire! You let the fire out! By
God, I'll teach you to do that again!"

He took a step to the door and seized the
walking stick which was standing behind it.

"I'll teach you to let the fire out!" he
said, rolling up his sleeve in order to give
his arm free play.

The little boy cried "*O, pa!*" and ran
whimpering round the table, but the man
followed him and caught him by the coat.
The little boy looked about him wildly but,
seeing no way of escape, fell upon his knees.

"Now, you'll let the fire out the next
time!" said the man, striking at him vigorously with the stick. "Take that, you little
whelp!"

The boy uttered a squeal of pain as the
stick cut his thigh. He clasped his hands
together in the air and his voice shook with
fright.

"O, pa!" he cried. "Don't beat me, pa!
And I'll . . . I'll say a *Hail Mary*[1] for you
. . . . I'll say a *Hail Mary* for you, pa, if you
don't beat me. . . . I'll say a *Hail Mary*. . . ."

[1] **Hail Mary**: Catholic prayer.

For Discussion

1. Farrington's actions at the end of
"Counterparts" are plainly unjust. What has
his son Tom done to provoke him? What is
he really angry and frustrated about?

2. Consider the title of this story. The
counterparts, of course, are Alleyne and Farrington. The former mimics: *"Mr. Shelley
said, sir. . . . Mr. Shelley says, sir"* (page 158).
The latter mimics: *"At the chapel. At the
chapel, if you please!"* (page 164). Physically
the two men are contrasted in virtually every
way — one burly and the other slight, one
moustached and the other clean-shaven, one
speaking with a Dublin accent and the other
with a North of Ireland accent, one the em-
ployee and the other the boss, one without
female companionship and the other accompanied by a perfumed lady. But despite these
contrasts, what similarities — in attitude and
relationship to those around them — do you
see between the two?

3. Farrington "was going to have a good
night of it" (page 161). What, in fact, is his
situation at the end of the night, waiting for
the Sandymount tram to take him home? Contrast his mood then with the earlier mood he
was feeling coming out of the pawn-office.
What specifically has happened in the interval
to change his mood so drastically?

4. **Setting.** The *setting* is the place and
time in which the experience related in a story,
play, or poem occurs. "Counterparts" is set in
early twentieth-century Dublin, and one of
Joyce's achievements here — as elsewhere
throughout his fiction — lies in bringing that
world vividly before the reader. The whining
match sellers at the door of the pub, the noises
of tram gongs and swishing trolleys, the rain
drizzling down on cold streets, all help to
create a particular city on the printed page.

What aspects of Dublin life struck you as most
unusual? On the basis of "Counterparts," what
would it be like to live there? Explain.

For Composition

Joyce's descriptive gifts are extraordinary.
Consider, as instances, the way he describes
Alleyne on page 157, and his description of the
young woman "out of the Tivoli" on page 163.
We see the latter clearly — how she is dressed,
how she moves — and we hear her unmistak-
able voice before she leaves.

1. **Description.** In a paragraph describe
someone you know well, using Joyce's descriptions as a model. The exercise will be
easier for you if you choose a person with
distinctive traits. In writing about him, avoid
mentioning at random whatever comes to
mind; instead, limit your description to significant details that let us see and hear the
individual in action. The description, though
brief, should also let us form an accurate
impression of your subject; that is, it should
let us understand him the way we come to
understand Alleyne very early in our encounter with him in "Counterparts."

2. **Analysis.** Farrington's reaction to his
defeat by Weathers at hand-wrestling *foreshadows* (that is, anticipates and prepares us
for) his behavior at the end of the story. In a
brief essay explain how Farrington's remark
to the curate, or publican, foreshadows what
happens at the conclusion of his night on the
town. Your remarks will concern the justice
of Farrington's responses in the two cases.

Words and Allusions

DIALECT. A dialect is a local or regional form
of language that differs noticeably from
standard usage in pronunciation, vocabulary,
or grammar, without becoming a separate language. In "Counterparts" Joyce uses a number of words and phrases that are not part of
American English. They are terms that reflect
the Dublin setting of the story. As used in
"Counterparts," what do the following words
mean: *touch* (for a drink, page 161), *bob*
(161), *nabs* (162), *tram* (162)?

César

The Yellow Buick

Karl Shapiro in "Auto Wreck" (page 155) and César in this sculpture are trying to deal with many of the same questions. In the past it was easy to find what was called the "picturesque," that is, what was considered a proper subject for a painter or sculptor. But the world has changed, and the environment of the artist has, to some observers, become degraded. To an artist like César, such degradation simply means that modern industry, commerce, and cities do not meet the old requirements for what is "picturesque" and that the term must be redefined so that what has been regarded as ugly becomes artistically usable.

Just as Shapiro makes a poem out of what was once regarded as "unpoetic," so César makes sculpture out of a crushed automobile. How prominent is this subject in our environment? César's inspiration comes from a relatively new technological development, the giant machines that crush scrapped and wrecked automobiles into the smallest possible regular mass of metal. Why are the size and regularity important? That regularity creates a recognizable shape which connects the crushed automobile with traditional sculpture. What is that shape?

Yet one of the most remarkable features of the modern visual environment is its nonregular randomness. The "strip" outside of most cities of any size is an obvious example. Here we find a collection of drive-in restaurants, gasoline stations, second-hand car lots, all marked by different sizes and shapes of neon signs. What other examples of visual randomness can you think of? What are the social and financial reasons behind such randomness?

César's sculpture reflects this randomness, yet you can also perceive a non-randomness — a design quality. In *The Yellow Buick* it can be found in the many parallel lines and in the implied red rectangle of the lower third of the front surface shown in the picture. The upper two-thirds implies a yellow rectangle, and the diagonal lines imply a rectangle with a different axis. At the top corners, the bits of blue suggest triangles that provide a frame by echoing the color of the base. What other suggestions of design can you find? Similarly, what suggestions of design do you find in the randomness of the "strip"?

The work is also colorful. The large areas of yellow give it a sense of life and emotional openness, and the white, the least aggressive of colors, is dominant. How would you feel if he had sprayed the whole thing with black?

In *The Yellow Buick,* then, we find suggestions of design amid randomness, and the further suggestion that the modern world offers a randomness that any other culture would have found intolerable. Some people object to this kind of sculpture since they turn to art to find an ordered world that they believe art is supposed to offer. But César's point is that randomness is neither good nor bad; it just is, and therefore it is a proper subject for artists to deal with.

MORSE PECKHAM

César (Baldaccini) (1921–   ) *The Yellow Buick,* compressed automobile. Museum of Modern Art, New York.

Dürer

Job and his Wife

As its title and content indicate, Dürer's painting illustrates The Book of Job (page 175). Dürer's problem in this painting was to present the whole story of Job, including the beginning of his sufferings as well as his reward for enduring them and accepting the will of God. The story of Job expresses the belief that man's powers to explain what happens to him are limited and stresses the necessity and desirability of accepting that fact. All this Dürer wished to include in his painting.

The central scene reflects the passage: "So . . . Satan . . . smote Job with sore boils from the sole of his foot unto his crown. . . . Then said his wife unto him, Dost thou still retain thine integrity? curse God, and die." In the background we see what preceded this event — the second affliction of Job: "The fire of God is fallen from heaven, and hath burned up the sheep, and the servants, and consumed them; and I only am escaped alone to tell thee." Here Dürer used an old medieval tradition of showing events separated by time in the same picture space and landscape. But how was he to show the outcome of the story?

He did so by changing the role of Job's wife. Instead of simply telling Job to curse God, she offers relief from his sufferings by pouring water on him to cool and bathe his skin broken out in boils. The significance of her action would be clear to any Christian observer of Dürer's time, according to the principle of typology. Typology is the study of similarities and analogies between characters and events in the Old and New Testaments to reveal the continuity of the Christian view of history. For example, in the Old Testament (Exodus 16), when the Israelites have escaped from Egypt and are journeying through the wilderness, they are fed by manna that falls from heaven. This event can be related to the scene in the New Testament (Matthew 15) where Jesus feeds a multitude with a few loaves and fishes. The two events can be viewed as parallel, or analogous, revealing the continuity of God's care for His people.

In like manner, the action of Job's wife in Dürer's painting reveals a link with the New Testament and thus with Christian doctrine. The water she is pouring over Job suggests the water of baptism that washes away man's sins and makes possible the salvation of his soul. Thus the story of Job is completed in Dürer's painting with water, the symbol of redemption, indicating Job's reconcilement with God.

The top of the painting suggests that it was used as an altarpiece. How does Dürer echo that shape in organizing the figures in the painting? What shape is suggested by the position of Job's body? Where else is that shape implied? Does the background, beyond the flames, appear calm or disturbed? What does this quality suggest?

MORSE PECKHAM

Albrecht Dürer (1471–1528) *Job and his Wife.* Frankfurt, Stadelsches Kunstinstitut.

Ambrogio Lorenzetti (active 1319–1348) *Allegory of Good Government*, fresco. Palazzo Pubblico, Siena.

Lorenzetti

Allegory of Good Government

This picture is one of a series printed on the walls of the council chamber of the city hall of Siena, Italy. In the fourteenth century, when these frescoes were done, Siena was an independent republic. Lorenzetti's task was to present in an allegory (see page 41), the principles by which justice is administered and a state kept in good order. The conception of justice here presented was influenced by Aristotle (page 190) and, of course, by Christian thought.

At the left Justice is enthroned as a queen. She is inspired by Divine Wisdom above her. Divine Wisdom holds a red covered Bible and a huge balance that rests on the head of Justice. On the left an angel leans out of one scale of the balance to decapitate one man and crown another. On the right an angel gives money and a sword to two figures. These actions represent Distributive Justice and Commutative Justice. What do these terms mean?

On the left, below Justice, sits Concord, the ability of individuals to cooperate. She holds two cords coming from the scales. The cords unite twenty-four citizens of Siena who march toward the feet of a majestic crowned figure. This figure symbolizes Siena, as, for example, the Statue of Liberty symbolizes the United States. Why are the cords attached to his scepter? He holds in his left hand an image of the Virgin Mary to whom Siena was dedicated, and at his feet are the wolf and the twins Romulus and Remus, the founders of Rome. The legend was that Senius, who founded Siena, was a son of Remus. Why would the Sienese want to relate the Roman legend to their own?

Above the figure of Siena are three angels representing the virtues of Faith, Hope, and Charity. How are they identified? Immediately next to Siena sit four more virtues. From the viewer's left they are Fortitude, Prudence, Magnanimity, and Temperance. What is the difference between these four virtues and the three virtues above?

The figure in white, further to the viewer's left, is Peace, the reward of good government. And to the extreme right is Legal Justice, the instrument of good government. Why is Legal Justice holding a crown and a severed head on her lap? In front of her are armed men on horseback and soldiers holding spears. These are the armed forces by which Siena maintains herself. In the lower right corner are a group of prisoners. Whom do they represent?

What does this painting suggest about the relationship of power and social organization to good government? If Lorenzetti had had a high narrow wall to paint on instead of a broad one, how do you think he would have arranged his figures?

In the same room with this painting are two other large frescoes. One represents the effects of good government in city and in country, and the other represents the effects of evil or unjust government dominated by tyranny. What is the difference between tyranny and the just exercise of power?

MORSE PECKHAM

Medieval Manuscript

Lucifer

The scene presented here is an illustration of the very end of Dante's *Inferno* (page 194). Dante and his guide Virgil have arrived at the last circle of hell, the circle of ice at the center of the earth in which the worst traitors are punished. The picture is a leaf from a manuscript done late in the fourteenth century in Naples, perhaps seventy years after the death of Dante in 1321. Printing had not yet been invented, and books were circulated in manuscript. Manuscripts were copied by scribes, and wealthy men often commissioned artists to decorate manuscripts of famous works with elaborate illustrations. The writing at the top of the page consists of the last six lines of the *Inferno* and a statement by the unknown scribe identifying the work and the author. Called the colophon, this statement was put at the end of manuscripts to indicate that the scribe had copied the entire work.

The problem of the unknown artist was to create a powerful and impressive design and at the same time to provide an accurate pictorial representation of what Dante had written. The problem gave him some difficulty. Dante describes the various traitors as buried in ice, and he has Lucifer (or Satan) — the rebel angel, the arch-traitor because he betrayed God — buried in ice up to the middle of his chest. Dante and Virgil climb down the body of Lucifer through the ice. When they pass the center of gravity and begin climbing up towards the opposite side of the earth, they see the lower half of Lucifer's body sticking up out of the ice on the other side. Moreover, Dante tells us that Lucifer had three wings and three faces, each looking in a different direction.

How did the artist solve the problem of making an impressive symmetrical design while retaining Dante's description? How does he handle the wings and the three heads? He presents the sinners in the positions Dante specifies, but he does not place them within the ice. Why not?

It is usually said that Lucifer's three faces represent an inversion of the attributes of God — hatred, impotence, and ignorance, instead of love, power, and wisdom. What other inversion do these three faces suggest? In heaven Lucifer was known as the most beautiful of the angels. Why, in the *Inferno*, does Dante call him ugly? Why does the artist make him hideously ugly? What does this difference reveal about the differing problems of poet and painter?

Lucifer is gnawing on three traitors — Judas, who betrayed Jesus, in the red center face, and Brutus and Cassius in the blue and green faces. (In Dante these faces are black and yellow, as they may once have been in this much-worn painting.) Brutus and Cassius are here because they betrayed Julius Caesar, regarded as the founder of the Roman Empire whose task was to protect the church. Why is Judas given the worst punishment?

MORSE PECKHAM

Lucifer from **Dante's** DIVINA COMMEDIA, medieval manuscript. Pierpont Morgan Library, New York.

Thou Art Indeed Just, Lord

GERARD MANLEY HOPKINS

From very early in his history, man has sought answers to the question of what sort of universe he lives in. Do things happen purely by chance, or is there justice behind events? If there is, why do wicked men succeed sometimes, and good men fail? The priest-poet Gerard Hopkins, a devout believer who had dedicated his life to God, was nevertheless moved to wonder about such matters in a poem that makes use of his characteristic rhythms and unusual word usage.

> Thou art indeed just, Lord, if I contend
> With thee; but, sir, so what I plead is just.
> Who do sinners' ways prosper? and why must
> Disappointment all I endeavor end?
>   Wert thou my enemy, O thou my friend,   5
> How wouldst thou worse, I wonder, than thou dost
> Defeat, thwart me? Oh, the sots* and thralls of lust
> Do in spare hours more thrive than I that spend,
> Sir, life upon thy cause. See, banks and brakes
> Now, leavèd how thick! lacèd they are again   10
> With fretty chervil, look, and fresh wind shakes
> Them; birds build — but not I build; no, but strain,
> Time's eunuch, and not breed one work that wakes.
> Mine, O thou lord of life, send my roots rain.

7. sots: drunkards.

For Discussion

1. Hopkins' phrasing, which requires attentive reading to understand, has had an important influence on modern poetry, although he himself died before the twentieth century began. If you do not already know what they mean, look up the following words: *thralls* (line 7), *chervil* (line 11), *eunuch* (line 13). Use context to help you determine which of the several dictionary meanings is appropriate for *brakes* (line 9) and *fretty* (line 11). "What I plead is just," the poet says in line 2. His plea takes the form of a series of questions extending into line 7. What is the gist of those questions?

2. At what time of year is the speaker of the poem addressing his remarks to God? What details tell you so? What does the speaker mean by the line on which the poem ends?

3. Hopkins chose to write his poetry in a rather unusual way, repeating the same number of stressed syllables in each line but varying the number of unstressed syllables. (Most regular, or *metrical*, verse, as you no doubt already know, repeats the same number of syllables, both stressed and unstressed, from line to line.) In this poem, there are five stressed syllables per line:

Thou art indeed just, Lord, if I contend

With thee; but, sir, so what I plead is just.

Why do sinners ways prosper? and why must

Disappointment all I endeavor end?

Notice that the meaning of the poem supports stress on *I* in line 4, though the same word is not stressed in line 2. See if you can indicate where the stresses might fall in lines 5 through 8 of the poem.

For Composition

1. **Paraphrase.** Set down a prose paraphrase of the first eight and a half lines of "Thou Art Indeed Just, Lord." Remember that the ideal paraphrase uses words different from the original to convey the meaning of the original as fully, accurately, and succinctly as possible.

2. **Comparison and Contrast.** Compare and contrast the sound of this poem with that of any regular metrical poem read earlier in this book; the poems by Keats (page 46) and Housman (page 145) would serve the purposes of the exercise.

About the Poet. Throughout his comparatively brief life, **Gerard Manley Hopkins** (1844–1889) was torn between his desire to write poems and his sense of duty in a life dedicated to God. This conflict "between his desire to be a saint and his desire to be an artist" was reflected in his ascetic life of self-denial and the delight in earthly things expressed in his verse. Hopkins entered the Roman Catholic Church in 1866, one year before his graduation from Oxford. When he joined the Jesuits in 1868, he burned his early poems and wrote no more for some years. It was not until 1918, nearly thirty years after his death, that his startlingly modern poems were brought before the public. As later editions of his poetry appeared, he was hailed by such important poets as W. H. Auden in the thirties and Dylan Thomas in the forties as their contemporary and their master — a twentieth-century poet born before his time.

FROM

The Book of Job

The eighteenth book of the Old Testament tells of the desperate ordeals of a man in the land of Uz — "greatest of all the men of the east." That man's name was Job. The Book of Job is part prose, but mostly poetry — and poetry of an extraordinary order: at times narrative, at times reflective, at times lyric. When it was written is not known; the fifth century B.C. is probably a reasonable guess. Who wrote it remains a mystery, as does the location of Job's homeland of Uz. Perhaps the account of Job's testing was contained in a familiar folktale that a brilliant poet was able to adapt to his own purposes. What is certain is that the poetry of *Job* is a glory of world literature — perhaps the most impressive poetry to be found anywhere in the Bible. And the questions that Job's ordeal raises — universal questions of justice — remain in all their profundity.

CHAPTER 1

There was a man in the land of Uz, whose name was Job; and that man was perfect and upright, and one that feared[1] God, and eschewed[2] evil. 2 And there were born unto him seven sons and three daughters. 3 His substance also was seven thousand sheep, and three thousand camels, and five hundred yoke of oxen, and five hundred she asses, and a very great household; so that this man was the greatest of all the men of the east. 4 And his sons went and feasted in their houses, every one his day; and sent and called for their three sisters to eat and to drink with them. 5 And it was so, when the days of their feasting were gone about, that Job sent and sanctified[3] them, and rose up early in the morning, and offered burnt offerings according to the number of them all: for Job said, It may be that my sons have sinned, and cursed God in their hearts. Thus did Job continually.

6 Now there was a day when the sons of God came to present themselves before the Lord, and Satan came also among them. 7 And the Lord said unto Satan, Whence comest thou? Then Satan answered the Lord, and said, From going to and fro in the earth, and from walking up and down in it. 8 And the Lord said unto Satan, Hast thou considered my servant Job, that there is none like him in the earth, a perfect and an upright man, one that feareth God, and escheweth evil? 9 Then Satan answered the Lord, and said, Doth Job fear God for nought?[4] 10 Hast not thou made an hedge about him, and about his house, and about all that he hath on every side? thou hast blessed the work of his hands, and his substance is increased in the land. 11 But put forth thine hand now, and touch all that he hath, and he will curse thee to thy face. 12 And the Lord said unto Satan, Behold, all that he hath is in thy power; only upon himself put not forth thine hand. So Satan went forth from the presence of the Lord.

13 And there was a day when his sons and his daughters were eating and drinking wine in their eldest brother's house: 14 And there came a messenger unto Job, and said, The oxen were plowing, and the asses feeding beside them: 15 And the Sabeans fell upon them, and took them away; yea, they have slain the servants with the edge of the sword; and I only am escaped alone to tell thee. 16 While he was yet speaking, there came also another, and said, The fire of God is fallen from

[1] **feared:** *here,* revered.
[2] **eschewed:** shunned, avoided.

[3] **sanctified:** blessed.
[4] **for nought:** for no reason.

ABOUT THE AUTHOR • We know nothing about the author of *Job*. Whoever he was, he apparently took material from an ancient folktale and created from it one of the most influential works in all literature. *Job* is one of the oldest books in the Bible, yet there is evidence that some of its dramatic dialogue comes from even earlier sources. The repeated refrain in the first chapter — "I only am escaped alone to tell thee" — suggests an origin in folk literature.

The Book of Job is unusual among books of the Bible in that it stresses questions more than answers. And the questions it raises have been asked by every generation of men down to the present day.

heaven, and hath burned up the sheep, and the servants, and consumed them; and I only am escaped alone to tell thee. 17 While he was yet speaking, there came also another, and said, The Chaldeans made out three bands, and fell upon the camels, and have carried them away, yea, and slain the servants with the edge of the sword; and I only am escaped alone to tell thee. 18 While he was yet speaking, there came also another, and said, Thy sons and thy daughters were eating and drinking wine in their eldest brother's house: 19 And, behold, there came a great wind from the wilderness, and smote the four corners of the house, and it fell upon the young men, and they are dead; and I only am escaped alone to tell thee. 20 Then Job arose, and rent his mantle,[1] and shaved his head, and fell down upon the ground, and worshiped, 21 And said, Naked came I out of my mother's womb, and naked shall I return thither: the Lord gave, and the Lord hath taken away; blessed be the name of the Lord. 22 In all this Job sinned not, nor charged[2] God foolishly.

CHAPTER 2

Again there was a day when the sons of God came to present themselves before the Lord, and Satan came also among them to present himself before the Lord. 2 And the Lord said unto Satan, From whence comest thou? And Satan answered the Lord, and said, From going to and fro in the earth, and from walking up and down in it. 3 And the Lord said unto Satan, Hast thou considered my servant Job, that there is none like him in the earth, a perfect and an upright man, one that feareth God, and escheweth evil? and still he holdeth fast his integrity, although thou movedst me against him, to destroy him without cause. 4 And Satan answered the Lord, and said, Skin for skin, yea, all that a man hath will he give for his life. 5 But put forth thine hand now, and touch his bone and his flesh, and he will curse thee to thy face. 6 And the Lord said unto Satan, Behold, he is in thine hand; but save his life.

7 So went Satan forth from the presence of the Lord, and smote Job with sore boils from the sole of his foot unto his crown. 8 And he took him a potsherd[3] to scrape himself withal, and he sat down among the ashes.

9 Then said his wife unto him, Dost thou still retain thine integrity? curse God, and die. 10 But he said unto her, Thou speakest as one of the foolish women speaketh. What? shall we receive good at the hand of God, and shall we not receive evil? In all this did not Job sin with his lips.

11 Now when Job's three friends heard of all this evil that was come upon him, they came every one from his own place; Eliphaz the Temanite,[4] and Bildad the Shuhite,[5] and Zophar the Naamathite:[6] for they had made an appointment together to come to mourn with him and to comfort him. 12 And when they lifted up their eyes afar off, and knew him not, they lifted up their voice, and wept; and they rent every one his mantle, and sprinkled dust upon their heads toward heaven. 13 So they sat down with him upon the ground seven days and seven nights, and none spake a word unto him: for they saw that his grief was very great.

[1] rent his mantle: tore his garment.
[2] charged: blamed.
[3] potsherd (pot'sherd): fragment of pottery.

[4] Eliphaz the Temanite: ə·lĭ'faz, tē'man·ĭt.
[5] Bildad the Shuhite: bĭl'dad, shū'hīt.
[6] Zophar the Naamathite: zō'fär, nā·am'ə·thĭt.

"So went Satan forth from the presence of the Lord, and smote Job with sore boils from the sole of his foot unto his crown." Job's affliction as depicted in a medieval manuscript.

CHAPTER 3

After this opened Job his mouth, and cursed his day.

2 And Job spake, and said,

3 Let the day perish wherein I was born, and the night in which it was said, There is a man child conceived.

4 Let that day be darkness; let not God regard it from above, neither let the light shine upon it.

5 Let darkness and the shadow of death stain it; let a cloud dwell upon it; let the blackness of the day terrify it.

6 As for that night, let darkness seize upon it; let it not be joined unto the days of the year, let it not come into the number of the months.

7 Lo, let that night be solitary, let no joyful voice come therein.

8 Let them curse it that curse the day, who are ready to raise up their mourning.

9 Let the stars of the twilight thereof be dark; let it look for light, but have none; neither let it see the dawning of the day:

10 Because it shut not up the doors of my mother's womb, nor hid sorrow from mine eyes.

11 Why died I not from the womb? why did I not give up the ghost when I came out of the belly?

12 Why did the knees prevent me? or why the breasts that I should suck?

13 For now should I have lain still and been quiet, I should have slept: then had I been at rest.

CHAPTER 4

Then Eliphaz the Temanite answered and said,

2 If we assay[1] to commune with thee, wilt thou be grieved? but who can withhold himself from speaking?

3 Behold, thou hast instructed many, and thou hast strengthened the weak hands.

4 Thy words have upholden him that was falling, and thou hast strengthened the feeble knees.

5 But now it is come upon thee, and thou

[1] **assay**: attempt.

faintest; it toucheth thee, and thou art troubled.

6 Is not this thy fear, thy confidence, thy hope, and the uprightness of thy ways?

7 Remember, I pray thee, who ever perished, being innocent? or where were the righteous cut off?

8 Even as I have seen, they that plow iniquity,[1] and sow wickedness, reap the same.

9 By the blast of God they perish, and by the breath of his nostrils are they consumed.

CHAPTER 5

Behold, happy is the man whom God correcteth: therefore despise not thou the chastening of the Almighty:

18 For he maketh sore, and bindeth up: he woundeth, and his hands make whole.

19 He shall deliver thee in six troubles: yea, in seven there shall no evil touch thee.

25 Thou shalt know also that thy seed shall be great, and thine offspring as the grass of the earth.

26 Thou shalt come to thy grave in a full age, like as a shock of corn[2] cometh in in his season.

27 Lo this, we have searched it, so it is; hear it, and know thou it for thy good.

CHAPTER 6

But Job answered and said,
2 Oh that my grief were thoroughly weighed, and my calamity laid in the balances together!

3 For now it would be heavier than the sand of the sea: therefore my words are swallowed up.[3]

[1] iniquity: sin.
[2] shock of corn: stalks of grain set upright in a field.
[3] my . . . up: i.e., I lack the words to express my grief.

4 For the arrows of the Almighty are within me, the poison whereof drinketh up my spirit: the terrors of God do set themselves in array against me.

8 Oh that I might have my request; and that God would grant me the thing that I long for!

9 Even that it would please God to destroy me; that he would let loose his hand, and cut me off!

24 Teach me, and I will hold my tongue: and cause me to understand wherein I have erred.

25 How forcible are right words! but what doth your arguing reprove?[4]

26 Do ye imagine to reprove words, and the speeches of one that is desperate, which are as wind?

27 Yea, ye overwhelm the fatherless, and ye dig a pit for your friend.

28 Now therefore be content, look upon me; for it is evident unto you if I lie.

29 Return, I pray you, let it not be iniquity; yea, return again, my righteousness is in it.

30 Is there iniquity in my tongue? cannot my taste discern perverse things?

CHAPTER 7

When I lie down, I say, When shall I arise, and the night be gone? and I am full of tossings to and fro unto the dawning of the day.

5 My flesh is clothed with worms and clods of dust; my skin is broken, and become loathsome.

6 My days are swifter than a weaver's shuttle, and are spent without hope.

7 O remember that my life is wind: mine eye shall no more see good.

8 The eye of him that hath seen me shall see me no more: thine eyes are upon me, and I am not.

9 As the cloud is consumed and vanisheth

[4] reprove: disprove.

away: so he that goeth down to the grave shall come up no more.

10 He shall return no more to his house, neither shall his place know him any more.

11 Therefore I will not refrain my mouth; I will speak in the anguish of my spirit; I will complain in the bitterness of my soul.

CHAPTER 8

Then answered Bildad the Shuhite, and said,

2 How long wilt thou speak these things? and how long shall the words of thy mouth be like a strong wind?

3 Doth God pervert[1] judgment? or doth the Almighty pervert justice?

4 If thy children have sinned against him, and he have cast them away for their transgression;[2]

5 If thou wouldest seek unto God betimes,[3] and make thy supplication to the Almighty;

6 If thou wert pure and upright; surely now he would awake for thee, and make the habitation of thy righteousness prosperous.

20 Behold, God will not cast away a perfect man, neither will he help the evil doers;

21 Till he fill thy mouth with laughing, and thy lips with rejoicing.

22 They that hate thee shall be clothed with shame; and the dwelling place of the wicked shall come to nought.

[1] **pervert**: misuse, misdirect.
[2] **transgression**: wrongdoing.
[3] **betimes**: soon.

CHAPTER 9

Then Job answered and said,

2 I know it is so of a truth: but how should man be just with God?

3 If he will contend with him, he cannot answer him one of a thousand.

4 He is wise in heart, and mighty in strength: who hath hardened himself against him, and hath prospered?

16 If I had called, and he had answered me; yet would I not believe that he had hearkened unto my voice.

17 For he breaketh me with a tempest, and multiplieth my wounds without cause.

18 He will not suffer me to take my breath, but filleth me with bitterness.

19 If I speak of strength, lo, he is strong: and if of judgment, who shall set me a time to plead?

20 If I justify myself, mine own mouth shall condemn me: if I say, I am perfect, it shall also prove me perverse.

21 Though I were perfect, yet would I not know my soul: I would despise my life.

22 This is one thing, therefore I said it, He destroyeth the perfect and the wicked.

CHAPTER 10

My soul is weary of my life; I will leave my complaint upon myself; I will speak in the bitterness of my soul.

2 I will say unto God, Do not condemn me; shew me wherefore thou contendest with me.

3 Is it good unto thee that thou shouldest oppress, that thou shouldest despise the work of thine hands, and shine upon the counsel of the wicked?

4 Hast thou eyes of flesh? or seest thou as man seeth?

5 Are thy days as the days of man? are thy years as man's days,

6 That thou inquirest after mine iniquity,

and searchest after my sin?

7 Thou knowest that I am not wicked; and there is none that can deliver out of thine hand.

15 If I be wicked, woe unto me; and if I be righteous, yet will I not lift up my head. I am full of confusion; therefore see thou mine affliction.

CHAPTER 11

Then answered Zophar the Naamathite, and said,

2 Should not the multitude of words be answered? and should a man full of talk be justified?

3 Should thy lies make men hold their peace? and when thou mockest, shall no man make thee ashamed?

4 For thou hast said, My doctrine is pure, and I am clean in thine eyes.

5 But oh that God would speak, and open his lips against thee;

6 And that he would shew thee the secrets of wisdom, that they are double to that which is! Know therefore that God exacteth of thee less than thine iniquity deserveth.

7 Canst thou by searching find out God? canst thou find out the Almighty unto perfection?

13 If thou prepare thine heart, and stretch out thine hands toward him;

14 If iniquity be in thine hand, put it far away, and let not wickedness dwell in thy tabernacles.

15 For then shalt thou lift up thy face without spot; yea, thou shalt be steadfast, and shalt not fear:

16 Because thou shalt forget thy misery, and remember it as waters that pass away:

20 But the eyes of the wicked shall fail, and they shall not escape, and their hope shall be as the giving up of the ghost.[1]

[1] hope . . . ghost: *i.e.,* their hope will die.

CHAPTER 12

And Job answered and said,
2 No doubt but ye are the people, and wisdom shall die with you.

3 But I have understanding as well as you; I am not inferior to you: yea, who knoweth not such things as these?

7 But ask now the beasts, and they shall teach thee; and the fowls of the air, and they shall tell thee:

8 Or speak to the earth, and it shall teach thee: and the fishes of the sea shall declare unto thee.

9 Who knoweth not in all these that the hand of the Lord hath wrought this?

10 In whose hand is the soul of every living thing, and the breath of all mankind.

CHAPTER 13

Lo, mine eye hath seen all this, mine ear hath heard and understood it.

2 What ye know, the same do I know also: I am not inferior unto you.

3 Surely I would speak to the Almighty, and I desire to reason with God.

13 Hold your peace, let me alone, that I may speak, and let come on me what will.

14 Wherefore do I take my flesh in my teeth, and put my life in mine hand?

15 Though he slay me, yet will I trust in him: but I will maintain mine own ways before him.

16 He also shall be my salvation.

CHAPTER 14

Man that is born of a woman is of few days, and full of trouble.

2 He cometh forth like a flower, and is cut down: he fleeth also as a shadow, and continueth not.

3 And dost thou open thine eyes upon such an one, and bringest me into judgment with thee?

4 Who can bring a clean thing out of an unclean? not one.

5 Seeing his days are determined, the number of his months are with thee, thou hast appointed his bounds that he cannot pass;

6 Turn from him, that he may rest, till he shall accomplish, as an hireling, his day.[1]

7 For there is hope of a tree, if it be cut down, that it will sprout again, and that the tender branch thereof will not cease.

8 Though the root thereof wax[2] old in the earth, and the stock thereof die in the ground;

9 Yet through the scent of water it will bud, and bring forth boughs like a plant.

10 But man dieth, and wasteth away: yea, man giveth up the ghost, and where is he?

11 As the waters fail from the sea, and the flood decayeth and drieth up:

12 So man lieth down, and riseth not: till the heavens be no more, they shall not awake, nor be raised out of their sleep.

13 O that thou wouldest hide me in the grave, that thou wouldest keep me secret, until thy wrath be past, that thou wouldest appoint me a set time, and remember me!

14 If a man die, shall he live again? all the days of my appointed time will I wait, till my change come.

15 Thou shalt call, and I will answer thee: thou wilt have a desire to the work of thine hands.

16 For now thou numberest my steps: dost thou not watch over my sin?

17 My transgression is sealed up in a bag, and thou sewest up mine iniquity.

18 And surely the mountain falling cometh to nought, and the rock is removed out of his place.

19 The waters wear the stones: thou washest away the things which grow out of the dust of the earth; and thou destroyest the hope of man.

20 Thou prevailest for ever against him, and he passeth: thou changest his countenance, and sendest him away.

21 His sons come to honor, and he knoweth it not; and they are brought low, but he perceiveth it not of them.

22 But his flesh upon him shall have pain, and his soul within him shall mourn.

CHAPTER 15

Then answered Eliphaz the Temanite, and said,

2 Should a wise man utter vain knowledge, and fill his belly with the east wind?[3]

3 Should he reason with unprofitable talk? or with speeches wherewith he can do no good?

4 Yea, thou castest off fear, and restrainest prayer before God.

5 For thy mouth uttereth thine iniquity, and thou choosest the tongue of the crafty.

6 Thine own mouth condemneth thee, and not I: yea, thine own lips testify against thee.

7 Art thou the first man that was born? or wast thou made before the hills?

8 Hast thou heard the secret of God? and dost thou restrain wisdom to thyself?

9 What knowest thou, that we know not? what understandest thou, which is not in us?

10 With us are both the gray-headed and very aged men, much elder than thy father.

11 Are the consolations of God small with thee? is there any secret thing with thee?

12 Why doth thine heart carry thee away? and what do thy eyes wink at,

---

[1] **till . . . day:** *i.e.*, till like one hired to do a job, he shall look for payment or reward for his labors.
[2] **wax:** grow.

[3] **fill . . . wind:** puff himself up with self-satisfaction.

13 That thou turnest thy spirit against God, and lettest such words go out of thy mouth?

14 What is man, that he should be clean? and he which is born of a woman, that he should be righteous?

15 Behold, he putteth no trust in his saints; yea, the heavens are not clean in his sight.

16 How much more abominable and filthy is man, which drinketh iniquity like water?

17 I will shew thee, hear me; and that which I have seen I will declare;

18 Which wise men have told from their fathers, and have not hid it:

19 Unto whom alone the earth was given, and no stranger passed among them.

20 The wicked man travaileth with pain all his days, and the number of years is hidden to the oppressor.

21 A dreadful sound is in his ears: in prosperity the destroyer shall come upon him.

CHAPTER 19

Then Job answered and said,
2 How long will ye vex my soul, and break me in pieces with words?

3 These ten times have ye reproached me: ye are not ashamed that ye make yourselves strange to me.

4 And be it indeed that I have erred, mine error remaineth with myself.

5 If indeed ye will magnify[1] yourselves against me, and plead against me my reproach:

6 Know now that God hath overthrown me, and hath compassed me with his net.

7 Behold, I cry out of wrong, but I am not heard: I cry aloud, but there is no judgment.

20 My bone cleaveth to my skin and to my flesh, and I am escaped with the skin of my teeth.

21 Have pity upon me, have pity upon me, O ye my friends; for the hand of God hath touched me.

22 Why do ye persecute me as God, and are not satisfied with my flesh?

23 Oh that my words were now written! oh that they were printed in a book!

24 That they were graven with an iron pen and lead in the rock for ever!

25 For I know that my redeemer liveth, and that he shall stand at the latter day upon the earth:

26 And though after my skin worms destroy this body, yet in my flesh shall I see God:

27 Whom I shall see for myself, and mine eyes shall behold, and not another; though my reins[2] be consumed within me.

CHAPTER 38

Then the Lord answered Job out of the whirlwind, and said,
2 Who is this that darkeneth counsel[3] by words without knowledge?

3 Gird up now thy loins[4] like a man; for I will demand of thee, and answer thou me.

4 Where wast thou when I laid the foundations of the earth? declare, if thou hast understanding.

5 Who hath laid the measures thereof, if thou knowest? or who hath stretched the line upon it?

6 Whereupon are the foundations thereof fastened? or who laid the corner stone thereof;

7 When the morning stars sang together,

[1] **magnify**: praise.

[2] **reins**: the kidneys, supposed to be the seat of knowledge, pleasure, and pain.

[3] **darkeneth counsel**: cloud or confuse the issue.

[4] **gird . . . loins**: Ancient Jews wore girdling belts only for a journey or for hard work.

"Then the Lord answered Job out of the whirlwind...." Engraving by the English poet and engraver, William Blake.

and all the sons of God shouted for joy?

16 Hast thou entered into the springs of the sea? or hast thou walked in the search of the depth?

17 Have the gates of death been opened unto thee? or hast thou seen the doors of the shadow of death?

18 Hast thou perceived the breadth of the earth? declare if thou knowest it all.

19 Where is the way where light dwelleth? and as for darkness, where is the place thereof,

20 That thou shouldest take it to the bound thereof, and that thou shouldest know the paths to the house thereof?

21 Knowest thou it, because thou wast then born? or because the number of thy days is great?

22 Hast thou entered into the treasures of the snow? or hast thou seen the treasures of the hail,

23 Which I have reserved against the time of trouble, against the day of battle and war?

24 By what way is the light parted, which scattereth the east wind upon the earth?

25 Who hath divided a watercourse for the overflowing of waters, or a way for the lightning of thunder;

26 To cause it to rain on the earth, where no man is; on the wilderness, wherein there is no man;

27 To satisfy the desolate and waste ground; and to cause the bud of the tender herb to spring forth?

39 Wilt thou hunt the prey for the lion? or fill the appetite of the young lions,

40 When they couch[1] in their dens, and abide in the covert[2] to lie in wait?

41 Who provideth for the raven his food? when his young ones cry unto God, they wander for lack of meat.

CHAPTER 39

Knowest thou the time when the wild goats of the rock bring forth? or canst thou mark when the hinds[3] do calve?

2 Canst thou number the months that they fulfil? or knowest thou the time when they bring forth?

13 Gavest thou the goodly wings unto the peacocks? or wings and feathers unto the ostrich?

[1] **couch**: lie down.
[2] **covert**: thicket.
[3] **hinds**: deer.

14 Which leaveth her eggs in the earth, and warmeth them in dust,

15 And forgetteth that the foot may crush them, or that the wild beast may break them.

19 Hast thou given the horse strength? hast thou clothed his neck with thunder?

20 Canst thou make him afraid as a grasshopper? the glory of his nostrils is terrible.

21 He paweth in the valley, and rejoiceth in his strength: he goeth on to meet the armed men.

22 He mocketh at fear, and is not affrighted; neither turneth he back from the sword.

23 The quiver rattleth against him, the glittering spear and the shield.

24 He swalloweth the ground with fierceness and rage: neither believeth he that it is the sound of the trumpet.

25 He saith among the trumpets, Ha, ha; and he smelleth the battle afar off, the thunder of the captains, and the shouting.

26 Doth the hawk fly by thy wisdom, and stretch her wings toward the south?

27 Doth the eagle mount up at thy command, and make her nest on high?

CHAPTER 40

Moreover the Lord answered Job, and said,

2 Shall he that contendeth with the Almighty instruct him? he that reproveth God, let him answer it.

3 Then Job answered the Lord, and said,

4 Behold, I am vile; what shall I answer thee? I will lay mine hand upon my mouth.

5 Once have I spoken; but I will not answer: yea, twice; but I will proceed no further.

6 Then answered the Lord unto Job out of the whirlwind, and said,

7 Gird up thy loins now like a man: I will demand of thee, and declare thou unto me.

8 Wilt thou also disannul[1] my judgment? wilt thou condemn me, that thou mayest be righteous?

9 Hast thou an arm like God? or canst thou thunder with a voice like him?

10 Deck thyself now with majesty and excellency; and array thyself with glory and beauty.

11 Cast abroad the rage of thy wrath: and behold every one that is proud, and abase him.

12 Look on every one that is proud, and bring him low; and tread down the wicked in their place.

13 Hide them in the dust together; and bind their faces in secret.

14 Then will I also confess unto thee that thine own right hand can save thee.

15 Behold now behemoth,[2] which I made with thee; he eateth grass as an ox.

16 Lo now, his strength is in his loins, and his force is in the navel of his belly.

17 He moveth his tail like a cedar:[3] the sinews of his stones are wrapped together.[4]

18 His bones are as strong pieces of brass; his bones are like bars of iron.

CHAPTER 41

Canst thou draw out leviathan[5] with an hook? or his tongue with a cord which thou lettest down?

2 Canst thou put an hook into his nose? or bore his jaw through with a thorn?

3 Will he make many supplications unto

---

[1] disannul: abolish.
[2] behemoth (bi·hē′məth; bē′ə·məth): large beast, perhaps the hippopotamus.
[3] cedar: evergreen tree, in the Bible a symbol of grandeur and might.
[4] sinews . . . together: his strength is protected.
[5] leviathan (lə·vī′ə·thən): aquatic beast, perhaps the whale or the crocodile.

thee? will he speak soft words unto thee?

4 Will he make a covenant[1] with thee? wilt thou take him for a servant for ever?

5 Wilt thou play with him as with a bird? or wilt thou bind him for thy maidens?

6 Shall the companions make a banquet of him? shall they part him among the merchants?

7 Canst thou fill his skin with barbed irons? or his head with fish spears?

8 Lay thine hand upon him, remember the battle, do no more.

9 Behold, the hope of him is in vain: shall not one be cast down[2] even at the sight of him?

10 None is so fierce that dare stir him up: who then is able to stand before me?

11 Who hath prevented me, that I

---

[1] **covenant:** formal agreement, contract.
[2] **cast down:** discouraged, humbled.

---

should repay him? whatsoever is under the whole heaven is mine.

CHAPTER 42

Then Job answered the Lord, and said, 2 I know that thou canst do everything, and that no thought can be withholden from thee.

3 Who is he that hideth counsel without knowledge? therefore have I uttered that I understood not; things too wonderful for me, which I knew not.

4 Hear, I beseech thee, and I will speak: I will demand of thee, and declare thou unto me.

5 I have heard of thee by the hearing of the ear: but now mine eye seeth thee.

6 Wherefore I abhor myself, and repent in dust and ashes.

---

7 And it was so, that after the Lord had spoken these words unto Job, the Lord said to Eliphaz the Temanite, My wrath is kindled against thee, and against thy two friends: for ye have not spoken of me the thing that is right, as my servant Job hath. 8 Therefore take unto you now seven bullocks[3] and seven rams, and go to my servant Job, and offer up for yourselves a burnt offering; and my servant Job shall pray for you: for him will I accept: lest I deal with you after your folly, in that ye have not spoken of me the thing which is right, like my servant Job. 9 So Eliphaz the Temanite and Bildad the Shuhite and Zophar the Naamathite went, and did according as the Lord commanded them: the Lord also accepted Job. 10 And the Lord turned[4] the captivity of Job, when he prayed for his friends: also the Lord gave Job twice as much as he had before. 11 Then came there unto him all his brethren, and all his sisters, and all they that had been of his acquaintance before, and did eat bread with him in his house: and they bemoaned[5] him, and comforted him over all the evil that the Lord had brought upon him: every man also gave him a piece of money, and every one an earring of gold. 12 So the Lord blessed the latter end of Job more than his beginning: for he had fourteen thousand sheep, and six thousand camels, and a thousand yoke of oxen, and a thousand she asses. 13 He had also seven sons and three daughters. 14 And he called the name of the first, Jemima; and the name of the second, Kezia; and the name of the third, Keren–happuch.[6] 15 And in all the land were no women found so fair as the

---

[3] **bullocks:** young bulls.
[4] **turned:** *here,* ended.

[5] **bemoaned:** expressed grief for.
[6] **Keren-happuch:** ker′ən-ha′puk.

daughters of Job: and their father gave them inheritance among their brethren.
16 After this lived Job an hundred and forty years, and saw his sons, and his sons'
sons, even four generations. 17 So Job died, being old and full of days.

For Discussion

1. Who is ultimately responsible for Job's torments? Consider the nature of God and his relationship to Satan. To what extent is Satan responsible? Reconsider the opening five verses of the book. Was Job's torment deserved? Why, then, was Job tormented?

2. How does Job respond to the disasters visited on his family and his possessions? After the first series of tests, a second test is imposed upon Job. Why? How does this test differ from the earlier ones? How does Job's wife react to his new torment? Job replies: "What? shall we receive good at the hand of God, and shall we not receive evil?" (page 177). What does he mean?

3. Three of Job's friends try to comfort him in his afflictions. How successful are they? Eliphaz first praises Job's goodness, but he then insists that Job has misunderstood God's justice. According to Eliphaz, how does God distribute rewards and punishments? Eliphaz goes on to suggest that Job should be "happy" because of his afflictions (page 179). Why?

4. In despair, Job longs for death — or for understanding of why he should be made to suffer: "Teach me, and I will hold my tongue: and cause me to understand wherein I have erred" (page 179). Bildad takes his turn at explaining God's ways (in Chapter 8, page 180). What is Bildad's explanation? Job replies: "This is one thing, therefore I said it, He destroyeth the perfect and the wicked" (page 180). What does he mean?

5. Zophar, annoyed at Job's persistence, gives Job a stern lecture in Chapter 11 (page 181). What does Zophar tell Job? What opinions about the condition of man does Job express in Chapter 14 (page 181)? To what extent do Job's words apply to man in the twentieth century?

6. In Chapter 15 (page 182) Eliphaz summarizes the opinions of Job's friends and adds a question about the nature of man. "What is man, that he should be clean? and he which is born of a woman, that he should be righteous?" (page 183). In other words, all men are naturally sinful. Thus, being human, Job must be sinful. How does Job accept this explanation?

7. Finally, God answers Job "out of the whirlwind," largely through a series of questions that all tend to make the same point. What sort of things does God ask Job about? What is the combined effect of these questions? What do they say about the nature of God and his relationship to man? How does Job respond to the words of God? How does God deal with Job? How does he treat Job's friends? How do you account for the difference?

8. Most of *Job* is poetry, but it is not the kind of poetry we are used to. English verse usually contains the same number of syllables in each line (meter), and it often repeats sounds at the ends of lines (rhyme.) Hebrew verse uses neither meter nor rhyme. It is distinguished by its use of parallel thoughts in successive lines or half lines. Consider the following examples:

Doth God pervert judgment? or doth the
    Almighty pervert justice?
But man dieth, and wasteth away; yea, man
    giveth up the ghost, and where is he?

In each line the second half of the line repeats what is said in the first. The same thought is expressed in each half line. Discuss the effect of this repetition: is it merely pleasing to the ear, or does it heighten and emphasize what the poet is saying? Most lines in Job contain this repetition, but others follow different patterns. What other kinds of lines do you find? How are they constructed?

For Composition

1. Argument. At one point Eliphaz suggests that a man should be grateful for being made to suffer: "Behold, happy is the man whom God correcteth: therefore despise not thou the chastening of the Almighty" (page 179). Discuss the assertion that suffering enlarges one's character, and that without some suffering in his life, man would be shallow and trivial. Draw upon the experience of Job as well as upon other reading and your own experience for concrete examples to support your argument.

2. Comparison and Contrast. Though their scope is entirely different, similarities can be found between the Book of Job and the brief poem by Hopkins on page 174. Point out these similarities.

3. Analysis. According to Mary Ellen Chase in *The Bible and the Common Reader*, the monologues of Job and the voice of God out of the whirlwind "form, without question, the most exalted poetry in the entire Bible." Reconsider the voice of God out of the whirlwind, and in a well-organized composition try to account for the merit Miss Chase finds in it. Do you find the language powerful and moving? Your analysis should at least touch upon matters of diction, imagery, and emotional power. The imagery, for example, spans an enormous range of human experience. What is the effect of this diversity? You will be able to appreciate the poetic qualities of the speech better if you read it aloud at least once before beginning your analysis.

4. Exposition. How relevant is Job's situation today? Explain what the Book of Job would be like if it were written today. What would Job's questions be? What answers would his friends give? What answers would God give? If you wish, put your explanation in the form of dialogue, as in the Book of Job.

5. For Research. Read Archibald MacLeish's play *J. B.* and explain how MacLeish has adapted the Book of Job to contemporary society.

Words and Allusions

CHANGES IN LANGUAGE. Languages, like people and societies, are constantly changing. Some words cease to be used, others acquire new meanings, and new words are added. The only languages that do not change are "dead" languages, such as Latin, no longer in daily use.

As the most widely read book for several centuries, the Bible is the source of many words and phrases that have become part of our language These have come from the King James version of the Bible — the translation commissioned by James I of England that was completed in 1611. Although many versions have followed, the widespread use of the King James version has had an influence on our language unmatched by any other translation. But the meanings of many words have changed over three hundred and fifty years. Study the following terms from *Job*. What do they mean in their original context? What words would we use today to express the same thoughts?

escheweth (1:8)	*wink* (15:12)
suffer (9:18)	*travaileth* (15:20)
perverse (9:20)	*reproveth* (40:2)
mock (11:3)	*covenant* (41:4)
prevail (14:20)	*prevent* (41:11)

ALLUSIONS. Many phrases in our language are allusions (page 53) to the Bible, but we do not realize their full force unless we are familiar with their sources. From the Book of Job, we have allusions that are direct quotations: "The Lord gave, and the Lord hath taken away" (1:21) and "the skin of my teeth" (19:20). What do these passages refer to in the story of Job? What do we mean when we use them today? When we say that someone has "the patience of Job," what kind of patience do we refer to? What do we mean when we refer to someone as "a Job's comforter"?

"Lucifer in Starlight"

GEORGE MEREDITH

Lucifer, prince of darkness cast down from Heaven because of his over-weening pride, rises from Hell in the following poem to challenge God once more.

On a starred night Prince Lucifer uprose.
Tired of his dark dominion swung the fiend
Above the rolling ball in cloud part screened,
Where sinners hugged their specter of repose.
Poor prey to his hot fit of pride were those.   5
And new upon his western wing he leaned,
Now his huge bulk o'er Afric's sands careened,
Now the black planet shadowed Arctic snows.
Soaring through wider zones that pricked his scars
With memory of the old revolt from Awe,   10
He reached a middle height, and at the stars,
Which are the brain of heaven, he looked, and sank.
Around the ancient track marched, rank on rank,
The army of unalterable law.

For Discussion

1. Why did Lucifer rise up from his "dark dominion"? At the "middle height . . . he looked, and sank." What caused him to sink back down into Hell? What kind of universe do the concluding lines of the poem imply?

2. A "specter" (line 4) is an insubstantial ghost. What is the "rolling ball" in line 3? Who are the "sinners" in line 4? Why is the repose that they are hugging in sleep spectral?

3. Consider the image of Satan ascending. In line 6 we are led to *feel* his ascent; what verb allows us to? What is the effect of "western" in place of, say, "left" (or "right")? Identify the "black planet" in line 8, and comment on the effectiveness of the imagery that line conveys.

4. The poem contains a number of examples of alliteration, and frequently their effect is to emphasize a phrase, as in "dark dominion." Point to another example. What vowel sound is repeated in the tremendous closing line of the poem? What is the effect of that assonance?

For Composition

In both *Job* and "Lucifer in Starlight" God is challenged, and the challenge is effectively met simply by His displaying the wonders of His universe.

• Argument. To what extent do we live in a harmonious universe? If the universe, taken as a whole, is characterized by order and harmony, can it be unjust? Or is injustice something that is simply apparent and temporary, and that will in time be balanced out on a cosmic scale of values? Draw upon your own readings in history, literature, and science, as well as upon convictions based on your experience, to discuss these difficult matters in a thoughtful composition. You may find that ideas contained in "Lucifer in Starlight" will provide you with a good starting point.

About the Poet. **George Meredith** (1828–1909) gained fame through his novels — *The Ordeal of Richard Feverel, The Egoist,* and others. Although he is still known primarily as a novelist, he cared more deeply about his poems, and some critics believe that his poetry may prove of more lasting worth than his novels. Especially noteworthy among his poems is a sequence of sixteen-line sonnets, entitled *Modern Love,* which together make up a kind of novel in verse. *Modern Love* reflects the unhappiness of Meredith's first marriage, but it moves beyond personal considerations to explore the whole question of delicate relationships in human love. "His best poems," writes one critic, "such as 'Love in the Valley,' 'Modern Love,' 'The Woods of Westermain,' 'Hymn to Color,' and 'Lucifer in Starlight,' endure for their startling imaginative and intellectual power."

FROM

The Nicomachean Ethics

ARISTOTLE

One major source of Western culture is the Hebraic-Christian tradition, from which has flowed such expressions of emotion and truth as the Book of Job and the poetry of Hopkins. It is a tradition much concerned with justice as a concept closely associated with guilt and punishment. But there is another great source of Western culture — the Graeco-Roman tradition — and from that classic source we may learn of justice as a concept quite distinct from the justice of Hebrews and Christians. Here, in explanation of the classic concept, is part of Aristotle's famous discussion of justice from Book V of his *Nicomachean Ethics,* written in the fourth century B.C. (Nicomachus, Aristotle's son, presumably edited the work; hence the title. Ethics, of course, is the study of good and bad, of what constitutes right and wrong behavior.)

Before beginning Aristotle's essay, you should be aware that his concept of virtue is a mean between extremes of action and feeling. By contrast, vice is excess or deficiency. Danger, for example, provokes fear. Too much fear leads to the vice of cowardice; too little leads to the vice of foolhardiness. The mean amount — the appropriate amount — of fear leads to the virtue of courage.

Notice, incidentally, that virtue in this sense has none of the religious overtones that it has acquired through Hebraic-Christian influences. Similarly, justice — for Aristotle and the classic world in general — has little to do with guilt and punishment, as you will see.

We come now to investigate justice and injustice. We have to consider the kinds of acts with which they deal, the sense in which justice is a mean,[1] and the extremes between which it is a mean. . . .

Let us first then ascertain all the various meanings of the word *unjust*. A man is unjust if he breaks the law of the land; he is unjust if he takes more than his fair share of anything. Clearly then the just man will be (1) one who keeps the law, (2) one who is fair. So what is just is (1) what is lawful, (2) what is fair; what is unjust is (1) what is unlawful, (2) what is unfair. . . .

The lawbreaker being, as we saw, unjust and the law-abiding person just, evidently any lawful act is in some sense just; for all the acts prescribed by legislative authority are lawful, and we call them all just. Laws dictate on all subjects that which is to the interest of the community as a whole, or of those who are its best or leading citizens, either in virtue or in any other way. Thus in one sense we apply the term *just* to everything that tends to create and conserve happiness and the elements of happiness in the body politic. The law commands us to act as a brave man, that is, not to leave the ranks, or run away, or throw down our arms; to act as a temperate man, that is, to abstain from adultery and outrage; and to act as a good-tempered man, that is, to abstain from violence and abuse. And so with all the other virtues and vices, it prescribes some acts and prohibits others, and does all this in a right spirit, if it is a right law, or in a spirit not equally right, if it is a law passed in the heat of the moment.

Justice then in this form is complete virtue, though not in an absolute sense, still so in relation to one's neighbors. Hence it is often regarded as the supreme virtue, "more

Nicomachean: pronounced ni·kom′ə·kē′an.
[1] mean: a middle point between extremes.

"The Nicomachean Ethics," pp. 156–162 from *Aristotle on Man in the Universe*, edited by Louise Ropes Loomis. Copyright 1943 by Walter J. Black, Inc. Reprinted by permission of the publisher.

> Every virtue is included in the idea of justice, and every just man is good.
> — Theognis

glorious than the star of eve or dawn"; or as the proverb runs,

"Justice is the summary of all virtue."

It is in the fullest sense complete virtue, for it is the exercise of complete virtue. It is complete because he who possesses it can practice virtue not merely in himself but towards his neighbors, and many people can be good at home but not in their relations with their neighbors. So there is truth in the saying of Bias that "office reveals the man," for a man in office is at once brought into relation and association with other men. For this same reason, justice alone of the virtues seems to mean the good of the other fellow, since it implies a relation to other people and works for the interest of someone else, whether our ruler or a simple fellow citizen. As then the worst of men is one who shows his depravity both in his own life and in his relation to his friends; so the best of men is one who shows his goodness not in his own life only but in his relation to others; for this is a difficult task.

Justice therefore, in this sense of the word, is not a part of virtue but the whole of virtue; its opposite, injustice, is not a part of vice but the whole of vice. If it be asked what is the difference between virtue and justice in this sense, the answer is clear from what we have already said. They are the same, but the idea of them is different; the state of character which, if regarded in its relation to others, is justice, if regarded absolutely as a moral state, is virtue.

But we are now to investigate the justice which is only a part of virtue; for there is such a justice, we believe. Similarly, there is a particular injustice which we must inquire into. That it does exist we may infer from the following fact. A person may display other forms of wickedness in his conduct, and yet, though he acts wrongly, not take more than properly belongs to him. He may, for example, throw away his shield out of cowardice, or use abusive language out of bad temper, or refuse money to a friend out of stinginess. And one who takes more than his share may do no other act of vice — certainly not all of them — yet plainly he is wicked in some way, for we condemn his act; in other words, he is unjust. There is then an injustice which is a part of injustice in the broader sense, and a use of the word *unjust* in which it is a part of the wider field of injustice as law-breaking. . . .

Evidently, then, besides injustice in the broader sense, there is another particular injustice, which has the same name because its definition falls under the same head, for both have to do with our relations to other people. But the latter is bent on getting honor or property or safety or whatever comprehensive name we may have for all these, and inspired by the pleasure of gain, whereas the former is concerned with the whole wide sphere of virtuous action. . . .

As the person who is unjust and the thing which is unjust are unfair or unequal, there is evidently a mean between the inequalities. This mean is what is fair or equal; for any kind of action that takes too much or too little may also take what is fair or equal. If then the unjust is the unequal, the just is the equal, as indeed everyone sees without argument.

And since the equal is a mean between two extremes, the just will be a mean. . . .

Injustice . . . means unfairness or inequality, and the endeavor of the judge is to equalize it. For when one person deals a blow and the other receives it, or one person kills and the other is killed, the suffering and the action are divided into unequal parts, and it is the effort of the judge to restore equality by the penalty he inflicts,

ABOUT THE AUTHOR • **Aristotle** (384–322 B.C.) was born in the little town of Stagira on the northern coast of the Aegean Sea. When he was seventeen, he was sent to Athens to study with Plato at his Academy. There Aristotle remained for twenty years as Plato's greatest pupil and as a master in his own right. He was the first philosopher to divide philosophy into separate branches, and in each branch he made major contributions to the thinking of all men who followed. Until well into the eighteenth century his classification of animals was regarded as complete and sufficient. Literary criticism began with his *Poetics*, still regarded as a central document. Political scientists owe their existence to Aristotle's belief that "man is a political animal." And ethical philosophers continue to debate Aristotle's concept of man as being capable of reason and self-rule and his doctrine of temperance rather than self-denial. Along with his teacher Plato, Aristotle is one of the chief builders of our view of man in the twentieth century.

since the penalty is so much subtracted from the aggressor's profit. For the term *profit* is applied generally in such cases, though it is not always strictly appropriate. For example, the "profit" is his who strikes the blow, and the "loss" is his who suffers it; at any rate, when the suffering is assessed in a court of law, the one is termed profit, and the other loss. The fair or the equal then is the mean between excess and defect. And the profit and the loss are excess and defect, though in opposite senses. More of the good and less of the evil are profit, and more of the evil and less of the good are loss. The mean between them is, as we said, the equal, which we call justice. Hence corrective justice is a mean between profit and loss.

This is the reason why, when people dispute, they have recourse to a judge; and to go to the judge is to go to justice, for the judge is set up to be a sort of personification of justice. And people look for the mean in a judge, and sometimes call judges "mediators,"[1] which implies that if they get the mean, they will get what is just.

[1] **mediators:** literally, those who occupy the middle position.

For Discussion

1. Aristotle makes a distinction between two kinds of justice. In one sense, what is just is what is lawful. What is the other sense of justice? What are examples of each kind of justice?

2. According to Aristotle, "any lawful act is in some sense just," for laws "dictate on all subjects that which is to the interest of the community as a whole." Is this claim always true? Does Aristotle admit any exceptions?

3. Justice and virtue, we are told, are closely related. What is that relationship? In general, virtues benefit their possessors. A man who possesses the virtue of courage is himself benefited by that virtue; a man who is temperate benefits himself by his moderation. In what way or ways does justice differ from these other virtues?

4. Injustice is what is unfair or unequal. The judge, who is responsible for coping with injustice, is sometimes called a mediator. What does the term *mediator* suggest about the proper role of a judge? Where is justice to be found?

For Composition

By illustrating and supporting a topic, *examples* provide an effective way to develop a paragraph or essay. Examples are especially useful when the subject under discussion is abstract, such as a discussion of justice, or truth, or beauty, or goodness.

● **Example.** In a brief composition restate Aristotle's conception of justice in your own words by providing examples to illustrate every aspect of that concept.

Words and Allusions

RELATED MEANINGS. Some words are clearly related although they may not be regarded as synonyms. Since such words are often misused, it is well to give them special attention. Distinguish between the words in each of the following pairs: *ethics* and *morality; virtue* and *temperance; vice* and *sin*. Then use each of the words in a sentence that makes its meaning clear.

ALLUSIONS. The term *Aristotelian* is an allusion (page 53) to a method of inquiry used by Aristotle. From what you have observed in this selection from *The Nicomachean Ethics*, how would you describe the Aristotelian *method?* Check your own description against an account in a dictionary, encyclopedia, or other source of your choice. How does the Aristotelian method of inquiry differ from that of Plato in, say, the "Allegory of the Cave" (page 49)?

FROM

The Inferno

DANTE ALIGHIERI

As *Don Quixote* (page 56) is unquestionably the greatest achievement of
Spanish literature, so the towering monument of Italian literature is Dante's
The Divine Comedy, a work in three parts that describes a man's journey through
Hell, Purgatory, and Heaven. Indeed, in the judgment of most critics, only the
work of Shakespeare bears comparison with Dante's marvelous poem. As the
poet and critic T. S. Eliot has written, "Dante and Shakespeare divide the
modern world between them, there is no third."

The first part of the *Comedy* (the word *Comedy* is used in the medieval sense
of a work that ends happily; the adjective *Divine* was affixed to the title not by
Dante himself but by admiring readers more than two hundred years after his
death) describes Hell — the Inferno — as a funnel-shaped opening of circles
descending to earth's dead center. The Florentine Dante Alighieri, in his
thirty-fifth year, on the day before Good Friday of 1300, has found himself
lost in a dark wood, from which he is rescued by the spirit of the Roman poet
Virgil (70–19 B.C.), sent at the request of Dante's beloved Beatrice, now dead,
to guide the poet on a journey unlike any that man has ever been permitted
to make before or will ever make again.

That journey, presented in a series of cantos, or chapters, is an allegory,
in which every concrete detail represents an abstraction. Dante himself, for
example, represents the Christian Sinner; Virgil represents Human Reason; and
Beatrice represents Divine Love or Grace. But the poem can be read with delight on the literal level, and the student encountering *The Divine Comedy* for
the first time will no doubt be well advised to read simply for what happens,
and for the unforgettable images that flash before him. In so doing he will
leave the allegorical meanings to enrich a second reading.

CANTO I

Midway in our life's journey, I went astray
   from the straight road and woke to find myself
   alone in a dark wood. How shall I say

what wood that was! I never saw so drear,
   so rank, so arduous a wilderness!   5
   Its very memory gives a shape to fear.

"The Inferno," Dante Alighieri, translation by John Ciardi of Cantos I, IV, and V published by Rutgers
University Press and copyright 1954 by John Ciardi. Reprinted by permission of the translator.

Death could scarce be more bitter than that place!
    But since it came to good, I will recount
    all that I found revealed there by God's grace.

How I came to it I cannot rightly say,   10
    so drugged and loose with sleep had I become
    when I first wandered there from the True Way.

But at the far end of that valley of evil
    whose maze had sapped my very heart with fear!
    I found myself before a little hill   15

and lifted up my eyes. Its shoulders glowed
    already with the sweet rays of that planet*
    whose virtue* leads men straight on every road,

and the shining strengthened me against the fright
    whose agony had wracked* the lake of my heart   20
    through all the terrors of that piteous night.

Just as a swimmer, who with his last breath
    flounders ashore from perilous seas, might turn
    to memorize the wide water of his death —

so did I turn, my soul still fugitive   25
    from death's surviving image, to stare down
    that pass that none had ever left alive.

And there I lay to rest from my heart's race
    till calm and breath returned to me. Then rose
    and pushed up that dead slope at such a pace   30

each footfall rose above the last. And lo!
    almost at the beginning of the rise
    I faced a spotted Leopard, all tremor and flow

and gaudy pelt.* And it would not pass, but stood
    so blocking my every turn that time and again   35
    I was on the verge of turning back to the wood.

This fell at the first widening of the dawn
    as the sun was climbing Aries with those stars
    that rode with him to light the new creation.*

---

17. **that planet:** the sun.   18. **virtue:** beneficent power.   20. **wracked:** tortured.   34. **pelt:** coat.   38–39. **sun . . . creation:** The sun was said to have been in the astrological sign of Aries at the time of the Creation.

Thus the holy hour and the sweet season   40
   of commemoration* did much to arm my fear
   of that bright murderous beast with their good omen.

Yet not so much but what I shook with dread
   at sight of a great Lion that broke upon me
   raging with hunger, its enormous head   45

held high as if to strike a mortal terror
   into the very air. And down his track,
   a She-Wolf drove upon me, a starved horror

ravening* and wasted beyond all belief.
   She seemed a rack* for avarice, gaunt and craving.   50
   Oh many the souls she has brought to endless grief!

She brought such heaviness upon my spirit
   at sight of her savagery and desperation,
   I died from every hope of that high summit.

And like a miser — eager in acquisition   55
   but desperate in self-reproach when Fortune's wheel
   turns to the hour of his loss — all tears and attrition

    40–41. **sweet . . . commemoration:** Easter   49. **ravening:** prowling for food.
50. **rack:** that which holds or contains.

ABOUT THE AUTHOR • Born in Florence of a noble family, **Dante Alighieri** (1265–1321), studied ancient authors at the University of Bologna. Taking Virgil as his model, he set out to create a Christian epic as great as Virgil's *Aeneid.* The result was the *Divina Commedia,* a work consisting of three parts — the *Inferno,* the *Purgatorio,* and the *Paradiso* (Hell, Purgatory, and Heaven). One of the enduring works in any language, Dante's *Divine Comedy* contains the essence of all knowledge available to medieval Europe.

During much of his life the poet was exiled from his beloved Florence for supporting the losing side in a Florentine civil war, one that ultimately involved several Popes and the rulers of the Holy Roman Empire. Dante hoped that his fame as the author of the *Divine Comedy* would eventually win him a pardon, but that hope did not prevent him from placing many of his religious and political enemies, including some who were still living, in the deepest and most uncomfortable regions of his *Inferno.*

". . . follow me and I will be your guide / and lead you forth through an eternal place." Virgil rescues Dante from the beasts that had threatened him in the "dark wood" and leads him to the entrance of the Inferno. From a fourteenth-century manuscript.

I wavered back; and still the beast pursued,
   forcing herself against me bit by bit
   till I slid back into the sunless wood.   60

And as I fell to my soul's ruin, a presence
   gathered before me on the discolored air,
   the figure of one who seemed hoarse from long silence.

At sight of him in that friendless waste I cried:
   "Have pity on me, whatever thing you are,   65
   whether shade* or living man." And it replied:

"Not man, though man I once was, and my blood
   was Lombard,* both my parents Mantuan.*
   I was born, though late, *sub Julio,** and bred

in Rome under Augustus* in the noon   70
   of the false and lying gods. I was a poet
   and sang of old Anchises' noble son*

who came to Rome after the burning of Troy.
   But you — why do *you* return to these distresses
   instead of climbing that shining Mount of Joy*   75

---

66. **shade:** spirit.   68. **Lombard:** Teutonic people settled in the Po valley.
Mantuan: Lombard city in northern Italy.   69. **sub Julio:** in the reign of
Julius Caesar.   70. **Augustus:** Augustus Caesar.   72. **old . . . son:** Aeneas.   75.
Mount of Joy: way towards Heaven.

197

which is the seat and first cause of man's bliss?"
"And are you then that Virgil and that fountain
of purest speech?" My voice grew tremulous:

"Glory and light of poets! now may that zeal
and love's apprenticeship that I poured out   80
on your heroic verses serve me well!

For you are my true master and first author,
the sole maker from whom I drew the breath
of that sweet style whose measures have brought me honor.

See there, immortal sage, the beast I flee.   85
For my soul's salvation, I beg you, guard me from her,
for she has struck a mortal tremor* through me."

And he replied, seeing my soul in tears:
"He must go by another way who would escape
this wilderness, for that mad beast that fleers*   90

before you there, suffers no man to pass.
She tracks down all, kills all, and knows no glut,*
but, feeding, she grows hungrier than she was.

She mates with any beast, and will mate with more
before the Greyhound* comes to hunt her down.   95
He will not feed on lands nor loot, but honor

and love and wisdom will make straight his way.
He will rise between Feltro and Feltro,* and in him
shall be the resurrection and new day

of that sad Italy for which Nisus died,   100
and Turnus, and Euryalus, and the maid Camilla.*
He shall hunt her through every nation of sick pride

till she is driven back forever to Hell
whence Envy first released her on the world.
Therefore, for your own good, I think it well   105

---

87. **mortal tremor**: *i.e.*, of fear. 90. **fleers**: grimaces. 92. **glut**: fullness.
95. **Greyhound**: probably refers to Can Grande della Scala, renowned Italian
leader of Dante's time. 98. **between . . . Feltro**: Della Scala was born in Verona,
which lies between the towns of Feltre and Montefeltro. 100–101. **Nisus . . .
Camilla**: All were killed in the war between the Latians and the Trojans in Virgil's
Aeneid.

you follow me and I will be your guide
and lead you forth through an eternal place.*
There you shall see the ancient spirits tried

in endless pain, and hear their lamentation
as each bemoans the second death* of souls.   110
Next you shall see upon a burning mountain*

souls in fire and yet content in fire,
knowing that whensoever it may be
they yet will mount into the blessed choir.*

To which, if it is still your wish to climb,   115
a worthier spirit* shall be sent to guide you.
With her shall I leave you, for the King of Time,

who reigns on high, forbids me to come there
since, living, I rebelled against his law.*
He rules the waters and the land and air   120

and there holds court, his city and his throne.
Oh blessed are they he chooses!" And I to him:
"Poet, by that God to you unknown,

lead me this way. Beyond this present ill
and worse to dread, lead me to Peter's gate*   125
and be my guide through the sad halls of Hell."

And he then: "Follow." And he moved ahead
in silence, and I followed where he led.

107. **eternal place**: Hell. 110. **second death**: damnation. 111. **burning mountain**: Dante's image of Purgatory. 114. **blessed choir**: souls in Heaven. 116. **worthier spirit**: Beatrice. 117–119. **King . . . law**: Since Virgil lived and died before Christ, he is not eligible for redemption through faith. 125. **Peter's gate**: Dante puts this gate at the entrance to Purgatory.

For Discussion

1. At what point in his life does Dante's ordeal begin? From what has he gone astray? What is the dark wood like in which he wanders? At sunrise he finds himself before a little hill. How does the hill look? What prevents him from ascending it? Falling back, Dante meets the Roman poet Virgil "in that friend-less waste." What does Virgil tell him? Where does Virgil propose to guide Dante?

2. The concrete details in Dante's poem carry allegorical meanings, and by examining these details in Canto I you can see how Dante's allegory works. Life, as many other poets have imagined it, is treated as a journey, and Dante is "midway" in that journey. Since man's life span, on the authority of the Bible, was be-

lieved to be three score years and ten, or seventy years, Dante is thirty-five years old — or "midway." What do you imagine is the allegorical meaning of the "straight road" from which he has strayed? The dark wood represents error, and here, as elsewhere, darkness represents the absence of God's light while the sun indicates its presence. The three beasts that Dante meets on the "little hill" have been variously identified — most often as Fraud (the Leopard); Violence (the Lion); and Incontinence (the She-Wolf), the failure to control one's senses or drives, such as gluttony or anger. Since it is the She-Wolf that drives Dante off the hill, we can assume that he is guilty of Incontinence, as all men are, not necessarily of Fraud or Violence. To overcome sin, one must first recognize it, and this recognition requires the use of reason. Thus Dante will be guided by Virgil, who represents Reason. Virgil (or Reason) can guide Dante through "an eternal place" (Hell), but Reason cannot lead man to salvation. For Dante to climb the mountain of Purgatory to the gate of Heaven will require the guidance of Beatrice (or Divine Love). How does Dante respond to Virgil's description of the journey before him? What does this response say about him?

Dante's journey begins on the Friday before Easter, in April of 1300. By the evening of that same day, Dante experiences grave doubts about the journey he has undertaken. Canto II tells of them: "Who could believe me worthy of the vision" — the vision that Virgil has promised to reveal. To reassure Dante, Virgil explains how he came to be Dante's guide. To Limbo, the region of Hell where the Roman poet ordinarily resides, had come a blessed and beautiful lady. The lady was Beatrice, Dante's beloved in life, dead now, who had come down from Heaven because her dearest friend had strayed from the True Way and needed guidance for his soul's salvation. In answer to her request, Virgil agreed to serve as Dante's guide through the regions where he must come to recognize sin so that he might be able to renounce it. Learning of Beatrice's concern for him and encouraged by Virgil's reassurance, Dante regains his earlier confidence "Now lead on," he tells Virgil, and Virgil turns to continue the journey that soon leads them to the very Gate of Hell.

In Canto III, Dante and Virgil come to the gate of Hell where they read:

I AM THE WAY INTO THE CITY OF WOE.
I AM THE WAY TO A FORSAKEN PEOPLE.
I AM THE WAY INTO ETERNAL SORROW. . . .
ABANDON ALL HOPE YE WHO ENTER HERE.

Just inside the gate of Hell, in the vestibule, they find the souls of sinners who have taken no side in the eternal war between God and Satan. Accordingly, those sinners are given no fixed place, even in Hell. They wander eternally in darkness, stung by swarms of wasps and hornets that represent their guilty consciences. Dante and Virgil come to the river Acheron where newly arrived souls of sinners wait for Charon, the boatman, to ferry them over to their places of punishment. As is true of all Christian inhabitants of Hell, these are the souls of sinners who died without repenting their sins and receiving absolution from the Church. Recognizing that Dante is alive, Charon does not want to let him board the boat, but Virgil forces him to take them both. At this point Dante faints and does not regain consciousness until he and his guide have crossed the river.

CANTO IV

A monstrous clap of thunder broke apart
    the swoon* that stuffed my head; like one awakened
    by violent hands, I leaped up with a start.

And having risen; rested and renewed,
    I studied out the landmarks of the gloom   5
    to find my bearings there as best I could.

And I found I stood on the very brink of the valley
    called the Dolorous Abyss, the desolate chasm
    where rolls the thunder of Hell's eternal cry,

so depthless-deep and nebulous and dim   10
    that stare as I might into its frightful pit
    it gave me back no feature and no bottom.

Death-pale, the Poet spoke: "Now let us go
    into the blind world waiting here below us.
    I will lead the way and you shall follow."   15

And I, sick with alarm at his new pallor,
    cried out, "How can I go this way when you
    who are my strength in doubt turn pale with terror?"

And he: "The pain of these below us here,
    drains the color from my face for pity,   20
    and leaves this pallor you mistake for fear.

Now let us go, for a long road awaits us."
    So he entered and so he led me in
    to the first circle and ledge of the abyss.

No tortured wailing rose to greet us here   25
    but sounds of sighing rose from every side,
    sending a tremor through the timeless air,

a grief breathed out of untormented sadness,
    the passive state of those who dwelled apart,
    men, women, children — a dim and endless congress.*   30

And the Master said to me: "You do not question
    what souls these are that suffer here before you?
    I wish you to know before you travel on

2. **swoon**: faintness. 30. **congress**: assembly.

that these were sinless. And still their merits fail,*
   for they lacked Baptism's grace, which is the door   35
   of the true faith *you* were born to. Their birth fell

before the age of the Christian mysteries,
   and so they did not worship God's Trinity
   in fullest duty. I am one of these.

For such defects are we lost, though spared the fire   40
   and suffering Hell in one affliction only:
   that without hope we live on in desire."

I thought how many worthy souls there were
   suspended in that Limbo, and a weight
   closed on my heart for what the noblest suffer.   45

"Instruct me, Master and most noble Sir,"
   I prayed him then, "better to understand
   the perfect creed that conquers every error:

has any, by his own or another's merit,
   gone ever from this place to blessedness?"   50
   He sensed my inner question and answered it:

"I was still new to this estate* of tears
   when a Mighty One* descended here among us,
   crowned with the sign of His victorious years.

He took from us the shade of our first parent,   55
   of Abel, his pure son, of ancient Noah,
   of Moses, the bringer of law, the obedient.

Father Abraham, David the King,
   Israel with his father and his children,
   Rachel, the holy vessel of His blessing,   60

and many more He chose for elevation
   among the elect.* And before these, you must know,
   no human soul had ever won salvation."

We had not paused as he spoke, but held our road
   and passed meanwhile beyond a press of souls   65
   crowded about like trees in a thick wood.

---

34. **their . . . fail:** to gain them entrance to Heaven.   52. **estate:** condition.
53. **Mighty One:** Christ.   55–62. **our . . . elect:** These were worthy of redemption because they had worshiped the True God in life.

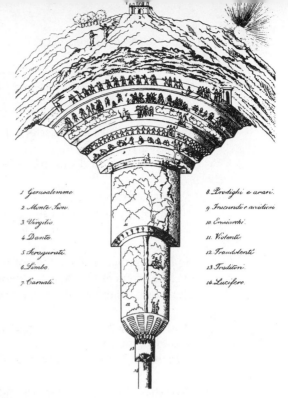

A diagram showing a side view of the circles of Hell. Virgil and Dante are at the upper left. Satan is seen at the lowest point in Hell at the center of the earth. From a nineteenth-century Italian edition of The Inferno.

1 *Gerusalemme*
2 *Monte Sion*
3 *Virgilio*
4 *Dante*
5 *Scapigurati*
6 *Limbo*
7 *Carnali*

8 *Prodighi e avari*
9 *Iracundi e accidiosi*
10 *Eresiarchi*
11 *Violenti*
12 *Fraudolenti*
13 *Traditori*
14 *Lucifero*

And we had not traveled far from where I woke
    when I made out a radiance before us
    that struck away a hemisphere* of dark.

We were still some distance back in the long night,   70
    yet near enough that I half-saw, half-sensed,
    what quality of souls lived in that light.

"O ornament of wisdom and of art,
    what souls are these whose merit lights their way
    even in Hell. What joy sets them apart?"   75

And he to me: "The signature of honor*
    they left on earth is recognized in Heaven
    and wins them ease in Hell out of God's favor."

And as he spoke a voice rang on the air:
    "Honor the Prince of Poets; the soul and glory   80
    that went from us returns. He is here! He is here!"

The cry ceased and the echo passed from hearing;
    I saw four mighty presences come toward us
    with neither joy nor sorrow in their bearing.

69. **hemisphere**: half-circle section.   76. **signature of honor**: high repute.

"Note well," my Master said as they came on,   85
  "that soul that leads the rest with sword in hand
  as if he were their captain and champion.

It is Homer, singing master of the earth.
  Next after him is Horace, the satirist,
  Ovid is third, and Lucan* is the fourth.   90

Since all of these have part in the high name
  the voice proclaimed, calling me Prince of Poets,
  the honor that they do me honors them."

So I saw gathered at the edge of light
  the masters of that highest school whose song   95
  outsoars all others like an eagle's flight.

And after they had talked together a while,
  they turned and welcomed me most graciously,
  at which I saw my approving Master smile.

And they honored me far beyond courtesy,   100
  for they included me in their own number,
  making me sixth in that high company.

So we moved toward the light, and as we passed
  we spoke of things as well omitted here
  as it was sweet to touch on there. At last   105

we reached the base of a great Citadel*
  circled by seven towering battlements
  and by a sweet brook flowing round them all.

This we passed over as if it were firm ground.
  Through seven gates I entered with those sages   110
  and came to a green meadow blooming round.

There with a solemn and majestic poise
  stood many people gathered in the light,
  speaking infrequently and with muted voice.

Past that enameled green we six withdrew   115
  into a luminous and open height
  from which each soul among them stood in view.

88–90. **Homer . . . Lucan:** the greatest of the ancient poets. 106. **great Citadel:** Dante's symbol for human reason.

And there directly before me on the green
    the master souls of time were shown to me.
    I glory in the glory I have seen!   120

Electra stood in a great company
    among whom I saw Hector and Aeneas
    and Caesar in armor with his falcon's eye.

I saw Camilla, and the Queen Amazon
    across the field. I saw the Latian King   125
    seated there with his daughter by his throne.

And the good Brutus who overthrew the Tarquin:
    Lucrezia, Julia, Marcia, and Cornelia;
    and, by himself apart, the Saladin.*

And raising my eyes a little I saw on high   130
    Aristotle, the master of those who know,
    ringed by the great souls of philosophy.

All wait upon him for their honor and his.
    I saw Socrates and Plato at his side
    before all others there. Democritus   135

who ascribes the world to chance, Diogenes,
    and with him there Thales, Anaxagoras,
    Zeno, Heraclitus, Empedocles.

And I saw the wise collector and analyst —
    Dioscorides I mean. I saw Orpheus there,   140
    Tully, Linus, Seneca the moralist,

Euclid the geometer, and Ptolemy,
    Hippocrates, Galen, Avicenna,
    and Averrhoës* of the Great Commentary.

I cannot count so much nobility;   145
    my longer theme pursues me so that often
    the word falls short of the reality.

The company of six is reduced by four.
    My Master leads me by another road
    out of that serenity to the roar   150

121–129. **Electra . . . Saladin:** all renowned heroes and heroines. 131–144.
Aristotle . . . Averrhoës: all famous philosophers and naturalists.

and trembling air of Hell. I pass from light
into the kingdom of eternal night.

For Discussion

1. Recovering from his swoon, Dante discovers that he is beyond Acheron in the first circle of Hell. This is Limbo, where reside the souls of pagans who lived virtuous lives but who died before the birth of Jesus; accordingly, they had no opportunity to accept him as their savior and thereby gain salvation. In this circle Virgil is ordinarily to be found with the other virtuous pagans of antiquity. How many names did you recognize? How are the virtuous pagans treated? What does this treatment indicate about Dante's attitude toward them? How is Dante received by the poets in Limbo? What does this reception say about him?

2. In Dante's *Inferno*, you will find not only that the punishment fits the crime (according to Dante's scale of values) but also that the condition of the sinners in Hell symbolically reflects their condition in life. Consider the virtuous pagans. They live in darkness except for the light of a "great Citadel" (line 106). This light represents the light of Reason, which pagans can possess. But we know that Reason is not enough to reach salvation. Thus their light is surrounded by darkness that indicates the absence of spiritual light, since they did not know the word of Jesus. In what other ways does their condition in Hell reflect their condition during their lives? For example, is there any indication that they suffer from guilty consciences?

CANTO V

So we went down to the second ledge alone;
   a smaller circle of so much greater pain
   the voice of the damned rose in a bestial moan.

There Minos* sits, grinning, grotesque, and hale.
   He examines each lost soul as it arrives   5
   and delivers his verdict with his coiling tail.

That is to say, when the ill-fated soul
   appears before him it confesses all,
   and that grim sorter of the dark and foul

decides which place in Hell shall be its end,   10
   then wraps his twitching tail about himself
   one coil for each degree it must descend.

The soul descends and others take its place:
   each crowds in its turn to judgment, each confesses,
   each hears its doom and falls away through space.   15

    4. **Minos**. in classical Greek mythology, a hero rather than a monster. Dante changes the myth to suit his own allegorical purposes.

"O you who come into this camp of woe,"
  cried Minos when he saw me turn away
  without awaiting his judgment, "watch where you go

once you have entered here, and to whom you turn!
  Do not be misled by that wide and easy passage!"   20
  And my Guide to him: "That is not your concern;

it is his fate to enter every door.
  This has been willed where what is willed must be,
  and is not yours to question. Say no more."

Now the choir of anguish, like a wound,   25
  strikes through the tortured air. Now I have come
  to Hell's full lamentation, sound beyond sound.

I came to a place stripped bare of every light
  and roaring on the naked dark like seas
  wracked by a war of winds. Their hellish flight   30

of storm and counterstorm through time foregone,
  sweeps the souls of the damned before its charge.
  Whirling and battering it drives them on,

and when they pass the ruined gap of Hell
  through which we had come, their shrieks begin anew.   35
  There they blaspheme the power of God eternal.

And this, I learned, was the never ending flight
  of those who sinned in the flesh, the carnal and lusty
  who betrayed reason to their appetite.

As the wings of wintering* starlings bear them on   40
  in their great wheeling flights, just so the blast
  wherries* these evil souls through time foregone.*

Here, there, up, down, they whirl and, whirling, strain
  with never a hope of hope to comfort them,
  not of release, but even of less pain.   45

As cranes* go over sounding their harsh cry,
  leaving the long streak of their flight in air,
  so come these spirits, wailing as they fly.

40. **wintering**: flying South for the winter. 42. **wherries**: carries swiftly.
foregone: forever. 46. **cranes**: large birds.

And watching their shadows lashed by wind, I cried:
    "Master, what souls are these the very air   50
    lashes with its black whips from side to side?"

"The first of these whose history you would know,"
    he answered me, "was Empress of many tongues.
    Mad sensuality corrupted her so

that to hide the guilt of her debauchery   55
    she licensed all depravity alike,
    and lust and law were one in her decree.

She is Semiramis* of whom the tale is told
    how she married Ninus and succeeded him
    to the throne of that wide land the Sultans hold.   60

The other is Dido;* faithless to the ashes
    of Sichaeus, she killed herself for love.
    The next whom the eternal tempest lashes

is sense-drugged* Cleopatra. See Helen there,
    from whom such ill arose. And great Achilles,*   65
    who fought at last with love in the house of prayer.

And Paris.* And Tristan."* As they whirled above
    he pointed out more than a thousand shades
    of those torn from the mortal life by love.

I stood there while my Teacher one by one   70
    named the great knights and ladies of dim time;
    and I was swept by pity and confusion.

At last I spoke: "Poet, I should be glad
    to speak a word with these two* swept together
    so lightly on the wind and still so sad."   75

And he to me: "Watch them. When next they pass,
    call to them in the name of love that drives
    and damns them here. In that name they will pause."

58. **Semiramis:** legendary queen of Assyria. 61. **Dido:** queen of Carthage, who broke her vow of faithfulness to the memory of her dead husband by falling in love with Aeneas, and by committing suicide when spurned by him. 64. **sense-drugged:** overcome by sensual appetite. 65. **Achilles:** Greek hero who agreed to desert and join Trojan forces because of his love for Polyxena, daughter of the Trojan leader Priam, but who was killed by Paris in the temple as he awaited his wedding. 67. **Paris:** Trojan hero whose elopement with Helen caused the Trojan war. **Tristan:** hero of medieval romance, who stole Isolde from her husband, King Mark. 74. **these two:** Paolo and Francesca.

Thus, as soon as the wind in its wild course
    brought them around, I called: "O wearied souls!   80
    if none forbid it, pause and speak to us."

As mating doves that love calls to their nest
    glide through the air with motionless raised wings,
    borne by the sweet desire that fills each breast —

Just so those spirits turned on the torn sky   85
    from the band where Dido whirls across the air;
    such was the power of pity in my cry.

"O living creature, gracious, kind, and good,
    going this pilgrimage through the sick night,
    visiting us who stained the earth with blood,   90

were the King of Time our friend, we would pray His peace
    on you who have pitied us. As long as the wind
    will let us pause, ask of us what you please.

The town where I was born lies by the shore
    where the Po descends into its ocean rest   95
    with its attendant streams in one long murmur.

Love, which in gentlest hearts will soonest bloom
    seized my lover with passion for that sweet body
    from which I was torn unshriven* to my doom.

Love, which permits no loved one not to love,   100
    took me so strongly with delight in him
    that we are one in Hell, as we were above.

Love led us to one death. In the depths of Hell
    Caïna* waits for him who took our lives."
    This was the piteous tale they stopped to tell.   105

And when I had heard those world-offended lovers
    I bowed my head. At last the Poet spoke:
    "What painful thoughts are these your lowered brow covers?"

When at length I answered, I began: "Alas!
    What sweetest thoughts, what green and young desire   110
    led these two lovers to this sorry pass."

99. **unshriven:** without having confessed and received pardon for his sins.
104. **Caïna:** a lower circle of Hell.

Then turning to those spirits once again,
   I said: "Francesca, what you suffer here
   melts me to tears of pity and of pain.

But tell me: in the time of your sweet sighs   115
   by what appearances found love the way
   to lure you to his perilous paradise?"

And she: "The double grief of a lost bliss
   is to recall its happy hour in pain.
   Your Guide and Teacher* knows the truth of this.   120

But if there is indeed a soul in Hell
   to ask of the beginning of our love
   out of his pity, I will weep and tell:

On a day for dalliance we read the rhyme
   of Lancelot, how love had mastered him.   125
   We were alone with innocence and dim time.

Pause after pause that high old story drew
   our eyes together while we blushed and paled;
   but it was one soft passage overthrew

our caution and our hearts. For when we read   130
   how her fond smile was kissed by such a lover,
   he who is one with me alive and dead

breathed on my lips the tremor of his kiss.
   That book, and he who wrote it, was a pander.*
   That day we read no further." As she said this,   135

the other spirit, who stood by her, wept
   so piteously, I felt my senses reel
   and faint away with anguish. I was swept

by such a swoon as death is, and I fell,
   as a corpse might fall, to the dead floor of Hell.   140

120. **Your Guide and Teacher:** Virgil.   134. **pander:** go-between.

For Discussion

1. What function does Minos serve at the entrance to the second circle? Minos is presented as a beast. Why is a beast appropriate here? The circle is "stripped bare of every light," and a strong wind whirls the sinners about continually. What, then, does their suffering consist of? Why is that punishment appropriate for the carnal sinners — for those "who betrayed reason to their appetite"? How does their condition in Hell reflect their condition in life?

2. Dante's meeting with Paolo and Francesca is one of the most famous encounters in the *Inferno*. Francesca explains how she and her husband's brother fell in love and as a result were murdered by her husband. How does Dante react to her story? What does his reaction indicate about his attitude toward love? Is there any conflict here between Dante's attitude and the inexorable laws of God that are reflected in the *Inferno?* What is recognizably human in Dante's attitude? According to the poem, what must he learn?

3. How just do you find the punishments that Dante has encountered so far? In discussing this question, you should keep in mind the relevant beliefs of Dante and his age: that the only way to spiritual truth and to Heaven is through belief in the divinity of Jesus; and that although love is a virtue, it must be controlled by the reason, which is God's greatest gift to man and which sets him apart from the rest of creation. Incidentally, since Paolo and Francesca were Christians, they could have avoided the sufferings of Hell if they had repented and sought salvation through their faith; but unfortunately they were murdered before they thought to repent. How just does their punishment appear in light of Dante's beliefs? How just does it appear today? What does the comparison suggest about the nature of justice?

4. The Divine Comedy is written in *terza rima,* or third rhyme: *a b a, b c b, c d c, d e d,* etc. Notice that each rhyme is repeated three times. This verse form is much easier to sustain in Italian than in English, since English has very few rhyming words compared to Italian. In what way has the translator, John Ciardi, modified Dante's rhyme scheme in this English verse translation?

For Composition

In all literary works there is a body of facts that must be grasped before the work can be understood. Dante's *Divine Comedy* is an allegory of almost endless meanings and implications, but the allegory is based on specific details, and it cannot be perceived without a grasp of those details.

1. Narrative. What happens to Dante in Cantos I through V? In your own words relate his actions and reactions as clearly as you can.

2. Description. Describe as accurately as you can the situation of the virtuous pagans and the carnal sinners. Be sure to include details of the setting in which each group appears.

3. Exposition. Explain the allegorical meanings and implications of either Canto I, Canto IV, or Canto V. Be sure to relate your explanation to specific details.

4. For Research. As Dante moves down toward the center of the earth, he observes a variety of sins and punishments, to which he reacts in various ways. In Cantos XXXII and XXXIII he finds those guilty of treachery in a circle called the Caïna (after Cain for his treachery to Abel). Find a copy of the entire *Inferno,* and compare and contrast Dante's treatment of the carnal sinners in Canto V with his treatment of the traitors in the later cantos. Include Dante's reactions to the two groups of sinners and whatever allegorical implications you can discover.

5. For Research. Find a copy of the entire *Inferno,* and consider Dante's arrangement of the whole range of sins. Prepare a report in which you discuss Dante's ordering of sins, from less to more serious, and his treatment of sinners at various levels. Consider also the shape of Hell as Dante conceives it and what that shape says about the number of sinners committing various sins. A drawing of the Inferno would be useful to accompany your discussion.

Words and Allusions

ALLUSIONS. The words *Dantean* or *Dantesque* allude to Dante's poem. From what you know of the poem, how would you explain these allusions (page 53)? The words *inferno* and *limbo* can refer directly to Dante's poem, but they are also used to refer to situations outside the poem. Use each word in a sentence that illustrates its general use while retaining the sense it has in Dante's poem.

The Divine Comedy

The opening cantos of *The Divine Comedy* provide only the faintest indication of the effect of the work as a whole. To read them and judge Dante's achievement thereby is like experiencing a few strong breezes and trying to describe a hurricane. Or better: it is like judging a finished mosaic on the basis of a handful of golden pieces that will fit eventually into a completed pattern.

The journey that Dante and Virgil make from Canto V of the *Inferno* onward leads them at first ever deeper into the darkness of Hell, down what in time will be revealed as nine levels, or terraces, where the sins of man are punished in ever increasing degrees of severity. Early in his journey, Dante feels pity for the sufferings of those whose souls are tormented. But as the descent continues, and he encounters the ever more grievous sins committed by the gluttonous, the hoarders and the wasteful, the wrathful and sullen, the heretics, the violent and fraudulent, the malicious, the hypocrites, the thieves, the evil counselors, the sowers of discord, and finally — worst of all — the treacherous, his heart hardens, and at one point he even adds to the suffering of a damned soul.

For allegorically he is making this journey to the center of the earth in order to learn to recognize sin. Unless the Christian — so the allegory is telling us — can recognize sin, he will not be able to renounce it, and true recognition of sin and of its consequences necessitates removing from our hearts all sympathy we might feel for those guilty of its commission. This is the hard lesson that Dante, under Virgil's guidance, learns in his descent.

Down go the voyagers, ever deeper into that dark pit, ever farther from God and the light of knowledge and grace, past souls buried in mire, or wrapped in flames, or bombarded with a mixture of stinking snow and freezing rain. In each case, the punishment is appropriate to the sin committed. The hoarders, for example, are a mob pitted against the wasters, both contending eternally over a boulderlike weight. Bubbles rise from slime beneath which the sullen are buried. Always the scene is created in unforgettable imagery, the sense of sight growing dimmer as the two poets descend, even as the sense of smell grows stronger.

Finally in the ninth and final level of Hell, in which the most extreme of sinners will be found, Satan himself, frozen with monstrous giants up to the waist in ice, gnaws perpetually on Brutus and Cassius, betrayers of Rome when they assassinated Caesar, and on Judas, betrayer of Jesus. These three, then, are the most profoundly sinful of all those who have ever lived, for they have betrayed those who would maintain God's order on earth through church and state.

Three: the number recurs throughout The Divine Comedy, not only in the *Inferno* but in all that follows. Jesus lived on earth for thirty-three years. There is an introductory canto to the *Inferno* (which you have read), then thirty-three cantos to describe Hell itself. Thirty-three more cantos describe Purgatory, and a final thirty-three describe Paradise. Three beasts obstruct Dante's passage to the Hill of Joy in Canto I. Three times three is nine, and there are nine circles in Hell, nine terraces on the Mountain of Purgatory, and nine spheres in the heavens of Paradise. Even the poem itself is rhymed in *terza rima*, each rhyme appearing three times and each stanza composed of three lines. In these and many other ways do the hundred cantos (ninety-nine plus the introductory) honor the Trinity that stood at the heart of Dante's Christian faith.

But to return to the journey. Sinners remain in Hell forever: "Abandon all hope, ye who enter here." Dante, though, is permitted to proceed, from the deepest level of Hell, at earth's dead center, out through a river that carries him and Virgil back to earth's crust, where, on the opposite side of the globe from where Jesus was crucified, rises the Mountain of Purgatory.

Now Dante's journey moves in the direction of ever increasing light. Virgil still guides him, up the nine terraces of the mountain, past singing choirs of angels and past the souls of those soon to be blessed: Statius, Hugh Capet, and others whose lives have been exemplary. But Virgil, the symbol of human reason, can guide the Christian only so far; reason alone will not admit the soul to Paradise. Divine Grace must do that, and in the allegory Grace, or Love, is represented by Dante's adored Beatrice, who finally appears before the poet at the gates of Paradise to lead him on.

They go upward together into the Ptolemaic heavens, into the nine spheres filled with music and beyond them to the Empyrean at their outer limits. There, exactly a week after the journey began, Dante reaches the realm of God's abode past time and motion. God in radiance that makes it all but impossible to see awaits Dante in the company of Jesus and the Virgin Mary, who receive the dazzled poet in a world where neither darkness nor the senses have any part. Here the poem ends, as far as is imaginable from the dark wood where it began.

What Longfellow called "This medieval miracle of song" ends and completes a form as bold and impressive as a cathedral — that only other product of the Middle Ages with which it can be fairly compared: equally bountiful in invention, equally solid in structure, equally delicate at the same time that it is overpowering. Indeed, in listing the three or four supreme triumphs of literary man — Homer, Plato, Shakespeare — Dante's name and his poem would be there, and the reader who finishes this extraordinary journey must echo the exclamation of the poet himself, in the company of the virtuous pagans at the first circle of the Inferno:

I glory in the glory I have seen!

• The word *universal* has been applied to Dante's poem, to indicate that his vision of mankind is relevant in all times and places whether or not one agrees with his particular religious doctrine. From what you know of *The Divine Comedy*, what aspects do you find relevant today? What aspects are no longer relevant?

In Summary

1. "Injustice is relatively easy to bear," according to H. L. Mencken; "what stings is justice." How would you interpret that remark? In what sense is the word *justice* being used there? In this section you have read a number of selections relating to questions of justice. In what ways have those selections enlarged your understanding of the concept? Your answer should refer to specific stories and poems, and you might also include a definition of justice as you understood the term before beginning the section, and your definition of justice as you understand the word now.

2. Imagine yourself charged with administering justice to some of the people you have come to know in the preceding pages. Invent a transgression for the dead man referred to in "The Isle of Portland" that would not contradict the poem. How would you punish that transgression? What punishment would be appropriate for Jim Kendall of "Haircut"? For Paul Dickson in the same story? What vice or sin would you identify as the one for which Farrington in "Counterparts" should be punished? If you were constructing a system like Dante's, where would you place Job in it? Be prepared to defend your administration of justice.

3. Consider the question of justice as it applies to selections read earlier (page 7–130). How just is the torment that the motorcyclist in "The Night Face Up" endures? What has he done to deserve his fate? Clearly, Young Goodman Brown made a pact with the Devil, agreeing to meet him in the forest in exchange for some benefits not specified in the story. What is the ultimate outcome of that meeting throughout the remainder of Goodman Brown's long life? Is his fate just? To what extent does Don Quixote deal justly with those he encounters early in his travels — at the inn and in the Andrés incident on the road? What justice is there in Peter Stockmann's position concerning the baths in *An Enemy of the People?* (Carefully think the matter through, instead of dismissing Peter's case out of hand.)

4. How specifically can you identify the setting of "Haircut"? (What state has a Northern Peninsula, how large is the barber's town, and about when would you guess the story takes place?) Define alliteration. How does it differ from assonance? What are the characteristics that most clearly distinguish Hebrew verse from English verse? The structure of "Counterparts" comes full-circle. Explain.

5. **Creative Writing.** As noted earlier (page 154), "Haircut" is written in the form of a monologue. Try your hand at telling a story that way, assuming a voice that is appropriate to your choice as speaker. But see how successfully you can imitate a voice other than your own. Think first of an anecdote or an experience that might form the basis of a short story, then imagine how someone with whose voice you are familiar might tell it. If the anecdote is one that the person you have chosen could be directly involved in, so much the better. A couple of pages should be enough to acquaint you with the challenges and the advantages of writing a story in the monologue form.

Reader's Choice

Aeschylus, *Oresteia.*

This great trilogy of ancient Greek drama — *Agamemnon, The Libation-Bearers,* and the *Eumenides* — tells of the murder of Agamemnon by his wife, Clytemnestra, her punishment at the hands of her son, Orestes, and the reconciliation of Orestes with the powers of justice.

Charles Dickens, *Bleak House*.

In an exposure of the absurdities of nineteenth-century British justice, a complicated suit involving a will, trusts, and missing heirs is finally settled after all of the inheritance has been dissipated through legal fees and court costs.

Victor Hugo, *Les Miserables*.

Jean Valjean, sent to the galleys for stealing bread to feed his starving family, escapes and attempts to lead a life of charity while pursued by those who place law above justice.

Franz Kafka, *The Trial*.

A young bank clerk, Joseph K, is accused of an unnamed crime by police from an unnamed court. Although K tries to argue his case, he is unable to communicate with his judges and is condemned and executed without knowing why.

Archibald MacLeish, *J.B.*

In a modern retelling of the story of Job in dramatic form, J.B., tested by God and the Devil, can accept the loss of his business, the death of his children, and agonizing pain, but insists on knowing the reason for his torment.

Herman Melville, *Billy Budd, Foretopman*.

Billy is tried for slaying the evil officer Claggart. Captain Vere must choose between the rigid law of the sea and Billy's moral innocence.

George Orwell, *Animal Farm*.

In resisting the exploitation of greedy human beings, animals overthrow their exploiters only to find themselves more harshly exploited by their revolutionary leaders.

Alan Paton, *Cry, The Beloved Country*.

A Zulu minister from a South African village loses his sister and his son to the corrupting forces of life in the city, but receives help and understanding from a white man his son has injured.

George Bernard Shaw, *Saint Joan*.

Prompted by her "voices" to lead the armies of France into battle against the English, Joan is betrayed, tried for heresy and witchcraft, and condemned to the stake.

Upton Sinclair, *The Jungle*.

A Bohemian workingman in the Chicago stockyards, learning of the filth and disease that is fed to people along with their breakfast sausage, joins the struggle of workers against their bosses.

Alexander Sozhnitsyn, *One Day in the Life of Ivan Denisovitch*.

A short novel by a former Soviet prisoner describes in terrifying detail the efforts by an inmate of one of Stalin's prison camps to survive one day at a time.

Richard Wright, *Native Son*.

In describing the career of a young Chicago Negro, Bigger Thomas, who commits two murders and is tried and executed, the novel asks who is really guilty, Bigger or the society that created him.

*This ancient Greek bronze figure, said to be either Posei-
don or Zeus, represents the traditional sense of greatness
derived from myth and legend.*

The Meaning of Greatness

When we apply the word *great* to a person seriously and not just colloquially ("a great guy" is not necessarily "a great man"), we usually mean one of two things. His accomplishments are so splendid that the world behaves as though they could only have resulted from some rare and special power in him, like Einstein and his physical theories. Or he may have no public accomplishment but be special for extraordinary personal and spiritual qualities, a perfect instance of this being the humble servant Félicité in Flaubert's "A Simple Heart" (page 266). In the highest instances of all, public accomplishment is at the same time a manifestation of the personal qualities, like Plato's Socrates in *The Apology* (page 245). Of course human affairs, if they are at all interesting, at all important, never are that tidy. Let us look at a few of the complications concerning greatness.

To begin with, there is the question of political power. It used to be that a man became the ruler of a powerful country simply by having been born the eldest son of the previous king. By the accident of birth he would be one of "the great of the earth," as the expression goes. But personally he might be stupid, weak, and petty, lacking any special talent, lacking what we commonly think of as true greatness.

Suppose, however, a man becomes a powerful ruler because of his own political or military skill and then rules that country disastrously, as Hitler and Stalin did. Not even their worst enemies would deny that such men were enormously astute and bold, as well as being famous and powerful. Yet are they "truly great"? Stephen Spender in his poem "I Think Continually of Those Who Were Truly Great" (page 243) would hardly say they are. Shelley in the sonnet "Ozymandias" (page 228) goes further yet. He implies that being a great and mighty ruler has, in itself, nothing to do with *true* greatness. "Look on my works, ye Mighty, and despair."

There is also the problem of mere fame. Often people confuse a man's fame with his greatness, and of course we would all like to think that fame is the just reward for greatness of accomplishment or of personal qualities. But unfortunately, only sometimes are things so justly ordered. Quite as often, fame is not the reward for anything more than a fad or an accident. In the 1930's, some people became famous by sitting on top of a flagpole for days and days, and they did this for no other reason than to become famous (and hopefully to pick up a little money). It is hard to think of many deeds less great than that. However, fame cannot be ignored in assessing a man's greatness. For though much fame is granted capriciously during a man's lifetime, there is also the fame which a man, or his work, is granted over the generations. After all the changes in fashion and custom and tradition, the names that weather the centuries are usually those of men who were truly great. Once again, we must remember that the word is used for some, such as Nero, who are mighty only in their wickedness.

There are all sorts of other obstructions between ordinary people and greatness. Perhaps the chief obstructors are those twins, envy and flattery. Envy hates the great for their very excellence and importance, while flattery lathers the great with such an excess of false praise that a reasonable person is likely to turn away in disgust. But it is possible to rise above these so as to be unaffected by them. Flattery and envy can both be thought of as tributes paid to greatness by those who are small of soul.

Most of us are not and never will be powerful, or highly gifted in some special way, or spiritually heroic. Then why does greatness in others, the very idea of human greatness, matter to us so much? Perhaps the root of our need for greatness to admire is that it extends our sense of human possibilities. God knows there is enough to be ashamed of and dissatisfied with in ourselves and the world we have made. But if you can feel in your heart, "He is like me but look what he has done," then you can imaginatively go beyond the limits of your own nature for a while and gratefully marvel at what it is to be a human being.

George P. Elliott

The Greatest Man in the World

JAMES THURBER

Our country has produced its share of heroes. Two who captured the hearts of all America did so by undertaking and successfully completing exceptionally difficult feats in the late 1920's. The shy, handsome young Charles Lindbergh, utterly alone, flew from New York across the Atlantic and landed in Paris May 21, 1927, thereby earning the proud and noisy acclaim not only of his countrymen but of all the world. Two years later Richard Byrd, a United States Naval aviator who earlier had flown to the North Pole and back, completed a flight to the South Pole — a dual achievement that none before him had even come close to matching. Yet great as they were, those great feats, by two appealing Americans, left plenty of room for other heroes who followed them, and worlds for other heroes to conquer.

Looking back on it now, from the vantage point of 1940, one can only marvel that it hadn't happened long before it did. The United States of America had been, ever since Kitty Hawk, blindly constructing the elaborate petard by which, sooner or later, it must be hoist.[1] It was inevitable that some day there would come roaring out of the skies a national hero of insufficient intelligence, background, and character successfully to endure the mounting orgies of glory prepared for aviators who stayed up a long time or flew a great distance. Both Lindbergh and Byrd, fortunately for national decorum and international amity, had been gentlemen; so had our other famous aviators. They wore their laurels gracefully, withstood the awful weather of publicity, married excellent women, usually of fine family, and quietly retired to private life and the enjoyment of their varying fortunes. No untoward[2] incidents, on a worldwide scale, marred the perfection of their conduct on the perilous heights of fame. The exception to the rule was, however, bound to occur and it did, in July, 1935, when Jack ("Pal") Smurch, erstwhile[3] mechanic's helper in a small garage in Westfield, Iowa, flew a secondhand, single-motored Bresthaven Dragon-Fly III monoplane all the way around the world, without stopping.

Never before in the history of aviation had such a flight as Smurch's ever been dreamed of. No one had even taken seriously the weird floating auxiliary gas tanks, invention of the mad New Hampshire professor of astronomy, Dr. Charles Lewis Gresham, upon which Smurch placed full reliance. When the garage worker, a slightly built, surly, unprepossessing young man of twenty-two, appeared at Roosevelt Field early in July, 1935, slowly chewing a great quid of scrap tobacco, and announced "Nobody ain't seen no flyin' yet," the newspapers touched briefly and satirically upon his projected twenty-five-thousand-mile flight. Aeronautical and automotive experts dismissed the idea curtly, implying that it

---

[1] petard . . . hoist: caught in its own trap.
[2] untoward: unseemly.

[3] erstwhile: former.

was a hoax, a publicity stunt. The rusty, battered, secondhand plane wouldn't go. The Gresham auxiliary tanks wouldn't work. It was simply a cheap joke.

Smurch, however, after calling on a girl in Brooklyn who worked in the flap-folding department of a large paper-box factory, a girl whom he later described as his "sweet patootie," climbed nonchalantly into his ridiculous plane at dawn of the memorable seventh of July, 1935, spit a curve of tobacco juice into the still air, and took off, carrying with him only a gallon of bootleg gin and six pounds of salami.

When the garage boy thundered out over the ocean the papers were forced to record, in all seriousness, that a mad, unknown young man — his name was variously misspelled — had actually set out upon a preposterous attempt to span the world in a rickety, one-engined contraption, trusting to the long-distance refueling device of a crazy schoolmaster. When, nine days later, without having stopped once, the tiny plane appeared above San Francisco Bay, headed for New York, spluttering and choking to be sure, but still magnificently and miraculously aloft, the headlines, which long since

had crowded everything else off the front page — even the shooting of the Governor of Illinois by the Capone gang — swelled to unprecedented size, and the news stories began to run to twenty-five and thirty columns. It was noticeable, however, that the accounts of the epoch-making flight touched rather lightly upon the aviator himself. This was not because facts about the hero as a man were too meager, but because they were too complete.

Reporters, who had been rushed out to Iowa when Smurch's plane was first sighted over the little French coast town of Serly-le-Mer, to dig up the story of the great man's life, had promptly discovered that the story of his life could not be printed. His mother, a sullen short-order cook in a shack restaurant on the edge of a tourists' camping ground near Westfield, met all inquiries as to her son with an angry "Ah, the hell with him; I hope he drowns." His father appeared to be in jail somewhere for stealing spotlights and laprobes from tourists' automobiles; his young brother, a weakminded lad, had but recently escaped from the Preston, Iowa, Reformatory and was already wanted in several Western towns for the theft of money-order blanks from post

ABOUT THE AUTHOR • James Thurber (1894–1961) had the gift of "seeing uncloudedly the ridiculous aspect" of life and of setting down his observations with a deceptively casual clarity and skill. Yet during much of his life as writer and artist — his drawings of sad dogs, unhappy men, and large determined women are unique — Thurber was almost blind.

One eye he had lost in his childhood. The other gradually deteriorated to one-eighth normal vision. Nevertheless, he continued until his death to produce vivid and witty prose. "There is an eerie, zany quality about his humor that hides a shiver under the laugh," one writer said of Thurber. "He is consciously whistling in a graveyard and the terror — which we all share — behind the mirth makes the mirth just so much the funnier."

offices. These alarming discoveries were still piling up at the very time that Pal Smurch, the greatest hero of the twentieth century, blear-eyed, dead for sleep, half-starved, was piloting his crazy junkheap high above the region in which the lamentable story of his private life was being unearthed, headed for New York and a greater glory than any man of his time had ever known.

The necessity for printing some account in the papers of the young man's career and personality had led to a remarkable predicament. It was of course impossible to reveal the facts, for a tremendous popular feeling in favor of the young hero had sprung up, like a grass fire, when he was halfway across Europe on his flight around the globe. He was, therefore, described as a modest chap, taciturn, blond, popular with his friends, popular with girls. The only available snapshot of Smurch, taken at the wheel of a phony automobile in a cheap photo studio at an amusement park, was touched up so that the little vulgarian[1] looked quite handsome. His twisted leer was smoothed into a pleasant smile. The truth was, in this way, kept from the youth's ecstatic compatriots; they did not dream that the Smurch family was despised and feared by its neighbors in the obscure Iowa town, nor that the hero himself, because of numerous unsavory exploits, had come to be regarded in Westfield as a nuisance and a menace. He had, the reporters discovered, once knifed the principal of his high school — not mortally, to be sure, but he had knifed him; and on another occasion, surprised in the act of stealing an altarcloth from a church, he had bashed the sacristan[2] over the head with a pot of Easter lilies; for each of these offenses he had served a sentence in the reformatory.

Inwardly, the authorities, both in New York and in Washington, prayed that an understanding Providence might, however awful such a thing seemed, bring disaster to the rusty, battered plane and its illustrious pilot, whose unheard-of flight had aroused the civilized world to hosannas[3] of hysterical praise. The authorities were convinced that the character of the renowned aviator was such that the limelight of adulation was bound to reveal him, to all the world, as a congenital hooligan mentally and morally unequipped to cope with his own prodigious fame. "I trust," said the Secretary of State, at one of many secret Cabinet meetings called to consider the national dilemma, "I trust that his mother's prayer will be answered," by which he referred to Mrs. Emma Smurch's wish that her son might be drowned. It was, however, too late for that — Smurch had leaped the Atlantic and then the Pacific as if they were millponds. At three minutes after two o'clock on the afternoon of July 17, 1935, the garage boy brought his idiotic plane into Roosevelt Field for a perfect three-point landing.

It had, of course, been out of the question to arrange a modest little reception for the greatest flier in the history of the world. He was received at Roosevelt Field with such elaborate and pretentious ceremonies as rocked the world. Fortunately, however, the worn and spent hero promptly swooned, had to be removed bodily from his plane, and was spirited from the field without having opened his mouth once. Thus he did not jeopardize the dignity of this first reception, a reception illumined by the presence of the Secretaries of War and the Navy, Mayor Michael J. Moriarity of New York, the Premier of Canada, Governors Fanniman, Groves, McFeely, and Critchfield, and a brilliant array of European diplomats. Smurch did not, in fact, come to in time to take part in the gigantic hullabaloo arranged at City Hall for the next day. He was rushed to a secluded nursing home and con-

---

[1] **vulgarian:** vulgar person.
[2] **sacristan:** sexton.
[3] **hosannas:** shouts of praise to God.

Welcome Home, *by the contemporary American painter Jack Levine, suggests the kind of welcome "Pal" Smurch expected after his dramatic flight around the world. In what ways does this scene reflect his expectations?*

fined in bed. It was nine days before he was able to get up, or to be more exact, before he was permitted to get up. Meanwhile the greatest minds in the country, in solemn assembly, had arranged a secret conference of city, state, and government officials, which Smurch was to attend for the purpose of being instructed in the ethics and behavior of heroism.

On the day that the little mechanic was finally allowed to get up and dress and, for the first time in two weeks, took a great chew of tobacco, he was permitted to receive the newspapermen — this by way of testing him out. Smurch did not wait for questions. "Youse guys," he said — and the *Times* man winced — "youse guys can tell the cockeyed world dat I put it over on Lindbergh, see? Yeh — an' made an ass o'

them two frogs." The "two frogs" was a reference to a pair of gallant French fliers who, in attempting a flight only halfway round the world, had, two weeks before, unhappily been lost at sea. The *Times* man was bold enough, at this point, to sketch out for Smurch the accepted formula for interviews in cases of this kind; he explained that there should be no arrogant statements belittling the achievements of other heroes, particularly heroes of foreign nations. "Ah, the hell with that," said Smurch. "I did it, see? I did it, an' I'm talkin' about it." And he did talk about it.

None of this extraordinary interview was, of course, printed. On the contrary, the newspapers, already under the disciplined direction of a secret directorate[1] created for

[1] **directorate :** board of directors.

the occasion and composed of statesmen and editors, gave out to a panting and restless world that "Jacky," as he had been arbitrarily nicknamed, would consent to say only that he was very happy and that anyone could have done what he did. "My achievement has been, I fear, slightly exaggerated," the *Times* man's article had him protest, with a modest smile. These newspaper stories were kept from the hero, a restriction which did not serve to abate the rising malevolence of his temper. The situation was, indeed, extremely grave, for Pal Smurch was, as he kept insisting, "rarin' to go." He could not much longer be kept from a nation clamorous to lionize[1] him. It was the most desperate crisis the United States of America had faced since the sinking of the Lusitania.[2]

On the afternoon of the twenty-seventh of July, Smurch was spirited away to a conference room in which were gathered mayors, governors, government officials, behaviorist psychologists, and editors. He gave them each a limp, moist paw and a brief unlovely grin. "Hah ya?" he said. When Smurch was seated, the Mayor of New York arose and, with obvious pessimism, attempted to explain what he must say and how he must act when presented to the world, ending his talk with a high tribute to the hero's courage and integrity. The Mayor was followed by Governor Fanniman of New York, who, after a touching declaration of faith, introduced Cameron Spottiswood, Second Secretary of the American Embassy in Paris, the gentleman selected to coach Smurch in the amenities of public ceremonies. Sitting in a chair, with a soiled yellow tie in his hand and his shirt open at the throat, unshaved, smoking

[1] lionize: treat as a celebrity.
[2] the ... Lusitania: In 1915, this nonmilitary liner was torpedoed and sunk by a German submarine; nearly twelve hundred civilians were killed, and the event aroused great anger against Germany.

> Fame has also this great drawback, that if we pursue it we must direct our lives in such a way as to please the fancy of men, avoiding what they dislike and seeking what is pleasing to them.
>
> — Benedict Spinoza

a rolled cigarette, Jack Smurch listened with a leer on his lips. "I get ya, I get ya," he cut in, nastily. "Ya want me to ack like a softy, huh? Ya want me to ack like that ——— baby-face Lindbergh, huh? Well, nuts to that, see?" Everyone took in his breath sharply; it was a sigh and a hiss. "Mr. Lindbergh," began a United States Senator, purple with rage, "and Mr. Byrd —" Smurch, who was paring his nails with a jackknife, cut in again. "Byrd!" he exclaimed. "Aw fa God's sake, *dat* big —" Somebody shut off his blasphemies with a sharp word. A newcomer had entered the room. Everyone stood up, except Smurch, who, still busy with his nails, did not even glance up. "Mr. Smurch," said someone, sternly, "the President of the United States!" It had been thought that the presence of the Chief Executive might have a chastening effect upon the young hero, and the former had been, thanks to the remarkable cooperation of the press, secretly brought to the obscure conference room.

A great, painful silence fell. Smurch looked up, waved a hand at the President. "How ya comin'?" he asked, and began rolling a fresh cigarette. The silence deepened. Someone coughed in a strained way. "Geez, it's hot, ain't it?" said Smurch. He loosened two more shirt buttons, revealing a hairy chest and the tattooed word "Sadie" enclosed in a stenciled heart. The great and important men in the room, faced by the most serious crisis in recent American history, exchanged worried frowns. Nobody seemed to know how to proceed. "Come awn, come awn," said Smurch. "Let's get the hell out of here! When do I start cuttin' in on de parties, huh? And what's they goin' to be *in* it?" He rubbed a thumb and forefinger together meaningly. "Money!" exclaimed a state senator, shocked, pale. "Yeh, money," said Pal, flipping his cigarette out of a window. "An' big money." He began rolling a fresh cigarette. "Big money," he repeated, frowning over the rice paper. He tilted back in his chair, and leered at each gentleman, separately, the leer of an animal that knows its power, the leer of a leopard loose in a bird-and-dog shop. "Aw fa God's sake, let's get some place where it's cooler," he said. "I been cooped up plenty for three weeks!"

Smurch stood up and walked over to an open window, where he stood staring down into the street, nine floors below. The faint shouting of newsboys floated up to him. He made out his name. "Hot dog!" he cried, grinning, ecstatic. He leaned out over the sill. "You tell 'em, babies!" he shouted down. "Hot diggity dog!" In the tense little knot of men standing behind him, a quick, mad impulse flared up. An unspoken word of appeal, of command, seemed to ring through the room. Yet it was deadly silent. Charles K. L. Brand, secretary to the Mayor of New York City, happened to be standing nearest Smurch; he looked inquiringly at the President of the United States. The President, pale, grim, nodded shortly. Brand, a tall, powerfully built man, once a tackle at Rutgers, stepped forward, seized the greatest man in the world by his left shoulder and the seat of his pants, and pushed him out the window.

"My God, he's fallen out the window!" cried a quick-witted editor.

"Get me out of here!" cried the President. Several men sprang to his side and he was hurriedly escorted out of a door toward a side entrance of the building. The editor of the Associated Press took charge, being

used to such things. Crisply he ordered certain men to leave, others to stay; quickly he outlined a story which all the papers were to agree on, sent two men to the street to handle that end of the tragedy, commanded a Senator to sob and two Congressmen to go to pieces nervously. In a word, he skillfully set the stage for the gigantic task that was to follow, the task of breaking to a grief-stricken world the sad story of the untimely, accidental death of its most illustrious and spectacular figure.

The funeral was, as you know, the most elaborate, the finest, the solemnest, and the saddest ever held in the United States of America. The monument in Arlington Cemetery, with its clean white shaft of marble and the simple device of a tiny plane carved on its base, is a place for pilgrims, in deep reverence, to visit. The nations of the world paid lofty tributes to little Jacky Smurch, America's greatest hero. At a given hour there were two minutes of silence throughout the nation. Even the inhabitants of the small, bewildered town of Westfield, Iowa, observed this touching ceremony; agents of the Department of Justice saw to that. One of them was especially assigned to stand grimly in the doorway of a little shack restaurant on the edge of the tourists' camping ground just outside the town. There, under his stern scrutiny, Mrs. Emma Smurch bowed her head above two hamburger steaks sizzling on her grill — bowed her head and turned away, so that the Secret Service man could not see the twisted, strangely familiar, leer on her lips.

For Discussion

1. "The Greatest Man in the World" first appeared in print in 1931. Is the account of "Pal" Smurch truth or fiction? How do you know?

2. Even while his amazing flight was in progress, "alarming discoveries" were being made about Aviator Smurch. What did reporters find when they visited his Iowa home? Why was it "impossible to reveal the facts" about Smurch's past? How were the authorities able to keep their secret about him from the American public?

3. If "Pal" Smurch were indeed the greatest man in the world, what constitutes greatness? Consider Smurch's personality and character. What, in general terms, had he done that would qualify him to be thought of as great? What qualities did he possess that, in your opinion, would deny him greatness?

4. **Satire, Types, and Stereotypes.** *Satire* is prose or verse that makes fun not of individuals but of institutions or customs or *types* of people. The purpose of satire (and "The Greatest Man in the World" is satirical) is to display weaknesses and folly in human behavior and attitudes. Clearly, then, a unique individual cannot be satirized, since he is unlike the rest of us. But mothers-in-law as a group, or absentminded professors as a type, or marriage as an institution can be satirized. Thus, in writing satire, authors rely on types; Smurch is a certain type of person rather than a complex individual full of contradictions. (Sometimes authors fall into the trap of inadvertently creating types where types are not appropriate. These *stereotypes* are a fault of characterization that lazily assumes that every detective must be hardboiled, every husband henpecked, and so on. Because they are unconvincing, stereotypes are a weakness in characterization; types, on the other hand, are a legitimate and necessary device in satire.)

Consider "The Greatest Man in the World." What does the story satirize? Are heroes as such what it is gently poking fun at? Or is it the attitude of the public toward its heroes? Obviously the latter, but how do you know? And specifically, what attitudes of the public toward its heroes are being pointed out as rather foolish?

5. Incidentally, "The Greatest Man in the World" raises the issue of justice. At a crucial moment in the story the President nods. What does the nod signify? To what extent can you justify the President's response? In answering, you will be probing some of the reasons why greatness matters, and why people naturally have a longing for examples of greatness in their midst.

For Composition

During his triumphal interview with the press, Smurch receives instructions in the accepted formula governing a hero's behavior before his public. Later, what emerges from that interview is a statement, purportedly by the daring aviator, that "My achievement has been, I fear, slightly exaggerated."

1. **Comparison and Contrast.** In a brief composition of two or three paragraphs, compare and contrast the nature of a public hero as implied on the one hand by the actions of the important officials surrounding Smurch, and by Smurch's own behavior on the other. Your composition should make clear the importance of such qualities as courage, modesty, forthrightness, and good sportsmanship in the makeup of a hero.

2. **Character Sketch.** Having examined "Pal" Smurch's behavior throughout the story, describe him in a character sketch. Refrain from exaggerating weaknesses and overlooking strengths. In other words, whether you like him or not, be fair in your evaluation of the "little mechanic."

Words and Allusions

ETYMOLOGY. The history of words — their origins and changes in form and meaning — is called *etymology*. What are the roots of the word *etymology?* The following words appear in Thurber's story: *laurels* (page 219), *quid* (219), *bootleg* (220), *snapshot* (221), *phony* (221), *nuisance* (221), *hosannas* (221), *hooligan* (221), *cockeyed* (222), *tattoo* (223). Using whatever sources you have available, find the origins of those words and relate the history of each to its meaning today.

Conversation with an American Writer

YEVGENY YEVTUSHENKO

A decade after the death of Joseph Stalin, it was still dangerous for Russians to criticize their government in even the mildest and most constructive way. Then a small band of Russian poets, including Yevgeny Yevtushenko, surprised the world by breaking into print with honest verses about what had been and still was happening in their homeland. Western observers expected such bold writers to be severely reprimanded by the Soviet Union. Some were, to be sure, but others seemed to get away with voicing their criticisms, and were even permitted to leave Russia and visit abroad. Yevtushenko himself came to America for a time; his warm reception here provides the occasion for the poem that follows.

"You're a fearless young man — "
                          they tell me. . . .
It's not true.
           I've never been fearless.
I've considered it unworthy, simply,
to sink to my colleagues' cowardice.

I didn't shake any sort of foundations.   5
Laughed at the false and pompous,
                     that's all.
Wrote — that's all.
               Never wrote denunciations.*
And tried to say
          just what I thought.

Yes,
    talented people I defended,
branded the incapable,
              into literature crawling,   10
but did this because, in general, one has to,
and now about my fearlessness they're talking.

7. **denunciations**: public condemnations.

Oh, with feelings of bitter shame
our descendants,
                    debunking* worthlessness,
will remember
            those times
                    so strange   15
when simple honesty
                    was called fearlessness.

14. **debunking**: exposing as sham.

For Discussion

1. According to the poem, what will future ages find strange about the world in which Yevtushenko lived? How will they feel about that world?

2. The poem suggests the kinds of subjects Yevtushenko has chosen to write about in his work. Has he written propaganda? Whom does his poetry criticize? Whom does it defend? Whom does it make fun of?

3. Greatness involves courage. "Pal" Smurch in the preceding story had courage, and he had plenty of arrogance too. By contrast, Yevtushenko's poem is modest. What statements in the poem convey the poet's modesty? Is modesty a necessary attribute of greatness? Discuss.

For Composition

You have already considered several ways of developing an expository paragraph or essay; for example, by telling a story to support a point (narration), by pointing out similarities and differences (comparison and contrast), or by classifying or dividing your subject (analysis). Frequently you will find it necessary to use *definition* in developing what you are saying. A definition may be brief or it may fill an entire essay or even a book. Abstractions, for instance, like beauty or democracy, usually require considerable space to define. Moreover, almost every writer using such terms carefully will need to define for his readers the precise sense in which he wants them to be understood.

● **Definition.** These first two selections have led you to think a little about what constitutes greatness. What attributes must a person possess in order to be regarded as great? Must he, for example, be modest? Write your own definition of *greatness*, clarifying your understanding of the term by mentioning specific examples of greatness that you have encountered in your reading or experience.

About the Poet. After the death of Stalin in 1953, the Soviet Union for a time underwent a period of liberalization in the arts known as "the Thaw." One of the youngest and most vigorous of the new Soviet poets was **Yevgeny Yevtushenko** (1933–   ), who before he was thirty was internationally known as the voice of the post-Stalin generation in Russia. "Let us be extremely outspoken," he proclaimed. In a famous poem, "Babi Yar," named after a place where the Nazis killed thousands of Jews in World War II, he condemns by implication anti-Semitism in Soviet Russia.

In recent years Yevtushenko's voice has been heard less often, but his vigorous and lyrical poetry and his *Precocious Autobiography* continue to circulate widely in his own country and in the West. From time to time he continues to speak out against injustice, most recently against the murder of Martin Luther King. "When I received this news," he wrote, "that same bullet entered me."

[Handwritten top margin: Rhymed Iambic Pentameter/Irony]
[Handwritten: *Illusory nature of power*]

Ozymandias

PERCY BYSSHE SHELLEY

One of the great Pharaohs of ancient Egypt was the haughty Rameses II,
called Ozymandias, who during his lifetime had his subjects erect at Thebes a
colossal statue in his honor.

[Handwritten annotations: speaker, Diction, slant rhyme]

I met a traveler from an antique* land   A
Who said: Two vast and trunkless legs of stone   B
Stand in the desert. Near them, on the sand,   A
Half sunk, a shattered visage lies, whose frown,   B
And wrinkled lip, and sneer of cold command,   A   5
Tell that its sculptor well those passions read   C
Which yet survive, stamped on these lifeless things, D
The hand that mocked them and the heart that fed   C
And on the pedestal these words appear —   E
My name is Ozymandias, king of kings: E   10
Look on my works, ye Mighty, and despair!   E
Nothing beside remains. Round the decay   F
Of that colossal wreck, boundless and bare   E
The lone and level sands stretch far away."   F

[Handwritten annotations: despise king, sculptor's statue in middle of kingdom, focal point, high opinion of himself, nothing left of kingdom, Imagery, sands of time, decay, eternity]

1. **antique**: ancient.

For Discussion

[Handwritten: *Echoes* — Rhyming!! — sound of words]

1. The pedestal of the ruined statue refers
to Ozymandias' "works." Why might those
works cause even the mighty of the world to
despair? What has become of those works?
What is the theme of "Ozymandias"?

2. Like such other abstractions as truth and
justice, greatness is difficult to define — and to
achieve. One reason why it is elusive is that
most of us have within ourselves traits that
limit our potential for greatness. Any cowardice in our make-up, for example, would impair
our abilities to do something great. Too much
common sense gets in the way of greatness;
common sense would have told "Pal" Smurch
not to fly around the world and would have
told the poet Yevtushenko either to praise his
government or keep his mouth shut. "Ozymandias" suggests another reason why some
people might consider greatness hardly worth
striving for. What is that reason?

3. **Sonnet.** No doubt you recognized this
poem as belonging to a special group called
sonnets. Earlier in this book you encountered
other examples of sonnets. Where? What are
the characteristics of a sonnet? Does Shelley's
sonnet fit those characteristics?

For Composition

● **Analysis.** Shelley's poem is filled with irony.
Point out the images that express that irony
and explain how they do so.

About the Poet. From his early days at Oxford, **Percy Bysshe Shelley** (1792–1822) took a
militant stand on the issues of his time. He
supported the Irish struggle for independence
from England and argued the cause of worker's rights in England. A radical poet as well
as a radical pamphleteer, he endures today
as the creator of such poems as "Prometheus
Unbound," "Ode to the West Wind," and the
elegy commemorating his friend John Keats,
"Adonais." Shelley lived a stormy, unsettled
life, a life that ended at twenty-nine when he
drowned while sailing his boat *Ariel* off the
coast of Italy.

[Handwritten bottom margin: alliteration - consonant rhyme (beginning), assonance - vowel rhyme, consonance - end rhyme]

228

The Myth of Sisyphus

ALBERT CAMUS

"The workman of today," according to the following rather difficult essay, "works every day in his life at the same tasks." Students may feel that the judgment describes their lot as well. What chances for greatness can such a routine fate provide? Indeed, isn't spending a life that way absurd? Yes, writes Camus, as absurd as the fate of Sisyphus, that mortal whom the gods condemned to an eternity of striving with all his strength for no purpose and toward no end. Yet absurd though it is — and even tragic — such a fate as Sisyphus' can also be seen as happy.

The gods had condemned Sisyphus to ceaselessly rolling a rock to the top of a mountain, whence the stone would fall back of its own weight. They had thought with some reason that there is no more dreadful punishment than futile and hopeless labor.

If one believes Homer, Sisyphus was the wisest and most prudent of mortals. According to another tradition, however, he was disposed to practice the profession of highwayman. I see no contradiction in this. Opinions differ as to the reasons why he became the futile laborer of the underworld. To begin with, he is accused of a certain levity[1] in regard to the gods. He stole their secrets. Aegina, the daughter of Aesopus, was carried off by Jupiter. The father was shocked by that disappearance and complained to Sisyphus. He, who knew of the abduction, offered to tell about it on condition that Aesopus would give water to the citadel of Corinth. To the celestial thunderbolts he preferred the benediction of water. He was punished for this in the underworld. Homer tells us also that Sisyphus had put Death in chains. Pluto could not endure the sight of his deserted, silent empire. He dispatched the god of war, who liberated Death from the hands of her conqueror.

It is said also that Sisyphus, being near to death, rashly wanted to test his wife's love. He ordered her to cast his unburied body into the middle of the public square. Sisyphus woke up in the underworld. And there, annoyed by an obedience so contrary to human love, he obtained from Pluto permission to return to earth in order to chastise his wife. But when he had seen again the face of this world, enjoyed water and sun, warm stones and the sea, he no longer wanted to go back to the infernal darkness. Recalls, signs of anger, warnings were of no avail. Many years more he lived facing the curve of the gulf, the sparkling sea, and the smiles of earth. A decree of the gods was necessary. Mercury came and seized the impudent man by the collar and, snatching him from his joys, led him forcibly back to the underworld, where his rock was ready for him.

You have already grasped that Sisyphus is the absurd hero. He *is*, as much through his passions as through his torture. His scorn of the gods, his hatred of death, and his passion for life won him that unspeakable penalty in which the whole being is exerted toward accomplishing nothing. This is the price that must be paid for the pas-

---

Sisyphus: pronounced sis′i·fəs.

[1] levity: disrespectful frivolity.

"All Sisyphus' silent joy is contained therein. His fate belongs to him. His rock is his thing." Sisyphus *by Titian.*

into them. As for this myth, one sees merely the whole effort of a body straining to raise the huge stone, to roll it and push it up a slope a hundred times over; one sees the face screwed up, the cheek tight against the stone, the shoulder bracing the clay-covered mass, the foot wedging it, the fresh starts with arms outstretched, the wholly human security of two earth-clotted hands. At the very end of his long effort measured by skyless space and time without depth, the purpose is achieved. Then Sisyphus watches the stone rush down in a few moments toward that lower world whence he will have to push it up again toward the summit. He goes back down to the plain.

It is during that return, that pause, that Sisyphus interests me. A face that toils so close to stones is already stone itself! I see that man going back down with a heavy yet measured step toward the torment of which he will never know the end. That hour like a breathing space which returns as surely as his suffering, that is the hour of consciousness. At each of those moments when he leaves the heights and gradually

sions of this earth. Nothing is told us about Sisyphus in the underworld. Myths are made for the imagination to breathe life

ABOUT THE AUTHOR • In his early writings **Albert Camus** (1913–1960) saw in the Sisyphus legend "the hopeless, meaningless, eternal uphill labor which is human life," but in later years he became more optimistic about man's destiny. "In the midst of winter," he declared, "I finally learned that there was in me an invincible summer." Born in Algeria of an Alsatian father and a Spanish mother, Camus came to literature by way of his interest in the theater, first as an actor in a small Algerian company and later as a playwright. He went to Paris in 1940 as a journalist, only to flee before the Nazis, but later he returned and edited a resistance newspaper. He first gained attention with his novel *The Stranger* in 1946; later he followed that success with *The Plague* and *The Fall*. He is author also of several plays, of which *Caligula* is the best known. Camus has been a great favorite with young people. His younger admirers have called him their "conscience . . . which is making a valiant effort to understand the age and to prepare a renascence from the ruins." Camus's life ended tragically at the age of forty-seven in an automobile accident.

sinks toward the lairs of the gods, he is superior to his fate. He is stronger than his rock.

If this myth is tragic, that is because its hero is conscious. Where would his torture be, indeed, if at every step the hope of succeeding upheld him? The workman of today works every day in his life at the same tasks, and this fate is no less absurd. But it is tragic only at the rare moments when it becomes conscious. Sisyphus, proletarian of the gods,[1] powerless and rebellious, knows the whole extent of his wretched condition: it is what he thinks of during his descent. The lucidity that was to constitute his torture at the same time crowns his victory. There is no fate that cannot be surmounted by scorn.

If the descent is thus sometimes performed in sorrow, it can also take place in joy. This word is not too much. Again I fancy Sisyphus returning toward his rock, and the sorrow was in the beginning. When the images of earth cling too tightly to memory, when the call of happiness becomes too insistent, it happens that melancholy rises in man's heart: this is the rock's victory, this is the rock itself. The boundless grief is too heavy to bear. These are our nights of Gethsemane.[2] But crushing truths perish from being acknowledged. Thus, Oedipus[3] at the outset obeys fate without knowing it. But from the moment he knows, his tragedy begins. Yet at the same moment, blind and desperate, he realizes that the only bond linking him to the world is the cool hand of a girl. Then a tremendous remark rings out: "Despite so many ordeals, my advanced age and the nobility of my soul make me conclude that all is well." Sophocles' Oedipus, like Dos-

[1] **proletarian . . . gods:** exploited by the gods.
[2] **Gethsemane:** scene of the agony of Jesus; *here,* intense suffering.
[3] **Oedipus:** protagonist of Sophocles' classic tragedy (see page 349).

> That man has shown himself great who has never grieved in evil days and never bewailed his destiny.
>
> — Seneca

toevsky's Kirilov, thus gives the recipe for the absurd victory. Ancient wisdom confirms modern heroism.

One does not discover the absurd without being tempted to write a manual of happiness. "What! by such narrow ways — ?" There is but one world, however. Happiness and the absurd are two sons of the same earth. They are inseparable. It would be a mistake to say that happiness necessarily springs from the absurd discovery. It happens as well that the feeling of the absurd springs from happiness. "I conclude that all is well," says Oedipus, and that remark is sacred. It echoes in the wild and limited universe of man. It teaches that all is not, has not been, exhausted. It drives out of this world a god who had come into it with dissatisfaction and a preference for futile sufferings. It makes of fate a human matter, which must be settled among men.

All Sisyphus' silent joy is contained therein. His fate belongs to him. His rock is his thing. Likewise, the absurd man, when he contemplates his torment, silences all the idols. In the universe suddenly restored to its silence, the myriad wondering little voices of the earth rise up. Unconscious, secret calls, invitations from all the faces, they are the necessary reverse and price of victory. There is no sun without shadow, and it is essential to know the night. The absurd man says yes and his effort will henceforth be unceasing. If there is a personal fate, there is no higher destiny, or at least there is but one which he concludes is inevitable and despicable. For the rest, he knows himself to be the master of his days. At that subtle moment when man glances backward over his life, Sisyphus returning toward his rock, in that slight pivoting he contemplates that series of unrelated actions which becomes his fate, created· by him, combined under his memory's eye and soon sealed by his death. Thus, convinced of the wholly human origin of all that is human, a blind man eager to see who knows that the night has no end, he is still on the go. The rock is still rolling.

I leave Sisyphus at the foot of the mountain! One always finds one's burden again. But Sisyphus teaches the higher fidelity that negates the gods and raises rocks. He too concludes that all is well. This universe henceforth without a master seems to him neither sterile nor futile. Each atom of that stone, each mineral flake of that night-filled mountain, in itself forms a world. The struggle itself toward the heights is enough to fill a man's heart. One must imagine Sisyphus happy.

For Discussion

1. You may find it necessary to reread this essay carefully two or three times to follow Camus's argument. Sisyphus he sees as in some ways like all the rest of us, engaged in a repeated cycle of labor that is ultimately pointless and futile. What portion of the cycle interests the author most? Why?

2. Camus suggests that only those people who are· conscious of the pattern of their lives — who can at times stand off from that pattern and see it for what it is — can be thought of as either tragic or happy. Most of us live the bulk of our lives day by day, imprisoned in the present, and it is only in those rare "hours of consciousness" that we rise above ourselves and become superior to our fate. What connection does the author find between happiness and an awareness of absurdity? Why does he feel that Sisyphus must be happy?

3. Though in some ways Sisyphus is like the rest of us, he is quite different from most of us, too. On earth Sisyphus was a hero, a man of great dimensions. What acts and attributes of his that support his heroism does the essay mention? Why was Sisyphus condemned to eternal punishment?

4. Many of us avert our gaze from what we make of life, preferring to live unquestioningly from day to day. The great man, however, does not. He is not afraid to confront the meaning of his life, even though the confrontation may be painful and filled with sorrow. But it may be joyful too. "The lucidity that was to constitute his torture at the same time crowns his victory" (page 231). Explain your understanding of that remark in the context in which it appears.

For Composition

"Myths are made for the imagination to breathe life into them." Camus proceeds to demonstrate what he means by describing Sisyphus at his labors: "the face screwed up, the cheek tight against the stone, the shoulder bracing. . . . "

1. **Description.** Choose a myth and breathe life into it. Icarus soaring toward the sun, Tantalus straining to quench his thirst and hunger, and Prometheus writhing on his rock are only three of the many mythical instances from which you might choose your subject. Make your description appeal to all the senses — how it would feel, taste, look, smell, and sound to be in the predicament you are describing.

2. **Argument.** In a brief composition present evidence to support your opinion that Sisyphus does or does not qualify as a heroic figure. Limit your evidence to what is contained in Camus's essay.

Words and Allusions

SPECIALIZATION OF MEANING. Sometimes a word that is broadly used is applied to a particular object or situation so that it takes on a specific meaning. For example, the word *deer* once referred to any animal, but it now refers to one kind of animal. This process is known as *specialization*.

Camus refers to Sisyphus as the "absurd

hero." What does the word *absurd* mean in everyday usage? In recent literature, stemming from the works of Camus and others, the word has taken on a special meaning — as in the "Theater of the Absurd." Using whatever reference books are available, together with your understanding of the essay, define *absurd* as it is used in recent literature.

ALLUSIONS. "These are our nights of Gethsemane," writes Camus on page 231 in words that allude to Jesus in the Garden of Gethsemane before the crucifixion. Read the following passages in the New Testament and explain what Camus means by his allusion to Gethsemane: Matthew 26: 36–45; Mark 14: 32–41; Luke 22: 39–46.

The Preacher: Ruminates Behind the Sermon

GWENDOLYN BROOKS

The demands of greatness are fearsome. The great man, Sisyphus-like, must suffer, and the example of Ozymandias suggests that all his vaunted achievements may in the end come to nothing. In addition, there is yet another aspect of greatness that the superior being must learn to accept.

I think it must be lonely to be God.
Nobody loves a master. No. Despite
The bright hosannas, bright dear-Lords, and bright
Determined reverence of Sunday eyes.

Picture Jehovah striding through the hall   5
Of His importance, creatures running out
From servant-corners to acclaim, to shout
Appreciation of His merit's glare.

But who walks with Him? — dares to take His arm,
To slap Him on the shoulder, tweak His ear,   10
Buy Him a Coca-Cola or a beer,
Pooh-pooh His politics, call Him a fool?

Perhaps — who knows? — He tires of looking down.
Those eyes are never lifted. Never straight.
Perhaps sometimes He tires of being great   15
In solitude. Without a hand to hold.

For Discussion

1. Who is the "I" of line 1? Under what circumstances is he thinking about God's position in the universe? What additional difficulty of greatness does this poem suggest — not only about God, but to some extent about any leader, such as the captain of a ship or the ruler of a country?

2. **Rhyme Scheme.** The pattern of rhyme that a given poem follows may be indicated by assigning a letter to the sound at the end of each line and repeating that letter when the sound is repeated at the end of any subsequent line. In "Ozymandias," for example, line 1 rhymes with lines 3 and 5; accordingly, the rhyme scheme of the first six lines would be indicated: *a b a c a d*. How would you indicate the rhyme scheme of "The Preacher: Ruminates Behind the Sermon"?

For Composition

To what extent does the image of God presented in this poem seem shocking? Does the title help justify that image?

● Argument. Carefully examine "The Preacher: Ruminates Behind the Sermon" and in a brief composition present reasons why it is or is not irreverent and sacrilegious.

About the Poet. **Gwendolyn Brooks** (1917–   ) published her first poem when she was thirteen years old. By the time she was seventeen, Miss Brooks was contributing regularly to the Negro newspaper *The Chicago Defender.* As she worked her way through college, she continued to write, joining a poetry workshop and winning four consecutive first prizes in the Midwestern Writers' Conferences. Since then Gwendolyn Brooks has won many other prizes for her poetry, including the Pulitzer Prize in 1950. Her courage in experimenting lends originality to her poetry. One critic has observed that she draws upon her experiences in such a way that they become "not merely personal or racial but universal."

The Angels

JOHN UPDIKE

Despite difficulties in pursuing it, greatness matters. Without examples of greatness, our lives would be much more narrow and constraining. For it is what the greatest people have achieved — in music, for example, and art, and literature — that makes known to the rest of us what man is capable of.

> They are above us all the time,
> the good gentlemen, Mozart and Bach,
> Scarlatti and Handel and Brahms,
> lavishing* measures of light down upon us,
> telling us, over and over, there is a realm   5
> above this plane* of silent compromise.

4. **lavishing:** bestowing profusely.   6. **plane:** *here,* level of existence.

"They are above us all the time, the good gentlemen . . . / telling us over and over, there is a realm / above this plane of silent compromise." Homage to Mozart *by the modern French painter Raoul Dufy.*

They are around us everywhere, the old seers,
Matisse and Vermeer, Cézanne and Piero,
greeting us echoing in subway tunnels,
springing like winter flowers from postcards   10
Scotch-Taped to white kitchen walls,
waiting larger than life in shadowy galleries
to whisper that edges of color
lie all about us innocent as grass.
They are behind us, beneath us,   15
the abysmal* books, Shakespeare and Tolstoy,
the Bible and Proust and Cervantes,
burning in memory like leaky furnace doors,
minepits of honesty from which we escaped   19
with dilated suspicions.* Love us, dead thrones,*
sing us to sleep, awaken our eyes,
comfort with terror our mortal afternoons.

16. **abysmal:** bottomless, unending. 20. **dilated suspicions:** expanded consciousness. **dead thrones:** "Thrones" are a class of angels; *thus,* angels of the past.

For Discussion

1. According to "The Angels," what function does art in its broadest sense play in the lives of sensitive human beings? Your answer may remind you of the closing lines of Keats' "Ode on a Grecian Urn" (page 46). What similarities do you see between the themes that that poem and this one develop?

2. "The Angels" is composed of four parts. Although you may not recognize every proper name alluded to, you will know enough of them to determine the focus of the first three parts of the poem. Identify the form of artistic expression (again, in the broadest sense) being referred to in the first part of the poem. At what line does the second part begin? What kind of artist is being referred

to there? What kind of artist is referred to in the third part?

3. **Paradox.** The fourth part begins in the middle of line 20, where the angels ("thrones" are a kind of angel) are addressed directly. The poem ends on an apparent contradiction: "comfort with terror." That phrase, which is a *paradox*, is apparently false (how can terror be a comfort?) but proves true on closer examination. Consider, for example, why people read murder mysteries or watch horror movies. Can you explain the meaning of the concluding thought in the poem?

For Composition

As suggested in the questions above, the structure of "The Angels" is carefully developed. Each of the three major sections begins "They are. . . ."

• **Analysis.** Write a brief paper that examines the relationship among the first three parts of "The Angels." You may want to develop your analysis by noting where each of the three parts is located with reference to mankind. Are those positions appropriate and justifiable?

About the Poet. **John Updike** (1932–   ), who was born in a small town in Pennsylvania, wrote his first novel, *The Poorhouse Fair,* in his early twenties; it is a sensitive description of life in an old people's home. Since then he has published several novels, collections of essays and stories, and two volumes of poetry. In 1964 his novel *The Centaur* received the National Book Award for fiction.

A poet even when writing prose, Updike gives all he writes rhythm and music. Some of his poetry is humorous, some satiric. Occasionally, as in "The Angels," he is serious. "His is what poetry . . . ought to be," writes one of his admirers, "playful, but elegant, sharp-eyed, witty."

FROM

On Heroes and Hero-Worship

THOMAS CARLYLE

Why does greatness matter? In the preceding poem John Updike has offered a personal answer — how greatness affects the private life of each individual. In the essay that follows, a portion of a series of important lectures delivered in the late 1830's, the Scottish historian Thomas Carlyle discusses how greatness matters to society as a whole.

We have undertaken to discourse here for a little on Great Men, their manner of appearance in our world's business, how they have shaped themselves in the world's history, what ideas men formed of them, what work they did; — on Heroes, namely, and on their reception and performance; what I call Hero-worship and the Heroic in human affairs. . . . A large topic; indeed, an illimitable one; wide as Universal History itself. For, as I take it, Universal History, the history of what man has accomplished in this world, is at bottom the History of the Great Men who have worked here. They were the leaders of men, these great ones; the modelers, patterns, and in a wide sense creators, of whatsoever the general mass of men contrived to do or to attain; all things that we see standing accomplished in the world are properly the outer material result, the practical realization and embodiment, of Thoughts that dwelt in the Great Men sent into the world: the soul of the whole world's history, it may justly be considered, were the history of these. Too clearly it is a topic we shall do no justice to in this place!

One comfort is that Great Men, taken up in any way, are profitable company. We cannot look, however imperfectly, upon a great man, without gaining something by him. He is the living light-fountain, which it is good and pleasant to be near. The light which enlightens, which has enlightened the darkness of the world; and this not as a kindled lamp only, but rather as a natural luminary[1] shining by the gift of Heaven; a flowing light-fountain, as I say, of native original insight, of manhood and heroic nobleness; — in whose radiance all souls feel that it is well with them. On any terms whatsoever, you will not grudge to wander in such neighborhood for a while. . . .

Society is founded on Hero-worship. All dignities of rank, on which human association rests, are what we may call a *Hero*archy (Government of Heroes), — or a Hierarchy,[2] for it is "sacred" enough withal! The Duke means *Dux*, Leader; King is *Kön-ning, Kan-ning*, Man that

Portrait of Thomas Carlyle by the American painter James McNeill Whistler.

knows or *cans*. Society everywhere is some representation, not *in*supportably inaccurate, of a graduated Worship of Heroes; — reverence and obedience done to men really great and wise. Not *in*supportably inaccurate, I say! They are all as bank notes,[3] these social dignitaries, all representing gold; — and several of them, alas, always are *forged* notes. We can do with some forged false notes; with a good many even; but not with all, or the most of them forged! No: there have to come revolutions then; cries of Democracy, Liberty, and Equality, and I know not what: — the notes being all false, and no gold to be had for *them*,

---

[1] **luminary:** body that gives off light, such as the sun.

[2] **Hierarchy:** from Greek *hieros*, meaning "sacred," and *archein*, meaning "to rule."

[3] **bank notes:** paper money.

people take to crying in their despair that there is no gold, that there never was any! — "Gold," Hero-worship, *is* nevertheless, as it was always and everywhere, and cannot cease till man himself ceases.

I am well aware that in these days Hero-worship, the thing I call Hero-worship, professes to have gone out, and finally ceased. This, for reasons which it will be worthwhile sometime to inquire into, is an age that as it were denies the existence of great men; denies the desirableness of great men. Show our critics a great man, a Luther[1] for example, they begin to what they call "account" for him; not to worship him, but take the dimensions of him, — and bring him out to be a little kind of man! He was the "creature of the Time," they say; the Time called him forth, the Time did everything, he nothing — but what we the little critic could have done too! This

seems to me but melancholy work. The Time call forth? Alas, we have known Times *call* loudly enough for their great man; but not find him when they called! He was not there; Providence[2] had not sent him; the Time, *calling* its loudest, had to go down to confusion and wreck because he would not come when called.

For if we will think of it, no Time need have gone to ruin, could it have *found* a man great enough, a man wise and good enough: wisdom to discern truly what the Time wanted, valor to lead it on the right road thither;[3] these are the salvation of any Time. But I liken common languid Times, with their unbelief, distress, perplexity, with their languid doubting characters and embarrassed[4] circumstances, impotently crumbling-down into ever worse distress towards final ruin; — all this I liken to dry

---

[1] **Luther:** sixteenth-century German leader of the Reformation.

[2] **Providence:** benevolent guidance of God or nature.

[3] **thither:** to there.

[4] **embarrassed:** *here,* impaired, troubled.

ABOUT THE AUTHOR • Thomas Carlyle (1795–1881) was a man of many moods. For example, he had a violent temper, but at times was capable of great restraint. He was most understanding when a large portion of his manuscript of *The French Revolution* lent to John Stuart Mill was burnt as waste paper by an illiterate housemaid. For a time he even refused Mill's offer of a hundred pounds to tide him over the rewriting.

Perhaps incidents like that one only reinforced Carlyle's distrust of the common people. Like Plato he doubted the ability of the masses to govern themselves. Unlike Plato, however, he placed his faith in the national deliverer, the strong man, the hero called forth by history to set events right.

A prodigious writer of history, biography, criticism, and philosophy, Carlyle as he grew older became consistently more suspicious of liberalism and social welfare. He is remembered not only for the content of his books but for the powerful irony and the verbal pyrotechnics with which he wrote them. His works include the philosophical *Sartor Resartus, On Heroes and Hero-Worship,* and the monumental *History of Frederick the Great.*

dead fuel, waiting for the lightning out of Heaven that shall kindle it. The great man, with his free force direct out of God's own hand, is the lightning. His word is the wise healing word which all can believe in. All blazes round him now, when he has once struck on it, into fire like his own. The dry moldering sticks are thought to have called him forth. They did want him greatly; but as to calling him forth — ! — Those are critics of small vision, I think, who cry: "See, is it not the sticks that made the fire?" No sadder proof can be given by a man of his own littleness than disbelief in great men. There is no sadder symptom of a generation than such general blindness to the spiritual lightning, with faith only in the heap of barren dead fuel. It is the last consummation[1] of unbelief. In all epochs of the world's history, we shall find the Great Man to have been the indispensable savior of his epoch; — the lightning, without which the fuel never would have burnt. The History of the World, I said already, was the Biography of Great Men.

Such small critics do what they can to promote unbelief and universal spiritual paralysis: but happily they cannot always completely succeed. In all times it is possible for a man to arise great enough to feel that they and their doctrines are chimeras[2] and cobwebs. And what is notable, in no time whatever can they entirely eradicate out of living men's hearts a certain altogether peculiar reverence for Great Men; genuine admiration, loyalty, adoration, however dim and perverted it may be. Hero-worship endures forever while man endures. Boswell venerates his Johnson,[3] right truly even in the eighteenth century.

[1] **consummation**: fulfillment.
[2] **chimeras** (kə·mēr′əz): impossible and foolish fancies.
[3] **Johnson**: Samuel Johnson, English author (1709–1784), subject of an admiring biography by his contemporary James Boswell.

> Great men are the tables of contents of mankind.
>
> — Friedrich Hebbel

The unbelieving French believe in their Voltaire;[4] and burst-out round him into very curious Hero-worship, in that last act of his life when they "stifle him under roses". . . .

Yes, from Norse Odin[5] to English Samuel Johnson, from the divine Founder of Christianity[6] to the withered Pontiff of Encyclopedism,[7] in all times and places, the Hero has been worshipped. It will ever be so. We all love great men; love, venerate, and bow down submissive before great men: nay can we honestly bow down to anything else? Ah, does not every true man feel that he is himself made higher by doing reverence to what is really above him? No nobler or more blessed feeling dwells in man's heart. And to me it is very cheering to consider that no skeptical logic, or general triviality, insincerity, and aridity of any Time and its influences can destroy this noble inborn loyalty and worship that is in man. In times of unbelief, which soon have to become times of revolution, much down-rushing sorrowful decay and ruin is visible to everybody. For myself in these days, I seem to see in this indestructibility of Hero-worship the everlasting adamant[8] lower than which the confused wreck of revolutionary things cannot fall. The confused wreck of things crumbling and even crashing and tumbling all round us in these

[4] **Voltaire**: eighteenth-century French philosopher satirist, historian, and dramatist.
[5] **Odin**: Scandinavian god of wisdom, poetry, war, the dead, and agriculture.
[6] **divine . . . Christianity**: *i.e.*, Jesus Christ.
[7] **withered . . . Encyclopedism**: Denis Diderot, eighteenth-century French man of letters.
[8] **adamant**: very hard substance.

revolutionary ages will get down so far; *no* farther. It is an eternal cornerstone, from which they can begin to build themselves up again. That man, in some sense or other, worships Heroes; that we all of us reverence and must ever reverence Great Men: this is, to me, the living rock amid all rushings-down whatsoever; — the one fixed point in modern revolutionary history, otherwise as if bottomless and shoreless.

For Discussion

1. "Universal History . . . is at bottom the History of the Great Men who have worked here." Yet according to Carlyle, the age in which he was writing (and many people say it about our own times) was an age that denied the existence of great men. How would the critics of Carlyle's day react when faced with an example of greatness — a Luther, for instance? Have you encountered similar reactions in judging the political and cultural heroes of our own day?

2. The essay implies two kinds of societies, or Times: the ordinary perplexed and languid times, and those times inspired by the actions of a hero. To what does the author compare ordinary times? To what does he compare the hero? How does Carlyle feel toward those who proclaim their disbelief in great men?

3. All religions are built on hero-worship, and so are all societies. In what way does the author use the abstractions of faith and loyalty to support that sweeping and impressive claim?

4. To be sure, not everyone whom the public worships as a hero is the genuine article; that is, some are frauds. Is it fatal to a society to have a few fraudulent heroes in its midst? What recourse does a society have to a situation in which most of its heroes prove to be false and unworthy?

5. **Style.** Style is the characteristic manner in which an author expresses himself. It includes considerations of diction, syntax, grammar, and punctuation. Carlyle has a style of writing all his own — a celebrated style that stimulates many readers and exasperates others. His habit of using capital letters with common nouns ("the Heroic," "Universal History," "Great Men") is a stylistic trait. His eccentric punctuation — exclamation points, dashes, and the like — is a characteristic of his style. And his fondness for metaphor to make abstractions concrete is a third stylistic attribute. One such comparison has been noted — that between heroes and lightning. What other comparison did you encounter in the essay, one having to do with counterfeit money? What other characteristics of Carlyle's style might be singled out for mention? Consider, for example, the presence or absence of rhetorical questions.

For Composition

As you know, you may develop a paragraph or essay by furnishing examples to illustrate and support your topic. Examples are particularly useful not only in explaining an abstraction concretely but also in clarifying a subject that may be unfamiliar to your reader.

1. **Example.** Can a single heroic figure change the direction in which his society is moving? Develop a brief composition by means of a specific historical example (Washington? Lincoln? Churchill?) to answer the question either negatively or affirmatively.

2. **Analysis.** "No nobler feeling than this of admiration for one higher than himself dwells in the breast of man." Yet there are risks involved in hero-worship. Write a brief, well-organized paper exploring what some of those risks might be.

Words and Allusions

ETYMOLOGY (page 225). According to Carlyle (page 237), "The Duke means *Dux*, Leader; King is *Kön-ning, Kan-ning*, Man that *knows* or *cans*." There are many words in English derived from *dux* or from the verb *ducere*, to lead, among them *produce, ductile, deduct*. List ten other words that have evolved from the Latin *dux* or *ducere* and explain their relationship to those words.

Is Carlyle's derivation of *King* as valid as his derivation of *Duke?* How do you know?

Heroes and Anti-Heroes

Writing as recently as 1959, the American historian Arthur Schlesinger, Jr., felt compelled to begin an essay: "Ours is an age without heroes." And indeed, others have identified these times of ours as the Age of the Anti-Hero, not only in America but throughout the globe.

We go to a movie. A famous Hollywood star, handsome and appealing, has been cast in a major role that will win our sympathy. What part does he play? Apparently a respected businessman, he turns out in fact to be a playboy, divorced from his wife and separated from his children, who spends most of his time taking lovely girls to dinner or racing his car over the sands of Cape Cod or sailing through the skies in his glider, or playing golf, or flying off to Switzerland. And where does he get the money for all this leisurely self-indulgence? Well, he is a thief. Although not the man who goes out and personally steals money, he is the brains behind a bank-robbing scheme so successful that in the course of the movie it lifts two million and more dollars from a Boston bank. In the final scene we witness our hero flying off to Europe once more, still smiling appealingly high overhead, having so thoroughly captured our sympathy that we feel relief at his having escaped all but unscathed after his misdeeds against society.

Nowadays, movies and television abound with heroes of the same stripe. What values do they exemplify? (Indeed, "hero" has become such an awkward word that it seems in some danger of dropping out of the language. Instead of the hero in fiction, we talk now about the "protagonist" — the major character pitched against his antagonist.) What values do such protagonists as the one in the movie exemplify? What strengths, if any, do they exhibit?

We must grant that the businessman-playboy-thief is handsome and physically sound; heroes for the most part have always been so. And he is young. And he is clever. But above all he is cool, emotionless, impossible to excite however tense a situation may become.

He may have other virtues, too, but it is the faults of such a character — as measured by almost every ethic or religion of the past — that seem so striking. Is the man courageous? He doesn't rob the bank himself, and he takes pains to protect himself from being linked in any way with the robbery. Others do his dirty work. Is he trustworthy? On the contrary, the man is a walking lie — totally different in fact from what he represents himself as being. He is rootless, sensual, self-indulgent, unprincipled, irresponsible, cynical, and for the most part bored with life. Yet he, and many other protagonists like him, claim our sympathy day after day in novels and plays, in movies and on television.

How can we account for the decline of the hero in the twentieth century? At least three intellectual influences have been recognized as contributing to that decline. The nineteenth-century naturalist Charles Darwin, in *On the Origin of Species* (1859), developed a scientific hypothesis that brought man down from his earlier position just a little lower than the angels, to the level of kinship with the apes. Sharing a common ancestry with orangutans and gorillas, which of us could expect to be heroic? Moreover, the political scientist Karl Marx, in *Das Kapital* (1867), exhibited man as a prisoner of vast historical forces, primarily economic. In contrast to Carlyle's feeling that history is the biography of great men, Marx felt that history is an economic record, as impersonal as a trend, unfolding independently of any one man's wishes or influence. Economic forces move history through cycles and stages no matter what any one individual might do. If so, where in such a world is there room for heroic acts? And finally, the psychoanalyst Sigmund Freud, in a series of studies around the beginning of the twentieth century, probed into the depths of man's subconscious and uncovered there motives for behavior quite different from those that appeared on the surface. The hero, under Freud's probing, turned out to be as vulnerable as are the rest of us.

The work of all three of these important thinkers has been challenged and modified, but the combined effect of their influence has altered our conception of ourselves. Other influences in modern times have helped erode man's confidence in his ability to affect the world he lives in. The dehumanizing industrial revolution, an enormous growth in population, two devastating and disillusioning world wars are only three of the many other phenomena that have made modern man a little more wary than was his ancestor about the credibility of the heroic ideal.

Yet there is consolation for those who deplore the absence of heroes in our time. Carlyle, as we have noticed, expressed doubts about his own age: "This . . . is an age that as it were denies the existence of great men; denies the desirableness of great men." But great men did live alongside Carlyle, and future historians will no doubt be able to identify great men in our own times. Nor perhaps should we take too seriously the tendency to glorify the man who outmaneuvers the system — the smoothly successful jewel thief or bank robber. Our is not the first age to celebrate the highwayman, the bold outlaw, the Robin Hood.

No, heroism and the virtues it extols — courage, wisdom, compassion, forbearance, idealism, imagination, originality, genius, grace — these are undoubtedly still very much alive in our society, and will endure as long as man does. Schlesinger himself, who had bemoaned the decline of heroes in 1959, must surely in the following year — with the election of John F. Kennedy to the Presidency of the United States — have changed his mind. For Kennedy was exactly the kind of heroic figure that Schlesinger had despaired of our times' producing; so that at least for the thousand days of his brief Presidency, the young chief executive's impact would have led the historian — a friend and warm admirer — to reverse his own earlier judgment that ours is an age without heroes.

1. What heroes do you find in literature, in movies, in television programs today? What are they like? Do they possess greatness as you understand that quality?

2. What is your concept of a hero, or heroine? What qualities must such a person possess? Is greatness among those qualities?

I Think Continually of Those Who Were Truly Great

STEPHEN SPENDER

The luckiest among us lead our lives in the company of great people. Not physically, of course — only the very luckiest can do that — but in the pages of books, on the surfaces of canvas, in the echoes of concert halls. Camus's essay earlier in this section implied a distinction between the harsh rock of earth underfoot and the liberating realms as Sisyphus ascends his mountain toward the sky. Spender's poem that follows makes a similar distinction, between the fog-imprisoned traffic of daily life and the sun-struck loveliness of greatness high on some mountain field, near the snow, near the sun.

I think continually of those who were truly great.
Who, from the womb, remembered the soul's history
Through corridors of light where the hours are suns,
Endless and singing. Whose lovely ambition
Was that their lips, still touched with fire,   5
Should tell of the Spirit, clothed from head to foot in song.
And who hoarded from the Spring branches
The desires falling across their bodies like blossoms.

What is precious, is never to forget   9
The essential delight of the blood drawn from ageless springs
Breaking through rocks in worlds before our earth.
Never to deny its pleasure in the morning simple light
Nor its grave evening demand for love.
Never to allow gradually the traffic to smother
With noise and fog, the flowering of the Spirit.   15

Near the snow, near the sun, in the highest fields,
See how these names are feted by the waving grass
And by the streamers of white cloud
And whispers of wind in the listening sky.
The names of those who in their lives fought for life,   20
Who wore at their hearts the fire's center.
Born of the sun, they traveled a short while toward the sun,
And left the vivid air signed with their honor.

For Discussion

1. The contemplation of greatness provides a liberation from the smothering fog and noise of daily life — through an ascent to another region, as pictured in the third stanza of the poem. How would you describe that region? Line 20 suggests what distinguishes the great man from his fellows. Explain your understanding of the line. Can you suggest any historical examples that might illustrate your explanation?

"*Near the snow, near the sun, in the highest fields. . . .*" *Ansel Adams*' Yosemite Point.

2. As Updike's poem expressed the importance of greatness in many private lives, and Carlyle's essay expressed the importance of greatness to society as a whole, so this poem of Spender's seems to voice what greatness means to a single, unique, and sensitive individual. Notice, in determining what the poem is concerned with, how important are the word choices in the first line. Suppose that line (and the title) had read: "Often I think of those who are great." Discuss the effect that the various diction changes would have in indicating the concerns of the poem.

3. **Denotation and Connotation.** Most words have both a literal, dictionary meaning — or *denotation* — and also various associations of meanings less precise than the literal. These overtones of meaning that a word suggests are called *connotations*. The term *swimming pool* denotes a cavity filled with purified water, but it connotes (according to each person's ex-

perience) good times and sunlight and happy fellowship and so on. Of course to a person who has experienced a tragedy at a swimming pool — the drowning of a loved one, for example — the connotations of the term would be altogether different.

Spender, for example, exploits connotations throughout this poem. In line 4, "singing" connotes joy and loveliness; the hours of a great man's life are as intense as sunlight and as joyful as song. What are the connotations of "fire" in line 5? Of "springs" in line 10?

For Composition

Both Updike's poem and Spender's are attempts to express why greatness matters. Although the poems share certain attitudes, in many ways they are quite different from each other.

● **Comparison and Contrast.** In a brief composition compare and contrast "The Angels" (page 234) and "I Think Continually of Those Who Were Truly Great." Before beginning to write, organize your insights in some logical manner — comparing and contrasting the styles of the two poets, for example, and their attitudes toward great achievements.

About the Poet. **Stephen Spender** (1909–   ) wrote lyric poetry while taking a militant stand against despotism. He was enrolled in many causes, marching with British workers during the depression years and defending Spain against Fascism in her Civil War of 1936–1939. In his eighteenth year Spender himself set up and printed a paper-bound pamphlet of his verse; five years later his volume *Poems* brought him renown as a poet. These showed the revolutionary fervor which caused critics to compare him to Shelley. The critic Louis Untermeyer has written of Spender: "there is always the . . . intense voice of something dearly held and deeply felt . . . an utterance which, achieving the high level of the lines beginning 'I think continually of those who were truly great,' is exalted and often noble." In addition to his poetry, Spender has written criticism, fiction, drama, and his autobiography *World Within World.*

Apology

PLATO

Examples of a few, rare men's lives have inspired others in ages and places far removed from their own. For many, Lincoln's life was such an example. Another was the life of Socrates, the Greek philosopher whose probing mind you encountered briefly earlier in this book (pages 49–53). Socrates merely talked. He wrote nothing. He was not a statesman, nor did he develop a systematic body of philosophic thought. He was assuredly not handsome, being squat and thick-nosed. Living into his seventies, he was poor most of his long life, and he died poor. Yet throughout the western world he is generally regarded as among the greatest men of all time.

His death occurred in Athens, in 399 B.C. Socrates was condemned to death — and paid the ultimate penalty — after having been tried on the charge of corrupting the minds of young people. How had he corrupted the youth of Athens? By teaching them to doubt and question and think for themselves. But those seemed dangerous skills to impart to young members of a state swept by turmoil, for Athens had only recently consumed its energies in fighting — and losing — the disastrous Peloponnesian War (431–404 B.C.). In the wake of that calamity a government of tyrants had ruled briefly, through terror, and were followed by successive oligarchies that held power insecurely and fearfully. Political chaos threatened, and it was under those circumstances that Socrates was summoned before the courts to answer charges of crimes against his state, brought by two men, Meletus (who is questioned by Socrates) and Anytus. His disciple Plato records what happened next. When his turn finally came to address the jury of his peers, Socrates spoke these words.

How you, O Athenians, have been affected by my accusers, I cannot tell; but I know that they almost made me forget who I was — so persuasively did they speak; and yet they have hardly uttered a word of truth. But of the many falsehoods told by them, there was one which quite amazed me — I mean when they said that you should be upon your guard and not allow yourselves to be deceived by the force of my eloquence. To say this, when they were certain to be detected as soon as I opened my lips and proved myself to be anything but a great speaker, did indeed appear to me most shameless — unless by the force of eloquence they mean the force of truth; for if such is their meaning, I admit that I am eloquent. But in how different a way from theirs! Well, as I was saying, they have scarcely spoken the truth at all; but from me you shall hear the whole truth: not, however, delivered after their manner in a set oration[1] duly ornamented with words and phrases. No, by heaven! but I shall use the words and arguments which occur to me at the moment; for I am confident in the justice of my cause. At my time of life I ought not to be appearing before you, O

Apology: *here,* formal defense.

[1] **set oration:** prepared speech.

245

men of Athens, in the character of a juvenile orator — let no one expect it of me. And I must beg of you to grant me a favor: If I defend myself in my accustomed manner, and you hear me using the words which I have been in the habit of using in the agora,[1] at the tables of the money changers, or anywhere else, I would ask you not to be surprised, and not to interrupt me on this account. For I am more than seventy years of age, and appearing now for the first time in a court of law, I am quite a stranger to the language of the place; and therefore I would have you regard me as if I were really a stranger, whom you would excuse if he spoke in his native tongue, and after the fashion of his country. Am I making an unfair request of you? Never mind the manner, which may or may not be good; but think only of the truth of my words, and give heed to that: let the speaker speak truly and the judge decide justly.

And first, I have to reply to the older charges and to my first accusers, and then I will go on to the later ones. For of old I have had many accusers, who have accused me falsely to you during many years; and I am more afraid of them than of Anytus[2]

[1] agora: market place.
[2] Anytus: one of Socrates' accusers.

and his associates, who are dangerous, too, in their own way. But far more dangerous are the others, who began when you were children, and took possession of your minds with their falsehoods, telling of one Socrates, a wise man, who speculated about the heaven above, and searched into the earth beneath, and made the worse appear the better cause. The disseminators[3] of this tale are the accusers whom I dread; for their hearers are apt to fancy that such inquirers do not believe in the existence of the gods. And they are many, and their charges against me are of ancient date, and they were made by them in the days when you were more impressible than you are now — in childhood, or it may have been in youth — and the cause when heard went by default, for there was none to answer. And hardest of all, I do not know and cannot tell the names of my accusers; unless in the chance case of a Comic poet.[4] All who from envy and malice have persuaded you — some of them having first convinced themselves — all this class of men are most difficult to deal with; for I cannot

[3] disseminators: spreaders.
[4] Comic poet: Aristophanes, satiric poet who had portrayed Socrates as a silly fraud in his comedy *The Clouds*.

ABOUT THE AUTHOR • Although the speaker in the *Apology* is Socrates, the author is **Plato**. As far as we know, Socrates never wrote down any of the wisdom for which he is famous. In Plato's dialogue, how much of the wisdom ascribed to Socrates is actually his, and how much is that of Plato, is impossible to say. According to tradition, Socrates was the teacher of Plato, who set down Socrates' words at his trial.

Both Socrates and Plato had angered two powerful factions in Athens, the Oligarchs, or dictators, who ruled the city for a time as puppets of the conquering Spartans (404 B.C.), and the Democrats, who had wrested control back from Sparta and the Oligarchs and sought to punish their supporters.

In 399 B.C., Socrates was accused of corrupting the young men of Athens and of not believing in the gods of the state. The *Apology* is his answer to these charges before a jury of his peers, 501 of them. The story of Socrates is continued in the *Crito*, where he explains why he should accept the verdict of the state, and in the *Phaedo*, which ends with a moving description of the death of Socrates.

have them up here, and cross-examine them, and therefore I must simply fight with shadows in my own defense, and argue when there is no one who answers. I will ask you then to assume with me, as I was saying, that my opponents are of two kinds; one recent, the other ancient: and I hope that you will see the propriety of my answering the latter first, for these accusations you heard long before the others, and much oftener.

Well, then, I must make my defense, and endeavor to clear away in a short time a slander which has lasted a long time. May I succeed, if to succeed be for my good and yours, or likely to avail me in my cause! The task is not an easy one; I quite understand the nature of it. And so leaving the event with God, in obedience to the law I will now make my defense.

I will begin at the beginning, and ask what is the accusation which has given rise to the slander of me, and in fact has encouraged Meletus to prefer this charge against me. Well, what do the slanderers say? They shall be my prosecutors, and I will sum up their words in an affidavit: "Socrates is an evil-doer, and a curious person, who searches into things under the earth and in heaven, and he makes the worse appear the better cause; and he teaches the aforesaid[1] doctrines to others." Such is the nature of the accusation: it is just what you have yourselves seen in the comedy of Aristophanes, who has introduced a man whom he calls Socrates, going about and saying that he walks in air, and talking a deal of nonsense concerning matters of which I do not pretend to know either much or little — not that I mean to speak disparagingly of anyone who is a student of natural philosophy.[2] I should be very sorry if Meletus could bring so grave a charge against me. But the simple truth is, O

Athenians, that I have nothing to do with physical speculations. Very many of those here present are witnesses to the truth of this, and to them I appeal. Speak then, you who have heard me, and tell your neighbors whether any of you have ever known me hold forth in few words or in many upon such matters. . . . You hear their answer. And from what they say of this part of the charge you will be able to judge of the truth of the rest.

As little foundation is there for the report that I am a teacher, and take money; this accusation has no more truth in it than the other. Although, if a man were really able to instruct mankind, to receive money for giving instruction would, in my opinion, be an honor to him. There is Gorgias of Leontium, and Prodicus of Ceos, and Hippias of Elis,[3] who go the round of the cities, and are able to persuade the young men to leave their own citizens by whom they might be taught for nothing, and come to them whom they not only pay, but are thankful if they may be allowed to pay them. There is at this time a Parian[4] philosopher residing in Athens, of whom I have heard; and I came to hear of him in this way: I came across a man who has spent a world of money on the Sophists,[5] Callias, the son of Hipponicus, and knowing that he had sons, I asked him: "Callias," I said, "if your two sons were foals or calves, there would be no difficulty in finding someone to put over them; we should hire a trainer of horses, or a farmer probably, who would improve and perfect them in their own proper virtue and excellence; but as they are human beings, whom are you thinking of placing over them? Is there anyone who understands human and political virtue?

[1] **aforesaid**: previously mentioned.
[2] **natural philosophy**: physical science.

[3] **Gorgias . . . Elis**: well-known professional teachers of the use of argument.
[4] **Parian**: from the island of Paros.
[5] **Sophists**: teachers of rhetoric, philosophy, and the art of successful living, famed for their subtle and often unsound reasoning.

You must have thought about the matter, for you have sons; is there anyone?" "There is," he said. "Who is he?" said I; "and of what country? and what does he charge?" "Evenus the Parian," he replied; "he is the man, and his charge is five minae."[1] — Happy is Evenus, I said to myself, if he really has this wisdom, and teaches at such a moderate charge. Had I the same, I should have been very proud and conceited; but the truth is that I have no knowledge of the kind.

I dare say, Athenians, that someone among you will reply, "Yes, Socrates, but what is the origin of these accusations which are brought against you; there must have been something strange which you have been doing? All these rumors and this talk about you would never have arisen if you had been like other men: tell us, then, what is the cause of them, for we should be sorry to judge hastily of you." Now I regard this as a fair challenge, and I will endeavor to explain to you the reason why I am called wise and have such an evil fame. Please to attend then. And although some of you may think that I am joking, I declare that I will tell you the entire truth. Men of Athens, this reputation of mine has come of a certain sort of wisdom which I possess. If you ask me what kind of wisdom, I reply, wisdom such as may perhaps be attained by man, for to that extent I am inclined to believe that I am wise, whereas the persons of whom I was speaking have a superhuman wisdom, which I may fail to describe, because I have it not myself; and he who says that I have, speaks falsely, and is taking away my character. And here, O men of Athens, I must beg you not to interrupt me, even if I seem to say something extravagant. For the word which I will speak is not mine. I will refer you to a witness who is worthy of credit; that witness shall be the God of Delphi[2] — he will tell you about my wisdom, if I have any, and of what sort it is. You must have known Chaerephon; he was early a friend of mine, and also a friend of yours, for he shared in the recent exile of the people, and returned with you. Well, Chaerephon, as you know, was very impetuous in all his doings, and he went to Delphi and boldly asked the oracle to tell him whether — as I was saying, I must beg you not to interrupt — he asked the oracle to tell him whether anyone was wiser than I was, and the Pythian prophetess[3] answered, that there was no man wiser. Chaerephon is dead himself; but his brother, who is in court, will confirm the truth of what I am saying.

Why do I mention this? Because I am going to explain to you why I have such an evil name. When I heard the answer, I said to myself, What can the god mean? and what is the interpretation of his riddle? for I know that I have no wisdom, small or great. What then can he mean when he says that I am the wisest of men? And yet he is a god, and cannot lie; that would be against his nature. After long consideration, I thought of a method of trying the question. I reflected that if I could only find a man wiser than myself, then I might go to the god with a refutation in my hand. I should say to him, "Here is a man who is wiser than I am; but you said that I was the wisest." Accordingly I went to one who had the reputation of wisdom, and observed him — his name I need not mention; he was a politician whom I selected for examination — and the result was as follows: When I began to talk with him, I could not help thinking that he was not really wise, although he was thought wise by many, and still wiser by himself; and thereupon I tried to explain to him that he thought himself wise, but

---

[1] **five minae:** in our money, about a hundred dollars.

[2] **God of Delphi:** Apollo.

[3] **Pythian prophetess:** priestess of Apollo, through whom his oracle spoke.

was not really wise; and the consequence was that he hated me, and his enmity was shared by several who were present and heard me. So I left him, saying to myself, as I went away: Well, although I do not suppose that either of us knows anything really beautiful and good, I am better off than he is — for he knows nothing, and thinks that he knows; I neither know nor think that I know. In this latter particular, then, I seem to have slightly the advantage of him. Then I went to another who had still higher pretensions to wisdom, and my conclusion was exactly the same. Whereupon I made another enemy of him, and of many others besides him.

Then I went to one man after another, being not unconscious of the enmity which I provoked, and I lamented and feared this: but necessity was laid upon me — the word of God, I thought, ought to be considered first. And I said to myself, Go I must to all who appear to know, and find out the meaning of the oracle. And I swear to you, Athenians, by the dog[1] I swear! — for I must tell you the truth — the result of my mission was just this: I found that the men most in repute were all but the most foolish; and that others less esteemed were really wiser and better. I will tell you the tale of my wanderings and of the Herculean labors,[2] as I may call them, which I endured only to find at last the oracle irrefutable. After the politicians, I went to the poets; tragic, dithyrambic,[3] and all sorts. And there, I said to myself, you will be instantly detected; now you will find out that you are more ignorant than they are. Accordingly, I took them some of the most elaborate passages in their own writings, and asked what was the meaning of them — thinking that they would teach me something. Will you believe me? I am almost ashamed to confess the truth, but I must say that there is hardly a person present who would not have talked better about their poetry than they did themselves. Then I knew that not by wisdom do poets write poetry, but by a sort of genius and inspiration; they are like diviners or soothsayers who also say many fine things, but do not understand the meaning of them. The poets appeared to me to be much in the same case; and I further observed that upon the strength of their poetry they believed themselves to be the wisest of men in other things in which they were not wise. So I departed, conceiving myself to be superior to them for the same reason that I was superior to the politicians.

At last I went to the artisans,[4] for I was conscious that I knew nothing at all, as I may say, and I was sure that they knew many fine things; and here I was not mistaken, for they did know many things of which I was ignorant, and in this they certainly were wiser than I was. But I observed that even the good artisans fell into the same error as the poets; because they were good workmen they thought that they also knew all sorts of high matters, and this defect in them overshadowed their wisdom; and therefore I asked myself on behalf of the oracle, whether I would like to be as I was, neither having their knowledge nor their ignorance, or like them in both; and I made answer to myself and to the oracle that I was better off as I was.

This inquisition has led to my having many enemies of the worst and most dangerous kind, and has given occasion also to many calumnies. And I am called wise, for my hearers always imagine that I myself possess the wisdom which I find wanting in others: but the truth is, O men of Athens,

[1] **by the dog:** a pseudo-oath; like saying "by gum."

[2] **Herculean labors:** Hercules is said to have performed twelve tasks of great difficulty and danger.

[3] **dithyrambic:** a type of short poem in a wild, inspired strain.

[4] **artisans:** skilled workers.

that God only is wise; and by his answer he intends to show that the wisdom of men is worth little or nothing; he is not speaking of Socrates; he is only using my name by way of illustration, as if he said, "He, O men, is the wisest, who, like Socrates, knows that his wisdom is in truth worth nothing." And so I go about the world, obedient to the god, and search and make inquiry into the wisdom of anyone, whether citizen or stranger, who appears to be wise; and if he is not wise, then in vindication of the oracle I show him that he is not wise; and my occupation quite absorbs me, and I have no time to give either to any public matter of interest or to any concern of my own, but I am in utter poverty by reason of my devotion to the god.

There is another thing: young men of the richer classes, who have not much to do, come about me of their own accord; they like to hear the pretenders examined, and they often imitate me, and proceed to examine others; there are plenty of persons, as they quickly discover, who think that they know something, but really know little or nothing; and then those who are examined by them instead of being angry with themselves are angry with me: "This confounded Socrates," they say; "this villainous misleader of youth!" — and then if somebody asks them, "Why, what evil does he practice or teach?" they do not know and cannot tell; but in order that they may not appear to be at a loss, they repeat the ready-made charges which are used against all philosophers about teaching things up in the clouds and under the earth, and having no gods, and making the worse appear the better cause; for they do not like to confess that their pretense of knowledge has been detected — which is the truth; and as they are numerous and ambitious and energetic, and are drawn up in battle array and have persuasive tongues, they have filled your ears with their loud and inveterate calumnies. And this is the reason why my three accusers, Meletus and Anytus and Lycon, have set upon me; Meletus, who has a quarrel with me on behalf of the poets; Anytus, on behalf of the craftsmen and politicians; Lycon, on behalf of the rhetoricians: and as I said at the beginning, I cannot expect to get rid of such a mess of calumny all in a moment. And this, O men of Athens, is the truth and the whole truth; I have concealed nothing, I have dissembled nothing. And yet, I know that my plainness of speech makes them hate me, and what is their hatred but a proof that I am speaking the truth? Hence has arisen the prejudice against me; and this is the reason of it, as you will find out either in this or in any future inquiry.

I have said enough in my defense against the first class of my accusers; I turn to the second class. They are headed by Meletus, that good man and true lover of his country, as he calls himself. Against these, too, I must try to make a defense. Let their affidavit be read; it contains something of this kind: It says that Socrates is a doer of evil, who corrupts the youth; and who does not believe in the gods of the state, but has other new divinities of his own. Such is the charge; and now let us examine the particular counts. He says that I am a doer of evil, and corrupt the youth; but I say, O men of Athens, that Meletus is a doer of evil, in that he pretends to be in earnest when he is only in jest, and is so eager to bring men to trial from a pretended zeal and interest about matters in which he really never had the smallest interest. And the truth of this I will endeavor to prove to you.

Come hither, Meletus, and let me ask a question of you. You think a great deal about the improvement of youth?

MELETUS. Yes, I do.

SOCRATES. Tell the judges, then, who is their improver; for you must know, as you

Rising above the modern city of Athens are the ancient ruins of the Acropolis (right).
The open space in the left foreground is the Agora, or marketplace.

have taken the pains to discover their corrupter, and are citing and accusing me before them. Speak, then, and tell the judges who their improver is. — Observe, Meletus, that you are silent, and have nothing to say. But is not this rather disgraceful, and a very considerable proof of what I was saying, that you have no interest in the matter? Speak up, friend, and tell us who their improver is.

MELETUS. The laws.

SOCRATES. But that, my good sir, is not my meaning. I want to know who the person is, who, in the first place, knows the laws.

MELETUS. The judges, Socrates, who are present in court.

SOCRATES. What, do you mean to say, Meletus, that they are able to instruct and improve youth?

MELETUS. Certainly they are.

SOCRATES. What, all of them, or some only and not others?

MELETUS. All of them.

SOCRATES. By the goddess Hera,[1] that is good news! There are plenty of improvers, then. And what do you say of the audience

[1] **Hera:** wife of Zeus, who was the chief of the Olympian gods

— do they improve them?

MELETUS. Yes, they do.

SOCRATES. And the senators?

MELETUS. Yes, the senators improve them.

SOCRATES. But perhaps the members of the assembly corrupt them? — or do they improve them?

MELETUS. They improve them.

SOCRATES. Then every Athenian improves and elevates them; all with the exception of myself; and I alone am their corrupter? Is that what you affirm?

MELETUS. That is what I stoutly affirm.

SOCRATES. I am very unfortunate if you are right. But suppose I ask you a question: How about horses? Does one man do them harm and all the world good? Is not the exact opposite the truth? One man is able to do them good, or at least not many; the trainer of horses, that is to say, does them good, and others who have to do with them rather injure them. Is not that true, Meletus, of horses, or of any other animals? Most assuredly it is; whether you and Anytus say yes or no. Happy indeed would be the condition of youth if they had one corrupter only, and all the rest of the world were their improvers. But you, Meletus, have sufficiently shown that you never had a thought about the young: your careless-ness is seen in your not caring about the very things which you bring against me.

And now, Meletus, I will ask you an-other question — by Zeus I will: Which is better, to live among bad citizens, or among good ones? Answer, friend, I say; the question is one which may be easily an-swered. Do not the good do their neigh-bors good, and the bad do them evil?

MELETUS. Certainly.

SOCRATES. And is there anyone who would rather be injured than benefited by those who live with him? Answer, my good friend, the law requires you to an-swer — does anyone like to be injured?

MELETUS. Certainly not.

SOCRATES. And when you accuse me of corrupting and deteriorating the youth, do you allege that I corrupt them intentionally or unintentionally?

MELETUS. Intentionally, I say.

SOCRATES. But you have just admitted that the good do their neighbors good, and the evil do them evil. Now, is that a truth which your superior wisdom has recog-nized thus early in life, and am I, at my age, in such darkness and ignorance as not to know that if a man with whom I have to live is corrupted by me, I am very likely to be harmed by him; and yet I corrupt him, and intentionally, too — so you say, al-though neither I nor any other human being is ever likely to be convinced by you. But either I do not corrupt them, or I corrupt them unintentionally; and on either view of the case you lie. If my offense is uninten-tional, the law has no cognizance[1] of unin-tentional offenses: you ought to have taken me privately, and warned and admonished me; for if I had been better advised, I should have left off doing what I only did unintentionally — no doubt I should; but you would have nothing to say to me and

refused to teach me. And now you bring me up in this court, which is a place not of instruction, but of punishment.

It will be very clear to you, Athenians, as I was saying, that Meletus has no care at all, great or small, about the matter. But still I should like to know, Meletus, in what I am affirmed to corrupt the young. I suppose you mean, as I infer from your indict-ment,[2] that I teach them not to acknowledge the gods which the state acknowledges, but some other new divinities or spiritual agencies in their stead. These are the lessons by which I corrupt the youth, as you say.

MELETUS. Yes, that I say, emphatically.

SOCRATES. Then, by the gods, Meletus, of whom we are speaking, tell me and the court, in somewhat plainer terms, what you mean! for I do not as yet understand whether you affirm that I teach other men to acknowledge some gods, and therefore that I do believe in gods, and am not an entire atheist — this you do not lay to my charge — but only you say that they are not the same gods which the city recog-nizes: the charge is that they are different gods. Or, do you mean that I am an atheist simply, and a teacher of atheism?

MELETUS. I mean the latter — that you are a complete atheist.

SOCRATES. What an extraordinary state-ment! Why do you think so, Meletus? Do you mean that I do not believe in the god-head[3] of the sun or moon, like other men?

MELETUS. I assure you, judges, that he does not: for he says that the sun is stone, and the moon earth.

SOCRATES. Friend Meletus, you think that you are accusing Anaxagoras[4] and you have but a bad opinion of the judges, if you fancy them illiterate to such a degree as not

[1] law . . . cognizance: law does not concern itself with.

[2] indictment: formal written statement charging a person with a crime.

[3] godhead: divine nature.

[4] Anaxagoras: philosopher-astronomer who had taught that the moon and sun were made of rocks and soil.

to know that these doctrines are found in the books of Anaxagoras the Clazomenian, which are full of them. And so, forsooth, the youth are said to be taught them by Socrates, when there are not unfrequently exhibitions of them at the theater (price of admission one drachma[1] at the most); and they might pay their money, and laugh at Socrates if he pretends to father these extraordinary views. And so, Meletus, you really think that I do not believe in any god?

MELETUS. I swear by Zeus that you believe absolutely in none at all.

SOCRATES. Nobody will believe you, Meletus, and I am pretty sure that you do not believe yourself. I cannot help thinking, men of Athens, that Meletus is reckless and impudent, and that he has written this indictment in a spirit of mere wantonness and youthful bravado. Has he not compounded a riddle, thinking to try me? He said to himself: I shall see whether the wise Socrates will discover my facetious contradiction, or whether I shall be able to deceive him and the rest of them. For he certainly does appear to me to contradict himself in the indictment as much as if he said that Socrates is guilty of not believing in the gods, and yet of believing in them — but this is not like a person who is in earnest.

I should like you, O men of Athens, to join me in examining what I conceive to be his inconsistency; and do you, Meletus, answer. And I must remind the audience of my request that they would not make a disturbance if I speak in my accustomed manner.

Did ever a man, Meletus, believe in the existence of human things, and not of human beings? . . . I wish, men of Athens, that he would answer, and not be always trying to get up an interruption. Did ever

any man believe in horsemanship, and not in horses? or in flute playing, and not in flute players? No, my friend; I will answer to you and to the court, as you refuse to answer for yourself. There is no man who ever did. But now please to answer the next question: Can a man believe in spiritual and divine agencies,[2] and not in spirits or demigods?

MELETUS. He cannot.

SOCRATES. How lucky I am to have extracted that answer, by the assistance of the court! But then you swear in the indictment that I teach and believe in divine or spiritual agencies (new or old, no matter for that); at any rate, I believe in spiritual agencies — so you say and swear in the affidavit; and yet if I believe in divine beings, how can I help believing in spirits or demigods; — must I not? To be sure I must; and therefore I may assume that your silence gives consent. Now what are spirits or demigods? are they not either gods or the sons of gods?

MELETUS. Certainly they are.

SOCRATES. But this is what I call the facetious riddle invented by you: the demigods or spirits are gods, and you say first that I do not believe in gods, and then again that I do believe in gods; that is, if I believe in demigods. For if the demigods are the illegitimate sons of gods, whether by the nymphs or by any other mothers, of whom they are said to be the sons — what human being will ever believe that there are no gods if they are the sons of gods? You might as well affirm the existence of mules, and deny that of horses and asses.[3] Such nonsense, Meletus, could only have been intended by you to make trial of me. You have put this into the indictment because you had nothing real of which to accuse me. But no one who has a particle of

---

[1] drachma: Greek coin, worth about twenty cents.

[2] agencies: *here,* person or thing through which power is exerted.

[3] You . . . asses: mules are born of the mating of a horse and an ass.

understanding will ever be convinced by you that the same men can believe in divine and superhuman things, and yet not believe that there are gods and demigods and heroes.

I have said enough in answer to the charge of Meletus: any elaborate defense is unnecessary; but I know only too well how many are the enmities which I have incurred, and this is what will be my destruction if I am destroyed — not Meletus, nor yet Anytus, but the envy and detraction of the world, which has been the death of many good men, and will probably be the death of many more; there is no danger of my being the last of them.

Someone will say: And are you not ashamed, Socrates, of a course of life which is likely to bring you to an untimely end? To him I may fairly answer: There you are mistaken: a man who is good for anything ought not to calculate the chance of living or dying; he ought only to consider whether in doing anything he is doing right or wrong — acting the part of a good man or of a bad. Whereas, upon your view, the heroes who fell at Troy were not good for much, and the son of Thetis[1] above all, who altogether despised danger in comparison with disgrace; and when he was so eager to slay Hector, his goddess mother said to him that if he avenged his companion Patroclus, and slew Hector, he would die himself — "Fate," she said, in these or the like words, "waits for you next after Hector"; he, receiving this warning, utterly despised danger and death, and instead of fearing them, feared rather to live in dishonor, and not to avenge his friend. "Let me die forthwith,"[2] he replies, "and be avenged of my enemy, rather than abide here by the beaked[3] ships, a laughingstock

---

[1] son of Thetis: Achilles.
[2] forthwith: immediately.
[3] beaked: Greek ships had beaklike metal beams projecting from the bow, with which they might pierce enemy ships.

---

and a burden of the earth." Had Achilles any thought of death and danger? For wherever a man's place is, whether the place which he has chosen or that in which he has been placed by a commander, there he ought to remain in the hour of danger; he should not think of death or of anything but of disgrace. And this, O men of Athens, is a true saying.

Strange, indeed, would be my conduct, O men of Athens, if I, who, when I was ordered by the generals whom you chose to command me at Potidaea and Amphipolis and Delium,[4] remained where they placed me, like any other man, facing death — if now, when, as I conceive and imagine, God orders me to fulfill the philosopher's mission of searching into myself and other men, I were to desert my post through fear of death, or any other fear, that would indeed be strange, and I might justly be arraigned in court for denying the existence of the gods, if I disobeyed the oracle because I was afraid of death, fancying that I was wise when I was not wise. For the fear of death is indeed the pretense of wisdom, and not real wisdom, being a pretense of knowing the unknown; and no one knows whether death, which men in their fear apprehend to be the greatest evil, may not be the greatest good. Is not this ignorance of a disgraceful sort, the ignorance which is the conceit that a man knows what he does not know? And in this respect only I believe myself to differ from men in general, and may perhaps claim to be wiser than they are: that whereas I know but little of the world below, I do not suppose that I know: but I do know that injustice and disobedience to a better, whether God or man, is evil and dishonorable, and I will never fear or avoid a possible good rather than a certain evil. And therefore if you

---

[4] Potidaea . . . Delium: campaigns in which Socrates had participated as a member of the Athenian infantry during the Peloponnesian War.

let me go now, and are not convinced by Anytus, who said that since I had been prosecuted I must be put to death (or if not, that I ought never to have been prosecuted at all); and that if I escape now, your sons will all be utterly ruined by listening to my words — if you say to me, Socrates, this time we will not mind Anytus, and you shall be let off, but upon one condition, that you are not to inquire and speculate in this way any more, and that if you are caught doing so again you shall die; if this was the condition on which you let me go, I should reply: Men of Athens, I honor and love you; but I shall obey God rather than you, and while I have life and strength I shall never cease from the practice and teaching of philosophy, exhorting anyone whom I meet and saying to him after my manner: "You, my friend — a citizen of the great and mighty and wise city of Athens — are you not ashamed of heaping up the greatest amount of money and honor and reputation, and caring so little about wisdom and truth and the greatest improvement of the soul, which you never regard or heed at all?" And if the person with whom I am arguing, says: "Yes, but I do care;" then I do not leave him or let him go at once; but I proceed to interrogate and examine and cross-examine him, and if I think that he has no virtue in him, but only says that he has, I reproach him with undervaluing the greater and overvaluing the less. And I shall repeat the same words to everyone whom I meet, young and old, citizen and alien, but especially to the citizens, inasmuch as they are my brethren. For know that this is the command of God; and I believe that no greater good has ever happened in the state than my service to the God. For I do nothing but go about persuading you all, old and young alike, not to take thought for your persons or your properties, but first and chiefly to care about the greatest improvement of the soul.

I tell you that virtue is not given by money, but that from virtue comes money and every other good of man, public as well as private. This is my teaching, and if this is the doctrine which corrupts the youth, I am a mischievous person. But if anyone says that this is not my teaching, he is speaking an untruth. Wherefore, O men of Athens, I say to you, do as Anytus bids or not as Anytus bids, and either acquit me or not; but which ever you do, understand that I shall never alter my ways, not even if I have to die many times.

Men of Athens, do not interrupt, but hear me; there was an understanding between us that you should hear me to the end; I have something more to say, at which you may be inclined to cry out; but I believe that to hear me will be good for you, and therefore I beg that you will not cry out. I would have you know that if you kill such an one as I am, you will injure yourselves more than you will injure me. Nothing will injure me, not Meletus nor yet Anytus — they cannot, for a bad man is not permitted to injure a better than himself. I do not deny that Anytus may, perhaps, kill him, or drive him into exile, or deprive him of civil rights; and he may imagine, and others may imagine, that he is inflicting a great injury upon him: but there I do not agree. For the evil of doing as he is doing — the evil of unjustly taking away the life of another — is greater far.

And now, Athenians, I am not going to argue for my own sake, as you may think, but for yours, that you may not sin against the God by condemning me, who am his gift to you. For if you kill me you will not easily find a successor to me, who, if I may use such a ludicrous figure of speech, am a sort of gadfly,[1] given to the state by God; and the state is a great and noble steed who is tardy in his motions owing to his very size, and requires to be stirred into life. I

[1] **gadfly**: biting insect.

am that gadfly which God has attached to the state, and all day long and in all places am always fastening upon you, arousing and persuading and reproaching you. You will not easily find another like me, and therefore I would advise you to spare me. I dare say that you may feel out of temper (like a person who is suddenly awakened from sleep), and you think that you might easily strike me dead as Anytus advises, and then you would sleep on for the remainder of your lives, unless God in his care of you sent you another gadfly. When I say that I am given to you by God, the proof of my mission is this: if I had been like other men, I should not have neglected all my own concerns or patiently seen the neglect of them during all these years, and have been doing yours, coming to you individually like a father or elder brother, exhorting you to regard virtue; such conduct, I say, would be unlike human nature. If I had gained anything, or if my exhortations had been paid, there would have been some sense in my doing so; but now, as you will perceive, not even the impudence of my accusers dares to say that I have ever exacted or sought pay of anyone; of that they have no witness. And I have a sufficient witness to the truth of what I say — my poverty.

Someone may wonder why I go about in private giving advice and busying myself with the concerns of others, but do not venture to come forward in public and advise the state. I will tell you why. You have heard me speak at sundry times and in divers places of an oracle or sign which comes to me, and is the divinity which Meletus ridicules in the indictment. This sign, which is a kind of voice, first began to come to me when I was a child; it always forbids but never commands me to do anything which I am going to do. This is what deters me from being a politician. And rightly, as I think. For I am certain, O men of Athens, that if I had engaged in politics,

I should have perished long ago, and done no good either to you or to myself. And do not be offended at my telling you the truth: for the truth is, that no man who goes to war with you or any other multitude, honestly striving against the many lawless and unrighteous deeds which are done in a state, will save his life: he who will fight for the right, if he would live even for a brief space, must have a private station[1] and not a public one.

I can give you convincing evidence of what I say, not words only, but what you value far more — actions. Let me relate to you a passage of my own life which will prove to you that I should never have yielded to injustice from any fear of death, and that as I should have refused to yield, I must have died at once. I will tell you a tale of the courts, not very interesting perhaps, but nevertheless true. The only office of state which I ever held, O men of Athens, was that of senator: the tribe Antiochis, which is my tribe, had the presidency at the trial of the generals who had not taken up the bodies of the slain after the battle of Arginusae; and you proposed to try them in a body, contrary to law, as you all thought afterwards; but at the time I was the only one of the Prytanes who was opposed to the illegality, and I gave my vote against you; and when the orators threatened to impeach and arrest me, and you called and shouted, I made up my mind that I would run the risk, having law and justice with me, rather than take part in your injustice because I feared imprisonment and death. This happened in the days of democracy. But when the oligarchy of the Thirty[2] was in power, they sent for me and four others into the rotunda,[3] and bade us bring Leon

[1] **station**: *here*, occupation.
[2] **oligarchy of the Thirty**: The Thirty Tyrants, appointed by Sparta over Athens after the final defeat of the city in 404 B.C.
[3] **rotunda**: Round Chamber; a building used as a government office.

the Salaminian from Salamis, as they wanted to put him to death. This was a specimen of the sort of commands which they were always giving with the view of implicating as many as possible in their crimes; and then I showed, not in word only but in deed, that, if I may be allowed to use such an expression, I cared not a straw for death, and that my great and only care was lest I should do an unrighteous or unholy thing. For the strong arm of that oppressive power did not frighten me into doing wrong; and when we came out of the rotunda the other four went to Salamis and fetched Leon, but I went quietly home. For which I might have lost my life, had not the power of the Thirty shortly afterwards come to an end. And many will witness to my words.

Now do you really imagine that I could have survived all these years, if I had led a public life, supposing that like a good man I had always maintained the right and had made justice, as I ought, the first thing? No indeed, men of Athens, neither I nor any other man. But I have been always the same in all my actions, public as well as private, and never have I yielded any base compliance to those who are slanderously termed my disciples, or to any other. Not that I have any regular disciples. But if anyone likes to come and hear me while I am pursuing my mission, whether he be young or old, he is not excluded. Nor do I converse only with those who pay; but anyone, whether he be rich or poor, may ask and answer me and listen to my words, and whether he turns out to be a bad man or a good one, neither result can be justly imputed[1] to me; for I never taught or professed to teach him anything. And if anyone says that he has ever learned or heard anything from me in private which all the world has not heard, let me tell you that he is lying.

But I shall be asked, Why do people

[1] **imputed**: attributed.

delight in continually conversing with you? I have told you already, Athenians, the whole truth about this matter: they like to hear the cross-examination of the pretenders to wisdom; there is amusement in it. Now this duty of cross-examining other men has been imposed upon me by God; and has been signified to me by oracles, visions, and in every way in which the will of divine power was ever intimated to anyone. This is true, O Athenians; or, if not true, would be soon refuted. If I am or have been corrupting the youth, those of them who are now grown up and have become sensible that I gave them bad advice in the days of their youth should come forward as accusers, and take their revenge; or if they do not like to come themselves, some of their relatives, fathers, brothers, or other kinsmen, should say what evil their families have suffered at my hands. Now is their time. Many of them I see in the court. There is Crito, who is of the same age and of the same deme[2] with myself, and there is Critobulus his son, whom I also see. Then again there is Lysanias of Sphettus, who is the father of Aeschines — he is present; and also there is Antiphon of Cephisus, who is the father of Epigenes; and there are the brothers of several who have associated with me. There is Nicostratus the son of Theosdotides, and the brother of Theodotus (now Theodotus himself is dead, and therefore he, at any rate, will not seek to stop him); and there is Paralus the son of Demodocus, who had a brother Theages; and Adeimantus the son of Ariston, whose brother Plato is present; and Aeantodorus, who is the brother of Apollodorus, whom I also see. I might mention a great many others, some of whom Meletus should have produced as witnesses in the course of his speech; and let him still produce them, if he has forgotten — I will make way for him. And let him say, if he has any testimony of the sort

[2] **deme**: unit of local government.

which he can produce. Nay, Athenians, the very opposite is the truth. For all these are ready to witness on behalf of the corrupter, of the injurer of their kindred, as Meletus and Anytus call me; not the corrupted youth only — there might have been a motive for that — but their uncorrupted elder relatives. Why should they too support me with their testimony? Why, indeed, except for the sake of truth and justice, and because they know that I am speaking the truth, and that Meletus is a liar.

Well, Athenians, this and the like of this is all the defense which I have to offer. Yet a word more. Perhaps there may be someone who is offended at me, when he calls to mind how he himself on a similar, or even a less serious occasion, prayed and entreated the judges with many tears, and how he produced his children in court, which was a moving spectacle, together with a host of relations and friends; whereas I, who am probably in danger of my life, will do none of these things. The contrast may occur to his mind, and he may be set against me, and vote in anger because he is displeased at me on this account. Now if there be such a person among you — mind, I do not say that there is — to him I may fairly reply: My friend, I am a man, and like other men, a creature of flesh and blood, and not "of wood or stone," as Homer says; and I have a family, yes, and sons, O Athenians, three in number, one almost a man, and two others who are still young; and yet I will not bring any of them hither in order to petition you for an acquittal. And why not? Not from any self-assertion[1] or want of respect for you. Whether I am or am not afraid of death is another question, of which I will not now speak. But, having regard to public opinion, I feel that such conduct would be discreditable to myself, and to you, and to the whole state. One who has reached my years, and who has a name for

[1] self-assertion: pride.

wisdom, ought not to demean himself. Whether this opinion of me be deserved or not, at any rate the world has decided that Socrates is in some way superior to other men. And if those among you who are said to be superior in wisdom and courage, and any other virtue, demean themselves in this way, how shameful is their conduct! I have seen men of reputation, when they have been condemned, behaving in the strangest manner: they seemed to fancy that they were going to suffer something dreadful if they died, and that they could be immortal if you only allowed them to live; and I think that such are a dishonor to the state, and that any stranger coming in would have said of them that the most eminent men of Athens, to whom the Athenians themselves give honor and command, are no better than women. And I say that these things ought not to be done by those of us who have a reputation; and if they are done, you ought not to permit them; you ought rather to show that you are far more disposed to condemn the man who gets up a doleful scene and makes the city ridiculous than him who holds his peace.

But, setting aside the question of public opinion, there seems to be something wrong in asking a favor of a judge, and thus procuring an acquittal, instead of informing and convincing him. For his duty is not to make a present of justice, but to give judgment; and he has sworn that he will judge according to the laws, and not according to his own good pleasure; and we ought not to encourage you, nor should you allow yourselves to be encouraged, in this habit of perjury — there can be no piety in that. Do not then require me to do what I consider dishonorable and impious and wrong, especially now, when I am being tried for impiety on the indictment of Meletus. For if, O men of Athens, by force of persuasion and entreaty I could overpower your oaths, then I should be teaching you to believe that there are no gods, and in defending should simply convict myself of the charge of not believing in them. But that is not so — far otherwise. For I do believe that there are gods, and in a sense higher than that in which any of my accusers believe in them. And to you and to God I commit my cause, to be determined by you as is best for you and me.

(He is convicted by the judges)

There are many reasons why I am not grieved, O men of Athens, at the vote of condemnation. I expected it, and am only surprised that the votes are so nearly equal; for I had thought that the majority against me would have been far larger, but now, had thirty votes gone over to the other side, I should have been acquitted. And I may say, I think, that I have escaped Meletus. I may say more; for without the assistance of Anytus and Lycon, anyone may see that he would not have had a fifth part of the votes, as the law requires, in which case he would have incurred a fine of a thousand drachmas.

And so he proposes death as the penalty. And what shall I propose on my part, O men of Athens? Clearly that which is my due. And what is my due? What return shall be made to the man who has never had the wit to be idle during his whole life; but has been careless of what the many care for — wealth, and family interests, and military offices, and speaking in the assembly, and magistracies,[1] and plots, and parties. Reflecting that I was really too honest a man to be a politician and live, I did not go where I could do no good to you or to myself; but where I could do the greatest good privately to every one of you, thither I went, and sought to persuade every man among you that he must look to himself, and seek virtue and wisdom before he looks to his private interests, and look to the state before he looks to the interests of the

state; and that this should be the order which he observes in all his actions. What shall be done to such an one? Doubtless some good thing, O men of Athens, if he has his reward; and the good should be of a kind suitable to him. What would be a reward suitable to a poor man who is your benefactor, and who desires leisure that he may instruct you? There can be no reward so fitting as maintenance in the Prytaneum.[2] O men of Athens, a reward which he deserves far more than the citizen who has won the prize at Olympia in the horse or chariot race, whether the chariots were drawn by two horses or by many. For I am in want, and he has enough; and he only gives you the appearance of happiness, and I give you the reality. And if I am to estimate the penalty fairly, I should say that maintenance in the Prytaneum is the just return.[3]

Perhaps you think that I am braving[4] you in what I am saying now, as in what I said before about the tears and prayers. But this is not so. I speak rather because I am convinced that I never intentionally wronged anyone, although I cannot convince you — the time has been too short; if there were a law at Athens, as there is in other cities, that a capital cause[5] should not be decided in one day, then I believe that I should have convinced you. But I cannot in a moment refute great slanders; and, as I am convinced that I never wronged another, I will assuredly not wrong myself. I will not say of myself that I deserve any evil, or propose any penalty. Why should I? Because I am afraid of the penalty of death which Meletus proposes? When I do not know whether death is a good or an evil, why should I propose a penalty which would

[1] **magistracies**: office of a magistrate.

[2] **Prytaneum**: public reception hall where heroes were entertained.

[3] **just return**: proper reward.

[4] **braving**: making a brave show to.

[5] **capital cause**: case in which the sentence is death.

Bust of Socrates by an unknown Greek sculptor.

certainly be an evil? Shall I say imprisonment? And why should I live in prison, and be the slave of the magistrates of the year — of the Eleven?[1] Or shall the penalty be a fine, and imprisonment until the fine is paid? There is the same objection. I should have to lie in prison, for money I have none, and cannot pay. And if I say exile (and this may possibly be the penalty which you will affix), I must indeed be blinded by the love of life, if I am so irrational as to expect that when you, who are my own citizens, cannot endure my discourses and words and have found them so grievous and odious that you will have no more of them, others are likely to endure me. No indeed, men of Athens, that is not very likely. And what a life should I lead, at my age, wandering from city to city, ever changing my place of exile, and always being driven out! For I

[1] **Eleven:** city police board, which executed court sentences.

am quite sure that wherever I go, there, as here, the young men will flock to me; and if I drive them away, their elders will drive me out at their request; and if I let them come, their fathers and friends will drive me out for their sakes.

Someone will say: Yes, Socrates, but cannot you hold your tongue, and then you may go into a foreign city, and no one will interfere with you? Now I have great difficulty in making you understand my answer to this. For if I tell you that to do as you say would be a disobedience to the God, and therefore that I cannot hold my tongue, you will not believe that I am serious; and if I say again that daily to discourse about virtue, and of those other things about which you hear me examining myself and others, is the greatest good of man, and the unexamined life is not worth living, you are still less likely to believe me. Yet I say what is true, although a thing of which it is hard for me to persuade you. Also, I have never been accustomed to think that I deserve to suffer any harm. Had I money I might have estimated the offense at what I was able to pay, and not have been much the worse. But I have none, and therefore I must ask you to proportion the fine to my means. Well, perhaps I could afford a mina, and therefore I propose that penalty: Plato, Crito, Critobulus, and Apollodorus, my friends here, bid me say thirty minae, and they will be the sureties. Let thirty minae be the penalty; for which sum they will be ample security to you.

(*He is sentenced to death*)

Not much time will be gained, O Athenians, in return for the evil name which you will get from the detractors of the city, who will say that you killed Socrates, a wise man; for they will call me wise, even although I am not wise, when they want to reproach you. If you had waited a little while, your desire would have been fulfilled in the course of nature. For I am far advanced in years, as you may perceive, and not far from death. I am speaking now not to all of you, but only to those who have condemned me to death. And I have another thing to say to them: You think that I was convicted because I had no words of the sort which would have procured my acquittal — I mean, if I had thought fit to leave nothing undone or unsaid. Not so; the deficiency which led to my conviction was not of words — certainly not. But I had not the boldness or impudence or inclination to address you as you would have liked me to do, weeping and wailing and lamenting, and saying and doing many things which you have been accustomed to hear from others, and which, as I maintain, are unworthy of me. I thought at the time that I ought not to do anything common or mean when in danger: nor do I now repent of the style of my defense; I would rather die having spoken after my manner, than speak in your manner and live. For neither in war nor yet at law ought I or any man to use every way of escaping death. Often in battle there can be no doubt that if a man will throw away his arms, and fall on his knees before his pursuers, he may escape death; and in other dangers there are other ways of escaping death, if a man is willing to say and do anything. The difficulty, my friends, is not to avoid death, but to avoid unrighteousness; for that runs faster than death. I am old and move slowly, and the slower runner has overtaken me, and my accusers are keen and quick, and the faster runner, who is unrighteousness, has overtaken them. And now I depart hence condemned by you to suffer the penalty of death — they too go their ways condemned by the truth to suffer the penalty of villainy and wrong; and I must abide by my award — let them abide by theirs. I suppose that these things may be regarded as fated — and I think that they are well.

And now, O men who have condemned me, I would fain prophesy to you; for I am about to die, and in the hour of death men are gifted with prophetic power. And I prophesy to you who are my murderers, that immediately after my departure punishment far heavier than you have inflicted on me will surely await you. Me you have killed because you wanted to escape the accuser, and not to give an account of your lives. But that will not be as you suppose: far otherwise. For I say that there will be more accusers of you than there are now; accusers whom hitherto I have restrained: and as they are younger they will be more inconsiderate with you, and you will be more offended at them. If you think that by killing men you can prevent someone from censuring[1] your evil lives, you are mistaken; that is not a way of escape which is either possible or honorable; the easiest and the noblest way is not to be disabling others, but to be improving yourselves. This is the prophecy which I utter before my departure to the judges who have condemned me.

Friends, who would have acquitted me, I would like also to talk with you about the thing which has come to pass, while the magistrates are busy, and before I go to the place at which I must die. Stay then a little, for we may as well talk with one another while there is time. You are my friends, and I should like to show you the meaning of this event which has happened to me. O my judges — for you I may truly call judges — I should like to tell you of a wonderful circumstance. Hitherto the divine faculty of which the internal oracle is the source[2] has constantly been in the habit of opposing me even about trifles, if I was going to make a slip or error in any matter; and now as you see there has come upon me that which may be thought, and is

[1] **censuring:** criticizing.
[2] **divine . . . source:** that is, conscience.

generally believed to be, the last and worst evil. But the oracle made no sign of opposition, either when I was leaving my house in the morning, or when I was on my way to the court, or while I was speaking, at anything which I was going to say; and yet I have often been stopped in the middle of a speech, but now in nothing I either said or did touching the matter in hand has the oracle opposed me. What do I take to be the explanation of this silence? I will tell you. It is an intimation that what has happened to me is a good, and that those of us who think that death is an evil are in error. For the customary sign would surely have opposed me had I been going to evil and not to good.

Let us reflect in another way, and we shall see that there is great reason to hope that death is a good; for one of two things — either death is a state of nothingness and utter unconsciousness, or, as men say, there is a change and migration of the soul from this world to another. Now if you suppose that there is no consciousness, but a sleep like the sleep of him who is undisturbed even by dreams, death will be an unspeakable gain. For if a person were to select the night in which his sleep was undisturbed even by dreams, and were to compare with this the other days and nights of his life, and then were to tell us how many days and nights he had passed in the course of his life better and more pleasantly than this one, I think that any man, I will not say a private man, but even the great king will not find many such days or nights, when compared with the others. Now if death be of such a nature, I say that to die is gain; for eternity is then only a single night. But if death is the journey to another place, and there, as men say, all the dead abide, what good, O my friends and judges, can be greater than this? If indeed when the pilgrim arrives in the world below, he is delivered from the professors of justice[1] in this world, and finds the true judges who are said to give judgment there, Minos and Rhadamanthus and Aecus and Triptolemus,[2] and other sons of God who were righteous in their own life, that pilgrimage will be worth making. What would not a man give if he might converse with Orpheus and Musaeus and Hesiod and Homer?[3] Nay, if this be true, let me die again and again. I myself, too, shall have a wonderful interest in there meeting and conversing with Palamedes, and Ajax the son of Telamon, and any other ancient hero who has suffered death through an unjust judgment; and there will be no small pleasure, as I think, in comparing my own sufferings with theirs. Above all, I shall then be able to continue my search into true and false knowledge; as in this world, so also in the next; and I shall find out who is wise, and who pretends to be wise, and is not. What would not a man give, O judges, to be able to examine the leader of the great Trojan expedition; or Odysseus or Sisyphus, or numberless others, men and women too! What infinite delight would there be in conversing with them and asking them questions! In another world they do not put a man to death for asking questions: assuredly not. For besides being happier than we are, they will be immortal, if what is said is true.

Wherefore, O judges, be of good cheer about death, and know of a certainty, that no evil can happen to a good man, either in life or after death. He and his are not neglected by the gods; nor has my own approaching end happened by mere chance. But I see clearly that the time had arrived when it was better for me to die and be released from trouble; wherefore the oracle

[1] **professors . . . justice:** those who claim to be just
[2] **Minos . . . Triptolemus:** mortal sons of Zeus who became judges in the Underworld.
[3] **Orpheus . . . Homer:** Greek poets and heroes.

gave no sign. For which reason, also, I am not angry with my condemners, or with my accusers; they have done me no harm, although they did not mean to do me any good; and for this I may gently blame them.

Still I have a favor to ask of them. When my sons are grown up, I would ask you, O my friends to punish them; and I would have you trouble them, as I have troubled you, if they seem to care about riches, or anything, more than about virtue; or if they pretend to be something when they are really nothing — then reprove them, as I have reproved you, for not caring about that for which they ought to care, and thinking that they are something when they are really nothing. And if you do this, both I and my sons will have received justice at your hands.

The hour of departure has arrived and we go our ways — I to die, and you to live. Which is better God only knows.

For Discussion

1. Through these speeches of Socrates, at an absolutely crucial instant in his life, you have the opportunity of confronting greatness directly. What characteristics of Socrates do the speeches reveal? Was he proud? Uncompromising? Independent? Did he have humor? Was he self-controlled? Law-abiding? Magnanimous? Refer to specific remarks that support your answers.

2. After the sentencing, how does the philosopher feel toward his accusers? Is he angry or spiteful or vengeful? How is his attitude to be accounted for? What surprises him most about the verdict?

3. There is reason to believe that his accusers wanted only to force Socrates to stop teaching. Accordingly, he might easily have saved his life by agreeing to go into exile. Why was he unwilling to do so? What penalty did he feel was appropriate to his "crimes"?

How would you characterize his manner before the court? How would you suppose that manner affected those who were judging him?

4. "Socrates," reads the charge in the affidavit, "is an evil-doer, and a curious person, who searches into things under the earth and in heaven, and he makes the worse appear the better cause; and he teaches the aforesaid doctrines to others." How does the accused answer the charge? How does he explain the fact that he has such an "evil name" among reputable citizens of Athens?

5. Socrates' attitude toward death has comforted numberless thousands of people since his time. What is that attitude? A man should not "calculate the chance of living or dying" (page 254). What motive should govern a man's actions instead?

6. Voicing a paradox, Socrates tells the court that "if you kill such an one as I am, you will injure yourselves more than you will injure me" (page 255). What does he mean? "Such an one as I am," according to Socrates himself, does "nothing but go about persuading you all, old and young alike, not to take thought for your persons or your properties." What should be your chief concern instead?

For Composition

In the midst of this inspiring defense one clause seems to leap from the page: ". . . if I say again that daily to discourse about virtue, and of those other things about which you hear me examining myself and others, is the greatest good of man, and that *the unexamined life is not worth living,* you are still less likely to believe me" (page 260).

1. **Analysis.** Clarify, through definition and example, your understanding of the famous Socratic sentiment that "the unexamined life is not worth living."

2. **Definition.** At one point Socrates compares himself to a "gadfly" (page 255). In a brief essay define the term *gadfly* in a way that makes the comparison intelligible.

3. **Argument.** How would Socrates fare in the world today? Consider the society in

which you live and other societies that you know of, and consider what you know about Socrates. Would he be welcomed or rejected? Give reasons to support your answer.

Words and Allusions

ALLUSIONS. Among allusions (page 53) that are made to Socrates are *Socratic method* and *Socratic irony*. The Socratic method can be seen in Socrates' cross-examination of Meletus (page 250). How would you describe the *Socratic method*? Check your description with whatever sources are available. (Socrates referred to his method of inquiry as *dialectic*. How is this word usually defined? What does it mean as used by Socrates?) Locate passages in the *Apology* where Socrates is being ironic. How would you describe *Socratic irony*?

COGNATES (page 22). The account of Socrates' trial is called the *Apology*. What is meant here by the word *apology*? Does Socrates apologize in the everyday sense of the term? What is an *apologia*? What are *apologetics*?

Professional teachers in ancient Greece were called *sophists*. The sophists became known as men clever in argument. From the noun *sophist* have come the nouns *sophistry* and *philosophy* and the adjective *sophisticated*. What does each of these words mean today, and how do they differ from the original meaning of *sophist*?

Frederick Douglass: 1817-1895

LANGSTON HUGHES

Born in Maryland, the son of a slave, Frederick Douglass escaped to freedom in 1838. Having taught himself to read and write, he became a day laborer in Massachusetts, where he soon was addressing a group opposed to slavery. His speech was a success; subsequently Douglass toured England as a lecturer, became a newspaper editor, and ended by serving as an official of the American government, most notably as minister to Haiti. His *Autobiography* tells the amazing story — of a man born with every disadvantage who through sheer strength of character made his life significant.

Douglass was someone who,
Had he walked with wary foot
And frightened tread,
From very indecision
Might be dead,   5
Might have lost his soul,
But instead decided to be bold
And capture every street
On which he set his feet,
To route each path   10
Toward freedom's goal,
To make each highway

Choose *his* compass' choice,
To all the world cried,
Hear my voice! . . .   15
Oh, to be a beast, a bird,
Anything but a slave! he said.

Who would be free
Themselves must strike
The first blow, he said.   20

He died in 1895.
He is not dead.

"*Who would be free / Themselves must strike the first blow, he said.*" An engraving of the black leader Frederick Douglass.

For Discussion

1. If Douglass had been a different sort he "Might be dead" now, according to line 5 of the poem. And yet he died in 1895. How do you account for the paradox that a man who died before the twentieth century is not yet dead?

2. What characteristics of the hero does the poem associate with Douglass? For instance, was he "wary" (line 2)? Is wariness, or caution, an heroic trait?

For Composition

Frederick Douglass' life is an inspiration to everyone — rich and poor, black and white alike.

1. **For Research.** Read two or more accounts, in encyclopedias and other sources (the *Autobiography* is one fascinating source), of Douglass' astonishing life. Prepare notes that might serve as the basis for an effective composition to present the chief facts of that life and clarify why it is relevant to our own times.

2. **Exposition.** In a brief composition of three or four paragraphs explain Douglass'

achievement with specific reference to the details that your research has uncovered.

About the Poet. **Langston Hughes** (1902–1967) is probably the most widely known American Negro poet. His verse articulates how it feels to be a Negro in America. In addition, he edited many anthologies by less well-known Negro poets and writers. As a satirist he created Jesse B. Semple — or Simple, as he is sometimes known — whose observations on race relations and mankind in general have delighted millions of readers.

Hughes began writing poetry in high school, and his broad experience from travel, his work as seaman, cook, and busboy, as well as his formal college training, helped him become one of the most successful authors in America. In 1929, after a brief apprenticeship, he began writing as a professional, producing — in addition to poetry — novels, short stories, plays, film scenarios, children's books, and articles. He translated poems by Cuban, Mexican, and Haitian poets. In later years Hughes became especially interested in Negro history. His poem about Frederick Douglass is a product of that interest.

A Simple Heart

GUSTAVE FLAUBERT

Félicité is a French word meaning happiness, bliss. It is the name, too, of the principal character in Flaubert's masterful story which you are about to read. Flaubert's Félicité was servant to a provincial French family through much of the nineteenth century. Like many other people, she led — despite her name — a life that only occasionally had moments of happiness in it, an obscure life of negligible consequences to her nation and the world. A simple heart she had, and a simple mind. Yet again like many other people, equally modest and unknown, Félicité lived out her long, quiet days in ways that partook of greatness.

I

Madame Aubain's servant Félicité[1] was the envy of the ladies[2] of Pont-l'Évêque for half a century.

She received four pounds a year. For that she was cook and general servant, and did the sewing, washing, and ironing; she could bridle a horse, fatten poultry, and churn butter — and she remained faithful to her mistress, unamiable as the latter was.

Mme. Aubain had married a gay bachelor without money who died at the beginning of 1809, leaving her with two small children and a quantity of debts. She then sold all her property except the farms of Toucques and Geffosses, which brought in two hundred pounds a year at most, and left her house in Saint-Melaine for a less expensive one that had belonged to her family and was situated behind the market.

The house had a slate roof and stood between an alley and a lane that went down to the river. There was an unevenness in the levels of the rooms which made you stumble. A narrow hall divided the kitchen from the "parlor" where Mme. Aubain spent her day, sitting in a wicker easy chair by the window. Against the panels, which were painted white, was a row of eight mahogany chairs. On an old piano under the barometer a heap of wooden and cardboard boxes rose like a pyramid. A stuffed armchair stood on either side of the Louis-Quinze[3] chimney piece, which was in yellow marble with a clock in the middle of it modeled like a temple of Vesta.[4] The whole room was a little musty, as the floor was lower than the garden.

The first floor began with "Madame's" room: very large, with a pale-flowered wallpaper and a portrait of "Monsieur" as a dandy of the period. It led to a smaller room, where there were two children's cots without mattresses. Next came the drawing room, which was always shut up and full of furniture covered with sheets. Then there was a corridor leading to a study. The shelves of a large bookcase were respectably lined with books and papers, and

[1] **Félicité:** pronounced fā·lē·cē·tā′.

[2] **envy . . . ladies:** *i.e.*, they wished they had employed her themselves.

"A Simple Heart," reprinted by permission of the publisher from *Three Tales* by Gustave Flaubert. Translated by Arthur McDowell. Published 1924 by Alfred A. Knopf, Inc.

[3] **Louis-Quinze** (kaⁿz): characteristic furniture style of the reign of King Louis XV of France.

[4] **Vesta:** Roman goddess of the hearth.

its three wings surrounded a broad writing table in darkwood. The two panels at the end of the room were covered with pen drawings, water-color landscapes, and engravings by Audran, all relics of better days and vanished splendor. Félicité's room on the top floor got its light from a dormer window, which looked over the meadows.

She rose at daybreak to be in time for Mass, and worked till evening without stopping. Then, when dinner was over, the plates and dishes in order, and the door shut fast, she thrust the log under the ashes and went to sleep in front of the hearth with her rosary in her hand. Félicité was the stubbornest of all bargainers; and as for cleanness, the polish on her saucepans was the despair of other servants. Thrifty in all things, she ate slowly, gathering off the table in her fingers the crumbs of her loaf — a twelve-pound loaf expressly baked for her, which lasted for three weeks.

At all times of year she wore a print handkerchief fastened with a pin behind, a bonnet that covered her hair, gray stockings, a red skirt, and a bibbed apron — such as hospital nurses wear — over her jacket.

Her face was thin and her voice sharp. At twenty-five she looked like forty. From fifty onwards she seemed of no particular age; and with her silence, straight figure, and precise movements she was like a woman made of wood, and going by clockwork.

La Cuisinière (*The Cook*), *an oil painting by Edouard Vuillard.*

II

She had had her love story like another.

Her father, a mason, had been killed by falling off some scaffolding. Then her mother died, her sisters scattered, and a farmer took her in and employed her, while she was still quite little, to herd the cows at pasture. She shivered in rags and would lie flat on the ground to drink water from the ponds; she was beaten for nothing, and finally turned out for the theft of a shilling which she did not steal. She went to another farm, where she became dairymaid; and as she was liked by her employers her companions were jealous of her.

One evening in August (she was then eighteen) they took her to the assembly at Colleville. She was dazed and stupefied in an instant by the noise of the fiddlers, the lights in the trees, the gay medley of dresses, the lace, the gold crosses, and the throng of people jigging all together. While she kept shyly apart a young man with a well-to-do air, who was leaning on the shaft of a cart and smoking his pipe, came up to ask her to dance. He treated her to cider, coffee, and cake, and bought her a silk handkerchief; and then, imagining she had guessed his meaning, offered to see her home. At the edge of a field of oats he pushed her roughly down. She was frightened and began to cry out; and he went off.

One evening later she was on the Beaumont road. A big hay wagon was moving slowly along; she wanted to get in front of it, and as she brushed past the wheels she recognized Theodore. He greeted her quite calmly, saying she must excuse it all because it was "the fault of the drink." She could not think of any answer and wanted to run away.

He began at once to talk about the harvest and the worthies[1] of the commune, for his father had left Colleville for the farm at Les Écots, so that now he and she were neighbors. "Ah!" she said. He added that they thought of settling him in life. Well, he was in no hurry; he was waiting for a wife to his fancy. She dropped her head; and then he asked her if she thought of marrying. She answered with a smile that it was mean to make fun of her.

"But I am not, I swear!" — and he passed his left hand round her waist. She walked in the support of his embrace; their steps grew slower. The wind was soft, the stars

[1] **worthies:** worthy people.

glittered, the huge wagonload of hay swayed in front of them, and dust rose from the dragging steps of the four horses. Then, without a word of command, they turned to the right. He clasped her once more in his arms, and she disappeared into the shadow.

The week after, Theodore secured some assignations[2] with her.

They met at the end of farmyards, behind a wall, or under a solitary tree. She was not innocent as young ladies are — she had learned knowledge from the animals — but her reason and the instinct of her honor would not let her fall. Her resistance exasperated Theodore's passion; so much so that to satisfy it — or perhaps quite artlessly — he made her an offer of marriage. She was in doubt whether to trust him, but he swore great oaths of fidelity.

Soon he confessed to something troublesome: the year before his parents had bought him a substitute for the army,[3] but any day he might be taken again, and the

[2] **assignations:** meetings.
[3] **bought . . . army:** Although the draft was universal, one could avoid service by paying another man to take his place.

ABOUT THE AUTHOR • **Gustave Flaubert** (1821–1880) was not so prolific a writer as his enormous reputation might suggest. One reason is that he was seldom satisfied with his work. He would write and rewrite, polishing each sentence to get it exactly as he wanted it. *Madame Bovary,* the novel for which he is best known, took him more than four years of constant work. It so engrossed him that he said at one point, "Madame Bovary, c'est moi" (Madame Bovary is myself), although later he so resented her popularity at the expense of his other writings that he wished he could buy all existing copies and "throw them . . . into the fire." Another work, *The Temptation of Saint Anthony,* he completely rewrote three times.

Like *Madame Bovary,* his story "A Simple Heart" is a relentlessly honest analysis of an individual human being. Despite his reputation as a meticulous artist in all of his writings, this story has been called "Flaubert's only perfect work of art."

idea of serving was a terror to him. Félicité took this cowardice of his as a sign of affection, and it redoubled hers. She stole away at night to see him, and when she reached their meeting place, Theodore racked her with his anxieties and urgings.

At last he declared that he would go himself to the prefecture[1] for information, and would tell her the result on the following Sunday, between eleven and midnight.

When the moment came she sped towards her lover. Instead of him she found one of his friends.

He told her that she would not see Theodore any more. To ensure himself against conscription[2] he had married an old woman, Madame Lehoussais, of Toucques, who was very rich.

There was an uncontrollable burst of grief. She threw herself on the ground, screamed, called to the God of mercy, and moaned by herself in the fields till daylight came. Then she came back to the farm and announced that she was going to leave; and at the end of the month she received her wages, tied all her small belongings with a handkerchief, and went to Pont-l'Évêque.

In front of the inn there she made inquiries of a woman in a widow's cap, who, as it happened, was just looking for a cook. The girl did not know much, but her willingness seemed so great and her demands so small that Mme. Aubain ended by saying: "Very well, then, I will take you."

A quarter of an hour afterwards Félicité was installed in her house.

She lived there at first in a tremble, as it were, at "the style of the house" and the memory of "Monsieur" floating over it all. Paul and Virginie, the first aged seven and the other hardly four, seemed to her beings of a precious substance; she carried them on her back like a horse; it was a sorrow to her that Mme. Aubain would not let her kiss them every minute. And yet she was happy there. Her grief had melted in the pleasantness of things all round.

Every Thursday regular visitors came in for a game of boston,[3] and Félicité got the cards and foot-warmers ready beforehand. They arrived punctually at eight and left before the stroke of eleven.

On Monday mornings the dealer who lodged in the covered passage spread out all his old iron on the ground. Then a hum of voices began to fill the town, mingled with the neighing of horses, bleating of lambs, grunting of pigs, and the sharp rattle of carts along the street. About noon, when the market was at its height, you might see a tall, hook-nosed old countryman with his cap pushed back making his appearance at the door. It was Robelin, the farmer of Geffosses. A little later came Liébard, the farmer from Toucques — short, red, and corpulent — in a gray jacket and gaiters shod with spurs.

Both had poultry or cheese to offer their landlord. Félicité was invariably a match for their cunning, and they went away filled with respect for her.

At vague intervals Mme. Aubain had a visit from the Marquis de Gremanville, one of her uncles, who had ruined himself by debauchery and now lived at Falaise on his last remaining morsel of land. He invariably came at the luncheon hour, with a dreadful poodle whose paws left all the furniture in a mess. In spite of efforts to show his breeding, which he carried to the point of raising his hat every time he mentioned "my late father," habit was too strong for him; he poured himself out glass after glass and fired off improper remarks. Félicité edged him politely out of the house — "You have had enough, Monsieur de Gremanville! Another time!" — and she shut the door on him.

She opened it with pleasure to M. Bourais,

<hr />

[1] **prefecture :** office of the chief magistrate.
[2] **conscription :** being drafted.
[3] **boston :** card game.

who had been a lawyer. His baldness, his white stock,[1] frilled shirt, and roomy brown coat, his way of rounding the arm as he took snuff — his whole person, in fact, created that disturbance of mind which overtakes us at the sight of extraordinary men.

As he looked after the property of "Madame" he remained shut up with her for hours in "Monsieur's" study, though all the time he was afraid of compromising himself. He respected the magistracy immensely, and had some pretensions to Latin.

To combine instruction and amusement he gave the children a geography book made up of a series of prints. They represented scenes in different parts of the world: cannibals with feathers on their heads, a monkey carrying off a young lady, Bedouins in the desert, the harpooning of a whale, and so on. Paul explained these engravings to Félicité; and that, in fact, was the whole of her literary education. The children's education was undertaken by Guyot, a poor creature employed at the town hall, who was famous for his beautiful hand and sharpened his penknife on his boots.

When the weather was bright the household set off early for a day at Geffosses Farm.

Its courtyard is on a slope, with the farmhouse in the middle, and the sea looks like a gray streak in the distance.

Félicité brought slices of cold meat out of her basket, and they breakfasted in a room adjoining the dairy. It was the only surviving fragment of a country house which was now no more. The wallpaper hung in tatters, and quivered in the drafts. Mme. Aubain sat with bowed head, overcome by her memories; the children became afraid to speak. "Why don't you play, then?" she would say, and off they went.

Paul climbed into the barn, caught birds,

played at ducks and drakes over the pond, or hammered with his stick on the big casks which boomed like drums. Virginie fed the rabbits or dashed off to pick cornflowers, her quick legs showing their embroidered little drawers.

One autumn evening they went home by the fields. The moon was in its first quarter, lighting part of the sky; and mist floated like a scarf over the windings of the Toucques. Cattle, lying out in the middle of the grass, looked quietly at the four people as they passed. In the third meadow some of them got up and made a half-circle in front of the walkers. "There's nothing to be afraid of," said Félicité, as she stroked the nearest on the back with a kind of crooning song; he wheeled round and the others did the same. But when they crossed the next pasture there was a formidable bellow. It was a bull, hidden by the mist. Mme. Aubain was about to run. "No! no! don't go so fast!" They mended their pace, however, and heard a loud breathing behind them which came nearer. His hoofs thudded on the meadow grass like hammers; why, he was galloping now! Félicité turned round, and tore up clods of earth with both hands and threw them in his eyes. He lowered his muzzle, waved his horns, and quivered with fury, bellowing terribly. Mme. Aubain, now at the end of the pasture with her two little ones, was looking wildly for a place to get over the high bank. Félicité was retreating, still with her face to the bull, keeping up a shower of clods which blinded him, and crying all the time, "Be quick! be quick!"

Mme. Aubain went down into the ditch, pushed Virginie first and then Paul, fell several times as she tried to climb the bank, and managed it at last by dint[2] of courage.

The bull had driven Félicité to bay against a rail fence; his slaver[3] was streaming

---

[1] **stock:** wide band worn around the neck.

[2] **dint:** force.

[3] **slaver:** saliva.

into her face; another second, and he would have gored her. She had just time to slip between two of the rails, and the big animal stopped short in amazement.

This adventure was talked of at Pont-l'Évêque for many a year. Félicité did not pride herself on it in the least, not having the barest suspicion that she had done anything heroic.

Virginie was the sole object of her thoughts, for the child developed a nervous complaint[1] as a result of her fright, and M. Poupart, the doctor, advised sea-bathing at Trouville. It was not a frequented place then. Mme. Aubain collected information, consulted Bourais, and made preparations as though for a long journey.

Her luggage started a day in advance, in Liébard's cart. The next day he brought round two horses, one of which had a lady's saddle with a velvet back to it, while a cloak was rolled up to make a kind of seat on the crupper of the other. Mme. Aubain rode on that, behind the farmer. Félicité took charge of Virginie, and Paul mounted M. Lechaptois' donkey, lent on condition that great care was taken of it.

The road was so bad that its five miles took two hours. The horses sank in the mud up to their pasterns, and their haunches jerked abruptly in the effort to get out; or else they stumbled in the ruts, and at other moments had to jump. In some places Liébard's mare came suddenly to a halt. He waited patiently until she went on again, talking·about the people who had properties along the road, and adding moral reflections to their history. So it was that as they were in the middle of Toucques, and passed under some windows bowered with nasturtiums, he shrugged his shoulders and said: "There's a Mme. Lehoussais lives there; instead of taking a young man she. . . ." Félicité did not hear the rest; the horses

were trotting and the donkey galloping. They all turned down a bypath; a gate swung open and two boys appeared; and the party dismounted in front of a manure heap at the very threshold of the farmhouse door.

When Mme. Liébard saw her mistress she gave lavish signs of joy. She served her a luncheon with a sirloin of beef, tripe, black-pudding, a fricassee of chicken, sparkling cider, a fruit tart, and brandied plums; seasoning it all with compliments to Madame, who seemed in better health; Mademoiselle, who was "splendid" now; and Monsieur Paul, who had "filled out" wonderfully. Nor did she forget their deceased grandparents, whom the Liébards had known, as they had been in the service of the family for several generations. The farm, like them, had the stamp of antiquity. The beams on the ceiling were worm-eaten, the walls blackened with smoke, and the windowpanes gray with dust. There was an oak dresser laden with every sort of useful article — jugs, plates, pewter bowls, wolf traps, and sheepshears; and a huge syringe[2] made the children laugh. There was not a tree in the three courtyards without mushrooms growing at the bottom of it or a tuft of mistletoe on its boughs. Several of them had been thrown down by the wind. They had taken root again at the middle; and all were bending under their wealth of apples. The thatched roofs, like brown velvet and of varying thickness, withstood the heaviest squalls. The cartshed, however, was falling into ruin. Mme. Aubain said she would see about it, and ordered the animals to be saddled again.

It was another half-hour before they reached Trouville. The little caravan dismounted to pass Écores — it was an overhanging cliff with boats below it — and three minutes later they were at the end of

---

[1] **child . . . complaint:** *i.e.*, her nerves were affected.

[2] **syringe:** device used to inject and withdraw fluids.

Women on a Beach at Trouville, *an oil painting by Claude Monet.*

the quay and entered the courtyard of the Golden Lamb, kept by good Mme. David.

From the first days of their stay Virginie began to feel less weak, thanks to the change of air and the effect of the sea-baths. These, for want of a bathing dress, she took in her chemise;[1] and her nurse dressed her afterwards in a coastguard's cabin which was used by the bathers.

In the afternoons they took the donkey and went off beyond the Black Rocks, in the direction of Hennequeville. The path climbed at first through ground with dells in it like the greensward[2] of a park, and then reached a plateau where grass fields and arable[3] lay side by side. Hollies rose stiffly out of the briary tangle at the edge of the road; and here and there a great withered tree made zigzags in the blue air with its branches.

[1] **chemise:** slip.
[2] **greensward:** land green with grass.
[3] **arable:** plowed and cultivated land.

They nearly always rested in a meadow, with Deauville on their left, Havre on their right, and the open sea in front. It glittered in the sunshine, smooth as a mirror and so quiet that its murmur was scarcely to be heard; sparrows chirped in hiding and the immense sky arched over it all. Mme Aubain sat doing her needlework; Virginie plaited rushes by her side; Félicité pulled up lavender, and Paul was bored and anxious to start home.

Other days they crossed the Toucques in a boat and looked for shells. When the tide went out sea urchins, starfish, and jellyfish were left exposed; and the children ran in pursuit of the foam flakes which scudded[4] in the wind. The sleepy waves broke on the sand and unrolled all along the beach; it stretched away out of sight, bounded on the land side by the dunes which parted it from the Marsh, a wide meadow shaped like an arena. As they came home that way,

[4] **scudded:** moved swiftly.

Trouville, on the hill slope in the background, grew bigger at every step, and its miscellaneous throng of houses seemed to break into a gay disorder.

On days when it was too hot they did not leave their room. From the dazzling brilliance outside light fell in streaks between the laths of the blinds. There were no sounds in the village; and on the pavement below not a soul. This silence round them deepened the quietness of things. In the distance, where men were calking,[1] there was a tap of hammers as they plugged the hulls,[2] and a sluggish breeze wafted up the smell of tar.

The chief amusement was the return of the fishing boats. They began to tack as soon as they had passed the buoys. The sails came down on two of the three masts; and they drew on with the foresail swelling like a balloon, glided through the splash of the waves, and when they had reached the middle of the harbor suddenly dropped anchor. Then the boats drew up against the quay. The sailors threw quivering fish over the side; a row of carts was waiting, and women in cotton bonnets darted out to take the baskets and give their men a kiss.

One of them came up to Félicité one day, and she entered the lodgings a little later in a state of delight. She had found a sister again — and then Nastasie Barette, "wife of Leroux," appeared, holding an infant at her breast and another child with her right hand, while on her left was a little cabin boy with his hands on his hips and a cap over his ear.

After a quarter of an hour Mme. Aubain sent them off; but they were always to be found hanging about the kitchen, or encountered in the course of a walk. The husband never appeared.

Félicité was seized with affection for them. She bought them a blanket, some shirts, and a stove; it was clear that they were making a good thing out of her. Mme. Aubain was annoyed by this weakness of hers, and she did not like the liberties taken by the nephew, who said "thee" and "thou"[3] to Paul. So as Virginie was coughing and the fine weather gone, she returned to Pont-l'Évêque.

There M. Bourais enlightened her on the choice of a boys' school. The one at Caen was reputed to be the best, and Paul was sent to it. He said his good-byes bravely, content enough at going to live in a house where he would have companions.

Mme. Aubain resigned herself to her son's absence as a thing that had to be. Virginie thought about it less and less. Félicité missed the noise he made. But she found an occupation to distract her; from Christmas onward she took the little girl to catechism every day.

III

After making a genuflexion[4] at the door she walked up between the double row of chairs under the lofty nave,[5] opened Mme. Aubain's pew, sat down, and began to look about her. The choir stalls were filled with the boys on the right and the girls on the left, and the curé[6] stood by the lectern. On a painted window in the apse the Holy Ghost looked down upon the Virgin. Another window showed her on her knees before the child Jesus, and a group carved in wood behind the altar shrine represented St. Michael overthrowing the dragon.

The priest began with a sketch of sacred history. The Garden, the Flood, the Tower of Babel, cities in flames, dying nations, and overturned idols passed like a dream before

[1] **calking**: stopping up and making tight against leakage.
[2] **plugged the hulls**: filled holes in the ship's body.
[3] **"thee" and "thou"**: intimate form of address in French.
[4] **genuflexion**: bending of the knee.
[5] **nave**: main part of the interior of a church.
[6] **curé**: parish priest.

her eyes; and the dizzying vision left her with reverence for the Most High and fear of his wrath. Then she wept at the story of the Passion. Why had they crucified Him, when He loved the children, fed the multitudes, healed the blind, and had willed, in His meekness, to be born among the poor, on the dungheap of a stable? The sowings, harvests, wine presses, all the familiar things the Gospel speaks of, were a part of her life. They had been made holy by God's passing; and she loved the lambs more tenderly for her love of the Lamb, and the doves because of the Holy Ghost.

She found it hard to imagine Him in person, for He was not merely a bird, but a flame as well, and a breath at other times. It may be His light, she thought, which flits at night about the edge of the marshes, His breathing which drives on the clouds, His voice which gives harmony to the bells; and she would sit rapt in adoration, enjoying the cool walls and the quiet of the church.

Of doctrines she understood nothing — did not even try to understand. The curé discoursed, the children repeated their lesson, and finally she went to sleep, waking up with a start when their wooden shoes clattered on the flagstones as they went away.

It was thus that Félicité, whose religious education had been neglected in her youth, learned the catechism by dint of hearing it; and from that time she copied all Virginie's observances, fasting as she did and confessing with her. On Corpus Christi Day they made a festal altar together.

The first communion loomed distractingly ahead. She fussed over the shoes, the rosary, the book and gloves; and how she trembled as she helped Virginie's mother to dress her!

All through the mass she was racked with anxiety. She could not see one side of the choir because of M. Bourais; but straight in front of her was the flock of maidens, with white crowns above their hanging veils, making the impression of a field of snow; and she knew her dear child at a distance by her dainty neck and thoughtful air. The bell tinkled. The heads bowed, and there was silence. As the organ pealed, singers and congregation took up the "Agnus Dei"; then the procession of the boys began, and after them the girls rose. Step by step, with their hands joined in prayer, they went towards the lighted altar, knelt on the first step, received the sacrament in turn, and came back in the same order to their places. When Virginie's turn came Félicité leaned forward to see her; and with the imaginativeness of deep and tender feeling it seemed to her that she actually was the child; Virginie's face became hers, she was dressed in her clothes, it was her heart beating in her breast. As the moment came to open her mouth she closed her eyes and nearly fainted.

She appeared early in the sacristy[1] next morning for Monsieur the curé to give her the communion. She took it with devotion, but it did not give her the same exquisite delight.

Mme. Aubain wanted to make her daughter into an accomplished person; and as Guyot could not teach her music or English she decided to place her in the Ursuline Convent at Honfleur as a boarder. The child made no objection. Félicité sighed and thought that Madame lacked feeling. Then she reflected that her mistress might be right; matters of this kind were beyond her.

So one day an old spring van drew up at the door, and out of it stepped a nun to fetch the young lady. Félicité hoisted the luggage onto the top, admonished the driver, and put six pots of preserves, a dozen pears, and a bunch of violets under the seat.

At the last moment Virginie broke into

[1] **sacristy**: vestry.

a fit of sobbing; she threw her arms round her mother, who kissed her on the forehead, saying over and over "Come, be brave! be brave!" The step was raised, and the carriage drove off.

Then Mme. Aubain's strength gave way; and in the evening all her friends — the Lormeau family, Mme. Lechaptois, the Rochefeuille ladies, M. de Houppeville, and Bourais — came in to console her.

To be without her daughter was very painful for her at first. But she heard from Virginie three times a week, wrote to her on the other days, walked in the garden, and so filled up the empty hours.

From sheer habit Félicité went into Virginie's room in the mornings and gazed at the walls. It was boredom to her not to have to comb the child's hair now, lace up her boots, tuck her into bed — and not to see her charming face perpetually and hold her hand when they went out together. In this idle condition she tried making lace. But her fingers were too heavy and broke the threads; she could not attend to anything, she had lost her sleep, and was, in her own words, "destroyed."

To "divert herself"[1] she asked leave to have visits from her nephew Victor.

He arrived on Sundays after mass, rosy-cheeked, bare-chested, with the scent of the country he had walked through still about him. She laid her table promptly and they had lunch, sitting opposite each other. She ate as little as possible herself to save expense, but stuffed him with food so generously that at last he went to sleep. At the first stroke of vespers she woke him up, brushed his trousers, fastened his tie, and went to church, leaning on his arm with maternal pride.

Victor was always instructed by his parents to get something out of her — a packet of moist sugar, it might be, a cake of soap, spirits, or even money at times. He

[1] **divert herself:** amuse herself.

brought his things for her to mend and she took over the task, only too glad to have a reason for making him come back.

In August his father took him off on a coasting voyage. It was holiday time, and she was consoled by the arrival of the children. Paul, however, was getting selfish, and Virginie was too old to be called "thou" any longer; this put a constraint and barrier between them.

Victor went to Morlaix, Dunkirk, and Brighton in succession and made Félicité a present on his return from each voyage. It was a box made of shells the first time, a coffee cup the next, and on the third occasion a large gingerbread man. Victor was growing handsome. He was well made, had a hint of a moustache, good honest eyes, and a small leather hat pushed backwards like a pilot's. He entertained her by telling stories embroidered with nautical terms.

On a Monday, July 14, 1819 (she never forgot the date), he told her that he had signed on for the big voyage and next night but one he would take the Honfleur boat and join his schooner, which was to weigh anchor from Havre before long. Perhaps he would be gone two years.

The prospect of this long absence threw Félicité into deep distress; one more good-by she must have, and on the Wednesday evening, when Madame's dinner was finished, she put on her clogs and made short work of the twelve miles between Pont-l'Évêque and Honfleur.

When she arrived in front of the Calvary[2] she took the turn to the right instead of the left, got lost in the timber yards, and retraced her steps; some people to whom she spoke advised her to be quick. She went all round the harbor basin full of ships, and knocked against hawsers;[3] then the ground fell away, lights flashed across each other,

[2] **Calvary:** open-air representation of the crucifixion of Christ.
[3] **hawsers:** ropes or cables.

and she thought her wits had left her, for she saw horses up in the sky.

Others were neighing by the quayside, frightened at the sea. They were lifted by a tackle[1] and deposited in a boat, where passengers jostled each other among cider casks, cheese baskets, and sacks of grain; fowls could be heard clucking, the captain swore; and a cabin boy stood leaning over the bows, indifferent to it all. Félicité, who had not recognized him, called "Victor!" and he raised his head; all at once, as she was darting forwards, the gangway was drawn back.

The Honfleur packet, women singing as they hauled it, passed out of harbor. Its framework creaked and the heavy waves whipped its bows. The canvas had swung round, no one could be seen on board now; and on the moon-silvered sea the boat made a black speck which paled gradually, dipped, and vanished.

As Félicité passed by the Calvary she had a wish to commend to God what she cherished most, and she stood there praying a long time with her face bathed in tears and her eyes towards the clouds. The town was asleep, coastguards were walking to and fro; and water poured without cessation through the holes in the sluice,[2] with the noise of a torrent. The clocks struck two.

The convent parlor would not be open before day. If Félicité were late Madame would most certainly be annoyed; and in spite of her desire to kiss the other child she turned home. The maids at the inn were waking up as she came in to Pont-l'Évêque.

So the poor slip of a boy was going to toss for months and months at sea! She had not been frightened by his previous voyages. From England or Brittany[3] you came back safe enough; but America, the colonies, the islands — these were lost in a dim region at the other end of the world.

Félicité's thoughts from that moment ran entirely on her nephew. On sunny days she was harassed by the idea of thirst; when there was a storm she was afraid of the lightning on his account. As she listened to the wind growling in the chimney or carrying off the slates she pictured him lashed by that same tempest, at the top of a shattered mast, with his body thrown backwards under a sheet of foam; or else (with a reminiscence of the illustrated geography) he was being eaten by savages, captured in a wood by monkeys, or dying on a desert shore. And never did she mention her anxieties.

Mme. Aubain had anxieties of her own, about her daughter. The good sisters found her an affectionate but delicate child. The slightest emotion unnerved her. She had to give up the piano.

Her mother stipulated for regular letters from the convent. She lost patience one morning when the postman did not come, and walked to and fro in the parlor from her armchair to the window. It was really amazing; not a word for four days!

To console Mme. Aubain by her own example Félicité remarked:

"As for me, Madame, it's six months since I heard. . . ."

"From whom, pray?"

"Why . . . from my nephew," the servant answered gently.

"Oh! your nephew!" And Mme. Aubain resumed her walk with a shrug of the shoulders, as much as to say: "I was not thinking of him! And what is more, it's absurd! A scamp of a cabin boy — what does he matter? . . . whereas my daughter . . . why, just think!"

Félicité, though she had been brought up on harshness, felt indignant with Madame — and then forgot. It seemed the simplest thing in the world to her to lose one's head

[1] **tackle** : lifting machine of ropes and pulleys.
[2] **sluice** : channel to drain excess water.
[3] **Brittany** : French peninsula between the English Channel and the Bay of Biscay.

over the little girl. For her the two children were equally important; a bond in her heart made them one, and their destinies must be the same.

She heard from the chemist[1] that Victor's ship had arrived at Havana. He had read this piece of news in a gazette.

Cigars — they made her imagine Havana as a place where no one does anything but smoke, and there was Victor moving among the Negroes in a cloud of tobacco. Could you, she wondered, "in case you needed," return by land? What was the distance from Pont-l'Évêque? She questioned M. Bourais to find out.

He reached for his atlas and began explaining the longitudes; Félicité's consternation provoked a fine pedantic smile. Finally he marked with his pencil a black, imperceptible point in the indentations of an oval spot, and said as he did so, "Here it is." She bent over the map; the maze of colored lines wearied her eyes without conveying anything; and on an invitation from Bourais to tell him her difficulty she begged him to show her the house where Victor was living. Bourais threw up his arms, sneezed, and laughed immensely: a simplicity like hers was a positive joy. And Félicité did not understand the reason; how could she when she expected, very likely, to see the actual image of her nephew — so stunted was her mind!

A fortnight afterwards Liébard came into the kitchen at market time as usual and handed her a letter from her brother-in-law. As neither of them could read she took it to her mistress.

Mme. Aubain, who was counting the stitches in her knitting, put the work down by her side, broke the seal of the letter, started, and said in a low voice, with a look of meaning:

"It is bad news . . . that they have to tell you. Your nephew. . . ."

[1] **chemist**: druggist.

He was dead. The letter said no more.

Félicité fell on to a chair, leaning her head against the wainscot;[2] and she closed her eyelids, which suddenly flushed pink. Then with bent forehead, hands hanging, and fixed eyes, she said at intervals:

"Poor little lad! poor little lad!"

Liébard watched her and heaved sighs. Mme. Aubain trembled a little.

She suggested that Félicité should go to see her sister at Trouville. Félicité answered by a gesture that she had no need.

There was a silence. The worthy Liébard thought it was time for them to withdraw.

Then Félicité said:

"They don't care, not they!"

Her head dropped again; and she took up mechanically, from time to time, the long needles on her worktable.

Women passed in the yard with a barrow of dripping linen.

As she saw them through the window-panes she remembered her washing; she had put it to soak the day before, today she must wring it out; and she left the room.

Her plank and tub were at the edge of the Toucques. She threw a pile of linen on the bank, rolled up her sleeves, and taking her wooden beater dealt lusty blows whose sound carried to the neighboring gardens. The meadows were empty, the river stirred in the wind; and down below long grasses wavered, like the hair of corpses floating in the water. She kept her grief down and was very brave until the evening; but once in her room she surrendered to it utterly, lying stretched on the mattress with her face in the pillow and her hands clenched against her temples.

Much later she heard, from the captain himself, the circumstances of Victor's end. They had bled him too much at the hospital for yellow fever. Four doctors held him at once. He had died instantly, and the chief had said:

[2] **wainscot**: paneled wall.

"Bah! there goes another!"

His parents had always been brutal to him. She preferred not to see them again; and they made no advances, either because they forgot her or from the callousness of the wretchedly poor.

Virginie began to grow weaker.

Tightness in her chest, coughing, continual fever, and veinings on her cheekbones betrayed some deep-seated complaint. M. Poupart had advised a stay in Provence. Mme. Aubain determined on it, and would have brought her daughter home at once but for the climate of Pont-l'Évêque.

She made an arrangement with a jobmaster,[1] and he drove her to the convent every Tuesday. There is a terrace in the garden, with a view over the Seine. Virginie took walks there over the fallen vine-leaves, on her mother's arms. A shaft of sunlight through the clouds made her blink sometimes, as she gazed at the sails in the distance and the whole horizon from the castle of Tancarville to the lighthouses at Havre. Afterwards they rested in the arbor. Her mother had secured a little cask of excellent Malaga; and Virginie, laughing at the idea of getting tipsy, drank a thimblefull of it, no more.

Her strength came back visibly. The autumn glided gently away. Félicité reassured Mme. Aubain. But one evening, when she had been out on a commission[2] in the neighborhood, she found M. Poupart's gig[3] at the door. He was in the hall, and Mme. Aubain was tying her bonnet.

"Give me my foot warmer, purse, gloves! Quicker, come!"

Virginie had inflammation of the lungs,[4] perhaps it was hopeless.

"Not yet!" said the doctor, and they both got into the carriage under whirling flakes of snow. Night was coming on and it was very cold.

Félicité rushed into the church to light a taper. Then she ran after the gig, came up with it in an hour, and jumped lightly in behind. As she hung on by the fringes a thought came into her mind: "The courtyard has not been shut up; supposing burglars got in!" And she jumped down.

At dawn next day she presented herself at the doctor's. He had come in and started for the country again. Then she waited in the inn, thinking that a letter would come by some hand or other. Finally, when it was twilight, she took the Lisieux coach.

The convent was at the end of a steep lane. When she was about halfway up it she heard strange sounds — a death bell tolling. "It is for someone else," thought Félicité, and she pulled the knocker violently.

After some minutes there was a sound of trailing slippers, the door opened ajar, and a nun appeared.

The good sister, with an air of compunction,[5] said that "she had just passed away." On the instant the bell of St. Leonard's tolled twice as fast.

Félicité went up to the second floor.

From the doorway she saw Virginie stretched on her back, with her hands joined, her mouth open, and head thrown back under a black crucifix that leaned towards her, between curtains that hung stiffly, less pale than was her face. Mme. Aubain, at the foot of the bed which she clasped with her arms, was choking with sobs of agony. The mother superior stood on the right. Three candlesticks on the chest of drawers made spots of red, and the mist came whitely through the windows. Nuns came and took Mme. Aubain away.

For two nights Félicité never left the dead child. She repeated the same prayers, sprinkled holy water over the sheets, came

[1] **jobmaster:** one who lets out carriages for hire.
[2] **commission:** errand.
[3] **gig:** carriage.
[4] **inflammation of the lungs:** pneumonia.

[5] **compunction:** remorse.

Burial at Ornans, *an oil painting by Gustave Courbet.*

and sat down again, and watched her. At the end of the first vigil she noticed that the face had grown yellow, the lips turned blue, the nose was sharper, and the eyes sunk in. She kissed them several times, and would not have been immensely surprised if Virginie had opened them again; to minds like hers the supernatural is quite simple. She made the girl's toilette, wrapped her in her shroud, lifted her down into her bier, put a garland on her head, and spread out her hair. It was fair, and extraordinarily long for her age. Félicité cut off a big lock and slipped half of it into her bosom, determined that she should never part with it.

The body was brought back to Pont-l'Évêque, as Mme. Aubain intended; she followed the hearse in a closed carriage.

It took another three-quarters of an hour after the mass to reach the cemetery. Paul walked in front, sobbing. M. Bourais was behind, and then came the chief residents, the women shrouded in black mantles, and Félicité. She thought of her nephew; and because she had not been able to pay these honors to him her grief was doubled, as though the one were being buried with the other.

Mme. Aubain's despair was boundless. It was against God that she first rebelled, thinking it unjust of Him to have taken her daughter from her — she had never done evil and her conscience was so clear! Ah, no! — she ought to have taken Virginie off to the south. Other doctors would have saved her. She accused herself now, wanted to join her child, and broke into cries of distress in the middle of her dreams. One dream haunted her above all. Her husband, dressed as a sailor, was returning from a long voyage, and shedding tears he told her that he had been ordered to take Virginie away. Then they consulted how to hide her somewhere.

She came in once from the garden quite upset. A moment ago — and she pointed out the place — the father and daughter had appeared to her, standing side by side, and they did nothing, but they looked at her.

For several months after this she stayed inertly in her room. Félicité lectured her gently; she must live for her son's sake, and for the other, in remembrance of "her."

"Her?" answered Mme. Aubain, as though she were just waking up. "Ah, yes! . . . yes! . . . You do not forget her!" This was an allusion to the cemetery, where she was strictly forbidden to go.

Félicité went there every day.

Precisely at four she skirted the houses, climbed the hill, opened the gate, and came to Virginie's grave. It was a little column of pink marble with a stone underneath and a garden plot enclosed by chains. The beds were hidden under a coverlet of flowers. She watered their leaves, freshened the gravel, and knelt down to break up the earth better. When Mme. Aubain was able to come there she felt a relief and a sort of consolation.

Then years slipped away, one like another, and their only episodes were the great festivals as they recurred — Easter, the Assumption, All Saints' Day. Household occurrences marked dates that were referred to afterwards. In 1825, for instance, two glaziers[1] whitewashed the hall; in 1827 a piece of the roof fell into the courtyard and nearly killed a man. In the summer of 1828 it was Madame's turn to offer the consecrated bread; Bourais, about this time, mysteriously absented himself; and one by one the old acquaintances passed away: Guyot, Liébard, Mme. Lechaptois, Robelin, and Uncle Gremanville, who had been paralyzed for a long time.

One night the driver of the mail coach announced the Revolution of July[2] in Pont-l'Évêque. A new sub-prefect[3] was appointed a few days later — Baron de Larsonnière, who had been consul in America, and brought with him, besides his wife, a sister-in-law and three young ladies, already growing up. They were to be seen about on their lawn, in loose blouses, and they had a Negro and a parrot. They paid a call on Mme. Aubain which she did not fail to return. The moment they were seen in the distance Félicité ran to let her mistress know. But only one thing could really move her feelings — the letters from her son.

He was swallowed up in a tavern life and could follow no career. She paid his debts, he made new ones; and the sighs that Mme. Aubain uttered as she sat knitting by the window reached Félicité at her spinning wheel in the kitchen.

They took walks together along the espaliered[4] wall, always talking of Virginie and wondering if such and such a thing would have pleased her and what, on some occasion, she would have been likely to say.

All her small belongings filled a cupboard in the two-bedded room. Mme. Aubain inspected them as seldom as she could. One summer day she made up her mind to it — and some moths flew out of the wardrobe.

Virginie's dresses were in a row underneath a shelf, on which there were three dolls, some hoops, a set of toy pots and pans, and the basin that she used. They took out her petticoats as well, and the stockings and handkerchiefs, and laid them out on the two beds before folding them up again. The sunshine lit up these poor things, bringing out their stains and the creases made by the body's movements. The air was warm and blue, a blackbird warbled, life seemed bathed in a deep sweetness. They found a little plush hat with thick, chestnut-colored pile; but it was eaten all over by moth. Félicité begged it for her own. Their eyes met fixedly and filled with tears; at last the mistress opened her arms, the servant threw herself into them, and they embraced each other, satisfying their

---

[1] **glaziers:** *here,* glazers, or whitewashers.
[2] **Revolution of July:** the French Revolution of 1830, which deposed Charles X, and created the July Monarchy under Louis Philippe, "the citizen king."
[3] **sub-prefect:** government official.

[4] **espaliered:** having a trellis or lattice.

grief in a kiss that made them equal.

It was the first time in their lives, Mme. Aubain's nature not being expansive. Félicité was as grateful as though she had received a favor, and cherished her mistress from that moment with the devotion of an animal and a religious worship.

The kindness of her heart unfolded.

When she heard the drums of a marching regiment in the street she posted herself at the door with a pitcher of cider and asked the soldiers to drink. She nursed cholera patients and protected the Polish refugees;[1] one of these even declared that he wished to marry her. They quarreled, however; for when she came back from the Angelus one morning she found that he had got into her kitchen and made himself a vinegar salad which he was quietly eating.

After the Poles came father Colmiche, an old man who was supposed to have committed atrocities in '93.[2] He lived by the side of the river in the ruins of a pigsty. The little boys watched him through the cracks in the wall, and threw pebbles at him which fell on the pallet where he lay constantly shaken by a catarrh; his hair was very long, his eyes inflamed, and there was a tumor on his arm bigger than his head. She got him some linen and tried to clean up his miserable hole; her dream was to establish him in the bakehouse,[3] without letting him annoy Madame. When the tumor burst she dressed it every day; sometimes she brought him cake, and would put him in the sunshine on a truss[4] of straw. The poor old man, slobbering and trembling, thanked her in his worn-out voice, was terrified that he might lose her, and stretched out his hands when he saw her go

---

[1] **Polish refugees:** persons fleeing from harsh punishment following the unsuccessful revolt of Poland against Russian rule in 1830.

[2] **'93:** 1793 was a period of extreme violence between contending political factions attempting to bring order to post-Revolutionary France.

[3] **bakehouse:** bakery.

[4] **truss:** tightly wrapped bundle.

---

away. He died; and she had a mass said for the repose of his soul.

That very day a great happiness befell her; just at dinnertime appeared Mme. de Larsonnière's Negro, carrying the parrot in its cage, with perch, chain, and padlock. A note from the baroness informed Mme. Aubain that her husband had been raised to a prefecture and they were starting that evening; she begged her to accept the bird as a memento and mark of her regard.

For a long time he had absorbed Félicité's imagination, because he came from America; and that name reminded her of Victor, so much so that she made inquiries of the Negro. She had once gone so far as to say "How Madame would enjoy having him!"

The Negro repeated the remark to his mistress; and as she could not take the bird away with her she chose this way of getting rid of him.

IV

His name was Loulou. His body was green and the tips of his wings rose-pink; his forehead was blue and his throat golden.

But he had the tiresome habits of biting his perch, tearing out his feathers, sprinkling his dirt about, and spattering the water of his tub. He annoyed Mme. Aubain, and she gave him to Félicité for good.

She endeavored to train him; soon he could repeat "Nice boy! Your servant, sir! Good morning, Marie!" He was placed by the side of the door, and astonished several people by not answering to the name Jacquot, for all parrots are called Jacquot. People compared him to a turkey and a log of wood, and stabbed Félicité to the heart each time. Strange obstinacy on Loulou's part! — directly you looked at him he refused to speak.

None the less he was eager for society; for on Sundays, while the Rochefeuille ladies, M. de Houppeville, and new familiars

— Onfroy the apothecary,[1] Monsieur Varin, and Captain Mathieu — were playing their game of cards, he beat the windows with his wings and threw himself about so frantically that they could not hear each other speak.

Bourais' face, undoubtedly, struck him as extremely droll. Directly he saw it he began to laugh — and laugh with all his might. His peals rang through the courtyard and were repeated by the echo; the neighbors came to their windows and laughed too; while M. Bourais, gliding along under the wall to escape the parrot's eye, and hiding his profile with his hat, got to the river and then entered by the garden gate. There was a lack of tenderness in the looks which he darted at the bird.

Loulou had been slapped by the butcher boy for making so free as to plunge his head into his basket; and since then he was always trying to nip him through his shirt. Fabu threatened to wring his neck, although he was not cruel, for all his tattooed arms and large whiskers. Far from it; he really rather liked the parrot, and in a jovial humor even wanted to teach him to swear. Félicité, who was alarmed by such proceedings, put the bird in the kitchen. His little chain was taken off and he roamed about the house.

His way of going downstairs was to lean on each step with the curve of his beak, raise the right foot, and then the left; and Félicité was afraid that these gymnastics brought on fits of giddiness. He fell ill and could not talk or eat any longer. There was a growth under his tongue, such as fowls have sometimes. She cured him by tearing the pellicle[2] off with her fingernails. Mr. Paul was thoughtless enough one day to blow some cigar smoke into his nostrils, and another time when Mme. Lormeau was teasing him with the end of her umbrella he snapped at the ferrule.[3] Finally he got lost.

Félicité had put him on the grass to refresh him, and gone away for a minute, and when she came back — no sign of the parrot! She began by looking for him in the shrubs, by the waterside, and over the roofs, without listening to her mistress's cries of "Take care, do! You are out of your wits!" Then she investigated all the gardens in Pont-l'Évêque, and stopped the passers-by. "You don't ever happen to have seen my parrot, by any chance, do you?" And she gave a description of the parrot to those who did not know him. Suddenly, behind the mills at the foot of the hill she thought she could make out something green that fluttered. But on the top of the hill there was nothing. A hawker[4] assured her that he had come across the parrot just before, at Saint-Melaine, in Mère Simon's shop. She rushed there; they had no idea of what she meant. At last she came home exhausted, with her slippers in shreds and despair in her soul; and as she was sitting in the middle of the garden seat at Madame's side, telling the whole story of her efforts, a light weight dropped on to her shoulder — it was Loulou! What on earth had he been doing? Taking a walk in the neighborhood, perhaps!

She had some trouble in recovering from this, or rather never did recover. As the result of a chill she had an attack of quinsy,[5] and soon afterwards an earache. Three years later she was deaf; and she spoke very loud, even in church. Though Félicité's sins might have been published in every corner of the diocese without dishonor to her or scandal to anybody, his Reverence the priest thought it right now to hear her confession in the sacristy only.

Imaginary noises in the head completed her upset. Her mistress often said to her, "Heavens! how stupid you are!" "Yes, Madame," she replied, and looked about for something.

---

[1] **apothecary**: pharmacist.
[2] **pellicle**: thin layer of skin.
[3] **ferrule**: ring of metal around the shaft of an umbrella.

[4] **hawker**: peddler.
[5] **quinsy**: severe inflammation of the throat.

Her little circle of ideas grew still narrower; the peal of church bells and the lowing of cattle ceased to exist for her. All living beings moved as silently as ghosts. One sound only reached her ears now — the parrot's voice.

Loulou, as though to amuse her, reproduced the click-clack of the turnspit, the shrill call of a man selling fish, and the noise of the saw in the joiner's[1] house opposite; when the bell rang he imitated Mme. Aubain's "Félicité! the door! the door!"

They carried on conversations, he endlessly reciting the three phrases in his repertory, to which she replied with words that were just as disconnected but uttered what was in her heart. Loulou was almost a son and a lover to her in her isolated state. He climbed up her fingers, nibbled at her lips, and clung to her kerchief: and when she bent her forehead and shook her head gently to and fro, as nurses do, the great wings of her bonnet and the bird's wings quivered together.

When the clouds massed and the thunder rumbled Loulou broke into cries, perhaps remembering the downpours in his native forests. The streaming rain made him absolutely mad; he fluttered wildly about, dashed up to the ceiling, upset everything, and went out through the window to dabble in the garden; but he was back quickly to perch on one of the firedogs and hopped about to dry himself, exhibiting his tail and his beak in turn.

One morning in the terrible winter of 1837 she had put him in front of the fireplace because of the cold. She found him dead, in the middle of his cage: head downwards, with his claws in the wires. He had died from congestion, no doubt. But Félicité thought he had been poisoned with parsley, and though there was no proof of any kind her suspicions inclined to Fabu.

She wept so piteously that her mistress said to her, "Well, then, have him stuffed!"

___
[1] **joiner's**: carpenter's.

She asked advice from the chemist, who had always been kind to the parrot. He wrote to Havre, and a person called Fellacher undertook the business. But as parcels sometimes got lost in the coach she decided to take the parrot as far as Honfleur herself.

Along the sides of the road were leafless apple trees, one after the other. Ice covered the ditches. Dogs barked about the farms; and Félicité, with her hands under her cloak, her little black sabots[2] and her basket, walked briskly in the middle of the road.

She crossed the forest, passed High Oak, and reached St. Gatien.

A cloud of dust rose behind her, and in it a mail coach, carried away by the steep hill, rushed down at full gallop like a hurricane. Seeing this woman who would not get out of the way, the driver stood up in front and the postilion[3] shouted too. He could not hold in his four horses, which increased their pace, and the two leaders were grazing her when he threw them to one side with a jerk of the reins. But he was wild with rage, and lifting his arm as he passed at full speed, gave her such a lash from waist to neck with his big whip that she fell on her back.

Her first act, when she recovered consciousness, was to open her basket. Loulou was happily none the worse. She felt a burn in her right cheek, and when she put her hands against it they were red; the blood was flowing.

She sat down on a heap of stones and bound up her face with her handkerchief. Then she ate a crust of bread which she had put in the basket as a precaution, and found a consolation for her wound in gazing at the bird.

When she reached the crest of Ecquemauville she saw the Honfleur lights sparkling in the night sky like a company of stars; beyond, the sea stretched dimly. Then a

___
[2] **sabots** (sa·bō′): wooden shoes.
[3] **postilion**: mail carrier.

faintness overtook her and she stopped; her wretched childhood, the disillusion of her first love, her nephew's going away, and Virginie's death all came back to her at once like the waves of an oncoming tide, rose to her throat, and choked her.

Afterwards, at the boat, she made a point of speaking to the captain, begging him to take care of the parcel, though she did not tell him what was in it.

Fellacher kept the parrot a long time. He was always promising it for the following week. After six months he announced that a packing case had started, and then nothing more was heard of it. It really seemed as though Loulou was never coming back. "Ah, they have stolen him!" she thought.

He arrived at last, and looked superb. There he was, erect upon a branch which screwed into a mahogany socket, with a foot in the air and his head on one side, biting a nut which the bird-stuffer — with a taste for impressiveness — had gilded.

Félicité shut him up in her room. It was a place to which few people were admitted, and held so many religious objects and miscellaneous things that it looked like a chapel and bazaar in one.

A big cupboard impeded you as you opened the door. Opposite the window commanding the garden a little round one looked into the court; there was a table by the folding bed with a water jug, two combs, and a cube of blue soap in a chipped plate. On the walls hung rosaries, medals, several benign Virgins, and a holy-water vessel made out of coconut; on the chest of drawers, which was covered with a cloth like an altar, was the shell box that Victor had given her, and after that a watering can, a toy balloon, exercise books, the illustrated geography, and a pair of young lady's boots; and, fastened by its ribbons to the nail of the looking glass, hung the little plush hat! Félicité carried observances of this kind so far as to keep one of Monsieur's frock coats. All the old rubbish which Mme. Aubain

did not want any longer she laid hands on for her room. That was why there were artificial flowers along the edge of the chest of drawers and a portrait of the Comte d'Artois in the little window recess.

With the aid of a bracket Loulou was established over the chimney, which jutted into the room. Every morning when she woke up she saw him there in the dawning light, and recalled old days and the smallest details of insignificant acts in a deep quietness which knew no pain.

Holding, as she did, no communication with anyone, Félicité lived as insensibly[1] as if she were walking in her sleep. The Corpus Christi processions[2] roused her to life again. Then she went round begging mats and candlesticks from the neighbors to decorate the altar they put up in the street.

In church she was always gazing at the Holy Ghost in the window, and observed that there was something of the parrot in him. The likeness was still clearer, she thought, on a crude color print representing the baptism of Our Lord. With his purple wings and emerald body he was the very image of Loulou.

She bought him, and hung him up instead of the Comte d'Artois, so that she could see them both together in one glance. They were linked in her thoughts; and the parrot was consecrated by his association with the Holy Ghost, which became more vivid to her eye and more intelligible. The Father could not have chosen to express Himself through a dove, for such creatures cannot speak; it must have been one of Loulou's ancestors, surely. And though Félicité looked at the picture while she said her prayers she swerved a little from time to time towards the parrot.

She wanted to join the Ladies of the

---

[1] **insensibly**: unconsciously.

[2] **Corpus Christi processions**: Roman Catholic feast, marked by devotional parades of holy symbols.

Virgin,[1] but Mme. Aubain dissuaded her.

And then a great event loomed up before them — Paul's marriage.

He had been a solicitor's clerk to begin with, and then tried business, the Customs, the Inland Revenue, and made efforts, even, to get into the Rivers and Forests. By an inspiration from heaven he had suddenly, at thirty-six, discovered his real line — the Registrar's Office. And there he showed such marked capacity that an inspector had offered him his daughter's hand and promised him his influence.

So Paul, grown serious, brought the lady to see his mother.

She sniffed at the ways of Pont-l'Évêque, gave herself great airs, and wounded Félicité's feelings. Mme. Aubain was relieved at her departure.

The week after came news of M. Bourais' death in an inn in Lower Brittany. The rumor of suicide was confirmed, and doubts arose as to his honesty. Mme. Aubain studied his accounts, and soon found out the whole tale of his misdoings — embezzled arrears,[2] secret sales of wood, forged receipts, etc. Besides that he had an illegitimate child, and "relations with a person at Dozulé."

These shameful facts distressed her greatly. In March 1853 she was seized with a pain in the chest; her tongue seemed to be covered with film, and leeches[3] did not ease the difficult breathing. On the ninth evening of her illness she died, just at seventy-two.

She passed as being younger, owing to the bands of brown hair which framed her pale, pock-marked face. There were few friends to regret her, for she had a stiffness of manner which kept people at a distance.

But Félicité mourned for her as one seldom mourns for a master. It upset her ideas

and seemed contrary to the order of things, impossible and monstrous, that Madame should die before her.

Ten days afterwards, which was the time it took to hurry there from Besançon, the heirs arrived. The daughter-in-law ransacked the drawers, chose some furniture, and sold the rest; and then they went back to their registering.

Madame's armchair, her small round table, her foot warmer, and the eight chairs were gone! Yellow patches in the middle of the panels showed where the engravings had hung. They had carried off the two little beds and the mattresses, and all Virginie's belongings had disappeared from the cupboard. Félicité went from floor to floor dazed with sorrow.

The next day there was a notice on the door, and the apothecary shouted in her ear that the house was for sale.

She tottered, and was obliged to sit down. What distressed her most of all was to give up her room, so suitable as it was for poor Loulou. She enveloped him with a look of anguish when she was imploring the Holy Ghost, and formed the idolatrous[4] habit of kneeling in front of the parrot to say her prayers. Sometimes the sun shone in at the attic window and caught his glass eye, and a great luminous ray shot out of it and put her in an ecstasy.

She had a pension of fifteen pounds a year which her mistress had left her. The garden gave her a supply of vegetables. As for clothes, she had enough to last her to the end of her days, and she economized in candles by going to bed at dusk.

---

[1] **Ladies of the Virgin:** a religious society.
[2] **arrears:** debts.
[3] **leeches:** blood-sucking worms used to bleed patients.
[4] **idolatrous:** worshiping idols.

She hardly ever went out, as she did not like passing the dealer's shop, where some of the old furniture was exposed for sale. Since her fit of giddiness she dragged one leg; and as her strength was failing Mère Simon, whose grocery business had collapsed, came every morning to split the wood and pump water for her.

Her eyes grew feeble. The shutters ceased to be thrown open. Years and years passed, and the house was neither let nor sold.

Félicité never asked for repairs because she was afraid of being sent away. The boards on the roof rotted; her bolster was wet for a whole winter. After Easter she spat blood.

Then Mère Simon called in a doctor. Félicité wanted to know what was the matter with her. But she was too deaf to hear, and the only word which reached her was "pneumonia." It was a word she knew, and she answered softly "Ah! like Madame," thinking it natural that she should follow her mistress.

The time for the festal shrines[1] was coming near. The first one was always at the bottom of the hill, the second in front of the post office, and the third towards the middle of the street. There was some rivalry in the matter of this one, and the women of the parish ended by choosing Mme. Aubain's courtyard.

The hard breathing and fever increased. Félicité was vexed at doing nothing for the altar. If only she could at least have put something there! Then she thought of the parrot. The neighbors objected that it would not be decent. But the priest gave her permission, which so intensely delighted her that she begged him to accept Loulou, her sole possession, when she died.

From Tuesday to Saturday, the eve of the festival, she coughed more often. By the evening her face had shriveled, her lips stuck to her gums, and she had vomitings; and at twilight next morning, feeling herself very low, she sent for a priest.

Three kindly women were round her during the extreme unction.[2] Then she announced that she must speak to Fabu. He arrived in his Sunday clothes, by no means at his ease in the funereal atmosphere.

"Forgive me," she said, with an effort to stretch out her arm; "I thought it was you who had killed him."

What did she mean by such stories? She suspected him of murder — a man like him! He waxed indignant, and was on the point of making a row.

"There," said the women, "she is no longer in her senses, you can see it well enough!"

Félicité spoke to shadows of her own from time to time. The women went away, and Mère Simon had breakfast. A little later she took Loulou and brought him close to Félicité with the words:

"Come, now, say good-by to him!"

Loulou was not a corpse, but the worms devoured him; one of his wings was broken, and the tow was coming out of his stomach. But she was blind now; she kissed him on the forehead and kept him close against her cheek. Mère Simon took him back from her to put him on the altar.

V

Summer scents came up from the meadows; flies buzzed; the sun made the river glitter and heated the slates. Mère Simon came back into the room and fell softly asleep.

She woke at the noise of bells; the people were coming out from vespers. Félicité's delirium subsided. She thought of the procession and saw it as if she had been there.

All the school children, the church

---

[1] **festal shrines:** temporary altars set up along the processional route.

[2] **extreme unction:** sacrament of the Catholic Church, customarily given to the dying.

singers, and the firemen walked on the pavement, while in the middle of the road the verger[1] armed with his hallebard[2] and the beadle[3] with a large cross advanced in front. Then came the schoolmaster, with an eye on the boys, and the sister, anxious about her little girls; three of the daintiest, with angelic curls, scattered rose petals in the air; the deacon controlled the band with outstretched arms; and two censer bearers[4] turned back at every step towards the Holy Sacrament, which was borne by Monsieur the curé, wearing his beautiful chasuble,[5] under a canopy of dark-red velvet held up by four churchwardens. A crowd of people pressed behind, between the white cloths covering the house walls, and they reached the bottom of the hill.

A cold sweat moistened Félicité's temples. Mère Simon sponged her with a piece of linen, saying to herself that one day she would have to go that way.

The hum of the crowd increased, was very loud for an instant, and then went further away.

A fusillade[6] shook the windowpanes. It was the postilions saluting the monstrance.[7] Félicité rolled her eyes and said as audibly as she could: "Does he look well?" The parrot was weighing on her mind.

Her agony began. A death rattle that grew more and more convulsed made her sides heave. Bubbles of froth came at the corners of her mouth and her whole body trembled.

Soon the booming of the ophicleides,[8]

[1] **verger**: church official who serves as usher.
[2] **hallebard**: weapon carried as a symbolic badge of office.
[3] **beadle**: minor parish official.
[4] **censer bearers**: those who carry the burning incense used in religious rituals.
[5] **chasuble**: priest's outer garment, worn for celebration of the Eucharist.
[6] **fusillade**: several shots fired in close succession.
[7] **monstrance**: vessel in which the consecrated Host is displayed.
[8] **ophicleides**: musical instruments producing deep tones.

the high voices of the children, and the deep voices of the men were distinguishable. At intervals all was silent, and the tread of feet, deadened by the flowers they walked on, sounded like a flock pattering on grass.

The clergy appeared in the courtyard. Mère Simon clambered on to a chair to reach the attic window, and so looked down straight upon the shrine. Green garlands hung over the altar, which was decked with a flounce of English lace. In the middle was a small frame with relics in it; there were two orange trees at the corners, and all along stood silver candlesticks and china vases, with sunflowers, lilies, peonies, foxgloves, and tufts of hortensia. This heap of blazing color slanted from the level of the altar to the carpet which went on over the pavement; and some rare objects caught the eye. There was a silver-gilt sugar basin with a crown of violets; pendants of Alençon stone glittered on the moss, and two Chinese screens displayed their landscapes. Loulou was hidden under roses and showed nothing but his blue forehead, like a plaque of lapis lazuli.[9]

The churchwardens, singers, and children took their places round the three sides of the court. The priest went slowly up the steps, and placed his great, radiant golden sun upon the lace. Everyone knelt down. There was a deep silence; and the censers glided to and fro on the full swing of their chains.

An azure vapor rose up into Félicité's room. Her nostrils met it; she inhaled it sensuously, mystically; and then closed her eyes. Her lips smiled. The beats of her heart lessened one by one, vaguer each time and softer, as a fountain sinks, an echo disappears; and when she sighed her last breath she thought she saw an opening in the heavens, and a gigantic parrot hovering above her head.

[9] **lapis lazuli** (lap′is laz′yü·lē): blue semiprecious stone.

For Discussion

1. "A Simple Heart" tells the story of one woman's life: "her wretched childhood, the disillusion of her first love, her nephew's going away." About that nephew, Mme. Aubain had once shrugged her shoulders, as much as to say, "What does he matter?" And the same might be said of Félicité herself: "What does she matter? Why go to the trouble of telling her life's story?" What justification can you see for Flaubert's having chosen Félicité's relatively uneventful and certainly unextraordinary life as a subject for fiction?

2. "Heavens! how stupid you are!" Mme. Aubain would often say to her servant, and indeed the woman was unlettered and without sophistication; she could hardly have been otherwise. Moreover, Mme. Aubain thought she was weak, permitting her nephew to take advantage of her. But what strengths, what virtues do you find in Félicité? Consider, for example, her behavior during the encounter with the bull, and her behavior to Father Colmiche, the old beggar who lived in the pigsty.

3. Félicité's childhood was miserable, devoid of love, and for the rest of her days she seemed in search of someone or something to love. Her youthful love affair ended in disillusionment. What happened to her lover Theodore? How did she learn of what he had done? How did she happen to secure work in the Aubain household?

4. With Mme. Aubain and her two children — and the memories of them collected like the paraphernalia in her upstairs room — Félicité lived out her humble days. Little Virginie was hardly four when the servant arrived. What kind of girl did Virginie grow into? What fate awaited her? What kind of life did Paul — seven when Félicité first saw him — grow up to lead?

5. The objects of Félicité's love — Theodore, Paul, Virginie, Victor, Mme. Aubain herself — gradually fell away, leaving the pitiful old woman with only a stuffed, threadbare parrot on which to expend her affection. How did the house itself change after Mme. Aubain's death? With what did Félicité finally come to identify the parrot? In what mood did she spend the final moment of her life?

6. Read through the following adjectives: sensitive, generous, loyal, uncomplaining, courageous, charitable, reverent, strong, kind. Which accurately describe aspects of Félicité's character? Mention details from the story that illustrate the qualities denoted by the adjectives you have chosen to apply to her.

7. **Point of View.** As used in analyzing imaginative literature, *point of view* refers to the position from which the events of a story are observed. If a character taking part in those events tells what happened, the story is said to be told from a *personal* point of view. "Haircut" (page 146) is an example. Alternatively, a story may be told from an *omniscient* point of view, allowing the author to stand off from the action and describe it not as it would appear to one of the characters in the story, but as it would appear to an all-knowing creator or observer above or outside the action. Both narrative methods have their advantages and disadvantages, of course. From which point of view — personal or omniscient — is "A Simple Heart" presented? What advantages can you suggest for telling a story this way? What disadvantages, in the hands of an unskillful writer?

For Composition

There is sadness in "A Simple Heart," and an absence of any glamor or sensation — in the sense in which those words are generally used. Unlike a Shakespearean hero, Félicité does not powerfully affect the lives of those around her, and when she dies, the world she leaves is not much changed. Yet the story has a haunting power about it, despite the absence of tension and excitement. Does the vividness of the individual scenes account for that power? Does the power come from the honesty with which Félicité's story is told?

1. **Argument.** In a brief composition, account as clearly as you can for the effectiveness of this story. Alternatively, if after a sensitive reading you find the story disappointing, explain specifically why you feel that it failed.

2. **Comparison and Contrast.** As an exercise in organization and expression, compare and contrast the character of Aviator Smurch in "The Greatest Man in the World" (page 219) with that of Félicité in "A Simple Heart." First jot down similarities and differences, then reduce your list by removing items that are so obvious as not to need mentioning. Limit your remarks to two or three paragraphs that include a consideration of the relationship between fame and virtue as exemplified in the two lives.

3. **Analysis.** Flaubert is a master of the telling detail that lets us experience characters and scenes unforgettably. Gremanville with his "dreadful poodle whose paws left all the furniture in a mess" and Guyot sharpening his penknife on his boots (page 270) are only two examples of details used skillfully to make characters credible and distinctive. Scenes, too, are made vivid by an appeal to more than one sense — that is, not only to the sense of sight but to the senses of hearing, smell, and touch as well.

Select from "A Simple Heart" one scene that struck you as particularly vivid. In a brief composition analyze the method and devices Flaubert used to make the scene memorable. Are the details that are mentioned distinctive? Are they described precisely? How many senses does the scene appeal to? Be as specific as possible.

Words and Allusions

MEANINGS IN NAMES. Although we believe that a name is simply a label that designates a person, we also believe that names have special meanings of their own. Thus we often say that a certain name is appropriate to a certain person and that another name is not. Since a parent names his child before he knows what the child will be like, the parent cannot know that the name will be appropriate. Writers, however, have more control. They know what their characters will be like, and they can name them accordingly. In Flaubert's story the name of his central character is significant. The name Félicité in French corresponds to the English word *felicity*. Do you find the name appropriate or inappropriate? Explain. Consider also the verb *felicitate* and the adjective *felicitous*. How do they relate to the noun *felicity*?

Antoine-Jean Gros (1771–1835) *Napoleon at Eylau.* Louvre, Paris.

Gros

Napoleon at Eylau

As he indicates in *On Heroes and Hero-Worship* (page 236), Thomas Carlyle saw Napoleon as an heroic figure. He compared him to the American frontiersman. Just as the frontiersman clears the woods to create a new civilization, Napoleon by carrying on the French Revolution was clearing away European feudalism so that a new and better social and political order might emerge.

By the time he painted this picture Baron Gros was one of Napoleon's official painters. His job was to help make Napoleon into a world-hero, a task he assumed with enthusiasm and conviction. As it happened, the battle of Eylau was not very successful. True, the opposing forces of Prussians and Russians withdrew, but Napoleon's losses were great. It was necessary to celebrate this indecisive battle by making Napoleon into something other than a military hero, or merely as a French conqueror, especially since on this occasion he had not conquered the enemy. He had merely made an orderly retreat.

In fact the battle was a kind of accident. Both armies were settling into winter quarters when an unplanned encounter started a struggle that lasted for several days. The campaign, however, was successfully concluded in the following spring; the Prussians were defeated and peace was made with Russia. Napoleon was at the height of his career, and it was desirable now to present him as an heroic peacemaker for Europe, most of which he had either conquered or subdued.

Gros dramatized the situation by emphasizing the extreme cold of the East Prussian plains, a cold with which his Parisian audience was unfamiliar. Napoleon, followed by his officers, visits the field on the day after the battle. It is covered with the frozen dead and the suffering wounded. But Napoleon is not presented as triumphing over his enemies, as in previous pictures of this sort. Rather, his right arm is stretched forth in an embracing and blessing gesture, and his eyes are raised to heaven. On the left a Lithuanian officer, recently Napoleon's enemy, responds by stretching forth one arm in salute and pressing the other to his heart. The former enemy soldier now recognizes Napoleon as the savior of Europe, one whom he wishes to serve.

The same theme is carried out in the lower right-hand corner. A wounded Prussian with a conical helmet is frightened by a Frenchman, probably a doctor, whose eager and friendly expression indicates that he wishes to help, not to hurt. This theme of reconciliation, and even change of loyalty, is further dramatized by the enemy soldier kneeling at Napoleon's stirrup, not in surrender, but in love and hope. Where else in the painting are these themes illustrated? What pictorial devices does Gros use to make Napoleon appear heroic? You have seen the same devices in movies, which took them from paintings like this.

MORSE PECKHAM

Raphael (Sanzio) (1483–1520) *The School of Athens*, fresco. Vatican, Rome.

Raphael

The School of Athens

Stephen Spender's poem "I Think Continually of Those Who Were Truly Great" (page 243) might have been inspired by this large wall-painting by Raphael. Spender's reference to those who "remembered the soul's history / Through corridors of light" could be an allusion to this painting, for Raphael presents a vast corridor of light, and one of his dominating figures is Plato, who above all men was concerned with remembering the soul's history.

The title of the painting refers to the great Greek philosophers who created the European mind and whose ideas are still the subject of passionate debate. Recognition of the importance of Greek philosophy and science was the achievement of the Italian world in which Raphael grew up. The ordered architecture of the painting, enclosed by the vaulting of the room in which the painting appears, creates a perfect setting for philosophers on the upper level and scientists on the lower to engage in their rational discussions. The architecture itself symbolizes the human reason.

In the center, from the viewer's left, are Plato and Aristotle. Plato holds the *Timaeus*, a work in which he presents his vision of the divine. In a niche in the wall to the left of him is a statue of Apollo, the god of the divine inspiration of poets. Aristotle holds his *Ethics* (page 190), and his goddess, Athene, stands in a corresponding niche to the right. Athene represents intelligence and social order. Considering the books they are holding, what is significant about the gestures each man is making with his right hand? Raphael was a master of the meaningful gesture. How are the interests of other figures indicated by gestures?

Lying on the steps is Diogenes, cynically suspicious of all rational efforts. His central position emphasizes his isolation. Why is he one of the few not engaged in discussion?

The group at the lower left surrounds Pythagoras, writing in a book. He saw in the relations of numbers and in musical harmonies the manifestation of divinity. To the right of Pythagoras, leaning on one arm, is probably Heraclitus, who saw reality not as fixed harmony but as constant change. How does his position in the painting suggest his point of view? The group at the right surrounds Euclid, demonstrating geometry with a compass. He represents the practical application of numerical relations. Why is Pythagoras on the Platonic side and Euclid on the Aristotelian?

The colors show the full range of the spectrum. How does this range relate to the subject of Raphael's painting? Raphael uses the recessive character of blue and the contrasting forward movement of yellow and brown to make the painting seem deeper. Why are Plato and Aristotle placed against the sky? How does the paving in the foreground help both the visual organization of the painting and the presentation of the subject?

MORSE PECKHAM

Jacques Louis David (1748–1825) *The Death of Socrates.* Metropolitan Museum, New York.

David

The Death of Socrates

In this painting David captures the grandeur of Socrates, as it appears in the *Apology* (page 245) and in Plato's dialogue *Phaedo,* which tells of Socrates' last discussion with his friends and of his death. The details are selected from different incidents in the *Phaedo.*

According to that dialogue more people were present than David shows, but he limits the characters in order not to lose the noble simplicity he was seeking. Socrates had been kept in chains until the morning of his execution, and when his friends joined him he had raised one leg up on the bed in order to massage it. His wife Xanthippe was present and hysterical, and he asked that she be taken home. We see her being led out in the background to the extreme left. What does her posture indicate? Phaedo sits to the right of Socrates. As Socrates requested, he controls his distress, but his powerful hand clutching Socrates' thigh shows his tension. Others react differently. The two young men above Phaedo are awestruck but scarcely aware of death, as the old man at the foot of the bed surely is. David used the standardized gestures of the stage conventions of his time. What emotions do the other figures show?

Socrates' right hand is reaching out for the cup of hemlock, to show that he drank it voluntarily, rather than postponing his death as long as possible. How does the light and shadow show that it is late afternoon? The executioner turns his head away to indicate his personal regret and distaste for his task. Socrates, still talking, raises his left arm and points to heaven, for his last discussion has been about why he believes in the immortality of the soul.

David wants to show the triumph of the rational mind and its superiority over blind faith. Thus there is nothing of Socrates' wit and humor and the many natural touches in the dialogue. He makes Socrates handsomer than he was and reduces everything in the setting to simple geometrical shapes. David's model for the garments is not the softness of traditional painting but the hardness of sculpture. Why are the curls in the hair so regular? Socrates' white costume indicates his innocence, and his naked torso is an ancient symbol for the nakedness of truth. The arrangement of the figures is also modeled on sculpture, as they might be seen in a Greek temple. Why are the colors sober and subdued?

To give life to the composition, David uses two devices of design. From the knee of the man seated at the left to the upraised hand of the man at the extreme right is implied a slanting line. The shadow on the wall joins with this to imply an immense triangle pointed to the right. This triangle at once organizes the scene visually and sets up a tension between the movement of the eye to the point of the triangle and the upright figure of Socrates. How does the tall torch help this tension? What does the deep perspective at the left contribute to the life of the painting?

MORSE PECKHAM

Daumier

The Washerwoman

In this painting and in "A Simple Heart" (page 266) Daumier and Flaubert solved the same problem — to give human dignity and greatness to ordinary working people. To do so, each had to create a new style. Traditional European painting had presented greatness by representing a great person, one defined as great by his social position and status — a king or nobleman, a saint or deity. The situation and the costume in which the figure appeared did most of the work with the aid of various other recognizable devices. Daumier used some of these devices and invented some of his own.

Greatness can be symbolized by making the figure appear monumental. This effect can be achieved by combining three principles of design. The figure must be simple, easily grasped by the eye and the mind. It must be large in relation to its surroundings. And it must give the impression of being larger than one would expect such a figure to be. Do you know of any buildings or statues that fulfill or violate these principles?

Daumier's first step was to divide his picture into three wide horizontal bands. The lowest includes the pavement of the street to which the washerwoman and her child are climbing and the shadow on the river Seine. The second consists of the sunlit part of the river and the wall of the embankment on the other side. The third combines the buildings and the sky. Why does he add a very narrow band of the wall parapet between the wide second and third bands? Next, he simplifies the buildings so that they seem one building instead of many. How does he do so? And why? Then he makes the human figures at the foot of the buildings very small to enhance the size of his main figures.

The setting is now ready for the washerwoman. By almost aligning her nose with her right arm, he makes her head into an almost perfect oval. An angle in her hair aligns her head with the tallest building, thus giving her figure added height. Why is she placed almost in the center of the painting? Instead of concealing the basket of clothes, or playing it down, Daumier gives it the brightest spot in the picture. What is the effect on the figure of placing the basket at hip level?

Next Daumier designs the woman and child in almost identical postures. Thus the larger figure is strengthened by reinforcement. In any monumental figure the neck is the weakest area. Thus Daumier has his woman lean forward to conceal that weak spot. That is why she is helping the child. What is added to the figure by the design of her arms? How does the color and lighting help make the figure monumental?

MORSE PECKHAM

Honoré Daumier (1808–1879) *The Washerwoman.* Metropolitan Museum, New York.

In Summary

1. "Some are born great, some achieve greatness, and some have greatness thrust upon them." The words are from Shakespeare's *Twelfth Night*. Explain your understanding of what the assertion means. In this section you have met a number of people who for one reason or another might be considered great: Félicité, Frederick Douglass, Socrates, the artists whom Updike mentions in "The Angels," Sisyphus, Ozymandias, even "Pal" Smurch in Thurber's story that opened the section. Which of these examples were born great, which achieved greatness, and which had greatness thrust upon them?

2. Consider once more the examples of greatness encountered in this section. Clearly what constitutes greatness remains difficult to determine. What about Ozymandias: on the evidence of Shelley's poem, what has Ozymandias done, other than become Pharaoh and have a statue erected, that would qualify him for greatness? And what of "Pal" Smurch? In short, examine the heroes represented in this section to arrive at your own opinion of what makes one man great and denies greatness to another. Although you will have earlier attempted to define greatness, that definition will necessarily be modified now by your having completed the section; Flaubert's story, for instance, might very well have provided you with new insights into the nature of heroism.

3. Extend the concept of greatness into other sections of the anthology that you have read. Is Dr. Stockmann in *An Enemy of the People* a hero? Is Don Quixote? Is the figure of Job heroic? In each instance, give reasons for answering as you have.

4. Distinguish between type and stereotype. Is Félicité a type, or is she presented to us as a distinctive individual? If the latter, what distinguishes her from thousands of other servants, past and present? From what point of view — personal or omniscient — is "The Greatest Man in the World" told? Poets, you have learned, exploit the connotations of words as well as their denotations. Consider the connotative values of Updike's diction in "The Angels." What, for example, are the connotations of "lavishing" (line 4)? Of "realm" (line 5)?

5. **Creative Writing.** Had Flaubert chosen to, he might have focused his presentation of Félicité on the incident in which, by blinding a wild bull, she saved her mistress and the two children (page 270). The justification for such a choice might have been that the event was the most important single happening in her life and therefore — more accurately than anything else she did before or after — showed her true character. Create that scene in two or three pages as vividly as you can. You should use dialogue appropriate to the people involved, and include imagery that appeals to all the senses. Alternatively, create in writing any other scene only implied in the section: the courtroom scene in which Socrates is speaking, Douglass' escape from slavery, or the childhood of "Pal" Smurch. Clearly some of those choices will require a little additional research, and all will require that you make good use of your imagination.

Reader's Choice

Chinua Achebe, *Things Fall Apart*.

Okonkwo, a harsh, proud man in an African village, is eventually destroyed along with the tribal world on which his strength is based.

Beowulf.

The oldest English epic tells of the hero Beowulf, who conquers with his bare hands the monster Grendel and Grendel's mother and later dies protecting his people from a fire-breathing dragon.

Willa Cather, *My Antonia*.

Set in the frontier days of Nebraska, the novel shows how greatness can be found in the life of a strong, enduring woman, whose yearning for a better life finds fulfillment in acceptance and love.

Joseph Conrad, *Lord Jim*.

A young seaman loses his chance for fame through an involuntary act of cowardice and exiles himself to the South Seas, where once again his honor is tested.

Henry Fielding, *Jonathan Wild, the Great*.

In this fictionalized biography of a famous English highwayman, Fielding spoofs at greatness and suggests that it is directly proportional to the size and number of crimes perpetrated by the hero.

F. Scott Fitzgerald, *The Great Gatsby*.

Born into a family of limited means, a young man accumulates enormous wealth, but what he wants is a girl he had won and lost.

The Epic of Gilgamesh.

A great Babylonian hero battles with men, giants, and gods before beginning his search for immortality in the country of Utnapishtim.

Homer, *The Iliad*.

The most famous epic of all tells the story of the closing weeks of the Trojan War, when the angry Achilles comes forth from his tent to avenge the death of his friend Patroclus with the blood of glorious Hector.

Kamala Markandaya, *Nectar in a Sieve*.

In this story of life in a rural Indian village success consists of the ability to endure despite incredible obstacles, and greatness appears in the dignity with which one meets those obstacles.

William Shakespeare, *Coriolanus*.

A patriotic but haughty aristocrat wins honor in battle for Rome but insults the populace and is driven from the city. In anger he joins the enemy and leads them against his fellow citizens.

George Bernard Shaw, *Arms and the Man*.

Raina Petkoff, daughter of a Bulgarian major, saves a professional soldier of the opposing army by hiding him in her boudoir. In the course of subsequent events she learns that most notions about war and warriors are romantic nonsense.

Stendhal, *The Red and the Black*.

Julien Sorel, a young divinity student, dreams of greatness and power. Calculating and determined, he uses others to serve his drive for power in the era following the fall of Napoleon.

John Millington Synge, *The Playboy of the Western World*.

In a comic Irish play, Christie Mahon, while resisting his father's demand that he marry an old widow, strikes his father in anger and fears he has killed him. While fleeing the law he is hailed as a hero and tries to live up to his new role.

Mark Twain, *The Adventures of Huckleberry Finn*.

Born in squalor, witness to corruption and moral degeneration, Huck escapes from both his drunken father's exploitation and Aunt Sally's middle-class morality to learn of dignity and human worth from a slave.

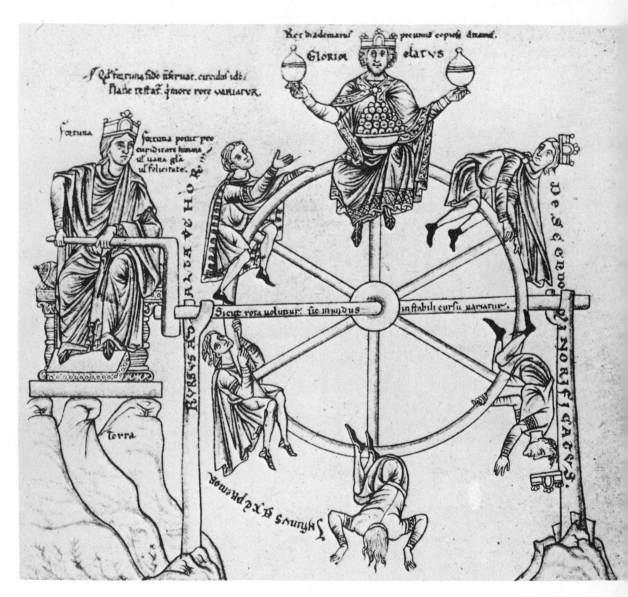

In this engraving from the twelfth century, Fortune turns
her wheel, and all men, including kings, rise and fall
accordingly.

Fate and Free Will

When we say an event was fated, we imply that some superior intelligence both knew ahead of time that it would happen and also caused, or at least allowed, it to happen as it did. The participants in the event could not have kept it from happening even if they had known about it beforehand, and in any case they were not consulted. Fate is not exactly the same as the gods or God. It is vague, dark, and yet powerful.

One way to imagine the relation between fate and a human event is to think of yourself high in a skyscraper looking down at two cars approaching a blind intersection at a high rate of speed. You know, as the drivers do not, that the cars are going to collide. Now suppose there are some electronic devices in each car to modify its acceleration and braking. The drivers do not know of these devices. You not only know about them, you remote-control them. You can let the two cars hit each other or prevent them from doing so, as you decide. Furthermore, whichever you decide, you will do it for your own reasons, not for the good of the drivers. You know little if anything about the drivers personally, and care less.

But now imagine yourself to be one of the drivers. You are driving your car according to the laws of mechanics and of the motor vehicle department, except that you are speeding. You do not know that your car is bugged in such a way that a remote observer can keep you from accelerating or stopping as you wish. When you see the other car at the intersection, you slam on the brakes. When your car does not stop as it should, you think this failure was caused by a mechanical defect and plain bad luck. Such a collision is ordinarily called an accident.

Did the drivers have any freedom of choice, or was the accident fated by the observer in the skyscraper? If you do not press this comparison too hard, it can help you imagine the relation of fate and free will to men's lives.

Fatalists say everything we do, including what we think we do freely, is caused and controlled. Libertarians say that in our inmost souls, in each individual's will, we are free to choose the right or the wrong path. Of

301

course they know that economic circumstances, luck, physical gifts, and cultural pressures mold every child and strongly influence the entire course of every person's life. But essentially, they believe, each of us controls and is responsible for most of what he does.

The whole question of fate and free will is one which, by its very nature, can never be resolved rationally. There can be no scientific proof, no experiment, which any reasonable person must accept as settling the matter. Yet it has long been, and remains, enormously important in literature as in life. Why?

There are two main reasons for its importance.

One is that people's attitude towards this problem will have much to do with whether they try to change the circumstances of their lives, especially with whether they try to improve the society they live in. If everything is fated, why bother to struggle? But if we are free, then we can, by our own decisions, change our world. Obviously the liberal attitude (*liber* is Latin for *free*) is dominant in the world, as it has been for nearly two centuries. But it certainly has not always been so, as you can see by reading the greatest of all plays which deal directly with the dilemma, *Oedipus the King* (page 349).

The other main reason for the importance of the problem is that people's attitudes towards it will essentially affect the way they assign moral responsibility for what happens. If an event, however cruel, was fated, then no person is responsible for it and no one is to blame. But if an event was at least in part freely willed, then the person or persons who did it are responsible to the extent that they willed it. Morality, the law, and psychology are all involved in trying to decide to just what extent an action was the responsibility of the person who did it. The very fact that we can rarely be absolutely sure of the degree of moral responsibility for what we have done keeps us interested in and talking about one another.

If we could answer such questions definitively, we would quit asking them, and life would be too dull for words.

George P. Elliott

How Much Land Does a Man Need?

LEO TOLSTOY

Presented with opportunities, we choose our destinies, thinking that we choose of our own free will. But — speaking through an idle conversation with some stranger, or maybe in the form of an old man holding his sides in laughter even as he promises us everything we want — is it fate that chooses for us?

1

An older sister from town came to visit her younger sister in the country. The elder had married a merchant in town; the younger a peasant in the country. Drinking tea, the sisters chatted. The elder began to brag — to boast of her life in town; how spaciously and comfortably she lived, how well she dressed the children, how nicely she ate and drank, and how she went for drives, excursions, and to the theater.

The younger sister became offended and began disparaging the merchant's life and exalting her peasant life.

"I wouldn't trade my life for yours," she said. "Our life is rough, I grant you, but we haven't a worry. You may live more neatly, and, perhaps, earn a lot at your trade, but you may lose it all. Remember the proverb: loss is gain's big brother. It often goes like that: one day you're rich and the day after, you're begging in the streets. But our peasant life is more stable: a meager life, but a long one. We won't be rich, but we'll always eat."

The old sister began to speak:

"Eat — like the pigs and calves! No elegance, no manners! No matter how hard your man works, you'll live and die in manure and so will your children!"

"What of it," said the younger; "that's our way. Our life may be hard, but we bow to no one, are afraid of no one, while you in town are surrounded by temptations. It's all right now, but tomorrow it may turn ugly — suddenly you'll find your man tempted by cards, or wine, or some young charmer, and everything will turn to ashes. That's what often happens, doesn't it?"

Pakhom, lying on top the stove, listened to the women babbling.

"It's the absolute truth," he said. "We're so busy tilling mother earth from infancy, we don't get such nonsense in our heads. There's just one trouble — too little land! If I had all the land I wanted, I wouldn't fear the Devil himself!"

The women finished their tea, chatted some more about dresses, cleared the dishes, and went to bed. But the Devil sitting behind the stove had heard everything. He was delighted that the peasant wife had induced her husband to boast and, particularly, to boast that if he had enough land even the Devil could not get him.

"All right," he thought, "we'll have a tussle, you and I; I'll give you plenty of land. And then I'll get you through your land."

2

Next to the peasants there lived a small landowner. She had three hundred and twenty-five acres of land. And she had always lived in peace with the peasants — never abusing them. Then she hired as overseer a retired soldier who began to harass the peasants with fines. No matter how careful Pakhom was, either his horses wandered into her oats, or his cattle got into her garden, or his calves strayed onto her meadow — and there was a fine for everything.

Pakhom would pay up and then curse and beat his family. Many were the difficulties Pakhom suffered all summer because of that overseer. Come winter, he was glad to stable the cattle — he begrudged them the fodder, but at least he was free from worry.

It was rumored that winter that the lady was selling her land, and that the innkeeper on the main road was arranging to buy it. The peasants heard this and groaned. "Well," they thought, "if the innkeeper gets the land, he'll pester us with worse fines than the lady. We can't get along without this land; we live too close."

A delegation of peasants representing the commune came to ask the lady not to sell the land to the innkeeper, but to give it to them. They promised to pay more. The lady agreed. The peasants started making arrangements for the commune to buy the land; they held one meeting and another meeting — but the matter was still unsettled. The Evil One divided them, and they were completely unable to agree. Then the peasants decided that each would buy individually as much as he could. To this, also, the lady agreed. Pakhom heard that his neighbor had bought fifty-five acres from the lady, and that she had loaned him half the money for a year. Pakhom became envious. "They're buying up all the land," he thought, "and I'll be left with nothing." He consulted his wife.

"People are buying," he said, "so we must buy about twenty-five acres, too. Otherwise we can't exist — the overseer is crushing us with fines."

They figured out how they could buy. They had one hundred rubles[1] put aside, and they sold the colt and half the bee swarm, hired out their son as a worker,

[1] **rubles:** Russian coins, each now worth about a dollar in American money.

ABOUT THE AUTHOR • **Leo Tolstoy** (1828–1910) is known both as Russia's greatest novelist and as a social and moral philosopher devoted to the alleviation of human suffering. Born the heir of wealthy landowners, Tolstoy served with distinction in the Russian army, retired to manage his family estates, and wrote *Anna Karenina,* the monumental *War and Peace,* and other shorter works. During those years he became acutely aware of questions regarding the meaning and purpose of life and created for himself a version of Christianity that answered his questions. He freed the serfs on his estates, worked in the fields with the peasants, and tried to live as simply as they did. In 1890 he gave away his lands to his wife and children and renounced all income from his writings so that he would own nothing. Twenty years later he left his home to seek freedom from all worldly attachments and to come closer to God. On his way to a monastery, he was taken ill and died in a small railway station.

borrowed from their brother-in-law, and raised half the money.

Pakhom gathered up the money, chose his land — forty acres including a little woods — and went to bargain with the lady. He drove a bargain for his forty acres, and sealed it with his hand and a deposit. They went to town and signed the deed with half the money paid down and the rest due in two years.

So Pakhom had his own land. He borrowed seed, sowed the land he had bought: it produced well. In a year, he had settled his debts with both the lady and his brother-in-law. And so Pakhom became a landowner: he plowed and sowed his own land, mowed hay on his own land, cut timber from his own land, and pastured his herd on his own land. When Pakhom went out to plow the land which he now owned forever, or when he happened to glance over the sprouting fields and meadows, he could not rejoice enough. It seemed to him that the grass grew and the flowers flowered in a new way. When he had walked across this land before, it had been land like any land; now it had become completely exceptional.

3

So Pakhom lived and was pleased. Everything would have been fine, had the peasants not begun trespassing on his fields and meadows. He begged them politely to stop, but the trespassing continued. Either the cowherds let the cattle into the meadows, or the horses got into the wheat while grazing at night. Time after time, Pakhom chased them out and forgave without pressing charges; then he became tired of it and started to complain to the district court. And he knew the peasants did not do these things deliberately, but only because they were crowded, yet he thought: "One still mustn't let them or they'll ravage everything. They must be taught."

To teach them, he sued once, and then again; one was fined, then another. Pakhom's neighbors began to hold a grudge against him; they started to trespass on purpose from time to time. One went to the grove at night and cut down a dozen linden trees for bast.[1] When Pakhom walked through the woods, he looked and saw a white glimmer. He approached — there lay the discarded peelings, and there stood the little stumps. If the villain had only cut the edges of the bush, or left one standing, but he had razed them all, one after the other. Pakhom was enraged. He thought and thought: "It must be Semon," he thought. He went to search Semon's farm, found nothing, and quarreled with him. And Pakhom was even more certain Semon had done it. He filed a petition. Semon was called into court. The case dragged on and on; the peasant was acquitted for lack of evidence. Pakhom felt even more wronged, and abused the elder and the judges.

"You're hand and hand with thieves," he said. "If you led honest lives, you wouldn't let thieves go free."

Pakhom quarreled with both the judges and his neighbors. The peasants started threatening to set fire to his place. Although Pakhom had more land than before, his neighbors were closing in on him.

Just then, there was a rumor that people were moving to new places. And Pakhom thought: "I have no reason to leave my land, but if some of us go, there'll be more space. I could take their land, add it to my place; life would be better. It's too crowded now."

Once when Pakhom was sitting at home, a peasant passing through dropped in. Pakhom put him up for the night, fed him, talked to him, and asked him where, pray, he came from. The peasant said he came from below, beyond the Volga, where he

---

[1] **bast**: woody fiber used in making rope and matting.

had been working. One thing led to another and the peasant gradually started telling how people were going there to settle. He told how his own people had gone there, joined the community, and divided off twenty-five acres a man.

"And the land is so good," he said, "that they sowed rye, and you couldn't see a horse in the stalks, it was so high; and so thick, that five handfuls make a sheaf. One peasant," he said, "who hadn't a thing but his bare hands, came there and now has six horses, two cows."

Pakhom's heart took fire. He was thinking: "Why be poor and crowded here if one can live well there? We'll sell the house and land here; with this money, I'll build myself a house there and set up a whole establishment. There's only trouble in this crowded place. But I had better make the trip and look into it myself."

That summer he got ready and went. He sailed down the Volga to Samara in a steamer, then walked four hundred versts[1] on foot. When he arrived, everything was just as described. The peasants were living amply on twenty-five acres per head, and they participated willingly in the activities of the community. And whoever had money could buy, in addition to his share, as much of the very best land as he wanted at a ruble an acre; you could buy as much as you wanted!

After finding out everything, Pakhom returned home and began selling all he owned. He sold the land at a profit, sold his own farm, sold his entire herd, resigned from the community, waited for spring, and set off with his family for the new place.

4

Pakhom arrived at the settlement with his family, and joined the community. He

[1] **versts:** Russian units of distance, each about two thirds of a mile.

stood the elders drinks and put all the papers in order. They accepted Pakhom, divided off one hundred and twenty-five acres of land in various fields as his portion for his family of five — in addition to the use of the pasture. Pakhom built himself a farm and acquired a herd. His part of the common land alone was three times as large as before. And the land was fertile. He lived ten times better than in the past. You had arable land and fodder at will. And you could keep as many cattle as you wanted.

At first, while he was busy building and settling himself, he was content; but after he became used to it, he felt crowded on this land, too. The first year, Pakhom sowed wheat on his share of the common land — it grew well. He wanted to sow wheat again, but there was not enough common land. And what there was, was not suitable. In that region, wheat is sown only on grassland or wasteland. They sow the land for a year or two, then leave it fallow until the grass grows back again. And there are many wanting that kind of land, and not enough of it for all. There were disputes over it, too; the richer peasants wanted to sow it themselvs, while the poor people wanted to rent it to dealers to raise tax money. Pakhom wanted to sow more. The following year, he went to a dealer and rented land from him for a year. He sowed more — it grew well; but it was far from the village — you had to cart it about fifteen versts. He saw the peasant-dealers living in farmhouses and growing rich. "That's the thing," thought Pakhom; "if only I could buy land permanently for myself and build a farmhouse on my land. Everything would be at hand." And Pakhom began pondering over how he could buy freehold land.

So Pakhom lived for three years. He rented land and sowed wheat on it. The years were good ones, and the wheat grew well, and the surplus money accumulated. But Pakhom found it annoying to rent land from people every year and to have to move from place to place. Whenever there was a good piece of land, the peasants immediately rushed to divide up everything; if Pakhom did not hurry to buy, he had no land to sow. The third year, he and a dealer rented part of the common pasture from some peasants; he had already plowed when the peasants sued and the work was wasted. "If it had been my own land," he thought, "I'd bow to no one and there'd be no trouble."

And Pakhom began to inquire where land could be bought permanently. And he came across a peasant. The peasant had bought one thousand three hundred and fifty acres, then gone bankrupt, and was selling cheaply. Pakhom began talking terms with him. They haggled and haggled and agreed on fifteen hundred rubles, half of it payable later. They had just reached an agreement when a traveling merchant stopped at the farm for something to eat. They drank and talked. The merchant said he was returning from the far-off Bashkir country.[1] There, he said, he bought thirteen thousand five hundred acres of land from the Bashkirs. And all for one thousand rubles. Pakhom began asking questions. The merchant recounted.

"You just have to be nice to the old men," he said. "I distributed about a hundred rubles' worth of oriental robes and carpets and a case of tea, and gave wine to whoever wanted it. And I got the land for less than ten kopecks[2] an acre." He showed Pakhom the deed. "The land," it read, "lies along a river, and the steppe is all grassland."

Pakhom began asking him how, where, and what.

"The land there — " said the merchant,

"you couldn't walk around it in a year. The Bashkirs own it all. And the people are as silly as sheep. You can almost get it free."

"Well," Pakhom thought, "why should I buy thirteen hundred and fifty acres for my thousand rubles and saddle myself with a debt as well, when I can really get something for a thousand rubles."

5

Pakhom asked the way to the Bashkirs and as soon as he had escorted the merchant to the door, he began getting ready to go himself. He left the house in his wife's charge, made preparations, and set off with his hired hand. They went to town, bought a case of tea, gifts, wine — everything just as the merchant had said. They traveled and traveled, traversing five hundred versts. The seventh fortnight, they arrived at a Bashkir camp. Everything was just as the merchant had said. They all lived in felt tents on the steppe[3] near a stream. They themselves neither plowed nor ate bread, but their cattle and horses wandered over the steppes in herds. Twice a day they drove the mares to the colts tethered behind the huts; they milked the mares and made kumiss[4] out of it. The women beat the kumiss and made cheese, while all the men did was drink tea and kumiss and eat mutton and play reed pipes. They were all polite and jolly and they made merry all summer. A completely backward people, with no knowledge of Russian, but friendly.

---

[1] **Bashkir country:** area between the Volga River and Ural Mountains, settled by a Turkish people.

[2] **kopecks:** Russian coins, each equal to a hundredth of a ruble.

[3] **steppe:** vast level and treeless plain.

[4] **kumiss:** drink made from mare's fermented milk.

As soon as the Bashkirs saw Pakhom, they came out of their tents and surrounded their guest. An interpreter was found; Pakhom told him he had come for land. The Bashkirs were delighted, seized Pakhom, conducted him to one of the best tents, placed him on a carpet, put feather pillows under him, sat down in a circle around him, and began serving him tea and kumiss. They slaughtered a sheep and fed him mutton. Pakhom fetched his gifts from the wagon and began distributing them among the Bashkirs. When Pakhom finished presenting his gifts to them, he divided up the tea. The Bashkirs were delighted. They jabbered and jabbered among themselves, then asked the interpreter to speak.

"They ask me to tell you that they like you," said the interpreter, "and that it is our custom to give a guest every satisfaction, and to render gifts in kind. You have presented us with gifts; now tell us what we have that you like, so we can give a gift to you."

"What I like most of all," said Pakhom, "is your land. Our land is crowded, and, furthermore, all of it has been tilled, while your land is plentiful and good. I've never seen the like."

The interpreter translated. The Bashkirs talked and talked among themselves. Pakhom did not understand what they were saying, but he saw that they were merry, were shouting something, and laughing. Then they became silent, turned to Pakhom, and the interpreter said, "They asked me to tell you that in return for your kindness they will be glad to give you as much land as you want. Just point it out and it will be yours."

They started to talk again and began to quarrel about something. Pakhom asked what the quarrel was about. And the interpreter said, "Some say the elder must be consulted about the land, that it can't be done without him. But others say it can be done."

The Bashkirs were still quarreling when, suddenly, out came a man in a fox fur cap. Everyone fell silent and stood up. And the interpreter said:

"That's the elder himself."

Pakhom immediately fetched the best robe and brought it to the elder along with five pounds of tea. The elder accepted and sat down in a seat of honor. And the Bashkirs immediately started telling him something. The elder listened and listened, requested silence with a nod, and said to Pakhom in Russian:

"Well," he said. "It can be done. Choose whatever you like. Land's plentiful."

"What does that mean: take what I want," thought Pakhom. "It has to be secured somehow. Or they'll say it's yours, then take it away."

"Thank you," he said, "for your kind words. You do have a lot of land, and I need only a little. But I'd like to know which is mine. It must be measured off somehow, and secured as mine. Our lives and deaths are in God's hands. What you, good people, are giving, your children may take back."

"You're right," said the elder; "it can be secured."

Pakhom said:

"I heard there was a merchant here. You gave him a little piece of land too, and made a deed. I should have the same thing."

The elder understood.

"It can all be done," he said. "We have a scribe, and we'll go to the town to affix the seals."

"And what is the price?" said Pakhom.

"We've only one price: a thousand rubles a day."

Pakhom did not understand.

"What kind of measure is that — a day? How many acres does it have?"

"That," he said, "we don't know. But we sell by the day; as much as you can walk around in a day is yours, and the price is a thousand rubles a day."

Pakhom was astonished.

"But look," he said, "a day's walking is a lot of land."

The elder laughed.

"It's all yours!" he said. "There's just one condition: if you're not back where you started in a day, your money is lost."

"And how," Pakhom said, "will you mark where I go?"

"Well, we'll stand on the spot you choose, and stay there while you walk off a circle; and you'll take a spade with you and, where convenient, dig holes to mark your path and pile the dirt up high; then we'll drive a plow from pit to pit. Make your circle wherever you want. What you walk around is all yours, as long as you're back where you started by sundown."

Pakhom was delighted. They decided to start off early. They chatted, drank more kumiss, ate mutton, drank tea again; night came on. They laid down a feather bed for Pakhom, and the Bashkirs dispersed, promising to assemble the next day at dawn to set out for the starting point before sunrise.

7

Pakhom lay on the feather bed, unable to sleep for thinking about the land. "I'll grab off a big piece of my own," he thought. "I can walk fifty versts in a day. The days are long now; there'll be quite a bit of land in fifty versts. What's poorest, I'll sell or let to the peasants, and I'll pick out the best to settle on myself. I'll get a plow and two oxen, and hire two laborers; I'll plow over a hundred acres and put cattle to graze on the rest."

All night Pakhom lay awake, drifting off to sleep only just before dawn. No sooner had he fallen asleep than he started to dream. He saw himself lying in the same hut and heard someone chuckling outside. And he wanted to see who was laughing, got up,

went out of the hut, and there sat the Bashkir elder himself in front of the hut with both hands holding his sides, rocking back and forth, laughing at something.

Pakhom approached him and asked: "What are you laughing at?" Then he saw that it was not the Bashkir elder, but the merchant of the other day who had come to him and told him about the land. And he had barely asked the merchant, "Have you been here long?" — when it was no longer the merchant, but the peasant who had come on foot from the south long ago. Then Pakhom saw that it was not the peasant, but the Devil himself, laughing, horns, hoofs, and all; and in front of him lay a barefoot man in shirt and trousers. And Pakhom looked closer to see what sort of man he was. He saw it was a corpse and that it was — he himself. Horrified, Pakhom woke up. "The things one dreams," he thought. He looked around; through the open door he saw the dawn; it was already turning white. "Must rouse the people," he thought; "time to go." Pakhom got up, woke his hired hand who was asleep in the wagon, ordered the horses harnessed, and went to wake the Bashkirs.

"It's time," he said, "to go to the steppe to measure off the land."

The Bashkirs got up, assembled everything, and the elder arrived. The Bashkirs began drinking kumiss again, and offered Pakhom tea, but he did not want to linger.

"If we're going, let's go," he said. "It's time."

8

The Bashkirs assembled, climbed on horseback and in wagons and set off. Meanwhile, Pakhom took a spade and set off with his laborer in his own wagon. They arrived at the steppe just as day was breaking. They went up a hillock[1] (known as a *shikhan* in Bashkir). The Bashkirs climbed out of their

---

[1] **hillock**: small hill.

"It was all grassland, level as the palm of the hand, black as a poppy seed. . . ." A nineteenth-century print of the Russian Steppes.

wagons, slid down from their horses, and gathered in a group. The elder went to Pakhom and pointed.

"There," he said; "everything the eye encompasses is ours. Take your pick."

Pakhom's eyes glowed. It was all grassland, level as the palm of the hand, black as a poppy seed, and wherever there was a hollow, there was grass growing chest-high.

The elder took off his fox cap and put it on the ground.

"That," he said, "will be the marker. Leave from here; return here. Whatever you walk around will be yours."

Pakhom drew out his money, placed it on the cap, unfastened his belt, took off his outer coat, girded his belt tightly over his stomach again, put a bag of bread inside his jacket, tied a flask of water to his belt, drew his bootlegs tight, took the spade from his laborer, and got set to go. He pondered and pondered over which direction to take — it was good everywhere. He was thinking: "It's all the same: I'll head toward the sunrise." He turned to face the sun and paced restlessly, waiting for it to appear over the horizon. He was thinking: "I must lose no time. And walking's easier while it's still cold." As soon as the sun's rays spurted over the horizon, Pakhom flung the spade over his shoulder and started off across the steppe.

He walked neither quickly nor slowly. He covered a verst; stopped, dug out a hole, and piled the turf up so it could be seen. He walked further. He loosened up and lengthened his stride. He covered still more ground; dug still another pit.

Pakhom glanced back. The *shikhan* was clearly visible in the sun, and the people stood there, and the hoops of the cart wheels glittered. Pakhom guessed that he had covered about five versts. It was getting warmer; he took off his jacket, flung it over his shoulder, and went on. He covered another five versts. It was warm. He glanced at the sun — already breakfast time.

"One lap finished," thought Pakhom. "But there are four in a day; it's too early to turn around yet. I'll just take my boots off." He sat down, took them off, stuck them in his belt, and went on. Walking became easier. He thought, "I'll just cover about five more versts, then start veering left. This is a very nice spot, too good to leave out. The farther away it is, the better it gets." He walked straight on. When he glanced around, the *shikhan* was barely visible, the people looked like black ants, and there was something faintly glistening on it.

"Well," thought Pakhom, "I've taken enough on this side; I must turn. Besides, I've been sweating — I'm thirsty." He stopped, dug a bigger hole, stacked the turf, untied his flask, and drank. Then he veered sharply to the left. On and on he went; the grass grew taller and it became hot.

Pakhom began to feel tired; he glanced at the sun — it was already lunch time. He stopped; sat on the ground; ate bread and drank water, but did not lie down. "Lie down and you'll fall asleep," he thought. After a while, he walked on. Walking was easy at first. Eating had increased his strength. But it had gotten very hot and he was becoming sleepy. Still he pressed on, thinking — an hour of suffering for a life-time of living.

He walked a long way in this direction too, and when he was about to turn left, he came to a damp hollow, too nice to over-look. "Flax[1] will grow well there," he thought. Again he went straight on. He took possession of the hollow, dug a hole beyond it, and turned the second corner. Pakhom glanced back at the *shikhan:* it was hazy from the heat, something seemed to be wavering in the air, and through the haze the people barely visible on top of the *shikhan* — fifteen versts away. "Well," thought Pakhom, "I've taken long sides, I must take this one shorter." As he walked the third side, he increased his stride. He looked at the sun — it was already approaching tea-time, and he had only covered two versts on the third side. And it was still fifteen versts to the starting point. "No," he thought, "I'll have a lopsided place, but I must go straight back so I'll arrive in time. And not take any more. There's lots of land already." Pakhom shoveled out a hole as quickly as he could and turned straight to-ward the *shikhan.*

9

As Pakhom walked straight toward the *shikhan,* he began having difficulties. He

[1] **flax:** plant from which linen thread and linseed oil are made.

was perspiring, and his bare legs were cut and bruised and were beginning to fail him. He wanted to rest but could not — other-wise he would not arrive before sunset. The sun would not wait; it continued sinking, sinking. "Ah," he thought, "if only I haven't made a mistake and taken too much! What if I don't make it?" He glanced ahead at the *shikhan,* looked at the sun: the starting point was far away, and the sun was nearing the horizon.

So Pakhom went on with difficulty; he kept increasing and increasing his stride. He walked, walked — and was still far away; he broke into a trot. He threw off his jacket, dropped his boots and flask; he threw off his cap, keeping only his spade to lean on. "Ah," he thought, "I've been too greedy, I've ruined the whole thing, I won't get there by sundown." And fear shortened his breath even more. Pakhom ran; his shirt and trousers clung to his body with sweat; his mouth was parched. His chest felt as though it had been inflated by the blacksmith's bel-lows; a hammer beat in his heart; and his legs no longer seemed to belong to his body — they were collapsing under him. Pakhom began to worry about dying of strain.

He was afraid of dying, but unable to stop. "I've run so far," he thought. "I'd be a fool to stop now." He ran and ran, and was very close when he heard a screeching — the Bashkirs shrieking at him — and his heart became even more inflamed by their cries. Pakhom pressed forward with his re-maining strength, but the sun was already reaching the horizon; and, slipping behind a cloud, it became large, red, and bloody. Now it was begining to go down. Although the sun was close to setting, Pakhom was no longer far from the starting point either. He could already see the people on the *shikhan* waving their arms at him, urging him on. He saw the fox cap on the ground and the money on it; and he saw the elder sitting on the ground, holding his sides with his hands. And Pakhom remembered his dream. "There is plenty of land," he thought, "if it please God to let me live on it. Oh, I've ruined myself," he thought. "I won't make it."

Pakhom glanced at the sun, but it had touched the earth and had already begun to slip behind the horizon which cut it into an arc. Pakhom overreached his remaining strength, driving his body forward so that his legs could barely move fast enough to keep him from falling. Just as Pakhom ran up to the base of the *shikhan*, it suddenly became dark. He glanced around — the sun had already set. Pakhom sighed. "My work has fallen through," he thought. He was about to stop when he heard the Bashkirs still shrieking. And he remembered that though it seemed below that the sun had set, it would still be shining on the top of the *shikhan*. Pakhom took a deep breath and ran up the *shikhan*. It was still light there. As Pakhom reached the top, he saw the elder sitting in front of the cap, chuckling, holding his sides with his hands. Pakhom remembered his dream and groaned; his legs gave way, and he fell forward, his hands touching the cap.

"Aiee, good man!" cried the elder. "You have acquired plenty of land!"

Pakhom's laborer ran to lift him, but the blood was flowing from his mouth and he lay dead.

The Bashkirs clicked their tongues in commiseration.

The laborer took up the spade, dug Pakhom a grave just long enough to reach from his feet to his head — six feet in all — and buried him.

———

For Discussion

1. The night before the most important day of his life, Pakhom has a ghastly dream. What does he dream? How does it happen that the dream comes true? To what extent is Pakhom himself responsible for what happens the following day?

2. Life is filled with accidents and temptations. "The instruments of darkness tell us truths," says Banquo in *Macbeth*, "Win us with honest trifles, to betray's In deepest consequence." Evil, in other words, lures us by means of innocuous and appealing gifts, only to betray us later, when it matters most. Discuss to what extent Banquo's thought is illustrated by what happens in Tolstoy's story.

3. The structure of "How Much Land Does a Man Need?" is based on the repetition of a pattern in Pakhom's life. Describe that pattern with reference to the following questions: what motivates Pakhom to want to move on? Should he, at any one time, have been happy with his present situation? What, specifically, leads him to want to improve that situation? How many times is the pattern repeated?

4. What is it that makes Pakhom overextend himself in the pacing off of the land that will be his? If you were to respond to the question of the title, how would you answer it ultimately? By contrast, how much land in life did Pakhom really need?

5. The style in which this story is told is one of extreme simplicity, making use of a great many concrete nouns and verbs, with the minimum of qualifying adjectives and adverbs. Point out examples to support that assertion. The effect of such a style is almost biblical, as though there is a truth embodied in Pakhom's experience that applies to all of us. How would you state that truth? Do you agree with it, as applied to lives in America in the second half of the twentieth century?

For Composition

We have been considering numerous ways to develop an initial statement into a paragraph or essay — by using examples, description, analysis, comparison and contrast, narrative, or definition. But in whatever way a composition is developed, it should have *unity;* that is, if it is to be effective, all the details it contains must be related to the overriding idea being communicated. For instance, if you are writing about the shifting American frontier, you should not include details about the Russian steppes unless you are prepared to show their relationship to the subject at hand.

1. **Description.** In a unified essay of two or three paragraphs, describe one of the El Dorados, or golden lands, that through the ages have lured men away from the security of their homes, as Pakhom was lured to the land where the rye grew so high that "they couldn't see a horse in the stalks." Perhaps some research will be necessary: you might describe Jamestown as imagined by English settlers before their arrival, or California in 1849, or Timbuktu, or any number of other locales that have haunted man's imagination. But after having described the place, reread your description and remove any details that do not contribute to the central impression of it you want to create. Strive, in other words, for an essay that has unity.

2. **Analysis.** Consider how Tolstoy creates the illusion of Pakhom's ordeal in hurrying toward the *shikhan* at the end (page 311). He does so by appealing to more than simply the sense of sight. Analyze the relevant passages and in a unified paragraph or two indicate the senses appealed to, illustrating your remarks with citations from the story.

Words and Allusions

LITERARY TERMS. Each special area of human knowledge has its own special terminology, and literature is no exception. To discuss literature intelligently requires an accurate use of literary terms. Some terms that often get confused are *allegory, fable, parable,* and *myth.* "How Much Land Does a Man Need?" is a parable. What is a parable? What other examples do you know of? What is *allegory, fable, myth?* Define each term and give examples. How do these terms relate to *parable*?

The Road Not Taken — Symbolic

ROBERT FROST

Most of us do exert some control over our destiny. In fact, we are constantly exercising our wills to shape our lives through a series of decisions made day by day, many of which may seem unimportant at the time we make them.

Two roads diverged in a yellow wood
And sorry I could not travel both
And be one traveler, long I stood
And looked down one as far as I could
To where it bent in the undergrowth;   5

Then took the other, as just as fair,
And having perhaps the better claim,
Because it was grassy and wanted wear;
Though as for that the passing there
Had worn them really about the same,   10

And both that morning equally lay
In leaves no step had trodden black.
Oh, I kept the first for another day!
Yet knowing how way leads on to way,
I doubted if I should ever come back.   15

[handwritten: Never come back to other road]

I shall be telling this with a sigh *[handwritten: wonders what he missed —regret (a little) CURIOSITY —wistful]*
Somewhere ages and ages hence:
Two roads diverged in a wood, and I —
I took the one less traveled by,
And that has made all the difference.   20

For Discussion

1. The subject of this poem is a man traveling through autumn woods and encountering a fork in the path he has been following. Which branch of the fork does he decide to follow? Why? What does he fancy will be the consequences of his decision? How will he regard it later?

2. The title of the poem is noteworthy. What is being emphasized? Why, do you suppose?

3. The subject of Frost's poem is a specific man in a wood choosing one path instead of another. In more general terms, what is the poem concerned with? How would you state its theme? Lines 14–15 contain a crucial thought, not only about paths in yellow woods but about decisions throughout life. Can you illustrate, from your reading or your own experience, the truth of those two lines?

4. In the context of what has gone before, how would you interpret the final line of the poem? Did the man freely choose the path he followed; that is, was his will free, or was he fated to choose as he did? Discuss.

5. **Meter, Foot, Scansion.** Some poems in English are written in free verse (page 24), but the majority are written in *meter;* that is, they follow a more or less regular pattern of sound that can be measured. Meter, then, is simply the measure of that sound, which can vary from poem to poem. The basic unit of meter is called a *foot,* consisting of one ac-

cented and one or more unaccented syllables. To indicate the meter of a line of verse, first transcribe the line by syllables:

Two   roads   di verged   in   a   yel low wood.

Mark the stressed syllables ′ :

Two   roads   di verged   in   a   yel low
wood.

Then mark the unstressed syllables ⌣ and separate the feet from each other with a diagonal, making sure that each foot contains one accented syllable:

Two   roads/   di verged/   in   a   yel/
low wood.

The process of indicating the meter of a poem in this manner is called *scansion.* To demonstrate your understanding of it, scan the remaining four lines of the opening stanza of Frost's poem. How regular is the meter in these lines?

For Composition

● **Autobiography.** We have all made choices that have affected our lives in various ways. Recall an important choice that you have made and explain how it has affected your life.

About the Poet. When **Robert Frost** (1874–1963) went to Dartmouth College, it was soon clear that an academic career was not for him. He was a drop-out long before the term was invented. After working as a mill hand, a teacher, a cobbler, and a small-town newspaperman, he spent eleven years on an isolated farm in New Hampshire, chopping, digging, thinking, and writing. In 1912 Frost and his wife sailed for England, and there he published his first collection of poems, *A Boy's Will*, in 1913. His second collection, *North of Boston*, followed a year later. Upon his return to the United States in 1915, he was famous. In his long life Frost won many honors for his poetry, including several Pulitzer Prizes, and honorary degrees from many colleges and universities.

Mr. Flood's Party

EDWIN ARLINGTON ROBINSON

One of the citizens of Tilbury Town in New England — that fictional town where people such as Richard Cory and Miniver Cheevy and Bewick Finzer lived — was an old man whose very name suggests the ups and downs of a life approaching a pathetic end.

Old Eben Flood, climbing alone one night
Over the hill between the town below
And the forsaken upland hermitage*
That held as much as he should ever know
On earth again of home, paused warily.   5
The road was his with not a native near;
And Eben, having leisure, said aloud,
For no man else in Tilbury Town to hear:

"Well, Mr. Flood, we have the harvest moon
Again, and we may not have many more;   10
The bird is on the wing, the poet says,
And you and I have said it here before.
Drink to the bird." He raised up to the light
The jug that he had gone so far to fill,
And answered huskily: "Well, Mr. Flood,   15
Since you propose it, I believe I will."

3. **hermitage**: solitary dwelling place.

Alone, as if enduring to the end
A valiant armor of scarred hopes outworn,
He stood there in the middle of the road
Like Roland's ghost* winding a silent horn.
Below him, in the town among the trees,
Where friends of other days had honored him,
A phantom salutation of the dead
Rang thinly till old Eben's eyes were dim.

Then, as a mother lays her sleeping child   25
Down tenderly, fearing it may awake,
He set the jug down slowly at his feet
With trembling care, knowing that most things break.
And only when assured that on firm earth
It stood, as the uncertain lives of men   30
Assuredly did not, he paced away,
And with his hand extended paused again:

"Well, Mr. Flood, we have not met like this
In a long time; and many a change has come
To both of us, I fear, since last it was   35
We had a drop together. Welcome home!"
Convivially returning with himself,
Again he raised the jug up to the light;
And with an acquiescent quaver said:
"Well, Mr. Flood, if you insist, I might.   40

"Only a very little, Mr. Flood —
For auld lang syne. No more, sir; that will do."
So, for the time, apparently it did,
And Eben evidently thought so too;
For soon amid the silver loneliness   45
Of night he lifted up his voice and sang,
Secure, with only two moons listening,
Until the whole harmonious landscape rang —

"For auld lang syne." The weary throat gave out,
The last word wavered, and the song was done.
He raised again the jug regretfully
And shook his head, and was again alone.
There was not much that was ahead of him,
And there was nothing in the town below —
Where strangers would have shut the many doors   55
That many friends had opened long ago.

20. **Roland's ghost:** Roland was a French hero of medieval legend.

For Discussion

1. By reading Robinson's poem carefully, you can come to understand a great deal about old Mr. Flood's life. Where is he heading when he pauses to have his party? Where has he been? Where are his friends now? There is irony in the mention of Eben's "leisure" (line 7). Explain.

2. Stanza 3 alludes to Roland, the heroic knight of medieval romance who, ambushed by Moslems in the Pyrenees, summoned Charlemagne to battle by blowing with his dying breath on an enchanted horn. What answer does Eben get from his own "silent" summons? How does it affect him? Line 18 refers metaphorically to hopes as armor. Against what might hopes protect one? Does Eben have any hopes left? Explain.

3. The plight of Eben Flood is pathetic, of course, and is made to seem all the more so by the gentle touches of humor throughout. Or perhaps you feel that the humor is inappropriate in describing a situation like this. Point to specific instances of humor in the poem, and discuss their effect on your attitude toward what is being described.

4. **Iambic Foot.** If you were to scan "Mr. Flood's Party," you would find one foot predominating, that of an unstressed syllable followed by a stressed syllable ⏑ ′:

⏑ ′ ⏑ ′ ⏑ ′ ⏑ ′ ⏑ ′
That held/as much/as he/should e/ver know

⏑ ′ ⏑ ′ ⏑ ′ ⏑ ′ ⏑ ′
On earth/a gain/of home/paused war/i ly.

Such a foot is called an *iamb;* it is by far the most frequently encountered foot in English metrical verse. Of course if every single foot in a given poem were iambic, the effect would very likely be monotonously singsong. Accordingly, variations from the basic foot will occur, but it is the kind of foot that predominates that determines the meter in which a poem is written. Scan the following lines from "Mr. Flood's Party," noting how many feet occur in each line: 6, 7, 9, 10, 11, 12, 14, 15, and 16. What kind of foot predominates in "The Road Not Taken"?

For Composition

Stanza 2 alludes to the poet Omar Khayyam, and specifically to a stanza in his poem *The Rubaiyat*:

Come, fill the Cup, and in the fire of spring
Your Winter-garment of Repentance fling;
    The Bird of Time has but a little way
To flutter — and the Bird is on the Wing.

1. **For Research.** Prepare notes to acquaint the class with *The Rubaiyat*. You will want to indicate not only what the title of the poem means and what the name of the man who originally wrote it means, but also when he wrote it, where, who translated it, what form it takes, its general theme, and some additional examples of stanzas that strike you as impressive. Is alluding to such a work appropriate in "Mr. Flood's Party"? Is Eben likely to have found the poem appealing?

2. **Analysis.** Analyze the fourth stanza of Robinson's poem in a brief composition. Your analysis should clarify what the simile comparing Eben's jug with a baby conveys, and what is suggested about Eben's earlier life by lines 28–31.

About the Poet. Although **Edwin Arlington Robinson** (1869–1935) began writing poems at the age of eleven and worked constantly at his poetry throughout his life, he remained almost unknown until he was fifty. Before then his few published poems had appeared in England, so that Americans who had heard of him thought he was English. When recognition came, however, it came swiftly, and for the last decade or so of his life Robinson shared with Robert Frost a reputation as America's greatest living poet.

Death of a Tsotsi

ALAN PATON

The voice that tells the following story is that of a principal of a boy's reformatory in South Africa. It is a disturbing story he tells — of the life and death of a young man who chose, of his own free will, to bind himself with chains.

Abraham Moletisane was his name, but no one ever called him anything but Spike. He was a true child of the city, gay, careless, plausible; but for all that he was easy to manage and anxious to please. He was clean though flashy in his private dress. The khaki shirts and shorts of the reformatory were too drab for him, and he had a red scarf and yellow handkerchief which he arranged to peep out of his shirt pocket. He also had a pair of black and white shoes and a small but highly colored feather in his cap. Now the use of private clothes, except after the day's work, was forbidden; but he wore the red scarf on all occasions, saying, with an earnest expression that changed into an enigmatic smile if you looked too long at him, that his throat was sore. That was a great habit of his, to look away when you talked to him, and to smile at some unseen thing.

He passed through the first stages of the reformatory very successfully. He had two distinct sets of visitors, one his hardworking mother and his younger sister, and the other a group of flashy young men from the city. His mother and the young men never came together, and I think he arranged it so. While we did not welcome his second set of visitors, we did not forbid

Tsotsi: hoodlum.

them so long as they behaved themselves; it was better for us to know about them than otherwise.

One day his mother and sister brought a friend, Elizabeth, who was a quiet and clean-looking person like themselves. Spike told me that his mother wished him to marry this girl, but that the girl was very independent, and refused to hear of it unless he reformed and gave up the company of the *tsotsis*.

"And what do you say, Spike?"

He would not look at me, but tilted his head up and surveyed the ceiling, smiling hard at it, and dropping his eyes but not his head to take an occasional glance at me. I did not know exactly what was in his mind, but it was clear to me that he was beginning to feel confidence in the reformatory.

"It doesn't help to say to her, just O.K., O.K.," he said. "She wants it done before everybody, as the Principal gives the first freedom."

"What do you mean, before everybody?"

"Before my family and hers."

"And are you willing?"

Spike smiled harder than ever at the ceiling, as though at some secret but delicious joy. Whether it was that he was savoring the delight of deciding his future, I do not know. Or whether he was savoring the

An outlying street in a South African city — a breeding ground for tsotsis.

delight of keeping guessing two whole families and the reformatory, I do not know either.

He was suddenly serious. "If I promise her, I'll keep it," he said. "But I won't be forced."

"No one's forcing you," I said.

He lowered his head and looked at me, as though I did not understand the ways of women.

Although Spike was regarded as a weak character, he met all the temptations of increasing physical freedom very successfully. He went to the free hostels, and after some months there he received the special privilege of special weekend leave to go home. He swaggered out, and he swaggered back, punctual to the minute. How he timed it I do not know, for he had no watch; but in all the months that he had the privilege, he was never late.

It was just after he had received his first special leave that one of his city friends was sent to the reformatory also. The friend's name was Walter, and within a week of his arrival he and Spike had a fight, and both were sent to me. Walter alleged that Spike had hit him first, and Spike did not deny it.

"Why did you hit him, Spike?"

"He insulted me, *meneer*."[1]

"How?"

At length he came out with it.

"He said I was reformed."

We could not help laughing at that, not much of course, for it was clear to me that Spike did not understand our laughter, and that he accepted it only because he knew we were well-disposed towards him.

"If I said you were reformed, Spike," I said, "would you be insulted?"

"No, meneer."

"Then why did he insult you?"

He thought that it was a difficult question. Then he said, "He did not mean anything good, meneer. He meant I was back to being a child."

"You are not," I said. "You are going forward to being a man."

[1] **meneer**: sir.

He was mollified by that, and I warned him not to fight again. He accepted my rebuke, but he said to me, "This fellow is out to make trouble for me. He says I must go back to the *tsotsis* when I come out."

I said to Walter, "Did you say that?"

Walter was hurt to the depths and said, "No, *meneer.*"

When they had gone I sent for de Villiers whose job it is to know every home in Johannesburg that has a boy at the reformatory. It was not an uncommon story, of a decent widow left with a son and daughter. She had managed to control the daughter, but not the son, and Spike had got in with a gang of *tsotsis;* as a result of one of their exploits he had found himself in court, but had not betrayed his friends. Then he had gone to the reformatory, which apart from anything it did itself, had enabled his mother to regain her hold on him, so that he had now decided to forsake the *tsotsis,* to get a job through de Villiers, and to marry the girl Elizabeth and live with her in his mother's house.

A week later Spike came to see me again.

"*The Principal must forbid these friends of Walter to visit the reformatory,*" he said.

"*Why, Spike?*"

"*They are planning trouble for me, meneer.*"

The boy was no longer smiling, but looked troubled, and I sat considering his request. I called in de Villiers, and we discussed it in Afrikaans,[1] which Spike understood. But we were talking a rather high Afrikaans[2] for him, and his eyes went from one face to the other, trying to follow what we said. If I forbade these boys to visit the reformatory, what help would that be to Spike? Would their resentment against him be any the less? Would they forget it because they did not see him? Might this not be a further cause for resentment against him? After all, one cannot remake the world; one can do all one can in a reformatory, but when the time comes, one

[1] **Afrikaans** (af'ri·känz'): language developed in the Republic of South Africa from seventeenth-century Dutch.

[2] **high Afrikaans**: complex and literary form of the language used by the more educated.

ABOUT THE AUTHOR • **Alan Paton** (1903–   ) was a schoolteacher and later a principal of a large reformatory near Johannesburg, South Africa, before becoming a novelist. It was not until after World War II, while traveling to visit reformatories in Europe and the United States, that Paton began to write the novel that made him world-famous. *Cry, the Beloved Country,* published in 1948, was hailed as "one of the best novels of our time." Within a few years it appeared on the stage as a musical drama, *Lost in the Stars,* and on the screen as a motion picture. Paton's second novel, *Too Late the Phalarope,* continued his concern with the "tragic plight of black-skinned people in a white man's world." In 1960 he published *Tales from a Troubled Land,* from which "Death of a Tsotsi" is taken. Banned in his own country but translated into many languages, Paton's books have carried his message to people all over the world.

has to take away one's hands. It was true that de Villiers would look after him, but such supervision had its defined limits. As I looked at the boy's troubled face, I also was full of trouble for him; for he had of his choice bound himself with chains, and now, when he wanted of his choice to put them off, he found it was not so easy to do. He looked at us intently, and I could see that he felt excluded, and wished to be brought in again.

"Did you understand what we said, Spike?"

"Not everything, meneer."

"I am worried about one thing," I said. "Which is better for you, to forbid these boys, or not to forbid them?"

"To forbid them," he said.

"They might say," I said, "Now he'll pay for this."

"The Principal does not understand," he said. "My time is almost finished at the reformatory. I don't want trouble before I leave."

"I'm not worried about trouble here," I said. "I'm worried about trouble outside."

He looked at me anxiously, as though I had not fully grasped the matter.

"I'm not worried about here," I said with asperity. "I can look after you here. If someone tries to make trouble, do you think I can't find the truth?"

He did not wish to doubt my ability, but he remained anxious.

"You still want me to forbid them?" I asked.

"Yes, meneer."

"Mr. de Villiers," I said, "find out all you can about these boys. Then let me know."

"And then," I said to Spike, "I'll talk to you about forbidding them."

"They're a tough lot," de Villiers told me later. "No parental control. In fact they have left home and are living with George, the head of the gang. George's mother is quite without hope for her son, but she's old now and depends on him. He gives her money, and she sees nothing, hears nothing, says nothing. She cooks for them."

"And they won't allow Spike to leave the gang?" I asked.

"I couldn't prove that, but it's a funny business. The reason why they don't want to let Spike go is because he has the brains and the courage. He makes the plans and they all obey him on the job But off the job he's nobody. Off the job they all listen to George."

"Did you see George?"

"I saw George," he said, "and I reckon he's a bad fellow. He's morose and sullen, and physically bigger than Spike."

"If you got in his way," he added emphatically, "he'd wipe you out — like that."

We both sat there rather gloomy about Spike's future.

"Spike's the best of the lot," he said. "It's tragic that he ever got in with them. Now that he wants to get out . . . well . . ."

He left his sentence unfinished.

"Let's see him," I said.

"We've seen these friends of Walter's" I said to Spike, "and we don't like them very much. But whether it will help to forbid their visits, I truly do not know. But I am willing to do what you say."

"We were all of us . . . bowed down by a knowledge that we lived in the shadow of a great danger. . . ."

"The Principal must forbid them," he said at once.

So I forbade them. They listened to me in silence, neither humble nor insolent, not affronted nor surprised; they put up no pleas or protests. George said, "Good, sir," and one by one they followed him out.

When a boy finally leaves the reformatory, he is usually elated, and does not hide his high spirits. He comes to the office for a final conversation, and goes off like one who has brought off an extraordinary coup.[1] But Spike was subdued.

"Spike," I said privately, with only de Villiers there, "are you afraid?"

He looked down at the floor and said, "I'm not afraid," as though his fear were

---

[1] **coup** (kü): sudden, brilliant action.

private also, and would neither be lessened nor made greater by confession.

He was duly married and de Villiers and I made him a present of a watch so that he could always be on time for his work. He had a good job in a factory in Industria, and worked magnificently; he saved money, and spent surprisingly little on clothes. But he had none of his old gaiety and attractive carelessness. He came home promptly, and once home, never stirred out.

It was summer when he was released, and with the approach of winter he asked if de Villiers would not see the manager of the factory, and arrange for him to leave half an hour earlier, so that he could reach his home before dark. But the manager said it was impossible, as Spike was on the kind of job that would come to a standstill if one man left earlier. De Villiers waited for him after work and he could see that the boy was profoundly depressed.

"Have they said anything to you?" de Villiers asked him.

The boy would not answer for a long time, and at last he said with a finality that was meant to stop further discussion, "They'll get me." He was devoid of hope, and did not wish to talk about it, like a man who has a great pain and does not wish to discuss it, but prefers to suffer it alone and silent. This hopelessness had affected his wife and mother and sister, so that all of them sat darkly and heavily. And de Villiers noted that there were new bars on every door and window. So he left darkly and heavily too, and Spike went with him to the little gate.

And Spike asked him, "Can I carry a knife?"

It was a hard question and the difficulty of it angered de Villiers, so that he said harshly, "How can I say that you can carry a knife?"

"You," said Spike, "my mother, my sister, Elizabeth."

He looked at de Villiers.

"I obey you all," he said, and went back into the house.

So still more darkly and heavily de Villiers went back to the reformatory, and sitting in my office, communicated his mood to me. We decided that he would visit Spike more often than he visited any other boy. This he did, and he even went to the length of calling frequently at the factory at five o'clock, and taking Spike home. He tried to cheer and encourage the boy, but the dark heavy mood could not be shifted.

One day Spike said to him, "I tell you, sir, you all did your best for me."

The next day he was stabbed to death just by the little gate.

In spite of my inside knowledge, Spike's death so shocked me that I could do no

work. I sat in my office, hopeless and defeated. Then I sent for the boy Walter.

"I sent for you," I said, "to tell you that Spike is dead."

He had no answer to make. Nothing showed in his face to tell whether he cared whether Spike were alive or dead. He stood there impassively, obedient and respectful, ready to go or ready to stand there for ever.

"He's dead," I said angrily. "He was killed. Don't you care?"

"I care," he said.

He would have cared very deeply, had I pressed him. He surveyed me unwinkingly, ready to comply with my slightest request. Between him and me there was an unbridgeable chasm; so far as I know there was nothing in the world, not one hurt or grievance or jest or sorrow, that could have stirred us both together.

Therefore I let him go.

De Villiers and I went to the funeral, and spoke words of sympathy to Spike's mother and wife and sister. But the words fell like dead things to the ground, for something deeper than sorrow was there. We were all of us, white and black, rich and poor, learned and untutored, bowed down by a knowledge that we lived in the shadow of a great danger, and were powerless against it. It was no place for a white person to pose in any mantle of power or authority; for this death gave the lie to both of them.

And this death would go on too, for nothing less than the reform of a society would bring it to an end. It was the menace of the socially frustrated, strangers

'on parole'

to mercy, striking like adders[1] for the dark reasons of ancient minds, at any who crossed their paths.

[1] **adders:** large, poisonous African snakes.

For Discussion

1. Sometime in the past, Spike "had of his choice bound himself with chains, and now, when he wanted of his choice to put them off, he found it was not so easy to do" (page 321). With what chains had he bound himself? Can you think of other "chains" that one might voluntarily put on, only to discover later that they cannot be easily removed?

2. Spike's relationship to the other tsotsis was an odd one, according to de Villiers. What was odd about it? Why did the gang not want to "let him go"? Why was Spike murdered? Who would you suspect was responsible for his murder?

3. How had a young man like Spike — gay, careless, plausible — come to be in the reformatory in the first place? After his release his life changed drastically. In what ways? How is the change to be accounted for?

4. Spike's fight with Walter in the reformatory grew out of an "insult." What was it? Why did the remark, coming from Walter, seem insulting? "You are going forward to being a man," the principal insists. What does he mean? How does the remark affect the boy?

5. "Death of a Tsotsi" is told from the personal point of view. In the course of the story, what opinion do you form of the narrator — the person who is telling it? Can you suggest advantages that grow out of telling this particular story this way, rather than from an omniscient point of view? Is the reader, for example, more deeply involved in the action than he would be otherwise? To indicate your awareness of the difference between the two narrative methods, briefly suggest the kinds of changes that would be necessary if the story were to be told from an omniscient point of view.

For Composition

A good way of attaining unity in a paragraph is by means of a *topic sentence*, which states the central idea that the paragraph is developing. Not every paragraph must have a topic sentence, but in order to strengthen the unity of your writing, it would no doubt be wise to use the device liberally. Although the topic sentence may come anywhere within the paragraph, by far the most frequent location for it is at the beginning.

1. **Argument.** In two or three unified paragraphs, consider alternatives by means of which Spike might have escaped his fate. Could he have gone away? Fought back? Hidden? Use topic sentences, and make sure that each topic sentence deals only with what is related to the central idea of each paragraph. Reread your composition and remove any details or sentences that weaken the unity of what you have written.

2. **Argument.** "After all, one cannot remake the world; one can do all one can in a reformatory, but when the time comes, one has to take away one's hands" (page 320). But did the principal do all he could for Spike? In a well-reasoned and unified essay, evaluate and draw conclusions about the course of conduct that the principal followed.

Words and Allusions

WORDS IN CONTEXT. Using a dictionary where necessary, determine from their context in the story the meanings of the following words that appear in "Death of a Tsotsi": *affronted* (page 322), *alleged* (319), *elated* (322), *enigmatic* (318), *mollified* (320), *morose* (321), *rebuke* (320), *savoring* (318). Use each word in a sentence of your own that illustrates the same meaning.

FOREIGN WORDS. Words from foreign languages often appear in newspapers and periodicals in the United States without becoming part of American English. Such words are not borrowed for use in our everyday language, but remain related to the country of their origin. The following words are common in stories about South Africa: *Boer, Kaffir, Bantu, apartheid.* What do the words mean?

Hay for the Horses

GARY SNYDER

[handwritten: visual / tactile / olfactory / kinetic — imagery]

Spike in the preceding story chose his fate to a very real extent. But fate will come, whether you make a choice or not.

[handwritten: speaker – young, male]

> He had driven half the night
> From far down San Joaquin
> Through Mariposa, up the
> Dangerous mountain roads,
> And pulled in at eight A.M.   5
> With his big truckload of hay behind the barn.
> With winch* and ropes and hooks
> We stacked the bales up clean
> To splintery redwood rafters
> High in the dark, flecks of alfalfa   10
> Whirling through shingle-cracks of light,
> Itch of haydust in the sweaty shirt and shoes.
> At lunchtime under Black oak
> Out in the hot corral,
> — The old mare nosing lunchpails,   15
> Grasshoppers crackling in the weeds—
> "I'm sixty-eight," he said,
> "I first bucked* hay when I was seventeen.
> I thought, that day I started,
> I sure would hate to do this all my life.   20
> And dammit, that's just what
> I've gone and done."

[handwritten annotations: harsh, tough / also admiration; pride; beautiful description; discomfort; discomfort; positive outlook; conflicting signals → gives end ironic twist - not good or bad, just is; FATE; inertia; ironic]

7. **winch:** machine for hoisting, operated by hand-cranking.   18. **bucked:** tossed.

For Discussion

1. The old fellow who had driven his load of hay up the dangerous mountain roads was nearing the end of a long life. How had he spent it? At seventeen he had bucked hay for the first time. If he hated it then, why do you suppose he went on doing it for all those years afterwards?

2. Clearly meter and rhyme alone do not make poetry, inasmuch as this poem, in free verse, has neither. But the lines do compress a great deal into a very small space, charging every word with more intensity of meaning than is ordinarily encountered in prose. The images, too, are more intensely and vividly felt and expressed than is usual in prose. Which images struck you most forcefully?

For Composition

It is almost as though an old man had wandered down that long path of life to which Frost refers in "The Road Not Taken," only in this instance there have been no forks in the path — or those that were there have been passed by unnoticed.

● **Comparison and Contrast.** Eben Flood (page 315), too, was an old man with a long life stretching behind him. What other similarities do you find between Flood and the man described in "Hay for the Horses"? What differences? In a unified composition consider the lives of the two men and the extent to which each man is responsible for what his life has turned out to be.

About the Poet. **Gary Snyder** (1930–   ) has worked as a logger in the United States and as a seaman on the various oceans of the world. He knows the Pacific Northwest and the legends of the American Indian, as well as the myths of Buddhism, which he studied in the Orient along with the Chinese and Japanese languages. His name is often associated with recent experimental writers in San Francisco who tend to reflect the philosophy of the Orient. Gary Snyder's two volumes of poetry are *Riprap*, which grew from his experience working in various parts of the world, and *Myths and Texts*, poetry of Pacific-coast life echoing the poet's protest against the destruction there of the wilderness areas and the wildlife.

The Bamboo Trick

ACHINTYA KUMAR SEN GUPTA

"I am the master of my fate," William Ernest Henley wrote defiantly in an oft-quoted poem of the nineteenth century. But was he? Are any of us? What do we have to say in choosing those all-important matters of time and place of birth? Who — if they could avoid it — would have chosen a fate that assumes the appalling burdens of growing up, say, in an impoverished village in modern India, where to eke out even a hand-to-mouth existence presents all but insurmountable obstacles not just every week, not simply every day, but hour by miserable hour?

The annual Gajan fair was being held in the maidan[1] at Khorogachi.

This year the fair wasn't much of a success, it hadn't drawn the usual crowds, and the variety of things offered for sale was poor: evil-smelling papadams[2] fried in rancid oil, popcorn and some hail-ridden green mangoes.[3] The scarcity of paper had banished the kites and the fluttering paper toys. Clay toys were there — dogs and cats, horses and elephants — all in one color, with only a dot or a line in black to denote an eye or the end of a tail. Then split-cane and bamboo baskets, fish traps etc. — small and large. Earthenware pots and pans, cups and plates. But the piles of handwoven towels in gay checks and the glitter of multi-colored glass bangles were missing.

[1] **maidan:** parade grounds.
[2] **papadams:** wafer-thin cakes of bread.

"The Bamboo Trick" by Achintya Kumar Sen Gupta, from *Green and Gold, Stories and Poems from Bengal* by Humayun Kabir. Reprinted by permission of Chapman and Hall, Ltd., copyright 1958. Copyright 1958 by Government of West Bengal, India.

[3] **mangoes:** tropical fruit.

Those who had come to the fair looked worn-out and lifeless, as if they had emerged more dead than alive from the bowels of some dark valley of fear. There was no gaiety either in their talk or in their walk. The clothes they wore were drab and shabby — on the verge of turning into rags.

The crowd was thickest under the pakur[1] tree and all the noise and tumult of the fair had concentrated there.

As I went forward, I heard a child wailing, "I'll fall, I'll die!" Eyes blind with streaming tears, he sobbed and wailed miserably. A little boy, six or seven years old, with arms and legs like brittle sticks, a strip of rag tied tightly below his waist, he looked as helpless as a fledgling fallen from its nest.

"What is it? Why is he crying?"

A bamboo trick was about to be performed, they informed me.

I didn't understand at first. Were they going to beat up the boy with a bamboo and was that why he sobbed so ceaselessly?

No, the bamboo wasn't going to be used for beating him, they explained. It was to be used for a trick — a trick we were shortly to see.

I knew that orders of attachment decreed by a court were sometimes executed by posting a notice on a bamboo pole near the property to be attached, with a beat of drums. But I was not aware of any other trick that could be performed with a piece of bamboo.

Someone asked, "Will the bamboo be planted in the ground?"

"Oh, no, this isn't an ordinary trick of that sort." Someone in the know explained in a tone of authority, "No, the old man will set it on his own tummy and the boy will climb the bamboo pole and go right up to the top. Then the boy will balance himself on the other end and lie on it face downwards. The bamboo pole will then start spinning, and the boy with his hands

¹ **pakur**: large, branching tropical tree.

> The poor man is never free; he serves in every country.
>
> — Voltaire

and legs hanging free will spin on top. I've seen them perform many times before."

"Is that the old man?"

"Yes, that's Mantaj."

The old man's body was shriveled like a piece of twisted rope, a few gray hairs jutted out from his chin. His chest was arched, moundlike, his stomach a concave hollow, and the little flesh he had hung loose from his bones. His deep-set eyes glittered in the afternoon sunshine. It was his eyes alone that gave evidence of whatever courage and skill he had.

The audience fanned out in a circle. Mantaj went round with an empty old tin mug hoping to collect a few coppers.

Someone scolded him: "The show isn't on yet and here you're asking for money!"

But how was the show to commence? The performer who was to do the act of climbing the pole was busy creating a rumpus with his wailing — "I'll fall, I'll die!"

"What is all this wailing for? If you are so jittery about falling, why come to perform?"

But Mantaj took no notice of the boy's howling. He went round with his tin mug assuring everyone that the show would certainly take place.

"This isn't their first performance, is it? Then why is the boy crying?" I asked the man standing next to me.

"He didn't perform before, he is a novice."

"Then who did it?"

"His elder brother — "

"No, no, this boy too has performed once or twice," someone else protested, "this boy climbed the bamboo when they gave a show during the Saraswati Puja, in the school

327

yard at Tentul. He isn't used to it yet, that day his performance consisted of just climbing up the bamboo. His elder brother is the real performer. But whatever you may say, I feel that the real credit for the trick goes to the man who spins the bamboo — Mantaj."

"Where's his brother?"

"I wish I knew!"

Not a solitary tinkle rang in Mantaj's mug. No one was prepared to part with a copper before the show commenced.

Having no other alternative, Mantaj went towards the boy. The boy screamed in fear as if he was facing a blank wall with a wild dog chasing behind him. "No, no, not I! I'll fall, I'll die — "

The father pulled the boy's hand roughly. He raised his hand to hit the boy.

"Pooh, see how frightened he is! Your father has shown this trick with many a grown-up young man on the bamboo, and now you think he can't manage you — a stripling of a boy!"

A part of the audience now began to scold the boy on behalf of the father.

Mantaj smiled. Long experience lent a keen edge to his smile.

"Supposing you do slip and fall, won't your father be able to catch you in his arms? Come along, now."

The man who was beating the tom-tom plied his sticks harder.

But the boy refused to budge. The sound of his wailing rose above the din of the fair.

So there was to be no bamboo trick! One, then another, began to slip away.

In exasperation Mantaj craned his neck and looked over the circle of the crowd. A little later, another boy came forward walking on weak, unsteady feet, a half-eaten papadam clutched in his hand.

"That's the brother!" some of the audience shouted.

A sickly looking ten-year-old boy with reedy arms and legs, a torn quilt wrapped round his body. All around his lips, on his cheeks and his chin were marks of cuts that had now become sores. A buzzing fly was worrying him as it settled again and again on the tip of his nose. His two big eyes held a blank meaningless look.

He went to his little brother and said, "Don't cry Akku, I'll climb the pole."

Akku quietened down and his tears dried up almost at once.

The crowd drew closer. The beat of the tom-tom became more frenzied.

Mantaj gathered together and tightened the bit of cloth that hung between his waist and knees. He placed the bamboo on his stomach, in the hollow of his navel. He muttered something indistinctly. Perhaps he sent up a prayer to his god. Then he touched the bamboo to his forehead. He now drew it close to his mouth, whispered something to it, then stroked it with his hands.

Nobody had ever seen him behave thus — so lacking in poise, as he was now.

"Come on, Imtaj," he called out to his elder son.

In a moment Imtaj whipped off the torn quilt from his body.

ABOUT THE AUTHOR • Achintya Kumar Sen Gupta was born in Noakhali, a district in East Bengal, now part of East Pakistan, in 1903. He is known as a writer of poetry and fiction both in the realistic tradition of the West and in the mythological tradition of classical Indian literature. "The Bamboo Trick" represents Sen Gupta's realistic approach in its depiction of poverty and suffering, two of India's most persistent foes.

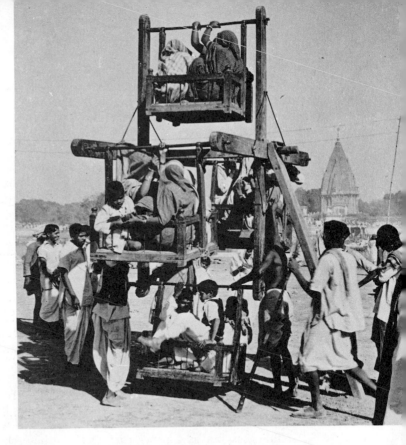

Hindu pilgrims ride a primitive Ferris wheel set up in an amusement area near a temple on the Ganges River in Benares, India.

It was as if something had hit me — I gasped in horror. The boy's chest and stomach were covered with sores which ran in long streaks. Scabs had formed on some, others were raw gaping wounds, some had festered and swelled with pus. That wretched fly had fetched a number of buzzing bluebottles to share his feast.

I felt a little relieved when the boy turned his back to me. His back was smooth, spotless.

"How did he get those sores? So many sores?" I asked.

Some of them knew, I learnt. On the festival of spring, while performing at the house of the zamindar[1] at Champali, Imtaj had slipped. The old man had just recovered from a bout of malaria and couldn't manage to get even a handful of cold wet rice while he was convalescing. That was the reason why he couldn't keep the bamboo balanced on his stomach. Where Imtaj fell, the

[1] zamindar: landowner.

ground was covered with gravel and broken tiles, and it had badly cut and bruised his chest and stomach. The boy had been out of sorts ever since.

"Won't you wrap yourself with that rag?" asked Mantaj.

"No." The boy rubbed both hands with dust and jumped up on the bamboo pole which by then rested on his father's stomach. With the suppleness of long practice, he began climbing up swiftly. Mantaj stood motionless, still, the bamboo gripped in both hands and pressed into the pit of his stomach.

"Let him see, let Akkas see, how willingly his brother has come to perform despite his sores!"

With his face turned upwards, Akkas or Akku stared at his brother. He had nothing to fear now. He could beat the tom-tom or go round with the mug if he so wished.

On reaching the top of the bamboo,

Imtaj paused for a moment, then he gathered his cloth together to fix the pole end against his stomach. His sores became visible again. The sight was unbearable. I turned to leave.

Somebody stopped me. He said, "When he lies stuck up on the pole like a frog, his arms and legs hanging loose, and starts spinning round and round in space, you won't see those sores any more!"

"Does the father turn the bamboo with his hands?"

"He turns the bamboo with his hands a few times, then stuck on his navel, it spins on its own momentum. That's really the trick."

Someone else cut in: "To display acrobatics on a bamboo planted in the ground has become out of date now — what's so clever about that?"

The bamboo in the meantime had started spinning in Mantaj's hand. The boy must have become very light after his fall, he was spinning as fast as a paper cartwheel. His arms and legs were spread out and his hideous sores were no longer visible. One could hardly make out whether it was a human being or bat or flying fox that was whirling in space.

My gaze had been fixed skywards, now I turned my eyes to Mantaj when he suddenly placed the revolving pole in his navel and let go his hands. The father's belly, rather than his son's, was a sight worth seeing. The son's stomach was a mass of sores, but the father's stomach was a great big hollow. This pit was not something contrived for the moment to dig in the bamboo. I felt this deep pit must have been there for a long, long time. And who knows what fiery churnstick was churning away inside that pit?

I could hardly believe my eyes when I saw how far back the bamboo end had pressed into his stomach. I had seen men with bellies flattened to their backs before

this. But now I saw a man who seemed to have no belly at all — the bamboo seemed to press straight into his back from the front. His very entrails had shriveled and disappeared nobody knew where. At each turn the bamboo clattered against his backbone.

What I was apprehending every moment came about, but it was not Imtaj who slipped, it was Mantaj who reeled and crashed to the ground. At the last moment he had held out his hands to catch the falling boy. But however frail the boy was, his father's arms were not strong enough to support him.

"Nowadays the old man seems to be slipping again and again. . . ." someone complained.

Mantaj squatted on his haunches with his head pressed into his hands, panting like a hard-run old horse. He was staring blankly at his empty mug.

No wonder he had taken round the mug before starting the performance. Had he obtained a few coppers, he could have eaten something — one or two papadams, or perhaps a few of the leathery batter-fried onion and brinjal slices selling nearby. A morsel of food could have made all the difference, it would perhaps have given some strength to his weary old arms. Long habit could train one to bear most things except perhaps to quench the pangs of hunger. The bamboo, the helpless arms, the son, the sores — one could face each in its turn with the courage that practice and experience endow — but hunger — it was unruly, ruthless.

The bamboo had skipped and fallen at a distance, and Imtaj still further away. The din of the crowd drowned his groans. Someone said, "He's finished." Said another: "His heart is still beating!"

There was a charitable hospital nearby. Some people carried Imtaj there, doing their best to avoid contact with his sores. The accident had just happened, the hospital could hardly dare turn away the patient. Had Imtaj gone there to have his sores attended to, they would have driven him away because Mantaj couldn't always pay the one-anna bit[1] they demanded for medicine. If half-an-anna or one anna came his way, was Mantaj to spend it on medicine for sores that covered the stomach or to soothe the sores that burned inside!

Mantaj sat grim and silent, but the younger boy began wailing at the top of his voice. I thought he was crying because of his brother.

But no, it was the same lament, in a still more helpless tone: "It's my turn now! It's my turn! I'm sure to fall, I'll die — "

Without a word Mantaj got up, took Akku by the hand and walked towards the hospital.

"I'll fall, I'll die!" What unseen god was being beseeched by a child's piteous wails — for a misery which knew no remedy.

Mantaj remained silent. His stony face looked cruel in its chill detachment. This hard cold silence was the only reply he could give his son. What else could he do? He must eat.

[1] **one-anna bit:** small coin worth a little more than an American cent.

For Discussion

1. What else could Mantaj do? Within that hollow stomach of his, "who knows what fiery churnstick was churning away?" The churnstick, of course, was hunger. Do you think the man was cruel by nature? If not, why did his face look "cruel in its chill detachment" when confronted by his son's piteous wails? To what extent is he responsible for the kind of life he leads?

2. To make what money he can, Mantaj has devised a trick different from what one might expect him to perform. Describe the trick. Why does he attempt to collect payment before performing it? What has been the fate of the elder son?

3. One of the agonies of an existence such as Mantaj's lies in the constant need to outdo one's previous performances. There is a desperation in such a fate; no longer will it do to repeat simply what you did yesterday, or what others are doing now. You must go further, trespassing on ever more dangerous grounds. What evidence of that pressure on the individual do you find in "The Bamboo Trick"? How do you account for the pressure?

4. "The Bamboo Trick" opens and closes with the tears of a six-year-old boy. Why is he crying? The narrator observes that the child looks "as helpless as a fledgling fallen from its nest" (page 327). What does he mean? In this instance why is the comparison particularly appropriate?

5. This is by no means a pleasant story, but it is moving, and it has the ring of truth about it. In part, that ring is sounded by the many images that allow us to see and hear what goes on at the annual Gajan fair. What atmosphere do the images in the second and third paragraphs of the story, taken together, create? What struck you as the most unforgettable image in this remarkable story?

For Composition

One of the rewards of reading literature lies in its capacity — by means of black marks on a white page — to re-create other worlds and other lives that transcend time and place.

1. **Description.** Write a unified essay of two or three paragraphs describing the world in which Mantaj and his two sons must fashion their lives. Work toward creating a single, focused effect by including only relevant details. And as you write, resist the temptation to incorporate whole phrases from the story in your own description.

2. **Analysis.** "Haircut" (page 146), "Death of a Tsotsi" (page 318), and "The Bamboo Trick" are all written from the personal point of view. In each case, what relationship does the person telling the story have to the action

he is describing? Who else within the stories might have been in a position to reveal the same action? What advantages are there in having a narrator related as these three are to the events being described? Discuss these matters in a composition, illustrating generalizations by means of examples from the three stories.

Words and Allusions

LINGUISTIC BORROWINGS. Ever since English became a distinct language, its users have been borrowing freely from other languages. Some words have come from conquerors of England, such as the Romans, various Germanic tribes, and the Norman French. Others have come from people conquered by the English. Whatever their source, these words have become an integral part of the language so that they no longer appear as foreign words.

For many years the English ruled India, and from India have come such words as *curry*, *pariah*, *khaki*, *bungalow*, and *dinghy*. What was the original meaning of each of those words? Use each in a sentence that illustrates its meaning in American English today.

A different kind of borrowing appears in phrases based on foreign customs or traditions. For example, we use the term "sacred cow." What is a sacred cow in India? What do we mean when we refer to someone or something as a "sacred cow"? In our use of the term, what attitude is implied toward Indian religious beliefs?

An Irish Airman Foresees His Death

WILLIAM BUTLER YEATS

The death foreseen in the title of this poem is that of Major Robert Gregory, who perished fighting in the First World War. He was the much-admired, only son of Lady Augusta Gregory. After the young flyer's death, Lady Gregory's celebrated friend William Butler Yeats — perhaps the greatest poet writing in English in the twentieth century — tried to articulate the reasons why a man of such promise would voluntarily give his life for a cause that he felt affected him only slightly.

> I know that I shall meet my fate
> Somewhere among the clouds above;
> Those that I fight I do not hate,
> Those that I guard I do not love;
> My country is Kiltartan Cross,   5
> My countrymen Kiltartan's poor,
> No likely end could bring them loss
> Or leave them happier than before.
> Nor law, nor duty bade me fight,
> Nor public men, nor cheering crowds,   10

A lonely impulse of delight
Drove to this tumult in the clouds;
I balanced all, brought all to mind,
The years to come seemed waste of breath,
A waste of breath the years behind   15
In balance with this life, this death.

For Discussion

1. In what mood did the speaker of the poem willingly assume the risks of being an airman in wartime? "Those" in line 3 are the Austrians and Germans primarily; "Those" in line 4 are the English. How would the war between those nations be likely to affect the speaker's countrymen? Who are those countrymen? What led the speaker to fight in the war?

2. **Trochaic Foot.** The reverse of the iamb is the *trochee*, an accented syllable followed by an unaccented one. Whole poems are written in trochaic meter; Poe's "The Raven" is an example:

Once u/pon a/ mid night/ drear y,/

while I/ pon dered,/ weak and/ wear y

O ver/ man y a/ quaint and/ cur ious/

vol ume/ of for/got ten/ lore. . . .

Moreover, within poems written predominantly in iambic meter, as is "An Irish Airman Foresees His Death," an occasional trochee provides an effective and emphatic way of varying the pattern. Line 1 of Yeats' poem, for example, contains four iambic feet, but line 2 contains one trochee and three iambs. Which foot in that line is the trochee? Is there a trochee in line 3? In line 4?

For Composition

The First World War was fought between 1914 and 1918, at a time when relations between England and Ireland were extremely tense. The story of those relations is a complicated and frequently tragic one that stretches far back into history. Indeed, the English and the Irish have reached some kind of reasonable settlement of their differences only in the last few decades.

1. **For Research.** Prepare notes on the relations between Ireland and England during the first thirty years of the twentieth century. All the complex details need not be included, but an indication of reasons for conflict between the two nations, the different interests each supported in the First World War, and the manner in which their abiding differences were finally resolved should appear in the notes you assemble.

2. **Exposition.** In an essay of two or three unified paragraphs, explain the dilemma in which a sensitive Irishman at the time of the First World War might have found himself placed. Your paper will draw both on the poem by Yeats and on your research.

About the Poet. **William Butler Yeats** (1865–1939), fighter for Irish independence from England, was recognized at his death as one of the supreme poets in the English language. Steeped in the traditions and mythologies of his native Ireland, Yeats wrote lyrically of the Celtic past in poems that expressed a mystic philosophy. When in his middle age he took up the cause of Irish freedom, he became an important force in the renaissance of Irish literature, writing and producing plays for the Abbey Theatre in Dublin and encouraging younger writers such as Sean O'Casey. As Yeats grew older, his many-sided career came to include politics as he served in the Irish Senate. Of his total work one biographer wrote: "It is difficult to think of any other poet writing in English who is so varied and so developed." Until his death, Yeats continued to grow as a poet, trimming away the non-essentials until only a stark and awesome truth remained.

The Kiss

ANTON CHEKHOV

Any profound story, play, or poem can be approached in a number of ways. "Young Goodman Brown," for instance, can profitably be read the way it was presented on page 26, as a story about truth, about appearance and reality. Or it may be considered as a story about justice: is it just that Goodman Brown's entire life be clouded by the errors of a single evening? Or it might even be seen as a story about the nature of greatness: was Brown, who finally saw more deeply into things than anyone else in Salem, greater than others?

"Young Goodman Brown" is a story about fate and free will, too. For it was Brown's fate to spend one night that would affect all the days and nights to follow — and ironically his fate was such that the crucial night might have been no more substantial than a dream.

Like Hawthorne's story, the story that follows can be approached from many directions. It is a haunting story about the Russian soldier Ryabovich, shy and clumsy, who quite unexpectedly one evening has a "little adventure." The adventure, as brief and anonymous as it is, nevertheless transforms him. Chekhov's story is about truth and justice and greatness. And it is about man's fate as well.

At eight o'clock on the evening of the twentieth of May all the six batteries[1] of the N—— Reserve Artillery Brigade halted for the night in the village of Mestechki on their way to camp. At the height of the general commotion, while some officers were busily occupied around the guns, and others, gathered together in the square near the church enclosure, were receiving the reports of the quartermasters, a man in civilian dress, riding a queer horse, came into sight round the church. The little dun-colored[2] horse with a fine neck and a short tail came, moving not straight forward, but as it were sideways, with a sort of dance step, as though it were being lashed about the legs. When he reached the officers the man on the horse took off his hat and said:

"His Excellency Lieutenant-General von Rabbeck, a local landowner, invites the officers to have tea with him this minute...."

The horse bowed, danced, and retired sideways; the rider raised his hat once more and in an instant disappeared with his strange horse behind the church.

"What the devil does it mean?" grumbled some of the officers, dispersing to their quarters. "One is sleepy, and here this von Rabbeck with his tea! We know what tea means."

The officers of all the six batteries remembered vividly an incident of the previous year, when during maneuvers they, together with the officers of a Cossack regi-

[1] **batteries**: basic units of field artillery.
[2] **dun-colored**: dull, grayish brown.

ment, were in the same way invited to tea by a count who had an estate in the neighborhood and was a retired army officer; the hospitable and genial count made much of them, dined and wined them, refused to let them go to their quarters in the village, and made them stay the night. All that, of course, was very nice — nothing better could be desired, but the worst of it was, the old army officer was so carried away by the pleasure of the young men's company that till sunrise he was telling the officers anecdotes of his glorious past, taking them over the house, showing them expensive pictures, old engravings, rare guns, reading them autograph letters from great people, while the weary and exhausted officers looked and listened, longing for their beds and yawning in their sleeves; when at last their host let them go, it was too late for sleep.

Might not this von Rabbeck be just such another? Whether he were or not, there was no help for it. The officers changed their uniforms, brushed themselves, and went all together in search of the gentleman's house. In the square by the church they were told they could get to his Excellency's by the lower road — going down behind the church to the river, walking along the bank to the garden, and there the alleys would take them to the house; or by the upper way — straight from the church by the road which, half a mile from the village, led right up to his Excellency's barns. The officers decided to go by the upper road.

"Which von Rabbeck is it?" they wondered on the way. "Surely not the one who was in command of the N—— cavalry division at Plevna?"

"No, that was not von Rabbeck, but simply Rabbe and no 'von.'"

"What lovely weather!"

At the first of the barns the road divided in two: one branch went straight on and vanished in the evening darkness, the other led to the owner's house on the right. The officers turned to the right and began to speak more softly. . . . On both sides of the road stretched stone barns with red roofs, heavy and sullen-looking, very much like barracks in a district town. Ahead of them gleamed the windows of the manor house.

"A good omen, gentlemen," said one of the officers. "Our setter leads the way; no doubt he scents game ahead of us! . . ."

Lieutenant Lobytko, who was walking in front, a tall and stalwart fellow, though entirely without mustache (he was over twenty-five, yet for some reason there was no sign of hair on his round, well-fed face), renowned in the brigade for his peculiar ability to divine the presence of women at a distance, turned round and said:

"Yes, there must be women here; I feel that by instinct."

On the threshold the officers were met by von Rabbeck himself, a comely looking man of sixty in civilian dress. Shaking hands with his guests, he said that he was very glad and happy to see them, but begged them earnestly for God's sake to excuse him for not asking them to stay the night; two sisters with their children, his brothers, and some neighbors, had come on a visit to him, so that he had not one spare room left.

The General shook hands with everyone, made his apologies, and smiled, but it was evident by his face that he was by no means so delighted as last year's count, and that he had invited the officers simply because, in his opinion, it was a social obligation. And the officers themselves, as they walked up the softly carpeted stairs, as they listened to him, felt that they had been invited to this house simply because it would have been awkward not to invite them; and at the sight of the footmen, who hastened to light the lamps at the entrance below and in the anteroom[1] above, they began to feel as though they had brought uneasiness and

---

[1] anteroom: hall; waiting room.

discomfort into the house with them. In a house in which two sisters and their children, brothers, and neighbors were gathered together, probably on account of some family festivity or event, how could the presence of nineteen unknown officers possibly be welcome?

Upstairs at the entrance to the drawing room the officers were met by a tall, graceful old lady with black eyebrows and a long face, very much like the Empress Eugénie.[1] Smiling graciously and majestically, she said she was glad and happy to see her guests, and apologized that her husband and she were on this occasion unable to invite *messieurs les officiers* to stay the night. From her beautiful majestic smile, which instantly vanished from her face every time she turned away from her guests, it was evident that she had seen numbers of officers in her day, that she was in no humor for them now, and if she invited them to her house and apologized for not doing more, it was

[1] **Empress Eugénie:** wife of Louis Napoleon of France.

only because her breeding and position in society required it of her.

When the officers went into the big dining room, there were about a dozen people, men and ladies, young and old, sitting at tea at the end of a long table. A group of men wrapped in a haze of cigar smoke was dimly visible behind their chairs; in the midst of them stood a lanky young man with red whiskers, talking loudly in English, with a burr. Through a door beyond the group could be seen a light room with pale blue furniture.

"Gentlemen, there are so many of you that it is impossible to introduce you all!" said the General in a loud voice, trying to sound very gay. "Make each other's acquaintance, gentlemen, without any ceremony!"

The officers — some with very serious and even stern faces, others with forced smiles, and all feeling extremely awkward — somehow made their bows and sat down to tea.

The most ill at ease of them all was

ABOUT THE AUTHOR • Grandson of a Russian serf who had bought his own freedom and son of an impoverished shopkeeper, **Anton Chekhov** (1860–1904) attended medical school and became a practicing physician. In order to support his family while pursuing his medical studies, he became a contributor to several humorous magazines. So successful were his literary efforts that writing gradually replaced the practice of medicine as his major occupation. By 1888 he had published three collections of stories, a novel, and a play that was produced in Moscow. Yet even after writing became his major source of income, he continued to practice medicine among the poor for no pay. He also devoted his efforts to improving education and to exposing and changing the conditions in which convicts were forced to live. His literary fame rests on the nearly one thousand stories he wrote during his twenties and the great plays, *The Sea Gull, Uncle Vanya, The Three Sisters,* and *The Cherry Orchard,* written during his last years. His career was cut short by tuberculosis, which had troubled him during most of his life and killed him at the age of forty-four.

Ryabovich — a short, somewhat stooped officer in spectacles, with whiskers like a lynx's.[1] While some of his comrades assumed a serious expression, while others wore forced smiles, his face, his lynxlike whiskers, and spectacles seemed to say, "I am the shyest, most modest, and most undistinguished officer in the whole brigade!" At first, on going into the room and later, sitting down at table, he could not fix his attention on any one face or object. The faces, the dresses, the cut-glass decanters of brandy, the steam from the glasses, the molded cornices[2] — all blended in one general impression that inspired in Ryabovich alarm and a desire to hide his head. Like a lecturer making his first appearance before the public, he saw everything that was before his eyes, but apparently only had a dim understanding of it (among physiologists[3] this condition, when the subject sees but does not understand, is called "mental blindness"). After a little while, growing accustomed to his surroundings, Ryabovich regained his sight and began to observe. As a shy man, unused to society, what struck him first was that in which he had always been deficient — namely, the extraordinary boldness of his new acquaintances. Von Rabbeck, his wife, two elderly ladies, a young lady in a lilac dress, and the young man with the red whiskers, who was, it appeared, a younger son of von Rabbeck, very cleverly, as though they had rehearsed it beforehand, took seats among the officers, and at once got up a heated discussion in which the visitors could not help taking part. The lilac young lady hotly asserted that the artillery had a much better time than the cavalry and the infantry, while von Rabbeck and the elderly ladies maintained the opposite. A brisk interchange followed.

Ryabovich looked at the lilac young lady who argued so hotly about what was unfamiliar and utterly uninteresting to her, and watched artificial smiles come and go on her face.

Von Rabbeck and his family skillfully drew the officers into the discussion, and meanwhile kept a sharp eye on their glasses and mouths, to see whether all of them were drinking, whether all had enough sugar, why someone was not eating cakes or not drinking brandy. And the longer Ryabovich watched and listened, the more he was attracted by this insincere but splendidly disciplined family.

After tea the officers went into the drawing room. Lieutenant Lobytko's instinct had not deceived him. There were a great many girls and young married ladies. The "setter" lieutenant was soon standing by a very young blonde in a black dress, and, bending over her jauntily, as though leaning on an unseen sword, smiled and twitched his shoulders coquettishly. He probably talked very interesting nonsense, for the blonde looked at his well-fed face condescendingly and asked indifferently, "Really?" And from that indifferent "Really?" the "setter," had he been intelligent, might have concluded that she would never call him to heel.

The piano struck up; the melancholy strains of a waltz floated out of the wide open windows, and everyone, for some reason, remembered that it was spring, a May evening. Everyone was conscious of the fragrance of roses, of lilac, and of the young leaves of the poplar. Ryabovich, who felt the brandy he had drunk, under the influence of the music stole a glance towards the window, smiled, and began watching the movements of the women, and it seemed to him that the smell of roses, of poplars, and lilac came not from the garden, but from the ladies' faces and dresses.

[1] **lynx's**: wildcat's.

[2] **cornices**: ornamental moldings along the top of a wall.

[3] **physiologists**: those who study the life processes.

Russian villagers pass by Anton Chekhov's country house, restored in 1960 as part of the hundredth-anniversary celebration of his birth.

Von Rabbeck's son invited a scraggy-looking[1] young lady to dance and waltzed round the room twice with her. Lobytko, gliding over the parquet[2] floor, flew up to the lilac young lady and whirled her away. Dancing began. . . . Ryabovich stood near the door among those who were not dancing and looked on. He had never once danced in his whole life, and he had never once in his life put his arm round the waist of a respectable woman. He was highly delighted that a man should in the sight of all take a girl he did not know round the waist and offer her his shoulder to put her hand on, but he could not imagine himself in the position of such a man. There were times when he envied the boldness and swagger of his companions and was inwardly wretched; the knowledge that he was timid, round-shouldered, and uninteresting, that he had a long waist and lynx-like whiskers deeply mortified him, but with years he had grown used to this feeling, and

now, looking at his comrades dancing or loudly talking, he no longer envied them, but only felt touched and mournful.

When the quadrille[3] began, young von Rabbeck came up to those who were not dancing and invited two officers to have a game at billiards. The officers accepted and went with him out of the drawing room. Ryabovich, having nothing to do and wishing to take at least some part in the general movement, slouched after them. From the big drawing room they went into the little drawing room, then into a narrow corridor with a glass roof, and thence into a room in which on their entrance three sleepy-looking footmen jumped up quickly from couches. At last, after passing through a long succession of rooms, young von Rabbeck and the officers came into a small room where there was a billiard table. They began to play.

Ryabovich, who had never played any game but cards, stood near the billiard table and looked indifferently at the players, while they in unbuttoned coats, with cues

[1] **scraggy-looking:** thin and bony in appearance.
[2] **parquet:** inlaid with woodwork in geometric designs.

[3] **quadrille:** form of square dancing.

in their hands, stepped about, made puns, and kept shouting out unintelligible words.

The players took no notice of him, and only now and then one of them, shoving him with his elbow or accidentally touching him with his cue, would turn round and say *"Pardon!"* Before the first game was over he was weary of it, and began to feel that he was not wanted and in the way. . . . He felt disposed to return to the drawing room and he went out.

On his way back he met with a little adventure. When he had gone halfway he noticed that he had taken a wrong turning. He distinctly remembered that he ought to meet three sleepy footmen on his way, but he had passed five or six rooms, and those sleepy figures seemed to have been swallowed up by the earth. Noticing his mistake, he walked back a little way and turned to the right; he found himself in a little room which was in semidarkness and which he had not seen on his way to the billiard room. After standing there a little while, he resolutely opened the first door that met his eyes and walked into an absolutely dark room. Straight ahead could be seen the crack in the doorway through which came a gleam of vivid light; from the other side of the door came the muffled sound of a melancholy mazurka.[1] Here, too, as in the drawing room, the windows were wide open and there was a smell of poplars, lilac, and roses. . . .

Ryabovich stood still in hesitation. . . . At that moment, to his surprise, he heard hurried footsteps and the rustling of a dress, a breathless feminine voice whispered "At last!" and two soft, fragrant, unmistakably feminine arms were clasped about his neck; a warm cheek was pressed against his, and simultaneously there was the sound of a kiss. But at once the bestower of the kiss uttered a faint shriek and sprang away from him, as it seemed to Ryabovich, with dis-

[1] **mazurka**: Polish dance, similar to the polka.

gust. He, too, almost shrieked and rushed towards the gleam of light at the door. . . .

When he returned to the drawing room his heart was palpitating and his hands were trembling so noticeably that he made haste to hide them behind his back. At first he was tormented by shame and dread that the whole drawing room knew that he had just been kissed and embraced by a woman. He shrank into himself and looked uneasily about him, but as he became convinced that people were dancing and talking as calmly as ever, he gave himself up entirely to the new sensation which he had never experienced before in his life. Something strange was happening to him. . . . His neck, round which soft, fragrant arms had so lately been clasped, seemed to him to be anointed with oil; on his left cheek near his mustache where the unknown had kissed him there was a faint chilly tingling sensation as from peppermint drops, and the more he rubbed the place the more distinct was the chilly sensation; all of him, from head to foot, was full of a strange new feeling which grew stronger and stronger. . . . He wanted to dance, to talk, to run into the garden, to laugh aloud. . . . He quite forgot that he was round-shouldered and uninteresting, that he had lynxlike whiskers and an "undistinguished appearance" (that was how his appearance had been described by some ladies whose conversation he had accidentally overheard). When von Rabbeck's wife happened to pass by him, he gave her such a broad and friendly smile that she stood still and looked at him inquiringly.

"I like your house immensely!" he said, setting his spectacles straight.

The General's wife smiled and said that the house had belonged to her father; then she asked whether his parents were living, whether he had long been in the army, why he was so thin, and so on. . . . After receiving answers to her questions, she went on, and after his conversation with her his smiles were more friendly than ever, and he thought he was surrounded by splendid people. . . .

At supper Ryabovich ate mechanically everything offered him, drank, and without listening to anything, tried to understand what had just happened to him. . . . The adventure was of a mysterious and romantic character, but it was not difficult to explain it. No doubt some girl or young married lady had arranged a tryst[1] with some man in the dark room; had waited a long time, and being nervous and excited had taken Ryabovich for her hero; this was the more probable as Ryabovich had stood still hesitating in the dark room, so that he, too, had looked like a person waiting for something. . . . This was how Ryabovich explained to himself the kiss he had received.

"And who is she?" he wondered, looking round at the women's faces. "She must be young, for elderly ladies don't arrange rendezvous. That she was a lady, one could tell by the rustle of her dress, her perfume, her voice. . . ."

His eyes rested on the lilac young lady, and he thought her very attractive; she had beautiful shoulders and arms, a clever face, and a delightful voice. Ryabovich, looking at her, hoped that she and no one else was his unknown. . . . But she laughed somehow artificially and wrinkled up her long nose, which seemed to him to make her look old. Then he turned his eyes upon the blonde in a black dress. She was younger, simpler, and more genuine, had a charming brow, and drank very daintily out of her wineglass. Ryabovich now hoped that it was she. But soon he began to think her face flat, and fixed his eyes upon the one next her.

"It's difficult to guess," he thought, musing. "If one were to take only the shoulders and arms of the lilac girl, add the brow of the blonde and the eyes of the one on the left of Lobytko, then. . . ."

[1] **tryst** (trist): lovers' secret meeting.

He made a combination of these things in his mind and so formed the image of the girl who had kissed him, the image that he desired but could not find at the table. . . .

After supper, replete and exhilarated, the officers began to take leave and say thank you. Von Rabbeck and his wife began again apologizing that they could not ask them to stay the night.

"Very, very glad to have met you, gentlemen," said von Rabbeck, and this time sincerely (probably because people are far more sincere and good-humored at speeding their parting guests than on meeting them). "Delighted. Come again on your way back! Don't stand on ceremony! Where are you going? Do you want to go by the upper way? No, go across the garden; it's nearer by the lower road."

The officers went out into the garden. After the bright light and the noise the garden seemed very dark and quiet. They walked in silence all the way to the gate. They were a little drunk, in good spirits, and contented, but the darkness and silence made them thoughtful for a minute. Probably the same idea occurred to each one of them as to Ryabovich: would there ever come a time for them when, like von Rabbeck, they would have a large house, a family, a garden — when they, too, would be able to welcome people, even though insincerely, feed them, make them drunk and contented?

Going out of the garden gate, they all began talking at once and laughing loudly about nothing. They were walking now along the little path that led down to the river and then ran along the water's edge, winding round the bushes on the bank, the gulleys, and the willows that overhung the water. The bank and the path were scarcely visible, and the other bank was entirely plunged in darkness. Stars were reflected here and there in the dark water; they quivered and were broken up — and from that alone it could be seen that the river was flowing rapidly. It was still. Drowsy sandpipers[1] cried plaintively on the farther bank, and in one of the bushes on the hither side a nightingale was trilling loudly, taking no notice of the crowd of officers. The officers stood round the bush, touched it, but the nightingale went on singing.

"What a fellow!" they exlaimed approvingly. "We stand beside him and he takes not a bit of notice! What a rascal!"

At the end of the way the path went up-hill, and, skirting the church enclosure, led into the road. Here the officers, tired with walking uphill, sat down and lighted their cigarettes. On the farther bank of the river a murky red fire came into sight, and having nothing better to do, they spent a long time in discussing whether it was a camp fire or a light in a window, or something else. . . . Ryabovich, too, looked at the light, and he fancied that the light looked and winked at him, as though it knew about the kiss.

On reaching his quarters, Ryabovich undressed as quickly as possible and got into bed. Lobytko and Lieutenant Merzlyakov — a peaceable, silent fellow, who was considered in his own circle a highly educated officer, and was always, whenever it was possible, reading *The Messenger of Europe*, which he carried about with him everywhere — were quartered in the same cottage with Ryabovich. Lobytko undressed, walked up and down the room for a long while with the air of a man who has not been satisfied, and sent his orderly for beer. Merzlyakov got into bed, put a candle by his pillow and plunged into *The Messenger of Europe*.

"Who was she?" Ryabovich wondered, looking at the sooty ceiling.

His neck still felt as though he had been anointed with oil, and there was still the chilly sensation near his mouth as though from peppermint drops. The shoulders and

[1] **sandpipers**: type of shore birds.

arms of the young lady in lilac, the brow and the candid eyes of the blonde in black, waists, dresses, and brooches, floated through his imagination. He tried to fix his attention on these images, but they danced about, broke up and flickered. When these images vanished altogether from the broad dark background which everyone sees when he closes his eyes, he began to hear hurried footsteps, the rustle of skirts, the sound of a kiss — and an intense baseless joy took possession of him. . . . Abandoning himself to this joy, he heard the orderly return and announce that there was no beer. Lobytko was terribly indignant, and began pacing up and down the room again.

"Well, isn't he an idiot?" he kept saying, stopping first before Ryabovich and then before Merzlyakov. "What a fool and a blockhead a man must be not to get hold of any beer! Eh? Isn't he a blackguard?"[2]

"Of course you can't get beer here," said Merzlyakov, not removing his eyes from *The Messenger of Europe*.

"Oh! Is that your opinion?" Lobytko persisted. "Lord have mercy upon us, if you dropped me on the moon I'd find you beer and women directly! I'll go and find some at once. . . . You may call me a rascal if I don't!"

He spent a long time in dressing and pulling on his high boots, then finished smoking his cigarette in silence and went out.

"Rabbeck, Grabbeck, Labbeck," he muttered, stopping in the outer room. "I don't care to go alone, damn it all! Ryabovich. wouldn't you like to go for a walk? Eh?"

Receiving no answer, he returned, slowly undressed, and got into bed. Merzlyakov sighed, put *The Messenger of Europe* away, and extinguished the light.

"H'm! . . ." muttered Lobytko, lighting a cigarette in the dark.

Ryabovich pulled the bedclothes over his head, curled himself up in bed, and tried to

[2] **blackguard** (blag'ĕrd): scoundrel.

gather together the flashing images in his mind and to combine them into a whole. But nothing came of it. He soon fell asleep, and his last thought was that someone had caressed him and made him happy — that something extraordinary, foolish, but joyful and delightful, had come into his life. The thought did not leave him even in his sleep.

When he woke up the sensations of oil on his neck and the chill of peppermint about his lips had gone, but joy flooded his heart just as the day before. He looked enthusiastically at the window frames, gilded by the light of the rising sun, and listened to the movement of the passers-by in the street. People were talking loudly close to the window. Lebedetzky, the commander of Ryabovich's battery, who had only just overtaken the brigade, was talking to his sergeant at the top of his voice, having lost the habit of speaking in ordinary tones.

"What else?" shouted the commander.

"When they were shoeing the horses yesterday, your Honor, they injured Pigeon's hoof with a nail. The vet put on clay and vinegar; they are leading him apart now. Also, your Honor, Artemyev got drunk yesterday, and the lieutenant ordered him to be put in the limber[1] of a spare gun-carriage."

The sergeant reported that Karpov had forgotten the new cords for the trumpets and the pegs for the tents, and that their Honors the officers had spent the previous evening visiting General von Rabbeck. In the middle of this conversation the red-bearded face of Lebedetzky appeared in the window. He screwed up his short-sighted eyes, looking at the sleepy faces of the officers, and greeted them.

"Is everything all right?" he asked.

"One of the horses has a sore neck from the new collar," answered Lobytko, yawning.

[1] limber: detachable, two-wheeled front part of a gun carriage.

The commander sighed, thought a moment, and said in a loud voice:

"I am thinking of going to see Alexandra Yevgrafovna. I must call on her. Well, good-by. I shall catch up with you in the evening."

A quarter of an hour later the brigade set off on its way. When it was moving along the road past the barns, Ryabovich looked at the house on the right. The blinds were down in all the windows. Evidently the household was still asleep. The one who had kissed Ryabovich the day before was asleep too. He tried to imagine her asleep. The wide-open window of the bedroom, the green branches peeping in, the morning freshness, the scent of the poplars, lilac, and roses, the bed, a chair, and on it the skirts that had rustled the day before, the little slippers, the little watch on the table — all this he pictured to himself clearly and distinctly, but the features of the face, the sweet sleepy smile, just what was characteristic and important, slipped through his imagination like quicksilver through the fingers. When he had ridden a third of a mile, he looked back: the yellow church, the house, and the river, were all bathed in light; the river with its bright green banks, with the blue sky reflected in it and glints of silver in the sunshine here and there, was very beautiful. Ryabovich gazed for the last time at Mestechki, and he felt as sad as though he were parting with something very near and dear to him.

And before him on the road were none but long familiar, uninteresting scenes. . . . To right and to left, fields of young rye and buckwheat with rooks[2] hopping about in them; if one looked ahead, one saw dust and the backs of men's heads; if one looked back, one saw the same dust and faces. . . . Foremost of all marched four men with sabers — this was the vanguard. Next came the singers, and behind them the trumpeters on horseback. The vanguard and the

[2] rooks: crows.

"To a civilian the long tedious procession which is a brigade on the move seems an intricate and unintelligible muddle. . . ."

singers, like torchbearers in a funeral procession, often forgot to keep the regulation distance and pushed a long way ahead. . . . Ryabovich was with the first cannon of the fifth battery. He could see all the four batteries moving in front of him. To a civilian the long tedious procession which is a brigade on the move seems an intricate and unintelligible muddle; one cannot understand why there are so many people round one cannon, and why it is drawn by so many horses in such a strange network of harness, as though it really were so terrible and heavy. To Ryabovich it was all perfectly comprehensible and therefore uninteresting. He had known for ever so long why at the head of each battery beside the officer there rode a stalwart noncom,[1] called bombardier; immediately behind him could be seen the horsemen of the first and then of the middle units. Ryabovich knew that of the horses on which they rode, those on the left were called one name, while those on the right were called another — it was all extremely uninteresting. Behind the

horsemen came two shaft-horses.[2] On one of them sat a rider still covered with the dust of yesterday and with a clumsy and funny-looking wooden guard on his right leg. Ryabovich knew the object of this guard, and did not think it funny. All the riders waved their whips mechanically and shouted from time to time. The cannon itself was not presentable. On the limber lay sacks of oats covered with a tarpaulin, and the cannon itself was hung all over with kettles, soldiers' knapsacks, bags, and looked like some small harmless animal surrounded for some unknown reason by men and horses. To the leeward of it marched six men, the gunners, swinging their arms. After the cannon there came again more bombardiers, riders, shaft-horses, and behind them another cannon, as unpresentable and unimpressive as the first. After the second came a third, a fourth; near the fourth there was an officer, and so on. There were six batteries in all in the brigade, and four cannon in each battery. The procession covered a third of a mile; it ended in a

[1] **noncom:** a noncommissioned officer.

[2] **shaft-horses:** horses pulling the gun.

string of wagons near which an extremely appealing creature — the ass, Magar, brought by a battery commander from Turkey — paced pensively, his long-eared head drooping.

Ryabovich looked indifferently ahead and behind him, at the backs of heads and at faces; at any other time he would have been half asleep, but now he was entirely absorbed in his new agreeable thoughts. At first when the brigade was setting off on the march he tried to persuade himself that the incident of the kiss could only be interesting as a mysterious little adventure, that it was in reality trivial, and to think of it seriously, to say the least, was stupid; but now he bade farewell to logic and gave himself up to dreams. . . . At one moment he imagined himself in von Rabbeck's drawing room beside a girl who was like the young lady in lilac and the blonde in black; then he would close his eyes and see himself with another, entirely unknown girl, whose features were very vague. In his imagination he talked, caressed her, leaned over her shoulder, pictured war, separation, then meeting again, supper with his wife, children. . . .

"Brakes on!" The word of command rang out every time they went downhill.

He, too, shouted "Brakes on!" and was afraid this shout would disturb his reverie and bring him back to reality. . . .

As they passed by some landowner's estate Ryabovich looked over the fence into the garden. A long avenue, straight as a ruler, strewn with yellow sand and bordered with young birch-trees, met his eyes. . . . With the eagerness of a man who indulges in daydreaming, he pictured to himself little feminine feet tripping along yellow sand, and quite unexpectedly had a clear vision in his imagination of her who had kissed him and whom he had succeeded in picturing to himself the evening before

at supper. This image remained in his brain and did not desert him again.

At midday there was a shout in the rear near the string of wagons:

"Attention! Eyes to the left! Officers!"

The general of the brigade drove by in a carriage drawn by a pair of white horses. He stopped near the second battery, and shouted something which no one understood. Several officers, among them Ryabovich, galloped up to him.

"Well? How goes it?" asked the general, blinking his red eyes. "Are there any sick?"

Receiving an answer, the general, a little skinny man, chewed, thought for a moment and said, addressing one of the officers:

"One of your drivers of the third cannon has taken off his leg-guard and hung it on the fore part of the cannon, the rascal. Reprimand him."

He raised his eyes to Ryabovich and went on:

"It seems to me your breeching[1] is too long."

Making a few other tedious remarks, the general looked at Lobytko and grinned.

"You look very melancholy today, Lieutenant Lobytko," he said. "Are you pining for Madame Lopuhova? Eh? Gentlemen, he is pining for Madame Lopuhova."

Madame Lopuhova was a very stout and very tall lady long past forty. The general, who had a predilection[2] for large women, whatever their ages, suspected a similar taste in his officers. The officers smiled respectfully. The general, delighted at having said something very amusing and biting, laughed loudly, touched his coachman's back, and saluted. The carriage rolled on. . . .

"All I am dreaming about now which seems to me so impossible and unearthly is really quite an ordinary thing," thought

---

[1] **breeching**: harness strap.
[2] **predilection**: preference.

Ryabovich, looking at the clouds of dust racing after the general's carriage. "It's all very ordinary, and everyone goes through it. . . . That general, for instance, was in love at one time; now he is married and has children. Captain Wachter, too, is married and loved, though the nape of his neck is very red and ugly and he has no waist. . . . Salmanov is coarse and too much of a Tartar,[1] but he had a love affair that has ended in marriage. . . . I am the same as everyone else, and I, too, shall have the same experience as everyone else, sooner or later. . . ."

And the thought that he was an ordinary person and that his life was ordinary delighted him and gave him courage. He pictured *her* and his happiness boldly, just as he liked. . . .

When the brigade reached their halting-place in the evening, and the officers were resting in their tents, Ryabovich, Merzlyakov, and Lobytko were sitting round a chest having supper. Merzlyakov ate without haste and, as he munched deliberately, read *The Messenger of Europe*, which he held on his knees. Lobytko talked incessantly and kept filling up his glass with beer, and Ryabovich, whose head was confused from dreaming all day long, drank and said nothing. After three glasses he got a little drunk, felt weak, and had an irresistible desire to relate his new sensations to his comrades.

"A strange thing happened to me at those von Rabbecks'," he began, trying to impart an indifferent and ironical tone to his voice. "You know I went into the billiard room. . . ."

He began describing very minutely the incident of the kiss, and a moment later relapsed into silence. . . . In the course of that moment he had told everything, and it

---

[1] **Tartar:** here, irritable and violent person.

What a man thinks of himself, that is what determines, or rather indicates, his fate.
— Henry David Thoreau

---

surprised him dreadfully to find out how short a time it took him to tell it. He had imagined that he could have been telling the story of the kiss till next morning. Listening to him, Lobytko, who was a great liar and consequently believed no one, looked at him skeptically and laughed. Merzlyakov twitched his eyebrows and, without removing his eyes from *The Messenger of Europe*, said:

"That's an odd thing! How strange! . . . throws herself on a man's neck, without addressing him by name. . . . She must have been some sort of lunatic."

"Yes, she must," Ryabovich agreed.

"A similar thing once happened to me," said Lobytko, assuming a scared expression. "I was going last year to Kovno. . . . I took a second-class ticket. The train was crammed, and it was impossible to sleep. I gave the guard half a ruble; he took my luggage and led me to another compartment. . . . I lay down and covered myself with a blanket. . . . It was dark, you understand. Suddenly I felt someone touch me on the shoulder and breathe in my face. I made a movement with my hand and felt somebody's elbow. . . . I opened my eyes and only imagine — a woman. Black eyes, lips red as a prime salmon, nostrils breathing passionately — a bosom like a buffer. . . ."

"Excuse me," Merzlyakov interrupted calmly, "I understand about the bosom, but how could you see the lips if it was dark?"

Lobytko began trying to put himself right and laughing at Merzlyakov's being so dull-witted. It made Ryabovich wince. He walked away from the chest, got into bed, and vowed never to confide again.

Camp life began. . . . The days flowed by, one very much like another. All those days Ryabovich felt, thought, and behaved as though he were in love. Every morning when his orderly handed him what he needed for washing, and he sluiced[1] his head with cold water, he recalled that there was something warm and delightful in his life.

In the evenings when his comrades began talking of love and women, he would listen, and draw up closer; and he wore the expression of a soldier listening to the description of a battle in which he has taken part. And on the evenings when the officers, out on a spree with the setter Lobytko at their head, made Don-Juanesque raids on the neighboring "suburb," and Ryabovich took part in such excursions, he always was sad, felt profoundly guilty, and inwardly begged *her* forgiveness. . . . In hours of leisure or on sleepless nights when he felt moved to recall his childhood, his father and mother — everything near and dear, in fact, he invariably thought of Mestechki, the queer horse, von Rabbeck, his wife who resembled Empress Eugénie, the dark room, the light in the crack of the door. . . .

On the thirty-first of August he was returning from the camp, not with the whole brigade, but with only two batteries. He was dreamy and excited all the way, as though he were going home. He had an intense longing to see again the queer horse, the church, the insincere family of the von Rabbecks, the dark room. The "inner voice," which so often deceives lovers, whispered to him for some reason that he would surely see her . . . And he was tortured by the questions: How would he meet her? What would he talk to her about? Had she forgotten the kiss? If the worst came to the worst, he thought, even if he did not meet

her, it would be a pleasure to him merely to go through the dark room and recall the past. . . .

Towards evening there appeared on the horizon the familiar church and white barns. Ryabovich's heart raced. . . . He did not hear the officer who was riding beside him and saying something to him, he forgot everything, and looked eagerly at the river shining in the distance, at the roof of the house, at the dovecote[2] round which the pigeons were circling in the light of the setting sun.

When they reached the church and were listening to the quartermaster, he expected every second that a man on horseback would come round the church enclosure and invite the officers to tea, but . . . the quartermaster ended his report, the officers dismounted and strolled off to the village, and the man on horseback did not appear.

"Von Rabbeck will hear at once from the peasants that we have come and will send for us," thought Ryabovich, as he went into the peasant cottage, unable to understand why a comrade was lighting a candle and why the orderlies were hastening to get the samovars going.

A crushing uneasiness took possession of him. He lay down, then got up and looked out of the window to see whether the messenger were coming. But there was no sign of him.

He lay down again, but half an hour later he got up and, unable to restrain his uneasiness, went into the street and strode towards the church. It was dark and deserted in the square near the church enclosure. Three soldiers were standing silent in a row where the road began to go downhill. Seeing Ryabovich, they roused themselves and saluted. He returned the salute and began to go down the familiar path.

On the farther bank of the river the

---

[1] **sluiced**: washed with flowing water.

[2] **dovecote**: small house for nesting pigeons.

whole sky was flooded with crimson: the moon was rising; two peasant women, talking loudly, were pulling cabbage leaves in the kitchen garden; beyond the kitchen garden there were some cottages that formed a dark mass. . . . Everything on the near side of the river was just as it had been in May: the path, the bushes, the willows overhanging the water . . . but there was no sound of the brave nightingale and no scent of poplar and young grass.

Reaching the garden, Ryabovich looked in at the gate. The garden was dark and still. . . . He could see nothing but the white stems of the nearest birch trees and a little bit of the avenue; all the rest melted together into a dark mass. Ryabovich looked and listened eagerly, but after waiting for a quarter of an hour without hearing a sound or catching a glimpse of a light, he trudged back. . . .

He went down to the river. The General's bathing cabin[1] and the bath-sheets on the rail of the little bridge showed white before him. . . . He walked up on the bridge, stood a little, and quite unnecessarily touched a sheet. It felt rough and cold. He looked down at the water. . . . The river ran rapidly and with a faintly audible gurgle round the piles of the bathing cabin. The red moon was reflected near the left bank; little ripples ran over the reflection, stretching it out, breaking it into bits, and seemed trying to carry it away. . . .

"How stupid, how stupid!" thought Ryabovich, looking at the running water. "How unintelligent it all is!"

Now that he expected nothing, the incident of the kiss, his impatience, his vague hopes and disappointment, presented themselves to him in a clear light. It no longer seemed to him strange that the General's messenger never came and that he would

---

[1] **bathing cabin**: building used for changing clothes when swimming.

never see the girl who had accidentally kissed him instead of someone else; on the contrary, it would have been strange if he had seen her. . . .

The water was running, he knew not where or why, just as it did in May. At that time it had flowed into a great river, from the great river into the sea; then it had risen in vapor, turned into rain, and perhaps the very same water was running now before Ryabovich's eyes again. . . . What for? Why?

And the whole world, the whole of life, seemed to Ryabovich an unintelligible, aimless jest. . . . And turning his eyes from the water and looking at the sky, he remembered again how Fate in the person of an unknown woman had by chance caressed him, he recalled his summer dreams and fancies, and his life struck him as extraordinarily meager, poverty-stricken, and drab. . . .

When he had returned to the cottage he did not find a single comrade. The orderly informed him that they had all gone to "General Fontryabkin, who had sent a messenger on horseback to invite them. . . ."

For an instant there was a flash of joy in Ryabovich's heart, but he quenched it at once, got into bed, and in his wrath with his fate, as though to spite it, did not go to the General's.

For Discussion

1. Should Ryabovich have followed the others to the General's at the end of the story? Why do you suppose he is feeling *wrathful* — intensely angry — toward his fate after the others leave? Shortly before, he has been seeing "his vague hopes and disappointment" in a clear light. Is he in fact seeing things clearly at that time, or was he seeing them clearly when he found delights wherever he looked? Discuss.

2. Two men among others experience an evening at the home of his excellency Lieutenant General von Rabbeck. One of the men is Lobytko. What sort of man is Lobytko? How does the evening affect him? How do you know? The other man is Ryabovich. In what ways does he differ from Lobytko? At the start how does the evening affect Ryabovich? How does he feel immediately after the party? What changes have occurred in his feelings by the following morning?

3. It was indeed an extraordinary adventure Ryabovich had. How does he explain it to himself? What do his fellow officers think when he tells them of it? What surprises him about the telling of the adventure? Whom does he suspect of having given him the kiss?

4. After having evoked the atmosphere of the evening at the von Rabbecks, Chekhov spends a considerable time describing the army brigade on the move as it sets off from Mestechki the following morning (page 342). To Ryabovich, the marching brigade was a sight "all perfectly comprehensible and therefore uninteresting." Would it be uninteresting to someone not familiar with it? What relationship do you see between that insight as related to the marching column of soldiers, and as related to the "little adventure" that befell Ryabovich at the von Rabbecks?

5. One of the concerns of this complex story has to do with the tendency of people to idealize the unusual — and to overlook entirely the miraculous aspects of whatever is familiar. Similarly, the story touches on the importance of illusion in our lives. Is Ryabovich better or worse off in that interval after the kiss and before his disenchantment at the end of the story?

6. As has been suggested, the story poses questions concerned with appearance and reality, with illusion and truth. What questions of justice are posed by the story? Is it just that Ryabovich's fate with women should be so different from that of Lobytko's? How is the difference to be accounted for? Is "The Kiss" about great men or ordinary ones? Ryabovich is extraordinary — that is, out of the ordinary. In what ways? Does that mean he is great?

For Composition

At one point in the story, Ryabovich admits to himself that his little adventure was in reality trivial "and to think of it seriously, to say the least, was stupid." Yet he does go on thinking of it, bidding farewell to logic and giving himself up to his dreams.

1. **Argument.** With all the pleasure his dreams bring him, making bearable a dreary and familiar routine and filling whole hours with happiness, why is Ryabovich unwilling at the end of the story to set out on yet another adventure with his fellow officers? In a unified essay consider the question, referring to the story and to other relevant reading or experience for specific support of your generalizations. In revising your essay, delete whatever does not relate to the major insights you are expressing.

2. **Analysis.** Ryabovich's thoughts voiced on page 344 are of crucial importance in understanding why his little adventure was so affecting: "All I am dreaming about now which seems to me so impossible and unearthly is really quite an ordinary thing. . . . " In a brief essay analyze the insight contained in that paragraph, explaining why a sentiment like the concluding one ("I am the same as everyone else. . . . ") should affect him as it does. Your analysis will necessarily comment on Ryabovich's character and life up to that moment, perhaps most relevantly as it was shown by his behavior upon arriving at the von Rabbecks'.

Words and Allusions

COGNATES (page 22). Early in "The Kiss," the elderly officer von Rabbeck entertains his guests by showing them, among other things, his collection of autograph letters. What is the origin of the word *autograph*, and what is its meaning in this context? What do the following related words mean: *holograph, grapheme, graphic, graphologist, demography*? Use each word in a sentence that illustrates its meaning.

Oedipus the King

SOPHOCLES

Near the middle of the fifth century B.C., the city-state of Athens, on the peninsula of Greece, was experiencing a golden age. Never before in history, perhaps never since, has a civilization achieved such heights. From that period have come not only the great classic architecture that stands today in Athens and — by means of imitations — throughout the Western world, but also a political system that has exerted profound influences down to our own times, as well as a dramatic literature that has yet to be surpassed. Indeed, one example of that literature, Sophocles' *Oedipus the King* (or *Oedipus Rex*) remains among the three or four greatest plays ever written; in Western culture only the supreme plays of the contemporary Athenian Aeschylus and those of Shakespeare bear comparison.

Oedipus the King is based on a legend with which Sophocles' audience was thoroughly familiar. His audience knew (as you should know in order to appreciate the play adequately) that the wandering Oedipus of Corinth had been made king of Thebes, north of Athens, for having solved a riddle that the monstrous sphinx was posing to every passerby: What walks on four feet in the morning, two in the afternoon, and three in the evening? Not to answer the riddle correctly meant death at the sphinx's claws. But Oedipus answered it: man, he said, who crawls as an infant, walks erect as an adult, and uses a cane in his old age. And with that answer the scourge of the city was lifted, and a grateful populace made the young stranger king, giving him as a bride the dead king Laius' wife Jocasta.

But Oedipus' fate, apparently so promising as the triumphant savior of a city and husband of a queen, was in reality black indeed. At the very height of his worldly success, he was some years later called upon to save his adopted city once more. A plague was raging through Thebes — and would rage until a mysterious crime was identified and atoned for. What was the crime that had outraged the gods? Who had committed it? No one knew, but the man who had saved the Thebans once might save them again. Accordingly, in supplication a group of citizens approached their king Oedipus, beseeching his aid. And it is at that moment that Sophocles' monumental drama of a man and his destiny begins.

CHARACTERS

OEDIPUS,[1] *King of Thebes*
PRIEST
CREON,[2] *Brother of Jocasta*

[1] **Oedipus**: pronounced ed'i·pəs.
[2] **Creon**: krē'on.

TEIRESIAS,[3] *an old blind prophet*
JOCASTA,[4] *wife of Oedipus*
MESSENGER
SHEPHERD
SERVANT
CHORUS

[3] **Teiresias**: tī·rē'sē·əs.
[4] **Jocasta**: jō·kas'tə.

Oedipus the King by Sophocles, trans. Kenneth Cavander. Published by Chandler Publishing Company, San Francisco. Copyright © 1961 by Chandler Publishing Company. Reprinted by permission.

In front of the palace of OEDIPUS *at Thebes. Near the altar stands the* PRIEST *with a large crowd of supplicants.*[1]

[*Enter* OEDIPUS.]

OEDIPUS. My children, why do you crowd
and wait at my altars?
Olive branches . . . and wreaths of sacred
flowers —
Why do you bring these, my people of
Thebes? Your streets
Are heavy with incense, solemn with
prayers for healing,
And when I heard your voices, I would
not let   5
My messengers tell me what you said. I
came
To be your messenger myself, Oedipus,
whose name
Is greatest known and greatest feared.

(*to* PRIEST) Will you tell me, then? You
have dignity enough
To speak for them all — is it fear that
makes you kneel   10
Before me, or do you need my help? I
am ready,
Whatever you ask will be done . . . Come,

[1] **supplicants:** persons humbly making requests.

I am not cold
Or dead to feeling — I will have pity on
you.

PRIEST. King Oedipus, our master in Thebes,
if you will look
At your altars, and at the ages of those
who kneel there,   15
You will see children, too small to fly far
from home;
You will see old men, slow with the years
they carry,
And priests — I am a priest of Zeus; and
you will see
The finest warriors you have; the rest of
your people
Kneel, praying, in the open city, in the
temples   20
Of Athene,[2] and in the shrine where we
keep a flame
Always alive and the ash whispers the
future.
Look about you. The whole city drowns
And cannot lift its hand from the storm
of death   24
In which it sinks; the green corn withers
In the fields, cattle die in the meadows,
Our wives weep in agony, and never give
birth!

[2] **Athene:** Greek goddess of wisdom.

ABOUT THE AUTHOR • Sophocles (496–406 B.C.) was one of the three great tragic poets of Athens, along with Aeschylus and Euripides, whose plays have continued to move modern audiences as they did those of ancient Greece. In the course of his long career, Sophocles performed as actor and producer as well as author. As a playwright he won twenty first prizes in the annual dramatic contests in Athens and was never less than second. Sophocles wrote over one hundred and twenty tragedies, but only seven have survived. Of these, the most widely known are the plays dealing with the story of Oedipus and his family — *Oedipus the King, Oedipus at Colonus,* and *Antigone. Oedipus the King* was held as a model for future playwrights by Aristotle in his *Poetics.* It is still our best model of classical tragedy, and it fascinates philosophers and psychiatrists by its remarkable insights into the nature of man.

Apollo[1] brings his fire like a drover[2] and
    herds us
Into death, and nature is at war with her-
    self.
Thebes is sick, every house deserted, and
    the blind   30
Prison of the dead grows rich with
    mourning
And our dying cries.
Eternal powers control our lives, and we
    do not
Think you are their equal; yet we pray
    to you, as your children,
Believing that you, more than any man,
    may direct   35
Events, and come to terms with the
    powers beyond us.
When the savage riddle of the Sphinx
    enslaved
Thebes, you came to set us free. We
Were powerless, we could not tell you
    how to answer her.
And now they say, and it is believed,
    that you   40
Were close to God when you raised our
    city from the dead.
Oedipus, we pray to your power, which
    can overcome
Sufferings we do not understand; guard
    us
From this evil. In heaven and earth there
    must
Be some answer to our prayer, and you
    may know it.   45
You have struggled once with the powers
    above us and been
Victorious; we trust that strength and be-
    lieve your words.
Oedipus, you are the royal glory of
    Thebes —
Give us life: Oedipus — think. Because
You overpowered the evil in the Sphinx
We call you saviour still. Must we re-
    member   51
Your reign for the greatness in which you

[1] **Apollo:** Greek god of the sun.
[2] **drover:** one who drives cattle or sheep.

began, and the sorrow
In which you ended? The country is
    sick, and you
Must heal us. You were once our luck,
    our fortune, the augury[3]
Of good we looked for in the world out-
    side. Fulfill   55
That augury now. You are king of
    Thebes, but consider:
Which is it better to rule — a kingdom?
    Or a desert?
What is a castle or a ship if there are
No men to give it life? Emptiness! Noth-
    ing!
OEDIPUS. My children, I know your sor-
    rows, I know why   60
You have come, and what you ask of me.
    I see
The pain of sickness in you all, and yet in
    all
That sickness, who is so sick as I? Each
Of you has one sorrow, his grief is his
    own —
But I must feel for my country, for my-
    self,   65
And for you. That is why you did not
    find me
Deaf or indifferent to your prayers. No,
I have spent many tears, and in my
    thoughts
Traveled long journeys. And then I saw
That we could be saved in one way only;
I took that way and sent Creon, my
    brother-   71
In-law, to the Oracle of Apollo,[4] there
The god will tell him how I can save the
    city —
The price may be an act of sacrifice, or
    perhaps
A vow, a prayer, will be enough. . . . But
    the days   75
Run on and the measure of time keeps
    pace with them

[3] **augury:** omen.
[4] **Oracle of Apollo:** shrine at Delphi where resided
a priestess of Apollo through whom the god was believed to speak; she gave advice and prophesied the
future to those who consulted the oracle.

People have right to know who King is...

And I begin to fear. What is he doing?
I did not think he would stay so long —
he should not
Stay so long! . . . But when he comes I
will do
Whatever the god commands; if I dis-
obeyed   80
It would be a sin.

PRIEST.   Heaven listened then;
This messenger says that Creon is returning.

OEDIPUS. My lord Apollo, let his news be
the shining sun
That answers our prayers and guides us
out of death!

PRIEST. I can see him now . . . the news
must be good.   85
Look, there is a crown of bay[1] thick with
flowers
Covering his hair.

OEDIPUS.   At last we shall know
the truth.
If I shout, he will hear me. . . . Creon!
My brother, son of Menoeceus, Lord of
Thebes,
What answer does Apollo send to us? Do
you bring   90
An answer?

[*Enter* CREON.]

CREON.   Our danger is gone. This
load of sorrow
Will be lifted if we follow the way
Where Apollo points.

OEDIPUS.   What does this mean?
I expected
Hope, or fear, but your answer gives me
neither.

CREON. I am ready to tell you my message
now, if you wish;   95
But they can hear us, and if we go inside. . . .

OEDIPUS. Tell me now and let them hear!
I must not think
Of myself; I grieve only when my peo-
ple suffer.

CREON. Then this is what I was told at
Delphi:
Our land is tainted. We carry the guilt in
our midst.   100
A foul disease, which will not be healed
unless
We drive it out and deny it life.

OEDIPUS.   But how
Shall we be clean? How did this happen
to us?

CREON. The crime of murder is followed by
a storm.
Banish the murder and you banish the
storm, kill   105
Again and you kill the storm.

OEDIPUS.   But Apollo
means
One man — who is this man?

CREON.   My lord,
There was once a king of Thebes; he was
our master
Before you came to rule our broken city.

OEDIPUS. I have heard of him. . . . I never
saw your king.   110

CREON. Now that he is dead your mission
from the god
Is clear: take vengeance on his murderers!

OEDIPUS. But where are they now? The
crime is old,
And time is stubborn with its secrets.
How   114
Can you ask me to find these men?

CREON.   The god said
You must search in Thebes; what is
hunted can
Be caught; only what we ignore escapes.

OEDIPUS. Where was the murder? Was
Laius[2] killed in the city?

---

[1] **crown of bay**: *i.e.*, the laurel wreath of victory.

[2] **Laius**: lā′i·əs.

"*When the savage riddle of the Sphinx enslaved / Thebes, you came to set us free.*" Oedipus and the Sphinx, *from a fifth-century Greek red-figure vase.*

Or did this happen in another country?

CREON.   He was traveling
 To Delphi, he said. But he never returned
  to the palace   120
 He left that day.

OEDIPUS.   Did no one see this?
 A messenger? The guard who watched
  his journey? You could
 Have questioned them.

CREON.   They were all killed, except
 One. He ran home in terror, and could
  only
 Repeat one thing.

OEDIPUS.   What did he repeat? 125
 Once we have learnt one thing, we may
  learn the rest.
 This hope is the beginning of other hopes.

CREON. He said they met some robbers who
  killed the king.
 He talked of an army, too strong for the
  servants of Laius.

OEDIPUS. Robbers would not dare to kill a
king — unless   130
They had bribes. They must have had
 bribes from the city! *maybe successor (creon)*
     had Laius murdered

CREON. We suspected that, but with Laius
 dead
We were defenseless against our troubles.

OEDIPUS.   Were
 Your troubles so great that they prevented you   134
 From knowing the truth? Your king had
  been murdered . . . !

CREON.   But the Sphinx
 Had a riddle to which there was no an-
  swer, and we thought
 Of our closest sorrows. We had no time
  for other
 Mysteries.

OEDIPUS. But I will begin again, and
  make your mysteries
 Plain. Apollo was right, and you were
  right,
 To turn my thoughts to the king who
  died. Now   140

You will see the measure of my power; I
come to defend you,
Avenging your country and the god
Apollo.
(*Aside*) If I can drive out this corruption
and make the city
Whole, I shall do more than save my
people,
Who are my friends, but still my subjects
— I shall save   145
Myself. For the knife that murdered
Laius may yet
Drink from my heart, and the debt I pay
to him
Lies to my own credit.[1]
My children, quickly, leave this altar and
take
Your branches. I will have the people of
Thebes assembled   150
To hear that I shall do all the god com-
mands.
And in the end we shall see my fortune
smiling
From heaven, or my fall.

[*Exit* OEDIPUS.]

PRIEST. Let us go, my sons; our king has
given the order
We came to hear. May Apollo, who sent
this answer   155
From his oracle, come to lay our sickness
To rest, and give us life.

[*Exeunt* PRIEST, CREON, *and some of the
elders.*]

[*Enter* CHORUS.]

CHORUS. From golden Delphi Apollo replies
to Thebes
And the words of heaven send a warning.
As a lyre[2] is strung and tightened, so we
Are tightened by fear.   161

As a lyre trembles, so we tremble at the
touch of fear.
Apollo, god of healing, god of newness,
We fear you, and the commands you send
to humble us.
Do you ask a new submission? Or is your
command   165
The same as we hear in every wind, and
every season, and every year?
Only the child of golden hope, whose
voice
Will never die, only the spirit of truth can
tell us.
First in my prayers is the goddess Athene,
the daughter of Zeus;
Second, her sister, Artemis,[3] who is queen
in Thebes,   170
For she sits at our country's heart, pure
and honored,
In a temple like the sun. And third in our
prayer
Is Phoebus Apollo,[4] whose arm reaches
over all the world.
Come three times to drive our wrongs
before you!   174
If ever in the past, when evil and blindness
Rose like a wave, when grief was burning
in our city,
If ever you banished that grief,
Come now to help us.

There is no numbering our sorrows;
The whole country is sick, and mortal
will and human mind   180
Are no weapons to defend us.
The great earth whom we call our
mother
Is barren and dead; women weep in the
pain of childbirth
But they fall sick and die.
Look, can you see the dying go following
each other,   185

---

[1] **Lies . . . credit:** *i.e.,* is to my own advantage.
[2] **lyre:** a harplike musical instrument.

[3] **Artemis:** goddess of the moon and hunting.
[4] **Phoebus Apollo:** *Phoebus* means "radiant" in Greek; this description was commonly applied to Apollo.

Gliding like gentle birds, quicker
Than the restless flash of fire that will
    never sleep,
The dying on their flight to the shore
Where evening sits like a goddess?   189
The city of the dying goes countless away
And the children of life fall to the earth,
The toys of death,
With no pity and no remembering tears.

In the rest of our city, wives and mothers
Stand grey at the altars,   195
Which tell us of a certainty resisting the
    seas of doubt;
They weep, pray, plead for release
From the harsh revenge which heaven
    brings.
A cry for healing rises and burns above
    the still crowd
That mourns in the city.   200
Send us strength that will look kindly on
    us,
Golden daughter of Zeus.
Ares, the god of war, confronts us, bitter
    in his cruelty,
And his shout burns like fire;
But his war is fought with no armor, and
    Ares   205
Carries no shield, for he brings his conflict
Into the moment of our birth and death.
Oh turn him flying down the winds, turn
    him
Back and dash him from our country
Into the wide chambers where Amphi-
    trite[1] sleeps,   210
Or to the lonely cliffs of Thrace where
    the seas
Allow no guests. For Ares comes to finish
The deadly work left undone by the
    night.
Zeus, you are the lord of lightning, lord
    of fire,
Destroy him with your thunder, crush
    our enemy!   215

[1] **Amphitrite** (am′fi·trī′tē): wife of Poseidon, god
of the sea.

Lord Apollo, god in the sun, we pray for
    your light;
Strike with your golden spears and your
    hands of fire,
Strike to protect us.
We pray for Artemis to bring her chaste
    fires,
Which we see her carry like a shining
    torch across   220
The mountains where the wolf runs.
I call you, the god with the golden crown,
Born in our country, Bacchus,
With the fire of wine in your cheek,
And the voice of wine in your shout,   225
Come with your pine branch burning,
    and your Maenads[2]
Following the light, the fire of heaven's
    madness
In their eyes, come to guard us against the
    treacherous power
Who goes to war with justice and the
    harmony of heaven!

[*Enter* OEDIPUS.]

OEDIPUS. You have told me of your need.
    Are you content   230
To hear me speak, obey my words, and
    work
To humor the sickness? . . . Then you
    will thrust away
The weight with which you struggle, and
    fulfill
Your need. I am a stranger to this story,
And to the crime; I have no signs to guide
    me,   235
And so if I am to trap this murderer, my
    hunt

[2] **Maenads** (mē′nadz): female attendants of
Bacchus, Greek god of wine.

Must follow every hope. I am speaking, then,
To every citizen of Thebes, and I shall not
Exempt myself, although I am a citizen only
In name, and not in blood.   240
Whoever knows the murderer of Laius, son
Of Labdacus, must make his knowledge mine.
It is the king's command! And if he is afraid,
Or thinks he will escape, I say to him, "Speak!
You will go into exile, but you will go un-harmed —   245
Banishment is all you have to fear."
Or if you know the assassin comes from another
Country, you must not be silent. I shall pay
The value of your knowledge, and your reward
Will be more than gratitude.   250
But if I find only silence, if you are afraid
To betray a friend or reveal yourself, and lock
The truth away, listen, this is my decree:
This murderer, no matter who he is, is banished
From the country where my power and my throne   255
Are supreme. No one must shelter him or speak to him;
When you pray to heaven, he must not pray with you;
When you sacrifice, drive him away, do not
Give him holy water, beat him from your doors!
He carries the taint of corruption with him — for so   260
The god Apollo has revealed to me. . . . You see
How I serve the god and revenge the king who died!

I curse that murderer; if he is alone, I curse him!
If he shares his guilt with others, I curse him! May   264
His evil heart beat out its years in sorrow,
Throughout his life may he breathe the air of death!
If I give him shelter, knowing who
He is, and let him feel the warmth of my fire,
I ask this punishment for myself.   269
This must be done! In every word I speak
I command obedience, and so does the god Apollo,
And so does your country, which a bar-ren sickness
And an angry heaven drag to death. But even
If it is not a god that comes to punish you
It would be shame to leave your land impure.   275
Your king was killed — he was a royal and noble
Man; hunt his murderer down!
I live in Laius' palace, my queen was once
The queen of Laius, and if his line had prospered   279
His children would have shared my love.
But now time has struck his head to earth
And in revenge I will fight for him as I
Would fight for my own father. My search will never
End until I take in chains the murderer
Of Laius, son of Labdacus. I pray heaven
That those who will not help me may watch the soil   286
They have ploughed crumble and turn black, let them see
Their women barren, let them be de-stroyed by the fury
That scourges[1] us, but may it rage more cruelly!
And for all the Thebans who will obey me gladly   290
I ask the strength of justice, and the power of heaven.

[1] **scourges**: punishes severely.

So we shall live in peace; so we shall be
   healed.

CHORUS. Your curse menaces me, my lord,
   if I lie.
I swear I did not kill him, nor can I tell
Who did. Apollo sent the reply, and
   Apollo   295
Should find the murderer.

OEDIPUS.   Yes, we believe
It is Apollo's task — but we cannot make
The gods our slaves; we must act for our-
   selves.

CHORUS.   Our next
Hope then, must be. . . .

OEDIPUS.   And every hope
You have. When I search, nothing escapes.   300

CHORUS. We know a lord who sees as clearly
   as the lord
Apollo — Teiresias; we could ask
   Teiresias, my king,
And be given the truth.

OEDIPUS.   Creon told me, and
   his advice
Did not lie idle for want of action. I have
   sent
Two servants. . . . It is strange they are
   not here.   305

CHORUS. And there are the old rumors —
   but they tell us nothing . . .

OEDIPUS. What do these rumors say? I must
   know
Everything.

CHORUS.   They say some travelers killed
   him.

OEDIPUS. I have heard that too. But the man
   who saw those travelers
Was never seen himself.

CHORUS.   The murderer will
   leave our country;   310
There is a part of every man that is ruled
By fear, and when he hears your curse. . . .

OEDIPUS.   A sentence

Holds no terror for the man who is not
   afraid
To kill.

CHORUS. But now he will be convicted.
   Look,
They are leading your priest to you;
   Teiresias comes.   315
When he speaks, it is the voice of heaven
That we hear.

[*Enter* TEIRESIAS, *guided by a boy.*]

OEDIPUS.   Teiresias, all things lie
In your power, for you have harnessed all
Knowledge and all mysteries; you know
   what heaven
Hides, and what runs in the earth below,
   and you   320
Must know, though you cannot see, the
   sickness with which
Our country struggles. Defend us, my
   lord, and save us —
We shall find no other defense or safety.
For Apollo — and yet you must have
   heard the message —
Apollo, whom we asked in our doubt,
   promised release —   325
But on one condition: that we find the
   murderers
Of Laius, and banish them, or repay the
   murder.
Teiresias, the singing birds will tell you
   of the future,
You have many ways of knowing the
   truth. Do not grudge
Your knowledge, but save yourself and
   your city, save me,   330
For murder defiles us all. Think of us
As your prisoners, whose lives belong to
   you!
To have the power and use that power
   for good
Is work to bring you honor.

TEIRESIAS.   When truth cannot help
The man who knows, then it brings
   terror. I knew   335

That truth, but I stifled it. I should not
have come.

OEDIPUS. What is it? You come as sadly as
despair.

TEIRESIAS. Send me away, I tell you! Then
it will be easy
For you to play the king, and I the priest.

OEDIPUS. This is no reply. You cannot love
Thebes — your own   340
Country, Teiresias — if you hide what
the gods tell you.

TEIRESIAS. I see your words guiding you on
the wrong
Path; I pray for my own escape.

OEDIPUS.   Teiresias!
You do not turn away if you know the
truth; we all
Come like slaves to a king with our
prayers to you.   345

TEIRESIAS. But you come without the truth,
and I can never
Reveal my own sorrows, lest they become
Yours.

OEDIPUS. You cannot? Then you know and
will not tell us!
Instead, you plan treason and the city's
death.

TEIRESIAS. I mean to protect us both from
pain. You search   350
And probe, and it is all wasted. I will not
tell you!

OEDIPUS. You demon! You soul of evil! You
would goad
A thing of stone to fury. Will you never
speak?
Can you feel, can you suffer? Answer
me, and end this!

TEIRESIAS. You see wrong in my mood, you
call me evil — blind   355
To the mood that settles in you and rages
there.

OEDIPUS. Rages! Yes, that is what your
words

Have done, when they shout your contempt for Thebes.

TEIRESIAS. The truth will come; my silence
cannot hide it.

OEDIPUS. And what must come is what you
must tell me.   360

TEIRESIAS. I can tell you no more, and on
this answer let
Your fury caper[1] like a beast.

OEDIPUS.   It is
A fury that will never leave me. Listen,
I know
What you are. I see now that you con-
spired to plan
This murder, and you committed it — all
but the stroke   365
That killed him. If you had eyes, I would
have said
The crime was yours alone.

TEIRESIAS.   Oedipus, I warn you!
Obey your own decree and the oath you
swore.
Never from this day speak to me, or to
these nobles;
You are our corruption, the unholiness in
our land.   370

OEDIPUS. How you must despise me to
flaunt your scorn like this,
Thinking you will escape. How?

TEIRESIAS.   I have escaped.
I carry the truth; it is my child, and
guards me.

OEDIPUS. Truth! Who taught you? Heaven
never taught you!

TEIRESIAS. You taught me; you forced me to
the point of speech.   375

OEDIPUS. Repeat your words, I do not remember this speech.

TEIRESIAS. You did not understand? Or do
you try to trap me?

OEDIPUS. I know nothing! Repeat your
truth!

---

[1] **caper**: prance.

TEIRESIAS. I said, you are the murderer you are searching for.

OEDIPUS. Again you attack me, but I will not forgive you again! 380

TEIRESIAS. Shall I say more to make your anger sprawl?

OEDIPUS. All you have breath for — it will all be useless.

TEIRESIAS. Then . . . you live with your dearest one in burning
Shame, and do not know it; nor can you see 384
The evil that surrounds you.

OEDIPUS. Do you think
You will always smile in freedom if you talk like this?

TEIRESIAS. If truth can give strength, I will.

OEDIPUS. It can —
But not to you; you have no truth. Your senses
Have died in you — ears: deaf! eyes: blind!

TEIRESIAS. Yes, be bitter, mock at me, poor Oedipus. 390
Soon they will all mock as bitterly as you.

OEDIPUS. You live in perpetual night; you cannot harm
Me, nor anyone who moves in the light.

TEIRESIAS. Your downfall
Will come, but I will not be the cause. Apollo 394
Is a great power; he watches over the end.

OEDIPUS. Did you or Creon plan this?

TEIRESIAS. Creon is not
Your enemy; you carry your enemy with you — in your soul.

OEDIPUS. We have wealth and power, the mind reaches higher, grows,
Breaks its own fetters, our lives are great and envied,
And the world rewards us — with spitefulness and hate! 400

Consider my power — I did not come begging, the city
Laid its submission in my hands as a gift.
Yes, for this power, Creon, my trusted, my first
Friend, goes like a thief behind my back,
Tries to exile me, and sends this wizard,
This patcher of threadbare stories, this cunning peddler 406
Of the future, with no eyes except
For money, and certainly no eyes for mysteries.
Tell me, tell me, when did you ever foretell the truth?
When the Sphinx howled her mockeries and riddles 410
Why could you find no answer to free the city?
Her question was too hard for the simple man,
The humble man; only heaven's wisdom could find
A reply. But you found none! Neither your birds
Above you, nor the secret voice of your inspiration 415
Sent you knowledge — then we saw what you were!
But I came, ignorant Oedipus, and silenced her,
And my only weapon was in my mind and my will;
I had no omens to teach me. And this is the man
You would usurp! You think, when Creon is king 420
You will sit close to the throne; but I think
Your plans to drive the accursed away will return
To defeat you, and to defeat their architect.
You are old, Teiresias, or else your prophetic wisdom 424
Would have been your death.

CHORUS. Your majesty, what he has said

And your reply — they were both born in anger.

We do not need this wildness; we ask the best

Fulfillment of Apollo's commands. This must be the search.

TEIRESIAS (*to* OEDIPUS). You flourish your power; but you must give me the right

To make my reply, and that will have equal power.   430

I have not lived to be your servant, but Apollo's;

Nor am I found in the list of those whom Creon

Protects. You call me blind, you jeer at me —

I say your sight is not clear enough to see

Who shares your palace, nor the rooms in which you walk,   435

Nor the sorrow about you. Do you know who gave you birth?

You are the enemy of the dead, and of the living,

And do not know it. The curse is a two-edged sword,

From your mother, from your father; the curse will hunt you,

Like a destruction, from your country. Now   440

You have sight, but then you will go in blindness;

When you know the truth of your wedding night

All the world will bear your crying to rest,

Every hill a Cithaeron[1] to echo you.

You thought that night was peace, like a gentle harbor —   445

But there was no harbor for that voyage, only grief.

Evil crowds upon you; you do not see

How it will level you with your children and reveal

[1] **Cithaeron** (si·thē′ron): mountain in Greece sacred to Bacchus.

Yourself as you truly are. Howl your abuse

At Creon and at me. . . . All men must suffer,   450

Oedipus, but none will find suffering more terrible

Than you.

OEDIPUS.   Must I bear this? Must I be silent?

Die! Go to your death! Leave my palace now!

Get away from me!

TEIRESIAS. Yet you called me here, or I would not have come.   455

OEDIPUS. If I had known you would talk in the raving language

Of a madman, I would never have sent for you.

TEIRESIAS. I am no more than you see. You see a madman,

The parents who gave you life saw a prophet.

OEDIPUS. My parents? Wait! Who were my parents?   460

TEIRESIAS. Today will be your parent, and your murderer.

OEDIPUS. Always riddles, always lies and riddles!

TEIRESIAS. You were best at solving riddles, were you not?

OEDIPUS. When you think of my greatness, it inspires your mockery.

TEIRESIAS. That greatness has conspired to be your traitor.   465

OEDIPUS. I saved this country, I care for nothing else.

TEIRESIAS. Then I shall go. . . . (*to his guide*) Boy, lead me away.

OEDIPUS. Yes, lead him. . . . You come and trouble me — you are nothing

But hindrance to my plans. Go, and I shall be safe.

The ancient Greek theater at Epidaurus.

TEIRESIAS. I came to speak, and I shall not
    leave until I speak.   470
  I need not cower at your frown, you can-
    not
  Harm me. This man for whom you
    search,
  Whom you threaten, and to the people
    call "the murderer
  Of Laius," this man is here, a stranger, a
    foreigner;
  But he will see his Theban blood, though
    he will not   475
  Have any joy at the discovery.
  He will be blind — though now he sees;
    a beggar —
  Though now he is rich, and he will go
    feeling
  Strange ground before him with a stick.
  He is a father to children — then he will
  Be called their brother; he is his mother's
    son —   481

Then he will be called her husband, then
He will be called his father's murderer.
Consider this when you walk between
    your palace walls;
If you find I have been false to you, then
    say   485
That all my prophetic wisdom is a lie.

    [*Exeunt all but the* CHORUS.]

CHORUS. In the rock at Delphi there is a cave
  Which is the mouth of heaven; now
  The cave warns us of one man, whose
    hands are red
  With murder, and whose actions   490
  Break the unspoken laws that shackle us.
  Time tells him now to escape,
  Faster than the jostling horses of the
    storm,
  For Apollo, the son of Zeus, leaps down
    on him,

foreshadowing

Armed with lightning, dressed in fire,
And the terrible avengers follow where
he goes,   496
The Furies[1] who never mistake and are
never cheated.
From the snow of Parnassus[2] over Delphi
the message
Gleamed and came shining to Thebes.
We must all hunt the murderer   500
Who hides from justice. Like a lonely
bull
He crosses and crosses our country,
through the harsh forests,
The hollows of the mountains, and the
rocks.
Sadly thinking and alone,
Sadly trying to escape   505
The words that came from Delphi, the
heart of the world.
But their wings are always beating in his
head.

The wisdom of the priest sets fear, fear,
beating in our blood;
Truth or lies, nothing comforts, nothing
denies.
The world is built out of our beliefs, 510
And when we lose those beliefs in doubt,
Our world is destroyed, and the present
and the past
Vanish into night.
We must have proof, a certainty that we
can touch   514
And feel, before we turn against Oedipus.
The land is peopled with rumors and
whispers —
They cannot make us avenge King Laius,
Whose death is guarded by such mystery.

All that men may do is watched and re-
membered
By Zeus, and by Apollo. But they are
gods;   520
Can any man, even the prophet, the priest,
Can even he know more than us?
And if he can, who will be judge of him,

1 **Furies**: avenging spirits in Greek mythology.
2 **Parnassus**: mountain in Greece sacred to Apollo.

and say he lied
Or spoke the truth.
Yet wisdom may come to us, not the wis-
dom that sees   525
How the world is ruled, but the wisdom
that guides
The modest life. In this alone we may
excel.
But the proof must be clear and certain,
Before I can accuse Oedipus.
Remember that the Sphinx came flying
To meet him, evil beyond our compre-
hension,   531
And we saw his wisdom then, we knew
and felt
The goodness of his heart towards our
country.
Thoughts cannot be guilty traitors to
such a man.

[*Enter* CREON.]

CREON. Lords of Thebes, this message has
called me here   535
In terror. . . . These crimes of which our
king accuses me —
No one would dare to think of them!
If he
Believes I could wrong him, or even speak
of wrong,
At such a time, when we are in such sor-
row,
Let me die! I have no wish to live out my
years   540
If I must live them suspected and despised.
I will not bear this slander, which is no
trifle
To forget, but the greatest injury — the
name
Of traitor. The people will call me that,
even
You will call me that!

CHORUS.   His fury mastered
him;   545
Perhaps he did not mean the charge.

CREON.   He said

To you all — you all heard — that the priest
Had been told to lie, and that I had planned the answer?

CHORUS. He said that, but I know he did not mean it.

CREON.   And when he
Accused me, he seemed master of his thoughts, and there was   550
Reason in his voice?

CHORUS.   I cannot remember,
I do not observe my king so closely. . . . But here
He comes from the palace himself to meet you.

[*Enter* OEDIPUS.]

OEDIPUS.   So,
My citizen, you have come to your king? Your eyes have great
Courage — they can look on my palace out of a murderer's   555
Face, a robber's face! Yes, I know you; You blaze, you thief of power. . . . In heaven's name
Tell me: when you planned to kill me, did you think I had
Become a coward or a fool? Did you think I would not
Notice your treason stalking me? Or were you sure   560
That if I knew, I would not dare defense?
See your insane attempt! You try to capture
Power, which must be hunted with armies and gold;
But no one will follow you, no one will make
You rich!

CREON.   Wait! You have accused, but you must not judge   565
Until you have heard my defense; I can reply.

OEDIPUS. You talk with the fangs of clever-

ness; but how
Can I understand? I understand only
That you are my enemy, and dangerous.

CREON. There is one thing I must say; hear it first.   570

OEDIPUS. One thing you must not say: "I am innocent."

CREON. You are stubborn, Oedipus, your will is too hard;
It is nothing to treasure, and you are wrong to think it is.

OEDIPUS. Treason, crimes against a brother, will not
Escape justice: you are wrong to think they will.   575

CREON. I do not quarrel with your talk of justice.
But tell me how I have harmed you: what is my crime?

OEDIPUS. Did you persuade me — perhaps you did not — to send for
The priest whom we used to worship for his wisdom?   579

CREON. And I still have faith in that advice.

OEDIPUS.   How long
Is it since Laius. . . .

CREON.   What has Laius to do
With this? I do not see. . . .

OEDIPUS.   Since he was hidden
From the living sun, since he was attacked and killed?

CREON. The years are old and the time is long since then.

OEDIPUS. Was Teiresias already a priest and prophet then?   585

CREON. As wise as now, and no less honored and obeyed.

OEDIPUS. But at the time he did not mention me?

CREON. I did not hear him. . . .

OEDIPUS.   But surely you tried to find
The murderer?

CREON.   We searched, of course, we could discover   589
Nothing.

OEDIPUS. If I was guilty, why did Teiresias
Not accuse me then? He must have
known, for he is wise.

CREON. I do not know. If I cannot know
the truth
I would rather be silent.

OEDIPUS.   But there is one truth
You will confess to; none knows it bet-
ter . . . ?

CREON. What is that? I shall deny noth-
ing. . . .   595

OEDIPUS. That only by some insidious plan
of yours
Could Teiresias ever say I murdered
Laius!

CREON. If he says that, I cannot unsay it for
him;
But give me an answer in return for mine.

OEDIPUS. Question till you have no questions left;   600
You cannot prove me a murderer.

CREON.   Now,
You have married my sister?

OEDIPUS.   I do not deny
it; the truth
Was in your question.

CREON.   You and she rule
This country, you are equal?

OEDIPUS.   If she has a wish
I grant it all to her.

CREON.   And am I not   605
Considered equal to you both?

OEDIPUS.   Yes, there

your friendship
Shows the face of evil it concealed.

CREON. No, reason to yourself as I have
reasoned.
First, imagine two ways of ruling, each
Bringing equal power. With one of these
fear   610
Never leaves you, but with the other you
sleep
Calm in the night. Who do you think
Would not choose the second? I feel no
ambition
To be the king, when I have the power of
a king.
For I have my place in the world, I know
it, and will not   615
Overreach myself. Now, you give me all
I wish, and no fear comes with the gift;
But if I were king myself, much more
would be forced
Upon me. Why should I love the throne
better
Than a throne's power and a throne's
majesty   620
Without the terrors of a throne? Now,
I may smile to all, and all will bow to me;
Those who need you petition me,
For I am their hopes of success. Is this
such a worthless
Life that I should exchange it for yours?
Treason   625
Is for those who cannot value what they
have.
I have never had longing thoughts about
your power,
Nor would I help a man who had. Send
To Delphi, make a test of me, ask the god
Whether my message was true, and if you
find   630
I have plotted with your priest, then you
may kill me —
I will be your authority, I will assent
When you decree my death. But do not
accuse me
Yet, when you know nothing. You
wrong your friends

To think them enemies, as much as you
    do wrong   635
To take enemies for friends. Think, be
    sure!
You banish life from your body — and
    life you love
Most dearly — by banishing a good
    friend.
Time will set this knowledge safely in
    your heart;
Time alone shows the goodness in a
    man —   640
One day is enough to tell you all his evil.

CHORUS. My king, a cautious man would
    listen; beware
Of being convinced too quickly. Sud-
    denness is not safety.

OEDIPUS. When the attack is quick and sud-
    den, and the plot
Runs in the darkness, my thoughts must
    be sudden   645
In reply. If I wait, sitting in silence,
He will have done his work, and I lost
My chance to begin.

CREON.   Your decision then!
    Will you
Banish me?

OEDIPUS.   No, not banishment; I
Will have your life! You must teach men
    the rewards   650
That I keep for the envious and the cruel.

CREON. Will you not listen to persuasion
    and the truth?

OEDIPUS. You will never persuade me that
    you speak the truth.

CREON. No, I can see you are blind to truth.

OEDIPUS.   I see
    Enough to guard my life.

CREON.   My life is as
    precious   655
  To me.

OEDIPUS. But you are a traitor!

CREON.   You know
    nothing!

OEDIPUS. Yet the king must rule.

CREON.   Not when the
    king is evil.

OEDIPUS. My city! My city!

CREON. It is my city too, do not forget that!

CHORUS. Stop, my lords! Look, here is
    Jocasta coming to you   660
From the palace, at the moment when she
    may help you
To bring this quarrel to rest.

[*Enter* JOCASTA.]

JOCASTA. My lords, it is pitiful to hear your
    senseless voices
Shouting and wrangling. Have you no
    shame? Our country
Is sick, and you go bustling about your
    private   665
Quarrels. My king, you must go inside,
    and you,
Creon, go to the palace. At this time
We have no troubles except the plague;
    all
Others are pretense.

CREON.   My sister, your sov-
    ereign, Oedipus,
Condemns me cruelly in his efforts to be
    just.   670
He will banish me, or murder me; in both
    he does wrong.

OEDIPUS. No, I have found a traitor, my
    queen, who plots
    Against my life.

CREON.   Never let me breathe
In freedom again, let me die under your
    curse,   674
If I am guilty of those crimes!

JOCASTA.   Oh, Oedipus,
    Believe him. Believe him for the sake of
    those words

That heaven witnessed; you have a duty
　　to that oath,
And to me, and to your people.

CHORUS. Obey her, my lord, I beg you; do
　　not be harsh,
Be wise.

OEDIPUS. Must I be ruled by you?　680

CHORUS. Creon was always wise and faith-
　　ful in the past; his oath was great
And you must respect it.

OEDIPUS. You know what you are asking?

CHORUS. 　　　　　　　　　　　I know.

OEDIPUS. Tell me, what do you advise?　684

CHORUS. He is your friend — that is a truth
As simple as the light of day;
But only confused and uncertain rumors
　　call him traitor;
No cause to rob him of his honor.

OEDIPUS. But listen, in asking this, you ask
For my banishment, or for my death.　690

CHORUS. No! By the sun who is prince of
　　the sky!
If that was ever my intention,
I pray for death, without friends on earth
Without love in heaven,
Death in pain and misery　　　695
Now, now, when the decaying earth eats
　　our lives
Away, will you add your quarrels to all
That we already suffer?

OEDIPUS. Let him go then; I shall die, I do
　　not care;
I shall be driven into banishment and dis-
　　grace.　　　　700
I do this for love and pity of you. For
　　him, I feel none;
Wherever he goes, he cannot escape my
　　hatred.

CREON. For you submission is a torment —
　　you do not hide it.
And when you force your way against
　　the world

You crush us all beneath you. Such
　　natures　　　705
Find their own company most terrible to
　　bear.
It is their punishment.

OEDIPUS. Leave my sight, then! Leave me to
　　myself!

CREON. I shall leave you. In all the time you
　　knew me,
You never understood me. . . . They see
　　my innocence.　　710

[Exit CREON.]

CHORUS. My queen, take our king to the
　　palace now.

JOCASTA. I must know what has happened.

CHORUS. Doubt and suspicion. Oedipus
　　spoke without thinking;
He was unjust, and Creon cannot bear in-
　　justice.

JOCASTA. Both were to blame?

CHORUS. 　　　　　　　　　Yes.

JOCASTA. 　　　　　　　　　　What was
　　said?　　　　715

CHORUS. The country is weary with sickness
　　already;
I am content, content to go no further
And let the evil rest.

OEDIPUS. You see what you have done, you
　　good,　　　719
Good adviser? My temper was a spear
And you have turned the edge and
　　blunted it.

CHORUS. Your majesty, I have repeated
　　many times —
But I tell you again;
I would have been robbed of all my
　　senses,
Emptied of all my reason,　　　725
If I caused your death.
You came like the wind we pray for in

danger,

When the storm was conquering us with
sorrows,

And carried our country into safety. Again

You may bring a spirit to guide us.   730

JOCASTA. But I still do not know why you
were quarreling, my king,

And I must know, for they talked of
your death.

OEDIPUS.   Jocasta,

You may command me when even my
people may not,

And I let Creon go. But he had conspired

Against me. . . .

JOCASTA.   Treason! Is this true?

Can you prove it?   735

OEDIPUS. He says I am Laius' murderer.

JOCASTA.   How

Can he know? Has he always known, or
has someone told him?

OEDIPUS. He sent that priest Teiresias, the
wicked Teiresias.

Creon's lips do not commit themselves to
words!

JOCASTA. Then set all this talk aside and
listen. I   740

Will teach you that no priest, no holy
magic

Can know your future or your destiny.
And my proof

Is as short as the stroke of a knife. Once,
an oracle

Came to Laius — I will not say it was
from

Apollo — but from Apollo's priests. It
told him   745

He was destined to be murdered by the
son that I

Would bear to him. But Laius, so they
say,

Was murdered by robbers from another
country at a place

Where three roads meet. A son was born

To us, but lived no more than three days.
Yes,   750

Laius pinned his ankles together and sent
him

Away to die on a distant, lonely mountain.

Once he was there, no power could make
him a murderer,

Nor make Laius die at the hands of his
son — .

And he feared that above anything in the
world.   755

You see how you may rely upon priests
and their talk

Of the future. Never notice them! When
god wishes

The truth discovered, he will easily work
his will.

OEDIPUS. As I listened, my queen, my
thoughts went reaching out

And touched on memories that make me
shudder . . .   760

JOCASTA. What memories? You stare as if
you were trapped.

OEDIPUS. You said — I heard you say — that
Laius' blood

Was spilt at a place where three roads
meet.

JOCASTA. We were all told that, and no one
has denied it.

OEDIPUS. And where is the place where this
happened?

JOCASTA.   The country   765

Is called Phocis; the road splits, to Delphi
And to Daulia.

OEDIPUS.   When did all this happen?

JOCASTA. The city was given the news a
little before
You became king of Thebes.

OEDIPUS.   God,   769

What do you hold prepared for me?

JOCASTA.   Oedipus!

What made you frown when I talked of

your becoming king?

OEDIPUS. Do not ask me yet. . . . Laius —
what was he like?

His appearance, his age, describe them to
me.

JOCASTA. He was tall, his hair beginning to
be flecked with a down

Of white; he was built like you. . . .

OEDIPUS.   Stop!
You torture me!   775

I have hurled myself blindly against un-
thinking

Fury and destruction!

JOCASTA.   How? I cannot bear
To watch you, my lord.

OEDIPUS.   So little hope is
frightening.

Listen, Teiresias the priest was not blind!

But one more answer, one more, will be
better proof.   780

JOCASTA. I dare not answer; but if my answers help you,

Ask.

OEDIPUS. When he left Thebes, was he alone,

Or did he have a company of men at arms

So that all could recognize he was a king?

JOCASTA. No, five were all the travelers, and
one   785

Was a herald. A single chariot carried
Laius. . . .

OEDIPUS. Yes! Now I see the truth. . . .

Who told you this?

JOCASTA. A servant, the only man who returned alive.

OEDIPUS. Is he still in the palace with us?

JOCASTA.   No, after

He escaped, and found that you were
king, and Laius   790

Dead, he implored me by my duty to a
suppliant[1]

To send him away. To the country, he
said, herding

<hr/>

[1] suppliant: supplicant.

Sheep on the hillsides, where he could
never see

The city he had left. . . . And I let him
go; he was

A good servant, deserving more than
this   795

Small favor.

OEDIPUS.   He must be found at once;
Can this be done?

JOCASTA. Yes, but why do you want him?

OEDIPUS. My queen, as I look into myself I
begin to fear;   799

I had no right to say those things, and so

I must see this man.

JOCASTA.   He will come. But I

Expect to be told your sorrows, my king,
when they weigh

So heavily.

OEDIPUS.   And I will not refuse you,
Jocasta.

I have come to face such thoughts, and
who should hear

Of them before you? I walk among   805
Great menaces.

My father is king of Corinth — Polybus;
my mother —

Merope from Doris. In Corinth I was
called

Their prince, their greatest noble, until

This happened to me — it was strange,
yet not   810

So strange as to deserve my thoughts so
much.

A man, stuffed with wine at a feast, called
out

To me as he drank. He said I was a son
only

In the imagination of my father. Anger

And pain would not let me rest that day;
the next   815

I went to my parents and questioned
them. They answered

The drunkard harshly for his insulting
story,

And for their sakes I was glad he lied.

Yet I always
Felt the wound, and the story spread in
  whispers.
At last I went to Delphi — my parents
  did not know —   820
But Apollo thought me unworthy of an
  answer
To that question. Instead he foretold
  many trials,
Many dangers, many sorrows. I was to be
My mother's husband, I was to murder
  my own
Father, my children would carry the guilt
  and none   825
Would dare look on them. When I heard
  this
I ran from my home and afterwards
  knew the land
Only by the stars that stood above it.
Never must I see the shame of that evil
  prophecy   829
Acted out by me in Corinth. I traveled
Until I came to this place where you say
  your king
Was killed. . . . My wife, this is the truth.
  . . . I will tell you. . . .
My journey brought me to the meeting
  of three roads;
And there a herald, and an old man who
  rode
A chariot drawn by mares, came towards
  me. . . .   835
Jocasta, the rider was like the man you
  described!
He and the herald, who went in front,
  tried
To force me out of their path. In a rage
  I struck
The one who touched me, the servant at
  the wheel.
The old man watched me, and waited till
  I was passing;   840
Then from the chariot he aimed at the
  crown of my head
With the twin prongs of his goad.[1] It was
  a costly

[1] **goad**: pointed rod used to urge on an animal.

Action! Slashing with my stick I cut at
  him
And my blow tumbled him backwards
  out of the chariot —
Then I killed them all! If this man I met
  may be said   845
To resemble Laius, to be, perhaps, Laius,
I stand condemned to more sorrow than
  any man,
More cursed by an evil power than any
  man.
No one in Thebes, no stranger, may
  shelter me
Or speak to me; they must hunt me from
  their doors.   850
And I, it was I, who cursed myself, cursed
  myself!
And the dead king's pillow is fouled by
  the touch
Of my murdering hands. Is the evil in
  my soul?
Is my whole nature tainted? Must I go
  into exile,
Never see my people again, nor turn
  home   855
And set foot in Corinth? — for if I do,
  I must wed
My mother, and kill my father — Poly-
  bus, who gave me
Life and youth. Can you see this hap-
  pen, and then
Deny that a cruel power has come to
  torture me?
No! You heavens, you pure light and
  holiness!   860
Let me die before that day, hide me
  before
I feel that black corruption in my soul!

CHORUS. My king, this is a frightening story.
  But hope,
Until you hear from the man who saw
  what happened.

OEDIPUS. Yes, that is all the hope I have.
  Oedipus   865
Waits for one man, and he is a shepherd.

JOCASTA. What makes you so eager for him
    to come?

OEDIPUS. I reason like this. We may find
    that his story
Matches yours. Then I shall be as free
As if this had never happened.

JOCASTA.   Was there
    anything in what   870
I said that could have such power?

OEDIPUS.   You said
He told you robbers murdered Laius. If
    he still
Says "robbers" and not "a robber," I am
    innocent.
One man cannot be taken for many.
But if he says a murderer, alone,   875
The guilt comes to rest on me.

JOCASTA.   But we all
Heard him say "robbers"; that is certain.
    He cannot
Unsay it. I am not alone, for the whole
    city heard.
But even if he swerves a little from his old
    account,   879
That will not prove you Laius' murderer,
Not in truth, not in justice. For Apollo
    said
He was to be killed by a son that was
    born to me. . . .
And yet my son, poor child, could not
    have killed him,
For he died first . . . but that shows the
    deceit
Of prophecies. They beckon at you, but
    I   885
Would fix my eyes ahead, and never look
    at them!

OEDIPUS. You are right. Nevertheless send
    someone
To bring me that servant; do not forget.

JOCASTA.   Yes,
I will send now. Let us go to the palace;
I would do nothing that could harm or
    anger you.   890

[*Exeunt all but the* CHORUS.]

CHORUS. All actions must beware of the
    powers beyond us, and each word
Must speak our fear of heaven. I pray
That I may live every hour in obedience.
The laws that hold us in subjection
Have always stood beyond our reach,
    conceived   895
In the high air of heaven. Olympus[1]
Was their sire, and no woman on earth
Gave them life. They are laws
That will never be lured to sleep in the
    arms of oblivion,
And in their strength heaven is great and
    cannot grow old.   900
Yet man desires to be more than man, to
    rule
His world for himself.
This desire, blown to immensity
On the rich empty food of its ambition,
Out of place, out of time,   905
Clambers to the crown of the rock, and
    stands there,
Tottering; then comes the steepling[2]
    plunge down to earth,
To the earth where we are caged and
    mastered.
But this desire may work for good
When it fights to save a country, and I
    pray   910
That heaven will not weaken it then.
For then it comes like a god to be our
    warrior
And we shall never turn it back.

Justice holds the balance of all things,
And we must fear her.   915
Do not despise the frontiers in which we
    must live,
Do not cross them, do not talk of them,
But bow before the places where the gods
    are throned.

[1] **Olympus**: mountain abode of the gods in Greek
mythology.
[2] **steepling**: sheer down.

Time will come with cruel vengeance on
    the man
Who disobeys; that is the punishment 920
For those who are proud and are more
    than men —
They are humbled.
If a man grows rich in defiance of this
    law,
If his actions trespass on a world that he
    should fear,
If he reaches after mysteries that no man
    should know,   925
No prayer can plead for him when the
    sword of heaven is raised.
If he were to glory in success
All worship would fall dumb.

Delphi is the heart of the world and holds
    its secrets;
The temple of Zeus, and Olympia, com-
    mand our prayers;   930
But we shall never believe again
Until the truth of this murder is known.
Let us be sure of our beliefs, give us proof.
Zeus, you may do your will; do not forget
    that you are immortal,   934
Your empire cannot die; hear our prayers.
For the oracle given to Laius in the years
    of the long past
Is dying and forgotten, wiped from the
    memory,
Apollo's glory turns to shadows,
And all divinity to ruin.

[*Enter* JOCASTA.]

JOCASTA. My lords, I have been summoned
    by my thoughts   940
To the temples of the gods, and I have
    brought
These garlands and this incense for an
    offering.
Oedipus is like a lonely bird among
The terrors that flock about his mind.
    He forgets
His wisdom, and no longer thinks the past

will guide him   945
When he tries to foresee the future. In-
    stead, he is
The slave of any word that talks of fear.
I try to reach him, to make him see that
    there is hope,
But it is useless; I have failed. And so I
    turn   949
To you, Apollo, nearest to us in Thebes,
A suppliant with prayers and gifts. Re-
    solve this doubt
By sending the truth. He is the guide and
    master
Of our ship. What shall we do when even
    he
Is struck into bewilderment?

[*Enter* MESSENGER.]

MESSENGER. I do not know this country.
    Will you show me the palace   955
Of King Oedipus? I must find King
    Oedipus. . . .
Do you know where he is?

CHORUS.   This is his pal-
    ace, sir.
He is inside, and you see his queen before
    you.

MESSENGER. Heaven give her and all she
    loves riches
And happiness if she is the queen of such
    a king.   960

JOCASTA. I return your greeting. You have
    spoken well and deserve
Well wishing. But what do you want
    with Oedipus?
Or do you bring a message for us?

MESSENGER.   A message
Of good, for your palace and your hus-
    band, my queen.

JOCASTA. What is it? Who sent you here?

MESSENGER.   I come from Corinth.   965
My story may be quickly told. You will
    be glad, of course,

For the news is glad, and yet . . . yet you
  may grieve.

JOCASTA. Well, what is this story with a
  double meaning?

MESSENGER. The people of Corinth — it was
  already announced
There — will make Oedipus their king.

JOCASTA.   But why?   970
  Your king is Polybus. He is wise,
  revered. . . .

MESSENGER. But no longer our king. Death
  hugs him to the earth.

JOCASTA. Is this true? Polybus is dead?

MESSENGER. By my hopes of living out my
  years, it is true.

JOCASTA. Servant, go, tell this to your
  master. Run!   975

  [*Exit* SERVANT.]

Where are the prophecies of heaven now?
  Always
Oedipus dreaded to kill this man, and hid
From him. But look, Polybus has been
  murdered
By the careless touch of time, and not by
  Oedipus.

  [*Enter* OEDIPUS.]

OEDIPUS. Dear Jocasta, dear wife, why have
  you called me   980
Here from the palace?

JOCASTA.   This man brings a
  message;
Listen, and then ask yourself what comes
Of the oracles from heaven that used to
  frighten us.

OEDIPUS. Who is this man? What has he to
  say to me?

JOCASTA. He comes from Corinth, and his
  message is the death   985

Of Polybus. You will never see Polybus
  again!

OEDIPUS. You said that, stranger? Let me
  hear you say that plainly.

MESSENGER. Since you force me to give that
  part of my message first,
I repeat, he walks among the dead.

OEDIPUS.   A plot?
Or did sickness conspire to kill him?

MESSENGER.   A small
  Touch on the balance sends old lives to
  sleep.   991

OEDIPUS. So, my poor father, sickness murdered you.

MESSENGER. And many years had measured
  out his life.

OEDIPUS. Oh look, look, who would listen
  to Apollo
Talking in his shrine at Delphi, or notice
  birds   995
That clamor to the air? They were the
  signs
That told me — and I believed — that I
  would kill
My father. But now he has the grave to
  protect him,
While I stand here, and I never touched a
  sword. . . .   999
Unless he died of longing to see me —
Then perhaps he died because of me. No!
Polybus lies in darkness, and all those
  prophecies
Lie with him, chained and powerless.

JOCASTA. I told you long ago how it would
  happen. . . .   1004

OEDIPUS. Yes, but I was led astray by fears.

JOCASTA. Then think no more of them;
  forget them all.

OEDIPUS. Not all. The marriage with my
  mother — I think of it.

JOCASTA. But is there anything a man need
  fear, if he knows

That chance is supreme throughout the world, and he cannot

See what is to come? Give way to the power   1010

Of events and live as they allow! It is best.

Do not fear this marriage with your mother. Many

Men have dreams, and in those dreams they wed

Their mothers. Life is easiest, if you do not try

To oppose these things that seem to threaten us.   1015

OEDIPUS. You are right, and I would agree with all

You say, if my mother were not alive. And though

You are right, I must fear. She is alive.

JOCASTA. Think of your father, and his grave.   1019

There is a light to guide you.

OEDIPUS.   It does guide me!

I know he. . . . But she is alive and I am afraid.

MESSENGER. You are afraid of a woman, my lord?

OEDIPUS. Yes,

Merope — Polybus was her husband.

MESSENGER. How can you be afraid of her?

OEDIPUS.   A prophecy warned me

To beware of sorrow. . . .

MESSENGER.   Can you speak of it, or are you   1025

Forbidden to talk of these things to others?

OEDIPUS. No,

I am not forbidden. The Oracle at Delphi

Has told me my destiny — to be my mother's husband

And my father's murderer. And so I left Corinth, many years ago and many   1030

Miles behind me. The world has rewarded me richly,

And yet all those riches are less than the sight

Of a parent's face.

MESSENGER.   And you went into exile because

You feared this marriage?

OEDIPUS.   And to save myself from becoming   1034

My father's murderer.

MESSENGER.   Then, my king,

I ought to have freed you from that fear since I

Wished to be thought your friend.

OEDIPUS.   Your reward

Will be measured by my gratitude.

MESSENGER.   I had hoped for reward

When you returned as king of your palace in Corinth.

OEDIPUS. I must never go where my parents are.

MESSENGER.   My son 1040

You do not know what you say; I see you do not.

OEDIPUS. How, sir? Tell me quickly.

MESSENGER.   . . . If you live in exile

Because of Polybus and Merope.

OEDIPUS.   Yes, and I live

In fear that Apollo will prove he spoke the truth.

MESSENGER. And it is from your parents that the guilt is to come?   1045

OEDIPUS. Yes, stranger, the fear never leaves my side.

MESSENGER. You have no cause to be afraid — do you know that?

OEDIPUS. No cause? But they were my parents — that is the cause!

MESSENGER. No cause, because they were

not your parents, Oedipus.

OEDIPUS. What do you mean? Polybus was
    not my father? 1050

MESSENGER. As much as I, and yet no more
    than I am.

OEDIPUS. How could my father be no more
    than nothing?

MESSENGER. But Polybus did not give you
    life, nor did I.

OEDIPUS. Then why did he call me son?

MESSENGER.   Listen, you were
    A gift that he took from my hands.

OEDIPUS.   A child 1055
    Given him by a stranger? But he loved me
    Dearly.

MESSENGER. He had no children, and so
    consented.

OEDIPUS. So you gave me to. . . . Had you
    bought me for your slave?
    Where did you find me?

MESSENGER.   You were lying
    beneath the trees
    In a glade upon Cithaeron.

OEDIPUS.   What were you
    doing on Cithaeron? 1060

MESSENGER. My flocks were grazing in the
    mountains;
    I was guarding them.

OEDIPUS.   Guarding your flocks
    — you were
    A shepherd, a servant!

MESSENGER.   It was in that ser-
    vice that I saved
    Your life, my child.

OEDIPUS.   Why? Was I hurt or
    sick
    When you took me home?

MESSENGER.   Your ankles will
    be my witness 1065
    That you would not have lived.

OEDIPUS.   Why do you

talk
    Of that? The pain is forgotten!

MESSENGER.   Your feet
    were pierced
    And clamped together. I set you free

OEDIPUS.   The child
    In the cradle had a scar — I still carry
    The shame of it.

MESSENGER.   You were named in re-
    membrance 1070
    Of that scar.[1]

OEDIPUS.   In heaven's name, who did
    this?
    My mother? My father?

MESSENGER.   I do not know.
    The man
    Who gave you to me knows more of the
    truth.

OEDIPUS. But you said you found me! Then
    it was not true. . . . 1074
    You had me from someone else?

MESSENGER.   Yes, another
    Shepherd gave me the child.

OEDIPUS.   Who? Can you
    Describe him?

MESSENGER. They said he was a servant of
    Laius.

OEDIPUS. Laius, who was once king of
    Thebes?

MESSENGER.   Yes,
    This man was one of his shepherds.

OEDIPUS.   Is he still
    Alive; could I see him?

MESSENGER. Your people here 1080
    Will know that best.

OEDIPUS.   Do any of you,
    My friends, know the shepherd he means?
    Has he
    Been seen in the fields, or in the palace?
    Tell me,

[1] **named . . . scar:** The Greek word for *Oedipus* means "swollen-footed."

Now! It is time these things were known!

CHORUS.   I think
He must be the man you were searching
    for, the one   1085
Who left the palace after Laius was killed.
But Jocasta will know as well as I.

OEDIPUS. My wife, you remember the man
    we sent for a little
Time ago? Is he the one this person
    means?

JOCASTA. Perhaps. . . . But why should he.
    . . . Think nothing of this!   1090
Do not idle with memories and stories. . . .

OEDIPUS. No, I have been given these signs,
    and I must
Follow them, until I know who gave me
    birth.

JOCASTA. No! Give up this search! I am
    tortured and sick
Enough. By the love of heaven, if you
    value life   1095

OEDIPUS. Courage! You are still a queen,
    though I discover
That I am three times three generations a
    slave.

JOCASTA. No, listen to me, I implore you!
    You must stop!

OEDIPUS. I cannot listen when you tell me to
    ignore the truth.

JOCASTA. But I know the truth, and I only
    ask you to save   1100
Yourself.

OEDIPUS.   I have always hated that way to
    safety!

JOCASTA. But evil lies in wait for you. . . .
    Oh, do not let him
Find the truth!

OEDIPUS.   Bring this shepherd to me,
And let her gloat over the riches of her
    ancestry.

JOCASTA. My poor child! Those are the
    only words   1105

I shall ever have for you. . . . I can speak
    no others!

[*Exit* JOCASTA.]

CHORUS. What is the torment that drives
    your queen so wildly
Into the palace, Oedipus? Her silence
    threatens
A storm. I fear some wrong. . . .

OEDIPUS.   Let the storm
Come if it will. I must know my birth,
I must know it, however humble. Perhaps
    she,   1111
For she is a queen, and proud, is ashamed
That I was born so meanly. But I consider
Myself a child of Fortune, and while she
    brings me
Gifts, I shall not lack honor. For she has
    given me   1115
Life itself; and my cousins, the months,
    have marked me
Small and great as they marched by. Such
Is my ancestry, and I shall be none
    other —
And I will know my birth!

CHORUS.   There are signs
Of what is to come, and we may read
    them,   1120
Casting our thoughts into the future,
And drawing in new knowledge.
For we have seen how the world goes
And we have seen the laws it obeys.
Cithaeron, mountain of Oedipus, the
    moon   1125
Will not rise in tomorrow's evening sky
Before our king calls you his true father,
His only nurse and mother — and then
You will have your greatest glory.
You will be honored with dances and
    choirs   1130
For your gentle kindness to our king —
    Hail
To the god Apollo! May he be content
With all our words.

[handwritten note: Jocasta wants him to save himself]

Pan walks among the mountains, and one
Of the immortal nymphs could have lain
    with him;   1135
Who was the goddess who became your
    mother, Oedipus?
Or was she the wife of Apollo, for he
    loves
The wild meadows and the long grass.
Or was it the prince of Cyllene, Hermes?
Or, Bacchus,[1] whose palace is the moun-
    tain top?   1140
Did he take you as a gift from the nymphs
    of Helicon,
With whom he plays through all his
    immortal years?

OEDIPUS. I never knew the shepherd or en-
    countered him,
My people, but the man I see there must
    be
The one we have been seeking. His age
    answers   1145
My riddle for me; it holds as many years
As our messenger's. And now I see that
    those
Who lead him are my servants. But you
    have known him
Before, you can tell me whether I am
    right.

CHORUS. Yes, we recognize him — the most
    faithful   1150
Of Laius' shepherds.

OEDIPUS.   And you, Corinthian,
You must tell me first. Is this the man
    you mean?

MESSENGER. It is; you see him there.

[*Enter* SHEPHERD.]

OEDIPUS.   You, sir,
    come to me,
Look me in the eyes, and answer all my
    questions!

[1] **Pan, Hermes, Bacchus:** Greek gods; legends of
unions between gods and mortal women were common in Greek mythology.

Did you once serve Laius?

SHEPHERD.   Yes, and I was
    born   1155
In his palace; I was not brought from an-
    other country . . . .

OEDIPUS. Your life? How were you em-
    ployed?

SHEPHERD.   Most
Of my life I watched his flocks.

OEDIPUS.   And where
Was their pasture? They had a favorite
    meadow?

SHEPHERD. Sometimes Cithaeron, sometimes
    the places near.   1160

OEDIPUS. Do you recognize this man? Did
    you see him on Cithaeron?

SHEPHERD. Why should anyone go there?
    Whom do you mean?

OEDIPUS. Here! Standing beside me. Have
    you ever met him?

SHEPHERD. I do not think so. . . . My mem-
    ory is not quick.

MESSENGER. We should not wonder at this,
    your majesty;   1165
But I shall remind him of all he has for-
    gotten.
I know that he remembers when for three
Whole years I used to meet him near
    Cithaeron,
Six months, from each spring to the rising
    of the Bear;
I had a single flock and he had two.   1170
Then, in the winters, I would take my
    sheep to their pens
While he went to the fields of Laius. . . .
Did this happen?
Have I told it as it happened, or have I
    not?

SHEPHERD. The time is long since then . . .
    yes, it is the truth.

MESSENGER. Good; now, tell me; you know
    the child you gave me . . . ?   1175

SHEPHERD. What is happening? What do these questions mean?

MESSENGER. Here is the child, my friend, who was so little then.

SHEPHERD. Damnation seize you! Can you not keep your secret?

OEDIPUS. Wait, Shepherd? Do not find fault; as I listened   1179
I found more fault in you than in him.

SHEPHERD.   What
Have I done wrong, most mighty king?

OEDIPUS.   You will not
Admit the truth about that child.

SHEPHERD.   He wastes
His time. He talks, but it is all lies.

OEDIPUS. When it would please me, you will not speak; but you will   1184
When I make you cry for mercy. . . .

SHEPHERD.   No, my king,
I am an old man — do not hurt me!

OEDIPUS (to guards). Take his arms and tie them quickly!

SHEPHERD.   But why,
Poor child? What more do you want to know?

OEDIPUS.   You gave
The boy to this Corinthian?

SHEPHERD.   Yes, I did. . . .
And I should have prayed for death that day.   1190

OEDIPUS. Your prayer will be answered now if you lie to me!

SHEPHERD. But you will surely kill me if I tell the truth.

OEDIPUS. He will drive my patience to exhaustion!

SHEPHERD.   No!
I told you now, I did give him the child.

OEDIPUS. Where did it come from? Your home? Another's?   1195

SHEPHERD. It was not mine, it was given to me.

OEDIPUS.   By someone
In the city? . . . I want to know the house!

SHEPHERD.   By all that is holy,
No more, your majesty, no more questions!

OEDIPUS.   You die
If I have to ask again!

SHEPHERD.   The child was born
In the palace of King Laius.

OEDIPUS.   By one of his slaves?   1200
Or was it a son of his own blood?

SHEPHERD.   My king,
How shall I tell a story of such horror?

OEDIPUS. And how shall I hear it? And yet I must, must hear.

SHEPHERD. The child was called his son. But your queen in the palace   1204
May tell you the truth of that most surely.

OEDIPUS. Jocasta gave you the child?

SHEPHERD.   Yes, my king.

OEDIPUS. Why? What were you to do?

SHEPHERD.   I was to destroy him.

OEDIPUS. The poor mother asked that?

SHEPHERD.   She was afraid.
A terrible prophecy. . . .

OEDIPUS.   What?

SHEPHERD.   There was
a story
That he would kill his parents.

OEDIPUS.   Why did you give   1210
The child away to this stranger?

SHEPHERD.   I pitied it,
My lord, and I thought he would take it
    to the far land
Where he lived. But he saved its life only
    for
Great sorrows. For if you are the man
    he says,
You must know your birth was watched
    by evil powers.   1215

OEDIPUS. All that was foretold will be made
    true! Light,
Now turn black and die; I must not look
    on you!
See, this is what I am; son of parents
I should not have known, I lived with
    those
I should not have touched, and murdered
    those   1220
A man must not kill!

[*Exit* OEDIPUS.]

CHORUS.   Every man who has
    ever lived
Is numbered with the dead; they fought
    with the world
For happiness, yet all they won
Was a shadow that slipped away to die.
And you, Oedipus, are all those men. I
    think of the power   1225
Which carried you to such victories and
    such misery
And I know there is no joy or triumph in
    the world.

Oedipus aimed beyond the reach of man
And fixed with his arrowing mind
Perfection and rich happiness.   1230
The Sphinx's talons were sharp with evil,
    she spoke in the mysteries
Of eternal riddles, and he came to destroy
    her,
To overcome death, to be a citadel

Of strength in our country.
He was called our king, and was   1235
The greatest noble in great Thebes.
And now his story ends in agony.
Death and madness hunt him,
Destruction and sorrow haunt him.
Now his life turns and brings the reward
    of his greatness   1240
Glorious Oedipus, son, and then father,
In the same chamber, in the same silent
    room,
Son and father in the same destruction;
Your marriage was the harvesting of
    wrong.
How could it hold you where your
    father lay,   1245
And bear you in such silence for such an
    end?

Child of Laius, I wish, I wish I had never
    known you,
For now there is only mourning, sorrow
    flowing
From our lips.   1249
And yet we must not forget the truth;
If we were given hope and life, it was
    your work.

[*Enter* SERVANT.]

SERVANT. My lords of Thebes, on whom rest
    all the honors
Of our country, when you hear what has
    happened,
When you witness it, how will you bear
    your grief   1254
In silence? Weep, if you have ever loved
The royal house of Thebes. For I do not
    think
The great streams of the Phasis or the
    Ister[1]
Could ever wash these walls to purity.
    But all

---

[1] **Phasis . . . Ister:** Ancient names of the Rion
River, in the U.S.S.R., and of the Danube River, in
central Europe, both of which flow into the Black
Sea.

The crimes they hide must glare out to
the light,
Crimes deliberate and considered. The
sorrows   1260
We choose ourselves bring the fiercest
pain!

CHORUS. We have seen great wrongs already, and they were frightening.
Do you bring new disasters?

SERVANT.   I bring a message
That I may tell, and you may hear, in a
few
Swift words. Jocasta is dead.   1265

CHORUS. Then she died in grief. What
caused her death?

SERVANT. It was her own will. Of that terrible act
The worst must remain untold, for I did
not watch it.
Yet you will hear what happened to our
poor queen
As far as memory guides me. When she
went   1270
Into the domed hall of the palace, whirled
On the torrent of her grief, she ran
straight
To her marriage chamber, both hands
clutched at her hair,
Tearing like claws. Inside, she crashed
shut the door
And shrieked the name Laius, Laius who
died   1275
So long ago. She talked to herself of the
son
She once bore, and of Laius murdered by
that son;
Of the mother who was left a widow, and
became
Wife and mother again in shame and
sorrow.
She wept for her marriage, in which her
husband gave   1280
To her a husband, and her children, children.

How her death followed I cannot tell
you. . . .
We heard a shout, and now Oedipus
blazed
And thundered through the door. I could
not see
How her sorrow ended, because he was
there,   1285
Circling in great mad strides, and we
watched
Him. He went round begging to each
Of us; he asked for a sword, he asked
to go
To his wife who was more than a wife,
to his mother in whom
His birth and his children's birth, like two
harvests   1290
From the same field, had been sown and
gathered. His grief
Was a raging madness, and some power
must have guided him —
It was none of us who were standing
there. He gave
A cry full of fear and anguish, then, as if
A ghost was leading him, he leaped
against the double   1295
Doors of Jocasta's room. The hinges
tilted
Full out of their sockets, and shattered
inside
The chamber — and there we saw his
wife, hanging
By her throat in the grip of a tall rope.
And when
He saw her, he shrieked like a wounded
beast, wrenched loose   1300
The knot that held her, and laid her on
the ground.
What followed was terrible to watch.
He ripped
The gold-worked brooches from her
robes — she wore them
As jewels — and raised them above his
head. Then he plunged them
Deep into the sockets of his eyes, shout-
ing   1305

Oedipus, masked and robed as in ancient Greek drama. From the Tyrone Guthrie production in Stratford, Ontario, in Canada.

That he would never look upon the wrongs
He had committed and had suffered. Now
In his blackness he must see such shapes as he deserved
And never look on those he loved. Repeating
This like a chant, he lifted his hands and stabbed   1310
His eyes, again and again. We saw his eyeballs
Fill with tears of blood that dyed his cheeks,
And a red stream pouring from his veins, dark
As the blood of life, thick as storming hail.

Yes, this is a storm that has broken, a storm   1315
That holds the queen and the king in its embrace.
They were rich and fortunate, and they were so
As we should wish to be. Now, in one day,
See how we must mourn them. The blind rush
To death, the shame, all the evils that we   1320
Have names for — they have escaped none!

CHORUS. Has our poor king found ease for his sorrow yet?

380

SERVANT. He shouts at us to open the doors and show

To all Thebes the murderer of his father

And his mother's. . . . his words are blasphemous, 1325

I dare not speak them. . . . He will be driven from Thebes,

Will not stay beneath this curse that he called upon

Himself. Yet he needs help and a guide. No one

Could bear that agony. . . . But he comes himself to show you;

The great doors of the palace open, and what you will see 1330

Will turn you away in horror — yet will ask for pity.

[*Enter* OEDIPUS.]

CHORUS. This suffering turns a face of terror to the world.

There is no story told, no knowledge born

That tells of greater sorrow.

Madness came striding upon you, Oedipus, 1335

The black, annihilating power that broods

And waits in the hand of time. . . .

I cannot look!

We have much to ask and learn and see.

But you blind us with an icy sword of terror. 1340

OEDIPUS. Where will you send this wreckage and despair of man?

Where will my voice be heard, like the wind drifting emptily

On the air. Oh you powers, why do you drive me on?

CHORUS. They drive you to the place of horror,

That only the blind may see, 1345

And only the dead hear of.

OEDIPUS. Here in my cloud of darkness there is no escape,

A cloud, thick in my soul, and there it dumbly clings;

That cloud is my own spirit

That now wins its fiercest battle and turns back 1350

To trample me. . . . The memory of evil can tear

Like goads of molten fire, and go deep,

Infinity could not be so deep.

CHORUS. More than mortal in your acts of evil.

More than mortal in your suffering, Oedipus. 1355

OEDIPUS. You are my last friend, my only help; you have

Waited for me, and will care for the eyeless body

Of Oedipus. I know you are there. . . . I know. . . .

Through this darkness I can hear your voice.

CHORUS. Oedipus, all that you do 1360

Makes us draw back in fear. How could you take

Such vivid vengeance on your eyes? What power lashed you on?

OEDIPUS. Apollo, my lords, Apollo sent this evil on me.

I was the murderer; I struck the blow. Why should I

Keep my sight? If I had eyes, what could delight them? 1365

CHORUS. It is so; it is as you say.

OEDIPUS. No, I can look on nothing. . . .

And I can love nothing — for love has lost

Its sweetness, I can hear no voice — for words

Are sour with hate. . . . Take stones and beat me 1370

From your country. I am the living curse, the source

Of sickness and death!

wants punishment

CHORUS. Your own mind, reaching after the secrets
Of the gods, condemned you to your fate.   1374
If only you had never come to Thebes. . . .

OEDIPUS. But when my feet were ground by iron teeth
That bolted me in the meadow grass,
A man set me free and ransomed me from death.
May hell curse him for that murderous kindness!
I should have died then   1380
And never drawn this sorrow on those I love
And on myself. . . .

CHORUS. Our prayers echo yours.

OEDIPUS. Nor killed my father,
Nor led my mother to the room where she gave me life.   1385
But now the gods desert me, for I am
Born of impurity, and my blood
Mingles with those who gave me birth.
If evil can grow with time to be a giant
That masters and usurps our world,   1390
That evil lords its way through Oedipus.

CHORUS. How can we say that you have acted wisely?
Is death not better than a life in blindness?

OEDIPUS. Do not teach me that this punishment is wrong —
I will have no advisers to tell me it is wrong!   1395
Why choke my breath and go among the dead
If I keep my eyes? For there I know I could not
Look upon my father or my poor mother. . . .
My crimes have been too great for such a death.
Or should I love my sight because it let me   1400
See my children? No, for then I would
Remember who their father was. My eyes
Would never let me love them, nor my city,
Nor my towers, nor the sacred images
Of gods. I was the noblest lord in Thebes,
But I have stripped myself of Thebes, and become   1406
The owner of all miseries. For I commanded
My people to drive out the unclean thing, the man
Heaven had shown to be impure in the house
Of Laius.   1410
I found such corruption in me — could I see
My people and not turn blind for shame? . . .
My ears are a spring, and send a river
Of sound through me; if I could have dammed that river
I would have made my poor body into a bolted prison   1415
In which there would be neither light nor sound.
Peace can only come if we shut the mind
Away from the sorrow in the world outside.
Cithaeron, why did you let me live? Why
Did you not kill me as I lay there? I would   1420
Have been forgotten, and never revealed the secret
Of my birth. Polybus, Corinth, the palace
They told me was my father's, you watched over
My youth, but beneath that youth's nobility lay
Corruption — you see it in my acts, in my blood!   1425
There are three roads, a hidden valley, trees,

And a narrow place where the roads meet
— they
Drink my blood, the blood I draw from
my father —
Do they remember me, do they remember what I did?
Do they know what next I did? . . . The
room, the marriage   1430
Room — it was there I was given life,
and now
It is there I give the same life to my
children.
The blood of brothers, fathers, sons, the
race
Of daughters, wives, mothers, all the
blackest
Shame a man may commit. . . . But I
must not name   1435
Such ugly crimes. Oh, you heavens, take
me
From the world and hide me, drown me
in oceans
Where I can be seen no more! Come, do
not fear
To touch a single unhappy man. Yes, a
man,
No more. Be brave, for my sufferings
can fall to no one   1440
But myself to bear!

CHORUS.   Oedipus, Creon came
While you were praying; he brings advice and help.
You can protect us no more, and we turn
to him.

OEDIPUS. What can I say to Creon? I have
given him
No cause to trust me or to listen. In all
I said   1445
Before, he has seen that I was wrong.

[*Enter* CREON *with* ANTIGONE *and* ISMENE.]

CREON. I have not come scorning or insult-

ing you, Oedipus,
For those wrongs. (*To servants*) Have
you no shame before
Your countrymen? At least show reverence to the sun's   1449
Flame that sends us life, and do not let
This curse lie open to disfigure heaven.
Neither earth, nor the pure falling rain,
nor light
May come near it. Take him to the palace now!
When evil grows in the family, only the
family
May hear of it and look without pollution.   1455

OEDIPUS. Creon, I thought. . . . but now you
have struck those fears
Away — you will be a gentle king.
But I ask one thing, and I ask it to help
you,
Not myself, for I am hated by powers
too strong
For us.

CREON.   What do you ask so eagerly?   1460

OEDIPUS. Banish me from the country now.
I must go
Where no one can see or welcome me
again.

CREON. I would have done so, Oedipus, but
first
I must know from Apollo what he commands.

OEDIPUS. But we have heard all his answer
— destroy the   1465
Parricide,[1] the unholiness, destroy me!

CREON. So it was said. . . . And yet we are
in such danger;
It is better to hear what we must do.

OEDIPUS.   Why need you
Go to Delphi for my poor body?

CREON. Delphi will never deceive us; you

───────

[1] **Parricide**: one who has murdered his parent.

know it speaks   1470
The truth.

OEDIPUS.   But Creon, I command you!
     . . . I will kneel
And pray to you. . . . Bury my queen as
     you wish
In her royal tomb; she is your sister
And it is her right. But as for myself, I
Must never think of entering my father's
     city   1475
Again, so long as its people live. Let me
Have no home but the mountains, where
     the hill
They call Cithaeron, my Cithaeron,
     stands.
There my mother and my father, while
They lived, decreed I should have my
     grave.   1480
My death will be a gift from them, for
     they
Have destroyed me. . . . And yet I know
     that sickness
Cannot break in and take my life, nothing
May touch me. I am sure of this, for each
     moment
Is a death, and I am kept alive only   1485
For the final punishment. . . . But let it go,
Let it go, I do not care what is done with
     me.
Creon, my sons will ask nothing more
     from you;
They are men, wherever they go they
     will take what they need
From life. But pity my two daughters,
     who will have   1490
No love. All that was owned by me, they
     shared,
And when I banqueted, they were always
     beside me.
You must become their father. . . . But
     let me touch them
And talk to them of our sorrows. Come,
     my lord,
Come, my noble kinsman, let me feel
     them   1495

In my arms and believe they are as much
     my own
As when I saw. . . . I cannot think. . . .
     Their weeping,
Their dear voices are near. Creon has
     pitied me
And given me my children. Is this true?

CREON. I sent for them; I know what joy
     they would give you   1500
And how you loved them once. Yes, it
     is true.

OEDIPUS. May heaven bless your life, and
     may the power
Watching us, guard you more safely on
     the throne
Than me. My children, where are you?
     Come near, come
To my hands; they are your brother's
     hands and they   1505
Went searching out and took your fa-
     ther's seeing
Eyes to darkness. I did not know my
     children,
And did not ask, but now the world may
     see
That I gave you life from the source that
     gave me mine.
Why is there no light? I cannot see you!
     . . . And tears   1510
Come when I think of the years you will
     have to live
In a cruel world. In the city they will
     shun you,
Fear your presence; when they feast and
     dance in the streets
You will not be allowed to watch, and
     they
Will send you weeping home. And when
     you come   1515
To the years of marriage, children, who
     will there be
So careless of his pride as to accept the
     shame
That glares on my birth and on yours?
     "Your father

Killed his father!" "Your father gave life
where he
Was given life, you are children where
he was once   1520
A child." That will be your humiliation!
And who will wed you?
No one, my daughters, there will be no
one, and I see
You must pine to death in lonely child-
lessness.   1524
Creon, you are their father, you alone.
For they have lost their parents. Do not
let them go
Into beggary and solitude — their blood
is yours.
I have nothing, but do not afflict them
with
My poverty. Have pity on them. See, so
young   1529
And robbed of all except your kindliness.
Touch me once, my lord, and give your
consent.
My children, I would have said much to
comfort
And advise you — but how could you
understand?
But pray, you must pray to live as the
world allows
And find a better life than the father
whom you follow.   1535

CREON. No more now. Go inside the palace.

OEDIPUS. It is hard, but I must obey.

CREON.   All
things are healed
By time.

OEDIPUS. But Creon, I demand one thing
before
I go.

CREON. What do you demand?

OEDIPUS.   Banishment!

CREON. Only heaven can answer your
prayer. When Apollo. . . .   1540

OEDIPUS. But Apollo can only detest me.

CREON. Then your prayer will be
The sooner heard.

OEDIPUS.   You mean what you
say?

CREON.   I cannot
Promise, when I see nothing certain.

OEDIPUS.   Now!
Exile me now!

CREON.   Go then, and leave your
children.   1545

OEDIPUS. You must not take them from me!

CREON.   You give
Commands as if you were king. You must
remember
Your rule is over, and it could not save
your life.

CHORUS. Men of Thebes, look at the king
who ruled
Your country; there is Oedipus.   1550
He knew how to answer the mystery
Of evil in the Sphinx, and was our greatest
lord.
We saw him move the world with his
will, and we envied him.
But look, the storm destroys him, the sea
Has come to defeat him.   1555
Remember that death alone can end all
suffering;
Go towards death, and ask for no greater
Happiness than a life
In which there has been no anger and no
pain.

For Discussion

1. "You are our corruption . . . ," the blind
Teiresias says to Oedipus early in the play
(page 358, line 370). And a few lines later he
says, ". . . you are the murderer you are search-

ing for." (line 379). Why does Oedipus not believe Teiresias? How does he account for Teiresias' accusation? What information leads Oedipus to believe he is the murderer? Who supplies that information?

2. A messenger arrives with good news for Oedipus. What is his message? When Oedipus expresses fears about returning to his former home, what does the messenger tell him? At what point does Jocasta try to prevent Oedipus from seeking further after the truth? How does Oedipus account for her behavior? Why was the shepherd sent for in the first place? What question is he asked when he arrives? The shepherd confirms Oedipus' worst fears. How? How does Jocasta react to the truth that has been uncovered? How does Oedipus? What will become of the king?

3. In this extraordinary sequence of events, a man attempting to escape his fate hurries directly toward it. The question arises: To what extent is Oedipus responsible for what happens to him? What kind of man is he? One can say that he is impulsive, or rash — as in fleeing Corinth and murdering a stranger on the road. He is also arrogant. Consider, for example, his remarks to Teiresias. What other evidence of impulsiveness and arrogance do you find in the play? Yet, is he not a good ruler, with the welfare of his people at heart? How does he respond to the request of the Priest in the opening lines of the play? Does he ever lie or try to evade the truth? Who, indeed, is most insistent about finding the truth? He tries to avoid his fate by fleeing from Corinth. Do you blame him for this? What attitude toward the gods does this act suggest?

4. What part do the gods play in the fall of Oedipus? They never appear, but they speak through the voice of the oracle of Apollo. How does the message of the oracle become known? We learn that Laius and Jocasta had heard the message before the events depicted in the play. What effect did the message have on them? How much did Oedipus know about the message of the oracle? What effect did it have upon him? The gods

clearly know what Oedipus' fate will be, but is there any evidence to suggest that they created his fate? Does Oedipus act of his own free will, or are his actions controlled by other powers?

5. Early in the play Oedipus says to Teiresias: "You live in perpetual night; you cannot harm / Me, nor anyone who moves in the light" (page 359, lines 392–393). Yet who at this point is truly blind — Teiresias or Oedipus? Oedipus' statement is ironic, as are many other statements in the play. In seeking the murderer of Laius, Oedipus says: "I will fight for him as I / Would fight for my own father" (page 356, lines 282–283). Explain the irony. The messenger from Corinth says of his message: ". . . the news is glad, and yet . . . yet you may grieve" (page 372, line 967). What news did he bring? His remark contains a double irony. Can you explain it?

6. *Oedipus the King* consists of six scenes or episodes separated by odes spoken by the chorus. In these odes the chorus comments on the action that is taking place, expressing questions, doubts, fears, and other reactions that would be shared by the audience. But the chorus (or a spokesman for the chorus) also appears as a character in the action. Examine several passages in which the chorus appears as a character and explain what kind of role it plays.

7. The play also contains conventional structural elements with which you are familiar. How is the exposition accomplished? Specifically, how is knowledge of the past brought into the action? Give an example. Where is the climax? Justify your choice. What complications precede the climax? What is the resolution of the action?

For Composition

As is true of any profound treatment of man's fate, *Oedipus the King* leads one to wonder about what kind of universe we live in. Are we simply cogs in a vast machine, destined to play out our lives in ways that have already been determined for us by superior powers? If the gods know what we are going to do before we do it, can our wills be free?

1. **Analysis.** Can a man be free to act as he chooses if a superior being knows how he will act beforehand? In an essay of two or three unified paragraphs, consider to what extent foreknowledge and free will are compatible. Develop your remarks around examples from your own experience or imagination. Imagine yourself, for example, in relation to a being of less developed intellect — a pet or a baby, for instance.

2. **Exposition.** What functions does the chorus serve in a Greek tragedy? By considering the relationship between the odes and the episodes, as well as the content of the odes themselves, explain the uses of the chorus as thoroughly as you can. Organize your essay in several paragraphs, each developing and illustrating one choral function. Support your explanation with examples from the text of the play.

3. **Analysis.** Most of the action in *Oedipus the King* is devoted to a search for truth — a search that culminates in Oedipus' discovery of who he is. In each scene something happens that moves Oedipus closer to the truth, yet there is always something that distracts him from it. Examine the action up to the time of Oedipus' discovery, and show how each scene both advances the search for truth and delays its discovery.

4. **Comparison and Contrast.** Compare and contrast the manner in which *Job* and *Oedipus the King* account for the existence of grief and suffering in the world. Does either suggest that there is a benevolent force ruling over us? Does either suggest that the force ruling the universe is powerless to prevent suffering? Discuss these matters in a unified essay that includes relevant quotations from the two works.

Words and Allusions

ALLUSIONS. *Oedipus the King* is the source of various allusions (page 53) that have become part of our language. An example is the term *Oedipal conflict* as used by Sigmund Freud. From your understanding of the play and from any other sources of information you may wish to consult, explain the meaning of *Oedipal conflict*. A related term is *Oedipus complex*. What does that term mean?

SYNONYMS (page 14). The following words relate to Teiresias and the role he plays in *Oedipus the King*, yet each differs slightly from the others in meaning: *augur, oracle, prophet, seer*. Explain how the words differ from each other, and use each one in a sentence that illustrates its meaning. (By the way, what is the difference between *prophesy* and *prophecy?*)

Aristotle on Tragedy

Since the days of ancient Greece, tragedy has been regarded as the highest form of literary art. But what is tragedy? Many definitions have been offered, but the most influential is the one presented by the philosopher Aristotle in his work entitled *Poetics*. Having read *Oedipus the King* (page 349), to which Aristotle frequently refers, you might now consider his definition of *tragedy* —not because it is the final word on the subject, but because it contains fundamental ideas with which all later definitions of tragedy must come to terms.

In the sixth chapter of the *Poetics*, Aristotle presents his definition:

> Tragedy . . . is an imitation of an action that is serious, complete, and of a certain magnitude; in language embellished with each kind of artistic ornament . . . in the form of action, not of narrative; with incidents arousing pity and fear, wherewith to accomplish its katharsis of such emotions.

Aristotle then goes on to explain his definition. Let us examine his explanation.

First of all, let us clarify several phrases. By "a certain magnitude" Aristotle refers to the scope of the action in a tragedy. There must be a convincing chain of events to change a given situation from good to bad fortune. In the phrase "language embellished" he indicates that tragedy should be expressed in poetry. And when he speaks of "the form of action, not of narrative," he means that the lines must be acted, not simply read.

Tragedy, according to Aristotle, is an *imitation*. It is not life itself; it is life imitated on a stage. Moreover, it is an imitation of an *action*, not merely a revelation of character, although character is expressed through action. Thus he regards the plot, "the structure of the incidents," as the most important part of a tragedy. Indeed, he tells us, "the plot ought to be so constructed that, even without the aid of the eye, he who hears the tale will thrill with horror and melt to pity at what takes place."

An effective plot, we are told, will be both "complete" and "complex." By "complete," Aristotle refers to the order of incidents. The plot must have "a beginning, a middle, and an end." That is, the beginning must be understandable without knowledge of earlier incidents and must lead naturally to what follows; the middle must follow from the beginning and point toward the end; and the end must follow naturally from what has gone before and conclude the action. Elementary, perhaps, but these are the requirements for a well constructed plot.

The plot should also be complex. A simple plot is one that moves in a straight line directly toward a conclusion. A complex plot is one that moves in various directions by means of what Aristotle calls *reversal* and *recognition*. *Reversal* "is a change by which the action veers round to its opposite" — as in *Oedipus the King*, where the accuser becomes the accused and the prosecutor becomes the defendant. *Recognition* "is a change from ignorance to knowledge." This, too, can affect the direction of the plot, as when Oedipus comes to realize who he actually is. According to Aristotle, these shifts in direction increase the tragic effect of the drama.

The word *serious* in the first line of Aristotle's definition refers both to the quality of the action and the characters involved. The action must end unhappily, but to be properly tragic it must have profound consequences involving people whose fate affects many beyond themselves. We may infer that Aristotle would find sadness in the death of a child in an automobile accident or of a policeman shot down in the line of duty, but he would not find these events tragic. Only in something as monumental as the assassination of a President, which alters all our lives, would he find the stuff of tragedy.

In Aristotle's day the appropriate tragic figure would be a king, but he must be one whose fate would excite feelings of pity and fear in the audience. Thus a virtuous man whose fortune changes from prosperity to adversity will not do. Such a fall merely shocks us. Nor is the fall of an evil man properly tragic. Such a fall can please our moral sense, but it does not create the effect of tragedy. The proper tragic figure, then, is one who is neither evil nor extremely virtuous, one "whose misfortune," in the words of Aristotle, "is brought about not by vice or depravity, but by some error or frailty."

Finally, Aristotle tells us, tragedy should arouse "pity and fear" through which it accomplishes "its katharsis of such emotions." The subject matter of tragedy is painful. Characters make mistakes, suffer, and are destroyed in various ways. Yet audiences regard tragedy as the highest form of theatrical experience. Why is this so? That was the question Aristotle asked himself, and his definition attempts to answer it.

Aristotle speaks constantly of pity and fear — the pity we feel for the tragic character and the fear that his fate arouses in us. The pity is obvious, and we fear that what can happen to him can happen to us also. But what makes the experience bearable, even exhilarating? According to Aristotle, great tragedy provokes those feelings so strongly that the audience expends its emotions in the theater and leaves having been purged of them at least temporarily.

In daily life we live constantly with occasions that evoke pity and fear — auto wrecks, deaths by cancer, wars, all the personal and social disasters that fill newspapers week after week. These events do not create the effect of tragedy that Aristotle speaks of, but once in a long while, we may be lucky enough to see represented on stage a structuring of disaster that purges our pity and fear, allowing us to depart more buoyantly than we had entered. Hence those feelings of exhilaration, even exaltation, that many have testified to experiencing in the presence of supreme tragic art when superlatively performed.

1. To what extent does *Oedipus the King* fit Aristotle's conception of tragedy?

2. What twentieth-century tragedies are you familiar with? To what extent do they conform to Aristotle's conception?

Pieter Bruegel the Elder (1525/30—1569) *Tower of Babel.* Kunsthistorisches Museum, Vienna.

Bruegel

Tower of Babel

In the Book of Genesis after the Flood, "the whole earth was of one language and one speech." And the people decided to make "a name" for themselves by building "a city and a tower, whose top may reach unto heaven." But the Lord said, "Behold, the people is one . . . and this they begin to do: and now nothing will be restrained from them, which they have imagined to do." So He "confounded their language" and "scattered them abroad from thence upon the face of all the earth."

It might sound as if the Lord were envious and afraid, but the point is that if nothing remained impossible, man would forget his Lord and Maker. The tendency of man to forget God is one of the recurring themes in the Bible, and in the stories of many other cultures man is punished for demanding more of life than he can obtain or manage. In the Biblical story excessive demand leads to failure of communication and cooperation, suggesting that society is possible only because people restrict their demands. Does Tolstoy suggest this in "How Much Land Does a Man Need" (page 303)?

Bruegel presents no indication of the ensuing punishment. He indicates only the extraordinary achievement by immensely filling out the short, simple Biblical account. The detail is so plentiful that the eye tends to get lost. One way to grasp the various details is to look at them through a tightly rolled-up tube of paper.

The emphasis of the painting is on the ingenuity of men. They have taken advantage of a mountain of rock to give their tower a firm anchorage and to simplify and shorten the building process. As the scene in the lower left corner shows, they have submitted to the control of a king in order to carry out their plan. They use not only brick but also cut stone, and they have fleets of ships and rafts to bring the materials they need as well as a fortress to protect their city and their tower. On the second turn of the winding platform an enormous crane is visible, modeled on the great crane of Bruges that was made a century before Bruegel painted but was still famous. What other labor-saving and labor-extending devices can you discover?

There are also signs of haste. Though supported by the rock, the unfinished right of the tower threatens the stability of the rest. Or is the core construction sufficiently strong to overcome this? Other signs of haste to get the tower completed are seen in the houses and shops built on the terrace of the tower. Why are they there? What other signs of haste are discoverable?

Yet all this marvelous cooperation, effort, and ingenuity are doomed. The power of the painting depends on the observer's sorrowful knowledge of the fate of the project combined with his interest in a tremendous human effort with which he is instinctively sympathetic. How can that tension between knowledge and sympathy be resolved?

MORSE PECKHAM

Vasarely

Folklore Planetaire — 0502

We usually think about fate and free will in philosophical language or in examples, such as Frost's poem "The Road Not Taken" (page 313). One kind of painting that emerged in the 1960's makes it possible to think about the problem in terms of seeing and to experience it through the act of seeing. If we look at these paintings, we become aware of an odd fact — that theories of fate and theories of free will both make sense.

These paintings are called "optical," or "op," paintings. Their subject is the visual experience they make possible, as this one does. The title, "Planetary Folklore," suggests that every human being on this planet has certain beliefs simply because he sees.

Vasarely depends on the fact that though we all see the same world, each of us sees it a bit differently, and we all interpret it in widely differing ways. In this painting there is nothing to interpret, though there would be nothing wrong in saying that it is colorful and lively, or that it is about the state of being colorful and lively. Such an emotional tone is very attractive, and Vasarely uses it so that the observer will not be put off by having to think about something disturbing or sad.

In the course of our lives each of us builds up certain expectancies about any situation we come to. When these expectancies are fulfilled, we think we are exercising our free will, because we feel we are controlling our perception of the situation. But when something happens that we do not expect, we feel that we are being controlled by something outside ourselves — by "fate." Can you think of examples of the shock you get when what happens is not what you expected?

One way of seeing this painting is to observe that most of the small squares are organized by color into large squares. A little off center is a large red square, and above it is a blue one. How many other large squares can you see? At the extreme right a blue square sits below a larger violet one. Are you tempted to see these two squares as one large oblong? Why?

Some of the small squares seem larger than others. Why? What happens if you place a ruler along the division between adjacent rows of squares? And are all the interior squares the same color? Do the frames make them only *seem* to be different colors?

The principle is clear. The painting introduces visual uncertainty and makes the observer feel he is losing control of his own visual acts. He expects a comprehensible design, but he cannot see the painting the way he wants to.

MORSE PECKHAM

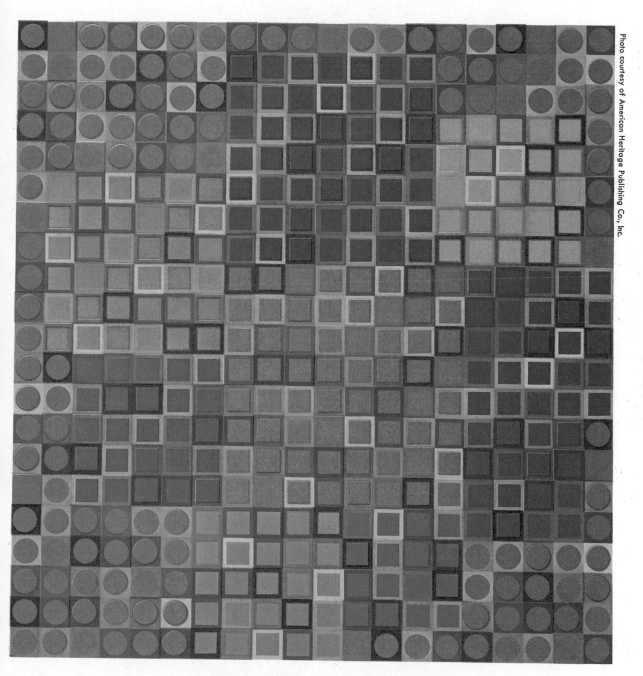

Victor Vasarely (1908–) *Folklore Planetaire-0502.*

Jan Steen (1626–1679) *The World Upside Down.* Kunsthistorisches Museum, Vienna.

Steen

The World Upside Down

"Mr. Flood's Party" (page 315) expresses a different attitude toward alcohol and its effect on the will than does this painting by Jan Steen. Does alcohol release the will from its inhibitions, or does it make it impossible to summon the will and concentrate it upon some meaningful activity? Taken together, the poem and the painting explore this question.

Steen wants to present a scene of confusion, but at the same time he wants the observer to know that it is such a scene. If the various incidents were scattered at random, there would be no tension between the character of the scene and the feeling that things have gotten out of hand. Consequently, he imposes a strong design upon his painting. Just off center he implies a large diamond shape. Follow the young man's leg up to his hip, then turn left at an acute angle along the highlights of his collar and face, parallel with the front edge of his jacket. Continue up to the violin and the dark patch of the violinist's hair. Turn again toward the left at an obtuse angle along the violinist's right shoulder past the collar of the sleeping woman's dress to the point where one hand rests upon the other. Turn again to the right at an acute angle along the fur edge of her jacket to the highlight on the bare arm of the drinking girl and down along her thigh to the young man's shoe. What other implied lines parallel the lines of the diamond shape?

Each line of the diamond shape points to other centers of interest — the overturned wine jug, wine running out of the cask, the roses in the young man's hand. The tight organization gives tension and force to the subject-matter. The expression on the girl's face, as well as her jug and glass, indicates that she is drunk. The dog is on the table eating the pie; the pig is in the parlor sniffing at a fallen rose. Pretzels and a pipe and playing cards are scattered on the floor. The violinist is playing to a sleeping woman. A crutch is in a hanging basket, out of reach of anyone who might need it. A monkey has stopped the clock. How many other absurdities can you find? Is there a similar basic absurdity in "Mr. Flood's Party"?

Further, all ages of man are present: children out of control, uninhibited youth, sleeping middle-age, and two old people. The old man, as we can tell from his hat, is a Puritan. He is puzzling over a book, probably the Bible, and is oblivious to the duck on his shoulder. The old woman, forgetting what was then thought of as the proper place of women, is laying down the law. Is Steen suggesting that absorption in religious argument makes people oblivious to the disorder around them?

MORSE PECKHAM

Da Verona

The Judgment of Paris

The subject of this painting and that of Sophocles' play *Oedipus the King* (page 349) both involve the problem of fate and free will. Throughout his life, Oedipus thought he was acting according to his own will, but, as he learned, his whole life was controlled by fate and the will of the gods. And so it was with Paris.

When Paris was born, his mother, Hecuba, dreamed that he would cause the destruction of Troy. To avoid this prophecy, Paris, like Oedipus, was exposed on a mountain to die, but survived and became a shepherd. Now Zeus, the chief Greek god, decided that mankind was becoming too numerous and determined to reduce their numbers by a destructive war. According to his plan, at a wedding-feast where gods and goddesses were assembled, the goddess Eris, or Discord, dropped a golden apple inscribed "To the fairest." Three goddesses claimed the apple — Hera, the goddess of wealth and power; Athene, the goddess of wisdom; and Aphrodite, the goddess of love.

Zeus decided that Paris should make the decision, and he sent Hermes, the messenger of the gods, to Paris to inform him of what he must do. The goddesses arrived, and each offered Paris a bribe. Paris accepted Aphrodite's offer of the most beautiful woman in the world. This was Helen, wife of Menelaus, a king of Greece. With the aid of Aphrodite, Paris eloped with Helen to the place of his birth, the city of Troy. In revenge, the Greeks attacked Troy, and after a long war destroyed the city and its people. Thus Paris, believing he was making a free choice, was actually carrying out the prophecy of his mother's dream and the will of Zeus.

This picture was probably made to be set into the elaborate paneling of some splendid Venetian room of the early sixteenth century. The painter cannot present the incidents one at a time as can the storyteller. He must present the whole story at once. Thus at the upper right Paris is seated on the ground surrounded by his flock. His shepherd's staff lies against one leg. Hermes, holding the messenger's wand he always carries, is explaining to Paris what he must do and is gesturing toward the three goddesses descending on a cloud. Above, the goddess Discord is shown just after she has thrown the golden apple which the three goddesses are looking at. Below in the center is the main scene where Paris is holding the apple, wondering what he should do, and the three goddesses are asking for it.

The problem of making an interesting composition for a circular painting is not easy. The artist uses the round apple in the center to reinforce the circularity of the painting, and he puts most of the scenes near the outer edge. In addition he puts a number of small figures next to the edge. How many of these can you identify? The small rectangular object at the left is probably a watering trough for the sheep. Can you fit the two small figures above it into the story, or into the design?

MORSE PECKHAM

Cecchino da Verona (active 1447–1480) *The Judgment of Paris.* National Museum, Florence.

In Summary

1. "I know that I shall meet my fate," Yeats' poem on page 332 begins. The word *fate* as there used means something close to "death," and indeed the term is frequently used in that sense. On the other hand, Chekhov seems to be using the word in a different sense when he writes of Ryabovich's "wrath with his fate" (page 347). Do you see a connection between the two meanings of *fate?* How would you define the term, as it applies to the selections you have just read?

2. A major problem posed by fate and free will is suggested in the essay on pages 301–302. If man's fate is predetermined by some superior power — or by one's chemical makeup or temperament or genes — there would seem to be nothing he can do about it. Consider "How Much Land Does a Man Need?" The devil is hiding behind the stove eavesdropping at the beginning of the story. Is it fated that the devil will make Pakhom do what he does? Does Pakhom in any way choose his fate? To what extent does Spike choose his in "Death of a Tsotsi"? Discuss.

3. Consider some of the other people you have met: the traveler at the fork in the path in Frost's poem, Eben Flood, the old man in "Hay for the Horses," Mantaj and Akku, the Irish airman Major Robert Gregory, Ryabovich, Oedipus. See if you can arrange those people on a scale that indicates the extent to which each one consciously chooses his fate. Where, for example, would Major Gregory be placed on such a scale in relation to Mantaj of "The Bamboo Trick"?

4. Fate plays a profound role in many of the selections you encountered earlier in this anthology. At the very beginning, to what extent is the cyclist in "The Night Face Up" (page 7) responsible for what happens to him? In other words, is he to blame for his fate? Could he have done anything to prevent the accident and its aftermath? Dr. Stockmann's fate is changed radically by what occurs in the course of *An Enemy of the People* (page 75). In what ways? To what extent is

he responsible for those changes? Considering the kind of man he is, do you think he could have prevented them? What is the fate of Jim Kendall in "Haircut" (page 146), and to what extent is he responsible for it? Farrington's fate in "Counterparts" (page 157) condemns him to an empty job and a meaningless round of pubs after his working day is done. How does his fate affect him? To what extent can he be blamed for it?

5. Death speaks, in Somerset Maugham's telling of a Middle Eastern folk tale: "There was a merchant in Bagdad who sent his servant to market to buy provisions and in a little while the servant came back, white and trembling, and said, Master, just now when I was in the market-place I was jostled by a woman in the crowd and when I turned I saw it was Death that jostled me. She looked at me and made a threatening gesture; now, lend me your horse, and I will ride away from this city and avoid my fate. I will go to Samarra and there Death will not find me. The merchant lent him his horse, and the servant mounted it, and he dug his spurs in its flanks and as fast as the horse could gallop he went. Then the merchant went down to the market-place and he saw me standing in the crowd and he came to me and said, Why did you make a threatening gesture to my servant when you saw him this morning? That was not a threatening gesture, I said, it was only a start of surprise. I was astonished to see him in Bagdad, for I had an appointment with him tonight in Samarra." What is the theme of this tale? To which of the selections you have read might the tale be most meaningfully compared? Explain.

6. What is a metrical foot? An iamb? A trochee? How would you define *topic sentence?* What characteristic distinguishes a unified paragraph from one that is not?

7. **Creative Writing.** Think of an occurrence with which you have firsthand acquaintance — because it happened either to you personally or to someone you know — and use it as the basis of a brief story that touches on some

aspect of fate. The story may, for example, illustrate the curious way in which something seemingly unimportant transforms one's life — a chance meeting, a change of plans, a letter, a casual suggestion that started you thinking and acting. You may prefer to write the story in the third person, and to change the details of setting and character in order to emphasize the role fate played in what happened. In other words, feel free to manipulate the basic material with which you are working in any way that will make the resulting story more effective. Four or five pages should be a reasonable length in which to develop characters and setting adequately and move the plot through the climax to some kind of resolution.

Reader's Choice

Ivo Andrić, *The Bridge on the Drina.*

In this novel from Yugoslavia, a bridge built by the Turks plays a major role in three centuries of conquest and oppression of the peoples who dwell near the bridge.

Anton Chekhov, *Uncle Vanya.*

A talented and intelligent steward of his brother-in-law's estate, Ivan Petrovitch has given up his own ambitions to support a man he comes to regard as a fraud.

Ecclesiastes.

What can a man achieve in life and what are the limitations upon his achievements? These questions are asked and answered in one of the most famous books of the Old Testament.

Euripides, *The Trojan Women.*

This ancient Greek tragedy deals with the fate of the survivors of Troy after its defeat in the Trojan War.

Johann Wolfgang von Goethe, *Faust.*

The most famous work of a great German author gives his version of the Faust legend — the story of a man who made a pact with the devil to achieve youth, power, and glory.

Thomas Hardy, *The Mayor of Casterbridge.*

Michael Henchard sells his wife and his only child to an unknown sailor and spends the rest of his life dealing with the effects of that desperate act.

André Malraux, *Man's Fate.*

A leading French writer tells of the Shanghai revolution of the 1920's, in which many good men were destroyed in a seemingly endless struggle for human liberation.

Christopher Marlowe, *Doctor Faustus.*

A major Elizabethan dramatist presents his version of the Faust legend — of a man who sells his soul to the devil in exchange for power through knowledge.

Erich Maria Remarque, *All Quiet on the Western Front.*

This classic anti-war novel of World War I asks why Germans must kill Frenchmen and Frenchmen kill Germans when all men want to live in peace.

William Shakespeare, *Macbeth.*

At the center of this tragedy is a man who kills to fulfill a prophecy of greatness, then continues to kill to forestall a prophecy of doom.

Leo Tolstoy, *War and Peace.*

This panoramic novel depicts Russia during the Napoleonic wars, with the destinies of men and women fulfilled against a background of violence and destruction.

Virgil, *The Aeneid.*

One of the few survivors of Troy, Aeneas rescues his father and goes forth to fulfill his destiny as the founder of Rome.

The African fetish figure represents Nature; the decorative offerings, an effort to control Nature's power.

Man and Nature

In one sense, man is a part of nature, so that everything human is also natural. But in the usual sense, nature is the visible world around us that exists independently of us. To the extent that the dog has been tamed by man, he is less natural than the wolf. For whatever natural reasons maize evolved ages ago, farmers now plant rows of hybrid corn for a purely human reason.

Most Americans now live in cities. For all too many of us, nature is something to take a vacation in or to glance at from a superhighway. We live remote from it and whizz through it in machines. Even when we are in it, we seldom wander far from a trail made and mapped by a forestry service, and we are likely to be equipped with guns, flashlights, and mosquito repellent. Man regards himself as nature's master. But he is uneasy about his mastery, for he knows that his control is imperfect and that his servant is far, far stronger than he.

Through science and technology, we harness the strength of rivers. We have eliminated polio almost entirely. We are poisoning the air we breathe. All the people now living could have an adequate diet. Life on earth could be exterminated. In other words, as master, man is not doing nature much good, and he is doing himself both great good and great harm.

But scientific mastery is only one approach to nature. It is certainly not one which has been congenial to poets, to creative writers generally. Not all poets love nature, of course, though a large number have done so. But poets, whether they profess their love of nature or not, feel connected with it, and connected in a way that is less scientific than religious, less intellectual than emotional. A scientist may or may not love nature, but his very enterprise is to study its mysteries in order to explain them so well that they will cease to be mysterious and will do what he wants them to do. The scientist's perfect language is mathematics. A poet wants to experience nature's mysteries, and to do this is very different from studying them. To study a thing is to master it, whereas to experience it is to take it into yourself. A poet does not think he can ever really understand the mysteries, and he does not think mathematical symbols really explain them. What he does want to understand is his relation to the mysteries. Scientific knowledge drives towards power. Poetic knowledge drives towards awe.

Awe is a combination of attraction and fear, implying reverence. The scientist who explores the ways of nature may marvel at them as a man, but as a scientist he seeks to explain them so that men may change them or use them. The writer, however, as writer, would rather bow in adoration, or even in horror, of nature than control or use it.

Sometimes a writer insists that nature is indifferent to mankind, as Crane does in "The Open Boat" (page 456). Yet in this story the characters' relation to nature is anything but indifferent and inhuman. They fear it; they marvel at it; it destroys some of them and threatens them all. Neither they nor Crane, nor we while we are reading the story, are indifferent to nature or to nature's indifference to us. Clark's "Hook" (page 431) is the life-story of a hawk. Yet the longer Clark talks about that bird, the more human Hook seems. A writer's medium is the ordinary language of his society, and, while it is natural for men to speak, nothing on earth is more exclusively and more intimately the creation of men than language. Just by using language a creative writer humanizes all things, and he certainly humanizes the nature to which he is so complexly connected.

George P. Elliott

A Sunrise on the Veld

DORIS LESSING

The veld is level grassland — a kind of vast meadow — located in areas of eastern and southern Africa. There is much beauty in it, at all times, in all seasons; and as is true of so many natural regions, there are things to fear within the veld as well.

Every night that winter he said aloud into the dark of the pillow: Half-past four! Half-past four! till he felt his brain had gripped the words and held them fast. Then he fell asleep at once, as if a shutter had fallen; and lay with his face turned to the clock so that he could see it first thing when he woke.

It was half-past four to the minute, every morning. Triumphantly pressing down the alarm knob of the clock, which the dark half of his mind had outwitted, remaining vigilant all night and counting the hours as he lay relaxed in sleep, he huddled down for a last warm moment under the clothes, playing with the idea of lying abed for this once only. But he played with it for the fun of knowing that it was a weakness he could defeat without effort; just as he set the alarm each night for the delight of the moment when he woke and stretched his limbs, feeling the muscles tighten, and thought: Even my brain — even that! I can control every part of myself.

Luxury of warm rested body, with the arms and legs and fingers waiting like soldiers for a word of command! Joy of knowing that the precious hours were given to sleep voluntarily! — for he had once stayed awake three nights running, to prove that he could, and then worked all day, refusing even to admit that he was tired; and now sleep seemed to him a servant to be commanded and refused.

The boy stretched his frame full length, touching the wall at his head with his hands, and the bedfoot with his toes; then he sprung out, like a fish leaping from water. And it was cold, cold.

He always dressed rapidly, so as to try and conserve his night-warmth till the sun rose two hours later; but by the time he had on his clothes his hands were numbed and he could scarcely hold his shoes. These he could not put on for fear of waking his parents, who never came to know how early he rose.

As soon as he stepped over the lintel,[1] the flesh of his soles contracted on the chilled earth, and his legs began to ache with cold. It was night: the stars were glittering, the trees standing black and still. He looked for signs of day, for the graying of the edge of a stone, or a lightening in the sky where the sun would rise, but there was nothing yet. Alert as an animal he crept past the dangerous window, standing poised with his hand on the sill for one proudly fastidious moment, looking in at the stuffy blackness of the room where his parents lay.

Feeling for the grass-edge of the path with his toes, he reached inside another

[1] lintel: threshold.

window further along the wall, where his gun had been set in readiness the night before. The steel was icy, and numbed fingers slipped along it, so that he had to hold it in the crook of his arm for safety. Then he tiptoed to the room where the dogs slept, and was fearful that they might have been tempted to go before him; but they were waiting, their haunches crouched in reluctance at the cold, but ears and swinging tails greeting the gun ecstatically. His warning undertone kept them secret and silent till the house was a hundred yards back: then they bolted off into the bush, yelping excitedly. The boy imagined his parents turning in their beds and muttering: Those dogs again! before they were dragged back in sleep; and he smiled scornfully. He always looked back over his shoulder at the house before he passed a wall of trees that shut it from sight. It looked so low and small, crouching there under a tall and brilliant sky. Then he turned his back on it, and on the frowsting[1] sleepers, and forgot them.

He would have to hurry. Before the light grew strong he must be four miles away; and already a tint of green stood in the hol-

low of a leaf, and the air smelled of morning and the stars were dimming.

He slung the shoes over his shoulder, veld *skoen*[2] that were crinkled and hard with the dews of a hundred mornings. They would be necessary when the ground became too hot to bear. Now he felt the chilled dust push up between his toes, and he let the muscles of his feet spread and settle into the shapes of the earth; and he thought: I could walk a hundred miles on feet like these! I could walk all day, and never tire!

He was walking swiftly through the dark tunnel of foliage that in daytime was a road. The dogs were invisibly ranging the lower travelways of the bush, and he heard them panting. Sometimes he felt a cold muzzle on his leg before they were off again, scouting for a trail to follow. They were not trained, but free-running companions of the hunt, who often tired of the long stalk before the final shots, and went off on their own pleasure. Soon he could see them, small and wild-looking in a wild strange light, now that the bush stood trembling on the verge of color, waiting for the sun to paint earth and grass afresh.

The grass stood to his shoulders; and the

---

[1] **frowsting**: lolling, lounging.

[2] **veld *skoen***: special shoes for walking on the veld.

ABOUT THE AUTHOR • Born of British parents in Iran, **Doris Lessing** (1919–   ) grew up in Southern Rhodesia and never even visited England until 1949. Her writings express her concern with two major issues — the conflict between the races in Africa and the problems of an intelligent woman seeking to maintain her identity in a man's world. Her *African Stories,* said the *Saturday Review,* are beautifully wrought "by a sensitive and thoughtful but fiercely honest writer whose humanity soon becomes as patent as her love of the sun-washed land where she spent her formative years." Playwright, poet, journalist, writer of fiction, Doris Lessing has been called by the *London Times* "not only the best *woman* novelist we have, but one of the most serious, intelligent, and honest writers of the whole post-war generation."

". . . the bush stood trembling on the verge of color, waiting for the sun to paint the earth and grass afresh."

trees were showering a faint silvery rain. He was soaked; his whole body was clenched in a steady shiver.

Once he bent to the road that was newly scored[1] with animal trails, and regretfully straightened, reminding himself that the pleasure of tracking must wait till another day.

He began to run along the edge of a field, noting jerkily how it was filmed over with fresh spiderweb, so that the long reaches of great black clods seemed netted in glistening gray. He was using the steady lope he had learned by watching the natives, the run that is a dropping of the weight of the body from one foot to the next in a slow balancing movement that never tires, nor shortens the breath; and he felt the blood pulsing down his legs and along his arms, and the exultation and pride of body mounted in him till he was shutting his teeth hard against a violent desire to shout his triumph.

Soon he had left the cultivated part of the farm. Behind him the bush was low and

black. In front was a long vlei,[2] acres of long pale grass that sent back a hollowing gleam of light to a satiny sky. Near him thick swathes of grass were bent with the weight of water, and diamond drops sparkled on each frond.

The first bird woke at his feet and at once a flock of them sprang into the air calling shrilly that day had come; and suddenly, behind him, the bush woke into song, and he could hear the guinea fowl calling far ahead of him. That meant they would now be sailing down from their trees into thick grass, and it was for them he had come: he was too late. But he did not mind. He forgot he had come to shoot. He set his legs wide, and balanced from foot to foot, and swung his gun up and down in both hands horizontally, in a kind of improvised exercise, and let his head sink back till it was pillowed in his neck muscles, and watched how above him small rosy clouds floated in a lake of gold.

Suddenly it all rose in him: it was un-

[1] **scored**: marked.

[2] **vlei** (vlī): low-lying land.

405

bearable. He leapt up into the air, shouting and yelling wild, unrecognizable noises. Then he began to run, not carefully, as he had before, but madly, like a wild thing. He was clean crazy, yelling mad with the joy of living and a superfluity of youth. He rushed down the vlei under a tumult of crimson and gold, while all the birds of the world sang about him. He ran in great leaping strides, and shouted as he ran, feeling his body rise into the crisp rushing air and fall back surely onto sure feet; and thought briefly, not believing that such a thing could happen to him, that he could break his ankle any moment, in this thick tangled grass. He cleared bushes like a duiker,[1] leapt over rocks; and finally came to a dead stop at a place where the ground fell abruptly away below him to the river. It had been a two-mile-long dash through waist-high growth, and he was breathing hoarsely and could no longer sing. But he poised on a rock and looked down at stretches of water that gleamed through stooping trees, and thought suddenly, I am fifteen! Fifteen! The words came new to him; so that he kept repeating them wonderingly, with swelling excitement; and he felt the years of his life with his hands, as if he were counting marbles, each one hard and separate and compact, each one a wonderful shining thing. That was what he was: fifteen years of this rich soil, and this slow-moving water, and air that smelt like a challenge whether it was warm and sultry at noon, or as brisk as cold water, like it was now.

There was nothing he couldn't do, nothing! A vision came to him, as he stood there, like when a child hears the word *eternity* and tries to understand it, and time takes possession of the mind. He felt his life ahead of him as a great and wonderful thing, something that was his; and he said aloud, with the blood rising to his head: all the great men of the world have been as I am now, and there is nothing I can't become, nothing I can't do; there is no country in the world I cannot make part of myself, if I choose. I contain the world. I can make of it what I want. If I choose, I can change everything that is going to happen: it depends on me, and what I decide now.

The urgency, and the truth and the courage of what his voice was saying exulted him so that he began to sing again, at the top of his voice, and the sound went echoing down the river gorge. He stopped for the echo, and sang again: stopped and shouted. That was what he was! — he sang, if he chose; and the world had to answer him.

And for minutes he stood there, shouting and singing and waiting for the lovely eddying[2] sound of the echo; so that his own new strong thoughts came back and washed round his head, as if someone were answering him and encouraging him; till the gorge was full of soft voices clashing back and forth from rock to rock over the river. And then it seemed as if there was a new voice. He listened, puzzled, for it was not his own. Soon he was leaning forward, all his nerves alert, quite still: somewhere close to him there was a noise that was no joyful bird, nor tinkle of falling water, nor ponderous movement of cattle.

There it was again. In the deep morning hush that held his future and his past, was a sound of pain, and repeated over and over: it was a kind of shortened scream, as if someone, something, had no breath to scream. He came to himself, looked about him, and called for the dogs. They did not appear: they had gone off on their own business, and he was alone. Now he was clean sober, all the madness gone. His heart beating fast, because of that frightened screaming, he stepped carefully off the rock

---

[1] **duiker** (dī′kər): small, horned antelope.

[2] **eddying**: whirling.

and went towards a belt of trees. He was moving cautiously, for not so long ago he had seen a leopard in just this spot.

At the edge of the trees he stopped and peered, holding his gun ready; he advanced, looking steadily about him, his eyes narrowed. Then, all at once, in the middle of a step, he faltered, and his face was puzzled. He shook his head impatiently, as if he doubted his own sight.

There, between two trees, against a background of gaunt black rocks, was a figure from a dream, a strange beast that was horned and drunken-legged, but like something he had never even imagined. It seemed to be ragged. It looked like a small buck that had black ragged tufts of fur standing up irregularly all over it, with patches of raw flesh beneath . . . but the patches of rawness were disappearing under moving black and came again elsewhere; and all the time the creature screamed, in small gasping screams, and leaped drunkenly from side to side, as if it were blind.

Then the boy understood: it *was* a buck.

He ran closer, and again stood still, stopped by a new fear. Around him the grass was whispering and alive. He looked wildly about, and then down. The ground was black with ants, great energetic ants that took no notice of him, but hurried and scurried towards the fighting shape, like glistening black water flowing through the grass.

And, as he drew in his breath and pity and terror seized him, the beast fell and the screaming stopped. Now he could hear nothing but one bird singing, and the sound of the rustling, whispering ants.

He peered over at the writhing blackness that jerked convulsively with the jerking nerves. It grew quieter. There were small twitches from the mass that still looked vaguely like the shape of a small animal.

It came into his mind that he should shoot it and end its pain; and he raised the gun. Then he lowered it again. The buck could no longer feel; its fighting was a mechanical protest of the nerves. But it was not that which made him put down the gun. It was a swelling feeling of rage and misery and

"Then the boy understood: it was *a buck"*—An African antelope.

protest that expressed itself in the thought: if I had not come it would have died like this: so why should I interfere? All over the bush things like this happen; they happen all the time; this is how life goes on, by living things dying in anguish. He gripped the gun between his knees and felt in his own limbs the myriad swarming pain[1] of the twitching animal that could no longer feel, and set his teeth, and said over and over again under his breath: I can't stop it. I can't stop it. There is nothing I can do.

He was glad that the buck was unconscious and had gone past suffering so that he did not have to make a decision to kill it even when he was feeling with his whole body: this is what happens, this is how things work.

It was right — that was what he was feeling. *It was right and nothing could alter it.*

The knowledge of fatality, of what has to be, had gripped him and for the first time in his life; and he was left unable to make any movement of brain or body, except to say: "Yes, yes. That is what living is." It had entered his flesh and his bones and grown in to the furthest corners of his brain and would never leave him. And at that moment he could not have performed the smallest action of mercy, knowing as he did, having lived on it all his life, the vast unalterable, cruel veld, where at any moment one might stumble over a skull or crush the skeleton of some small creature.

Suffering, sick, and angry, but also grimly satisfied with his new stoicism, he stood there leaning on his rifle, and watched the seething black mound grow smaller. At his feet, now, were ants trickling back with pink fragments in their mouths, and there was a fresh acid smell in his nostrils. He sternly controlled the uselessly convulsing muscles of his empty stomach, and reminded himself: the ants must eat too! At the same time he found that the tears were streaming

down his face, and his clothes were soaked with the sweat of that other creature's pain.

The shape had grown small. Now it looked like nothing recognizable. He did not know how long it was before he saw the blackness thin, and bits of white showed through, shining in the sun — yes, there was the sun, just up, glowing over the rocks. Why, the whole thing could not have taken longer than a few minutes.

He began to swear, as if the shortness of the time was in itself unbearable, using the words he had heard his father say. He strode forward, crushing ants with each step, and brushing them off his clothes, till he stood above the skeleton, which lay sprawled under a small bush. It was clean-picked. It might have been lying there years, save that on the white bone were pink fragments of gristle. About the bones ants were ebbing away, their pincers full of meat.

The boy looked at them, big black ugly insects. A few were standing and gazing up at him with small glittering eyes.

"Go away!" he said to the ants, very coldly. "I am not for you — not just yet, at any rate. Go away." And he fancied that the ants turned and went away.

He bent over the bones and touched the sockets in the skull; that was where the eyes were, he thought incredulously, remembering the liquid dark eyes of a buck. And then he bent the slim foreleg bone, swinging it horizontally in his palm.

That morning, perhaps an hour ago, this small creature had been stepping proud and free through the bush, feeling the chill on its hide even as he himself had done, exhilarated by it. Proudly stepping the earth, tossing its horns, frisking a pretty white tail, it had sniffed the cold morning air. Walking like kings and conquerors it had moved through this free-held bush, where each blade of grass grew for it alone, and where the river ran pure sparkling water for its slaking.

And then — what had happened? Such a swift surefooted thing could surely not be

---

[1] **myriad swarming pain**: *i.e.*, the pain from countless individual ant bites.

trapped by a swarm of ants?

The boy bent curiously to the skeleton. Then he saw that the back leg that lay uppermost and strained out in the tension of death, was snapped midway in the thigh, so that broken bones jutted over each other uselessly. So that was it! Limping into the ant-masses, it could not escape, once it had sensed the danger. Yes, but how had the leg been broken? Had it fallen, perhaps? Impossible, a buck was too light and graceful. Had some jealous rival horned it?

What could possibly have happened? Perhaps some Africans had thrown stones at it, as they do, trying to kill it for meat, and had broken its leg. Yes, that must be it.

Even as he imagined the crowd of running, shouting natives, and the flying stones, and the leaping buck, another picture came into his mind. He saw himself, on any one of these bright ringing mornings, drunk with excitement, taking a snap shot at some half-seen buck. He saw himself with the gun lowered, wondering whether he had missed or not; and thinking at last that it was late, and he wanted his breakfast, and it was not worthwhile to track miles after an animal that would very likely get away from him in any case.

For a moment he would not face it. He was a small boy again, kicking sulkily at the skeleton, hanging his head, refusing to accept the responsibility.

Then he straightened up, and looked down at the bones with an odd expression of dismay, all the anger gone out of him. His mind went quite empty: all around him he could see trickles of ants disappearing into the grass. The whispering noise was faint and dry, like the rustling of a cast snakeskin.

At last he picked up his gun and walked homewards. He was telling himself half defiantly that he wanted his breakfast. He was telling himself that it was getting very hot, much too hot to be out roaming the bush.

> The universe is not hostile, nor is it friendly. It is simply indifferent.
>
> — John Haynes Holmes

Really, he was tired. He walked heavily, not looking where he put his feet. When he came within sight of his home, he stopped, knitting his brows. There was something he had to think out. The death of that small animal was a thing that concerned him, and he was by no means finished with it. It lay at the back of his mind uncomfortably.

Soon, the very next morning, he would get clear of everybody and go to the bush and think about it.

For Discussion

1. "For a moment he would not face it. He was a small boy again, kicking sulkily at the skeleton, hanging his head, refusing to accept the responsibility." What responsibility was he shirking? What was he reluctant to face? The death of a small animal troubled the boy, we are told, and he would have to think more about it very soon. Why do you suppose the incident of the buck's death disturbed him so? In what directions do you think his later thoughts about the animal's death moved?

2. The story opens with a boy's going to sleep. In what mood does he sleep and wake up in the early hours of the morning? For what purpose does he leave the house? In what mood does he enter the veld? Once there, he suddenly "leapt up into the air, shouting and yelling wild, unrecognizable noises. Then he began to run, not carefully as he had before, but madly, like a wild thing" (page 406). How is his conduct at that moment to be accounted for? What shatters the mood that that conduct expresses?

3. This apparently simple story is in fact quite complex, incorporating all the shifting

and sometimes contradictory feelings of a human being towards the natural world of which he finds himself a part. What similarities do you observe between the life of the buck and the boy's experience? The boy "ran in great leaping strides, and shouted as he ran, feeling his body rise into the crisp rushing air and fall back surely onto sure feet; and thought briefly . . . that he could break his ankle any moment, in this thick tangled grass" (page 406). What may we assume might have happened if in fact he had broken his ankle that morning? To what extent was it true that "There was nothing he couldn't do, nothing!" (page 406)?

4. **Visual, Tactile, Olfactory, and Auditory Imagery.** The story so vividly creates the natural world of the veld that we come to know what it would feel like, sound like, look like to be there ourselves. Sensory images are responsible for the vividness: *visual* images (appealing to our sense of sight), *tactile* images (of touch), *olfactory* images (of smell), *auditory* images (of sound or hearing). Consider, for example, the boy's encounter with the buck. In that scene what sights are memorable? What sounds? What smell? What tactile images accompany his reminder to himself that "the ants must eat too" (page 408)?

5. "A Sunrise on the Veld" touches on the question of fate and free will that you have considered earlier. "The knowledge of fatality, of what has to be, had gripped him and for the first time in his life" (page 408). Does the story maintain that a person is free to control his fate? Or is his fate entirely out of his hands? Or — a third possibility — is the story saying something about fate and free will more complicated than either of those two alternatives? Discuss.

For Composition

To be effective, a composition must as you know be *unified*. And it must be *coherent*. Unity refers to the relevance of each sentence to the central thought of a paragraph, or of each paragraph to the central thought of an essay. *Coherence*, on the other hand, refers to the sequence of sentences within a para-graph, or paragraphs within an essay. That sequence should be logical and clear. The short paragraph on page 405 ("Soon he had left . . . sparkled on each frond") is unified around the idea of describing the boy's progress through new surroundings. The sentences might be shifted without destroying the unity of the paragraph (all of them would still relate to the same central idea), but shifting them would most likely destroy the coherence.

1. **Analysis.** Analyze the placement of the four sentences that make up the paragraph in "A Sunrise on the Veld" referred to above. Why are they in the order in which they occur? Suppose the first sentence were moved farther into the paragraph, say, between what is now the second and third sentences. What effect would the move have on the unity of the paragraph? On its coherence? Illustrate your analysis with specific references.

2. **Comparison and Contrast.** In a unified and coherent composition of three or four paragraphs, compare and contrast the boy's relationship to the natural world around him with the relationship of the buck to his that same morning but "perhaps an hour ago" (page 408). What similarities exist between the two creatures? What differences?

Words and Allusions

ANTONYMS. Words of opposite meanings are called *antonyms*. Although he does not use these words, the boy in "A Sunrise on the Veld" sees nature at first as *benevolent*, but before the end of the story, nature appears to him as *malevolent*. Use each word in a sentence that illustrates its meaning.

LINGUISTIC BORROWING (page 332). The words *benevolent* and *malevolent* are taken from Latin. They combine the Latin words *bene* and *male* with *volent*. What are the meanings of those Latin words? Do the same meanings carry over into English? The word *voluntarily* appears in Miss Lessing's story on page 403. How is *voluntarily* related to *benevolent*?

Stanzas from the Gitanjali

RABINDRANATH TAGORE

Nature affects our moods in many ways. On rare occasions it can affect us in a way that is almost overwhelming, when — like the boy yelling in unbearable joy in the preceding story — we feel such a oneness with it that we all but merge with our surroundings, transported beyond our limitations. The feeling is difficult to describe, but that many have felt it is undeniable. Here is how one great Indian poet and mystic has put it in words.

LXIX

The same stream of life that runs through my veins night and day runs through the world and dances in rhythmic measures.

It is the same life that shoots in joy through the dust of the earth in numberless blades of grass and breaks into tumultuous waves of leaves and flowers.

It is the same life that is rocked in the ocean-cradle of birth and of death, in ebb and in flow.

I feel my limbs are made glorious by the touch of this world of life. And my pride is from the life-throb of ages dancing in my blood this moment.

LXX

Is it beyond thee to be glad with the gladness of this rhythm? to be tossed and lost and broken in the whirl of this fearful joy?

All things rush on, they stop not, they look not behind, no power can hold them back, they rush on.

Keeping steps with that restless, rapid music, seasons come dancing and pass away — colors, tunes, and perfumes pour in endless cascades in the abounding joy that scatters and gives up and dies every moment.

Gitanjali: pronounced jē·tän·jäl·ē.
Rabindranath Tagore: rə·bēn′drə·nät′ tä′gōr; tə·gōr′.

For Discussion

1. *Gitanjali,* the name of the work from which these two stanzas come, is a Bengali word meaning "song offerings." One might think of them as brief outbursts of feeling — lyrics or psalms to express emotions intensely experienced. The two stanzas view nature in a unified way; that is, all the images contribute to evoking a single aspect of nature. Is it nature as soother, or nature as threatener, or nature as life-giver, or what? What do the images — of a stream and a dance and waves and a rocking cradle and a whirlpool and a cascade and the like — have in common?

2. **Kinetic Imagery.** In addition to the kinds of imagery considered on page 410, there is

yet another — imagery that describes movement, the imagery that would describe a man running with all his might, or lifting a huge rock with every muscle straining, or leaping high to clear an obstacle in his way. Much kinetic imagery is communicated by verbs: *crouch*, *bound*, *scamper*, *scuttle*, *tumble*, and many others. What kinetic imagery do you encounter in these stanzas from the *Gitanjali?*

For Composition

In Stanza LXX Tagore refers to the rhythm of life as "this fearful joy." "Fearful joy" is a figure of speech known as *oxymoron*, in which two terms are combined that in ordinary usage are regarded as contrary.

• **Analysis.** Examine both stanzas and explain why "fearful joy" is an appropriate response to life as described here.

About the Poet. Grandson of a Bengal prince, **Rabindranath Tagore** (1861–1941) studied law in England, but returned to India to manage his father's estates and begin the two careers that were to make him famous, as author and as teacher. He began by writing poems in imitation of the ancient poets of India, but soon he was writing tales, parables, and plays about the everyday lives of people he had come to know. In 1901 he established a school in Bengal which later became an international institute. While lecturing in the United States in 1913, he was awarded the Nobel Prize of some $40,000, which he donated to his school. He was knighted by the British in 1915, but rejected the honor in protest against British suppression of Indians.

The Force That Through the Green Fuse Drives the Flower

DYLAN THOMAS

A sense of oneness with nature can cause a man to rejoice in the harmony that exists between himself and his surroundings. But that same sense of oneness can affect a man altogether differently. Instead of joy it can create feelings of dread. For the same force that withers a fragile flower will age and wither us all.

The force that through the green fuse* drives the flower
Drives my green age; that blasts the roots of trees
Is my destroyer.
And I am dumb to tell the crooked rose
My youth is bent by the same wintry fever.   5

1. **fuse**: casing, tube.

The force that drives the water through the rocks
Drives my red blood; that dries the mouthing streams
Turns mine to wax.
And I am dumb to mouth unto my veins
How at the mountain spring the same mouth sucks.   10

The hand that whirls the water in the pool
Stirs the quicksand; that ropes the blowing wind
Hauls my shroud sail.
And I am dumb to tell the hanging man
How of my clay is made the hangman's lime.   15

The lips of time leech* to the fountain head;
Love drips and gathers, but the fallen blood
Shall calm her sores.
And I am dumb to tell a weather's wind
How time has ticked a heaven round the stars.   20

And I am dumb to tell the lover's tomb
How at my sheet goes the same crooked worm.

16. **leech:** feed on the substance of.

For Discussion

1. This poem exemplifies the highly distinctive style of Dylan Thomas. What characteristics of that style strike you most forcefully? Although individual lines and images may be ambiguous and obscure, the overall meaning is clear. How is nature being regarded here: as healer, soother, destroyer, inspirer, or what? How would you paraphrase "And I am dumb . . ."?

2. Thomas' diction is rich with connotations; indeed, his meaning is perhaps more clearly conveyed on a connotative level than on the denotative. "Green" suggests youth and vitality: "He's still green"; "green grass and leaves"; etc. A "fuse" is long and slender like the stalk of a flower; it connotes brief time, the destructive force of dynamite, and the like. The force in nature that is pushing the bud through the stem to flower is also pushing my life through youth to old age; and that force is destructive. Discuss the connotations of "wintry" (line 5). Of "fever." Comment on the juxtaposition of those two words. How would you paraphrase the closing two lines of the first stanza?

3. In order to extend your appreciation of Thomas' unique expression, consider another series of images and what they connote. (Each imaginative rereading of the poem will yield additional meanings and enlarge your appreciation, as the obscurities become clearer.) In lines 16–18 love is being treated as a kind of wound. A serene temperament that falls in love abruptly finds his peace of mind disturbed, much as a healthy skin punctured becomes charged with cellular disturbances designed to fight off the ill effects of the wound — hence, swelling and tenderness. Love, then, "drips and gathers," but as one grows older ("the fallen blood") the passions subside and grow calm. Time, in the line that opens the stanza, is seen as a leech sucking strength from life. In the second stanza, in what sense might water penetrate rocks? How are blood and water comparable? Why are streams that have gone dry appropriately regarded as "mouthing" (line 7)?

For Composition

"A Sunrise on the Veld" (page 403) incorporates two attitudes toward experiencing a close kinship with nature: one a sense of great power and exaltation, the other a realization of the mortality and perishableness of all natural things.

● **Comparison and Contrast.** In a unified and coherent essay that makes specific reference to lines in each poem, compare and contrast the attitudes expressed about man and his relationship to the natural world in Tagore's stanzas (page 411) and those of Dylan Thomas.

About the Poet. **Dylan Thomas** (1914–1953) was born in a village in Wales and died in New York City while on a poetry-reading tour of the United States. Much of Thomas' prose deals with his childhood and adolescence, particularly "A Child's Christmas in Wales" and *Portrait of the Artist as a Young Dog.* His radio play *Under Milk Wood* describes life in a Welsh village not unlike the one in which he grew up.

The body of Dylan Thomas' poetry is not large, but shortly before his death one critic found sufficient merit in his *Collected Poems* to acclaim him as "the greatest living poet in the English language." Thomas is still a favorite poet, especially among young people. He is vivid in his use of imagery, passionate and intense in his range of language. His poems are meant to be read aloud, but no one can read them as he read and recorded them in a rich, rolling baritone that captures the powerful rhythms in his lines.

Lines

Composed a Few Miles Above Tintern Abbey, on Revisiting the Banks of the Wye During a Tour, July 13, 1798

WILLIAM WORDSWORTH

The unwieldy title of this great reflective poem is generally shortened to "Tintern Abbey," although that ruined structure beside the Wye River in southeastern Wales is never mentioned within the poem itself. What provoked these lines, as the title suggests, was a walking trip Wordsworth took in his late twenties, in company with his beloved younger sister Dorothy. On the trip they revisited the beautiful Wye valley, which the poet had last seen five years earlier.

> Five years have passed; five summers, with the length
> Of five long winters! and again I hear
> These waters, rolling from their mountain-springs
> With a soft inland murmur. — Once again
> Do I behold these steep and lofty cliffs, 5
> That on a wild secluded scene impress
> Thoughts of more deep seclusion; and connect
> The landscape with the quiet of the sky.

The day is come when I again repose
Here, under this dark sycamore, and view   10
These plots of cottage-ground, these orchard-tufts,
Which at this season, with their unripe fruits,
Are clad in one green hue, and lose themselves
'Mid groves and copses.* Once again I see
These hedge-rows,* hardly hedge-rows, little lines   15
Of sportive* wood run wild: these pastoral farms,
Green to the very door; and wreaths of smoke
Sent up, in silence, from among the trees!
With some uncertain notice, as might seem
Of vagrant dwellers in the houseless woods,   20
Or of some Hermit's cave, where by his fire
The Hermit sits alone.
               These beauteous forms,
Through a long absence, have not been to me
As is a landscape to a blind man's eye:
But oft, in lonely rooms, and 'mid the din   25
Of towns and cities, I have owed to them
In hours of weariness, sensations sweet,
Felt in the blood, and felt along the heart;
And passing even into my purer mind,
With tranquil restoration: — feelings too   30
Of unremembered pleasure: such, perhaps,
As have no slight or trivial influence
On that best portion of a good man's life,
His little, nameless, unremembered, acts
Of kindness and of love. Nor less, I trust,   35
To them I may have owed another gift,
Of aspect more sublime; that blessed mood,
In which the burthen* of the mystery
In which the heavy and the weary weight
Of all this unintelligible world,   40
Is lightened: — that serene and blessed mood,
In which the affections* gently lead us on, —
Until, the breath of this corporeal* frame
And even the motion of our human blood
Almost suspended, we are laid asleep   45
In body, and become a living soul:
While with an eye made quiet by the power
Of harmony, and the deep power of joy,
We see into the life of things.

---

14. **copses**: thickets of small trees or shrubs. 15. **hedge-rows**: row of shrubs forming a fence. 16. **sportive**: playful. 38. **burthen**: burden. 42. **affections**: feelings. 43. **corporeal**: bodily.

If this
Be but a vain belief, yet, oh! how oft —   50
In darkness and amid the many shapes
Of joyless daylight; when the fretful stir
Unprofitable, and the fever of the world,
Have hung upon the beatings of my heart —
How oft, in spirit, have I turned to thee,   55
O sylvan Wye! thou wanderer thro' the woods,
How often has my spirit turned to thee!

And now, with gleams of half-extinguished thought,
With many recognitions dim and faint,
And somewhat of a sad perplexity,   60
The picture of the mind revives again:
While here I stand, not only with the sense
Of present pleasure, but with pleasing thoughts
That in this moment there is life and food
For future years. And so I dare to hope,   65
Though changed, no doubt, from what I was when first
I came among these hills; when like a roe*
I bounded o'er the mountains, by the sides
Of the deep rivers, and the lonely streams,
Wherever nature led: more like a man   70

67. **roe**: deer.

Flying from something that he dreads, than one
Who sought the thing he loved. For nature then
(The coarser pleasures of my boyish days,
And their glad animal movements all gone by)
To me was all in all. — I cannot paint   75
What then I was. The sounding cataract*
Haunted me like a passion: the tall rock,
The mountain, and the deep and gloomy wood,
Their colors and their forms, were then to me
An appetite; a feeling and a love,   80
That had no need of a remoter charm,
By thought supplied, nor any interest
Unborrowed from the eye. — That time is past,
And all its aching joys are now no more,
And all its dizzy raptures. Not for this   85
Faint I, nor mourn nor murmur; other gifts
Have followed; for such loss, I would believe,
Abundant recompense. For I have learned
To look on nature, not as in the hour
Of thoughtless youth; but hearing oftentimes   90
The still, sad music of humanity,
Nor harsh nor grating, though of ample power
To chasten and subdue. And I have felt
A presence that disturbs me with the joy
Of elevated thoughts; a sense sublime   95
Of something far more deeply interfused,*
Whose dwelling is the light of setting suns,
And the round ocean and the living air,
And the blue sky, and in the mind of man:
A motion and a spirit, that impels   100
All thinking things, all objects of all thought,
And rolls through all things. Therefore am I still
A lover of the meadows and the woods,
And mountains; and of all that we behold
From this green earth; of all the mighty world   105
Of eye, and ear, — both what they half create,
And what perceive; well pleased to recognize
In nature and the language of the sense,
The anchor of my purest thoughts, the nurse,
The guide, the guardian of my heart, and soul   110
Of all my moral being.
                    Nor perchance,
If I were not thus taught, should I the more
Suffer my genial spirits* to decay:
For thou art with me here upon the banks

76. **cataract**: large waterfall. 96. **interfused**: intermingled. 113. **genial spirits**:
natural disposition.

Of this fair river; thou my dearest Friend,   115
My dear, dear Friend; and in thy voice I catch
The language of my former heart, and read
My former pleasures in the shooting lights
Of thy wild eyes. Oh! yet a little while
May I behold in thee what I was once,   120
My dear, dear Sister! and this prayer I make,
Knowing that Nature never did betray
The heart that loved her; 'tis her privilege,
Through all the years of this our life, to lead
From joy to joy: for she can so inform   125
The mind that is within us, so impress
With quietness and beauty, and so feed
With lofty thoughts, that neither evil tongues,
Rash judgments, nor the sneers of selfish men,
Nor greetings where no kindness is, nor all   130
The dreary intercourse* of daily life,
Shall e'er prevail against us, or disturb
Our cheerful faith, that all which we behold
Is full of blessings. Therefore let the moon
Shine on thee in thy solitary walk;   135
And let the misty mountain-winds be free
To blow against thee: and, in after years,
When these wild ecstasies shall be matured
Into a sober pleasure; when thy mind
Shall be a mansion for all lovely forms,   140
Thy memory be as a dwelling-place
For all sweet sounds and harmonies; oh! then,
If solitude, or fear, or pain, or grief,
Should be thy portion, with what healing thoughts
Of tender joy wilt thou remember me,   145
And these my exhortations! Nor, perchance —
If I should be where I no more can hear
Thy voice, nor catch from thy wild eyes these gleams
Of past existence — wilt thou then forget
That on the banks of this delightful stream   150
We stood together; and that I, so long
A worshiper of Nature, hither came
Unwearied in that service; rather say
With warmer love — oh! with far deeper zeal
Of holier love. Nor wilt thou then forget,   155
That after many wanderings, many years
Of absence, these steep woods and lofty cliffs,
And this green pastoral landscape, were to me
More dear, both for themselves and for thy sake!

131. **intercourse**: communication.

For Discussion

1. Though stated in relatively simple language, the insights within this poem are profound; the more you reread and ponder the stanzas, the more you will come to appreciate what they express. Wordsworth, one of the four or five greatest English poets, is above all a poet of nature, and "Tintern Abbey" is among his most moving statements of what nature has meant to him. The first stanza describes the scene that provokes the poem. What are the characteristics of that scene?

2. Though five years have passed since the scene was last visited, the poet tells us that it has often been pictured in his mind's eye. Under what circumstances? The "beauteous forms" of the landscape (line 22) have furnished him with two gifts. What are they?

3. Perhaps the second gift is only fanciful, "a vain belief" (line 50). Nevertheless, the poet has frequently thought of this specific manifestation of the beauty of nature in moods of weariness and discouragement. Now, standing before the landscape itself, he experiences not only present pleasure but something else as well. What?

4. Lines 65 through 111 develop a contrast between the poet's attitude toward nature as a child and his attitude as a grown man. How do the two attitudes differ? How does he feel about the change in attitude that the years have brought? In other words, what has been lost (line 87), and what has recompensed him for that loss?

5. In the eyes and bearing of his younger sister, who accompanies him, the poet is reminded of his own youthful attitudes toward nature. What advice does he offer her from line 134 on? What benefits does he suggest she will receive from following his advice?

6. **Blank Verse.** "Tintern Abbey" is written in a verse form that has been used to express some of the greatest poetry in English: Shakespeare's mature plays and Milton's epic *Paradise Lost*, to mention obvious examples. The form is called *blank verse*, and its characteristics are three: it is unrhymed; it is written in iambic feet; and there are five feet to each line. Do not confuse *blank* verse, which is *unrhymed iambic pentameter*, with *free* verse (the verse form in which, among others you have read, "The Wayfarer," "Dover Beach," "Auto Wreck," "The Angels," and "Hay for the Horses" are written). Scan four or five lines of "Tintern Abbey" to demonstrate your understanding of the requirements of blank verse.

For Composition

To achieve coherence, whether in prose or poetry, ideas must be presented in a logical sequence, and the relationship between successive ideas must be clear. Clarity is gained in part by repeating some element of one sentence in the following one: "That time is past," writes Wordsworth (line 83), referring back to an idea developed earlier in the stanza, and the reference makes the connection between ideas clear. Again, transitional expressions provide an effective means of linking ideas: "And so I dare to hope," Wordsworth tells us in line 65, the *so* (like *thus* and *consequently* and *therefore*) demonstrating that what is being introduced will draw a conclusion from what has gone before.

1. **Analysis.** Demonstrate your understanding of principles of coherence by writing a composition of four or five paragraphs that show specifically how ideas are connected in "Tintern Abbey." Make sure your own writing is coherent as you develop and illustrate your insights.

2. **Argument.** On the basis of your experience, support or refute Wordsworth's implication that the way a young boy or girl experiences nature is quite different from the way a more mature person does. If you feel there is a difference, you will want to clarify it by means of examples and narration — presumably an illustrative personal anecdote or two.

About the Poet. **William Wordsworth** (1770–1850) began his literary career as a revolutionary in politics and poetry. A supporter of the French Revolution and the rights of man,

Wordsworth wrote about common people in what he asserted was their natural language instead of the highly stylized diction typical of eighteenth-century verse. With the rise of Napoleon, Wordsworth became disillusioned with revolutionary politics and turned for solace and inspiration to the world of nature.

From childhood memories and fresh perceptions, he evolved a mystical view of the natural world that he expressed in some of the greatest poetry in the English language. He died as Poet Laureate of England many years after he had written the poems for which he is remembered.

FROM

Nature

RALPH WALDO EMERSON

Wordsworth's ideas expressed at the very end of the eighteenth century had profound influences on the century that followed. In America, for instance, the New England essqyist and philosopher Ralph Waldo Emerson set down variations of what the earlier English poet had written in verse. The relationship between the two writers was not so close as the preceding statement perhaps implies; Emerson's inspiration came from many other sources as well. But you will find in the following essay many thoughts that Wordsworth would very likely have shared.

To go into solitude, a man needs to retire as much from his chamber as from society. I am not solitary whilst I read and write, though nobody is with me. But if a man would be alone, let him look at the stars. The rays that come from those heavenly worlds will separate between him and what he touches. One might think the atmosphere was made transparent with this design, to give man, in the heavenly bodies, the perpetual presence of the sublime. Seen in the streets of cities, how great they are! If the stars should appear one night in a thousand years, how would men believe and adore; and preserve for many generations the remembrance of the city of God which had been shown! But every night come out these envoys[1] of beauty, and light the universe with their admonishing smile.

The stars awaken a certain reverence, because though always present, they are inaccessible; but all natural objects make a kindred[2] impression, when the mind is open to their influence. Nature never wears a mean appearance. Neither does the wisest man extort her secret, and lose his curiosity by finding out all her perfection. Nature never became a toy to a wise spirit. The flowers, the animals, the mountains, reflected the wisdom of his best hour, as much

[1] **envoys**: messengers, representatives.
[2] **kindred**: similar.

as they had delighted the simplicity of his childhood.

When we speak of nature in this manner, we have a distinct but most poetical sense in the mind. We mean the integrity[1] of impression made by manifold[2] natural objects. It is this which distinguishes the stick of timber of the woodcutter from the tree of the poet. The charming landscape which I saw this morning is indubitably made up of some twenty or thirty farms. Miller owns this field, Locke that, and Manning the woodland beyond. But none of them owns the landscape. There is a property in the horizon which no man has but he whose eye can integrate all the parts, that is, the poet. This is the best part of these men's farms, yet to this their warranty deeds give no title.[3]

To speak truly, few adult persons can see nature. Most persons do not see the sun. At least they have a very superficial seeing. The sun illuminates only the eye of the man, but shines into the eye and the heart of the child. The lover of nature is he whose inward and outward senses are still truly adjusted to each other; who has retained the spirit of infancy even into the era of manhood. His intercourse with heaven and earth becomes part of his daily food. In the presence of nature a wild delight runs through the man, in spite of real sorrows. Nature says — he is my creature, and mauger[4] all his impertinent[5] griefs, he shall be glad with me. Not the sun or the summer alone, but every hour and season yields its tribute of delight; for every hour and change corresponds to and authorizes a different state of the mind, from breathless noon to grimmest midnight. Nature is a setting that fits equally well a comic or a

"Standing on the bare ground . . . I become a transparent eyeball. . . ." Cartoon by Thomas Cranch.

mourning piece. In good health, the air is a cordial[6] of incredible virtue. Crossing a bare common,[7] in snow puddles, at twilight, under a clouded sky, without having in my thoughts any occurrence of special good fortune, I have enjoyed a perfect exhilaration. I am glad to the brink of fear. In the woods, too, a man casts off his years, as the snake his slough,[8] and at what period soever of life is always a child. In the woods is perpetual youth. Within these plantations of God, a decorum[9] and sanctity reign, a perennial festival is dressed, and the guest sees not how he should tire of them in a thousand years. In the woods, we return to reason and faith. There I feel that nothing can befall me in life — no disgrace, no calamity (leaving me my eyes), which nature cannot repair. Standing on the bare ground — my head bathed by the blithe air and uplifted into infinite space — all mean egotism vanishes. I become a transparent eyeball; I am nothing; I see all; the currents

---

[1] **integrity**: entirety.

[2] **manifold**: many and varied.

[3] **title**: right to ownership.

[4] **mauger**: in spite of.

[5] **impertinent**: *here,* having no meaning or importance.

[6] **cordial**: stimulating medicine or drink.

[7] **common**: open public land.

[8] **slough** (sluf): outer layer of skin which is periodically cast off.

[9] **decorum**: orderliness.

> Everything in Nature contains all the hidden powers of Nature. Everything is all made of one hidden stuff.
>
> — Ralph Waldo Emerson

of the Universal Being circulate through me; I am part or parcel of God. The name of the nearest friend sounds then foreign and accidental: to be brothers, to be acquaintances, master or servant, is then a trifle and a disturbance. I am the lover of uncontained and immortal beauty. In the wilderness, I find something more dear and connate[1] than in streets or villages. In the tranquil landscape, and especially in the distant line of the horizon, man beholds somewhat as beautiful as his own nature.

The greatest delight which the fields and woods minister is the suggestion of an occult[2] relation between man and the vegetable. I am not alone and unacknowledged. They nod to me, and I to them. The waving of the boughs in the storm is new to me and old. It takes me by surprise, and yet is

[1] **connate**: close, sympathetic.
[2] **occult**: hidden, concealed.

not unknown. Its effect is like that of a higher thought or a better emotion coming over me, when I deemed I was thinking justly or doing right.

Yet it is certain that the power to produce this delight does not reside in nature, but in man, or in a harmony of both. It is necessary to use these pleasures with great temperance. For nature is not always tricked[3] in holiday attire, but the same scene which yesterday breathed perfume and glittered as for the frolic of the nymphs is overspread with melancholy today. Nature always wears the colors of the spirit. To a man laboring under calamity, the heat of his own fire hath sadness in it. Then there is a kind of contempt of the landscape felt by him who has just lost by death a dear friend. The sky is less grand as it shuts down over less worth in the population.

[3] **tricked**: dressed up.

For Discussion

1. Emerson's prose is not easy reading; each sentence is made to bear a heavy load of mean-

ABOUT THE AUTHOR • Nearly a century after his death, **Ralph Waldo Emerson** (1803–1882) remains for many the greatest American thinker and writer. Descended from early Puritans, Emerson was inspired by Oriental and European thought as well as by the common sense and rugged wisdom of New England. He began his career as a teacher and minister, but by 1832 he had left the Unitarian pulpit to study and to write. Although deeply concerned with social questions, such as the abolition movement, Emerson was not an activist like his friend Thoreau. As poet, essayist, and lecturer, he served more as a prophet, a seeker after truth, a "preacher to the world." In such essays as "The American Scholar" and "Self-Reliance" he preached values that Americans have come to regard as peculiarly their own. Emerson was a dreamer who soared high but retained contact with the earth. He is among the most quoted of the world's great minds.

ing. But again and again what is said is surprising and memorable. Suppose, the essayist suggests, the stars "should appear one night in a thousand years." How would that appearance affect us? He implies a contrast between the world wherein "Miller owns this field, Locke that," and the world that an extremely sensitive person — a poet — perceives. Clarify the distinction between the two views of nature. What is the one calamity that could befall the essayist, the loss of which nature could not repair? Why does he make that exception?

2. Notice the similarities between the ideas expressed in this celebrated essay and in Wordsworth's great poem written some thirty or forty years earlier. In the world of nature, Emerson reports, "I have enjoyed a perfect exhilaration. I am glad to the brink of fear." Wordsworth wrote:

> "Nature never did betray
> The heart that loved her; 'tis her privilege,
> Through all the years of this our life, to lead
> From joy to joy...."

Again, Emerson writes that "To speak truly, few adult persons can see nature." Would Wordsworth have agreed? Support your answer specifically. Would the English poet have agreed with Emerson's assertion that "The flowers, the animals, the mountains, reflected the wisdom of [the wisest man's] best hour, as much as they had delighted the simplicity of his childhood" (page 420)?

3. **Tone.** *Tone* refers to the attitude that a speaker takes toward what he is saying; accordingly, adjectives like *angry, outraged, indignant, jubilant, ironic, amused,* and *solemn* may appropriately be used to describe the tone of a particular piece of writing. Often, as in this essay, the author and the speaker whose attitude determines the tone are one (whereas in a play, tones vary among many speakers, but the author himself never speaks). Tone is conveyed primarily by diction. If I refer to the *cold, bleak, distant* stars overhead that make me feel *tiny* and *unimportant,* I am conveying a different attitude toward the subject of stars than is Emerson when he speaks of "these envoys of beauty," lighting "the universe with their admonishing smile." Consider the first paragraph of the essay. Which words go farthest toward revealing the attitude the writer is taking toward his subject? What is the tone of Emerson's initial remarks about the natural world?

For Composition

Emerson's distinctive prose style is characterized not only by sentences heavily packed with meaning, but also by such devices as abundance of metaphor (stars are "envoys of beauty"; the air is a "cordial"), the unexpected juxtaposition of abstract and concrete words, or of sublime and humble ones ("This [property of natural beauty] is the best part of these men's farms, yet to this their warranty-deeds give no title"), and a fondness for aphorisms, or brief memorable generalizations ("Nature always wears the colors of the spirit").

1. **Analysis.** Analyze Emerson's prose style in a coherent and unified composition that makes use of a number of specific illustrations to support the characteristics noted. You may choose to end your essay by drawing certain conclusions about the effectiveness of his style.

2. **Comparison and Contrast.** Reconsider the ideas expressed in Wordsworth's "Tintern Abbey," and in a coherent essay compare and contrast them with those expressed in Emerson's "Nature."

Words and Allusions

WORDS IN CONTEXT. In different contexts (page 131) the word *nature* and its derivatives take on different meanings.

1. What does *nature* mean in the following contexts: the beauties of *nature,* human *nature,* the *nature* of the thing, an evil *nature,* the laws of *nature?*

2. Explain the use of the word *natural* in each of the following: *natural* ability, *natural* resources, *natural* boundaries, *natural* rights, *natural* causes, *natural* science. What is the difference between *natural* and *unnatural* behavior?

Give Me the Splendid Silent Sun

WALT WHITMAN

The debate between the virtues of city and country life has gone on for centuries. On the basis of his essay "Nature," Emerson was clearly on the side of the country, with its solitude, peace, and opportunities to observe God's handiwork in order to restore one's soul. Emerson's is not the only possible attitude, however. His nineteenth-century contemporary, Walt Whitman, reveals early in the following poem a sensitivity to the appeal of nature, yet his temperament finally resists that appeal, for what seem to him good reasons.

1

Give me the splendid silent sun with all his beams full-dazzling,
Give me juicy autumnal fruit ripe and red from the orchard,
Give me a field where the unmow'd grass grows,
Give me an arbor, give me the trellis'd grape,
Give me fresh corn and wheat, give me serene-moving animals teaching content,   5
Give me nights perfectly quiet as on high plateaus west of the Mississippi, and I
      looking up at the stars,
Give me odorous at sunrise a garden of beautiful flowers where I can walk undis-
      turb'd,
Give me for marriage a sweet-breath'd woman of whom I should never tire,
Give me a perfect child, give me away aside from the noise of the world a rural
      domestic life,
Give me to warble spontaneous songs recluse by myself, for my own ears only,   10
Give me solitude, give me Nature, give me again O Nature your primal* sanities!

These demanding to have them, (tired with ceaseless excitement, and rack'd by the
      war-strife,)
These to procure incessantly asking, rising in cries from my heart,
While yet incessantly asking still I adhere to my city,
Day upon day and year upon year O city, walking your streets,   15
Where you hold me enchain'd a certain time refusing to give me up,
Yet giving to make me glutted, enrich'd of soul, you give me forever faces;
(O I see what I sought to escape, confronting, reversing my cries,
I see my own soul trampling down what it ask'd for.)

2

Keep your splendid silent sun,   20
Keep your woods O Nature, and the quiet places by the woods,
Keep your fields of clover and timothy, and your corn fields and orchards,
Keep the blossoming buckwheat fields where the Ninth-month* bees hum;
Give me faces and streets — give me these phantoms incessant and endless along the
      trottoirs!*

11. **primal**: first, most important.   23. **Ninth-month**: September.   24. **trottoirs**: sidewalks.

Give me interminable eyes — give me women — give me comrades and lovers by
    the thousand! 25
Let me see new ones every day — let me hold new ones by the hand every day!
Give me such shows —give me the streets of Manhattan!
Give me Broadway, with the soldiers marching — give me the sound of the trum-
    pets and drums!
(The soldiers in companies or regiments — some starting away, flush'd and reckless,
Some, their time up, returning with thinn'd ranks, young, yet very old, worn,
    marching, noticing nothing;) 30
Give me the shores and wharves heavy-fringed with black ships!
O such for me! O an intense life, full to repletion and varied!
The life of the theater, barroom, huge hotel, for me!
The saloon of the steamer! the crowded excursion for me! the torchlight proces-
    sion!
The dense brigade bound for the war, with high piled military wagons following;
People, endless, streaming, with strong voices, passions, pageants, 36
Manhattan streets with their powerful throbs, with beating drums as now,
The endless and noisy chorus, the rustle and clank of muskets, (even the sight of
    the wounded,)
Manhattan crowds, with their turbulent musical chorus!
Manhattan faces and eyes forever for me. 40

Brooklyn Bridge *by the contemporary American painter
Joseph Stella.*

For Discussion

1. The poem is divided into two stanzas. Are the tones of the two stanzas similar? Their content is, of course, utterly different. What appeal do the images in the first stanza have for the speaker? What is it that appeals to him in the images of the second stanza?

2. Is the poem an expression of feeling by someone at present in the city or in the country? How do you know? Lines 12–19 provide the turning point. How is the shift in attitude — "reversing my cries" — that makes up the second stanza accounted for?

3. **Apostrophe.** *Apostrophe*, a figure of speech frequently encountered in poetry, directly addresses something inanimate as though it could hear, or something or someone absent as though it were present. Keats directly addresses, or apostrophizes, the Grecian urn (page 46): "Thou still unravished bride of quietness. . . ." Similarly, Whitman here addresses Nature directly in line 11. Where else in the poem do you find an example of apostrophe? What is the effect of the device? (You may find it helpful to consider the line rewritten with the direct address altered to remove the apostrophe: "Give me solitude, give me Nature, give me again Nature's primal sanities!")

4. Is this poem written in blank verse or free verse? Explain. What are the characteristics of the verse form?

For Composition

To understand a poem fully, it is sometimes helpful to know when it was written. "Give Me the Splendid Silent Sun" was written in 1865.

1. **Exposition.** Explain to what extent the date of composition of "Give Me the Splendid Silent Sun" is reflected in the content. Cite specific lines from the poem to make your explanation clear.

2. **Comparison and Contrast.** In a coherent and unified composition of three or four paragraphs, compare and contrast the arguments in favor of city living and those in favor of country living, using Whitman's poem to suggest strengths and weaknesses on both sides of the issue. What does a confirmed city-dweller find missing in the country? Why is the rural person often suspicious of people from the city?

3. **Argument.** Emerson, who initially was very much impressed with Walt Whitman's poetry, found some of his poems unsatisfying: "I expect [Whitman] to make the songs of the nation," he wrote, "but he seems to be content to make the inventories." In a coherent composition support or refute Emerson's charge against Whitman on the basis of "Give Me the Splendid Silent Sun." (You will want to be sure you know what an inventory is, of course.) Your composition may reasonably take the form, at least in part, of an analysis of Whitman's verse style in order to appreciate why you find his poetry either effective or ineffective.

About the Poet. **Walt Whitman** (1819–1892) has been called by Mark Van Doren "the most original and passionate of American poets." In his free verse, he brought to American literature a new poetic voice that has continued long after his death to echo in the poems of his successors.

Born in Brooklyn, which was then a sparse grouping of villages and farms, Whitman grew up with a deep interest in the creatures of land and ocean. He worked on newspapers as printer and reporter, taught school, and studied literature and philosophy. When his poems first appeared in *Leaves of Grass* in 1855, they were greeted with silence by the common men they celebrated. Before his death, however, he had been accepted by the literate public as "the Good Gray Poet," an authentic voice of America.

The Intruder

CAROLYN KIZER

Nature is by no means always lovable and soothing. Nor is it always beautiful.

My mother — preferring the strange to the tame:
Dove-note, bone marrow, deer dung,
Frog's belly distended with finny young,
Leaf-mold wilderness, hare-bell, toadstool,
Odd, small snakes roving through the leaves,   5
Metallic beetles rambling over stones: all
Wild and natural! — flashed out her instinctive love, and quick, she
Picked up the fluttering, bleeding bat the cat laid at her feet,
And held the little horror to the mirror, where
He gazed on himself, and shrieked like an old screen door far off.   10

Depended from her pinched thumb, each wing
Came clattering down like a small black shutter.
Still tranquil, she began, "It's rather sweet. . . ."
The soft mouse body, the hard feral* glint
In the caught eyes. Then we saw,   15
And recoiled: lice, pallid, yellow,
Nested within the wing-pits, cosily sucked and snoozed.
The thing dropped from her hands, and with its thud,
Swiftly, the cat, with a clean careful mouth
Closed on the soiled webs, growling, took them out to the back stoop.   20

But still, dark blood, a sticky puddle on the floor
Remained, of all my mother's tender, wounding passion
For a whole wild, lost, betrayed and secret life
Among its dens and burrows, its clean stones,
Whose denizens* can turn upon the world   25
With spitting tongue, an odor, talon, claw,
To sting or soil benevolence, alien
As our clumsy traps, our random scatter of shot.
She swept to the kitchen. Turning on the tap,
She washed and washed the pity from her hands.   30

14. **feral**: savage.   25. **denizens**: inhabitants.

The savage beauty of Nature is portrayed in Winslow Homer's painting Fox Hunt, *showing starving crows pursuing a fox who desperately tries to flee through the deep snow.*

For Discussion

1. The mother of the speaker in the poem prefers "the strange to the tame." What are her feelings when she first sees the bat that the cat brings in? What does she do with the bat? What remark does she make? The remark is interrupted. By what?

2. The closing image of the poem explains the mother's initial attitude toward the bat while at the same time dramatizing her feelings about the experience after it has ended. How does she feel toward the "strange" world that the bat sheltered — that gruesome aspect of nature that "cosily sucked and snoozed"?

3. The incident recorded in the poem is a specific instance of a general attribute of wild nature,

> Whose denizens can turn upon the world
> With spitting tongue, an odor, talon, claw,
> To sting or soil benevolence. . . .

Explain the meaning of these crucial lines (25–27). What happens finally to the bat?

4. **Onomatopoeia.** As you know, *onomatopoeia* refers to words that imitate the sounds they describe — *buzz, hum, knock,* and the like. What examples of onomatopoeia do you find in "The Intruder"? What do such words add to the effect of the poem?

For Composition

Tone is expressed primarily by the writer's choice of imagery and diction. The tone of this poem shifts with the shifting attitude of the speaker's mother to the bat she first holds, then releases.

● **Analysis.** Analyze the successive tones of the poem, avoiding such general adjectives as *happy* and *sad* in favor of more precise descriptions like *outraged, angered, repulsed, sympathetic, curious, disgusted,* and the like. Indicate, by quoting specific phrases, the means by which the tone is conveyed as the poem proceeds.

About the Poet. **Carolyn Kizer** (19?–   ) was born in Spokane, Washington, and studied at Sarah Lawrence College and Columbia University. In 1959 she founded the literary magazine *Poetry North West* which features the work of western American poets. She has taught poetry and conducted workshops in New York City and Pakistan, where she served with the Department of State. Recently she has served as program director for literature of the National Council of the Arts. Of her poetry the *Saturday Review* has said: "Her witty urbanity and sophistication cut savagely through all sentimental disguises." Of herself she is reported to have said: "Everyone has faults; mine is writing poems."

Nature and the Needs of Man

If someone says "What a beautiful tree!" what he means by "beautiful" depends on his viewpoint. If he is a botanist he probably means that it is a fine specimen of a particular kind of tree; if he is a lumberman, he may see the tree as good building material; if he is a painter, he sees it as a fine subject for painting. Or, if he views the tree in a religious context, he may mean that the tree symbolizes for him the perfection of God as shown in the world.

Thus man's view of nature is affected by his needs and his beliefs. One of his most important needs is to make sense out of his experience with the world. After his immediate needs of food and shelter are satisfied, such understanding is perhaps his most important need. When man is no longer hungry, he begins to discover a variety of taste pleasures; when he is protected from the elements, he begins to discover ways of making his shelter pleasant, even beautiful. Thus he creates a new need — the need to understand how his various interests are related and what his ultimate interests are. In gratifying that need, he turns to religion and philosophy, ways of relating himself psychologically to the world so that his deep need to organize his interests in nature may be gratified.

We can see this process at work in ancient Greek culture and literature. Homer's *Iliad* contains numerous word-pictures of man in peaceful activity, in contrast to the war that is the main subject of that epic. Each of these vignettes shows man in nature engaged in cultivating the soil and caring for and using his domesticated animals. The ancient Greeks saw nature as something to satisfy their basic needs and interests, yet they also found ways to organize their experience to make sense out of it. They did so by assigning the powers of nature to various gods and goddesses, and they related themselves to the natural world through these deities. Demeter, for example, was goddess of harvest and hearth, the source of food and shelter. Proserpine was goddess of the seasons, and her story explained man's changing experience with the elements.

To believe in one God, however, as opposed to believing in many, is to assert that all man's interests and needs can be reconciled and organized into one unifying need, the need to understand himself and the world he lives in. For everyone until a few hundred years ago, that world was the world of nature. Nowadays there are people who have lived all their lives in large cities without ever having seen what all human beings until recently have always seen — the heavens crowded with stars. Artificial illumination, smog, and other man-made products separate man from such natural phenomena as the stars. But until recently, through all the ages man has existed, "the world he lives in" meant "nature." His conception of God, therefore, included his understanding of nature and his relationship to it.

In the Middle Ages, European thinking was dominated by a belief in original sin. Adam and Eve had disobeyed God, the ultimate power that makes sense out of the world He created. All men inherit that sin and thus fall into error in relating themselves to God's world. God had made that world beautiful, but Satan uses that beauty to tempt man away from God and his true interests. Thus the beauty of nature was regarded as dangerous, and artists could create images of plants and animals only on the capitals of columns in churches or on the margins of prayer books where the curse upon such images would be removed. Moreover, the earth itself suffered from man's original sin, falling into a process of steady aging and decay. Mountains were thought hideous, the wrinkles of an aging earth.

About four hundred years ago, however, a new conception of nature began to emerge. Part of the medieval conception had been that Jesus had died to redeem man from his own evil nature and from the fallen world in a spiritual life thereafter. The new conception was that man could help redeem himself, in part at least, by understanding nature, by studying it and using it. And the notion soon appeared that the world itself, instead of reflecting man's evil nature, reflected the glory and perfection of God. Thus God had created mountains as something sublimely beautiful for man to enjoy as symbols of His majesty. Nature could be used to gratify man's interests as well as his needs, for in nature man could detect the power of God that made sense out of his world.

Seen in this light, the natural world became valuable for its own sake. Painters began to paint landscapes, flowers, fruit, vegetables, fish. A systematic investigation of nature was begun that became modern science. By the end of the eighteenth century, it appeared to radical thinkers that all man's powers derived from nature and that original sin was merely a way of indicating man's failure to attune himself perfectly to nature.

But within the nineteenth century yet another view of nature developed. Close examination of the natural world revealed that man's interests and nature's are different. In its drive for survival nature does not observe the ethical and spiritual considerations with which man shapes his world. Nature, in the words of Tennyson, is "red in tooth and claw," whereas man is set above and apart from nature because of his intellectual and spiritual culture. Given that division, God is conceived of in various ways — sometimes as the power that unifies man and nature in a way that can be experienced but not intellectually grasped, sometimes as identical with human culture and its history. And artists depict the natural world in ways that reflect man's purely human interests. Separated from nature, man now sees it as something that is at once the source of his frustrations and gratifications — wintry blasts that block his actions and summer sunshine that provides refreshment and pleasure. Thus, modern religion and philosophy, art and literature have become continuously more deeply absorbed with what is purely human, with those qualities of man that set him apart from nature. Nature is seen only as providing the material for realizing those qualities.

1. According to this essay, what changes have occurred in man's view of nature?
2. From your own observation, what would you say is man's view of nature today?

Hook

WALTER VAN TILBURG CLARK

Man shares this planet with thousands and hundreds of thousands of other kinds of creatures. How might the world look from their point of view — a nonhuman point of view different from our own? In providing an answer to that question in the story that follows, Walter Van Tilburg Clark tells us much about the laws of nature by which every being, man included, lives.

I

Hook, the hawks' child, was hatched in a dry spring among the oaks beside the seasonal river, and was struck from the nest early. In the drouth his single-willed parents had to extend their hunting ground by more than twice, for the ground creatures upon which they fed died and dried by the hundreds. The range became too great for them to wish to return and feed Hook, and when they had lost interest in each other they drove Hook down into the sand and brush and went back to solitary courses over the bleaching hills.

Unable to fly yet, Hook crept over the ground, challenging all large movements with recoiled head, erected, rudimentary wings, and the small rasp of his clattering beak. It was during this time of abysmal ignorance and continual fear that his eyes took on the first quality of a hawk, that of being wide, alert, and challenging. He dwelt, because of his helplessness, among the rattling brush which grew between the oaks and the river. Even in his thickets and near the water, the white sun was the dominant presence. Except in the dawn, when the land wind stirred, or in the late afternoon, when the sea wind became strong enough to penetrate the half-mile inland to this turn in the river, the sun was the major force, and everything was dry and motionless under it. The brush, small plants and trees alike husbanded[1] the little moisture at their hearts; the moving creatures waited for dark, when sometimes the sea fog came over and made a fine, soundless rain which relieved them.

The two spacious sounds of his life environed Hook at this time. One was the great rustle of the slopes of yellowed wild wheat, with over it the chattering rustle of the leaves of the California oaks, already as harsh and individually tremulous as in autumn. The other was the distant whisper of the foaming edge of the Pacific, punctuated by the hollow shoring[2] of the waves. But these Hook did not yet hear, for he was attuned by fear and hunger to the small, spasmodic rustlings of live things. Dry, shrunken, and nearly starved, and with his plumage delayed, he snatched at beetles, dragging in the sand to catch them. When swifter and stronger birds and animals did not reach them first, which was seldom, he ate the small, silver fish left in the mud by the failing river. He watched, with nearly chattering beak, the quick, thin lizards pause, very alert, and raise and lower themselves, but could not catch them because he had to raise his wings to move rapidly, which startled them.

Only one sight and sound not of his world of microscopic necessity was forced upon Hook. That was the flight of the big

[1] **husbanded:** used carefully.
[2] **shoring:** hitting the shore.

gulls from the beaches, which sometimes, in quealing play, came spinning back over the foothills and the river bed. For some inherited reason, the big, ship-bodied birds did not frighten Hook, but angered him. Small and chewed-looking, with his wide, already yellowing eyes glaring up at them, he would stand in an open place on the sand in the sun and spread his shaping wings and clatter his bill like shaken dice. Hook was furious about the swift, easy passage of gulls.

His first opportunity to leave off living like a ground owl came accidentally. He was standing in the late afternoon in the red light under the thicket, his eyes half-filmed with drowse and the stupefaction of starvation, when suddenly something beside him moved, and he struck, and killed a field mouse driven out of the wheat by thirst. It was a poor mouse, shriveled and lice-ridden, but in striking, Hook had tasted blood, which raised nest memories and restored his nature. With started neck plumage and shining eyes, he tore and fed. When the

mouse was devoured, Hook had entered hoarse adolescence. He began to seek with a conscious appetite, and to move more readily out of shelter. Impelled by the blood appetite, so glorious after his long preservation upon the flaky and bitter stuff of bugs, he ventured even into the wheat in the open sun beyond the oaks, and discovered the small trails and holes among the roots. With his belly often partially filled with flesh, he grew rapidly in strength and will. His eyes were taking on their final change, their yellow growing deeper and more opaque, their stare more constant, their challenge less desperate. Once during this transformation, he surprised a ground squirrel, and although he was ripped and wing-bitten and could not hold his prey, he was not dismayed by the conflict, but exalted. Even while the wing was still drooping and the pinions[1] not grown back, he was excited by other ground squirrels and pursued them futilely, and was angered by their dusty escapes. He realized that his

[1] **pinions**: end parts of a bird's wings.

ABOUT THE AUTHOR • Although **Walter Van Tilburg Clark** (1909–1971) set most of his fiction in the far West, he was born in New York State, studied in New England, and taught for ten years in New York. While he was teaching he was also writing, and by 1945 he had published the novel *The City of Trembling Leaves,* a number of short stories, and *The Ox-Bow Incident,* which has become a contemporary classic both as a novel and as a film. He then turned to full-time writing, but he published relatively little after his third novel, *The Track of the Cat,* in 1950. Clark made few public appearances. Among things he disliked he once listed many that relate to contemporary urban life: "popular music, slanted journalism, advertising English, radio serials, big cities, hurry, political speeches, cover girls in the flesh or on paper, and all theories, political, historical, religious, or literary, which pretend to authority and finality." He found more of value in the mountains and forests of Nevada. He moved there in 1962 and became writer-in-residence at the University of Nevada in Reno.

world was a great arena for killing, and felt the magnificence of it.

The two major events of Hook's young life occurred in the same day. A little after dawn he made the customary essay and succeeded in flight. A little before sunset, he made his first sustained flight of over two hundred yards, and at its termination struck and slew a great buck squirrel whose thrashing and terrified gnawing and squealing gave him a wild delight. When he had gorged on the strong meat, Hook stood upright, and in his eyes was the stare of the hawk, never flagging in intensity but never swelling beyond containment. After that the stare had only to grow more deeply challenging and more sternly controlled as his range and deadliness increased. There was no change in kind. Hook had mastered the first of the three hungers which are fused into the single, flaming will of a hawk, and he had experienced the second.

The third and consummating hunger did not awaken in Hook until the following spring, when the exultation of space had grown slow and steady in him, so that he swept freely with the wind over the miles of coastal foothills, circling, and ever in sight of the sea, and used without struggle the warm currents lifting from the slopes, and no longer desired to scream at the range of his vision, but intently sailed above his shadow swiftly climbing to meet him on the hillsides, sinking away and rippling across the brush-grown canyons.

That spring the rains were long, and Hook sat for hours, hunched and angry under their pelting, glaring into the fogs of the river valley, and killed only small, drenched things flooded up from their tunnels. But when the rains had dissipated, and there were sun and sea wind again, the game ran plentiful, the hills were thick and shining green, and the new river flooded about the boulders where battered turtles climbed up to shrink and sleep. Hook then was

scorched by the third hunger. Ranging farther, often forgetting to kill and eat, he sailed for days with growing rage, and woke at night clattering on his dead tree limb, and struck and struck and struck at the porous wood of the trunk, tearing it away. After days, in the draft of a coastal canyon miles below his own hills, he came upon the acrid taint he did not know but had expected, and sailing down it, felt his neck plumes rise and his wings quiver so that he swerved unsteadily. He saw the unmated female perched upon the tall and jagged stump of a tree that had been shorn by storm, and he stopped, as if upon game. But she was older than he, and wary of the gripe of his importunity, and banked off screaming, and he screamed also at the intolerable delay.

At the head of the canyon, the screaming pursuit was crossed by another male with a great wing-spread, and the light golden in the fringe of his plumage. But his more skillful opening played him false against the ferocity of the twice-balked Hook. His rising maneuver for position was cut short by Hook's wild, upward swoop, and at the blow he raked desperately and tumbled off to the side. Dropping, Hook struck him again, struggled to clutch, but only raked and could not hold, and, diving, struck once more in passage, and then beat up, yelling triumph, and saw the crippled antagonist side-slip away, half-tumble once, as the ripped wing failed to balance, then steady and glide obliquely into the cover of brush on the canyon side. Beating hard and stationary in the wind above the bush that covered his competitor, Hook waited an instant, but when the bush was still, screamed again, and let himself go off with the current, reseeking, infuriated by the burn of his own wounds, the thin choke-thread of the acrid taint.

On a hilltop projection of stone two miles inland, he struck her down, gripping her

"Hook was master of the sky and the hills of his range. His flight became a lovely and certain thing. . . . He could sail for hours. . . ."

rustling body with his talons, beating her wings down with his wings, belting her head when she whimpered or thrashed, and at last clutching her neck with his hook and, when her coy struggles had given way to stillness, succeeded.

In the early summer, Hook drove the three young ones from their nest, and went back to lone circling above his own range. He was complete.

II

Throughout that summer and the cool, growthless weather of the winter, when the gales blew in the river canyon and the ocean piled upon the shore, Hook was master of the sky and the hills of his range. His flight became a lovely and certain thing, so that he played with the treacherous currents of the air with a delicate ease surpassing that of the gulls. He could sail for hours, searching the blanched grasses below him with telescopic eyes, gaining height against the wind, descending in mile-long, gently declining swoops when he curved and rode back, and never beating either wing. At the swift passage of his shadow within their vision, gophers, ground squirrels, and rab-

bits froze, or plunged gibbering into their tunnels beneath matted turf. Now, when he struck, he killed easily in one hard-knuckled blow. Occasionally, in sport, he soared up over the river and drove the heavy and weaponless gulls downstream again, until they would no longer venture inland.

There was nothing which Hook feared now, and his spirit was wholly belligerent, swift and sharp, like his gaze. Only the mixed smells and incomprehensible activities of the people at the Japanese farmer's home, inland of the coastwise highway and south of the bridge across Hook's river, troubled him. The smells were strong, unsatisfactory and never clear, and the people, though they behaved foolishly, constantly running in and out of their built-up holes, were large, and appeared capable, with fearless eyes looking up at him, so that he instinctively swerved aside from them. He cruised over their yard, their gardens, and their bean fields, but he would not alight close to their buildings.

But this one area of doubt did not interfere with his life. He ignored it, save to look upon it curiously as he crossed, his afternoon shadow sliding in an instant over the chicken-and-crate-cluttered yard, up the side of the unpainted barn, and then out again smoothly, just faintly, liquidly rippling over the furrows and then over the stubble of the grazing slopes. When the season was dry, and the dead earth blew on the fields, he extended his range to satisfy his great hunger, and again narrowed it when the fields were once more alive with the minute movements he could not only see but anticipate.

Four times that year he was challenged by other hawks blowing up from behind the coastal hills to scud[1] down his slopes, but two of these he slew in mid-air, and saw hurtle down to thump on the ground and lie still while he circled, and a third, whose wing he tore, he followed closely to earth and beat to death in the grass, making the crimson jet out from its breast and neck into the pale wheat. The fourth was a strong flier and experienced fighter, and theirs was a long, running battle, with brief, rising flurries of striking and screaming, from which down and plumage soared off.

Here, for the first time, Hook felt doubts, and at moments wanted to drop away from the scoring, burning talons and the twisted hammer strokes of the strong beak, drop away shrieking, and take cover and be still. In the end, when Hook, having outmaneuvered his enemy and come above him, wholly in control, and going with the wind, tilted and plunged for the death rap, the other, in desperation, threw over on his back and struck up. Talons locked, beaks raking, they dived earthward. The earth grew and spread under them amazingly, and they were not fifty feet above it when Hook, feeling himself turning toward the underside, tore free and beat up again on heavy, wrenched wings. The other, stroking swiftly, and so close to down that he lost wing plumes to a bush, righted himself and planed up, but flew on lumberingly between the hills and did not return. Hook

[1] **scud:** move swiftly.

screamed the triumph, and made a brief pretense of pursuit, but was glad to return, slow and victorious, to his dead tree.

In all these encounters Hook was injured, but experienced only the fighter's pride and exultation from the sting of wounds received in successful combat. And in each of them he learned a new skill. Each time the wounds healed quickly, and left him a more dangerous bird.

In the next spring, when the rains and the night chants of the little frogs were past, the third hunger returned upon Hook with a new violence. In his quest, he came into the taint of a young hen. Others too were drawn by the unnerving perfume, but only one of them, the same with which Hook had fought his great battle, was a worthy competitor. This hunter drove off two, while two others, game but neophytes,[2] were glad enough that Hook's impatience would not permit him to follow and kill. Then the battle between the two champions fled inland, and was a tactical marvel, but Hook lodged the neck-breaking blow, and struck again as they dropped past the treetops. The blood had already begun to pool on the gray, fallen foliage as Hook flapped up between branches, too spent to cry his victory. Yet his hunger would not let him rest until, late in the second day, he drove the female to ground, among the laurels of a strange river canyon.

When the two fledglings of this second brood had been driven from the nest, and Hook had returned to his own range, he was not only complete, but supreme. He slept without concealment on his bare limb, and did not open his eyes when, in the night, the heavy-billed cranes coughed in the shadows below him.

III

The turning point of Hook's career came that autumn, when the brush in the canyons

[2] **neophytes:** beginners.

rustled dryly and the hills, mowed close by the cattle, smoked under the wind as if burning. One midafternoon, when the black clouds were torn on the rim of the sea and the surf flowered white and high on the rocks, raining in over the low cliffs, Hook rode the wind diagonally across the river mouth. His great eyes, focused for small things stirring in the dust and leaves, over-looked so large and slow a movement as that of the Japanese farmer rising from the brush and lifting the two black eyes of his shotgun. Too late Hook saw and, startled, swerved, but wrongly. The surf muffled the reports, and nearly without sound, Hook felt the minute whips of the first shot, and the astounding, breath-breaking blow of the second.

Beating his good wing, tasting the blood that quickly swelled into his beak, he tumbled off with the wind and struck into the thickets on the far side of the river mouth. The branches tore him. Wild with rage, he thrust up and clattered his beak, challenging, but when he had fallen over twice, he knew that the trailing wing would not carry, and then heard the boots of the hunter among the stones in the river bed and, seeing him loom at the edge of the bushes, crept back among the thickest brush and was still. When he saw the boots stand before him, he reared back, lifting his good wing and cocking his head for the serpent-like blow, his beak open but soundless, his great eyes hard and very shining. The boots passed on. The Japanese farmer, who believed that he had lost chickens, and who had cunningly observed Hook's flight for many afternoons, until he could plot it, did not greatly want a dead hawk.

When Hook could hear nothing but the surf and the wind in the thicket, he let the sickness and shock overcome him. The fine film of the inner lid dropped over his big eyes. His heart beat frantically, so that it made the plumage of his shot-aching breast throb. His own blood throttled his breath-

ing. But these things were nothing compared to the lightning of pain in his left shoulder, where the shot had bunched, shattering the airy bones so the pinions trailed on the ground and could not be lifted. Yet, when a sparrow lit in the bush over him, Hook's eyes flew open again, hard and challenging, his good wing was lifted and his beak strained open. The startled sparrow darted piping out over the river.

Throughout that night, while the long clouds blew across the stars and the wind shook the bushes about him, and throughout the next day, while the clouds still blew and massed until there was no gleam of sun-light on the sand bar, Hook remained sta-tionary, enduring his sickness. In the second evening, the rains began. First there was a long, running patter of drops upon the beach and over the dry trees and bushes. At dusk there came a heavier squall, which did not die entirely, but slacked off to a con-tinual, spaced splashing of big drops, and then returned with the front of the storm. In long, misty curtains, gust by gust, the rain swept over the sea, beating down its heaving, and coursed up the beach. The little jets of dust ceased to rise about the drops in the fields, and the mud began to gleam. Among the boulders of the river bed, darkling pools grew slowly.

Still Hook stood behind his tree from the wind, only gentle drops reaching him, fall-ing from the upper branches and then again from the brush. His eyes remained closed, and he could still taste his own blood in his mouth, though it had ceased to come up freshly. Out beyond him, he heard the storm changing. As rain conquered the sea, the heave of the surf became a hushed sound, often lost in the crying of the wind. Then gradually, as the night turned toward morn-ing, the wind also was broken by the rain. The crying became fainter, the rain settled toward steadiness, and the creep of the waves could be heard again, quiet and reg-ular upon the beach.

At dawn there was no wind and no sun, but everywhere the roaring of the vertical, relentless rain. Hook then crept among the rapid drippings of the bushes, dragging his torn sail, seeking better shelter. He stopped often and stood with the shutters of film drawn over his eyes. At midmorning he found a little cave under a ledge at the base of the sea cliff. Here, lost without branches and leaves about him, he settled to await improvement.

When, at midday of the third day, the rain stopped altogether, and the sky opened before a small, fresh wind, letting light through to glitter upon a tremulous sea, Hook was so weak that his good wing trailed also to prop him upright, and his open eyes were lusterless. But his wounds were hardened, and he felt the return of hunger. Beyond his shelter, he heard the gulls flying in great numbers and crying their joy at the cleared air. He could even hear, from the fringe of the river, the ecstatic and unstinted bubblings and chirpings of the small birds. The grassland, he felt, would be full of the stirring anew of the close-bound life, the undrowned insects clicking as they dried out, the snakes slithering down, heads half erect, into the grasses where the mice, gophers, and ground squirrels ran and stopped and chewed and licked themselves smoother and drier.

With the aid of this hunger, and on the crutches of his wings, Hook came down to stand in the sun beside his cave, whence he could watch the beach. Before him, in ellipses on tilting planes, the gulls flew. The surf was rearing again, and beginning to shelve and hiss on the sand. Through the white foam-writing it left, the long-billed pipers twinkled in bevies,[1] escaping each wave, then racing down after it to plunge their fine drills into the minute double holes were the sand crabs bubbled. In the third row of breakers two seals lifted sleek, streaming heads and barked, and over them,

[1] **bevies**: groups.

trailing his spider legs, a great crane flew south. Among the stones at the foot of the cliff, small red and green crabs made a little, continuous rattling and knocking. The cliff swallows glittered and twanged on aerial forays.

The afternoon began auspiciously for Hook also. One of the two gulls which came squabbling above him dropped a freshly caught fish to the sand. Quickly Hook was upon it. Gripping it, he raised his good wing and cocked his head with open beak at the many gulls which had circled and come down at once toward the fall of the fish. The gulls sheered off, cursing raucously. Left alone on the sand, Hook devoured the fish and, after resting in the sun, withdrew again to his shelter.

IV

In the succeeding days, between rains, he foraged on the beach. He learned to kill and crack the small green crabs. Along the edge of the river mouth, he found the drowned bodies of mice and squirrels and even sparrows. Twice he managed to drive feeding gulls from their catch, charging upon them with buffeting wing and clattering beak. He grew stronger slowly, but the shot sail continued to drag. Often, at the choking thought of soaring and striking and the good, hot-blood kill, he strove to take off, but only the one wing came up, winnowing with a hiss, and drove him over onto his side in the sand. After these futile trials, he would rage and clatter. But gradually he learned to believe that he could not fly, that his life must now be that of the dis-

437

charged nestling again. Denied the joy of space, without which the joy of loneliness was lost, the joy of battle and killing, the blood lust, became his whole concentration. It was his hope, as he charged feeding gulls, that they would turn and offer battle, but they never did. The sandpipers, at his approach, fled peeping, or, like a quiver of arrows shot together, streamed out over the surf in a long curve. Once, pent beyond bearing, he disgraced himself by shrieking challenge at the businesslike heron which flew south every evening at the same time. The heron did not even turn his head, but flapped and glided on.

Hook's shame and anger became such that he stood awake at night. Hunger kept him awake also, for these little leavings of the gulls could not sustain his great body in its renewed violence. He became aware that the gulls slept at night in flocks on the sand, each with one leg tucked under him. He discovered also that the curlews and the pipers, often mingling, likewise slept, on the higher remnant of the bar. A sensation of evil delight filled him in the consideration of protracted striking among them.

There was only half of a sick moon in a sky of running but far-separated clouds on the night when he managed to stalk into the center of the sleeping gulls. This was light enough, but so great was his vengeful pleasure that there broke from him a shrill scream of challenge as he first struck. Without the power of flight behind it, the blow was not murderous, and this newly discovered impotence made Hook crazy, so that he screamed again and again as he struck and tore at the felled gull. He slew the one, but was twice knocked over by its heavy flounderings, and all the others rose above him, weaving and screaming, protesting in the thin moonlight. Wakened by their clamor, the wading birds also took wing, startled and plaintive. When the beach was quiet again, the flocks had settled elsewhere, beyond his pitiful range, and he was left alone beside the single kill. It was a disappointing victory. He fed with lowering spirit.

Thereafter, he stalked silently. At sunset he would watch where the gulls settled along the miles of beach, and after dark he would come like a sharp shadow among them, and drive with his hook on all sides of him, till the beatings of a poorly struck victim sent the flock up. Then he would turn vindictively upon the fallen and finish them. In his best night, he killed five from one flock. But he ate only a little from one, for the vigor resulting from occasional repletion strengthened only his ire, which became so great at such a time that food revolted him. It was not the joyous, swift, controlled hunting anger of a sane hawk, but something quite different, which made him dizzy if it continued too long, and left him unsatisfied with any kill.

Then one day, when he had very nearly struck a gull while driving it from a gasping yellowfin, the gull's wing rapped against him as it broke for its running start, and, the trailing wing failing to support him, he was knocked over. He flurried awkwardly in the sand to regain his feet, but his mastery of the beach was ended. Seeing him, in clear sunlight, struggling after the chance blow, the gulls returned about him in a flashing cloud, circling and pecking on the wing. Hook's plumage showed quick little jets of irregularity here and there. He reared back, clattering and erecting the good wing, spreading the great, rusty tail for balance. His eyes shone with a little of the old pleasure. But it died, for he could reach none of them. He was forced to turn and dance awkwardly on the sand, trying to clash bills with each tormentor. They banked up quealing and returned, weaving about him in concentric and overlapping circles. His scream was lost in their clamor, and he appeared merely to be hopping

"Hook screamed the triumph, and made a brief pretense of pursuit, but was glad to return, slow and victorious, to his dead tree."

clumsily with his mouth open. Again he fell sideways. Before he could right himself, he was bowled over, and a second time, and lay on his side, twisting his neck to reach them and clappering in blind fury, and was struck three times by three successive gulls, shrieking their flock triumph.

Finally he managed to roll to his breast, and to crouch with his good wing spread wide and the other stretched nearly as far, so that he extended like a gigantic moth, only his snake head, with its now silent scimitar,[1] erect. One great eye blazed under its level brow, but where the other had been was a shallow hole from which thin blood trickled to his russet gap.

In this crouch, by short stages, stopping repeatedly to turn and drive the gulls up, Hook dragged into the river canyon and under the stiff cover of the bitter-leafed laurel. There the gulls left him, soaring up

[1] **scimitar:** curved sword (*here,* meaning his pointed beak).

with great clatter of their valor. Till nearly sunset Hook, broken spirited and enduring his hardening eye socket, heard them celebrating over the waves.

When his will was somewhat replenished, and his empty eye socket had stopped the twitching and vague aching which had forced him often to roll ignominiously to rub it in the dust, Hook ventured from the protective lacing of his thicket. He knew fear again, and the challenge of his remaining eye was once more strident, as in adolescence. He dared not return to the beaches, and with a new, weak hunger, the home hunger, enticing him, made his way by short hunting journeys back to the wild wheat slopes and the crisp oaks. There was in Hook an unwonted sensation now, that of the ever-neighboring possibility of death. This sensation was beginning, after his period as a mad bird on the beach, to solidify him into his last stage of life. When, during his slow homeward passage, the gulls wafted inland over him, watching the earth with curious, miserish eyes, he did not cower, but neither did he challenge, either by opened beak or by raised shoulder. He merely watched carefully, learning his first lessons in observing the world with one eye.

At first the familiar surroundings of the bend in the river and the tree with the dead limb to which he could not ascend, aggravated his humiliation, but in time, forced to live cunningly and half-starved, he lost much of his savage pride. At the first flight of a strange hawk over his realm, he was wild at his helplessness, and kept twisting his head like an owl, or spinning in the grass like a small and feathered dervish,[1] to keep the hateful beauty of the wind-rider in sight. But in the succeeding weeks, as one after another coasted his beat, his resentment declined, and when one of the raiders, a haughty yearling,[2] sighted his up-staring eye, and plunged and struck him dreadfully, and failed to kill him only because he dragged under a thicket in time, the second of his great hungers was gone. He had no longer the true lust to kill, no joy of battle, but only the poor desire to fill his belly.

Then truly he lived in the wheat and the brush like a ground owl, ridden with ground lice, dusty or muddy, ever half-starved, forced to sit for hours by small holes for petty and unsatisfying kills. Only once during the final months before his end did he make a kill where the breath of danger recalled his valor, and then the danger was such as a hawk with wings and eyes would scorn. Waiting beside a gopher hole, surrounded by the high, yellow grass, he saw the head emerge, and struck, and was amazed that there writhed in his clutch the neck and dusty coffin-skull of a rattlesnake. Holding his grip, Hook saw the great, thick body slither up after, the tip an erect,

strident blur, and writhe on the dirt of the gopher's mound. The weight of the snake pushed Hook about, and once threw him down, and the rising and falling whine of the rattles made the moment terrible, but the vaulted mouth, gaping from the closeness of Hook's gripe, so that the pale, envenomed sabers stood out free, could not reach him. When Hook replaced the grip of his beak with the grip of his talons, and was free to strike again and again at the base of the head, the struggle was over. Hook tore and fed on the fine, watery flesh, and left the tattered armor and the long, jointed bone for the marching ants.

When the heavy rains returned, he ate well during the period of the first escapes from flooded burrows, and then well enough, in a vulture's way, on the drowned creatures. But as the rains lingered, and the burrows hung full of water, and there were no insects in the grass and no small birds sleeping in the thickets, he was constantly hungry, and finally unbearably hungry. His sodden and ground-broken plumage stood out raggedly about him, so that he looked fat, even bloated, but underneath it his skin clung to his bones. Save for his great talons and clappers, and the rain in his down, he would have been like a handful of air. He often stood for a long time under some bush or ledge, heedless of the drip, his one eye filmed over, his mind neither asleep or awake, but between. The gurgle and swirl of the brimming river, and the sound of chunks of the bank cut away to splash and dissolve in the already muddy flood, became familiar to him, and yet a torment, as if that great, ceaselessly working power of water ridiculed his frailty, within which only the faintest spark of valor still glimmered. The last two nights before the rain ended, he huddled under the floor of the bridge on the coastal highway, and heard the palpitant[3] thunder of motors swell and

---

[1] **dervish**: member of a Muslim religious sect who practice whirling as a religious act.
[2] **yearling**: one-year-old.
[3] **palpitant**: vibrating.

roar over him. The trucks shook the bridge so that Hook, even in his famished lassitude,[1] would sometimes open his one great eye wide and startled.

V

After the rains, when things became full again, bursting with growth and sound, the trees swelling, the thickets full of song and chatter, the fields, turning green in the sun, alive with rustling passages, and the moonlit nights strained with the song of the peepers all up and down the river and in the pools in the fields, Hook had to bear the return of the one hunger left him. At times this made him so wild that he forgot himself and screamed challenge from the open ground. The fretfulness of it spoiled his hunting, which was now entirely a matter of patience. Once he was in despair, and lashed himself through the grass and thickets, trying to rise when that virgin scent drifted for a few moments above the current of his own river. Then, breathless, his beak agape, he saw the strong suitor ride swiftly down on the wind over him, and heard afar the screaming fuss of the harsh wooing in the alders.[2] For that moment even the battle heart beat in him again. The rim of his good eye was scarlet, and a little bead of new blood stood in the socket of the other. With beak and talon, he ripped at a fallen log, and made loam and leaves fly from about it.

But the season of love passed over to the nesting season, and Hook's love hunger, unused, shriveled in him with the others, and there remained in him only one stern quality befitting a hawk, and that the negative one, the remnant, the will to endure. He resumed his patient, plotted hunting, now along a field of the Japanese farmer, but ever within reach of the river thickets.

Growing tough and dry again as the summer advanced, inured to the family of the farmer, whom he saw daily, stooping and scraping with sticks in the ugly, open rows of their fields, where no lovely grass rustled and no life stirred save the shameless gulls, which walked at the heels of the workers, gobbling the worms and grubs as they turned up, Hook became nearly content with his shard[3] of life. The only longing or resentment to pierce him was that which he suffered occasionally when forced to hide at the edge of the mile-long bean field from the wafted cruising and the restive, down-bent gaze of one of his own kind. For the rest, he was without flame, a snappish, dust-colored creature, fading into the grasses he trailed through, and suited to his petty ways.

At the end of that summer, for the second time in his four years, Hook underwent a drouth. The equinoctial[4] period passed without a rain. The laurel and the rabbit-brush dropped dry leaves. The foliage of the oaks shriveled and curled. Even the night fogs in the river canyon failed. The farmer's red cattle on the hillside lowed constantly, and could not feed on the dusty stubble. Grass fires broke out along the highway, and ate fast in the wind, filling the hollows with the smell of smoke, and died in the dirt of the shorn hills. The river made no sound. Scum grew on its vestigial pools, and turtles died and stank among the rocks. The dust rode before the wind, and ascended and flowered to nothing between the hills, and every sunset was red with the dust in the air. The people in the farmer's house quarreled, and even struck one another. Birds were silent, and only the hawks flew much. The animals lay breathing hard for very long spells, and ran and crept jerkily. Their flanks were fallen in, and their eyes were red.

---

[1] **lassitude**: weakness, weariness.
[2] **alders**: trees of the birch family.

[3] **shard**: fragment.
[4] **equinoctial**: occurring during the equinox, September 22–23.

At first Hook gorged at the fringe of the grass fires on the multitudes of tiny things that came running and squeaking. But thereafter there were the blackened strips on the hills, and little more in the thin, crackling grass. He found mice and rats, gophers and ground squirrels, and even rabbits, dead in the stubble and under the thickets, but so dry and fleshless that only a faint smell rose from them, even on the sunny days. He starved on them. By early December he had wearily stalked the length of the eastern foothills, hunting at night to escape the voracity of his own kind, resting often upon his wings. The queer trail of his short steps and great horned toes zigzagged in the dust and was erased by the wind at dawn. He was nearly dead, and could make no sound through the horn funnels of his clappers.

Then one night the dry wind brought him, with the familiar, lifeless dust, another familiar scent, troublesome, mingled and unclear. In his vision-dominated brain he remembered the swift circle of his flight a year past, crossing in one segment, his shadow beneath him, a yard cluttered with crates and chickens, a gray barn and then again the plowed land and the stubble. Traveling faster than he had for days, impatient of his shrunken sweep, Hook came down to the farm. In the dark wisps of cloud blown among the stars over him, but no moon, he stood outside the wire of the chicken run. The scent of fat and blooded birds reached him from the shelter, and also within the enclosure was water. At the breath of the water, Hook's gorge contracted, and his tongue quivered and clove in its groove of horn. But there was the wire. He stalked its perimeter and found no opening. He beat it with his good wing, and felt it cut but not give. He wrenched at it with his beak in many places, but could not tear it. Finally, in a fury which drove the thin blood through him, he leaped repeatedly against it, beating and

clawing. He was thrown back from the last leap as from the first, but in it he had risen so high as to clutch with his beak at the top wire. While he lay on his breast on the ground, the significance of this came upon him.

Again he leapt, clawed up the wire, and, as he would have fallen, made even the dead wing bear a little. He grasped the top and tumbled within. There again he rested flat, searching the dark with quick-turning head. There was no sound or motion but the throb of his own body. First he drank at the chill metal trough hung for the chickens. The water was cold, and loosened his tongue and his tight throat, but it also made him drunk and dizzy, so that he had to rest again, his claws spread wide to brace him. Then he walked stiffly, to stalk down the scent. He trailed it up the runway. Then there was the stuffy, body-warm air, acrid with droppings, full of soft rustlings as his talons clicked on the board floor. The thick, white shapes showed faintly in the darkness. Hook struck quickly, driving a hen to the floor with one blow, its neck broken and stretched out stringily. He leaped the still pulsing body, and tore it. The rich, streaming blood was overpowering to his dried senses, his starved, leathery body. After a few swallows, the flesh choked him. In his rage, he struck down another hen. The urge to kill took him again, as in those nights on the beach. He could let nothing go. Balked of feeding, he was compelled to slaughter. Clattering, he struck again and again. The henhouse was suddenly filled with the squawking and helpless rushing and buffeting of the terrified, brainless fowls.

Hook reveled in mastery. Here was game big enough to offer weight against a strike, and yet unable to soar away from his blows. Turning in the midst of the turmoil, cannily, his fury caught at the perfect pitch, he struck unceasingly. When the hens finally discovered the outlet, and streamed into the yard, to run around the fence, beating and squawking, Hook followed them, scraping down the incline, clumsy and joyous. In the yard, the cock, a bird as large as he, and much heavier, found him out and gave valiant battle. In the dark, and both earthbound, there was little skill, but blow upon blow, and only chance parry.[1] The still-squawking hens pressed into one corner of the yard. While the duel went on, a dog, excited by the sustained scuffling, began to bark. He continued to bark, running back and forth along the fence on one side. A light flashed on in an uncurtained window of the farmhouse, and streamed whitely over the crates littering the ground.

Enthralled by his old battle joy, Hook knew only the burly cock before him. Now, in the farthest reach of the window light, they could see each other dimly. The Japanese farmer, with his gun and lantern, was already at the gate when the finish came. The great cock leapt to jab with his spurs and, toppling forward with extended neck as he fell, was struck and extinguished. Blood had loosened Hook's throat. Shrilly he cried his triumph. It was a thin and exhausted cry, but within him as good as when he shrilled in mid-air over the plummeting descent of a fine foe in his best spring.

The light from the lantern partially blinded Hook. He first turned and ran directly from it, into the corner where the hens were huddled. They fled apart before his charge. He essayed the fence, and on the second try, in his desperation, was out. But in the open dust, the dog was on him, circling, dashing in, snapping. The farmer, who at first had not fired because of the chickens, now did not fire because of the dog, and, when he saw that the hawk was unable to fly, relinquished the sport to the dog, holding the lantern up in order to see better. The light showed his own flat,

[1] **parry**: skillful turning aside of a blow.

broad, dark face as sunken also, the cheekbones very prominent, and showed the torn-off sleeves of his shirt and the holes in the knees of his overalls. His wife, in a stained wrapper, and barefooted, heavy black hair hanging around a young, passionless face, joined him hesitantly, but watched, fascinated and a little horrified. His son joined them too, encouraging the dog, but quickly grew silent. Courageous and cruel death, however it may afterward sicken the one who has watched it, is impossible to look away from.

In the circle of the light, Hook turned to keep the dog in front of him. His one eye gleamed with malevolence. The dog was an Airedale, and large. Each time he pounced, Hook stood ground, raising his good wing, the pinions newly torn by the fence, opening his beak soundlessly, and, at the closest approach, hissed furiously, and at once struck. Hit and ripped twice by the whetted horn, the dog recoiled more quickly from several subsequent jumps and, infuriated by his own cowardice, began to bark wildly. Hook maneuvered to watch him, keeping his head turned to avoid losing the foe on the blind side. When the dog paused, safely away, Hook watched him quietly, wing partially lowered, beak closed, but at the first move again lifted the wing and gaped. The dog whined, and the man spoke to him encouragingly. The awful sound of his voice made Hook for an instant twist his head to stare up at the immense figures behind the light. The dog again sallied, barking, and Hook's head spun back. His wing was bitten this time, and with a furious side-blow, he caught the dog's nose. The dog dropped him with a yelp, and

443

then, smarting, came on more warily, as Hook propped himself up from the ground again between his wings. Hook's artificial strength was waning, but his heart still stood to the battle, sustained by a fear of such dimension as he had never known before, but only anticipated when the arrogant young hawk had driven him to cover. The dog, unable to find any point at which the merciless, unwinking eye was not watching him, the parted beak waiting, paused and whimpered again.

"Oh, kill the poor thing," the woman begged.

The man, though, encouraged the dog again, saying, "Sick him; sick him."

The dog rushed bodily. Unable to avoid him, Hook was bowled down, snapping and raking. He left long slashes, as from the blade of a knife, on the dog's flank, but before he could right himself and assume guard again, was caught by the good wing and dragged, clattering, and seeking to make a good stroke from his back. The man followed them to keep the light on them, and the boy went with him, wetting his lips with his tongue and keeping his fists closed tightly. The woman remained behind, but could not help watching the diminished conclusion.

In the little, palely shining arena, the dog repeated his successful maneuver three times, growling but not barking, and when Hook thrashed up from the third blow, both wings were trailing, and dark, shining streams crept on his black-fretted[1] breast from the shoulders. The great eye flashed more furiously than it ever had in victorious battle, and the beak still gaped, but there was no more clatter. He faltered when turning to keep front; the broken wings played him false even as props. He could not rise to use his talons.

The man had tired of holding the lantern up, and put it down to rub his arm. In the

___

[1] **black-fretted:** crossed with black markings.

low, horizontal light, the dog charged again, this time throwing the weight of his forepaws against Hook's shoulder, so that Hook was crushed as he struck. With his talons up, Hook raked at the dog's belly, but the dog conceived the finish, and furiously worried the feathered bulk. Hook's neck went limp, and between his gaping clappers came only a faint chittering, as from some small kill of his own in the grasses.

In this last conflict, however, there had been some minutes of the supreme fire of the hawk whose three hungers are perfectly fused in the one will; enough to burn off a year of shame.

Between the great sails the light body lay caved and perfectly still. The dog, smarting from his cuts, came to the master and was praised. The woman, joining them slowly, looked at the great wingspread, her husband raising the lantern that she might see it better.

"Oh, the brave bird," she said.

For Discussion

1. **Plot.** The *plot* — or series of events that make up the action — of this story is simple indeed. Why was Hook so early on his own? What two major events occurred in his young life? What was the turning point of Hook's career? For a while after that event, Hook was master of the beach. What brought an end to that mastery? What changes had occurred in him by the time he returned to the familiar surroundings of the bend in the river and the tree with the dead limb? What kind of life did he live in the months before his death? What was it that drove him to his death?

2. To what extent is the woman's comment at the end of the story justified? What is described here is a life from beginning to end — not a human life, but it nevertheless affects us powerfully. Is it because we personify Hook, seeing in him all the nobility and valor of battered maturity — powers failing yet the fail-

ures gallantly coped with as a creature ages? To what extent does the author invest the hawk with human characteristics? What emotions does the hawk experience in the course of the story? Do they seem credible, or do they seem too "humanized" for a wild animal to feel?

3. If the story strikes you as successful, it will be because you believe it — that this, indeed, is what it must be like to be born a hawk and live out a hawk's life. What three hungers drive the bird? Notice that sense impressions pervade his awareness. Does intellect ever motivate his actions? That is, does he ever reason out how he should behave?

4. The story is all the more effective because the point of view from which it is told is for the most part consistent. Almost everything we learn is from Hook's point of view: ". . . the people, though they behaved foolishly, constantly running in and out of their built-up holes, were large, and appeared capable, with fearless eyes looking up at him, so that he instinctively swerved aside from them. He cruised over their yard, their gardens, and their bean fields, but he would not alight close to their buildings" (page 434). What are the "built-up holes"? At least once, to be sure, the author departs from Hook's point of view. "The Japanese farmer, who believed that he had lost chickens, and who had cunningly observed Hook's flight for many afternoons, until he could plot it, did not greatly want a dead hawk" (page 436). Is the sentence from Hook's point of view? Explain. Why is the information that the sentence furnishes included?

5. What aspects of nature does "Hook" illustrate? Images make concrete certain abstract ideas about the natural world we live in. Comment on aspects implicit in details from the hawk's life; for example, "Hook tore and fed on the fine, watery flesh, and left the tattered armor and the long, jointed bone for the marching ants" (page 440); "The river made no sound. Scum grew on its vestigial pools, and turtles died and stank among the rocks" (page 441). Is nature seen here as cruel? As beautiful? As reasonable? As just? Discuss.

For Composition

Narratives, as you know (page 74), are most frequently written in chronological order, making use of such transitional expressions as *later, meanwhile, the following day, at sunset, afterwards,* and *gradually* to clarify the time sequence.

1. **Analysis.** Consider Section II of "Hook." It gains in coherence because — as elsewhere in the story — the order of events is clear. In a brief composition examine the chronological order of that section, and explain the means by which the author has conveyed the chronology clearly.

2. **Argument.** Many of the events in this story could have been told from the point of view of a human being. From whose? How would the change have changed the story itself? In a composition of five or six paragraphs indicate the kinds of changes such a shift in point of view would entail. What incidents could remain. Which would have to be omitted? What would be the consequences of the omissions?

Words and Allusions

DERIVATION. Although Hook takes joy in killing, Clark's story seems to emphasize that in nature the battle for survival is *amoral* rather than *immoral*. These words have been formed by *derivation* — that is, by the addition of a prefix or suffix to an existing word, called a stem. What is the difference in meaning between the two words, and how is that difference created? Use each word in a sentence that illustrates its meaning.

WORDS IN CONTEXT. Working from context, but using a dictionary if necessary, find the meaning of each of the following words from "Hook," and illustrate the meanings by using each word in a sentence of your own: *spasmodic* (page 431), *stupefaction* (432), *importunity* (433), *neophyte* (435), *auspiciously* (437), *repletion* (438), *strident* (439), *palpitant* (440), *lassitude* (441), *cannily* (442).

Henri Rousseau (1844–1910) *Jungle with Setting Sun.* Kunstmuseum, Basel, Switzerland.

Rousseau

Jungle with Setting Sun

This picture interprets man's relationship to nature in a variety of ways. For one thing, in a setting of magnificent forest, bursting with vitality, a leopard is attacking a man. Amid all that splendor one part of nature is being destroyed by another, as in the experience of the boy in Doris Lessing's "A Sunrise on the Veld" (page 403). Man, Rousseau seems to be saying, is a part of the natural world just as animals and plants are, and constant destruction is as much a part of nature as constant creation. How does the absence of distinguishing features in the human figure contribute to this theme and its pictorial presentation?

Rousseau is technically called a "primitive." That is, he was an artist with no *formal* training in painting, who did not learn the traditional ways by which the natural world is represented. To see what this means, compare Rousseau's painting with that by Friedrich (page 450) or that by Watteau (page 620), both of whom had formal training. What differences do you find?

Traditional ways of painting are conventions — that is, established ways of representing objects — but they are by no means the only ways or even the "true" ways. The primitive painter, not having learned the conventions, sees aspects of the world which the conventions do not reproduce. Particularly, he sees structure and pattern. At first Rousseau was derided, but before his death, painters trained in the conventions but weary of them recognized his "natural" genius. Among them was Picasso, and if you look at his *Girl before a Mirror* (page 695), you will see the same interest in structure and pattern. Then compare both paintings with a patchwork quilt. What other "popular" arts of this sort can you think of that show the same interest in bold patterning and clear structure?

Rousseau's jungle is strange because the plants he presents do not in nature grow together in the same soil or climate. He saw such plants in hothouses. What plants can you recognize?

The quite clear organization of the painting and its abstract quality are characteristic of all primitive thinking. Its heavy patterning comes out in the thick grasslike plants in the foreground, in the grouping of cacti in the center, in the line of yellow and pink flowers right across the middle (can you identify them?). It is also seen in the nearly symmetrical placement of the two tall trees and in the red sun, just off exact center. Why do you think the tops of the trunks of the trees appear mutilated? Despite this heavy patterning, Rousseau refuses to be exactly symmetrical, a refusal that indicates his "natural" genius for pictorial variety.

MORSE PECKHAM

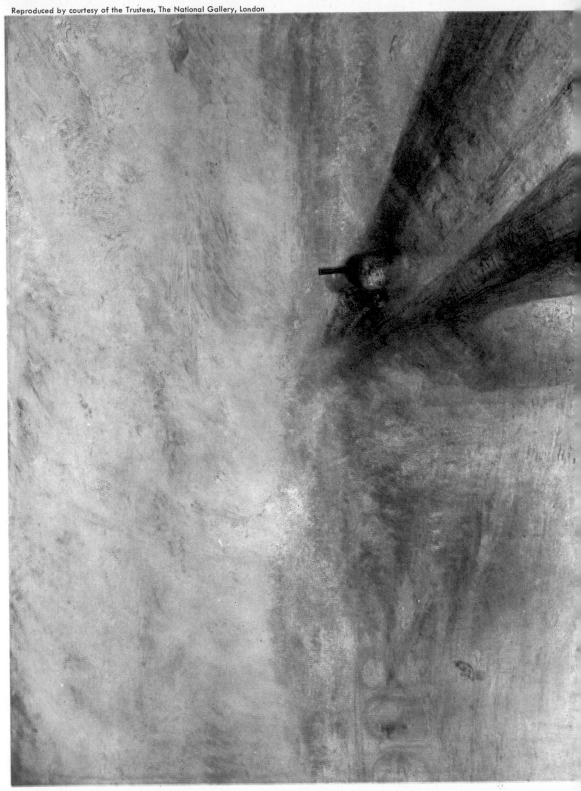

Joseph M. W. Turner (1775–1851) *Rain, Steam and Speed.* National Gallery, London.

Turner

Rain, Steam, and Speed

Both Dylan Thomas' poem "The Force That Through the Green Fuse Drives the Flower" (page 412) and Turner's painting *Rain, Steam, and Speed* are responses to the same experience and the same problem. Man uses the forces of nature for his own purposes; yet man is part of nature and he, too, is subject to its forces. The problem for both Thomas and Turner was to express this contradictory situation.

Turner helps us to understand the problem by his title. Rain is a natural product, and so is steam. But steam is also a natural force harnessed by man and put to work. The result is the speed of the railroad train. With the invention of the machine, man has greatly increased his control over nature, but to maintain that control, he must depend more than ever before on natural forces. The machine at once separates man from nature and enriches his relationship to it. One of the most original things about Turner's painting is that he introduced modern machinery and technology into landscape painting.

The principal oddity in Turner's painting is that we can see the fire in the engine firebox through the front of the engine. No railroad engine was ever built like this. In reality only the fireman can see the fire, and only from the back of the engine. This puzzle at once tells us that the painting is concerned with a problem. Turner wishes to bring out forcefully that man has mastered the fire and put it to use by making it turn water into steam in order to power an engine and pull a train. Where else in the train do you see man-made light? Yet the scene is one of uncontrolled water, fire's antithesis, water in its natural state, the rain and the wide river crossed by man-made bridges. The whirling of the storm reminds us that man has under his control only a minute fragment of nature. Thus the engine and train are small, and the smaller bridge to the left tells us that when seen in perspective, the larger bridge rushing toward us will also be submerged in the larger grandeur of nature.

So the visibility of the fire suggests that the forces man controls always threaten to get out of control, a point emphasized by the frailness of the boat on the majestic river, which Turner makes seem mightier than the river Thames really is. The fire and the train lights, like the bridges, stress the perilousness of man's safety in this elemental wildness. To Turner the cold grays and blues and the green-gray of the river were "minus" colors, colors of negative emotion, restless and anxious and susceptible to disturbance and trouble. The nonrealistic visibility of the engine's fire, then, is the ambiguity of man's relation to nature. He must dominate it, but his dominance is minute and fragile, and these vast forces, at once his friend and his enemy, always threaten to overwhelm him.

MORSE PECKHAM

Caspar David Friedrich (1774–1840) *Floating Clouds*. Hamburger Kunsthalle, Hamburg.

Friedrich

Floating Clouds

Friedrich lived at almost exactly the same time as Wordsworth (page 414). One a German and the other an Englishman, neither ever knew of the other's existence, yet their feelings about nature and themselves were remarkably alike. This picture of clouds and mountains with plains beyond, as seen from the top of a mountain or near the top of a mountain, can make one feel that there is something particularly significant about the little pond in the foreground. This feeling is quite justified. How is the feeling intensified by the design of the picture?

In one of Friedrich's paintings a monk is alone by the seashore. In another a man alone on a mountainside is looking at a rainbow. In still another a man stands by a small pool looking at a mountain landscape. In almost all of his paintings we see only the backs of human figures. When they stand sideways, their faces are turned away. In Wordsworth's "Tintern Abbey" the speaker is alone before nature; in Friedrich's paintings the observer is similarly alone as he contemplates the natural world. Friedrich once wrote: "You call me an enemy of mankind because I avoid company. You are wrong. I love you. But in order not to hate men, I must abstain from their society."

Now we can understand the little pond in the center of this painting. It is Friedrich himself, but so detached from mankind that he is not even in human form. He has become merely an eye, but an eye of the spirit. For him, as for Wordsworth, to turn away from man was to turn toward nature, and, like Wordsworth, the meaning he could not find in social relationships he found in the natural world, particularly in the world of mountains and sky.

That is why there is such a sharp distinction between the green of the mountaintop and the blue of the landscape. The green is man, and the blue is nature, withdrawn from man and awe-inspiring. But the green earth is also nature. Man is part of nature and also different from nature. As the pond-eye tells us, man is conscious of this ambiguous relationship. In this situation what is suggested by the drifting clouds that obscure the landscape? Does the light that strikes both the pond and a river in the landscape directly above it suggest that in spite of their differences, man and nature have something in common? What other forms are common to both parts of the painting?

The painting is organized in three wide horizontal bands that create a sense of calm. Yet there is also disturbance created by the diagonal lines of the clouds. What does this tension between calm and disturbance suggest about man's relationship to nature? In what ways are the shapes of the rocks in the foreground echoed in the mountains in the blue landscape?

MORSE PECKHAM

Frederic E. Church (1826–1900) *Rainy Season in the Tropics.*
Collection of Mr. and Mrs. J. William Middendorf II, New York.

Church

Rainy Season in the Tropics

Frederic Church greatly admired Emerson, and his painting was influenced by that admiration. In "Nature" (page 420) Emerson says, "the power to produce this delight does not reside in nature, but in man, or in harmony of both." To create that harmony between man and nature was Church's ambition.

Emerson also said: "few adult persons can see nature. . . . The lover of nature is he . . . who has retained the spirit of infancy even into the era of manhood." To capture the fresh vision of a child, Church had to look at nature in a new way, and he had to paint in a new way. There is hardly a detail to be found in the landscape of Watteau's *A Pilgrimage to Cythera* (page 620) that cannot be found in paintings from the preceding two centuries. There is hardly a detail in Church's painting that had appeared in any earlier painting.

Before Church, American painters felt they had to go to Europe to learn. Church went instead to South America and to Jamaica, where he found the inspiration for this painting. To look at nature as if he had never seen it before was Church's ideal. But no one looks at anything without some notion, conscious or unconscious, of what he is going to see. We see pretty much what we expect to see, and that is the reason none of us sees very accurately. Church looked at a landscape no artist had painted and tried to see it with a fresh eye. He also wished to paint what he saw with complete accuracy. How well do you think he succeeded? Does this painting look like an actual landscape? Would a camera record all the details Church includes? The painting is seven feet by nearly five feet. How would looking at the original affect your feeling about it?

To achieve harmony between man and nature, Church also wanted to express human feelings that give a natural scene its emotional character. It has been said that this painting expresses his consolation after the loss of two children and his joy at the end of the American Civil War. What elements in the painting do you find especially consoling or joyous?

The landscape is seen at the end of a storm. The rainbow is an ancient symbol of peace and reconciliation — as it appeared to Noah after the Flood. Would the rainbow be as effective here if it were less symmetrically placed? The only human figures are travelers with their horses on a primitive road, at the lower right-hand corner in a patch of sunlight. Does the common metaphor of life as a road to be traveled have any bearing here? There is a patch of blue in the sky above. The most intense spot of light is in the ravine. The tallest mountain inside the rainbow rises like the facade of a cathedral and has almost the symmetry of a man-made monument. Why is a higher mountain suggested outside the rainbow?

MORSE PECKHAM

453

Autumn

ALEXANDER   SERGEYEVICH   PUSHKIN

From earliest times man has observed parallels between human life and
nature's seasons. Spring is birth and summer fullness. Afterwards comes the
old age of autumn, prefacing winter's chill death. But whether death hovers
over autumn or not, not everyone sees it as a season of sadness. Here is a
poem that expresses a freshly felt attitude toward a seasonal phenomenon
with which all of us are annually made familiar.

October at last has come! The thicket has shaken
The last leaf lingering down from the naked branch.
Autumn is breathing cold, the road is frozen —
The brook still runs with a murmur behind the mill,
But the pond is still; my neighbor is up and away   5
With a hunt, away to the farthest dreaming field,
Where the winter wheat will suffer from his mad sport,
And the bark of dogs will startle the forest oaks.

It is my time now! I never could love the spring,
The dragging thaw, the mud, the stench — I am sick   10
In spring: my blood's astray, my mind is oppressed
With a yearning pain. Winter is better for me.
I love the serious snow-fields under the moon!
How the light run of the sled is swift and free,   14
And the warm hand of a love down under the sables warm! . . .

And Oh the fun, to be shod with the sharpened steel,
And glide on the glassy face of the standing river!
The shining alarm of a winter holiday!
But still there's a limit in things! —A half year's snow —
Even at last to the old cave-dweller, the bear,   20
It is long enough! You cannot forever and ever
Slide in a sled with the beautiful young Armida,
Or sulk behind double glass by a friendly stove. . . .

They commonly scold the last days of autumn: to me,
My reader and friend, they are dear; their beauty is quiet,   25
Their modesty brilliant; they draw me to them like a child
Whom the family does not love. I will tell you frankly:
Of all the seasons of time I can love but one;
I find in her — I am not a vainglorious lover,
Though willful of fancy — I find in my love much good.   30

How shall I tell you? She ravishes me
As a dying virgin, perhaps, might ravish you.
Condemned, and bending meekly, and murmuring not.
Not angry — a smile on the fading lips —
She does not perceive the abysmal opening mouth   35
Of the tomb — the purplish light on her features, plays —
Today she is here — she lives — and tomorrow not.

Sweet mournful days, charm of the dreaming eyes,
Your beauty is dear to me that says farewell!
I love the sumptuous decline of nature's life,   40
The tents of forest adorned with purple and gold,
And loud with the sound of the faster breath of the wind,
A billowy curtain of fog concealing the sky,
And the sun's rare beam, and the early frost,
And the threat of the gray-head winter standing off! . . .   45

With every autumn that comes I bloom again;
It is good for my health, it is good, this Russian cold;
I fall afresh in love with the habit of being;
Sleep flies early, and hunger is in its place,
The blood romps joyfully through my heart,   50
Desire seethes up — I laugh again, I am young,
I am living life — such is my organism
(If you will excuse me, please, the prosaism).

So saddle my horse; and into the plentiful open
With fluttering mane he will carry me flying, and under   55
His body his glittering hoofs will ring like a tune
Through the frozen valley, will crackle and crash on the ice —
Till the brief day dies! And then the chimney, forgotten,
Will waken again with fire — will pour sharp light,
Or dimly glow, while I sit reading long,   60
And nourishing the long thoughts in my soul. . . .

For Discussion

1. Pushkin's poem was translated by the American Max Eastman. Notice how promptly an attitude toward autumn is established. What is the effect of "at last" in line 1? The first stanza is filled with imagery. What is the effect of the kinetic imagery at the end of line 5? Of the auditory imagery in the final line of the stanza?

2. The poem expresses feelings about spring and winter as well. What are the speaker's objections to spring? Is stanza 3 about fall or winter? Explain the speaker's feelings about winter as a season.

3. The last days of autumn have an appeal for the speaker that he expresses as a simile. How do they appeal to him? Autumn itself he personifies as a dying virgin. In what sense is the season "condemned" (line 33)? In what sense is it "bending meekly, and murmuring not"? Consider the other attributes of autumn that the personification suggests — innocence, beauty, a smiling countenance. To what ex-

tent are they justified? In terms of the metaphor, what is the "abysmal opening mouth / Of the tomb" (lines 35–36)?

4. The closing stanzas convey the effect of autumn on the speaker. How does the season affect him? How is winter viewed at the end of the poem? Contrast that view with the personification of it in line 45.

For Composition

The poem is unusually rich in metaphorical language; examples of simile, metaphor, and personification abound.

• **Exposition.** Demonstrate your understanding of figurative language in a coherent composition of four or five paragraphs that distinguish among the kinds of comparisons found in "Autumn." Illustrate your remarks with examples from the poem.

About the Poet. **Alexander Pushkin** (1799–1837), the greatest Russian poet of the nineteenth century, was proud of his African ancestry, inherited from an Ethiopian great-grandfather who had been a high-ranking official in the Czar's court. Pushkin was raised by French-speaking parents (to imitate the French was stylish among Russian aristocrats) and learned his Russian from servants. He was only fifteen when his first poem was published in an influential Russian magazine. By the time he was eighteen he was a widely known poet. A political revolutionary, Pushkin was frequently in trouble with the authorities and banished to the provinces. A turbulent figure to the end, he lost his life in a duel. His narrative poem, *Eugene Onegin,* generally regarded as his greatest work, was set to music by the composer Tchaikovsky; and Pushkin's historical drama *Boris Godunov* was made into an opera by Mussorgsky.

The Open Boat

A Tale Intended to Be After the Fact: Being the Experience of Four Men from the Sunk Steamer Commodore.

STEPHEN CRANE

There is no last word to be spoken on nature. Crane's great story that follows, based on his own chilling experiences off the Florida coast after a shipwreck on New Year's Day, 1897, may not resolve all the complexities of nature, but it expresses many of those complexities concretely and memorably in the episode described. It is a simple episode — of four men whose lives are abruptly jeopardized — yet for all its surface simplicity, the meanings beneath the surface are as profound as the sea itself.

I

None of them knew the color of the sky. Their eyes glanced level, and were fastened upon the waves that swept toward them. These waves were of the hue of slate, save for the tops, which were of foaming white, and all of the men knew the colors of the sea. The horizon narrowed and widened, and dipped and rose, and at all times its edge was jagged with waves that seemed thrust up in points like rocks.

Many a man ought to have a bathtub larger than the boat which here rode upon the sea. These waves were most wrongfully and barbarously abrupt and tall, and each froth-top was a problem in small-boat navigation.

The cook squatted in the bottom, and looked with both eyes at the six inches of gunwale[1] which separated him from the ocean. His sleeves were rolled over his fat forearms, and the two flaps of his unbuttoned vest dangled as he bent to bail out the boat. Often he said, "Gawd! that was a narrow clip." As he remarked it he invariably gazed eastward over the broken sea.

The oiler, steering with one of the two oars in the boat, sometimes raised himself suddenly to keep clear of water that swirled in over the stern. It was a thin little oar, and it seemed often ready to snap.

The correspondent, pulling at the other oar, watched the waves and wondered why he was there.

The injured captain, lying in the bow, was at this time buried in that profound dejection and indifference which comes, temporarily at least, to even the bravest and most enduring when, willy-nilly, the firm fails, the army loses, the ship goes down. The mind of the master of a vessel is rooted deep in the timbers of her, though he command for a day or a decade; and this captain had on him the stern impression of a scene in the grays of dawn of seven turned faces, and later a stump of a topmast with a white ball on it, that slashed to and fro at the waves, went low and lower, and down. Thereafter there was something strange in his voice. Although steady, it was deep with mourning, and of a quality beyond oration or tears.

"Keep 'er a little more south, Billie," said he.

[1] gunwale (gun'əl): upper edge of a boat's side.

The Commodore *disaster, as reported in the* New York Journal, *January 3, 1897.*

"A little more south, sir," said the oiler in the stern.

A seat in this boat was not unlike a seat upon a bucking bronco, and, by the same token, a bronco is not much smaller. The craft pranced and reared and plunged like an animal. As each wave came, and she rose for it, she seemed like a horse making at a fence outrageously high. The manner of her scramble over these walls of water is a mystic thing, and, moreover, at the top of them were ordinarily these problems in white water, the foam racing down from the summit of each wave, requiring a new leap, and a leap from the air. Then, after scornfully bumping a crest, she would slide and race and splash down a long incline, and arrive bobbing and nodding in front of the next menace.

A singular disadvantage of the sea lies in the fact that, after successfully surmounting one wave, you discover that there is another behind it, just as important and just as nervously anxious to do something effective in the way of swamping[1] boats. In a ten-foot dinghy one can get an idea of the resources of the sea in the line of waves that is not probable to the average experience, which is never at sea in a dinghy. As each slaty wall of water approached, it shut all else from the view of the men in the boat, and it was not difficult to imagine that this particular wave was the final outburst of the ocean, the last effort of the grim water. There was a terrible grace in the move of the waves, and they came in silence, save for the snarling of the crests.

In the wan light the faces of the men must have been gray. Their eyes must have glinted in strange ways as they gazed steadily astern.[2] Viewed from a balcony, the whole thing would, doubtless, have been weirdly picturesque. But the men in the boat had no time to see it, and if they had

[1] **swamping**: filling with water and sinking.
[2] **astern**: toward the rear of the boat.

had leisure, there were other things to occupy their minds. The sun swung steadily up the sky, and they knew it was broad day because the color of the sea changed from slate to emerald-green streaked with amber lights, and the foam was like tumbling snow. The process of the breaking day was unknown to them. They were aware only of this effect upon the color of the waves that rolled toward them.

In disjointed sentences the cook and the correspondent argued as to the difference between a life-saving station and a house of refuge. The cook had said: "There's a house of refuge just north of the Mosquito Inlet Light, and as soon as they see us they'll come off in their boat and pick us up."

"As soon as who see us?" said the correspondent.

"The crew," said the cook.

"Houses of refuge don't have crews," said the correspondent. "As I understand them, they are only places where clothes and grub are stored for the benefit of shipwrecked people. They don't carry crews."

"Oh, yes, they do," said the cook.

"No, they don't," said the correspondent.

"Well, we're not there yet, anyhow," said the oiler in the stern.

"Well," said the cook, "perhaps it's not a

ABOUT THE AUTHOR • Stephen Crane (1871–1900) made a permanent place for himself in literature before he was twenty-five, and died before he was thirty. His early realistic masterpiece, *Maggie: A Girl of the Streets*, reflected the human misery in New York's Bowery section. The equally realistic *The Red Badge of Courage*, the Civil War novel that made him famous, was written without his having ever witnessed a single battle. In his last years Crane became a successful war correspondent and covered campaigns in Greece and in Cuba. On his first trip to Cuba, his ship was wrecked, and he spent four days in a lifeboat, an experience that contributed to his death by tuberculosis, but that also resulted in his great short story, "The Open Boat."

house of refuge that I'm thinking of as being near Mosquito Inlet Light; perhaps it's a life-saving station."

"We're not there yet," said the oiler in the stern.

II

As the boat bounced from the top of each wave the wind tore through the hair of the hatless men, and as the craft plopped her stern down again the spray slashed past them. The crest of each of these waves was a hill, from the top of which the men surveyed for a moment a broad, tumultuous expanse, shining and wind-riven.[1] It was probably splendid, it was probably glorious, this play of the free sea, wild with lights of emerald and white and amber.

"Bully good thing it's an onshore wind," said the cook. "If not, where would we be? Wouldn't have a show."

"That's right," said the correspondent.

The busy oiler nodded his assent.

Then the captain, in the bow, chuckled in a way that expressed humor, contempt, tragedy, all in one. "Do you think we've got much of a show now, boys?" said he.

Whereupon the three were silent, save for a trifle of hemming and hawing. To express any particular optimism at this time they felt to be childish and stupid, but they all doubtless possessed this sense of the situation in their minds. A young man thinks doggedly at such times. On the other hand, the ethics of their condition was decidedly against any open suggestion of hopelessness. So they were silent.

"Oh, well," said the captain, soothing his children, "we'll get ashore all right."

But there was that in his tone which made them think; so the oiler quoth, "Yes! if this wind holds."

The cook was bailing. "Yes! if we don't catch hell in the surf."

[1] **wind-riven**: divided by the wind.

Canton-flannel gulls flew near and far. Sometimes they sat down on the sea, near patches of brown seaweed that rolled over the waves with a movement like carpets on a line in a gale. The birds sat comfortably in groups, and they were envied by some in the dinghy, for the wrath of the sea was no more to them than it was to a covey of prairie chickens[2] a thousand miles inland. Often they came very close and stared at the men with black, beadlike eyes. At these times they were uncanny and sinister in their unblinking scrutiny, and the men hooted angrily at them, telling them to be gone. One came, and evidently decided to alight on the top of the captain's head. The bird flew parallel to the boat, and did not circle, but made short sidelong jumps in the air in chicken fashion. His black eyes were wistfully fixed upon the captain's head. "Ugly brute," said the oiler to the bird. "You look as if you were made with a jack-knife." The cook and the correspondent swore darkly at the creature. The captain naturally wished to knock it away with the end of the heavy painter,[3] but he did not dare do it, because anything resembling an emphatic gesture would have capsized this freighted[4] boat; and so, with his open hand, the captain gently and carefully waved the gull away. After it had been discouraged from the pursuit the captain breathed easier on account of his hair, and others breathed easier because the bird struck their minds at this time as being somehow gruesome and ominous.

In the meantime the oiler and the correspondent rowed; and also they rowed. They sat together in the same seat, and each rowed an oar. Then the oiler took both oars; then the correspondent took both oars; then the oiler; then the correspondent. They rowed

[2] **prairie chickens**: kind of ground-dwelling game birds.

[3] **painter**: rope used for fastening the boat.

[4] **freighted**: loaded, weighed down.

and they rowed. The very ticklish part of the business was when the time came for the reclining one in the stern to take his turn at the oars. By the very last star of truth, it is easier to steal eggs from under a hen than it was to change seats in the dinghy. First the man in the stern slid his hand along the thwart[1] and moved with care, as if he were of Sèvres.[2] Then the man in the rowing seat slid his hand along the other thwart. It was all done with the most extraordinary care. As the two sidled past each other, the whole party kept watchful eyes on the coming wave, and the captain cried: "Look out, now! Steady, there!"

The brown mats of seaweed that appeared from time to time were like islands, bits of earth. They were traveling, apparently, neither one way nor the other. They were, to all intents, stationary. They informed the men in the boat that it was making progress slowly toward the land.

The captain, rearing cautiously in the bow after the dinghy soared on a great swell, said that he had seen the lighthouse at Mosquito Inlet. Presently the cook remarked that he had seen it. The correspondent was at the oars then, and for some reason he too wished to look at the lighthouse; but his back was toward the far shore, and the waves were important, and for some time he could not seize an opportunity to turn his head. But at last there came a wave more gentle than the others, and when at the crest of it he swiftly scoured the western horizon.

"See it?" said the captain.

"No," said the correspondent, slowly; "I didn't see anything."

"Look again," said the captain. He pointed. "It's exactly in that direction."

At the top of another wave the correspondent did as he was bid, and this time his eyes chanced on a small, still thing on the edge of the swaying horizon. It was precisely like the point of a pin. It took an anxious eye to find a lighthouse so tiny.

"Think we'll make it, Captain?"

"If this wind holds and the boat don't swamp, we can't do much else," said the captain.

The little boat, lifted by each towering sea and splashed viciously by the crests, made progress that in the absence of seaweed was not apparent to those in her. She seemed just a wee thing wallowing miraculously, top up, at the mercy of five oceans. Occasionally a great spread of water, like white flames, swarmed into her.

"Bail her, cook," said the captain, serenely.

"All right, Captain," said the cheerful cook.

III

It would be difficult to describe the subtle brotherhood of men that was here established on the seas. No one said that it was so. No one mentioned it. But it dwelt in the boat, and each man felt it warm him. They were a captain, an oiler, a cook, and a correspondent, and they were friends — friends in a more curiously ironbound degree than may be common. The hurt captain, lying against the water jar in the bow, spoke always in a low voice and calmly; but he could never command a more ready and swiftly obedient crew than the motley three of the dinghy. It was more than a mere recognition of what was best for the common safety. There was surely in it a quality that was personal and heartfelt. And after this devotion to the commander of the boat, there was this comradeship, that the correspondent, for instance, who had been taught to be cynical of men, knew even at the time was the best experience of his life. But no one said that it was so. No one mentioned it.

---

[1] **thwart**: brace extending across the boat.
[2] **Sèvres**: very delicate kind of china.

"I wish we had a sail," remarked the captain. "We might try my overcoat on the end of an oar, and give you two boys a chance to rest." So the cook and the correspondent held the mast and spread wide the overcoat; the oiler steered; and the little boat made good way with her new rig. Sometimes the oiler had to scull[1] sharply to keep a sea from breaking into the boat, but otherwise sailing was a success.

Meanwhile the lighthouse had been growing slowly larger. It had now almost assumed color, and appeared like a little gray shadow on the sky. The man at the oars could not be prevented from turning his head rather often to try for a glimpse of this little gray shadow.

At last, from the top of each wave, the men in the tossing boat could see land. Even as the lighthouse was an upright shadow on the sky, this land seemed but a long black shadow on the sea. It certainly was thinner than paper. "We must be about opposite New Smyrna," said the cook, who had coasted this shore often in schooners. "Captain, by the way, I believe they abandoned that life-saving station there about a year ago."

"Did they?" said the captain.

The wind slowly died away. The cook and the correspondent were not now obliged to slave in order to hold high the oar; but the waves continued their old impetuous swooping at the dinghy, and the little craft, no longer under way, struggled woundily over them. The oiler or the correspondent took the oars again.

Shipwrecks are apropos[2] of nothing. If men could only train for them and have them occur when the men had reached pink condition, there would be less drowning at sea. Of the four in the dinghy none had slept any time worth mentioning for two days and two nights previous to embarking in the dinghy, and in the excitement of clambering about the deck of a foundering ship they had also forgotten to eat heartily.

For these reasons, and for others, neither the oiler nor the correspondent was fond of rowing at this time. The correspondent wondered ingenuously how in the name of all that was sane could there be people who thought it amusing to row a boat. It was not an amusement; it was a diabolical punishment, and even a genius of mental aberrations could never conclude that it was anything but a horror to the muscles and a crime against the back. He mentioned to the boat in general how the amusement of rowing struck him, and the weary-faced oiler smiled in full sympathy. Previously to the foundering, by the way, the oiler had worked double watch in the engine room of the ship.

"Take her easy now, boys," said the captain. "Don't spend yourselves. If we have to run a surf you'll need all your strength, because we'll sure have to swim for it. Take your time."

Slowly the land arose from the sea. From a black line it became a line of black and a line of white — trees and sand. Finally the captain said he could make out a house on the shore. "That's the house of refuge, sure," said the cook. "They'll see us before long and come out after us."

The distant lighthouse reared high. "The keeper ought to be able to make us out now, if he's looking through a glass," said the captain. "He'll notify the life-saving people."

"None of those other boats could have got ashore to give word of the wreck," said the oiler, in a low voice, "else the lifeboat would be out hunting us."

Slowly and beautifully the land loomed out of the sea. The wind came again. It had veered from the northeast to the southeast. Finally a new sound struck the ears of the

---

[1] scull: stroke with an oar.
[2] apropos (ap·rə·pō′): suitable to the occasion or subject.

men in the boat. It was the low thunder of the surf on the shore. "We'll never be able to make the lighthouse now," said the captain. "Swing her head a little more north, Billie."

"A little more north, sir," said the oiler.

Whereupon the little boat turned her nose once more down the wind, and all but the oarsman watched the shore grow. Under the influence of this expansion, doubt and direful apprehension were leaving the minds of the men. The management of the boat was still most absorbing, but it could not prevent a quiet cheerfulness. In an hour, perhaps, they would be ashore.

Their backbones had become thoroughly used to balancing in the boat, and they now rode this wild colt of a dinghy like circus men. The correspondent thought that he had been drenched to the skin, but happening to feel in the top pocket of his coat, he found therein eight cigars. Four of them were soaked with sea water; four were perfectly scatheless. After a search, somebody produced three dry matches; and thereupon the four waifs rode in their little boat and, with an assurance of an impending rescue shining in their eyes, puffed at the big cigars, and judged well and ill of all men. Everybody took a drink of water.

IV

"Cook," remarked the captain, "there don't seem to be any signs of life about your house of refuge."

"No," replied the cook. "Funny they don't see us!"

A broad stretch of lowly coast lay before the eyes of the men. It was of low dunes topped with dark vegetation. The roar of the surf was plain, and sometimes they could see the white lip of a wave as it spun up the beach. A tiny house was blocked out black upon the sky. Southward, the slim lighthouse lifted its little gray length.

Tide, wind, and waves were swinging the dinghy northward. "Funny they don't see us," said the men.

The surf's roar was here dulled, but its tone was nevertheless thunderous and and mighty. As the boat swam over the great rollers the men sat listening to this roar. "We'll swamp sure," said everybody.

It is fair to say here that there was not a life-saving station within twenty miles in either direction; but the men did not know this fact, and in consequence they made dark and opprobrious[1] remarks concerning the eyesight of the nation's lifesavers. Four scowling men sat in the dinghy, and surpassed records in the invention of epithets.

"Funny they don't see us."

The lightheartedness of a former time had completely faded. To their sharpened minds it was easy to conjure pictures of all kinds of incompetency and blindness and, indeed, cowardice. There was the shore of the populous land, and it was bitter and bitter to them that from it came no sign.

"Well," said the captain, ultimately, "I suppose we'll have to make a try for ourselves. If we stay out here too long, we'll none of us have strength left to swim after the boat swamps."

And so the oiler, who was at the oars, turned the boat straight for the shore. There was a sudden tightening of muscles. There was some thinking.

"If we don't all get ashore," said the captain — "if we don't all get ashore, I suppose you fellows know where to send news of my finish?"

They then briefly exchanged some addresses and admonitions. As for the reflections of the men, there was a great deal of rage in them. Perchance they might be formulated thus: "If I am going to be drowned — if I am going to be drowned, why, in the name of seven mad gods who rule the sea, was I allowed to come thus far and contemplate sand and trees? Was I

[1]opprobrious: abusive.

brought here merely to have my nose dragged away as I was about to nibble the sacred cheese of life? It is preposterous! If this old ninny-woman, Fate, cannot do better than this, she should be deprived of the management of men's fortunes. She is an old hen who knows not her intention. If she has decided to drown me, why did she not do it in the beginning, and save me all this trouble? The whole affair is absurd. . . . But no; she cannot mean to drown me. She dare not drown me. She cannot drown me. Not after all this work!" Afterward the man might have had an impulse to shake his fist at the clouds. "Just you drown me, now, and then hear what I call you!"

The billows that came at this time were more formidable. They seemed always just about to break and roll over the little boat in a turmoil of foam. There was a preparatory and long growl in the speech of them. No mind unused to the sea would have concluded that the dinghy could ascend these sheer heights in time. The shore was still afar. The oiler was a wily surfman. "Boys," he said swiftly, "she won't live three minutes more, and we're too far out to swim. Shall I take her to sea again, Captain?"

"Yes; go ahead!" said the captain.

This oiler, by a series of quick miracles and fast and steady oarsmanship, turned the boat in the middle of the surf and took her safely to sea again.

There was a considerable silence as the boat bumped over the furrowed sea to deeper water. Then somebody in gloom spoke: "Well, anyhow, they must have seen us from the shore by now."

The gulls went in slanting flight up the wind toward the gray, desolate east. A squall, marked by dingy clouds, and clouds brick red, like smoke from a burning building, appeared from the southeast.

"What do you think of those lifesaving people? Ain't they peaches?"

"Funny they haven't seen us."

"Maybe they think we're out here for sport! Maybe they think we're fishin'. Maybe they think we're damned fools."

It was a long afternoon. A changed tide tried to force them southward, but wind and wave said northward. Far ahead, where coastline, sea, and sky formed their mighty angle, there were little dots which seemed to indicate a city on the shore.

"St. Augustine?"

The captain shook his head. "Too near Mosquito Inlet."

And the oiler rowed, and then the correspondent rowed; then the oiler rowed. It was a weary business. The human back can become the seat of more aches and pains than are registered in books for the composite anatomy of a regiment. It is a limited area, but it can become the theater[1] of innumerable muscular conflicts, tangles, wrenches, knots, and other comforts.

"Did you ever like to row, Billie?" asked the correspondent.

"No," said the oiler; "hang it!"

When one exchanged the rowing seat for a place in the bottom of the boat, he suffered a bodily depression that caused him to be careless of everything save an obligation to wiggle one finger. There was cold sea water swashing to and fro in the boat, and he lay in it. His head, pillowed on a thwart, was within an inch of the swirl of a wave-crest, and sometimes a particularly obstrep-

[1] **theater:** *here,* place where action is carried on.

463

erous sea came inboard and drenched him once more. But these matters did not annoy him. It is almost certain that if the boat had capsized he would have tumbled comfortably out upon the ocean as if he felt sure that it was a great, soft mattress.

"Look! There's a man on the shore!"

"Where?"

"There! See 'im? See 'im?"

"Yes, sure! He's walking along."

"Now he's stopped. Look! He's facing us!"

"He's waving at us!"

"So he is! By thunder!"

"Ah, now we're all right! Now we're all right! There'll be a boat out here for us in half an hour."

"He's going on. He's running. He's going up to that house there."

The remote beach seemed lower than the sea, and it required a searching glance to discern the little black figure. The captain saw a floating stick, and they rowed to it. A bath towel was by some weird chance in the boat, and tying this on the stick, the captain waved it. The oarsman did not dare turn his head, so he was obliged to ask questions.

"What's he doing now?"

"He's standing still again. He's looking, I think. . . . There he goes again — toward the house. . . . Now he's stopped again."

"Is he waving at us?"

"No, not now; he was, though."

"Look! There comes another man!"

"He's running."

"Look at him go, would you!"

"Why, he's on a bicycle. Now he's met the other man. They're both waving at us. Look!"

"There comes something up the beach."

"What the devil is that thing?"

"Why, it looks like a boat."

"Why, certainly, it's a boat."

"No; it's on wheels."

"Yes, so it is. Well, that must be the lifeboat. They drag them along the shore on a wagon."

"That's the lifeboat, sure."

"No, by ——, it's — an omnibus."[1]

"I tell you it's a lifeboat."

"It is not! It's an omnibus. I can see it plain. See? One of these big hotel omnibuses."

"By thunder, you're right. It's an omnibus, sure as fate. What do you suppose they are doing with an omnibus? Maybe they are going around collecting the life crew, hey?"

"That's it, likely. Look! There's a fellow waving a little black flag. He's standing on the steps of the omnibus. There come those other two fellows. Now they're all talking together. Look at the fellow with the flag. Maybe he ain't waving it!"

"That ain't a flag, is it? That's his coat. Why, certainly, that's his coat."

"So it is; it's his coat. He's taken it off and is waving it around his head. But would you look at him swing it!"

"Oh, say, there isn't any lifesaving station there. That's just a winter resort hotel omnibus that has brought over some of the boarders to see us drown."

"What's that idiot with the coat mean? What's he signaling, anyhow?"

"It looks as if he were trying to tell us to go north. There must be a lifesaving station up there."

"No; he thinks we're fishing. Just giving us a merry hand. See? Ah, there, Willie!"

"Well, I wish I could make something out of those signals. What do you suppose he means?"

"He don't mean anything; he's just playing."

"Well, if he'd just signal us to try the surf again, or to go to sea and wait, or go north, or go south, or go to hell, there would be

---

[1] **omnibus**: bus.

some reason in it. But look at him! He just stands there and keeps his coat revolving like a wheel. The ass!"

"There come more people."

"Now there's quite a mob. Look! Isn't that a boat?"

"Where? Oh, I see where you mean. No, that's no boat."

"That fellow is still waving his coat."

"He must think we like to see him do that. Why don't he quit it? It don't mean anything."

"I don't know. I think he is trying to make us go north. It must be that there's a lifesaving station there somewhere."

"Say, he ain't tired yet. Look at 'im wave!"

"Wonder how long he can keep that up. He's been revolving his coat ever since he caught sight of us. He's an idiot. Why aren't they getting men to bring a boat out? A fishing boat — one of those big yawls — could come out here all right. Why don't he do something?"

"Oh, it's all right now."

"They'll have a boat out here for us in less than no time, now that they've seen us."

A faint yellow tone came into the sky over the low land. The shadows on the sea slowly deepened. The wind bore coldness with it, and the men began to shiver.

"Holy smoke!" said one, allowing his voice to express his impious mood, "if we keep on monkeying out here! If we've got to flounder out here all night!"

"Oh, we'll never have to stay here all night! Don't you worry. They've seen us now, and it won't be long before they'll come chasing out after us."

The shore grew dusky. The man waving a coat blended gradually into this gloom, and it swallowed in the same manner the omnibus and the group of people. The spray, when it dashed uproariously over the side, made the voyagers shrink and swear like men who were being branded.

"I'd like to catch the chump who waved the coat. I feel like soaking him one, just for luck."

"Why? What did he do?"

"Oh, nothing, but then he seemed so damned cheerful."

In the meantime the oiler rowed, and then the correspondent rowed, and then the oiler rowed. Gray-faced and bowed forward, they mechanically, turn by turn, plied the leaden oars. The form of the lighthouse had vanished from the southern horizon, but finally a pale star appeared, just lifting from the sea. The streaked saffron[1] in the west passed before the all-merging darkness, and the sea to the east was black.. The land had vanished, and was expressed only by the low and drear thunder of the surf.

"If I am going to be drowned — if I am going to be drowned, why, in the name of the seven mad gods who ruled the sea, was I allowed to come thus far and contemplate sand and trees? Was I brought here merely to have my nose dragged away as I was about to nibble the sacred cheese of life?"

The patient captain, drooped over the water jar, was sometimes obliged to speak to the oarsman.

"Keep her head up! Keep her head up!"

"Keep her head up, sir." The voices were weary and low.

This was surely a quiet evening. All save the oarsman lay heavily and listlessly in the boat's bottom. As for him, his eyes were just capable of noting the tall black waves that swept forward in a most sinister silence, save for an occasional subdued growl of a crest.

The cook's head was on a thwart, and he looked without interest at the water under his nose. He was deep in other scenes. Finally he spoke. "Billie," he murmured

[1] **saffron**: yellowish-orange color.

dreamfully, "what kind of pie do you like best?"

V

"Pie!" said the oiler and the correspondent, agitatedly. "Don't talk about those things, blast you!"

"Well," said the cook, "I was just thinking about ham sandwiches, and — "

A night on the sea in an open boat is a long night. As darkness settled finally, the shine of the light, lifting from the sea in the south, changed to a full gold. On the northern horizon a new light appeared, a small bluish gleam on the edge of the waters. These two lights were the furniture[1] of the world. Otherwise there was nothing but waves.

Two men huddled in the stern, and distances were so magnificent in the dinghy that the rower was enabled to keep his feet partly warm by thrusting them under his companions. Their legs indeed extended far under the rowing seat until they touched the feet of the captain forward. Sometimes, despite the efforts of the tired oarsman, a wave came piling into the boat, an icy wave of the night, and the chilling water soaked them anew. They would twist their bodies for a moment and groan, and sleep the dead sleep once more, while the water in the boat gurgled about them as the craft rocked.

The plan of the oiler and the correspondent was for one to row until he lost the ability, and then arouse the other from his sea-water couch in the bottom of the boat.

The oiler plied the oars until his head drooped forward and the overpowering sleep blinded him; and he rowed yet afterward. Then he touched a man in the bottom of the boat, and called his name. "Will you spell me for a little while?" he said meekly.

"Sure, Billie," said the correspondent, awakening and dragging himself to a sitting

[1] **furniture** : necessary equipment.

position. They exchanged places carefully, and the oiler, cuddling down in the sea water at the cook's side, seemed to go to sleep instantly.

The particular violence of the sea had ceased. The waves came without snarling. The obligation of the man at the oars was to keep the boat headed so that the tilt of the rollers would not capsize her, and to preserve her from filling when the crests rushed past. The black waves were silent and hard to be seen in the darkness. Often one was almost upon the boat before the oarsman was aware.

In a low voice the correspondent addressed the captain. He was not sure that the captain was awake, although this iron man seemed to be always awake. "Captain, shall I keep her making for that light north, sir?"

The same steady voice answered him. "Yes. Keep it about two points off the port bow."[2]

The cook had tied a life belt around himself in order to get even the warmth which this clumsy cork contrivance could donate, and he seemed almost stovelike when a rower, whose teeth invariably chattered wildly as soon as he ceased his labor, dropped down to sleep.

The correspondent, as he rowed, looked down at the two men sleeping under foot. The cook's arm was around the oiler's shoulders, and, with their fragmentary clothing and haggard faces, they were the babes of the sea — a grotesque rendering of the old babes in the wood.

Later he must have grown stupid at his work, for suddenly there was a growling of water, and a crest came with a roar and a swash into the boat, and it was a wonder that it did not set the cook afloat in his life-belt. The cook continued to sleep, but the oiler sat up, blinking his eyes and shaking with the new cold.

[2] **port bow** : front left part of boat.

"Oh, I'm awful sorry, Billie," said the correspondent, contritely.

"That's all right, old boy," said the oiler, and lay down again and was asleep.

Presently it seemed that even the captain dozed, and the correspondent thought that he was the one man afloat on all the oceans. The wind had a voice as it came over the waves, and it was sadder than the end.

There was a long, loud swishing astern of the boat, and a gleaming trail of phosphorescence,[1] like blue flame, was furrowed on the black waters. It might have been made by a monstrous knife.

Then there came a stillness, while the correspondent breathed with the open mouth and looked at the sea.

Suddenly there was another swish and another long flash of bluish light, and this time it was alongside the boat, and might almost have been reached with an oar. The correspondent saw an enormous fin speed like a shadow through the water, hurling the crystalline[2] spray and leaving the long glowing trail.

The correspondent looked over his shoulder at the captain. His face was hidden, and he seemed to be asleep. He looked at the babes of the sea. They certainly were asleep. So, being bereft of sympathy, he leaned a little way to one side and swore softly into the sea.

But the thing did not then leave the vicinity of the boat. Ahead or astern, on one side or the other, at intervals long or short, fled the long sparkling streak, and there was to be heard the whiroo of the dark fin. The speed and power of the thing was greatly to be admired. It cut the water like a gigantic and keen projectile.

The presence of this biding[3] thing did not affect the man with the same horror that it would if he had been a picnicker. He

[1] **phosphorescence**: glowing light.
[2] **crystalline**: clear, transparent.
[3] **biding**: waiting.

simply looked at the sea dully and swore in an undertone.

Nevertheless, it is true that he did not wish to be alone with the thing. He wished one of his companions to awake by chance and keep him company with it. But the captain hung motionless over the water jar, and the oiler and the cook in the bottom of the boat were plunged in slumber.

VI

"If I am going to be drowned — if I am going to be drowned — if I am going to be drowned, why, in the name of the seven mad gods who rule the sea, was I allowed to come thus far and contemplate sand and trees?"

During this dismal night, it may be remarked that a man would conclude that it was really the intention of the seven mad gods to drown him, despite the abominable injustice of it. For it was certainly an abominable injustice to drown a man who had worked so hard, so hard. The man felt it would be a crime most unnatural. Other people had drowned at sea since galleys swarmed with painted sails, but still —

When it occurs to a man that nature does not regard him as important, and that she feels she would not maim the universe by disposing of him, he at first wishes to throw bricks at the temple, and he hates deeply the fact that there are no bricks and no temples. Any visible expression of nature would surely be pelleted with his jeers.

Then, if there be no tangible thing to hoot, he feels, perhaps, the desire to confront a personification and indulge in pleas, bowed to one knee, and with hands supplicant, saying, "Yes, but I love myself."

A high cold star on a winter's night is the word he feels that she says to him. Thereafter he knows the pathos of his situation.

The men in the dinghy had not discussed these matters, but each had, no doubt, reflected upon them in silence and according to his mind. There was seldom any expression upon their faces save the general one of complete weariness. Speech was devoted to the business of the boat.

To chime the notes of his emotion, a verse mysteriously entered the correspondent's head. He had even forgotten that he had forgotten this verse, but it suddenly was in his mind.

A soldier of the Legion lay dying in Algiers;
There was lack of woman's nursing, there was dearth of woman's tears;
But a comrade stood beside him, and he took that comrade's hand,
And he said, "I never more shall see my own, my native land."

In his childhood the correspondent had been made acquainted with the fact that a soldier of the Legion lay dying in Algiers, but he had never regarded it as important. Myriads of his schoolfellows had informed him of the soldier's plight, but the dinning had naturally ended by making him perfectly indifferent. He had never considered it his affair that a soldier of the Legion lay dying in Algiers, nor had it appeared to him as a matter for sorrow. It was less to him than breaking of a pencil's point.

Now, however, it quaintly came to him as a human, living thing. It was no longer merely a picture of a few throes in the breast of a poet, meanwhile drinking tea and warming his feet at the grate; it was an actuality — stern, mournful, and fine.

The correspondent plainly saw the soldier. He lay on the sand with his feet out straight and still. While his pale left hand was upon his chest in an attempt to thwart the going of his life, the blood came between his fingers. In the far Algerian distance, a city of low square forms was set against a sky that was faint with the last sunset hues. The correspondent, plying the oars and dreaming of the slow and slower movements of the lips of the soldier, was moved by a profound and perfectly impersonal comprehension. He was sorry for the soldier of the Legion who lay dying in Algiers.

The thing which had followed the boat and waited had evidently grown bored at the delay. There was no longer to be heard the slash of the cutwater,[1] and there was no longer the flame of the long trail. The light in the north still glimmered, but it was apparently no nearer to the boat. Sometimes the boom of the surf rang in the correspondent's ears, and he turned the craft seaward then and rowed harder. Southward, some one had evidently built a watch fire on the beach. It was too low and too far to be seen, but it made a shimmering, roseate[2] reflection upon the bluff back of it, and this could be discerned from the boat. The wind came stronger, and sometimes a wave suddenly raged out like a mountain cat, and there was to be seen the sheen and sparkle of a broken crest.

The captain, in the bow, moved on his water jar and sat erect. "Pretty long night," he observed to the correspondent. He looked at the shore. "Those life-saving people take their time."

"Did you see that shark playing around?"

"Yes, I saw him. He was a big fellow, all right."

"Wish I had known you were awake."

Later the correspondent spoke into the bottom of the boat.

"Billie!" There was a slow and gradual disentanglement. "Billie, will you spell me?"

"Sure," said the oiler.

As soon as the correspondent touchèd the cold, comfortable sea water in the bottom of the boat and had huddled close to the cook's life belt he was deep in sleep, despite the fact that his teeth played all the popular airs. This sleep was so good to him that it was but a moment before he heard a voice

---

[1] **cutwater**: front of a boat's prow.
[2] **roseate**: rosy.

". . . at all times its edge was jagged with waves that seemed thrust up in points like rocks." Kissing the Moon, *by Winslow Homer.*

call his name in a tone that demonstrated the last stages of exhaustion. "Will you spell me?"

"Sure, Billie."

The light in the north had mysteriously vanished, but the correspondent took his course from the wide-awake captain.

Later in the night they took the boat farther out to sea, and the captain directed the cook to take one oar at the stern and keep the boat facing the seas. He was to call out if he should hear the thunder of the surf. This plan enabled the oiler and the correspondent to get respite together. "We'll give those boys a chance to get into shape again," said the captain. They curled down and, after a few preliminary chatterings and trembles, slept once more the dead sleep. Neither knew they had bequeathed[1] to the cook the company of another shark,

[1] **bequeathed:** *here,* transmitted.

or perhaps the same shark.

As the boat caroused on the waves, spray occasionally bumped over the side and gave them a fresh soaking, but this had no power to break their repose. The ominous slash of the wind and the water affected them as it would have affected mummies.

"Boys," said the cook, with the notes of every reluctance in his voice, "she's drifted in pretty close. I guess one of you had better take her to sea again." The correspondent, aroused, heard the crash of the toppled crests.

As he was rowing, the captain gave him some whisky and water, and this steadied the chills out of him. "If I ever get ashore and anybody shows me even a photograph of an oar — "

At last there was a short conversation.

"Billie! . . . Billie, will you spell me?"

"Sure," said the oiler.

VII

When the correspondent again opened his eyes, the sea and the sky were each of the gray hue of the dawning. Later, carmine[1] and gold was painted upon the waters. The morning appeared finally, in its splendor, with a sky of pure blue, and the sunlight flamed on the tips of the waves.

On the distant dunes were set many little black cottages, and a tall white windmill reared above them. No man, nor dog, nor bicycle appeared on the beach. The cottages might have formed a deserted village.

The voyagers scanned the shore. A conference was held in the boat. "Well," said the captain, "if no help is coming, we might better try a run through the surf right away. If we stay out here much longer we will be too weak to do anything for ourselves at all." The others silently acquiesced in this reasoning. The boat was headed for the beach. The correspondent wondered if none ever ascended the tall wind tower, and if then they never looked seaward. This tower was a giant, standing with its back to the plight of the ants. It represented in a degree, to the correspondent, the serenity of nature amid the struggles of the individual — nature in the wind, and nature in the vision of men. She did not seem cruel to him then, nor beneficent, nor treacherous, nor wise. But she was indifferent, flatly indifferent. It is, perhaps, plausible that a man in this situation, impressed with the unconcern of the universe, should see the innumerable flaws of his life and have them taste wickedly in his mind and wish for another chance. A distinction between right and wrong seems absurdly clear to him, then, in this new ignorance of the grave edge, and he understands that if he were given another opportunity he would mend his conduct and his words, and be better and brighter during an introduction or at a tea.

"Now, boys," said the captain, "she is

[1] **carmine**: rich crimson color.

going to swamp sure. All we can do is to work her in as far as possible, and then when she swamps, pile out and scramble for the beach. Keep cool now, and don't jump until she swamps sure."

The oiler took the oars. Over his shoulders he scanned the surf. "Captain," he said, "I think I'd better bring her about, and keep her head-on to the seas, and back her in."

"All right, Billie," said the captain. "Back her in." The oiler swung the boat then, and, seated in the stern, the cook and the correspondent were obliged to look over their shoulders to contemplate the lonely and indifferent shore.

The monstrous inshore rollers heaved the boat high until the men were again enabled to see the white sheets of water scudding up the slanted beach. "We won't get in very close," said the captain. Each time a man could wrest his attention from the rollers, he turned his glance toward the shore, and in the expression of the eyes during this contemplation there was a singular quality. The correspondent, observing the others, knew that they were not afraid, but the full meaning of their glances was shrouded.

As for himself, he was too tired to grapple fundamentally with the fact. He tried to coerce his mind into thinking of it, but the mind was dominated at this time by the muscles, and the muscles said they did not care. It merely occurred to him that if he should drown it would be a shame.

There were no hurried words, no pallor, no plain agitation. The men simply looked at the shore. "Now, remember to get well clear of the boat when you jump," said the captain.

Seaward the crest of a roller suddenly fell with a thunderous crash, and the long white comber came roaring down upon the boat.

"Steady now," said the captain. The men were silent. They turned their eyes from the shore to the comber and waited. The boat slid up the incline, leaped at the furious top, bounced over it, and swung down the long back of the wave. Some water had been shipped, and the cook bailed it out.

But the next crest crashed also. The tumbling, boiling flood of white water caught the boat and whirled it almost perpendicular. Water swarmed in from all sides. The correspondent had his hands on the gunwale at this time, and when the water entered at that place he swiftly withdrew his fingers, as if he objected to wetting them.

The little boat, drunken with this weight of water, reeled and snuggled deeper into the sea.

"Bail her out, cook! Bail her out!" said the captain.

"All right, Captain," said the cook.

"Now, boys, the next one will do for us sure," said the oiler. "Mind to jump clear of the boat."

The third wave moved forward, huge, furious, implacable. It fairly swallowed the dinghy, and almost simultaneously the men tumbled into the sea. A piece of life belt had lain in the bottom of the boat, and as the correspondent went overboard he held this to his chest with his left hand.

The January water was icy, and he reflected immediately that it was colder than he had expected to find it off the coast of Florida. This appeared to his dazed mind as a fact important enough to be noted at the time. The coldness of the water was sad; it was tragic. This fact was somehow mixed and confused with his opinion of his own situation so that it seemed almost a proper reason for tears. The water was cold.

When he came to the surface he was conscious of little but the noisy water. Afterward he saw his companions in the sea. The oiler was ahead in the race. He was swimming strongly and rapidly. Off to the correspondent's left, the cook's great white and corked back bulged out of the water;

and in the rear the captain was hanging with his one good hand to the keel[1] of the overturned dinghy.

There is a certain immovable quality to a shore, and the correspondent wondered at it amid the confusion of the sea.

It seemed also very attractive; but the correspondent knew that it was a long journey, and he paddled leisurely. The piece of life preserver lay under him, and sometimes he whirled down the incline of a wave as if he were on a hand sled.

But finally he arrived at a place in the sea where travel was beset with difficulty. He did not pause swimming to inquire what manner of current had caught him, but there his progress ceased. The shore was set before him like a bit of scenery on a stage, and he looked at it, and understood with his eyes each detail of it.

As the cook passed, much farther to the left, the captain was calling to him, "Turn over on your back, cook! Turn over on your back and use the oar."

"All right, sir." The cook turned on his back, and, paddling with an oar, went ahead as if he were a canoe.

Presently the boat also passed to the left of the correspondent, with the captain clinging with one hand to the keel. He would have appeared like a man raising himself to look over a board fence if it were not for the extraordinary gymnastics of the boat. The correspondent marveled that the captain could still hold to it.

They passed on nearer to shore, — the oiler, the cook, the captain — and following them went the water jar, bouncing gaily over the seas.

[1] keel: plate lengthwise along a boat's bottom.

The correspondent remained in the grip of this strange new enemy, a current. The shore, with its white slope of sand and its green bluff, topped with little silent cottages, was spread like a picture before him. It was very near to him then, but he was impressed as one who, in a gallery, looks at a scene from Brittany or Algiers.

He thought: "I am going to drown? Can it be possible? Can it be possible? Can it be possible?" Perhaps an individual must consider his own death to be the final phenomenon of nature.

But later a wave perhaps whirled him out of this small deadly current, for he found suddenly that he could again make progress toward the shore. Later still he was aware that the captain, clinging with one hand to the keel of the dinghy, had his face turned away from the shore and toward him, and was calling his name. "Come to the boat! Come to the boat!"

In his struggle to reach the captain and the boat, he reflected that when one gets properly wearied drowning must really be a comfortable arrangement — a cessation of hostilities accompanied by a large degree of relief; and he was glad of it, for the main thing in his mind for some moments had been horror of the temporary agony; he did not wish to be hurt.

Presently he saw a man running along the shore. He was undressing with most remarkable speed. Coat, trousers, shirt, everything flew magically off him.

"Come to the boat!" called the captain.

"All right, Captain." As the correspondent paddled, he saw the captain let himself down to bottom and leave the boat. Then the correspondent performed his one little marvel of the voyage. A large wave caught him and flung him with ease and supreme speed completely over the boat and far beyond it. It struck him even then as an event in gymnastics and a true miracle of the sea. An overturned boat in the surf is not a plaything to a swimming man.

The correspondent arrived in water that reached only to his waist, but his condition did not enable him to stand for more than a moment. Each wave knocked him into a heap, and the undertow pulled at him.

Then he saw the man who had been running and undressing, and undressing and running, come bounding into the water. He dragged ashore the cook, and then waded toward the captain; but the captain waved him away and sent him to the correspondent. He was naked — naked as a tree in winter; but a halo was about his head, and he shone like a saint. He gave a strong pull, and a long drag, and a bully heave at the correspondent's hand. The correspondent, schooled in the minor formulae,[1] said, "Thanks, old man." But suddenly the man cried, "What's that?" He pointed a swift finger. The correspondent said, "Go."

In the shallows, face downward, lay the oiler. His forehead touched sand that was periodically, between each wave, clear of the sea.

The correspondent did not know all that transpired afterward. When he achieved safe ground he fell, striking the sand with each particular part of his body. It was as if he had dropped from a roof, but the thud was grateful to him.

It seems that instantly the beach was populated with men with blankets, clothes, and flasks, and women with coffee pots and all the remedies sacred to their minds. The welcome of the land to the men from the sea was warm and generous; but a still and dripping shape was carried slowly up the beach, and the land's welcome for it could only be the different and sinister hospitality of the grave.

When it came night, the white waves paced to and fro in the moonlight, and the wind brought the sound of the great sea's voice to the men on shore, and they felt that they could then be interpreters.

---

[1] **minor formulae**: *i.e.*, of etiquette.

For Discussion

1. After their ordeal, the survivors "felt that they could then be interpreters." Interpreters of what? Only *then*, however — not before. In order to understand life, the story suggests, one must experience it — and the same is true of literature. What causes the correspondent to reconsider the bit of doggerel from his childhood about the soldier of the Legion? How had he felt about the soldier before? How does he feel about him now? What does the difference suggest about the importance of profound experience in understanding what one sees, hears, and reads? Why do you suppose the correspondent regarded the ordeal he was going through "even at the time" as "the best experience of his life" (page 460)?

2. Only one of the characters in this story is named. Who? At the end of the story, the oiler dies. How do you account for his death? Would the story have been as effective if no one had died at the end? Suppose the captain had died, and the others had lived. What would that outcome have suggested about the universe we live in — that is, about Nature?

3. Among other things, the story is about men facing the ultimate test, and one of the triumphs of "The Open Boat" lies in the honesty with which it reports on what it would be like to face death squarely. We believe, as we read, that yes, it would be like this — at least for people of the correspondent's temperament. Section VI, specifically, opens with an examination of the shifting attitudes of the correspondent toward his fate. How does he feel about being threatened with death? At the climax of the experience, moments and even seconds away from having to leap into the water, how does the correspondent feel about the death that may very well be waiting for him there? What are his feelings once he hits the water? "Perhaps," we are told, "an individual must consider his own death to be the final phenomenon of nature" (page 472). Explain what the comment means.

4. The death that does occur is to some extent foreshadowed, or anticipated. On page 461 we learn that the oiler, who does much of the rowing, worked double-watch just before the shipwreck, and immediately after we are given that information, we hear the captain urging the rowers not to exhaust themselves: "If we have to run a surf you'll need all your strength, because we'll sure have to swim for it." Nevertheless, there is irony in the oiler's death, while the others survive. Nature itself, the story seems to be saying, behaves ironically, nearly killing them all, for instance, within full sight of land and safety, and finally destroying the young one and letting the old one live. Irony pervades the situation from the start, where the four desperate men in the dinghy look "picturesque" (page 458), amid surroundings that are "probably splendid . . . probably glorious, this play of the free sea, wild with lights of emerald and white and amber" (page 458). What other ironies do you find in the situation of the four men adrift?

5. Stylistically, the irony is reflected in both understatement and overstatement. As for the latter, the gulls were "uncanny and sinister," and distances in the ten-foot boat were "magnificent." But more characteristically, Crane makes use of understatement. He refers to a "singular disadvantage" of the sea (page 459), when what is meant literally is something like an overwhelming cause of despair about the sea. Neither the oiler nor the correspondent, we are told, "was fond of rowing at this time," when what is meant literally is that both of them loathed, detested, and abominated rowing. What other examples of understatement struck you most forcefully?

For Composition

Similes, you remember, are stated comparisons introduced by *like, as,* or *than.* Examples of similes making use of each of those conjunctions occur in "The Open Boat." The craft on which the four men rode "plunged *like* an animal" (page 457). The gulls sat on the water, and "the wrath of the sea was no more to them *than* it was to a covey of prairie chickens" (page 459). In shifting position in the boat, the man in the stern "moved with care, *as* if he were of Sèvres," that is, of very fragile china.

1. **Analysis.** Examine the highly metaphorical content of Crane's prose style, clarifying the kinds of metaphors he uses and commenting — in a coherent essay of four or five paragraphs — on the effect of a style that depends to such an extent on comparisons. Is it effective or not?

2. **Analysis.** Analyze the structure of this story, commenting on the amount of time it occupies, what each of the seven parts contributes to the whole, and how the author has managed to keep what is essentially a static situation dramatic and interesting over such a considerable length of space.

Words and Allusions

ETYMOLOGY (page 225). On page 459 of "The Open Boat" a flock of seagulls is described as staring at the men in a *sinister* manner. What does *sinister* mean in that context? The word *sinister* is taken from Latin, where it means "left side" or "left hand." Using whatever sources you find necessary, explain how *sinister* has come to mean what it does today. Using the same sources, explain how the word *dexterity* has arrived at its present meaning, deriving as it does from the Latin word *dexter* which means "right hand."

WORDS IN CONTEXT (page 131). Explain the meanings of the following words as they are used in "The Open Boat": *picturesque* (458), *singular* (458), *ominous* (459), *ingenuously* (461), *diabolical* (461), *direful* (462), *admonitions* (462), *preposterous* (463), *obstreperous* (463), *contritely* (467).

In Summary

1. Facing the ultimate ordeal, the correspondent in "The Open Boat" formed an answer to that tantalizing question about man and nature: Is nature man's friend or enemy? "She did not seem cruel to him then, nor beneficent, nor treacherous, nor wise. But she was indifferent, flatly indifferent" (page 470). In which of the selections in this section are cruel aspects of nature exposed? Which dwell on beneficent aspects? Which reveal treacherous aspects of nature? Do any present nature as wise? Which of these attitudes toward nature seem to you nearest the truth? Support your answer specifically.

2. How does Nature regard man, Crane asks: "A high cold star on a winter's night is the word he feels that she says to him" (page 467). Explain what that "word" means. Contrast it with the stars to which Emerson directs our attention at the beginning of "Nature" (page 420). How do you think the author of "Autumn" would most likely regard those stars that Crane speaks of? On what do you base your opinion? How would the boy in "A Sunrise on the Veld," rising at half-past four and starting out from home on a winter's morning, regard them overhead?

3. Nature plays an important role in some of the selections read earlier in the anthology. Is the part it plays significant in "Dover Beach"? In "Young Goodman Brown"? In "Ozymandias"? In "How Much Land Does a Man Need?" In each case, justify your answer. With which of the attitudes toward nature expressed in this section do you think the author of *Job* would most likely have sympathized?

4. What is tactile imagery? How does it differ from kinetic imagery? Give examples of each. Distinguish between unity and coherence. Between free verse and blank verse. Define tone.

5. **Creative Writing.** "Autumn" (page 454) and "The Open Boat" (page 456) present unusually vivid examples of description — of a season in the case of the poem, of a day and a night and another day at sea in the case of the story. Other selections contain comparably vivid descriptions: in "Hook" and "A Sunrise on the Veld," to mention only two examples.

Compose a description of your own, of perhaps three hundred words of prose, or fewer of poetry. Whether poetry or prose, what you write should make whatever use is appropriate of the models mentioned above. For instance, you may choose to celebrate a season other than autumn. Think concretely of imagery that will evoke the season by appealing to several senses, and select details to include that will convey your attitude toward the season, whether favorable or unfavorable. You may want to use metaphorical language to make what may be unfamiliar to your reader clear and memorable. And be willing to revise, working always in the direction of greater coherence, unity, and vividness.

Reader's Choice

Pearl Buck, *The Good Earth*.

Wang Lung, a Chinese peasant, with his wife O-Lan, rises from poverty to wealth through hard work and his love of the soil.

Walter Van Tilburg Clark, *The Track of the Cat*.

A family of brothers pursues a great black panther during a blizzard from which only death can return.

Joseph Conrad, *Heart of Darkness*.

Marlow tells the story of Kurtz, the brilliant European adventurer who went into the Congo to bring enlightenment to its people but succumbed to the power of the jungle.

Daniel Defoe, *Robinson Crusoe*.

A young man, shipwrecked on a deserted island for twenty-four years, conquers the elements through ingenuity, as he conquers loneliness through strength of will.

William Faulkner, *The Bear*.

Young Ike McCaslin is initiated into the life of the hunter and joins the hunt for a huge bear that has never been brought to bay.

William Golding, *Lord of the Flies*.

A band of British schoolboys, stranded on an island uninhabited by adults, tries to organize a society but reverts to savagery.

Thomas Hardy, *The Return of the Native*.

Clym Yeobright returns from Paris to found a school on Egdon Heath. There he becomes a furze-cutter and a preacher among a people held forever in their natural surroundings.

W. H. Hudson, *Green Mansions*.

An English writer tells the story of Rima, a half-wild girl of the South American jungle, whom the Indians regard as a spirit of the forest.

Ole Rölvaag, *Giants in the Earth*.

A Norwegian couple from Minnesota migrates to the Dakota territory to dig a life out of the harsh and treeless land.

Antoine de Saint-Exupéry, *Wind, Sand, and Stars*.

An airmail pilot, in the early days of flight, records his responses to the wonders of sky and earth.

John Steinbeck, *The Grapes of Wrath*.

A rebellion of nature against man's abuse begins a tragic tale of social conflict.

Henry Thoreau, *Walden*.

Thoreau tells of his effort to free himself from dependence on material possessions by living alone in a natural setting with the bare essentials of life.

The Indian god Krishna, representing the force of good, subdues a serpent-demon by dancing on its heads.

Good and Evil

The great question is: who, or what, is responsible?

An earthquake ruins a city and kills 70,000 people. If a supernatural being caused that earthquake, then it makes sense to suspect that he is evil. If he did it for the purpose of ruining and killing, and only for that purpose, then surely he is an evil being, a demon.

But Jews and Christians believe their God is good. Because he created nature, it too is good, even including an earthquake. But, you say, maybe the devil caused this particular harm, putting a good thing to an evil use. However, this theory gets you into trouble, because God is so much more powerful than the devil that He would have to give him permission to do the harm. In *Job* (page 175) God did give the devil such permission, but to an ultimately good end. If God is all-powerful, it does not finally matter whether our suffering is caused by devils or by natural forces. Either way, He is ultimately responsible. If God is good too, then He makes us suffer for our own good. Our suffering is punishment for our trespasses against His law.

According to the Bible, there are two main events in the history of mankind. The first is Adam and Eve's transgression against God's one prohibition. Before they learned the difference between good and evil by doing that forbidden act, there was no suffering or death. After that, they and their descendants — all mankind — had to suffer and to die. The second main event according to the Bible is the coming of the Messiah to redeem mankind from this sin and suffering. The root difference between the faith of the Jews and that of the Christians is that Jews believe the Messiah has not yet come, whereas Christians believe that Jesus was the Messiah.

Let's go back to that earthquake. If this suffering was caused solely by natural forces, then it makes no sense to say it was evil. Natural forces in themselves are neither evil nor good. They just are. This is the scientific explanation of what happens. Damage, pain, illness, death, all are natural and only natural. No one is responsible for having willed them to exist.

For some thinkers, not even the crimes and injuries which men commit can be called evil. Everyone agrees, of course, that a man is not responsible for anything he does for reasons over which he has no control, including a monstrous murder committed while he was insane. But how are we to define *insane?* According to these thinkers, the very fact a man commits a murder proves he was insane, at least at the time he did it. Of course, it is logically impossible to be free to do a good act unless you were also free to do a bad one instead. Without evil, there can be no good in human actions. For these thinkers, there are health and sickness, comfort and pain, well-adjusted and anti-social behavior, but no good or evil.

But most people, thinking of the treacheries, wars, injustices, lies, cheats with which human life is afflicted, believe that there is plenty of man-made evil in the world, as well as much man-made good. This means that there is a terrible mystery at our very hearts. Sometimes we harm others because we can not help it, as in an accident. Sometimes we inflict pain on them for their own good, as a parent spanks a disobedient child or as a surgeon cuts out an appendix. Sometimes we hurt them for our own pleasure, as conquerors do. But often we suspect that the rational cause was not enough to explain fully *what I did, what they did.* There was more to it than we understand. There seems to be, in men individually and in men collectively, an ineradicable will to do evil for its own sake, freely, for no other reason than just to do it, but also to refrain from doing evil and to do positive good.

Writers, artists, philosophers, all thoughtful people are endlessly fascinated by this doubleness in our hearts as it manifests itself in what we say and do, in the ways we look and move, in the customs we make and break.

George P. Elliott

Parable of the Family That Dwelt Apart

E. B. WHITE

The difference between good and evil seems at first glance a distinction easy enough to make. Good people do good things. Isn't it clearly a good thing, for instance, to lend a hand to others?

On a small, remote island in the lower reaches of Barnetuck Bay there lived a family of fisherfolk by the name of Pruitt. There were seven of them, and they were the sole inhabitants of the place. They subsisted on canned corn, canned tomatoes, pressed duck, whole-wheat bread, terrapin,[1] Rice Krispies, crabs, cheese, queen olives, and homemade wild-grape preserve. Once in a while Pa Pruitt made some whiskey and they all had a drink.

They liked the island and lived there from choice. In winter, when there wasn't much doing, they slept the clock around, like so many bears. In summer they dug clams and set off a few pinwheels and salutes on July 4th. No case of acute appendicitis had ever been known in the Pruitt household, and when a Pruitt had a pain in his side he never even noticed whether it was the right side or the left side, but just hoped it would go away, and it did.

One very severe winter Barnetuck Bay froze over and the Pruitt family was marooned. They couldn't get to the mainland by boat because the ice was too thick, and they couldn't walk ashore because the ice was too treacherous. But inasmuch as no Pruitt had anything to go ashore for, except

mail (which was entirely second class), the freeze-up didn't make any difference. They stayed indoors, kept warm, and ate well, and when there was nothing better to do, they played crokinole.[2] The winter would have passed quietly enough had not someone on the mainland remembered that the Pruitts were out there in the frozen bay. The word got passed around the county and finally reached the Superintendent of State Police, who immediately notified Pathé News and the United States Army. The Army got there first, with three bombing planes from Langley Field, which flew low over the island and dropped packages of dried apricots and bouillon cubes, which the Pruitts didn't like much. The newsreel plane, smaller than the bombers and equipped with skis, arrived next and landed on a snow-covered field on the north end of the island. Meanwhile, Major Bulk, head of the state troopers, acting on a tip that one of the Pruitt children had appendicitis, arranged for a dog team to be sent by plane from Laconia, New Hampshire, and also dispatched a squad of troopers to attempt a crossing of the bay. Snow began falling at sundown, and during the night three of the rescuers lost their lives about half a mile from shore, trying to jump from one ice cake to another.

The plane carrying the sled dogs was over

[1] **terrapin:** turtle meat.

[2] **crokinole:** game in which disks are snapped from the edge of a table to a mark in the center.

southern New England when ice began forming on its wings. As the pilot circled for a forced landing, a large meat bone which one of the dogs had brought along got wedged in the socket of the main control stick, and the plane went into a steep dive and crashed against the side of a powerhouse, instantly killing the pilot and all the dogs, and fatally injuring Walter Ringstead, 7, of 3452 Garden View Avenue, Stamford, Conn.

Shortly before midnight, the news of the appendicitis reached the Pruitt house itself, when a chartered autogiro[1] from Hearst's International News Service made a landing in the storm and reporters informed Mr. Pruitt that his oldest boy, Charles, was ill and would have to be taken to Baltimore for an emergency operation. Mrs. Pruitt remonstrated, but Charles said his side did hurt a little, and it ended by his leaving in the giro. Twenty minutes later another plane came in, bearing a surgeon, two trained nurses, and a man from the National Broadcasting Company, and the second Pruitt boy, Chester, underwent an exclusive

appendectomy in the kitchen of the Pruitt home, over the Blue Network. This lad died, later, from eating dried apricots too soon after his illness, but Charles, the other boy, recovered after a long convalescence and returned to the island in the first warm days of spring.

He found things much changed. The house was gone, having caught fire on the third and last night of the rescue when a flare dropped by one of the departing planes lodged in a bucket of trash on the piazza.[2] After the fire, Mr. Pruitt had apparently moved his family into the emergency shed which the radio announcers had thrown up, and there they had dwelt under rather difficult conditions until the night the entire family was wiped out by drinking a ten-percent solution of carbolic acid which the surgeon had left behind and which Pa Pruitt had mistaken for grain alcohol.

Barnetuck Bay seemed a different place to Charles. After giving his kin decent burial, he left the island of his nativity and went to dwell on the mainland.

---

[1] **autogiro :** type of aircraft similar to a helicopter.

[2] **piazza :** porch.

ABOUT THE AUTHOR • Elwyn Brooks White (1899–) was born in Mount Vernon, New York, and attended Cornell University. In 1925, after a few years of newspaper work, he joined the staff of a new magazine called *The New Yorker.* It was here in writing weekly essays that he developed his highly individual style — "those silver and crystal sentences," James Thurber called them, "which have a ring like nobody else's sentences in the world." In 1938 White moved to the Maine coast where he wrote for *Harper's Magazine* a monthly column called *One Man's Meat.* The essays were published in book form under the same title. A later collection, *The Second Tree from the Corner,* won praise for White as "the finest essayist in the United States." In his writings White appears as an amused spectator of life and a gently ironic commentator on human weaknesses. "Humor," he once wrote, "plays close to the big hot fire which is truth, and the reader often feels the heat."

For Discussion

1. Plato's parable of the cave (page 49) tells a story to clarify a complex point. More frequently, as with those that Jesus told, parables teach a lesson; they are little stories from which conclusions about ethics and morality can be drawn. Unlike fables, which generally tell stories involving animals, parables tell their stories about humans, and the lesson to be derived from a parable is usually more profound than that of a fable. What would you say is the lesson — the theme, if you prefer — to be extracted from this parable of the Pruitts?

2. Why were the Pruitts on the island in Barnetuck Bay in the first place? The freezing-over of the bay sets in motion the catastrophes that befall them. Why do the family not simply leave the island? What causes people on the mainland to set forth to help them? What, specifically, are the consequences of that help?

3. There are elements of satire in White's parable. What follies of human behavior are being satirized?

For Composition

Fables end with morals that are stated; parables usually do not.

● **Argument.** In a coherent and unified essay of two or three paragraphs, indicate what the moral of E. B. White's parable might be, supporting your choice with specific references to the selection.

Words and Allusions

DOUBLETS. When two or more words come into a language from the same source but by different routes, they are referred to as *doublets*. For example, *parable*, *parabola*, and *palaver* all can be traced to the same Greek word; but *parable* came into English from Middle French, and *palaver* from Latin. What do *parable*, *parabola*, and *palaver* have in common that would suggest a common origin?

I Called the Devil and He Came

HEINRICH HEINE

Evil consequences can flow from the best of intentions; wanting to do good is not enough. Nor is it enough to trust the surface appearances of things to determine accurately what is good, what is evil. Appearances may deceive.

I called the devil and he came;
And then I saw, with a wondering gaze,
He was not hideous, he was not lame,
But a genial man with charming ways.
A man in the very flush of his prime;   5
Experienced, suave, and in touch with his time.

"Ich rief den Teufel und er kam" from *Heinrich Heine: Paradox and Poet, the Poems*, translated and edited by Louis Untermeyer, copyright 1937 by Harcourt Brace Jovanovich, Inc., renewed 1965 by Louis Untermeyer, reprinted by permission of the publisher.

As a diplomat, his talent is great,
And he speaks wisely of Church and the State.
True, he is pale; but it's little wonder,
For Sanskrit* and Hegel* he's staggering under. 10
His favorite poet is still Fouqué;*
As critic he finds that the work is a bother,
So Hecaté* now, his beloved grandmother,
Has taken the task and enjoys it, they say.
My legal studies called forth his laudation;* 15
He too, in his youth, found them quaint recreation.
He said that my friendship could never be
Too dear for him, and bowed to me,
And asked had we not met some place — 19
Perhaps the ambassador's? And with that sentence
I looked more closely at his face,
And recognized an old acquaintance.

10. **Sanskrit:** classical literary language of ancient India. **Hegel:** German philosopher (1770-1831). 11. **Fouqué:** German Romantic writer (1777-1843). 13. **Hecaté:** in Greek mythology, witch goddess of the lower world. 15. **laudation:** praise.

For Discussion

1. Heine's poem introduces us to that embodiment of evil, the devil himself. What are his characteristics as here presented? What does his being "in the very flush of his prime" tell us about evil? What does the fact that he was met earlier "Perhaps [at] the ambassador's" tell us? What does the final line "And recognized an old acquaintance" suggest about the pervasiveness of evil?

2. The devil is "Experienced, suave, and in touch with his time." What does his genial and charming manner suggest about the true nature of evil? Does it help explain the temptations to which people succumb? Can you think of examples of recognized evils that are not outwardly "hideous" (line 3)?

For Composition

The devil of Heine's poem bears affinities to the gentleman young Goodman Brown encountered in the forest near Salem Village (page 27).

• **Comparison and Contrast.** In a unified and coherent composition compare and contrast the two embodiments of evil created by Hawthorne and Heine. Cite relevant passages from "Young Goodman Brown" and "I Called the Devil and He Came" to support your comparison.

About the Poet. **Heinrich Heine** (1797–1856), one of the most popular and influential writers of his day, is still regarded as one of Germany's greatest poets. As a child he received both a Jewish and a Catholic education; in his twenties he was converted to Catholicism. An intense liberal, he fought for intellectual and political freedom both in Germany and in France, where he spent much of his youth in exile. During the Hitler regime Heine's books were publicly burned, not only because their author had been born a Jew, but because of their vigorous support of political liberty and social justice for all men.

The False Gems

GUY DE MAUPASSANT

No doubt you are familiar with Maupassant's celebrated story "The Neck-lace," about a woman who borrows jewels from a friend, loses them, then works the rest of her life to repay the loss, only to discover at the last that the jewels were imitation. Here is another, perhaps more subtle, story by the same author — set in the same world of Paris in the second half of the nine-teenth century. It, too, involves two women, a husband, and some jewelry.

M. Lantin had met the young woman at a soiree[1] at the home of the assistant chief of his bureau and at first sight had fallen madly in love with her.

She was the daughter of a country physi-cian who had died some months previously. She had come to live in Paris with her mother, who visited much among her ac-quaintances, in the hope of making a favor-able marriage for her daughter. They were poor and honest, quiet and unaffected.

The young girl was a perfect type of the virtuous woman whom every sensible young man dreams of one day winning for life. Her simple beauty had the charm of angelic modesty, and the imperceptible smile which constantly hovered about her lips seemed to be the reflection of a pure and lovely soul. Her praises resounded on every side. People were never tired of saying: "Happy the man who wins her love! He could not find a better wife."

Now M. Lantin enjoyed a snug little in-come of seven hundred dollars and, thinking he could safely assume the responsibilities of matrimony, proposed to this model young girl and was accepted.

He was unspeakably happy with her; she governed his household so cleverly and eco-nomically that they seemed to live in luxury. She lavished the most delicate attentions on her husband, coaxed and fondled him, and the charm of her presence was so great that six years after their marriage M. Lantin dis-covered that he loved his wife even more than during the first days of their honey-moon.

He only felt inclined to blame her for two things: her love of the theater and a taste for false jewelry. Her friends (she was ac-quainted with some officers' wives) fre-quently procured for her a box at the theater, often for the first representations of the new plays, and her husband was obliged to accompany her, whether he willed or not, to these amusements, though they bored him excessively after a day's labor at the office.

After a time M. Lantin begged his wife to get some lady of her acquaintance to accom-pany her. She was at first opposed to such an arrangement, but, after much persuasion on his part, she finally consented — to the infinite delight of her husband.

Now with her love for the theater came also the desire to adorn her person. True her costumes remained as before, simple and in the most correct taste, but she soon began to ornament her ears with huge rhinestones[2] which glittered and sparkled like real dia-monds. Around her neck she wore strings of false pearls, and on her arms bracelets of imitation gold.

Guy de Maupassant: pronounced gē də mō′pə·sän.
[1] soiree: evening party.

[2] rhinestones: artificial gems of glass made to resemble diamonds.

[handwritten: mockery —or— still ♡ in relationship]

Her husband frequently remonstrated with her, saying:

"My dear, as you cannot afford to buy real diamonds, you ought to appear adorned with your beauty and modesty alone, which are the rarest ornaments of your sex."

But she would smile sweetly and say:

"What can I do? I am so fond of jewelry. It is my only weakness. We cannot change our natures."

Then she would roll the pearl necklaces around her fingers and hold up the bright gems for her husband's admiration, gently coaxing him.

"Look! Are they not lovely? One would swear they were real."

M. Lantin would then answer smilingly:

"You have Bohemian[1] tastes, my dear."

Often of an evening, when they were enjoying a tête-à-tête[2] by the fireside, she would place on the tea table the leather box containing the "trash," as M. Lantin called it. She would examine the false gems with a passionate attention, as though they were in some way connected with a deep and secret joy, and she often insisted on passing a neck-

---

[1] **Bohemian**: unconventional, arty.

[2] **tête-à-tête** (tāt′ə·tāt′; in French, te′tä′tet′): private, intimate conversation between two people.

---

lace around her husband's neck and, laughing heartily, would exclaim: "How droll[3] you look!" Then she would throw herself into his arms and kiss him affectionately.

One evening in winter she attended the opera and on her return was chilled through and through. The next morning she coughed, and eight days later she died of inflammation of the lungs.[4]

M. Lantin's despair was so great that his hair became white in one month. He wept unceasingly; his heart was torn with grief, and his mind was haunted by the remembrance, the smile, the voice — by every charm of his beautiful dead wife.

Time, the healer, did not assuage his grief. Often during office hours, while his colleagues were discussing the topics of the day, his eyes would suddenly fill with tears, and he would give vent to his grief in heart-rending sobs. Everything in his wife's room remained as before her decease, and here he was wont to seclude himself daily and think of her who had been his treasure — the joy of his existence.

But life soon became a struggle. His income, which in the hands of his wife had

---

[3] **droll** (drōl): amusing.

[4] **inflammation of the lungs**: pneumonia.

ABOUT THE AUTHOR · **Guy de Maupassant** (1850–1893) produced nearly three hundred short stories, six novels, several plays, a volume of poetry, three travel books, and nearly three hundred articles in journals and newspapers during his brief lifetime. Born to affluent parents in Normandy, Maupassant became the godson of the novelist Gustave Flaubert. Under the tutelage of his famous godfather, he trained for his career as an author, a career launched with the publication of "Boule de suif" a few weeks before Flaubert's death in 1880. Tolstoy described *Une Vie*, Maupassant's first novel, as "perhaps the best French novel since Victor Hugo's *Les Misérables*." Other critics have compared Maupassant favorably with Balzac, Stendhal, and Flaubert.

"Her friends . . . frequently procured for her a box at the theater . . . and her husband was obliged to accompany her . . . to these amusements, though they bored him excessively. . . ."

covered all household expenses, was now no longer sufficient for his own immediate wants, and he wondered how she could have managed to buy such excellent wines and such rare delicacies, things which he could no longer 'procure with his modest resources.

He incurred some debts and was soon reduced to absolute poverty. One morning, finding himself without a cent in his pocket, he resolved to sell something, and immediately the thought occurred to him of disposing of his wife's paste jewels. He cherished in his heart a sort of rancor against the false gems. They had always irritated

him in the past, and the very sight of them spoiled somewhat the memory of his lost darling.

To the last days of her life she had continued to make purchases, bringing home new gems almost every evening. He decided to sell the heavy necklace which she seemed to prefer and which, he thought, ought to be worth about six or seven francs, for although paste it was, nevertheless, of very fine workmanship.

He put it in his pocket and started out in search of a jeweler's shop. He entered the first one he saw, feeling a little ashamed to expose his misery and also to offer such a worthless article for sale.

"Sir," he said to the merchant, "I would like to know what this is worth."

The man took his necklace, examined it, called his clerk and made some remarks in an undertone; then he put the ornament back on the counter and looked at it from a distance to judge of the effect.

M. Lantin was annoyed by all this detail and was on the point of saying: "Oh! I know well enough it is not worth anything," when the jeweler said: "Sir, that necklace is worth from twelve to fifteen thousand francs,[1] but I could not buy it unless you tell me now whence it comes."

The widower opened his eyes wide and remained gaping, not comprehending the merchant's meaning. Finally he stammered: "You say — are you sure?" The other replied dryly: "You can search elsewhere and see if anyone will offer you more. I consider it worth fifteen thousand at the most. Come back here if you cannot do better."

M. Lantin, beside himself with astonishment, took up the necklace and left the store. He wished time for reflection.

Once outside, he felt inclined to laugh and said to himself: "The fool! Had I only taken him at his word! That jeweler cannot distinguish real diamonds from paste."[2]

A few minutes after, he entered another store in the Rue de la Paix. As soon as the proprietor glanced at the necklace he cried out:

"Ah, *parbleu!*[3] I know it well; it was bought here."

M. Lantin was disturbed and asked:

"How much is it worth?"

"Well, I sold it for twenty thousand francs. I am willing to take it back for eighteen thousand when you inform me, according to our legal formality, how it

comes to be in your possession."

This time M. Lantin was dumfounded. He replied:

"But — but — examine it well. Until this moment I was under the impression that it was paste."

Said the jeweler:

"What is your name, sir?"

"Lantin — I am in the employ of the minister of the interior. I live at Number 16 Rue des Martyrs."

The merchant looked through his books, found the entry and said: "That necklace was sent to Madame Lantin's address, 16 Rue des Martyrs, July 20, 1876."

The two men looked into each other's eyes — the widower speechless with astonishment, the jeweler scenting a thief. The latter broke the silence by saying:

"Will you leave this necklace here for twenty-four hours? I will give you a receipt."

"Certainly," answered M. Lantin hastily. Then, putting the ticket in his pocket, he left the store.

He wandered aimlessly through the streets, his mind in a state of dreadful confusion. He tried to reason, to understand. He could not afford to purchase such a costly ornament. Certainly not. But then it must have been a present! — a present! — a present from whom? Why was it given her?

He stopped and remained standing in the middle of the street. A horrible doubt entered his mind — she? Then all the other gems must have been presents too! The earth seemed to tremble beneath him; the tree before him was falling; throwing up his arms, he fell to the ground, unconscious. He recovered his senses in a pharmacy into which the passers-by had taken him and was then taken to his home. When he arrived he shut himself up in his room and wept until nightfall. Finally, overcome with fatigue, he threw himself on the bed, where he passed an uneasy, restless night.

---

[1] **francs**: basic French monetary unit.

[2] **paste**: hard, bright glass, used in making artificial jewels.

[3] *parbleu!*: Heavens!

The following morning he arose and prepared to go to the office. It was hard to work after such a shock. He sent a letter to his employer, requesting to be excused. Then he remembered that he had to return to the jeweler's. He did not like the idea, but he could not leave the necklace with that man. So he dressed and went out.

It was a lovely day; a clear blue sky smiled on the busy city below, and men of leisure were strolling about with their hands in their pockets.

Observing them, M. Lantin said to himself: "The rich, indeed, are happy. With money it is possible to forget even the deepest sorrow. One can go where one pleases and in travel find that distraction which is the surest cure for grief. Oh, if I were only rich!"

He began to feel hungry, but his pocket was empty. He again remembered the necklace. Eighteen thousand francs! Eighteen thousand francs! What a sum!

He soon arrived in the Rue de la Paix, opposite the jeweler's. Eighteen thousand francs! Twenty times he resolved to go in, but shame kept him back. He was hungry, however, very hungry, and had not a cent in his pocket. He decided quickly, ran across the street in order not to have time for reflection and entered the store.

The proprietor immediately came forward and politely offered him a chair; the clerks glanced at him knowingly.

"I have made inquiries, Monsieur Lantin," said the jeweler, "and if you are still resolved to dispose of the gems I am ready to pay you the price I offered."

"Certainly, sir," stammered M. Lantin.

Whereupon the proprietor took from a drawer eighteen large bills, counted and handed them to M. Lantin, who signed a receipt and with a trembling hand put the money into his pocket.

As he was about to leave the store he turned toward the merchant, who still wore

> Inability to tell good from evil is the greatest worry of man's life.
>
> — Cicero

the same knowing smile, and, lowering his eyes, said:

"I have — I have other gems which I have received from the same source. Will you buy them also?"

The merchant bowed: "Certainly, sir."

M. Lantin said gravely: "I will bring them to you." An hour later he returned with the gems.

The large diamond earrings were worth twenty thousand francs; the bracelets, thirty-five thousand; the rings, sixteen thousand; a set of emeralds and sapphires, fourteen thousand; a gold chain with solitaire pendant,[1] forty thousand — making the sum of one hundred and forty-three thousand francs.

The jeweler remarked jokingly:

"There was a person who invested all her earnings in precious stones."

M. Lantin replied seriously:

"It is only another way of investing one's money."

That day he lunched at Voisin's[2] and drank wine worth twenty francs a bottle. Then he hired a carriage and made a tour of the Bois, and as he scanned the various turnouts[3] with a contemptuous air he could hardly refrain from crying out to the occupants:

"I, too, am rich! I am worth two hundred thousand francs."

Suddenly he thought of his employer. He drove up to the office and entered gaily, saying:

---

[1] **solitaire pendant:** single jewel hanging from a chain.

[2] **Voisin's:** elegant and expensive Parisian restaurant.

[3] **turnouts:** carriages with their horses.

"Sir, I have come to resign my position. I have just inherited three hundred thousand francs."

He shook hands with his former colleagues and confided to them some of his projects for the future; then he went off to dine at the Café Anglais.[1]

He seated himself beside a gentleman of aristocratic bearing and during the meal informed the latter confidentially that he had just inherited a fortune of four hundred thousand francs.

For the first time in his life he was not bored at the theater and spent the remainder of the night in a gay frolic.

Six months afterward he married again. His second wife was a very virtuous woman with a violent temper. She caused him much sorrow.

[1] **Café Anglais:** another elegant and famed restaurant.

For Discussion

1. The jewels belonging to his dead wife, M. Lantin discovers, were given to her: "a present! — a present from whom?" What is the answer? How does the discovery immediately affect him? How long does that first reaction last? What is his mood subsequently?

2. The outcome of "The False Gems" explains several little mysteries raised earlier. Lantin's first wife "would examine the false gems with a passionate attention, as though they were in some way connected with a deep and secret joy" (page 484). Comment on the remark in the light of what you know by the end of the story. M. Lantin wondered after his wife's death "how she could have managed to buy such excellent wines and such rare delicacies." How had she?

3. M. Lantin married twice, the second time to "a very virtuous woman," the first time to "a perfect type of the virtuous woman whom

every sensible young man dreams of one day winning for life." Of the two, which was the better wife? Defend your answer.

4. Literature is concerned primarily with emotion, and most literature is a chronicle of feeling, whether expressed as verse or fiction, as a lyric poem or (the case here) a story. Notice that again and again we are told of M. Lantin's feelings: "He was unspeakably happy"; "she finally consented — to the infinite delight of her husband"; "M. Lantin was annoyed . . ."; "M. Lantin, beside himself with astonishment . . ."; "Twenty times . . . shame kept him back." The list of citations could be extended. History records fact; literature records reactions to facts. Mention several other instances in the story where strong emotion, provoked by events, is specifically identified.

For Composition

Analysis, as you have discovered, is the process of examining something in order to understand it. If the something being analyzed is a single entity — a wristwatch or Shakespeare's life, for instance — analysis is a matter of *division* into parts. If, on the other hand, analysis of many entities is being undertaken — the works of Shakespeare or the flora of the American Southwest — the process is one of *classification*.

• **Analysis.** In a coherent and specific composition, analyze the sources of M. Lantin's happiness that derive from his marriage to his first wife. Consider the happiness she brings him both during her lifetime and afterwards. Is your analysis one of division or of classification? Explain.

Words and Allusions

CONNOTATION. Words may have the same denotations, but their connotations may differ greatly (page 37). Here are a list of words that denote falseness: *fake, artificial, phoney, imitation, unreal, sham, synthetic, fraudulent.* Which of these words has the most favorable connotation? Which has the least favorable? Arrange them in an order that moves from most favorable to least favorable.

Snake

D. H. LAWRENCE

Man has pictured evil in many shapes. The devil himself assumed a serpent's form in the Garden of Eden, and most of us even now, whether justly or unjustly, feel at the sight of a snake — that slithery, strange whiplash — a feeling that Emily Dickinson called "zero at the bone." Yet the chill feeling may not be entirely one of revulsion. At the same time that we are repelled, we may be involuntarily attracted too.

A snake came to my water-trough
On a hot, hot day, and I in pyjamas for the heat,
To drink there.

In the deep, strange-scented shade of the great dark carob-tree*
I came down the steps with my pitcher   5
And must wait, must stand and wait, for there he was at the trough before me.

He reached down from a fissure* in the earth-wall in the gloom
And trailed his yellow-brown slackness soft-bellied down, over the edge of the
      stone trough
And rested his throat upon the stone bottom,
And where the water had dripped from the tap, in a small clearness,   10
He sipped with his straight mouth,
Softly drank through his straight gums, into his slack long body,
Silently.

Someone was before me at my water-trough,
And I, like a second comer, waiting.   15

He lifted his head from his drinking, as cattle do,
And looked at me vaguely, as drinking cattle do,
And flickered his two-forked tongue from his lips, and mused a moment,
And stooped and drank a little more,
Being earth-brown, earth-golden from the burning bowels of the earth   20
On the day of Sicilian July, with Etna* smoking.

The voice of my education said to me
He must be killed,
For in Sicily the black, black snakes are innocent, the gold are venomous.

4. **carob-tree**: evergreen tree of the Mediterranean area. 7. **fissure**: crack. 21. **Etna**: volcanic mountain in eastern Sicily.

And voices in me said, If you were a man 25
You would take a stick and break him now, and finish him off.

But must I confess how I liked him,
How glad I was he had come like a guest in quiet, to drink at my water-trough
And depart peaceful, pacified, and thankless,
Into the burning bowels of this earth? 30

Was it cowardice, that I dared not kill him?
Was it perversity,* that I longed to talk to him?
Was it humility, to feel so honored?
I felt so honored.

And yet those voices: 35
If you were not afraid, you would kill him!

And truly I was afraid, I was most afraid,
But even so, honored still more
That he should seek my hospitality
From out the dark door of the secret earth. 40

He drank enough
And lifted his head, dreamily, as one who has drunken,
And flickered his tongue like a forked night on the air, so black;
Seeming to lick his lips,
And looked around like a god, unseeing, into the air, 45
And slowly turned his head,
And slowly, very slowly, as if thrice adream,
Proceeded to draw his slow length curving round
And climb again the broken bank of my wall-face.

And as he put his head into that dreadful hole, 50
And as he slowly drew up, snake-easing his shoulders, and entered farther,
A sort of horror, a sort of protest against his withdrawing into that horrid black
    hole,
Deliberately going into the blackness, and slowly drawing himself after,
Overcame me now his back was turned.

I looked round, I put down my pitcher, 55
I picked up a clumsy log
And threw it at the water-trough with a clatter.

I think it did not hit him,
But suddenly that part of him that was left behind convulsed in undignified haste,
Writhed like lightning, and was gone 60

32. **perversity**: obstinacy, contrariness.

Into the black hole, the earth-lipped fissure in the wall-front.
At which, in the intense still noon, I stared with fascination.

And immediately I regretted it.
I thought how paltry, how vulgar, what a mean act!
I despised myself and the voices of my accursed human education.   65

And I thought of the albatross,*
And I wished he would come back, my snake.

For he seemed to me again like a king,
Like a king in exile, uncrowned in the underworld,
Now due to be crowned again.   70

And so, I missed my chance with one of the lords
Of life.
And I have something to expiate;*
A pettiness.

> 66. **albatross**: seabird; *here*, a reference to Samuel Taylor Coleridge's *The Rime of the Ancient Mariner*.   73. **expiate**: atone for.

For Discussion

1. The snake's appearance at the water-trough provokes in the speaker a number of responses. What are they? In what way does the snake challenge the speaker's manliness? Finally the speaker does respond to the challenge by throwing the "clumsy log." What makes him do it?

2. Because of its position, the final line gains emphasis. Why do you suppose the speaker regards his own act toward the snake as "petty"?

3. "And so I missed my chance with one of the lords / Of life," the speaker remarks (lines 71–72). How do you suppose he imagines he should have conducted himself? The speaker "longed to talk to him" (line 32). In what sense might "talk" be used there?

4. From very early in man's experience snakes have been associated with evil. In this instance education taught the speaker to kill the snake at the water-trough, and for what seem good reasons. Why should the snake have been killed? What case can be made for allowing the snake to live? Did the speaker in fact regard the snake as evil? Explain.

5. Consider the diction that describes the snake. Which words — nouns, adjectives, verbs — seem to you especially effective in showing the snake's appearance and movements? Is the poem in free verse, blank verse, or rhymed metrical verse? Explain.

For Composition

Line 66 refers to the albatross, a great sea bird that figures prominently in *The Rime of the Ancient Mariner*, by Samuel Taylor Coleridge (1772–1834). There, a crewman for no apparent reason shoots and kills the great bird as it flies over the ship, and the consequences of that senseless killing of one of God's creatures extend through the rest of his life.

1. **For Research.** Read *The Rime of the Ancient Mariner* and prepare notes on which an oral report or written essay might be based. Your notes should briefly retell the story the mariner tells, should interpret that story as well as you are able, and should indicate something about the nature of the poem as a poem.

Appropriate quotations will strengthen your remarks, and you should indicate how an acquaintance with the poem elucidates the meaning of Lawrence's "Snake."

2. **Argument.** "The snake is an envoy from the natural world — neither evil nor good, but assuredly beautiful. Lawrence's poem is really about the conflict between instinct and learning, between man's instinctive responses to beauty and his learned and quite different responses to the world around him." In a coherent and unified essay of three or four paragraphs, consider the quoted judgment, supporting or refuting it on the basis of the effect of the poem as a whole as well as specific citations from it.

About the Poet. **D. H. Lawrence** (1885–1930)

was born in Nottingham, England, the son of a coal miner and a schoolteacher. Taught to read by his mother, he attended high school and university with the intention of becoming a teacher himself. But abandoning that when his first novel was published in 1911, he devoted the rest of his life to writing fiction and poetry. A controversial and frequently banned author, Lawrence is best known for his novels. His writing often explores sexual themes, although his own life was extremely temperate and austere. He was fascinated by nature, particularly by animals, a fascination reflected in his poetry. As one critic notes, he "makes us feel the intensity of life in the natural world." In his poetry "birds, beasts, and flowers have a glowing vigor." Lawrence died at forty-four in a French sanitorium after years of suffering from tuberculosis.

Rashomon

RYUNOSUKE AKUTAGAWA

The preceding selection suggests that a man's instincts may not agree with what his reason tells him is evil. But the question of distinguishing good from evil presents other perplexities. Suppose, for instance, there is no choice in the matter: commit evil or die. That situation is posed in the following grim story set in twelfth-century Kyoto, ancient capital of Japan. The Rashomon of the story was the great city gate, built in 789, and at the time of the events described here, in bad repair and all but abandoned.

It was a chilly evening. A servant of a samurai[1] stood under the Rashomon, waiting for a break in the rain.

No one else was under the wide gate. On

the thick column, its crimson lacquer rubbed off here and there, perched a cricket. Since the Rashomon stands on Sujaku Avenue, a few other people at least in sedge[2] hat or nobleman's headgear, might have been expected to be waiting there for a break in the rain storm. But no one was near except this man.

For the past few years the city of Kyoto

Rashomon: rä′shō·mōn′.
Ryunosuke Akutagawa: pronounced rī·ü·nō′s′ke′ ä·kü′tä·gä′wä.
[1] **samurai:** Japanese military officer.

"Rashomon," from *Rashomon* by Ryunosuke Akutagawa. Permission by Liveright, Publishers, New York. Copyright 1952 by Liveright Publishing Corp.

[2] **sedge:** coarse grass.

had been visited by a series of calamities, earthquakes, whirlwinds, and fires, and Kyoto had been greatly devastated. Old chronicles say that broken pieces of Buddhist images and other Buddhist objects, with their lacquer, gold, or silver leaf worn off, were heaped up on roadsides to be sold as firewood. Such being the state of affairs in Kyoto, the repair of the Rashomon was out of the question. Taking advantage of the devastation, foxes and other wild animals made their dens in the ruins of the gate, and thieves and robbers found a home there too. Eventually it became customary to bring unclaimed corpses to this gate and abandon them. After dark it was so ghostly that no one dared approach.

Flocks of crows flew in from somewhere. During the daytime these cawing birds circled round the ridgepole[1] of the gate. When the sky overhead turned red in the afterlight of the departed sun, they looked like so many grains of sesame[2] flung across the gate. But on that day not a crow was to be seen, perhaps because of the lateness of the hour. Here and there the stone steps, beginning to crumble, and with rank grass growing in their crevices, were dotted with the white droppings of crows. The servant, in a worn blue kimono, sat on the seventh and highest step, vacantly watching the rain. His attention was drawn to a large pimple irritating his right cheek.

As has been said, the servant was waiting for a break in the rain. But he had no particular idea of what to do after the rain stopped. Ordinarily, of course, he would have returned to his master's house, but he had been discharged just before. The prosperity of the city of Kyoto had been rapidly declining, and he had been dismissed by his master, whom he had served many years, because of the effects of this decline. Thus, confined by the rain, he was at a loss to

know where to go. And the weather had not a little to do with his depressed mood. The rain seemed unlikely to stop. He was lost in thoughts of how to make his living tomorrow, helpless incoherent thoughts protesting an inexorable fate. Aimlessly he had been listening to the pattering of the rain on the Sujaku Avenue.

The rain, enveloping the Rashomon, gathered strength and came down with a pelting sound that could be heard far away. Looking up, he saw a fat black cloud impale itself on the tips of the tiles jutting out from the roof of the gate.

He had little choice of means, whether fair or foul, because of his helpless circumstances. If he chose honest means, he would undoubtedly starve to death beside the wall or in the Sujaku gutter. He would be brought to this gate and thrown away like a stray dog. If he decided to steal. . . . His mind, after making the same detour time and again, came finally to the conclusion that he would be a thief.

But doubt returned many times. Though determined that he had no choice, he was still unable to muster enough courage to justify the conclusion that he must become a thief.

After a loud fit of sneezing he got up slowly. The evening chill of Kyoto made him long for the warmth of a brazier.[3] The wind in the evening dusk howled through the columns of the gate. The cricket which had been perched on the crimson-lacquered column was already gone.

Ducking his neck, he looked around the

---

[1] **ridgepole:** top beam.
[2] **sesame:** flat seeds.

[3] **brazier:** metal container holding burning coals.

gate, and drew up the shoulders of the blue kimono which he wore over his thin underwear. He decided to spend the night there, if he could find a secluded corner sheltered from wind and rain. He found a broad lacquered stairway leading to the tower over the gate. No one would be there, except the dead, if there were any. So, taking care that the sword at his side did not slip out of the scabbard, he set foot on the lowest step of the stairs.

A few seconds later, halfway up the stairs, he saw a movement above. Holding his breath and huddling catlike in the middle of the broad stairs leading to the tower, he watched and waited. A light coming from the upper part of the tower shone faintly upon his right cheek. It was the cheek with the red, festering pimple visible under his stubbly whiskers. He had expected only dead people inside the tower, but he had only gone up a few steps before he noticed a fire above, about which someone was moving. He saw a dull, yellow, flickering light which made the cobwebs hanging from the ceiling glow in a ghostly way. What sort of person would be making a light in the Rashomon . . . and in a storm? The unknown, the evil terrified him.

As quietly as a lizard, the servant crept up to the top of the steep stairs. Crouching on all fours, and stretching his neck as far as possible, he timidly peeped into the tower.

As rumor had said, he found several corpses strewn carelessly about the floor. Since the glow of the light was feeble, he could not count the number. He could only see that some were naked and others clothed. Some of them were women, and all were lolling on the floor with their mouths open or their arms outstretched showing no more signs of life than so many clay dolls. One would doubt that they had even been alive, so eternally silent they were. Their shoulders, breasts, and torsos stood out in the dim light, other parts vanished in shadow. The offensive smell of these decomposed corpses brought his hand to his nose.

The next moment his hand dropped and he stared. He caught sight of a ghoulish form bent over a corpse. It seemed to be an old woman, gaunt, gray-haired, and nunnish in appearance. With a pine torch in her right hand, she was peeping into the face of a corpse which had long black hair.

Seized more with horror than curiosity, he even forgot to breathe for a time. He felt the hair of his head and body stand on end. As he watched, terrified, she wedged

ABOUT THE AUTHOR • Ryunosuke Akutagawa (1892–1927) was a Japanese writer whose poems, essays, and stories have been widely translated into English. Before his suicide at age thirty-five, Akutagawa had been a teacher and newspaperman as well as a widely acclaimed author. In his stories, he creates a supernatural and surrealistic atmosphere of nightmare quality. His best-known story, "Rashomon," and another of his stories, "In the Grove," provided the basis for the motion picture Rashomon, which won first prize at the Venice Film Festival in 1951; Rashomon has also been produced as a play in the United States.

the torch between two floor boards and, laying hands on the head of the corpse, began to pull out the long hairs one by one, as a monkey kills the lice of her young. The hair came out smoothly with the movement of her hands.

As the hair came out, fear faded from his heart, and his hatred toward the old woman mounted. It grew beyond hatred, becoming a consuming antipathy[1] against all evil. At this instant if anyone had brought up the question of whether he would starve to death or become a thief — the question which had occurred to him a little while ago — he would not have hesitated to choose death. His hatred toward evil flared up like the piece of pine wood which the old woman had stuck in the floor.

He did not know why she pulled out the hair of the dead. Accordingly, he did not know whether her case was to be put down as good or bad. But in his eyes, pulling out the hair of the dead in the Rashomon on this stormy night was an unpardonable crime. Of course it never entered his mind that a little while ago he had thought of becoming a thief.

Then, summoning strength into his legs, he rose from the stairs and strode, hand on sword, right in front of the old creature. The hag turned, terror in her eyes, and sprang up from the floor, trembling. For a small moment she paused, poised there, then lunged for the stairs with a shriek.

"Wretch! Where are you going?" he shouted, barring the way of the trembling hag who tried to scurry past him. Still she attempted to claw her way by. He pushed her back to prevent her . . . they struggled, fell among the corpses, and grappled there. The issue was never in doubt. In a moment he had her by the arm, twisted it, and forced her down to the floor. Her arms

[1] **antipathy**: hatred.

were all skin and bones, and there was no more flesh on them than on the shanks of a chicken. No sooner was she on the floor than he drew his sword and thrust the silver-white blade before her very nose. She was silent. She trembled as if in a fit, and her eyes were open so wide that they were almost out of their sockets, and her breath came in hoarse gasps. The life of this wretch was his now. This thought cooled his boiling anger and brought a calm pride and satisfaction. He looked down at her, and said in a somewhat calmer voice:

"Look here, I'm not an officer of the High Police Commissioner. I'm a stranger who happened to pass by this gate. I won't bind you or do anything against you, but you must tell me what you're doing up here."

Then the old woman opened her eyes still wider, and gazed at his face intently with the sharp red eyes of a bird of prey. She moved her lips, which were wrinkled into her nose, as though she were chewing something. Her pointed Adam's apple moved in her thin throat. Then a panting sound like the cawing of a crow came from her throat:

"I pull the hair . . . I pull out the hair . . . to make a wig."

Her answer banished all unknown from their encounter and brought disappointment. Suddenly she was only a trembling old woman there at his feet. A ghoul no longer: only a hag who makes wigs from the hair of the dead — to sell, for scraps of food. A cold contempt seized him. Fear left his heart, and his former hatred entered.

Rashomon Gate, the setting of Akutagawa's story, no longer exists. But similar gates, serving as entrances to temple and palace grounds, can be seen in many parts of Japan. Pictured here is the Chion-in Temple Gate in Kyoto.

These feelings must have been sensed by the other. The old creature, still clutching the hair she had pulled off the corpse, mumbled out these words in her harsh broken voice:

"Indeed, making wigs out of the hair of the dead may seem a great evil to you, but these that are here deserve no better. This woman, whose beautiful black hair I was pulling, used to sell cut and dried snake flesh at the guard barracks, saying that it was dried fish. If she hadn't died of the plague, she'd be selling it now. The guards liked to buy from her, and used to say her fish was tasty. What she did couldn't be wrong, because if she hadn't, she would have starved to death. There was no other choice. If she knew I had to do this in order to live, she probably wouldn't care."

He sheathed his sword, and, with his left hand on its hilt, he listened to her medi-tatively. His right hand touched the big pimple on his cheek. As he listened, a certain courage was born in his heart — the courage which he had not had when he sat under the gate a little while ago. A strange power was driving him in the opposite direction of the courage which he had had when he seized the old woman. No longer did he wonder whether he should starve to death or become a thief. Starvation was so far from his mind that it was the last thing that would have entered it.

"Are you sure?" he asked in a mocking tone, when she finished talking. He took his right hand from his pimple, and, bending forward, seized her by the neck and said sharply:

"Then it's right if I rob you. I'd starve if I didn't."

He tore her clothes from her body and

kicked her roughly down on the corpses as she struggled and tried to clutch his leg. Five steps, and he was at the top of the stairs. The yellow clothes he had wrested off her were under his arm, and in a twinkling he had rushed down the steep stairs into the abyss of night. The thunder of his descending steps pounded in the hollow tower, and then it was quiet.

Shortly after that the hag raised up her body from the corpses. Grumbling and groaning, she crawled to the top stair by the still flickering torchlight, and through the gray hair which hung over her face, she peered down to the last stair in the torch light.

Beyond this was only darkness . . . unknowing and unknown.

For Discussion

1. Is the servant of this story a good man or an evil one? What leads him to kick the old woman down, tear off her clothes, and flee? At the end, how does the old woman respond to what has happened to her?

2. What I'm doing, the old woman says, "may seem a great evil to you, but these that are here deserve no better." What reasons does she offer to support that attitude? Do you agree with what she is saying? Would you have been convinced, had you been hearing her argument face to face?

3. Like begets like. In what way is that truism applicable to the events in "Rashomon"? Can a society survive if right is defined as the servant defines it late in this story?

4. Again notice how literature chronicles feeling. The servant is in turn terrified, horrified, and filled with hatred by what he is experiencing. What other emotions does he feel in the course of his encounter with the old woman? What emotions might she be feeling at the same time?

For Composition

"He had little choice of means, whether fair or foul, because of his helpless circumstances. If he chose honest means, he would undoubtedly starve to death. . . . His mind, after making the same detour time and again, came finally to the conclusion that he would be a thief."

1. **Analysis.** In a brief composition consider the irony of the servant's attitude as expressed in the citation above, in the light of his response to the old woman's activities discovered a few moments later.

2. **Argument.** Does the plight of the servant in twelfth-century Japan have any relevance to life in modern America? In a coherent and unified essay discuss the relevance of "Rashomon" to life today. One persuasive way to develop the argument would be through the use of example.

Words and Allusions

LITERARY TERMS (page 313) 1. The crows flying about the gate of the city in "Rashomon" are carrion eaters, harbingers of death. Along with the broken idols, the wild beasts, and the crumbling masonry of the gate, they serve as symbols of death and decay. What does the word *symbol* denote in literature? Use the word in a sentence to illustrate its meaning.

2. The term *pathetic fallacy* refers to the attribution of human traits to inanimate or natural objects. For example, Akutagawa describes how "the wind in the evening dusk howled through the columns of the gate." What other examples of the pathetic fallacy do you find in the story? What is the difference between the terms *pathetic fallacy* and *personification?*

Good and Evil Reconsidered

FRIEDRICH NIETZSCHE

Some of the most disturbing reflections on the nature of evil and good are contained in the works of the brilliant late-nineteenth-century German philosopher Friedrich Nietzsche. It was Nietzsche who, in frequently aphoristic and compelling prose, developed the concept of the superman. "I am writing," he proclaimed in his *The Will to Power*, "for a race of men which does not yet exist: for 'the lords of the earth.'" Meanwhile, in the world that does exist, he distinguished in good patrician fashion between masters (or lords) and slaves (or dependents), to whom good and evil mean quite different things. Hence, questions of morality he found to be relative, and he proceeded to demonstrate the consequences of that conviction in writings that were intended to be read only by the lords themselves — those few outstanding people in every culture for whom, Nietzsche felt, different rules should apply. What follows is an extract from his work *Beyond Good and Evil*, written in 1885.

By examining the many finer and baser moral systems that have influenced and still influence the world, I have found that certain traits regularly reappear in combination, until finally two basic types have been revealed to me and a basic difference has emerged. There is a master morality and a slave morality. Let me add at once that all higher and more complex cultures make an effort to combine both moral systems. Usually the systems get tangled and misunderstood. Indeed, now and then they even lodge together in the same people, in the same single soul.

The differences in moral values depend on whether they come from a ruling class, comfortably aware of its detachment from its inferiors, or from the inferiors, slaves and dependents of all kinds. In the first case, if the rulers determine moral values, the idea

Friedrich Nietzsche: pronounced frē′drik nē′chə.

of "good" means a lofty, proud state of the soul which serves to distinguish and determine those of rank. The man of rank cuts himself off from creatures in whom the opposite of such a proud, lofty soul appears. He detests them. One understands at once that for this higher moral type, the contrast between "good" and "wicked" is the same as the contrast between "noble" and "common."

The contrast between today's so-called good and so-called evil has another origin, for which let us hate the cowardly, jittery, petty man thinking only of security; also the suspicious man with his covert glances, the slavish doglike kind of man who lets himself be whipped, the wheedling flatterer; and above all the liar. A basic belief of all aristocrats is that the common people are liars.

"We honest ones." — Thus the nobles of ancient Greece described themselves. It is perfectly clear that the standards of moral values were first of all for men, then were later led astray and applied to actions. Thus it is a serious error for historians of morality to start by asking such questions as, "Why should an action involving fellow feeling be praised?"

The noble man looks to himself as the arbiter[1] of values, has no need to be adjudged[2] good. He decrees: "What is harmful to me is in itself harmful." He knows it is he himself who lends the highest values to things, that he is the arbiter of values. He honors everything that he finds in himself. Such a morality is self-en-nobling.

In the forefront of this morality stands a taste for monopoly,[3] for power that wants to overflow, for joy at the breaking point, for experience of great wealth that can grant or deprive. The noble man does help unfortunates, but hardly or not at all from fellow feeling, rather from an impulse prompted by the abundance of his power. The noble man honors what is powerful in himself, for he who has power over himself understands what to say and when to guard his tongue, struggles against his own nature with harsh, hard joy, and has reverence for all that is harsh and hard. "Wotan set a hard heart within my breast," says an old Scandinavian saga. Thus the soul of a proud Viking is truly described. Such a man is proud of not being bred for fellow feeling, for the saga's hero continues warningly, "He whose heart is not hard in youth will never have a hard heart." The noble, brave men who think this way are the farthest off from that kind of moral standard that sees signs of virtue in fellow feeling, in doing good deeds for others, or in being neutral.

Belief in one's self, pride in one's self, irony toward and a basic hatred of so-called selflessness belong as clearly to master moral-

[1] **arbiter**: person authorized to judge.
[2] **adjudged**: regarded as.
[3] **monopoly**: exclusive control.

> The greater part of what my neighbors call good I believe in my soul to be bad, and if I repent of anything, it is very likely to be my good behavior.
>
> — Henry David Thoreau

ity as do quiet contempt for and distrust of fellow feeling and so-called warm hearts. The powerful know what to honor. It is their art, their province of knowledge. Typical of the morality of the powerful is a deep respect for their forefathers and for the past (all justice rests upon this dual respect), belief in the past and prejudice in its favor. And if, demoralized[4] by so-called modern ideas, common men believe almost instinctively in so-called Progress and in a so-called Future, and more and more fail to respect the past, the low origin of these so-called modern ideas has in this way amply betrayed itself.

Master morality is alien and painful to present taste in the harshness of its principles, requiring a man to owe allegiance only to his equals. Here is how fellow feeling fits in: with all creatures of lower rank, with all that is alien, a man may deal as he thinks good or "as his heart wills it," at all events beyond the common standards of good and evil. The need and ability for greater gratitude and greater hate, both among equals only, the refinements of revenge, the idea of delicacy of friendship, a certain compulsion to have enemies (as a sort of release for affectation, envy, viciousness, insolence, in effect, to be able to be a good friend): all these things are typical traits of master morality which, as has been implied, is not the morality of so-called modern ideas. Therefore it is hard to accept today, also hard to uncover and to explain.

The second kind of morality, slave moral-

[4] **demoralized**: having had their morals corrupted.

ity, is quite the opposite. Suppose the beaten, the crushed, the suffering, the enslaved, the self-ignorant, the exhausted set up a standard of good and evil. What will the pattern of their moral values be? Probably the expression of a gloomy distrust of man's entire state. Perhaps a condemnation of man himself together with his state. The slave's viewpoint condemns the virtues of the powerful. He has skepticism, distrust, a refinement of distrust against all the "good" that ought to be honored. He has to persuade himself that joy itself is not proper. Instead, those traits that serve to ease the existence of sufferers are pushed out in front and spotlighted. Fellow feeling, the obliging helping hand, the warm heart, patience, industry, humility, friendliness, all these come to be honored, for these are the necessary traits of slave morality and provide almost its only means of coping with the pressures of life.

Slave morality is essentially based on security. Here is the source for the creation of that famous contrast between so-called good and so-called evil. The so-called evil of slave morality includes power, awesomeness, a certain terror, elegance and strength, all really unworthy of being despised. According to slave morality, so-called evil inspires fear. According to master morality, it is the "good" man who inspires fear, and wishes to do so, while the "wicked" man shows himself to be detestable. The contrast is at its sharpest when so-called good, according to the standards of slave morality, takes on an odor of the contemptible, delicate, and well deserved, because the good of the slavish way of thinking belongs of necessity to the purposeless man. He is good-natured, easy to betray, perhaps a little stupid, a goodfellow.

Above all, where slave morality dominates, language narrows and the words "good" and "stupid" come together. A final basic difference: the desire for liberty, the instinct for playing and for all other aspects of the whims of freedom, belong of necessity to slave morality and morals; while art and a passionate devotion to duty form the standard condition of an aristocratic system of thought and values.

ABOUT THE AUTHOR • **Friedrich Nietzsche** (1844–1900) profoundly influenced twentieth-century philosophy and left his mark upon art, music, literature, and perhaps the history of Europe. The son of a Protestant clergyman, Nietzsche rejected his heritage when he encountered the pessimistic philosophy of Arthur Schopenhauer and the music of Richard Wagner. Christianity became for him "a slave revolt against everything superior," a philosophy that teaches men to die, not to live. For Nietzsche, morality had to be based upon power. In his doctrine of the Übermensch, the superman above common morality, he celebrated power in a strong, hypnotic style, which becomes at times almost lyrical. Beyond Good and Evil urges philosophers to tear down rational systems of thought and reach the irrational human level beneath. Before his career ended in madness, Nietzsche had clearly foreshadowed the Nazi belief in a master race that nearly destroyed Europe.

For Discussion

1. Before evaluating the merit of Nietzsche's argument, it is important that first you be sure you understand it. Nietzsche himself was a brilliant philologist and historian, and much of his inspiration grew out of his study of the classical world of ancient Greece. In time he came to feel that good and evil were not absolute, but relative; what was good for one person or culture was not necessarily good for another. Moreover, he felt that to speak of good and bad actions was misleading, even erroneous. The concepts of good and evil should be applied to men, not actions: "It is perfectly clear that the standards of moral values were first of all for men, then were later led astray and applied to actions." Between what two basic types of morality does this selection from *Beyond Good and Evil* distinguish? Are both found in complex cultures? Can both be found in the same individual?

2. The noble man — the master, the lord — lives by a set of values different from what the mass of men live by. For the noble man, who finally decides what is good? He may be a philanthropist, helping less fortunate people. For what reason would he do so? Of the following qualities, which would the noble man feel were good, which evil: wealth, liberty, joy, humility, friendliness, power, strength, awesomeness, aloofness, good nature?

3. How does Nietzsche account for the development of what he calls slave morality? By slaves he means, as he says, "dependents of all kinds," as distinguished from independent masters — the mighty of any culture. Who or what was responsible for the standards of good and evil that such a slave morality identifies? How do the moralities of slave and master differ in their attitude toward past and present? Toward security?

4. With which morality — slave or master — does Nietzsche sympathize? The tone with which he describes the two kinds of moralities reveals his attitude toward them. In general what is that tone: deferential, wry, disdainful, haughty, ingratiating, sardonic, or what? Point to diction that reveals the tone most forcefully.

For Composition

Goodness, Nietzsche seems to be saying, is equivalent to greatness, and whatever qualities permit a man to be great — to control himself and dominate others, to lead instead of follow — are good.

1. **Analysis.** In a unified and coherent essay of four or five paragraphs, classify and illustrate the attributes of good and evil for both slave and master moralities, as Nietzsche here expounds them.

2. **Analysis.** Consider the example of Dr. Stockmann at the end of Ibsen's *An Enemy of the People* (page 130). The strongest man in the world, he tells us, "is the man who stands alone." In a well-organized paper of three or four paragraphs, consider to what extent Dr. Stockmann at the conclusion of the play exemplifies the values of leader morality as Nietzsche defines them in this essay.

3. **Argument.** Frequently we do seem to talk one way about goodness and act another way altogether. In an essay that makes use of specific examples, apply Nietzsche's insights to athletic contests. In the midst of play, how are such qualities as joy, strength, humility, helpfulness, and the like regarded? Which would your coach and teammates regard as good?

Words and Allusions

DERIVATIONS (page 445). The following words are derived from *moral: morals, morality, moralize, demoralize.* Use each word in a sentence that will make its meaning clear. Is *morale* derived from *moral?* What does *morale* mean?

Genesis: The Garden of Eden

Let us return to the origin of evil as the Hebraic-Christian tradition narrates it. Lawrence's snake (page 489) can lead us there, back through its ancestry in time to the very beginnings, not long after God had created the heaven and the earth, had brought light to them, and formed — as the first chapter of the Book of Genesis says — man out of the dust of the ground "and breathed into his nostrils the breath of life."

Now the serpent was more subtil[1] than any beast of the field which the Lord God had made. And he said unto the woman, Yea, hath God said, Ye shall not eat of every tree of the garden? 2 And the woman said unto the serpent, We may eat of the fruit of the trees of the garden: 3 But of the fruit of the tree which is in the midst of the garden, God hath said, Ye shall not eat of it, neither shall ye touch it, lest ye die. 4 And the serpent said unto the woman, Ye shall not surely die: 5 For God doth know that in the day ye eat thereof, then your eyes shall be opened, and ye shall be as gods, knowing good and evil. 6 And when the woman saw that the tree was good for food, and that it was pleasant to the eyes, and a tree to be desired to make one wise, she took of the fruit thereof, and did eat, and gave also unto her husband with her; and he did eat. 7 And the eyes of them both were opened, and they knew that they were naked; and they sewed fig leaves together, and made themselves aprons.

8 And they heard the voice of the Lord God walking in the garden in the cool of the day: and Adam and his wife hid themselves from the presence of the Lord God amongst the trees of the garden. 9 And the Lord God called unto Adam, and said unto him, Where art thou? 10 And he said, I heard thy voice in the garden, and I was afraid, because I was naked; and I hid

myself. 11 And he said, Who told thee that thou wast naked? Hast thou eaten of the tree, whereof I commanded thee that thou shouldest not eat? 12 And the man said, The woman whom thou gavest to be with me, she gave me of the tree, and I did eat. 13 And the Lord God said unto the woman, What is this that thou hast done? And the woman said, The serpent beguiled[2] me, and I did eat. 14 And the Lord God said unto the serpent, Because thou hast done this, thou art cursed above all cattle, and above every beast of the field; upon thy belly shalt thou go, and dust shalt thou eat all the days of thy life: 15 And I will put enmity between thee and the woman, and between thy seed and her seed; it shall bruise thy head, and thou shalt bruise his heel. 16 Unto the woman he said, I will greatly multiply thy sorrow and thy conception;[3] in sorrow thou shalt bring forth children; and thy desire shall be to thy husband, and he shall rule over thee. 17 And unto Adam he said, Because thou hast hearkened[4] unto the voice of thy wife, and hast eaten of the tree, of which I commanded thee, saying, Thou shalt not eat of it: cursed is the ground for thy sake; in sorrow shalt thou eat of it all the days of thy life; 18 Thorns also and thistles shall it bring

[1] **subtil**: crafty, sly.

[2] **beguiled**: deceived.
[3] **multiply ... conception**: make childbearing painful.
[4] **hearkened**: heeded.

forth to thee; and thou shalt eat the herb of the field; 19 In the sweat of thy face shalt thou eat bread, till thou return unto the ground; for out of it wast thou taken: for dust thou art, and unto dust shalt thou return.

20 And Adam called his wife's name Eve;[1] because she was the mother of all living. 21 Unto Adam also and to his wife did the Lord God make coats of skins, and clothed them. 22 And the Lord God said, Behold, the man is become as one of us, to know good and evil: and now, lest he put forth his hand, and take also of the tree of life, and eat, and live for ever: 23 Therefore the Lord God sent him forth from the garden of Eden, to till the ground from whence he was taken. 24 So he drove out the man; and he placed at the east of the garden of Eden Cherubims, and a flaming sword which turned every way, to keep the way of the tree of life.

[1] **Eve:** The Hebrew name, Haiya, means "life."

For Discussion

1. This portion of *Genesis* narrates the events surrounding man's original sin, the single most significant occurrence in the Old Testament. Satan, in the form of a serpent, beguiled Eve to taste of the fruit of the tree of the knowledge of good and evil. How did he convince her to do so? Did Adam taste of the fruit of the tree? How did God discover their transgression?

2. Three kinds of punishment God inflicted on the offenders. What punishment did the serpent receive? What was the woman's punishment? The man's? What aspects of life today do these punishments explain? Why did God expel Adam and Eve from the Garden of Eden?

3. Notice that God's words to the three offenders are in verse. What are the characteristics of Hebraic verse (page 187)? To what extent do the passages illustrate those characteristics? Be specific.

For Composition

The first two chapters of *Genesis* tell of the creation of man and his earliest, cataclysmic transgression. Human origins are thus accounted for in the Hebraic-Christian tradition, one of the two dominant sources of western culture. The other source, of course, is the Graeco-Roman tradition.

1. **Précis.** Read the opening chapters of the Bible, and briefly summarize the contents of the first chapter of *Genesis*. The ideal précis, or succinct summary, reports on important events in the order in which they occur in the original, avoiding excessive elaboration and the overuse of direct quotation.

2. **For Research.** Prepare notes from which may be developed an oral talk or written paper on the origins of humanity according to the Graeco-Roman tradition. Your notes will include identification of Uranus, Gaia, Cronus, the Titans, Zeus, Prometheus, and the activities of those various individuals with regard to man.

3. **Comparison and Contrast.** In a coherent paper compare and contrast the Greek and Hebraic accounts of the creation of the earth and man's place in it, developing the notes assembled in the preceding assignment.

Words and Allusions

COGNATES (page 22). The word *genesis* came into English through Latin from a Greek word meaning "to be born." It appears as a root in the following words: *genetics, progenitor, primogeniture, congenital, genealogy.* What do those words mean? Use each in a sentence to illustrate its meaning.

DOUBLETS. In the Book of Genesis, the serpent is said to be "more subtil than any beast in the field." The word *subtil* appears in dictionaries today as *subtile. Subtile* clearly suggests *subtle.* What does each word mean, and how are they related? Are they doublets (page 481)?

Paradise Lost: Book IX

JOHN MILTON

Sometime shortly before 1667, John Milton, after a lifetime of preparation and several years of composition, finally concluded the greatest epic poem in the English language. *Paradise Lost*, the work he had first planned a quarter of a century earlier, was published that year — an epic unlike any before. Its subject was not the adventures of a hero in battle or on the frontiers of the known world, as were earlier poems like Homer's *Iliad* and *Odyssey* and Virgil's *Aeneid* and the anonymous Anglo-Saxon *Beowulf*. Instead, Milton chose a subject he identifies in the opening verses of the poem as

> . . . man's first disobedience and the fruit
> Of that forbidden tree whose mortal taste
> Brought death into the world and all our woe,
> With loss of Eden. . . .

He will retell the story, he says, in order to

> . . . assert Eternal Providence,
> And justify the ways of God to men.

The epic unfolds in twelve books, the climax of which occurs in Book IX. For his source, the poet used primarily the account of the creation given in Genesis 1–3, as well as hints of the downfall of Satan, first of angels, in Isaiah 14:12–15, and — for the rebellion of Satan against God and the battle in Heaven thereby provoked — Revelation 12:7–9. Many commentators had elaborated those cryptic texts by the time Milton lived, so that he was able to draw not only on the words of the Bible but on the numerous interpretations that those words had provoked over the intervening centuries.

Briefly, earlier books of *Paradise Lost* tell of the consequences of the revolt against God by Satan and his angels. Thrown into Hell, they gather to debate their next move, determining in time to investigate rumors of a new world peopled by new beings of God's creation. Satan departs upward from Hell to investigate the rumors alone, and for that purpose makes his way to Eden, where he is able to penetrate the dreams of one of the new creatures, Eve, before being discovered by the heavenly angel Gabriel and driven from the Garden. But Satan's threat against man is by no means ended with that angelic discovery and dismissal. In Book IX, after the customary epic invocation of some forty-seven lines, the narration resumes.

The sun was sunk, and after him the star
Of Hesperus,* whose office is to bring
Twilight upon the earth, short arbiter*

'Twixt day and night, and now from end to
end
Night's hemisphere had veiled the horizon
round,   5
When Satan, who late fled before the threats

1–2. **star Of Hesperus:** evening star. 3. **arbiter:** judge.

Ancient legend says that the snake, symbol of evil, once walked upright. More intelligent than other animals, it envied man and so plotted his downfall. This sixth century B.C. snake has the forelegs of a lion, the hind legs of an eagle, and the darting tongue of a snake.

Of Gabriel* out of Eden, now improved*
In meditated fraud and malice, bent
On man's destruction, maugre* what might
   hap
Of heavier on himself,* fearless returned. 10
By night he fled, and at midnight returned
From compassing the earth, cautious of day,
Since Uriel,* regent of the sun, descried
His entrance, and forewarned the Cherubim
That kept their watch; thence full of an-
   guish driv'n,   15
The space of seven continued nights he rode
With darkness, thrice the equinoctial line*
He circled, four times crossed the car of

Night*
From pole to pole, traversing each colure;*
On the eighth returned, and on the coast
   averse*   20
From entrance or Cherubic watch, by
   stealth
Found unsuspected way. There was a
   place —
Now not, though sin, not time, first wrought
   the change —
Where Tigris*at the foot of Paradise
Into a gulf shot under ground, till part 25
Rose up a fountain by the Tree of Life;
In with the river sunk, and with it rose

7. Gabriel: an angel of God. This incident is described in Book IV. improved: made more intense. 9. maugre: in spite of. 9–10. what . . . himself: what further punishments he might incur for himself. 13. Uriel: an archangel (in Book IV). 17. equinoctial line: the sun's path.

18. the car of Night: *i.e.,* night as it moves around the earth. 19. colure: circle of longitude. 20. averse: opposite. 24. Tigris: The Tigris River borders the Mesopotamian Valley, believed to have been the birthplace of civilization. Milton follows earlier Biblical commentaries in locating Eden on this site.

Satan, involved* in rising mist, then sought
Where to lie hid; sea he had searched and
   land
From Eden over Pontus,* and the pool   30
Maeotis,* up beyond the river Ob;*
Downward as far antarctic; and in length
West from Orontes*to the ocean barred
At Darien,* thence to the land where flows
Ganges and Indus.* Thus the orb he
   roamed   35
With narrow search, and with inspection
   deep
Considered every creature, which of all
Most opportune might serve his wiles, and
   found
The serpent subtlest beast of all the field.
Him after long debate, irresolute   40
Of the thoughts revolved, his final sentence*
   chose
Fit vessel, fittest imp* of fraud, in whom
To enter, and his dark suggestions hide
From sharpest sight; for in the wily snake,

Whatever sleights none would suspicious
   mark,   45
As from his wit and native subtlety
Proceeding, which, in other beasts observed,
Doubt might beget of diabolic pow'r
Active within beyond the sense of brute.
Thus he resolved, but first from inward
   grief   50
His bursting passion into plaints* thus
   poured:
   "O earth, how like to heav'n, if not pre-
   ferred
More justly, seat worthier of gods, as built
With second thoughts, reforming what was
   old!
For what God after better worse would
   build?   55
Terrestrial heav'n danced round by other
   heav'ns
That shine, yet bear their bright officious*
   lamps,
Light above light, for thee alone, as seems,
In thee concentring all their precious beams
Of sacred influence! As God in heav'n   60
Is center, yet extends to all, so thou
Centring receiv'st from all those orbs; in
   thee,

---

28. **involved**: wreathed. 30. **Pontus**: the Black Sea. 31. **Maeotis**: Sea of Azov. **Ob**: Obi River, in Siberia. 33. **Orontes**: river in Syria. 34. **Darien**: Isthmus of Panama. 35. **Ganges and Indus**: *i.e.*, India and Southern Asia. 41. **sentence**: judgment. 42. **imp**: offspring.

51. **plaints**: lamentations. 57. **officious**: dutiful.

ABOUT THE AUTHOR • John Milton (1608–1674) was a man of epic proportions. A remarkably learned individual schooled in Latin, Greek, Italian, and Hebrew, and possessing in himself most of the knowledge of his age, Milton also possessed a lyric power and an eloquence that elevated his poetry above that of most other poets in any language. In addition to being England's greatest epic poet, Milton was a Puritan revolutionary and a political leader. A rebel under Oliver Cromwell, he served as Latin secretary for foreign affairs to the Lord Protector, and survived the public burning of his pamphlets and prose works after the return of Charles II. Husband to three wives and father of three daughters, he did not have a high regard for women, as can be seen in many of his works. *Paradise Lost* was written after he had become totally blind in the service of the Commonwealth.

Not in themselves, all their known virtue
appears
Productive in herb, plant, and nobler birth
Of creatures animate with gradual life   65
Of growth, sense, reason, all summed up in
man.
With what delight could I have walked thee
round,
If I could joy in aught, sweet interchange
Of hill and valley, rivers, woods, and plains,
Now land, now sea, and shores with forest
crowned,   70
Rocks, dens, and caves; but I in none of
these
Find place or refuge; and the more I see
Pleasures about me, so much more I feel
Torment within me, as from the hateful
siege
Of contraries,* all good to me becomes   75
Bane,* and in heav'n much worse would be
my state.
But neither here seek I, no nor in heav'n
To dwell, unless by mast'ring heav'n's Su-
preme;*
Nor hope to be myself less miserable
By what I seek, but others to make such   80
As I, though thereby worse to me re-
dound.*
For only in destroying I find ease
To my relentless thoughts; and him de-
stroyed,
Or won to what may work his utter loss,
For whom all this was made, all this will
soon   85
Follow, as to him linked in weal* or woe;
In woe then, that destruction wide may
range.
To me shall be the glory sole among
The infernal* Powers, in one day to have
marred
What he, Almighty styled, six nights and
days   90

Continued making, and who knows how
long
Before had been contriving? Though per-
haps
Not longer than since I in one night freed
From servitude inglorious well-nigh half
Th' angelic name, and thinner left the
throng   95
Of his adorers.* He to be avenged,
And to repair his numbers thus impaired,
Whether such virtue spent of old now failed
More angels to create, if they at least
Are his created, or to spite us more,   100
Determined to advance into our room
A creature formed of earth, and him endow,
Exalted* from so base original,*
With heav'nly spoils,* our spoils. What he
decreed
He effected;* man he made, and for him
built   105
Magnificent this world, and earth his seat,
Him lord pronounced, and, O indignity!
Subjected to his service angel wings,
And flaming ministers to watch and tend
Their earthy charge. Of these the vigi-
lance   110
I dread, and to elude, thus wrapped in mist
Of midnight vapor glide obscure,* and pry
In every bush and brake, where hap may
find
The serpent sleeping, in whose mazy folds
To hide me, and the dark intent I bring.   115
O foul descent! that I who erst* contended
With Gods to sit the highest, am now con-
strained
Into a beast, and mixed with bestial slime,
This essence to incarnate and imbrute,*
That to the height of deity aspired;   120
But what will not ambition and revenge
Descend to? Who aspires must down as low

74–75. **siege Of contraries:** location of conflicting
feelings. 76. **Bane:** source of harm. 78: **mast'ring
heav'n's Supreme:** *i.e.,* by overthrowing God and
ruling in His place. 81. **redound:** reflects back.
86. **weal:** well-being. 89. **infernal:** of Hell.

93–96. **since . . . adorers:** Earlier Books describe
how Satan, then an angel himself, organized and led
a rebellion of angels against God's rule. 103.
Exalted: raised higher. **so base original:** *i.e.,* the
dust from which man was formed. 104. **spoils:**
riches taken by force in war. 105. **effected:** accomplished. 112. **obscure:** concealed. 116. **erst:**
formerly. 119. **imbrute:** make bestial.

As high he soared, obnoxious* first or last
To basest things. Revenge, at first though
    sweet,
Bitter ere long back on itself recoils;   125
Let it; I reck* not, so it light well aimed,
Since higher I fall short, on him who next
Provokes my envy, this new favorite
Of Heav'n, this man of clay, son of despite,*
Whom us the more to spite his Maker
    raised   130
From dust: spite then with spite is best re-
    paid."
    So saying, though each thicket dank or
    dry,
Like a black mist low creeping, he held on
His midnight search, where soonest he might
    find
The serpent. Him fast sleeping soon he
    found   135
In labyrinth of many a round self-rolled,
His head the midst, well stored with subtle
    wiles;
Not yet in horrid shade or dismal den,
Nor nocent* yet, but on the grassy herb
Fearless, unfeared, he slept. In at his mouth
The Devil entered, and his brutal sense,   141
In heart or head, possessing soon inspired
With act intelligential,* but his sleep
Disturbed not, waiting close* th' approach
    of morn.
    Now whenas sacred light began to
    dawn   145
In Eden on the humid flow'rs, that breathed
Their morning incense, when all things that
    breathe
From th' earth's great altar send up silent
    praise
To the Creator, and his nostrils fill
With grateful smell, forth came the human
    pair   150
And joined their vocal worship to the quire*
Of creatures wanting* voice; that done,
    partake

The season, prime for sweetest scents and
    airs;
Then cómmune* how that day they best
    may ply
Their growing work; for much their work
    outgrew   155
The hands' dispatch* of two gard'ning so
    wide.
And Eve first to her husband thus began:
    "Adam, well may we labor still to dress*
This garden, still to tend plant, herb, and
    flow'r,
Our pleasant task enjoined,* but till more
    hands   160
Aid us, the work under our labor grows,
Luxurious by restraint;* what we by day
Lop* overgrown, or prune, or prop, or bind,
One night or two with wanton growth
    derides,*
Tending to wild. Thou therefore now ad-
    vise   165
Or hear what to my mind first thoughts
    present:
Let us divide our labors, thou where choice
Leads thee, or where most needs, whether to
    wind
The woodbine* round this arbor, or direct
The clasping ivy where to climb, while I   170
In yonder spring of roses intermixed
With myrtle, find what to redress till noon.
For while so near each other thus all day
Our task we choose, what wonder if so near
Looks intervene and smiles, or object
    new   175
Casual discourse draw on, which intermits*
Our day's work, brought to little, though
    begun
Early, and th' hour of supper comes un-
    earned."
    To whom mild answer Adam thus re-
    turned:

---

123. **obnoxious**: exposed. 126. **reck**: care. 129. **despite**: scorn, insult. 139. **nocent**: harmful. 143. **intelligential**: having intelligence. 144. **close**: hidden. 151. **quire**: choir. 152. **wanting**: lacking.

154. **cómmune**: think and converse about. 156. **dispatch**: performance. 158. **dress**: cultivate. 160. **enjoined**: commanded. 162. **luxurious by restraint**: Plants that are pruned and flowers that are picked tend to grow even more vigorously afterwards. 163. **lop**: trim. 164. **derides**: mocks. 169. **woodbine**: ivy. 176. **intermits**: interrupts.

"Sole Eve, associate sole,* to me beyond 180
Compare above all living creatures dear,
Well hast thou motioned, well thy thoughts
    employed
How we might best fulfill the work which
    here
God hath assigned us, nor of me shalt pass
Unpraised; for nothing lovelier can be
    found   185
In woman, than to study household good,
And good works in her husband to promote.
Yet not so strictly hath our Lord imposed
Labor, as to debar* us when we need
Refreshment, whether food, or talk be-
    tween,   190
Food of the mind, or this sweet intercourse
Of looks and smiles, for smiles from reason
    flow,
To brute denied, and are of love the food,
Love not the lowest end of human life.
For not to irksome toil, but to delight   195
He made us, and delight to reason joined.
These paths and bowers doubt not but our
    joint hands
Will keep from wilderness with ease, as
    wide
As we need walk, till younger hands ere
    long
Assist us. But if much convérse* per-
    haps   200
Thee satiate, to short absence I could yield.
For solitude sometimes is best society,
And short retirement urges sweet return.
But other doubt possesses me, lest harm
Befall thee severed from me; for thou
    know'st   205
What hath been warned us, what malicious
    foe,
Envying our happiness, and of his own
Despairing, seeks to work us woe and shame
By sly assault; and somewhere nigh* at hand
Watches, no doubt, with greedy hope to
    find   210

His wish and best advantage, us asunder,*
Hopeless to circumvent* us joined, where
    each
To other speedy aid might lend at need;
Whether his first design be to withdraw
Our fealty* from God, or to disturb   215
Conjugal* love, than which perhaps no bliss
Enjoyed by us excites his envy more;
Or this,* or worse, leave not the faithful side
That gave thee being, still shades thee and
    protects.
The wife, where danger or dishonor
    lurks,   220
Safest and seemliest* by her husband stays,
Who guards her, or with her the worst
    endures."
    To whom the virgin* majesty of Eve,
As one who loves, and some unkindness
    meets,
With sweet austere composure thus re-
    plied: 225
    "Offspring of heav'n and earth, and all
        earth's lord,
That such an enemy we have, who seeks
Our ruin, both by thee informed I learn,
And from the parting angel overheard
As in a shady nook I stood behind,   230
Just then returned at shut of evening flow'rs.
But that thou shouldst my firmness therefore
    doubt
To God or thee, because we have a foe
May tempt it, I expected not to hear.
His violence thou fear'st not, being such 235
As we, not capable of death or pain,
Can either not receive, or can repel.
His fraud is then thy fear, which plain infers
Thy equal fear that my firm faith and love
Can by his fraud be shaken or seduced;   240
Thoughts, which how found they harbor in
    thy breast,
Adam, misthought* of her to thee so dear?"

180. **associate sole**: only companion. 189. **debar**:
prohibit. 200. **convérse**: conversation. 209. **nigh**:
near.

211. **asunder**: apart. 212. **circumvent**: catch
in a trap, outwit. 215. **fealty**: loyalty. 216.
conjugal: of marriage. 218. **Or this**: whether this
(is his plan). 221. **seemliest**: most suitably and
properly. 223. **virgin**: innocent. 242. **misthought**:
misjudgment.

To whom with healing words Adam replied:

"Daughter of God and man, immortal Eve,
For such thou art, from sin and blame entire,*   245
Not diffident of* thee do I dissuade
Thy absence from my sight, but to avoid
Th' attempt itself, intended by our foe.
For he who tempts, though in vain, at least asperses*
The tempted with dishonor foul, supposed   250
Not incorruptible of faith, not proof
Against temptation. Thou thyself with scorn
And anger wouldst resent the offered wrong,
Though ineffectual found. Misdeem not then,
If such affront I labor to avert   255
From thee alone, which on us both at once
The enemy, though bold, will hardly dare,
Or daring, first on me th' assault shall light.
Nor thou his malice and false guile contemn;*
Subtle he needs must be, who could seduce   260
Angels, nor think superfluous other's aid.
I from the influence of thy looks receive
Access* in every virtue, in thy sight
More wise, more watchful, stronger, if need were
Of outward strength; while shame, thou looking on,   265
Shame to be overcome or overreached,
Would utmost vigor raise, and raised unite.
Why shouldst not thou like sense within thee feel
When I am present, and thy trial choose
With me, best witness of thy virtue tried?"
So spake domestic Adam in his care   271
And matrimonial love; But Eve, who thought

245. **entire**: free. 246. **diffident of**: lacking faith in. 249. **asperses**: slanders. 259. **contemn**: scorn, treat with contempt. 263. **Access**: increase.

Less* attributed to her faith sincere,
Thus her reply with accent sweet renewed:
"If this be our condition, thus to dwell
In narrow circuit straitened* by a foe,   276
Subtle or violent, we not endued*
Single with like defense, wherever met,
How we are happy, still in fear of harm?
But harm precedes not sin: only our foe 280
Tempting affronts us with his foul esteem
Of our integrity; his foul esteem
Sticks no dishonor on our front,* but turns
Foul on himself; then wherefore shunned or feared
By us? Who rather double honor gain   285
From his surmise proved false, find peace within,
Favor from Heav'n, our witness, from th' event.
And what is faith, love, virtue, unassayed
Alone, without exterior help sustained?
Let us not then suspect our happy state 290
Left so imperfect by the Maker wise
As not secure to single or combined.*
Frail is our happiness, if this be so,
And Eden were no Eden thus exposed."
To whom thus Adam fervently replied:
"O woman, best are all things as the will 296
Of God ordained them; his creating hand
Nothing imperfect or deficient left
Of all that he created, much less man,
Or aught* that might his happy state secure,   300
Secure from outward force: within himself
The danger lies, yet lies within his power;
Against his will he can receive no harm.
But God left free the will, for what obeys
Reason is free, and reason he made right, 305
But bid her well beware, and still erect,*
Lest by some fair appearing good surprised
She dictate false, and misinform the will
To do what God expressly hath forbid.

273. **less**: too little. 276. **straitened**: confined.
277. **endued**: provided with. 283. **front**: brow.
292. **secure . . . combined**: safe singly or together.
300. **aught**: anything. 306. **still erect**: always alert.

One story concerning Milton reported that he would wake in the middle of the night and dictate parts of Paradise Lost to his daughters. This story inspired this painting by the nineteenth-century French artist Eugène Delacroix.

Not then mistrust, but tender love enjoins, 310
That I should mind* thee oft, and mind thou me.
Firm we subsist, yet possible to swerve,
Since reason not impossibly may meet
Some specious object by the foe suborned,
And fall into deception unaware, 315
Not keeping strictest watch, as she was warned.
Seek not temptation then, which to avoid
Were better, and most likely if from me
Thou sever not; trial will come unsought.
Wouldst thou approve* thy constancy, approve 320
First thy obedience; th' other who can know,
Not seeing thee attempted, who attest?
But if thou think trial unsought may find
Us both securer* than thus warned thou seem'st,
Go, for thy stay, not free, absents thee more;* 325

Go in thy native innocence, rely
On what thou hast of virtue, summon all,
For God towards thee hath done his part, do thine."
   So spake the patriarch* of mankind, but Eve
Persisted; yet submiss,* though last, replied: 330
   "With thy permission then, and thus forewarned,
Chiefly by what thy own last reasoning words
Touched only, that our trial, when least sought,
May find us both perhaps far less prepared,
The willinger I go, nor much expect 335
A foe so proud will first the weaker seek;
So bent, the more shall shame him his repulse."
   Thus saying, from her husband's hand her hand
Soft she withdrew, and like a wood-nymph* light,

311. **mind**: remind. 320. **approve**: give proof of. 324. **securer**: *here*, less on guard. 325. **for . . . more**: I feel even more distant from you when I know that you remain with me against your wishes.

329. **patriarch**: father and founder. 330. **submiss**: submissively. 339. **wood-nymph**: in classical mythology, a minor nature goddess, represented as a lovely and graceful maiden living in forest groves.

511

Oread or Dryad, or of Delia's train   340
Betook her to the groves, but Delia's self
In gait surpassed the goddess-like deport,*
Though not as she with bow and quiver
   armed,
But with such gard'ning tools as art yet
   rude,*
Guiltless of fire had formed, or angels
   brought.   345
To Pales, or Pomona, thus adorned,
Likest she seemed, Pomona when she fled
Vertumnus, or to Ceres in her prime,
Yet virgin of Proserpina from Jove.*
Her long with ardent look his eye pursued
Delighted, but desiring more her stay.   351
Oft he to her his charge of quick return
Repeated, she to him as oft engaged*
To be returned by noon amid the bow'r,
And all things in best order to invite   355
Noontide repast,* or afternoon's repose.
O much deceived, much failing, hapless*
   Eve,
Of thy presumed return! event perverse!
Thou never from that hour in Paradise
Found'st either sweet repast or sound re-
   pose,   360
Such ambush hid among sweet flow'rs and
   shades
Waited with hellish rancor imminent
To intercept thy way, or send thee back
Despoiled* of innocence, of faith, of bliss.
For now, and since first break of dawn the
   Fiend,   365
Mere serpent in appearance, forth was come,
And on his quest, where likeliest he might
   find
The only two of mankind, but in them
The whole included race, his purposed*
   prey.
In bow'r and field he sought, where any
   tuft   370

Of grove or garden-plot more pleasant lay,
Their tendance or plantation for delight;
By fountain or by shady rivulet
He sought them both, but wished his hap*
   might find
Eve separate; he wished, but not with
   hope   375
Of what so seldom chanced, when to his
   wish,
Beyond his hope, Eve separate he spies,
Veiled in a cloud of fragrance, where she
   stood,
Half spied, so thick the roses bushing round
About her glowed, oft stooping to sup-
   port   380
Each flow'r of slender stalk, whose head
   though gay
Carnation, purple, azure, or specked with
   gold,
Hung drooping unsustained; them she up-
   stays
Gently with myrtle band, mindless* the
   while,
Herself, though fairest unsupported flow'r,
From her best prop so far, and storm so
   nigh.   386
Nearer he drew, and many a walk traversed
Of stateliest covert, cedar, pine, or palm,
Then voluble* and bold, now hid, now seen
Among thick-woven arborets* and flow'rs
Imbordered on each bank, the hand* of
   Eve: 391
Spot more delicious than those gardens
   feigned*
Or* of revived Adonis,* or renowned
Alcinous, host of old Laertes' son,*
Or that, not mystic,* where the sapient

342. **deport:** bearing. 344. **rude:** rough in workmanship. 346–349. **Pales . . . Jove:** references to
various classical goddesses associated with nature.
353. **engaged:** pledged. 356. **repast:** meal. 357.
hapless: unfortunate. 364. **despoiled:** robbed. 369.
purposed: intended.

374. **hap:** luck. 384. **mindless:** careless, heedless. 389. **voluble:** rolling. 390. **arborets:** shrubs.
391. **hand:** handiwork. 392. **feigned:** fictitious.
393. **Or:** either.   **revived Adonis:** The feast of
Adonis, a beautiful young man beloved of Venus
in classical mythology, was celebrated for eight
days during which quickly growing plants were
sown, tended, permitted to wither, and then thrown
into the sea—this final act being the symbolic re-
counting of the death and resurrection of Adonis.
394. **Laertes' son:** Odysseus. 395. **mystic:** mythical.

king* 395
Held dalliance with his fair Egyptian
   spouse.
Much he the place admired, the person
   more.
As one who long in populous city pent,
Where houses thick and sewers annoy the
   air,
Forth issuing on a summer's morn to breathe
Among the pleasant villages and farms 401
Adjoined, from each thing met conceives*
   delight,
The smell of grain, or tedded* grass, or
   kine,*
Or dairy, each rural sight, each rural sound;
If chance with nymph-like step fair virgin
   pass, 405
What pleasing seemed, for* her now pleases
   more,
She most, and in her look sums all delight:
Such pleasure took the Serpent to behold
This flow'ry plat,* the sweet recess* of Eve
Thus early, thus alone; her heav'nly form
Angelic, but more soft and feminine, 411
Her graceful innocence, her every air
Of gesture or least action overawed
His malice, and with rapine* sweet bereaved
His fierceness of the fierce intent it brought.
That space the Evil One abstracted* stood
From his own evil, and for the time re-
   mained
Stupidly good, of enmity disarmed, 418
Of guile, of hate, of envy, of revenge;
But the hot hell that always in him burns, 420
Though in mid-heav'n, soon ended his de-
   light,
And tortures him now more, the more he
   sees
Of pleasure not for him ordained; then soon
Fierce hate he recollects, and all his thoughts
Of mischief, gratulating,* thus excites: 425

395. **sapient king**: Solomon. 402. **conceives**: creates. 403. **tedded**: spread out to dry. **kine**: cows.
406. **for**: because of. 409. **plat**: plot of ground. **recess**: retreat. 414. **rapine**: plunder. 416. **abstracted**:
removed, withdrawn in mind. 425. **gratulating**:
repaying.

"Thoughts, whither have ye led me, with
   what sweet
Compulsion thus transported to forget
What hither brought us? Hate, not love,
   nor hope
Of Paradise for hell, hope here to taste
Of pleasure, but all pleasure to destroy, 430
Save what is in destroying; other joy
To me is lost. Then let me not let pass
Occasion which now smiles: behold alone
The woman, opportune* to all attempts,
Her husband, for I view far round, not
   nigh, 435
Whose higher intellectual more I shun,
And strength, of courage haughty, and of
   limb
Heroic built, though of terrestrial mold,
Foe not informidable, exempt from wound,*
I not; so much hath hell debased, and pain
Enfeebled me, to what I was in heav'n. 441
She fair, divinely fair, fit love for gods,
Not terrible, though terror be in love
And beauty, not approached by stronger
   hate,
Hate stronger, under show of love well
   feigned, 445
The way which to her ruin now I tend."
   So spake the Enemy of mankind, enclosed
In serpent, inmate* bad, and toward Eve
Addressed his way, not with indented*
   wave,
Prone on the ground, as since, but on his
   rear, 450
Circular base of rising folds, that tow'red
Fold above fold a surging maze; his head
Crested aloft, and carbuncle* his eyes;
With burnished neck of verdant gold, erect
Amidst his circling spires, that on the
   grass 455
Floated redundant.* Pleasing was his shape,
And lovely, never since of serpent kind
Lovelier; not those that in Illyria changed

434. **opportune**: conveniently situated. 439. **exempt from wound**: See line 236. 448. **inmate**:
occupant. 449. **indented**: zigzag. 453. **carbuncle**:
deep red. 456. **redundant**: with wavy motion.

Hermióne and Cadmus, or the god
In Epidaurus; nor to which transformed 460
Ammonian Jove, or Capitoline was seen,
He with Olympias, this with her who bore
Scipio, the highth of Rome.* With tract
   oblique*
At first, as one who sought accéss, but
   feared
To interrupt, sidelong he works his way. 465
As when a ship by skilful steersman wrought
Nigh river's mouth or foreland, where the
   wind
Veers oft, as oft so steers, and shifts her sail,
So varied he, and of his tortuous train
Curled many a wanton* wreath in sight of
   Eve,   470
To lure her eye; she busied heard the sound
Of rustling leaves, but minded not, as used
To such disport* before her through the
   field
From every beast, more duteous at her call
Then at Circean call the herd dis-
   guised.*   475
He bolder now, uncalled before her stood,
But as in gaze admiring. Oft he bowed
His turret* crest, and sleek enameled neck,
Fawning, and licked the ground whereon
   she trod.
His gentle dumb expression turned at length
The eye of Eve to mark his play; he glad 481
Of her attention gained, with serpent tongue
Organic, or impulse of vocal air,*
His fraudulent temptation thus began:
   "Wonder not, sovran* mistress, if per-
   haps   485
Thou canst, who art sole wonder, much less
   arm

458–463. **Illyria . . . Rome**: reference to various classical legends of metamorphosis into serpent form. 463. **With tract oblique**: in an indirect route. 470. **wanton**: luxurious. 473. **disport**: frolic. 474–475. **more : . . disguised**: Homer's *Odyssey* describes the fawning devotion of Ulysses' crew, changed by Circe into swine, to their mistress and captor. 478. **turret**: towering. 482–483. **serpent . . . air**: Because the serpent itself lacked the power of speech, Satan had to use the former's tongue as an instrument (organ) to simulate speech. 485. **sovran**: sovereign.

Thy looks, the heav'n of mildness, with dis-
   dain,
Displeased that I approach thee thus, and
   gaze
Insatiate, I thus single, nor have feared
Thy awful* brow, more awful thus re-
   tired.   490
Fairest resemblance of thy Maker fair,
Thee all things living gaze on, all things
   thine
By gift, and thy celestial beauty adore,
With ravishment* beheld, there best beheld
Where universally admired; but here   495
In this enclosure wild, these beasts among,
Beholders rude, and shallow to discern
Half what in thee is fair, one man except,
Who sees thee? (and what is one?) who
   shouldst be seen
A goddess among gods, adored and served
By angels numberless, thy daily train."* 501
   So glozed* the Tempter, and his proem*
   tuned;
Into the heart of Eve his words made way,
Though at the voice much marveling; at
   length
Not unamazed she thus in answer spake: 505
   "What may this mean? Language of man
   pronounced
By tongue of brute, and human sense ex-
   pressed?
The first at least of these I thought denied
To beasts, whom God on their creation-day
Created mute to all articulate sound; 510
The latter I demur,* for in their looks
Much reason, and in their actions oft ap-
   pears.
Thee, Serpent, subtlest beast of all the field
I knew, but not with human voice endued;
Redouble then this miracle, and say, 515
How cam'st thou speakable* of mute, and
   how
To me so friendly grown above the rest

490. **awful**: worthy of reverence. 494. **ravishment**: rapture. 501. **train**: group of attendants. 502. **glozed**: flattered. **proem**: introduction. 511. **demur**: am in doubt about. 516. **speakable**: able to speak.

Of brutal kind, that daily are in sight?
Say, for such wonder claims attention due."
　To whom the guileful Tempter thus re-
　　plied:　　　　　　　　　　　　520
"Empress of this fair world, resplendent*
　Eve,
Easy to me it is to tell thee all
What thou command'st, and right thou
　shouldst be obeyed.
I was at first as other beasts that graze
The trodden herb, of abject thoughts and
　low,　　　　　　　　　　　　525
As was my food, nor aught but food dis-
　cerned
Or sex, and apprehended* nothing high:
Till on a day roving the field, I chanced
A goodly tree far distant to behold,　　529
Loaden with fruit of fairest colors mixed,
Ruddy and gold. I nearer drew to gaze;
When from the boughs a savory odor
　blown,
Grateful to appetite, more pleased my sense
Than smell of sweetest fennel* or the teats
Of ewe or goat dropping with milk at
　ev'n,　　　　　　　　　　　　535
Unsucked of lamb or kid,* that tend their
　play.
To satisfy the sharp desire I had
Of tasting those fair apples, I resolved
Not to defer;* hunger and thirst at once, 539
Powerful persuaders, quickened at the scent
Of that alluring fruit, urged me so keen.
About the mossy trunk I wound me soon,
For high from ground the branches would
　require
Thy utmost reach or Adam's: round the tree
All other beasts that saw, with like desire 545
Longing and envying stood, but could not
　reach.
Amid the tree now got, where plenty hung
Tempting so nigh, to pluck and eat my fill
I spared not, for such pleasure till that hour

At feed or fountain never had I found.　550
Sated at length, ere long I might perceive
Strange alteration in me, to degree
Of reason in my inward powers, and speech
Wanted not long, though to this shape re-
　tained.
Thenceforth to speculations high or deep 555
I turned my thoughts, and with capacious*
　mind
Considered all things visible in heav'n,
Or earth, or middle,* all things fair and
　good;
But all that fair and good in thy divine
Semblance, and in thy beauty's heav'nly
　ray　　　　　　　　　　　　560
United I beheld; no fair to thine
Equivalent or second, which compelled
Me thus, though importune* perhaps, to
　come
And gaze, and worship thee of right de-
　clared
Sovran of creatures, universal dame."*　565
　So talked the spirited* sly Snake; and Eve
Yet more amazed unwary thus replied:
　"Serpent, thy overpraising leaves in doubt
The virtue of that fruit, in thee first proved.
But say, where grows the tree, from hence
　how far?　　　　　　　　　　570
For many are the trees of God that grow
In Paradise, and various, yet unknown
To us; in such abundance lies our choice
As leaves a greater store of fruit untouched,
Still hanging incorruptible,* till men　575
Grow up to their provision,* and more
　hands
Help to disburden Nature of her bearth."*
　To whom the wily Adder, blithe and glad:
"Empress, the way is ready, and not long,
Beyond a row of myrtles, on a flat,　580
Fast by a fountain, one small thicket past

---

521. **resplendent**: full of spendor.　527. **apprehended**: understood.　534. **fennel**: an aromatic
herb.　534–536. **teats . . . kid**: According to popular
legend, snakes suck milk from sheep and goats.
539. **defer**: delay.

556. **capacious**: able to contain a great deal.
558. **middle**: the air.　563. **importune**: annoying,
troublesome.　565. **universal dame**: mistress of
the universe.　566. **spirited**: possessed by a spirit.
575. **incorruptible**: incapable of rotting.　575–576.
men . . . provision: there is a population proportionate to what has been provided.　577. **bearth**:
birth, what is born.

Of blowing myrrh and balm;* if thou accept
My conduct,* I can bring thee thither soon."
    "Lead then," said Eve. He leading swiftly
    rolled   584
In tangles, and made intricate seem straight,
To mischief swift. Hope elevates, and joy
Brightens his crest, as when a wand'ring
    fire,*
Compact of unctuous vapor, which the
    night
Condenses, and the cold environs round,
Kindled through agitation to a flame,   590
Which oft, they say, some evil Spirit attends,
Hovering and blazing with delusive light,
Misleads th' amazed night-wanderer from
    his way
To bogs and mires, and oft through pond or
    pool,
There swallowed up and lost, from succor
    far.   595
So glistered* the dire Snake, and into fraud
Led Eve our credulous mother, to the tree
Of prohibition, root of all our woe;
Which when she saw, thus to her guide she
    spake:
    "Serpent, we might have spared our com-
        ing hither,   600
Fruitless to me, though fruit be here to
    excess,
The credit of whose virtue rest with thee,
Wondrous indeed, if cause of such effects.
But of this tree we may not taste nor touch;
God so commanded, and left that com-
    mand   605
Sole daughter of his voice; the rest, we live
Law to ourselves, our reason is our law."
    To whom the Tempter guilefully replied:
"Indeed? Hath God then said that of the
    fruit
Of all these garden trees ye shall not eat, 610
Yet lords declared of all in earth or air?"

To whom thus Eve yet sinless: "Of the
    fruit
Of each tree in the garden we may eat,
But of the fruit of this fair tree amidst
The garden, God hath said, 'Ye shall not
    eat   615
Thereof, nor shall ye touch it, lest ye die.' "
    She scarce had said, though brief, when
        now more bold
The Tempter, but with show of zeal and
    love
To man, and indignation at his wrong,   619
New part puts on,* and as to passion moved,
Fluctuates disturbed, yet comely, and in act
Raised, as of some great matter to begin.
As when of old some orator renowned
In Athens or free Rome, where eloquence
Flourished, since mute, to some great cause
    addressed,   625
Stood in himself collected, while each part,
Motion, each act won audience ere the
    tongue,
Sometimes in highth began, as no delay
Of preface brooking* through his zeal of
    right: 629
So standing, moving, or to highth upgrown,
The Tempter all impassioned thus began:
    "O sacred, wise, and wisdom-giving Plant,
Mother of science,* now I feel thy power
Within me clear, not only to discern
Things in their causes, but to trace the
    ways   635
Of highest agents, deemed however wise.
Queen of this universe, do not believe
Those rigid threats of death; ye shall not
    die:
How should ye? By the fruit? It gives you
    life
To knowledge; by the Threat'ner? Look on
    me,   640
Me who have touched and tasted, yet both
    live,
And life more perfect have attained than
    fate

---

582. **blowing myrrh and balm**: blossoming aromatic
shrubs. 582–583. **if . . . conduct**: if you will permit
me to lead you there. 587. **wand'ring fire**: Marsh
gas, or the "will-o'-the-wisp," is a flamelike phosphorescence due to the combustion of gases; according to superstition these fires are evil spirits intent
on misleading wanderers. 596. **glistered**: sparkled.

620. **new part puts on**: acts out a new role.
629. **brooking**: enduring. 633. **science**: knowledge.

Meant me, by vent'ring* higher than my lot.
Shall that be shut to man, which to the beast
Is open? Or will God incense* his ire   645
For such a petty trespass, and not praise
Rather your dauntless virtue, whom the pain
Of death denounced, whatever thing death
  be,
Deterred not from achieving what might
  lead
To happier life, knowledge of good and
  evil?   650
Of good, how just? Of evil, if what is evil
Be real, why not known, since easier
  shunned?
God therefore cannot hurt ye, and be just;
Not just, not God; not feared then, nor
  obeyed: 654
Your fear itself of death removes the fear.
Why then was this forbid? Why but to
  awe,
Why but to keep ye low and ignorant,
His worshipers? He knows that in the day
Ye eat thereof, your eyes that seem so clear,
Yet are but dim, shall perfectly be then 660
Opened and cleared, and ye shall be as gods,
Knowing both good and evil as they know.
That ye should be as gods, since I as man,
Internal man,* is but proportion meet,
I of brute human, ye of human gods.   665
So ye shall die perhaps, by putting off
Human, to put on gods, death to be wished,
Though threatened, which no worse than
  this can bring.
And what are gods that man may not be-
  come
As they, participating godlike food?   670
The gods are first, and that advantage use
On our belief, that all from them proceeds;
I question it, for this fair earth I see,
Warmed by the sun, producing every kind,
Them nothing. If they all things, who
  enclosed   675

Knowledge of good and evil in this tree,
That whoso eats thereof, forthwith* attains
Wisdom without their leave? And wherein
  lies
Th' offense, that man should thus attain to
  know?
What can your knowledge hurt him, or this
  tree   680
Impart against his will, if all be his?
Or is it envy, and can envy dwell
In heav'nly breasts? These, these and many
  more
Causes import* your need of this fair fruit.
Goddess humane,* reach then, and freely
  taste!"   685
  He ended, and his words replete with
    guile
Into her heart too easy entrance won.
Fixed on the fruit she gazed, which to
  behold
Might tempt alone, and in her ears the sound
Yet rung of his persuasive words, im-
  pregned*   690
With reason, to her seeming, and with truth;
Meanwhile the hour of noon drew on, and
  waked
An eager appetite, raised by the smell
So savory of that fruit, which with desire,
Inclinable* now grown to touch or taste, 695
Solicited her longing eye; yet first
Pausing a while, thus to herself she mused:
  "Great are thy virtues, doubtless, best of
    fruits,
Though kept from man, and worthy to be
  admired,
Whose taste, too long forborne,* at first
  assay*   700
Gave elocution* to the mute, and taught
The tongue not made for speech to speak
  thy praise.
Thy praise he also who forbids thy use
Conceals not from us, naming thee the Tree

643. vent'ring: venturing. 645. incense: fill with
wrath.   664. Internal man: See line 553; Satan
argues that if the fruit elevated him one step up
the ladder in perception (from animal to human),
it will correspondingly elevate Adam and Eve from
human to godlike understanding.

677. forthwith: immediately. 684. import: indicate, prove. 685. humane: probably "human."
690. impregned (im·prēnd′): filled. 695. inclinable: easily inclined. 700. forborne: refrained
from, avoided. assay: try. 701. elocution: power
of speech.

Of Knowledge, knowledge both of good
    and evil;   705
Forbids us then to taste, but his forbidding
Commends* thee more, while it infers the
    good
By thee communicated, and our want;
For good unknown sure is not had, or had
And yet unknown, is as not had at all.   710
In plain* then, what forbids he but to know,
Forbids us good, forbids us to be wise?
Such prohibitions bind not. But if Death
Bind us with after-bands, what profits then
Our inward freedom? In the day we eat 715
Of this fair fruit, our doom is, we shall die.
How dies the Serpent? He hath eat'n and
    lives,
And knows, and speaks, and reasons, and
    discerns,
Irrational till then. For us alone
Was death invented? Or to us denied   720
This intellectual food, for beasts reserved?
For beasts it seems; yet that one beast which
    first
Hath tasted, envies not, but brings with joy
The good befall'n him, author unsuspect,*
Friendly to man, far from deceit or guile. 725
What fear I then, rather what know to fear
Under this ignorance of good and evil,
Of God or death, of law or penalty?
Here grows the cure of all, this fruit divine,
Fair to the eye, inviting to the taste,   730
Of virtue to make wise; what hinders then
To reach, and feed at once both body and
    mind?"
    So saying, her rash hand in evil hour
Forth reaching to the fruit, she plucked, she
    eat.*
Earth felt the wound, and Nature from her
    seat   735
Sighing through all her works gave signs of
    woe,
That all was lost. Back to the thicket slunk
The guilty Serpent, and well might, for Eve

Intent now wholly on her taste, naught
    else   739
Regarded; such delight till then, as seemed,
In fruit she never tasted, whether true
Or fancied so, through expectation high
Of knowledge, nor was Godhead* from her
    thought.
Greedily she engorged* without restraint,
And knew not eating death. Satiate at
    length,   745
And heightened as with wine, jocund and
    boon,*
Thus to herself she pleasingly began:
    "O sovran, virtuous, precious of all trees
In Paradise, of operation blest   749
To sapience,* hitherto obscured, infamed,*
And thy fair fruit let hang, as to no end
Created; but henceforth my early care,
Not without song, each morning, and due
    praise,
Shall tend thee, and the fertile burden ease
Of thy full branches offered free to all; 755
Till dieted by* thee I grow mature
In knowledge, as the gods who all things
    know;
Though others envy what they cannot give;
For had the gift been theirs, it had not here
Thus grown. Experience, next to thee I
    owe,   760
Best guide; not following thee, I had re-
    mained
In ignorance; thou open'st wisdom's way,
And giv'st accéss, though secret she retire.
And I perhaps am secret;* Heav'n is high,
High and remote to see from thence dis-
    tinct   765
Each thing on earth; and other care perhaps
May have diverted from continual watch
Our great Forbidder, safe* with all his spies
About him. But to Adam in what sort 769
Shall I appear? Shall I to him make known

---

707. **Commends**: recommends. 711. **plain**: plain terms. 724. **author unsuspect**: authority not to be suspected. 734. **eat**: ate.

743. **Godhead**: "godhood"; the state of being a god. 744. **engorged**: devoured. 746. **jocund and boon**: cheerful and merry. 749–750: of . . . **sapience**: gifted with power to give wisdom. 750. **infamed**: given an evil reputation. 756. **dieted by**: having eaten. 764. **secret**: unseen, hidden. 768. **safe**: harmless.

As yet my change, and give him to partake
Full happiness with me, or rather not,
But keep the odds of knowledge in my
  power
Without copartner? So to add what wants
In female sex, the more to draw his love, 775
And render me more equal, and perhaps,
A thing not undesirable, sometime
Superior; for inferior who is free?
This may be well. But what if God have
  seen,
And death ensue? Then I shall be no
  more,   780
And Adam wedded to another Eve
Shall live with her enjoying, I extinct;
A death to think. Confirmed then I resolve,
Adam shall share with me in bliss or woe.
So dear I love him, that with him all
  deaths   785
I could endure, without him live no life."
    So saying, from the tree her step she
      turned,
But first low reverence done, as to the
  power
That dwelt within, whose presence had
  infused
Into the plant sciential sap, derived   790
From nectar, drink of gods. Adam the while
Waiting desirous her return, had wove
Of choicest flow'rs a garland to adorn
Her tresses, and her rural labors crown,   794
As reapers oft are wont their harvest queen.
Great joy he promised to his thoughts, and
  new
Solace in her return, so long delayed;
Yet oft his heart, divine of* something ill,
Misgave* him; he the falt'ring measure* felt;
And forth to meet her went, the way she
  took   800
That morn when first they parted. By the
  Tree
Of Knowledge he must pass; there he her
  met,
Scarce from the tree returning; in her hand

A bough of fairest fruit that downy smiled,
New gathered, and ambrosial smell dif-
  fused.   805
To him she hasted; in her face excuse
Came prologue, and apology to prompt,
Which with bland words at will she thus
  addressed:
    "Hast thou not wondered, Adam, at my
      stay?
Thee I have missed, and thought it long,
  deprived   810
Thy presence, agony of love till now
Not felt, nor shall be twice, for never more
Mean I to try what rash untried I sought,
The pain of absence from thy sight. But
  strange
Hath been the cause, and wonderful to
  hear: 815
This tree is not as we are told, a tree
Of danger tasted,* nor to evil unknown
Op'ning the way, but of divine effect
To open eyes, and make them gods who
  taste;
And hath been tasted such. The Serpent
  wise,   820
Or not restrained as we, or not obeying,
Hath eaten of the fruit, and is become
Not dead, as we are threatened, but thence-
  forth
Endued with human voice and human sense,
Reasoning to admiration,* and with me   825
Persuasively hath so prevailed, that I
Have also tasted, and have also found
Th' effects to correspond, opener mine eyes,
Dim erst, dilated* spirits, ampler heart,
And growing up to Godhead; which for
  thee   830
Chiefly I sought, without thee can despise.
For bliss, as thou hast part, to me is bliss;
Tedious, unshared with thee, and odious
  soon.
Thou therefore also taste, that equal lot*
May join us, equal joy, as equal love;   835
Lest thou not tasting, different degree

---

798. **divine of**: foreseeing. 799. **misgave him**: caused him fear and doubt. **falt'ring measure**: uneven beat (of his heart).

817. **tasted**: if tasted. 825. **to admiration**: to the point of seeming wondrous. 829. **dilated**: made larger. 834. **equal lot**: the same fate.

Disjoin* us, and I then too late renounce
Deity for thee, when fate will not permit."
    Thus Eve with count'nance blithe her
      story told;
But in her cheek distemper* flushing
    glowed.   840
On th' other side, Adam, soon as he heard
The fatal trespass done by Eve, amazed,
Astonied* stood and blank, while horror
    chill
Ran through his veins, and all his joints
    relaxed;
From his slack hand the garland wreathed
    for Eve   845
Down dropped, and all the faded roses shed.
Speechless he stood and pale, till thus at
    length
First to himself he inward silence broke:
    "O fairest of creation, last and best
Of all God's works, creature in whom
    excelled   850
Whatever can to sight or thought be
    formed,
Holy, divine, good, amiable, or sweet!
How art thou lost, how on a sudden lost,
Defaced, deflow'red,* and now to death
    devote!*
Rather how hast thou yielded to trans-
    gress   855
The strict forbiddance, how to violate
The sacred fruit forbidd'n! Some cursèd
    fraud
Of enemy hath beguiled thee, yet unknown,
And me with thee hath ruined, for with thee
Certain my resolution is to die;   860
How can I live without thee, how forgo
Thy sweet converse and love so dearly
    joined,
To live again in these wild woods forlorn?
Should God create another Eve, and I
Another rib afford, yet loss of thee   865
Would never from my heart; no, no! I feel
The link of nature draw me: flesh of flesh,

---

837. **Disjoin:** separate. 840. **distemper:** fever.
843. **Astonied:** dazed. 854. **deflow'red:** spoiled.
devote: doomed.

Bone of my bone thou art, and from thy
    state
Mine never shall be parted, bliss or woe."
    So having said, as one from sad dismay 870
Recomforted, and after thoughts disturbed
Submitting to what seemed remédiless,
Thus in calm mood his words to Eve he
    turned:
    "Bold deed thou hast presumed, adven-
    t'rous Eve,
And peril great provoked, who thus hast
    dared   875
Had it been only coveting to eye
That sacred fruit, sacred to abstinence,
Much more to taste it under ban to touch.
But past who can recall, or done undo?
Not God omnipotent, nor fate. Yet so   880
Perhaps thou shalt not die; perhaps the fact
Is not so heinous now, foretasted fruit,
Profaned first by the Serpent, by him first
Made common and unhallowed ere our
    taste,
Nor yet on him found deadly; he yet
    lives,   885
Lives, as thou saidst, and gains to live as man
Higher degree of life, inducement strong
To us, as likely tasting to attain
Proportional ascent, which cannot be
But to be gods, or angels, demi-gods.   890
Nor can I think that God, Creator wise,
Though threat'ning, will in earnest* so
    destroy
Us his prime creatures, dignified so high,
Set over all his works, which in our fall,
For us created, needs with us must fail,   895
Dependent made; so God shall uncreate,
Be frustrate,* do, undo, and labor lose,
Not well conceived of God, who though his
    power
Creation could repeat, yet would be loth
Us to abolish, lest the Adversary*   900
Triumph and say: 'Fickle their state whom
    God
Most favors, who can please him long? Me

---

892. **in earnest:** really. 897. **frustrate:** frustrated. 900. **Adversary:** Satan.

first
He ruined, now mankind; whom will he
    next?'
Matter of scorn not to be given the Foe;
However, I with thee have fixed my lot, 905
Certain* to undergo like doom: if death
Consort with* thee, death is to me as life;
So forcible within my heart I feel
The bond of nature draw me to my own,
My own in thee, for what thou art is
    mine; 910
Our state cannot be severed; we are one,
One flesh; to lose thee were to lose myself."
    So Adam, and thus Eve to him replied:
"O glorious trial of exceeding love,
Illustrious evidence, example high! 915
Engaging* me to emulate, but short
Of thy perfection, how shall I attain,
Adam? From whose dear side I boast me
    sprung,
And gladly of our union hear thee speak,
One heart, one soul in both; whereof good
    proof 920
This day affords, declaring thee resolved,
Rather than death or aught than death more
    dread
Shall separate us, linked in love so dear,
To undergo with me one guilt, one crime,
If any be, of tasting this fair fruit, 925
Whose virtue (for of good still good pro-
    ceeds,
Direct, or by occasion) hath presented
This happy trial of thy love, which else
So eminently never had been known.
Were it I thought death menaced would
    ensue 930
This my attempt, I would sustain alone
The worst, and not persuade thee, rather die
Deserted, than oblige* thee with a fact
Pernicious* to thy peace, chiefly assured
Remarkably so late of thy so true, 935
So faithful love unequaled; but I feel

Far otherwise th' event, not death, but life
Augmented,* opened eyes, new hopes, new
    joys,
Taste so divine, that what of sweet before
Hath touched my sense, flat seems to this
    and harsh. 940
On my experience, Adam, freely taste,
And fear of death deliver to the winds."
    So saying, she embraced him, and for joy
Tenderly wept, much won that he his love
Had so ennobled, as of choice to incur 945
Divine displeasure for her sake, or death.
In recompense (for such compliance bad
Such recompense best merits) from the
    bough
She gave him of that fair enticing fruit
With liberal hand. He scrupled* not to
    eat 950
Against his better knowledge, not deceived,
But fondly overcome with female charm.
Earth trembled from her entrails,* as again
In pangs, and Nature gave a second groan;
Sky loured* and, muttering thunder, some
    sad drops 955
Wept at completing of the mortal sin
Original; while Adam took no thought,
Eating his fill, nor Eve to iterate*
Her former trespass feared, the more to
    soothe
Him with her loved society, that now 960
As with new wine intoxicated both
They swim in mirth, and fancy that they
    feel
Divinity within them breeding wings
Wherewith to scorn the earth. But that
    false fruit
Far other operation first displayed, 965
Carnal* desire inflaming: he on Eve
Began to cast lascivious* eyes, she him
As wantonly repaid; in lust they burn,
Till Adam thus 'gan Eve to dalliance move:

906. **Certain:** resolved. 907. **Consort with:** accompanies. 916. **Engaging:** binding. 933. **oblige:** involve in guilt. 934. **Pernicious:** causing destruction.

938. **Augmented:** made larger. 950. **scrupled:** hesitated because of doubt. 953. **entrails:** inner parts. 955. **loured:** appeared black and threatening. 958. **iterate:** repeat. 966. **Carnal:** sensual. 967. **lascivious:** lustful.

"Eve, now I see thou art exact of taste, 970
And elegant, of sapience no small part;
Since to each meaning savor we apply,
And palate call judicious;* I the praise
Yield thee, so well this day thou hast pur-
veyed.*
Much pleasure we have lost, while we ab-
stained   975
From this delightful fruit, nor known till
now
True relish, tasting; if such pleasure be
In things to us forbidden, it might be wished
For this one tree had been forbidden ten.
But come, so well refreshed, now let us
play,   980
As meet is, after such delicious fare;
For never did thy beauty since the day
I saw thee first and wedded thee, adorned
With all perfections, so inflame my sense
With ardor to enjoy thee, fairer now   985
Than ever, bounty of this virtuous tree."
    So said he, and forbore not glance or toy
Of amorous intent, well understood
Of Eve, whose eye darted contagious fire.
Her hand he seized, and to a shady bank, 990
Thick overhead with verdant roof em-
bow'red,
He led her nothing loth,* flow'rs were the
couch,
Pansies, and violets, and asphodel,
And hyacinth, earth's freshest softest lap.
There they their fill of love and love's
disport   995
Took largely, of their mutual guilt the seal,
The solace of their sin, till dewy sleep
Oppressed them, wearied with their amo-
rous play.
Soon as the force of that fallacious* fruit,
That with exhilarating vapor bland   1000
About their spirits had played, and inmost
powers
Made err, was now exhaled, and grosser
sleep

Bred of unkindly* fumes, with conscious
dreams
Encumbered, now had left them, up they
rose
As from unrest, and each the other view-
ing,   1005
Soon found their eyes how opened, and
their minds
How darkened; innocence, that as a veil
Had shadowed them from knowing ill, was
gone;
Just confidence, and native righteousness,
And honor from about them, naked left 1010
To guilty Shame; he* covered, but his robe
Uncovered more. So rose the Danite strong,
Herculean Samson, from the harlot-lap
Of Philistéan Dálilah, and waked
Shorn of his strength, they destitute and
bare   1015
Of all their virtue. Silent, and in face
Confounded,* long they sat, as strucken
mute,
Till Adam, though not less than Eve
abashed,
At length gave utterance to these words
constrained: 1019
    "O Eve, in evil hour thou didst give ear
To that false worm, of whomsoever taught
To counterfeit man's voice, true in our fall,
False in our promised rising; since our eyes
Opened we find indeed, and find we know
Both good and evil, good lost and evil
got,   1025
Bad fruit of knowledge, if this be to know,
Which leaves us naked thus, of honor void,
Of innocence, of faith, of purity,
Our wonted ornaments now soiled and
stained,
And in our faces evident the signs   1030
Of foul concupiscence;* whence evil store,
Even shame, the last of evils; of the first
Be sure then. How shall I behold the face
Henceforth of God or angel, erst with joy

972-973. **Since . . . judicious:** a play on the literal and figurative meanings of "taste." 974. **pur-veyed:** supplied (food). 992. **nothing loth:** not reluctant. 999. **fallacious:** deceptive.

1003. **unkindly:** unnatural. 1011. **he:** shame. 1017. **Confounded:** ashamed. 1031. **concupiscence:** lust.

Expulsion from the Garden of Eden *by the nineteenth-century American painter Thomas Cole.*

And rapture so oft beheld? Those heav'nly shapes 1035
Will dazzle now this earthly, with their blaze
Insufferably bright. O might I here
In solitude live savage, in some glade
Obscured, where highest woods impenetrable
To star or sunlight, spread their umbrage* broad 1040
And brown* as evening! Cover me, ye pines,
Ye cedars, with innumerable boughs
Hide me, where I may never see them more.
But let us now, as in bad plight, devise 1044
What best may for the present serve to hide
The parts of each from other that seem most
To shame obnoxious,* and unseemliest seen,
Some tree whose broad smooth leaves together sewed,
And girded on our loins, may cover round
Those middle parts, that this newcomer, Shame, 1050
There sit not, and reproach us as unclean."
So counseled he, and both together went
Into the thickest wood; there soon they chose
The fig-tree, not that kind for fruit renowned, 1054
But such as at this day to Indians known
In Malabar or Deccan* spreads her arms
Branching so broad and long, that in the ground
The bended twigs take root, and daughters grow
About the mother tree, a pillared shade
High overarched, and echoing walks between; 1060
There oft the Indian herdsman shunning heat
Shelters in cool, and tends his pasturing herds
At loop-holes cut through thickest shade. Those leaves
They gathered, broad as Amazonian targe,*
And with what skill they had, together sewed, 1065
To gird their waist, vain covering if to hide
Their guilt and dreaded shame, O how unlike
To that first naked glory! Such of late
Columbus found th' American so girt
With feathered cincture,* naked else and wild 1070
Among the trees on isles and woody shores.

1056. **Malabar, Deccan**: areas in southern India. 1064. **targe**: shield. Amazon women warriors of Greek mythology carried heavy shields. 1070. **cincture**: belt.

1040. **umbrage**: shade. 1041. **brown**: shadowy, dark. 1047. **To shame obnoxious**: liable to shame.

Thus fenced, and as they thought, their
  shame in part
Covered, but not at rest or ease of mind,
They sat them down to weep; nor only tears
Rained at their eyes, but high winds worse
  within   1075
Began to rise, high passions, anger, hate,
Mistrust, suspicion, discord, and shook sore
Their inward state of mind, calm region
  once
And full of peace, now tossed and turbulent;
For understanding ruled not, and the
  will   1080
Heard not her lore,* both in subjection now
To sensual appetite, who from beneath
Usurping over sovran reason claimed
Superior sway. From thus distempered
  breast,
Adam, estranged* in look and altered
  style,   1085
Speech intermitted* thus to Eve renewed:
  "Would thou hadst hearkened to my
    words, and stayed
With me, as I besought* thee, when that
  strange
Desire of wand'ring this unhappy morn,
I know not whence possessed thee; we had
  then   1090
Remained still happy, not as now, despoiled
Of all our good, shamed, naked, miserable.
Let none henceforth seek needless cause to
  approve
The faith they owe;* when earnestly they
  seek
Such proof, conclude they then begin to
  fail."   1095
  To whom, soon moved with touch of
    blame, thus Eve:
"What words have passed thy lips, Adam
  severe!
Imput'st* thou that to my default,* or will

1080–1081. **will . . . lore:** *i.e.,* the will did not act
in response to understanding, but to sensual appetite. 1085. **estranged:** become unfriendly and
distant. 1086. **intermitted:** stopped for a time.
1088. **besought:** begged. 1094. **owe:** own, possess.
1098. **Imput'st:** attribute, blame on. **default:**
failure to be somewhere.

Of wand'ring, as thou call'st it, which who
  knows
But might as ill have happened thou being
  by,   1100
Or to thyself perhaps? Hadst thou been
  there,
Or here th' attempt, thou couldst not have
  discerned
Fraud in the Serpent, speaking as he spake;
No ground of enmity between us known
Why he should mean me ill, or seek to
  harm.   1105
Was I to have never parted from thy side?
As good have grown there still a lifeless rib.
Being as I am, why didst not thou, the head,
Command me absolutely not to go,
Going into such danger as thou saidst?   1110
Too facile* then, thou didst not much gain-
  say,*
Nay didst permit, approve, and fair dismiss.
Hadst thou been firm and fixed in thy dis-
  sent,
Neither had I transgressed, nor thou with
  me."
  To whom then first incensed Adam re-
    plied: 1115
"Is this the love, is this the recompense
Of mine to thee, ingrateful Eve, expressed
Immutable when thou wert lost, not I,
Who might have lived and joyed immortal
  bliss,
Yet willingly chose rather death with
  thee?   1120
And am I now upbraided, as the cause
Of thy transgressing? Not enough severe,
It seems, in thy restraint. What could I
  more?
I warned thee, I admonished thee, foretold
The danger, and the lurking enemy   1125
That lay in wait; beyond this had been
  force,
And force upon free will hath here no place.
But confidence then bore thee on, secure
Either to meet no danger, or to find
Matter of glorious trial; and perhaps   1130

1111. **facile:** easy to influence. **gainsay:** oppose,
forbid.

I also erred in overmuch admiring
What seemed in thee so perfect, that I
    thought
No evil durst* attempt thee, but I rue*
That error now, which is become my crime,
And thou th' accuser. Thus it shall be-
    fall   1135
Him who to worth in women overtrusting
Lets her will rule; restraint she will not
    brook,
And left to herself, if evil thence ensue,*
She first his weak indulgence will accuse."

    Thus they in mutual accusation spent 1140
The fruitless hours, but neither self-con-
    demning,
And of their vain contést appeared no end.

1133. **durst:** dared, **rue:** regret. 1138. **ensue:**
result.

For Discussion

1. It might be helpful to consider Book IX
of *Paradise Lost* as falling into three parts: the
section that precedes Satan's temptation of
Eve, the temptation itself, and the aftermath.
As for the first of the three, how did Satan
enter Eden? His speech at lines 52–131 explores his motives for behaving as he does,
against both God and man. What are those
motives? Why does he pick the snake as the
"Fit vessel" for his plan?

2. Adam and Eve we encounter discussing
"how that day they best may ply / Their
growing work" (154–155). Why does Eve
want to divide their labors? What is Adam's
response to her suggestion that each of them
go his separate way? His response offends
Eve. Why? In lines 275–294 she argues her
position eloquently, if erroneously. What is
the gist of her argument? Adam's fervent reply
from line 296 on lies at the heart of the theme
of *Paradise Lost*. How does Eve answer his
reasoning?

3. The second large portion of the book is
concerned with the temptation itself. How is
Satan first affected by the sight of Eve's loveliness? Why is he particularly eager to exploit
this opportunity with Eve alone, rather than

with Adam? As a snake he approaches Eve—
but as a snake unlike the kind we know. Describe him. How does he behave? To what
proverbial weaknesses of women does he appeal in the speech beginning at line 485? Eve
is amazed that the snake can speak. How is his
gift of speech accounted for?

4. Before the tree of the knowledge of good
and evil Eve hesitates. Why? What arguments
does Satan bring forth to tempt her to taste of
the fruit? Notice that he professes "show of
zeal and love / To man, and indignation at his
wrong" (618–619). What "wrong"? How does
the serpent answer Eve's fears of impending
death? How does he reassure her that God
cannot hurt her? After elaborately rationaliz-
ing her act in advance (lines 698–732) Eve eats
of the fruit. Is this the climax of the book?
Explain.

5. The aftermath of Eve's sin is a compen-
dium of the seven deadly sins of pride, greed,
lust, envy, sloth, anger, and gluttony. How
does she show greed? How sloth—or laziness?
How envy? Eve protests that she would not
try to persuade Adam to eat of the fruit if she
suspected "death menaced would ensue" (930).
Compare her thoughts at line 779 and following: Is she telling Adam the truth? Why does
he taste of the fruit? What are the immediate
consequences of their defiance of God? How
do they feel and behave upon awakening from
their sleep?

6. Three books of *Paradise Lost* conclude
the epic. In them God sends His son to judge
the transgressors; Adam and Eve beseech his
intercession on their behalf; the Son of God
does intercede, and the Father forgives the
erring humans but dismisses them from Paradise. Moreover, because of their act, Sin and
Death make their way into the world, and
from Hell a bridge is built across Chaos so that
Satan and all his cohorts can enter the world
of man. The poem ends as the angel Michael,
bearing a flaming sword, leads Adam and Eve
from the Garden:

The world was all before them, where to
    choose
Their place of rest, and Providence their
    guide;
They, hand in hand, with wandering steps

and slow,
Through Eden took their solitary way.

7. Having reviewed the content of the epic, look more closely at the ideas expressed in Book IX. Adam's speech at lines 296–328 bears careful consideration, because it expresses one resolution of those recurring problems that surround good and evil, fate and free will. If God is all-good and all-powerful, how can man be blamed for what he does, since man can act only by God's leave? How does Adam account for man's responsibility for whatever evil he may be guilty of? Reason says to shun evil. Man has the gift of reason to rely on, so why need he fear evil at all? Why does Adam urge Eve to "Seek not temptation" (line 317)?

8. Another expression of ideas concerning good and evil that merits close consideration is that of Satan at lines 632–685. By striving for the knowledge of good and evil, he tells Eve, man will earn God's praise for his "dauntless virtue." According to Satan, what was God's motive for forbidding man to taste of the fruit of knowledge in the first place? By tasting the fruit, Eve will come to know what is good—and that outcome must be just (line 650). Why? Why, according to Satan, should she desire to know evil as well? The argument at lines 663–665 is particularly weak. Can you see the fallacy in it?

9. Though the themes of *Paradise Lost* are profound and inexhaustible, the value of the work as poetry must not be disregarded. In what verse form is it written? Illustrate your answer. The epic was composed in an unusual way. In middle age Milton went blind, so in order to write *Paradise Lost* he was forced to conceive and memorize lines of verse in the evening and dictate them to friends the following day. It is hardly surprising to discover that the poem as a consequence is rich in imagery that appeals to senses other than that of sight. The perfumes of the tree of knowledge are one memorable instance of such an appeal. What other images of sound, smell, taste, and touch struck you forcefully? Images of sight, of course, do appear—in the description of the serpent, for instance. What other visual imagery seemed especially effective?

10. **Epic.** *Epic*, a Greek word meaning "tale," has come to be applied to a kind of narrative poetry treating a subject and theme of national or universal significance involving characters of superhuman dimensions engaged in heroic actions, the whole expressed in dignified, often exalted, language. Milton's literary epic makes use of most of the characteristics of classical epics of Homer and Virgil. There is the invocation to the muses. There are the heroic roll calls, the boastings, the apostrophes (as, for example, at lines 357–364), the elaborate similes (lines 466–471), and a structure that begins *in medias res*—in the middle of things—then recapitulates in flashback. *Paradise Lost*, to be specific, begins after Satan and his angels have been thrown into the flaming lake of Hell, and it is only in Books V and VI that we learn of the actions preceding that event. What is the effect of the apostrophe at line 748 and following? What other elaborate similes (often called *Homeric similes*) did you encounter in this portion of *Paradise Lost*?

For Composition

1. **Analysis.** A number of influences contribute to make Eve succumb to the serpent's wiles. In a coherent essay that quotes judiciously from the poem, analyze the different reasons why Eve finally ate of the fruit of the tree of knowledge. Consider both her physical and mental states at the time of the transgression.

2. **Exposition.** Milton's verse style makes abundant use of classical allusion, which served effectively to communicate meaning to educated readers of his day. Many such allusions are lost on us now, but a few minutes spent with a classical dictionary or a heavily annotated edition of the poem will restore some of the effects of allusion to a modern reader. In a clearly written essay explain the classical allusions at lines 338–349 and 393–396.

3. **Comparison and Contrast.** Book IX of *Paradise Lost* enlarges specifically on Genesis 3:1–7; the verses appear on page 502. Compare and contrast Milton's version of the Fall of Man with the account in Genesis. In what ways has the poet most notably departed from the source he was following?

Fact, Myth, and Truth

The opening selections of this anthology, which explored some aspects of truth, by no means exhausted that tantalizing subject. "Water boils at 212° F." True or false? It depends. In Denver, a mile high, the statement is false; at sea level, it is true, provided we all agree what F stands for, what the superscript ° means, and what the rest of the words in the statement denote. But facts — a kind of truth — are slippery. The fact that water flows downhill can be verified to most people's satisfaction by pouring water down a number of hills, but what practical test is there to verify that the square root of nine is three? That it is considered to be so is a convention we have agreed to agree on, though any other convention about that square root, if consistently followed, would work as well.

All this is by way of suggesting that fact and truth are not always identical. Nor should we assume that the only kind of truth we can rely on is the truth embodied in cold, hard fact. Consider the following for a moment.

It is a truth about human life — has been and no doubt always will be — that a young man of great gifts must sooner or later make a choice, and in doing so he closes the door on alternative choices. He may devote all his talent to becoming, say, a great soldier, and with diligence he may enjoy success. Or he may devote his talent to becoming a politician, and assuming he is willing to make the necessary sacrifices of time and energy, he may very well succeed there. Or he may concentrate all his gifts on becoming a playboy and *bon vivant*, and no doubt he will have success there too, always of course at the cost of realizing his potential in other areas of endeavor. Most of us can do only so much in one lifetime, and to do anything extremely well takes something close to total commitment.

Insight into this truth is expressed in one of the great myths of classical antiquity. At a feast of the gods on Mount Olympus, the uninvited goddess of discord, Eris, mischievously threw onto the table an apple labeled "For the Fairest." Three feminine hands reached for it. One hand belonged to Hera, wife of the supreme god, Zeus. The second belonged to the goddess of wisdom and valor, Athene. And the third was the hand of Aphrodite, goddess of love. Which of the three goddesses was the fairest in fact? To whom should the apple be given?

To decide, the handsomest of mortals, Paris, was brought to the feast, where each of the three goddesses promised rewards to him if he would give the apple to her. Hera would see that he enjoyed transcendent success in statecraft; Athene would make of him an unexampled warrior hero; and Aphrodite would furnish him success in love beyond that of any other mortal. Paris, as you may know, gave the apple to Aphrodite, and from that choice reaped the reward of Helen, most beautiful of women, with all the consequences — including the fall of Troy and the destruction of his family — that flowed therefrom.

Whether or not there was ever a man named Paris, there is truth in the myth that is as valid as fact, and more affecting. Myth, then, collects the diverse experience of the race of man and fashions it into memorable and enduring form.

Consider some selections you have read. Although they are not myths in the strict sense of the word, they contain truths as solid as facts but embrace more of man's experience. Although the Pruitts and their island may never have existed outside of E. B. White's story (page 479), is it not true that men often do evil with the best of intentions? Whether or not the incident described in "Rashomon" (page 492) ever occurred, the story dramatizes an eternal problem about the effect of circumstances on man's behavior.

What is true about the Garden of Eden and the events we are told took place there? Some people read the account in *Genesis* as factual truth, but it is hardly necessary to insist on literal accuracy to appreciate the profound mythical truths of the story told simply in *Genesis* and more elaborately in *Paradise Lost*. The temptation to rise above one's place in the universe, to which Eve succumbed, is a universal human experience. And Adam's loyalty to Eve, his desire to remain with her whatever the consequences, reflects another and perhaps more admirable human trait. Less admirable, but just as human, is their effort to convince themselves that what they have done is right despite all evidence to the contrary. We can recognize these and other truths in the story, although we have never known a world literally like that of Adam and Eve.

Perhaps the most profound aspect of the story lies in God's commandment that man not eat the fruit of the tree of knowledge and man's breaking of that commandment. We assume the value of knowledge, but many of the most able observers of man's progress wonder, as they ponder the future, whether what lies before us is ultimately good or evil. Has our knowledge outgrown our ability to use it wisely? As we learn how to destroy the inhabitants of the earth, and as we hover on the brink of discovering how to create life itself, we might find more significance in the ancient story of the fall of man than we had realized.

"I only have time for facts," the innocent often say. "No time for make-believe." But fiction — the best of it — isn't make-believe. It is often the more enduring reality, and because it contains truth, it goes beyond personal and national boundaries. Thus, one need not be a Greek to recognize truth in *Oedipus the King*, or a Roman Catholic to be astonished by the accuracy of vision in *The Divine Comedy*. Nor does one have to insist on a literal interpretation of Christian doctrine in order to find profound truths about man and his fate in *Paradise Lost*.

1. Although facts are not the only form of truth, they are extremely important. What is a fact? What is the importance of facts in your everyday life? What is the relationship between facts and ideas? Between facts and opinions?

2. Is man essentially good? Or is he essentially evil? To what extent can facts help you to answer those questions? Will your final answer be a fact?

[handwritten top: ways speaker conveys his attitude about subject. Include use of imagery & diction that convey attitude]

Original Sin

ROBINSON JEFFERS

[handwritten: hyphenated-compounds (man-brained, flag-flower) 2 words becoming 1]

A twentieth-century American poet has absorbed the lessons of psychology and anthropology, but those modern sciences offer him little comfort about the human condition. In the following poem he envisages a moment in man's long past when innocence was lost and the first sin committed, in Eden-like surroundings bathed in "the intense color and nobility of sunrise."

[handwritten: still animal / until killed / overall disgust]

The man-brained and man-handed ground-ape, physically
The most repulsive of all hot-blooded animals
Up to that time of the world: they had dug a pitfall*
And caught a mammoth, but how could their sticks and stones
Reach the life in that hide? They danced around the pit, shrieking   5
With ape excitement, flinging sharp flints in vain, and the stench of their bodies
Stained the white air of dawn; but presently one of them
Remembered the yellow dancer, wood-eating fire
That guards the cave-mouth: he ran and fetched him, and others
Gathered sticks at the wood's edge; they made a blaze   10
And pushed it into the pit, and they fed it high, around the mired sides
Of their huge prey. They watched the long hairy trunk
Waver over the stifle-trumpeting* pain,
And they were happy.

        Meanwhile the intense color and nobility of sunrise,
Rose and gold and amber, flowed up the sky. Wet rocks were shining, a little wind
Stirred the leaves of the forest and the marsh flag-flowers; the soft valley between
    the low hills   16
Became as beautiful as the sky; while in its midst, hour after hour, the happy
    hunters
Roasted their living meat slowly to death.

           These are the people.
This is the human dawn. As for me, I would rather
Be a worm in a wild apple than a son of man.   20
But we are what we are, and we might remember
Not to hate any person, for all are vicious;
And not to be astonished at any evil, all are deserved;
And not fear death; it is the only way to be cleansed.

[handwritten annotations: bad Picture — narrative; direct statement/contrast; stark contrast of images!; acceptance don't hate — not better than anyone (pot/kettle black)]

3. **pitfall**: lightly covered pit, used as a trap for animals. 13. **stife-trumpeting**: proclaiming suffering.

529

[handwritten bottom: dawn of man ⇒ evil is nature; not a learned behavior]

For Discussion

1. According to this account, what form did man's first sin take? The poem is in three parts, the first describing an action-filled scene involving "ground-apes" and a trapped mammoth. What is the effect of the second part on the first? The third part gives the speaker's reaction to what he has described. What is his attitude toward man? Toward evil? Toward hate? Toward death?

2. How is "happy" in line 14 emphasized? The word seems almost commonplace in this context; one might have expected a more charged adjective—"jubilant," "elated," "exultant." But the very ordinariness of "happy"— the vagueness of it—suggests the scorn of the speaker for the attitude of his primeval ancestors toward what they had done. What other diction best conveys the speaker's scorn?

3. Is this poem written in blank verse or free verse? Explain.

For Composition

The title invites parallels between the scene here being described and the account of man's fall given in the Book of Genesis (page 502).

1. **Comparison and Contrast.** What similarities and differences do you find between Jeffers' account of the origins of sin and that of Genesis? In a specific and coherent paper compare and contrast the two accounts. Notice the description at the center of the poem (lines 14–18), and the connotations of lines 19–20: "As for me, I would rather / Be a worm in a wild apple than a son of man. . . ."

2. **Argument.** In a well-organized essay supported by specific examples, justify or refute the attitude toward man expressed in "Original Sin." Your essay should avoid merely stating an opinion, developing instead some sort of systematic survey—however brief—of man's influence on his surroundings through history.

About the Poet. **Robinson Jeffers** (1887–1962) celebrated in drama and in poetry the individual hero who confronts the mass and the destructive spirit which lurks beneath the surface of man's civilization. Jeffers preferred relative isolation in his personal life. He chose for his symbols the hawk, the wild but solitary spirit of man, and the rooted, ageless earth. Summarizing his beliefs, he once wrote, "Humanity is needless." As Horace Gregory and Marya Zaturenska noted, however, his philosophy may have less endurance "than those gifts which enabled him to create parables of human blindness and suffering."

Mario and the Magician

THOMAS MANN

The following story is set at a seaside resort called Torre di Venere — the Tower of Venus — south of Rome on the west coast of Italy, in the late 1920's. That era, between two world wars, was one of uncertainty in much of Europe. But in Italy itself, uncertainty had apparently given way to the rise of *Il Duce* — The Leader — Benito Mussolini, strong-man founder of modern fascism. It was the boast of the fascists, a totalitarian party deriving strength at the start from small shopkeepers and the so-called lower-middle class, that they

Thomas Mann: pronounced tō'mäs män'.

had made the trains run on time — had brought order out of chaos. But fascism, with its cruelties, its tyrannies, its strutting goon squads, set an ominous example for the rest of Europe, an example that Thomas Mann's own countryman Adolf Hitler was even at the time of the story emulating successfully in his drive to gain power in Germany.

Mussolini was destined to end his days ignominiously murdered and displayed in a Milan filling station as an object of derision to all his countrymen. But his career up to that time had been a dramatic one — comic, repulsive, awesome, impressive, disgusting in turn. To know something of fascism and *Il Duce* adds greatly to the meaning of the story that follows. Yet a knowledge of the rise and fall of the tyranny in Italy — so like tyrannies elsewhere before and since — is not indispensable to appreciating the profound insights into goodness and evil that "Mario and the Magician" affords.

The atmosphere of Torre di Venere[1] remains unpleasant in the memory. From the first moment the air of the place made us uneasy, we felt irritable, on edge; then at the end came the shocking business of Cipolla,[2] that dreadful being who seemed to incorporate, in so fateful and so humanly impressive a way, all the peculiar evilness of the situation as a whole. Looking back, we had the feeling that the horrible end of the affair had been preordained and lay in the nature of things; that the children had to be present at it was an added impropriety, due to the false colors in which the weird creature presented himself. Luckily for them, they did not know where the comedy left off and the tragedy began; and we let them remain in their happy belief that the whole thing had been a play up till the end.

Torre di Venere lies some fifteen kilometers[3] from Portoclemente, one of the most popular summer resorts on the Tyrrhenian Sea.[4] Portoclemente is urban and elegant and full to overflowing for months on end. Its gay and busy main street of shops and hotels runs down to a wide sandy beach covered with tents and pennanted sand castles and sunburnt humanity, where at all times a lively social bustle reigns, and much noise. But this same spacious and inviting fine-sanded beach, this same border of pine grove and near, presiding mountains, continues all the way along the coast. No wonder then that some competition of a quiet kind should have sprung up further on. Torre di Venere — the tower that gave the town its name is gone long since, one looks for it in vain — is an offshoot of the larger resort, and for some years remained an idyll for the few, a refuge for more unworldly spirits. But the usual history of such places repeated itself: peace has had to retire further along the coast, to Marina Petriera and dear knows where else. We all know how the world at once seeks peace and puts her to flight — rushing upon her in the fond idea that they two will wed, and where she is, there it can be at home. It will even set up its Vanity Fair[5] in a spot and be capable of thinking that peace is still by its side. Thus Torre — though its atmosphere so far is more modest and contemplative than that of Portoclemente — has been quite taken up,

---

[1] **Torre di Venere**: literally, Tower of Venus.

[2] **Cipolla**: chē·pō′lä.

[3] **kilometers**: European unit of measurement, equal to about five eighths of a mile.

[4] **Tyrrhenian Sea**: part of the Mediterranean Sea.

[5] **Vanity Fair**: Bunyan's *Pilgrim's Progress* describes this allegorical fair established by devils, at which were sold honors, kingdoms, and pleasures.

by both Italians and foreigners. It is no longer the thing to go to Portoclemente — though still so much the thing that it is as noisy and crowded as ever. One goes next door, so to speak: to Torre. So much more refined, even, and cheaper to boot.[1] And the attractiveness of these qualities persists, though the qualities themselves long ago ceased to be evident. Torre has got a Grand Hotel. Numerous pensions[2] have sprung up, some modest, some pretentious. The people who own or rent the villas and pinetas[3] overlooking the sea no longer have it all their own way on the beach. In July and August it looks just like the beach at Portoclemente: it swarms with a screaming, squabbling, merrymaking crowd, and the sun, blazing down like mad, peels the skin off their necks. Garish little flat-bottomed boats rock on the glittering blue, manned by children, whose mothers hover afar and fill the air with anxious cries of Nino! and Sandro! and Bice! and Maria! Peddlers step across the legs of recumbent sun-bathers, selling flowers and corals, oysters, lemonade, and *cornetti al burro*,[4] and crying their wares in

[1] **to boot**: in addition.
[2] **pensions** (pän′syōn′): boardinghouses in Continental Europe.
[3] **pinetas**: pine groves.
[4] *cornetti al burro*: crescent rolls with butter.

the breathy, full-throated southern voice.

Such was the scene that greeted our arrival in Torre: pleasant enough, but after all, we thought, we had come too soon. It was the middle of August, the Italian season was still at its height, scarcely the moment for strangers to learn to love the special charms of the place. What an afternoon crowd in the cafés on the front! For instance, in the Esquisito, where we sometimes sat and were served by Mario, that very Mario of whom I shall have presently to tell. It is well-nigh impossible to find a table; and the various orchestras contend together in the midst of one's conversation with bewildering effect. Of course, it is in the afternoon that people come over from Portoclemente. The excursion is a favorite one for the restless denizens[5] of that pleasure resort, and a Fiat motorbus plies to and fro, coating inch thick with dust the oleander[6] and laurel hedges along the highroad — a notable if repulsive sight.

Yes, decidedly one should go to Torre in September, when the great public has left. Or else in May, before the water is warm enough to tempt the Southerner to bathe. Even in the before and after seasons Torre

[5] **denizens**: inhabitants.
[6] **oleander**: an evergreen shrub.

ABOUT THE AUTHOR • **Thomas Mann** (1875–1955) is the outstanding German novelist of the twentieth century. Author of *Buddenbrooks, Joseph and His Brothers, Dr. Faustus,* and many other well-known novels, Mann began as a believer in the civilizing destiny of Germany, but he uncovered the decay within the German intellectual and middle classes in *The Magic Mountain,* and symbolically represented the evils of dictatorship in "Mario and the Magician." Mann received the Nobel Prize for Literature in 1929. With the Nazi rise to power in 1933, he fled to America, where he lectured at Princeton and continued writing. Later he lived in Switzerland and lectured in East and West Germany. His career spanned the period in which German industry and military might rose and fell under the Kaiser, and rose and fell again under Nazism.

is not empty, but life is less national and more subdued. English, French, and German prevail under the tent awnings and in the pension dining rooms; whereas in August — in the Grand Hotel, at least, where, in default of[1] private addresses, we had engaged rooms — the stranger finds the field so occupied by Florentine and Roman society that he feels quite isolated and even temporarily *déclassé*.[2]

We had, rather to our annoyance, this experience on the evening we arrived, when we went in to dinner and were shown to our table by the waiter in charge. As a table, it had nothing against it, save that we had already fixed our eyes upon those on the veranda beyond, built out over the water, where little red-shaded lamps glowed — and there were still some tables empty, though it was as full as the dining room within. The children went into raptures at the festive sight, and without more ado we announced our intention to take our meals by preference in the veranda. Our words, it appeared, were prompted by ignorance; for we were informed, with somewhat embarrassed politeness, that the cosy nook outside was reserved for the clients of the hotel: *ai nostri clienti*.[3] Their clients? But we were their clients. We were not tourists or trippers,[4] but boarders for a stay of some three or four weeks. However, we forbore to press for an explanation of the difference between the likes of us and that clientèle to whom it was vouchsafed[5] to eat out there in the glow of the red lamps, and took our dinner by the prosaic common light of the dining room chandelier — a thoroughly ordinary and monotonous hotel bill of fare, be it said. In Pensione Eleonora, a few steps landward,[6] the table,[7] as we were to discover, was much better.

And thither it was that we moved, three or four days later, before we had had time to settle in properly at the Grand Hotel. Not on account of the veranda and the lamps. The children, straightway on the best of terms with waiters and pages, absorbed in the joys of life on the beach, promptly forgot those colorful seductions. But now there arose, between ourselves and the veranda clientèle — or perhaps more correctly with the compliant management — one of those little unpleasantnesses which can quite spoil the pleasure of a holiday. Among the guests were some high Roman aristocracy, a Principe[8] X and his family. These grand folk occupied rooms close to our own, and the Principessa,[9] a great and a passionately maternal lady, was thrown into a panic by the vestiges of a whooping cough which our little ones had lately got over, but which now and then still faintly troubled the unshatterable slumbers of our youngest-born. The nature of this illness is not clear, leaving some play for the imagination. So we took no offense at our elegant neighbor for clinging to the widely held view that whooping cough is acoustically contagious[10] and quite simply fearing lest her children yield to the bad example set by ours. In the fullness of her feminine self-confidence she protested to the management, which then, in the person of the proverbial[11] frock-coated manager, hastened to represent to us, with many expressions of regret, that under the circumstances they were obliged to transfer us to the annex. We did our best to assure him that the disease was in its very last stages, that it was actually over, and presented no danger of infection to anybody. All that we gained was permission to bring the case before the

---

[1] **in default of**: through lack of.
[2] *déclassé* (dā′klä′sā′): lowered in social status.
[3] *ai nostri clienti*: for our customers.
[4] **trippers**: travelers.
[5] **vouchsafed**: granted.
[6] **landward**: *i.e.*, farther from the seashore.
[7] **table**: food.

[8] **Principe**: Prince.
[9] **Principessa**: Princess.
[10] **acoustically contagious**: *i.e.*, one can catch the disease if he is within hearing distance of the cough.
[11] **proverbial**: traditional.

hotel physician — not one chosen by us — by whose verdict we must then abide. We agreed, convinced that thus we should at once pacify the Princess and escape the trouble of moving. The doctor appeared, and behaved like a faithful and honest servant of science. He examined the child and gave his opinion: the disease was quite over, no danger of contagion was present. We drew a long breath and considered the incident closed — until the manager announced that despite the doctor's verdict it would still be necessary for us to give up our rooms and retire to the *dépendance*.[1] Byzantinism[2] like this outraged us. It is not likely that the Principessa was responsible for the willful breach of faith. Very likely the fawning management had not even dared to tell her what the physician said. Anyhow, we made it clear to his understanding that we preferred to leave the hotel altogether and at once — and packed our trunks. We could do so with a light heart, having already set up casual friendly relations with Casa Eleonora. We had noticed its pleasant exterior and formed the acquaintance of its proprietor, Signora Angiolieri, and her husband: she slender and black-haired, Tuscan[3] in type, probably at the beginning of the thirties, with the dead ivory complexion of the southern woman, he quiet and bald and carefully dressed. They owned a larger establishment in Florence and presided only in summer and early autumn over the branch in Torre di Venere. But earlier, before her marriage, our new landlady had been companion, fellow-traveler, wardrobe mistress, yes, friend, of Eleonora Duse[4] and manifestly regarded that period as the crown of her career. Even at our first visit she spoke of it with animation. Numerous photo-

graphs of the great actress, with affectionate inscriptions, were displayed about the drawing room, and other souvenirs of their life together adorned the little tables and étagères.[5] This cult of a so interesting past was calculated, of course, to heighten the advantages of the signora's present business. Nevertheless our pleasure and interest were quite genuine as we were conducted through the house by its owner and listened to her sonorous and staccato Tuscan voice relating anecdotes of that immortal mistress, depicting her suffering saintliness, her genius, her profound delicacy of feeling.

Thither, then, we moved our effects, to the dismay of the staff of the Grand Hotel, who, like all Italians, were very good to children. Our new quarters were retired and pleasant, we were within easy reach of the sea through the avenue of young plane trees that ran down to the esplanade.[6] In the clean, cool dining room Signora Angiolieri daily served the soup with her own hands, the service was attentive and good, the table capital. We even discovered some Viennese acquaintances, and enjoyed chatting with them after luncheon, in front of the house. They, in their turn, were the means of our finding others — in short, all seemed for the best, and we were heartily glad of the change we had made. Nothing was now wanting to a holiday of the most gratifying kind.

And yet no proper gratification ensued. Perhaps the stupid occasion of our change of quarters pursued us to the new ones we had found. Personally, I admit that I do not easily forget these collisions with ordinary humanity, the naïve misuse of power, the injustice, the sycophantic corruption. I dwelt upon the incident too much, it irritated me in retrospect — quite futilely, of course, since such phenomena are only all too natural and all too much the rule. And we had not broken off relations with the

---

[1] *dépendance* (dā'päⁿ-däⁿs') : annex.
[2] **Byzantinism** : *here,* the subordination of the truth to practical concerns.
[3] **Tuscan** : characteristic of inhabitants of Tuscany, a territory in western Italy.
[4] **Eleonora Duse** (dü'zā) : great Italian actress of the late nineteenth and early twentieth centuries.

[5] **étagères** (ā'tä'zher') : sets of shelves.
[6] **esplanade** : open space of ground along a shore.

Grand Hotel. The children were as friendly as ever there, the porter mended their toys, and we sometimes took tea in the garden. We even saw the Principessa. She would come out, with her firm and delicate tread, her lips emphatically corallined,[1] to look after her children, playing under the supervision of their English governess. She did not dream that we were anywhere near, for so soon as she appeared in the offing[2] we sternly forbade our little one even to clear his throat.

The heat — if I may bring it in evidence — was extreme. It was African. The power of the sun, directly one left the border of the indigo-blue wave, was so frightful, so relentless, that the mere thought of the few steps between the beach and luncheon was a burden, clad though one might be only in pyjamas. Do you care for that sort of thing? Weeks on end? Yes, of course, it is proper to the south, it is classic weather, the sun of Homer, the climate wherein human culture came to flower — and all the rest of it. But after a while it is too much for me, I reach a point where I begin to find it dull. The burning void of the sky, day after day, weighs one down; the high coloration, the enormous naïveté of the unrefracted light — they do, I dare say, induce lightheartedness, a carefree mood born of immunity from downpours and other meteorological caprices. But slowly, slowly, there makes itself felt a lack: the deeper, more complex needs of the northern soul remain unsatisfied. You are left barren — even, it may be, in time, a little contemptuous. True, without that stupid business of the whooping cough I might not have been feeling these things. I was annoyed, very likely I wanted to feel them and so half-unconsciously seized upon an idea lying ready to hand to induce, or if not to induce, at least to justify and strengthen, my attitude. Up to this point, then, if you

like, let us grant some ill will on our part. But the sea; and the mornings spent extended upon the fine sand in face of its eternal splendors — no, the sea could not conceivably induce such feelings. Yet it was none the less true that, despite all previous experience, we were not at home on the beach, we were not happy.

It was too soon, too soon. The beach, as I have said, was still in the hands of the middle-class native. It is a pleasing breed to look at, and among the young we saw much shapeliness and charm. Still, we were necessarily surrounded by a great deal of very average humanity — a middle-class mob, which, you will admit, is not more charming under this sun than under one's own native sky. The voices these women have! It was sometimes hard to believe that we were in the land which is the western cradle of the art of song. *"Fuggièro!"* I can still hear that cry, as for twenty mornings long I heard it close behind me, breathy, fullthroated, hideously stressed, with a harsh open *e*, uttered in accents of mechanical despair. *"Fuggièro! Rispondi almeno!"* Answer when I call you! The *sp* in *rispondi* was pronounced like *shp*, as Germans pronounce it; and this, on top of what I felt already, vexed my sensitive soul. The cry was addressed to a repulsive youngster whose sunburn had made disgusting raw sores on his shoulders. He outdid anything I have ever seen for ill-breeding, refractoriness,[3] and temper, and was a great coward to boot, putting the whole beach in an uproar, one day, because of his outrageous sensitiveness to the slightest pain. A sand crab had pinched his toe in the water, and the minute injury made him set up a cry of heroic proportions — the shout of an antique hero in his agony — that pierced one to the marrow and called up visions of some frightful tragedy. Evidently he considered himself not only wounded, but poisoned as well; he crawled out on the

---

[1] **corallined**: colored a yellowish red.
[2] **offing**: near distance.

[3] **refractoriness**: obstinacy, stubbornness.

sand and lay in apparently intolerable anguish, groaning *"Ohi!"* and *"Ohimè"*[1] and
threshing about with arms and legs to ward
off his mother's tragic appeals and the questions of the bystanders. An audience gathered round. A doctor was fetched — the
same who had pronounced objective judgment on our whooping cough — and here
again acquitted himself[2] like a man of science. Good-naturedly he reassured the boy,
telling him that he was not hurt at all, he
should simply go into the water again to
relieve the smart. Instead of which, Fuggièro was borne off the beach, followed by
a concourse[3] of people. But he did not fail
to appear next morning, nor did he leave off
spoiling our children's sand castles. Of
course, always by accident. In short, a perfect terror.

And this twelve-year-old lad was prominent among the influences that, imperceptibly at first, combined to spoil our
holiday and render it unwholesome. Somehow or other, there was a stiffness, a lack
of innocent enjoyment. These people stood
on their dignity — just why, and in what
spirit, it was not easy at first to tell. They
displayed much self-respectingness; towards
each other and towards the foreigner their
bearing was that of a person newly conscious of a sense of honor. And wherefore?
Gradually we realized the political implications and understood that we were in the
presence of a national ideal. The beach, in
fact, was alive with patriotic children — a
phenomenon as unnatural as it was depressing. Children are a human species and a
society apart, a nation of their own, so to
speak. On the basis of their common form
of life, they find each other out with the
greatest ease, no matter how different their
small vocabularies. Ours soon played with
natives and foreigners alike. Yet they were
plainly both puzzled and disappointed at

times. There were wounded sensibilities,
displays of assertiveness — or rather hardly
assertiveness, for it was too self-conscious
and too didactic to deserve the name. There
were quarrels over flags, disputes about authority and precedence. Grown-ups joined
in, not so much to pacify as to render judgment and enunciate principles. Phrases were
dropped about the greatness and dignity of
Italy, solemn phrases that spoiled the fun.
We saw our two little ones retreat, puzzled
and hurt, and were put to it to explain the
situation. These people, we told them, were
just passing through a certain stage, something rather like an illness, perhaps; not very
pleasant, but probably unavoidable.

We had only our own carelessness to
thank that we came to blows in the end with
this "stage" — which, after all, we had seen
and sized up long before now. Yes, it came
to another "cross-purposes," so evidently
the earlier ones had not been sheer accident.
In a word, we became an offense to the
public morals. Our small daughter — eight
years old, but in physical development a
good year younger and thin as a chicken —
had had a good long bathe and gone playing
in the warm sun in her wet costume. We
told her that she might take off her bathing
suit, which was stiff with sand, rinse it in
the sea, and put it on again, after which she
must take care to keep it cleaner. Off goes
the costume and she runs down naked to
the sea, rinses her little jersey, and comes
back. Ought we to have foreseen the outburst of anger and resentment which her
conduct, and thus our conduct, called forth?
Without delivering a homily[4] on the subject, I may say that in the last decade our
attitude towards the nude body and our
feelings regarding it have undergone, all
over the world, a fundamental change.
There are things we "never think about"
any more, and among them is the freedom
we had permitted to this by no means provocative little childish body. But in these

---

[1] *Ohi!* . . . *Ohimè!:* Ah! . . . Alas!
[2] **acquitted himself:** behaved.
[3] **concourse:** throng.
[4] **homily:** sermon.

parts it was taken as a challenge. The patriotic children hooted. Fuggièro whistled on his fingers. The sudden buzz of conversation among the grown people in our neighborhood boded no good. A gentleman in city togs, with a not very apropos[1] bowler hat on the back of his head, was assuring his outraged womenfolk that he proposed to take punitive measures; he stepped up to us, and a philippic[2] descended on our unworthy heads, in which all the emotionalism of the sense-loving south spoke in the service of morality and discipline. The offense against decency of which we had been guilty was, he said, the more to be condemned because it was also a gross ingratitude and an insulting breach of his country's hospitality. We had criminally injured not only the letter and spirit of the public bathing regulations, but also the honor of Italy; he, the gentleman in the city togs, knew how to defend that honor and proposed to see to it that our offense against the national dignity should not go unpunished.

We did our best, bowing respectfully, to give ear to this eloquence. To contradict the man, overheated as he was, would probably be to fall from one error into another. On the tips of our tongues we had various answers: as, that the word "hospitality," in its strictest sense, was not quite the right one, taking all the circumstances into consideration. We were not literally the guests of Italy, but of Signora Angiolieri, who had assumed the role of dispenser of hospitality some years ago on laying down that of familiar friend to Eleonora Duse. We longed to say that surely this beautiful country had not sunk so low as to be reduced to a state of hypersensitive prudishness. But we confined ourselves to assuring the gentleman that any lack of respect, any provocation on our parts, had been the furthest from our thoughts. And as a miti-

gating circumstance we pointed out the tender age and physical slightness of the little culprit. In vain. Our protests were waved away, he did not believe in them; our defense would not hold water. We must be made an example of. The authorities were notified, by telephone, I believe, and their representative appeared on the beach. He said the case was *"molto grave."*[3] We had to go with him to the Municipio[4] up in the Piazza,[5] where a higher official confirmed the previous verdict of *"molto grave,"* launched into a stream of the usual didactic phrases — the selfsame tune and words as the man in the bowler hat — and levied a fine and ransom of fifty lire.[6] We felt that the adventure must willy-nilly[7] be worth to us that much of a contribution to the economy of the Italian government; paid, and left. Ought we not at this point to have left Torre as well?

If we only had! We should thus have escaped that fatal Cipolla. But circumstances combined to prevent us from making up our minds to a change. A certain poet says that it is indolence that makes us endure uncomfortable situations. The *aperçu*[8] may serve as an explanation for our inaction. Anyhow, one dislikes voiding[9] the field immediately upon such an event. Especially if sympathy from other quarters encourages one to defy it. And in the Villa Eleonora, they pronounced as with one voice upon the injustice of our punishment. Some Italian after-dinner acquaintances found that the episode put their country in a very bad light, and proposed taking the man in the bowler hat to task, as one fellow-citizen to another. But the next day he and his party had vanished from the beach. Not on our account, of course. Though it might

[1] **apropos:** appropriate to the occasion.
[2] **philippic:** bitter verbal attack.

[3] *molto grave:* very serious.
[4] **Municipio:** town hall.
[5] **Piazza:** open public square.
[6] **lire:** basic Italian monetary unit.
[7] **willy-nilly:** whether one wishes it or not.
[8] *aperçu* (ä′pär′su′): insight.
[9] **voiding:** leaving.

be that the consciousness of his impending departure had added energy to his rebuke; in any case his going was a relief. And, furthermore, we stayed because our stay had by now become remarkable in our own eyes, which is worth something in itself, quite apart from the comfort or discomfort involved. Shall we strike sail,[1] avoid a certain experience so soon as it seems not expressly calculated to increase our enjoyment or our self-esteem? Shall we go away whenever life looks like turning in the slightest uncanny, or not quite normal, or even rather painful and mortifying? No, surely not. Rather stay and look matters in the face, brave them out; perhaps precisely in so doing lies a lesson for us to learn. We stayed on and reaped as the awful reward of our constancy the unholy and staggering experience with Cipolla.

I have not mentioned that the after season had begun, almost on the very day we were disciplined by the city authorities. The worshipful gentleman in the bowler hat, our denouncer, was not the only person to leave the resort. There was a regular exodus, on every hand you saw luggage carts on their way to the station. The beach denationalized itself. Life in Torre, in the cafés and the pinetas, became more homelike and more European. Very likely we might even have eaten at a table in the glass veranda, but we refrained, being content at Signora Angiolieri's — as content, that is, as our evil star would let us be. But at the same time with this turn for the better came a change in the weather: almost to an hour it showed itself in harmony with the holiday calendar of the general public. The sky was overcast; not that it grew any cooler, but the unclouded heat of the entire eighteen days since our arrival, and probably long before that, gave place to a stifling sirocco[2] air, while from time to time a little ineffectual rain sprinkled the velvety surface of the beach. Add to which, that two-thirds of our intended stay at Torre had passed. The colorless, lazy sea, with sluggish jellyfish floating in its shallows, was at least a change. And it would have been silly to feel retrospective longings after a sun that had caused us so many sighs when it burned down in all its arrogant power.

At this juncture, then, it was that Cipolla announced himself. Cavaliere[3] Cipolla he was called on the posters that appeared one day stuck up everywhere, even in the dining room of Pensione Eleonora. A traveling virtuoso,[4] an entertainer, "*forzatore, illusionista, prestidigatore*,"[5] as he called himself, who proposed to wait upon the highly respectable population of Torre di Venere with a display of extraordinary phenomena of a mysterious and staggering kind. A conjuror![6] The bare announcement was enough to turn our children's heads. They had never seen anything of the sort, and now our present holiday was to afford them this new excitement. From that moment on they besieged us with prayers to take tickets for the performance. We had doubts, from the first, on the score of[7] the lateness of the hour, nine o'clock; but gave way, in the idea that we might see a little of what Cipolla had to offer, probably no great matter, and then go home. Besides, of course, the children could sleep late next day. We bought four tickets of Signora Angiolieri herself, she having taken a number of the stalls[8] on commission to sell them to her guests. She could not vouch for the man's performance, and we had no great expectations. But we were conscious of a need for diversion, and the children's violent curiosity proved catching.

---

[1] **strike sail**: give up.

[2] **sirocco**: hot and oppressive.

[3] **Cavaliere** (kä′vä·lyä′rä): title for member of the nobility.

[4] **virtuoso**: skilled performer.

[5] *forzatore, illusionista, prestidigatore:* master, illusionist, sleight-of-hand expert.

[6] **conjuror**: magician.

[7] **on the score of**: because of.

[8] **stalls**: seats.

The Cavaliere's performance was to take place in a hall where during the season there had been a cinema with a weekly program. We had never been there. You reached it by following the main street under the wall of the *"palazzo,"* a ruin with a "For sale" sign, that suggested a castle and had obviously been built in lordlier days. In the same street were the chemist, the hairdresser, and all the better shops; it led, so to speak, from the feudal past the bourgeois into the proletarian, for it ended off between two rows of poor fishing huts, where old women sat mending nets before the doors. And here, among the proletariat, was the hall, not much more, actually, than a wooden shed, though a large one, with a turreted entrance, plastered on either side with layers of gay placards. Some while after dinner, then, on the appointed evening, we wended our way thither in the dark, the children dressed in their best and blissful with the sense of so much irregularity. It was sultry, as it had been for days; there was heat lightning now and then, and a little rain; we proceeded under umbrellas. It took us a quarter of an hour.

Our tickets were collected at the entrance, our places we had to find ourselves. They were in the third row left, and as we sat down we saw that, late though the hour was for the performance, it was to be interpreted with even more laxity. Only very slowly did an audience — who seemed to be relied upon to come late — begin to fill the stalls. These comprised the whole auditorium; there were no boxes. This tardiness gave us some concern. The children's cheeks were already flushed as much with fatigue as with excitement. But even when we entered, the standing room at the back and in the side aisles was already well occupied. There stood the manhood of Torre di Venere, all and sundry, fisherfolk, rough-and-ready youths with bare forearms crossed over their striped jerseys. We were well pleased with the presence of this native

assemblage, which always adds color and animation to occasions like the present; and the children were frankly delighted. For they had friends among these people — acquaintances picked up on afternoon strolls to the further ends of the beach. We would be turning homeward, at the hour when the sun dropped into the sea, spent with the huge effort it had made and gilding with reddish gold the oncoming surf; and we would come upon bare-legged fisherfolk standing in rows, bracing and hauling with long-drawn cries as they drew in the nets and harvested in dripping baskets their catch, often so scanty, of *frutta di mare.*[1] The children looked on, helped to pull, brought out their little stock of Italian words, made friends. So now they exchanged nods with the "standing room" clientèle; there was Guiscardo, there Antonio, they knew them by name and waved and called across in half-whispers, getting answering nods and smiles that displayed rows of healthy white teeth. Look, there is even Mario, Mario from the Esquisito, who brings us the chocolate. He wants to see the conjuror, too, and he must have come early, for he is almost in front; but he does not see us, he is not paying attention; that is a way he has, even though he is a waiter. So we wave instead to the man who lets out the little boats on the beach; he is there too, standing at the back.

It had got to a quarter past nine, it got to almost half past. It was natural that we should be nervous. When would the children get to bed? It had been a mistake to bring them, for now it would be very hard to suggest breaking off their enjoyment before it had got well under way. The stalls had filled in time; all Torre, apparently, was there: the guests of the Grand Hotel, the guests of Villa Eleonora, familiar faces from the beach. We heard English and German and the sort of French that Rumanians speak with Italians. Madame Angiolieri herself sat

[1] *frutta di mare:* literally, fruit of the sea.

two rows behind us, with her quiet, bald-headed spouse, who kept stroking his moustache with the two middle fingers of his right hand. Everybody had come late, but nobody too late. Cipolla made us wait for him.

He made us wait. This is probably the way to put it. He heightened the suspense by his delay in appearing. And we could see the point of this, too — only not when it was carried to extremes. Towards half past nine the audience began to clap — an amiable way of expressing justifiable impatience, evincing as it does an eagerness to applaud. For the little ones, this was a joy in itself — all children love to clap. From the popular sphere came loud cries of *"Pronti!" "Cominciamo!"*[1] And lo, it seemed now as easy to begin as before it had been hard. A gong sounded, greeted by the standing rows with a many-voiced "Ah-h!" and the curtains parted. They revealed a platform furnished more like a schoolroom than like the theater of a conjuring performance — largely because of the blackboard in the left foreground. There was a common yellow hat-stand, a few ordinary straw-bottomed chairs, and further back a little round table holding a water carafe[2] and glass, also a tray with a liqueur glass and a flask of pale yellow liquid. We had still a few seconds of time to let these things sink in. Then, with no darkening of the house, Cavaliere Cipolla made his entry.

He came forward with a rapid step that expressed his eagerness to appear before his public and gave rise to the illusion that he had already come a long way to put himself at their service — whereas, of course, he had only been standing in the wings. His costume supported the fiction. A man of an age hard to determine, but by no means young; with a sharp, ravaged face, piercing eyes, compressed lips, small black waxed moustache, and a so-called imperial[3] in the curve between mouth and chin. He was dressed for the street with a sort of complicated evening elegance, in a wide black pelerine[4] with velvet collar and satin lining; which, in the hampered state of his arms, he held together in front with his white-gloved hands. He had a white scarf round his neck; a top hat with a curving brim sat far back on his head. Perhaps more than anywhere else the eighteenth century is still alive in Italy, and with it the charlatan[5] and mountebank[6] type so characteristic of the period. Only there, at any rate, does one still encounter really well-preserved specimens. Cipolla had in his whole appearance much of the historic type; his very clothes helped to conjure up the traditional figure with its blatantly, fantastically foppish[7] air. His pretentious costume sat upon him, or rather hung upon him, most curiously, being in one place drawn too tight, in another a mass of awkward folds. There was something not quite in order about his figure, both front and back — that was plain later on. But I must emphasize the fact that there was not a trace of personal jocularity or clownishness in his pose, manner, or behavior. On the contrary, there was complete seriousness, an absence of any humorous appeal; occasionally even a cross-grained pride, along with that curious, self-satisfied air so characteristic of the deformed. None of all this, however, prevented his appearance from being greeted with laughter from more than one quarter of the hall.

All the eagerness had left his manner. The swift entry had been merely an expression of energy, not of zeal. Standing at the footlights he negligently drew off his gloves, to display long, yellow hands, one of them

---

[1] *Pronti! . . . Cominciamo!:* ready! . . . let's begin!
[2] **carafe** (kə·raf′): decanter.
[3] **imperial:** small pointed beard.
[4] **pelerine:** cape.
[5] **charlatan** (shär′lə·tən): person who pretends to have knowledge or power that he does not have.
[6] **mountebank:** quack.
[7] **foppish:** vain and affected.

adorned with a seal ring with a lapis lazuli[1] in a high setting. As he stood there, his small hard eyes, with flabby pouches beneath them, roved appraisingly about the hall, not quickly, rather in a considered examination, pausing here and there upon a face with his lips clipped together, not speaking a word. Then with a display of skill as surprising as it was casual, he rolled his gloves into a ball and tossed them across a considerable distance into the glass on the table. Next from an inner pocket he drew forth a packet of cigarettes; you could see by the wrapper that they were the cheapest sort the government sells. With his fingertips he pulled out a cigarette and lighted it, without looking, from a quick-firing benzine[2] lighter. He drew the smoke deep into his lungs and let it out again, tapping his foot, with both lips drawn in an arrogant grimace and the gray smoke streaming out between broken and saw-edged teeth.

With a keenness equal to his own his audience eyed him. The youths at the rear scowled as they peered at this cocksure creature to search out his secret weaknesses. He betrayed none. In fetching out and putting back the cigarettes, his clothes got in his way. He had to turn back his pelerine, and in so doing revealed a riding-whip with a silver claw-handle that hung by a leather thong from his left forearm and looked decidedly out of place. You could see that he had on not evening clothes but a frock coat, and under this, as he lifted it to get at his pocket, could be seen a striped sash worn about the body. Somebody behind me whispered that this sash went with his title of Cavaliere. I give the information for what it may be worth — personally, I never heard that the title carried such insignia with it. Perhaps the sash was sheer pose, like the way he stood there, without a word, casually and

arrogantly puffing smoke into his audience's face.

People laughed, as I said. The merriment had become almost general when somebody in the "standing seats," in a loud, dry voice, remarked: *"Buona sera."*[3]

Cipolla cocked his head. "Who was that?" asked he, as though he had been dared. "Who was that just spoke? Well? First so bold and now so modest? *Paura,*[4] eh?" He spoke with a rather high, asthmatic voice, which yet had a metallic quality. He waited.

"That was me," a youth at the rear broke into the stillness, seeing himself thus challenged. He was not far from us, a handsome fellow in a woolen shirt, with his coat hanging over one shoulder. He wore his curly, wiry hair in a high, disheveled mop, the style affected by the youth of the awakened Fatherland; it gave him an African appearance that rather spoiled his looks. *"Bè!"*[5] That was me. It was your business to say it first, but I was trying to be friendly."

More laughter. The chap had a tongue in his head. *"Ha sciolto la scilinguágnolo,"*[6] I heard near me. After all, the retort was deserved.

"Ah, bravo!" answered Cipolla. "I like you, *giovanotto.*[7] Trust me, I've had my eye on you for some time. People like you are just in my line. I can use them. And you are the pick of the lot, that's plain to see. You do what you like. Or is it possible you have ever not done what you liked — or even, maybe, what you didn't like? What somebody else liked, in short? Hark ye, my friend, that might be a pleasant change for you, to divide up the willing and the doing and stop tackling both jobs at once. Division of labor, *sistema americano,*

---

[1] **lapis lazuli** (lap′is laz′yü·lē): blue semiprecious stone.
[2] **benzine:** type of fuel.
[3] *Buona sera:* good evening.
[4] *Paura:* fear.
[5] *Bè!:* Good!
[6] *Ha . . . scilinguágnolo:* He has a ready tongue.
[7] *giovanotto:* young man.

sa'![1] For instance, suppose you were to show your tongue to this select and honorable audience here — your whole tongue, right down to the roots?"

"No, I won't," said the youth, hostilely. "Sticking out your tongue shows a bad bringing-up."

"Nothing of the sort," retorted Cipolla. "You would only be *doing* it. With all due respect to your bringing-up, I suggest that before I count ten, you will perform a right turn and stick out your tongue at the company here further than you knew yourself that you could stick it out."

He gazed at the youth, and his piercing eyes seemed to sink deeper into their sockets. "*Uno!*" said he. He had let his riding-whip slide down his arm and made it whistle once through the air. The boy faced about and put out his tongue, so long, so extendedly, that you could see it was the very uttermost in tongue which he had to offer. Then turned back, stony-faced, to his former position.

"That was me," mocked Cipolla, with a jerk of his head towards the youth. "*Bè!* That was me." Leaving the audience to enjoy its sensations, he turned towards the little round table, lifted the bottle, poured out a small glass of what was obviously cognac, and tipped it up with a practiced hand.

The children laughed with all their hearts. They had understood practically nothing of what had been said, but it pleased them hugely that something so funny should happen, straightaway, between that queer man up there and somebody out of the audience. They had no preconception of what an "evening" would be like and were quite ready to find this a priceless beginning. As for us, we exchanged a glance, and I remember that involuntarily I made with my lips the sound that Cipolla's whip had made when it cut the air. For the rest, it was plain that people did not know what to make of a preposterous beginning like this to a sleight-of-hand performance. They could not see why the *giovanotto*, who after all in a way had been their spokesman, should suddenly have turned on them to vent his incivility. They felt that he had behaved like a silly ass and withdrew their countenances from him in favor of the artist, who now came back from his refreshment table and addressed them as follows:

"Ladies and gentlemen," said he, in his wheezing, metallic voice, "you saw just now that I was rather sensitive on the score of the rebuke this hopeful young linguist saw fit to give me" — "*questo linguista di belle speranze*"[2] was what he said, and we all laughed at the pun. "I am a man who sets some store by himself, you may take it from me. And I see no point in being wished a good-evening unless it is done courteously and in all seriousness. For anything else there is no occasion. When a man wishes me a good-evening he wishes himself one, for the audience will have one only if I do. So this lady-killer of Torre di Venere" (another thrust) "did well to testify that I have one tonight and that I can dispense with any wishes of his in the matter. I can boast of having good evenings almost without exception. One not so good does come my way now and again, but very seldom. My calling is hard and my health not of the best. I have a little physical defect which prevented me from doing my bit in the war for the greater glory of the Fatherland. It is perforce[3] with my mental and spiritual parts that I conquer life — which after all only means conquering oneself. And I flatter myself that my achievements have aroused interest and respect among the educated public. The leading newspapers have lauded me, the *Corriere della Sera*[4] did me the courtesy of calling me a phenomenon,

---

[1] *sistema americano, sa'!*: that's the American way.

[2] *di belle speranze*: either "hopeful" or "conceited."

[3] **perforce**: of necessity.

[4] *Corriere della Sera*: Evening Courier.

and in Rome the brother of the *Duce* honored me by his presence at one of my evenings. I should not have thought that in a relatively less important place" (laughter here, at the expense of poor little Torre) "I should have to give up the small personal habits which brilliant and elevated audiences had been ready to overlook. Nor did I think I had to stand being heckled by a person who seems to have been rather spoilt by the favors of the fair sex." All this of course at the expense of the youth whom Cipolla never tired of presenting in the guise of *donnaiuolo*[1] and rustic Don Juan. His persistent thin-skinnedness and animosity were in striking contrast to the self-confidence and the worldly success he boasted of. One might have assumed that the *giovanotto* was merely the chosen butt of Cipolla's customary professional sallies,[2] had not the very pointed witticisms betrayed a genuine antagonism. No one looking at the physical parts of the two men need have been at a loss for the explanation, even if the deformed man had not constantly played on the other's supposed success with the fair sex. "Well," Cipolla went on, "before beginning our entertainment this evening, perhaps you will permit me to make myself comfortable."

And he went towards the hat stand to take off his things.

"*Parla benissimo*,"[3] asserted somebody in our neighborhood. So far, the man had done nothing; but what he had said was accepted as an achievement, by means of that he had made an impression. Among southern peoples speech is a constituent[4] part of the pleasure of living, it enjoys far livelier social esteem than in the north. That national cement, the mother tongue, is paid symbolic honors down here, and there is something blithely symbolical in the plea-

sure people take in their respect for its forms and phonetics. They enjoy speaking, they enjoy listening; and they listen with discrimination. For the way a man speaks serves as a measure of his personal rank; carelessness and clumsiness are greeted with scorn, elegance and mastery are rewarded with social éclat.[5] Wherefore the small man too, where it is a question of getting his effect, chooses his phrase nicely and turns it with care. On this count, then, at least, Cipolla had won his audience; though he by no means belonged to the class of men which the Italian, in a singular mixture of moral and aesthetic judgments, labels "*simpatico*."[6]

After removing his hat, scarf, and mantle he came to the front of the stage, settling his coat, pulling down his cuffs with their large cuff buttons, adjusting his absurd sash. He had very ugly hair; the top of his head, that is, was almost bald, while a narrow, black-varnished frizz of curls ran from front to back as though stuck on; the side hair, likewise blackened, was brushed forward to the corners of the eyes — it was, in short, the hairdressing of an old-fashioned circus-director, fantastic, but entirely suited to his outmoded personal type and worn with so much assurance as to take the edge off the public's sense of humor. The little physical defect of which he had warned us was now all too visible, though the nature of it was even now not very clear: the chest was too high, as is usual in such cases; but the corresponding malformation of the back did not sit between the shoulders, it took the form of a sort of hips or buttocks hump, which did not indeed hinder his movements but gave him a grotesque and dipping stride at every step he took. However, by mentioning his deformity beforehand he had broken the shock of it, and a delicate propriety of feeling appeared to reign throughout the hall.

[1] *donnaiuolo:* ladykiller, flirt.
[2] **sallies**: thrusts.
[3] *Parla benissimo:* he speaks very well.
[4] **constituent**: elemental, basic.

[5] éclat (ā·klä′): success.
[6] *simpatico:* congenial.

"At your service," said Cipolla. "With your kind permission, we will begin the evening with some arithmetical tests."

Arithmetic? That did not sound much like sleight-of-hand. We began to have our suspicions that the man was sailing under a false flag, only we did not yet know which was the right one. I felt sorry on the children's account; but for the moment they were content simply to be there.

The numerical test which Cipolla now introduced was as simple as it was baffling. He began by fastening a piece of paper to the upper right-hand corner of the blackboard; then lifting it up, he wrote something underneath. He talked all the while, relieving the dryness of his offering by a constant flow of words, and showed himself a practiced speaker, never at a loss for conversational turns of phrase. It was in keeping with the nature of his performance, and at the same time vastly entertained the children, that he went on to eliminate the gap between stage and audience, which had already been bridged over by the curious skirmish with the fisher lad: he had representatives from the audience mount the stage, and himself descended the wooden steps to seek personal contact with his public. And again, with individuals, he fell into his former taunting tone. I do not know how far that was a deliberate feature of his system; he preserved a serious, even a peevish air, but his audience, at least the more popular section, seemed convinced that that was all part of the game. So then, after he had written something and covered the writing by the paper, he desired that two persons should come up on the platform and help to perform the calculations. They would not be difficult, even for people not clever at figures. As usual, nobody volunteered, and Cipolla took care not to molest the more select portion of his audience. He kept to the populace. Turning to two sturdy young louts standing behind us, he beckoned them to the front, encouraging and scolding by turns. They should not stand there gaping, he said, unwilling to oblige the company. Actually, he got them in motion; with clumsy tread they came down the middle aisle, climbed the steps, and stood in front of the blackboard, grinning sheepishly at their comrades' shouts and applause. Cipolla joked with them for a few minutes, praised their heroic firmness of limb and the size of their hands, so well calculated to do this service for the public. Then he handed one of them the chalk and told him to write down the numbers as they were called out. But now the creature declared that he could not write! *"Non so scrivere,"*[1] said he in his gruff voice, and his companion added that neither did he.

God knows whether they told the truth or whether they wanted to make game of Cipolla. Anyhow, the latter was far from sharing the general merriment which their confession aroused. He was insulted and disgusted. He sat there on a straw-bottomed chair in the center of the stage with his legs crossed, smoking a fresh cigarette out of his cheap packet; obviously it tasted the better for the cognac he had indulged in while the yokels were stumping up the steps. Again he inhaled the smoke and let it stream out between curling lips. Swinging his leg, with his gaze sternly averted from the two shamelessly chuckling creatures and from the audience as well, he stared into space as one who withdraws himself and his dignity from the contemplation of an utterly despicable phenomenon.

"Scandalous," said he, in a sort of icy snarl. "Go back to your places! In Italy everybody can write — in all her greatness there is no room for ignorance and unenlightenment. To accuse her of them, in the hearing of this international company, is a cheap joke, in which you yourselves cut a very poor figure and humiliate the government and the whole country as well. If it is true that Torre di Venere is indeed the last

[1] *Non so scrivere:* I don't know how to write.

refuge of such ignorance, then I must blush to have visited the place — being, as I already was, aware of its inferiority to Rome in more than one respect —"

Here Cipolla was interrupted by the youth with the Nubian[1] coiffure and his jacket across his shoulder. His fighting spirit, as we now saw, had only abdicated[2] temporarily, and he now flung himself into the breach in defense of his native heath. "That will do," said he loudly. "That's enough jokes about Torre. We all come from the place and we won't stand strangers making fun of it. These two chaps are our friends. Maybe they are no scholars, but even so they may be straighter than some folks in the room who are so free with their boasts about Rome, though they did not build it either."

That was capital. The young man had certainly cut his eyeteeth.[3] And this sort of spectacle was good fun, even though it still further delayed the regular performance, It is always fascinating to listen to an altercation.[4] Some people it simply amuses, they take a sort of killjoy pleasure in not being principals. Others feel upset and uneasy, and my sympathies are with these latter, although on the present occasion I was under the impression that all this was part of the show — the analphabetic[5] yokels no less than the *giovanotto* with the jacket. The children listened well pleased. They understood not at all, but the sound of the voices made them hold their breath. So this was a "magic evening" — at least it was the kind they have in Italy. They expressly found it "lovely."

Cipolla had stood up and with two of his scooping strides was at the footlights.

"Well, well, see who's here!" said he with grim cordiality. "An old acquaintance! A young man with his heart at the end of his tongue" (he used the word *linguaccia*, which means a coated tongue, and gave rise to much hilarity). "That will do, my friends," he turned to the yokels. "I do not need you now, I have business with this deserving young man here, *con questo torregiano di Venere*, this tower of Venus, who no doubt expects the gratitude of the fair as a reward for his prowess —"

"*Ah, non scherziamo!*[6] We're talking earnest," cried out the youth. His eyes flashed, and he actually made as though to pull off his jacket and proceed to direct methods of settlement.

Cipolla did not take him too seriously. We had exchanged apprehensive glances; but he was dealing with a fellow countryman and had his native soil beneath his feet. He kept quite cool and showed complete mastery of the situation. He looked at his audience, smiled, and made a sideways motion of the head towards the young cockerel[7] as though calling the public to witness how the man's bumptiousness only served to betray the simplicity of his mind. And then, for the second time, something strange happened, which set Cipolla's calm superiority in an uncanny light, and in some mysterious and irritating way turned all the explosiveness latent in the air into matter for laughter.

Cipolla drew still nearer to the fellow, looking him in the eye with a peculiar gaze. He even came halfway down the steps that led into the auditorium on our left, so that he stood directly in front of the troublemaker, on slightly higher ground. The riding-whip hung from his arm.

"My son, you do not feel much like joking," he said. "It is only too natural, for anyone can see that you are not feeling too well. Even your tongue, which leaves something to be desired on the score of cleanliness, indicates acute disorder of the gastric

---

[1] **Nubian**: African.
[2] **abdicated**: surrendered.
[3] **had . . . eyeteeth**: was very clever.
[4] **altercation**: argument.
[5] **analphabetic**: illiterate.

[6] *non scherziamo:* let us not joke.
[7] **cockerel**: arrogant, vain person (literally, rooster).

system. An evening entertainment is no place for people in your state; you yourself, I can tell, were of several minds whether you would not do better to put on a flannel bandage and go to bed. It was not good judgment to drink so much of that very sour white wine this afternoon. Now you have such a colic[1] you would like to double up with the pain. Go ahead, don't be embarrassed. There is a distinct relief that comes from bending over, in cases of intestinal cramp."

He spoke thus, word for word, with quiet impressiveness and a kind of stern sympathy, and his eyes, plunged the while deep in the young man's, seemed to grow very tired and at the same time burning above their enlarged tear ducts — they were the strangest eyes, you could tell that not manly pride alone was preventing the young adversary from withdrawing his gaze. And presently, indeed, all trace of its former arrogance was gone from the bronzed young face. He looked open-mouthed at the Cavaliere and the open mouth was drawn in a rueful smile.

"Double over," repeated Cipolla. "What else can you do? With a colic like that you *must* bend. Surely you will not struggle against the performance of a perfectly natural action just because somebody suggests it to you?"

Slowly the youth lifted his forearms, folded and squeezed them across his body; it turned a little sideways, then bent, lower and lower, the feet shifted, the knees turned inward, until he had become a picture of writhing pain, until he all but groveled upon the ground. Cipolla let him stand for some seconds thus, then made a short cut through the air with his whip and went with his scooping stride back to the little table, where he poured himself out a cognac.

"*Il boit beaucoup*,"[2] asserted a lady behind us. Was that the only thing that struck her? We could not tell how far the audience

[1] colic: acute abdominal pain.
[2] *Il boit beaucoup:* He drinks a lot.

grasped the situation. The fellow was standing upright again, with a sheepish grin — he looked as though he scarcely knew how it had all happened. The scene had been followed with tense interest and applauded at the end; there were shouts of "*Bravo, Cipolla!*" and "*Bravo, giovanotto!*" Apparently the issue of the duel was not looked upon as a personal defeat for the young man. Rather the audience encouraged him as one does an actor who succeeds in an unsympathetic role. Certainly his way of screwing himself up with cramp had been highly picturesque, its appeal was directly calculated to impress the gallery — in short, a fine dramatic performance. But I am not sure how far the audience was moved by that natural tactfulness in which the south excels, or how far it penetrated into the nature of what was going on.

The Cavaliere, refreshed, had lighted another cigarette. The numerical tests might now proceed. A young man was easily found in the back row who was willing to write down on the blackboard the numbers as they were dictated to him. Him too we knew; the whole entertainment had taken on an intimate character through our acquaintance with so many of the actors. This was the man who worked at the greengrocer's in the main street; he had served us several times, with neatness and dispatch. He wielded the chalk with clerkly confidence, while Cipolla descended to our level and walked with his deformed gait through the audience, collecting numbers as they were given, in two, three, and four places, and calling them out to the grocer's assistant, who wrote them down in a column. In all this, everything on both sides was calculated to amuse, with its jokes and its oratorical asides. The artist could not fail to hit on foreigners, who were not ready with their figures, and with them he was elaborately patient and chivalrous, to the great amusement of the natives, whom he reduced to confusion in their turn, by making them

translate numbers that were given in English or French. Some people gave dates concerned with great events in Italian history. Cipolla took them up at once and made patriotic comments. Somebody shouted "Number one!" The Cavaliere, incensed at this as at every attempt to make game of him, retorted over his shoulder that he could not take less than two-place figures. Whereupon another joker cried out "Number two!" and was greeted with the applause and laughter which every reference to natural functions is sure to win among southerners.

When fifteen numbers stood in a long straggling row on the board, Cipolla called for a general adding-match. Ready reckoners might add in their heads, but pencil and paper were not forbidden. Cipolla, while the work went on, sat on his chair near the blackboard, smoked and grimaced, with the complacent, pompous air cripples so often have. The five-place addition was soon done. Somebody announced the answer, somebody else confirmed it, a third had arrived at a slightly different result, but the fourth agreed with the first and second. Cipolla got up, tapped some ash from his coat, and lifted the paper at the upper right-hand corner of the board to display the writing. The correct answer, a sum close on a million, stood there; he had written it down beforehand.

Astonishment, and loud applause. The children were overwhelmed. How had he done that, they wanted to know. We told them it was a trick, not easily explainable offhand. In short, the man was a conjuror. This was what a sleight-of-hand evening was like, so now they knew. First the fisherman had cramp, and then the right answer was written down beforehand — it was all simply glorious, and we saw with dismay that despite the hot eyes and the hand of the clock at almost half past ten, it would be very hard to get them away. There would be tears. And yet it was plain that this magician did not "magick" — at least not in the accepted sense, of manual dexterity — and that the entertainment was not at all suitable for children. Again, I do not know, either, what the audience really thought. Obviously there was grave doubt whether its answers had been given of "free choice"; here and there an individual might have answered of his own motion, but on the whole Cipolla certainly selected his people and thus kept the whole procedure in his own hands and directed it towards the given result. Even so, one had to admire the quickness of his calculations, however much one felt disinclined to admire anything else about the performance. Then his patriotism, his irritable sense of dignity — the Cavaliere's own countrymen might feel in their element with all that and continue in a laughing mood; but the combination certainly gave us outsiders food for thought.

Cipolla himself saw to it — though without giving them a name — that the nature of his powers should be clear beyond a doubt to even the least-instructed person. He alluded to them, of course, in his talk — and he talked without stopping — but only in vague, boastful, self-advertising phrases. He went on awhile with experiments on the same lines as the first, merely making them more complicated by introducing operations in multiplying, subtracting, and dividing; then he simplified them to the last degree in order to bring out the method. He simply had numbers "guessed" which were previously written under the paper; and the guess was nearly always right. One guesser admitted that he had had in mind to give a certain number, when Cipolla's whip went whistling through the air, and a quite different one slipped out, which proved to be the "right" one. Cipolla's shoulders shook. He pretended admiration for the powers of the people he questioned. But in all his compliments there was something fleering[1] and derogatory; the victims could scarcely have relished them much, although they smiled, and although they might easily have set down some part of the applause to their own credit. Moreover, I had not the impression that the artist was popular with his public. A certain ill will and reluctance were in the air, but courtesy kept such feelings in check, as did Cipolla's competency and his stern self-confidence.

[1] fleering: mocking.

Even the riding-whip, I think, did much to keep rebellion from becoming overt.

From tricks with numbers he passed to tricks with cards. There were two packs, which he drew out of his pockets, and so much I still remember, that the basis of the tricks he played with them was as follows: from the first pack he drew three cards and thrust them without looking at them inside his coat. Another person then drew three out of the second pack, and these turned out to be the same as the first three — not invariably all the three, for it did happen that only two were the same. But in the majority of cases Cipolla triumphed, showing his three cards with a little bow in acknowledgment of the applause with which his audience conceded his possession of strange powers — strange whether for good or evil. A young man in the front row, to our right, an Italian, with proud, finely chiseled features, rose up and said that he intended to assert his own will in his choice and consciously to resist any influence, of whatever sort. Under these circumstances, what did Cipolla think would be the result? "You will," answered the Cavaliere, "make my task somewhat more difficult thereby. As for the result, your resistance will not alter it in the least. Freedom exists, and also the will exists; but freedom of the will does not exist, for a will that aims at its own freedom aims at the unknown. You are free to draw or not to draw. But if you draw, you will draw the right cards — the more certainly, the more willfully obstinate your behavior."

One must admit that he could not have chosen his words better, to trouble the waters and confuse the mind. The refractory youth hesitated before drawing. Then he pulled out a card and at once demanded to see if it was among the chosen three. "But why?" queried Cipolla. "Why do things by halves?" Then, as the other defiantly insisted, "E servito,"[2] said the juggler, with a

[2] E servito: that's enough.

gesture of exaggerated servility; and held out the three cards fanwise, without looking at them himself. The left-hand card was the one drawn.

Amid general applause, the apostle of freedom sat down. How far Cipolla employed small tricks and manual dexterity to help out his natural talents, the deuce only knew. But even without them the result would have been the same: the curiosity of the entire audience was unbounded and universal, everybody both enjoyed the amazing character of the entertainment and unanimously conceded the professional skill of the performer. *"Lavora bene,"*[1] we heard, here and there in our neighborhood; it signified the triumph of objective judgment over antipathy and repressed resentment.

After his last, incomplete, yet so much the more telling success, Cipolla had at once fortified himself with another cognac. Truly he did "drink a lot," and the fact made a bad impression. But obviously he needed the liquor and the cigarettes for the replenishment of his energy, upon which, as he himself said, heavy demands were made in all directions. Certainly in the intervals he looked very ill, exhausted and hollow-eyed. Then the little glassful would redress[2] the balance, and the flow of lively, self-confident chatter run on, while the smoke he inhaled gushed out gray from his lungs. I clearly recall that he passed from the card tricks to parlor games — the kind based on certain powers which in human nature are higher or else lower than human reason: on intuition and "magnetic" transmission; in short, upon a low type of manifestation.[3] What I do not remember is the precise order things came in. And I will not bore you with a description of these experiments; everybody knows them, everybody has at one time or another taken part in this finding of hidden articles, this blind carrying out of

a series of acts, directed by a force that proceeds from organism to organism by unexplored paths. Everybody has had his little glimpse into the equivocal,[4] impure, inexplicable nature of the occult, has been conscious of both curiosity and contempt, has shaken his head over the human tendency of those who deal in it to help themselves out with humbuggery,[5] though, after all, the humbuggery is no disproof whatever of the genuineness of the other elements in the dubious amalgam.[6] I can only say here that each single circumstance gains in weight and the whole greatly in impressiveness when it is a man like Cipolla who is the chief actor and guiding spirit in the sinister business. He sat smoking at the rear of the stage, his back to the audience while they conferred. The object passed from hand to hand which it was his task to find, with which he was to perform some action agreed upon beforehand. Then he would start to move zigzag through the hall, with his head thrown back and one hand outstretched, the other clasped in that of a guide who was in the secret but enjoined to keep himself perfectly passive, with his thoughts directed upon the agreed goal. Cipolla moved with the bearing typical in these experiments: now groping upon a false start, now with a quick forward thrust, now pausing as though to listen and by sudden inspiration correcting his course. The roles seemed reversed, the stream of influence was moving in the contrary direction, as the artist himself pointed out, in his ceaseless flow of discourse. The suffering, receptive, performing part was now his, the will he had before imposed on others was shut out, he acted in obedience to a voiceless common will which was in the air. But he made it perfectly clear that it all came to the same thing. The capacity for self-surrender, he said, for becoming a tool, for the most un-

---

[1] *Lavora bene:* he works well.
[2] **redress:** correct.
[3] **manifestation:** public demonstration of powers.

[4] **equivocal:** uncertain.
[5] **humbuggery:** fraud, deceit.
[6] **amalgam:** combination.

conditional and utter self-abnegation,[1] was but the reverse side of that other power to will and to command. Commanding and obeying formed together one single principle, one indissoluble[2] unity; he who knew how to obey knew also how to command, and conversely; the one idea was comprehended[3] in the other, as people and leader were comprehended in one another. But that which was *done*, the highly exacting and exhausting performance, was in every case his, the leader's and mover's, in whom the will became obedience, the obedience will, whose person was the cradle and womb of both, and who thus suffered enormous hardship. Repeatedly he emphasized the fact that his lot was a hard one — presumably to account for his need of stimulant and his frequent recourse to the little glass.

Thus he groped his way forward, like a blind seer, led and sustained by the mysterious common will. He drew a pin set with a stone out of its hiding place in an Englishwoman's shoe, carried it, halting and pressing on by turns, to another lady — Signora Angiolieri — and handed it to her on bended knee, with the words it had been agreed he was to utter. "I present you with this in token of my respect," was the sentence. Their sense was obvious, but the words themselves not easy to hit upon, for the reason that they had been agreed on in French; the language complication seemed to us a little malicious, implying as it did a conflict between the audience's natural interest in the success of the miracle, and their desire to witness the humiliation of this presumptuous man. It was a strange sight: Cipolla on his knees before the signora, wrestling, amid efforts at speech, after knowledge of the preordained words. "I must say something," he said, "and I feel clearly what it is I must say. But I also feel that if it passed my lips it would be wrong.

Be careful not to help me unintentionally!" he cried out, though very likely that was precisely what he was hoping for. "*Pensez très fort*," he cried all at once, in bad French, and then burst out with the required words — in Italian, indeed, but with the final substantive pronounced in the sister tongue, in which he was probably far from fluent: he said *vénération* instead of *venerazione*, with an impossible nasal. And this partial success, after the complete success before it, the finding of the pin, the presentation of it on his knees to the right person — was almost more impressive than if he had got the sentence exactly right, and evoked bursts of admiring applause.

Cipolla got up from his knees and wiped the perspiration from his brow. You understand that this experiment with the pin was a single case, which I describe because it sticks in my memory. But he changed his method several times and improvised a number of variations suggested by his contact with his audience; a good deal of time thus went by. He seemed to get particular inspiration from the person of our landlady; she drew him on to the most extraordinary displays of clairvoyance.[4] "It does not escape me, madame," he said to her, "that there is something unusual about you, some special and honorable distinction. He who has eyes to see descries about your lovely brow an aureola[5] — if I mistake not, it once was stronger than now — a slowly paling radiance . . . hush, not a word! Don't help me. Beside you sits your husband — yes?" He turned towards the silent Signor Angiolieri. "You are the husband of this lady, and your happiness is complete. But in the midst of this happiness memories rise . . . the past, signora, so it seems to me, plays an important part in your present. You knew a king . . . has not a king crossed your path in bygone days?"

---

[1] **self-abnegation**: giving up one's freedom.
[2] **indissoluble**: lasting.
[3] **comprehended**: included.

[4] **clairvoyance**: ability to see things that are not in sight.
[5] **aureola**: radiance encircling the head; halo.

"No," breathed the dispenser of our midday soup, her golden-brown eyes gleaming in the noble pallor of her face.

"No? No, not a king; I meant that generally, I did not mean literally a king. Not a king, not a prince, and a prince after all, a king of a loftier realm; it was a great artist, at whose side you once — you would contradict me, and yet I am not wholly wrong. Well, then! It was a woman, a great, a world-renowned woman artist, whose friendship you enjoyed in your tender years, whose sacred memory overshadows and transfigures your whole existence. Her name? Need I utter it, whose fame has long been bound up with the Fatherland's, immortal as its own? Eleonora Duse," he finished, softly and with much solemnity.

The little woman bowed her head, overcome. The applause was like a patriotic demonstration. Nearly everyone there knew about Signora Angiolieri's wonderful past; they were all able to confirm the Cavaliere's intuition — not least the present guests of Casa Eleonora. But we wondered how much of the truth he had learned as the result of professional inquiries made on his arrival. Yet I see no reason at all to cast doubt, on rational grounds, upon powers which, before our very eyes, became fatal to their possessor.

At this point there was an intermission. Our lord and master withdrew. Now I confess that almost ever since the beginning of my tale I have looked forward with dread to this moment in it. The thoughts of men are mostly not hard to read; in this case they are very easy. You are sure to ask why we did not choose this moment to go away — and I must continue to owe you an answer. I do not know why. I cannot defend myself. By this time it was certainly eleven, probably later. The children were asleep. The last series of tests had been too long, nature had had her way. They were sleeping in our laps, the little one on mine, the boy on his mother's. That was, in a way, a

consolation; but at the same time it was also ground for compassion and a clear leading to take them home to bed. And I give you my word that we wanted to obey this touching admonition, we seriously wanted to. We roused the poor things and told them it was now high time to go. But they were no sooner conscious than they began to resist and implore — you know how horrified children are at the thought of leaving before the end of a thing. No cajoling[1] has any effect, you have to use force. It was so lovely, they wailed. How did we know what was coming next? Surely we could not leave until after the intermission; they liked a little nap now and again — only not go home, only not go to bed, while the beautiful evening was still going on!

We yielded, but only for the moment, of course — so far as we knew — only for a little while, just a few minutes longer. I cannot excuse our staying, scarcely can I even understand it. Did we think, having once said A, we had to say B — having once brought the children hither we had to let them stay? No, it is not good enough. Were we ourselves so highly entertained? Yes, and no. Our feelings for Cavaliere Cipolla were of a very mixed kind, but so were the feelings of the whole audience, if I mistake not, and nobody left. Were we under the sway of a fascination which emanated from this man who took so strange a way to earn his bread; a fascination which he gave out independently of the program and even between the tricks and which paralyzed our resolve? Again, sheer curiosity may account for something. One was curious to know how such an evening turned out; Cipolla in his remarks having all along hinted that he had tricks in his bag stranger than any he had yet produced.

But all that is not it — or at least it is not all of it. More correct it would be to answer the first question with another. Why had we not left Torre di Venere itself before

[1] **cajoling**: coaxing.

now? To me the two questions are one and the same, and in order to get out of the impasse I might simply say that I had answered it already. For, as things had been in Torre in general: queer, uncomfortable, troublesome, tense, oppressive, so precisely they were here in this hall tonight. Yes, more than precisely. For it seemed to be the fountainhead of all the uncanniness and all the strained feelings which had oppressed the atmosphere of our holiday. This man whose return to the stage we were awaiting was the personification of all that; and, as we had not gone away in general, so to speak, it would have been inconsistent to do it in the particular case. You may call this an explanation, you may call it inertia, as you see fit. Any argument more to the purpose I simply do not know how to adduce.[1]

Well, there was an interval of ten minutes, which grew into nearly twenty. The children remained awake. They were enchanted by our compliance, and filled the break to their own satisfaction by renewing relations with the popular sphere, with Antonio, Guiscardo, and the canoe man. They put their hands to their mouths and called messages across, appealing to us for the Italian words. "Hope you have a good catch tomorrow, a whole netful!" They called to Mario, Esquisito Mario: "*Mario, una cioccolata e biscotti!*"[2] And this time he heeded and answered with a smile: "*Subito, signorini!*"[3] Later we had reason to recall this kindly, if rather absent and pensive smile.

Thus the interval passed, the gong sounded. The audience, which had scattered in conversation, took their places again, the children sat up straight in their chairs with their hands in their laps. The curtain had not been dropped. Cipolla came forward again, with his dipping stride, and began to introduce the second half of the program with a lecture.

Let me state once for all that this self-confident cripple was the most powerful hypnotist I have ever seen in my life. It was pretty plain now that he threw dust in the public eye and advertised himself as a prestidigitator on account of police regulations which would have prevented him from making his living by the exercise of his powers. Perhaps this eyewash is the usual thing in Italy; it may be permitted or even connived at by the authorities. Certainly the man had from the beginning made little concealment of the actual nature of his operations; and this second half of the program was quite frankly and exclusively devoted to one sort of experiment. While he still practiced some rhetorical circumlocutions,[4] the tests themselves were one long series of attacks upon the will power, the loss or compulsion of volition.[5] Comic, exciting, amazing by turns, by midnight they were still in full swing; we ran the gamut of all the phenomena this natural-unnatural field has to show, from the unimpressive at one end of the scale to the monstrous at the other. The audience laughed and applauded as they followed the grotesque details; shook their heads, clapped their knees, fell very frankly under the spell of this stern, self-assured personality. At the same time I saw signs that they were not quite complacent, not quite unconscious of the peculiar ignominy which lay, for the individual and for the general, in Cipolla's triumphs.

Two main features were constant in all the experiments: the liquor glass and the claw-handled riding-whip. The first was always invoked to add fuel to his demoniac fires; without it, apparently, they might have burned out. On this score we might even have felt pity for the man; but the whistle of his scourge,[6] the insulting symbol of his domination, before which we all

---

[1] **adduce** : give as a reason.
[2] *una cioccolata e biscotti:* cocoa and cookies.
[3] *Subito, signorini:* right away, young people.

[4] **circumlocutions**: roundabout, elaborate phrasings.
[5] **volition**: will.
[6] **scourge**: whip.

cowered, drowned out every sensation save a dazed and outbraved submission to his power. Did he then lay claim to our sympathy to boot? I was struck by a remark he made — it suggested no less. At the climax of his experiments, by stroking and breathing upon a certain young man who had offered himself as a subject and already proved himself a particularly susceptible one, he had not only put him into the condition known as deep trance and extended his insensible body by neck and feet across the backs of two chairs, but had actually sat down on the rigid form as on a bench, without making it yield. The sight of this unholy figure in a frock coat squatted on the stiff body was horrible and incredible; the audience, convinced that the victim of this scientific diversion must be suffering, expressed its sympathy: *"Ah, poveretto!"* Poor soul, poor soul! *"Poor soul!"* Cipolla mocked them, with some bitterness. "Ladies and gentlemen, you are barking up the wrong tree. *Sono io il poveretto.* I am the person who is suffering, I am the one to be pitied." We pocketed the information. Very good. Maybe the experiment was at his expense, maybe it was he who had suffered the cramp when the *giovanotto* over there had made the faces. But appearances were all against it; and one does not feel like saying *poveretto* to a man who is suffering to bring about the humiliation of others.

I have got ahead of my story and lost sight of the sequence of events. To this day my mind is full of the Cavaliere's feats of endurance; only I do not recall them in their order — which does not matter. So much I do know: that the longer and more circumstantial tests, which got the most applause, impressed me less than some of the small ones which passed quickly over. I remember the young man whose body Cipolla converted into a board, only because of the accompanying remarks which I have quoted. An elderly lady in a cane-seated chair was lulled by Cipolla in the delusion that she was on a voyage to India and gave a voluble account of her adventures by land and sea. But I found this phenomenon less impressive than one which followed immediately after the intermission. A tall, well-built, soldierly man was unable to lift his arm, after the hunchback had told him that he could not and given a cut through the air with his whip. I can still see the face of that stately, mustachioed colonel smiling and clenching his teeth as he struggled to regain his lost freedom of action. A staggering performance! He seemed to be exerting his will, and in vain; the trouble, however, was probably simply that he could not will. There was involved here that recoil of the will upon itself which paralyzes choice — as our tyrant had previously explained to the Roman gentleman.

Still less can I forget the touching scene, at once comic and horrible, with Signora Angiolieri. The Cavaliere, probably in his first bold survey of the room, had spied out her ethereal lack of resistance to his power. For actually he bewitched her, literally drew her out of her seat, out of her row, and away with him whither he willed. And in order to enhance his effect, he bade Signor Angiolieri call upon his wife by her name, to throw, as it were, all the weight of his existence and his rights in her into the scale, to rouse by the voice of her husband everything in his spouse's soul which could shield her virtue against the evil assaults of magic. And how vain it all was! Cipolla was standing at some distance from the couple, when he made a single cut with his whip through the air. It caused our landlady to shudder violently and turn her face towards him. "Sofronia!" cried Signor Angiolieri — we had not known that Signora Angiolieri's name was Sofronia. And he did well to call, everybody saw that there was no time to lose. His wife kept her face turned in the direction of the diabolical Cavaliere, who with his ten long yellow fingers was making passes at his victim, moving backwards as he did so, step by step. Then Signora Angiolieri, her pale face gleaming, rose up from her seat, turned right round, and began to glide after him. Fatal and forbidding sight! Her face as though moonstruck, stiff-armed, her lovely hands lifted a little at the wrists, the feet as it were together, she seemed to float slowly out of her row and after the tempter. "Call her, sir, keep calling," prompted the redoubtable man. And Signor Angiolieri, in a weak voice, called: "Sofronia!" Ah, again and again he called; as his wife went further off he even curved one hand round his lips and beckoned with the other as he called. But the poor voice of love and duty echoed unheard, in vain, behind the lost one's back; the signora swayed along, moonstruck, deaf, enslaved; she glided into the middle aisle and down it towards the fingering hunchback, towards the door. We were convinced, we were driven to the conviction, that she would have followed her master, had he so willed it, to the ends of the earth.

"*Accidente!*[1]" cried out Signor Angiolieri, in genuine affright, springing up as the exit was reached. But at the same moment the Cavaliere put aside, as it were, the triumphal crown and broke off. "Enough, signora, I thank you," he said, and offered his arm to lead her back to her husband. "Signor," he greeted the latter, "here is your wife. Unharmed, with my compliments, I give her into your hands. Cherish with all the strength of your manhood a treasure which is so wholly yours, and let your zeal be quickened by knowing that there are powers stronger than reason of virtue, and not always so magnanimously ready to relinquish their prey!"

Poor Signor Angiolieri, so quiet, so bald! He did not look as though he would know how to defend his happiness, even against powers much less demoniac than these which were now adding mockery to frightfulness. Solemnly and pompously the Cava-

liere retired to the stage, amid applause to which his eloquence gave double strength. It was this particular episode, I feel sure, that set the seat upon his ascendancy.[2] For now he made them dance, yes, literally; and the dancing lent a dissolute, abandoned, topsy-turvy air to the scene, a drunken abdication of the critical spirit which had so long resisted the spell of this man. Yes, he had had to fight to get the upper hand — for instance against the animosity of the young Roman gentleman, whose rebellious spirit threatened to serve others as a rallying-point. But it was precisely upon the importance of example that the Cavaliere was so strong. He had the wit to make his attack at the weakest point and to choose as his first victim that feeble, ecstatic youth whom he had previously made into a board. The master had but to look at him, when this young man would fling himself back as though struck by lightning, place his hands rigidly at his sides, and fall into a state of military somnambulism,[3] in which it was plain to any eye that he was open to the most absurd suggestion that might be made to him. He seemed quite content in his abject state, quite pleased to be relieved of the burden of voluntary choice. Again and again he offered himself as a subject and gloried in the model facility he had in losing consciousness. So now he mounted the platform, and a single cut of the whip was enough to make him dance to the Cavaliere's orders, in a kind of complacent ecstasy, eyes closed, head nodding, lank limbs flying in all directions.

It looked unmistakably like enjoyment, and other recruits were not long in coming forward: two other young men, one humbly and one well dressed, were soon jigging alongside the first. But now the gentleman from Rome bobbed up again, asking defiantly if the Cavaliere would engage to make him dance too, even against his will.

---

[1] *Accidente!*: the devil!

[2] **ascendancy**: domination.

[3] **somnambulism**: sleepwalking.

"Even against your will," answered Cipolla, in unforgettable accents. That frightful *"anche se non vuole"* still rings in my ears. The struggle began. After Cipolla had taken another little glass and lighted a fresh cigarette he stationed the Roman at a point in the middle aisle and himself took up a position some distance behind him, making his whip whistle through the air as he gave the order: *"Balla!"*[1] His opponent did not stir. *"Balla!"* repeated the Cavaliere incisively, and snapped his whip. You saw the young man move his neck round in his collar; at the same time one hand lifted slightly at the wrist, one ankle turned outward. But that was all, for the time at least; merely a tendency to twitch, now sternly repressed, now seeming about to get the upper hand. It escaped nobody that here a heroic obstinacy, a fixed resolve to resist, must needs be conquered; we were beholding a gallant effort to strike out and save the honor of the human race. He twitched but danced not; and the struggle was so prolonged that the Cavaliere had to divide his attention between it and the stage, turning now and then to make his riding-whip whistle in the direction of the dancers, at it were to keep them in leash. At the same time he advised the audience that no fatigue was involved in such activities, however long they went on, since it was not the automatons up there who danced, but himself. Then once more his eye would bore itself into the back of the Roman's neck and lay siege to the strength of purpose which defied him.

One saw it waver, that strength of purpose, beneath the repeated summons and whip-crackings. Saw with an objective interest which yet was not quite free from traces of sympathetic emotion — from pity, even from a cruel kind of pleasure. If I understand what was going on, it was the negative character of the young man's fighting position which was his undoing. It is likely that *not* willing is not a practicable

state of mind; *not* to want to do something may be in the long run a mental content impossible to subsist on. Between not willing a certain thing and not willing at all — in other words, yielding to another person's will — there may lie too small a space for the idea of freedom to squeeze into. Again, there were the Cavaliere's persuasive words, woven in among the whip-crackings and commands, as he mingled effects that were his own secret with others of a bewilderingly psychological kind. *"Balla!"* said he. "Who wants to torture himself like that? Is forcing yourself your idea of freedom? *Una ballatina!*[2] Why, your arms and legs are aching for it. What a relief to give way to them — there, you are dancing already! That is no struggle any more, it is a pleasure!" And so it was. The jerking and twitching of the refractory youth's limbs had at last got the upper hand; he lifted his arms, then his knees, his joints quite suddenly relaxed, he flung his legs and danced, and amid bursts of applause the Cavaliere led him to join the row of puppets on the stage. Up there we could see his face as he "enjoyed" himself; it was clothed in a broad grin and the eyes were half-shut. In a way, it was consoling to see that he was having a better time than he had had in the hour of his pride.

His "fall" was, I may say, an epoch. The ice was completely broken, Cipolla's triumph had reached its height. The Circe's wand, that whistling leather whip with the claw handle, held absolute sway. At one time — it must have been well after midnight — not only were there eight or ten persons dancing on the little stage, but in the hall below a varied animation reigned, and a long-toothed Anglo-Saxoness in a pince-nez left her seat of her own motion to perform a tarantella[3] in the center aisle. Cipolla was lounging in a cane-seated chair at the left of the stage, gulping down the

[1] *Balla!*: dance!

[2] *Una ballatina*: a dance.
[3] tarantella: a fast, whirling dance.

smoke of a cigarette and breathing it impudently out through his bad teeth. He tapped his foot and shrugged his shoulders, looking down upon the abandoned scene in the hall; now and then he snapped his whip backwards at a laggard upon the stage. The children were awake at the moment. With shame I speak of them. For it was not good to be here, least of all for them; that we had not taken them away can only be explained by saying that we had caught the general devil-may-careness of the hour. By that time it was all one. Anyhow, thank goodness, they lacked understanding for the disreputable side of the entertainment, and in their innocence were perpetually charmed by the unheard-of indulgence which permitted them to be present at such a thing as a magician's "evening." Whole quarter-hours at a time they drowsed on our laps, waking refreshed and rosy-cheeked, with sleep-drunken eyes, to laugh to bursting at the leaps and jumps the magician made those people up there make. They had not thought it would be so jolly; they joined with their clumsy little hands in every round of applause. And jumped for joy upon their chairs, as was their wont, when Cipolla beckoned to their friend Mario from the Esquisito, beckoned to him just like a picture in a book, holding his hand in front of his nose and bending and straightening the forefinger by turns.

Mario obeyed. I can see him now going up the stairs to Cipolla, who continued to beckon him, in that droll, picture-book sort of way. He hesitated for a moment at first; that, too, I recall quite clearly. During the whole evening he had lounged against a wooden pillar at the side entrance, with his arms folded, or else with his hands thrust into his jacket pockets. He was on our left, near the youth with the militant hair, and had followed the performance attentively, so far as we had seen, if with no particular animation and God knows how much comprehension. He could not much relish being summoned thus, at the end of the evening. But it was only too easy to see why he obeyed. After all, obedience was his calling in life; and then, how should a simple lad like him find it within his human capacity to refuse compliance to a man so throned and crowned as Cipolla at that hour? Willy-nilly he left his column and with a word of thanks to those making way for him he mounted the steps with a doubtful smile on his full lips.

Picture a thickset youth of twenty years, with clipped hair, a low forehead, and heavy-lidded eyes of an indefinite gray, shot with green and yellow. These things I knew from having spoken with him, as we often had. There was a saddle of freckles on the flat nose, and the whole upper half of the face retreated behind the lower, and that again was dominated by thick lips that parted to show the salivated[1] teeth. These thick lips and the veiled look of the eyes lent the whole face a primitive melancholy — it was that which had drawn us to him from the first. In it was not the faintest trace of brutality — indeed, his hands would have given the lie to such an idea, being unusually slender and delicate even for a southerner. They were hands by which one liked being served.

We knew him humanly without knowing him personally, if I may make that distinction. We saw him nearly every day, and felt a certain kindness for his dreamy ways, which might at times be actual inattentiveness, suddenly transformed into a redeeming zeal to serve. His mien[2] was serious, only the children could bring a smile to his face. It was not sulky, but uningratiating, without intentional effort to please — or, rather, it seemed to give up being pleasant in the conviction that it could not succeed. We should have remembered Mario in any case, as one of those homely recollections of travel which often stick in the mind better

---

[1] **salivated**: covered with saliva.
[2] **mien**: manner.

than more important ones. But of his circumstances we knew no more than that his father was a petty clerk in the Municipio and his mother took in washing.

His white waiter's-coat became him better than the faded striped suit he wore, with a gay colored scarf instead of a collar, the ends tucked into his jacket. He neared Cipolla, who however did not leave off that motion of his finger before his nose, so that Mario had to come still closer, right up to the chair seat and the master's legs. Whereupon the latter spread out his elbows and seized the lad, turning him so that we had a view of his face. Then gazed him briskly up and down, with a careless, commanding eye.

"Well, *ragazzo mio*,[1] how comes it we make acquaintance so late in the day? But believe me, I made yours long ago. Yes, yes, I've had you in my eye this long while and known what good stuff you were made of. How could I go and forget you again? Well, I've had a good deal to think about. . . . Now tell me, what is your name? The first name, that's all I want."

"My name is Mario," the young man answered, in a low voice.

"Ah, Mario. Very good. Yes, yes, there is such a name, quite a common name, a classic name too, one of those which preserve the heroic traditions of the Fatherland. *Brava! Salve!*" And he flung up his arm slantingly above his crooked shoulder, palm outward, in the Roman salute. He may have been slightly tipsy by now, and no wonder; but he spoke as before, clearly, fluently, and with emphasis. Though about this time there had crept into his voice a gross, autocratic note, and a kind of arrogance was in his sprawl.

"Well, now, Mario *mio*," he went on, "it's a good thing you came this evening, and that's a pretty scarf you've got on; it is becoming to your style of beauty. It must stand you in good stead with the girls, the

pretty pretty girls of Torre — "

From the row of youths, close by the place where Mario had been standing, sounded a laugh. It came from the youth with the militant hair. He stood there, his jacket over his shoulder, and laughed outright, rudely and scornfully.

Mario gave a start. I think it was a shrug, but he may have started and then hastened to cover the movement by shrugging his shoulders, as much as to say that the neckerchief and the fair sex were matters of equal indifference to him.

The Cavaliere gave a downward glance.

"We needn't trouble about him," he said. "He is jealous, because your scarf is so popular with the girls, maybe partly because you and I are so friendly up here. Perhaps he'd like me to put him in mind of his colic — I could do it free of charge. Tell me, Mario. You've come here this evening for a bit of fun — and in the daytime you work in an ironmonger's shop?"[2]

"In a café," corrected the youth.

"Oh, in a café. That's where Cipolla nearly came a cropper![3] What you are is a cup-bearer, a Ganymede — I like that, it is another classical allusion — *Salvietta!*" Again the Cavaliere saluted, to the huge gratification of his audience.

Mario smiled too. "But before that," he interpolated, in the interest of accuracy, "I worked for a while in a shop in Portoclemente." He seemed visited by a natural desire to assist the prophecy by dredging out its essential feaures.

"There, didn't I say so? In an ironmonger's shop?"

"They kept combs and brushes," Mario got round it.

"Didn't I say that you were not always a Ganymede? Not always at the sign of the serviette?[4] Even when Cipolla makes a mistake, it is a kind that makes you believe in

[1] *ragazzo mio:* my boy.

[2] **ironmonger's shop:** hardware store.

[3] **came a cropper:** made a mistake.

[4] **serviette:** napkin.

him. Now tell me: Do you believe in me?"

An indefinite gesture.

"A halfway answer," commented the Cavaliere. "Probably it is not easy to win your confidence. Even for me, I can see, it is not so easy. I see in your features a reserve, a sadness, *un tratto di malinconia*[1] . . . tell me" (he seized Mario's hand persuasively) "have you troubles?"

"*Nossignore*,"[2] answered Mario, promptly and decidedly.

"You *have* troubles," insisted the Cavaliere, bearing down the denial by the weight of his authority. "Can't I see? Trying to pull the wool over Cipolla's eyes, are you? Of course, about the girls — it is a girl, isn't it? You have love troubles?"

Mario gave a vigorous head shake. And again the *giovanotto's* brutal laugh rang out. The Cavaliere gave heed. His eyes were roving about somewhere in the air; but he cocked an ear to the sound, then swung his whip backwards, as he had once or twice before in his conversation with Mario, that none of his puppets might flag in their zeal. The gesture had nearly cost him his new prey: Mario gave a sudden start in the direction of the steps. But Cipolla had him in his clutch.

"Not so fast," said he. "That would be fine, wouldn't it? So you want to skip, do you, Ganymede, right in the middle of the fun, or, rather, when it is just beginning? Stay with me, I'll show you something nice. I'll convince you. You have no reason to worry, I promise you. This girl — you know her and others know her too — what's her name? Wait! I read the name in your eyes, it is on the tip of my tongue and yours too — "

"Silvestra!" shouted the *giovanotto* from below.

The Cavaliere's face did not change.

"Aren't there the forward people?" he asked, not looking down, more as in undisturbed converse with Mario. "Aren't there the young fighting-cocks that crow in season and out? Takes the word out of your mouth, the conceited fool, and seems to think he has some special right to it. Let him be. But Silvestra, your Silvestra — ah, what a girl that is! What a prize! Brings your heart into your mouth to see her walk or laugh or breathe, she is so lovely. And her round arms when she washes, and tosses her head back to get the hair out of her eyes! An angel from paradise!"

Mario stared at him, his head thrust forward. He seemed to have forgotten the audience, forgotten where he was. The red rings round his eyes had got larger, they looked as though they were painted on. His thick lips parted.

"And she makes you suffer, this angel," went on Cipolla, "or, rather, you make yourself suffer for her — there is a difference, my lad, a most important difference, let me tell you. There are misunderstandings in love, maybe nowhere else in the world are there so many. I know what you are thinking: what does this Cipolla, with his little physical defect, know about love? Wrong, all wrong, he knows a lot. He has a wide and powerful understanding of its workings, and it pays to listen to his advice. But let's leave Cipolla out, cut him out altogether and think only of Silvestra, your peerless Silvestra! What! Is she to give any young gamecock the preference, so that he can laugh while you cry? To prefer him to a chap like you, so full of feeling and so sympathetic? Not very likely, is it? It is impossible — we know better, Cipolla and she. If I were to put myself in her place and choose between the two of you, a tarry lout like that — a codfish, a sea-urchin — and a Mario, a knight of the serviette, who moves among gentlefolk and hands round refreshments with an air — my word, but my heart would speak in no uncertain tones — it knows to whom I gave it long ago. It is time that he should see and understand, my

---

[1] *un tratto di malinconia:* a dash of melancholy.
[2] *Nossignore:* no, sir.

chosen one! It is time that you see me and recognize me, Mario, my beloved! Tell me, who am I?"

It was grisly, the way the betrayer made himself irresistible, wreathed and coquetted with his crooked shoulder, languished with the puffy eyes, and showed his splintered teeth in a sickly smile. And alas, at his beguiling words, what was come of our Mario? It is hard for me to tell, hard as it was for me to see; for here was nothing less than an utter abandonment of the inmost soul, a public exposure of timid and deluded passion and rapture. He put his hands across his mouth, his shoulders rose and fell with his pantings. He could not, it was plain, trust his eyes and ears for joy, and the one thing he forgot was precisely that he could not trust them. "Silvestra!" he breathed, from the very depths of his vanquished heart.

"Kiss me!" said the hunchback. "Trust me, I love thee. Kiss me here." And with the tip of his index finger, hand, arm, and little finger outspread, he pointed to his cheek, near the mouth. And Mario bent and kissed him.

It had grown very still in the room. That was a monstrous moment, grotesque and thrilling, the moment of Mario's bliss. In that evil span of time, crowded with a sense of the illusiveness of all joy, one sound became audible, and that not quite at once, but on the instant of the melancholy and ribald meeting between Mario's lips and the repulsive flesh which thrust itself forward for his caress. It was the sound of a laugh, from the *giovanotto* on our left. It broke into the dramatic suspense of the moment, coarse, mocking, and yet — or I must have been grossly mistaken — with an undertone of compassion for the poor, bewildered, victimized creature. It had a faint ring of that "*Poveretto*" which Cipolla had declared was wasted on the wrong person, when he claimed the pity for his own.

The laugh still rang in the air when the recipient of the caress gave his whip a little swish, low down, close to his chair leg, and Mario started up and flung himself back. He stood in that posture staring, his hands one over the other on those desecrated lips. Then he beat his temples with his clenched fists, over and over; turned and staggered down the steps, while the audience applauded, and Cipolla sat there with his hands in his lap, his shoulders shaking. Once below, and even while in full retreat, Mario hurled himself round with legs flung wide apart; one arm flew up, and two flat shattering detonations crashed through applause and laughter.

There was instant silence. Even the dancers came to a full stop and stared about, struck dumb. Cipolla bounded from his seat. He stood with his arms spread out, slanting as though to ward everybody off, as though next moment he would cry out: "Stop! Keep back! Silence! What was that?" Then, in that instant, he sank back in his seat, his head rolling on his chest; in the next he had fallen sideways to the floor, where he lay motionless, a huddled heap of clothing, with limbs awry.

The commotion was indescribable. Ladies hid their faces, shuddering, on the breasts of their escorts. There were shouts for a doctor, for the police. People flung themselves on Mario in a mob, to disarm him, to take away the weapon that hung from his fingers — that small, dull-metal, scarcely pistol-shaped tool with hardly any barrel — in how strange and unexpected a direction had fate leveled it!

And now — now finally, at last — we took the children and led them towards the exit, past the pair of *carabinieri*[1] just entering. Was that the end, they wanted to know, that they might go in peace? Yes, we assured them, that was the end. An end of horror, a fatal end. And yet a liberation — for I could not, and I cannot, but find it so!

[1] *carabinieri:* policemen.

For Discussion

1. A story as complex and profound as this must be thoroughly comprehended before it can be understood. Comprehension is a matter of noting what happens and what details are mentioned and emphasized. At the very beginning we are told that the story will concern "the shocking business of Cipolla, that dreadful being who seemed to incorporate . . . all the peculiar evilness of the situation as a whole." Yet the first of the two major portions of "Mario and the Magician" does not seem to concern Cipolla at all. It describes, instead, apparently trivial events during the narrator's stay with his family at Torre di Venere before the magician's arrival. What little incident distressed the family on the evening of their arrival in Torre? Why were they obliged to move three or four days later from their rooms in the Grand Hotel? "It is not likely that the Principessa was responsible for the willful breach of faith" (page 534). Who was?

2. Even after having moved to the Casa Eleonora, and "despite all previous experience, we were not at home on the beach, we were not happy" (page 535). How is their dissatisfaction accounted for? What kinds of quarrels arose among the children? In time, the narrator's small daughter commits an "offense against decency." What are the consequences of that "offense"? Why, at that point, did the narrator not take his family away from Torre? That vital question is considered throughout the paragraph on page 537. It deserves careful consideration, as an explanation of why people endure an unpleasant situation rather than take steps to alter it.

3. It is that question—of why the narrator remained—that links the first major part of the story with the second, the arrival and performance of Cipolla. In both, there are good reasons to forsake an environment that is uninviting and even unpleasant; yet the narrator and his family remain, first in the town, then in the auditorium. Once inside the latter, the effect is more like a schoolroom than a theater. Cipolla keeps his audience waiting. Describe his appearance when he finally does arrive. The youths at the rear "peered at this cocksure creature to search out his secret weaknesses" (page 541). Did they find any?

4. Billed in advance as a prestidigitator—one who performs sleight-of-hand tricks—Cipolla in fact does tricks of quite a different nature. But before beginning them, he deals with a chap who "had a tongue in his head" (page 541). Why is Cipolla offended by the youth? How does he handle him? What effect does the trick have on the audience? On the narrator's children? The tricks that follow begin quite innocently. What is the first one? "And then, for the second time, something strange happened" (page 545). What was it? The audience soon has to concede that Cipolla possesses "strange powers—strange whether for good or evil" (page 548). Passing from card tricks to parlor games, the magician finally encounters Signora Angiolieri, "the dispenser of our midday soup." What effect does his identification of her past have on her? On the audience?

5. What follows after the intermission brings the action rapidly to its shocking climax and denouement. The second half of the program, more sinister than the first, is "quite frankly and exclusively devoted to one sort of experiment" (page 552). What sort? A "stately, mustachioed colonel" attempts in a memorable scene to defy Cipolla. How? What happens to him? Equally horrifying is the scene involving Signora Angiolieri. Under Cipolla's influence how does she respond to "the poor voice of love and duty" that is her husband's? A third ghastly exhibition is put on by a gentleman of "rebellious spirit" from Rome. Describe it. How does the narrator account for the triumph of Cipolla over the audience? Against which group had he "had the wit to make his attack" first?

6. At last Mario is summoned up the stairs to Cipolla. What characteristics of the waiter does the narrator remark on? In other words, what are Mario's strengths and weaknesses? His final gestures and expression on stage are "nothing less than an utter abandonment of the inmost soul, a public exposure of timid and deluded passion and rapture" (page 559). Where is the climax of the story? Defend your answer. What is the narrator's enduring attitude toward the denouement?

7. **Symbol.** In literature a *symbol* is an object that suggests meanings beyond its literal one. Throughout "Mario and the Magician" occurs mention of objects that gradually assume overtones beyond the merely literal. Cipolla's whip, for example, finally comes—as we encounter it again and again—to symbolize the force of tyranny, just as the excessive liquor and cigarettes that sustain the hypnotist may be regarded (from the point of view of the proper narrator especially) as symbols of the corruption that nourishes his diabolical gifts. Clearly the story is about more than simply an isolated theatrical experience in an Italian resort town of the twenties, and one reason it successfully radiates outward from that specific event to penetrate our own lives lies in its effective use of symbol. The whooping cough (page 533) comes to symbolize any essentially harmless attribute against which other people irrationally discriminate. Similarly, the veranda is every discriminatory country club or fraternity in whatever society. What might the "*palazzo*," a ruin now for sale, symbolize (page 539)? Consider the symbolism in the route one follows to get to Cipolla's performance: "from the feudal past the bourgeois into the proletarian." What are the symbolic overtones of the detail about the sash Cipolla wears, as first described (page 541)?

8. The story, then, is about much more than a single, isolated incident. It is about modern tyrannies everywhere, humorless, arrogant, undeniably spellbinding, quick to take offense, jingoistic, and exerting power finally over all classes in a society. What, according to the outcome of the story, will finally, inevitably defeat such tyrannies over the minds and hearts of men?

For Composition

Even a passing acquaintance with the rise and fall of fascism and the goals the movement espoused adds enormously to an appreciation of "Mario and the Magician."

1. **For Research.** Take notes on the characteristics of the fascist movement in Italy in the third and fourth decades of the twentieth century. Your research should encompass the character and impact, on his countrymen and the world, of Benito Mussolini, and if you can discover indications of what it felt like to live under fascism, so much the better. Be prepared to relate your researches to details contained in Mann's story.

2. **Character Sketch.** In a coherent essay of several paragraphs compose a character sketch of Cipolla. Briefly consider his appearance, but concentrate on what his behavior tells us about him. For instance, does he have a sense of humor? Notice, incidentally, that his character is not static: it develops—or we see more of it—as the story proceeds, until finally there creeps "into his voice a gross, autocratic note, and a kind of arrogance" is in his sprawl (page 557).

3. **Comparison and Contrast.** Specifically compare and contrast the character of Cipolla with that of Mario. To what extent is the comparison equivalent to a comparison between good and evil?

4. **Argument.** Throughout, Cipolla—emblem of the tyrant—declares that what he is doing hurts him more than it does his victims. "But appearances were all against it; and one does not feel like saying *poveretto* to a man who is suffering to bring about the humiliation of others" (page 553). In a well-organized paper that refers to specific examples of totalitarian rulers, support or refute Cipolla's claim that he suffers more than his subjects.

Words and Allusions

ETYMOLOGY (page 225). 1. In Thomas Mann's story, Cipolla symbolizes a fascist dictator. The words *fascist* and *fascism* have an interesting history. Trace the history of *fascism* from its Latin origins to its use in the twentieth century as the name of a political movement. What does *fascism* mean today?

2. A synonym (page 14) for *magic* is *prestidigitation*, and a synonym for *magician* is *prestidigitator*. What roots combine to make *prestidigitator*? What do those roots mean? Are the words *prestige* and *prestigious* related in any way to *prestidigitator*? Do you find any relationship between the original meaning of *prestige* and its meaning today?

Burning of the Sanjo Palace, mid-13th century, Kamakura Romantic, Japanese scroll, Museum of Fine Arts, Boston.

Japanese Scroll

Burning of the Sanjo Palace

The Burning of the Sanjo Palace was an incident that occurred in 1160 during the Heiji Rebellion. This rebellion, which constituted a struggle for power between two rival clans, was one of the reasons for the terrible conditions that form the setting for Akutagawa's story "Rashomon" (page 492). This picture is a section of a long scroll painting that depicts that rebellion.

At the time of the rebellion the Emperor was a puppet in the hands of the chief of the Taira clan, the traditional enemy of the Minamoto clan. The Minamotos tried to capture and imprison this Emperor so that they could place their own Emperor on the throne and rule through him. This attempt was called the Heiji Rebellion. The Minamoto clan was defeated, and the Tairas continued to rule with such tyranny and greed that Kyoto was economically almost ruined, thus accounting for the dreadful conditions described in "Rashomon."

The scene shown here comes near the beginning of a magnificent scroll painting of the Rebellion that dates from the thirteenth century. Chinese and Japanese scroll paintings were very long. This one is about twenty-three feet. The scenes are viewed from right to left as the scroll is unrolled, thus creating a sense of motion. You can get some idea of what examining such a scroll is like if you place a piece of paper over the whole painting and move it steadily and slowly to the left.

In the scenes immediately preceding this one, the Minamotos have stormed the palace of the Emperor, have captured him, and are preparing to carry him off. Meanwhile, their soldiers are killing the Taira soldiers and followers and have set the palace on fire. Thus as the scroll is unrolled the capture of the Emperor is followed by the terrible fire. One sees first the tongues of flame, then the billows of fire-reddened smoke and boiling flames. Visible are the dark roof of the palace, a corner pavilion, and a connecting corridor. Japanese palaces were built as covered corridors connecting larger rooms or pavilions. Thus fire could run rapidly all through the wooden palace.

The defending Taira warriors are in red armor, and the attacking Minamotos in light brown. In unrolling the scroll, one sees first the isolated killing at the lower right, then the heads of soldiers, and finally the general struggle. What separate incidents of that struggle can you make out? Japanese art shows an astonishing capacity to present extremes of great violence together with the beauty of perfect calm. Here the long lines of the buildings and the ordered architecture are contrasted with the visually confusing battle and fire. Do you find the same elements in "Rashomon"?

MORSE PECKHAM

Masaccio

The Expulsion from Paradise

This painting is one of a series by three different artists, painted on the walls of a chapel in Florence. The chapel is dedicated to Saint Peter, and all the scenes but two are devoted to his life. At one end of the series we see the temptation of Adam and Eve, and at the other end their expulsion from the Garden of Eden — both paintings inspired by the story in "Genesis" (page 502).

As Masaccio's painting is placed, Adam and Eve appear to be walking into the chapel, toward the scenes of Saint Peter's life. The reason for this position is found in Christian doctrine. According to that doctrine, Adam and Eve committed the original sin which all men have inherited. Because of their sinful natures all men became alienated from God. But Jesus died to redeem men from sin, and Saint Peter was given the keys to Paradise with the power to admit those whose souls have been redeemed by faith. Thus Adam and Eve, expelled from the Garden of Eden and conscious only of their present anguish, are moving toward their redemption.

This is one of the most important paintings in European art. Before Masaccio, painters had depended upon conventional but unrealistic figures to present ideas in their works, but Masaccio established a new principle, that to convey an idea the painting must have a convincing appearance of the visible world. Thus he does his utmost to paint his figures as much like real human beings as possible. Do you find any place where he has been unsuccessful? Observe how he molds the bodies through the use of shadows. Remembering that light is an ancient symbol for divinity and divine grace, why is it significant that the light in the painting comes from the direction of the chapel?

Masaccio wished also to emphasize the importance of what had happened to man and to bring out the greatness that God had given man but that Adam and Eve had lost through their sin. He does this by making the figures very large in relation to the size of the painting and by giving them a power in their stride that in another moment will carry them out of the picture. He thus achieves a vitality unexpected in this scene.

The angel is the color of fire. (The chapel was damaged by smoke from a fire in the church. The original colors were much brighter.) From the gate of the Garden radiate lines of force that symbolize the divine energy that has driven Adam and Eve forth. The angel's sword reiterates this force. Yet the angel's face is filled with sorrow and pity, and the angel's arms reach out as if to embrace them.

There is a striking contrast between the reactions of Adam and Eve to their shame and punishment. What is the difference? What does this difference suggest about the emotional reactions of men and women?

MORSE PECKHAM

Masaccio (1401–1428) *The Expulsion from Paradise,*
fresco. Brancacci Chapel, Sta. Maria del Carmine, Florence.

Rouault

First Sinners

This painting is intended to illustrate one of a series of poems, entitled *Passion,* by André Suarès, on the suffering and crucifixion of Jesus. In the poem a man and woman are digging three graves. They are approached by a tramp who asks them why they are digging three. They answer that two are for themselves and that the third is perhaps for him, for he looks evil and smells of blood. He admits that he is Cain, the first murderer and their first child. For they are Adam and Eve.

This incident, invented by the poet, and Rouault's painting deal in an unusual way with the same questions Milton was concerned with in *Paradise Lost* (page 504) — how evil came into the world, why all men have inherited their sinful state, and how their sin is to be redeemed. The poem Rouault was working with interprets the Biblical story in terms of Christian doctrine. Adam and Eve brought sin into the world, and part of their punishment was death. Although they died a long time ago, they continue to live in every man since every man inherits their sinful nature. Cain, however, the first murderer, was condemned to wander the earth, and God put a mark on him so that no man would kill him. Thus, he, too, lives on as a symbol of man's sinful nature. But the three graves mentioned in the poem tell us that Adam, Eve, and Cain can all die, and their deaths indicate a change in the history of man. This change comes about through the sacrifice of Jesus, whose death offers man the possibility of freeing himself from sin and entering heaven. Thus the incident illustrated by Rouault implies the whole story of sin and redemption.

Rouault presents Adam and Eve in ordinary laborer's clothes. Adam wears a workingman's blue trousers and what we call a T-shirt. Eve is dressed as a working woman with her hair bound in a cloth. Almost all pictures of Adam and Eve present them as very beautiful, but Rouault presents them as ordinary men and women, not at all attractive. How does this presentation relate to the theme of inherited sin?

In the upper right-hand corner is a square of blue, a symbol of heaven. The light area in the center suggests the sunrise, a symbol of the redemption of man from sin.

The painting gains religious emphasis by its resemblance to the stained glass windows of early medieval cathedrals, that is, through patches of color outlined in black. Of course, Rouault does not directly imitate stained glass. The areas of color are larger, and they show mixtures of colors. The black borders are not sharp, but are irregular, even smeared. Why does he not imitate stained glass exactly? Nevertheless, the black borders make the patches of color glow more intensely, and thus give a splendor to the ordinary human beings Rouault paints. What does this splendor suggest?

MORSE PECKHAM

Georges Rouault (1871–1958) *First Sinners*. Valley House Gallery, Dallas.

Peter Blume (1906—   ) *The Eternal City.* Museum of Modern Art, New York.

Blume

The Eternal City

The Eternal City (a name for Rome) was inspired by exactly the same situation as Thomas Mann's *Mario and the Magician* (page 530) — Italy under the fascist dictatorship of Benito Mussolini. Mann published his story in 1929, and Blume was in Rome in 1932.

Blume's painting is an allegory (page 41) that presents a particular moment in history with allusions to Italy's marvelous and tragic past. The most prominent shape is the papier-mâché head of the jack-in-the-box Mussolini. Why is the head made of papier-mâché? The way the head is mounted, it must project in front of the picture plane. Its contrast with the deep and exaggerated perspective of the rest of the picture indicates that it does not belong there. Who releases a jack-in-the-box? Why?

In the foreground is a heap of ruins of ancient Roman statues and architecture, a comment on the "eternal" city. Behind these fragments are the ruined subterranean chambers of the Coliseum where in the past human victims were held until they were sacrificed in various games. Here we see figures, lost as if in a labyrinth, struggling to get out. Just beneath the head of Mussolini stands a well-dressed couple who gaze admiringly, even adoringly, at the jack-in-the-box. How do they differ from the other figures in the painting? What do you make of their attitude?

To the left of the ruined statues, the poverty of Italy is indicated by a crippled beggar. Above him is a religious shrine of Jesus as the Man of Sorrows — he who takes on himself the sufferings of mankind — made of gold and surrounded with rich offerings. The wall enclosing the side of the shrine is ancient stonework built by the Etruscans, predecessors of the Romans, and below is a section of typical ancient Roman brick. Just beyond is a bit of wall with two brick columns like that at Ostia, the ancient seaport of Rome, excavated and restored at great expense on Mussolini's orders. What comment does this imply? On the right is the towered Capitol, a medieval-renaissance building erected on ancient and crumbling foundations. What should we make of this fact?

The stagelike platform in back is identifiable as the Roman Forum, the ancient place of public assembly. Blume makes it difficult to decide what kind of agitation and struggle is going on here. However, the mounted figures are Mussolini's fascist troops. Men are arguing with them, and women are approaching them on hands and knees. What else can you make out? Does Blume suggest that in these particular ruins there is still genuine human life? Is the smallness of the figures here significant? What does the total picture suggest about life in Italy under the rule of Mussolini? Do you find any connections with Mann's story?

MORSE PECKHAM

In Summary

1. Consider some of the many lives encountered in this section: specifically, those of Cipolla, Mario, the ground-apes at their pitfall, Lucifer, Eve, Adam, the servant and the old woman inside the Rashomon gate, the speaker in "The Snake," M. Lantin and his two wives, the Pruitts and their helpers. Other characters appear in the selections, but focusing on those mentioned, which seems most fully to embody a valid concept of goodness? Defend your answer by defining goodness as you understand the term, noting how your choice fulfills the definition and how the others fall short. To what extent are goodness and greatness synonymous? Discuss by means of specific illustrations from the section.

2. Which of the characters listed above most fully embodies your concept of evil? Define evil, illustrating the definition both positively and negatively (what evil is *not*) by means of the characters encountered in the section. Is there a difference between evil and weakness? In what ways might Milton's Lucifer and Heine's devil be compared and contrasted?

3. Questions of good and evil figure significantly in selections earlier in the anthology. Consider the part it plays in the worlds of *An Enemy of the People* (page 75), "Haircut" (146), "Counterparts" (157), *Inferno* (194), and "A Simple Heart" (266). In which is goodness most clearly exemplified? Which presents the most memorable portrait of evil? Are questions of good and evil relevant to a consideration of "Mr. Flood's Party" (page 315)? To "The Open Boat" (456)? Discuss.

4. How do fables and parables differ? How do the two forms resemble each other? What is a précis? An epic? How would you define Homeric simile? Symbol? Illustrate your definition of symbol with an example, not previously discussed, from "Mario and the Magician."

5. **Creative Writing.** Some of the force of Mann's great story derives from the point of view from which it is told—that of a rather aristocratic foreigner and family man. Suppose the same events had been reported from the point of view of one of the children. In a composition of two or three pages describe and narrate one of Cipolla's several tricks as it would be perceived by a child of Mann's narrator. Try to enter completely into the child's consciousness, noting details that he would likely observe, and using a style appropriate to the new narrator. Would the tone, or attitude toward the proceedings, be the same as that of Mann's narrator? If not, adjust the tone appropriately. And create the atmosphere of the scene by appealing to more than simply the sense of sight.

Reader's Choice

Honoré de Balzac, *Le Père Goriot.*

In a society that worships wealth, old Goriot gives up everything he has for the sake of his selfish and ungrateful daughters, then dies attended by strangers.

Albert Camus, *The Stranger.*

Condemned for murder, partly because of his total indifference to accepted social and religious values, Meursault discovers value in the fact of life itself.

Fyodor Dostoyevsky, *Crime and Punishment*.

Raskolnikov, an impoverished student, kills an old pawnbroker and her sister in the belief that his intellectual superiority justifies his crime.

Graham Greene, *The Power and the Glory*.

A cowardly, drunken priest, while fleeing from religious persecution in Mexico, turns from concern with himself and faces a martyr's death.

Richard Hughes, *A High Wind in Jamaica*.

A family of children on their way home to England from the West Indies are captured by pirates who are eventually destroyed by their victims.

Henry James, *The Turn of the Screw*.

A governess struggles to save the souls of two children who she believes are under the evil influence of the ghosts of their former governess and of the former steward of the estate.

Nikos Kazantzakis, *The Greek Passion*.

Greek villagers in an impoverished and oppressed region of Turkey take up roles in a passion play about the persecution of Jesus and eventually perform the same roles in real life.

Molière, *Le Tartuffe*.

Worming his way into the confidence of a wealthy but foolish man, a religious hypocrite tries to win the man's daughter and wife and evict him from his property.

William Shakespeare, *King Lear*.

An elderly king proposes to divide his kingdom among his three daughters, thus beginning a chain of destructive events for himself and others.

Ignazio Silone, *Bread and Wine*.

An Italian exile from fascism returns to his native province disguised as a priest but flees in disillusionment from both his fascist enemies and the communist underground.

Sophocles, *Antigone*.

A daughter of Oedipus comes into conflict with her uncle, King Creon, over his decree that her rebel brother Polynices be denied burial.

J. R. R. Tolkien, *The Lord of the Rings*.

Frodo, a jolly and contented hobbit, is given the dire responsibility of returning the ring of power and evil to the dark fires of Mordor in which it was forged.

War, the ultimate expression of hate, inspired this litho-graph of a loving mother protecting her children. Seedcorn Must Not Be Ground, *by Kaethe Kollwitz.*

Love and Hate

Love is attraction. Before science divided things up so rationally, philosophers and poets said that love was more than just human. Men have always loved nature or parts of nature — blossoming flowers, song birds, swift horses. And we believe some creatures, dogs especially, love us. Love could be natural and supernatural as well. Men have believed that even the force which makes apples fall from trees is a manifestation of divine love through nature, not merely of the law of gravity. The pagan gods sometimes loved men, sometimes hated them, sometimes were indifferent to them, just as these same gods loved, hated, or were indifferent to one another. The greatest of Christian philosophical poets, Dante, ended his masterpiece *The Divine Comedy* with these words: "Now my desire and will, like a wheel that spins with even motion, were revolved by the Love that moves the sun and the other stars." This Love is God, and we know it as it moves all things, including man's own spirit.

However, for us moderns overwhelmingly, as for most people all the time, love means attraction between people and especially between two individuals. It is an emotion which makes you want to be near, see, touch another. It is one of the great goods of life.

That seems easy enough to understand, but in actuality, as everyone knows, love is endlessly bewildering and mysterious and complicated. For we are such complex creatures, we human beings, and love is so strong and pervasive a force in us that all our spiritual life is touched by it and touches it in turn. It is even directly connected with what is ordinarily called its opposite, hate.

But there are opposites and opposites. Love and hate seem poles apart, but all you have to do is to change perspective in order to see how much they have in common. Think of love-hate together, and then oppose them to indifference. If a boy loves a girl who does not return his affection, it is quite possible that he would rather have her hate him than have her coldly indifferent to him. For hate, though painful, is a kind of connection, and disconnection can be worse than pain.

Love is an attraction that wishes another well, whereas hate is an attraction that wishes another harm. Love grieves when the other suffers, whereas hate rejoices. Yet it is inevitable that love will be mixed with bad feelings towards the beloved person, with anger especially. Of course you can be angry with another without the love between you being endangered. The question is not whether you feel anger but what you do with it. In that strange, true poem "A Poison Tree" (page 602), Blake shows us the different uses love and hate make of anger. Freely released by love, the anger flies away. Hidden and buried by hate, it bears poisonous fruit.

When love does not free itself sufficiently from other strong and destructive emotions, it can become perverse and tormented as in Faulkner's horror story "A Rose for Emily" (page 630). It can turn into its antagonist, hatred, as in Browning's "My Last Duchess" (page 604). Indeed, sometimes one can love another and hate him at the same time. You can see this occasionally between parents and children, though they may not admit to themselves just how much hate is mixed in with their love. And you can see it quite often between lovers who are ill-matched. Their heads tell them one thing, their hearts another. Two thousand years ago the Latin poet Catullus gave this contradiction its classical statement.

> I hate and I love. Perhaps you ask how that can be.
> I do not know; yet I feel it. And it tortures me.

Imagine two boys who are best friends, furiously wrestling. Is it love that is locking them into each other's arms, or hate, or anger? Or all three at once? Can you tell which? Can the boys themselves be sure?

George P. Elliott

Judas

FRANK O'CONNOR

To feel an emotion as strong as love means getting involved, deeply so.
It means absorbing yourself in someone else's life. And such a preoccupation
with one person is likely to be at the expense of others. So Jerry Moynihan,
the young Irishman who tells the following story, discovered during a night
that he would remember for a very long time.

Sure you won't be late, Jerry?" said the
mother and I going out. *Irish Idiom*
"Am I ever late?" said I, and I laughed.

That was all we said, Michael John, but it
stuck in my mind. As I was going down the
road, I was thinking it was months since I'd
taken her to the pictures. Of course, you
might think that funny, but after the
father's death we were thrown together a
lot. And I knew she hated being alone in
the house after dark.

At the same time I had my own troubles.
You see, Michael John, being an only child
I never knocked round the way other fellows did. All the fellows in the office went
out with girls, or at any rate they let on
they did. They said "Who was the old doll
I saw you with last night, Jerry? You'd
better mind yourself, or you'll be getting
into trouble." To hear them you'd imagine
there was no sport in the world, only girls,
and that they'd always be getting you into
trouble. Paddy Kinnane, for instance, talked
like that, and he never saw the way it upset
me. I think he thought it was a great compliment. It wasn't until years after that I
began to suspect that Paddy's acquaintance
with girls was about of one kind with my
own.

Then I met Kitty Doherty. Kitty was a
hospital nurse, and all the chaps in the office said a fellow should never go with
hospital nurses. Ordinary girls were bad
enough, but nurses were a fright — they
knew too much. I knew when I met Kitty
that that was a lie. She was a well-educated
superior girl; she lived up the river in a
posh[1] locality, and her mother was on all
sorts of councils and committees. Kitty was
small and wiry; a good-looking girl, always
in good humor, and when she talked, she
hopped from one thing to another like a
robin on a frosty morning.

I used to meet her in the evening up the
river road, as if I was walking there by
accident and very surprised to see her.
"Fancy meeting you!" I'd say or "Well,
well, isn't this a great surprise!" Mind you,
it usually was, for, no matter how much I
was expecting her, I was never prepared for
the shock of her presence. Then we'd stand
talking for half an hour and I'd see her
home. Several times she asked me in, but I
was too nervous. I knew I'd lose my head,
break the china, use some dirty word, and
then go home and cut my throat. Of course,
I never asked her to come to the pictures or
anything of the sort. She was above that.
My only hope was that if I waited long
enough, I might be able to save her from
drowning or the white slavers or something
else dramatic, which would show in a mod-

[1] **posh**: luxurious, fashionable.

est and dignified way how I felt about her. At the same time I had a bad conscience because I knew I should stay at home more with the mother, but the very thought that I might be missing an opportunity of fishing Kitty out of the river would spoil a whole evening on me.

That night in particular I was nearly distracted. It was three weeks since I'd seen Kitty. I was sure that, at the very least, she was dying and asking for me, and that no one knew my address. A week before, I had felt I simply couldn't bear it any longer, so I had made an excuse and gone down to the post office. I rang up the hospital and asked for Kitty. I fully expected them to say in gloomy tones that Kitty had died half an hour before, and got the shock of my life when the girl at the other end asked my name. I lost my head. "I'm afraid I'm a stranger to Miss Doherty," I said with an embarrassed laugh, "but I have a message for her from a friend."

Then I grew completely panic-stricken. What could a girl like Kitty make of a damned, deliberate lie like that? What else was it but a trap laid by an old and cunning hand? I held the receiver out and looked at it as if it was someone whose neck I was going to wring. "Moynihan," I said to it, "you're mad. An asylum, Moynihan, is the only place for you."

I heard Kitty's voice, not in my ear at all, but in the telephone booth as though she were standing before me, and nearly dropped the receiver in terror. Then I raised it and asked in what I thought of as a French accent: "Who is dat speaking, please?" "This is Kitty Doherty," she replied impatiently. "Who are you?"

That was exactly what I was wondering myself. "I am Monsieur Bertrand," I went on cautiously. "I am afraid I have the wrong number. I am so sorry." Then I put down the receiver carefully and thought how nice it would be if only I had a penknife handy to cut my throat with. It's funny, but from the moment I met Kitty I was always coveting sharp things like razors and penknives.

After that an awful idea dawned on me. Of course, I should have thought of it before, but, as you can see, I wasn't exactly knowledgeable where girls were concerned. I began to see that I wasn't meeting Kitty for the very good reason that Kitty didn't want to meet me. What her reason was, I could only imagine, but imagination was my strong point. I examined my conscience to see what I might have said to her. I remembered every remark I had made. The reason was only too clear. Every single remark I had made was either brutal, indecent, or disgusting. I had talked of Paddy Kinnane as

ABOUT THE AUTHOR • **Frank O'Connor** (1903–1966) was born in Cork, Ireland, the son of poor parents who could not afford to give him a university education. O'Connor worked for a time as a librarian and briefly directed the Abbey Theatre. He collaborated on several plays, but his special medium was the short story. For O'Connor, storytelling was "the nearest thing one can get to the quality of a pure lyric poem." In addition to many volumes of short stories, O'Connor wrote several books of verse, a critical study of Ivan Turgenev, and a study of Michael Collins and the Irish Revolution.

a fellow who "went with dolls." What could a pure-minded girl think of a chap who naturally used such a phrase except — what unfortunately was quite true — that he had a mind like a cesspit.

But this evening I felt more confident. It was a lovely summer evening with views of hillsides and fields between the gaps in the houses, and it raised my spirits. Perhaps I was wrong; perhaps she hadn't noticed or understood my filthy conversation, perhaps we might meet and walk home together. I walked the full length of the river road and back, and then started to walk it again. The crowds were thinning out as fellows and girls slipped off up the lanes or down to the river bank, courting. As the streets went out like lamps about me, my hopes sank lower and lower. I saw clearly that she was avoiding me; that she knew I was not the quiet, good-natured fellow I let on to be, but a volcano of brutality and lust. "Lust, lust, lust!" I hissed to myself, clenching my fists. I could have forgiven myself anything but the lust.

Then I glanced up and saw her on a tram.[1] I instantly forgot about the lust and smiled and waved my cap to her, but she was looking ahead and didn't see me. I raced after the car, intending to jump onto it, to sit in one of the back seats on top where she would not see me, and then say in astonishment as she got off, "Fancy meeting you here!" But as if the driver knew what was in my mind, he put on speed, and the old tram went tossing and screeching down the one straight bit of road in the town, and I stood panting in the roadway, smiling as though missing a tram were the best joke in the world, and wishing all the time that I had a penknife and the courage to use it. My position was hopeless!

Then I must have gone a bit mad — really mad, I mean — for I started to race the tram. There were still lots of people out

[1] tram: streetcar.

walking, and they stared after me in an incredulous way, so I lifted my fists to my chest in the attitude of a professional runner and dropped into what I fondly hoped would look like a comfortable stride and delude them into the belief that I was in training for a big race. By the time I was finished, I *was* a runner, and full of indignation against the people who still continued to stare at me.

Between my running and the tram's halts I just managed to keep it in view as far as the other side of town. When I saw Kitty get off and go up a hilly street, I collapsed and was only just able to drag myself after her. When she went into a house on a terrace, I sat on the high curb with my head between my knees until the panting stopped. At any rate I felt safe. I could afford to rest, could walk up and down before the house until she came out, and accost her with an innocent smile and say "Fancy meeting you!"

But my luck was dead out that night. As I was walking up and down, close enough to the house to keep it in view but not close enough to be observed from the windows, I saw a tall man strolling up at the opposite side of the road and my heart sank. It was Paddy Kinnane.

"Hallo, Jerry," he chuckled with that knowing grin he put on whenever he wanted to compliment you on being discovered in a compromising situation. "What are you doing here?"

"Just waiting for a chap I had a date with, Paddy," I said, trying to sound casual.

"Looks more as if you were waiting for an old doll, to me," Paddy said flatteringly. "Still waters run deep. When are you supposed to be meeting him?"

Cripes, I didn't even know what the time was!

"Half eight," I said at random.

"Half eight?" said Paddy. " 'Tis nearly nine now."

"Ah, he's a most unpunctual fellow," I said. "He's always the same. He'll turn up all right."

"I may as well wait with you," said Paddy, leaning against the wall and taking out a packet of cigarettes. "You might find yourself stuck by the end of the evening. There's people in this town that have no consideration for anyone."

That was Paddy all out: a heart of gold; no trouble too much for him if he could do you a good turn — I'd have loved to strangle him.

"Ah, to hell with him!" I said impatiently. "I won't bother waiting. It only struck me this minute that I have another appointment up the Western Road. You'll excuse me now, Paddy. I'll tell you all about it another time."

And away I went hell-for-leather[1] to the tram. I mounted it and went on to the terminus,[2] near Kitty's house. There, at least, Paddy Kinnane could not get at me. I sat on the river wall in the dusk. The moon was rising, and every quarter of an hour a tram came grunting and squeaking over the old bridge and went blackout while the conductor switched his trolley. Each time I got off the wall and stood on the curb in the moonlight, searching for Kitty among the passengers. Then a policeman came along, and, as he seemed to be watching me, I slunk slowly off up the hill and stood against a wall in shadow. There was a high wall at the other side of the road as well, and behind it the roof of a house was cut out of the sky in moonlight. Every now and then a tram came in and people passed, and the snatches of conversation I caught were like the warmth from an open door to the heart of a homeless man. It was quite clear now that my position was hopeless. If Kitty had walked or been driven, she could have reached home from the opposite direction. She could be at home in bed by now. The last tram came and went, and still there was no Kitty, and still I hung on despairingly. While one glimmer of a chance remained I could not go home.

Then I heard a woman's step. I couldn't even pretend to myself that it might be Kitty until she suddenly shuffled past me with that hasty little walk of hers. I started and called her name. She glanced quickly over her shoulder and, seeing a man emerge from the shadow, took fright and ran. I ran too, but she put on speed and began to outdistance me. At that I despaired. I stood on the pavement and shouted after her at the top of my voice.

"Kitty! Kitty, for God's sake, wait!"

She ran a few steps farther and then halted incredulously. She looked back, and then turned and slowly retraced her steps.

"Jerry Moynihan!" she whispered in astonishment. "What are you doing here?"

I was summoning strength to tell her that I had happened to be taking a stroll in that direction and was astonished to see her when I realized the improbability of it and began to cry instead. Then I laughed. It was hysteria, I suppose. But Kitty had had a bad fright and, now she was getting over it, she was as cross as two sticks.

"What's wrong with you, I say?" she snapped. "Are you out of your mind or what?"

"But I didn't see you for weeks," I burst out.

"I know," she replied. "I wasn't out. What about it?"

"I thought it might be something I said to you," I said desperately.

"What did you say?" she asked in bewilderment, but I couldn't repeat the hideous things I had already said. Perhaps, after all, she hadn't noticed them!

"How do I know?"

"Oh, it's not that," she said impatiently. "It's just Mother."

"Why?" I asked almost joyously. "Is there something wrong with her?"

---

[1] **hell-for-leather**: with utmost speed.
[2] **terminus**: station at the end of the line.

"Ah, no, but she made such a fuss about it. I felt it wasn't worth it."

"A fuss? What did she make a fuss about?"

"About you, of course," Kitty said in exasperation.

"But what did I do?" I asked, clutching my head. This was worse than anything I had ever imagined. This was terrible!

"You didn't do anything, but people were talking about us. And you wouldn't come in and be introduced like anyone else. I know she's a bit of a fool, and her head is stuffed with old nonsense about her family. I could never see that they were different to anyone else, and anyway she married a commercial traveler[1] herself, so she has nothing to talk about. Still, you needn't be so superior."

I felt cold shivers run through me. I had thought of Kitty as a secret between God, herself, and me, and assumed that she only knew the half of it. Now it seemed I didn't even know the half. People were talking about us! I was superior! What next?

"But what has she against me?" I asked despairingly.

"She thinks we're doing a tangle, of course," snapped Kitty as if she was astonished at my stupidity, "and I suppose she imagines you're not grand enough for a great-great grandniece of Daniel O'Connell.[2] I told her you were above that sort of thing, but she wouldn't believe me. She said I was a deep, callous, crafty little intriguer and I hadn't a drop of Daniel O'Connell's blood in my veins." Kitty giggled at the thought of herself as an intriguer, and no wonder.

"That's all she knows," I said despairingly.

"I know," Kitty agreed. "She has no sense. And anyway she has no reason to think I'm telling lies. Cissy and I always

---

[1] **commercial traveler**: traveling salesman.
[2] **Daniel O'Connell**: Irish political leader (1775–1847), who worked for the independence of Ireland from Great Britain.

---

had fellows, and we spooned[3] with them all over the shop under her very nose, so I don't see why she thinks I'm trying to conceal anything."

At this I began to laugh like an idiot. This was worse than appalling. This was a nightmare. Kitty, whom I had thought so angelic, talking in cold blood about "spooning" with fellows all over the house. Even the bad women in the books I had read didn't talk about love-making in that cold-blooded way. Madame Bovary herself had at least the decency to pretend that she didn't like it. It was another door opening on the outside world, but Kitty thought I was laughing at her and started to apologize.

"Of course, I had no sense at the time," she said. "You were the first fellow I met that treated me properly. The others only wanted to fool around, and now, because I don't like it, Mother thinks I'm into something ghastly. I told her I liked you better than any fellow I knew, but that I'd grown out of all that sort of thing."

"And what did she say to that?" I asked fiercely. I was beginning to see that imagination wasn't enough; that all round me there was an objective reality that was a thousand times more nightmarish than any fantasy of my own. I couldn't hear enough about it, though at the same time it turned my stomach.

"Ah, I told you she was silly," Kitty said in embarrassment.

"Go on!" I shouted. "I want to know."

"Well," said Kitty with a demure grin, "she said you were a deep, designing guttersnipe[4] who knew exactly how to get round

---

[3] **spooned**: necked.
[4] **guttersnipe**: slum child (contemptuous term).

---

featherpated[1] little idiots like me. . . . You see, it's quite hopeless. The woman is common. She doesn't understand."

"Oh, God!" I said almost in tears. "I only wish she was right."

"Why do you wish she was right?" Kitty asked with real curiosity.

"Because then I'd have some chance of you," I said.

"Oh!" said Kitty, as if this was news to her. "To tell you the truth," she added after a moment, "I thought you were a bit keen at first, but then I wasn't sure. When you didn't kiss me or anything, I mean."

"God," I said bitterly, "when I think what I've been through in the past few weeks!"

"I know," said Kitty, biting her lip. "I was a bit fed up too."

Then we said nothing for a few moments.

"You're sure you mean it?" she asked suspiciously.

"But I tell you I was on the point of committing suicide," I said angrily.

"What good would that be?" she asked with another shrug, and this time she looked at me and laughed outright — the little jade!

I insisted on telling her about my prospects. She didn't want to hear about my prospects; she wanted me to kiss her, but that seemed to me a very sissy sort of occupation, so I told her just the same, in the intervals. It was as if a stone had been lifted off my heart, and I went home in the moonlight, singing. Then I heard the clock strike, and the singing stopped. I remembered the mother's "Sure you won't be late?" and my own "Am I ever late?" This was desperation too, but of a different sort.

The door was ajar and the kitchen in darkness. I saw her sitting before the fire by herself, and just as I was about to throw my arms round her, I smelt Kitty's perfume and was afraid to go near her. God help

[1] featherpated: silly.

us, as though that would have told her anything!

"Hullo, Mum," I said with a nervous laugh, rubbing my hands. "You're all in darkness."

"You'll have a cup of tea?" she said.

"I might as well."

"What time is it?" she said, lighting the gas. "You're very late."

"I met a fellow from the office," I said, but at the same time I was stung by the complaint in her tone.

"You frightened me," she said with a little whimper. "I didn't know what happened you. What kept you at all?"

"Oh, what do you think?" I said, goaded by my own sense of guilt. "Drinking and blackguarding[2] as usual."

I could have bitten my tongue off as I said it; it sounded so cruel, as if some stranger had said it instead of me. She turned to me with a frightened stare as if she were seeing the stranger too, and somehow I couldn't bear it.

"God Almighty!" I said. "A fellow can have no life in his own house."

I went hastily upstairs, lit the candle, undressed, and got into bed. A chap could be a drunkard and blackguard and not be made to suffer what I was being made to suffer for being out late one single night. This, I felt, was what you got for being a good son.

"Jerry," she called from the foot of the stairs, "will I bring you up your cup?"

"I don't want it now, thanks," I said.

I heard her sigh and turn away. Then she locked the doors, front and back. She didn't wash up, and I knew that my cup of tea was standing on the table with a saucer on top in case I changed my mind. She came slowly upstairs and her walk was that of an

[2] **blackguarding** (blag′ĕrd·ing): behaving as a scoundrel.

old woman. I blew out the candle before she reached the landing, in case she came in to ask if I wanted anything else, and the moonlight came in the attic window and brought me memories of Kitty. But every time I tried to imagine her face as she grinned up at me, waiting for me to kiss her, it was the mother's face that came up instead, with that look like a child's when you strike him for the first time — as if he suddenly saw the stranger in you. I remembered all our life together from the night my father died; our early Mass on Sunday; our visits to the pictures, and our plans for the future, and Christ! Michael John, it was as if I was inside her mind while she sat by the fire waiting for the blow to fall. And now it had fallen, and I was a stranger to her, and nothing I could ever do would make us the same to one another again. There was something like a cannonball stuck in my chest, and I lay awake till the cocks started crowing. Then I could bear it no longer. I went out on the landing and listened.

"Are you awake, Mother?" I asked in a whisper.

"What is it, Jerry?" she replied in alarm, and I knew that she hadn't slept any more than I had.

"I only came to say I was sorry," I said, opening the door of her room, and then as I saw her sitting up in bed under the Sacred Heart lamp, the cannonball burst inside me and I began to cry like a kid.

"Oh, child, child, child!" she exclaimed, "what are you crying for at all, my little boy?" She spread out her arms to me. I went to her and she hugged me and rocked me as she did when I was only a nipper. "Oh, oh, oh," she was saying to herself in a whisper, "my storeen bawn, my little man!" — all the names she hadn't called me in years. That was all we said. I couldn't bring myself to tell her what I had done, nor could she confess to me that she was jealous: all she could do was to try and comfort me for the way I'd hurt her, to make up to me for the nature she had given me. "My storeen bawn!" she said. "My little man!"

For Discussion

1. Consider the title. Who was the historical Judas? With what is the name synonymous? At the end, Jerry confesses that "I couldn't bring myself to tell her what I'd done." What had he done that would hurt his mother so? But what else could he have done? Do you see the ambiguity implicit in the title? Certainly "villainous" Jerry is the Judas, but the question is: whom might he betray? His mother? Kitty? Himself? What should his next step be?

2. Like so many stories, this one gains from a second reading. The mother's plight, as revealed in the first paragraph, is made all the more poignant after the reader has experienced the ending. What circumstances have drawn her and Jerry unusually close together? What parallels do you find between the position of Kitty in her household and Jerry in his? What differences exist between the two situations?

3. The relationship between Kitty and Jerry was for a long time in danger of never getting off the ground. As far as Jerry was concerned, what impeded its progress? How did Kitty interpret his actions and attitude toward her? Did their relationship — and the confusions that attended it — strike you as convincing? What finally cleared up the confusions?

4. **Hyperbole.** *Hyperbole* (hī·pėr′bə·lē), a figure of speech frequently encountered in prose and poetry, denotes exaggeration for purposes of humor or emphasis. "His desperation gave him the strength of an ox": not literally, of course, but the exaggeration is effective. Similarly, the appealing tone of "Judas" is owing in part to hyperbole: "I knew I'd lose my head, break the china, use some dirty word,

and then go home and cut my throat." Again, of course not really, but the effect does add to the humor. Where else in the story did you encounter hyperbole?

For Composition

Much of the charm of "Judas" arises from the personality and character of the young man from whose point of view the story is told. But on the basis of what we learn of Kitty — spirited, quick, and articulate herself — we can be sure an equally warm story, full of exasperations and misunderstandings, could be told from her point of view.

1. **Analysis.** In a composition of three or four paragraphs consider the values and disadvantages of telling the events in "Judas" from Kitty's point of view. What might be gained thereby? What would be lost? You might choose to illustrate your insights by writing a couple of paragraphs of the story as Kitty might tell it.

2. **Comparison and Contrast.** The setting of this story is similar to that of "Counterparts" (page 157); Joyce and O'Connor were fellow countrymen, each with a sharp eye for physical details of the world they knew firsthand. Identify and illustrate the characteristics of these two stories that would indicate that their settings are similar. What major differences between the settings do you discover?

Words and Allusions

COGNATES (page 22). In "Judas" we read of people staring "in an incredulous way" (page 577). What is the difference between *incredulous* and *incredible*? Both words come from the Latin *credere*, to believe. The following words also come from that source: *creed, credit, credentials, accreditation, creditable.* Explain what each word has to do with the concept of belief.

ETYMOLOGY (page 225). Using a good dictionary, show how *deliberate* (page 576) evolved from the Latin word for "scales," *demure* (page 579) from an old French word meaning "ripe," and *curiosity* from the Latin word for "care."

Love Song

FLAVIEN RANAIVO

Many poets have striven to express the elusive qualities of love — to define just what love is. Here is one definition by a Madagascar poet, in the form of a request that moves by analogy and negation: "Love is not like this, nor should it be like this. Instead, to be true, it should be like this."

Do not love me, my friend,
Like your shadow —
Shadows fade in the evening
And I will hold you
Until the cock crows.   5

"Love Song," by Flavien Ranaivo, translated by Miriam Koshland, from *Poems from Black Africa*, edited by Langston Hughes. Copyright © 1963 by Langston Hughes. Reprinted by permission of Indiana University Press.

Do not love me like pepper —
It makes my belly hot.
I cannot eat pepper
When I am hungry.   9

Do not love me like a pillow —
One would meet in sleep
And not see each other
During the day.

Love me like a dream —
For dreams are your life   15
In the night
And my hope in the day.

For Discussion

1. "Love Song" has a delicate structure composed of four stanzas, the first three of which compare love to a shadow, pepper, and a pillow. What inadequacy in love does each comparison reveal? What qualities of a dream make the love that resembles it whole and satisfying?

2. The culture out of which "Love Song" grows is different from American culture as generally represented on television, in magazines, and at the movies. Does the poem transcend those differences, or do your own experiences with life make it difficult, if not impossible, to understand what is being said? What overtones of a less complex and industrialized culture do you find in the poem?

For Composition

Effective expository writing should have unity. It should have coherence. And, finally, it should distribute *emphasis* appropriately, so that what is less important is subordinated to what is more so. There are several ways to emphasize an important detail or insight, one of which is by position: what is first said and what is said last are often remembered after what has gone between them has been forgotten.

1. Analysis.   Which of the four concepts expressed in this poem is most important? In a brief composition identify the most important concept, justify your choice, and account for the position in which it has been placed.

2. Argument.   "Love me like a dream," the poet says, and yet there are connotations to dreams — connotations not stressed here — that might lead some friends and lovers to object to the simile. In a paper that explores two or three such connotations, present an argument that either refutes or supports the closing assertion of the poem.

About the Poet. **Flavien Ranaivo** (1914–   ) was born on the island of Madagascar, now part of the Malagasy Republic. The author of a popular volume of poems entitled *L'Ombre et la Vent*, which was published in the capital city Tananarive, Ranaivo combines in his poetry what one observer has called a "lounging gait" and "a delightful impudence of language." The "slangy insolent tone of his verse" has been described as "an authentic inspiration from the popular vernacular songs of the island."

creatures, nature images

→ unexpressed; unrequited love *
— detail, word of ♥, darling
— not his right to express ♥
esp. @ funeral

Elegy for Jane

My Student, Thrown by a Horse — subtitle

THEODORE ROETHKE

An *elegy* is a poem expressing grief, usually over the death of a loved one. And love, like grief, goes everywhere — from parent to child, from man to woman, and even from one with no "rights" in the matter to another who may not have been aware at all of the innocent love she inspired.

talking about her

usually shy
intrigued by own thoughts

I remember the neckcurls, limp and damp as tendrils;*
And her quick look, a sidelong pickerel* smile;
And how, once startled into talk, the light syllables leaped for her,
And she balanced in the delight of her thought,
A wren, happy, tail into the wind,   5
Her song trembling the twigs and small branches.
The shade sang with her;
The leaves, their whispers turned to kissing;
And the mold* sang in the bleached valleys under the rose.   9

when she gets excited, everyone else does too

harmonious w/ nature

Oh, when she was sad, she cast herself down into such a pure depth,
Even a father could not find her:
Scraping her cheek against straw;
Stirring the clearest water.

talking to her

My sparrow, you are not here,
Waiting like a fern, making a spiny shadow.
The sides of wet stones cannot console me,   15
Nor the moss, wound with the last light.

went to visit grave, her spirits not there — no consolation in stones/earth

loves her; sorrow over death
college student

If only I could nudge you from this sleep,
My maimed darling, my skittery pigeon.
Over this damp grave I speak the words of my love: 20
I, with no rights in this matter,
Neither father nor lover.

Roethke: pronounced ret′kə.   1. **tendrils:** threadlike parts of a climbing plant.
2. **pickerel:** darting fish.   9. **mold:** earth.

For Discussion

protector; teacherly love

1. A teacher expresses his grief for the death of a student. Why does he say he has "no rights in this matter"? What matter?

2. The first two stanzas evoke an impression of Jane, to whom the poem is addressed. What is the combined effect that she created on the speaker?

3. Notice in the opening stanza the preponderance of kinetic imagery — imagery expressed in diction that communicates a sense of movement: "quick look," "startled into talk," "syllables leaped for her." What other examples do you observe? Considering the moment when and place where the stanza is represented as being uttered, there is a poignant irony in such imagery. Where is the poem spoken? Why are such memories as the first stanza mentions particularly poignant?

4. The poem is filled with images from nature — flora and fauna both: pickerel, wren, pigeon, rose, fern, moss. What do such images contribute to the effect of the poem? Do they reveal anything about Jane as a person?

For Composition

A careful rereading of "Elegy for Jane" will disclose a remarkably complete picture of the girl to whom these lines pay tribute.

• **Character Sketch.** In a well-substantiated composition characterize the Jane of this poem. Limit yourself to description and character traits that can be supported by details mentioned in the poem itself (don't overlook the title), and end the essay with a consideration of the detail that you think is most essential to defining Jane's individuality.

About the Poet. As early as the seventh grade, **Theodore Roethke** (1908–1963) wanted to become a writer. Encouraged at Harvard by the poet Robert Hillyer, Roethke turned to poetry and continued writing during a teaching career at Bennington College, Pennsylvania State University, and the University of Washington. As teacher and poet, he won the praise of his students and several notable awards, including a Guggenheim Award in 1945 and a Pulitzer Prize in 1954. A hearty individual who appeared to love life despite his frequent depressions, Roethke wrote verse inspired by what Stanley Kunitz called "a ferocity of imagination" which "makes most modern poetry seem pale and tepid in comparison."

Of Love

FRANCIS BACON

Not everyone regards love as a blessing. Indeed, the ardent, romantic lover who pines away, unable to focus his mind on anything but the loved one, has long been recognized as a figure in part comic, in part pathetic.

The stage is more beholding[1] to Love than the life of man. For as to the stage, love is ever matter of comedies, and now and then of tragedies, but in life it doth much mischief, sometimes like a siren,[2] sometimes like a fury. You may observe that amongst all the great and worthy per-

[1] **beholding:** indebted.

[2] **siren:** In Greek mythology, Sirens were monsters who lured mariners to destruction by the sweetness of their singing.

sons (whereof the memory remaineth, either ancient or recent) there is not one that hath been transported to the mad degree of love, which shews that great spirits and great business do keep out this weak passion. You must except[1] nevertheless Marcus Antonius, the half partner of the empire of Rome, and Appius Claudius, the decemvir[2] and lawgiver; whereof the former was indeed a voluptuous man, and inordinate, but the latter was an austere and wise man; and therefore it seems (though rarely) that love can find entrance not only into an open heart, but also into a heart well fortified, if watch be not well kept. It is a poor saying of Epicurus, *Satis magnum alter alteri theatrum sumus,*[3] as if man, made for the contemplation of heaven and all noble objects, should do nothing but kneel before a little idol, and make himself a subject, though not of the mouth (as beasts are), yet of the eye, which was given him for higher purposes. It is a strange thing to note the excess of this passion, and how it braves[4] the nature and value of things, by this; that the speaking in a perpetual hyperbole is comely in nothing but in love. Neither is it merely in the phrase, for whereas it hath been well said that the archflatterer, with whom all the petty flatterers have intelligence,[5] is a man's self, certainly the lover is more. For there was never proud man thought so absurdly well of himself as the lover doth of the person loved; and therefore it was well said, *That it is impossible to love and to be wise.* Neither doth this weakness appear to others only, and not to the party loved, but to the loved most of all, except the love be reciproque.[6] For it is a true rule that love is ever rewarded either with the reciproque or with an inward and secret contempt. By how much the more men ought to beware of this passion, which loseth not only other things but itself. As for the other losses, the poet's relation doth well figure them; that he that preferred Helena,[7] quitted the

---

[1] **except:** make an exception of.
[2] **decemvir:** one of a body of ten magistrates who ruled ancient Rome.
[3] *Satis . . . sumus:* Each of us is to the other a sufficiently large theater.

[4] **braves:** insults.
[5] **have intelligence:** get information.
[6] **reciproque:** reciprocal.
[7] **Helena:** reference is to Virgil's *Aeneid;* Paris, son of the king of Troy, brought about the Trojan war by abducting the beautiful Helen.

ABOUT THE AUTHOR • Scientist, philosopher, statesman, and essayist, **Sir Francis Bacon** (1561–1626) was in many ways the embodiment of the Renaissance man. Praised for his intellectual and artistic prowess, he collected numerous honors and titles during his lifetime. He also acquired powerful enemies, including Queen Elizabeth I, and was discredited and even imprisoned on a charge of bribery. Later cleared of the charges, he devoted his life to the discovery of truth and laid the foundations for experimental science and the scientific method. Even his death involved the pursuit of truth; he contracted pneumonia while studying the effects of cold on the preservation of poultry.

gifts of Juno and Pallas.[1] For whosoever esteemeth too much of amorous affection quitteth both riches and wisdom. This passion hath his floods in the very times of weakness, which are great prosperity and great adversity, though this latter hath been less observed, both which times kindle love, and make it more fervent, and therefore shew it to be the child of folly. They do best, who if they cannot but admit love, yet make it keep quarter,[2] and sever it wholly from their serious affairs and actions of life, for if it check[3] once with business, it troubleth men's fortunes, and maketh men that they can no ways be true to their own ends. I know not how, but martial men are given to love; I think it is but as they are given to wine, for perils commonly ask to be paid in pleasures. There is in man's nature a secret inclination and motion towards love of others, which if it be not spent upon some one or a few, doth naturally spread itself towards many, and maketh men become humane and charitable, as it is seen sometime in friars. Nuptial[4] love maketh mankind; friendly love perfecteth it; but wanton love corrupteth and embaseth[5] it.

[1] **Juno and Pallas:** goddesses of marriage and wisdom, respectively.
[2] **quarter:** its proper place.
[3] **check:** interfere.
[4] **Nuptial:** of marriage.
[5] **embaseth:** makes base, degrades.

For Discussion

1. The essay ends by elaborating a distinction. By nuptial love, Bacon refers of course to married love, which produces children — hence, "maketh mankind." What does he mean by friendly love? "There is in man's nature a secret inclination and motion towards love of others, which if it be not spent upon some one or a few, doth naturally spread itself toward many." Explain the assertion. What is meant by wanton love?

2. It is wanton love that "doth much mischief." History, according to Bacon, only rarely (in the case of Mark Antony, for one) records cases of any great and worthy person "transported to the mad degree of love." In fact, "it is impossible to love and to be wise." How does Bacon substantiate that assertion?

3. What, according to the essay, is the proper object of man's love and attention? What is the "little idol" before which the romantic lover worships? Love may be reciprocated — that is, returned. But when love is not "reciproque," how, according to the essay, does the object of love receive the attention of the lover? Speaking "in a perpetual hyperbole is comely in nothing but in love." Paraphrase what Bacon is saying in that assertion.

For Composition

"This passion hath his floods in the very times of weakness, which are great prosperity and great adversity...."

1. **Exposition.** In a brief composition using examples, explain the meaning of the quoted passage. Your explanation should clarify why prosperity and adversity are "weaknesses," and should furnish instances of both states and their effect on love, as drawn from reading, personal knowledge, or imagination.

2. **Argument.** What case can be made for the kind of intense emotional love that Bacon's essay attacks? In a thoughtful composition, support or refute the case that Bacon makes against romantic love.

Words and Allusions

HOMOPHONES. Words that are pronounced alike but differ in meaning, derivation, or spelling are called *homophones*. Bacon refers to his brief essays as *counsels*. *Counsel* and *council* sound alike, although they differ in spelling. How do they differ in meaning and derivation? What are homonyms and homographs?

DERIVATION (page 445). Bacon speaks of love that "embaseth" (587). Related words in use now are *abase* and *debase*. How do those words differ? Which is closer to Bacon's meaning?

Love and Bread

AUGUST STRINDBERG

Amor vincit omnia: love conquers all. Does it, though? There is no question about the power of love, but can love overcome all obstacles that stand in its way?

The assistant had not thought of studying the price of wheat before he called on the major to ask him for the hand of his daughter; but the major had studied it.

"I love her," said the assistant.

"What's your salary?" said the old man.

"Well, twelve hundred crowns, at present; but we love one another. . . ."

"That has nothing to do with me; twelve hundred crowns is not enough."

"And then I make a little in addition to my salary, and Louisa knows that my heart. . . ."

"Don't talk nonsense! How much in addition to your salary?"

He seized paper and pencil.

"And my feelings. . . ."

"How much in addition to your salary?"

And he drew hieroglyphics[1] on the blotting paper.

"Oh! We'll get on well enough, if only. . . ."

"Are you going to answer my question or not? How much in addition to your salary? Figures! figures, my boy! Facts!"

"I do translations at ten crowns a sheet; I give French lessons, I am promised proofcorrecting. . . ."[2]

"Promises aren't facts! Figures, my boy! Figures! Look here, now, I'll put it down. What are you translating?"

"What am I translating? I can't tell you straight off."

"You can't tell me straight off? You are engaged on a translation, you say; can't you tell me what it is? Don't talk such rubbish!"

"I am translating Guizot's *History of Civilization,* twenty-five sheets."

"At ten crowns a sheet makes two hundred and fifty crowns. And then?"

"And then? How can I tell beforehand?"

"Indeed, can't you tell beforehand? But you ought to know. You seem to imagine that being married simply means living together and amusing yourselves! No, my dear boy, there will be children, and children require feeding and clothing."

"There needn't be babies directly, if one loves *as we love* one another."

"How the dickens do you love one another?"

"*As we love* one another." He put his hand on his waistcoat.

"And won't there be any children if people love as you love? You must be mad! But you are a decent, respectable member of society, and therefore I'll give my consent; but make good use of the time, my boy, and increase your income, for hard times are coming. The price of wheat is rising."

The assistant grew red in the face when he heard the last words, but his joy at the old man's consent was so great that he seized his hand and kissed it. Heaven knew how happy he was! When he walked for the first time down the street with his future bride on his arm, they both radiated light; it seemed to them that the passersby stood

---

[1] **hieroglyphics:** *here,* doodles.
[2] **proofcorrecting:** reading printer's proof in order to spot mistakes and correct them.

still and lined the road in honor of their triumphal march; and they walked along with proud eyes, squared shoulders and elastic steps.

In the evening he called at her house; they sat down in the center of the room and read proofs; she helped him. "He's a good sort," chuckled the old man. When they had finished, he took her in his arms and said: "Now we have earned three crowns," and then he kissed her. On the following evening they went to the theater and he took her home in a cab, and that cost twelve crowns.

Sometimes, when he ought to have given a lesson in the evening, he (is there anything a man will not do for love's sake?) canceled his lesson and took her out for a walk instead.

But the wedding day approached. They were very busy. They had to choose the furniture. They began with the most important purchases. Louisa had not intended to be present when he bought the bedroom furniture, but when it came to the point, she went with him. They bought two beds, which were, of course to stand side by side. The furniture had to be walnut, every single piece real walnut. And they must have spring mattresses covered with red and white striped tick;[1] and bolsters[2] filled with down; and two eiderdown[3] quilts, exactly alike. Louisa chose blue, because she was very fair.

They went to the best stores. They could not do without a red hanging-lamp and a Venus made of plaster of paris. Then they bought a dinner service; and six dozen differently shaped glasses with cut edges; and knives and forks, grooved and engraved with their initials. And then the kitchen utensils! Mama had to accompany them to see to those.

And what a lot he had to do besides!

There were bills to accept, journeys to the banks and interviews with tradespeople and artisans;[4] a flat had to be found, and curtains had to be put up. He saw to everything. Of course he had to neglect his work; but once he was married, he would soon make up for it.

They were only going to take two rooms to begin with, for they were going to be frightfully economical. And as they were only going to have two rooms, they could afford to furnish them well. He rented two rooms and a kitchen on the first floor in Government Street, for six hundred crowns. When Louisa remarked that they might just as well have taken three rooms and a kitchen on the fourth floor for five hundred crowns, he was a little embarrassed; but what did it matter if only they loved one another? Yes, of course, Louisa agreed, but couldn't they have loved one another just as well in four rooms at a lower rent, as in three at a higher? Yes, he admitted that he had been foolish, but what *did* it matter so long as they loved one another?

The rooms were furnished. The bedroom looked like a little temple. The two beds stood side by side, like two carriages. The rays of the sun fell on the blue eiderdown quilt, the white, white sheets and the little pillow slips which an elderly maiden aunt had embroidered with their monogram; the latter consisted of two huge letters, formed of flowers, joined together in one single embrace, and kissing here and there, wherever they touched, at the corners. The bride had her own little alcove, which was screened off by a Japanese screen. The drawing room, which was also dining room, study, and morning room, contained her piano (which had cost twelve hundred crowns), his writing table with twelve pigeonholes (every single piece of it real walnut), a pier glass,[5] armchairs; a sideboard and a dining table. "It looks as if nice peo-

---

[1] **tick**: cloth covering.
[2] **bolsters**: long, narrow pillows.
[3] **eiderdown**: soft breast feathers of a duck.

[4] **artisans**: skilled workmen.
[5] **pier glass**: tall mirror.

ple lived here," they said, and they could not understand why people wanted a separate dining room, which always looked so cheerless with its cane chairs.

The wedding took place on a Saturday. Sunday dawned, the first day of their married life. Oh! what a life it was! Wasn't it lovely to be married! Wasn't marriage a splendid institution! One was allowed one's own way in everything, and parents and relations came and congratulated one into the bargain.

At nine o'clock in the morning their bedroom was still dark. He wouldn't open the shutters to let in daylight, but relighted the red lamp, which threw its bewitching light on the blue eiderdown, the white sheets, a little crumpled now, and the Venus made of plaster of paris, who stood there rosy-red and without shame. And the red light also fell on his little wife, who nestled in her pillows with a look of contrition, and yet so refreshed as if she had never slept so well in all her life. There was no traffic in the street today, for it was Sunday, and the church bells were calling people to the morning service with exulting, eager voices, as if they wanted all the world to come to church and praise Him who had created men and women.

He whispered to his little bride to shut her eyes so that he might get up and order breakfast. She buried her head in the pillows, while he slipped on his dressing gown and went behind the screen to dress.

A broad radiant path of sunlight lay on the sitting room floor; he did not know whether it was spring or summer, autumn or winter; he only knew that it was Sunday! His bachelor life was receding into the background like something ugly and dark; the sight of his little home stirred his heart with a faint recollection of the home of his childhood, and at the same time held out a glorious promise for the future.

How strong he felt! The future appeared to him like a mountain coming to meet him. He would breathe on it, and the mountain would fall down at his feet like sand; he would fly away, far above gables and chimneys, holding his little wife in his arm.

He collected his clothes which were scattered all over the room; he found his white necktie hanging on a picture frame; it looked like a big white butterfly.

ABOUT THE AUTHOR • An enormously prolific writer of essays, novels, short stories, plays, and pamphlets, **August Strindberg** (1849–1912) is best known as Sweden's greatest playwright. Born the illegitimate son of a maid-servant who later married his father, Strindberg had an insecure and unhappy personal life. He fought bitterly with his aristocratic first wife, and eventually divorced her after fourteen years of marriage. Following two divorces in the 1890's, Strindberg suffered much emotional disturbance. During this period of distress, he became fascinated with mysticism and alchemy. When his emotional crisis finally passed, he began a new phase of creative life. The character of his writing shifted from the cold and bitter realism of his novel *The Red Room* and his play *Miss Julie,* to *The Spook Sonata* — perhaps the strangest and one of the most influential of Strindberg's plays — which anticipates modern expressionist drama.

"'They think we are out on the spree,' he laughed. 'What fun! What madness!' But his wife did not like it. They had a big bill to pay." Breakfast in Ledoyen's Restaurant, *by the Swedish artist Hugo Birger.*

He went into the kitchen. How the new copper vessels sparkled, the new tin kettles shone! And all this belonged to him and to her! He called the maid, who came out of her room in her petticoat. But he did not notice it, nor did he notice that her shoulders were bare. For him there was but one woman in all the world. He spoke to the girl as a father would to his daughter. He told her to go to the restaurant and order breakfast, at once, a first-rate breakfast. Porter and Burgundy![1] The manager knew his taste. She was to give him his regards.

He went out of the kitchen and knocked at the bedroom door.

"May I come in?"

There was a little startled scream.

"Oh, no, darling, wait a bit!"

He laid the breakfast table himself. When the breakfast was brought from the restaurant, he served it on her new breakfast set. He folded the dinner napkins according to all the rules of art. He wiped the wine glasses, and finally took her bridal bouquet and put it in a vase before her place.

When she emerged from her bedroom in her embroidered morning gown and stepped into the brilliant sunlight, she felt just a tiny bit faint; he helped her into the arm-

[1] **Porter and Burgundy:** types of ale and wine.

chair, made her drink a little liqueur out of a liqueur glass, and eat a caviar sandwich.

What fun it all was! One could please oneself when one was married. What would Mama have said if she had seen her daughter drinking liqueurs at this hour of the morning!

He waited on her as if she were still his fiancée. What a breakfast they were having on the first morning after their wedding! And nobody had a right to say a word. Everything was perfectly right and proper, one could enjoy oneself with the very best of consciences, and that was the most delightful part of it all. It was not for the first time that he was eating such a breakfast, but what a difference between then and now! He had been restless and dissatisfied then; he could not bear to think of it, now. And as he drank a glass of genuine Swedish porter after the oysters, he felt the deepest contempt for all bachelors.

"How stupid of people not to get married! Such selfishness! They ought to be taxed like dogs."

"I'm sorry for those poor men who haven't the means to get married," replied his demure little wife kindly, "for I am sure, if they had the means, they would all get married."

A little pang shot through the assistant's heart; for a moment he felt afraid, lest he had been a little too venturesome. All his happiness rested on the solution of a financial problem, and if, if.... Pooh! A glass of Burgundy! Now he would work! They should see!

"Game? With cranberries and cucumbers!" The young wife was a little startled, but it was really delicious.

"Lewis, darling," she put a trembling little hand on his arm, "can we afford it?"

Fortunately she said "we."

"Pooh! It doesn't matter for once! Later on we can dine on potatoes and herrings."

"Can you eat potatoes and herrings?"

"I should think so!"

"When you have been drinking more than is good for you, and expect a beefsteak after the herring?"

"Nonsense! Nothing of the kind! Your health, sweetheart! The game is excellent! So are these artichokes!"

"No, but you are mad, darling! Artichokes at this time of the year! What a bill you will have to pay!"

"Bill! Aren't they good? Don't you think that it is glorious to be alive? Oh! It's splendid, splendid!"

At six o'clock in the afternoon a carriage drove up to the front door. The young wife would have been angry if it had not been so pleasant to loll luxuriously on the soft cushions, while they were being slowly driven to the Deer Park.

"It's just like lying on a couch," whispered Lewis.

She playfully hit his fingers with her sunshade. Mutual acquaintances bowed to them from the footpath. Friends waved their hands to him as if they were saying:

"Hallo! you rascal, you have come into a fortune!"

How small the passersby looked, how smooth the street was, how pleasant their ride on springs and cushions!

Life should always be like that.

It went on for a whole month. Balls, visits, dinners, theaters. Sometimes, of course, they remained at home. And at home it was more pleasant than anywhere else. How lovely, for instance, to carry off one's wife from her parents' house, after supper, without saying as much as "by your leave," put her into a closed carriage, slam the door, nod to her people and say: "Now we're off home, to our own four walls! And there we'll do exactly what we like!"

And then to have a little supper at home and sit over it, talking and gossiping until the small hours of the morning.

Lewis was always very sensible at home, at least in theory. One day his wife put him to the test by giving him salt salmon, potatoes boiled in milk, and oatmeal soup for dinner. Oh! how he enjoyed it! He was sick of elaborate menus.

On the following Friday, when she again suggested salt salmon for dinner, Lewis came home, carrying two ptarmigans![1] He called to her from the threshold:

"Just imagine, Lou, a most extraordinary thing happened! A most extraordinary thing!"

"Well, what is it?"

"You'll hardly believe me when I tell you that I bought a brace[2] of ptarmigans, bought them myself at the market for — guess!"

His little wife seemed more annoyed than curious.

"Just think! One crown the two!"

"I have bought ptarmigans at eightpence the brace; but — " she added in a more conciliatory tone, so as not to upset him altogether, "that was in a very cold winter."

"Well, but you must admit that I bought them very cheaply."

Was there anything she would not admit in order to see him happy?

She had ordered boiled groats[3] for dinner,

---

[1] **ptarmigans**: type of game birds.
[2] **brace**: pair.
[3] **groats**: coarsely cracked grain.

as an experiment. But after Lewis had eaten a ptarmigan, he regretted that he could not eat as much of the groats as he would have liked, in order to show her that he was really very fond of groats. He liked groats very much indeed — milk did not agree with him after his attack of ague. He couldn't take milk, but groats he would like to see on his table every evening, every blessed evening of his life, if only she wouldn't be angry with him.

And groats never again appeared on his table.

When they had been married for six weeks, the young wife fell ill. She suffered from headaches and sickness. It could not be anything serious, just a little cold. But this sickness? Had she eaten anything which had disagreed with her? Hadn't all the copper vessels new coatings of tin? He sent for the doctor. The doctor smiled and said it was all right.

"What was all right? Oh! Nonsense! It wasn't possible. How could it have been possible? No, surely, the bedroom paper was to blame. It must contain arsenic. Let us send a piece to the chemist's at once and have it tested."

"Entirely free from arsenic," reported the chemist.

"How strange! No arsenic in the wallpapers?"

The young wife was still ill. He consulted a medical book and whispered a question in her ear. "There now! a hot bath!"

Four weeks later the midwife declared that everything was "as it should be."

"As it should be? Well, of course! Only it was somewhat premature!"

But as it could not be helped, they were delighted. Fancy, a baby! They would be papa and mama! What should they call him? For, of course, it would be a boy. No doubt, it would.

But now she had a serious conversation with her husband! There had been no translating or proofcorrecting since their mar-

riage. And his salary alone was not sufficient.

"Yes, they had given no thought to the morrow. But, dear me, one was young only once! Now, however, there would be a change."

On the following morning the assistant called on an old schoolfriend, a registrar, to ask him to stand security[1] for a loan.

"You see, my dear fellow, when one is about to become a father, one has to consider how to meet increasing expenses."

"Quite so, old man," answered the registrar, "therefore I have been unable to get married. But you are fortunate in having the means."

The assistant hesitated to make his request. How could he have the audacity to ask this poor bachelor to help him to provide the expenses for the coming event? This bachelor, who had not the means to found a family of his own? He could not bring himself to do it.

When he came home to dinner, his wife told him that two gentlemen had called to see him.

What did they look like? Were they young? Did they wear eyeglasses? Then there was no doubt, they were two lieutenants, old friends of his whom he had met at Waxholm.

"No, they couldn't have been lieutenants; they were too old for that."

Then he knew; they were old college friends from Upsala, probably P. who was a lecturer, and O. who was a curate, now. They had come to see how their old pal was shaping as a husband.

"No, they didn't come from Upsala, they came from Stockholm."

The maid was called in and cross-examined. She thought the callers had been shabbily dressed and had carried sticks.

"Sticks! I can't make out what sort of people they can have been. Well, we'll

[1] **stand security:** declare himself ready to pay the money if the borrower fails to do so.

know soon enough, as they said they would call again. But to change the subject, I happened to see a basket of hothouse strawberries at a really ridiculous price; it really is absurd! Just imagine, hothouse strawberries at one and sixpence a basket! And at this time of the year!"

"But, my darling, what is this extravagance to lead to?"

"It'll be all right. I have got an order for a translation this very day."

"But you are in debt, Lewis?"

"Trifles! Mere nothings! It'll be all right when I take up a big loan, presently."

"A loan! But that'll be a new debt!"

"True! But there'll be easy terms! Don't let's talk business now! Aren't these strawberries delicious? What? A glass of sherry with them would be tip-top. Don't you think so? Lina, run round to the stores and fetch a bottle of sherry, the best they have."

After his afternoon nap, his wife insisted on a serious conversation.

"You won't be angry, dear, will you?"

"Angry? I! Good heavens, no! Is it about household expenses?"

"Yes! We owe money at the stores! The butcher is pressing for payment; the man from the livery stables has called for his money; it's most unpleasant."

"Is that all? I shall pay them to the last farthing tomorrow. How dare they worry you about such trifles? They shall be paid tomorrow, but they shall lose a customer. Now, don't let's talk about it any more. Come out for a walk. No carriage! Well, we'll take the car to the Deer Park, it will cheer us up."

They went to the Deer Park. They asked for a private room at the restaurant, and people stared at them and whispered.

"They think we are out on the spree," he laughed. "What fun! What madness!"

But his wife did not like it.

They had a big bill to pay.

"If only we had stayed at home! We might have bought such a lot of things for the money."

Months elapsed. The great event was coming nearer and nearer. A cradle had to be bought, and baby clothes. A number of things were wanted. The young husband was out on business all day long. The price of wheat had risen. Hard times were at hand. He could get no translations, no proofcorrecting. Men had become materialists. They didn't spend money on books, they bought food. What a prosaic[1] period they were living in! Ideals were melting away, one after the other, and ptarmigans were not to be had under two crowns the brace. The livery stables would not provide carriages for nothing for the cab-proprietors had wives and families to support, just as everybody else; at the stores cash had to be paid for goods. Oh! what realists they all were!

The great day had come at last. It was evening. He must run for the midwife. And while his wife suffered all the pangs of childbirth, he had to go down into the hall and pacify the creditors.

At last he held a daughter in his arms. His tears fell on the baby, for now he realized his responsibility, a responsibility which he was unable to shoulder. He made new resolutions. But his nerves were unstrung. He was working at a translation which he seemed unable to finish, for he had to be constantly out on business.

He rushed to his father-in-law, who was staying in town, to bring him the glad news.

"We have a little daughter!"

"Well and good," replied his father-in-law; "can you support a child?"

"Not at present; for heaven's sake, help us, father!"

"I'll tide you over your present difficulties. I can't do more. My means are only sufficient to support my own family."

The patient required chickens, which he bought himself at the market, and wine at

---

[1] **prosaic**: unpoetic, matter-of-fact.

six crowns the bottle. It had to be the very best.

The midwife expected a hundred crowns. "Why should we pay her less than others? Hasn't she just received a check for a hundred crowns from the captain?"

Very soon the young wife was up again. She looked like a girl, as slender as a willow, a little pale, it was true, but the pallor suited her.

The old man called and had a private conversation with his son-in-law.

"No more children, for the present," he said, "or you'll be ruined."

"What language from a father! Aren't we married! Don't we love one another? Aren't we to have a family?"

"Yes, but not until you can provide for them. It's all very fine to love one another, but you mustn't forget that you have responsibilities."

His father-in-law, too, had become a materialist. Oh! what a miserable world it was! A world without ideals!

The home was undermined, but love survived, for love was strong, and the hearts of the young couple were soft. The bailiff,[1] on the contrary, was anything but soft. Distraint[2] was imminent, and bankruptcy threatened. Well, let them distrain then!

The father-in-law arrived with a large traveling coach to fetch his daughter and grandchild. He warned his son-in-law not to show his face at his house until he could pay his debts and make a home for his wife and child. He said nothing to his daughter, but it seemed to him that he was bringing home a girl who had been led astray. It was as if he had lent his innocent child to a casual admirer and now received her back "dishonored." She would have preferred to stay with her husband, but he had no home to offer her.

And so the husband of one year's stand-

The Borrower, *by the nineteenth-century Swedish artist August Jernberg.*

ing was left behind to watch the pillaging of his home, if he could call it his home, for he had paid for nothing. The two men with spectacles carted away the beds and bedclothes; the copper kettles and tin vessels; the dinner set, the chandelier and the candlesticks; everything, everything!

He was left alone in the two empty, wretched rooms! If only *she* had been left to him! But what should she do here, in these empty rooms? No, she was better off where she was! She was being taken care of.

Now the struggle for a livelihood began in bitter earnest. He found work at a daily paper as a proofcorrector. He had to be at the office at midnight; at three in the morning his work was done. He did not lose his

---

[1] **bailiff:** sheriff's assistant.
[2] **Distraint:** seizing property as payment for a debt.

berth,[1] for bankruptcy had been avoided, but he had lost all chance of promotion.

Later on he is permitted to visit wife and child once a week, but he is never allowed to see her alone. He spends Saturday night in a tiny room, close to his father-in-law's bedroom. On Sunday morning he has to return to town, for the paper appears on Monday morning. . . . He says good-by to his wife and child, who are allowed to accompany him as far as the garden gate, he waves his hand to them once more from the furthest hillock, and succumbs to his wretchedness, his misery, his humiliation. And she is no less unhappy.

He has calculated that it will take him twenty years to pay his debts. And then? Even then he cannot maintain a wife and child. And his prospects? He has none! If his father-in-law should die, his wife and child would be thrown on the street; he cannot venture to look forward to the death of their only support.

Oh! How cruel it is of nature to provide food for all her creatures, leaving the children of men alone to starve! Oh! How cruel, how cruel! that life has not ptarmigans and strawberries to give to all men. How cruel! How cruel!

[1] **berth**: position, job.

For Discussion

1. At the end of the story, Lewis, who assumed that nothing but bliss would flow from his marriage, is so deeply in debt that it will take him twenty years to pay off his creditors. In what other unfortunate ways has his life been affected? Whom or what does Lewis blame? There is irony in the closing sentence. Explain.

2. How do you account for the downfall of the marriage described in "Love and Bread"? Given the characters of Lewis and Louisa, could such a fate as the one that befalls them

have been avoided? To answer, you will need to reconsider each step of the way in their downward descent. Which of the two characters is less prudent? Does the story offer any explanation for their lack of prudence?

3. "Love and Bread" is set in Sweden around the turn of the century. For America of the 1970's does the story have any meaning? Is it still possible for young married people to find themselves in the position of Lewis and Louisa at the end of the story? Is it easier now — or more difficult — to live beyond one's means than it seems to have been at the time and in the place the story describes?

For Composition

Emphasis is partly a matter of *proportion*. The point or detail that is written about at greater length will receive more emphasis than the one that is briefly mentioned.

● **Analysis.** What was wrong with the marriage of Lewis and Louisa? In an essay of several paragraphs, examine their marriage to discover what made it fail. Be specific, quoting from the story to support your remarks. Try to develop two or three distinct points. For emphasis the least important point should come first and be treated only briefly, whereas the most important should be dealt with in more detail and at the end.

Words and Allusions

GENERALIZATION OF MEANING. Some words begin with a restricted meaning and gradually acquire a more generalized one. The word *clerk*, for example, once referred to a man who was studying for the priesthood — a man who could read and write. Now, however, the meaning of *clerk* is more general. It can refer to a bookkeeper or to someone who waits on customers in a store.

On page 588 of "Love and Bread" the assistant is described as drawing hieroglyphics on a blotter. According to its roots, what does *hieroglyphics* mean? Has that meaning become generalized? A related word is *hierarchy*. What was its original meaning? How is it used today?

Walking Asleep

FEDERICO GARCÍA LORCA

At the heart of love lies a mystery: what is it that draws two people together, sometimes against all reason? Indeed, a mysterious love pervades the
following Spanish gypsy ballad. The mood is haunting, and the passions are
obviously overwhelming. But what is the story the ballad tells?

Green as I would have you be.
Green wind. Green boughs.
The boat on the sea
And the horse on the mountain.
With shadow around her waist   5
She is dreaming at her railing,
Green flesh, green hair,
Eyes of frozen silver.
Green as I would have you be.
Under the gypsy moon,   10
Things are watching her,
Things she cannot see.

Green as I would have you be.
Great stars of hoar-frost*
Come with the shadowy fish   15
That opens the road of dawn.
The fig-tree rubs the wind
On its abrasive boughs;
The mountain, catamount,*   19
Thrusts out her sharpened thorns.
Who's coming? By what road?
She lingers at her railing,
Green flesh, green hair,
Dreams of the bitter sea.

"Old man, I'd like to change   25
My pony for your house,
My saddle for your mirror,
My dagger for your blanket.
Old man, I come bleeding   29

From Cabra's* mountain passes."

"If I could, my lad,
We might strike a bargain,
But I hardly know who I am,
Nor is my house my own."

"Old man, I'd like to die   35
Decently in my bed
Of steel, if that could be,
Between the linen sheets.
My wound,— or don't you see?—
Reaches from chest to throat."   40

"Three hundred crimson roses
Stain your white shirt red;.
The blood smells and oozes
Around the swathing bands.*
But I hardly know who I am,   45
Nor is my house my own."

"Let me climb at least
To the high railing;
Let me climb, I pray,
To the green railing,   50
The moon's balustrade*
By the sounding water."

Now they both are climbing
To the high railing,
Leaving a bloody trail,   55

Federico García Lorca: pronounced fä·dä·rē′kō gär·thē′ä lōr′kä. 14. **hoar-frost**:
white, frozen dew. 19. **catamount**: type of wildcat. 30. **Cabra**: city in southern
Spain. 44. **swathing bands**: bandages. 51. **balustrade**: fence.

"Walking Asleep," by Federico García Lorca, from *Gypsy Ballads of García Lorca*, translated by Rolfe
Humphries. Copyright © 1954 by Rolfe Humphries. Reprinted by permission of Indiana University Press.

Leaving a trail of tears.
Little tinny lights
Wink across the roof-tops:
A thousand crystal timbrels*
Wound the early dawn.   60

Green as I would have you be.
Green wind. Green boughs.
Both of them are climbing.
The wind leaves in the mouth
A rare and generous savor,*   65
Gall* and mint and basil.*
"Old man! Where is she tell me,
Tell me where she is,
That bitter girl, your daughter?"
"How long she waited for you! 70
How long, how vainly leaning,
Bright face, dark hair,
At this green railing!"

Over the cistern's* face
Sways the gypsy lass.   75
Green flesh, green hair,
Eyes of frozen silver.
An icicle of moonlight
Holds her over the water.
Night becomes familiar,   80
A homely little plaza.
Drunken Civil Guards
Hammer on the door.

Green as I would have you be.
Green wind. Green boughs. 85
The boat on the sea,
And the horse on the mountain.

59. **timbrels**: tambourines. 65. **savor**: particular or distinctive flavor. 66. **gall**: bitter fluid. **basil**: aromatic herb. 74. **cistern**: tank in which rain water is collected for use.

Marc Chagall's Vase of Flowers at Night *evokes the dreamlike quality of this poem.*

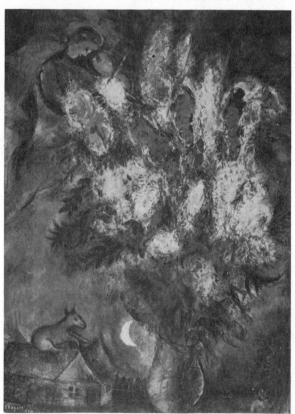

For Discussion

1. This most famous poem by the most famous of modern Spanish poets has been translated by Rolfe Humphries in the version here printed. Its Spanish title — *"Romance sonámbulo"* — means literally "Somnambulist (Sleepwalking) Ballad," and indeed there is about the whole a dreamlike, at times nightmarish, quality. But what happens? Beginning at line 25 a young man speaks to an old man. In what condition does the young man arrive on the scene? Why might he want to trade his pony for the old man's house, his dagger for the old man's blanket? Where do the two men go together? Can the old man help the young man? What does the old man say about his daughter?

2. The opening and closing lines of the poem, uttered by an unknown speaker, provide a commentary on the brief dialogue. The opening lines speak of a girl waiting for someone, and the closing lines describe the girl swaying, or hanging, over the water in the moonlight, with "Drunken Civil Guards" knocking on the door. What has happened to the girl? Whom do the guards wish to arrest?

3. Much of the content of the poem is expressed through imagery. The poem opens with an image of greenness that recurs in later lines. To García Lorca, as to many other poets, green symbolizes the forces of life, youth, birth, rebirth, as opposed, for example, to the moon of line 10 and the moonlight of line 78. What does the moon suggest in this context? Other recurring images are the boat and the horse (lines 3–4). What do those images suggest? Do they suggest that the young man is a smuggler? Can the entire poem be read as the dream of a dying, or dead, man?

4. García Lorca's unusual images seem at first startling, but on reflection, an imaginative reader finds them often astonishingly accurate. A mountain (lines 19–20) is seen as a great cat about to leap, and indeed the thorny mountains of Spain, looming over one as though with claws bared, might accurately be thought of that way. What other metaphors struck you as unusual? Try to justify them. For example, what justification is there for seeing lights at a distance as "tinny" (line 57)?

For Composition

No two readers will agree precisely on what is going on in "Walking Asleep."

1. **Exposition.** In a coherent and unified composition furnish an interpretation that will explain to your own satisfaction the events stated or implied in "Walking Asleep." The explanation should account for such details as the old man's bemusement (lines 33–34, 45–46), the young man's wounds, the Civil Guards' knocks, and the gypsy girl's disappearance.

2. **Analysis.** Emphasis is a matter of proportion, of placement, and of *repetition*. In a unified essay analyze the repetition that occurs in the poem. What, specifically, is repeated? Why? Does the effect of a phrase that is repeated vary as the poem proceeds?

About the Poet. A major Spanish poet and playwright, **Federico García Lorca** (1899–1936) was murdered by fascist soldiers during the Spanish Civil War. His poems and plays celebrate his love for his homeland, where his works are still banned by the Spanish government. García Lorca was formally educated in Madrid and learned music from his famous godfather, the composer Manuel de Falla. He traveled widely throughout the world and was in residence at Columbia University in New York from 1929 to 1930. Inspired by days spent strolling through Harlem, he wrote a collection, *The Poet in New York*, that shows the influence of the blues and other rhythms of black people in America. García Lorca later returned to Spain to write such major plays as *Blood Wedding, Yerma,* and *The House of Bernarda Alba.*

Edward

There are many similarities between "Walking Asleep" and the traditional ballads of English literature. Both create a highly charged and mysterious atmosphere in which much is left unsaid. Both tell stories, frequently through dialogue. And both make use of repetition and refrain, the meaning of which changes as the poem progresses. Here, for comparison, is a famous Scottish ballad of the Middle Ages, about people whose emotions are as strong as those of the Spanish gypsies.

"Why dois your brand* sae drap wi bluid,
     Edward, Edward?
Why dois your brand sae drap wi bluid,
 And why sae sad gang* yee O?"
"O I hae killed my hauke sae guid,   5
     Mither, mither,
O I hae killed my hauke sae guid,
 And I had nae mair bot hee* O."

"Your haukis bluid was nevir sae reid,*
     Edward, Edward, 10
Your haukis bluid was never sae reid,
 My deir son I tell thee O."
"O I hae killed my reid-roan steid,*
     Mither, mither,
O I hae killed my reid-roan steid,   15
 That erst* was sae fair and frie O."

"Your steid was auld, and ye hae gat mair,
     Edward, Edward,
Your steid was auld, and ye hae gat mair;
 Sum other dule* ye drie* O."   20
"O I hae killed my fadir* deir,
     Mither, mither,
O I hae killed my fadir deir,
 Alas, and wae* is mee O!"

"And whatten penance wul ye drie for that, 25
     Edward, Edward?
And whatten penance wul ye drie, for that?
 My deir son, now tell me O."
"Ile set my feit in yonder boat,
     Mither, mither, 30
Ile set my feit in yonder boat,
 And Ile fare ovir the sea O."

"And what wul ye doe wi your towirs and your ha,*
     Edward, Edward?
And what wul ye doe wi your towirs and your ha, 35
 That were sae fair to see O?"
"Ile let thame stand tul they doun fa,*
     Mither, mither,

---

1. **brand**: sword.   4. **gang**: go.   8. **I ... hee**: he was my only one.   9. **reid**: red.
13. **steid**: steed, horse.   16. **erst**: once.   20. **dule**: grief.   **drie**: undergo, suffer.
21. **fadir**: father.   24. **wae**: woe.   33. **ha**: hall, manorhouse.   37. **fa**: fall.

Ile let thame stand tul they doun fa,
    For here nevir mair maun* I bee O."   40

"And what wul ye leive to your bairns* and your wife,
        Edward, Edward?
And what wul ye leive to your bairns and your wife,
    Whan ye gang ovir the sea O?"
"The warldis* room, late them beg thrae* life,   45
        Mither, mither,
The warldis room, late them beg thrae life,
    For thame nevir mair wul I see O."

"And what wul ye leive to your ain* mither deir,
        Edward, Edward?   50
And what wul ye leive to your ain mither deir?
    My deir son, now tell me O."
"The curse of hell frae* me sall* ye beir,
        Mither, mither,
The curse of hell frae me sall ye beir,   55
    Sic counseils* ye gave to me O."

40. **maun**: must. 41. **bairns**: children. 45. **warldis**: world's. **thrae**: through.
49. **ain**: own. 53. **frae**: from. **sall**: shall. 56. **Sic counseils**: such counsel.

This illustration from a thirteenth-century German manuscript shows a knight such as Edward confronting a woman who might be his mother.

For Discussion

1. What "counseils" did the mother give Edward? What does he give her in return?

2. The winds of strong emotion swirl through this poem as they do through García Lorca's gypsy ballad; but in the case of "Edward" the strongest emotion is not love but hate. And the hate seems justified, for Edward's act has destroyed his life. What will become of him? Of his possessions? Of his wife and children?

3. How does Edward first explain the blood on his sword? What is his second explanation for it? How do you account for his delay in admitting whose blood is on the sword? The single word "deir" (line 21) is enormously moving. What does it reveal?

For Composition

Emphasize what is most important by putting it first or last. The rule holds true in a sentence, in a paragraph, or in an entire paper. Of course in a paper if you state your most interesting and significant point first, everything that follows is likely to seem anticlimactic, whereas if you arrange your points in an ascending order of importance, moving from least to most important, the paper will become more interesting as it proceeds. In making a comparison and contrast, for instance, first decide which is more interesting — the similarities or the differences between the two items being compared. Then begin with the less interesting and proceed from there.

● **Comparison and Contrast.** In a well-organized paper compare and contrast "Edward" and "Walking Asleep." You may want to consider such matters as the emotions expressed, the presence or absence of violence, the explicitness of the stories, and — in terms of style and form — the presence or absence of dialogue, repetition, and memorable imagery. In your paper arrange your points in an ascending order of importance.

About the Poet. This version of the anonymous narrative song "Edward" is taken from F. J. Child's collection *The English and Scottish Ballads.* Like many other famous English ballads, "Edward" was composed between 1200 and 1700 and was passed down from singer to singer. First printed in Bishop Thomas Percy's collection of folk ballads, *Reliques of Ancient English Poetry,* "Edward" was later brought by Scottish and English immigrants to the American frontier. A version of this song can still be heard in the mountains of Kentucky and Tennessee.

A Poison Tree

WILLIAM BLAKE

The other side of love is hate, and those two powerful emotions resemble each other in certain surprising ways. At first glance it might seem that love Is creative and that hate is destructive; but love, too, can destroy. And hate can be creative, as William Blake's celebrated parable about a poison tree makes clear.

> I was angry with my friend:
> I told my wrath, my wrath did end.
> I was angry with my foe:
> I told it not, my wrath did grow.
>
> And I water'd it in fears,   5
> Night and morning with my tears;
> And I sunnèd it with smiles,
> And with soft deceitful wiles.*

8. **wiles:** tricks.

And it grew both day and night,
Till it bore an apple bright;   10
And my foe beheld it shine,
And he knew that it was mine,

And into my garden stole
When the night had veil'd the pole:
In the morning, glad, I see   15
My foe outstretch'd beneath the tree.

For Discussion

1. Angered by something his friend has done, the speaker in the poem discusses the matter with the friend — and the anger dies. What happens to the anger he feels for his foe? How does he behave toward his foe while the consequences of his anger are developing? What form do those consequences take in the poem? How does the foe react? Considering the title, interpret what has happened by the final line.

2. According to the poem, repressed hatred — hatred bottled up — creates, but creates in order to destroy. What keeps the hate alive and growing? That is, how is it nourished and watered? What moves the enemy to enter the garden by nightfall — in other words, put himself in the speaker's power?

3. Three lines of this poem are iambic. Which ones? Do you feel the effect of them, when contrasted with the sound of the remaining verses? In what metrical foot are the other lines written? The three exceptions provide an effect of regularity restored — and rather a feeling of relief. Are such effects appropriate, considering the sense of the lines?

4. **Tetrameter, Pentameter, Hexameter.** The number of feet in a line of verse is recorded by means of special terms. If five feet appear in the line (whether the feet are iambic, trochaic, anapestic, or whatever), the line is a *pentameter*. If four occur, the line is a *tetrameter*. If six occur, the line is a *hexameter*. Rarely does English verse have fewer than four feet in a line, and rarely are there more than six feet. How many feet occur in each line of "A Poison Tree"? Is the poem then written in iambic pentameters, in trochaic hex-ameters, in anapestic tetrameters, or what?

For Composition

Blake's poem tells a story in general terms, but only the addition of specific details — names, setting, the particular offense that provoked the anger, and the like — would be needed to expand the poem into a fully developed narrative, with exposition, development, climax, and denouement.

● **Narrative.** From your own experience, your reading, or your imagination, tell a story that will illustrate "A Poison Tree." If your narrative is based on an actual event, you might prefer to fictionalize names. If the experience being described happened to you, you might want to tell of it in the third person. But however you handle the assignment, in the course of it you should demonstrate your understanding of the truth of Blake's insight about the consequences of repressing anger.

About the Poet. **William Blake** (1757–1827) earned his living as an artist and illustrator but has won his greatest fame as a poet. His reputation was largely established by two collections of poems, *Songs of Innocence,* published in 1789, and *Songs of Experience* which appeared five years later. Largely ignored during his lifetime, these two volumes present Blake's diametrically opposed visions of the human soul, divine love and sympathy in *Innocence,* and corruption and evil in *Experience.* In later poems, the poet became more obscure and mystical, so engrossed in the world of the spirit that his patient wife once remarked, "I have little of Mr. Blake's company; he is always in Paradise."

My Last Duchess

ROBERT BROWNING

Handwritten left margin: *sending message - I want my new wife to be like this...

WARNING

The speaker of the following monologue, set in Renaissance Italy, is the Duke of Ferrara, encountered as he is addressing an envoy sent to work out the details of the duke's approaching marriage to a count's daughter. The conference has been briefly interrupted by the duke's desire to show his visitor a portrait of his former wife — "my last duchess." And as the two of them look at the picture together while the duke reminisces, the envoy — and the reader — learn as much about the speaker as about his subject.

Handwritten: Negotiation for $

Handwritten left margin: *900 yr old name
*ruthless

Handwritten vertical left margin: Setting: walking w/ envoy-discussing dowry. Not getting what he wants. hints at murder → bargaining tool

That's my last Duchess painted on the wall,
Looking as if she were alive. I call
That piece a wonder, now: Fra Pandolf's* hands
Worked busily a day, and there she stands.
Will't please you sit and look at her? I said   5
"Fra Pandolf" by <u>design</u>, for never read   *Handwritten:* → on purpose
Strangers like you that pictured countenance,
The depth and passion of its earnest glance,
But to myself they turned (since none puts by   *Handwritten:* only he opens curtain
The curtain I have drawn for you, but I)   10
And seemed as they would ask me, if they durst,
How such a glance came there; so, not the first   *Handwritten:* expression on face
Are you to turn and ask thus. Sir, 'twas not
Her husband's presence only, called that spot
Of joy into the Duchess' cheek: perhaps   15
Fra Pandolf chanced to say, "Her mantle laps
Over my lady's wrist too much," or "Paint
Must never hope to reproduce the faint
Half-flush that dies along her throat"; such stuff
Was courtesy, she thought, and cause enough   20
For calling up that spot of joy. She had
A heart — how shall I say? — too soon made glad,
Too easily impressed; she liked whate'er
She looked on, and her looks went everywhere.
Sir, 'twas all one! My favor at her breast,   *Handwritten:* → necklace   25
The dropping of the daylight in the west,
The bough of cherries some officious fool
Broke in the orchard for her, the white mule
She rode with round the terrace — all and each
Would draw from her alike the approving speech,   30
Or blush, at least. She thanked men — good! but thanked

3. **Fra Pandolf**: Brother Pandolf, the ficticious artist-monk who painted the picture.

Handwritten bottom: *why is he showing the envoy the picture?
*why does he show the 2nd piece of art?

Somehow — I know not how — as if she ranked
My gift of a nine-hundred-years-old name
With anybody's gift. Who'd stoop to blame
This sort of trifling?* Even had you skill   35
In speech — (which I have not) — to make your will
Quite clear to such an one, and say, "Just this
Or that in you disgusts me; here you miss,
Or there exceed the mark" — and if she let
Herself be lessoned so, nor plainly set   40
Her wits to yours, forsooth, and made excuse,
— E'en then would be some stooping; and I choose
Never to stoop. Oh sir, she smiled, no doubt,
Whene'er I passed her; but who passed without
Much the same smile? This grew; I gave commands;   45
Then all smiles stopped together. There she stands
As if alive. Will't please you rise? We'll meet
The company below, then. I repeat,
The Count your master's known munificence*
Is ample warrant that no just pretense*   50
Of mine for dowry will be disallowed;*
Though his fair daughter's self, as I avowed
At starting, is my object. Nay, we'll go
Together down, sir. Notice Neptune, though,
Taming a sea horse, thought a rarity,   55
Which Claus of Innsbruck* cast in bronze for me!

35. **trifling**: playing.   49. **munificence**: generosity.   50. **pretense**: claim.
51. **disallowed**: refused.   56. **Claus of Innsbruck**: fictitious sculptor.

For Discussion

1. Fifty-six lines of verse are all that is needed for us to understand fully the duke, his former wife, and their life together. Lines 2 and 47 suggest that the duchess is dead. What is suggested by "I gave commands; / Then all smiles stopped together" (lines 45–46)? What was it about his last duchess that displeased the duke? Did he make known his displeasure to her? What lines provide the answer?

2. The look on the face in the painting — "The depth and passion of its earnest glance" — is the look a young lady might give her lover. Hence the duke feels it necessary to explain that the painter was a monk (lines 5–6), therefore a celibate, so that there could have been no love affair in progress between painter and subject. What, according to the duke, provoked the intense expression on the duchess' face? What did the duke object to about the duchess' smiles? Is there any evidence that the duchess was guilty of anything?

3. Consider the image of Neptune and the sea horse that ends the poem. How does it relate to the story the duke tells?

4. The poem covers a wide range of tonal effects. At the beginning the tone is cordial and gracious — a host attending to his guest. Where does anger show through the veneer of cordiality? Where does disgust? Where does a tone of icy cruelty show through? What other tones of voice do you hear?

5. "My Last Duchess" is a *dramatic monologue*, dramatic because of the articulated emo-

tional interaction between two characters, a monologue because only one of the characters' voices is heard. Browning wrote a number of famous dramatic monologues, most of them in blank verse. Is "My Last Duchess" in blank verse? Explain.

For Composition

The character of a complex and sophisticated person is revealed in these fifty-six lines of verse — and revealed in all its horror.

● Character Sketch. Compose a character sketch of the Duke of Ferrara, limiting yourself to the five or six most significant traits of his character. Include both positive and negative traits, and arrange them in an ascending order of importance, illustrating each one specifically. Is the duke generous, egocentric, cultivated, well-spoken, imaginative, cruel, possessive, urbane, insensitive, or what?

About the Poet. Born the son of a successful businessman, **Robert Browning** (1812–1889) was well educated in the classics, music, and art. After proving to his father that he was not suited to a business career, he devoted the rest of his life to poetry. Browning was successful in handling many verse forms; however, his chief contribution to English poetry is the dramatic monologue, a vivid composition in which the speaker creates the drama by suggesting a situation in which others are present, characterizing himself in natural but carefully disciplined verse. "My Last Duchess" is a classic example of this form. Others are "Andrea del Sarto," "Fra Lippo Lippi," and "The Bishop Orders His Tomb at Saint Praxed's Church." Browning is remembered, too, for the letters and poems that he exchanged with Elizabeth Barrett Browning during their courtship and marriage. Their moving love story has formed the basis of several plays and novels.

One Intoxicating Evening of Spring Breeze

YÜ TA-FU

A far distance, both in space and time, separates Ferrara's ducal palace of the Renaissance from a Shanghai slum in our own century. Humanity connects them, but is it only in the leisure of the former world that the intensities of love and hate can ripen?

I

For a half year I lived in Shanghai,[1] out of work, and because of this I changed my lodgings three times. At first I lived in a room like a birdcage on Bubbling Well Road, an unguarded prison where the sun never shone. With the exception of a few tailors who were as ferocious as bandits and marauders,[2] the inmates of this unguarded prison were mostly pitiable unknown scholars. That was why I gave the place the title of Yellow Grub-street. After I had stayed in this Grub-street for one month, the rent suddenly went up. Then I, with a few torn books, had to move into a small inn somewhere near the racecourse.

Yü Ta-fu: pronounced yù dä-fü.
[1] Shanghai: seaport city in China.

[2] marauders: those who roam in search of plunder.

Rear view of houses in Shanghai's slums, before World War II.

Here too I met with certain pressures and coercions which forced me to move again. This time I found and moved into a tiny room in the slums opposite Jih-hsin Lane on Dent Road at the north end of the Garden Bridge.

The houses on this side of Dent Road stood no higher than twenty feet. I lived in the loft, which was extremely small and low. If I had stood up and stretched my arms, my two hands would have gone through the dusty gray roof.

From the lane in front of the house I came through the front door to enter first the landlord's room. Then I had to edge my way through heaps of rags, old tins and bottles, and other junk, to walk a few steps, after which I came to a rickety ladder leaning against the wall. By means of this ladder I could get up to the dark opening only two square feet in extent, which led to the upper floor. This floor was really only a small, dark loft, but the landlord had partitioned it into two tiny rooms. The outer room was let to a woman who worked in the N. Cigarette Company; I lived in the room near the trap door. As the other tenant had to go through my room, my monthly rent was a few dimes cheaper.

My landlord was an old man, fifty or so,

with a bent back. There was a dark oily gleam on his greenish-yellow face. His eyes were unequal in size, and his cheekbones were protruding. The lines on his forehead and face were filled with coal dust, which seemed indelible despite his daily morning wash. He got up between eight and nine every morning and in a fit of coughing left the house, shouldering two bamboo baskets. Usually he returned at three or four in the same afternoon, shouldering the same baskets, empty. Occasionally he came back with a load of those rags, broken bottles, and other junk. On these evenings, he would buy himself a few ounces of wine and, sitting on the edge of the bed, would curse roundly in an incomprehensible language.

I met my fellow-lodger in the adjacent room on the afternoon I moved in. At five o'clock, when the spring day was approaching evening, I lighted a candle and began to arrange the books I had brought with me from the inn, making two piles, one large and one small. Then I put two twenty-four-inch picture frames on the top of the large pile. Because all my furniture had been sold, this pile of books and picture frames would serve as a desk during the day and a bed at night. After the picture frames had been placed, I sat down on the small pile of books, facing the desk, which was made of the larger pile of books, and smoked, with my back towards the door. As I smoked and stared at the candle light, suddenly I heard a rustling under the trap door. I looked round but could see only the enlarged projecting shadow of my own head. But my sense of hearing told me plainly that someone was coming up. I stared at the darkness for a few seconds and then saw a pale white round face and the upper body of a slender woman emerge before my eyes. When I had first come to look for a room, the landlord had told me that besides himself there was only a woman worker who lived upstairs. I at once took the room, because, first of all, I liked the low rent and, second, I was glad there were no other women or children in the house. As she came up the ladder, I stood up and nodded.

"Excuse me," I said. "I moved in today. I hope you'll look after me."

She made no answer but opened her big dark eyes and looked at me intensely. Then she went to her door, unlocked it, and went in. Although that was all I saw at my first encounter with her, for some unknown reason I felt that she was a pitiable woman. Her high-bridged nose, her pale round face, and her small slender figure all seemed to give the impression that she was a pitiful soul. However, at that time I had too many worries about my own livelihood to spare much pity on a woman worker who was not out of work. For a few more moments, I sat motionless on the small pile of books, staring at the candlelight.

I had lived in the slums for more than a week. Every day when she went to work at seven in the morning and returned after six in the evening, she could find me sitting dumbly[1] on the pile of books, facing the candle or the oil lamp. Perhaps her curiosity was aroused by my keeping to myself in such a manner, as if I were stupid and dumb. One day when she came up the stairs, I stood up as usual to let her pass. When she came to my side, she suddenly stopped and took a look at me.

"What books are you reading every day?" she asked in a halting, timid voice.

(She spoke a soft Soochow dialect, but my feeling on hearing this voice could not be expressed, and I can only translate her words into ordinary speech.)

When I heard her question, my face flushed. The fact was that, though I had spread out several foreign books before me, as I sat there dumbly day in and day out, my brain was completely confused, and I could not read a single sentence or even a single word. Sometimes I let my imagination fill the empty space between the lines with strange forms and shapes. At other times I only opened the books and took a look at their illustrations, from which I conjured up some fantastic images. Because of

---

[1] **dumbly**: without speaking.

ABOUT THE AUTHOR • Novelist, short-story writer, and literary critic, **Yü Ta-fu** (1896–1945) extended the psychological and moral frontiers of Chinese fiction by stressing human weaknesses in his stories. *Ch'en Lun*, his first publication, enraged moralists who regarded the stories in the volume as decadent and corrupting. Others, however, have found moral sensibility in the hero of his stories, as well as kindness and ultimate decency. Yü Ta-fu, who had read widely in European and Japanese fiction, became a newspaper editor in Singapore in 1938. After the bombing of Pearl Harbor, he fled to Sumatra, living under a different name until he was killed by Japanese gendarmes in 1945.

insomnia and malnutrition, I was actually ill. Moreover, since the padded gown on my back — my only property — was too shabby for words, I could not go out in the daytime, and in my room, without any sunlight, I had to light a candle or the oil lamp all the time, so that my eyes and legs too were withered and shrunken. Under such circumstances, when I heard her question, how could I keep from blushing?

"I'm not reading," I answered vaguely. "But if I just sat here dumbly without doing anything, it would look so silly. That is why I spread out a few books."

When she heard my words, she looked at me closely with a puzzled expression, and then went back to her room.

It would be untrue to say that during these days I had not tried to find a job or that I had not done anything. Now and then, when my brain became a little bit clearer, I had translated a few French and English poems, as well as several German short stories, around four thousand words each. At night, when everybody was asleep, I silently went out to mail them to some new publishers. Since I felt that I had no hope of getting a job, the only thing I could do was to try and make use of my dried-up brains. If luckily my translations met with the approval of the editors and were published, I'd receive a few dollars in payment. Since I had moved to Dent Road, and she had first talked to me, I had already mailed out translations three or four times.

II

Living amidst the turmoil of foreign concessions[1] in Shanghai, one hardly noticed the passing of the days or the changing of the seasons. After I moved to the Dent Road slums, I only felt that my shabby padded gown became heavier and warmer day by day.

"Spring must have grown quite old!" I thought.

[1] concessions: stores, booths.

But I, with my empty purse, could not take a trip anywhere. All I could do was to sit dumbly by the lamp in my dark room day and night. One day — it might have been late afternoon — I was sitting there as usual when my fellow-lodger in the adjacent room suddenly came upstairs, carrying two paper parcels in her hand. When I stood up to let her pass, she put one of the parcels on my desk.

"This is a bit of grape-jam bread; you may keep it and eat it tomorrow," she said. "I've bought some bananas, too. Will you come into my room and eat them with me?"

I held the paper parcel for her while she unlocked the door and invited me into her room. We had been fellow-lodgers for a number of days, and it seemed she had come to trust me as an honest and sincere man. The suspicion and fear on her face the first time she saw me had completely vanished. Entering her room, I noticed that it was not yet dark outside, because in her room there was a window facing the south. Reflecting rays of sunlight projected through the window and revealed that in the tiny room there were a bed made of two planks, a small black lacquered table, a wooden trunk, and a round stool. Though there was no bed curtain, two clean blue cotton quilts were folded on the bed. A small tin case on the table probably held her combs and other toilet things; on the tin case there were a good many spots. Picking up some old pieces of clothing from the round stool and putting them on the bed, she invited me to sit down. I felt a little embarrassed by the warm, hospitable fuss she made for me.

"We are fellow-lodgers," said I. "You need not be so polite to me."

"I'm not," she said. "But you always stand up when I come through to let me pass. I really feel very much obliged."

She opened the parcel as she spoke, offered me a banana, and peeled one for herself. As we ate, sitting on the bed, we began to talk.

"Why do you stay at home all the time instead of going out to get some work?" she asked.

"I wonder that, myself," I answered, "but though I've looked round, I've been unable to find a job."

"Have you any friends?"

"I did have friends, but at a time like this they won't communicate with me."

"Have you ever entered any school?"

"Yes. I've had some years in a foreign school."

"Where is your family? Why don't you go home?"

Her questioning suddenly made me aware of my present condition. Since last year, I had simply been dispirited and listless, every day, and had almost forgotten such questions as "Who am I?" "What kind of environment am I now facing?" or "Am I sad or happy in heart?" Now I recollected all the hardships I had encountered during the past six months. After hearing her question, I could only stare at her dumbly, unable to say a word for some time. Seeing my expression, she thought that I was a homeless wanderer. A look of loneliness was reflected on her face.

"Ah! You're like me!" said she with a slight sigh.

Then she lapsed into silence. I saw that the rims of her eyes were wet and red, so I tried to change the subject.

"What kind of work are you doing in the factory?" I asked.

"Cigarette wrapping."

"How many hours do you work?"

"From seven in the morning till six in the evening, with an hour's break for lunch. We work ten hours a day. We have to do the lot, or they will deduct money from our wages."

"How much will be deducted, then?"

"Nine dollars a month. Three dollars for tens — that is, three cents an hour."

"How much do you pay for food?"

"Four dollars a month."

"According to this computation, if you don't rest an hour, then you're left with five dollars, besides money for food. Is that enough for you to pay rent and buy clothes?"

"Of course it's not enough! And the foreman there is so. . . . Oh, I — I hate that factory very much. Do you smoke?"

"Yes, I smoke."

"I wish you wouldn't! If you must, please don't smoke my factory's cigarettes. I really hate it, everything about it."

I saw her gnash her teeth in anger, and realized that she did not want to talk any more. Then I ate up the banana and looked around. I noticed that her room was getting dark too. I got up, thanked her, and went back to my own room.

Usually, because she was tired after her work, she went to bed as soon as she returned; that night she seemed not to go to sleep until after midnight. After that evening, she always said a few words to me on her return, and I learned all about her.

Her name was Chen Erh-mei,[1] and she was a native of Tungshiang, Soochow, but she had been brought up in one of the villages outside Shanghai. Her father had also worked in the cigarette factory, but he had died last autumn. She and her father had originally shared this same tiny room and had gone together to the factory every day. Now she was all by herself. For the first month or so after her father's death she used to weep in the morning on the way to the factory and in the evening on her return home. She was now only seventeen, and had no brothers or sisters or near kin. The old man downstairs had taken full charge of her father's funeral and burial, for which he had been entrusted with fifteen dollars left by her father before his death.

"The old man downstairs is a good man," she told me. "He has never had any bad intentions towards me, so I have been able to stay here as I did when my father was

[1] **Chen Erh-mei:** pronounced jun ur-mā.

living. One of the foreman in the factory, a man by the name of Li, is very wicked. He knows that my father is dead, and he tries to flirt with me every day."

I knew all about her and her father. However, who was her mother? Was she dead or alive? If alive, where was she now? As to these questions, she never touched upon them when we talked.

III

The weather seemed to have changed. During the past few days, the stuffy, dim, little room — my lone world — had become as close and hot as a damp steam oven. It was so oppressive it made me dizzy, so that I felt like fainting. At the juncture of spring and summer, I usually suffered from a nervous sickness which, particularly in this kind of weather, drove me half crazy. So during these days I usually went out to take a walk at night, when the streets were quiet. Strolling alone, under the narrow strip of deep blue sky, I gazed at the stars, while I entertained boundless, fantastic ideas. This was beneficial to my health. On the intoxicating[1] evenings of spring breeze, when there was nothing to be done, I often roamed until it was nearly dawn before I went back. After these exhausting strolls, I could sleep till noon the next day, sometimes even later, and, in fact, till it was nearly time for Erh-mei to return from work. Because of these hours of good sleep, my physical condition gradually improved. Ordinarily, my stomach could digest not more than a pound of bread, but since I had begun my midnight strolling exercise, my appetite had improved until I found myself eating nearly twice as much. Though financially this was a setback, yet my brain, being thus nourished, seemed to be able to concentrate much better. After these night strolls and before I went to bed, I managed to write a couple of short stories

[1] **intoxicating**: raising the spirits.

in the style of Edgar Allan Poe. Reading them over, I thought they weren't too bad. After making several corrections and recopying them, I mailed them out. Though I entertained a light hope in my mind, yet I thought of my former translations which I had sent out without receiving any news. So after a few days, I forgot them too.

As for my neighbor, Erh-mei, in these days when she went out to work in the morning I was usually sound asleep; only when she returned after work in the afternoon did I occasionally see her. However, for some unknown reason, her attitude towards me had reverted to that of fear and suspicion with which she met me the first time. Sometimes she looked at me intensely, her dark glittering eyes, filled with tears, seeming to scold me and to advise me.

About twenty days or so had passed since I had moved into the slums. One afternoon when I had just lighted the candle and was reading a novel which I had bought at a secondhand bookstore, Erh-mei rushed up the stairs.

"There's a messenger downstairs," she said to me, "who wants you to get a letter with your seal."

When she spoke to me, the expression of suspicion and fear on her face was more evident than ever. She seemed to be saying, "Oh, you have been found out!" I was rather annoyed at this attitude of hers.

"What letter have I?" I said sharply. "It can't be mine."

When she heard my angry reply, she seemed to be triumphant, and a cold smile leaped to her face.

"Go and have a look yourself!" said she. "You alone know your own affairs."

Meanwhile I heard the postman downstairs at the gate calling impatiently, "Registered letter!"

When I got the letter and read it, my heart began to thump. One of my translations of German short stories had been published in a magazine, and in the letter was enclosed a money order for five dollars. My purse was actually getting empty, and the five dollars meant that I need not worry over payment of the rent which was due at the end of the month and would have some money left to buy my food for several days. The need I had for this five dollars was greater than anyone would imagine.

The next afternoon I went to the post office and cashed the money order. After walking on the street a short while under the bright sun, I suddenly felt that my body was dripping with perspiration. Looking at the people around me and then at myself, I unconsciously lowered my head. Trickles of sweat on my head and neck were pouring down drop by drop like heavy rain. When I strolled at midnight, there was no sun, and the chilly spring cool before dawn still lingered over the quiet and silent streets and alleys; therefore the shabby padded gown that was my only wear was not so incompatible with the season. But now it was mid-afternoon on a warm spring day, and I had not had the sense to notice it but had gone striding down the street in the same old attire. When I compared myself with my fellow creatures on the street, who had adapted themselves to the changes of the season, how ashamed I was of my own appearance! At that moment I forgot the rent that was due in a few days and the fast-emptying savings in my purse and went slowly to the clothes store on Cha Road.

As I had not been out in broad daylight for a long time, I now felt for a moment that I had entered paradise when I saw automobiles and rickshaws[1] rushing down the streets with beautifully clothed young men and women in them, and the luxurious and dazzling windows of the silk shops and jewelers', and heard the noisy and confusing human voices like the buzz of beehives, footsteps, and the bells and horns of vehicles. I forgot my own existence and would

[1] **rickshaws:** small, two-wheeled Oriental carriages, drawn by men.

Front view of houses in Shanghai's slums, before World War II.

have liked to sing and dance as merrily as my countrymen. Unconsciously, I began to hum a long-forgotten tune from some Peking opera. But this momentary fantasy of *nirvana*[2] was suddenly shattered by the sharp notes of a bell when I tried to cross the street and turn to Cha Road. I raised my head to look up and saw that a trackless tram was rushing towards me and the fat driver, leaning out, was staring at me angrily.

"You pig! Have no eyes?" he scolded. "If you get killed, let a yellow dog take the blame!"

I dumbly stood there, to see the trackless tram passing away in a cloud of dust and turning towards the north. I did not know why, but I found myself bursting into peals of laughter. All too soon I noticed that

[2] *nirvana:* in Buddhism, the state of perfect blessedness achieved by the extinction of individual existence.

passersby were staring at me in astonishment, and I went off with a very red face towards Cha Road.

I went into a few clothes stores, asked the prices of a couple of lined garments, and offered a price I could afford. All the clerks of these stores behaved as if they had been trained by one master. They all frowned on me and joked with me.

"You're not joking, are you?" said they. "If you can't afford to buy anything, don't bother us."

I went on from store to store until I got to a small store a long way down Fifth Road. Realizing that it was impossible to get a lined garment for what I could afford to pay, I bought an unlined garment of glazed cotton cloth, and changed into it then and there. Carrying my old padded gown wrapped up in a parcel, I walked silently homewards.

"The money won't be enough, anyway, to buy anything, so I might as well use it up," I thought. Meanwhile, I remembered the bread and banana Erh-mei had given me, and without a second thought I went straight to a confectioner's and bought a dollar's worth of chocolate, cakes, and various other eatables. As I stood waiting for the counter hand to wrap it up, I remembered that I hadn't had a bath for more than a month; so I decided to take advantage of the opportunity to have one.

When I had had my bath and returned to Dent Road with my two parcels — the candy and the old gown — the stores on both sides of the street had turned on their lights. There were few people on the street, and a cold evening breeze swept in from the bund. I shivered in the cold air. I went back to my room, lighted the candle and looked towards Erh-mei's door, only to find that she had not yet returned. I was very hungry then but I did not like to open the parcel of candies, because I wanted to wait for her return and share with her. I picked up a book to read, swallowing my saliva all the while. I kept on waiting and waiting, but Erh-mei did not return. Finally my fatigue overcame me, and I dozed off against the books. The sound of Erh-mei's return roused me. I noticed that the candle had burnt down two inches, and I asked her what time it was.

"The ten o'clock siren's just gone."

"Why are you back so late today?"

"They made us do night work because the sales have gone up. Though I get extra pay, I get too tired."

"You could refuse to do overtime, then."

"There aren't enough workers, so I have to work."

When she said this, suddenly a tear trickled down her cheek. I thought she was crying from exhaustion and felt not only a deep sympathy but also a certain thrill at discovering that she was still such a child. I opened the parcel and offered her some candies. While she ate, I tried to comfort her.

"You are not used to night work; that's why you feel so tired," I said. "When you get used to it, it's really nothing."

She sat down silently on the desk made of books and nibbled at a chocolate, but her eyes turned to me several times as if she had something to tell me.

"Is there something in your mind?" I said, to encourage her.

After a short pause, she started to speak falteringly.

"I — I — have been wanting to ask you something for a long time," she said. "These past few days, you've been going out every night. Have you made friends with bad men?"

I was very surprised at her words. She seemed to have suspected me of mixing with thieves and gangsters since I had been going out at night. When she saw that I was struck dumb, she thought that she had actually found out what I had been doing. Then she began to talk to me.

"Do you have to eat such good food and

wear such good clothes?" she said with a gentle voice. "Don't you know what you are doing is very risky? If you were caught, how could you save your face? Let's forget what is past, but I just want you to reform from now on."

I only stared at her with my mouth agape,[1] because her thoughts were so strange and unexpected that I did not know how to explain. She was silent for a few seconds and then went on talking to me.

"Now take your smoking, for instance," she continued. "If you stopped smoking you'd be able to save a few coppers.[2] I've already told you not to smoke, particularly not the cigarettes made in my factory. But you won't listen."

When she said this, again she shed a few tears. I knew that her tears came at the thought of her hated N. factory, but my heart would not let me think that way; I preferred to think that these tears were shed for the sake of admonishing me. I kept on thinking quietly until her nerves calmed down. Then I explained to her the source of the registered letter of yesterday, and told her about how I had cashed the money order to buy things, and finally about my nervousness and why I had to go out for walks at night. When she listened to my explanation, she believed me, and her cheeks suddenly became pink as I finished. With her eyes on the desk, she seemed to be bashful.

"Oh, I was wrong to blame you!" she said. "Please don't mind what I said. I did not have any evil intention. Because your behavior was very strange, I thought of evils. If you really studied hard, wouldn't it be very fine? That thing you just mentioned — whatever it was that you sold for five dollars — if you could do one of those every day, wouldn't it be fine?"

When I saw her simplicity and purity, a certain inconceivable sentiment suddenly swept through my mind. I wanted to stretch out my arms and embrace her, but my reasoning power restrained me from doing this, saying, "You must not commit a sin! You know your present situation! Do you want to kill this pure, simple girl by poison? Devil, devil, you have no right at present to love!"

Full of emotion, I closed my eyes for a few seconds, but under the command of my reasoning power I opened them again. Then the place around me looked brighter, and I smiled gently at her.

"It's getting late," said I. "You had better go to bed! You've got to go to work tomorrow. From today, I promise you, I'll stop smoking."

Listening to me, she stood up and went back to her room in a happy mood.

When she was gone, I lighted another candle and quietly thought over many things:

"The fruits of my labor brought me this five dollars for the first time, but I have already spent three dollars. In addition to the one dollar I had, only two or three dimes will be left after the rent is paid. What shall I do?

"I could pawn my old padded gown, but I am afraid that no pawnshop will take it.

"The girl is really pitiful, but my own situation is even worse than hers. She does not want to work, but she has to do overtime. I want to find work, but I cannot get any.

"Perhaps I could do some manual work. Oh, my two weak wrists could not even bear the weight of a rickshaw.

"Commit suicide! If I had had the courage, I could have done so long ago. However, the fact that I am still thinking of these two words at present shows that I haven't lost all my ambition!

"Ha, ha! What was it the trackless tram-driver said today?

" 'Yellow dog!' Yellow dog is a good term."

---

[1] **agape**: open wide.
[2] **coppers**: pennies.

My mind went over many scattered unconnected thoughts, but I could not think of any good way to get out of my present poverty. A siren from a factory sounded; it must have been midnight. I stood up and changed into my shabby old gown. Then I blew out the candle and went out for my walk.

All the people of the slums were sleeping quietly. Opposite the slums, in the modern buildings of the block of Jih-Hsin Lane, a few homes were still bright with colored lights. The strains of balalaika[1] and snatches of soft melancholy song drifted across the chilly night into my ear. This was probably a young homeless Russian girl, singing for her living. Overhead, grayish-white clouds covered the sky, piling up heavily like decaying corpses. Because of the gaps in the clouds a few stars could be seen, but even the scraps of dark sky around these stars seemed to contain limitless sadness.

[1] **balalaika:** Russian stringed instrument, similar to a guitar.

For Discussion

1. "Do you want to kill this pure, simple girl by poison?" the narrator demands of himself at a crucial moment in the story. "Devil, devil, you have no right at present to love!" Why not? What would be the consequences of his allowing the relationship with Erh-mei to develop?

2. On his nightly walk afterwards, the narrator sees only a few homes brightly lit. And, too, "a few stars could be seen, but even the scraps of dark sky around these stars seemed to contain limitless sadness," even as the slums with all the quietly sleeping people seemed to contain limitless sadness beyond the homes "still bright with colored lights." What is the effect of the imagery contained in the last paragraph? Does it establish a mood of serenity, nostalgia, resurging strength, loneliness, kinship that joins all humanity together, or what?

3. The story opens with images almost as memorable as those with which it closes. Consider the description of the house on Dent Road in which the narrator found a room to live. "From the lane in front of the house I came through the front door to enter first the landlord's room" (page 607). What diction allows you best to see the house and perceive its atmosphere? In the paragraph that follows, how, in general terms, is the landlord pictured? That is, what effect does he create on you? How, specifically, is the effect achieved?

4. The presence of Chen Erh-mei, and the questions she asks the narrator, "suddenly made me aware of my present condition" (page 610). What is that condition? How is it to be accounted for — through laziness, ineptitude, or through some other means? How might the narrator escape from his present condition? Explain your answer.

For Composition

There is at least one similarity between Lewis in "Love and Bread" (page 588) and the narrator of "One Intoxicating Evening of Spring Breeze." Both make a living of sorts from translating foreign literature. Are there other similarities?

1. **Comparison and Contrast.** In a coherent essay comment on similarities and significant differences between Strindberg's story and Yü Ta-fu's. On what terms may the two stories most reasonably be compared? Do both tell of relationships between a man and a woman that are foredoomed?

2. **Argument.** "The situation in 'One Intoxicating Evening of Spring Breeze' is in no way relevant to life in America in this affluent age of ours." Support or refute that assertion by means of specific examples and data. You may need to do a little research to develop the paper authoritatively.

Words and Allusions

DERIVATION. Like the imprudent assistant in "Love and Bread," the central character in this Chinese story does translations. What is the derivation (page 445) of *translate*? How is it related to *dilate, elate, relate*?

Sandro Botticelli (1444/5–1510) *Mars and Venus.* National Gallery, London.

616

Botticelli

Mars and Venus

This painting presents an attitude toward love that is expressed in Bacon's essay "Of Love" (page 585), written a hundred years or so after Botticelli painted. "I know not how," Bacon writes, "but martial men are given to love." In Roman mythology, Mars was the god of war and Venus the goddess of love, and Venus was married to Vulcan, the divine smith, who was lame. Venus and Mars had a secret affair, but Vulcan caught them in a net and exposed them to the laughter of the gods. According to Bacon, "wanton love corrupteth and embaseth" — as we can see in the sleeping Mars who should be ready always for action and war.

Late in the fifteenth century, Botticelli lived and worked in Florence, one of the most beautiful and, then, one of the wealthiest cities of Europe. He and his contemporaries celebrated the splendor of simply being alive and happy, but they also thought deeply about the meaning of life. And in later years Botticelli turned his back on pagan themes and painted only religious pictures. The painting before us reflects his concern with moral questions.

The usual companions of Venus are Amoretti, little loves, such as those seen in Watteau's *A Pilgrimage to Cythera* (page 620). These are the winged, laughing children who symbolize the fruitfulness of love. But here Botticelli does something strange and unusual. Instead of Amoretti he presents little satyr children, half human and half goat, symbols of lust and animality. They are playing with Mars' helmet and spear, and in the lower right-hand corner with his armor. Thus "wanton love corrupteth and embaseth" by bringing the human down to the animal level. Botticelli further emphasizes this debasement by painting the figure of Mars without his usual heavy muscles and powerful frame, by making him appear almost effeminate. In what details of his figure is this quality brought out?

The theme is stressed in an unexpected way in the figure of Venus. Usually in such scenes she is presented as unclothed, but here she is fully dressed. In Botticelli's time the tradition was to paint sacred or divine love as a naked figure to express love's true nature, as in the phrase *naked truth*. Profane, or earthly, love was painted as a clothed figure to symbolize the idea that the world conceals divine truth in false garments, however beautiful. In Christian allegory Mars often represents the power and majesty of God, but here the awake and triumphant Venus has degraded Mars from his divine status.

The strange long narrow shape of this painting on wood suggests the reasons for its creation. It was probably painted for the front of a *cassone*, the great wooden chest in which Florentine brides kept their trousseaus. Why would this painting be appropriate for that purpose?

MORSE PECKHAM

Bronzino

Eleanora of Toledo

Bronzino's painting is related to Browning's "My Last Duchess" (page 604). This particular Duchess (Eleanora was Duchess of Florence), her husband, Cosimo (Duke of Florence and later Grand Duke of Tuscany), and Browning's Duke (Alfonso II, last Duke of Ferrara) were connected in curious and complicated ways. To understand something about them will help in understanding both this painting and Browning's poem.

Cosimo de Medici, a distant relation of the *great* Medici of Florence, intrigued his way into becoming head of state of the Florentine Republic and had himself declared Duke of Florence. Among the royalty of Italy he was regarded as an upstart, and to help gain acceptance, he managed to marry the very wealthy Eleanora of Toledo, the daughter of the Spanish Marquess who ruled the southern half of Italy for the Spanish monarchy. Bronzino's portrait shows Eleanora with her first child — later Francis I of Tuscany — about three years after her marriage.

Eleanora also had a daughter who some years later was married to Alfonso II of Ferrara — Browning's Duke. This daughter was the Duke's first wife, and she died a few years later. She may have been Browning's "Last Duchess," for rumor had it that she had been poisoned by her husband. Of Alfonso's three wives, she is the most likely possibility.

It is relevant to note that Alfonso was bitterly envious of Cosimo, his father-in-law, who had become increasingly powerful, while Alfonso, also an independent ruler, was no longer politically important. He had no political or economic power to justify his magnificent court. Yet his was the oldest and proudest noble family in all of Europe, while Cosimo, growing richer all the time, was not truly a member of the nobility. Does this explain anything about the attitude of Browning's Duke?

Bronzino's task — as was often the task of a painter in his day — was to execute in this portrait a work of propaganda art to support and justify Cosimo's claim to royal status. The portrait is not of Eleanora as a person, but of Eleanora as the Duchess of Florence. It is her role as Duchess that is important here. Does the presence of her child say anything about her fulfillment of that role?

The portrait shows what a great lady of the Italian aristocracy in the sixteenth century ought to look like, and the bearing she ought to have. Bronzino's severe style makes her look like a statue. The metallic-like costume is magnificent but is without warmth. This is what Browning's Duke wanted his wife to be, insisted *his* wife should be. But although she was, probably, Eleanora's daughter, she refused to be or could not be what he wanted.

MORSE PECKHAM

Agnolo Bronzino (1503–1575) *Eleonora of Toledo.* Uffizi Gallery, Florence.

Antoine Watteau (1684–1721) *A Pilgrimage to Cythera.* Louvre, Paris.

Watteau

A Pilgrimage to Cythera

Cythera is a Greek island dedicated to Venus (or Aphrodite), the goddess of love. It is her home and stands for a place in which lovers are completely happy.

Watteau's painting relates to Donne's poem "The Canonization" in that both use religion to express attitudes toward love. The relationship between religion and love is very old, and the same words are often used in both. A religious person "adores" God when he prays, and a lover "adores" his beloved. What other words do you find in the vocabularies of both religion and love?

Donne says that he and his beloved will be "canonized," that is, recognized as "saints of love." Watteau presents his lovers as pilgrims and their voyage as a pilgrimage. That is why the men in his painting are wearing short capes of various colors. These are survivals of the long capes that were worn by medieval pilgrims on their journeys to shrines of saints or to Rome or Jerusalem. Some of the men are carrying long staffs that were also part of the traveling equipment of pilgrims. Flying cupids are the messengers of Venus, and one cupid hangs onto a staff. When a medieval pilgrim took a long journey to the very popular shrine of Saint James at Compostella, in the northwestern corner of Spain, he brought back a seashell as a souvenir and proof of his journey. Thus shells became the badges of pilgrims. Where in Watteau's painting do you find a shell? Why is it placed where it is?

That this is the island of Venus is indicated by the statue of Venus at the right. Strictly speaking it is a *herm*, a tall base which has part of a statue on top. Roses grow round the herm, for roses are the flowers of Venus and thus of love. The roses, the rich vegetation, and the beauty of the landscape suggest that all aspects of love are part of the bountiful productivity of nature.

However, at the lower left we see a dead tree and a dead branch, and above we see rocky cliffs. Why do we have these symbols of death and difficulty in contrast to the warmth and richness in the rest of the painting? A clue may be found if we begin at the far right with the cupid wearing a pilgrim's cape and move to the left across the picture. Each pair of lovers appears less closely related than the preceding pair, and at the left are groups of lovers in conversation. Moreover, the colors change as we move from right to left. The pink of the roses on the herm is repeated in strong, bright colors in the clothes of the lovers closest to the herm. As we move to the left, the colors become darker and less distinct. Is there a suggestion here of a contrast between the warmth and intimacy of love and the lack of these qualities in ordinary social life? Does this explain why the ship is at the extreme left, between the dead tree below and the rocky cliff above?

The tall peaks of the mountains in the background suggest aspiration and self-assertion. How do these qualities relate to the main part of the painting?

MORSE PECKHAM

Albright

That Which I Should Have Done I Did Not Do

The title of this painting is the only direct clue the artist gives us to its meaning. Albright set the door up in his studio in its frame, attached the wreath to the door, and worked at the painting for ten years. It is a picture of decay, and of the arresting of decay.

If we ask who the "I" of the title is, the best answer seems to be that it is a universal "I." This is what everyone says to himself, at one time or other, and the older he gets the more often he is likely to say it. With this admission comes awareness that the past is irrecoverable and unchangeable, and that one's life is in large part a history of opportunities missed and duties neglected. The painting afflicts us with the sense that our failures are forever, and it forces us to remember what we would prefer to forget. Just as Emily, in Faulkner's story "A Rose for Emily" (page 630), forced herself to remember what she had done and confined herself to her own living tomb, Albright's painting suggests that the memory of our failures can destroy our hopes for realizing our dreams.

The first thing to notice is that the door and its frame are richly carved. This is the kind of woodwork to be found only in certain houses built by wealthy people in such a city as Chicago during the latter part of the nineteenth century. It is likely that Albright found the door after the area had become a slum and the house for which it was built had been torn down. Doors have a double function. They are a means of communication and a means of separation. Doors are to go through, to be opened or closed. But here is a door that no one will ever go through again, at least no one who is on the other side of it, as the funeral wreath tells us.

Albright emphasizes the decay in several ways. The panels are all distorted from their proper rectangular shapes, and the sides of the door are bulging outward. The varnish is cracking and peeling. The effect is one of slow but inevitable collapse. The wreath with its cheap ribbon of gauze has begun to wilt and will soon decay. Is there nobody left to remove it?

The major puzzle in the picture is the hand. The lace cuff suggests that it belongs to a woman. Is it holding a handkerchief? But whose hand is it? Has someone come to visit and discovered death? Is someone turning away, the hand lingering in sad regret? Or is it the hand of the dead person we suspect is on the other side of the door? The effect of decay is overwhelming. Does the presence of the hand relieve or lighten it? Or does it make it worse?

The decaying doorway with the wilting wreath can be viewed as a symbol of life itself. This, Albright seems to say, is what human life really is.

MORSE PECKHAM

Ivan Albright (1897–   ) *That Which I Should Have Done I Did Not Do.* Art Institute of Chicago.   623

Varieties of Love

The Chinese story "One Intoxicating Evening of Spring Breeze" (page 606) seems in many ways strange. Its title, the leisurely pace at which it proceeds, and the indecisiveness with which it seems to conclude are all alien to the traditional conventions of western storytelling. But perhaps strangest of all is the central relationship depicted in the story. Does boy love girl? Does girl love boy? What happens between them in the end? Having reached that end, we are apt to come away from the story vaguely dissatisfied, wondering, "Is that all?"

Part of our perplexity arises from our having brought to the story certain expectations about what it should concern, how it should develop, and when it should conclude. Romantic love we recognize at once as a fitting topic for fiction so that as soon as we encounter the characters of a lonely boy and a lonely girl sharing adjacent cubicles in a rooming house, we expect the story not only to concern itself with their relationship, but to proceed in exploring that relationship in one of several well-established ways. After all, isn't it human nature to fall in love, and isn't the chronicle that records that inevitable journey down the unsmooth paths of love timelessly interesting and universally applicable?

The answer — to both parts of the question — is no. Why we, the products of a specific culture, feel as we do about love has to do with an accident of history that has profoundly affected western attitudes toward the relationship between the sexes. On the southern coast of France as relatively recently as the twelfth century, for reasons still not wholly understood, what is called *courtly love* developed. In that one area of southern France there were knights without land who congregated within the castle of their lord and formed a society that developed a culture of its own. Within that special society of feudal lords and ladies, men far outnumbered women. Knights, sworn to allegiance, served their lord and — when he was off in battle or on pilgrimages — his lady. She could command them; they would obey her, and would rival one another for her favor. With plenty of leisure time on their hands, members of that society worked out an intricate system defining the roles of lords and ladies in their relationships with one another. The result was that romantic emotions became idealized in a code of behavior that has been described by C. S. Lewis in *The Allegory of Love:*

> The lover is always abject. Obedience to his lady's lightest wish, however whimsical, and silent acquiescence in her rebukes, however unjust, are the only virtues he dares to claim. There is a service of love closely modeled on the service which a feudal vassal owes to his lord. The lover is the lady's "man."

In time, rules governing the relationship between knight and lady were codified in verse, spread by wandering troubadours all over Europe. And it is those romances, or stories of courtly love, descending through Arthurian legend and Chaucer and Shakespeare, that determined the subject matter and tone of most novels of the nineteenth and twentieth centuries. These were the novels the middle class read and sought to pattern their lives after.

But it has not always been so, even in western culture. Literature written before the twelfth century shows little interest in exploring the relationship between a man and a woman. In medieval epic and legend — in *Beowulf*, for example — the nature of heroism and loyalty receives immeasurably more attention than does the nature of love. And as for ancient Greece and Rome, in neither culture were human relationships viewed through clouds of romance. Far from the notion of Hollywood movies "that romantic love is the only possible basis for a happy and lasting marriage," H. D. F. Kitto reminds us, was the view of the ancient Greek. "He was aware of the force of 'romantic' love," writes Kitto in his study *The Greeks*, but he "generally represented it as a destructive thing."

The Greeks, then, would agree with Francis Bacon about the harmful effects of romantic passion; indeed, the two outstanding classical women who "fall in love" — Phaedra and Dido — are invariably depicted as in the throes of a kind of madness, and their end is prompt and catastrophic. Nor, for that matter, would other cultures, influenced by other traditions or occupied with more urgent problems, find what Bacon has to say in his essay "Of Love" (page 585) unintelligible.

Differences in ideas about love, as about many other things, are no doubt narrowing under such influences as the movies and increased mobility of the world's populations; and it is interesting to speculate on what the long-range effects of that narrowing will be. But meanwhile, stories like "One Intoxicating Evening" exist — stories that depart from our traditional attitudes and preconceptions. If we insist on prejudging such stories, we cannot hope to understand them. If we decide too soon that we know what they are about, assuming complacently that the attitudes of all cultures toward fundamental matters concerning the human condition must be identical to our own, then our comprehension is bound to be superficial.

All of which raises a broader question about the value of reading literature outside the bounds of our own culture. Given our limited vision and the preconceptions our own environment necessarily thrusts upon us, can we ever hope to understand literature that grows out of experiences so vastly different from our own? Perhaps not fully; we might as well admit that. But we can understand a great deal if we make the effort. For the moral here is not to avoid reading foreign literature. As the world grows smaller, mutual understanding becomes increasingly urgent. The moral is simply to read the literature of other cultures with deference and an open mind.

1. In an encyclopedia or other appropriate source, look up *courtly love*, and list other aspects not noted here. What aspects of courtly love do you find in *Don Quixote* (page 56)?

2. What aspects of courtly love are present in society today? What aspects are not present? How do you account for the change?

*[handwritten: Metaphysical Poets – revolutionized romantic poetry – form & imagry / comparison
* archaic language
* inversion]*

The Canonization

JOHN DONNE

Is romantic love to be commended? To all discussion of that question John Donne might well have replied with the outburst that begins the following poem. "The Canonization" is a defense of love that ends finally with the lovers placed in the catalogue of saints, to be venerated and invoked by others through all eternity.

[handwritten: make fun of me for this not ↲]

For God's sake hold your tongue, and let me love;
    Or chide* my palsy, or my gout,*
My five gray hairs, or ruined fortune flout;*
    With wealth your state, your mind with arts improve,
      Take you a course, get you a place, *[handwritten: (job)]*
      Observe his Honor, or his Grace,   5
Or the king's real,* or his stampèd face *[handwritten: (coins)]*
    Contemplate; what you will, approve,
    So you will let me love.

[handwritten right margin: criticize me for something else, & get a life]

[handwritten left margin: rhetorical questions - love doesn't hurt anybody]

Alas, alas, who's injured by my love?   10
    What merchant's ships have my sighs drowned?
Who says my tears have overflowed his ground?
    When did my colds a forward spring remove?* *[handwritten: winter]*
      When did the heats which my veins fill
      Add one more to the plaguy bill?*   15
Soldiers find wars, and lawyers find out still
    Litigious* men, which quarrels move,
    Though she and I do love.

Call us what you will, we are made such by love;
    Call her one, me another fly, *[handwritten: moths]*
We're tapers too, and at our own cost die,*   20 *[handwritten: candles — candles burn themselves]*
    And we in us find th' eagle and the dove.* *[handwritten: strength / peace]*
[handwritten: resurrection] The Phoenix* riddle hath more wit
    By us; we two being one, are it.
So to one neutral thing both sexes fit,
    We die and rise the same, and prove   25
    Mysterious by this love.

[handwritten right margin: die to themselves, become one]

Donne: pronounced dun. **Canonization:** being declared a saint; glorification. 2. **chide:** scold. **palsy, gout:** minor diseases. 3. **flout:** show scorn for. 7. **real** (rā·äl′): coin. **stampèd face:** *i.e.*, on coins. 13. **colds . . . remove:** chills delay an early spring. 15. **plaguy bill:** weekly list of deaths from the plague issued during epidemics. 17. **litigious:** given to carrying on lawsuits. 20–21. **Call . . . die:** we are like flies that burn in a candle's flame; we are also like the candle itself, self-consuming. 22. **eagle, dove:** symbols of constancy and love. 23. **Phoenix:** fabulous bird; only one ever existed at a time; it died, self-consumed in flame, and from its ashes arose a new phoenix.

*[handwritten: * conceit - interesting, clever comparisons]*

We can die by it, if not live by love,
　　And if unfit for tombs and hearse — *famous people*
　　Our *legend* be, it will be fit for verse;　　　　30 — *story*
And if no piece of chronicle* we prove,
　　We'll build in sonnets pretty rooms; — *as much a tribute*
　　As well a well-wrought urn becomes — *as tombs*
The greatest ashes, as half-acre tombs,
　　And by these hymns, all shall approve　　　　35
　　Us canonized for love; — *become saints*

people will recognize

And thus invoke us: "You whom reverend love
　　Made one another's hermitage;*
You, to whom love was peace, that now is rage;　　39
　　Who did the whole world's soul contract, and drove
　　Into the glasses of your eyes
　　(So made such mirrors, and such spies,
That they did all to you epitomize),
Countries, towns, courts: beg from above
　　A pattern of your love!"*　　　　45

people will ask "how did you do it?"

31. **chronicle**: prose history. 38. **hermitage**: secluded retreat. 45. **pattern** . . . love: *i.e.,* a love like that of the speaker and his sweetheart.

For Discussion

1. A poem as compressed and complex as this one requires close and imaginative reading — and rereading. In the first stanza, the speaker asks to be let alone with his love, suggests other things he might be scolded for and things that others might do to improve themselves. What might he be scolded for? What might others do to improve themselves? To whom is the opening stanza addressed? What complaint is it answering?

2. "Who's injured by my love," the speaker asks in the second stanza. Of what injuries does he profess himself to be innocent? How will soldiers and lawyers be affected if "she and I do love"?

3. In the third stanza the speaker characterizes his love in a series of images — insects and tapers consumed in flame, eagle and dove, and the Phoenix. What aspects of love do these images suggest? The fourth stanza considers the social usefulness of love. It may not be appropriate for chronicles — that is, history — but it will be recorded in other forms. What

are the "hymns all shall approve"? And what will be the result of these hymns?

4. "You" in line 37 refers to the sainted lovers, who are asked to beg from heaven "A pattern of your love" for all to follow. The image in lines 40–43 is of two lovers so self-absorbed that they look at no one but each other, and in so doing see the whole world in each others' faces and reflected in each others' eyes.

5. Having considered the meaning of the poem, reread it yet again, preferably aloud, to appreciate qualities of the verse. What meter predominates? The first line is pentameter. Is the second line? Are the concluding lines of each stanza metrically identical? Does each stanza contain the same number of lines? Is the rhyme scheme consistent from stanza to stanza? The poem contains hyperbole. Point out examples.

For Composition

Donne's metaphors are celebrated for their unexpectedness as well as their precision. At line 21 he compares the lovers to tapers. The passions of love are hot as the candle flame; both are self-consuming; both die finally and become cold. Indeed, both tend to last only briefly, yet while they burn, they light up their surroundings.

• **Analysis.** In a thoughtful paper of three or four coherent paragraphs, analyze one of the metaphors that appear in "The Canonization." Your analysis should justify the metaphor by examining similarities between the two objects being compared, for emphasis placing the most interesting similarity last.

About the Poet. **John Donne** (1572–1631) has been both praised and attacked for his highly individual style of writing. Born in London the son of a prosperous merchant, Donne was raised in a Roman Catholic family and failed to receive a degree from Oxford because he re-

fused to recognize the supremacy of the Church of England. He eventually conformed, however, and rose to become a great preacher and the dean of St. Paul's Cathedral. Known during his earlier years as a dandy and a wit, Donne was described by Sir Richard Baker as "not dissolute, but very neat, a great visiter of Ladies, a great frequenter of Playes, a great writer of conceited Verses." Donne studied law and seemed destined for a brilliant diplomatic career before his elopement with Anne More, the niece of his employer, ruined this possibility. Under pressure from King James, Donne was ordained in the church, after which time he wrote little poetry. He never wrote for publication but to please himself and his friends. His poems are direct and personal, and are noted for brilliant images and daring paradoxes.

Sonnet 116

WILLIAM SHAKESPEARE

Undoubtedly the most discussed collection of lyric poetry in the language is that of the sonnets of William Shakespeare. In Sonnet 116 Shakespeare provides a definition of love to which his contemporary Francis Bacon might have objected, but with which John Donne — another great contemporary — would surely have concurred.

> Let me not to the marriage of true minds
> Admit impediments. Love is not love
> Which alters when it alteration finds,
> Or bends with the remover to remove.
> O, no! it is an ever-fixèd mark
> That looks on tempests* and is never shaken;
> It is the star to every wandering bark,*

6. **tempests**: storms. 7. **bark**: sailing ship.

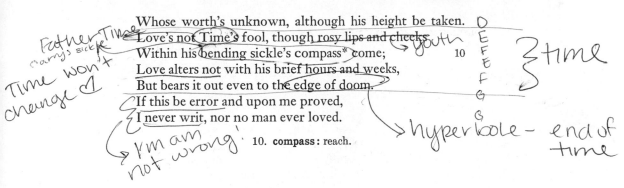

Whose worth's unknown, although his height be taken.
Love's not Time's fool, though rosy lips and cheeks
Within his bending sickle's compass* come;   10
Love alters not with his brief hours and weeks,
But bears it out even to the edge of doom.
If this be error and upon me proved,
I never writ, nor no man ever loved.

Father Time marries sickle
Time won't change it
I am not wrong

youth
time
hyperbole — end of time

10. **compass:** reach.

For Discussion

1. The sonnet suggests several attributes of true love — for example, that it is constant, not altering when situations change. In what different ways is the idea of love's constancy expressed? What similarities are there between true love and the pole star, by which sailors navigate at sea?

2. What other traits of true love does the poem identify?

3. **Petrarchan and Shakespearean Sonnets.** A sonnet is a poem of fourteen lines written in iambic pentameter. Two kinds predominate: the Petrarchan (or Italian) and the Shakespearean (or English). Differences between the two are noticeable in their rhyme scheme. The *Petrarchan* ("Thou Art Indeed Just, Lord," page 174, is an example) tends to have one set of rhymes in the first eight lines, a different set in the last six; and frequently the meaning reinforces the division after the eighth line. That is, the first eight lines may develop a scene or insight that the last six will modify sharply, perhaps by contradiction. What is the rhyme scheme of a *Shakespearean* sonnet? The example here expresses love's constancy in three different ways, then concludes with a comment in the last two lines. Does the rhyme scheme bear that structure out?

For Composition

Paraphrasing can be a useful exercise in clari-fying your understanding of a difficult poem. The ideal paraphrase follows the original closely, substituting synonymous terms to explain difficult diction and rearranging syntax to elucidate meaning.

1. **Paraphrase.** Write a paraphrase of Sonnet 116. Rearrange syntax where appropriate ("If this is a mistake, and *proved against me* . . ."), and write in prose sentences, not lines of verse.

2. **Analysis.** What values of Sonnet 116 are lost in the paraphrase? In a composition containing specific illustration, discuss what a poem conveys beyond its paraphrasable content.

About the Poet. Widely recognized as one of the greatest writers in any language, **William Shakespeare** (1564–1616) was hailed by his contemporary Ben Jonson as "not of an age, but for all time." Although best known for his plays, Shakespeare was also a master of the sonnet form. Of the one hundred and fifty sonnets he wrote, some describe the attractiveness of a young man, whereas others deal with an unknown lady, often called by critics the Dark Lady of the Sonnets. A love triangle involving two men and a woman appears in several sonnets, and others lament the ravages of time while praising the permanence of love and poetry. Whether they reflect events in their author's life or not, they are among the treasures of English verse.

A Rose for Emily

WILLIAM FAULKNER

Extreme love and extreme hate — hate and love raised to a superhuman level — both presuppose extraordinary capacities. We average mortals may not be capable of either, but clearly the one who can love with fever intensity can also hate with an iciness of glacial dimensions. Such a one was Miss Emily Grierson, last of the high and mighty Griersons, who lived and died in William Faulkner's fictional town of Jefferson, in northern Mississippi.

I

When Miss Emily Grierson died, our whole town went to her funeral: the men through a sort of respectful affection for a fallen monument, the women mostly out of curiosity to see the inside of her house, which no one save an old manservant — a combined gardener and cook — had seen in at least ten years.

It was a big, squarish frame house that had once been white, decorated with cupolas[1] and spires and scrolled balconies in the heavily lightsome style of the seventies, set on what had once been our most select street. But garages and cotton gins had encroached and obliterated even the august names of that neighborhood; only Miss Emily's house was left, lifting its stubborn and coquettish decay above the cotton wagons and the gasoline pumps — an eyesore among eyesores. And now Miss Emily had gone to join the representatives of those august names where they lay in the cedar-bemused cemetery among the ranked and anonymous graves of Union and Confederate soldiers who fell at the battle of Jefferson.

Alive, Miss Emily had been a tradition, a duty, and a care; a sort of hereditary obligation upon the town, dating from that day in 1894 when Colonel Sartoris, the mayor — he who fathered the edict that no Negro woman should appear on the streets without an apron — remitted her taxes, the dispensation dating from the death of her father on into perpetuity.[2] Not that Miss Emily would have accepted charity. Colonel Sartoris invented an involved tale to the effect that Miss Emily's father had loaned money to the town, which the town, as a matter of business, preferred this way of repaying. Only a man of Colonel Sartoris' generation and thought could have invented it, and only a woman could have believed it.

When the next generation, with its more modern ideas, became mayors and aldermen, this arrangement created some little dissatisfaction. On the first of the year they mailed her a tax notice. February came, and there was no reply. They wrote her a formal letter, asking her to call at the sheriff's office at her convenience. A week later the mayor wrote her himself, offering to call or to send his car for her, and received in reply a note on paper of an archaic shape, in a thin, flowing calligraphy[3] in faded ink, to the effect that she no longer went out at all. The tax notice was also enclosed, without comment.

[1] cupolas : small domes on a roof.

[2] into perpetuity : lasting forever.
[3] calligraphy : beautiful handwriting.

They called a special meeting of the Board of Aldermen. A deputation waited upon her, knocked at the door through which no visitor had passed since she ceased giving china-painting lessons eight or ten years earlier. They were admitted by the old Negro into a dim hall from which a stairway mounted into still more shadow. It smelled of dust and disuse — a close, dank smell. The Negro led them into the parlor. It was furnished in heavy, leather-covered furniture. When the Negro opened the blinds of one window, they could see that the leather was cracked; and when they sat down, a faint dust rose sluggishly about their thighs, spinning with slow motes in the single sun-ray. On a tarnished gilt easel before the fireplace stood a crayon portrait of Miss Emily's father.

They rose when she entered — a small, fat woman in black, with a thin gold chain descending to her waist and vanishing into her belt, leaning on an ebony cane with a tarnished gold head. Her skeleton was small and spare; perhaps that was why what would have been merely plumpness in another was obesity in her. She looked bloated, like a body long submerged in motionless water, and of that pallid hue. Her eyes, lost in the fatty ridges of her face, looked like two small pieces of coal pressed into a lump of dough as they moved from one face to another while the visitors stated their errand.

She did not ask them to sit. She just stood in the door and listened quietly until the spokesman came to a stumbling halt. Then they could hear the invisible watch ticking at the end of the gold chain.

Her voice was dry and cold. "I have no taxes in Jefferson. Colonel Sartoris explained it to me. Perhaps one of you can gain access to the city records and satisfy yourselves."

"But we have. We are the city authorities, Miss Emily. Didn't you get a notice from the sheriff, signed by him?"

"I received a paper, yes," Miss Emily said.

"Perhaps he considers himself the sheriff. . . . I have no taxes in Jefferson."

"But there is nothing on the books to show that, you see. We must go by the — "

"See Colonel Sartoris. I have no taxes in Jefferson."

"But, Miss Emily — "

"See Colonel Sartoris." (Colonel Sartoris had been dead almost ten years.) "I have no taxes in Jefferson. Tobe!" The Negro appeared. "Show these gentlemen out."

II

So she vanquished them, horse and foot, just as she had vanquished their fathers thirty years before about the smell. That was two years after her father's death and a short time after her sweetheart — the one we believed would marry her — had deserted her. After her father's death she went out very little; after her sweetheart went away, people hardly saw her at all. A few of the ladies had the temerity to call, but were not received, and the only sign of life about the place was the Negro man — a young man then — going in and out with a market basket.

"Just as if a man — any man — could keep a kitchen properly," the ladies said; so they were not surprised when the smell developed. It was another link between the gross, teeming world and the high and mighty Griersons.

A neighbor, a woman, complained to the mayor, Judge Stevens, eighty years old.

"But what will you have me do about it, madam?" he said.

"Why, send her word to stop it," the woman said. "Isn't there a law?"

"I'm sure that won't be necessary," Judge Stevens said. "It's probably just a snake or a rat that nigger of hers killed in the yard. I'll speak to him about it."

The next day he received two more complaints, one from a man who came in diffident deprecation.[1] "We really must do

[1] **deprecation**: protest.

something about it, Judge. I'd be the last one in the world to bother Miss Emily, but we've got to do something." That night the board of Aldermen met — three graybeards and one younger man, a member of the rising generation.

"It's simple enough," he said. "Send her word to have her place cleaned up. Give her a certain time to do it in, and if she don't. . . ."

"Dammit, sir," Judge Stevens said, "will you accuse a lady to her face of smelling bad?"

So the next night, after midnight, four men crossed Miss Emily's lawn and slunk about the house like burglars, sniffing along the base of the brickwork and at the cellar openings while one of them performed a regular sowing motion with his hand out of a sack slung from his shoulder. They broke open the cellar door and sprinkled lime there, and in all the outbuildings. As they recrossed the lawn, a window that had been dark was lighted and Miss Emily sat in it, the light behind her, and her upright torso motionless as that of an idol. They crept quietly across the lawn and into the shadow of the locusts that lined the street. After a

week or two the smell went away.

That was when people had begun to feel really sorry for her. People in our town, remembering how old lady Wyatt, her great-aunt, had gone completely crazy at last, believed that the Griersons held themselves a little too high for what they really were. None of the young men were quite good enough for Miss Emily and such. We had long thought of them as a tableau: Miss Emily a slender figure in white in the background, her father a spraddled[1] silhouette in the foreground, his back to her and clutching a horsewhip, the two of them framed by the back-flung front door. So when she got to be thirty and was still single, we were not pleased exactly, but vindicated; even with insanity in the family she wouldn't have turned down all of her chances if they had really materialized.

When her father died, it got about that the house was all that was left to her; and in a way, people were glad. At last they could pity Miss Emily. Being left alone, and a pauper, she had become humanized. Now she too would know the old thrill and the old despair of a penny more or less.

[1] **spraddled:** with legs spread.

ABOUT THE AUTHOR • **William Faulkner** (1897–1962), the descendant of Southern families prominent before the Civil War, wrote the chronicles of Yoknapatawpha County, a mythical county in Mississippi, based on the Oxford of his boyhood, and created the Sartoris family which closely resembled his own. Most of Faulkner's work deals with the decay of the old planter class in the South after the Civil War, particularly with their conflict of racial pride with the realization that their wealth and power was derived from the enslavement and exploitation of Negroes. Faulkner has been acclaimed for his innovations in fiction, but he once told a college class that he had "never given the subject of form a single thought." "If a story is in you," he said, "it has got to come out." A man with limited formal education who spent most of his life in Oxford, Faulkner made one of his few trips abroad in 1950 when he visited Sweden to accept the Nobel Prize for Literature.

The day after his death all the ladies prepared to call at the house and offer condolence and aid, as is our custom. Miss Emily met them at the door, dressed as usual and with no trace of grief on her face. She told them that her father was not dead. She did that for three days, with the ministers calling on her, and the doctors, trying to persuade her to let them dispose of the body. Just as they were about to resort to law and force, she broke down, and they buried her father quickly.

We did not say she was crazy then. We believed she had to do that. We remembered all the young men her father had driven away, and we knew that with nothing left, she would have to cling to that which had robbed her, as people will.

III

She was sick for a long time. When we saw her again, her hair was cut short, making her look like a girl, with a vague resemblance to those angels in colored church windows — sort of tragic and serene.

The town had just let the contracts for paving the sidewalks, and in the summer after her father's death they began the work. The construction company came with niggers and mules and machinery, and a foreman named Homer Barron, a Yankee — a big, dark, ready man, with a big voice and eyes lighter than his face. The little boys would follow in groups to hear him cuss the niggers, and the niggers singing in time to the rise and fall of picks. Pretty soon he knew everybody in town. Whenever you heard a lot of laughing anywhere about the square, Homer Barron would be in the center of the group. Presently we began to see him and Miss Emily on Sunday afternoons driving in the yellow-wheeled buggy and the matched team of bays from the livery stable.

At first we were glad that Miss Emily would have an interest, because the ladies all said, "Of course a Grierson would not think

seriously of a Northerner, a day laborer." But there were still others, older people, who said that even grief could not cause a real lady to forget *noblesse oblige*[1] — without calling it *noblesse oblige*. They just said, "Poor Emily. Her kinsfolk should come to her." She had some kin in Alabama; but years ago her father had fallen out with them over the estate of old lady Wyatt, the crazy woman, and there was no communication between the two families. They had not even been represented at the funeral.

And as soon as the old people said, "Poor Emily," the whispering began. "Do you suppose it's really so?" they said to one another. "Of course it is. What else could . . . ." This behind their hands; rustling of craned silk and satin behind jalousies[2] closed upon the sun of Sunday afternoon as the thin, swift clop-clop-clop of the matched team passed: "Poor Emily."

She carried her head high enough — even when we believed that she was fallen. It was as if she demanded more than ever the recognition of her dignity as the last Grierson; as if it had wanted that touch of earthiness to reaffirm her imperviousness. Like when she bought the rat poison, the arsenic. That was over a year after they had begun to say "Poor Emily," and while the two female cousins were visiting her.

"I want some poison," she said to the druggist. She was over thirty then, still a slight woman, though thinner than usual, with cold, haughty black eyes in a face the flesh of which was strained across the temples and about the eyesockets as you imagine a lighthouse-keeper's face ought to look. "I want some poison," she said.

"Yes, Miss Emily. What kind? For rats and such? I'd recom — "

"I want the best you have. I don't care what kind."

The druggist named several. "They'll kill

---

[1] *noblesse oblige* (nō′bles′ ō′blēzh′): nobility obligates; *i.e.*, the idea that people of high social position should behave nobly.

[2] **jalousies**: shutters.

My Forebears Were Pioneers, *by the American Philip Evergood, shows the superficial dignity and the impenetrability to change of a woman much like Faulkner's Emily.*

anything up to an elephant. But what you want is — "

"Arsenic," Miss Emily said. "Is that a good one?"

"Is . . . arsenic? Yes, ma'am. But what you want — "

"I want arsenic."

The druggist looked down at her. She looked back at him, erect, her face like a strained flag. "Why, of course," the druggist said. "If that's what you want. But the law requires you to tell what you are going to use it for."

Miss Emily just stared at him, her head tilted back in order to look him eye for eye, until he looked away and went and got the arsenic and wrapped it up. The Negro delivery boy brought her the package; the druggist didn't come back. When she opened the package at home there was written on the box, under the skull and bones: "For rats."

IV

So the next day we all said, "She will kill herself"; and we said it would be the best thing. When she had first begun to be seen with Homer Barron, we had said, "She will marry him." Then we said, "She will persuade him yet," because Homer himself had remarked — he liked men, and it was known that he drank with the younger men in the Elks' Club — that he was not a marrying man. Later we said, "Poor Emily," behind the jalousies as they passed on Sunday afternoon in the glittering buggy, Miss Emily with her head high and Homer Barron with his hat cocked and a cigar in his teeth, reins and whip in a yellow glove.

Then some of the ladies began to say that it was a disgrace to the town and a bad example to the young people. The men did not want to interfere, but at last the ladies forced the Baptist minister — Miss Emily's people were Episcopal — to call upon her. He would never divulge what happened during that interview, but he refused to go back again. The next Sunday they again drove about the streets, and the following day the minister's wife wrote to Miss Emily's relations in Alabama.

So she had blood-kin under her roof again, and we sat back to watch developments. At first nothing happened. Then we were sure that they were to be married. We learned that Miss Emily had been to the jeweler's and ordered a man's toilet set in silver, with the letters H.B. on each piece. Two days later we learned that she had bought a complete outfit of men's clothing, including a nightshirt, and we said, "They are married." We were really glad. We were glad because the two female cousins were even more Grierson than Miss Emily had ever been.

So we were not surprised when Homer Barron — the streets had been finished some time since — was gone. We were a little disappointed that there was not a public blowing-off, but we believed that he had gone on to prepare for Miss Emily's coming, or to give her a chance to get rid of the cousins. (By that time it was a cabal,[1] and we were all Miss Emily's allies to help circumvent the cousins.) Sure enough, after another week they departed. And, as we had expected all along, within three days Homer Barron was back in town. A neighbor saw the Negro man admit him at the kitchen door at dusk one evening.

And that was the last we saw of Homer Barron. And of Miss Emily for some time. The Negro man went in and out with the market basket, but the front door remained closed. Now and then we would see her at a window for a moment, as the men did that night when they sprinkled the lime, but for almost six months she did not appear on the streets. Then we knew that this was to be expected too; as if that quality of her father which had thwarted her woman's life so many times had been too virulent and too furious to die.

When we next saw Miss Emily, she had grown fat and her hair was turning gray. During the next few years it grew grayer and grayer until it attained an even pepper-and-salt iron-gray, when it ceased turning. Up to the day of her death at seventy-four it was still that vigorous iron-gray, like the hair of an active man.

From that time on her front door remained closed, save for a period of six or seven years, when she was about forty, during which she gave lessons in china-painting. She fitted up a studio in one of the downstairs rooms, where the daughters and granddaughters of Colonel Sartoris' contemporaries were sent to her with the same regularity and in the same spirit that they were sent on Sundays with a twenty-five cent piece for the collection plate. Meanwhile her taxes had been remitted.

Then the newer generation became the backbone and the spirit of the town, and the painting pupils grew up and fell away and did not send their children to her with boxes of color and tedious brushes and pictures cut from the ladies' magazines. The front door closed upon the last one and remained closed for good. When the town got free postal delivery Miss Emily alone refused to let them fasten the metal numbers above her door and attach a mailbox to it. She would not listen to them.

Daily, monthly, yearly we watched the Negro grow grayer and more stooped, going in and out with the market basket. Each December we sent her a tax notice, which would be returned by the post office a week later, unclaimed. Now and then we would see her in one of the downstairs windows — she had evidently shut up the top floor of the house — like the carven torso of an idol in a niche, looking or not looking at us, we could never tell which. Thus she passed from generation to generation — dear, inescapable, impervious, tranquil, and perverse.

And so she died. Fell ill in the house filled with dust and shadows, with only a doddering Negro man to wait on her. We did not even know she was sick; we had long since given up trying to get any information from the Negro. He talked to no one, probably not even to her, for his voice had grown harsh and rusty, as if from disuse.

She died in one of the downstairs rooms, in a heavy walnut bed with a curtain, her gray head propped on a pillow yellow and moldy with age and lack of sunlight.

---

[1] **cabal**: small group of persons joined in a secret scheme.

V

The Negro met the first of the ladies at the front door and let them in, with their hushed, sibilant[1] voices and their quick, curious glances, and then he disappeared. He walked right through the house and out the back and was not seen again.

The two female cousins came at once. They held the funeral on the second day, with the town coming to look at Miss Emily beneath a mass of bought flowers, with the crayon face of her father musing profoundly above the bier and the ladies sibilant and macabre; and the very old men — some in their brushed Confederate uniforms — on the porch and the lawn, talking of Miss Emily as if she had been a contemporary of theirs, believing that they had danced with her and courted her perhaps, confusing time with its mathematical progression, as the old do, to whom all the past is not a diminishing road, but, instead, a huge meadow which no winter ever quite touches, divided from them now by the narrow bottleneck of the most recent decade of years.

Already we knew that there was one room in that region above stairs which no one had seen in forty years, and which would have to be forced. They waited until Miss Emily was decently in the ground before they opened it.

The violence of breaking down the door seemed to fill this room with pervading dust. A thin, acrid pall[2] as of the tomb seemed to lie everywhere upon this room decked and furnished as for a bridal: upon the valance curtains of faded rose color, upon the rose-shaded lights, upon the dressing table, upon the delicate array of crystal and the man's toilet things backed with tarnished silver, silver so tarnished that the monogram was obscured. Among them lay a collar and tie, as if they had just been removed, which, lifted, left upon the surface a pale crescent in the dust. Upon a chair hung the suit, carefully folded; beneath it the two mute shoes and the discarded socks.

The man himself lay in the bed.

For a long while we just stood there, looking down at the profound and fleshless grin. The body had apparently once lain in the attitude of an embrace, but now the long sleep that outlasts love, that conquers even the grimace of love, had cuckolded[3] him. What was left of him, rotted beneath what was left of the nightshirt, had become inextricable[4] from the bed in which he lay; and upon him and upon the pillow beside him lay that even coating of the patient and biding dust.

Then we noticed that in the second pillow was the indentation of a head. One of us lifted something from it, and leaning forward, that faint and invisible dust dry and acrid in the nostrils, we saw a long strand of iron-gray hair.

[3] **cuckolded**: betrayed.
[4] **inextricable**: that cannot be disentangled.

[1] **sibilant**: making a hissing sound.
[2] **pall** (pôl): dark, gloomy covering.

For Discussion

1. This story is many things. For one thing it is a horror story, containing mystery and murder. What letters appeared in the monogram on the man's toilet things discovered in Miss Grierson's upstairs room? What happened to Homer Barron? Why?

2. To understand "A Rose for Emily" fully, chronology is important. When did Miss Emily cut her hair? How much time had elapsed after her father's death before she met Homer Barron? When did Homer appear on the scene for the last time? For how long? When did the incidents involving the smell occur? When did Miss Emily's hair turn gray?

3. From whose point of view is the story told? What attitude in his town does the narrator represent? The attitude he feels toward Miss Emily may be inferred from the tone he uses to express himself. Is it a tone of outrage, of disgust, of abhorrence, of pity, of admira-

tion, of awe, or what? Point to specific diction that supports your answer. What is the effect of the title in conveying the narrator's attitude? What are the connotations of *rose*?

4. The horrifying denouement indicates a very sick mind, to be sure, but a mind capable of the most extreme passions — of hatred and of love. Twice before in the story the ending is prepared for. On what two occasions earlier was Miss Grierson unwilling or unable to make a distinction between the dead and the living?

5. This many-sided story is also a symbolic representation of the corruption of older values by the new. As in all of Faulkner's work, the past constantly invades the present and serves as a standard against which the present is measured. Once an impressive home, the Grierson mansion stands now as "an eyesore among eyesores," even as the last of the Griersons — grown obese and senile — hangs on into the third decade of the twentieth century. The new generation among whom she finds herself has "more modern ideas" (page 630). How do those ideas differ from the older ones? What values of an earlier age are implied elsewhere in the story? What attitudes — one cannot call them values — does Homer Barron represent by contrast?

6. "A Rose for Emily" was first published in 1931. Its evocation of setting — a small Mississippi town in the early part of the present century — is observed with a sharp and sympathetic eye and portrayed with an accurate attention to local details and ways of speaking. Accordingly, the word *nigger* appears. Is it applied to Miss Emily's manservant? The term is offensive, but then to refined Southern ears the term Yankee (as opposed to Northerner) is pejorative — that is, degrading. Can you account for Faulkner's use of these terms in this context? Does his use of them adversely affect your appreciation of the story?

For Composition

We come to know people by what they say and do. In the case of Miss Emily Grierson, she says little enough to her neighbors, but by the end of the story, her character is revealed full-length.

1. **Character Sketch.** Compose a character sketch of Miss Emily Grierson, concentrating on the four or five elements in her character that strike you as most significant. Arrange the details in some meaningful order — from most obvious to least obvious, from faults to strengths, from least significant to most significant. And make sure that each detail is supported by specific reference to her behavior as revealed in the story.

2. **Analysis.** Faulkner's writing style is individual and justly famous. Among its characteristics are a plentiful use of adjectives, a balance of short sentences with long ones, a mixing of the abstract and general thought with the concrete image, a generous use of metaphor, and a richness of descriptive detail. Analyze Faulkner's style as revealed in "A Rose for Emily," and illustrate your analysis with citations from the story. You may wish to take a specific paragraph as the basis for your paper, or you may prefer to take characteristics (abundance of adjectives, for one example) and illustrate them from various parts of the story. In the case of the adjectives, are the ones used just and accurate? Are Homer Barron's two shoes at the end of the story more effective and affecting for being "mute"? What is the effect of the adjective "discarded," with "socks," in the same sentence (page 636)? Is the adjective superfluous?

Words and Allusions

WORDS IN CONTEXT (page 131). From their context in the story, find the meanings of the following words: *edict* (page 630), *diffident* (631), *divulge* (634), *virulent* (635), *impervious* (635), *tranquil* (635), *perverse* (635), *macabre* (636), *acrid* (636). Check your findings in a dictionary. Then use each word in a sentence that illustrates its meaning.

DOUBLETS. The word *perpetuity* (page 630) has an interesting relationship with the word *petulant*. They are doublets (page 481) from the Latin *petere*, to seek. Trace the relationship of these words to their present-day meanings. While consulting a dictionary, see whether or not *perpetuate* and *perpetrate* are related.

In Summary

1. As a means of putting the selections in this section in a new perspective, determine how many different kinds of love are represented. In which selections is love between an adult and a younger person (mother and son, for example) depicted? Which deals with love between the individual and all mankind? Which deals with love between man and woman? In the last-named instance, which of the selections seem to depict the most profound relationship between a man and a woman? Defend your answer with reference not only to your choice but to the relevant selections that you rejected.

2. Where love is, hate is often not far away. Which of the selections in the section deal directly with aspects of hate? In some of those selections the cause of the hatred is unspecified. In others, what provokes the hate is clear. Identify the hatred and its source in "A Rose for Emily." In "One Intoxicating Evening of Spring Breeze," why does Chen Erh-mei hate her employer? Why does the Duke of Ferrara hate the memory of his former Duchess? Are the reasons for the hatred identified in "Edward"? In "A Poison Tree"? Which selection seems most graphically to represent the emotion of hate?

3. Love and hate play decisive roles in earlier selections in the anthology. What part do they play in "Mario and the Magician"? In Book IX of *Paradise Lost?* In *Oedipus the King?* In "Counterparts"? In "Haircut"? In what other selections does love or hate figure prominently?

4. Define elegy. What are the characteristics of a ballad? Distinguish between Petrarchan and Shakespearean sonnet forms. How many feet are in a hexameter line? A tetrameter line? A pentameter line? What is hyperbole? Illustrate your answer. In what ways is emphasis most effectively achieved in composition?

5. **Creative Writing.** Faulkner's powers of description are formidable. Consider, for example, the description of Miss Emily Grierson confronting the deputation from the Board of Aldermen (page 631):

They rose when she entered — a small, fat woman in black, with a thin gold chain descending to her waist and vanishing into her belt, leaning on an ebony cane with a tarnished gold head. Her skeleton was small and spare; perhaps that was why what would have been merely plumpness in another was obesity in her. She looked bloated, like a body long submerged in motionless water, and of that pallid hue. Her eyes, lost in the fatty ridges of her face, looked like two small pieces of coal pressed into a lump of dough as they moved from one face to another while the visitors stated their errand.

Earlier (page 37) you developed a description — but not of a person. Now try your hand at describing a person in a way that creates a clear impression on the reader. Faulkner could serve as one model, but there are others in the section — for instance, the landlord at the beginning of "One Intoxicating Evening of Spring Breeze." In every effective description, notice that details are selected to create an effect, and that of the hundreds of possible details that might be mentioned about anyone, most are omitted as either insignificant or irrelevant. Pick a person, then, about whom you feel strongly, preferably someone of a distinctive appearance, and convey your feelings without stating them directly. Rather, evoke them through the details you choose to describe. The description, which may include dialogue and some representation of behavior, need not be long — two or three paragraphs might do. But be willing to revise to sharpen the image, and don't hesitate to replace a descriptive detail if you think of one that would convey the same impression more effectively.

Reader's Choice

Charlotte Brontë, *Jane Eyre*.

A young governess falls in love with her employer, Mr. Rochester, but finds her romance blocked by a secret that lies behind a locked door.

Emily Brontë, *Wuthering Heights*.

A story set in the lonely English moors tells of the passionate attraction between Catherine Earnshaw and the wild, uncouth Heathcliff, a passion that extends beyond the grave and disturbs the lives of those who follow.

Euripides, *Medea*.

When Jason deserts the sorceress Medea for a political marriage with the daughter of King Creon, the passion of Medea turns from love to hate with disastrous consequences for those around her.

Gustave Flaubert, *Madame Bovary*.

A sentimental woman of the French middle class, growing tired of her dull marriage to a country doctor, yearns for romance and falls victim to the reality created by her dreams.

Nathaniel Hawthorne, *The Scarlet Letter*.

Hester Prynne, punished for adultery by the citizens of Salem, watches in silent horror the evil wrought by the hate of her diabolical husband.

Henrik Ibsen, *Hedda Gabler*.

A strong-willed woman, bored with her husband, exerts her power over her former lover, destroying him and eventually herself.

W. Somerset Maugham, *Of Human Bondage*.

An artistically talented medical student falls desperately in love with a waitress who mocks him mercilessly for his weakness.

Arthur Miller, *Death of a Salesman*.

Willy Loman, whose dreams of glory have been destroyed, is forced to look at the real reasons behind his own failure and that of his sons.

Yukio Mishima, *The Sound of Waves*.

In a story of first love in a Japanese fishing village, a boy and girl remain true to themselves and to each other although various forces combine to drive them apart.

Thakazhi Sivasankara Pillai, *Chemmeen*.

Set in a fishing village in India, the love between Karuthamma and Pareekutti endures despite social taboos, religious differences, folk superstitions, and economic necessities.

Jean Racine, *Phèdre*.

Based on *Hippolytus*, by Euripides, this French tragedy tells of Phèdre's passion for her stepson and the destruction wrought by that passion.

William Shakespeare, *Othello*.

Deceived into believing that the wife he loves has betrayed him, a black general of the Venetian army destroys his wife and himself to retrieve his honor.

Leo Tolstoy, *Anna Karenina*.

A beautiful young woman forsakes her husband and son for a handsome officer who eventually abandons her to neglect and scorn.

Edith Wharton, *Ethan Frome*.

Chained by circumstances to his unlovely and unloved wife, Zeena, Ethan tries to escape through his love for Mattie, but succeeds only in tightening his chains.

Nobody Knows Himself, *one of a series
of etchings by the Spanish artist Goya.*

The Question of Identity

Who are you?" What a simple-minded question that seems to be! How easy to answer! But perhaps the answer is harder to come by than one might think.

To begin with, you can point to yourself — that is, to your body. "This is who I am." But that is only a beginning, for, though everyone has a body, no one is just a body. One looks at an unknown corpse and says, "Who *were* you?"

You can give your name. "I am Eva Carducci." But there are probably several Eva Carduccis in the world. Even if you are the only one, you may think your name is merely attached to you like a label. Suppose you marry Adolf Stein. Is Eva, or Mrs. Adolf Stein, the same as Eva Carducci? Not quite the same. But did the change of name change the person's identity? Common sense says, "Of course not." But we are not just creatures of common sense; we also feel as though we believed that words have magical power. For example, many names come from words which originally meant something favorable, as though what the name means might become part of the person who is given the name. "Eva" means "life-giving" and "Adolf" means "noble wolf." Names are also used (or not used) because of famous people or characters, as though something of their quality might carry over in the name. "Eva" became popular in America in the second half of the nineteenth century because of the heroine of an enormously popular novel, *Uncle Tom's Cabin*. After Hitler, it is not likely that many Israeli boys will ever be named "Adolf."

Who you are depends greatly on the way other people treat you. As James Baldwin (page 662) has said so eloquently, the identity of a black American is profoundly modified by the attitudes of white Americans, who are the majority and who have most of the political and economic power in our society. These attitudes are embodied in our language: Negro, nigger, nigra, black, Afro-American, Afro. Who you are depends in good part on who society says you are.

"I am Eva Carducci, twenty-nine years old, single, white, Democrat, Catholic. I am a file clerk at B & S Sheet Metal Co., my social security number is 565-03-3029, and I live at 6329 Piedmont Ave." This sounds like a pretty thorough identification. But Auden's "The Unknown Citizen" (page 675) was identified in this same way, yet remained, according to the poet, unknown. In the twentieth century, there are a great many "unknown citizens."

Just as we wonder what is really there in all the facts and figures by which society identifies a person, so we wonder what is really in his body that makes him himself. Sometimes we meet people who seem to lack this mysterious inner identity, such as idiots, those whom old age has deprived of their faculties, or the abjectly insane. We say that they are "not all there." Something essential is missing.

Suppose a catastrophe hits a man, even a prince. He may be so shaken, as Hamlet (page 726) was, that he is no longer sure what is what. Usually, when Hamlet is behaving madly with others, we the audience know he is putting it on; but sometimes in his torment of doubt (why does *he* see his father's ghost, but *his mother* not see it?), we are not sure just how sane he is and we suspect he is not sure either. He asks himself who he is. Sometimes he is convinced he is the righteous avenger of his father's murder. But, because of the doubtful evidence, he is not absolutely sure that that is what he is. If he is not an avenger, he is a murderer, and he seems to be a mere murderer when he kills Polonius. Is he a coward when he refuses to kill Claudius at prayer? Yet Hamlet acts like a brave man against Laertes in the end. Tormented by such uncertainties as to his identity, Hamlet is "beside himself," "out of his mind," "no longer himself."

In the fluid, changing, troubled world we twentieth century Americans live in, no one can be as sure of his identity as people used to be in stabler traditional societies. *Hamlet* is the most modern of Shakespeare's plays.

George P. Elliott

Paul's Case

WILLA CATHER

Everyone knows of cases like Paul's. Although Willa Cather's story that follows first appeared in 1905, it remains as timely as the most recent high-school faculty meeting, during which yet another problem-student's seemingly inexplicable behavior was just yesterday discussed.

It was Paul's afternoon to appear before the faculty of the Pittsburgh High School to account for his various misdemeanors. He had been suspended a week ago, and his father had called at the Principal's office and confessed his perplexity about his son. Paul entered the faculty room suave and smiling. His clothes were a trifle outgrown, and the tan velvet on the collar of his open overcoat was frayed and worn; but for all that there was something of the dandy about him, and he wore an opal pin in his neatly knotted black four-in-hand,[1] and a red carnation in his buttonhole. This latter adornment the faculty somehow felt was not properly significant of the contrite spirit befitting a boy under the ban of suspension.

Paul was tall for his age and very thin, with high, cramped shoulders and a narrow chest. His eyes were remarkable for a certain hysterical brilliancy, and he continually used them in a conscious, theatrical sort of way, peculiarly offensive in a boy. The pupils were abnormally large, as though he were addicted to belladonna, but there was a glassy glitter about them which that drug does not produce.

When questioned by the Principal as to why he was there, Paul stated, politely enough, that he wanted to come back to school. This was a lie, but Paul was quite accustomed to lying; found it, indeed, indispensable for overcoming friction. His teachers were asked to state their respective charges against him, which they did with such a rancor and aggrievedness as evinced that this was not a usual case. Disorder and impertinence were among the offenses named, yet each of his instructors felt that it was scarcely possible to put into words the real cause of the trouble, which lay in a sort of hysterically defiant manner of the boy's; in the contempt which they all knew he felt for them, and which he seemingly made not the least effort to conceal. Once, when he had been making a synopsis of a paragraph at the blackboard, his English teacher had stepped to his side and attempted to guide his hand. Paul had started back with a shudder and thrust his hands violently behind him. The astonished woman could scarcely have been more hurt and embarrassed had he struck at her. The insult was so involuntary and definitely personal as to be unforgettable. In one way and another, he had made all his teachers, men and women alike, conscious of the same feeling of physical aversion. In one class he habitually sat with his hand shading his eyes; in another he always looked out of the window during the recitation; in another he made a running commentary on the lecture, with humorous intent.

His teachers felt this afternoon that his whole attitude was symbolized by his shrug

[1] four-in-hand: necktie.

"Paul's Case," reprinted from *Youth and the Bright Medusa* by Willa Cather, courtesy of Alfred A. Knopf, Inc.

and his flippantly red carnation flower, and they fell upon him without mercy, his English teacher leading the pack. He stood through it smiling, his pale lips parted over his white teeth. (His lips were continually twitching, and he had a habit of raising his eyebrows that was contemptuous and irritating to the last degree.) Older boys than Paul had broken down and shed tears under that ordeal, but this set smile did not once desert him, and his only sign of discomfort was the nervous trembling of the fingers that toyed with the buttons of his overcoat, and an occasional jerking of the other hand which held his hat. Paul was always smiling, always glancing about him, seeming to feel that people might be watching him and trying to detect something. This conscious expression, since it was as far as possible from boyish mirthfulness, was usually attributed to insolence or "smartness."

As the inquisition proceeded, one of his instructors repeated an impertinent remark of the boy's, and the Principal asked him whether he thought that a courteous speech to make to a woman. Paul shrugged his shoulders slightly and his eyebrows twitched.

"I don't know," he replied. "I didn't mean to be polite or impolite, either. I guess it's a sort of way I have, of saying things regardless."

The Principal asked him whether he didn't think that a way it would be well to get rid of. Paul grinned and said he guessed so. When he was told that he could go, he bowed gracefully and went out. His bow was like a repetition of the scandalous red carnation.

His teachers were in despair, and his drawing master voiced the feeling of them all when he declared there was something about the boy which none of them understood. He added: "I don't really believe that smile of his comes altogether from insolence; there's something sort of haunted about it. The boy is not strong, for one thing. There is something wrong about the fellow."

The drawing master had come to realize that, in looking at Paul, one saw only his white teeth and the forced animation of his eyes. One warm afternoon the boy had gone to sleep at his drawing board, and his master had noted with amazement what a white, blue-veined face it was; drawn and wrinkled like an old man's about the eyes, the lips twitching even in his sleep.

His teachers left the building dissatisfied and unhappy; humiliated to have felt so vindictive toward a mere boy, to have uttered

ABOUT THE AUTHOR · Though born in Virginia, **Willa Cather** (1876–1947) grew up on a ranch in Nebraska, and later attended the state university there. After college she worked as a newspaper correspondent in Pittsburgh before turning briefly to high-school teaching, where she encountered the experience that inspired "Paul's Case." Miss Cather's poetry and short stories brought her public attention and the invitation to become managing editor of McClure's Magazine. With the publication of O Pioneers! in 1913, she devoted her life to traveling and writing. Most of the novels and short stories that followed reflect her love of the prairie and of the Southwest.

this feeling in cutting terms, and to have set each other on, as it were, in the gruesome game of intemperate reproach. One of them remembered having seen a miserable street cat set at bay by a ring of tormentors.

As for Paul, he ran down the hill whistling the Soldiers' Chorus from *Faust*,[1] looking wildly behind him now and then to see whether some of his teachers were not there to witness his lightheartedness. As it was now late in the afternoon and Paul was on duty that evening as usher at Carnegie Hall, he decided that he would not go home to supper.

When he reached the concert hall the doors were not yet open. It was chilly outside, and he decided to go up into the picture gallery — always deserted at this hour — where there were some of Raffelli's[2] gay studies of Paris streets and an airy blue Venetian scene or two that always exhilarated him. He was delighted to find no one in the gallery but the old guard, who sat in the corner, a newspaper on his knee, a black patch over one eye and the other closed. Paul possessed himself of the place and walked confidently up and down, whistling under his breath. After a while he sat down before a blue Rico[3] and lost himself. When he bethought him to look at his watch, it was after seven o'clock, and he rose with a start and ran downstairs, making a face at Augustus Caesar, peering out from the cast room,[4] and an evil gesture at the Venus of Milo as he passed her on the stairway.

When Paul reached the ushers' dressing room, half a dozen boys were there already, and he began excitedly to tumble into his uniform. It was one of the few that at all approached fitting, and Paul thought it very becoming — though he knew the tight, straight coat accentuated his narrow chest,

about which he was exceedingly sensitive. He was always excited while he dressed, twanging all over to the tuning of the strings and the preliminary flourishes of the horns in the music room; but tonight he seemed quite beside himself, and he teased and plagued the boys until, telling him that he was crazy, they put him down on the floor and sat on him.

Somewhat calmed by his suppression, Paul dashed out to the front of the house to seat the early comers. He was a model usher. Gracious and smiling he ran up and down the aisles. Nothing was too much trouble for him; he carried messages and brought programs as though it were his greatest pleasure in life, and all the people in his section thought him a charming boy, feeling that he remembered and admired them. As the house filled, he grew more and more vivacious and animated, and the color came to his cheeks and lips. It was very much as though this were a great reception and Paul were the host. Just as the musicians came out to take their places, his English teacher arrived with checks for the seats which a prominent manufacturer had taken for the season. She betrayed some embarrassment when she handed Paul the tickets, and a *hauteur*[5] which subsequently made her feel very foolish. Paul was startled for a moment, and had the feeling of wanting to put her out; what business had she here among all these fine people and gay colors? He looked her over and decided that she was not appropriately dressed and must be a fool to sit downstairs in such togs.[6] The tickets had probably been sent her out of kindness, he reflected, as he put down a seat for her, and she had about as much right to sit there as he had.

When the symphony began, Paul sank into one of the rear seats with a long sigh of relief, and lost himself as he had done before the Rico. It was not that symphonies,

[1] *Faust*: famous opera by Gounod.
[2] **Raffelli**: early twentieth-century French painter.
[3] **Rico**: nineteenth-century Spanish painter.
[4] **cast room**: dressing room for the members of the company.

[5] *hauteur* (hō·tür'): haughtiness, disdainful pride.
[6] **togs**: clothes.

as such, meant anything in particular to Paul, but the first sigh of the instruments seemed to free some hilarious spirit within him; something that struggled there like the Genius[1] in the bottle found by the Arab fisherman. He felt a sudden zest of life; the lights danced before his eyes and the concert hall blazed into unimaginable splendor. When the soprano soloist came on, Paul forgot even the nastiness of his teacher's being there, and gave himself up to the peculiar intoxication such personages always had for him. The soloist chanced to be a German woman, by no means in her first youth, and the mother of many children; but she wore a satin gown and a tiara,[2] and she had that indefinable air of achievement, that world-shine upon her, which always blinded Paul to any possible defects.

After a concert was over, Paul was often irritable and wretched until he got to sleep — and tonight he was even more than usually restless. He had the feeling of not being able to let down; of its being impossible to give up this delicious excitement which was the only thing that could be called living at all. During the last number he withdrew and, after hastily changing his clothes in the dressing room, slipped out to the side door where the singer's carriage stood. Here he began pacing rapidly up and down the walk, waiting to see her come out.

Over yonder the Schenley, in its vacant stretch, loomed big and square through the fine rain, the windows of its twelve stories glowing like those of a lighted cardboard house under a Christmas tree. All the actors and singers of any importance stayed there when they were in the city, and a number of the big manufacturers of the place lived there in the winter. Paul had often hung about the hotel, watching the people go in and out, longing to enter and leave schoolmasters and dull care behind him for ever.

At last the singer came out, accompanied by the conductor, who helped her into her carriage and closed the door with a cordial *auf wiedersehen*,[3] — which set Paul to wondering whether she were not an old sweetheart of his. Paul followed the carriage over

[1] **Genius**: genie.

[2] **tiara**: crownlike headdress of jewels.

[3] *auf wiedersehen* (ouf vē'dėr·zā'ən): German expression for "until we meet again"; farewell.

to the hotel, walking so rapidly as not to be far from the entrance when the singer alighted and disappeared behind the swinging glass doors which were opened by a Negro in a tall hat and a long coat. In the moment that the door was ajar, it seemed to Paul that he, too, entered. He seemed to feel himself go after her up the steps, into the warm, lighted building, into an exotic, a tropical world of shiny, glistening surfaces and basking ease. He reflected upon the mysterious dishes that were brought into the dining room, the green bottles in buckets of ice, as he had seen them in the supper party pictures of the Sunday supplement. A quick gust of wind brought the rain down with sudden vehemence, and Paul was startled to find that he was still outside in the slush of the gravel driveway; that his boots were letting in the water and his scanty overcoat was clinging wet about him; that the lights in front of the concert hall were out, and that the rain was driving in sheets between him and the orange glow of the windows above him. There it was, what he wanted — tangibly before him, like the fairy world of a Christmas pantomime; as the rain beat in his face, Paul wondered whether he were destined always to shiver in the black night outside, looking up at it.

He turned and walked reluctantly toward the car tracks. The end had to come sometime; his father in his nightclothes at the top of the stairs, explanations that did not explain, hastily improvised fictions that were forever tripping him up, his upstairs room and its horrible yellow wallpaper, the creaking bureau with the greasy plush collar box, and over his painted wooden bed the pictures of George Washington and John Calvin, and the framed motto, "Feed my Lambs," which had been worked in red worsted by his mother, whom Paul could not remember.

Half an hour later, Paul alighted from the Negley Avenue car and went slowly down one of the side streets off the main thoroughfare. It was a highly respectable street, where all the houses were exactly alike, and where business men of moderate means begot and reared large families of children, all of whom went to Sabbath school and learned the shorter catechism, and were interested in arithmetic; all of whom were as exactly alike as their homes, and of a piece with the monotony in which they lived. Paul never went up Cordelia Street without a shudder of loathing. His home was next the house of the Cumberland minister. He approached it tonight with the nerveless sense of defeat, the hopeless feeling of sinking back forever into ugliness and commonness that he had always had when he came home. The moment he turned into Cordelia Street he felt the waters close above his head. After each of these orgies of living, he experienced all the physical depression which follows a debauch;[1] the loathing of respectable beds, of common food, of a house permeated by kitchen odors; a shuddering repulsion for the flavorless, colorless mass of everyday existence; a morbid desire for cool things and soft lights and fresh flowers.

The nearer he approached the house, the more absolutely unequal Paul felt to the sight of it all; his ugly sleeping chamber; the cold bathroom with the grimy zinc tub, the cracked mirror, the dripping spiggots; his father, at the top of the stairs, his hairy legs sticking out from his nightshirt, his feet thrust into carpet slippers. He was so much later than usual that there would certainly be inquiries and reproaches. Paul stopped short before the door. He felt that he could not be accosted by his father tonight; that he could not toss again on that miserable bed. He would not go in. He would tell his father that he had no carfare, and it was raining so hard he had gone home with one of the boys and stayed all night.

[1] **debauch:** corrupt, dissipated behavior.

Meanwhile, he was wet and cold. He went around to the back of the house and tried one of the basement windows, found it open, raised it cautiously, and scrambled down the cellar wall to the floor. There he stood, holding his breath, terrified by the noise he had made; but the floor above him was silent, and there was no creak on the stairs. He found a soap box, and carried it over to the soft ring of light that streamed from the furnace door, and sat down. He was horribly afraid of rats, so he did not try to sleep, but sat looking distrustfully at the dark, still terrified lest he might have awakened his father. In such reactions, after one of the experiences which made days and nights out of the dreary blanks of the calendar, when his senses were deadened, Paul's head was always singularly clear. Suppose his father had heard him getting in at the window and had come down and shot him for a burglar? Then, again, suppose his father had come down, pistol in hand, and he had cried out in time to save himself, and his father had been horrified to think how nearly he had killed him? Then, again, suppose a day should come when his father would remember that night, and wish there had been no warning cry to stay his hand? With this last supposition Paul entertained himself until daybreak.

The following Sunday was fine; the sodden November chill was broken by the last flash of autumnal summer. In the morning Paul had to go to church and Sabbath school, as always. On seasonable Sunday afternoons the burghers of Cordelia Street usually sat out on their front "stoops," and talked to their neighbors on the next stoop, or called to those across the street in neighborly fashion. The men sat placidly on gay cushions placed upon the steps that led down to the sidewalk, while the women, in their Sunday "waists,"[1] sat in rockers on the cramped porches, pretending to be greatly

[1] **waists**: blouses.

at their ease. The children played in the streets; there were so many of them that the place resembled the recreation grounds of a kindergarten. The men on the steps — all in their shirt sleeves, their vests unbuttoned — sat with their legs well apart, their stomachs comfortably protruding, and talked of the prices of things, or told anecdotes of the sagacity of their various chiefs and overlords. They occasionally looked over the multitude of squabbling children, listened affectionately to their high-pitched, nasal voices, smiling to see their own proclivities reproduced in their offspring, and interspersed their legends of the iron kings with remarks about their sons' progress at school, their grades in arithmetic, and the amounts they had saved in their toy banks.

On this last Sunday of November, Paul sat all the afternoon on the lowest step of his "stoop," staring into the street, while his sisters, in their rockers, were talking to the minister's daughters next door about how many shirtwaists they had made in the last week, and how many waffles someone had eaten at the last church supper. When the weather was warm, and his father was in a particularly jovial frame of mind, the girls made lemonade, which was always brought out in a red glass pitcher, ornamented with forget-me-nots in blue enamel. This the girls thought very fine, and the neighbors joked about the suspicious color of the pitcher .

Today Paul's father, on the top step, was talking to a young man who shifted a restless baby from knee to knee. He happened to be the young man who was daily held up to Paul as a model, and after whom it was his father's dearest hope that he would pattern. This young man was of a ruddy complexion, with a compressed red mouth, and faded, nearsighted eyes, over which he wore thick spectacles, with gold bows that curved about his ears. He was clerk to one of the magnates of a great steel corporation, and was looked upon in Cordelia Street as a young man with a future. There was a story that, some five years ago — he was now barely twenty-six — he had been a trifle "dissipated," but in order to curb his appetites and save the loss of time and strength that a sowing of wild oats might have entailed, he had taken his chief's advice, oft reiterated to his employees, and at twenty-one had married the first woman whom he could persuade to share his fortunes. She happened to be an angular schoolmistress, much older than he, who also wore thick glasses, and who had now borne him four children, all nearsighted, like herself.

The young man was relating how his chief, now cruising in the Mediterranean, kept in touch with all the details of the business, arranging his office hours on his yacht just as though he were at home, and "knocking off work enough to keep two stenographers busy." His father told, in turn, the plan his corporation was considering, of putting in an electric railway plant at Cairo. Paul snapped his teeth; he had an awful apprehension that they might spoil it all before he got there. Yet he rather liked to hear these legends of the iron kings, that were told and retold on Sundays and holidays; these stories of palaces in Venice, yachts on the Mediterranean, and high play at Monte Carlo appealed to his fancy, and he was interested in the triumphs of cash boys[1] who had become famous, though he had no mind for the cash-boy stage.

After supper was over, and he had helped to dry the dishes, Paul nervously asked his father whether he could go to George's to get some help in his geometry, and still more nervously asked for carfare. This latter request he had to repeat, as his father, on principle, did not like to hear requests for money, whether much or little. He asked Paul whether he could not go to some boy who lived nearer, and told him that he

[1] **cash boys:** messengers who carry customers' money.

ought not to leave his schoolwork until Sunday; but he gave him the dime. He was not a poor man, but he had a worthy ambition to come up in the world. His only reason for allowing Paul to usher was that he thought a boy ought to be earning a little.

Paul bounded upstairs, scrubbed the greasy odor of the dishwater from his hands with the ill-smelling soap he hated, and then shook over his fingers a few drops of violet water from the bottle he kept hidden in his drawer. He left the house with his geometry conspicuously under his arm, and the moment he got out of Cordelia Street and boarded a downtown car, he shook off the lethargy of two deadening days, and began to live again.

The leading juvenile of the permanent stock company which played at one of the downtown theaters was an acquaintance of Paul's, and the boy had been invited to drop in at the Sunday-night rehearsals whenever he could. For more than a year Paul had spent every available moment loitering about Charley Edwards' dressing room. He had

A Pittsburgh street, where "women . . . sat in rockers on the cramped porches. . . . "

won a place among Edwards' following not only because the young actor, who could not afford to employ a dresser, often found him useful, but because he recognized in Paul something akin to what churchmen term "vocation."

It was at the theater and at Carnegie Hall that Paul really lived; the rest was but a sleep and a forgetting. This was Paul's fairy tale, and it had for him all the allurement of a secret love. The moment he inhaled the gassy, painty, dusty odor behind the scenes, he breathed like a prisoner set free, and felt within him the possibility of doing or saying splendid, brilliant things. The moment the cracked orchestra beat out the overture from *Martha*,[1] or jerked at the serenade from *Rigoletto*,[2] all stupid and ugly things slid from him, and his senses were deliciously, yet delicately, fired.

Perhaps it was because, in Paul's world, the natural nearly always wore the guise of ugliness, that a certain element of artificiality seemed to him necessary in beauty. Perhaps it was because his experience of life elsewhere was so full of Sabbath-school picnics, petty economies, wholesome advice as to how to succeed in life, and the unescapable odors of cooking, that he found this existence so alluring, these smartly clad men and women so attractive, that he was so moved by these starry apple orchards that bloomed perennially under the limelight.

It would be difficult to put it strongly enough how convincingly the stage entrance of that theater was for Paul the actual portal of Romance. Certainly none of the company ever suspected it, least of all Charley Edwards. It was very like the old stories that used to float about London of fabulously rich Jews, who had subterranean halls, with palms, and fountains, and soft lamps and richly appareled women who never saw the disenchanting light of London day. So,

in the midst of that smoke-palled city, enamored of figures and grimy toil, Paul had his secret temple, his wishing-carpet, this bit of blue-and-white Mediterranean shore bathed in perpetual sunshine.

Several of Paul's teachers had a theory that his imagination had been perverted by garish fiction; but the truth was, he scarcely ever read at all. The books at home were not such as would either tempt or corrupt a youthful mind, and as for reading the novels that some of his friends urged upon him — well, he got what he wanted much more quickly from music; any sort of music, from an orchestra to a barrel organ. He needed only the spark, the indescribable thrill that made his imagination master of his senses, and he could make plots and pictures enough of his own. It was equally true that he was not stagestruck — not, at any rate, in the usual acceptation[3] of that expression. He had no desire to become an actor, any more than he had to become a musician. He felt no necessity to do any of these things; what he wanted was to see, to be in the atmosphere, float on the wave of it, to be carried out, blue league after blue league, away from everything.

After a night behind the scenes, Paul found the schoolroom more than ever repulsive; the bare floors and naked walls; the prosy men who never wore frock coats, or violets in their buttonholes; the women with their dull gowns, shrill voices, and pitiful seriousness about prepositions that govern the dative. He could not bear to have the other pupils think, for a moment, that he took these people seriously; he must convey to them that he considered it all trivial, and was there only by way of a joke, anyway. He had autograph pictures of all the members of the stock company, which he showed his classmates, telling them the most incredible stories of his familiarity with these people, of his acquaintance with the soloists

[1] *Martha*: opera by Friedrich von Flotow.
[2] *Rigoletto*: opera by Giuseppe Verdi.

[3] **acceptation**: generally accepted meaning.

who came to Carnegie Hall, his suppers with them, and the flowers he sent them. When these stories lost their effect, and his audience grew listless, he would bid all the boys good-by, announcing that he was going to travel for a while; going to Naples, to California, to Egypt. Then, next Monday, he would slip back, conscious and nervously smiling; his sister was ill, and he would have to defer his voyage until spring.

Matters went steadily worse with Paul at school. In the itch to let his instructors know how heartily he despised them, and how thoroughly he was appreciated elsewhere, he mentioned once or twice that he had no time to fool with theorems; adding — with a twitch of the eyebrows and a touch of that nervous bravado which so perplexed them — that he was helping the people down at the stock company; they were old friends of his.

The upshot of the matter was, that the Principal went to Paul's father, and Paul was taken out of school and put to work. The manager at Carnegie Hall was told to get another usher in his stead; the doorkeeper at the theater was warned not to admit him to the house; and Charley Edwards remorsefully promised the boy's father not to see him again.

The members of the stock company were vastly amused when some of Paul's stories reached them — especially the women. They were hard-working women, most of them supporting indolent husbands or brothers, and they laughed rather bitterly at having stirred the boy to such fervid and florid inventions. They agreed with the faculty and with his father, that Paul's was a bad case.

The eastbound train was ploughing through a January snowstorm; the dull dawn was beginning to show gray when the engine whistled a mile out of Newark. Paul started up from the seat where he had lain curled in uneasy slumber, rubbed the breath-misted window glass with his hand, and peered out. The snow was whirling in curling eddies[1] above the white bottom lands, and the drifts lay already deep in the fields and along the fences, while here and there the long dead grass and dried weed stalks protruded black above it. Lights shone from the scattered houses, and a gang of laborers who stood beside the track waved their lanterns.

Paul had slept very little, and he felt grimy and uncomfortable. He had made the all-night journey in a day coach because he was afraid if he took a Pullman,[2] he might be seen by some Pittsburgh businessman who had noticed him in Denny & Carson's office. When the whistle woke him, he clutched quickly at his breast pocket, glancing about him with an uncertain smile. But the little, clay-bespattered Italians were still sleeping, the slatternly women across the aisle were in open-mouthed oblivion, and even the crumby, crying babies were for the nonce[3] stilled. Paul settled back to struggle with his impatience as best he could.

When he arrived at the Jersey City station, he hurried through his breakfast, manifestly ill at ease and keeping a sharp eye about him. After he reached the Twenty-third Street station, he consulted a cabman, and had himself driven to a men's furnishing[4] establishment which was just opening for the day. He spent upward of two hours there, buying with endless reconsidering and great care. His new street suit he put on in the fitting room; the frock coat and dress clothes he had bundled into the cab with his new shirts. Then he drove to a hatter's and a shoe house. His next errand was at Tiffany's,[5] where he selected silver

[1] **eddies**: whirlpools.
[2] **Pullman**: railroad car with seats that can be made up into berths for sleeping.
[3] **nonce**: time being.
[4] **furnishing**: clothing.
[5] **Tiffany's**: famous and expensive jewelry store.

mounted brushes and a scarf pin. He would not wait to have his silver marked, he said. Lastly, he stopped at a trunk shop on Broadway, and had his purchases packed into various traveling bags.

It was a little after one o'clock when he drove up to the Waldorf,[1] and, after settling with the cabman, went into the office. He registered from Washington; said his mother and father had been abroad, and that he had come down to await the arrival of their steamer. He told his story plausibly and had no trouble, since he offered to pay for them in advance, in engaging his rooms; a sleeping room, sitting room and bath.

Not once, but a hundred times Paul had planned this entry into New York. He had gone over every detail of it with Charley Edwards, and in his scrap book at home there were pages of description about New York hotels, cut from the Sunday papers.

When he was shown to his sitting room on the eighth floor, he saw at a glance that everything was as it should be; there was but one detail in his mental picture that the place did not realize, so he rang for the bell boy and sent him down for flowers. He moved about nervously until the boy returned, putting away his new linen and fingering it delightedly as he did so. When the flowers came, he put them hastily into water, and then tumbled into a hot bath. Presently he came out of his white bathroom, resplendent in his new silk underwear, and playing with the tassels of his red robe. The snow was whirling so fiercely outside his windows that he could scarcely see across the street; but within, the air was deliciously soft and fragrant. He put the violets and jonquils on the tabouret[2] beside the couch, and threw himself down with a long sigh, covering himself with a Roman blanket. He was thoroughly tired; he had been in such haste, he had stood

up to such a strain, covered so much ground in the last twenty-four hours, that he wanted to think how it had all come about. Lulled by the sound of the wind, the warm air, and the cool fragrance of the flowers, he sank into deep, drowsy retrospection.

It had been wonderfully simple; when they had shut him out of the theater and concert hall, when they had taken away his bone, the whole thing was virtually determined. The rest was a mere matter of opportunity. The only thing that at all surprised him was his own courage — for he realized well enough that he had always been tormented by fear, a sort of apprehensive dread that, of late years, as the meshes of the lies he had told closed about him, had been pulling the muscles of his body tighter and tighter. Until now, he could not remember a time when he had not been dreading something. Even when he was a little boy, it was always there — behind him, or before, or on either side. There had always been the shadowed corner, the dark place into which he dared not look, but from which something seemed always to be watching him — and Paul had done things that were not pretty to watch, he knew.

But now he had a curious sense of relief, as though he had at last thrown down the gauntlet[3] to the thing in the corner.

Yet it was but a day since he had been sulking in the traces;[4] but yesterday afternoon that he had been sent to the bank with Denny & Carson's deposit, as usual — but this time he was instructed to leave the book to be balanced. There was above two thousand dollars in checks, and nearly a thousand in the bank notes[5] which he had taken from the book and quietly transferred to his pocket. At the bank he had made out a new deposit slip. His nerves had been steady enough to permit of his returning to

---

[1] **Waldorf:** elegant and fashionable New York hotel.
[2] **tabouret:** low, ornamental table.

[3] **thrown . . . gauntlet:** challenged to combat.
[4] **traces:** harnesses.
[5] **bank notes:** form of paper money.

the office, where he had finished his work and asked for a full day's holiday tomorrow, Saturday, giving a perfectly reasonable pretext. The bank book, he knew, would not be returned before Monday or Tuesday, and his father would be out of town for the next week. From the time he slipped the bank notes into his pocket until he boarded the night train for New York, he had not known a moment's hesitation.

How astonishingly easy it had all been; here he was, the thing done; and this time there would be no awakening, no figure at the top of the stairs. He watched the snow flakes whirling by his window until he fell asleep.

When he awoke, it was four o'clock in the afternoon. He bounded up with a start; one of his precious days gone already! He spent nearly an hour in dressing, watching every stage of his toilet carefully in the mirror. Everything was quite perfect; he was exactly the kind of boy he had always wanted to be.

When he went downstairs, Paul took a carriage and drove up Fifth Avenue toward the Park. The snow had somewhat abated; carriages and tradesmen's wagons were hurrying soundlessly to and fro in the winter twilight; boys in woolen mufflers were shoveling off the doorsteps; the avenue stages made fine spots of color against the white street. Here and there on the corners whole flower gardens blooming behind glass windows, against which the snowflakes stuck and melted; violets, roses, carnations, lilies of the valley — somehow vastly more lovely and alluring that they blossomed thus unnaturally in the snow. The Park itself was a wonderful stage winter-piece.

When he returned, the pause of the twilight had ceased, and the tune of the streets had changed. The snow was falling faster, lights streamed from the hotels that reared their many stories fearlessly up into the storm, defying the raging Atlantic winds. A long, black stream of carriages poured down the avenue, intersected here and there by other streams, tending horizontally. There were a score of cabs about the entrance of his hotel, and his driver had to wait. Boys in livery[1] were running in and out of the awning stretched across the sidewalk, up and down the red velvet carpet laid from the door to the street. Above, about, within it all, was the rumble and roar, the hurry and toss of thousands of human beings as hot for pleasure as himself, and on every side of him towered the glaring affirmation of the omnipotence of wealth.

The boy set his teeth and drew his shoulders together in a spasm of realization; the plot of all dramas, the text of all romances, the nerve-stuff of all sensations was whirling about him like the snowflakes. He burnt like a faggot[2] in a tempest.[3]

When Paul came down to dinner, the music of the orchestra floated up the elevator shaft to greet him. As he stepped into the thronged corridor, he sank back into one of the chairs against the wall to get his breath. The lights, the chatter, the perfumes, the bewildering medley[4] of color — he had, for a moment, the feeling of not being able to stand it. But only for a moment; these were his own people, he told himself. He went slowly about the corridors, through the writing rooms, smoking rooms, reception rooms, as though he were exploring the chambers of an enchanted palace, built and peopled for him alone.

When he reached the dining room, he sat down at a table near a window. The flowers, the white linen, the many-colored wine glasses, the gay toilettes of the women, the low popping of corks, the undulating repetitions of the *Blue Danube* from the orchestra, all flooded Paul's dream with be-

---

[1] **livery:** identifying uniform.
[2] **faggot:** bundle of twigs used as fuel.
[3] **tempest:** *here,* violent wind.
[4] **medley:** mixture.

wildering radiance. When the roseate[1] tinge of his champagne was added — that cold, precious, bubbling stuff that creamed and foamed in his glass — Paul wondered that there were honest men in the world at all. This was what all the world was fighting for, he reflected; this was what all the struggle was about. He doubted the reality of his past. Had he ever known a place called Cordelia Street, a place where fagged[2] looking businessmen boarded the early car? Mere rivets[3] in a machine they seemed to Paul, — sickening men, with combings of children's hair always hanging to their coats, and the smell of cooking in their clothes. Cordelia Street — Ah, that belonged to another time and country! Had he not always been thus, had he not sat here night after night, from as far back as he could remember, looking pensively over just such shimmering textures, and slowly twirling the stem of a glass like this one between his thumb and middle finger? He rather thought he had.

He was not in the least abashed or lonely. He had no especial desire to meet or to know any of these people; all he demanded was the right to look on and conjecture, to watch the pageant. The mere stage properties were all he contended for. Nor was he lonely later in the evening, in his loge at the Opera. He was entirely rid of his nervous misgivings, of his forced aggressiveness, of the imperative desire to show himself different from his surroundings. He felt now that his surroundings explained him. Nobody questioned the purple;[4] he had only to wear it passively. He had only to glance down at his dress coat to reassure himself that here it would be impossible for anyone to humiliate him.

He found it hard to leave his beautiful sitting room to go to bed that night, and sat long watching the raging storm from his turret[5] window. When he went to sleep, it was with the lights turned on in his bedroom; partly because of his old timidity, and partly so that, if he should wake in the night, there would be no wretched moment of doubt, no horrible suspicion of yellow wallpaper, or of Washington and Calvin above his bed.

On Sunday morning the city was practically snowbound. Paul breakfasted late, and in the afternoon he fell in with a wild San Francisco boy, a freshman at Yale, who said he had run down for a "little flyer" over Sunday. The young man offered to show Paul the night side of the town, and the two boys went off together after dinner, not returning to the hotel until seven o'clock the next morning. They had started out in the confiding warmth of a champagne friendship, but their parting in the elevator was singularly cool. The freshman pulled himself together to make his train, and Paul went to bed. He awoke at two o'clock in the afternoon, very thirsty and dizzy, and rang for ice water, coffee, and the Pittsburgh papers.

On the part of the hotel management, Paul excited no suspicion. There was this to be said for him, that he wore his spoils with dignity and in no way made himself conspicuous. His chief greediness lay in his ears and eyes, and his excesses were not offensive ones. His dearest pleasures were the gray winter twilights in his sitting room; his quiet enjoyment of his flowers, his clothes, his wide divan,[6] his cigarette and his sense of power. He could not remember a time when he had felt so at peace with himself. The mere release from the necessity of petty lying, lying every day and every day, restored his self-respect. He had never lied for pleasure, even at school; but to make himself noticed and admired, to assert

---

[1] **roseate**: rosy.
[2] **fagged**: tired.
[3] **rivets**: metal bolts.
[4] **the purple**: symbol of luxury and power.

[5] **turret**: tower.
[6] **divan**: large, low sofa.

his difference from other Cordelia Street boys; and he felt a good deal more manly, more honest, even, now that he had no need for boastful pretensions, now that he could, as his actor friends used to say, "dress the part." It was characteristic that remorse did not occur to him. His golden days went by without a shadow, and he made each as perfect as he could.

On the eighth day after his arrival in New York, he found the whole affair exploited in the Pittsburgh papers, exploited with a wealth of detail which indicated that local news of a sensational nature was at a low ebb. The firm of Denny & Carson announced that the boy's father had refunded the full amount of his theft, and that they had no intention of prosecuting. The Cumberland minister had been interviewed, and expressed his hope of yet reclaiming the motherless lad, and Paul's Sabbath school teacher declared that she would spare no effort to that end. The rumor had reached Pittsburgh that the boy had been seen in a New York hotel, and his father had gone East to find him and bring him home.

Paul had just come in to dress for dinner; he sank into a chair, weak in the knees, and clasped his head in his hands. It was to be worse than jail, even; the tepid waters of Cordelia Street were to close over him finally and forever. The gray monotony stretched before him in hopeless, unrelieved years; Sabbath school, Young People's Meeting, the yellow-papered room, the damp dish towels; it all rushed back upon him with sickening vividness. He had the old feeling that the orchestra had suddenly stopped, the sinking sensation that the play was over. The sweat broke out on his face, and he sprang to his feet, looking about him with his white, conscious smile, and winked at himself in the mirror. With something of the childish belief in miracles with which he had so often gone to class, all his lessons unlearned, Paul dressed and dashed whistling

> To understand oneself is the classic form of consolation; to elude oneself is the romantic.
>
> — George Santayana

down the corridor to the elevator.

He had no sooner entered the dining room and caught the measure of the music, than his remembrance was lightened by his old elastic power of claiming the moment, mounting with it, and finding it all sufficient. The glare and glitter about him, the mere scenic accessories had again, and for the last time, their old potency. He would show himself that he was game, he would finish the thing splendidly. He doubted, more than ever, the existence of Cordelia Street, and for the first time he drank his wine recklessly. Was he not, after all, one of these fortunate beings? Was he not still himself, and in his own place? He drummed a nervous accompaniment to the music and looked about him, telling himself over and over that it had paid.

He reflected drowsily, to the swell of the violin and the chill sweetness of his wine, that he might have done it more wisely. He might have caught an outbound steamer and been well out of their clutches before now. But the other side of the world had seemed too far away and too uncertain then; he could not have waited for it; his need had been too sharp. If he had to choose over again, he would do the same thing tomorrow. He looked affectionately about the dining room, now gilded with a soft mist. Ah, it had paid indeed!

Paul was awakened next morning by a painful throbbing in his head and feet. He had thrown himself across the bed without undressing, and had slept with his shoes on. His limbs and hands were lead heavy, and his tongue and throat were parched. There came upon him one of those fateful attacks of clearheadedness that never occurred except when he was physically exhausted and his nerves hung loose. He lay still and closed his eyes and let the tide of realities wash over him.

His father was in New York; "stopping at some joint or other," he told himself. The memory of successive summers on the front stoop fell upon him like a weight of black water. He had not a hundred dollars left; and he knew now, more than ever, that money was everything, the wall that stood between all he loathed and all he wanted. The thing was winding itself up; he had thought of that on his first glorious day in New York, and had even provided a way to snap the thread. It lay on his dressing table now; he had got it out last night when he came blindly up from dinner — but the shiny metal hurt his eyes, and he disliked the look of it, anyway.

He rose and moved about with a painful effort, succumbing now and again to attacks of nausea. It was the old depression exaggerated; all the world had become Cordelia Street. Yet somehow he was not afraid of anything, was absolutely calm; perhaps because he had looked into the dark corner at last, and knew. It was bad enough, what he saw there; but somehow not so bad as his long fear of it had been. He saw everything clearly now. He had a feeling that he had made the best of it, that he had lived the sort of life he was meant to live, and for half an hour he sat staring at the revolver. But he told himself that was not the way, so he went downstairs and took a cab to the ferry.

When Paul arrived at Newark, he got off the train and took another cab, directing the driver to follow the Pennsylvania tracks out of the town. The snow lay heavy on the roadways and had drifted deep in the open fields. Only here and there the dead grass or dried weed stalks projected, singularly black, above it. Once well into the country, Paul dismissed the carriage and walked, floundering along the tracks, his mind a medley of irrelevant things. He seemed to hold in his brain an actual picture of everything he had seen that morning. He remembered every feature of both his drivers, the toothless old woman from whom he had bought the red flowers in his coat, the agent from whom he had got his ticket, and all of his fellow-passengers on the ferry. His mind, unable to cope with vital matters near at hand, worked feverishly and deftly at sorting and grouping these images. They made for him a part of the ugliness of the world, of the ache in his head, and the bitter burning on his tongue. He stooped and put a handful of snow into his mouth as he walked, but that, too, seemed hot. When he reached a little hillside, where the tracks ran through a cut some twenty feet below him, he stopped and sat down.

The carnations in his coat were drooping with the cold, he noticed; all their red glory over. It occurred to him that all the flowers he had seen in the show windows that first night must have gone the same way, long before this. It was only one splendid breath they had, in spite of their brave mockery at the winter outside the glass. It was a losing game in the end, it seemed, this revolt against the homilies[1] by which the world is run. Paul took one of the blossoms carefully from his coat and scooped a little hole in the snow, where he covered it up. Then he dozed a while, from his weak condition, seeming insensible to the cold.

The sound of an approaching train woke him, and he started to his feet, remembering only his resolution, and afraid lest he should be too late. He stood watching the approaching locomotive, his teeth chattering, his lips drawn away from them in a frightened smile; once or twice he glanced nervously sidewise, as though he were being watched. When the right moment came, he

[1] **homilies**: tedious and solemn moral talk.

jumped. As he fell, the folly of his haste occurred to him with merciless clearness, the vastness of what he had left undone. There flashed through his brain, clearer than ever before, the blue of Adriatic[1] water, the yellow of Algerian[2] sands.

He felt something strike his chest — his body was being thrown swiftly through the air, on and on, immeasurably far and fast, while his limbs gently relaxed. Then, because the picture-making mechanism was crushed, the disturbing visions flashed into black, and Paul dropped back into the immense design of things.

[1] **Adriatic:** of a part of the Mediterranean Sea.
[2] **Algerian:** of Algeria, a country in North Africa.

For Discussion

1. In New York at last, everything was perfect; Paul "was exactly the kind of boy he had always wanted to be" (page 653). In other words, he felt he had discovered his identity — found out who he really was. What kind of life did Paul want to lead? What kind of person did he want to be?

2. To understand Paul's case, it is vital to understand thoroughly the boy himself. Was he an artistic genius frustrated by an ugly environment and surrounded by people who didn't appreciate his gifts? What were the boy's goals? To be an actor? A musician? What kind of reading did he do?

3. Paul's behavior in high school was compounded of aggressiveness and indifference. How does the story account for that behavior? During his youth the boy had grown "quite accustomed to lying" (page 643). Why did he resort to lies? What would have been the consequences of his telling the truth?

4. The boy's father holds before him a particular young man — a clerk — as a model. What attributes of the model young man win the father's approval? Are the attributes worthy of imitation? Discuss.

5. What is it that finally drives Paul to New York? Under different circumstances, would it have been possible for him to have survived in the world of Cordelia Street? What he learned from the newspaper finally determined him to commit suicide. Why? If Denny & Carson, from whom he had embezzled funds, had decided to press charges, would Paul's response have been the same?

6. Though focusing on Paul, Willa Cather tells her story from the omniscient point of view. The third paragraph, for example, informs the reader of feelings of Paul's teachers about his conduct — an awareness the boy himself would have been able only to surmise. One advantage of the omniscient point of view becomes obvious at the end. Explain.

7. The story could have been told, with certain changes, from the point of view of Paul's father, or the principal, or even a clerk at the Waldorf. Each would have entailed using the personal point of view. What effect would the use of these narrators have on the tone of the story?

For Composition

Clearly much of Paul's confusion about who he was arose from his having lived in an environment that seemed foreign and repugnant to him. During the course of the story we learn a great deal about the home in which Paul grew up.

1. **Description.** In a coherent essay of three or four paragraphs describe Paul's house on Cordelia Street. Draw from the entire story, being careful not to overlook such specific details as the appearance of the cellar (page 648) and the pictures over the boy's bed (page 647).

2. **Argument.** "Paul's suicide was by no means inevitable; someone willing to take the trouble to understand the boy could have helped make his life bearable and even rewarding." In a thoughtful paper that draws on the story for substantiation, support or refute that assertion.

3. **Character Sketch.** Write a character sketch of Paul, including details of his ap-

pearance, manner, and motivations for behaving as he does.

Words and Allusions

CHANGES IN LANGUAGE (page 188). Although Willa Cather lived well into the twentieth century, a number of words in "Paul's Case," some of them slang, are now obsolete. What is the common term today for each of the following: *dandy* (page 643), *spiggots* (647), *toilet* (653), *fagged* (654)?

ALLUSIONS (page 53). The word *jovial* (page 648) is an allusion to the Roman god Jupiter, or Jove. It refers to the quality of good humor attributed by astrologists to those born under the influence of the planet Jupiter. Each of the following words also alludes to a Roman or Greek god: *mercurial, martial, panic, saturnine, cereal, atlas, herculean, janitor.* Explain the relationship between each word and the deity to which it refers.

Who Are You?

ANDREY VOZNESENSKY

Who are you: a son, a student, a brother, a customer, a coward, an athlete, a genius? In the following poem, by a contemporary Russian poet, a series of striking images present the fragments that together form identity.

Who are we — poker chips or giants?
Genius in the bloodstream of the planets.
No "physicists," no "lyricists"* exist —
Just pygmies or poets!

Independent of our works the epoch   5
Vaccinated us like smallpox.
Flabbergastingly: "Who are you?"
We're as worn out as race tracks.

Who are you? Who are you? Then suddenly — no? . . .
On Venus an overcoat's irritating!   10
Starlings strive their best to crow.
Architects to be poet-creators!

And thawing their palms,
Poetesses run to be pedlars!*

Voznesensky: pronounced väz′nə·sen′skē.   3. **lyricists:** writers of lyrics; lyric poets.   14. **Poetesses . . . pedlars:** allusion to Bella Akhmadulina, who was at one time a salesgirl.

But what about you? ...   15
What month is it —
You aim at the stars, but sweep the puddles.
School finished with, pigtails cut,
Became a salesgirl — then chucked that.

But, between Stoleshnikov* kiosks*   20
As if again playing "It,"
Panting and puffing you stand
A deer,
     a tigress,
          a dim-wit!   25
Who are you? Who?! — You look with longing
Into books, windows — but where are you meanwhile? —
You recline, as to a telescope,
To masculine eyes watching immobile. ...

I wander with you, Vera, Vega! ...   30
For, 'midst an avalanche let loose,
I too am an abominable snowman
Absolutely elusive.

20. **Stoleshnikov:** Moscow street. **kiosks:** billboards.

For Discussion

1. These verses, as ambiguous as identity itself, gradually yield meaning the more they are pondered. The opening question defines the contrasts that the remainder of the poem develops. Poker chips, like pawns on a chessboard or keys on a piano, are passive objects that others manipulate for their ends. By contrast, what are the connotations of "giants"?

2. Lines 5 and 6 suggest that a person's identity depends to some extent on the times in which he lives. This "epoch" of ours appears to proceed independently of individual desires or aspirations; indeed, events that are beyond our influencing profoundly affect our identity. Our sensitivities may be altered, so that we become "as worn out as race tracks." And few have the strength to be loyal to their own natures: "Starlings strive their best to crow" (line 11). What other images in the poem express the betrayal of one's own identity in favor of some other calling?

3. "I too," the speaker concludes, "am an abominable snowman / Absolutely elusive." What are the traits of the Abominable Snowman, that creature of the Tibetan highlands? In what sense does the speaker compare himself to this creature?

4. **Parallelism, Antithesis.** *Parallelism* is a rhetorical device in which two or more balancing ideas or details are expressed in similar form or grammatical structure. The device lends strength and coherence to Voznesensky's poem: "Starlings strive their best to crow" is followed by the parallel assertion that "Architects [strive their best] to be poet-creators!" (lines 11–12). What other parallel constructions do you find in the poem? When those constructions involve opposites that are set side by side, the device is called *antithesis*. In one sense, the antithesis of a giant — huge, active, significant — might be the trivial, passive, and insignificant poker chip of line 1. Where else in the poem do you encounter antithesis?

For Composition

One aspect of Voznesensky's style as evidenced by this poem is a fondness for parallelism and antithesis. In addition, he makes generous use of exclamations and interrogations, and his thoughts are expressed in images that leap boldly from one frame of reference to another altogether different, the leap being signaled sometimes by a dash that marks an interruption.

• **Analysis.** Analyze and illustrate characteristics of Voznesensky's style in "Who Are You?" Arrange the attributes in a coherent order, and in the course of your composition consider to what extent Voznesensky's style is appropriate to the subject of the poem.

About the Poet. **Andrey Voznesensky** (1933–) has sought vigorously to free Russian poetry from the restrictions placed upon it during the Stalin era. An ardent defender of the literary artist, Voznesensky writes in defense of the free human spirit with an insistence that has frequently brought him into conflict with Soviet authorities. In its original language, Voznesensky's verse is rich in metaphor, slang, scientific and technical language, and humor. Enormously popular in Russia, where his books are best-sellers and his speaking engagements draw huge crowds, Voznesensky has been called by the American poet Robert Lowell "one of the greatest living poets in any language."

The Waste Places

JAMES STEPHENS

Life is a journey; and though no traveler is omnipotent, the kind of journey
it turns out to be depends at least to some extent on the person who makes it.

As a naked man I go
    Through the desert sore afraid,
Holding up my head, although
    I am as frightened as a maid.

The couching* lion there I saw   5
    From barren rocks lift up his eye,
He parts the cactus with his paw,
    He stares at me as I go by.

He would follow on my trace
    If he knew I was afraid,   10
If he knew my hardy face
    Hides the terrors of a maid.

5. **couching**: waiting in ambush to attack.

In the night he rises, and
    He stretches forth, he snuffs the air,
He roars and leaps along the sand,   15
    He creeps and watches everywhere.

His burning eyes, his eyes of bale,*
    Through the darkness I can see;
He lashes fiercely with his tail,
    He would love to spring at me.   20

I am the lion in his lair,
    I am the fear that frightens me,
I am the desert of despair,
    And the nights of agony.

Night or day, whate'er befall,   25
    I must walk that desert land,
Until I can dare to call
    The lion out to lick my hand.

17. **bale**: evil.

For Discussion

1. The sixth stanza of the poem interprets all that has gone before. Consider carefully what has been revealed to that point. A man walks through life naked — that is, exposed, vulnerable, defenseless. Through what kind of landscape, specifically, does he pass? In daylight he is aware of a lion watching him. Is the lion crouching to spring? What does the lion do? When night falls, what actually happens?

2. The identity of the speaker embraces a number of contradictions. How does he appear on the exterior? How does he feel inside? Clearly the lion, emerging during the speaker's "nights of agony," is a symbol, as is the desert landscape. What might the lion symbolize?

3. Of the several general statements below, which comes closest to conveying adequately the central theme of "The Waste Places" as you understand it?

a. Even someone who seems perfectly assured and composed is likely to be subject to private torments.
b. One's identity comprises many apparently contradictory aspects.
c. Anyone who is a prey to his fears is doomed to live in solitude.
d. A person at the mercy of his fears leads a barren and profitless life.
e. Fear will follow us wherever we go.
f. Man's conscious self must learn to control his subconscious.

If none of the items above states the theme to your satisfaction, state it in an assertion of your own.

For Composition

The journey that Paul made through life in Willa Cather's story (page 643) was quite different from that of the speaker in "The Waste Places."

● **Comparison and Contrast.** Compare those attributes of Paul's life that are relevant to the life depicted in James Stephens' poem. For example, did Paul go through life "sore afraid" (line 2)? If not, what adjective would best characterize his attitude? Does "desert" accurately convey the world of Cordelia Street? If not, what environment would you suggest as an alternative?

About the Poet. Dedicated to "giving Ireland a new mythology," **James Stephens** (1882–1950) turned his boundless energy in various directions. Author of many collections of verse and several volumes of fiction, he was a popularizer of Irish folk music and an authority on Gaelic art. Steeped in the Irish past, he also found time to work for the establishment of the Irish Free State in the 1920's.

FROM

Notes of a Native Son

JAMES BALDWIN

External circumstances can transform identity. An acquaintance, an event, a condition, a status can all contribute to molding any one of us into shapes beyond our power to affect. From an eloquent and powerful collection of his essays comes this account of the pressures in the midst of which James Baldwin fashioned his own impressive identity.

On the 29th of July, in 1943, my father died. On the same day, a few hours later, his last child was born. Over a month before this, while all our energies were concentrated in waiting for these events, there had been, in Detroit, one of the bloodiest race riots of the century. A few hours after my father's funeral, while he lay in state in the undertaker's chapel, a race riot broke out in Harlem. On the morning of the 3rd of August, we drove my father to the graveyard through a wilderness of smashed plate glass.

The day of my father's funeral had also been my nineteenth birthday. As we drove him to the graveyard, the spoils of injustice, anarchy, discontent, and hatred were all around us. It seemed to me that God himself had devised, to mark my father's end, the most sustained and brutally dissonant[1] of codas.[2] And it seemed to me, too, that the violence which rose all about us as my father left the world had been devised as a corrective for the pride of his eldest son. I had declined to believe in that apocalypse[3] which had been central to my father's vision; very well, life seemed to be saying, here is something that will certainly pass for an apocalypse until the real thing comes along. I had inclined to be contemptuous of my father for the conditions of his life, for the conditions of our lives. When his life had

[1] **dissonant:** full of conflict, not harmonious.
[2] **codas:** in music, formal closes of compositions.
[3] **apocalypse:** prophetic disclosure, revelation.

ended, I began to wonder about that life and also, in a new way, to be apprehensive about my own.

I had not known my father very well. We had got on badly, partly because we shared, in our different fashions, the vice of stubborn pride. When he was dead, I realized that I had hardly ever spoken to him. When he had been dead a long time, I began to wish I had. It seems to be typical of life in America, where opportunities, real and fancied, are thicker than anywhere else on the globe, that the second generation has no time to talk to the first. No one, including my father, seems to have known exactly how old he was, but his mother had been born during slavery. He was of the first generation of free men. He, along with thousands of other Negroes, came North after 1919, and I was part of that generation which had never seen the landscape of what Negroes sometimes call the Old Country.

He had been born in New Orleans and had been a quite young man there during the time that Louis Armstrong,[1] a boy, was running errands for the dives and honky-tonks of what was always presented to me as one of the most wicked of cities — to this day, whenever I think of New Orleans, I also helplessly think of Sodom and Gomorrah. My father never mentioned Louis Armstrong, except to forbid us to play his records; but there was a picture of him on our wall for a long time. One of my father's strong-willed female relatives had placed it there and forbade my father to take it down. He never did, but he eventually maneuvered her out of the house, and when, some years later, she was in trouble and near death, he refused to do anything to help her.

He was, I think, very handsome. I gather this from photographs and from my own memories of him, dressed in his Sunday best and on his way to preach a sermon somewhere, when I was little. Handsome, proud and ingrown, "like a toenail," somebody said. But he looked to me, as I grew older,

[1] **Louis Armstrong:** famous jazz musician.

"Over a month before this . . . there had been, in Detroit, one of the bloodiest race riots of the century." Detroit in June, 1943.

like pictures I had seen of African tribal chieftains: he really should have been naked, with war paint on and barbaric mementos, standing among spears. He could be chilling in the pulpit and indescribably cruel in his personal life, and he was certainly the most bitter man I have ever met; yet it must be said that there was something else in him, buried in him, which lent him his tremendous power and, even, a rather crushing charm. It had something to do with his blackness, I think — he was very black — with his blackness and his beauty, and with the fact that he knew that he was black but did not know that he was beautiful. He claimed to be proud of his blackness, but it had also been the cause of much humiliation and it had fixed bleak boundaries to his life. He was not a young man when we were growing up, and he had already suffered many kinds of ruin; in his outrageously demanding and protective way he loved his children, who were black like him and menaced, like him; and all these things sometimes showed in his face when he tried, never to my knowledge with any success, to establish contact with any of us. When he took one of his children on his knee to play, the child always became fretful and began to cry; when he tried to help one of us with our homework, the absolutely unabating tension which emanated from him caused our minds and our tongues to become paralyzed, so that he, scarcely knowing why, flew into a rage, and the child, not knowing why, was punished. If it ever entered his head to bring a surprise home for his children, it was, almost unfailingly, the wrong surprise, and even the big watermelons he often brought home on his back in the summer time led to the most appalling scenes. I do not remember, in all those years, that one of his children was ever glad to see him come home. From what I was able to gather of his early life, it seemed that this inability to establish contact with other people had always marked him and had been one of the things which had driven him out of New Orleans. There was something in him, therefore, groping and tentative, which was never expressed and which was buried with him. One saw it most clearly when he was facing new people and hoping to impress them. But he never did, not for long. We went from church to smaller and more improbable church, he found himself in less and less demand as a minister, and by the time he died none of his friends had come to see him for a long time. He had lived and died in an intolerable bitterness of spirit, and it frightened me, as we drove him to the graveyard through those unquiet, ruined streets, to see

ABOUT THE AUTHOR • Novelist, short-story writer, and essayist, **James Baldwin** (1924—   ) has, in the words of Kay Boyle, "told us things about ourselves with such clarity that we had to raise our hands to shield our eyes from the sudden light." Born the son of a Harlem preacher, Baldwin was a preacher himself until he began writing at the age of seventeen. Since that time, he has won innumerable fellowships, including the Saxton Fellowship awarded for an early version of *Go Tell It On the Mountain*. Baldwin, Edmund Wilson has noted, is "not only one of the best Negro writers that we have ever had in this country, but one of the best writers that we have."

how powerful and overflowing this bitterness could be and to realize that this bitterness now was mine.

When he died, I had been away from home for a little over a year. In that year I had had time to become aware of the meaning of all my father's bitter warnings, had discovered the secret of his proudly pursed lips and rigid carriage; I had discovered the weight of white people in the world. I saw that this had been for my ancestors and now would be for me an awful thing to live with and that the bitterness which had helped to kill my father could also kill me.

He had been ill a long time — in the mind, as we now realized, reliving instances of his fantastic intransigence[1] in the new light of his affliction and endeavoring to feel a sorrow for him which never, quite, came true. We had not known that he was being eaten up by paranoia,[2] and the discovery that his cruelty, to our bodies and our minds, had been one of the symptoms of his illness was not, then, enough to enable us to forgive him. The younger children felt, quite simply, relief that he would not be coming home anymore. My mother's observation that it was he, after all, who had kept them alive all these years meant nothing because the problems of keeping children alive are not real for children. The older children felt, with my father gone, that they could invite their friends to the house without fear that their friends would be insulted or, as had sometimes happened with me, being told that their friends were in league with the devil and intended to rob our family of everything we owned. (I didn't fail to wonder, and it made me hate him, what on earth we owned that anybody else would want.)

His illness was beyond all hope of healing before anyone realized that he was ill. He had always been so strange and had lived,

like a prophet, in such unimaginably close communion with the Lord that his long silences, which were punctuated by moans and hallelujahs and snatches of old songs while he sat at the living room window, never seemed odd to us. It was not until he refused to eat because, he said, his family was trying to poison him, that my mother was forced to accept as a fact what had, until then, been only an unwilling suspicion. When he was committed, it was discovered that he had tuberculosis and, as it turned out, the disease of his mind allowed the disease of his body to destroy him. For the doctors could not force him to eat, either, and, though he was fed intravenously it was clear from the beginning that there was no hope for him.

In my mind's eye I could see him, sitting at the window, locked up in his terrors; hating and fearing every living soul including his children who had betrayed him, too, by reaching towards the world which had despised him. There were nine of us. I began to wonder what it could have felt like for such a man to have had nine children whom he could barely feed. He used to make little jokes about our poverty, which never, of course, seemed very funny to us; they could not have seemed very funny to him, either, or else our all too feeble response to them would never have caused such rages. He spent great energy and achieved, to our chagrin, no small amount of success in keeping us away from the people who surrounded us, people who had all-night rent parties to which we listened when we should have been sleeping, people who cursed and drank and flashed razor blades on Lenox Avenue. He could not understand why, if they had so much energy to spare, they could not use it to make their lives better. He treated almost everybody on our block with a most uncharitable asperity,[3] and neither they, nor, of course, their chil-

[1] **intransigence**: refusal to compromise.
[2] **paranoia**: mental disorder characterized by delusions of persecution.
[3] **asperity**: harshness.

dren, were slow to reciprocate.[1]

The only white people who came to our house were welfare workers and bill collectors. It was almost always my mother who dealt with them, for my father's temper, which was at the mercy of his pride, was never to be trusted. It was clear that he felt their very presence in his home to be a violation: this was conveyed by his carriage, almost ludicrously stiff, and by his voice, harsh and vindictively polite. When I was around nine or ten, I wrote a play which was directed by a young, white schoolteacher, a woman, who then took an interest in me, and gave me books to read and, in order to corroborate[2] my theatrical bent,[3] decided to take me to see what she somewhat tactlessly referred to as "real" plays. Theatergoing was forbidden in our house, but, with the really cruel intuitiveness of a child, I suspected that the color of this woman's skin would carry the day for me. When, at school, she suggested taking me to the theater, I did not, as I might have done if she had been a Negro, find a way of discouraging her, but agreed that she should pick me up at my house one evening. I then, very cleverly, left all the rest to my mother, who suggested to my father, as I knew she would, that it would not be very nice to let such a kind woman make the trip for nothing. Also, since it was a schoolteacher, I imagine that my mother countered the idea of sin with the idea of "education," which word, even with my father, carried a kind of bitter weight.

Before the teacher came my father took me aside to ask *why* she was coming, what *interest* she could possibly have in our house, in a boy like me. I said I didn't know, but I, too, suggested that it had something to do with education. And I understood that my father was waiting for me to say something

—I didn't quite know what; perhaps that I wanted his protection against this teacher and her "education." I said none of these things, and the teacher came and we went out. It was clear, during the brief interview in our living room, that my father was agreeing very much against his will and that he would have refused permission if he had dared. The fact that he did not dare caused me to despise him: I had no way of knowing that he was facing in that living room a wholly unprecedented and frightening situation.

Later, when my father had been laid off from his job, this woman became very important to us. She was really a very sweet and generous woman and went to a great deal of trouble to be of help to us, particularly during one awful winter. My mother called her by the highest name she knew: she said she was a "christian." My father could scarcely disagree, but during the four or five years of our relatively close association he never trusted her and was always trying to surprise in her open, Midwestern face the genuine, cunningly hidden, and hideous motivation. In later years, particularly when it began to be clear that this "education" of mine was going to lead me to perdition,[4] he became more explicit and warned me that my white friends in high school were not really my friends and that I would see, when I was older, how white people would do anything to keep a Negro down. Some of them could be nice, he admitted, but none of them were to be trusted, and most of them were not even nice. The best thing was to have as little to do with them as possible. I did not feel this way, and I was certain, in my innocence, that I never would.

But the year which preceded my father's death had made a great change in my life. I had been living in New Jersey, working in defense plants, working and living among

---

[1] **reciprocate**: act in the same way.
[2] **corroborate**: strengthen, support.
[3] **bent**: enthusiasm, interest.
[4] **perdition**: damnation.

"I saw . . . that the bitterness which had helped to kill my father could also kill me." An untitled woodcut by the American Negro artist Sylvester Britton.

southerners, white and black. I knew about the south, of course, and about how southerners treated Negroes and how they expected them to behave, but it had never entered my mind that anyone would look at me and expect *me* to behave that way. I learned in New Jersey that to be a Negro meant, precisely, that one was never looked at but was simply at the mercy of the reflexes the color of one's skin caused in other people. I acted in New Jersey as I had always acted, that is, as though I thought a great deal of myself — I had to *act* that way — with results that were, simply, unbelievable. I had scarcely arrived before I had earned the enmity, which was extraordinarily ingenious, of all my superiors and nearly all my co-workers. In the beginning, to make matters worse, I simply did not know what was happening. I did not know what I had done, and I shortly began to wonder what *anyone* could possibly do, to bring about such unanimous, active, and unbearably vocal hostility. I knew about jim crow,[1] but I had never experienced it. I went to the same self-service restaurant three

times and stood with all the Princeton boys before the counter, waiting for a hamburger and coffee; it was always an extraordinarily long time before anything was set before me; but it was not until the fourth visit that I learned that, in fact, nothing had ever been set before me: I had simply picked something up. Negroes were not served there, I was told, and they had been waiting for me to realize that I was always the only Negro present. Once I was told this, I determined to go there all the time. But now they were ready for me and, though some dreadful scenes were subsequently enacted in that restaurant, I never ate there again.

It was the same story all over New Jersey, in bars, bowling alleys, diners, places to live. I was always being forced to leave, silently, or with mutual imprecations.[2] I very shortly became notorious and children giggled behind me when I passed and their elders whispered or shouted — they really believed that I was mad. And it did begin to work on my mind, of course; I began to be afraid to go anywhere, and to compensate for this I went places to which I really should not have

[1] **jim crow:** discrimination against, and segregation of, Negroes.

[2] **imprecations:** curses.

gone and where, God knows, I had no desire to be. My reputation in town naturally enhanced my reputation at work, and my working day became one long series of acrobatics designed to keep me out of trouble. I cannot say that these acrobatics succeeded. It began to seem that the machinery of the organization I worked for was turning over, day and night, with but one aim: to eject me. I was fired once, and contrived, with the aid of a friend from New York, to get back on the payroll; was fired again, and bounced back again. It took a while to fire me for the third time, but the third time took. There were no loopholes anywhere. There was not even any way of getting back inside the gates.

That year in New Jersey lives in my mind as though it were the year during which, having an unsuspected predilection for it, I first contracted some dread, chronic disease, the unfailing symptom of which is a kind of blind fever, a pounding in the skull and fire in the bowels. Once this disease is contracted, one can never be really carefree again, for the fever, without an instant's warning, can recur at any moment. It can wreck more important things than race relations. There is not a Negro alive who does not have this rage in his blood — one has the choice, merely, of living with it consciously or surrendering to it. As for me this fever has recurred in me, and does, and will until the day I die.

My last night in New Jersey, a white friend from New York took me to the nearest big town, Trenton, to go to the movies and have a few drinks. As it turned out, he also saved me from, at the very least, a violent whipping. Almost every detail of that night stands out very clearly in my memory. I even remember the name of the movie we saw because its title impressed me as being so patly ironical. It was a movie about the German occupation of France, starring Maureen O'Hara and Charles Laughton and called *This Land Is Mine*. I remember the name of the diner we walked into when the movie ended: it was the "American Diner." When we walked in, the counterman asked what we wanted, and I remember answering with the casual sharpness which had become my habit: "We want a hamburger and a cup of coffee, what do you think we want?" I do not know why, after a year of such rebuffs, I so completely failed to anticipate his answer, which was, of course, "We don't serve Negroes here." This reply failed to discompose[1] me, at least for the moment. I made some sardonic comment about the name of the diner, and we walked out into the streets.

This was the time of what was called the "brown-out," when the lights in all American cities were very dim. When we reentered the streets, something happened to me which had the force of an optical illusion, or a nightmare. The streets were very crowded and I was facing north. People were moving in every direction, but it seemed to me, in that instant, that all of the people I could see, and many more than that, were moving toward me, against me, and that everyone was white. I remember how their faces gleamed. And I felt, like a physical sensation, a *click* at the nape of my neck as though some interior string connecting my head to my body had been cut. I began to walk. I heard my friend call after me, but I ignored him. Heaven only knows what was going on in his mind, but he had the good sense not to touch me — I don't know what would have happened if he had — and to keep me in sight. I don't know what was going on in my mind, either; I certainly had no conscious plan. I wanted to do something to crush these white faces, which were crushing me. I walked for perhaps a block or two until I came to an enor-

[1] **discompose:** ruffle, agitate.

mous, glittering, and fashionable restaurant in which I knew not even the intercession of the Virgin would cause me to be served. I pushed through the doors and took the first vacant seat I saw, at a table for two, and waited.

I do not know how long I waited and I rather wonder, until today, what I could possibly have looked like. Whatever I looked like, I frightened the waitress who shortly appeared, and the moment she appeared, all of my fury flowed towards her. I hated her for her white face, and for her great, astounded, frightened eyes. I felt that if she found a black man so frightening I would make her fright worthwhile.

She did not ask me what I wanted, but repeated, as though she had learned it somewhere, "We don't serve Negroes here." She did not say it with the blunt, derisive hostility to which I had grown so accustomed, but, rather, with a note of apology in her voice, and fear. This made me colder and more murderous than ever. I felt I had to do something with my hands. I wanted her to come close enough for me to get her neck between my hands.

So I pretended not to have understood her, hoping to draw her closer. And she did step a very short step closer, with her pencil poised incongruously over her pad, and repeated the formula: ". . . don't serve Negroes here."

Somehow, with the repetition of that phrase, which was already ringing in my head like a thousand bells of a nightmare, I realized that she would never come any closer and that I would have to strike from a distance. There was nothing on the table but an ordinary water mug half full of water, and I picked this up and hurled it with all my strength at her. She ducked and it missed her and shattered against the mirror behind the bar. And, with that sound, my frozen blood abruptly thawed, I re-

He is strong who conquers others; he who conquers himself is mighty.

— Lao-tzu

turned from wherever I had been, I *saw*, for the first time, the restaurant, the people with their mouths open, already, as it seemed to me, rising as one man, and I realized what I had done, and where I was, and I was frightened. I rose and began running for the door. A round, potbellied man grabbed me by the nape of the neck just as I reached the doors and began to beat me about the face. I kicked him and got loose and ran into the streets. My friend whispered, "*Run!*" and I ran.

My friend stayed outside the restaurant long enough to misdirect my pursuers and the police, who arrived, he told me, at once. I do not know what I said to him when he came to my room that night. I could not have said much. I felt, in the oddest, most awful way, that I had somehow betrayed him. I lived it over and over and over again, the way one relives an automobile accident after it has happened and one finds oneself alone and safe. I could not get over two facts, both equally difficult for the imagination to grasp, and one was that I could have been murdered. But the other was that I had been ready to commit murder. I saw nothing very clearly, but I did see this: that my life, my *real* life, was in danger, and not from anything other people might do but from the hatred I carried in my own heart.

For Discussion

1. Before his father's death, young James Baldwin had been away from home for a little over a year. "In that year I had had time to

669

become aware of all my father's bitter warnings, had discovered the secret of his proudly pursed lips and rigid carriage" (page 665). What was the secret the young man discovered? Where and how had he spent that year?

2. This account focuses on two different people — Baldwin's father and Baldwin himself. In the course of the account the behavior of both of them, at different times, verges on madness. Shortly before his death, what form did the father's madness assume? Why did it go unrecognized so long?

3. Young Baldwin's hurling of the pitcher at the waitress in the fashionable restaurant is hardly rational behavior, and circumstances surrounding it — the hallucinations, the aggressiveness, the condition approaching a blackout — suggest an interval of severe mental disturbance. Are the two conditions, father's and son's, related? Are their causes identical? What profound difference distinguishes the way each responds to what afflicts him?

4. James Baldwin's talents brought him, as a child, to the attention of a white schoolteacher — "a very sweet and generous woman." It was her presence in the Baldwin household that presented his father with "a wholly unprecedented and frightening situation" (page 666). Why unprecedented? What was frightening about it? How did the father react to the situation? How did his reaction affect his son?

5. Baldwin's sensitivity and skill with language evoke a clear and unforgettable picture of the father. What traits of character distinguish the man from others? What specific examples and incidents does the author include to support his analysis of his father? He says, for instance, that his father was cruel. If you believe what Baldwin says, it is because he has supported the assertion with examples. What examples?

6. What is the tone of this essay — angry, compassionate, embittered, outraged, solemn, despairing, or what? Mention specific examples of diction that convey the tone most effectively.

For Composition

"I learned in New Jersey that to be a Negro meant, precisely, that one was never looked at but was simply at the mercy of the reflexes the color of one's skin caused in other people" (page 667).

1. Argument. In a coherent paper supported by concrete examples, consider the effect on an individual of having his identity denied, of being "never looked at," of being — in Ralph Ellison's phrase — an Invisible Man. How might one respond to such treatment? Are any of the responses Baldwin's? What effect would such treatment have on one's sense of his own identity?

2. Analysis. Analyze the relationships between the two parts that make up this essay. What connects the part concerned with the father with that concerned with the son? Are the two situations parallel? If so, in what ways? Illustrate your insights about the structure of the essay, and arrange the insights in a logical and coherent manner.

3. Definition. As you no doubt recognized, this essay exemplifies a type of writing called *autobiography*. Define the term and explain how it differs from biography, pointing out the advantages and limitations of each form.

Words and Allusions

EUPHEMISM. On page 666 Baldwin uses the word *perdition* as a euphemism for *hell*. A *euphemism* is an agreeable or inoffensive synonym (page 14) that is substituted for one regarded as disagreeable or offensive. Thus we say *odor* instead of *smell*, to *pass away* instead of to *die*. What other euphemisms can you think of? Is Baldwin's use of "chronic disease" and "blind fever" (page 668) euphemistic?

ALLUSION (page 53). Baldwin speaks of "that apocalypse which had been central to my father's vision" (page 662). The word *apocalypse* is an allusion to the New Testament. Identify the allusion, and show how it relates to the scene Baldwin is describing.

Once Upon a Time

GABRIEL OKARA

As Baldwin's essay suggests, identity is not static; it changes with circumstances and the passing of time. Here a Nigerian poet expresses an insight about differences that come over a person as he grows older — almost any person, almost anywhere.

Once upon a time, son
they used to laugh with their hearts
and laugh with their eyes;
but now they only laugh with their teeth,
while their ice-block-cold eyes   5
search behind my shadow.

There was a time indeed
they used to shake hands with their hearts;
but that's gone, son.
Now they shake hands without hearts   10
while their left hands search
my empty pockets.

"Feel at home," "Come again,"
they say, and when I come
again and feel   15
at home, once, twice,
there will be no thrice —
for then I find doors shut on me.

So I have learned many things, son.
I have learned to wear many faces   20
like dresses — homeface,
officeface, streetface, hostface, cock-
tailface, with all their conforming smiles
like a fixed portrait smile.

And I have learned too   25
to laugh with only my teeth
and shake hands without my heart.
I have also learned to say, "Goodbye,"
when I mean "Goodriddance";
to say "Glad to meet you,"   30
without being glad; and to say "It's been
nice talking to you," after being bored.

But believe me, son.
I want to be what I used to be
when I was like you. I want   35
to unlearn all these muting things.
Most of all, I want to relearn
how to laugh, for my laugh in the mirror
shows only my teeth like a snake's bare fangs!

So show me, son,   40
how to laugh; show me how
I used to laugh and smile
once upon a time when I was like you.

For Discussion

1. The poem develops a contrast between past and present. In what ways does the behavior of people in the past differ from their behavior toward the speaker now? How has the speaker's behavior changed? How is that change to be accounted for?

2. Near the end of the poem the speaker expresses a wish "to unlearn all these muting things" (line 36). What he may be referring to by "muting things" are all those compromises, concessions, and little hypocrisies by which the business of the world gets done. To whom does he turn for help in "unlearning" what his experience has taught him is the safest way to behave?

For Composition

To what extent is the change that comes over the speaker of this poem an inevitable part of growing older? Children can be brutally frank to the point of cruelty, but can society function if adults invariably say exactly what they think at any given instant?

• Argument. In a well-organized essay examine the cases to be made for and against rigorous honesty of expression in the mature individual. Should he always "be himself"? Where does tact end and hypocrisy begin?

About the Poet. **Gabriel Okara,** a press officer at the Nigerian Information Service at Enugu, is one of Nigeria's outstanding poets. His poetry, described as "sensitive and strange and semi-mystic to the Western reader," has been translated into several languages, including Hebrew. Okara, who has also written a novel and translations of the folklore of his Ijaw heritage, has given readings in Africa, Europe, and the United States.

Talking Myself to Sleep at One More Hilton

JOHN CIARDI

Roots nourish a tree, determining to a large extent how it will grow. People have roots too, although more and more often in our mobile and rapidly changing society a single life — uprooted — is lived in many different places. What effect does such movement have on one's identity?

I have a country but no town.
Home ran away from me. My trees
ripped up their white roots and lay down.
Bulldozers cut my lawn. All these
are data toward some sentiment   5
like money: God knows where it went.

There was a house as sure as time.
Sure as my father's name and grave.
Sure as trees for me to climb.
Sure as behave and misbehave.   10
Sure as lamb stew. Sure as sin.
As warts. As games. As a scraped shin.

There was a house, a chicken run,
a garden, guilt, a rocking chair.
I had six dogs and every one   15
was killed in traffic. I knew where
their bones were once. Now I'm not sure.
Roses used them for manure.

There was a house early and late.
One day there came an overpass.   20
It snatched the stew right off my plate.
It snatched the plate. A whiff of gas
blew up the house like a freak wind.
I wonder if I really mind.

My father died. My father's house   25
fell out of any real estate.
My dogs lie buried where time was
when time still flowed, where now a slate

Hilton: one of a world-wide chain of hotels.   **Ciardi:** pronounced chärd′ē.

stiff river loops, called Exit Nine.
Why should I mind? It isn't mine.　　　　30

I have the way I think I live.
The doors of my expense account
open like arms when I arrive.
There is no cloud I cannot mount
and sip good bourbon as I ride.　　　　35
My father's house is Hilton-wide.

What are old dog bones? Were my trees
still standing would I really care?
What's the right name for this disease
of wishing they might still be there　　　　40
if I went back, though I will not
and never meant to? — Smash the pot,

knock in the windows, blow the doors.
I am not and mean not to be
what I was once. I have two shores　　　　45
five hours apart, soon to be three.
And home is anywhere between.
Sure as the airport limousine,

sure as credit, sure as a drink,
as the best steak you ever had,　　　　50
as thinking — when there's time to think —
it's good enough. At least not bad.
Better than dog bones and lamb stew.
It does. Or it will have to do.

For Discussion

1. At present, what position does the speaker of this poem occupy in his society? How do you know? What is his attitude toward the life he is now leading, as compared with the life of his childhood?

2. "Country" is one of the central concepts developed in the poem, along with the parallel concepts of "town" and "house." How has the speaker's understanding of each concept changed as he has matured? What happened to the speaker's birthplace? To the neighborhood in which he grew up? "In my Father's house are many mansions," Jesus said (John 14:2). Consider the irony of line 36. What is the speaker's "house" now?

3. Discuss the different effects of these titles:
   a. "Talking Myself to Sleep at One More Hilton"
   b. "Talking Myself to Sleep at the Hilton"
   c. "Drifting Off to Sleep at the Elegant New Hilton."

For Composition

In both "Once Upon a Time" and "Talking Myself to Sleep at One More Hilton" a mature man looks at his life now and compares it with his childhood.

• **Comparison and Contrast.** In a thoughtful and well-organized essay compare and contrast the poem by Ciardi with the one by Okara. If similarities seem more interesting than differences, deal with the differences first. Otherwise, reverse the arrangement. Present details in some logical way, considering both speakers' attitudes toward changes that have occurred in their lives, as well as their attitudes toward their society and their own childhoods.

About the Poet. A Bostonian by birth, **John Ciardi** (1916–) graduated *magna cum laude* from Tufts University, and won the Hopwood Major Award in Poetry while in graduate school at Michigan. After World War II, Ciardi taught at Harvard and Rutgers Universities, devoting his summers to the Bread Loaf Writers Conference at Middlebury College in Vermont. He became poetry editor for the *Saturday Review* in 1956, where he caused considerable controversy by reviewing his own poetry. During recent years, Ciardi has been in great demand as a lecturer and reader at college conferences and other gatherings. In addition to his highly acclaimed translation of Dante's *Divine Comedy*, Ciardi has written several volumes of poetry, critical works, and prize-winning poetry for children.

The Unknown Citizen

W. H. AUDEN

The identity of the individual often appears threatened in our complex, modern world. The sheer numbers of people and their organization into ever larger social groups — huge schools and universities, gigantic corporations and industrial enterprises, larger and ever larger governments — tend to diminish the importance of any one person by reducing him to the level of a statistic.

(To JS/07/M/378
This Marble Monument
Is Erected by the State)

He was found by the Bureau of Statistics to be
One against whom there was no official complaint,
And all the reports on his conduct agree
That, in the modern sense of an old-fashioned word, he was a saint,
For in everything he did he served the Greater Community.   5
Except for the War till the day he retired
He worked in a factory and never got fired,
But satisfied his employers, Fudge Motors Inc.

Yet he wasn't a scab* or odd in his views,
For his Union reports that he paid his dues, 10
(Our report on his Union shows it was sound)
And our Social Psychology workers found
That he was popular with his mates and liked a drink.
The Press are convinced that he bought a paper every day
And that his reactions to advertisements were normal in every way. 15
Policies taken out in his name prove that he was fully insured,
And his Health-card shows he was once in hospital but left it cured.
Both Producers Research and High-Grade Living declare
He was fully sensible to the advantages of the Installment Plan
And had everything necessary to the Modern Man, 20
A phonograph, a radio, a car and a frigidaire.
Our researchers into Public Opinion are content
That he held the proper opinions for the time of year;
When there was peace, he was for peace; when there was war, he went.
He was married and added five children to the population, 25
Which our Eugenist says was the right number for a parent of his generation,
And our teachers report that he never interfered with their education.
Was he free? Was he happy? The question is absurd:
Had anything been wrong, we should certainly have heard.

9. **scab**: worker who refuses to join a union.

For Discussion

1. The unknown citizen commemorated in Auden's poem was a "saint" (line 4). In what sense? What aspects of his conduct were saintly? Why is the term *saint*, in the context of this poem, considered old-fashioned?

2. The various reports on the citizen suggest that he "had everything necessary to the Modern Man." What are those necessities? Of course the citizen did not have everything. What dimensions and qualities were missing from his life?

3. "The Unknown Citizen" makes use of a jingle-like rhythm and rhymes that are for the most part flat and predictable. Is the language metaphorical? Is the diction, in general, fresh and arresting? Is it closer to the language of committees and reports than to that of poetry? Who or what is the source of the poem; that is, who is the "speaker"? Would an artful, sophisticated, and poetically accomplished expression be appropriate here?

For Composition

Auden's poem makes effective use of verbal irony, which exploits a contrast between what a word means literally and what it suggests. The reports, for example, state that the citizen left the hospital "cured" (line 17), whereas what was really wrong with his life was beyond medical treatment.

● **Analysis.** In a unified essay of four or five paragraphs analyze examples of verbal irony in "The Unknown Citizen." Such terms as "saint" (line 4) and "necessary" (line 20) have been touched upon briefly in the questions, but you may choose to examine them more thoroughly. Make clear how the literal meaning of each term you discuss differs from its larger meanings.

About the Poet. Born in England and educated at Oxford, **W. H. Auden** (1907–1973) became a permanent resident of the United States in 1939. A prolific writer, Auden wrote long and short poems, verse drama, light verse, occasional verse, songs, opera libretti, political odes and epistles and, between poems, hundreds of essays and articles on subjects ranging from Shakespeare to detective novels. Many of Auden's best-known poems were written during his younger days, when he diagnosed the social ills of England in devastating satires of the middle-class technological man. Later his poetic interests shifted, but he continued to write poetry of startling originality, poetry both lyrical and learned.

A Hunger Artist

FRANZ KAFKA

One man may be many things — part animal, part spirit; part body, part soul; part beast, part ascetic. In addition, if he has the special talents of an artist, he performs as he must, but in ways that distinguish and therefore isolate him from the rest of humanity. These contradictions, with others, are expressed in the following memorable story, typical of the work of Franz Kafka, who had the gift of describing in meticulous detail the most outlandish occurrences as though they were altogether ordinary.

During these last decades the interest in professional fasting has markedly diminished. It used to pay very well to stage such great performances under one's own management, but today that is quite impossible. We live in a different world now. At one time the whole town took a lively interest in the hunger artist; from day to day of his fast the excitement mounted; everybody wanted to see him at least once a day; there were people who bought season tickets for the last few days and sat from morning till night in front of his small barred cage; even in the nighttime there were visiting hours, when the whole effect was heightened by torch flares; on fine days the cage was set out in the open air, and then it was the children's special treat to see the hunger artist; for their elders he was often just a joke that happened to be in fashion, but the children stood open-mouthed, holding each other's hands for greater security, marveling at him as he sat there pallid in black tights, with his ribs sticking out so prominently, not even on a seat but down among straw on the ground, sometimes giving a courteous nod, answering questions with a constrained smile, or perhaps stretching an arm through the bars so that one might feel how thin it was, and then again withdrawing deep into himself, paying no attention to anyone or anything, not even to the all-important striking of the clock that was the only piece of furniture in his cage, but merely staring into vacancy with half-shut eyes, now and then taking a sip from a tiny glass of water to moisten his lips.

Besides casual onlookers there were also relays of permanent watchers selected by the public, usually butchers, strangely enough, and it was their task to watch the hunger artist day and night, three of them at a time, in case he should have some secret recourse to nourishment. This was nothing but a formality, instituted to reassure the masses, for the initiates[1] knew well enough that during his fast the artist would never in any circumstances, not even under forcible compulsion, swallow the smallest morsel of food; the honor of his profession forbade it. Not every watcher, of course, was capable of understanding this, there were often groups of night watchers who were very lax in carrying out their duties and deliberately

[1] **initiates**: those who are familiar with the rites and customs of a club, etc.

huddled together in a retired corner to play cards with great absorption, obviously intending to give the hunger artist the chance of a little refreshment, which they supposed he could draw from some private hoard. Nothing annoyed the artist more than such watchers; they made him miserable; they made his fast seem unendurable; sometimes he mastered his feebleness sufficiently to sing during their watch for as long as he could keep going, to show them how unjust their suspicions were. But that was of little use; they only wondered at his cleverness in being able to fill his mouth even while singing. Much more to his taste were the watchers who sat close up to the bars, who were not content with the dim night lighting of the hall but focused him in the full glare of the electric pocket torch given them by the impresario.[2] The harsh light did not trouble him at all, in any case he could never sleep properly, and he could always drowse a little, whatever the light, at any hour, even when the hall was thronged with noisy onlookers. He was quite happy at the prospect of spending a sleepless night with such

[2] **impresario**: manager.

ABOUT THE AUTHOR • Born in Prague of an affluent Czech family, **Franz Kafka** (1883–1924) studied law and did most of his writing while working in an insurance office. Very little of his work was published during his lifetime, but the novels, stories, and journals that appeared after his death clearly reveal, in the words of one critic, his "surpassing originality as an innovator in creative method." The nightmare world of his novels *The Castle* and *The Trial*, in which an ordinary citizen is manipulated without explanation by impersonal forces, has startling relevance to subsequent history. Kafka died of tuberculosis at a relatively early age, but his accomplishments during his brief career have had an enormous influence on contemporary literature.

watchers; he was ready to exchange jokes with them, to tell them stories out of his nomadic[1] life, anything at all to keep them awake and demonstrate to them again that he had no eatables in his cage and that he was fasting as not one of them could fast. But his happiest moment was when the morning came and an enormous breakfast was brought them, at his expense, on which they flung themselves with the keen appetite of healthy men after a weary night of wakefulness. Of course there were people who argued that this breakfast was an unfair attempt to bribe the watchers, but that was going rather too far, and when they were invited to take on a night's vigil without a breakfast, merely for the sake of the cause, they made themselves scarce, although they stuck stubbornly to their suspicions.

Such suspicions, anyhow, were a necessary accompaniment to the profession of fasting. No one could possibly watch the hunger artist continuously, day and night, and so no one could produce firsthand evidence that the fast had really been rigorous and continuous; only the artist himself could know that, he was therefore bound to be the sole completely satisfied spectator of his own fast. Yet for other reasons he was never satisfied; it was not perhaps mere fasting that had brought him to such skeleton thinness that many people had regretfully to keep away from his exhibitions, because the sight of him was too much for them, perhaps it was dissatisfaction with himself that had worn him down. For he alone knew, what no other initiate knew, how easy it was to fast. It was the easiest thing in the world. He made no secret of this, yet people did not believe him; at the best they set him down as modest. Most of them, however, thought he was out for publicity or else was some kind of cheat who found it easy to fast because he had dis-

[1] **nomadic:** wandering.

covered a way of making it easy, and then had the impudence to admit the fact, more or less. He had to put up with all that, and in the course of time had got used to it, but his inner dissatisfaction always rankled, and never yet, after any term of fasting — this must be granted to his credit — had he left the cage of his own free will. The longest period of fasting was fixed by his impresario at forty days, beyond that term he was not allowed to go, not even in great cities, and there was good reason for it, too. Experience had proved that for about forty days the interest of the public could be stimulated by a steadily increasing pressure of advertisement, but after that the town began to lose interest, sympathetic support began notably to fall off; there were of course local variations as between one town and another or one country and another, but as a general rule forty days marked the limit. So on the fortieth day the flower-bedecked cage was opened, enthusiastic spectators filled the hall, a military band played, two doctors entered the cage to measure the results of the fast, which were announced through a megaphone, and finally two young ladies appeared, blissful at having been selected for the honor, to help the hunger artist down the few steps leading to a small table on which was spread a carefully chosen invalid repast. And at this very moment the artist always turned stubborn. True, he would entrust his bony arms to the outstretched helping hands of the ladies bending over him, but stand up he would not. Why stop fasting at this particular moment, after forty days of it? He had held out for a long time, an illimitably long time; why stop now, when he was in his best fasting form, or rather, not yet quite in his best fasting form? Why should he be cheated of the fame he would get for fasting longer, for being not only the record hunger artist of all time, which presumably he was already, but for beating his own record by a performance beyond human imagination, since he felt that there were no limits to his capacity for fasting? His public pretended to admire him so much, why should it have so little patience with him; if he could endure fasting longer, why shouldn't the public endure it? Besides, he was tired, he was comfortable sitting in the straw, and now he was supposed to lift himself to his full height and go down to a meal the very thought of which gave him a nausea that only the presence of the ladies kept him from betraying, and even that with an effort. And he looked up into the eyes of the ladies who were apparently so friendly and in reality so cruel, and shook his head, which felt too heavy on its strengthless neck. But then there happened yet again what always happened. The impresario came forward, without a word — for the band made speech impossible — lifted his arms in the air above the artist, as if inviting Heaven to look down upon its creature here in the straw, this suffering martyr, which indeed he was, although in quite another sense; grasped him round the emaciated waist, with exaggerated caution, so that the frail condition he was in might be appreciated; and committed him to the care of the blenching[1] ladies, not without secretly giving him a shaking so that his legs and body tottered and swayed. The artist now submitted completely; his head lolled on his breast as if it had landed there by chance; his body was hollowed out; his legs in a spasm of self-preservation clung close to each other at the knees, yet scraped on the ground as if it were not really solid ground; as if they were only trying to find solid ground; whole weight of his body, a featherweight after all, relapsed[2] onto one of the ladies, who, looking round for help and panting a

[1] blenching: becoming pale.
[2] relapsed: fell back.

little — this post of honor was not at all what she had expected it to be — first stretched her neck as far as she could to keep her face at least free from contact with the artist, then finding this impossible, and her more fortunate companion not coming to her aid but merely holding extended on her own trembling hand the little bunch of knucklebones that was the artist's, to the great delight of the spectators burst into tears and had to be replaced by an attendant who had long been stationed in readiness. Then came the food, a little of which the impresario managed to get between the artist's lips, while he sat in a kind of half-fainting trance, to the accompaniment of cheerful patter designed to distract the public's attention from the artist's condition; after that, a toast was drunk to the public, supposedly prompted by a whisper from the artist in the impresario's ear; the band confirmed it with a mighty flourish, the spectators melted away, and no one had any cause to be dissatisfied with the proceedings, no one except the hunger artist himself, he only, as always.

So he lived for many years, with small regular intervals of recuperation, in visible glory, honored by the world, yet in spite of that troubled in spirit, and all the more troubled because no one would take his trouble seriously. What comfort could he possibly need? What more could he possibly wish for? And if some good-natured person, feeling sorry for him, tried to console him by pointing out that his melancholy was probably caused by fasting, it could happen, especially when he had been fasting for some time, that he reacted with an outburst of fury and to the general alarm began to shake the bars of his cage like a wild animal. Yet the impresario had a way of punishing these outbreaks which he rather enjoyed putting into operation. He would apologize publicly for the artist's behavior, which was only to be excused, he admitted, because of the irritability caused by fasting; a condition hardly to be understood by well-fed people; then by natural transition he went on to mention the artist's equally incomprehensible boast that he could fast for much longer than he was doing; he praised the high ambition, the good will, the great self-denial undoubtedly implicit in such a statement; and then quite simply countered it by bringing out photographs, which were also on sale to the public, showing the artist on the fortieth day of a fast lying in bed almost dead from exhaustion. This perversion of the truth, familiar to the artist though it was, always unnerved him afresh and proved too much for him. What was a consequence of the premature ending of his fast was here presented as the cause of it! To fight against this lack of understanding, against a whole world of non-understanding, was impossible. Time and again in good faith he stood by the bars listening to the impresario, but as soon as the photographs appeared he always let go and sank with a groan back on to his straw, and the reassured public could once more come close and gaze at him.

A few years later when the witnesses of such scenes called them to mind, they often failed to understand themselves at all. For meanwhile the aforementioned change in public interest had set in; it seemed to happen almost overnight; there may have been profound causes for it, but who was going to bother about that; at any rate the pampered hunger artist suddenly found himself deserted one fine day by the amusement seekers, who went streaming past him to other more favored attractions. For the last time the impresario hurried him over half Europe to discover whether the old interest might still survive here and there; all in vain; everywhere, as if by secret agreement, a positive revulsion from professional fasting

was in evidence. Of course it could not really have sprung up so suddenly as all that, and many premonitory[1] symptoms which had not been sufficiently remarked or suppressed during the rush and glitter of success now came retrospectively to mind, but it was now too late to take any countermeasures. Fasting would surely come into fashion again at some future date, yet that was no comfort for those living in the present. What, then, was the hunger artist to do? He had been applauded by thousands in his time and could hardly come down to showing himself in a street booth at village fairs, and as for adopting another profession, he was not only too old for that but too fanatically devoted to fasting. So he took leave of the impresario, his partner in an unparalleled career, and hired himself to a large circus; in order to spare his own feelings he avoided reading the conditions of his contract.

A large circus with its enormous traffic in replacing and recruiting men, animals, and apparatus can always find a use for people at any time, even for a hunger artist, provided of course that he does not ask too much, and in this particular case anyhow it was not only the artist who was taken on but his famous and long-known name as well. Indeed, considering the peculiar nature of his performance, which was not impaired by advancing age, it could not be objected that here was an artist past his prime, no longer at the height of his professional skill, seeking a refuge in some quiet corner of a circus; on the contrary, the hunger artist averred[2] that he could fast as well as ever, which was entirely credible. He even alleged that if he were allowed to fast as he liked, and this was at once promised him without more ado, he could astound the world by establishing a record never yet achieved, a

[1] **premonitory**: warning in advance.
[2] **averred**: claimed.

statement which certainly provoked a smile among the other professionals, since it left out of account the change in public opinion, which the hunger artist in his zeal conveniently forgot.

He had not, however, actually lost his sense of the real situation and took it as a matter of course that he and his cage should be stationed, not in the middle of the ring as a main attraction, but outside, near the animal cages, on a site that was after all easily accessible. Large and gaily painted placards made a frame for the cage and announced what was to be seen inside it. When the public came thronging out in the intervals to see the animals, they could hardly avoid passing the hunger artist's cage and stopping there for a moment. Perhaps they might even have stayed longer had not those pressing behind them in the narrow gangway, who did not understand why they should be held up on their way towards the excitements of the menagerie, made it impossible for anyone to stand gazing quietly for any length of time. And that was the reason why the hunger artist, who had of course been looking forward to these visiting hours as the main achievement of his life, began instead to shrink from them. At first he could hardly wait for the intervals; it was exhilarating to watch the crowds come streaming his way, until only too soon — not even the most obstinate self-deception, clung to almost consciously, could hold out against the fact — the conviction was borne in upon him that these people, most of them, to judge from their actions, again and again, without exception, were all on their way to the menagerie. And the first sight of them from the distance remained the best. For when they reached his cage he was at once deafened by the storm of shouting and abuse that arose from the two contending factions, which renewed themselves continuously, of those who wanted to stop and stare at him — he soon began to dislike them more than the others — not out of real interest but only out of obstinate self-assertiveness, and those who wanted to go straight on to the animals. When the first great rush was past, the stragglers came along, and these, whom nothing could have prevented from stopping to look at him as long as they had breath, raced past with long strides, hardly even glancing at him, in their haste to get to the menagerie in time. And all too rarely did it happen that he had a stroke of luck, when some father of a family fetched up before him with his children, pointed a finger at the hunger artist and explained at length what the phenome-. non meant, telling stories of earlier years when he himself had watched similar but much more thrilling performances, and the children, still rather uncomprehending, since neither inside nor outside school had they been sufficiently prepared for this lesson — what did they care about fasting? — yet showed by the brightness of their intent eyes that new and better times might be coming. Perhaps, said the hunger artist to himself many a time, things would be a little better if his cage were set not quite so near the menagerie. That made it too easy for people to make their choice, to say nothing of what he suffered from the stench of the menagerie, the animals' restlessness by night, the carrying past of raw lumps of flesh for the beasts of prey, the roaring at feeding times, which depressed him continually. But he did not dare to lodge a complaint with the management; after all, he had the animals to thank for the troops of people who passed his cage, among whom there might always be one here and there to take an interest in him, and who could tell where they might seclude him if he called attention to his existence and thereby to the fact that, strictly speaking, he was only an impediment on the way to the menagerie.

A small impediment, to be sure; one that

grew steadily less. People grew familiar with the strange idea that they could be expected, in times like these, to take an interest in a hunger artist, and with this familiarity the verdict went out against him. He might fast as much as he could, and he did so; but nothing could save him now, people passed him by. Just try to explain to anyone the art of fasting! Anyone who has no feeling for it cannot be made to understand it. The fine placards grew dirty and illegible, they were torn down; the little notice board telling the number of fast days achieved, which at first was changed carefully every day, had long stayed at the same figure, for after the first few weeks even this small task seemed pointless to the staff; and so the artist simply fasted on and on, as he had once dreamed of doing, and it was no trouble to him, just as he had always foretold, but no one counted the days, no one, not even the artist himself, knew what records he was already breaking, and his heart grew heavy. And when once in a time some leisurely passer-by stopped, made merry over the old figure on the board and spoke of swindling, that was in its way the stupidest lie ever invented by indifference and inborn malice, since it was not the hunger artist who was cheating, he was working honestly, but the world was cheating him of his reward.

Many more days went by, however, and that too came to an end. An overseer's eye fell on the cage one day and he asked the attendants why this perfectly good stage should be left standing there unused with dirty straw inside it; nobody knew, until one man, helped out by the notice board, remembered about the hunger artist. They poked into the straw with sticks and found him in it. "Are you still fasting?" asked the overseer, "when on earth do you mean to stop?" "Forgive me, everybody," whispered the hunger artist; only the overseer, who had his ear to the bars, understood him.

"Of course," said the overseer, and tapped his forehead with a finger to let the attendants know what state the man was in, "we forgive you." "I always wanted you to admire my fasting," said the hunger artist. "We do admire it," said the overseer, affably. "But you shouldn't admire it," said the hunger artist. "Well then we don't admire it," said the overseer, "but why shouldn't we admire it?" "Because I have to fast, I can't help it," said the hunger artist. "What a fellow you are," said the overseer, "and why can't you help it?" "Because," said the hunger artist, lifting his head a little and speaking, with his lips pursed, as if for a kiss, right into the overseer's ear, so that no syllable might be lost, "because I couldn't find the food I liked. If I had found it, believe me, I should have made no fuss and stuffed myself like you or anyone else." These were his last words, but in his dimming eyes remained the firm, though no longer proud, persuasion that he was still continuing to fast.

"Well, clear this out now!" said the overseer, and they buried the hunger artist, straw and all. Into the cage they put a young panther. Even the most insensitive felt it refreshing to see this wild creature leaping around the cage that had so long been dreary. The panther was all right. The food he liked was brought him without hesitation by the attendants; he seemed not even to miss his freedom; his noble body, furnished almost to the bursting point with all that it needed, seemed to carry freedom around with it too; somewhere in his jaws it seemed to lurk; and the joy of life streamed with such ardent passion from his throat that for the onlookers it was not easy to stand the shock of it. But they braced themselves, crowded round the cage, and did not want ever to move away.

For Discussion

1. The question of identifying who the hunger artist is lies at the heart of appreciating Kafka's story. A literal reading will hardly make that identification clear, yet an understanding of what the story literally says is necessary before the meaning can be extended. Literally, the hunger artist is a man who makes a public spectacle of himself by fasting over long periods. At the beginning of the story what is the attitude of people toward the hunger artist? How is that attitude different from what it once had been? The hunger artist sits in a cage. What furniture is in the cage? Who guards the cage? The fasts last for forty days only. Why? What happens at the end of each fasting period?

2. At the literal level still, the multitude is seen in time to abandon the hunger artist in favor of other spectacles. Accordingly, he is reduced to appearing as a sideshow feature in a circus. Where is his cage placed? Who comes to look at him? What finally spells his doom? His dying words are a confession. What does he confess? At last the cage encloses a new attraction. What is it? How do the multitudes respond to it?

3. The faster is identified as an artist, and artists — composers, poets, painters, and others with special creative gifts — are different from ordinary people. Their difference isolates them. How is that isolation symbolized in the story? The achievement of art — writing a novel, developing the skill to paint a great picture — requires dedication and discipline, and the hunger artist has those qualities. How do you know? What various attitudes does the multitude have toward what the artist is doing? In general, what insights about the relationship of the artist to society are developed in the story?

4. At another level, the story may be read as an allegory of man's dual nature. Caged within a single life are impulses toward both the bestial and the spiritual. One, pertaining to the senses, is nourished by the appetites; the other, pertaining to the sensibilities, is nourished by the soul. How are these contrasting aspects of a single identity symbolized in the story? What is the story suggesting about the fate of a life of the mind that is divorced entirely from matter?

5. At yet another level the story conveys religious meanings. In olden times people went to church every day, but now they prefer to flock to other spectacles. In attempting to take its place in the secularized world that resembles a circus, amid "the stench of the menagerie, the animals' restlessness by night, the carrying past of raw lumps of flesh for the beasts of prey, the roaring at feeding times," religion serves as "only an impediment on the way to the menagerie." About religious matters, as about art, "Anyone who has no feeling for it cannot be made to understand it" (page 683). What other insights about religion in times past and in the present does the story convey?

6. **Verisimilitude.** A creative author usually seeks to convince the reader of the factual truth of what his story conveys, even if — indeed, especially if — the story is fiction. The quality of apparent truthfulness, or *verisimilitude*, can be obtained in a number of ways — for example, by filling the story with precise facts (street addresses, dates, first names and middle initials), as though in an effort to be scrupulously accurate. A story as fantastic as "A Hunger Artist" gains from Kafka's attentions to effect of verisimilitude, as in the precise description of the hunger artist's appearance, sitting in his cage "pallid in black tights, with his ribs sticking out so prominently, not even on a seat but down among straw on the ground, sometimes giving a courteous nod, answering questions with a constrained smile . . . ." (page 677). Give other examples within

the story that contribute to the verisimilitude — examples that make you, in Coleridge's phrase, willingly suspend your disbelief, at least temporarily.

For Composition

Up to this point the discussion has suggested three directions in which the meaning of "A Hunger Artist" might be extended beyond the literal. The story might be read as a religious allegory, as an allegory of the position of the artist in society, and as an allegory of man's dual nature that partakes of both mind and matter.

● Analysis.   In an essay supported by specific examples, develop in detail one of the three interpretations mentioned. Regarding the story at the religious level, for instance, what is suggested by such insights as the following: "for their elders he was often just a joke that happened to be in fashion, but the children stood open-mouthed holding each other's hands for greater security. . . . "?

Words and Allusions

HOMOGRAPHS.   Words that are spelled alike but differ in derivation, meaning, or pronunciation are called *homographs*. In Kafka's story *fast* refers to abstaining from food. How many other uses of this spelling can you find? How do these homographs differ?

DOUBLETS (page 481).   The word *feast* is almost an antonym of *fast* as it is used in Kafka's story. Are the two words related? Are they doublets?

The Hollow Men

T. S. ELIOT

Identity implies substance. To be sure, some observers have felt that people in our own century of the committee and the anti-hero lack the substantiality of people in earlier ages. Among those observers, T. S. Eliot has expressed what seemed to him to be the spiritual emptiness of men's lives in the twentieth century. The poem that follows is difficult, partly because it imitates the inarticulateness of the people it describes and partly because of Eliot's frequent allusions to the works of other writers. Despite the problems, the poem will speak to you if you read it attentively two or three times, responding in any ways that the diction and imagery suggest are appropriate.

Mistah Kurtz — he dead.
A penny for the Old Guy

I

We are the hollow men
We are the stuffed men
Leaning together

Headpiece filled with straw. Alas!
Our dried voices, when   5
We whisper together
Are quiet and meaningless

As wind in dry grass
Or rats' feet over broken glass
In our dry cellar   10

Shape without form, shade without color,
Paralyzed force, gesture without motion;

Those who have crossed
With direct eyes, to death's other Kingdom
Remember us — if at all — not as lost   15
Violent souls, but only
As the hollow men
The stuffed men.

II

Eyes I dare not meet in dreams
In death's dream kingdom   20
These do not appear:
There, the eyes are
Sunlight on a broken column
There, is a tree swinging
And voices are   25
In the wind's singing
More distant and more solemn
Than a fading star.

Let me be no nearer
In death's dream kingdom   30
Let me also wear
Such deliberate disguises
Rat's coat, crowskin, crossed staves*
In a field
Behaving as the wind behaves   35
No nearer —

Not that final meeting
In the twilight kingdom

III

This is the dead land
This is cactus land   40
Here the stone images

33. **staves**: staffs.

Are raised, here they receive
The supplication of a dead man's hand
Under the twinkle of a fading star.

Is it like this   45
In death's other kingdom
Waking alone
At the hour when we are
Trembling with tenderness
Lips that would kiss   50
Form prayers to broken stone.

IV

The eyes are not here
There are no eyes here
In this valley of dying stars
In this hollow valley   55
This broken jaw of our lost kingdoms

In this last of meeting places
We grope together
And avoid speech   59
Gathered on this beach of the tumid* river

Sightless, unless
The eyes reappear
As the perpetual star
Multifoliate* rose
Of death's twilight kingdom   65
The hope only
Of empty men.

V

*Here we go round the prickly pear
Prickly pear prickly pear
Here we go round the prickly pear*   70
At five o'clock in the morning.

Between the idea
And the reality
Between the motion
And the act   75

60. **tumid**: swollen.
64. **multifoliate**: having many leaves.

"*Let me also wear ... deliberate disguises.*" Double Self-Portrait *by the American artist Ben Shahn.*

Falls the Shadow

       For Thine is the Kingdom

Between the conception
And the creation
Between the emotion   80
And the response
Falls the Shadow

       Life is very long

Between the desire
And the spasm   85
Between the potency
And the existence

Between the essence
And the descent
Falls the Shadow   90

       For Thine is the Kingdom

For Thine is
Life is
For Thine is the

This is the way the world ends   95
This is the way the world ends
This is the way the world ends
Not with a bang but a whimper.

For Discussion

1. In five parts, "The Hollow Men" explores the lives led by empty people in a world as vacant and unproductive as a desert. The poem opens with two parallel statements. Are they antithetical? In what sense might a person be hollow and stuffed at the same time? The men and the sterile aridity of their surroundings are evoked throughout Part I: they *lean together*, rather than stand up; they *whisper* rather than speak out. What diction conveys the dryness of their world? What is the effect of the absence of moisture?

2. Lines 13 and following introduce the concerns of death, while suggesting a contrast between the hollow men and those who, having died before them, have gone with direct eyes to meet their fate. Do such people — "lost / Violent souls" — remember the people now living? If so, how? Death's other Kingdom (line 14) differs from death's dream kingdom (line 20), perhaps in the way that what is real may differ from what is imagined, or as Hell differs from Heaven. How does the speaker of Part II dream of death? Does the first stanza of the part evoke, through image and rhythm, a harsh desert land? The speaker shies away from thoughts of death. Why, do you suppose? What familiar object is suggested by "crossed staves / In a field"? Does the answer help explain the apparent paradox in the opening two lines of the poem?

3. Images recur. Eyes (line 19), which see things as they are, contrast with the sightlessness of the hollow men (line 61). Desert images early in the poem appear again in Part III, where they are spread under "the twinkle of a fading star." Is it like this in Hell, the speaker wonders at lines 45–46. Like what?

4. The stars of lines 28, 44, and 63 allude to Dante's *Divine Comedy* (page 212). In *The Inferno*, the condemned will never see stars again. Moreover, each of the three parts of the *Comedy* ends on *stars*, which come to represent increasing spiritual knowledge as Dante's own journey toward Paradise takes

him from the depths of Hell ever nearer them. In Eliot's world, by contrast, the stars are dying. What is the effect of that adjective, and of "fading"? Line 60 incorporates another allusion to *The Inferno*, Canto III. Explain.

5. At the summit of Dante's vision is the multifoliate rose (line 64), an image of God at the blinding center and the souls of the redeemed clustered like petals around Him. Will the hollow men ever be able to see such a stunning and imaginative vision as the rose represents? Is the answer clear-cut, or is "twilight" ambiguous?

6. The opening of Part V alludes to a familiar nursery rhyme. What different connotations do you associate with "mulberry bush" in the original rhyme, and "prickly pear" in this alteration? Who are "we" as the nursery rhyme has been refashioned? The activity depicted seems childish and pointless. Notice that line 72 and following develop ideas expressed in lines 11–12. How do you interpret the Shadow that falls between the thought and act? The italicized indentations seem to represent abortive prayers, as though the speaker were trying hard to articulate a spiritual thought and finding it impossible. The poem in time runs down like a record on a faulty phonograph. How does the final thought support that effect?

7. Two quotations, called epigraphs, precede the poem. One refers to the practice in England, corresponding roughly to our Halloween, in which on a November anniversary children build stuffed effigies of Guy Fawkes, an early seventeenth-century "lost, violent soul" who tried unsuccessfully to blow up Parliament; the children beseech passers-by to give them a penny as a tribute to their dummy of the Old Guy. What connection do you see between Guy Fawkes, his effigy, and the Hollow Men?

8. The other epigraph is more complicated. It comes from *Heart of Darkness*, a novella by Joseph Conrad that describes the disintegration of a high-minded individual who goes mad within the heart of Africa. The narrator

of the story has mixed feelings about this man Kurtz: bestial he became, and excessive, yet he looked at life directly and lived his life with courage. His final words had been "The horror! The horror!" But Kurtz "had summed up — he had judged. 'The horror!' He was a remarkable man. After all, this was the expression of some sort of belief; it had candor, it had conviction, it had a vibrating note of revolt in its whisper. . . . " At least, the narrator feels, Kurtz had the courage to look life squarely in the face and live with what he saw there, however horrible that might have been. Do you see the relationship between Kurtz and his kind on the one hand, and the hollow men on the other?

9. **Dactyl.** This metrical foot derives its name from the Greek word for "finger." A finger has a long joint and two shorter ones; the dactyl has a stressed syllable followed by two unstressed ones:

We are the / hol low men

Whole poems may be written in dactylic feet:

This is the/ for est pri/me val. The/

mur mur ing/ pines and the/ hem locks

The line opens Longfellow's *Evangeline,* a poem written entirely in dactylic hexameters. How does dactylic differ from anapestic? In "The Hollow Men," what other isolated dactylic feet do you find? Consider, for example, lines 3 and 11.

For Composition

Eliot's poem was written in 1925. To what extent is its description of modern man — hollow, secularized, spiritually bankrupt, without direction to his life — applicable a half-century later?

1. **Analysis.** In a brief but coherent and well-supported paper, explain what attributes of the hollow men are identified in the poem. They speak softly, for example; they have shape but no form, and whatever force they have is paralyzed (lines 6, 11, and 12).

2. **Argument.** To what extent is modern society populated by "hollow men"? In an essay that makes use of specific examples, support or refute the assertion: "Eliot's poem accurately describes the lives that most people continue to lead today."

3. **Comparison and Contrast.** In an essay that quotes appropriately from both poems, compare and contrast Auden's unknown citizen with Eliot's hollow men.

About the Poet. Poet, playwright, and critic, **T. S. Eliot** (1888–1965) was born in St. Louis but became a British subject in 1927. Educated at Harvard, the Sorbonne, and Oxford, Eliot worked as an English schoolmaster and as a bank clerk before joining a publishing firm with which he was associated for the rest of his life. He began writing poetry while at Harvard, where he discovered the French symbolist poets and adapted many of their conventions to English verse. Writing in an unusual rhyming free verse, Eliot produced highly disciplined poems, such as *The Waste Land* and "The Love Song of J. Alfred Prufrock," that departed from traditional forms. For his work as a "trailblazing pioneer of modern poetry," he was awarded the Nobel Prize in 1948. In later years he received public acclaim for his verse dramas.

Munch

The Scream

This painting can be seen as a kind of footnote to Willa Cather's "Paul's Case" (page 643), as the direct expression of what Paul feels. The painting gives us no reason for the cry because what Munch was trying to do was to catch in paint pure emotion, divorced as much as possible from any situation and separated from any specific cause. Yet the character of the emotion would be incomprehensible if he gave no clues at all.

The first thing to observe is that Munch has used lines, both straight and curved, on such a large scale that they clearly have a purpose beyond that of simply representing objects. The two kinds of lines are kept in separate areas of the picture — straight lines on the bridge and curved lines in the background. The figures on the bridge, however, appear in both kinds of lines and extend into both areas.

Directly before us is the screaming figure (man or woman? Does it make any difference?) who is all curved lines. Behind are two more figures, almost all vertical straight lines. The emotion, then, is signified by the curved lines. From the screamer, waves of emotion spread out and completely dominate the landscape so that the landscape becomes a mere extension and repetition of the cry. The sunset repeats the same curved lines. In how many other ways are these curves repeated?

Munch wishes to indicate that it is the emotion of the screamer that infects the landscape, not the other way round. Thus the lower part of the harbor in the background instead of being a part of endless waves is a self-contained oval. Moreover, the ships are riding peacefully. The cry issues from a distorted oval mouth and skull-like face. This repetition of shapes in mouth and harbor suggests that the cry bursts out of a tortured human being but is absorbed into the landscape.

The curved and wavy lines identify the landscape with emotion. The straight lines of the bridge and the two figures on it suggest a contrast to that emotion. Bridges have two characteristics. Since they connect places, they are symbols of communication. But they are also worlds in themselves, like ships. On a bridge one feels separate from the world, and for that reason a bridge can be frightening, a prison. The screamer has turned his back on the bridge and on the two figures, and is stopping his ears. Thus it appears that the straight lines contain the situation that terrifies the screamer. Do the two figures appear sinister or threatening? Why, or why not?

The deep blues and greens of the screamer and of the landscape suggest the repression of emotion. The red of the sky is traditionally used to suggest a bursting forth of repressed emotion, as in the red flag of revolution. All these colors appear also on the bridge, whose straight lines are the screamer's emotional prison. Thus it appears that the screamer is the source of the fear that he is trying to escape.

MORSE PECKHAM

Edvard Munch (1863–1944) *The Scream.* National Museum, Oslo.

/ Courbet

The Violincellist

This painting is an attempt to answer Voznesensky's question "Who Are You?" (page 658). In the poem we read of "Architects [striving] to be poet-creators." If the line were changed to "Painters striving to be musicians," it would apply precisely to this painting, for it is a self-portrait of Courbet posing as a cellist.

In his twenties Courbet painted a whole series of self-portraits. One shows him with a dog at the mouth of a cave in the mountains. Beside him are a walking stick and a book, and he is holding a pipe, which for many years had been a symbol of the meditative, noncommunicative man. He looks out from the painting with the utmost arrogance. In another he is posing as a self-absorbed guitarist in medieval costume, again in a forest. A third also shows him in medieval costume in the same kind of setting. This painting is known as "The Sculptor" and also as "The Poet." In the last two paintings he is trying out historical poses in order to isolate himself from his contemporary world so that he can become aware of himself and define himself. Do you or your contemporaries ever try out various costumes for the same purpose? It is significant that in these two paintings Courbet poses in several artistic roles. As a painter — one artistic role — he is trying to feel what it is like to be some other kind of artist in order to determine what an artist is, regardless of what art he practices.

In the next of this series of self-portraits something quite different appears. His hair is tousled, his shirt collar is open, and he gives the impression of one quite indifferent to middle-class attitudes. This painting forms a contrast with the earlier self-portraits in which he is dressed very elegantly. Here again he is with a pipe, but he is smoking it, not holding it. It is an ordinary workingman's pipe, and it is clear that Courbet wishes to identify himself with workingmen.

Yet that mode of self-identification did not satisfy him either, and in the next year he once again portrayed himself as a musician. But the painting before us, *The Violincellist,* is very different from the earlier ones. The face is troubled, in contrast with the arrogant assurance of some portraits and the easy confidence of the year before. The brow is deeply lined, and the eyes are sunk in shadow. What does the sidelong glance suggest? Notice the almost deformed shape of the left hand. How does this relate to playing a cello?

Of all Courbet's self-portraits, this is by far the darkest. A profound melancholy pervades the picture, coming from the sadness of the face, the large areas of darkness, and the cello itself. For the cello has a low, solemn, melancholy sound. It is often opposed in orchestration, for example, to the lighter brilliance of the violin.

MORSE PECKHAM

Gustave Courbet (1819–1877) *The Violincellist.* National Museum, Stockholm.   693

Picasso

Girl before a Mirror

Artists use various means to explore visually the problem ot identity. They paint self-portraits or pictures of themselves painting self-portraits. They also like to paint themselves and other people looking into mirrors. Picasso's *Girl before a Mirror* is an example of a long series of such paintings.

In their interest in themselves, artists are just like everyone else, except that their talents and training make it possible for them to do something for themselves that others have to depend on artists to do. What is the difference between looking at yourself in a mirror and looking at a portrait of yourself? To ask "Who am I?" means, among other things, to ask: "What do I look like to other people? How do they perceive me and define me?" James Baldwin's "Notes of a Native Son" (page 662) is a literary treatment of this problem. He uses his father, and also white people, to see and identify himself. Do you think it significant that he breaks a mirror?

Since the invention of photography, artists have been freed from making conventional portraits. They can turn more directly to an interpretation of the self. Here Picasso is concerned with something that happens when we see ourselves. The mirror is the long oval shape at the right, and the girl's arm extends across it, as if she were embracing her image or trying, perhaps, to integrate it with herself. Her real face, on the left, shows that she indeed has a problem of integration. The profile is simple, almost naturalistic, and highly regular. But the oval that encloses it includes half of another face. This second half-face reflects an unintegrated aspect of her personality. The lips and cheek are red; the face is yellow. The effect is one of great vigor, emphasized by the dark green of the eye. But why does the black eyeball have no pupil?

The face in the mirror is quite different. The dominant colors are murky blues, violets, blacks, and purples — all colors of emotional disturbance and repression. The two faces on the left are now almost completely integrated in the profile in the mirror. But has anything been lost, left out? Does the girl see herself as attractive as she really is? What effect does her divided personality have on her image of herself? Again, in the face in the mirror there is no pupil in the eye.

The rest of her body is white with light green stripes. These are colors of emotional ease. But here again the lack of integration is brought out by the disharmony between her actual body and its reflection in the mirror. Can you see how even the squares and circles of the wallpaper background express this struggle toward integration?

MORSE PECKHAM

Pablo Picasso (1881–1973) *Girl before a Mirror.* Museum of Modern Art, New York.

Eugène Delacroix (1798–1863) *Hamlet and Horatio in the Graveyard.* Louvre, Paris.

Delacroix

Hamlet and Horatio in the Graveyard

Delacroix was obsessed with *Hamlet* (page 726), and he painted him a number of times. Contemporary artists, writers, and musicians felt the same attraction. Berlioz set several scenes of the play to music, and Tschaikowsky wrote a symphonic poem. The conception of Hamlet as a man attempting to establish his own identity comes from the period of Delacroix.

Several times Delacroix painted the scene of Hamlet and Horatio in the graveyard. At the time this was felt to be a crucial scene in Shakespeare's play because a man can be said to be truly aware of his own identity only when he has truly faced his own death.

In this painting Delacroix created an interlocking problem of color and design. He wanted Hamlet, if not in the traditional black, at least in some color that would serve the function of black in relation to other colors. He chose a deep blue, one with very little white in it — a color at the negative or emotionally repressive end of the color range. For Horatio, less withdrawn than Hamlet, he wanted a less repressive color. Thus Horatio appears not only in Hamlet's blue but also in a rich red —a more emotionally assertive color. But this combination created a problem, in that the red tended to make Horatio appear the dominant figure. To establish which was truly the dominant figure, Delacroix repeated the figures in the towers of Elsinore. The taller tower is at the right, just as Hamlet is, and to the left of the lower tower reflecting Horatio is the long line of a gabled roof which emphasizes still further the height of the dominant tower. Horatio is given such importance in the scene because his friendship is essential to Hamlet's efforts to define his identity.

To avoid making the figures of Hamlet and Horatio inert, Delacroix places them off center and twists the figure of Horatio. Horatio's movement is emphasized by the funeral procession with Ophelia's casket, a line that is continued in the row of cypresses on the opposite side of the painting, and in the posture of the gravedigger near the trees. In front of this gravedigger appears a small wedge of lighted ground. One line of this wedge is continued up the low hill in front of the funeral procession. The other line moves toward the feet of Horatio and Hamlet and continues from there. What shape or design is created by these lines? How does this design help concentrate our attention on the two central figures? How does Delacroix prevent this design from becoming too obvious and distracting attention away from the central figures?

Finally, in addition to the somber melancholy of Hamlet, Delacroix wanted to suggest Hamlet's vitality and power of language. How does he accomplish this in color and in gesture?

MORSE PECKHAM

The Secret Sharer

JOSEPH CONRAD

Times of crisis reveal a person's true nature. In the safety of his own living room he may talk bravely enough, but how well will he acquit himself when, alone and exposed and gripped with fear, he has to act? The following impressive story explores the complexities of one man's identity as exhibited under the pressures that surround the assuming of his first command at sea.

On my right hand there were lines of fishing stakes resembling a mysterious system of half-submerged bamboo fences, incomprehensible in its division of the domain of tropical fishes, and crazy of aspect as if abandoned forever by some nomad tribe of fishermen now gone to the other end of the ocean; for there was no sign of human habitation as far as the eye could reach. To the left a group of barren islets, suggesting ruins of stone walls, towers, and blockhouses, had its foundations set in a blue sea that itself looked solid, so still and stable did it lie below my feet; even the track of light from the westering sun shone smoothly, without that animated glitter which tells of an imperceptible ripple. And when I turned my head to take a parting glance at the tug which had just left us anchored outside the bar, I saw the straight line of the flat shore joined to the stable sea, edge to edge, with a perfect and unmarked closeness, in one leveled floor half brown, half blue under the enormous dome of the sky. Corresponding in their insignificance to the islets of the sea, two small clumps of trees, one on each side of the only fault in the impeccable joint, marked the mouth of the river Meinam[1] we had just left on the first preparatory stage of our homeward journey; and, far back on the inland level, a larger and loftier mass, the grove surrounding the great Paknam pagoda,[2] was the only thing on which the eye could rest from the vain task of exploring the monotonous sweep of the horizon. Here and there gleams as of a few scattered pieces of silver marked the windings of the great river; and on the nearest of them, just within the bar, the tug steaming right into the land became lost to my sight, hull[3] and funnel[4] and masts, as though the impassive earth had swallowed her up without an effort, without a tremor. My eye followed the light cloud of her smoke, now here, now there, above the plain, according to the devious curves of the stream, but always fainter and farther away, till I lost it at last behind the miter-shaped[5] hill of the great pagoda. And then I was left alone with my ship, anchored at the head of the Gulf of Siam.

She floated at the starting point of a long journey, very still in an immense stillness, the shadows of her spars[6] flung far to the eastward by the setting sun. At that moment I was alone on her decks. There was not a sound in her — and around us nothing moved, nothing lived, not a canoe on the

[1] **Meinam:** river in southern Thailand.

[2] **Paknam pagoda:** famous temple in the port city of Samut Prakan.

[3] **hull:** frame or body of a ship.

[4] **funnel:** smokestack.

[5] **miter-shaped:** coming to a peaked point at the front and back.

[6] **spars:** poles and masts supporting the sails.

water, not a bird in the air, not a cloud in the sky. In this breathless pause at the threshold of a long passage we seemed to be measuring our fitness for a long and arduous enterprise, the appointed task of both our existences to be carried out, far from all human eyes, with only sky and sea for spectators and for judges.

There must have been some glare in the air to interfere with one's sight, because it was only just before the sun left us that my roaming eyes made out beyond the highest ridge of the principal islet of the group something which did away with the solemnity of perfect solitude. The tide of darkness flowed on swiftly; and with tropical suddenness a swarm of stars came out above the shadowy earth, while I lingered yet, my hand resting lightly on my ship's rail as if on the shoulder of a trusted friend. But, with all that multitude of celestial bodies staring down at one, the comfort of quiet communion with her was gone for good. And there were also disturbing sounds by this time — voices, footsteps forward; the steward flitted along the main deck, a busily ministering spirit; a hand bell tinkled urgently under the poop deck. . . .[1]

I found my two officers waiting for me near the supper table, in the lighted cuddy.[2] We sat down at once, and as I helped the chief mate, I said:

"Are you aware that there is a ship anchored inside the islands? I saw her mastheads above the ridge as the sun went down."

He raised sharply his simple face, overcharged by a terrible growth of whisker, and emitted his usual ejaculations: "Bless my soul, sir! You don't say so!"

My second mate was a round-cheeked, silent young man, grave beyond his years, I thought; but as our eyes happened to meet

[1] **poop deck:** raised deck at the back section of a ship.
[2] **cuddy:** small room on a ship.

I detected a slight quiver on his lips. I looked down at once. It was not my part to encourage sneering on board my ship. It must be said, too, that I knew very little of my officers. In consequence of certain events of no particular significance, except to myself, I had been appointed to the command only a fortnight before. Neither did I know much of the hands forward.[3] All these people had been together for eighteen months or so, and my position was that of the only stranger on board. I mention this because it has some bearing on what is to follow. But what I felt most was my being a stranger to the ship; and if all the truth must be told, I was somewhat of a stranger to myself. The youngest man on board (barring the second mate), and untried as yet by a position of the fullest responsibility, I was willing to take the adequacy of the others for granted. They had simply to be equal to their tasks; but I wondered how far I should turn out faithful to that ideal conception of one's own personality every man sets up for himself secretly.

Meantime the chief mate, with an almost visible effect of collaboration on the part of his round eyes and frightful whiskers, was trying to evolve a theory of the anchored ship. His dominant trait was to take all things into earnest consideration. He was of a painstaking turn of mind. As he used to say, he "liked to account to himself" for practically everything that came in his way, down to a miserable scorpion he had found in his cabin a week before. The why and the wherefore of that scorpion — how it got on board and came to select his room rather than the pantry (which was a dark place and more what a scorpion would be partial to), and how on earth it managed to drown itself in the inkwell of his writing desk — had exercised him infinitely. The ship

[3] **forward:** the crew customarily lived at the front of the ship, or *forward*.

within the islands was much more easily accounted for; and just as we were about to rise from the table he made his pronouncement. She was, he doubted not, a ship from home lately arrived. Probably she drew too much water to cross the bar except at the top of spring tides. Therefore she went into that natural harbor to wait for a few days in preference to remaining in an open roadstead.

"That's so," confirmed the second mate, suddenly, in his slightly hoarse voice. "She draws over twenty feet. She's the Liverpool ship *Sephora* with a cargo of coal. Hundred and twenty-three days from Cardiff."

We looked at him in surprise.

"The tugboat skipper told me when he came on board for your letters, sir," explained the young man. "He expects to take her up the river the day after tomorrow."

After thus overwhelming us with the extent of his information he slipped out of the cabin. The mate observed regretfully that he "could not account for that young fellow's whims." What prevented him telling us all about it at once, he wanted to know.

I detained him as he was making a move. For the last two days the crew had had plenty of hard work, and the night before they had very little sleep. I felt painfully that I — a stranger — was doing something unusual when I directed him to let all hands turn in without setting an anchor watch. I proposed to keep on deck myself till one o'clock or thereabouts. I would get the second mate to relieve me at that hour.

"He will turn out the cook and the steward[1] at four," I concluded, "and then give you a call. Of course at the slightest sign of any sort of wind we'll have the hands up and make a start at once."

He concealed his astonishment. "Very well, sir." Outside the cuddy he put his head in the second mate's door to inform him of my unheard-of caprice to take a five hours' anchor watch on myself. I heard the other raise his voice incredulously: "What? The captain himself?" Then a few more murmurs, a door closed, then another. A few moments later I went on deck.

My strangeness, which had made me sleepless, had prompted that unconventional arrangement, as if I had expected in those solitary hours of the night to get on terms with the ship of which I knew nothing, manned by men of whom I knew very little more. Fast alongside a wharf, littered like

---

[1] steward: officer in charge of food supplies.

ABOUT THE AUTHOR • The son of a Polish nobleman, Teodor Jósef Konrad Korzeniowski, or **Joseph Conrad** (1857–1924), was fascinated by England, which to him seemed a nation of sea-faring adventurers. Leaving Poland at seventeen, Conrad went to sea, serving first on a French merchantman and later on English vessels. While serving as captain or mate of various ships, he began writing novels in English, a language he could not even speak until his twenties. Later he left the sea to assume a full-time writing career, producing such works as *Heart of Darkness*, *Victory*, and *Lord Jim*. Conrad's mature novels are concerned with problems of guilt, the effects of isolation, and the psychology of man's secret inner self.

any ship in port with a tangle of unrelated things, invaded by unrelated shore people, I had hardly seen her yet properly. Now, as she lay cleared for sea, the stretch of her main deck seemed to me very fine under the stars. Very fine, very roomy for her size, and very inviting. I descended the poop and paced the waist, my mind picturing to myself the coming passage through the Malay Archipelago,[1] down the Indian Ocean, and up the Atlantic. All its phases were familiar enough to me, every characteristic, all the alternatives which were likely to face me on the high seas — everything! . . . except the novel responsibility of command. But I took heart from the reasonable thought that the ship was like other ships, the men like other men, and that the sea was not likely to keep any special surprises expressly for my discomfiture.

Arrived at that comforting conclusion, I bethought myself of a cigar and went below to get it. All was still down there. Everybody at the after end of the ship was sleeping profoundly. I came out again on the quarterdeck,[2] agreeably at ease in my sleeping suit on that warm breathless night, barefooted, a glowing cigar in my teeth, and, going forward, I was met by the profound silence of the fore[3] end of the ship. Only as I passed the door of the forecastle[4] I heard a deep, quiet, trustful sigh of some sleeper inside. And suddenly I rejoiced in the great security of the sea as compared with the unrest of the land, in my choice of that untempted life presenting no disquieting problems, invested with an elementary moral beauty by the absolute straightforwardness of its appeal and by the singleness of its purpose.

The riding light in the fore-rigging[5] burned with a clear, untroubled, as if symbolic, flame, confident and bright in the mysterious shades of the night. Passing on my way aft[6] along the other side of the ship, I observed that the rope side ladder, put over, no doubt, for the master of the tug when he came to fetch away our letters, had not been hauled in as it should have been. I became annoyed at this, for exactitude in small matters is the very soul of discipline. Then I reflected that I had myself peremptorily dismissed my officers from duty, and by my own act had prevented the anchor watch being formally set and things properly attended to. I asked myself whether it was wise ever to interfere with the established routine of duties even from the kindest of motives. My action might have made me appear eccentric. Goodness only knew how that absurdly whiskered mate would "account" for my conduct, and what the whole ship thought of that informality of their new captain. I was vexed with myself.

Not from compunction certainly, but, as it were mechanically, I proceeded to get the ladder in myself. Now a side ladder of that sort is a light affair and comes in easily, yet my vigorous tug, which should have brought it flying on board, merely recoiled upon my body in a totally unexpected jerk. What the devil! . . . I was so astounded by the immovableness of that ladder that I remained stock-still, trying to account for it to myself like that imbecile mate of mine. In the end, of course, I put my head over the rail.

The side of the ship made an opaque belt of shadow on the darkling glassy shimmer of the sea. But I saw at once something elongated and pale floating very close to the ladder. Before I could form a guess a faint flash of phosphorescent light, which seemed

---

[1] **Malay Archipelago:** chain of islands extending from the southernmost part of the Asiatic mainland to a point north of eastern Australia.

[2] **quarterdeck:** section of the upper deck, usually reserved for officers.

[3] **fore:** front.

[4] **forecastle** (fōk′s′l, fōr′kas″l): front part of the ship, where sailors' quarters are located.

[5] **fore-rigging:** ropes supporting the front sails of a ship.

[6] **aft:** toward the back of the ship.

to issue suddenly from the naked body of a man, flickered in the sleeping water with the elusive, silent play of summer lightning in a night sky. With a gasp I saw revealed to my stare a pair of feet, the long legs, a broad livid back immersed right up to the neck in a greenish cadaverous glow. One hand, awash, clutched the bottom rung of the ladder. He was complete but for the head. A headless corpse! The cigar dropped out of my gaping mouth with a tiny plop and a short hiss quite audible in the absolute stillness of all things under heaven. At that I suppose he raised up his face, a dimly pale oval in the shadow of the ship's side. But even then I could only barely make out down there the shape of his black-haired head. However, it was enough for the horrid, frost-bound sensation which had gripped me about the chest to pass off. The moment of vain exclamations was past, too. I only climbed on the spare spar and leaned over the rail as far as I could, to bring my eyes nearer to that mystery floating alongside.

As he hung by the ladder, like a resting swimmer, the sea lightning played about his limbs at every stir; and he appeared in it ghastly, silvery, fishlike. He remained as mute as a fish, too. He made no motion to get out of the water, either. It was inconceivable that he should not attempt to come on board, and strangely troubling to suspect that perhaps he did not want to. And my first words were prompted by just that troubled incertitude.

"What's the matter?" I asked in my ordinary tone, speaking down to the face upturned exactly under mine.

"Cramp," it answered, no louder. Then slightly anxious, "I say, no need to call anyone."

"I was not going to," I said.

"Are you alone on deck?"

"Yes."

I had somehow the impression that he was on the point of letting go the ladder to swim away beyond my ken — mysterious as he came. But, for the moment, this being appearing as if he had risen from the bottom of the sea (it was certainly the nearest land to the ship) wanted only to know the time. I told him. And he, down there, tentatively:

"I suppose your captain's turned in?"

"I am sure he isn't," I said.

He seemed to struggle with himself, for I heard something like the low, bitter murmur of doubt. "What's the good?" His next words came out with a hesitating effort.

"Look here, my man. Could you call him out quietly?"

I thought the time had come to declare myself.

"*I* am the captain."

I heard a "By Jove!" whispered at the level of the water. The phosphorescence flashed in the swirl of the water all about his limbs, his other hand seized the ladder.

"My name's Leggatt."

The voice was calm and resolute. A good voice. The self-possession of that man had somehow induced a corresponding state in myself. It was very quietly that I remarked:

"You must be a good swimmer."

"Yes. I've been in the water practically since nine o'clock. The question for me now is whether I am to let go this ladder and go on swimming till I sink from exhaustion, or — to come on board here."

I felt this was no mere formula of desperate speech, but a real alternative in the view of a strong soul. I should have gathered from this that he was young; indeed, it is only the young who are ever confronted by such clear issues. But at the time it was pure intuition on my part. A mysterious communication was established already between us two — in the face of that silent, darkened tropical sea. I was young, too; young enough to make no comment. The man in the water began suddenly to climb up the ladder, and I hastened away from the rail to fetch some clothes.

Before entering the cabin I stood still, listening in the lobby at the foot of the stairs.

A faint snore came through the closed door of the chief mate's room. The second mate's door was on the hook, but the darkness in there was absolutely soundless. He, too, was young and could sleep like a stone. Remained the steward, but he was not likely to wake up before he was called. I got a sleeping suit out of my room and, coming back on deck, saw the naked man from the sea sitting on the main hatch, glimmering white in the darkness, his elbows on his knees and his head in his hands. In a moment he had concealed his damp body in a sleeping suit of the same gray-stripe pattern as the one I was wearing and followed me like my double on the poop. Together we moved right aft, barefooted, silent.

"What is it?" I asked in a deadened voice, taking the lighted lamp out of the binnacle,[1] and raising it to his face.

"An ugly business."

He had rather regular features; a good mouth; light eyes under somewhat heavy, dark eyebrows; a smooth, square forehead; no growth on his cheeks; a small, brown mustache, and a well-shaped, round chin. His expression was concentrated, meditative, under the inspecting light of the lamp I held up to his face; such as a man thinking hard in solitude might wear. My sleeping suit was just right for his size. A well-knit young fellow of twenty-five at most. He caught his lower lip with the edge of white, even teeth.

"Yes," I said, replacing the lamp in the binnacle. The warm, heavy tropical night closed upon his head again.

"There's a ship over there," he murmured.

"Yes, I know. The *Sephora*. Did you know of us?"

"Hadn't the slightest idea. I am the mate of her —" He paused and corrected himself. "I should say I *was*."

"Aha! Something wrong?"

"Yes. Very wrong indeed. I've killed a man."

[1] **binnacle**: case enclosing the ship's compass.

"What do you mean? Just now?"

"No, on the passage. Weeks ago. Thirty-nine south.[2] When I say a man —"

"Fit of temper," I suggested, confidently.

The shadowy, dark head, like mine, seemed to nod imperceptibly above the ghostly gray of my sleeping suit. It was, in the night, as though I had been faced by my own reflection in the depths of a somber and immense mirror.

"A pretty thing to have to own up to for a Conway[3] boy," murmured my double, distinctly.

"You're a Conway boy?"

"I am," he said, as if startled. Then, slowly . . . . "Perhaps you too —"

It was so; but being a couple of years older I had left before he joined. After a quick interchange of dates a silence fell; and I thought suddenly of my absurd mate with his terrific whiskers and the "Bless my soul — you don't say so" type of intellect. My double gave me an inkling of his thoughts by saying:

"My father's a parson in Norfolk.[4] Do you see me before a judge and jury on that charge? For myself I can't see the necessity. There are fellows that an angel from heaven — And I am not that. He was one of those creatures that are just simmering all the time with a silly sort of wickedness. Miserable devils that have no business to live at all. He wouldn't do his duty and wouldn't let anybody else do theirs. But what's the good of talking! You know well enough the sort of ill-conditioned snarling cur —"[5]

He appealed to me as if our experiences had been as identical as our clothes. And I knew well enough the pestiferous[6] danger of such a character where there are no means of legal repression. And I knew well enough also that my double there was no

[2] **Thirty-nine south**: location given in latitude.
[3] **Conway**: preparatory school in England.
[4] **Norfolk**: county in southeastern England.
[5] **cur**: mongrel dog; *thus*, contemptible person.
[6] **pestiferous**: evil, harmful.

homicidal ruffian. I did not think of asking him for details, and he told me the story roughly in brusque, disconnected sentences. I needed no more. I saw it all going on as though I were myself inside that other sleeping suit.

"It happened while we were setting a reefed foresail,[1] at dusk. Reefed foresail! You understand the sort of weather. The only sail we had left to keep the ship running; so you may guess what it had been like for days. Anxious sort of job, that. He gave me some of his cursed insolence at the sheet. I tell you I was overdone with this terrific weather that seemed to have no end to it. Terrific, I tell you — and a deep ship. I believe the fellow himself was half crazed with funk.[2] It was no time for gentlemanly reproof, so I turned round and felled him like an ox. He up and at me. We closed just as an awful sea made for the ship. All hands saw it coming and took to the rigging, but I had him by the throat, and went on shaking him like a rat, the men above us yelling, 'Look out! Look out!' Then a crash as if the sky had fallen on my head. They say that for over ten minutes hardly anything was to be seen of the ship — just the three masts and a bit of the forecastle head and of the poop all awash driving along in a smother of foam. It was a miracle that they found us, jammed together behind the forebits.[3] It's clear that I meant business, because I was holding him by the throat still when they picked us up. He was black in the face. It was too much for them. It seems they rushed us aft together, gripped as we were, screaming 'Murder!' like a lot of lunatics, and broke into the cuddy. And the ship running for her life, touch and go all the time, any minute her last in a sea fit to turn your hair gray only a-looking at

it. I understand that the skipper, too, started raving like the rest of them. The man had been deprived of sleep for more than a week, and to have this sprung on him at the height of a furious gale nearly drove him out of his mind. I wonder they didn't fling me overboard after getting the carcass of their precious shipmate out of my fingers. They had rather a job to separate us, I've been told. A sufficiently fierce story to make an old judge and a respectable jury sit up a bit. The first thing I heard when I came to myself was the maddening howling of that endless gale, and on that the voice of the old man. He was hanging on to my bunk, staring into my face out of his sou'-wester.[4]

"'Mr. Leggatt, you have killed a man. You can act no longer as chief mate of this ship.'"

His care to subdue his voice made it sound monotonous. He rested a hand on the end of the skylight to steady himself with, and all that time did not stir a limb, so far as I could see. "Nice little tale for a quiet tea party," he concluded in the same tone.

One of my hands, too, rested on the end of the skylight; neither did I stir a limb, so far as I knew. We stood less than a foot from each other. It occurred to me that if old "Bless my soul — you don't say so" were to put his head up the companion and catch sight of us, he would think he was seeing double, or imagine himself come upon a scene of weird witchcraft; the strange captain having a quiet confabulation[5] by the wheel with his own gray ghost. I became very much concerned to prevent anything of the sort. I heard the other's soothing undertone.

"My father's a parson in Norfolk," it said. Evidently he had forgotten he had told me this important fact before. Truly a nice little tale.

"You had better slip down into my state-

---

[1] **reefed foresail**: main sail tied down to reduce the area exposed to the wind.

[2] **funk**: panic.

[3] **forebits**: heavy beams for holding cables, toward the front of the ship.

[4] **sou'wester**: waterproof oilskin rain hat.

[5] **confabulation**: chat.

room now," I said, moving off stealthily. My double followed my movements; our bare feet made no sound; I let him in, closed the door with care, and, after giving a call to the second mate, returned on deck for my relief.

"Not much sign of any wind yet," I remarked when he approached.

"No, sir. Not much," he assented, sleepily, in his hoarse voice, with just enough deference, no more, and barely suppressing a yawn.

"Well, that's all you have to look out for. You have got your orders."

"Yes, sir."

I paced a turn or two on the poop and saw him take up his position face forward with his elbow in the ratlines[1] of the mizzen-rigging[2] before I went below. The mate's faint snoring was still going on peacefully. The cuddy lamp was burning over the table on which stood a vase with flowers, a polite attention from the ship's provision merchant —the last flowers we should see for the next three months at the very least. Two bunches of bananas hung from the beam symmetrically, one on each side of the rudder[3] casing. Everything was as before in the ship — except that two of her captain's sleeping suits were simultaneously in use, one motionless in the cuddy, the other keeping very still in the captain's stateroom.

It must be explained here that my cabin had the form of the capital letter L, the door being within the angle and opening into the short part of the letter. A couch was to the left, the bed-place to the right; my writing desk and the chronometers' table[4] faced the door. But anyone opening it, unless he stepped right inside, had no view of what I call the long (or vertical) part of the letter.

[1] **ratlines**: small ropes which serve as a ladder for climbing the rigging.
[2] **mizzen-rigging**: ropes and chains used for supporting and working the stern mast.
[3] **rudder**: instrument used for steering.
[4] **chronometers' table**: table holding the instrument used on ships to determine longitude.

It contained some lockers surmounted by a bookcase; and a few clothes, a thick jacket or two, caps, oilskin coat, and such like, hung on hooks. There was at the bottom of that part a door opening into my bathroom, which could be entered also directly from the saloon. But that way was never used.

The mysterious arrival had discovered the advantage of this particular shape. Entering my room, lighted strongly by a big bulkhead lamp swung on gimbals[5] above my writing desk, I did not see him anywhere till he stepped out quietly from behind the coats hung in the recessed part.

"I heard somebody moving about, and went in there at once," he whispered.

I, too, spoke under my breath.

"Nobody is likely to come in here without knocking and getting permission."

He nodded. His face was thin and the sunburn faded, as though he had been ill. And no wonder. He had been, I heard presently, kept under arrest in his cabin for nearly seven weeks. But there was nothing sickly in his eyes or in his expression. He was not a bit like me, really; yet, as we stood leaning over my bed-place, whispering side by side, with our dark heads together and our backs to the door, anybody bold enough to open it stealthily would have been treated to the uncanny sight of a double captain busy talking in whispers with his other self.

"But all this doesn't tell me how you came to hang on to our side ladder," I inquired, in the hardly audible murmurs we used, after he had told me something more of the proceedings on board the *Sephora* once the bad weather was over.

"When we sighted Java Head[6] I had had time to think all those matters out several times over. I had six weeks of doing nothing else, and with only an hour or so every evening for a tramp on the quarterdeck."

He whispered, his arms folded on the side

[5] **gimbals**: pair of rings attached to the ceiling.
[6] **Java Head**: westernmost point of Indonesia, in Indian Ocean.

of my bed-place, staring through the open port. And I could imagine perfectly the manner of this thinking out — a stubborn if not a steadfast operation; something of which I should have been perfectly incapable.

"I reckoned it would be dark before we closed with the land," he continued, so low that I had to strain my hearing, near as we were to each other, shoulder touching shoulder almost. "So I asked to speak to the old man. He always seemed very sick when he came to see me — as if he could not look me in the face. You know, that foresail saved the ship. She was too deep to have run long under bare poles. And it was I that managed to set it for him. Anyway, he came. When I had him in my cabin — he stood by the door looking at me as if I had the halter around my neck already — I asked him right away to leave my cabin door unlocked at night while the ship was going through Sunda Straits. There would be the Java coast within two or three miles, off Angier Point. I wanted nothing more. I've had a prize for swimming my second year in the Conway."

"I can believe it," I breathed out.

"God only knows why they locked me in every night. To see some of their faces you'd have thought they were afraid I'd go about at night strangling people. Am I a murdering brute? Do I look it? By Jove! if I had been he wouldn't have trusted himself like that into my room. You'll say I might have chucked him aside and bolted out, there and then — it was dark already. Well, no. And for the same reason I wouldn't think of trying to smash the door. There would have been a rush to stop me at the noise, and I did not mean to get into a confounded scrimmage.[1] Somebody else might have got killed — for I would not have broken out only to get chucked back, and I did not want any more of that work. He refused, looking more sick than ever. He was afraid

[1] **scrimmage**: rough-and-tumble fight.

of the men, and also of that old second mate of his who had been sailing with him for years — a gray-headed old humbug;[2] and his steward, too, had been with him devil knows how long — seventeen years or more —a dogmatic sort of loafer who hated me like poison, just because I was the chief mate. No chief mate ever made more than one voyage in the *Sephora*, you know. Those two old chaps ran the ship. Devil only knows what the skipper wasn't afraid of (all his nerve went to pieces altogether in that hellish spell of bad weather we had) — of what the law would do to him — of his wife, perhaps. Oh, yes! she's on board. Though I don't think she would have meddled. She would have been only too glad to have me out of the ship in any way. The 'brand of Cain' business, don't you see. That's all right. I was ready enough to go off wandering on the face of the earth — and that was price enough to pay for an Abel of that sort. Anyhow, he wouldn't listen to me. 'This thing must take its course. I represent the law here.' He was shaking like a leaf. 'So you won't?' 'No!' 'Then I hope you will be able to sleep on that,' I said, and turned my back on him. 'I wonder that *you* can,' cries he, and locks the door.

"Well, after that, I couldn't. Not very well. That was three weeks ago. We have had a slow passage through the Java Sea; drifted about Carimata for ten days. When we anchored here they thought, I suppose, it was all right. The nearest land (and that's five miles) is the ship's destination; the consul would soon set about catching me; and there would have been no object in bolting to these islets there. I don't suppose there's a drop of water on them. I don't know how it was, but tonight that steward, after bringing me my supper, went out to let me eat it, and left the door unlocked. And I ate it — all there was, too. After I had finished I strolled out on the quarterdeck. I don't know that I meant to do anything. A

[2] **humbug**: dishonest person.

breath of fresh air was all I wanted, I believe. Then a sudden temptation came over me. I kicked off my slippers and was in the water before I had made up my mind fairly. Somebody heard the splash and they raised an awful hullabaloo. 'He's gone! Lower the boats! He's committed suicide! No, he's swimming.' Certainly I was swimming. It's not so easy for a swimmer like me to commit suicide by drowning. I landed on the nearest islet before the boat left the ship's side. I heard them pulling about in the dark, hailing, and so on, but after a bit they gave up. Everything quieted down and the anchorage became as still as death. I sat down on a stone and began to think. I felt certain they would start searching for me at daylight. There was no place to hide on those stony things — and if there had been, what would have been the good? But now I was clear of that ship, I was not going back. So after a while I took off all my clothes, tied them up in a bundle with a stone inside, and dropped them in the deep water on the outer side of that islet. That was suicide enough for me. Let them think what they liked, but I didn't mean to drown myself. I meant to swim till I sank — but that's not the same thing. I struck out for another of these little islands, and it was from that one that I first saw your riding light. Something to swim for. I went on easily, and on the way I came upon a flat rock a foot or two above water. In the daytime, I dare say, you might make it out with a glass from your poop. I scrambled up on it and rested myself for a bit. Then I made another start. That last spell must have been over a mile."

His whisper was getting fainter and fainter, and all the time he stared straight out through the porthole, in which there was not even a star to be seen. I had not interrupted him. There was something that made comment impossible in his narrative, or perhaps in himself; a sort of feeling, a quality, which I can't find a name for. And when he ceased, all I found was a futile whisper: "So you swam for our light?"

"Yes — straight for it. It was something to swim for. I couldn't see any stars low down because the coast was in the way, and I couldn't see the land, either. The water was like glass. One might have been swimming in a confounded thousand-feet deep cistern[1] with no place for scrambling out anywhere; but what I didn't like was the notion of swimming round and round like a crazed bullock before I gave out; and as I didn't mean to go back. . . . No. Do you see me being hauled back, stark naked, off one of these little islands by the scruff of the neck and fighting like a wild beast? Somebody would have got killed for certain, and I did not want any of that. So I went on. Then your ladder — "

"Why didn't you hail the ship?" I asked, a little louder.

He touched my shoulder lightly. Lazy footsteps came right over our heads and stopped. The second mate had crossed from the other side of the poop and might have been hanging over the rail, for all we knew.

"He couldn't hear us talking — could he?" My double breathed into my very ear, anxiously.

His anxiety was an answer, a sufficient answer, to the question I had put to him. An answer containing all the difficulty of that situation. I closed the porthole quietly, to make sure. A louder word might have been overheard.

"Who's that?" he whispered then.

"My second mate. But I don't know much more of the fellow than you do."

And I told him a little about myself. I had been appointed to take charge while I least expected anything of the sort, not quite a fortnight ago. I didn't know either the ship or the people. Hadn't had the time in port to look about me or size anybody up. And as to the crew, all they knew was that I was appointed to take the ship home. For the rest, I was almost as much of a stranger on

[1] cistern: tank in which water is stored.

Self-Portrait *by the Italian artist Giorgio De Chirico.*

board as himself, I said. And at the moment I felt it most acutely. I felt that it would take very little to make me a suspect person in the eyes of the ship's company.

He had turned about meantime; and we, the two strangers in the ship, faced each other in identical attitudes.

"Your ladder—" he murmured, after a silence. "Who'd have thought of finding a ladder hanging over at night in a ship anchored out here! I felt just then a very unpleasant faintness. After the life I've been leading for nine weeks, anybody would have got out of condition. I wasn't capable of swimming round as far as your rudder chains. And, lo and behold! there was a ladder to get hold of. After I gripped it I said to myself, 'What's the good?' When I saw a man's head looking over I thought I would swim away presently and leave him shouting — in whatever language it was. I didn't mind being looked at. I — I liked it. And then you speaking to me so quietly — as if you had expected me — made me hold on a little longer. It had been a confounded lonely time — I don't mean while swimming. I was glad to talk a little to somebody that didn't belong to the *Sephora*. As to asking

for the captain, that was a mere impulse. It could have been no use, with all the ship knowing about me and the other people pretty certain to be round here in the morning. I don't know — I wanted to be seen, to talk with somebody, before I went on. I don't know what I would have said. . . . 'Fine night, isn't it?' or something of the sort."

"Do you think they will be round here presently?" I asked with some incredulity.

"Quite likely," he said, faintly.

He looked extremely haggard all of a sudden. His head rolled on his shoulders.

"H'm. We shall see then. Meantime get into that bed," I whispered. "Want help? There."

It was a rather high bed-place with a set of drawers underneath. This amazing swimmer really needed the lift I gave him by seizing his leg. He tumbled in, rolled over on his back, and flung one arm across his eyes. And then, with his face nearly hidden, he must have looked exactly as I used to look in that bed. I gazed upon my other self for a while before drawing across carefully the two green serge curtains which ran on a brass rod. I thought for a moment of pin-

708

ning them together for greater safety, but I sat down on the couch, and once there I felt unwilling to rise and hunt for a pin. I would do it in a moment. I was extremely tired, in a peculiarly intimate way, by the strain of stealthiness, by the effort of whispering and the general secrecy of this excitement. It was three o'clock by now and I had been on my feet since nine, but I was not sleepy; I could not have gone to sleep. I sat there, fagged out, looking at the curtains, trying to clear my mind of the confused sensation of being in two places at once, and greatly bothered by an exasperating knocking in my head. It was a relief to discover suddenly that it was not in my head at all, but on the outside of the door. Before I could collect myself the words "Come in" were out of my mouth, and the steward entered with a tray, bringing in my morning coffee. I had slept, after all, and I was so frightened that I shouted, "This way! I am here, steward," as though he had been miles away. He put down the tray on the table next the couch and only then said, very quietly, "I can see you are here, sir." I felt him give me a keen look, but I dared not meet his eyes just then. He must have wondered why I had drawn the curtains of my bed before going to sleep on the couch. He went out, hooking the door open as usual.

I heard the crew washing decks above me. I knew I would have been told at once if there had been any wind. Calm, I thought, and I was doubly vexed. Indeed, I felt dual more than ever. The steward reappeared suddenly in the doorway. I jumped up from the couch so quickly that he gave a start.

"What do you want here?"

"Close your port,[1] sir — they are washing decks."

"It is closed," I said, reddening.

"Very well, sir." But he did not move from the doorway and returned my stare

[1] **port**: window.

in an extraordinary, equivocal manner for a time. Then his eyes wavered, all his expression changed, and in a voice unusually gentle, almost coaxingly:

"May I come in to take the empty cup away, sir?"

"Of course!" I turned my back on him while he popped in and out. Then I unhooked and closed the door and even pushed the bolt. This sort of thing could not go on very long. The cabin was as hot as an oven, too. I took a peep at my double, and discovered that he had not moved, his arm was still over his eyes; but his chest heaved; his hair was wet; his chin glistened with perspiration. I reached over him and opened the port.

"I must show myself on deck," I reflected.

Of course, theoretically, I could do what I liked, with no one to say nay to me within the whole circle of the horizon; but to lock my cabin door and take the key away I did not dare. Directly I put my head out of the companion I saw the group of my two officers, the second mate barefooted, the chief mate in long india-rubber boots, near the break of the poop, and the steward halfway down the poop ladder talking to them eagerly. He happened to catch sight of me and dived, the second ran down on the main deck shouting some order or other, and the chief mate came to meet me, touching his cap.

There was a sort of curiosity in his eye that I did not like. I don't know whether the steward had told them that I was "queer" only, or downright drunk, but I know the man meant to have a good look at me. I watched him coming with a smile which, as he got into point-blank range, took effect and froze his very whiskers. I did not give him time to open his lips.

"Square the yards by lifts and braces[2] before the hands go to breakfast."

It was the first particular order I had

[2] **Square . . . braces**: fasten the sails down.

given on board that ship; and I stayed on deck to see it executed, too. I had felt the need of asserting myself without loss of time. That sneering young cub got taken down a peg or two on that occasion, and I also seized the opportunity of having a good look at the face of every foremast man as they filed past me to go to the after braces. At breakfast time, eating nothing myself, I presided with such frigid dignity that the two mates were only too glad to escape from the cabin as soon as decency permitted; and all the time the dual working of my mind distracted me almost to the point of insanity. I was constantly watching myself, my secret self, as dependent on my actions as my own personality, sleeping in that bed, behind that door which faced me as I sat at the head of the table. It was very much like being mad, only it was worse because one was aware of it.

I had to shake him for a solid minute, but when at last he opened his eyes it was in the full possession of his senses, with an inquiring look.

"All's well so far," I whispered. "Now you must vanish into the bathroom."

He did so, as noiseless as a ghost, and I then rang for the steward, and facing him boldly, directed him to tidy up my stateroom while I was having my bath — "and be quick about it." As my tone admitted of no excuses, he said, "Yes, sir," and ran off to fetch his dustpan and brushes. I took a bath and did most of my dressing, splashing, and whistling softly for the steward's edification, while the secret sharer of my life stood drawn up bolt upright in that little space, his face looking very sunken in daylight, his eyelids lowered under the stern, dark line of his eyebrows drawn together by a slight frown.

When I left him there to go back to my room the steward was finishing dusting. I sent for the mate and engaged him in some insignificant conversation. It was, as it were,

trifling with the terrific character of his whiskers; but my object was to give him an opportunity for a good look at my cabin. And then I could at last shut, with a clear conscience, the door of my stateroom and get my double back into the recessed part. There was nothing else for it. He had to sit still on a small folding stool, half smothered by the heavy coats hanging there. We listened to the steward going into the bathroom out of the saloon, filling the water bottles there, scrubbing the bath, setting things to rights, whisk, bang, clatter — out again into the saloon — turn the key — click. Such was my scheme for keeping my second self invisible. Nothing better could be contrived under the circumstances. And there we sat; I at my writing desk ready to appear busy with some papers, he behind me, out of sight of the door. It would not have been prudent to talk in daytime; and I could not have stood the excitement of that queer sense of whispering to myself. Now and then, glancing over my shoulder, I saw him far back there, sitting rigidly on the low stool, his bare feet close together, his arms folded, his head hanging on his breast — and perfectly still. Anybody would have taken him for me.

I was fascinated by it myself. Every moment I had to glance over my shoulder. I was looking at him when a voice outside the door said:

"Beg pardon, sir."

"Well!" . . . I kept my eyes on him, and so, when the voice outside the door announced, "There's a ship's boat coming our way, sir," I saw him give a start — the first movement he had made for hours. But he did not raise his bowed head.

"All right. Get the ladder over."

I hesitated. Should I whisper something to him? But what? His immobility seemed to have been never disturbed. What could I tell him he did not know already? . . . Finally I went on deck.

II

The skipper of the *Sephora* had a thin red whisker all round his face, and the sort of complexion that goes with hair of that color; also the particular, rather smeary shade of blue in the eyes. He was not exactly a showy figure; his shoulders were high, his stature but middling — one leg slightly more bandy than the other. He shook hands, looking vaguely around. A spiritless tenacity[1] was his main characteristic, I judged. I behaved with a politeness which seemed to disconcert him. Perhaps he was shy. He mumbled to me as if he were ashamed of what he was saying; gave his name (it was something like Archbold — but at this distance of years I hardly am sure), his ship's name, and a few other particulars of that sort, in the manner of a criminal making a reluctant and doleful confession. He had had terrible weather on the passage out — terrible — terrible — wife aboard, too.

By this time we were seated in the cabin and the steward brought in a tray with a bottle and glasses. "Thanks! No." Never took liquor. Would have some water, though. He drank two tumblerfuls. Terrible thirsty work. Ever since daylight had been exploring the islands round his ship.

"What was that for — fun?" I asked, with an appearance of polite interest.

"No!" He sighed. "Painful duty."

As he persisted in his mumbling and I wanted my double to hear every word, I hit upon the notion of informing him that I regretted to say I was hard of hearing.

"Such a young man, too!" he nodded, keeping his smeary blue, unintelligent eyes fastened upon me. What was the cause of it — some disease? he inquired, without the least sympathy and as if he thought that, if so, I'd got no more than I deserved.

"Yes; disease," I admitted in a cheerful

[1] **tenacity**: persistence.

tone which seemed to shock him. But my point was gained, because he had to raise his voice to give me his tale. It is not worthwhile to record that version. It was just over two months since all this had happened, and he had thought so much about it that he seemed completely muddled as to its bearings, but still immensely impressed.

"What would you think of such a thing happening on board your own ship? I've had the *Sephora* for these fifteen years. I am a well-known shipmaster."

He was densely distressed — and perhaps I should have sympathized with him if I had been able to detach my mental vision from the unsuspected sharer of my cabin as though he were my second self. There he was on the other side of the bulkhead, four or five feet from us, no more, as we sat in the saloon. I looked politely at Captain Archbold (if that was his name), but it was the other I saw, in a gray sleeping suit, seated on a low stool, his bare feet close together, his arms folded, and every word said between us falling into the ears of his dark head bowed on his chest.

"I have been at sea now, man and boy, for seven-and-thirty years, and I've never heard of such a thing happening in an English ship. And that it should be my ship. Wife on board, too."

I was hardly listening to him.

"Don't you think," I said, "that the heavy sea which, you told me, came aboard just then might have killed the man? I have seen the sheer weight of sea kill a man very neatly, by simply breaking his neck."

"Good God!" he uttered, impressively, fixing his smeary blue eyes on me. "The sea! No man killed by the sea ever looked like that." He seemed positively scandalized at my suggestion. And as I gazed at him, certainly not prepared for anything original on his part, he advanced his head close to mine and thrust his tongue out at me so suddenly that I couldn't help starting back.

After scoring over my calmness in this graphic[1] way he nodded wisely. If I had seen the sight, he assured me, I would never forget it as long as I lived. The weather was too bad to give the corpse a proper sea burial. So next day at dawn they took it up on the poop, covering its face with a bit of bunting;[2] he read a short prayer, and then, just as it was, in its oilskins and long boots, they launched it amongst those mountainous seas that seemed ready every moment to swallow up the ship herself and the terrified lives on board of her.

"That reefed foresail saved you," I threw in.

"Under God — it did," he exclaimed fervently. "It was by a special mercy, I firmly believe, that it stood some of those hurricane squalls."

"It was the setting of that sail which —" I began.

"God's own hand in it," he interrupted me. "Nothing less could have done it. I don't mind telling you that I hardly dared give the order. It seemed impossible that we could touch anything without losing it, and then our last hope would have been gone."

The terror of that gale was on him yet. I let him go on for a bit, then said, casually — as if returning to a minor subject:

"You were very anxious to give up your mate to the shore people, I believe?"

He was. To the law. His obscure tenacity on that point had in it something incomprehensible and a little awful; something, as it were, mystical, quite apart from his anxiety that he should not be suspected of "countenancing[3] any doings of that sort." Seven-and-thirty virtuous years at sea, of which over twenty of immaculate command, and the last fifteen in the *Sephora*, seemed to have laid him under some pitiless obligation.

[1] **graphic**: vivid.
[2] **bunting**: strip of cloth.
[3] **countenancing**: approving, supporting.

"And you know," he went on, groping shamefacedly amongst his feelings, "I did not engage that young fellow. His people had some interest with my owners. I was in a way forced to take him on. He looked very smart, very gentlemanly, and all that. But do you know — I never liked him, somehow. I am a plain man. You see, he wasn't exactly the sort for the chief mate of a ship like the *Sephora*."

I had become so connected in thoughts and impressions with the secret sharer of my cabin that I felt as if I, personally, were being given to understand that I, too, was not the sort that would have done for the chief mate of a ship like the *Sephora*. I had no doubt of it in my mind.

"Not at all the style of man. You understand," he insisted, superfluously, looking hard at me.

I smiled urbanely. He seemed at a loss for a while.

"I suppose I must report a suicide."

"Beg pardon?"

"Sui-cide! That's what I'll have to write to my owners directly I get in."

"Unless you manage to recover him before tomorrow," I assented, dispassionately. . . . "I mean, alive."

He mumbled something which I really did not catch, and I turned my ear to him in a puzzled manner. He fairly bawled:

"The land — I say, the mainland is at least seven miles off my anchorage."

"About that."

My lack of excitement, of curiosity, of surprise, of any sort of pronounced interest, began to arouse his distrust. But except for the felicitous pretense of deafness I had not tried to pretend anything. I had felt utterly incapable of playing the part of ignorance properly, and therefore was afraid to try. It is also certain that he had brought some ready-made suspicions with him, and that he viewed my politeness as a strange and unnatural phenomenon. And yet how else could I have received him? Not heartily! That was impossible for psychological reasons, which I need not state here. My only object was to keep off his inquiries. Surlily? Yes, but surliness might have provoked a point-blank question. From its novelty to him and from its nature, punctilious courtesy was the manner best calculated to restrain the man. But there was the danger of his breaking through my defense bluntly. I could not, I think, have met him by a direct lie, also for psychological (not moral) reasons. If he had only known how afraid I was of his putting my feeling of identity with the other to the test! But, strangely enough — (I thought of it only afterward) — I believe that he was not a little disconcerted by the reverse side of that weird situation, by something in me that reminded him of the man he was seeking — suggested a mysterious similitude to the young fellow he had distrusted and disliked from the first.

However that might have been, the silence was not very prolonged. He took another oblique step.

"I reckon I had no more than a two-mile pull to your ship. Not a bit more."

"And quite enough, too, in this awful heat," I said.

Another pause full of mistrust followed. Necessity, they say, is mother of invention, but fear, too, is not barren of ingenious suggestions. And I was afraid he would ask me point-blank for news of my other self.

"Nice little saloon, isn't it?" I remarked, as if noticing for the first time the way his eyes roamed from one closed door to the other. "And very well fitted out, too. Here, for instance," I continued, reaching over the back of my seat negligently and flinging the door open, "is my bathroom."

He made an eager movement, but hardly gave it a glance. I got up, shut the door of the bathroom, and invited him to have a look round, as if I were very proud of my accommodation. He had to rise and be shown round, but he went through the business without any raptures whatever.

"And now we'll have a look at my stateroom," I declared, in a voice as loud as I dared to make it, crossing the cabin to the starboard[1] side with purposely heavy steps.

He followed me in and gazed around. My intelligent double had vanished. I played my part.

"Very convenient — isn't it?"

"Very nice. Very comf. . . ." He didn't finish, and went out brusquely as if to escape from some unrighteous wiles of mine. But it was not to be. I had been too frightened not to feel vengeful; I felt I had him on the run, and I meant to keep him on the run. My polite insistence must have had something menacing in it, because he gave in suddenly. And I did not let him off a single item; mate's room, pantry, storerooms, the very sail locker which was also under the poop — he had to look into them all. When at last I showed him out on the quarterdeck he drew a long, spiritless sigh, and mumbled dismally that he must really be going back to his ship now. I desired my mate, who had joined us, to see to the captain's boat.

The man of whiskers gave a blast on the whistle which he used to wear hanging round his neck, and yelled, *Sephora's away!* My double down there in my cabin must have heard, and certainly could not feel more relieved than I. Four fellows came running out from somewhere forward and went over the side, while my own men, appearing on deck too, lined the rail. I escorted my visitor to the gangway ceremoniously, and nearly overdid it. He was a tenacious beast. On the very ladder he lingered, and in that unique, guiltily conscientious manner of sticking to the point:

---

[1] **starboard**: right-hand side of the ship.

"I say . . . you . . . you don't think that —"

I covered his voice loudly:

"Certainly not. . . . I am delighted. Good-by."

I had an idea of what he meant to say, and just saved myself by the privilege of defective hearing. He was too shaken generally to insist, but my mate, close witness of that parting, looked mystified and his face took on a thoughtful cast. As I did not want to appear as if I wished to avoid all communication with my officers, he had the opportunity to address me.

"Seems a very nice man. His boat's crew told our chaps a very extraordinary story, if what I am told by the steward is true. I suppose you had it from the captain, sir?"

"Yes. I had a story from the captain."

"A very horrible affair — isn't it, sir?"

"It is."

"Beats all these tales we hear about murders in Yankee ships."

"I don't think it beats them. I don't think it resembles them in the least."

"Bless my soul — you don't say so! But of course I've no acquaintance whatever with American ships, not I, so I couldn't go against your knowledge. It's horrible enough for me. . . . But the queerest part is that those fellows seemed to have some idea the man was hidden aboard here. They had really. Did you ever hear of such a thing?"

"Preposterous — isn't it?"

We were walking to and fro athwart[1] the quarterdeck. No one of the crew forward could be seen (the day was Sunday), and the mate pursued:

"There was some little dispute about it. Our chaps took offense. 'As if we would harbor a thing like that,' they said. 'Wouldn't you like to look for him in our coal hole?' Quite a tiff.[2] But they made it up in the end. I suppose he did drown himself. Don't you, sir?"

[1] athwart: across.
[2] tiff: quarrel.

"I don't suppose anything."

"You have no doubt in the matter, sir?"

"None whatever."

I left him suddenly. I felt I was producing a bad impression, but with my double down there it was most trying to be on deck. And it was almost as trying to be below. Altogether a nerve-trying situation. But on the whole I felt less torn in two when I was with him. There was no one in the whole ship whom I dared take into my confidence. Since the hands had got to know his story, it would have been impossible to pass him off for anyone else, and an accidental discovery was to be dreaded now more than ever. . . .

The steward being engaged in laying the table for dinner, we could talk only with our eyes when I first went down. Later in the afternoon we had a cautious try at whispering. The Sunday quietness of the ship was against us; the stillness of air and water around her was against us; the elements, the men were against us — everything was against us in our secret partnership; time itself — for this could not go on forever. The very trust in Providence was, I suppose, denied to his guilt. Shall I confess that this thought cast me down very much? And as to the chapter of accidents which counts for so much in the book of success, I could only hope that it was closed. For what favorable accident could be expected?

"Did you hear everything?" were my first words as soon as we took up our position side by side, leaning over my bed-place.

He had. And the proof of it was his earnest whisper, "The man told you he hardly dared to give the order."

I understood the reference to be to that saving foresail.

"Yes. He was afraid of it being lost in the setting."

"I assure you he never gave the order. He may think he did, but he never gave it. He stood there with me on the break of the poop after the maintopsail blew away, and whimpered about our last hope — positively whimpered about it and nothing else — and the night coming on! To hear one's skipper go on like that in such weather was enough to drive any fellow out of his mind. It worked me up into a sort of desperation. I just took it into my own hands and went away from him, boiling, and —. But what's the use telling you? *You* know! . . . Do you think that if I had not been pretty fierce with them I should have got the men to do anything? Not it! The bosun[1] perhaps? Perhaps! It wasn't a heavy sea — it was a sea gone mad! I suppose the end of the world will be something like that; and a man may have the heart to see it coming once and be done with it — but to have to face it day after day — I don't blame anybody. I was precious little better than the rest. Only — I was an officer of that old coal-wagon, anyhow —"

"I quite understand," I conveyed that sincere assurance into his ear. He was out of breath with whispering; I could hear him pant slightly. It was all very simple. The same strung-up force which had given twenty-four men a chance, at least, for their lives, had, in a sort of recoil, crushed an unworthy mutinous existence.

But I had no leisure to weigh the merits of the matter — footsteps in the saloon, a heavy knock. "There's enough wind to get under way with, sir." Here was the call of a new claim upon my thoughts and even upon my feelings.

"Turn the hands up," I cried through the door. "I'll be on deck directly."

I was going out to make the acquaintance of my ship. Before I left the cabin our eyes met — the eyes of the only two strangers on board. I pointed to the recessed part where the little campstool awaited him and laid my finger on my lips. He made a gesture — somewhat vague — a little mysterious, ac-

companied by a faint smile, as if of regret.

This is not the place to enlarge upon the sensations of a man who feels for the first time a ship move under his feet to his own independent word. In my case they were not unalloyed.[2] I was not wholly alone with my command; for there was that stranger in my cabin. Or rather, I was not completely and wholly with her. Part of me was absent. That mental feeling of being in two places at once affected me physically as if the mood of secrecy had penetrated my very soul. Before an hour had elapsed since the ship had begun to move, having occasion to ask the mate (he stood by my side) to take a compass bearing[3] of the Pagoda, I caught myself reaching up to his ear in whispers. I say I caught myself, but enough had escaped to startle the man. I can't describe it otherwise than by saying that he shied.[4] A grave, preoccupied manner, as though he were in possession of some perplexing intelligence, did not leave him henceforth. A little later I moved away from the rail to look at the compass with such a stealthy gait that the helmsman[5] noticed it — and I could not help noticing the unusual roundness of his eyes. These are trifling instances, though it's to no commander's advantage to be suspected of ludicrous eccentricities. But I was also more seriously affected. There are to a seaman certain words, gestures, that should in given conditions come as naturally, as instinctively, as the winking of a menaced eye. A certain order should spring on to his lips without thinking; a certain sign should get itself made, so to speak, without reflection. But all unconscious alertness had abandoned me. I had to make an effort of will to recall myself back (from the cabin) to the conditions of the moment. I felt that I was ap-

[1] **bosun**: petty officer in charge of the crew.

[2] **unalloyed**: unmixed.
[3] **take . . . bearing**: calculate its position.
[4] **shied**: recoiled.
[5] **helmsman**: man who steers the ship.

pearing an irresolute commander to those people who were watching me more or less critically.

And, besides, there were the scares. On the second day out, for instance, coming off the deck in the afternoon (I had straw slippers on my bare feet) I stopped at the open pantry door and spoke to the steward. He was doing something there with his back to me. At the sound of my voice he nearly jumped out of his skin, as the saying is, and incidentally broke a cup.

"What on earth's the matter with you?" I asked, astonished.

He was extremely confused. "Beg your pardon, sir. I made sure you were in your cabin."

"You see I wasn't."

"No, sir. I could have sworn I had heard you moving in there not a moment ago. It's most extraordinary . . . very sorry, sir."

I passed on with an inward shudder. I was so identified with my secret double that I did not even mention the fact in those scanty, fearful whispers we exchanged. I suppose he had made some slight noise of some kind or other. It would have been miraculous if he hadn't at one time or another. And yet, haggard as he appeared, he looked always perfectly self-controlled, more than calm — almost invulnerable. On my suggestion he remained almost entirely in the bathroom, which, upon the whole, was the safest place. There could be really no shadow of an excuse for anyone ever wanting to go in there, once the steward had done with it. It was a very tiny place. Sometimes he reclined on the floor, his legs bent, his head sustained on one elbow. At others I would find him on the campstool, sitting in his gray sleeping suit and with his cropped dark hair like a patient, unmoved convict. At night I would smuggle him into my bed-place, and we would whisper together, with the regular footfalls of the officer of the watch passing and repassing over our heads. It was an in-

finitely miserable time. It was lucky that some tins of fine preserves were stowed in a locker in my stateroom; hard bread I could always get hold of; and so he lived on stewed chicken, paté de foie gras, asparagus, cooked oysters, sardines — on all sorts of abominable sham[1] delicacies out of tins. My early morning coffee he always drank; and it was all I dared do for him in that respect.

Every day there was the horrible maneuvering to go through so that my room and then the bathroom should be done in the usual way. I came to hate the sight of the steward, to abhor the voice of that harmless man. I felt that it was he who would bring on the disaster of discovery. It hung like a sword over our heads.

The fourth day out, I think (we were then working down the east side of the Gulf of Siam, tack for tack,[2] in light winds and smooth water) — the fourth day, I say, of this miserable juggling with the unavoidable, as we sat at our evening meal, that man, whose slightest movement I dreaded, after putting down the dishes ran up on deck busily. This could not be dangerous. Presently he came down again; and then it appeared that he had remembered a coat of mine which I had thrown over a rail to dry after having been wetted in a shower which had passed over the ship in the afternoon. Sitting stolidly at the head of the table I became terrified at the sight of the garment on his arm. Of course he made for my door. There was no time to lose.

"Steward," I thundered. My nerves were so shaken that I could not govern my voice and conceal my agitation. This was the sort of thing that made my terrifically whiskered mate tap his forehead with his forefinger. I had detected him using that gesture while talking on deck with a confidential air to the carpenter. It was too far

---

[1] sham: not genuine.
[2] tack for tack: in zigzag movements to maneuver the ship against the wind.

to hear a word, but I had no doubt that this pantomime could only refer to the strange new captain.

"Yes, sir," the pale-faced steward turned resignedly to me. It was this maddening course of being shouted at, checked without rhyme or reason, arbitrarily chased out of my cabin, suddenly called into it, sent flying out of his pantry on incomprehensible errands, that accounted for the growing wretchedness of his expression.

"Where are you going with that coat?"

"To your room, sir."

"Is there another shower coming?"

"I'm sure I don't know, sir. Shall I go up again and see, sir?"

"No! never mind."

My object was attained, as of course my other self in there would have heard everything that passed. During this interlude my two officers never raised their eyes off their respective plates; but the lip of that confounded cub, the second mate, quivered visibly.

I expected the steward to hook my coat on and come out at once. He was very slow about it; but I dominated my nervousness sufficiently not to shout after him. Suddenly I became aware (it could be heard plainly enough) that the fellow for some reason or other was opening the door of the bathroom. It was the end. The place was literally not big enough to swing a cat in. My voice died in my throat and I went stony all over. I expected to hear a yell of surprise and terror, and made a movement, but had not the strength to get on my legs. Everything remained still. Had my second self taken the poor wretch by the throat? I don't know what I would have done next moment if I had not seen the steward come out of my room, close the door, and then stand quietly by the sideboard.[1]

Saved, I thought. But, no! Lost! Gone! He was gone!

[1] sideboard: serving table.

I laid my knife and fork down and leaned back in my chair. My head swam. After a while, when sufficiently recovered to speak in a steady voice, I instructed my mate to put the ship round at eight o'clock himself.

"I won't come on deck," I went on. "I think I'll turn in, and unless the wind shifts I don't want to be disturbed before midnight. I feel a bit seedy."

"You did look middling bad a little while ago," the chief mate remarked without showing any great concern.

They both went out, and I stared at the steward clearing the table. There was nothing to be read on that wretched man's face. But why did he avoid my eyes, I asked myself. Then I thought I should like to hear the sound of his voice.

"Steward!"

"Sir!" Startled as usual.

"Where did you hang up that coat?"

"In the bathroom, sir." The usual anxious tone. "It's not quite dry yet, sir."

For some time longer I sat in the cuddy. Had my double vanished as he had come? But of his coming there was an explanation, whereas his disappearance would be inexplicable. . . . I went slowly into my dark room, shut the door, lighted the lamp, and for a time dared not turn round. When at last I did I saw him standing bolt upright in the narrow recessed part. It would not be true to say I had a shock, but an irresistible doubt of his bodily existence flitted through my mind. Can it be, I asked myself, that he is not visible to other eyes than mine? It was like being haunted. Motionless, with a grave face, he raised his hands slightly at me in a gesture which meant clearly, "Heavens! what a narrow escape!" Narrow indeed. I think I had come creeping quietly as near insanity as any man who has not actually gone over the border. That gesture restrained me, so to speak.

The mate with the terrific whiskers was now putting the ship on the other tack. In the moment of profound silence which follows upon the hands going to their stations I heard on the poop his raised voice: "Hard alee!"[1] and the distant shout of the order repeated on the maindeck. The sails, in that light breeze, made but a faint fluttering noise. It ceased. The ship was coming round slowly; I held my breath in the renewed stillness of expectation; one wouldn't have thought that there was a single living soul on her decks. A sudden brisk shout, "Mainsail haul!" broke the spell, and in the noisy cries and rush overhead of the men running away with the main brace we two, down in my cabin, came together in our usual position by the bed-place.

He did not wait for my question. "I heard him fumbling here and just managed to squat myself down in the bath," he whispered to me. "The fellow only opened the door and put his arm in to hang the coat up. All the same —"

"I never thought of that," I whispered back, even more appalled than before at the closeness of the shave, and marveling at that something unyielding in his character which was carrying him through so finely. There was no agitation in his whisper. Whoever was being driven distracted, it was not he. He was sane. And the proof of his sanity was continued when he took up the whispering again.

"It would never do for me to come to life again."

It was something that a ghost might have said. But what he was alluding to was his old captain's reluctant admission of the theory of suicide. It would obviously serve his turn — if I had understood at all the view which seemed to govern the unalterable purpose of his action.

"You must maroon me as soon as ever you can get amongst these islands off the Cambodje shore," he went on.

"Maroon you! We are not living in a

boy's adventure tale," I protested. His scornful whispering took me up.

"We aren't indeed! There's nothing of a boy's tale in this. But there's nothing else for it. I want no more. You don't suppose I am afraid of what can be done to me? Prison or gallows or whatever they may please. But you don't see me coming back to explain such things to an old fellow in a wig and twelve respectable tradesmen, do you? What can they know whether I am guilty or not — or of *what* I am guilty, either? That's my affair. What does the Bible say? 'Driven off the face of the earth.' Very well. I am off the face of the earth now. As I came at night so I shall go."

"Impossible!" I murmured. "You can't."

"Can't? . . . Not naked like a soul on the Day of Judgment. I shall freeze on to this sleeping suit. The Last Day is not yet — and . . . you have understood thoroughly. Didn't you?"

I felt suddenly ashamed of myself. I may say truly that I understood — and my hesitation in letting that man swim away from my ship's side had been a mere sham sentiment, a sort of cowardice.

"It can't be done now till next night," I breathed out. "The ship is on the offshore tack and the wind may fail us."

"As long as I know that you understand," he whispered. "But of course you do. It's a great satisfaction to have got somebody to understand. You seem to have been there on purpose." And in the same whisper, as if we two whenever we talked had to say things to each other which were not fit for the world to hear, he added, "It's very wonderful."

We remained side by side talking in our secret way — but sometimes silent or just exchanging a whispered word or two at long intervals. And as usual he stared through the port. A breath of wind came now and again into our faces. The ship might have been moored[2] in dock, so gently and on an

---

[1] **Hard alee**: steer sharply in the direction in which the wind is blowing.

[2] **moored**: anchored and fastened to the shore.

even keel[1] she slipped through the water, that did not murmur even at our passage, shadowy and silent like a phantom sea.

At midnight I went on deck, and to my mate's great surprise put the ship round on the other tack. His terrible whiskers flitted round me in silent criticism. I certainly should not have done it if it had been only a question of getting out of that sleepy gulf as quickly as possible. I believe he told the second mate, who relieved him, that it was a great want of judgment. The other only yawned. That intolerable cub shuffled about so sleepily and lolled against the rails in such a slack, improper fashion that I came down on him sharply.

"Aren't you properly awake yet?"

"Yes, sir! I am awake."

"Well, then, be good enough to hold yourself as if you were. And keep a look-out. If there's any current we'll be closing with some islands before daylight."

The east side of the gulf is fringed with islands, some solitary, others in groups. On the blue background of the high coast where they seem to float on silvery patches of calm water, arid and gray, or dark green and rounded like clumps of evergreen bushes, with the larger ones, a mile or two long, showing the outlines of ridges, ribs of gray rock under the dark mantle of matted leafage. Unknown to trade, to travel, almost to geography, the manner of life they harbor is an unsolved secret. There must be villages — settlements of fishermen at least — on the largest of them, and some communication with the world is probably kept up by native craft. But all that forenoon, as we headed for them, fanned along by the faintest of breezes, I saw no sign of man or canoe in the field of the telescope I kept on pointing at the scattered group.

At noon I gave no orders for a change of course, and the mate's whiskers became much concerned and seemed to be offering themselves unduly to my notice. At last I said:

"I am going to stand right in. Quite in — as far as I can take her."

The stare of extreme surprise imparted an air of ferocity also to his eyes, and he looked truly terrific for a moment.

"We're not doing well in the middle of the gulf," I continued, casually. "I am going to look for the land breezes tonight."

"Bless my soul! Do you mean, sir, in the dark amongst the lot of all of them islands and reefs and shoals?"[2]

"Well — if there are any regular land breezes at all on this coast one must get close inshore to find them, mustn't one?"

"Bless my soul!" he exclaimed again under his breath. All that afternoon he wore a dreamy, contemplative appearance which in him was a mark of perplexity. After dinner I went into my stateroom as if I meant to take some rest. There we two bent our dark heads over a half-unrolled chart lying on my bed.

"There," I said. "It's got to be Koh-ring. I've been looking at it ever since sunrise. It has got two hills and a low point. It must be inhabited. And on the coast opposite there is what looks like the mouth of a biggish river — with some town, no doubt, not far up. It's the best chance for you that I can see."

"Anything. Koh-ring let it be."

He looked thoughtfully at the chart as if surveying chances and distances from a lofty height — and following with his eyes his own figure wandering on the blank land of Cochin-China, and then passing off that piece of paper clean out of sight into uncharted regions. And it was as if the ship had two captains to plan her course for her. I had been so worried and restless running up and down that I had not had the patience to dress that day. I had remained in my

---

[1] on . . . keel: with an even, steady, smooth motion.

[2] reefs and shoals: ridges of sand and rock lying at or near the surface of the water.

sleeping suit, with straw slippers and a soft floppy hat. The closeness of the heat in the gulf had been most oppressive, and the crew were used to see me wandering in that airy attire.

"She will clear the south point as she heads now," I whispered into his ear. "Goodness only knows when, though, but certainly after dark. I'll edge her in to half a mile, as far as I may be able to judge in the dark —"

"Be careful," he murmured, warningly — and I realized suddenly that all my future, the only future for which I was fit, would perhaps go irretrievably to pieces in any mishap to my first command.

I could not stop a moment longer in the room. I motioned him to get out of sight and made my way on the poop. That unplayful cub had the watch. I walked up and down for a while thinking things out, then beckoned him over.

"Send a couple of hands to open the two quarterdeck ports," I said, mildly.

He actually had the impudence, or else so forgot himself in his wonder at such an incomprehensible order, as to repeat:

"Open the quarterdeck ports! What for, sir?"

"The only reason you need concern yourself about is because I tell you to do so. Have them open wide and fastened properly."

He reddened and went off, but I believe made some jeering remark to the carpenter as to the sensible practice of ventilating a ship's quarterdeck. I know he popped into the mate's cabin to impart the fact to him because the whiskers came on deck, as it were by chance, and stole glances at me from below — for signs of lunacy or drunkenness, I suppose.

A little before supper, feeling more restless than ever, I rejoined, for a moment, my second self. And to find him sitting so quietly was surprising, like something against nature, inhuman.

I developed my plan in a hurried whisper. "I shall stand in as close as I dare and then put her round. I shall presently find means to smuggle you out of here into the sail locker, which communicates with the lobby. But there is an opening, a sort of square for hauling the sails out, which gives straight on the quarterdeck and which is never closed in fine weather, so as to give air to the sails. When the ship's way is deadened in stays and all the hands are aft at the main braces you shall have a clear road to slip out and get overboard through the open quarterdeck port. I've had them both fastened up. Use a rope's end to lower yourself into the water so as to avoid a splash — you know. It could be heard and cause some beastly complication."

He kept silent for a while, then whispered, "I understand."

"I won't be there to see you go," I began with an effort. "The rest . . . I only hope I have understood, too."

"You have. From first to last," and for the first time there seemed to be a faltering, something strained in his whisper. He caught hold of my arm, but the ringing of the supper bell made me start. He didn't, though; he only released his grip.

After supper I didn't come below again till well past eight o'clock. The faint, steady breeze was loaded with dew; and the wet, darkened sails held all there was of propelling power in it. The night, clear and starry, sparkled darkly, and the opaque, lightless patches shifting slowly against the low stars were the drifting islets. On the port bow there was a big one more distant and shadowily imposing by the great space of sky it eclipsed.

On opening the door I had a back view of my very own self looking at a chart. He had come out of the recess and was standing near the table.

"Quite dark enough," I whispered.

He stepped back and leaned against my bed with a level, quiet glance. I sat on the couch. We had nothing to say to each other. Over our heads the officer of the watch moved here and there. Then I heard him move quickly. I knew what that meant. He was making for the companion; and presently his voice was outside my door.

"We are drawing in pretty fast, sir. Land looks rather close."

"Very well," I answered. "I am coming on deck directly."

I waited till he was gone out of the cuddy, then rose. My double moved too. The time had come to exchange our last whispers, for neither of us was ever to hear each other's natural voice.

"Look here!" I opened a drawer and took out three sovereigns. "Take this, anyhow. I've got six and I'd give you the lot, only I must keep a little money to buy some fruit and vegetables for the crew from native boats as we go through Sunda Straits."

He shook his head.

"Take it," I urged him, whispering desperately. "No one can tell what —"

He smiled and slapped meaningly the only pocket of the sleeping jacket. It was not safe, certainly. But I produced a large old silk handkerchief of mine, and tying the three pieces of gold in a corner, pressed it on him. He was touched, I suppose, because he took it at last and tied it quickly round his waist under the jacket, on his bare skin.

Our eyes met; several seconds elapsed, till, our glances still mingled, I extended my hand and turned the lamp out. Then I passed through the cuddy, leaving the door of my room wide open. . . . "Steward!"

He was still lingering in the pantry in the greatness of his zeal, giving a rub-up to a plated cruet[1] stand the last thing before going to bed. Being careful not to wake up the mate, whose room was opposite, I spoke in an undertone.

He looked round anxiously. "Sir!"

"Can you get me a little hot water from

[1] **cruet:** small glass serving bottle.

the galley?"

"I am afraid, sir, the galley fire's been out for some time now."

"Go and see."

He fled up the stairs.

"Now," I whispered, loudly, into the saloon — too loudly, perhaps, but I was afraid I couldn't make a sound. He was by my side in an instant — the double captain slipped past the stairs — through the tiny dark passage . . . a sliding door. We were in the sail locker, scrambling on our knees over the sails. A sudden thought struck me. I saw myself wandering barefooted, bareheaded, the sun beating on my dark poll. I snatched off my floppy hat and tried hurriedly in the dark to ram it on my other self. He dodged and fended off silently. I wonder what he thought had come to me before he understood and suddenly desisted. Our hands met gropingly, lingered united in a steady, motionless clasp for a second. . . . No word was breathed by either of us when they separated.

I was standing quietly by the pantry door when the steward returned.

"Sorry, sir. Kettle barely warm. Shall I light the spirit lamp?"

"Never mind."

I came out on deck slowly. It was now a matter of conscience to shave the land as close as possible — for now he must go overboard whenever the ship was put in stays. Must! There could be no going back for him. After a moment I walked over to leeward and my heart flew into my mouth at the nearness of the land on the bow. Under any other circumstances I would not have held on a minute longer. The second mate had followed me anxiously.

I looked on till I felt I could command my voice.

"She will weather," I said then in a quiet tone.

"Are you going to try that, sir?" he stammered out incredulously.

I took no notice of him and raised my

tone just enough to be heard by the helmsman.

"Keep her good full."

"Good full, sir."

The wind fanned my cheek, the sails slept, the world was silent. The strain of watching the dark loom of the land grow bigger and denser was too much for me. I had shut my eyes — because the ship must go closer. She must! The stillness was intolerable. Were we standing still?

When I opened my eyes the second view started my heart with a thump. The black southern hill of Koh-ring seemed to hang right over the ship like a towering fragment of the everlasting night. On that enormous mass of blackness there was not a gleam to be seen, not a sound to be heard. It was gliding irresistibly toward us and yet seemed already within reach of the hand. I saw the vague figures of the watch grouped in the waist, gazing in awed silence.

"Are you going on, sir?" inquired an unsteady voice at my elbow.

I ignored it. I had to go on.

"Keep her full. Don't check her way. That won't do now," I said warningly.

"I can't see the sails very well," the helmsman answered me, in strange, quavering tones.

Was she close enough? Already she was, I won't say in the shadow of the land, but in the very blackness of it, already swallowed up as it were, gone too close to be recalled, gone from me altogether.

"Give the mate a call," I said to the young man who stood at my elbow as still as death. "And turn all hands up."

My tone had a borrowed loudness reverberated from the height of the land. Several voices cried out together: "We are all on deck, sir."

Then stillness again, with the great shadow gliding closer, towering higher, without a light, without a sound. Such a hush had fallen on the ship that she might have been a bark of the dead floating in slowly under the very gate of Erebus.[1]

"My God! Where are we?"

It was the mate moaning at my elbow. He was thunderstruck, and as it were deprived of the moral support of his whiskers. He clapped his hands and absolutely cried out, "Lost!"

"Be quiet," I said sternly.

He lowered his tone, but I saw the shadowy gesture of his despair. "What are we doing here?"

"Looking for the land wind."

He made as if to tear his hair, and addressed me recklessly.

"She will never get out. You have done it, sir. I knew it'd end in something like this. She will never weather, and you are too close now to stay. She'll drift ashore before she's round. O my God!"

I caught his arm as he was raising it to batter his poor devoted head, and shook it violently.

"She's ashore already," he wailed, trying to tear himself away.

"Is she? . . . Keep good full there!"

"Good full, sir," cried the helmsman in a frightened, thin, childlike voice.

I hadn't let go the mate's arm and went on shaking it. "Ready about, do you hear? You go forward" — shake — "and stop there" — shake — "and hold your noise" — shake — "and see these head sheets properly overhauled" — shake, shake — shake.

And all the time I dared not look toward the land lest my heart should fail me. I released my grip at last and he ran forward as if fleeing for dear life.

I wondered what my double there in the sail locker thought of this commotion. He was able to hear everything — and perhaps he was able to understand why, on my conscience, it had to be thus close — no less. My first order "Hard alee!" re-echoed omi-

---

[1] **gate of Erebus:** in classical mythology, the entrance to the Underworld, through which the spirits of the dead pass.

nously under the towering shadow of Koh-ring as if I had shouted in a mountain gorge. And then I watched the land intently. In that smooth water and light wind it was impossible to feel the ship coming-to. No! I could not feel her. And my second self was making now ready to slip out and lower himself overboard. Perhaps he was gone already . . . ?

The great black mass brooding over our very mastheads began to pivot away from the ship's side silently. And now I forgot the secret stranger ready to depart, and remembered only that I was a total stranger to the ship. I did not know her. Would she do it? How was she to be handled?

I swung the mainyard and waited helplessly. She was perhaps stopped, and her very fate hung in the balance, with the black mass of Koh-ring like the gate of the everlasting night towering over her taffrail. What would she do now? Had she way on her yet? I stepped to the side swiftly, and on the shadowy water I could see nothing except a faint phosphorescent flash revealing the glassy smoothness of the sleeping surface. It was impossible to tell — and I had not learned yet the feel of my ship. Was she moving? What I needed was something easily seen, a piece of paper, which I could throw overboard and watch. I had nothing on me. To run down for it I didn't dare. There was no time. All at once my strained, yearning stare distinguished a white object floating within a yard of the ship's side. White on the black water. A phosphorescent flash passed under it. What was that thing? . . . I recognized my own floppy hat. It must have fallen off his head . . . and he didn't bother. Now I had what I wanted — the saving mark for my eyes. But I hardly thought of my other self, now gone from the ship, to be hidden forever from all friendly faces, to be a fugitive and a vagabond[1] on the earth, with no brand of the curse[2] on his sane forehead to stay a slaying hand . . . too proud to explain.

And I watched the hat — the expression of my sudden pity for his mere flesh. It had been meant to save his homeless head from the dangers of the sun. And now — behold — it was saving the ship, by serving me for a mark to help out the ignorance of my strangeness. Ha! It was drifting forward, warning me just in time that the ship had gathered sternway.

"Shift the helm," I said in a low voice to the seaman standing still like a statue.

The man's eyes glistened wildly in the binnacle light as he jumped round to the other side and spun round the wheel.

I walked to the break of the poop. On the overshadowed deck all hands stood by the forebraces waiting for my order. The stars ahead seemed to be gliding from right to left. And all was so still in the world that I heard the quiet remark "She's round," passed in a tone of intense relief between two seamen.

"Let go and haul."

The foreyards ran round with a great noise, amidst cheery cries. And now the frightful whiskers made themselves heard giving various orders. Already the ship was drawing ahead. And I was alone with her. Nothing! no one in the world should stand now between us, throwing a shadow on the way of silent knowledge and mute affection, the perfect communion of a seaman with his first command.

Walking to the taffrail, I was in time to make out, on the very edge of a darkness thrown by a towering black mass like the very gateway of Erebus — yes, I was in time to catch an evanescent glimpse of my white hat left behind to mark the spot where the secret sharer of my cabin and of my thoughts, as though he were my second self, had lowered himself into the water to take his punishment: a free man, a proud swimmer striking out for a new destiny.

---

[1] **vagabond**: wandering beggar.

[2] **brand . . . curse**: the mark of Cain, Genesis 4: 15.

For Discussion

1. "The Secret Sharer" is the story of a young man's assumption of his first command, and the peculiar events that befall him at the outset of a voyage that will take his sailing vessel from the South China Sea homeward toward England. How does it happen that the captain himself is the one who discovers the stranger clinging to the rope ladder? Why does the captain hide Leggatt, rather than turn him over to the *Sephora?* What effect does Leggatt's presence on board have on the way the narrator discharges his new duties as captain? What finally becomes of Leggatt? "I wondered what my double there in the sail locker thought of this commotion. He was able to hear everything — and perhaps he was able to understand why, on my conscience, it had to be thus close — no less" (page 722). Why, indeed, did the captain take the ship so close into shore? Was it because Leggatt would not otherwise have been able to make good his escape?

2. At the literal level, Conrad's famous story is an adventure tale, and at that level it has its share of suspense, misunderstandings, and conflict. Why do the captain's steward and mates think he is crazy? Describe the scheme by which the secret sharer's presence on board is kept from the crew. Why is it vital that his presence not be suspected? In the interview with the captain of the *Sephora,* why does the narrator resort· to studied politeness in responding to questions put to him? What would have been the consequences of responding in any other way? At one point, when the steward goes into the captain's bathroom with the wet coat, discovery seems inevitable. How does Leggatt escape detection on that occasion?

3. Although a splendid sea yarn, "The Secret Sharer" is much more than that. It has profound things to say about the dual nature each of us possesses — our public side and our private side, our conscious and our subconscious. Consider Leggatt carefully. Although his resemblance to the narrator is stressed repeatedly, we are told at one point that "He was not a bit like me, really" (page 705). How do the two men differ? The question deserves careful thought. Which one is the more violent? Which is the more assured and confident? Which is the more mysterious? Support your responses by referring to specific details in the story.

4. Leggatt killed a man, but he also saved a ship — and all the other lives on it. Or put the other way, he saved a ship, but he also killed a man. If the secret sharer, whose presence is so distracting to the narrator, is seen as a symbol of the captain's own darker nature, the story becomes something more than a diverting anecdote involving a curious coincidence. It becomes a kind of parable or allegory of everyman's reactions to independence and responsibility. Under stress, from out of the watery depths of his subconscious a man may discover a part of himself he did not know existed before. That part may be what will give him the strength not to behave as the *Sephora*'s captain behaved in his crisis — whimpering, unable to speak or act. On the other hand, no man can exercise responsibility effectively if his own inner nature is torn in two; hence, Leggatt's presence on board makes the narrator-captain take at last an extraordinary risk before the ship is finally rid of the secret sharer. What impressions do you suppose the mates and crew would have of their captain on that long voyage home, after the escapade under the towering shadow of Koh-ring? What had the captain learned from the experience?

5. For his part, the narrator in Conrad's story more than once stresses that moving the ship in close to shore was like approaching death itself, "with the black mass of Koh-ring like the gate of the everlasting night towering over her taffrail." What are the captain's feelings as he sees the ship finally drawing ahead, moving out of danger? From that point, does he bring the ship home safely, or can you tell?

6. Not only does "The Secret Sharer" explore profound psychological insights; it also treats some of the most abiding themes in literature. Fate and free will is one such theme. Leggatt may be a free man, "a proud

swimmer striking out for a new destiny," but a captain of a vessel is not free: "Of course, theoretically, I could do what I liked, with no one to say nay to me within the whole circle of the horizon" (page 709); but why are theory and practice in this instance necessarily different? That is, why must someone in absolute power, if he is to behave responsibly, control his actions? In what ways must they be controlled?

7. In considering Leggatt's crime, the question of justice arises. He is unwilling to explain to an "old fellow in a wig and twelve respectable tradesmen" what he has done. Why does he refuse to have his case judged back home in England? Should he be punished? Will he be? Of the other themes treated in this anthology — truth, greatness, man and nature, good and evil, love and hate — which seem most applicable to the story? Does the question of what is true or real arise? What does the story suggest about what constitutes greatness? Does it suggest anything about the ambiguities of good and evil?

8. Conrad's allegory is all the more effective because he insists on the factualness of what he is relating. He achieves verisimilitude by precise detail ("As he used to say, he 'liked to account to himself' for practically everything that came in his way, down to a miserable scorpion he had found in his cabin a week before") and by such means as pretending to forget certain minor matters: "gave his name (it was something like Archbold — but at this distance of years I hardly am sure). . . ." In what other ways does the author achieve verisimilitude in "The Secret Sharer"?

For Composition

To what extent does "The Secret Sharer" develop the anecdote suggested in Stephens' "The Waste Places" (page 660)?

1. Comparison and Contrast. Compare and contrast the ideas implicit in Conrad's story and Stephens' poem. Does fear play a part in both? Do both concern themselves with learning to control one's nature? How do the settings of the two works compare? Arrange your insights logically, and illustrate them specifically.

2. Argument. "From the point of view of his crew, the new captain's behavior during the first days of his command were irresponsible and inexcusable." In a well-reasoned paper support or refute that judgment.

3. Character Sketch. Characterize the new captain, developing late in the essay those attributes you feel are most important. Justify why you have chosen each attribute by citing details or quotations from the story, and develop more profound attributes at greater length.

4. Comparison and Contrast. Compare and contrast Leggatt and the captain. Both, for example, are strangers on the ship — and the only strangers aboard. In what other ways do they resemble each other? In what ways do they differ?

Words and Allusions

AMELIORATIVE AND PEJORATIVE MEANINGS. When the meaning of a word changes from unfavorable to favorable, the word is said to have an *ameliorative* meaning. The word *enthusiasm*, for example, once indicated an unfavorable condition, much like *fanaticism*, but it gradually acquired a favorable, or ameliorative, meaning. Conversely, when the meaning of a word moves from neutral or favorable to unfavorable, it is said to have a *pejorative* meaning. *Dictator*, for example, once referred to someone who possessed absolute power. It now suggests one who misuses power. What other examples of either process can you think of?

The captain in Conrad's story is aware that his actions make him appear *eccentric*. What is the root meaning of *eccentric*? How is it used in mathematics and science? How is it generally used? Is it an example of ameliorative or of pejorative meaning?

SPECIALIZATION OF MEANING (page 232). The word *phenomenon* appears on page 712. What was its original meaning? How is it used today?

Hamlet

WILLIAM SHAKESPEARE

Along with *King Lear, Hamlet* is generally regarded as one of the two greatest plays in the English language. Written about 1600, the play unfolds a story of murder and revenge. It is set at the royal castle of Elsinore, in Denmark, during some unspecified time in the Middle Ages, and it opens not long after the death of a beloved Danish king. The dead king's brother Claudius now rules the land, while the dead king's son — named like his father, Hamlet, — broods in a fit of depression so deep that it alarms all those about him. Besides his father's death, Hamlet is grieved by another event: his mother, the former king's widow, has seen fit to marry, in less than two months' time, her brother-in-law, the new king Claudius.

Many of Shakespeare's plays move freely from place to place, but *Hamlet* takes place entirely in and around Elsinore. The atmosphere within the castle is one of treachery and deceit. People dissemble; spies spy and are spied upon; every curtain may hide its eavesdropper. There is madness in Elsinore, and conspiracies, and murders that cry for vengeance. Into that tormented world characters come — and some are able to depart. But the spectator remains at the castle from start to finish, seeing its great hall within, its more intimate rooms, and even the windswept parapets high overhead, where the watch is stationed through nights of bitter chill — and where the play begins.

DRAMATIS PERSONAE

HAMLET, *only son of the late King Hamlet.*
CLAUDIUS, *King of Denmark; brother of the former king.*
GERTRUDE, *widow of the former king; now wife of Claudius.*
GHOST *of the dead king.*
POLONIUS, *Lord High Chamberlain.*
LAERTES, *son of Polonius.*
OPHELIA, *daughter of Polonius; beloved by Prince Hamlet.*
HORATIO, *loyal friend to Prince Hamlet.*
ROSENCRANTZ ⎱ *false friends to*
GUILDENSTERN ⎰ *Prince Hamlet.*

OSRIC, *a foolish courtier.*
FORTINBRAS, *Prince of Norway.*
VOLTIMAND ⎱ *Ambassadors to Norway.*
CORNELIUS ⎰
MARCELLUS ⎱
BERNARDO ⎱ *sentinels.*
FRANCISCO ⎰
REYNALDO, *servant to Polonius.*
TWO CLOWNS, *gravediggers.*
TROUPE OF CITY PLAYERS, *on tour.*
Lords, Ladies, Ambassadors, Priests, Captain, Soldiers, Sailors, a mob of Danes, Messengers, and Attendants.

THE SCENE — *Elsinore, in Denmark*

Act I

SCENE I. *Elsinore. The sentinel's plat-form before the royal castle.*

FRANCISCO, *a sentinel with lantern in hand and partisan* on shoulder, walks back and forth.* BERNARDO, *the relief-sentinel, enters.*

BERNARDO. Who's there?

FRANCISCO. Nay, answer me. Stand and un-fold yourself!

BERNARDO. Long live the king!

FRANCISCO. Bernardo?

BERNARDO. He.   5

FRANCISCO. You come most carefully upon your hour.

BERNARDO. 'Tis now struck twelve. Get thee to bed, Francisco.

FRANCISCO. For this relief much thanks. 'Tis bitter cold,
And I am sick at heart.   9

BERNARDO. Have you had quiet guard?

FRANCISCO.   Not a mouse stirring.

BERNARDO. Well, good night.
If you do meet Horatio and Marcellus,
The rivals* of my watch, bid them make haste.
[*Enter* MARCELLUS *and* HORATIO.]

FRANCISCO. I think I hear them. Stand ho!
Who is there?   14

HORATIO. Friends to this ground.

MARCELLUS.   And liegemen to the Dane.*

FRANCISCO. Give you good night.

MARCELLUS. O! — Farewell, honest soldier.
Who hath reliev'd you?

FRANCISCO.   Bernardo hath my place.
Give you good night.
[*Exit.*]

MARCELLUS. Holla? — Bernardo?

BERNARDO.   Say,

What! is Horatio there?

HORATIO.   A piece of him.

BERNARDO. Welcome, Horatio. Welcome, good Marcellus.   20

MARCELLUS. What, has this thing appear'd again tonight?

BERNARDO. I have seen nothing.

MARCELLUS. Horatio says 'tis but our fan-tasy,
And will not let belief take hold of him
Touching this dreaded sight, twice seen of us.   25
Therefore I have entreated him along
With us to watch the minutes of this night,
That, if again this apparition come
He may approve* our eyes and speak to it.   29

HORATIO. Tush! tush! 'twill not appear!

BERNARDO.   Sit down awhile,
And let us once again assail your ears,
That are so fortified against our story,
What we, two nights, have seen.

HORATIO.   Well, sit we down,
And let us hear Bernardo speak of this.

BERNARDO. Last night of all,   35
When yond same star, that's westward from the pole,*
Had made his course t' illume that part of heaven
Where now it burns, Marcellus and my-self,
The bell then beating one —
[*Enter* GHOST.]

MARCELLUS. Peace! Break thee off! Look, where it comes again!   40

BERNARDO. In the same figure, like the king that's dead.

MARCELLUS. Thou art a scholar;* speak to it, Horatio.

BERNARDO. Looks it not like the king? Mark it, Horatio.

SCENE I. **partisan**: spearlike weapon; a pike or halberd. 13. **rivals**: partners. 15. **the Dane**: the Danish king.

29. **approve**: confirm. 36. **pole**: the North or Pole Star. 42. **scholar**: man who speaks Latin, the language used to drive out evil spirits.

HORATIO. Most like. It harrows me with
fear and wonder. 44

BERNARDO. It would be spoke to.*

MARCELLUS. Question it, Horatio.

HORATIO. What art thou that usurp'st this
time of night,

Together with that fair and warlike form

In which the majesty of buried Denmark*

Did sometimes march? By heaven I
charge thee, speak! 49

MARCELLUS. It is offended.

BERNARDO. See, it stalks away.

HORATIO. Stay! Speak, speak. I charge
thee, speak!

[*Exit* GHOST.]

MARCELLUS. 'Tis gone, and will not answer.

BERNARDO. How now, Horatio! You
tremble and look pale!

Is not this something more than fantasy?

What think you on't? 55

HORATIO. Before my God, I might not this
believe

Without the sensible and true avouch

Of mine own eyes.

MARCELLUS. Is it not like the king?

HORATIO. As thou art to thyself.

Such was the very armor he had on 60

When he the ambitious Norway com-
bated.

So frown'd he once, when in an angry
parle*

He smote the sledded Polack* on the ice.
'Tis strange!

MARCELLUS. Thus twice before, and jump*
at this dead hour, 65

With martial stalk hath he gone by our
watch.

HORATIO. In what particular thought to
work I know not;

But in the gross and scope* of my opinion,

This bodes some strange eruption* to our
state.

MARCELLUS. Good now, sit down; and tell
me, he that knows, 70

Why this same strict and most observant
watch

So nightly toils* the subject of the land,

And why such daily cast of brazen cannon,

And foreign mart* for implements of
war;

Why such impress* of shipwrights, whose
sore task 75

45. **would be spoke to:** The popular belief was that a ghost could not speak unless first spoken to. 48. **buried Denmark:** the buried king of Denmark.

62. **parle:** conference. 63. **Polack:** the King of Poland. The elder Hamlet, angered in the conference, probably struck him with his glove or hand. 65. **jump:** exactly. 68. **gross and scope:** general drift. 69. **eruption:** sudden calamity. 72. **toils:** fatigues. 74. **mart:** purchase. 75. **impress:** impressment, enforced service.

ABOUT THE AUTHOR • Although most of the plays of his contemporaries are remembered only by scholars, the plays of **William Shakespeare** (1564–1616) continue to excite millions of playgoers every year. It is said that not a day goes by in which Shakespeare is not being performed professionally somewhere in the world. Easily adaptable to the new media of film and television, *Hamlet, Macbeth, Othello, King Lear,* and other of Shakespeare's plays are continually presented in ever-changing interpretations. Shakespeare is truly a world figure whose imagination, psychological insight, and brilliant language continue to illuminate the human condition.

Does not divide the Sunday from the week.

What might be toward* that this sweaty haste

Doth make the night joint-laborer with the day?

Who is't that can inform me?

HORATIO.   That can I;

At least, the whisper goes so. Our last king —   80

Whose image even but now appear'd to us —

Was, as you know, by Fortinbras of Norway,

Thereto prick'd on by a most emulate pride,

Dar'd to the combat; in which our valiant Hamlet —

For so this side of our known world esteem'd him —   85

Did slay this Fortinbras; who, by a seal'd compact,

Well ratified by law and heraldry,*

Did forfeit, with his life, all those his lands

Which he stood seiz'd of* to the conqueror;   89

Against the which a moiety competent*

Was gagèd* by our king — which had return'd

To the inheritance of Fortinbras

Had he been vanquisher, as, by the same covenant

And carriage* of the article design'd,

His fell to Hamlet. Now, sir, young Fortinbras,   95

Of unimprovèd mettle* hot and full,

Hath in the skirts of Norway here and there

Shark'd up* a list of lawless resolutes,

For food and diet,* to some enterprise

That hath a stomach* in't; which is no other,   100

As it doth well appear unto our state,*

But to recover of us, by strong hand

And terms compulsatory, those foresaid lands

So by his father lost. And this, I take it,

Is the main motive of our preparations,

The source of this our watch, and the chief head   106

Of this post-haste and romage* in the land.

BERNARDO. I think it be no other but e'en so.

Well may it sort* that his portentous figure

Comes armed through our watch, so like the king   110

That was and is the question of these wars.

HORATIO. A mote it is to trouble the mind's eye.

In the most high and palmy state of Rome,

A little ere the mightiest Julius fell,

The graves stood tenantless, and the sheeted dead   115

Did squeak and gibber in the Roman streets.

As stars with trains of fire,* and dews of blood,

Disasters in the sun; and the moist star*

Upon whose influence Neptune's empire stands

Was sick almost to doomsday with eclipse.   120

And even the like precurse* of fierce events —

As harbingers preceding still* the fates

And prologue to the omen coming on —

---

77. **toward**: in preparation. 87. **by law and heraldry**: by the formalities of civil law (with bonds, signatures, and seals), and by the Heraldic Court, which governed matters of chivalry. 89. **seiz'd of**: possessed of. 90. **moiety competent**: equivalent portion (of land). 91. **gagèd**: pledged. 94. **carriage**: specified terms as carried by the signed document. 96. **unimprovèd mettle**: untried courage. 98. **Shark'd up**: collected without discrimination.

99. **For food and diet**: without other pay than their keep. 100. **stomach**: courage (suggested by "food and diet"). 101. **state**: government. 107. **romage**: bustle. 109. **Well may it sort**: it may well be on this account. 117. **stars with trains of fire**: meteors. 118. **moist star**: the moon. 121. **precurse**: forerunners. 122. **still**: always.

Have heaven and earth together demon-
strated
Unto our climature and countrymen. 125
[*Re-enter the* GHOST.]
But soft, behold! Lo, where it comes
again!
I'll cross it,* though it blast me.
Stay, illusion!
If thou hast any sound or use of voice,
Speak to me. 129
If there be any good thing to be done,
That may to thee do ease and grace to
me,
Speak to me.
If thou art privy to thy country's fate,
Which happily* foreknowing may avoid,
O, speak! 135
Or if thou hast uphoarded in thy life
Extorted treasure in the womb of earth —
For which, they say, you spirits oft walk
in death —
Speak of it!
[*Cock crows.*]
Stay and speak! — Stop it, Marcellus.
MARCELLUS. Shall I strike at it with my
partisan? 140
HORATIO. Do, if it will not stand.
BERNARDO. 'Tis here!
HORATIO. 'Tis here!
[*Exit* GHOST.]
MARCELLUS. 'Tis gone!
We do it wrong, being so majestical,
To offer it the show of violence;
For it is, as the air, invulnerable, 145
And our vain blows malicious mockery.
BERNARDO. It was about to speak when the
cock crew.
HORATIO. And then it started like a guilty
thing
Upon a fearful summons. I have heard,
The cock, that is the trumpet to the
morn, 150
Doth with his lofty and shrill-sounding
throat

Awake the god of day; and at his warn-
ing,
Whether in sea or fire, in earth or air,
The extravagant and erring* spirit hies
To his confine; and of the truth herein 155
This present object made probation.*
MARCELLUS. It faded on the crowing of
the cock.
Some say that ever 'gainst that season
comes
Wherein our Savior's birth is celebrated,
The bird of dawning singeth all night
long; 160
And then, they say, no spirit dare walk
abroad,
The nights are wholesome, then no
planets strike,*
No fairy takes,* nor witch hath power to
charm,
So hallow'd and so gracious is the time.
HORATIO. So have I heard, and do in part
believe it. 165
But look, the morn in russet mantle clad
Walks o'er the dew of yon high eastern
hill.
Break we our watch up. And by my ad-
vice
Let us impart what we have seen tonight
Unto young Hamlet; for, upon my life,
This spirit, dumb to us, will speak to
him. 171
Do you consent we shall acquaint him
with it,
As needful in our loves, fitting our duty?
MARCELLUS. Let's do't, I pray. And I this
morning know
Where we shall find him most con-
veniently. 175
[*Exeunt.*]

SCENE II. *A room of state in the castle.*

127. **I'll cross it:** To step into the path of a ghost
was to invite disaster. 134. **happily:** haply, perhaps.

154. **extravagant and erring:** wandering and
roaming. 155–156. **of the truth . . . probation:** the
truth of this is proved by this latest demonstration.
162. **strike:** exert an evil influence. 163. **takes:**
does mischief.

[A flourish of trumpets. Enter KING CLAUDIUS, QUEEN GERTRUDE, PRINCE HAMLET, POLONIUS, LAERTES, CORNELIUS, VOLTIMAND, *Lords, Ladies, Attendants. The* KING *and* QUEEN *take their places on the throne.]*

KING. Though yet of Hamlet our dear brother's death
The memory be green, and that it us befitted
To bear our hearts in grief, and our whole kingdom
To be contracted in one brow of woe,
Yet so far hath discretion fought with nature   5
That we with wisest sorrow think on him
Together with remembrance of ourselves.
Therefore, our sometime sister,* now our queen,
The imperial jointress* to this warlike state,
Have we, as 'twere with a defeated joy —   10
With an auspicious* and a dropping eye,
With mirth in funeral and with dirge in marriage,
In equal scale weighing delight and dole —
Taken to wife. Nor have we herein barr'd
Your better wisdoms, which have freely gone   15
With this affair along. For all, our thanks.
Now follows that you know: young Fortinbras,
Holding a weak supposal of our worth,
Or thinking by our late dear brother's death   19
Our state to be disjoint and out of frame,
Colleaguèd* with the dream of his advantage,

He hath not fail'd to pester us with message
Importing the surrender of those lands
Lost by his father, with all bonds of law,
To our most valiant brother. So much for him.   25
[Enter VOLTIMAND *and* CORNELIUS.]
Now for ourself, and for this time of meeting.
Thus much the business is: we have here writ
To Norway, uncle of young Fortinbras —
Who, impotent and bed-rid, scarcely hears
Of this his nephew's purpose — to suppress   30
His further gait* herein, in that the levies,
The lists, and full proportions,* are all made
Out of his subject. And we here dispatch
You, good Cornelius, and you, Voltimand,
For bearers of this greeting to old Norway,   35
Giving to you no further personal power
To business with the king more than the scope
Of these delated articles* allow. (*Hands them papers.*)
Farewell, and let your haste commend your duty.
CORNELIUS. ⎱ In that, and all things, will
VOLTIMAND. ⎰ we show our duty.   40
KING. We doubt it nothing. Heartily farewell.
[Exeunt CORNELIUS *and* VOLTIMAND.]
And now, Laertes, what's the news with you?
You told us of some suit; what is't, Laertes?
You cannot speak of reason to the Dane
And lose your voice.* What wouldst thou beg, Laertes,   45

8. **sometime sister:** former sister-in-law. 9. **jointress:** woman who inherits her husband's estate. 11. **auspicious:** joyful. 21. **Colleaguèd:** joined.

31. **gait:** proceeding. 32. **proportions:** provisions. 38. **delated articles:** detailed documents. 45. **lose your voice:** waste your breath.

That shall not be my offer, not thy asking?
The head is not more native to the heart,
The hand more instrumental to the mouth,
Than is the throne of Denmark to thy father. 49
What wouldst thou have, Laertes?
LAERTES.   Dread my lord,
Your leave and favor to return to France;
From whence though willingly I came to Denmark
To show my duty in your coronation,
Yet now, I must confess, that duty done,
My thoughts and wishes bend again toward France, 55
And bow them to your gracious leave and pardon.*
KING. Have you your father's leave? What says Polonius?
POLONIUS. He hath, my lord, wrung from me my slow leave
By laborsome petition, and at last
Upon his will I seal'd my hard consent. 60
I do beseech you, give him leave to go.
KING. Take thy fair hour, Laertes. Time be thine,
And thy best graces spend it at thy will.
But now, my cousin* Hamlet, and my son —
HAMLET (*Aside*). A little more than kin, and less than kind.* 65
KING. How is it that the clouds still hang on you?
HAMLET. Not so, my lord; I am too much i' the sun.*
QUEEN. Good Hamlet, cast thy nighted color off,
And let thine eye look like a friend on Denmark.
Do not forever with thy vailèd* lids 70
Seek for thy noble father in the dust.

56. **pardon:** permission to depart. 64. **cousin:** near kinsman; here, nephew. 65. **kind:** kindly in feeling, as by kind (nature) a son would be to his father. 67. **i' the sun:** a pun on "sonship," and the "sunshine of royal attention." 70. **vailèd:** lowered.

Thou know'st 'tis common: all that live must die,
Passing through nature to eternity.
HAMLET. Ay, madam, it is — "common."
QUEEN.   If it be,
Why seems it so particular with thee? 75
HAMLET. "Seems," madam! Nay, it is. I know not "seems."
'Tis not alone my inky cloak, good mother,
Nor customary suits of solemn black,
Nor windy suspiration of forced breath,
No, nor the fruitful river in the eye, 80
Nor the dejected havior of the visage,
Together with all forms, modes, shows of grief,
That can denote me truly. These indeed "seem,"
For they are actions that a man might play;
But I have that within which passeth show — 85
These but the trappings and the suits of woe.
KING. 'Tis sweet and commendable in your nature, Hamlet,
To give these mourning duties to your father.
But, you must know, your father lost a father;
That father lost, lost his; and the survivor bound 90
In filial obligation for some term
To do obsequious* sorrow: but to persever
In obstinate condolement* is a course
Of impious stubbornness. 'Tis unmanly grief. 94
It shows a will most incorrect to heaven,
A heart unfortified, a mind impatient,
An understanding simple and unschool'd:*
For, what we know must be, and is as common

92. **obsequious:** proper to obsequies, or funeral ceremonies. 93. **condolement:** grief. 97. **unschool'd:** undisciplined.

As any the most vulgar* thing to sense,
Why should we, in our peevish opposi-
tion,   100
Take it to heart? Fie! 'Tis a fault to
heaven,
A fault against the dead, a fault to nature,
To reason most absurd, whose common
theme
Is "death of fathers," and who still hath
cried,
From the first corse till he that died
today,   105
"This must be so." We pray you, throw
to earth
This unprevailing woe — and think of us
As of a father. For, let the world take
note,
You are the most immediate* to our
throne,
And with no less nobility of love   110
Than that which dearest father bears his
son
Do I impart* toward you. For your
intent
In going back to school in Wittenberg,
It is most retrograde* to our desire,
And, we beseech you, bend you to
remain   115
Here, in the cheer and comfort of our
eye,
Our chiefest courtier, cousin, and — our
son.
QUEEN. Let not thy mother lose her
prayers, Hamlet:
I pray thee, stay with us. Go not to
Wittenberg.
HAMLET. I shall in all my best obey you,
madam.   120
KING. Why, 'tis a loving and a fair reply!
Be as ourself in Denmark. Madam, come;
This gentle and unforc'd accord of
Hamlet
Sits smiling to my heart; in grace whereof,

No jocund health that Denmark drinks
today   125
But the great cannon to the clouds shall
tell,
And the king's rouse* the heavens shall
bruit* again,
Re-speaking earthly thunder. Come;
away.
[*Exeunt all except* HAMLET.]
HAMLET. O, that this too too solid flesh
would melt,
Thaw, and resolve itself into a dew!   130
Or that the Everlasting had not fix'd
His canon* 'gainst self-slaughter! O God!
God!
How weary, stale, flat, and unprofitable
Seem to me all the uses* of this world!
Fie on't! ah, fie! 'tis an unweeded garden
That grows to seed; things rank and gross
in nature   136
Possess it merely.* — That it should come
to this!
But two months dead! nay, not so much,
not two.
So excellent a king, that was to this
Hyperion* to a satyr; so loving to my
mother   140
That he might not beteem* the winds of
heaven
Visit her face too roughly. — Heaven and
earth!
Must I remember? — Why, she would
hang on him
As if increase of appetite had grown
By what it fed on; and yet, within a
month —   145
Let me not think on't! — Frailty, thy
name is woman! —
A little month! or ere those shoes were
old
With which she follow'd my poor
father's body,
Like Niobe, all tears, why she, even she —

99. **vulgar**: common. 109. **immediate**: closest
(in influence and power; also as successor). 112.
impart: give a share (of royal power). 114. **retrograde**: diametrically opposed.

127. **rouse**: full draught of liquor. **bruit**: echo.
132. **canon**: law. 134. **uses**: customs, employ-
ments. 137. **merely**: absolutely, completely. 140.
Hyperion: the sun god, a model of beauty. 141.
beteem: permit.

O God, a beast that wants discourse of
reason*   150
Would have mourn'd longer! — married
with mine uncle,
My father's brother, but no more like my
father
Than I to Hercules. — Within a month!
Ere yet the salt of most unrighteous tears
Had left the flushing in her gallèd*
eyes,   155
She married. O, most wicked speed to
post
With such dexterity to incestuous*
sheets!
It is not, nor it cannot come to good —
But break my heart, for I must hold my
tongue.   159

[*Enter* HORATIO, MARCELLUS, *and*
BERNARDO.]

HORATIO. Hail to your lordship!
HAMLET.   I am glad to see you well —
Horatio! or I do forget myself.
HORATIO. The same, my lord, and your
poor servant ever.
HAMLET. Sir, my good friend — I'll
change* that name with you.
And what make you from Wittenberg,
Horatio? —
Marcellus?   165
MARCELLUS. My good lord.
HAMLET. I am very glad to see you. (*To*
BERNARDO) Good even, sir. —
But what, in faith, make you from Wit-
tenberg?
HORATIO. A truant disposition, good my
lord.
HAMLET. I would not hear your enemy say
so;   170
Nor shall you do mine ear that violence
To make it truster* of your own report
Against yourself. I know you are no
truant.
But what is your affair in Elsinore?

We'll teach you to drink deep ere you
depart!   175
HORATIO. My lord, I came to see your
father's funeral.
HAMLET. I pray thee, do not mock me,
fellow student.
I think it was to see my mother's wed-
ding.
HORATIO. Indeed, my lord, it follow'd hard
upon.
HAMLET. Thrift, thrift, Horatio! the fu-
neral bak'd meats   180
Did coldly furnish forth the marriage
tables.
Would I had met my dearest* foe in
heaven
Ere I had ever seen that day, Horatio!
My father! methinks I see my father —
HORATIO. O, where, my lord?
HAMLET.   In my mind's eye, Horatio.
HORATIO. I saw him once. He was a goodly
king.   186
HAMLET. He was a man! Take him for all
in all,
I shall not look upon his like again.
HORATIO. My lord, I think I saw him yes-
ternight.
HAMLET. Saw? Who?   190
HORATIO. My lord, the king your father.
HAMLET.   The king my father!
HORATIO. Season your admiration* for a
while
With an attent ear, till I may deliver,
Upon the witness of these gentlemen, 194
This marvel to you.
HAMLET.   For God's love, let me hear!
HORATIO. Two nights together had these
gentlemen,
Marcellus and Bernardo, on their watch,
In the dead waste and middle of the night.
Been thus encounter'd: a figure, like your
father,
Armed at points* exactly, cap-a-pe,* 200

150. **discourse of reason**: faculty of reasoning.
155. **gallèd**: sore (from weeping). 157. **incestuous**:
Canon law considered marriage with a deceased
brother's widow to be incestuous. 163. **change**:
exchange. 172. **truster**: one who believes.

182. **dearest**: used of any intense personal feeling;
here, most hated. 192. **Season your admiration**:
moderate your astonishment. 200. **at points**: at all
points. **cap-a-pe**: from head to foot.

Appears before them, and with solemn
    march
Goes slow and stately by them. Thrice
    he walk'd
By their oppress'd and fear-surprisèd
    eyes,
Within his truncheon's* length, whilst
    they, distill'd
Almost to jelly with the act of fear,   205
Stand dumb and speak not to him. This
    to me
In dreadful secrecy impart they did,
And I with them the third night kept the
    watch,
Where, as they had deliver'd, both in
    time,
Form of the thing, each word made true
    and good,   210
The apparition comes. I knew your
    father;
These hands are not more like.

HAMLET.   But where was this?
MARCELLUS. My lord, upon the platform
    where we watch'd.
HAMLET. Did you not speak to it?
HORATIO.   My lord, I did;
    But answer made it none. Yet once me-
      thought   215
    It lifted up its head and did address
    Itself to motion like as it would speak;
    But even then the morning cock crew
      loud,
    And at the sound it shrunk in haste away
    And vanish'd from our sight.
HAMLET.   'Tis very strange.
HORATIO. As I do live, my honor'd lord, 'tis
    true;   221
    And we did think it writ down in our
      duty
    To let you know of it.
HAMLET. Indeed, indeed, sirs, but this
    troubles me.   224
    Hold you the watch tonight?
MARCELLUS. ⎫
BERNARDO. ⎬   We do, my lord.
HAMLET. Arm'd, say you?

204. **truncheon**: staff.

MARCELLUS. ⎫
BERNARDO. ⎬   Arm'd, my lord.
HAMLET.   From top to toe?
MARCELLUS. ⎫
BERNARDO. ⎬ My lord, from head to foot.
HAMLET. Then saw you not his face?
HORATIO. O yes, my lord; he wore his
    beaver* up.
HAMLET. What, look'd he frowningly? 230
HORATIO. A countenance more in sorrow
    than in anger.
HAMLET. Pale or red?
HORATIO. Nay, very pale.
HAMLET.   And fix'd his eyes upon you?
HORATIO. Most constantly.
HAMLET.   I would I had been there.
HORATIO. It would have much amaz'd
    you.   235
HAMLET. Very like; very like. Stay'd it
    long?
HORATIO. While one with moderate haste
    might tell a hundred.
MARCELLUS. ⎫
BERNARDO. ⎬ Longer, longer.
HORATIO. Not when I saw it.
HAMLET.   His beard was grizzled,* no?
HORATIO. It was, as I have seen it in his
    life,   240
    A sable* silver'd.
HAMLET.   I will watch tonight.
    Perchance 'twill walk again.
HORATIO.   I warrant it will.
HAMLET. If it assume my noble father's
    person,
    I'll speak to it though hell itself should
      gape
    And bid me hold my peace! I pray you
      all,   245
    If you have hitherto conceal'd this sight,
    Let it be tenable* in your silence still;
    And whatsoever else shall hap tonight,
    Give it an understanding, but no tongue:
    I will requite your loves. So, fare you
      well.   250

229. **beaver**: visor. 239. **grizzled**: gray. 241.
sable: black. 247. **tenable**: held, kept.

Upon the platform, 'twixt eleven and twelve,

I'll visit you.

ALL.   Our duty to your honor.

HAMLET. Your love, as mine to you. Farewell.

[*Exeunt* HORATIO, MARCELLUS, *and* BERNARDO.]

My father's spirit — in arms! All is not well.

I doubt* some foul play. Would the night were come!   255

Till then sit still, my soul. Foul deeds will rise,

Though all the earth o'erwhelm them, to men's eyes.

[*Exit.*]

SCENE III. *A room in* POLONIUS' *house.*

[*Enter* LAERTES *and* OPHELIA.]

LAERTES. My necessaries are embark'd. Farewell.

And sister, as the winds give benefit,

And convoy* is assistant, do not sleep,

But let me hear from you.

OPHELIA.   Do you doubt that?

LAERTES. For Hamlet, and the trifling of his favor,   5

Hold it a fashion and a toy in blood,

A violet in the youth of primy* nature,

Forward,* not permanent; sweet, not lasting,

The perfume and suppliance* of a minute,   9

No more.

OPHELIA. No more but so?

LAERTES.   Think it no more:

For nature, crescent,* does not grow alone

In thews* and bulk, but, as this temple* waxes,

The inward service of the mind and soul

Grows wide withal. Perhaps he loves you now,

And now no soil nor cautel* doth besmirch   15

The virtue of his will; but you must fear,

His greatness weigh'd, his will is not his own,

For he himself is subject to his birth.

He may not, as unvalu'd persons do,

Carve for himself; for on his choice depends   20

The safety and the health of the whole state,

And therefore must his choice be circumscrib'd

Unto the voice and yielding of that body

Whereof he is the head. Then, if he says he loves you,   24

It fits your wisdom so far to believe it

As he in his particular act and place*

May give his saying deed; which is no further

Than the main voice of Denmark goes withal.

Then weigh what loss your honor may sustain   29

If with too credent ear you list his songs,

Or lose your heart, or your chaste treasure open

To his unmaster'd* importunity.

Fear it, Ophelia! fear it, my dear sister,

And keep you in the rear of your affection,

Out of the shot and danger of desire.   35

The chariest* maid is prodigal enough

If she unmask her beauty to the moon.

Virtue itself 'scapes not calumnious strokes.

The canker* galls the infants of the spring

---

255. **doubt**: suspect.

3. **convoy**: conveyance (*i.e.*, a ship). 7. **primy**: of the springtime. 8. **Forward**: premature. 9. **suppliance**: pastime. 11. **crescent**: growing.

12. **thews**: muscles. **temple**: body. 15. **cautel**: deceit. 26. **place**: social station. 32. **unmaster'd**: uncontrolled. 36. **chariest**: shyest. 39. **canker**: cankerworm.

Too oft before their buttons* be dis-
clos'd,   40
And in the morn and liquid dew of youth
Contagious blastments are most immi-
nent.
Be wary then. Best safety lies in fear:
Youth to itself rebels, though none else
near.
OPHELIA. I shall the effect of this good
lesson keep   45
As watchman to my heart. But, good my
brother,
Do not, as some ungracious pastors* do,
Show me the steep and thorny way to
heaven,
Whilst, like a puff'd and reckless libertine,
Himself the primrose path of dalliance
treads,   50
And recks not his own rede.*
LAERTES.   O, fear me not.
I stay too long. But here my father
comes.
  [*Enter* POLONIUS.]
A double blessing is a double grace;
Occasion smiles upon a second leave.
POLONIUS. Yet here, Laertes! Aboard,
aboard, for shame!   55
The wind sits in the shoulder of your sail,
And you are stay'd for! There — my
blessing with thee.
And these few precepts in thy memory
See thou character.* Give thy thoughts
no tongue,   59
Nor any unproportion'd* thought his act.
Be thou familiar, but by no means vulgar.
The friends thou hast, and their adoption
tried,
Grapple them to thy soul with hoops of
steel;
But do not dull thy palm* with entertain-
ment
Of each new-hatch'd, unfledg'd comrade.

Beware   65
Of entrance to a quarrel; but, being in,
Bear't that th' oppos'd may beware of
thee.
Give every man thine ear, but few thy
voice;
Take each man's censure,* but reserve
thy judgment.   69
Costly thy habit as thy purse can buy —
But not express'd in fancy; rich, not
gaudy;
For the apparel oft proclaims the man,
And they in France of the best rank and
station
Are most select and generous chief in
that.
Neither a borrower nor a lender be;   75
For loan oft loses both itself and friend,
And borrowing dulls the edge of hus-
bandry.*
This above all: to thine own self be true,
And it must follow, as the night the day,
Thou canst not then be false to any man.
Farewell! My blessing season* this in
thee!   81
LAERTES. Most humbly do I take my leave,
my lord.
POLONIUS. The time invites you. Go, your
servants tend.
LAERTES. Farewell, Ophelia, and remember
well   84
What I have said to you.
OPHELIA.   'Tis in my memory lock'd,
And you yourself shall keep the key of it.
LAERTES. Farewell!
  [*Exit.*]
POLONIUS. What is't, Ophelia, he hath said
to you?
OPHELIA. So please you, something touch-
ing the Lord Hamlet.
POLONIUS. Marry, well bethought!   90
'Tis told me he hath very oft of late
Given private time to you, and you your-
self

---

40. **buttons**: buds. 47. **ungracious pastors**: cler-
ics lacking spiritual grace. 51. **rede**: advice.
59. **character**: inscribe. 60. **unproportion'd**: un-
balanced. 64. **dull thy palm**: make your palm
callous by too much handshaking.

69. **censure**: opinion. 77. **husbandry**: thrift.
81. **season**: ripen.

Have of your audience been most free
   and bounteous.
If it be so — as so tis put on me,
And that in way of caution — I must tell
   you,   95
You do not understand yourself so clearly
As it behooves my daughter and your
   honor.
What is between you? Give me up the
   truth!
OPHELIA. He hath, my lord, of late made
   many tenders*
Of his affection to me.   100
POLONIUS. Affection! Pooh! You speak
   like a green girl,
Unsifted* in such perilous circumstance.
Do you believe his "tenders," as you call
   them?
OPHELIA. I do not know, my lord, what I
   should think.
POLONIUS. Marry, I'll teach you! think
   yourself a baby   105
That you have ta'en his "tenders" for
   true pay,
Which are not sterling. "Tender" your-
   self more dearly,
Or — not to crack the wind* of the poor
   phrase.
Running it thus — you'll "tender" me a
   fool.
OPHELIA. My lord, he hath importun'd me
   with love   110
In honorable fashion —
POLONIUS. Ay, "fashion" you may call it.
   Go to! Go to!
OPHELIA. And hath given countenance to
   his speech, my lord,
With almost all the holy vows of heaven.
POLONIUS. Ay, springes to catch wood-
   cocks!* I do know,   115
When the blood burns, how prodigal the
   soul
Lends the tongue vows. These blazes,
   daughter,
Giving more light than heat — extinct in
   both,
Even in their promise as it is a-making —
You must not take for fire. From this
   time   120
Be somewhat scanter of your maiden
   presence;
Set your entreatments* at a higher rate
Than a command to parley. For Lord
   Hamlet,
Believe so much in him, that he is young,
And with a larger tether may he walk 125
Than may be given you. In few, Ophelia,
Do not believe his vows, for they are
   brokers,*
Not of that dye which their investments*
   show,
But mere implorators of unholy suits, 129
Breathing like sanctified and pious bawds
The better to beguile. That is for all:*
I would not, in plain terms, from this
   time forth
Have you so slander any moment's
   leisure
As to give words or talk with the Lord
   Hamlet.
Look to't, I charge you! Come your
   ways.   135
OPHELIA. I shall obey, my lord.
   [*Exeunt.*]

SCENE IV. *The sentinel's platform.*

[*Enter* HAMLET, HORATIO, *and* MAR-
CELLUS.]

HAMLET. The air bites shrewdly; it is very
   cold.

---

99. **tenders:** offers. But Polonius plays on the
term in lines 106, 107, and 109 where it means (1)
"counters" (or chips), (2) "hold" (or regard), and
(3) "present me with," respectively. 102. **Unsifted:**
inexperienced. 108. **crack the wind:** as of a horse, by
running too fast and far. 115. **springes to catch
woodcocks:** snares to catch simpletons.

122. **entreatments:** interviews. 127. **brokers:**
panders. 128. **investments:** vestments, garments.
131. **for all:** final.

A motion picture crew at Kronborg Castle, Elsinore, the setting of Shakespeare's play.

HORATIO. It is a nipping and an eager* air.

HAMLET. What hour now?

HORATIO. I think it lacks of twelve.

MARCELLUS. No, it is struck.

HORATIO. Indeed? I heard it not. Then it
   draws near the season   5
   Wherein the spirit held his wont to walk.
   [*The roll of kettledrums, a flourish of
   trumpets, and two cannon shot off
   within.*]
   What does this mean, my lord?

HAMLET. The king doth wake* tonight,
   and takes his rouse,*
   Keeps wassail,* and the swaggering up-
   spring* reels;
   And, as he drains his draughts of Rhenish
   down,   10
   The kettledrum and trumpet thus bray
   out
   The triumph* of his pledge.

HORATIO. Is it a custom?

HAMLET. Ay, marry, is't,
   But to my mind — though I am native
   here   14
   And to the manner born — it is a custom

More honor'd in the breach than the ob-
servance.
This heavy-headed revel east and west
Makes us traduc'd and tax'd of other
   nations.
They clepe* us drunkards, and with
   swinish phrase   19
Soil our addition;* and, indeed, it takes
From our achievements, though per-
   form'd at height,
The pith and marrow of our attribute.*
So, oft it chances in particular men,
That for some vicious mole* of nature
   in them,
As in their birth — wherein they are not
   guilty,   25
Since nature cannot choose his origin —
By the o'ergrowth of some complexion,*
Oft breaking down the pales and forts of
   reason,
Or by some habit that too much o'er-
   leavens
The form of plausive* manners, that
   these men,   30
Carrying, I say, the stamp of one defect—

---

2. **eager:** sharp. 8. **wake:** hold revels. **takes his rouse:** carouses. 9. **Keeps wassail:** revels in drink. **up-spring:** drunken dance. 12. **triumph:** achievement, feat (at downing a cup of wine in one draught).

19. **clepe:** call. 20. **addition:** reputation, an honorary title. 22. **our attribute:** the reputation ascribed to us. 24. **mole:** blemish. 27. **complexion:** natural disposition. 30. **plausive:** pleasing.

Being nature's livery, or fortune's star*—
Their virtues else, be they as pure as
grace,
As infinite as man may undergo —
Shall, in the general censure, take cor-
ruption   35
From that particular fault. The dram of
e'il
Doth all the noble substance of a doubt*
To his own scandal.
    [*Enter* GHOST.]
HORATIO.   Look, my lord, it comes!
HAMLET. Angels and ministers of grace
defend us! —
Be thou a spirit of health* or goblin
damn'd,   40
Bring with thee airs from heaven or blasts
from hell,
Be thy intents wicked or charitable,
Thou comest in such a questionable*
shape
That I will speak to thee. I'll call thee
"Hamlet,"
"King," "Father," "Royal Dane" — O,
answer me!   45
Let me not burst in ignorance, but tell
Why thy canoniz'd* bones, hearsèd in
death,
Have burst their cerements;* why the
sepulcher
Wherein we saw thee quietly inurn'd
Hath op'd his ponderous and marble
jaws   50
To cast thee up again. What may this
mean,
That thou, dead corse, again in complete
steel

Revisit'st thus the glimpses of the moon,
Making night hideous, and we fools of
nature
So horridly to shake our disposition   55
With thoughts beyond the reaches of our
souls?
Say, why is this? Wherefore? What
should we do?
    [*The* GHOST *beckons* HAMLET.]
HORATIO. It beckons you to go away with
it,
As if it some impartment* did desire
To you alone.
MARCELLUS.   Look, with what courteous
action   60
It waves you to a more removèd ground.
But do not go with it.
HORATIO.   No, by no means.
HAMLET. It will not speak. Then will I
follow it.
HORATIO. Do not, my lord.
HAMLET.   Why, what should be the fear?
I do not set my life at a pin's fee,   65
And for my soul, what can it do to that,
Being a thing immortal as itself?
It waves me forth again. I'll follow it.
HORATIO. What if it tempt you toward the
flood, my lord?
Or to the dreadful summit of the cliff 70
That beetles* o'er his base into the sea,
And there assume some other horrible
form
Which might deprive your sovereignty
of reason*
And draw you into madness? Think
of it.   74
The very place puts toys of desperation,*
Without more motive, into every brain
That looks so many fathoms to the sea
And hears it roar beneath.
HAMLET. It waves me still. — Go on; I'll
follow thee.

---

32. **fortune's star**: One's temperament was supposed to be determined by the planet under which
he was born. **36–37. The dram . . . doubt**: Although the metaphor of these lines is difficult to
paraphrase precisely, the gist is clear: the smallest
amount of evil is all that is needed to taint a wholesome thing. **40. spirit of health**: sound, good.
Some spirits were malignant — devils in disguise.
43. questionable: provoking questioning. **47. canoniz'd**: consecrated. **48. cerements**: linen grave-
clothes; shroud.

59. **impartment**: communication. **71. beetles**:
juts. **73. deprive your sovereignty of reason**:
destroy the sovereignty of your reason. **75. toys
of desperation**: impulse to reckless behavior (*i.e.*,
suicide).

MARCELLUS. You shall not go, my lord!

HAMLET.   Hold off your hands! 80

HORATIO. Be rul'd. You shall not go!

HAMLET.   My fate cries out,
And makes each petty artery in this body
As hardy as the Nemean lion's* nerve.*
Still am I call'd. — Unhand me, gentle-
    men!
By heaven, I'll make a ghost of him that
    lets* me! 85
I say, away! [*He breaks from them.*] Go
    on. I'll follow thee.
    [*Exeunt* GHOST *and* HAMLET.]

HORATIO. He waxes desperate with imag-
    ination.

MARCELLUS. Let's follow. 'Tis not fit thus
    to obey him.

HORATIO. Have after. To what issue will
    this come?

MARCELLUS. Something is rotten in the state
    of Denmark. 90

HORATIO. Heaven will direct it.

MARCELLUS.   Nay, let's follow him.
    [*Exeunt.*]

SCENE V. *Another part of the platform.*

[*Enter* GHOST *and* HAMLET.]

HAMLET. Whither wilt thou lead me?
    Speak. I'll go no further.

GHOST. Mark me.

HAMLET.   I will.

GHOST.   My hour is almost come
When I to sulphurous and tormenting
    flames
Must render up myself.

HAMLET.   Alas! poor ghost!

GHOST. Pity me not, but lend thy serious
    hearing 5
To what I shall unfold.

HAMLET.   Speak. I am bound to hear.

GHOST. So art thou to revenge, when thou

shalt hear!

HAMLET. What?

GHOST. I am thy father's spirit,
Doom'd for a certain term to walk the
    night, 10
And for the day confin'd to fast* in fires,
Till the foul crimes* done in my days of
    nature
Are burnt and purg'd away. But that I
    am forbid
To tell the secrets of my prison house,*
I could a tale unfold whose lightest word
Would harrow up thy soul, freeze thy
    young blood, 16
Make thy two eyes, like stars, start from
    their spheres,
Thy knotted and combinèd locks to part
And each particular hair to stand on end
Like quills upon the fretful porpentine.*
But this eternal blazon* must not be 21
To ears of flesh and blood. List, Hamlet!
    O, list!
If thou didst ever thy dear father love —

HAMLET. O God!

GHOST. Revenge his foul and most unnat-
    ural murder! 25

HAMLET. Murder!

GHOST. Murder — most foul, as in the best
    it is,
But this most foul, strange, and unnatural.

HAMLET. Haste me to know't, that I with
    wings as swift
As meditation or the thoughts of love 30
May sweep to my revenge!

GHOST.   I find thee apt.
And duller shouldst thou be than the fat*
    weed
That roots itself in ease on Lethe* wharf
Wouldst thou not stir in this! Now,
    Hamlet, hear:
'Tis given out that, sleeping in mine or-
    chard, 35

11. **fast:** do penance. 12. **crimes:** sins. 14. **prison house:** purgatory. 20. **porpentine:** porcupine. 21. **eternal blazon:** revelation of things eternal. 32. **fat:** soft, flabby, limp (hence, spiritless). 33. **Lethe:** the river of forgetfulness.

83. **Nemean lion:** lion slain by Hercules as one of his twelve labors. **nerve:** sinew. 85. **lets:** hinders.

A serpent stung me; so the whole ear of
    Denmark
Is by a forgèd process* of my death
Rankly abus'd. But know, thou noble
    youth,
The serpent that did sting thy father's
    life
Now wears his crown.
HAMLET.   O my prophetic soul! 40
    My uncle?
GHOST. Ay. That incestuous, that adulter-
    ate* beast,
With witchcraft of his wit, with traitor-
    ous gifts —
O wicked wit and gifts, that have the
    power 44
So to seduce! — won to his shameful lust
The will of my most seeming-virtuous
    queen.
O, Hamlet, what a falling-off was there,
From me, whose love was of that dignity
That it went hand in hand even with the
    vow 49
I made to her in marriage, and to decline
Upon a wretch whose natural gifts were
    poor
To those of mine!
But virtue, as it never will be mov'd,
Though lewdness court it in a shape of
    heaven,* 54
So lust, though to a radiant angel link'd,
Will sate itself in a celestial bed,
And prey on garbage. —
But, soft! methinks I scent the morning
    air.
Brief let me be. Sleeping within mine or-
    chard —
My custom always in the afternoon — 60
Upon my secure* hour thy uncle stole
With juice of cursed hebona* in a vial,
And in the porches of mine ears did pour

The leperous distilment, whose effect 64
Holds such an enmity with blood of man
That swift as quicksilver it courses
    through
The natural gates and alleys of the body,
And with a sudden vigor it doth posset*
And curd, like eager* droppings into
    milk,
The thin and wholesome blood. So did
    it mine, 70
And a most instant tetter* bark'd about
Most lazarlike* with vile and loathsome
    crust
All my smooth body.
Thus was I, sleeping, by a brother's hand
Of life, of crown, of queen at once dis-
    patch'd, 75
Cut off even in the blossoms of my sin,
Unhousel'd, disappointed, unanel'd,*
No reckoning made, but sent to my ac-
    count
With all my imperfections on my head.
HAMLET. O, horrible! O, horrible! most
    horrible! 80
GHOST. If thou hast nature in thee, bear it
    not!
Let not the royal bed of Denmark be
A couch for luxury and damnèd incest!
But howsover thou pursuest this act,
Taint not thy mind, nor let thy soul con-
    trive 85
Against thy mother aught. Leave her to
    heaven,
And to those thorns that in her bosom
    lodge
To prick and sting her. — Fare thee well
    at once!
The glowworm shows the matin to be
    near
And 'gins to pale his uneffectual fire. 90
Adieu, adieu, adieu! Remember me.
    [Exit.]

---

37. **forgèd process**: falsified account. 42. **adult-erate**: adulterous. 54. **a shape of heaven**: a heavenly disguise, the form of an angel. 61. **secure**: free from apprehension or fear. 62. **hebona**: ebony, the sap of which was thought to be poisonous.

68. **posset**: curdle. 69. **eager**: sour. 71. **tetter**: eruption of the skin. 72. **lazarlike**: resembling leprosy. 77. **Unhousel'd, disappointed, unanel'd**: without having received the eucharist, not made ready, unanointed with extreme unction.

HAMLET. O all you host of heaven! — O earth! — What else?

And shall I couple hell? O fie! — Hold, hold, my heart!

And you, my sinews, grow not instant old,

But bear me stiffly up. (*Rises*) Remember thee? 95

Ay, thou poor ghost, while memory holds a seat

In this distracted globe.* Remember thee?

Yea, from the table* of my memory

I'll wipe away all trivial fond* records,

All saws* of books, all forms, all pressures* past 100

That youth and observation copied there,

And thy commandment, all alone, shall live

Within the book and volume of my brain

Unmix'd with baser matter: yes, by heaven! —

O most pernicious woman! — 105

O villain! villain! smiling damnèd villain!

My tables — meet it is I set it down

That one may smile, and smile, and be a villain —

At least I'm sure it may be so in Denmark.

So, uncle, there you are! Now to my word:* 110

It is "Adieu, adieu! Remember me!" —

I have sworn't.

HORATIO (*within*). My lord, my lord!

MARCELLUS (*within*). Lord Hamlet!

HORATIO (*within*). Heaven secure him.

MARCELLUS (*within*). So be it! 114

HORATIO (*within*). Hillo! ho ho! My lord!

HAMLET. Hillo, ho, ho, boy! come, bird, come!*

[*Enter* HORATIO *and* MARCELLUS.]

MARCELLUS. How is't, my noble lord?

HORATIO.　　　　　What news, my lord?

97. **globe**: head. 98. **table**: table-book, notebook. 99. **fond**: foolish. 100. **saws**: wise sayings. **pressures**: things impressed or inscribed (in a tablebook). 110. **word**: command. 116. **Hillo . . . come**: the cry of the falconer to the hawk.

HAMLET. O, wonderful!

HORATIO. Good my lord, tell it.

HAMLET.　　　　　No, you will reveal it.

HORATIO. Not I, my lord, by heaven!

MARCELLUS.　　　　　Nor I, my lord. 120

HAMLET. How say you, then, would heart of man once think it! —

But you'll be secret?

HORATIO. ⎫
MARCELLUS. ⎭ Ay, by heaven, my lord.

HAMLET. There's ne'er a villain dwelling in all Denmark —

But he's an arrant knave.

HORATIO. There needs no ghost, my lord, come from the grave 125

To tell us this.

HAMLET. Why, right, you are i' the right.

And so, without more circumstance at all,

I hold it fit that we shake hands and part.

You, as your business and desire shall point you — 129

For every man hath business and desire,

Such as it is — and, for mine own poor part,

Look you, I'll go pray.

HORATIO. These are but wild and whirling words, my lord.

HAMLET. I am sorry they offend you, heartily;

Yes, faith, heartily.

HORATIO. There's no offense, my lord. 135

HAMLET. Yes, by Saint Patrick, but there is, Horatio!

And much offense, too. Touching this vision here,

It is an honest* ghost, that let me tell you.

For your desire to know what is between us,

O'ermaster't as you may. And now, good friends, 140

As you are friends, scholars, and soldiers,

Give me one poor request.

HORATIO. What is't, my lord? we will.

HAMLET. Never make known what you have seen tonight.

138. **honest**: genuine.

HORATIO. }
MARCELLUS. } My lord, we will not.

HAMLET. Nay, but swear't.

HORATIO. In faith, 145
My lord, not I.

MARCELLUS. Nor I, my lord — in faith.

HAMLET. Upon my sword.*

MARCELLUS. We have sworn,
my lord, already.

HAMLET. Indeed, upon my sword, indeed.

GHOST (*beneath*). Swear!

HAMLET. Ah, ha, boy! say'st thou so? Art
thou there, truepenny?* — 150
Come on! you hear this fellow in the
cellerage.
Consent to swear.

HORATIO. Propose the oath, my lord.

HAMLET. Never to speak of this that you
have seen.
Swear by my sword.

GHOST (*beneath*). Swear! 155

HAMLET. *Hic et ubique?** then we'll shift
our ground.
Come hither, gentlemen,
And lay your hands again upon my
sword.
Never to speak of this that you have
heard:
Swear by my sword. 160

GHOST (*beneath*). Swear!

HAMLET. Well said, old mole! Canst work
i' the earth so fast?
A worthy pioner!* — Once more remove, good friends.

HORATIO. O day and night, but this is
wondrous strange!

HAMLET. And therefore as a stranger give
it welcome. 165
There are more things in heaven and
earth, Horatio,
Than are dreamt of in your philosophy.*

147. **sword**: The sword, by reason of its hilt, was regularly employed as the symbol of the cross. 150. **truepenny**: honest old fellow. 156. *Hic et ubique*: here and everywhere. 163. **pioner**: one who digs a trench (a military term). 167. **your philosophy**: this philosophy that people make so much of.

But come.
Here, as before, never, so help you mercy,
How strange or odd soe'er I bear my-
self — 170
As I perchance hereafter shall think meet
To put an antic* disposition on —
That you, at such times seeing me, never
shall,
With arms encumber'd* thus, or this
head-shake,
Or by pronouncing of some doubtful
phrase 175
As "Well, well, we know," or "We could,
an if we would,"
Or "If we list to speak," or "There be, an
if they might,"
Or such ambiguous giving-out, to note
That you know aught of me. This not
to do,
So grace and mercy at your most need
help you, 180
Swear!

GHOST (*beneath*). Swear!

HAMLET. Rest, rest, perturbèd spirit!
[*They swear.*]
So, gentlemen,
With all my love I do commend me to
you; 184
And what so poor a man as Hamlet is
May do to express his love and friending
to you,
God willing, shall not lack. Let us go in
together.
And still your fingers on your lips, I pray.
The time is out of joint. O cursèd spite
That ever I was born to set it right! 190
Nay, come, let's go together.
[*Exeunt.*]

172. **antic**: fantastic. 174. **encumber'd**: folded, as in superior knowledge.

For Discussion

1. The question of identity is posed in the very first words spoken in the play. Describe as precisely as you can the mood of the open-

ing scene. Where and when does it take place? A ghost has already twice appeared before the watch. The ghost of whom? Why is Hamlet's friend Horatio present? On its third appearance how does the ghost conduct itself? For Horatio, that appearance "bodes some strange eruption to our state" (I, i, 69). Denmark at that moment is, as it were, mobilizing all its forces. For what purpose? Horatio resolves to tell Hamlet about the ghost. Why?

2. Contrast makes drama effective. Consider the contrasts between Scenes i and ii: one is dark, fearful, private, cold; the other begins in an atmosphere that is bright, relaxed, social, warm. In what other ways may the two scenes be contrasted? Having reminded his court of its concurrence in his marriage to Gertrude (ii, 14–16), Claudius proceeds to deal with outstanding matters one at a time. How does he deal with the Norway threat? With Laertes? All this while, Hamlet will have been on stage, to one side. How is he dressed? What is his mood? The King attempts at line 87 and following to reason with him. What argument does Claudius offer there? What does he beseech Hamlet to do? How does Hamlet respond? To whom does he speak? What is the effect of his reply at line 120?

3. Left alone on the stage after the King and his court depart, Hamlet speaks his first soliloquy (ii, 129–159). What does the soliloquy reveal about his state of mind and the causes for it? When Horatio enters, how does Hamlet receive him and his companions? The short speeches from line 225 on would accelerate the pace of that portion of the scene, adding to the excitement. Hamlet resolves to watch for the ghost's next appearance. In parting, what does he urge his companions to do?

4. Again, after the tension of Scene ii, notice the effect of the opening of Scene iii. What is the mood there? What impression does Ophelia make upon you? Does she have spirit, wit? Is she appealing? Polonius' advice to his departing son (iii, 58 ff) is often quoted approvingly. What do you think of his "few precepts"? By the end of the scene Polonius has forbidden his daughter to speak with

Hamlet again. Why does he do so? On the evidence of this scene, what sort of person does Polonius seem to be?

5. When the ghost reappears in Scene iv, Hamlet's friends urge him not to follow it. What do they fear? Despite their protests, Hamlet does go where the ghost beckons, and there learns the cause of his father's death. At Scene v, line 25, the word "murder" would receive ominous stress; until that point Hamlet might have suspected foul play, but could not have been sure of it. Whom does the ghost charge with murder? Hamlet has suspected as much. How do you know? How was the murder committed? The ghost calls for vengeance. What does he say about Gertrude? Near the end of the scene, to what does Hamlet require his friends to swear? Why?

6. *Hamlet*, like Shakespeare's other mature plays, is written predominantly in blank verse. Define blank verse. In what ways does the dramatist vary the basic blank-verse pattern?

Act II

SCENE I. *A room in Polonius' house.*

[*Enter* POLONIUS *and his servant* REYNALDO.]

POLONIUS. Give him this money and these notes, Reynaldo.
REYNALDO. I will, my lord.
POLONIUS. You shall do marvelous wisely, good Reynaldo,
Before you visit him, to make inquiry
Of his behavior.
REYNALDO.   My lord, I did intend it. 5
POLONIUS. Marry, well said, very well said.
Look you, sir,
Inquire me first what Danskers* are in Paris,
And how, and who, what means, and

7. **Danskers**: Danes

where they keep,*
What company, at what expense; and
   finding
By this encompassment and drift* of
   question   10
That they do know my son, come you
   more nearer
Than your particular demands will touch
   it.
Take you, as 'twere, some distant knowl-
   edge of him,
As thus: "I know his father and his
   friends,
And, in part, him." — Do you mark this,
   Reynaldo?   15
REYNALDO. Ay, very well, my lord.
POLONIUS. "And, in part, him; but," you
   may say, "not well.
But if't be he I mean, he's very wild,
Addicted" — so and so. And there put
   on him
What forgeries* you please; marry, none
   so rank   20
As may dishonor him — take heed of
   that! —
But, sir, such wanton, wild, and usual slips
As are companions noted and most known
To youth and liberty.
REYNALDO.   As gaming, my lord?
POLONIUS. Ay, or drinking, fencing, swear-
   ing, quarreling —   25
Drabbing.* You may go so far.
REYNALDO. My lord! that would dishonor
   him.
POLONIUS. Faith, no, as you may season* it
   in the charge.
You must not put another scandal on
   him,
That he is open to incontinency —   30
That's not my meaning. But breathe* his
   faults so quaintly*
That they may seem the taints of liberty,
The flash and outbreak of a fiery mind,

A savageness in unreclaimèd blood,*
Of general assault.*
REYNALDO.   But, my good lord — 35
POLONIUS. Wherefore should you do this?
REYNALDO.   Ay, my lord;
I would know that.
POLONIUS.   Marry, sir, here's my drift,
And I believe it is a fetch of warrant.*
You laying these slight sullies on my son,
As 'twere a thing a little soil'd i' the
   working* —   40
Mark you,
Your party in converse — him you would
   sound —
Having ever seen in the prenominate*
   crimes
The youth you breathe of guilty, be
   assur'd   44
He closes with you in this consequence:*
"Good sir," or so, or "Friend," or "Gen-
   tleman,"
According to the phrase or the addition*
Of man and country —
REYNALDO.   Very good, my lord.
POLONIUS. And then, sir — does he this —
   he does — What was I about to say? 50
By the mass, I was about to say some-
   thing! Where did I leave?
REYNALDO. At "closes in the consequence,"
At "friend or so," and "gentleman."
POLONIUS. At "closes in the consequence"
   — Ay, marry!   55
He closes with you thus: "I know the
   gentleman;
I saw him yesterday, or t'other day,
Or then, or then, with such, or such; and,
   as you say,
There was he gaming; there o'ertook in's
   rouse;*

34. **unreclaimèd blood**: untamed youth (*cf.*
"wild oats"). 35. **Of general assault**: common to
young men in general. 38. **a fetch of warrant**: a
sure or guaranteed device. 40. **a thing . . . working**:
a young man a little contaminated by his contact
with the world. 43. **prenominate**: previously mentioned. 45. **closes . . . consequence**: agrees with
you in this conclusion. 47. **addition**: style of
address. 58. **o'ertook in's rouse**: overcome by
drink.

8. **keep**: reside. 10. **encompassment and drift**:
roundabout method. 20. **forgeries**: invented
wrongdoings. 26. **Drabbing**: wenching. 28. **Season**: soften. 31. **breathe**: whisper. **quaintly**:
delicately.

There, falling out at tennis"; or per-
chance,   60
"I saw him enter such a house of sale,"
Videlicet,* a brothel, or so forth.
See you now —
Your bait of falsehood takes this carp of
truth.   64
And thus do we of wisdom and of reach,
With windlasses,* and with assays of
bias,*
By indirections find directions out,
So, by my former lecture and advice,
Shall you my son. You have me, have you
not?   69
REYNALDO. My lord, I have.
POLONIUS.   God be wi' you;
fare you well!
REYNALDO (leaving). Good my lord.
POLONIUS. Observe his inclination in your-
self.
REYNALDO. I shall, my lord.
POLONIUS. And let him ply his music.*
REYNALDO.   Well, my lord.
POLONIUS. Farewell!
    [Exit REYNALDO.]
    [Enter OPHELIA.]
    How now, Ophelia! What's the matter?
OPHELIA. Oh, my lord! my lord! I have
been so affrighted!   76
POLONIUS. With what, in the name of God?
OPHELIA. My lord, as I was sewing in my
closet,
Lord Hamlet, with his doublet* all un-
brac'd,*
No hat upon his head, his stockings
foul'd,   80
Ungarter'd, and down-gyvèd* to his an-
kle,
Pale as his shirt, his knees knocking each
other,

And with a look so piteous in purport
As if he had been loosèd out of hell   84
To speak of horrors, he comes before me.
POLONIUS. Mad for thy love?
OPHELIA.   My lord, I do not know,
But truly, I do fear it.
POLONIUS.   What said he?
OPHELIA. He took me by the wrist, and
held me hard.
Then goes he to the length of all his arm,
And, with his other hand thus o'er his
brow,   90
He falls to such perusal of my face
As he would draw it. Long stay'd he so.
At last, a little shaking of mine arm,
And thrice his head thus waving up and
down,   94
He rais'd a sigh so piteous and profound
That it did seem to shatter all his bulk
And end his being. That done, he lets
me go;
And, with his head over his shoulder
turn'd,
He seem'd to find his way without his
eyes,
For out o'doors he went without their
help,   100
And to the last bended their light on me.
POLONIUS. Come, go with me. I will go seek
the king.
This is the very ecstasy* of love,
Whose violent property fordoes* itself
And leads the will to desperate under-
takings   105
As oft as any passion under heaven
That does afflict our natures. I am sorry.
What, have you given him any hard
words of late?
OPHELIA. No, my good lord; but — as you
did command —
I did repel his letters and denied   110
His access to me.
POLONIUS.   That hath made him mad.

---

62. **Videlicit:** namely. 66. **windlasses:** winding
turns. **assays of bias:** a term used in bowling, when
the bowl is made to run in an oblique line. 74. **let
him ply his music:** give him rope, let him sow his
wild oats. 79. **doublet:** jacket. **unbrac'd:** unlaced.
81. **down-gyvèd:** fallen down, like gyves, or fetters,
on a prisoner's legs.

---

103. **ecstasy:** madness, insanity. 104. **property
fordoes:** quality destroys.

I am sorry that with better heed and
    judgment
I had not quoted* him. I fear'd he did
    but trifle,
And meant to wrack thee. But beshrew
    my jealousy!
It seems it is as proper to our age   115
To cast beyond ourselves* in our opin-
    ions
As it is common for the younger sort
To lack discretion. Come, go we to the
    king.
This must be known; which, being kept
    close, might move
More grief to hide than hate to utter
    love.*   120
Come.
[*Exeunt.*]

SCENE II. *A room in the castle.*

[*Enter* KING, QUEEN, ROSENCRANTZ,
GUILDENSTERN, *and Attendants.*]

KING. Welcome, dear Rosencrantz and
    Guildenstern!
Moreover that we much did long to see
    you,
The need we have to use you did pro-
    voke
Our hasty sending. Something have you
    heard   4
Of Hamlet's transformation — so I call it,
Since nor the exterior nor the inward man
Resembles that it was. What it should be,
More than his father's death, that thus
    hath put him
So much from the understanding of him-
    self,   .   9
I cannot dream of. I entreat you both,
That, being of so young days brought up

with him
And since so neighbor'd to his youth and
    humor,*
That you vouchsafe your rest* here in
    our court
Some little time; so by your companies
To draw him on to pleasures, and to
    gather   15
So much as from occasion you may glean,
Whether aught to us unknown afflicts
    him thus,
That, open'd, lies within our remedy.
QUEEN. Good gentlemen, he hath much
    talk'd of you,
And sure I am two men there are not
    living   20
To whom he more adheres. If it will
    please you
To show us so much gentry* and good
    will
As to expend your time with us awhile
For the supply and profit of our hope,   24
Your visitation shall receive such thanks
As fits a king's remembrance.
ROSENCRANTZ.   Both your majesties
Might, by the sovereign power you have
    of us,
Put your dread pleasures more into com-
    mand
Than to entreaty.
GUILDENSTERN.   But we both obey,
And here give up ourselves in the full
    bent*   30
To lay our service freely at your feet
To be commanded.
KING. Thanks, Rosencrantz and gentle
    Guildenstern.
QUEEN. Thanks, Guildenstern and gentle
    Rosencrantz.
And I beseech you instantly to visit   35
My too much changèd son. — Go, some
    of you,
And bring these gentlemen where Ham-
    let is.

---

113. **quoted**: understood. 116. **cast beyond ourselves**: to overshoot ourselves. Polonius has been
unnecessarily suspicious of Hamlet's character.
119–120. Polonius' meaning is that while to tell the
King of Hamlet's love for Ophelia may anger him,
to conceal it would lead to even greater grief.

12. **humor**: disposition. 13. **vouchsafe your rest**:
consent to stay. 22. **gentry**: courtesy. 30. **in the
full bent**: completely (a term in archery).

GUILDENSTERN. Heavens make our presence and our practices
Pleasant and helpful to him!

QUEEN.   Ay, amen!
[*Exeunt* ROSENCRANTZ, GUILDENSTERN, *and Attendants*.]
[*Enter* POLONIUS.]

POLONIUS. The ambassadors from Norway, my good lord,   40
Are joyfully return'd.

KING. Thou still hast been the father of good news.

POLONIUS. Have I, my lord? Assure you, my good liege,
I hold my duty, as I hold my soul,   44
Both to my God and to my gracious king.
And I do think — or else this brain of mine
Hunts not the trail* of policy so sure
As it hath us'd to do — that I have found
The very cause of Hamlet's lunacy.

KING. O, speak of that! that do I long to hear.   50

POLONIUS. Give first admittance to the ambassadors.
My news shall be the fruit* to that great feast.

KING. Thyself do grace to them and bring them in.
[*Exit* POLONIUS.]
He tells me, my sweet queen, that he hath found
The head and source of all your son's distemper.   55

QUEEN. I doubt it is no other but the main —
His father's death, and our o'erhasty marriage.

KING. Well, we shall sift him.
[*Re-enter* POLONIUS, *with* VOLTIMAND *and* CORNELIUS.]
           Welcome, my good friends!
Say, Voltimand, what from our brother Norway?

VOLTIMAND. Most fair return of greetings and desires.*   60
Upon our first,* he sent out to suppress
His nephew's levies, which to him appear'd
To be a preparation* 'gainst the Polack,
But, better look'd into, he truly found
It was against your highness; whereat griev'd   65
That so his sickness, age, and impotence
Was falsely borne in hand,* sends out arrests
On Fortinbras; which he, in brief, obeys,
Receives rebuke from Norway, and, in fine,*   69
Makes vow before his uncle never more
To give th' assay of arms against your majesty.
Whereon old Norway, overcome with joy,
Gives him three thousand crowns in annual fee,
And his commission to employ those soldiers,   74
So levied as before, against the Polack;
With an entreaty, herein further shown,
(*Gives a paper.*)
That it might please you to give quiet pass
Through your dominions for this enterprise,
On such regards of safety and allowance
As therein are set down.

KING.   It likes us well;   80
And at our more consider'd time we'll read,
Answer, and think upon this business:
Meantime we thank you for your well-took labor.
Go to your rest; at night we'll feast together.
Most welcome home!
[*Exeunt* VOLTIMAND *and* CORNELIUS.]

60. **desires:** the conventional wishes for good health and happiness contained in Claudius' communication to old Norway. 61. **our first:** our first interview. 63. **preparation:** organized military force. 67. **borne in hand:** received. 69. **in fine:** in the end.

47. **Hunts not the trail:** The image is that of a hound following the scent. 52. **fruit:** dessert.

POLONIUS.   This business is well ended.   85
My liege, and madam, to expostulate
What majesty should be, what duty is,
Why day is day, night night, and time is
    time,
Were nothing but to waste night, day,
    and time.
Therefore, since brevity is the soul of
    wit,   90
And tediousness the limbs and outward
    flourishes,
I will be brief. Your noble son is mad.
Mad call I it; for, to define true madness,
What is't but to be nothing else but mad?
But let that go.
QUEEN.   More matter, with less art.   95
POLONIUS. Madam, I swear I use no art at
    all.
That he is mad, 'tis true: 'tis true 'tis pity;
And, pity 'tis 'tis true — a foolish figure!
But farewell it, for I will use no art.
Mad let us grant him, then. And now
    remains   100
That we find out the cause of this
    effect—
Or rather say, the cause of this defect;
For this effect-defective comes by cause.
Thus it remains, and the remainder thus.
Perpend!*   105
I have a daughter — have while she is
    mine —
Who, in her duty and obedience, —
    mark! —
Hath given me this. Now gather, and
    surmise!
    [Reads the letter.]
*To the celestial, and my soul's idol, the
    most beautified Ophelia,* —   110
That's an ill phrase, a vile phrase; "beauti-
fied" is a vile phrase. But you shall hear.
Thus:
*In her excellent white bosom, these.**
QUEEN (reaching for the letter). Came this
    from Hamlet to her?   115

POLONIUS. Good madam, stay awhile. I
    will be faithful.
    [Reads.]
*Doubt thou the stars are fire;
    Doubt that the sun doth move;
Doubt truth to be a liar;
    But never doubt I love.*   120
*O dear Ophelia! I am ill at these num-
bers:* I have not art to reckon my groans;
but that I love thee best, O most best!
believe it. Adieu.*   124
    *Thine evermore, most dear lady, whilst
        this machine* is to him,
                            Hamlet.*
This, in obedience, hath my daughter
    shown me;
And more above, hath his solicitings,
As they fell out by time, by means, and
    place,   130
All given to mine ear.
KING.   But how hath she
    Receiv'd his love?
POLONIUS.   What do you think of me?
KING. As of a man faithful and honorable.
POLONIUS. I would fain prove so. But what
    might you think,
When I had seen this hot love on the
    wing —   135
As I perceiv'd it, I must tell you that,
Before my daughter told me — what
    might you,
Or my dear majesty your queen here,
    think,
If I had play'd the desk or table-book,*
Or given my heart a winking mute and
    dumb,   140
Or look'd upon this love with idle sight?
What might you think? No, I went
    round* to work,
And my young mistress thus I did be-
    speak:

105. **Perpend:** Mark my words.   114. **these:**
The conventional ending was "deliver these."

122. **numbers:** verses, versifying.   The term
derives from the number of metrical feet in a line of
verse.   126. **machine:** the body.   Hamlet's com-
plimentary close is in the artificial style of the
sixteenth century.   139. **play'd ... table-book:**
a passive receiver of secrets. 142. **round:** vigorously.

"Lord Hamlet is a prince, out of thy
   star;*
This must not be!" And then I precepts
   gave her,   145
That she should lock herself from this
   resort,
Admit no messengers, receive no tokens.
Which done, she took the fruits of my
   advice;
And he, repulsed — a short tale to make—
Fell into a sadness, then into a fast, 150
Thence to a watch,* thence into a weak-
   ness,
Thence to a lightness,* and, by this
   declension,
Into the madness wherein now he raves
And all we wail for!
KING (to GERTRUDE). Do you think 'tis
   this?
QUEEN. It may be, very like.   155
POLONIUS. Hath there been such a time —
   I'd fain know that —
That I have positively said, " 'Tis so,"
When it prov'd otherwise?
KING.   Not that I know.
POLONIUS. Take this from this, if this be
   otherwise.
   [Points to his head and shoulder.]
If circumstances lead me, I will find 160
Where truth is hid, though it were hid
   indeed
Within the center!*
KING.   How may we try it further?
POLONIUS. You know sometimes he walks
   four hours together
Here in the lobby.
QUEEN.   So he does indeed.
POLONIUS. At such a time I'll loose my
   daughter to him.   165
Be you and I behind an arras then.
Mark the encounter. If he love her not,
And be not from his reason fallen thereon,

Let me be no assistant for a state,   169
But keep a farm and carters.
KING.   We will try it.
   [Enter HAMLET, reading a book.]
QUEEN. But look, where sadly the poor
   wretch comes reading.
POLONIUS. Away, I do beseech you both,
   away!
   I'll board* him presently.* O, give me
   leave.
   [Exeunt KING and QUEEN.]
How does my good Lord Hamlet?
HAMLET. Well, God-a-mercy.   175
POLONIUS. Do you know me, my lord?
HAMLET. Excellent well. You are a fish-
   monger.
POLONIUS. Not I, my lord!   179
HAMLET. Then I would you were so
   honest* a man.
POLONIUS. "Honest," my lord?
HAMLET. Ay, sir. To be honest, as this
   world goes, is to be one man picked out
   of ten thousand.   185
POLONIUS. That's very true, my lord.
HAMLET. For, if the sun breed maggots in
   a dead dog, being a good kissing carrion.*
   — Have you a daughter?
POLONIUS. I have, my lord.   190
HAMLET. Let her not walk i' the sun.* Con-
   ception is a blessing, but not as your
   daughter may conceive. Friend, look to't.
POLONIUS (aside). How say you by that?
   Still harping on my daughter! Yet 195
   he knew me not at first; he said I was a
   fishmonger. He is far gone, far gone!
   And truly, in my youth I suffered much
   extremity for love — very near this. I'll
   speak to him again. — What do you 200
   read, my lord?
HAMLET. Words, words, words.
POLONIUS. What is the matter, my lord?

144. out of thy star: beyond you in rank and
fortune (things determined by one's natal star).
151. watch: state of sleeplessness. 152. lightness:
of mind, lightheadedness. 162. center: of the
earth.

173. board: accost. The image is nautical: to
board an enemy ship in attack. presently: at once.
181. honest: having honorable motives, with a
glance at the common meaning of the word,
"chaste." 188. good kissing carrion: carrion good
to kiss. 191. i' the sun: abroad.

HAMLET. Between who?

POLONIUS. I mean the matter that you 205 read, my lord.

HAMLET. Slanders, sir; for the satirical rogue says here that old men have gray beards, that their faces are wrinkled, their eyes purging thick amber or plum- 210 tree gum, and that they have a plentiful lack of wit, together with most weak hams. All which, sir, though I most powerfully and potently believe, yet I hold it not honesty to have it thus 215 set down; for you yourself sir, should be old as I am — if, like a crab, you could go backward.

POLONIUS (aside). Though this be madness, yet there is method in't. — will 220 you walk out of the air, my lord?

HAMLET. Into my grave?

POLONIUS. Indeed, that is out o' the air. [Aside] How pregnant* sometimes his replies are! a happiness* that often 225 madness hits on, which reason and sanity could not so prosperously be delivered of. I will leave him and suddenly contrive the means of meeting between him and my daughter. — My honorable lord, 230 I will most humbly take my leave of you.

HAMLET. You cannot, sir, take from me anything that I will more willingly part withal — except my life, except my life, except my life. 235

POLONIUS. Fare you well, my lord.

HAMLET. These tedious old fools!

[Enter ROSENCRANTZ and GUILDEN-STERN.]

POLONIUS. You go to seek the Lord Hamlet? there he is.

ROSENCRANTZ (to POLONIUS). God 240 save you, sir!

[Exit POLONIUS.]

GUILDENSTERN. Mine honored lord!

ROSENCRANTZ. My most dear lord!

HAMLET. My excellent good friends! How dost thou, Guildernstern? Ah, 245 Rosencrantz! Good lads, how do ye both?

ROSENCRANTZ. As the indifferent* children of the earth.

GUILDENSTERN. Happy in that we are not over-happy.

On Fortune's cap we are not the very button. 250

HAMLET. Nor the soles of her shoe?

ROSENCRANTZ. Neither, my lord. . . .

HAMLET. What news?

ROSENCRANTZ. None, my lord, but that the world's grown honest. 255

HAMLET. Then is doomsday near. But your news is not true. Let me question more in particular. What have you, my good friends, deserved at the hands of Fortune, that she sends you to prison 260 hither?

GUILDENSTERN. Prison, my lord!

HAMLET. Denmark's a prison.

ROSENCRANTZ. Then is the world one.

HAMLET. A goodly one; in which 265 there are many confines, wards and dungeons, Denmark being one o' the worst.

ROSENCRANTZ. We think not so, my lord.

HAMLET. Why, then 'tis none to you; for there is nothing either good or bad 270 but thinking makes it so. To me it is a prison.

ROSENCRANTZ. Why, then, your ambition makes it one. 'Tis too narrow for your mind. 275

HAMLET. O God, I could be bounded in a nutshell and count myself a king of infinite space, were it not that I have bad dreams.

GUILDENSTERN. Which dreams, in- 280 deed, are ambition; for the very substance of the ambitious is merely the shadow of a dream.

HAMLET. A dream itself is but a shadow.

ROSENCRANTZ. Truly, and I hold am- 285 bition of so airy and light a quality that it

224. **pregnant**: full of meaning. 225. **happiness**: apt turn of phrase.

248. **indifferent**: ordinary.

is but a shadow's shadow.

HAMLET. Then are our beggars bodies, and our monarchs and outstretched heroes the beggars' shadows.* Shall we 290 to the court? for, by my fay, I cannot reason.

ROSENCRANTZ. ⎫
GUILDENSTERN. ⎬ We'll wait upon you.

HAMLET. No such matter! I will not sort you with the rest of my servants; 295 for, to speak to you like an honest man, I am most dreadfully attended.* — But, in the beaten way of friendship, what make you at Elsinore?

ROSENCRANTZ. To visit you, my lord; 300 no other occasion.

HAMLET. Beggar that I am, I am even poor in thanks; but I thank you; and sure, dear friends, my thanks are too dear a half-penny.* — Were you not sent for? 305 Is it your own inclining? Is it a free visitation? Come, come, deal justly with me. Come, come! Nay, speak.

GUILDENSTERN. What should we say, my lord? 310

HAMLET. Why, anything — but to the purpose. You were sent for; and there is a kind of confession in your looks which your modesties have not craft enough to color. I know the good king 315 and queen have sent for you.

ROSENCRANTZ. To what end, my lord?

HAMLET. That you must teach me. — But let me conjure you: By the rights of our fellowship, by the consonancy of our 320 youth, by the obligation of our ever-preserved love, and by what more dear a better proposer could charge you withal, be even and direct with me, whether you were sent for or no! 325

ROSENCRANTZ (aside to GUILDENSTERN).

What say you?

HAMLET (aside). Nay, then, I have an eye of you. — If you love me, hold not off. 330

GUILDENSTERN. My lord, we were sent for.

HAMLET. I will tell you why; so shall my anticipation prevent your discovery,* and your secrecy to the king and queen molt no feather. I have of late — but 335 wherefore I know not — lost all my mirth, forgone all custom of exercises; and indeed it goes so heavily with my disposition that this goodly frame, the earth, seems to me a sterile promontory; 340 this most excellent canopy, the air, look you, this brave* o'erhanging firmament, this majestical roof fretted with golden fire* — why, it appears no other thing to me but a foul and pestilent con- 345 gregation of vapors. What a piece of work is a man! how noble in reason! how infinite in faculty! in form and moving, how express* and admirable! in action how like an angel! in apprehen- 350 sion* how like a god: the beauty of the world, the paragon of animals! And yet to me, what is this quintessence of dust? man delights not me. — No, nor woman neither, though by your smiling 355 you seem to say so.

ROSENCRANTZ. My lord, there was no such stuff in my thoughts.

HAMLET. Why did you laugh then, when I said, "Man delights not me"? 360

ROSENCRANTZ. To think, my lord, if you delight not in man, what lenten* entertainment the players shall receive from you. We coted* them on the way, and hither are they coming to offer you 365 service.

288–290. **Then are our beggars ... shadows:** by your reasoning beggars (being ambitionless) must have substance (bodies) and great men be mere shadows. 297. **dreadfully attended:** Hamlet is aware of his uncle's suspicion and surveillance. 304–305. **a halfpenny:** at a halfpenny.

333. **prevent your discovery:** forestall your disclosure. 342. **brave:** handsome, gorgeous. 343–344. **golden fire:** the stars. 349. **express:** well-framed. 351. **apprehension:** the act of grasping with the intellect; understanding. 362. **lenten:** meager. Plays were forbidden by law during Lent. 364. **coted:** passed.

HAMLET. He that plays the king shall be welcome, his majesty shall have tribute of me; the adventurous knight shall use his foil and target; the lover shall not 370 sigh gratis; the humorous man* shall end his part in peace; the clown shall make those laugh whose lungs are tickle o' the sere;* and the lady shall say her mind freely, or the blank verse shall halt 375 for't. What players are they?

ROSENCRANTZ. Even those you were wont to take such delight in, the tragedians of the city.

HAMLET. How chances it they travel? 380 Their residence,* both in reputation and profit, was better both ways.

ROSENCRANTZ. I think their inhibition* comes by the means of the late innovation.* 385

HAMLET. Do they hold the same estimation they did when I was in the city? Are they so followed?

ROSENCRANTZ. No, indeed they are not!

HAMLET. How comes it? Do they 390 grow rusty?

ROSENCRANTZ. Nay, their endeavor keeps in the wonted pace; but there is, sir, an aerie* of children, little eyases,* that cry out on the top of question,* and are 395 most tyrannically clapped for't. These are now the fashion, and so berattle the "common stages"* — so they call them

— that many wearing rapiers* are afraid of goose quills,* and dare scarce 400 come thither.

HAMLET. What! are they children? Who maintains 'em? How are they escoted?* Will they pursue the quality* no longer than they can sing? Will they not 405 say afterwards, if they should grow themselves to "common" players — as it is most like if their means are no better — their writers do them wrong to make them exclaim against their own suc- 410 cession?

ROSENCRANTZ. Faith, there has been much to-do on both sides; and the nation holds it no sin to tarre* them to controversy. There was, for a while, no money 415 bid for argument* unless the poet and the player went to cuffs in the question.

HAMLET. Is it possible!

GUILDENSTERN. O! there has been much throwing about of brains. 420

HAMLET. Do the boys carry it away?

ROSENCRANTZ. Ay, that they do, my lord — Hercules and his load,* too.

HAMLET. It is not very strange; for my uncle is King of Denmark, and those 425 that would make mows* at him while my father lived, give twenty, forty, fifty, an hundred ducats apiece for his picture in little. 'Sblood,* there is something in this more than natural, if philosophy 430 could find it out.

[*A flourish within, announcing the arrival of the players.*]

GUILDENSTERN. There are the players.

HAMLET. Gentlemen, you are welcome to Elsinore. Your hands, come. The appur-

---

371. **humorous man**: a man in whom one "humor" dominates. According to an ancient theory there are four principal fluids (humors) in the body that determine one's disposition: blood, phlegm, bile, and choler. 373–374. **tickle o' the sere**: quick on the trigger. 381. **residence**: continuance in the city at their large theater. 383. **their inhibition**: the closing of their city theater. 384–385. **late innovation**: Companies of child actors were growing popular and giving serious competition to the adult troupes in London. 394. **aerie**: brood. **eyases**: nestlings, unfledged hawks. 394–395. **cry out . . . question**: exclaim in shrill tones on matters in debate. 398. **"common stages"**: The child-actors occupied a "private" theater and gave performances before a more or less aristocratic audience; the adult actors occupied "common" theaters and played before the rascality of London.

399. **many wearing rapiers**: gallants. 400. **goose quills**: the pens of the dramatists writing for the child-actors, particularly Ben Jonson. 403. **escoted**: paid. 404. **quality**: the profession of acting. 414. **tarre**: urge on (used for dogs in a fight). 416. **argument**: plot, a play. 423. **Hercules and his load**: the Globe Theater, which had before its door as a sign Hercules bearing the world upon his shoulders. 426. **mows**: grimaces. 429. **'Sblood**: by God's blood.

tenancc* of welcome is fashion and 435
ceremony; let me comply with you in
this garb,* lest my extent* to the players
(which I tell you must show fairly outward) should more appear like entertainment than yours. You are wel- 440
come. — But my uncle-father and aunt-
mother are deceived.

GUILDENSTERN. In what, my dear lord?

HAMLET. I am but mad north-northwest:
when the wind is southerly I know 445
a hawk* from a handsaw.

[*Enter* POLONIUS.]

POLONIUS. Well be with you, gentlemen!

HAMLET. Hark you, Guildenstern — and
you, too — at each ear a hearer. (*Aside
to them*) That great baby you see 450
there is not yet out of his swaddling
clouts.

ROSENCRANTZ. Happily he's the second
time come to them; for they say an old
man is twice a child. 455

HAMLET. I will prophesy he comes to tell
me of the players. Mark it. (*Aloud*)
You say right, sir; o' Monday morning;
'twas so, indeed. 459

POLONIUS. My lord, I have news to tell you.

HAMLET. My lord, I have news to tell you.
When Roscius* was an actor in Rome —

POLONIUS. The actors are come hither, my
lord!

HAMLET. Buzz, buzz! 465

POLONIUS. Upon my honor —

HAMLET. Then came each actor on his ass.

POLONIUS. The best actors in the world,
either for tragedy, comedy, history, pastoral, pastoral-comical, historical- 470
pastoral, tragical-historical, tragical-comi-
cal-historical-pastoral, scene individable,

or poem unlimited.* Seneca* cannot be
too heavy, nor Plautus* too light. For the
law of writ and the liberty,* these 475
are the only men —

HAMLET. O Jephthah,* judge of Israel,
what a treasure hadst thou!

POLONIUS. What a treasure had he, my
lord? 480

HAMLET. Why —
*One fair daughter and no more,
   The which he loved passing well.*

POLONIUS (*Aside*). Still on my daugh- 484
ter!

HAMLET. Am I not i' the right, old
Jephthah?

POLONIUS. If you call me Jephthah, my
lord, I have a daughter that I love passing
well. 490

HAMLET. Nay, that follows not.

POLONIUS. What follows, then, my lord?

HAMLET. Why —
As by lot, God wot.
And then, you know — 495
It came to pass, as most like it was.
The first row of the pious chanson* will
show you more; for look where my
abridgment* comes.

[*Enter the Players.*]

You are welcome, masters! Wel- 500
come, all! I am glad to see thee well.
Welcome, good friends! O, my old friend,
why, thy face is valanced* since I saw thee
last: comest thou to beard me in Denmark? (*To the boy-actor*) What, 505
my young lady and mistress? By'r lady,

---

435. **appurtenance**: companion, adjunct. 436–437.
comply . . . garb: welcome you (*lit.*, observe the
forms of courtesy with you) in this fashion. 437.
extent: extending of courtesy. 446. **hawk**: The term
can refer both to a bird and to a kind of pickax.
462. **Roscius**: one of the most famous comic actors
of ancient time.

472–473. **individable . . . unlimited**: An "undivid-
able" scene would observe the classical unities of
time, place, and action; an "unlimited" poem would
be free of such restrictions. 473. **Seneca**: Roman
tragic dramatist. 474. **Plautus**: Roman comic dramatist. 474–475. **the law of writ and the liberty**:
The contrast is probably between academic (classical) plays and more loosely written (modern) ones.
477. **Jephthah**: a judge of Israel who was compelled
to sacrifice a beloved daughter. 497. **chanson**:
song. (The ballad of Jephthah will be found in
Child's *English and Scottish Ballads*.) 499. **abridgment**: curtailment of my conversation with you.
503. **valanced**: bearded.

your ladyship is nearer heaven than when I saw you last, by the altitude of a chopine.* Pray God your voice, like a piece of uncurrent gold, be not cracked 510 within the ring.* — Masters, you are all welcome. We'll e'en to't like French falconers, fly at anything we see. We'll have a speech straight. (*To the First Player*) Come, give us a taste of 515 your quality. Come, a passionate speech.

FIRST PLAYER. What speech, my good lord?

HAMLET. I heard thee speak me a speech once, but it was never acted; or, if 520 it was, not above once, for the play, I remember, pleased not the million — 'twas caviare to the general;* but it was — as I received it and others whose judgments in such matters cried in the top of 525 mine — an excellent play, well digested in the scenes, set down with as much modesty as cunning. I remember one said there were no sallets* in the lines to make the matter savory, nor no matter in 530 the phrase that might indict the author of affectation, but called it an honest method, as wholesome as sweet, and by very much more handsome than fine.* One speech in it I chiefly loved. 535 'Twas Aeneas' tale to Dido, and thereabout of it especially where he speaks of Priam's slaughter.* If it live in your memory, begin at this line — let me see — let me see — 540
The rugged Pyrrhus, like the Hyrcanian beast, —*
'Tis not so. — It begins with Pyrrhus. —
*The rugged Pyrrhus, he, whose sable arms,**

Black as his purpose, did the night resemble
When he lay couchèd in the ominous horse, 545
Hath now this dread and black complexion smear'd
With heraldry more dismal; head to foot
Now is he total gules,* horridly trick'd*
With blood of fathers, mothers, daughters, sons,
Bak'd and impasted with the parching streets 550
That lend a tyrannous and damnèd light
To their vile murders. Roasted in wrath and fire,
And thus o'ersizèd* with coagulate gore,
With eyes like carbuncles,* the hellish Pyrrhus
Old grandsire Priam seeks. 555*
So proceed you.

POLONIUS. 'Fore God, my lord, well spoken, with good accent and good discretion.

FIRST PLAYER. *Anon he finds him, 560
Striking too short at Greeks; his antique sword,
Rebellious to his arm, lies where it falls,
Repugnant to command.* Unequal match'd,
Pyrrhus at Priam drives, in rage strikes wide;
But with the whiff and wind of his fell sword 565
The unnervèd* father falls. Then senseless Ilium,*
Seeming to feel this blow, with flaming top
Stoops to his base, and with a hideous crash
Takes prisoner Pyrrhus' ear. For lo! his sword, 569
Which was declining on the milky head*

---

509. **chopine**: thick-soled shoe. 510-511. **cracked ...ring**: A crack extending within outer ring of a coin rendered the coin illegal. When the boy's voice cracked, he could no longer act the woman's part in plays. 523. **caviare to the general**: too choice for the multitude. 529. **sallets**: spicy sayings. 534. **handsome than fine**: elegant than showy. 538. **Priam's slaughter**: death of Priam, king of Ilium. 541. **Hyrcanian beast**: tiger. 543. **sable arms**: black insignia on shield.

548. **gules**: red (a term in heraldry). **trick'd**: painted (a term in heraldry). 553. **o'ersizèd**: smeared over. 554. **carbuncles**: precious stones of a red, fiery color. 563. **Repugnant to command**: disobedient. 566. **unnervèd**: weak, through exhaustion. **Ilium**: Troy.

Of reverend Priam, seem'd i' the air to
stick.
So; as a painted* tyrant, Pyrrhus stood,
And, like a neutral to his will and matter,*
Did nothing. 574
But, as we often see, against some storm,
A silence in the heavens, the rack* stand
still,
The bold winds speechless, and the orb
below
As hush as death, anon the dreadful
thunder
Doth rend the region; so, after Pyrrhus'
pause, 579
A rousèd vengeance sets him new awork.
And never did the Cyclops' hammers fall
On Mars's armor, forg'd for proof eterne,
With less remorse than Pyrrhus' bleeding
sword
Now falls on Priam.
Out, out, thou strumpet Fortune! All
you gods, 585
In general synod take away her power,
Break all the spokes and fellies* from her
wheel,
And bowl the round nave* down the hill
of heaven
As low as to the fiends!

POLONIUS. This is too long. 590

HAMLET. It shall to the barber's, with your
beard. — Prithee, say on. He's for a jig*
or a tale of bawdry, or he sleeps. Say on.
Come to Hecuba.

FIRST PLAYER. *But who, O! who had seen*
the mobled* queen — 595

HAMLET. The "mobled queen"?

POLONIUS. That's good! "Mobled queen"
is good.

FIRST PLAYER. *Run barefoot up and down,*
threatening the flames

With bisson rheum,* a clout* upon that
head 600
Where late the diadem stood, and for a
robe,
About her lank and all o'er-teemèd* loins
A blanket, in the alarm of fear caught
up —
Who this had seen, with tongue in venom
steep'd,
'Gainst Fortune's state* would treason
have pronounc'd 605
But if the Gods themselves did see her
then,
When she saw Pyrrhus make malicious
sport
In mincing with his sword her husband's
limbs,
The instant burst of clamor that she
made —
Unless things mortal move them not at
all — 610
Would have made milch* the burning
eyes of heaven
And passion in the gods.

POLONIUS. Look, whe'r he has not turned
his color and has tears in's eyes! Prithee,
no more. 615

HAMLET. 'Tis well. I'll have thee speak out
the rest soon. (*To* POLONIUS) Good my
lord, will you see the players well bestowed?* Do you hear, let them be well
used; for they are the abstracts and 620
brief chronicles of the time. After your
death you were better have a bad epitaph
than their ill report while you live.

POLONIUS. My lord, I will use them according to their desert. 625

HAMLET. God's bodikins, man, much
better! Use every man after his desert,
and who should 'scape whipping? Use
them after your own honor and dignity:
the less they deserve, the more 630
merit is in your bounty. Take them in.

572. **painted:** pictured. 573. **neutral to his will**
and matter: indifferent to his purpose and his task.
576. **rack:** cloud. 587. **fellies:** curved pieces of
wood forming the circular rim of a wheel. 588.
nave: hub. 592. **jig:** comic performance, of dancing and singing, by clowns, usually given at the
close of a play. 595. **mobled:** with head muffled
in a scarf.

600. **bisson rheum:** blinding tears. **clout:** rag.
602. **all o'er-teemèd:** overproductive of children.
605. **state:** government, management. 611. **milch:**
moist. 619. **bestowed:** lodged.

POLONIUS. Come, sirs.

HAMLET. Follow him, friends. We'll hear a play tomorrow.

> [*Exeunt all but the First Player.*]

Dost thou hear me, old friend? Can 635 you play *The Murder of Gonzago?*

FIRST PLAYER. Ay, my lord.

HAMLET. We'll ha't tomorrow night. You could, for a need, study a speech of some dozen or sixteen lines which I would 640 set down and insert in't, could you not?

FIRST PLAYER. Ay, my lord.

HAMLET. Very well. Follow that lord, and look you mock him not.

> [*Exit First Player.*]

(*To* ROSENCRANTZ *and* GUILDENSTERN)

My good friends, I'll leave you till 645 night. You are welcome to Elsinore.

ROSENCRANTZ. Good my lord—

> [*Exeunt* ROSENCRANTZ *and* GUILDENSTERN.]

HAMLET. Ay, so; God be wi' ye! Now I am alone.

O, what a rogue and peasant* slave am I!
Is it not monstrous that this player here,   650
But in a fiction, in a dream of passion,
Could force his soul so to his own conceit*
That from her working all his visage wann'd,
Tears in his eyes, distraction in's aspect,
A broken voice, and his whole function* suiting   655
With forms to his conceit? And all for nothing!
For Hecuba!
What's Hecuba to him, or he to Hecuba,
That he should weep for her? What would he do   659
Had he the motive and the cue for passion
That I have! He would drown the stage with tears,
And cleave the general ear* with horrid speech,
Make mad the guilty and appall the free,*
Confound the ignorant, and amaze indeed
The very faculties of eyes and ears.   665
Yet I—
A dull and muddy-mettled rascal, peak,*
Like John-a-dreams, unpregnant of my cause,
And can say nothing! no, not for a king.
Upon whose property and most dear life
A damn'd defeat was made! Am I a coward?   671
Who calls me villain? breaks my pate across?
Plucks off my beard and blows it in my face?
Tweaks me by the nose? gives me the lie i' the throat
As deep as to the lungs? Who does me this?   675
Ha!—
'Swounds,* I should take it, for it cannot be
But I am pigeon-liver'd and lack gall
To make oppression bitter—or ere this
I should have fatted all the region kites*
With this slave's offal! Bloody, bawdy villain!   681
Remorseless, treacherous, lecherous, kindless* villain!
O, vengeance!—
Why, what an ass am I! This is most brave   684
That I, the son of a dear father murder'd,
Prompted to my revenge by heaven and hell,
Must, like a whore, unpack my heart with words,
And fall a-cursing like a very drab,
A scullion!—Fie upon't! Foh!
About,* my brain!—H'm—I have heard   690
That guilty creatures sitting at a play

---

649. **peasant**: base (with the connotation of *serf*). 652. **conceit**: idea, conception. 655. **function**: action in general. 662. **general ear**: public audience. 663. **free**: innocent. 667. **peak**: mope. 677. **'Swounds** (zounds): by God's wounds. 680. **region kites**: kites of the air. 682. **kindless**: unnatural. 690. **About**: get to work.

Have by the very cunning of the scene

Been struck so to the soul that presently*

They have proclaim'd their malefactions;

For murder, though it have no tongue,
will speak   695

With most miraculous organ. I'll have
these players

Play something like the murder of my
father

Before mine uncle. I'll observe his looks.

I'll tent him to the quick.* If he but
blench*

I know my course! The spirit that I have
seen   700

May be the devil — and the devil hath
power

T' assume a pleasing shape; yea, and perhaps

Out of my weakness, and my melancholy —

As he is very potent with such spirits —

Abuses me to damn me. I'll have grounds

More relative* than this. The play's the
thing   706

Wherein I'll catch the conscience of the
king.

[*Exit.*]

693. **presently**: immediately. 699. **tent him to
the quick**: probe him to the living, sensitive flesh.
blench: flinch his eyes. 706. **relative**: pertinent.

For Discussion

1. Act II opens on a note of intrigue: Polonius is discovered arranging for someone to
spy on his absent son. As Reynaldo departs,
Ophelia enters. What news of Hamlet does
she bring her father? How does he respond
to the news?

2. The opening of the second scene of Act
II parallels the first. In what way? What does
the King ask Rosencrantz and Guildenstern to
do? Polonius arrives with important news; he
has discovered the "very cause of Hamlet's

lunacy" (ii, 49). What does the Queen think
is the cause? What is Polonius' explanation
for Hamlet's behavior? The King wants
proof. How does Polonius propose to test his
theory? The early portions of the scene return to the Norway question raised in Act I,
Scene ii. How is that threat to the peace of
Denmark here resolved?

3. Rosencrantz and Guildenstern encounter
Hamlet, who before long leads them to admit
that they "were sent for" (ii, 331). To the
prince they suggest that his ambition is the
cause of his discontent. Ambition for what?
How does Hamlet answer the charge? The
arrival of the players provides him with an
opportunity to put a plan into motion. For
what purpose? What is the plan? The soliloquy at Scene ii, line 648 and following, expresses a self-evaluation. What about himself
distresses Hamlet? Is he a coward? Is he insensitive? As you continue reading, try to arrive
at an understanding of the kind of person Hamlet is, and of what motivates him to behave as
he does.

4. In traditional drama, the playwright never
speaks in his own voice. Instead, as in life,
each person in a play should speak with a style
of his own. Consider the ways in which
Claudius, Rosencrantz and Guildenstern, Polonius, and Hamlet speak. What characteristics do you notice in the speech of each of
these characters? Illustrate your remarks with
examples.

Act III

SCENE I. *A room in the castle.*

[*Enter* KING, QUEEN, POLONIUS,
OPHELIA, ROSENCRANTZ *and* GUILDEN-
STERN.]

KING. And can you by no drift of circumstance*

1. **drift of circumstance**: device of beating about
the bush.

Get from him why he puts on this con-
fusion,*
Grating so harshly all his days of quiet
With turbulent and dangerous lunacy?
ROSENCRANTZ. He does confess he feels
himself distracted,   5
But from what cause he will by no means
speak.
GUILDENSTERN. Nor do we find him for-
ward to be sounded,
But with a crafty madness keeps aloof
When we would bring him on to some
confession   9
Of his true state.
QUEEN.   Did he receive you well?
ROSENCRANTZ. Most like a gentleman.
GUILDENSTERN. But with much forcing of
his disposition.
ROSENCRANTZ. Niggard of question,* but
of our demands
Most free in his reply.
QUEEN.   Did you assay* him
To any pastime?   15
ROSENCRANTZ. Madam, it so fell out that
certain players
We o'er-raught* on the way. Of these
we told him,
And there did seem in him a kind of joy
To hear of it. They are about the
court,   19
And, as I think, they have already order
This night to play before him.
POLONIUS.   'Tis most true;
And he beseech'd me to entreat your
majesties
To hear and see the matter.
KING. With all my heart; and it doth much
content me
To hear him so inclin'd.   25
Good gentlemen, give him a further edge
And drive his purpose on to these de-

lights.
ROSENCRANTZ. We shall, my lord.
  [*Exeunt* ROSENCRANTZ *and* GUILDEN-
STERN.]
KING.   Sweet Gertrude, leave us too;
For we have closely sent for Hamlet
hither,
That he, as 'twere by accident, may
here   30
Affront* Ophelia.
Her father and myself, lawful espials,*
Will so bestow ourselves that, seeing un-
seen,
We may of their encounter frankly
judge,
And gather by him, as he is behav'd,   35
If't be the affliction of his love or no
That thus he suffers for.
QUEEN.   I shall obey you. —
And for your part, Ophelia, I do wish
That your good beauties be the happy
cause
Of Hamlet's wildness; so shall I hope your
virtues   40
Will bring him to his wonted way again,
To both your honors.
OPHELIA.   Madam, I wish it may.
  [*Exit* QUEEN.]
POLONIUS. Ophelia, walk you here. — Gra-
cious, so please you,
We will bestow ourselves. (*To* OPHELIA)
Read on this book,   44
That show of such an exercise* may color
Your loneliness. — We are oft to blame
in this,
'Tis too much prov'd, that with devo-
tion's visage
And pious action we do sugar o'er
The devil himself.
KING (*aside*).   O, 'tis too true!
How smart a lash that speech doth give
my conscience!   50
The harlot's cheek, beautied with plaster-
ing art,

<hr>

2. **puts on this confusion**: behaves in this distracted way. The metaphor is borrowed from the
act of dressing, but it does not here imply that
Hamlet's "confusion" is feigned. 13. **Niggard of
question**: indisposed to start conversation. 14.
assay: tempt. 17. **o'er-raught**: overtook.

31. **Affront**: come face to face with. 32. **espials**:
spies. 45. **exercise**: religious devotion.

Is not more ugly to the thing that helps it
Than is my deed to my most painted
   word.
O heavy burden!
POLONIUS. I hear him coming. Let's with-
   draw, my lord.   55
   [*Exeunt* KING *and* POLONIUS.]
   [*Enter* HAMLET.]
HAMLET. To be, or not to be — that is the
   question:
Whether 'tis nobler in the mind to suffer
The slings and arrows of outrageous for-
   tune,
Or to take arms against a sea of troubles,
And by opposing, end them. To die —
   to sleep —   60
No more; and by a sleep to say we end
The heartache and the thousand natural
   shocks
That flesh is heir to — 'tis a consumma-
   tion
Devoutly to be wish'd. To die — to sleep.
To sleep — perchance to dream! Ay,
   there's the rub!   65
For in that sleep of death what dreams
   may come,
When we have shuffled off this mortal
   coil,*
Must give us pause. There's the respect
That makes calamity of so long life.*
For who would bear the whips and scorns
   of time,   70
The oppressor's wrong, the proud man's
   contumely,
The pangs of despis'd love, the law's de-
   lay,
The insolence of office,* and the spurns
That patient merit of the unworthy takes,
When he himself might his quietus make
With a bare bodkin?* Who would far-
   dels* bear,   76

To grunt and sweat under a weary life,
But that the dread of something after
   death,
The undiscover'd country, from whose
   bourn*
No traveler returns, puzzles the will,   80
And makes us rather bear those ills we
   have
Than fly to others that we know not of?
Thus conscience does make cowards of
   us all,
And thus the native hue* of resolution
Is sicklied o'er with the pale cast of
   thought,   85
And enterprises of great pith and moment
With this regard their currents turn awry
And lose the name of action. — Soft you
   now!
The fair Ophelia! Nymph, in thy orisons
Be all my sins remember'd.
OPHELIA.   Good my lord,   90
   How does your honor for this many a
   day?
HAMLET. I humbly thank you, well — well
   — well.
OPHELIA. My lord, I have remembrances of
   yours
That I have longed to re-deliver;
I pray you, now receive them.
HAMLET.   No, not I!   95
   I never gave you aught.
OPHELIA. My honor'd lord, you know right
   well you did,
And with them words of so sweet breath
   compos'd
As made the things more rich. Their
   perfume lost,   99
Take these again; for to the noble mind
Rich gifts wax poor when givers prove
   unkind. —
There, my lord.
HAMLET. Ha! ha! — are you honest?*
OPHELIA. My lord!

---

67. **mortal coil**: turmoil of life; also the body, conceived of a a coil of rope entwining the soul. 69. **of so long life**: so long-lived (makes us endure calamity). 73. **office**: office holders considered as a type. 76. **bodkin**: dagger. **fardels**: burdens.

79. **bourn**: boundary. 84. **native hue**: natural and healthy ruddy complexion. 103. **honest**: virtuous, chaste.

HAMLET. Are you fair? 105

OPHELIA. What means your lordship?

HAMLET. That if you be honest and fair, your honesty should admit no discourse to your beauty.

OPHELIA. Could beauty, my lord, have 110 better commerce* than with honesty?

HAMLET. Ay, truly; for the power of beauty will sooner transform honesty from what it is to a bawd than the force of honesty can translate beauty into 115 his likeness. This was sometime a paradox, but now the time gives it proof. — I did love you once.

OPHELIA. Indeed, my lord, you made me believe so. 120

HAMLET. You should not have believed me! for virtue cannot so inoculate our old stock but we shall relish of it.* I loved you not.

OPHELIA. I was the more deceived. 125

HAMLET. Get thee to a nunnery. Why wouldst thou be a breeder of sinners? I am myself indifferent* honest, but yet I could accuse me of such things that it were better my mother had not 130 borne me. I am very proud, revengeful, ambitious; with more offenses at my beck than I have thoughts to put them in, imagination to give them shape, or time to act them in. What should such 135 fellows as I do crawling between heaven and earth? We are arrant knaves, all. Believe none of us. Go thy ways to a nunnery. — Where's your father?

OPHELIA. At home, my lord. 140

HAMLET. Let the doors be shut upon him, that he may play the fool nowhere but in's own house. Farewell.

OPHELIA. O! help him, you sweet heavens!

HAMLET. If thou dost marry, I'll give 145 thee this plague for thy dowry: be thou as chaste as ice, as pure as snow, thou shalt not escape calumny. Get thee to a nunnery, go! Farewell. Or, if thou wilt needs marry, marry a fool; for wise 150 men know well enough what monsters* you make of them. To a nunnery, go; and quickly too. Farewell.

OPHELIA. O heavenly powers, restore him!

HAMLET. I have heard of your paint- 155 ings, too, well enough. God hath given you one face, and you make yourselves another. You jig, you amble,* and you lisp; you nickname God's creatures, and make your wantonness your igno- 160 rance.* Go to, I'll no more on't! it hath made me mad. I say, we will have no more marriages. Those that are married already — all but one — shall live; the rest shall keep as they are. To a 165 nunnery, go!

[*Exit.*]

OPHELIA. O, what a noble mind is here o'erthrown!

The courtier's, soldier's, scholar's, eye, tongue, sword;

The expectancy and rose of the fair state,

The glass of fashion, and the mold of form,* 170

The observ'd of all observers — quite, quite down!

And I, of ladies most deject and wretched,

That suck'd the honey of his music vows,

Now see that noble and most sovereign reason,

Like sweet bells jangled, out of tune and harsh; 175

That unmatch'd form and feature of blown* youth

Blasted with ecstasy.* O! woe is me

111. **commerce**: dealings. 122–123. **cannot . . . of it**: cannot, by grafting, so change our sinful nature (corrupted by the original sin of Adam) that we shall not still retain the taint. The figure is that of a fruit tree on which a better shoot has been grafted. The fruit, says Hamlet, will still taste of the old stock. 128. **indifferent**: fairly, reasonably.

151. **monsters**: A husband whose wife was false to him was said to have horns on his head. 158. **amble**: walk in an affected way. 159–161. **you nickname . . . ignorance**: you give affected names to ordinary things, and pretend that this is not affectation but simple ignorance about vulgar matters. 170. **mold of form**: model of social behavior. 176. **blown**: in full blossom. 177. **ecstasy**: insanity.

To have seen what I have seen, see what
I see!

[*Re-enter* KING *and* POLONIUS.]

KING. Love? his affections* do not that
way tend;

Nor what he spake, though it lack'd form
a little, 180

Was not like madness. There's something in his soul

O'er which his melancholy sits on brood;

And I do doubt* the hatch and the disclose*

Will be some danger. Which for to
prevent,

I have in quick determination 185

Thus set it down: he shall with speed to
England

For the demand of our neglected tribute.

Haply the seas, and countries different,

With variable objects, shall expel

This something-settled matter in his
heart, 190

Whereon his brains still beating puts him
thus

From fashion of himself. What think you
on't?

POLONIUS. It shall do well. But yet do I
believe

The origin and commencement of his
grief

Sprung from neglected love. — How
now, Ophelia! 195

You need not tell us what Lord Hamlet
said;

We heard it all. — My lord, do as you
please;

But, if you hold it fit, after the play

Let his queen mother all alone entreat
him

To show his grief. Let her be round*
with him; 200

And I'll be plac'd, so please you, in the
ear

Of all their conference. If she find* him

179. **affections**: mental disposition. 183. **doubt**:
suspect. **disclose**: breaking out from the egg.
200. **round**: plainspoken. 202. **find**: find out,
discover.

not,

To England send him, or confine him
where

Your wisdom best shall think.

KING.   It shall be so.

Madness in great ones must not un-
watch'd go. 205

[*Exeunt.*]

SCENE II. *A hall in the castle.*

[*Enter* HAMLET *and* PLAYERS.]

HAMLET. Speak the speech, I pray you, as
I pronounced it to you, trippingly on the
tongue. But if you mouth it, as many of
our players do, I had as lief the town
crier spoke my lines. Nor do not saw 5
the air too much with your hand, thus,
but use all gently; for in the very torrent,
tempest, and (as I may say) whirlwind
of your passion, you must acquire and
beget a temperance that may give it 10
smoothness. O, it offends me to the soul
to hear a robustious periwig-pated* fellow tear a passion to tatters, to very rags,
to split the ears of the groundlings,* who
for the most part are capable of 15
nothing but inexplicable dumb shows and
noise. I would have such a fellow
whipped for o'erdoing Termagant.* It
out-herods Herod.* Pray you, avoid it.

FIRST PLAYER. I warrant your honor. 20

HAMLET. Be not too tame neither, but let
your own discretion be your tutor. Suit
the action to the word, the word to the
action; with this special observance, that
you o'erstep not the modesty* of 25
nature. For anything so overdone is from
the purpose of playing, whose end, both

12. **periwig-pated**: wig-wearing. 14. **groundlings**: the rabble, which paid only a penny for
admission and stood on the ground in the open-air
"yard" of the theater. 18. **Termagant**: Saracen
god represented in the early drama as a ranting
boaster. 19. **out-herods Herod**: In the early Bible
plays, Herod raged with unrestrained violence. 25.
modesty: propriety.

at the first and now, was and is, to hold, as 'twere, the mirror up to nature: to show virtue her own feature, scorn 30 her own image, and the very age and body of the time his form and pressure.* Now, this overdone, or come tardy off, though it make the unskilful* laugh, cannot but make the judicious grieve; 35 the censure of the which one must in your allowance o'erweigh a whole theatre of others. O, there be players that I have seen play — and heard others praise, and that highly — not to speak it pro- 40 fanely,* that, neither having the accent of Christians, nor the gait of Christian, pagan, nor man, have so strutted and bellowed that I have thought some of nature's journeymen* had made men, 45 and not made them well, they imitated humanity so abominably.

FIRST PLAYER. I hope we have reformed that indifferently with us.

HAMLET. O, reform it altogether! And 50 let those that play your clowns speak no more than is set down for them;* for there be of them that will themselves laugh to set on some quantity of barren* spectators to laugh too, though in 55 the mean time some necessary question of the play be then to be considered. That's villainous, and shows a most pitiful ambition in the fool that uses it. Go, make you ready. 60

[*Exeunt Players.*]

[*Enter* POLONIUS, ROSENCRANTZ, *and* GUILDENSTERN.]

How now, my lord? Will the king hear this piece of work?

POLONIUS. And the queen too, and that presently.

HAMLET. Bid the players make haste. 65

32. **pressure**: image, impress. 34. **unskilful**: undiscriminating. 40–41. **not to speak it profanely**: not intending, in what I am about to say, any disrespect to the Divine Being. 45. **journeymen**: craftsmen not yet masters of their trade. 51–52. **clowns . . . them**: Clowns were accustomed to extemporize humor to please the groundlings. 54. **barren**: empty-headed.

[*Exit* POLONIUS.]

Will you two help to hasten them?

ROSENCRANTZ. ⎫
GUILDENSTERN. ⎬ We will, my lord.

[*Exeunt* ROSENCRANTZ *and* GUILDENSTERN.]

HAMLET. What, ho, Horatio!

[*Enter* HORATIO.]

HORATIO. Here, sweet lord, at your service.

HAMLET. Horatio, thou art e'en as just a man 70
As e'er my conversation cop'd withal.*

HORATIO. O! my dear lord.

HAMLET.   Nay, do not think I flatter;
For what advancement may I hope from thee,
That no revenue hast but thy good spirits
To feed and clothe thee? Why should the poor be flatter'd? 75
No, let the candied tongue lick absurd pomp,
And crook the pregnant hinges* of the knee
Where thrift may follow fawning. Dost thou hear?
Since my dear soul was mistress of her choice
And could of men distinguish, her election 80
Hath seal'd thee for herself. For thou hast been
As one, in suff'ring all, that suffers nothing;
A man that fortune's buffets and rewards.
Hath ta'en with equal thanks; and bless'd are those
Whose blood* and judgment are so well co-mingled 85
That they are not a pipe for Fortune's finger
To sound what stop she please. Give me that man
That is not passion's slave, and I will wear him

71. **conversation cop'd withal**: intercourse with others encountered. 77. **pregnant hinges**: supple joints. 85. **blood**: emotional nature.

In my heart's core, ay, in my heart of
heart,

As I do thee. — Something too much of
this.   90

There is a play tonight before the king.

One scene of it comes near the circumstance

Which I have told thee of my father's
death.

I prithee, when thou seest that act afoot,

Even with the very comment of thy
soul   95

Observe mine uncle! If his occulted*
guilt

Do not itself unkennel in one speech,

It is a damnèd ghost that we have seen,

And my imaginations are as foul

As Vulcan's stithy.* Give him heedful
note;   100

For I mine eyes will rivet to his face,

And after we will both our judgments
join

In censure of his seeming.*

HORATIO.   Well, my lord,

If he steal aught the whilst this play is
playing,

And 'scape detecting, I will pay the
theft.   105

HAMLET. They are coming to the play. I
must be idle.*

Get you a place.

[*A Danish march. Enter attendants
carrying torches. A flourish of trumpets. Enter* KING, QUEEN, POLONIUS,
OPHELIA, ROSENCRANTZ, GUILDEN-
STERN, *Lords and Ladies of the court.*]

KING. How fares* our cousin Hamlet?

HAMLET. Excellent, i' faith, of the chameleon's dish;* I eat the air, promise-   110
crammed. You cannot feed capon so!

KING. I have nothing with this answer,
Hamlet; these words are not mine.

HAMLET. No, nor mine now. (*To* POLO-
NIUS) My lord, you played once i'   115
the university, you say?

POLONIUS. That did I, my lord, and was
accounted a good actor.

HAMLET. And what did you enact?

POLONIUS. I did enact Julius Caesar. I   120
was killed i' the Capitol. Brutus killed me.

HAMLET. It was a brute part of him to kill
so capital a calf there. Be the players
ready?

ROSENCRANTZ. Ay, my lord. They stay   125
upon your patience.

QUEEN. Come hither, my dear Hamlet, sit
by me.

HAMLET. No, good mother, here's metal
more attractive.   130

[*Sitting down at* OPHELIA's *feet.*]

POLONIUS (*To the* KING). O ho! do you
mark that?

HAMLET. Lady, shall I lie in your lap?

OPHELIA. No, my lord!   134

HAMLET. I mean, my head upon your lap?

OPHELIA. Ay, my lord. . . . You are merry,
my lord.

HAMLET. Who, I?

OPHELIA. Ay, my lord.

HAMLET. O God, your only jig-   140
maker!* What should a man do but be
merry? For look you how cheerfully my
mother looks, and my father died within
's two hours.

OPHELIA. Nay, 'tis twice two months,   145
my lord.

HAMLET. So long? Nay then, let the devil
wear black, for I'll have a suit of sables.*
O heavens! die two months ago, and not
forgotten yet? Then there's hope a   150
great man's memory may outlive his life
half a year — but, by 'r lady, he must
build churches then, or else shall he suffer
not thinking on, with the hobbyhorse,*

---

96. occulted: hidden. 100. stithy: smithy. 103.
censure of his seeming: judgment of his appearance.
106. be idle: play the madman. 108. fares:
Claudius uses the word in the sense of *does*, Hamlet
in the sense of *feeds*. 109–110. chameleon's dish:
chameleons were said to feed on air.

141. jig-maker: stage-clown, who amused the
rabble with jigs. 148. sables: black (like the devil).
Hamlet's madness still has method in it. 154.
hobbyhorse: mock figure strapped around the waist
of a performer in the morris dance.

whose epitaph is (*Singing*) *For O,*   155
for O, the hobbyhorse is forgot!

[*Hautboys play. The dumb-show
enters.*]

Enter a KING *and a* QUEEN, *very lov-
ingly; the* QUEEN *embracing him and he
her. She kneels, and makes show of pro-
testation unto him. He takes her up, and
declines his head upon her neck. He lays
him down upon a bank of flowers. She,
seeing him asleep, leaves him. Anon
comes in a fellow, takes off his crown,
kisses it, and pours poison in the* KING's
ears, and exit. The QUEEN *returns, finds
the* KING *dead, and makes passionate action. The poisoner, with some two or
three mutes, comes in again, seeming to
lament with her. The dead body is carried away. The poisoner wooes the*
QUEEN *with gifts. She seems loath and
unwilling awhile, but in the end accepts
his love.*

[*Exeunt; the music ceases.*]

OPHELIA. What means this, my lord?

HAMLET. Marry, this is miching mallecho;*
it means mischief.

OPHELIA. Belike this show imports the   160
argument* of the play?

[*Enter a* PLAYER *as* PROLOGUE.]

HAMLET. We shall know by this fellow.
The players cannot keep counsel; they'll
tell all.

OPHELIA. Will he tell us what this   165
show meant?

HAMLET. Ay, or any show that you'll show
him. Be not you asham'd to show, he'll
not shame to tell you what it means.

OPHELIA. You are naught, you are   170
naught! I'll mark the play.

PROLOGUE. *For us and for our tragedy,
Here stooping to your clemency,
We beg your hearing patiently.*

[*Bows, and goes out.*]

HAMLET. Is this a prologue, or the   175

158. **miching mallecho:** hidden mischief. 161.
argument: plot.

posy of a ring?*

OPHELIA. 'Tis brief, my lord.

HAMLET. As woman's love!

[*Enter two* PLAYERS, *as* PLAYER KING
and PLAYER QUEEN.]

PLAYER KING. *Full thirty times hath
Phoebus' cart* gone round
Neptune's salt wash and Tellus' orbèd
ground,*   180
And thirty dozen moons with borrow'd
sheen
About the world have times twelve
thirties been,
Since love our hearts and Hymen* did
our hands
Unite commutual in most sacred bands.*

PLAYER QUEEN. *So many journeys may the
sun and moon*   185
*Make us again count o'er ere love be
done!
But, woe is me! you are so sick of late,
So far from cheer and from your former
state,
That I distrust* you. Yet, though I dis-
trust,
Discomfort you, my lord, it nothing
must;*   190
*For women's fear and love holds quan-
tity* —
In neither aught, or in extremity.*
Now, what my love is, proof hath made
you know;
And as my love is siz'd, my fear is so.
Where love is great, the littlest doubts are
fear;*   195
*Where little fears grow great, great love
grows there.*

PLAYER KING. *Faith, I must leave thee,
love, and shortly too;*

176. **posy of a ring:** very short verse inscribed
within finger ring. 179. **Phoebus' cart:** the sun.
180. **Tellus' orbèd ground:** the earth. 183.
Hymen: the god of marriage. 189. **distrust you:**
am fearful for your health. 191. **holds quantity:**
are proportionate to each other. 192. **In . . .
extremity:** there is nothing of either, or an extreme
of both.

My operant* powers their functions
   leave to do:
And thou shalt live in this fair world be-
   hind,   199
Honor'd, belov'd; and haply, one as kind
For husband shalt thou —
PLAYER QUEEN.   O, confound the rest!
Such love must needs be treason in my
   breast.
In second husband let me be accurst!
None wed the second but who kill'd the
   first.   204
HAMLET (aside). Wormwood, wormwood!
PLAYER QUEEN. The instances* that second
   marriage move
Are base respects* of thrift but none of
   love.
A second time I kill my husband dead
When second husband kisses me in bed!
PLAYER KING. I do believe you think what
   now you speak;   210
But what we do determine oft we break.
Purpose is but the slave to memory,
Of violent birth, but poor validity;
Which now, like fruit unripe, sticks on
   the tree,   214
But fall unshaken when they mellow be.
Most necessary 'tis that we forget
To pay ourselves what to ourselves is
   debt:
What to ourselves in passion we propose,
The passion ending, doth the purpose
   lose.
The violence of either grief or joy   220
Their own enactures with themselves
   destroy.
Where joy most revels grief doth most
   lament;
Grief joys, joy grieves, on slender acci-
   dent.
This world is not for aye, nor 'tis not
   strange
That even our loves should with our

fortunes change;   225
For 'tis a question left us yet to prove
Whether love lead fortune or else fortune
   love.
The great man down, you mark his
   favorite flies;
The poor advanc'd makes friends of
   enemies.   229
And hitherto doth love on fortune tend,
For who not needs shall never lack a
   friend;
And who in want a hollow friend doth
   try
Directly seasons* him his enemy.
But — orderly to end where I begun —
Our wills and fates do so contrary run   235
That our devices still are overthrown;
Our thoughts are ours, their ends none of
   our own.
So think thou wilt no second husband
   wed;
But die thy thoughts when thy first lord
   is dead.
PLAYER QUEEN. Nor earth to me give food,
   nor heaven light!   240
Sport and repose lock from me day and
   night!
To desperation turn my trust and hope!
An anchor's cheer* in prison be my
   scope!
Each opposite that blanks* the face of
   joy
Meet what I would have well and it
   destroy!   245
Both here and hence pursue me lasting
   strife
If, once a widow, ever I be wife.
HAMLET. If she should break it now!
PLAYER KING. 'Tis deeply sworn! Sweet,
   leave me here awhile;
My spirits grow dull, and fain I would
   beguile   250
The tedious day with sleep.

---

198. **operant**: that operate, and so maintain life.
206. **instances**: motives. 207. **respects**: considerations.

233. **seasons**: hardens, matures. 243. **anchor's
cheer**: hermit's meager fare. 244. **opposite that
blanks**: contrary event that makes pale.

[*Lies down.*]

PLAYER QUEEN.   *Sleep rock thy brain,*
And never come mischance between us
        twain!
        [*Exit.*]

HAMLET. Madam, how like you this play?

QUEEN. The lady doth protest too much,
methinks.   255

HAMLET. O, but she'll keep her word!

KING. Have you heard the argument? Is
there no offense in't?

HAMLET. No, no! They do but jest! —
poison in jest. No offense i' the   260
world.

KING. What do you call the play?

HAMLET. "The Mousetrap." Marry, how?
Tropically.* This play is the image of a
murder done in Vienna. Gonzago   265
is the duke's name; his wife, Baptista.
You shall see anon 'tis a knavish piece of
work; but what of that? Your majesty,
and we that have free souls, it touches us
not. Let the galled jade* wince!   270
our withers are unwrung.*

        [*Enter* PLAYER *as* LUCIANUS.]

This is one Lucianus, nephew to the king.

OPHELIA. You are as good as a chorus,* my
lord.

HAMLET. I could interpret between   275
you and your love, if I could see the
puppets dallying.

OPHELIA. You are keen, my lord, you are
keen.

HAMLET. It would cost you a groaning   280
to take off my edge.

OPHELIA. Still better, and worse.

HAMLET. So you must take your husbands.
— Begin, murderer! Pox, leave thy
damnable faces, and begin! Come;   285
the croaking raven doth bellow for revenge!

LUCIANUS. *Thoughts black, hands apt,*
        drugs fit, and time agreeing;
Confederate season, else no creature see-
        ing.
Thou mixture rank, of midnight weeds
        collected,   290
With Hecate's* ban thrice blasted, thrice
        infected,
Thy natural magic and dire property
On wholesome life usurp immediately.
        [*Pours the poison into the sleeper's*
        ears.]

HAMLET. He poisons him — i' the garden
— for's estate. (*The* KING *shows* 295
alarm.) His name's Gonzago. The story
is extant, and writ in very choice Italian.
You shall see anon how the murderer gets
the love of Gonzago's wife.

OPHELIA. The king rises.   300

HAMLET. What! frighted with false fire?

QUEEN. How fares my lord?

POLONIUS. Give o'er the play.

KING. Give me some light! Away!

ALL. Lights! lights! lights!   305
        [*Exeunt all except* HAMLET *and*
        HORATIO.]

HAMLET (*sings*).
Why, let the stricken deer go weep,
        The hart ungallèd play;
For some must watch, while some must
        sleep:
        So runs the world away.

Would not this, sir, and a forest of   310
feathers,* if the rest of my fortunes turn
Turk* with me, with two Provincial
roses* on my razed shoes, get me a fellowship in a cry* of players, sir?

HORATIO. Half a share.*   315

264. **Tropically:** by a trope, or figure of speech,
with a hidden meaning.   270. **galled jade:** sore or
skinned horse.   271. **unwrung:** not chafed or rubbed.
273. **chorus:** In Elizabethan plays a chorus was
often fetched in to explain what would otherwise not
be understood.

291. **Hecate:** in Greek mythology, a goddess
associated with sorcery and witchcraft.   310–311. **a**
forest of feathers: Plumes were often part of an
actor's costume.   311–312. **turn Turk:** turn to the
bad.   312–313. **Provincial roses:** rosettes as large
as the double-rose called the Provincial rose.   314.
cry: pack.   315. **share:** The more important actors
in a troupe divided the profits of their acting by a
system of shares, the best actor usually enjoying a
whole share.

HAMLET. A whole one, I — (*Sings.*)
> *For thou dost know, O Damon* dear,*
> *This realm dismantled was*
> *Of Jove himself; and now reigns here*
> *A very, very — pajock.**   320

HORATIO. You might have rhymed.*

HAMLET. O good Horatio! I'll take the ghost's word for a thousand pound! Didst perceive?

HORATIO. Very well, my lord.   325

HAMLET. Upon the talk of the poisoning?

HORATIO. I did very well note him.

HAMLET. Ah, ha! — Come, some music! Come, the recorders! (*Sings*)
> *For if the king like not the comedy,*   330
> *Why then, belike — he likes it not,*
>   *perdy.**

Come, some music!

[*Re-enter* ROSENCRANTZ *and* GUILDEN-
STERN.]

GUILDENSTERN. Good my lord, vouchsafe me a word with you.

HAMLET. Sir, a whole history.   335

GUILDENSTERN. The king, sir —

HAMLET. Ay, sir, what of him?

GUILDENSTERN. Is in his retirement marvelous distemper'd.

HAMLET. With drink, sir?   340

GUILDENSTERN. No, my lord, rather with choler.*

HAMLET. Your wisdom should show itself more richer to signify this to his doctor; for, for me to put him to his purga-   345 tion would perhaps plunge him into far more choler.

GUILDENSTERN. Good my lord, put your discourse into some frame, and start not so wildly from my affair.   350

HAMLET. I am tame, sir; pronounce.

GUILDENSTERN. The queen your mother, in most great affliction of spirit, hath sent me to you —

HAMLET. You are welcome!   355

GUILDENSTERN. Nay, good my lord, this courtesy is not of the right breed. If it shall please you to make me a wholesome answer, I will do your mother's commandment; if not, your pardon   360 and my return shall be the end of my business.

HAMLET. Sir, I cannot.

GUILDENSTERN. What, my lord?

HAMLET. Make you a wholesome   365 answer; my wit's diseas'd. But, sir, such answer as I can make, you shall command — or rather, as you say, my mother. Therefore, no more, but to the matter. My mother, you say —   370

ROSENCRANTZ. Then thus she says: your behavior hath struck her into amazement and admiration.*

HAMLET. O wonderful son, that can so astonish a mother! But is there no   375 sequel at the heels of this mother admiration? Impart.

ROSENCRANTZ. She desires to speak with you in her closet ere you go to bed.

HAMLET. We shall obey, were she ten   380 times our mother.
Have you any further trade* with us?

ROSENCRANTZ. My lord, you once did love me.

HAMLET. So I do still, by these pickers   385 and stealers.*

ROSENCRANTZ. Good my lord, what is your cause of distemper? You do surely bar the door upon your own liberty, if you deny your griefs to your friend.   390

HAMLET. Sir, I lack advancement.

ROSENCRANTZ. How can that be when you have the voice of the king himself for your succession in Denmark?

HAMLET. Ay, sir, but "While the grass   395

---

317. **Damon**: alluding to Horatio; the friendship of Damon and Pythias was famous in literature. 320. **pajock**: peacock. 321. **You might have rhymed**: *i.e.*, rhymed *was* with *ass*. 331. **perdy**: by God (French: *par dieu*). 342. **choler**: anger. Hamlet then jests on the other meaning of the word, biliousness.

373. **admiration**: astonishment. 382. **trade**: business. Hamlet's choice of the word gives offense to Rosencrantz. 385–386. **pickers and stealers**: holding up his ten fingers.

grows" — the proverb is something musty.*

[*Enter one with recorders.*]

O! the recorders; let me see one. (*To* ROSENCRANTZ *and* GUILDENSTERN) To withdraw with you — why did you 400 go about to recover the wind of me,* as if you would drive me into a toil?

GUILDENSTERN. O my lord, if my duty be too bold, my love is too unmannerly.

HAMLET. I do not well understand 405 that. Will you play upon this pipe?

GUILDENSTERN. My lord, I cannot.

HAMLET. I pray you.

GUILDENSTERN. Believe me, I cannot.

HAMLET. I do beseech you! 410

GUILDENSTERN. I know no touch of it, my lord.

HAMLET. 'Tis as easy as lying. Govern these ventages* with your finger and thumb, give it breath with your 415 mouth, and it will discourse most eloquent music. Look you, these are the stops.

GUILDENSTERN. But these cannot I command to any utt'rance of harmony; 420 I have not the skill.

HAMLET. Why, look you now, how unworthy a thing you make of me! You would play upon me; you would seem to know my stops; you would pluck 425 out the heart of my mystery; you would sound me from my lowest note to the top of my compass. And there is much music, excellent voice, in this little organ, yet cannot you make it speak. 430 'Sblood! do you think I am easier to be played on than a pipe? Call me what instrument you will, though you can fret me, you cannot play upon me. —

[*Enter* POLONIUS.]

God bless you, sir! 435

POLONIUS. My lord, the queen would speak with you, and presently.

HAMLET. Do you see yonder cloud that's almost in shape of a camel?

POLONIUS. By the mass! and 'tis like a 440 camel, indeed.

HAMLET. Methinks it is like a weasel.

POLONIUS. It is backed like a weasel.

HAMLET. Or like a whale?

POLONIUS. Very like a whale! 445

HAMLET. Then I will come to my mother by and by.* (*Aside*) They fool me to the top of my bent. (*Aloud*) I will come by and by.

POLONIUS. I will say so. 450

HAMLET. "By and by" is easily said. — Leave me, friends.

[*Exeunt all but* HAMLET.]

'Tis now the very witching time of night,
When churchyards yawn, and hell itself breathes out
Contagion to this world. Now could I drink hot blood 455
And do such bitter business as the day
Would quake to look on! — Soft! now to my mother.
O heart, lose not thy nature! let not ever
The soul of Nero* enter this firm bosom.
Let me be cruel, not unnatural; 460
I will speak daggers to her, but use none.
My tongue and soul in this be hypocrites:
How in my words soever she be shent,*
To give them seals* never, my soul, consent!

[*Exit.*]

SCENE III. *A room in the castle.*

[*Enter* KING, ROSENCRANTZ, *and* GUILDENSTERN.]

397. The old proverb runs: "Whylst grace doth grow, oft starves the silly steed." 401. **to recover the wind of me:** to keep on the downwind side of an animal that is to be driven into a trap, so that it cannot be warned by its sense of smell. 414. **ventages:** vents or stops on the recorder, a musical instrument something like a flute.

447. **by and by:** at once. 459. **Nero:** who killed his mother. 463. **shent:** brought to destruction. 464. **seals:** execution, as by affixing seals to a document.

KING. I like him not, nor stands it safe with us

    To let his madness range. Therefore prepare you;

    I your commission will forthwith dispatch,

    And he to England shall along with you.

    The terms of our estate* may not endure   5

    Hazard so near us as doth hourly grow

    Out of his lunacies.

GUILDENSTERN. We will ourselves provide.

    Most holy and religious fear it is

    To keep those many many bodies safe

    That live and feed upon your majesty.   10

ROSENCRANTZ. The single and peculiar life* is bound

    With all the strength and armor of the mind

    To keep itself from noyance;* but much more

    That spirit upon whose weal depend and rest   14

    The lives of many. The cease of majesty*

    Dies not alone, but like a gulf* doth draw

    What's near it with it. It is a massy wheel,

    Fix'd on the summit of the highest mount,

    To whose huge spokes ten thousand lesser things

    Are mortis'd and adjoin'd; which, when it falls,   20

    Each small annexment, petty consequence,

    Attends the boisterous ruin. Never alone

    Did the king sigh, but with a general groan.

KING. Arm you,* I pray you, to this speedy voyage;

    For we will fetters put upon this fear,   25

    Which now goes too free-footed.

ROSENCRANTZ.   ⎫
GUILDENSTERN. ⎬   We will haste us.

    [*Exeunt* ROSENCRANTZ *and* GUILDENSTERN.]

    [*Enter* POLONIUS.]

POLONIUS. My lord, he's going to his mother's closet.

    Behind the arras I'll convey myself

    To hear the process.* I'll warrant she'll tax him home,

    And, as you said—and wisely was it said—   30

    'Tis meet that some more audience than a mother

    (Since nature makes them partial) should o'erhear

    The speech, of vantage.* Fare you well, my liege.

    I'll call upon you ere you go to bed   34

    And tell you what I know.

KING.   Thanks, dear my lord.

    [*Exit* POLONIUS.]

    O, my offense is rank, it smells to heaven!

    It hath the primal eldest curse upon't,

    A brother's murder!—Pray can I not:

    Though inclination be as sharp as will,

    My stronger guilt defeats my strong intent;   40

    And, like a man to double business bound,

    I stand in pause where I shall first begin,

    And both neglect.—What if this cursèd hand

    Were thicker than itself with brother's blood,

    Is there not rain enough in the sweet heavens   45

    To wash it white as snow? Whereto serves mercy

    But to confront the visage of offense?

    And what's in prayer but this two-fold force,

    To be forestallèd ere we come to fall,

    Or pardon'd, being down? Then, I'll look up;   50

---

5. **terms of our estate:** circumstances of my exalted rank. 11. **single and peculiar life:** individual and private person. 13. **noyance:** harm. 15. **cease of majesty:** death of a king. 16. **gulf:** whirlpool. 24. **Arm you:** make preparations.

29. **process:** proceeding. 33. **of vantage:** from a vantage point.

"Now might I do it pat, now he is praying."

My fault is past. — But, O, what form of
    prayer
Can serve my turn? "Forgive me my foul
    murder"?
That cannot be, since I am still possess'd
Of those effects for which I did the mur-
    der,
My crown, mine own ambition, and my
    queen.   55
May one be pardon'd and retain the
    offense?
In the corrupted currents of this world
Offense's gilded hand may shove by
    justice;
And oft 'tis seen the wicked prize itself
Buys out the law. But 'tis not so
    above.   60
There, is no shuffling; there, the action
    lies
In his true nature, and we ourselves com-
    pell'd
Even to the teeth and forehead of our
    faults
To give in evidence. — What then?

What rests?*
Try what repentance can? What can it
    not?   65
Yet what can it, when one cannot re-
    pent? —
O wretched state! O bosom black as
    death!
O limèd* soul that, struggling to be free,
Art more engaged! Help, angels! —
    Make assay;*
Bow, stubborn knees; and heart with
    strings of steel   70
Be soft as sinews of the newborn babe!
All may be well.
    [*Kneels.*]
    [*Enter* HAMLET, *behind.*]
HAMLET. Now might I do it pat, now he is
    praying. —
And now I'll do't. And so he goes to
    heaven,
And so am I reveng'd. — That would be
    scann'd:*   75
A villain kills my father; and for that,
I, his sole son, do this same villain send
To heaven. —
Why, this is hire and salary, not revenge!
He took my father grossly, full of
    bread,   80
With all his crimes broad blown,* as flush
    as May;
And how his audit stands, who knows
    save heaven?
But in our circumstance and course of
    thought,
'Tis heavy with him. And am I then re-
    veng'd,   84
To take him in the purging of his soul,
When he is fit and season'd for his pas-
    sage?
No. (*Sheathes his sword.*)
Up, sword, and know thou a more horrid
    hent!*

64. **rests:** remains. 68. **limèd:** caught as with
birdlime. 69. **assay:** attempt. 75. **scann'd:** carefully scrutinized. 81. **broad blown:** in full bloom.
88. **hent:** intention, design.

When he is drunk asleep, or in his rage,
Or in the incestuous pleasure of his
    bed,   90
At game, a-swearing, or about some act
That has no relish of salvation in't.
Then trip him, that his heels may kick at
    heaven,
And that his soul may be as damn'd and
    black
As hell, whereto it goes! — My mother
    stays. —   95
This physic but prolongs thy sickly days.
    [*Exit.*]
KING (*rising*). My words fly up, my
    thoughts remain below.
Words without thoughts never to heaven
    go.
    [*Exit.*]

SCENE IV. *The* QUEEN'S *private apartment.*

[*Enter* QUEEN *and* POLONIUS.]

POLONIUS. He will come straight. Look you
    lay home to him.
Tell him his pranks have been too broad
    to bear with,
And that your Grace hath screen'd and
    stood between
Much heat and him. I'll silence me e'en
    here.
Pray you, be round with him!   5
HAMLET (*within*). Mother, mother,
    mother!
QUEEN. I'll warrant you; fear me not.
    Withdraw; I hear him coming.
    [POLONIUS *hides behind the arras.*]
    [*Enter* HAMLET.]
HAMLET. Now, mother, what's the matter?
QUEEN. Hamlet, thou hast thy father much
    offended.
HAMLET. Mother, you have my father
    much offended.   10

QUEEN. Come, come, you answer with an
    idle tongue.
HAMLET. Go, go, you question with a
    wicked tongue.
QUEEN. Why, how now — Hamlet!
HAMLET.   What's the matter now?
QUEEN. Have you forgot me?
HAMLET.   No, by the rood,* not so!
    You are "the Queen," your husband's
        brother's wife,   15
    And — would it were not so! — you are
        my mother.
QUEEN. Nay then, I'll set those to you that
    can speak.
    [*Starts toward the door.* HAMLET
    seizes her, and forces her into a chair.]
HAMLET. Come, come, and sit you down.
    You shall not budge!
    You go not till I set you up a glass
    Where you may see the inmost part of
        you.   20
QUEEN. What wilt thou do? Thou wilt not
    murder me?
    Help, help, ho!
POLONIUS (*behind*). What, ho! help! help!
    help!
HAMLET (*draws*). How now, a rat? Dead,
    for a ducat! dead!
    [*Makes a pass through the arras.*]
POLONIUS (*behind*). O, I am slain!
QUEEN. O me! what hast thou done?   25
HAMLET. Nay, I know not. — Is it the
    king?
QUEEN. O! what a rash and bloody deed is
    this!
HAMLET. A bloody deed — almost as bad,
    good mother,
    As kill a king and marry with his
        brother.   29
QUEEN. As kill a king!
HAMLET.   Ay, lady, 'twas my word.
    [*Lifts up the arras and discovers*
    POLONIUS.]
    Thou wretched, rash, intruding fool,
        farewell!

14. **rood**: cross.

I took thee for thy better. Take thy
    fortune;
Thou find'st to be too busy is some
    danger. —
Leave wringing of your hands. Peace!
    Sit you down
And let me wring your heart; for so I
    shall,   35
If it be made of penetrable stuff;
If damnèd custom have not brass'd it so
That it is proof and bulwark against
    sense.
QUEEN. What have I done, that thou dar'st
    wag thy tongue
In noise so rude against me?
HAMLET.   Such an act 40
That blurs the grace and blush of
    modesty;
Calls virtue hypocrite; takes off the rose*
From the fair forehead of an innocent
    love
And sets a blister* there; makes marriage
    vows   44
As false as dicers' oaths! O, such a deed
As from the body of contraction* plucks
The very soul, and sweet religion makes
A rhapsody* of words! Heaven's face
    doth glow;
Yea, this solidity and compound mass,*
With tristful visage, as against the
    doom,   50
Is thought-sick at the act!
QUEEN.   Ay me, what act,
That roars so loud and thunders in the
    index?
HAMLET. Look here, upon this picture, and
    on this,
The counterfeit presentment of two
    brothers.
See what a grace was seated on this
    brow: 55

Hyperion's curls, the front of Jove him-
    self,
An eye like Mars, to threaten and com-
    mand,
A station* like the herald Mercury
New lighted on a heaven-kissing hill —
A combination and a form, indeed,   60
Where every god did seem to set his seal
To give the world assurance of a man.
This was your husband. Look you now,
    what follows.
Here is your husband, like a mildew'd
    ear
Blasting his wholesome brother! Have
    you eyes?   65
Could you on this fair mountain leave to
    feed,
And batten* on this moor? Ha! have
    you eyes?
You cannot call it love; for at your age
The heyday in the blood is tame, it's
    humble,
And waits upon the judgment; and what
    judgment   70
Would step from this to this? Sense*
    sure you have,
Else could you not have motion; but sure
    that sense
Is apoplex'd: for madness would not err,
Nor sense to ecstasy was ne'er so thrall'd
But it reserv'd some quantity of choice 75
To serve in such a difference.* What
    devil was't
That thus hath cozen'd you at hoodman-
    blind?
Eyes without feeling, feeling without
    sight,
Ears without hands or eyes, smelling sans
    all,
Or but a sickly part of one true sense 80

---

42. **rose**: beauty. 44. **blister**: Women convicted of adultery were branded on the forehead (*cf.* Hawthorne's *The Scarlet Letter*). 46. **contraction**: the act of forming the marriage contract. 48. **rhapsody**: senseless outpouring. 49. **solidity . . . mass**: the earth, which was supposed to grow sick and feverish at Doomsday.

58. **station**: bearing. 67. **batten**: feed gluttonously. 71. **Sense**: the faculty of perception, including the five senses. 72–76. **that sense . . . difference**: Your senses must be paralyzed, for insanity would never lead you to such a mistaken judgment. It would never undermine the five senses so completely that they could not perceive so enormous a difference.

Could not so mope.*
O shame! where is thy blush? Rebellious
    hell,
If thou canst mutine in a matron's bones,
To flaming youth let virtue be as wax
And melt in her own fire. Proclaim no
    shame   85
When the compulsive ardor gives the
    charge,*
Since frost itself as actively doth burn,
And reason panders will.*

QUEEN.   O Hamlet, speak no more!
Thou turn'st mine eyes into my very soul,
And there I see such black and grainèd*
    spots   90
As will not leave their tinct.

HAMLET.   Nay, but to live
In the rank sweat of an enseamèd bed,
Stew'd in corruption, honeying and mak-
    ing love
Over the nasty sty!

QUEEN.   O, speak to me no more!
These words like daggers enter in mine
    ears.   95
No more, sweet Hamlet!

HAMLET.   A murderer and a villain!
A slave that is not twentieth part the tithe
Of your precedent lord! A vice* of
    kings!
A cutpurse of the empire and the rule,
That from a shelf the precious diadem
    stole,   100
And put it in his pocket! —

QUEEN.   No more!

[*Enter* GHOST.]

HAMLET. A king of shreds and patches! —
Save me and hover o'er me with your
    wings,
You heavenly guards! — What would
    your gracious figure?

QUEEN. Alas, he's mad!   105

HAMLET. Do you not come your tardy son
    to chide,

That, laps'd in time and passion,* lets go
    by
The important acting of your dread com-
    mand?
O, say!

GHOST.   Do not forget. This visitation
Is but to whet thy almost blunted pur-
    pose.   110
But look, amazement on thy mother sits.
O, step between her and her fighting soul!
Conceit* in weakest bodies strongest
    works.
Speak to her, Hamlet.

HAMLET.   How is it with you, lady?

QUEEN. Alas, how is't with you,   115
That you do bend your eye on vacancy,
And with the incorporal air do hold dis-
    course?
Forth at your eyes your spirits wildly
    peep;
And as the sleeping soldiers in the alarm,
Your bedded hairs, like life in excre-
    ments,*   120
Start up and stand on end. O gentle son,
Upon the heat and flame of thy dis-
    temper
Sprinkle cool patience. — Whereon do
    you look?

HAMLET. On him! on him! Look you, how
    pale he glares!
His form and cause conjoin'd, preaching
    to stones,   125
Would make them capable.* (*To the*
    GHOST) Do not look upon me,
Lest with this piteous action you convert
My stern effects.* Then what I have to
    do
Will want true color — tears perchance
    for blood.   129

QUEEN. To whom do you speak this?

HAMLET.   Do you see nothing there?

QUEEN. Nothing at all; yet all that is I see.

---

81. **so mope:** be so stupid. 86. **gives the charge:** leads the attack. 88. **panders will:** acts as a procurer for desire. 90. **grainèd:** dyed in grain, *i.e.*, in fast colors. 98. **vice:** the fool and mischief-maker in old morality plays.

107. **laps'd in time and passion:** having let the moment slip and passion cool. 113. **Conceit:** imagination. 120. **excrements:** outgrowths on the body; here, hair. 126. **capable:** an echo of the Biblical phrase: "The very stones should cry out." 128. **effects:** action.

HAMLET. Nor did you nothing hear?

QUEEN.   No, nothing but ourselves.

HAMLET. Why, look you there! Look how
it steals away!

My father, in his habit* as he liv'd!

Look where he goes, even now, out at
the portal.   135

[*Exit* GHOST.]

QUEEN. This is the very coinage of your
brain.

This bodiless creation* ecstasy

Is very cunning in.

HAMLET. Ecstasy?

My pulse, as yours, doth temperately
keep time,   140

And makes as healthful music. It is not
madness

That I have utter'd. Bring me to the
test,*

And I the matter will reword which madness

Would gambol from. Mother, for love
of grace

Lay not that flattering unction* to your
soul,   145

That not your trespass but my madness
speaks.

It will but skin and film the ulcerous
place,

Whiles rank corruption, mining all
within,

Infects unseen. Confess yourself to
heaven;

Repent what's past, avoid what is to
come;   150

And do not spread the compost on the
weeds

To make them ranker. Forgive me this
my virtue;*

For in the fatness of these pursy times

Virtue itself of vice must pardon beg —

Yea, curb* and woo for leave to do him
good.   155

QUEEN. O Hamlet! thou hast cleft my heart
in twain!

HAMLET. O, throw away the worser part
of it,

And live the purer with the other half.

Good night — But go not to mine uncle's
bed.

Assume a virtue, if you have it not.   160

That monster, custom, who all sense*
doth eat,

Of habits devil, is angel yet in this,

That to the use of actions fair and good

He likewise gives a frock or livery

That aptly is put on. Refrain tonight, 165

And that shall lend a kind of easiness

To the next abstinence; the next more
easy:

For use almost can change the stamp of
nature,

And either master the devil or throw
him out

With wondrous potency. — Once more,
good night;   170

And when you are desirous to be bless'd,

I'll blessing beg of you. For this same
lord,

I do repent; but heaven hath pleas'd it so,

To punish me with this, and this with me,

That I must be their scourge and
minister.   175

I will bestow him, and will answer well

The death I gave him. — So, again, good
night.

I must be cruel only to be kind;

Thus bad begins, and worse remains behind.   179

One word more, good lady.

QUEEN.   What shall I do?

HAMLET. Not this, by no means, that I bid
you do:

Let the bloat king tempt you again to
bed;

---

134. **habit**: dress. 137. **bodiless creation**: hallucination. 142. **the test**: of rephrasing a sentence
involving abstract thought. 145. **unction**: salve.
152. **my virtue**: my assumption of virtue in this
preaching to you.

155. **curb**: bow as in petition. 161. **sense**:
sensibility.

Pinch wanton on your cheek; call you his
    mouse;
And let him, for a pair of reechy kisses,
Or paddling in your neck with his damn'd
    fingers   185
Make you to ravel all this matter out,
That I essentially am not in madness,
But mad in craft. 'Twere good you let
    him know;
For who that's but a queen, fair, sober,
    wise,
Would from a paddock,* from a bat,
    a gib,*   190
Such dear concernings hide? Who would
    do so?
No, in despite of sense and secrecy,
Unpeg the basket on the house's top,
Let the birds fly, and like the famous
    ape,   194
To try conclusions, in the basket creep,
And break your own neck down.
QUEEN. Be thou assur'd, if words be made
    of breath,
And breath of life, I have no life to
    breathe
What thou hast said to me.
HAMLET. I must to England; you know
    that?
QUEEN.   Alack!   200
I had forgot. 'Tis so concluded on.
HAMLET. There's letters seal'd; and my two
    school fellows —
Whom I will trust as I will adders
    fang'd —
They bear the mandate. They must
    sweep my way,
And marshal me to knavery. Let it
    work!   205
For 'tis the sport to have the enginer*
Hoist with his own petar;* and 't shall
    go hard
But I will delve one yard below their

190. **paddock**: toad. **gib**: tomcat. 206. **enginer**:
one who constructs military engines. 207. **petar**:
an engine of war, bellshaped, filled with gunpowder
and exploded with a fuse.

mines,
And blow them at the moon. O, 'tis most
    sweet,
When in one line two crafts directly
    meet.   210
This man shall set me packing.
I'll lug the guts into the neighbor room.—
Mother, good night. — Indeed this coun-
    selor
Is now most still, most secret, and most
    grave,
Who was in life a foolish prating
    knave.   215
Come, sir, to draw toward an end with
    you —
Good night, mother.
    [*Exeunt severally*, HAMLET *dragging in
    the body of* POLONIUS.]

For Discussion

1. Spies are making their report at the start
of Act III, and soon afterward Polonius is
baiting his trap, setting up the encounter between his daughter and Hamlet. In doing so,
he gives Ophelia a book of devotions that she
is to pretend to be reading. The action causes
him a moment's remorse (III, i, 46–49). Why?
How do his words affect the King? Hamlet
enters and speaks the soliloquy beginning, "To
be, or not to be." What arguments do his
thoughts assemble to discourage him from
suicide? That he should be contemplating
such an act at all indicates, of course, his desperate state of mind. How does he behave
toward Ophelia? Ophelia remembers Hamlet's
earlier identity — what he once had been (i,
167 ff). How does she account for his present
behavior? How does that behavior affect
Claudius? Polonius?

2. The second scene of Act III presents
"The Mousetrap," the play within a play, by
which Hamlet will test the King's guilt or
innocence. How does Claudius respond to the
play? At what point does he respond most
dramatically? During the excitement that fol-

lows, Guildenstern and Rosencrantz summon Hamlet to his mother's chamber, where she has retired "in most great affliction of spirit." But before answering the summons, Hamlet accuses the two courtiers of seeking to make an "unworthy" thing of him (ii, 422). How? The exchange is a crucial one; it has to do with using people as means to your ends or as ends in themselves. Does it suggest reasons to explain Hamlet's tardiness in carrying out the ghost's command of revenge? Discuss.

3. In Scene iii Hamlet has his opportunity; the King is alone, unarmed, unguarded, and his guilt is beyond question. Why, then, does the prince refrain from killing him? What does the long speech beginning at Scene iii, line 36, reveal about Claudius?

4. The intense, closing scene of Act III begins with murder. Why does Hamlet strike through the arras? How does the discovery of Polonius' body affect him? In arguing with his mother, the prince contrasts Claudius with the former king, and his words move Gertrude profoundly. The ghost's appearance interrupts them. Why has the ghost come? What leads the Queen to think her son is mad? At the end of the act does she still think so? By then, what has been revealed about the fate that lies in store for Hamlet? Where must he go? Who will accompany him?

5. Shakespeare's language is richly metaphorical, making full use of simile, personification, apostrophe, and other figurative devices to extend meaning far beyond the literal. Take any speech of over five lines in this act and comment on the effectiveness of the metaphors it contains. Are they appropriate to the character speaking them?

Act IV

SCENE I. *A room in the castle.*

[*Enter* QUEEN *to* KING, ROSENCRANTZ, *and* GUILDENSTERN.]

KING (*to the* QUEEN). There's matter in these sighs, these profound heaves.
You must translate; 'tis fit we understand them.
Where is your son?
QUEEN (*to* ROSENCRANTZ *and* GUILDEN-
STERN). Bestow this place on us a little while.
[*Exeunt* ROSENCRANTZ *and* GUILDEN-
STERN.]
Ah, my good lord, what have I seen to-
night!   5
KING. What, Gertrude? How does Ham-
let?
QUEEN. Mad as the sea and wind when both contend
Which is the mightier! In his lawless fit,
Behind the arras hearing something stir,
Whips out his rapier, cries, "A rat! a rat!"   10
And, in this brainish apprehension,* kills
The unseen good old man.
KING.   O heavy deed! —
It had been so with us had we been there!
His liberty is full of threats to all,
To you yourself, to us, to everyone.   15
Alas, how shall this bloody deed be an-
swered?
It will be laid to us, whose providence
Should have kept short, restrain'd, and out of haunt,*
This mad young man. But so much was our love,
We would not understand what was most fit,   20
But, like the owner of a foul disease,
To keep it from divulging, let it feed
Even on the pith of life. Where is he gone?
QUEEN. To draw apart the body he hath kill'd;
O'er whom his very madness, like some ore   25
Among a mineral* of metals base,

---

11. **brainish apprehension:** brainsick notion.
18. **out of haunt:** out of association with others.
25–26. **ore Among a mineral:** vein of gold in a mine.

Shows itself pure. He weeps for what is
done.
KING. O Gertrude, come away!
The sun no sooner shall the mountains
touch
But we will ship him hence; and this vile
deed   30
We must, with all our majesty and skill,
Both countenance and excuse. — Ho.
Guildenstern!
[Re-enter ROSENCRANTZ and GUILDEN-
STERN.]
Friends both, go join you with some fur-
ther aid:
Hamlet in madness hath Polonius slain,
And from his mother's closet hath he
dragg'd him.   35
Go seek him out; speak fair, and bring
the body
Into the chapel. I pray you, haste in this.
[Exeunt ROSENCRANTZ and GUILDEN-
STERN.]
Come, Gertrude, we'll call up our wisest
friends,
And let them know both what we mean
to do
And what's untimely done. So, haply,
slander —   40
Whose whisper o'er the world's diameter,
As level as the cannon to his blank*
Transports his poison'd shot, may miss
our name
And hit the woundless air. O, come
away!
My soul is full of discord and dismay.   45
[Exeunt.]

SCENE II. *A hall in the castle.*

[*Enter* HAMLET.]

HAMLET. Safely stowed.
ROSENCRANTZ. } (*within*). Hamlet! Lord
GUILDENSTERN. } Hamlet!

42. **blank:** the white center of the target.

HAMLET. But soft, what noise? Who calls
on Hamlet?
O, here they come.
[*Enter* ROSENCRANTZ, GUILDENSTERN,
and Attendants.]
ROSENCRANTZ. What have you done, my
lord, with the dead body?   5
HAMLET. Compounded it with dust,
whereto 'tis kin.
ROSENCRANTZ. Tell us where 'tis, that we
may take it thence
And bear it to the chapel.   10
HAMLET. Do not believe it.
ROSENCRANTZ. Believe what?
HAMLET. That I can keep your counsel and
not mine own. Besides, to be demanded
of a sponge! what replication* should   15
be made by the son of a king?
ROSENCRANTZ. Take you me for a sponge,
my lord?
HAMLET. Ay, sir, that soaks up the king's
countenance,* his rewards, his   20
authorities.* But such officers do the
king best service in the end: he keeps
them, like an ape, in the corner of his
jaw; first mouthed, to be last swallowed.
When he needs what you have   25
gleaned, it is but squeezing you — and,
sponge, you shall be dry again.
ROSENCRANTZ. I understand you not, my
lord.
HAMLET. I am glad of it: "a knavish   30
speech sleeps in a foolish ear."
ROSENCRANTZ. My lord, you must tell us
where the body is, and go with us to the
king.
HAMLET. The body is with the king,   35
but the king is not with the body. The
king is a thing —
GUILDENSTERN. A thing, my lord!
HAMLET. Of nothing. Bring me to him.
Hide fox, and all after!   40

[*Exeunt.*]

15. **replication:** reply. 20. **countenance:** favor,
patronage. 21. **authorities:** delegated powers.

SCENE III. *A room in the castle.*

[*Enter* KING.]

KING. I have sent to seek him and to find
    the body.
  How dangerous is it that this man goes
    loose!
  Yet must not we put the strong law on
    him:
  He's loved of the distracted multitude,
  Who like not in their judgment, but their
    eyes;*   5
  And where 'tis so, the offender's scourge
    is weigh'd,
  But never the offense. To bear* all
    smooth and even,
  This sudden sending him away must seem
  Deliberate pause.* Diseases desperate
    grown
  By desperate appliance are reliev'd,   10
  Or not at all.
      [*Enter* ROSENCRANTZ.]
          How now! what hath befall'n?

ROSENCRANTZ. Where the dead body is be-
    stow'd, my lord,
  We cannot get from him.

KING.   But where is he?

ROSENCRANTZ. Without, my lord, guarded,
    to know your pleasure.

KING. Bring him before us.   15

ROSENCRANTZ. Ho, Guildenstern! Bring in
    my lord.
    [*Enter* GUILDENSTERN *and* HAMLET.]

KING. Now, Hamlet, where's Polonius?

HAMLET. At supper.

KING. At supper! Where?

HAMLET. Not where he eats, but where   20
  he is eaten: a certain convocation of politic worms* are e'en at him. Your worm
  is your only emperor for diet: we fat all

creatures else to fat us, and we fat ourselves for maggots. Your fat king and   25
your lean beggar is but variable service*
— two dishes, but to one table. That's
the end.

KING. Alas, alas!

HAMLET. A man may fish with the   30
worm that hath eat of a king, and eat of
the fish that hath fed of that worm.

KING. What dost thou mean by this?

HAMLET. Nothing, but to show you how a
king may go a progress* through the   35
guts of a beggar.

KING. Where is Polonius?

HAMLET. In heaven. Send thither to see.
If your messenger find him not there, seek
him i' the other place yourself. But,   40
indeed, if you find him not within this
month, you shall nose him as you go up
the stairs into the lobby.

KING (*to some Attendants*). Go seek him
there.   45

HAMLET. He will stay till you come!
    [*Exeunt Attendants.*]

KING. Hamlet, this deed, for thine especial
    safety —
  Which we do tender,* as we dearly grieve
  For that which thou hast done — must
    send thee hence
  With fiery quickness. Therefore prepare
    thyself.   50
  The bark is ready and the wind at help,
  The associates tend, and everything is
    bent
  For England.

HAMLET.   For England?

KING.   Ay, Hamlet.

HAMLET.   Good.

KING. So is it, if thou knew'st our purposes.

HAMLET. I see a cherub* that sees   55
them! (*To* ROSENCRANTZ *and* GUILDEN-
STERN) But come, for England! (*To the*

---

5. **Who . . . eyes:** whose judgment is based on
mere appearances. 7. **bear:** carry out. 9. **pause:**
planning. 21–22. **convocation . . . worms:** a gibe
at Polonius' attempts at crafty policy, and an
allusion to the famous assembly known as the
Diet of Worms.

26. **variable service:** different courses. 35. **progress:** a term applied to the magnificent journeys of
royalty through the country. 48. **tender:** hold
dear. 55. **cherub:** angel of knowledge.

KING) Farewell, dear mother.

KING. Thy loving father, Hamlet.

HAMLET. My mother — father and 60
mother is man and wife, man and wife is
one flesh; and so, my mother. (*To* Ro-
SENCRANTZ *and* GUILDENSTERN) Come,
for England!

[*Exit.*]

KING. Follow him at foot. Tempt him with
speed aboard. 65

Delay it not; I'll have him hence tonight.

Away! for everything is seal'd and done

That else leans on the affair. Pray you,
make haste.

[*Exeunt* ROSENCRANTZ *and* GUILDEN-
STERN.]

And, England, if my love thou hold'st at
aught —

As my great power thereof may give
thee sense, 70

Since yet thy cicatrice* looks raw and red

After the Danish sword, and thy free awe

Pays homage to us — thou mayst not
coldly set*

Our sovereign process;* which imports at
full,

By letters conjuring* to that effect, 75

The present* death of Hamlet. Do it,
England,

For like the hectic* in my blood he rages,

And thou must cure me. Till I know 'tis
done,

Howe'er my haps,* my joys were ne'er
begun.

[*Exit.*]

SCENE IV. *A plain in Denmark.*

[*Enter* FORTINBRAS, *a* CAPTAIN, *and a
troop of soldiers, with drums, marching.*]

71. cicatrice : scar. 73. set : disregard. 74. process : command. 75. conjuring : solemnly charging.
76. present : instant. 77. hectic : fever. 79. my
haps : the fortunes that fall to me.

FORTINBRAS. Go, captain, from me greet the
Danish king.

Tell him that, by his licence, Fortinbras

Claims the conveyance of a promis'd
march

Over his kingdom. You know the rendezvous. 4

If that his majesty would aught with us,

We shall express our duty in his eye;

And let him know so.

CAPTAIN. I will do't, my lord.

FORTINBRAS (*to the soldiers*). Go softly*
on.

[*Exeunt all but* CAPTAIN.]

[*Enter* HAMLET, ROSENCRANTZ, GUIL-
DENSTERN, *and Attendants.*]

HAMLET. Good sir, whose powers are
these?

CAPTAIN. They are of Norway, sir. 10

HAMLET. How purpos'd, sir, I pray you?

CAPTAIN. Against some part of Poland.

HAMLET. Who commands them, sir?

CAPTAIN. The nephew to old Norway,
Fortinbras.

HAMLET. Goes it against the main* of Poland, sir, 15

Or for some frontier?

CAPTAIN. Truly to speak, and with no addition,*

We go to gain a little patch of ground

That hath in it no profit but the name.

To pay five ducats, five, I would not
farm* it; 20

Nor will it yield to Norway or the Pole

A ranker rate* should it be sold in fee.

HAMLET. Why, then, the Polack never will
defend it.

CAPTAIN. Yes, 'tis already garrison'd.

HAMLET. Two thousand souls and twenty
thousand ducats 25

Will not debate the question of this straw!

This is the imposthume* of much wealth
and peace,

8. softly : slowly. 15. main : mainland. 17. with
no addition : plainly. 20. farm : rent. 22. ranker
rate : greater sum. 27. imposthume : abscess, ulcer.

That inward breaks, and shows no cause
without

Why the man dies. — I humbly thank
you, sir.

CAPTAIN. God be wi' you, sir.

[*Exit.*]

ROSENCRANTZ.   Will't please you go, my
lord?   30

HAMLET. I'll be with you straight. Go a
little before.

[*Exeunt all except* HAMLET.]

How all occasions do inform against me,
And spur my dull revenge! What is a
man,
If his chief good and market* of his time
Be but to sleep and feed? a beast, no more.
Sure He that made us with such large dis-
course,*   36
Looking before and after, gave us not
That capability and godlike reason
To fust* in us unus'd. Now, whether
it be   39
Bestial oblivion, or some craven scruple
Of thinking too precisely on the event —
A thought which, quarter'd, hath but one
part wisdom
And ever three parts coward — I do not
know
Why yet I live to say "This thing's to do,"
Sith I have cause, and will, and strength,
and means   45
To do't. Examples gross* as earth exhort
me.
Witness this army of such mass and
charge,*
Led by a delicate and tender prince,
Whose spirit, with divine ambition puff'd,
Makes mouths at the invisible event,*   50
Exposing what is mortal and unsure
To all that fortune, death, and danger
dare —
Even for an eggshell! Rightly to be great

Is not to stir without great argument.*
But greatly to find quarrel in a straw   55
When honor's at the stake. How stand
I, then,
That have a father kill'd, a mother stain'd,
Excitements of my reason and my blood,
And let all sleep? while, to my shame, I
see
The imminent death of twenty thousand
men   60
That for a fantasy and trick of fame*
Go to their graves like beds, fight for a
plot
Whereon the numbers · cannot try the
cause,
Which is not tomb enough and conti-
nent*
To hide the slain! O, from this time
forth,   65
My thoughts be bloody, or be nothing
worth!

[*Exit.*]

SCENE V. *A room in the castle.*

[*Enter* QUEEN, HORATIO, *and a Gentleman.*]

QUEEN. I will not speak with her.

GENTLEMAN. She is importunate, indeed
distract.
Her mood will needs be pitied.

QUEEN.   What would she have?

GENTLEMAN. She speaks much of her
father; says she hears
There's tricks i' the world, and hems, and
beats her heart;   5
Spurns enviously at straws;* speaks things
in doubt,
That carry but half sense. Her speech is
nothing,
Yet the unshapèd use of it doth move

---

34. **market:** profit. 36. **discourse:** faculty of
reasoning. 39. **fust:** grow moldy. 46. **gross:** large,
obvious. 47. **charge:** cost. 50. **Makes mouths
at the invisible event:** makes scornful faces at (is
contemptuous of) the unseen outcome.

54. **argument:** cause. 61. **trick of fame:** trifle
of reputation. 64. **continent:** receptacle.
6. **Spurns enviously at straws:** objects spitefully
to trifles.

The hearers to collection;* they aim at it,
And botch the words up fit to their own
   thoughts; 10
Which, as her winks and nods and gestures yield them,
Indeed would make one think there might
   be thought,
Though nothing sure, yet much unhappily.

HORATIO. 'Twere good she were spoken
   with, for she may strew
Dangerous conjectures in ill-breeding
   minds. 15

QUEEN. Let her come in.
   [*Exeunt* HORATIO *and Gentleman.*]
To my sick soul — as sin's true nature
   is —
Each toy* seems prologue to some great
   amiss.
So full of artless jealousy* is guilt,
It spills* itself in fearing to be spilt. 20
   [*Re-enter* HORATIO *and Gentleman
   with* OPHELIA, *distracted.*]

OPHELIA. Where is the beauteous majesty
   of Denmark?

QUEEN. How now, Ophelia?

OPHELIA (*sings*).
   How should I your true love know
     From another one? 25
   *By his cockle hat and staff,**
     *And his sandal shoon.**

QUEEN. Alas, sweet lady, what imports this
   song?

OPHELIA. Say you? Nay, pray you, 30
   mark: (*Sings*)
   He is dead and gone, lady,
     He is dead and gone;
   At his head a grass-green turf,
     At his heels a stone. 35
O, ho!

QUEEN. Nay, but Ophelia —

OPHELIA. Pray you, mark: (*Sings*)
White his shroud as the mountain snow —
   [*Enter* KING.]

QUEEN (*aside to him*). Alas, look here, 40
   my lord!

OPHELIA.   *Larded* with sweet flowers;*
     *Which bewept to the grave did
       not go*
     With true-love showers.

KING. How do you, pretty lady? 45

OPHELIA. Well, God dild* you. They say
   the owl was a baker's daughter.* Lord,
   we know what we are, but know not
   what we may be. God be at your table!

KING. Conceit* upon her father. 50

OPHELIA. Pray you, let's have no words of
   this; but when they ask you what it
   means, say you this: (*Sings*)

   Tomorrow is Saint Valentine's day,
     All in the morning betime, 55
   And I a maid at your window
     To be your Valentine.

   Then up he rose and donn'd his clo'es
     And dupp'd the chamber door,
   Let in the maid, that out a maid 60
     Never departed more.

.   .   .   .

KING. How long hath she been thus?

OPHELIA. I hope all will be well. We must
   be patient; but I cannot choose but weep
   to think they should lay him i' the 65
   cold ground. My brother shall know of
   it. And so, I thank you for your good
   counsel. — Come, my coach! — Good
   night, ladies. Good night, sweet ladies.
   Good night! Good night! 70
   [*Exit.*]

KING. Follow her close; give her good
   watch, I pray you.
   [*Exeunt* HORATIO *and Gentleman.*]

---

9. **collection**: putting things together and finding some sort of meaning in them. 18. **toy**: trifle. 19. **artless jealousy**: unreasonable suspicion. 20. **spills**: destroys. 26. **cockle hat and staff**: signs of the pilgrim. The male lover was conventionally represented as a pilgrim, his lady as the saint; *cf. Romeo and Juliet*, I.v. 27. **shoon**: shoes.

42. **Larded**: bedecked. 46. **dild**: yield; *i.e.,* reward. 47. **baker's daughter**: There were several old ballads on the story of how a certain baker's daughter was turned into an owl for denying bread to Jesus. 50. **Conceit**: brooding.

O, this is the poison of deep grief; it
  springs
All from her father's death. O Gertrude,
  Gertrude,
When sorrows come, they come not sin-
  gle spies,   74
But in battalions! First, her father slain;
Next, your son gone — and he most vio-
  lent author
Of his own just remove; the people mud-
  died,
Thick, and unwholesome in their thoughts
  and whispers
For good Polonius' death — and we have
  done but greenly
In hugger-mugger* to inter him; poor
  Ophelia   80
Divided from herself and her fair judg-
  ment,
Without the which we are pictures, or
  mere beasts;
Last, and as much containing as all these,
Her brother is in secret come from
  France,
Feeds on his wonder, keeps himself in
  clouds,*   85
And wants not buzzers to infect his ear
With pestilent speeches of his father's
  death,
Wherein necessity, of matter beggar'd,*
Will nothing stick* our person to arraign
In ear and ear. O my dear Gertrude,
  this,   90
Like to a murd'ring-piece,* in many
  places
Gives me a superfluous death.
  [A noise within.]
QUEEN.   Alack! what noise is this?
KING. Where are my Switzers? Let them
  guard the door!
  [Enter a Gentleman in haste.]

What is the matter?
GENTLEMAN.   Save yourself, my lord!
The ocean, overpeering of his list,* 95
Eats not the flats with more impetuous
  haste
Than young Laertes, in a riotous head,*
O'erbears your officers. The rabble call
  him lord,
And, as the world were now but to be-
  gin,   99
Antiquity forgot, custom not known,
The ratifiers and props of every word,
They cry, "Choose we! Laertes shall be
  king!"
Caps, hands, and tongues applaud it to
  the clouds,
"Laertes shall be king! Laertes king!"
QUEEN. How cheerfully on the false trail
  they cry!   105
O, this is counter,* you false Danish dogs!
  [Noise within of crashing doors.]
KING. The doors are broke.
  [Enter LAERTES, with drawn sword, a
  mob of Danes at his back.]
LAERTES. Where is the king? — Sirs, stand
  you all without.
DANES. No, let's come in!
LAERTES.   I pray you, give me leave.
DANES. We will! we will!   110
  [They retire.]
LAERTES. I thank you. Keep the door. O
  thou vile king,
Give me my father!
QUEEN.   Calmly, good Laertes.
LAERTES. That drop of blood that's calm
  proclaims me bastard!
Cries cuckold to my father, brands the
  harlot
Even here between the chaste unsmirchèd
  brows   115
Of my true mother.
KING.   What is the cause, Laertes,
That thy rebellion looks so giantlike? —

---

80. **hugger-mugger**: haste and secrecy. 85. **in clouds**: wrapped in dark suspicions. 88. **of matter beggar'd**: unprovided with facts. 89. **Will nothing stick**: will not hesitate. 91. **murd'ring-piece**: cannon loaded with a scattering shot.

95. **list**: shore, boundary. 97. **head**: mob. 106. **counter**: a hunting term, when dogs follow the trail in the wrong direction.

Let him go, Gertrude; do not fear* our
person:
There's such divinity doth hedge a king,
That treason can but peep to what it
would,   120
Acts little of his will. — Tell me, Laertes,
Why thou art thus incens'd. — Let him
go, Gertrude. —
Speak, man.

LAERTES. Where's my father?

KING.   Dead.

QUEEN.   But not by him.

KING. Let him demand his fill.   125

LAERTES. How came he dead? I'll not be
juggled with.
To hell, allegiance! vows, to the blackest
devil!
Conscience and grace, to the profoundest
pit!
I dare damnation! To this point I stand,
That both the worlds I give to negli-
gence,   130
Let come what comes; only I'll be re-
veng'd,
Most thoroughly for my father!

KING.   Who shall stay you?

LAERTES. My will, not all the world!
And for my means, I'll husband them so
well
They shall go far with little.

KING.   Good Laertes,   135
If you desire to know the certainty
Of your dear father's death, is't writ in
your revenge
That, swoopstake,* you will draw both
friend and foe,
Winner and loser?

LAERTES. None but his enemies.

KING.   Will you know them then?   140

LAERTES. To his good friends thus wide I'll
ope my arms,
And, like the kind life-rendering pelican,*

Repast them with my blood.

KING.   Why, now you speak
Like a good child and a true gentleman.
That I am guiltless of your father's death,
And am most sensibly in grief for it,   146
It shall as level to your judgment pierce
As day does to your eye.

DANES (within).   Let her come in.

LAERTES. How now! what noise is that?
    [Re-enter OPHELIA.]
O heat, dry up my brains! Tears seven
times salt   150
Burn out the sense and virtue* of mine
eye!
By heaven, thy madness shall be paid by
weight,
Till our scale turn the beam. O rose of
May!
Dear maid, kind sister, sweet Ophelia! —
O heavens! is't possible a young maid's
wits   155
Should be as mortal as an old man's life?
Nature is fine in love,* and where 'tis fine
It sends some precious instance of itself
After the thing it loves.*

OPHELIA (sings).
    They bore him barefac'd on the bier; 160
    Hey non nonny, nonny, hey nonny;
    And in his grave rain'd many a tear.
        Fare you well, my dove!

LAERTES. Hadst thou thy wits, and didst
persuade revenge, it could not move   165
thus.

OPHELIA. You must sing, *"A-down a-
down!"* and you, *"Call him a-down-a!"*
O how the wheel becomes it! It is the
false steward that stole his master's   170
daughter.

LAERTES. This nothing's more than matter.

OPHELIA (to LAERTES). There's rosemary;

---

118. **fear**: fear for. 138. **swoopstake**: a game in
which the winner sweeps all the stakes; hence,
indiscriminately. 142. **life-rendering pelican**: It
was formerly supposed that the pelican fed its young
with its own blood.

151. **virtue**: faculty, power. 157. **fine in love**:
refined, or exalted, by love. 157–159. **where 'tis
fine . . . loves**: The meaning is that just as a highly
refined substance is sensitive to a force of attraction,
so a part of Ophelia's pure nature (her mind and
sanity) has followed "the thing it loves" (her father).

that's for remembrance. Pray you, love, remember. And there is pansies; 175 that's for thoughts.

LAERTES. A document* in madness — "thoughts" and "remembrance" fitted.

OPHELIA (*to the* KING). There's fennel* for you, and columbines;* there's rue* 180 for you; and here's some for me. We may call it herb of grace o' Sundays. — O! you must wear your rue with a difference. There's a daisy.* I would give you some violets,* but they withered 185 all when my father died. They say he made a good end. (*Sings*)
For bonny sweet Robin is all my joy.

LAERTES. Thought and affliction, passion, hell itself,
She turns to favor and to prettiness. 190

OPHELIA (*sings*).
And will he not come again?
And will he not come again?
  No, no, he is dead!
  Go to thy deathbed,
He never will come again! 195

His beard was as white as snow,
All flaxen was his poll.
  He is gone, he is gone,
  And we cast away moan.
God ha' mercy on his soul! 200
And of all Christian souls, I pray God.
God be wi' ye!
  [*Exit.*]

LAERTES. Do you see this, O God?

KING. Laertes, I must commune with* your grief,
Or you deny me right. Go but apart, 205
Make choice of whom your wisest friends you will,
And they shall hear and judge 'twixt you and me.

If by direct or by collateral hand
They find us touch'd, we will our kingdom give,
Our crown, our life, and all that we call ours, 210
To you in satisfaction; but if not,
Be you content to lend your patience to us,
And we shall jointly labor with your soul
To give it due content.*

LAERTES.   Let this be so.
His means of death, his obscure burial, 215
No trophy, sword, nor hatchment* o'er his bones,
No noble rite nor formal ostentation,
Cry to be heard, as 'twere from heaven to earth,
That I must call 't in question

KING.   So you shall;
And where the offense is let the great ax fall. 220
I pray you go with me.
  [*Exeunt.*]

SCENE VI. *A room in the castle.*

[*Enter* HORATIO *and a Servant.*]

HORATIO. What are they that would speak with me?

SERVANT. Sailors, sir. They say they have letters for you.

HORATIO. Let them come in.
  [*Exit Servant.*]
I do not know from what part of the world
I should be greeted, if not from Lord Hamlet. 5
  [*Enter Sailors.*]

FIRST SAILOR. God bless you, sir.

HORATIO. Let Him bless thee too.

FIRST SAILOR. He shall, sir, an't please Him.

---

177. **document**: lesson. 179. **fennel**: the emblem of flattery. 180. **columbines**: the emblem of ingratitude. **rue**: the emblem of repentance and sorrow. 184. **daisy**: the emblem of faithlessness. 185. **violets**: the emblem of faithfulness. 204. **commune with**: have a share in.

214. **content**: satisfaction (through due revenge on the guilty one). 216. **hatchment**: tablet bearing the coat of arms of the dead.

There's a letter for you, sir; it comes
from the ambassador that was bound   10
for England —if your name be Horatio,
as I am let to know it is.

HORATIO (*Opens the letter and reads*).
Horatio,

When thou shalt have overlooked   15
this, give these fellows some means to the
king; they have letters for him. Ere we
were two days old at sea, a pirate of very
warlike appointment gave us chase. Find-
ing ourselves too slow of sail, we put   20
on a compelled valor, and in the grapple
I boarded them. On the instant they got
clear of our ship, so I alone became their
prisoner. They have dealt with me like
thieves of mercy, but they knew   25
what they did — I am to do a good turn
for them. Let the king have the letters I
have sent, and repair thou to me with as
much haste as thou wouldst fly death. I
have words to speak in thine ear will   30
make thee dumb; yet are they much too
light for the bore* of the matter. These
good fellows will bring thee where I am.
Rosencrantz and Guildenstern hold their
course for England. Of them I have   35
much to tell thee. Farewell.

> *He that thou knowest thine,*
> > *Hamlet.*

Come, I will give you way for these your
letters,
And do't the speedier that you may direct
me   40
To him from whom you brought them.
[*Exeunt.*]

SCENE VII. *A room in the castle.*

[*Enter* KING *and* LAERTES.]

KING. Now must your conscience my ac-
quittance seal,

And you must put me in your heart for
friend,
Sith you have heard, and with a knowing
ear;
That he which hath your noble father
slain   4
Pursu'd my life.

LAERTES.   It well appears. But tell me
Why you proceeded not against these
feats
So crimeful and so capital in nature,
As by your safety, wisdom, all things else,
You mainly were stirr'd up.

KING.   O, for two special reasons,
Which may to you, perhaps, seem much
unsinew'd,   10
And yet to me they are strong. The queen
his mother
Lives almost by his looks; and for my-
self —
My virtue or my plague, be it either
which —
She's so conjunctive* to my life and soul,
That, as the star moves not but in his
sphere,   15
I could not but by her. The other motive
Why to a public count* I might not go
Is the great love the general gender* bear
him;
Who, dipping all his faults in their affec-
tion,
Would, like the spring that turneth wood
to stone,   20
Convert his gyves* to graces; so that my
arrows,
Too slightly timber'd for so loud* a wind,
Would have reverted to my bow again,
And not where I had aim'd them.

LAERTES. And so have I a noble father
lost,   25

32. **bore**: caliber (here, "importance").

14. **conjunctive**: united; with a glance at the
astronomical meaning as applied to heavenly
bodies; hence the references to "star" and "sphere"
in the next line.   17. **count**: reckoning.   18. **general gender**: the common people.   21. **gyves**:
fetters.   22. **loud**: violent, with a suggestion of the
noisy clamor of a mob.

A sister driven into desperate terms,
Whose worth — if praises may go back
    again —
Stood challenger-on-mount of all the age
For her perfections. But my revenge will
    come.
KING. Break not your sleeps for that. You
    must not think   30
That we are made of stuff so flat and dull
That we can let our beard be shook with
    danger
And think it pastime. You shortly shall
    hear more.
I lov'd your father, and we love ourself,
And that, I hope, will teach you to
    imagine —   35
    [Enter a Messenger.]
How now! What news?
MESSENGER. Letters, my lord, from Hamlet:
This to your majesty; this to the queen.
KING. From Hamlet! Who brought them?
MESSENGER. Sailors, my lord, they say; I
    saw them not.
They were given me by Claudio; he re-
    ceiv'd them   40
Of him that brought them.
KING.   Laertes, you shall hear them. —
Leave us.
    [Exit Messenger.]
    [Reads.]
High and Mighty:
    You shall know I am set naked* on
your kingdom. Tomorrow shall I 45
beg leave to see your kingly eyes; when I
shall (first asking your pardon thereunto)
recount the occasions of my sudden and
more strange return.
                  Hamlet 50
What should this mean? Are all the rest
    come back?
Or is it some abuse, and no such thing?
LAERTES. Know you the hand?
KING. 'Tis Hamlet's character.*—"Naked!"
And in a postscript here he says, "alone."
Can you advise me?   55

44. **naked:** destitute. 53. **character:** handwriting.

LAERTES. I'm lost in it, my lord. But let him
    come!
It warms the very sickness in my heart
That I shall live and tell him to his teeth,
"Thus did'st thou!"
KING.   If it be so,* Laertes —
As how should it be so? — How other-
    wise? —   60
Will you be rul'd by me?
LAERTES.   Ay, my lord,
So you will not o'errule me to a peace.
KING. To thine own peace. If he be now
    return'd.
As checking at* his voyage, and that he
    means
No more to undertake it, I will work
    him   65
To an exploit, now ripe in my device,
Under the which he shall not choose but
    fall;
And for his death no wind of blame shall
    breathe,
But even his mother shall uncharge the
    practice*   69
And call it accident.
LAERTES.   My lord, I will be rul'd;
The rather, if you could devise it so
That I might be the organ.
KING.   It falls right.
You have been talk'd of since your travel
    much,
And that in Hamlet's hearing, for a
    quality
Wherein they say you shine. Your sum
    of parts   75
Did not together pluck such envy from
    him
As did that one; and that, in my regard,
Of the unworthiest siege.*
LAERTES.   What part is that, my lord?
KING. A very riband in the cap of youth —
Yet needful, too; for youth no less be-
    comes   80

59. **If it be so:** *i.e.,* that Hamlet returns. 64.
checking at: recoiling from, shying at (a hawking
term). 69. **uncharge the practice:** free the stratagem from all blame. 78. **siege:** rank, importance.

The light and careless livery* that it
   wears
Than settled age his sables and his weeds,*
Importing health and graveness. Two
   months since
Here was a gentleman of Normandy.
I've seen myself, and serv'd against, the
   French,   85
And they can well on horseback; but this
   gallant
Had witchcraft in't. He grew unto his
   seat,
And to such wondrous doing brought his
   horse,
As he had been incorps'd and demi-
   natur'd*
With the brave beast. So far he topp'd
   my thought,   90
That I, in forgery* of shapes and tricks,
Come short of what he did.
LAERTES.   A Norman was't?
KING. A Norman.
LAERTES. Upon my life, Lamord!
KING.   The very same.
LAERTES. I know him well. He is the brooch
   indeed   95
And gem of all the nation.
KING. He made confession of you;*
   And gave you such a masterly report
   For art and exercise in your defense —
   And for your rapier most especially— 100
   That he cried out 'twould be a sight in-
   deed
   If one could match you. The scrimers*
   of their nation,
   He swore, had neither motion, guard, nor
   eye,
   If you oppos'd them. Sir, this report of
   his
   Did Hamlet so envenom with his envy 105

That he could nothing do but wish and
   beg
Your sudden coming o'er to play with
   him.
Now, out of this —
LAERTES.   What out of this, my lord?
KING. Laertes, was your father dear to you?
   Or are you, like the painting of a sor-
   row,   110
   A face without a heart?
LAERTES.   Why ask you this?
KING. Not that I think you did not love
   your father,
   But that I know love is begun by time,*
   And that I see, in passages of proof,
   Time qualifies the spark and fire of it. 115
   There lives within the very flame of love
   A kind of wick or snuff that will abate it;
   And nothing is at a like goodness still,
   For goodness, growing to a plurisy,*
   Dies in his own too-much. That we
   would do,   120
   We should do when we would, for this
   "would" changes,
   And hath abatements and delays as many
   As there are tongues, are hands, are acci-
   dents;
   And then this "should" is like a spend-
   thrift sigh,*
   That hurts by easing. But to the quick o'
   the ulcer: 125
   Hamlet comes back — What would you
   undertake
   To show yourself your father's son in
   deed
   More than in words?
LAERTES.   To cut his throat i' the church!
KING. No place, indeed, should murder
   sanctuarize;*
   Revenge should have no bounds. But,
   good Laertes,   130

---

81. **livery**: clothes distinctive of a group. 82.
his sables and his weeds: its warm furs and dignified
clothes. 89. **incorps'd and demi-natur'd**: of the
same body and almost the same nature (as his horse).
91. **forgery**: invention. 97. **made confession of
you**: acknowledged your excellence. 102. **scrimers**:
fencers.

113. **is begun by time**: has a beginning, and hence
is subject to time. 119. **plurisy**: excess. 124.
spendthrift sigh: It was believed that the sigh eased
grief by drawing blood from the heart to the hurt of
the body as a whole. 129. **sanctuarize**: give the
protection of sanctuary to.

Will you do this? Keep close within your
    chamber.
Hamlet return'd shall know you are come
    home.
We'll put on those shall praise your excel-
    lence,
And set a double varnish on the fame
The Frenchman gave you; bring you, in
    fine, together   135
And wager on your heads. He, being
    remiss,
Most generous, and free from all contriv-
    ing,
Will not peruse the foils; so that with
    ease,
Or with a little shuffling, you may choose
A sword unbated,* and, in a pass of prac-
    tice,*   140
Requite him for your father.
LAERTES.   I will do't!
And for that purpose I'll anoint my
    sword.
I bought an unction of a mountebank,
So mortal that, but dip a knife in it,
Where it draws blood no cataplasm* so
    rare,   145
Collected from all simples* that have
    virtue
Under the moon, can save the thing from
    death
That is but scratch'd withal. I'll touch
    my point
With this contagion, that, if I gall him
    slightly,   149
It may be death.
KING.   Let's further think of this;
Weigh what convenience both of time
    and means
May fit us to our shape.* If this should
    fail,
And that our drift look through our bad
    performance,

'Twere better not assay'd. Therefore this
    project
Should have a back, or second, that might
    hold   155
If this should blast in proof.* Soft! — let
    me see. —
We'll make a solemn wager on your cun-
    nings —
I ha't!
When in your motion you are hot and
    dry —
As make your bouts more violent to that
    end —   160
And that he calls for drink, I'll have pre-
    par'd him
A chalice for the nonce, whereon but
    sipping,
If he by chance escape your venom'd
    stuck,*
Our purpose may hold there. —
[Enter QUEEN.]
                   How now, sweet queen!
QUEEN. One woe doth tread upon another's
    heel,   165
So fast they follow. — Your sister's
    drown'd, Laertes.
LAERTES. Drown'd! O! where?
QUEEN. There is a willow* grows aslant a
    brook,
That shows his hoar leaves in the glassy
    stream;
There with fantastic garlands did she
    come,   170
Of crowflowers, nettles, daisies, and long
    purples,
That liberal shepherds give a grosser
    name,
But our cold maids do "dead men's
    fingers" call them.
There, on the pendent boughs her coronet
    weeds
Clambering to hang, an envious sliver*
    broke,   175

---

140. **unbated**: not blunted, as foils were, with a button on the end; *i.e.*, Laertes was to use a real sword instead of a foil. **pass of practice**: treacherous thrust. 145. **cataplasm**: poultice. 146. **simples**: herbs. 152. **shape**: plan, design.

156. **blast in proof**: fail in actual trial. 163. **stuck**: thrust. 168. **willow**: The willow was the common symbol of forsaken love. 175. **sliver**: branch.

Ophelia, *by the nineteenth-century English painter John Everett Millais.*

When down her weedy trophies and her-
    self
Fell in the weeping brook. Her clothes
    spread wide,
And, mermaidlike, awhile they bore her
    up;
Which time she chanted snatches of old
    tunes,
As one incapable of her own distress, 180
Or like a creature native and indued
Unto that element. But long it could not
    be
Till that her garments, heavy with their
    drink,
Pull'd the poor wretch from her melodi-
    ous lay   184
To muddy death.
LAERTES.   Alas! then she is drown'd?
QUEEN. Drown'd, drown'd.
LAERTES. Too much of water hast thou,
    poor Ophelia,
And therefore I forbid my tears. — But
    yet
It is our trick;* nature her custom holds,
189. **trick:** way.

Let shame say what it will. — When
    these* are gone   190
The woman will be out. — Adieu, my
    lord!
I have a speech of fire that fain would
    blaze,
But that this folly douts* it.
    [*Exit.*]
KING.   Let's follow, Gertrude.
How much I had to do to calm his rage!
Now fear I this will give it start again; 195
Therefore let's follow.
    [*Exeunt.*]

190. **these:** these tears.   193. **douts:** extin-
guishes.

For Discussion

1. From the opening of Act IV the King is
certain that Hamlet means to kill him: "It
had been so with us," he realizes, "had we
been there" where Polonius was hiding, behind the arras (IV, i, 13). What steps does he

take to protect himself from Hamlet's vengeance? Why does he not simply have the prince put to death? What reasons does he offer Hamlet for sending him to England?

2. In Scene iv Hamlet utters the famous soliloquy beginning "How all occasions do inform against me" (iv, 32 ff). What effect does the example of Fortinbras' march on "a little patch of ground" have on the prince? What change comes over him in the course of the speech?

3. The pathetic spectacle of Ophelia's madness opens Scene v. What has driven her mad? "When sorrows come," the King remarks, "they come not single spies, / But in battalions" (v, 74–75). To what sorrows specifically does he refer? Laertes' violent approach interrupts the exchange between Claudius and Gertrude. What has caused the young man's outrage, evident the moment he enters? Against whom is that outrage initially directed? Ophelia's re-entry adds to her brother's grief and desperation, so that Claudius wisely takes him aside. In the interval of the King's explanation to Laertes, we move briefly to another part of the castle. What does the note Horatio receives reveal about the fate of Hamlet on his voyage toward England? What questions does it leave unanswered?

4. In Scene vii, Laertes is revealed as completely under Claudius' influence — a tool in the King's hands, a means to his ends. Notice the young man's outburst at Scene vii, line 128. After reconsidering Hamlet's behavior in Act III, Scene iii, comment on the irony of Laertes' remark. What plan does the King propose for dealing with Hamlet? How does Laertes refine the plan? The Queen's reappearance concludes the act. What, specifically, is the doleful news she brings?

5. Clearly tone is of prime importance in reading drama effectively. Different speeches must be read in different ways, depending on the emotions implicit in the words on the page. Consider Act IV, Scene iii, the scene in which the King questions Hamlet about Polonius' whereabouts. In what tone would the King speak? In what tone would Hamlet reply?

Act V

SCENE I. *A day later. A churchyard.*

[*Enter two* CLOWNS, *with spades and pickaxes.*]

FIRST CLOWN. Is she to be buried in Christian burial* that wilfully seeks her own salvation?

SECOND CLOWN. I tell thee she is; and therefore make her grave straight:* 5
the crowner* hath sat on her, and finds it Christian burial.

FIRST CLOWN. How can that be, unless she drowned herself in her own defense?

SECOND CLOWN. Why, 'tis found so. 10

FIRST CLOWN. It must be *se offendendo;* * it cannot be else. For here lies the point: if I drown myself wittingly, it argues an act; and an act hath three branches; it is — to act, to do, and to perform: 15 argal* she drowned herself wittingly.

SECOND CLOWN. Nay, but hear you, Goodman Delver, —

FIRST CLOWN. Give me leave. — Here lies the water; good. Here stands the 20 man; good. If the man go to this water, and drown himself, it is, will-he-nill-he, he goes — mark you that! But if the water come to him and drown him, he drowns not himself: argal, he that is 25 not guilty of his own death, shortens not his own life.

SECOND CLOWN. But is this law?

FIRST CLOWN. Ay, marry, is't — crowner's quest* law. 30

SECOND CLOWN. Will you ha' the truth on't? If this had not been a gentlewoman,

2. **Christian burial**: Burial within the churchyard was denied to suicides. 5. **straight**: straightaway. 6. **crowner**: coroner. 11. *se offendendo*: The clown means to say *se defendendo*, in self-defense. 16. **argal**: the clown's perversion of the Latin *ergo*, therefore. 30. **quest**: inquest.

she should have been buried out o' Christian burial.

FIRST CLOWN. Why, there thou sayest! 35
And the more pity that great folk should
have countenance* in this world to drown
or hang themselves more than their even*
Christian. — Come, my spade. (*Hands
him a spade.*) There is no ancient 40
gentlemen but gardeners, ditchers, and
grave-makers. They hold up Adam's profession.

SECOND CLOWN. Was he a gentleman?

FIRST CLOWN. A' was the first that ever 45
bore arms.

SECOND CLOWN. Why, he had none.

FIRST CLOWN. What! art a heathen? How
dost thou understand the Scripture? The
Scripture says Adam digged. Could 50
he dig without arms? I'll put another
question to thee; if thou answerest me not
to the purpose, confess thyself —

SECOND CLOWN. Go to!

FIRST CLOWN. What is he that builds 55
stronger than either the mason, the shipwright, or the carpenter?

SECOND CLOWN. The gallows-maker; for
that frame outlives a thousand tenants.

FIRST CLOWN. I like thy wit well, in 60
good faith. The gallows does well. But
how does it well? it does well to those that
do ill. Now thou dost ill to say the gallows is built stronger than the church:
argal, the gallows may do well to thee. 65
To't again, come!

SECOND CLOWN. Who builds stronger than
a mason, a shipwright, or a carpenter?

FIRST CLOWN. Ay, tell me that, and unyoke.* 70

SECOND CLOWN. Marry, now I can tell!

FIRST CLOWN. To't!

SECOND CLOWN. Mass, I cannot tell.

[*Enter at a distance* HAMLET *and*
HORATIO.]

FIRST CLOWN. Cudgel thy brains no more
about it, for your dull ass will not 75

37. **countenance**: privilege. 38. **even**: fellow
equal. 70. **unyoke**: call it a day.

mend his pace with beating; and when
you are asked this question next, say "a
grave-maker"; the houses that he makes
last till doomsday. — Go, get thee to
Yaughan; fetch me a stoup of liquor. 80

[*Exit Second Clown.*]

FIRST CLOWN (*digs and sings*).
In youth, when I did love, did love,
  Methought it was very sweet,
To contract — o — the time for — a —
  my behove,
  O! methought there — a — was nothing — a — meet.

HAMLET. Has this fellow no feeling of 85
his business, that he sings at grave-making?

HORATIO. Custom hath made it in him a
property of easiness.*

HAMLET. 'Tis e'en so. The hand of 90
little employment hath the daintier sense.

FIRST CLOWN (*sings*).
  But age, with his stealing steps,
    Hath claw'd me in his clutch,
  And hath shipped me intil the land,
    As if I had never been such. 95

[*Throws up a skull.*]

HAMLET. That skull had a tongue in it, and
could sing once. How the knave jowls*
it to the ground, as if it were Cain's jawbone, that did the first murder! This
might be the pate of a politician, 100
which this ass now o'er-offices, one that
would circumvent* God, might it not?

HORATIO. It might, my lord.

HAMLET. Or of a courtier, which could say
"Good morrow, sweet lord! how 105
dost thou, good lord?" This might be my
Lord Such-a-one, that praised my Lord
Such-a-one's horse, when he meant to beg
it, might it not?

HORATIO. Ay, my lord. 110

HAMLET. Why, e'en so! and now my Lady
Worm's chapless,* and knocked about

89. **property of easiness**: quality that comes
easily. 97. **jowls**: dashes. 102. **circumvent**: get
the better of by outwitting. 112. **chapless**: lacking
a lower jaw.

the mazzard* with a sexton's spade.
Here's fine revolution, an we had the
trick to see't. Did these bones cost 115
no more than the breeding but to play at
loggats* with 'em? Mine ache to think
on't.

FIRST CLOWN (sings).

> A pickaxe and a spade, a spade
> For and a shrouding sheet; 120
> O! a pit of clay for to be made
> For such a guest is meet.

[Throws up another skull.]

HAMLET. There's another. Why might not
that be the skull of a lawyer? Where be
his quiddities* now? his quillets,* his 125
cases, his tenures, and his tricks? Why
does he suffer this rude knave now to
knock him about the sconce with a dirty
shovel, and will not tell him of his action
of battery? Hum! This fellow might 130
be in's time a great buyer of land, with
his statutes, his recognizances, his fines,
his double vouchers, his recoveries. Is this
the fine* of his fines, and the recovery of
his recoveries, to have his fine pate 135
full of fine dirt? Will his vouchers vouch
him no more of his purchases, and double
ones too, than the length and breadth of
a pair of indentures? The very con-
veyances of his lands will hardly lie 140
in this box; and must the inheritor himself
have no more, ha?

HORATIO. Not a jot more, my lord.

HAMLET. Is not parchment made of sheep-
skins? 145

HORATIO. Ay, my lord, and of calfskins too.

HAMLET. They are sheep and calves which
seek out assurance* in that. — I will speak
to this fellow. Whose grave's this,
sirrah? 150

FIRST CLOWN. Mine, sir.

[Sings.]

> O! a pit of clay for to be made
> For such a guest is meet.

HAMLET. I think it be thine indeed, for
thou liest* in't. 155

FIRST CLOWN. You lie out on't sir, and
therefore 'tis not yours. For my part, I
do not lie in't, and yet it is mine.

HAMLET. Thou dost lie in't, to be in't and
say it is thine: 'tis for the dead, not 160
for the quick;* therefore thou liest.

FIRST CLOWN. 'Tis a quick lie, sir 'twill
away again from me to you.

HAMLET. What man dost thou dig it for?

FIRST CLOWN. For no man, sir. 165

HAMLET. What woman, then?

FIRST CLOWN. For none, neither.

HAMLET. Who is to be buried in't?

FIRST CLOWN. One that was a woman, sir;
but, rest her soul, she's dead. 170

HAMLET. How absolute* the knave is! We
must speak by the card,* or equivocation
will undo us. By the Lord, Horatio, these
three years I have taken note of it, the
age is grown so picked* that the toe 175
of the peasant comes so near the heel of
the courtier he galls his kibe.* — How
long hast thou been a grave-maker?

FIRST CLOWN. Of all the days i' the year,
I come to't that day that our last 180
King Hamlet overcame Fortinbras.

HAMLET. How long is that since?

FIRST CLOWN. Cannot you tell that? Every
fool can tell that! It was the very day that
young Hamlet was born — he that is 185
mad, and sent into England.

HAMLET. Ay, marry, why was he sent into
England?

FIRST CLOWN. Why, because a' was mad.
A' shall recover his wits there; or, if 190

---

113. **mazzard**: head. 117. **loggats**: a game in which loggats (pear-shaped, and hence suggesting a skull) were hurled at a stake fixed in the ground. 125. **quiddities**: subtleties in argument. **quillets**: nice verbal distinctions. 134. **fine**: a law term, with a pun, "the end." 148. **assurance**: in law, the conveyance of lands by deed; with a pun on "se-curity."

155. **liest**: are. Several puns are made on the verb "lie" in its various senses, "to be," "to reside," "to tell a falsehood." 161. **quick**: living. 171. **absolute**: exact. 172. **by the card**: exactly to the point, as by a compass. 175. **picked**: particular, fastidious. 177. **kibe**: sore on the back of the heel.

a' do not, tis no great matter there.

HAMLET. Why?

FIRST CLOWN. 'Twill not be seen in him there; there the men are as mad as he.

HAMLET. How came he mad?   195

FIRST CLOWN. Very strangely, they say.

HAMLET. How strangely?

FIRST CLOWN. Faith, e'en with losing his wits.

HAMLET. Upon what ground?   200

FIRST CLOWN. Why, here in Denmark. I have been sexton here, man and boy, thirty years.*

HAMLET. How long will a man lie i' the earth ere he rot?   205

FIRST CLOWN. Faith, if a' be not rotten before a' die — as we have many pocky corses nowadays that will scarce hold the laying in — a' will last you some eight year, or nine year. A tanner will last   210 you nine year.

HAMLET. Why he more than another?

FIRST CLOWN. Why, sir, his hide is so tanned with his trade that a' will keep out water a great while; and your water   215 is a sore decayer of your whoreson dead body. Here's a skull now: this skull hath lain you i' the earth three-and-twenty years.

HAMLET. Whose was it?   220

FIRST CLOWN. A whoreson mad fellow's it was! Whose do you think it was?

HAMLET. Nay, I know not.

FIRST CLOWN. A pestilence on him for a mad rogue! 'A poured a flagon of   225 Rhenish on my head once. This same skull, sir, was Yorick's skull, the king's jester.

HAMLET. This!

FIRST CLOWN. E'en that.   230

HAMLET. Let me see. (*Takes the skull.*) Alas, poor Yorick! I knew him, Horatio — a fellow of infinite jest, of most excellent fancy. He hath borne me on his back a thousand times — and now   235

how abhorred in my imagination it is! My gorge rises at it. Here hung those lips that I have kissed I know not how oft. Where be your gibes now? your gambols? your songs? your flashes of   240 merriment that were wont to set the table on a roar? Not one now, to mock your own grinning? quite chapfallen? Now get you to my lady's chamber, and tell her, let her paint an inch thick, to   245 this favor* she must come. Make her laugh at that! — Prithee, Horatio, tell me one thing.

HORATIO. What's that, my lord?

HAMLET. Dost thou think Alexander   250 looked o' this fashion i' the earth?

HORATIO. E'en so.

HAMLET. And smelt so? pah!
    [*Throws down the skull.*]

HORATIO. E'en so, my lord.

HAMLET. To what base uses we may   255 return, Horatio! Why may not imagination trace the noble dust of Alexander, till he find it stopping a bunghole?

HORATIO. 'Twere to consider too curiously,* to consider so.   260

HAMLET. No, faith, not a jot! But to follow him thither, with modesty* enough, and likelihood to lead it, as thus: Alexander died; Alexander was buried; Alexander returneth into dust; the dust is   265 earth; of earth we make loam; and why of that loam whereto he was converted might they not stop a beer barrel?

Imperious Caesar, dead and turn'd to clay,

Might stop a hole to keep the wind away.   270

O, that that earth, which kept the world in awe,

Should patch a wall to expel the winter's flaw!*

But soft! but soft! Aside! Here comes the king.
    [*Enter Priests, etc., in procession; bell*

201–203. This line fixes Hamlet's age.

246. **favor:** appearance.   260. **curiously:** minutely.   262. **modesty:** moderation.   272. **flaw:** gust.

tolling; the corpse of OPHELIA *borne in,*
LAERTES, KING, QUEEN, *Lords, etc.,*
following.]

The queen, the courtiers? Who is that
they follow?

And with such maimèd* rites? This doth
betoken   275

The corse they follow did with desp'rate
hand

Fordo its own life. 'Twas of some estate.

Couch* we awhile and mark.

[*He retires with* HORATIO.]

LAERTES. What ceremony else?

HAMLET.   That is Laertes —

A very noble youth. Mark.   280

LAERTES. What ceremony else?

FIRST PRIEST. Her obsequies have been as
far enlarg'd

As we have warrantise. Her death was
doubtful,

And, but that great command o'ersways
the order,

She should in ground unsanctified have
lodg'd   285

Till the last trumpet; for charitable
prayers,

Shards,* flints, and pebbles should be
thrown on her.

Yet here she is allow'd her virgin crants,*

Her maiden strewments, and the bringing home*

Of bell and burial.   290

LAERTES. Must there no more be done?

FIRST PRIEST.   No more be done.

We should profane the service of the dead

To sing a requiem and such rest to her

As to peace-parted souls.

LAERTES.   Lay her i' the earth;

And from her fair and unpolluted flesh

May violets spring! — I tell thee, churlish
priest,   296

A minist'ring angel shall my sister be

When thou liest howling.*

HAMLET.   What! the fair Ophelia?

QUEEN (*scattering flowers*). Sweets to the
sweet. Farewell!

I hop'd thou shouldst have been my
Hamlet's wife;   300

I thought thy bride-bed to have deck'd,
sweet maid,

And not t'have strewed thy grave.

LAERTES.   O, treble woe

Fall ten times treble on that cursèd head

Whose wicked deed thy most ingenious
sense*

Depriv'd thee of! — Hold off the earth
awhile,   305

Till I have caught her once more in mine
arms.

[*Leaps into the grave.*]

Now pile your dust upon the quick and
dead,

Till of this flat a mountain you have made

To o'ertop old Pelion* or the skyish head

Of blue Olympus!

HAMLET (*advancing*). What is he whose
grief   310

Bears such an emphasis? whose phrase of
sorrow

Conjures the wandering stars,* and makes
them stand

Like wonder-wounded hearers? This is I,
Hamlet, the Dane!

[*Leaps into the grave.*]

LAERTES (*seizing him by the throat*). The
devil take thy soul!

HAMLET. Thou pray'st not well.   315

I prithee, take thy fingers from my throat;

For though I am not splenetive and rash,

Yet have I in me something dangerous,

Which let thy wiseness fear. Hold off
thy hand!   319

[*They struggle in the grave.*]

KING. Pluck them asunder.

---

275. **maimèd**: incomplete. 278. **Couch**: hide.
287. **Shards**: fragments of pottery. 288. **crants**:
garlands, usually made of white paper, carried at the
funerals of young girls or virgins. 289. **bringing
home**: The image is that of bringing a bride from
the church to her future home.

298. **howling**: *i.e.*, in hell's torments. 304. **ingenious sense**: finely endowed mind. 309. **Pelion**:
In Greek mythology the giants piled Mount Pelion
on Mount Ossa (line 339) in an attempt to reach
Olympus, home of the gods. 312. **wandering stars**:
planets.

QUEEN.   Hamlet! Hamlet!

ALL. Gentlemen!

[*The Attendants part them, and they
come out of the grave.*]

HORATIO.   Good my lord, be quiet.

HAMLET. Why, I will fight with him upon
        this theme

Until my eyelids will no longer wag.

QUEEN. O, my son, what theme?

HAMLET. I lov'd Ophelia. Forty thousand
        brothers   325

Could not, with all their quantity of love,

Make up my sum! — What wilt thou do
        for her?

KING. O, he is mad, Laertes.

QUEEN. For love of God, forbear him.

HAMLET. 'Swounds, show me what thou'lt
        do!   330

Woo't weep? woo't fight, woo't fast?
        woo't tear thyself?

Woo't drink up eisel?* eat a crocodile?

I'll do't! Dost thou come here to whine?

To outface me with leaping in her grave?

Be buried quick with her, and so will I!

And if thou prate of mountains, let them
        throw   336

Millions of acres on us, till our ground,

Singeing his pate against the burning
        zone,*

Make Ossa like a wart! Nay, an thou'lt
        mouth,   339

I'll rant as well as thou!

QUEEN.   This is mere madness;

And thus a while the fit will work on him.

Anon, as patient as the female dove

When that her golden couplets* are dis-
        clos'd,

His silence will sit drooping.

HAMLET.   Hear you, sir;

What is the reason that you use me
        thus?   345

I lov'd you ever. — But it is no matter.

Let Hercules himself do what he may,

The cat will mew and dog will have his
        day.

[*Exit.*]

KING. I pray you, good Horatio, wait upon
        him.

[*Exit* HORATIO.]

(*Aside to* LAERTES) Strengthen your pa-
        tience in our last night's speech;   350

We'll put the matter to the present
        push.* —

Good Gertrude, set some watch over
        your son.

This grave shall have a living* monument.

(*Aside to* LAERTES) An hour of quiet
        shortly shall we see;

Till then, in patience our proceeding
        be.   355

[*Exeunt.*]

SCENE II. *A hall in the castle.*

[*Enter* HAMLET *and* HORATIO.]

HAMLET. So much for this, sir. Now shall
        you see the other.

You do remember all the circumstance?

HORATIO. Remember it, my lord!

HAMLET. Sir, in my heart there was a kind
        of fighting

That would not let me sleep; methought
        I lay   5

Worse than the mutines in the bilboes.*
        Rashly —

And prais'd be rashness for it; let us know,

Our indiscretion sometimes serves us well

When our deep plots do pall, and that
        should learn us   9

There's a divinity that shapes our ends,

Rough-hew them how we will —

HORATIO.   That is most certain.

HAMLET. Up from my cabin,

---

332. **eisel**: vinegar. 338. **burning zone**: sun's
orbit. 343. **golden couplets**: The pigeon lays two
eggs, and the young when "disclosed" (hatched out
of the shell) are covered with a yellow down.

351. **present push**: immediate execution. 353.
living: enduring.
6. **bilboes**: The bilbo was a long iron bar, fixed
to the floor, and equipped with shackles into which
the ankles of mutinous sailors were fitted.

My sea-gown scarf'd about me, in the dark

Grop'd I to find out them; had my desire;

Finger'd their packet; and, in fine, withdrew   15

To mine own room again, making so bold —

My fears forgetting manners — to unseal

Their grand commission. Where I found Horatio, —

O royal knavery! — an exact* command,

Larded with many several sorts of reasons   20

Importing Denmark's health, and England's too,

With, ho! such bugs and goblins in my life,*

That, on the supervise, no leisure bated,*

No, not to stay the grinding of the ax,   24

My head should be struck off.

HORATIO.   Is't possible!

HAMLET. Here's the commission; read it at more leisure.

But wilt thou hear me how I did proceed?

HORATIO. I beseech you.

HAMLET. Being thus benetted round with villainies,

Ere I could make a prologue to my brains   30

They* had begun the play. I sat me down,

Devis'd a new commission, wrote it fair.

I once did hold it, as our statists do,

A baseness to write fair,* and labor'd much

How to forget that learning; but, sir, now   35

It did me yeoman's service. Wilt thou know

The effect of what I wrote?

HORATIO.   Ay, good my lord.

HAMLET. An earnest conjuration from the king,

As England was his faithful tributary,

As love between them like the palm should flourish,   40

As peace should still her wheaten garland wear,

And stand a comma* 'tween their amities,

And many suchlike "As"es of great charge,

That, on the view and knowing of these contents,   44

Without debatement further more or less,

He should the bearers put to sudden death,

Not shriving time* allow'd.

HORATIO.   How was this seal'd?

HAMLET. Why, even in that was heaven ordinant.

I had my father's signet in my purse,

Which was the model of that Danish seal;   50

Folded the writ up in form of the other,

Subscrib'd it, gave't the impression, plac'd it safely,

The changeling never known. Now, the next day

Was our sea-fight; and what to this was sequent

Thou know'st already.   55

HORATIO. So Guildenstern and Rosencrantz go to't.

HAMLET. Why, man, they did make love to this employment!

They are not near my conscience; their defeat

Does by their own insinuation* grow.

'Tis dangerous when the baser nature* comes   60

Between the pass* and fell-incensèd points

---

19. **exact:** strict. 22. **such bugs . . . life:** such bug-bears and imagined terrors if I were allowed to live. 23. **bated:** allowed. 31. **They:** *i.e.,* "my brains." 34. **write fair:** To write a clear and beautiful hand, such as official scribes were required to write, might place a gentleman under suspicion of professionalism.

42. **comma:** as opposed to a period, indicating continuity. 47. **shriving time:** time to receive absolution (forgiveness for sins) through confession. 59. **insinuation:** meddling; literally, winding themselves into the affair. 60. **baser nature:** inferior person. 61. **pass:** thrust.

Of mighty opposites.*

HORATIO. Why, what a king is this!

HAMLET. Does it not, thinks't thee, stand
    me now upon —

He that hath kill'd my king, and whor'd
    my mother,

Popp'd in between the election and my
    hopes,*   65

Thrown out his angle for my proper life,

And with such cozenage* — is't not per-
    fect conscience

To quit him with this arm? And is't not
    to be damn'd

To let this canker of our nature come

In further evil?   70

HORATIO. It must be shortly known to him
    from England

What is the issue of the business there.

HAMLET. It will be short; the interim is
    mine,

And a man's life's no more than to say
    "One." —

But I am very sorry, good Horatio,   75

That to Laertes I forgot myself;

For by the image of my cause I see

The portraiture of his. I'll court his
    favors.

But, sure, the bravery* of his grief did
    put me   79

Into a tow'ring passion! —

HORATIO. Peace! Who comes here?

    [*Enter* OSRIC, *a gallant.*]

OSRIC. Your lordship is right welcome back
to Denmark.

HAMLET. I humbly thank you, sir. (*Aside
to* HORATIO) Dost know this waterfly?

HORATIO (*aside to* HAMLET). No, my   85
good lord.

HAMLET (*aside to* HORATIO). Thy state is
the more gracious, for 'tis a vice to know
him. He hath much land, and fertile. Let
a beast be lord of beasts, and his crib   90

shall stand at the king's mess.* 'Tis a
chough* — but, as I say, spacious in the
possession of dirt.

OSRIC. Sweet lord, if your lordship were at
leisure, I should impart a thing to you   95
from his majesty.

HAMLET. I will receive it, sir, with all diligence of spirit. Put your bonnet to his
right use; 'tis for the head.*

OSRIC. I thank your lordship, 'tis very   100
hot.

HAMLET. No, believe me, 'tis very cold;
the wind is northerly.

OSRIC. It is indifferent cold — my lord —
indeed —   105

HAMLET. But yet methinks it is very sultry
and hot for my complexion.

OSRIC. Exceedingly, my lord! It is very
sultry — as 'twere — I cannot tell how.
But, my lord, his majesty bade me   110
signify to you that he has laid a great
wager on your head. Sir, this is the
matter —

HAMLET. I beseech you, remember.

    [HAMLET *moves him to put on his hat.*]

OSRIC. Nay, good my lord. For mine   115
ease, in good faith. Sir, here is newly
come to court Laertes — believe me, an
absolute gentleman, full of most excellent
differences, of very soft society, and great
showing. Indeed, to speak feelingly   120
of him, he is the card or calendar* of
gentry; for you shall find in him the continent* of what part a gentleman would
see.

---

62. **opposites:** opponents. 65. **the election and my
hopes:** Claudius did not usurp the throne but had
himself chosen by the court. The kingship was
elective. 67. **cozenage:** fraud, treachery. 79.
bravery: ostentation, showy character.

89–91. **Let . . . mess:** Let an ass be rich in
possessions, and he will be admitted into the highest
circles of society. 92. **chough:** foolish chattering
bird. 98–99. **bonnet . . . head:** Courtesy required
a man to remove his hat in the presence of a superior,
and equally required the person so honored to give
permission for the hat to be replaced. Osric's reply
is essentially discourteous in that it implies that
he had removed his hat not as a compliment but
because of the hot weather. Hamlet thereupon
beat him at his own game, but it is Osric who
ultimately wins this contest. 121. **card or calendar:** mariner's compass, or guide (index). 123.
continent: that which comprises or sums up.

HAMLET. Sir, his definement suffers no 125
perdition in you, though I know to
divide him inventorially would dizzy the
arithmetic of memory and yet but yaw
neither in respect of his quick sail, but, in
the verity of extolment, I take him 130
to be a soul of great article, and his in-
fusion of such dearth and rareness as, to
make true diction of him, his semblable
is his mirror, and who else would trace
him, his umbrage, nothing more. 135

OSRIC. Your lordship speaks most infallibly
of him.

HAMLET. The concernancy,* sir? Why do
we wrap the gentleman in our more rawer
breath? 140

OSRIC. Sir?

HORATIO. Is't not possible to understand in
another tongue?* You will to't, sir,
really.

HAMLET. What imports the nomina- 145
tion* of this gentleman?

OSRIC. Of Laertes?

HORATIO (aside to Hamlet). His purse is
empty already; all's golden words are
spent. 150

HAMLET. Of him, sir.

OSRIC. I know you are not ignorant —

HAMLET. I would you did, sir; yet, in faith,
if you did, it would not much approve*
me. Well, sir? 155

OSRIC. You are not ignorant of what excellence Laertes is —

HAMLET. I dare not confess that, lest I
should compare with him in excellence;
but to know a man well, were to 160
know himself.

OSRIC. I mean, sir, for his weapon. But in
the imputation laid on him by them, in
his meed* he's unfellowed.

HAMLET. What's his weapon? 165

OSRIC. Rapier and dagger.

HAMLET. That's two of his weapons — but
well.

OSRIC. The king, sir, hath wagered with
him six Barbary horses; against the 170
which he has imponed,* as I take it, six
French rapiers and poniards, with their
assigns,* as girdle, hangers, and so. Three
of the carriages, in faith, are very dear to
fancy, very responsive* to the hilts, 175
most delicate carriages, and of very liberal
conceit.*

HAMLET. What call you the "carriages"?

HORATIO (aside to HAMLET). I knew you
must be edified by the margent,* ere 180
you had done.

OSRIC. The "carriages," sir, are the
hangers.*

HAMLET. The phrase would be more ger-
mane to the matter if we could carry 185
cannon by our sides; I would it might be
"hangers" till then. But on! Six Barbary
horses against six French swords, their
assigns, and three liberal-conceited carriages: that's the French bet against 190
the Danish. Why is this all "imponed,"
as you call it?

OSRIC. The king, sir, hath laid that in a
dozen passes between yourself and him,
he shall not exceed you three hits; 195
he hath laid on twelve for nine. And it
would come to immediate trial, if your
lordship would vouchsafe the answer.*

HAMLET. How if I answer no?

OSRIC. I mean, my lord, the opposition 200
of your person in trial.

HAMLET. Sir, I will walk here in the hall.
If it please his majesty, 'tis the breathing
time* of day with me. Let the foils be
brought, the gentleman willing, and 205
the king hold his purpose. I will win for
him if I can; if not, I will gain nothing
but my shame and the odd hits.

138. **concernancy**: relevance. 142-143. **Is't ...
tongue**: Can't you understand your own lingo when
somebody else speaks it? 146. **nomination**: mention.
154. **approve**: commend. 164. **meed**: excellence.

171. **imponed**: staked. 173. **assigns**: a legal term,
appurtenances. 175. **responsive**: becoming. 176-
177. **liberal conceit**: elaborate design. 180. **margent**:
explanatory notes printed in the margin. 183.
hangers: straps by which the rapier was suspended, often richly decorated. 198. **answer**:
encounter; Hamlet wilfully misinterprets. 203–204.
breathing time: time for recreation.

OSRIC. Shall I redeliver you e'en so?

HAMLET. To this effect, sir, after what 210
flourish your nature will.

OSRIC. I commend my duty to your lordship.

HAMLET. Yours, yours.

[*Exit* OSRIC.]

He does well to commend it himself; 215
there are not tongues else for's turn.

HORATIO. This lapwing runs away with the
shell on his head.*

HAMLET. He did comply* with his dug before he sucked it. Thus has he — 220
and many more of the same bevy that I
know the drossy age dotes on — only got
the tune of the time and outward habit
of encounter,* a kind of yesty collection* which carries them through 225
and through the most fond and winnowed
opinions;* and do but blow them to their
trial — the bubbles arc out.

[*Enter a Lord.*]

LORD. My lord, his majesty commended
him to you by young Osric, who 230
brings back to him that you attend him
in the hall. He sends to know if your
pleasure hold to play with Laertes, or
that you will take longer time.

HAMLET. I am constant to my pur- 235
poses; they follow the king's pleasure. If
his fitness speaks, mine is ready, now or
whensoever, provided I be so able as now.

LORD. The king and queen and all are coming down. 240

HAMLET. In happy time.

LORD. The queen desires you to use some
gentle entertainment to Laertes before
you fall to play.

HAMLET. She well instructs me. 245

[*Exit Lord.*]

HORATIO. You will lose this wager, my lord.

HAMLET. I do not think so. Since he went
into France, I have been in continual
practice. I shall win at the odds. — But
thou wouldst not think how ill all's 250
here about my heart. But it is no matter.

HORATIO. Nay, good my lord.

HAMLET. It is but foolery, but it is such a
kind of gaingiving* as would perhaps
trouble a woman. 255

HORATIO. If your mind dislike anything,
obey it. I will forestall their repair hither
and say you are not fit.

HAMLET. Not a whit — we defy augury.
There's a special providence in the 260
fall of a sparrow. If it be now, 'tis not to
come; if it be not to come, it will be now;
if it be not now, yet it will come: the
readiness is all. Since no man has aught
of what he leaves,* what is't to leave 265
betimes? Let be.

[*Enter* KING, QUEEN, LAERTES, OSRIC,
*Lords, etc.; Attendants with table, foils,
flagons of wine.*]

KING. Come, Hamlet; come and take this
hand from me.

[*The* KING *puts* LAERTES's *hand into*
HAMLET's.]

HAMLET. Give me your pardon, sir. I've
done you wrong;

But pardon't, as you are a gentleman.

This presence* knows, 270

And you must needs have heard, how I
am punish'd

With sore distraction. What I have done

That might your nature, honor, and exception

Roughly awake, I here proclaim was madness.

Was't Hamlet wrong'd Laertes? Never
Hamlet. 275

If Hamlet from himself be ta'en away,

217-218. **lapwing...head**: It was the general notion that the newly hatched lapwing ran about with the shell still upon its head; hence, a young upstart. 219. **comply**: observe forms of ceremonious polite-ness. 224. **encounter**: social usage. 224-225. **yesty collection**: collection of light social behaviors which are, like bubbles, pretty but empty. 226-227. **fond and winnowed opinions**: foolish and accepted arbiters of elegance.

254. **gaingiving**: misgiving. 264-265. **Since ... leaves**: since the things of this world are no part of a man's real self. 270. **presence**: the court.

And when he's not himself does wrong
    Laertes,
Then Hamlet does it not. Hamlet denies
    it.
Who does it then? His madness. If't be
    so,   279
Hamlet is of the faction that is wrong'd;
His madness is poor Hamlet's enemy.
Sir, in this audience,
Let my disclaiming from a purpos'd evil
Free me so far in your most generous
    thoughts,
That I have shot mine arrow o'er the
    house   285
And hurt my brother.

LAERTES.   I am satisfied in nature,
Whose motive in this case should stir me
    most
To my revenge. But in my terms of
    honor
I stand aloof and will no reconcilement
Till by some elder masters, of known
    honor,   290
I have a voice and precedent of peace,*
To keep my name ungor'd. But till that
    time
I do receive your offer'd love like love,
And will not wrong it.

HAMLET.   I embrace it freely,
And will this brother's wager frankly
    play. —   295
Give us the foils. (To LAERTES) Come
    on!

LAERTES.   Come, one for me.

HAMLET. I'll be your foil, Laertes. In mine
    ignorance
Your skill shall, like a star i' the darkest
    night,
Stick fiery off indeed.

LAERTES.   You mock me, sir.

HAMLET. No, by this hand.   300

KING. Give them the foils, young Osric.
                Cousin Hamlet,
You know the wager?

291. **voice and precedent of peace**: authority and
precedent in the accepted rules of honor to make
my peace with you.

HAMLET.   Very well, my lord.
Your Grace hath laid the odds o' the
    weaker side.

KING. I do not fear it; I have seen you both:
But since he is better'd, we have therefore
    odds.   305

LAERTES. This is too heavy; let me see an-
    other.

HAMLET. This likes me well. — These foils
    have all a length?
[They prepare to play.]

OSRIC. Ay, my good lord.

KING. Set me the stoups of wine upon that
    table.
If Hamlet give the first or second hit, 310
Or quit in answer of the third exchange,*
Let all the battlements their ordnance
    fire;
The king shall drink to Hamlet's better
    breath,
And in the cup an union* shall he throw,
Richer than that which four successive
    kings   315
In Denmark's crown have worn. Give
    me the cups;
And let the kettle* to the trumpets speak,
The trumpets to the cannoneer without,
The cannons to the heavens, the heavens
    to earth,
"Now the king drinks to Hamlet!" —
    Come, begin.   320
And you, the judges, bear a wary eye.
[The Judges, OSRIC and HORATIO, take
    their stand. HAMLET and LAERTES as-
    sume the dueling posture.]

HAMLET. Come on, sir.

LAERTES.   Come, my lord.
[They begin to play.]

HAMLET.   One.

LAERTES.   No.

HAMLET.   Judgment!

OSRIC. A hit, a very palpable hit.

LAERTES.   Well; again!

311. **quit . . . exchange**: repay Laertes with a
hit in the third bout. 314. **union**: unusually fine
and perfectly spherical pearl. 317. **kettle**: kettledrum.

KING. Stay, give me drink. — Hamlet, this
  pearl is thine.   324
  [*Drops a pearl into the cup.*]
  Here's to thy health!
  [*Pretends to drink.*]
                          Give him the cup.
  [*The Attendant offers the cup to* HAM-
  LET. *The kettledrums roll, the trumpets
  sound, and the cannons roar within.*]
HAMLET. I'll play this bout first; set it by
  awhile. —
  Come!
  [*They begin the second bout.*]
                  Another hit; what say you?
LAERTES. A touch, a touch, I do confess.
KING. Our son shall win.
QUEEN.   He's fat,* and scant of breath.
  Here, Hamlet, take my napkin, rub thy
  brows.   330
  The queen carouses to thy fortune,
  Hamlet.
HAMLET. Good madam!
KING.   Gertrude, do not drink!
QUEEN. I will, my lord! I pray you, pardon
  me.
  [*Drinks.*]
KING (*aside*). It is the poison'd cup. It is
  too late!
  [*She offers the cup to* HAMLET.]
HAMLET. I dare not drink yet, madam; by
  and by.   335
QUEEN. Come, let me wipe thy face.
LAERTES (*to the* KING). My lord, I'll hit
  him now.
KING (*to Laertes*).   I do not think't.
LAERTES (*aside*). And yet 'tis almost 'gainst
  my conscience.
HAMLET. Come, for the third! Laertes,
  you but dally.   339
  I pray you, pass with your best violence.
  I am afeard you make a wanton* of me.
LAERTES. Say you so? come on.
  [*The third bout is begun.*]
OSRIC. Nothing, neither way.
LAERTES. Have at you now!

329. **fat**: not in good physical condition; soft.
341. **wanton**: child.

[LAERTES *wounds* HAMLET. *In the
  scuffle they exchange weapons.* HAM-
  LET *wounds* LAERTES.]
KING.   Part them! They are incens'd.
HAMLET. Nay, come again!
  [*The* QUEEN *falls.*]
OSRIC.   Look to the queen there, ho!
HORATIO. They bleed on both sides. (*To*
  HAMLET) How is it, my lord?   346
OSRIC. How is it, Laertes?
LAERTES. Why, as a woodcock to mine
  own springe,* Osric;
  I am justly kill'd with mine own treach-
  ery.   349
HAMLET. How does the queen?
KING.   She swounds to see them bleed.
QUEEN. No, no; the drink! the drink! — O
  my dear Hamlet! —
  The drink! the drink! I am poison'd.
  [*Dies.*]
HAMLET. O villainy! Ho, let the door be
  lock'd!
  [HORATIO *leaps to the door and locks
  it.*]
  Treachery! Seek it out!
  [LAERTES *falls.*]
LAERTES. It is here, Hamlet. Hamlet, thou
  art slain.   355
  No medicine in the world can do thee
  good.
  In thee there is not half an hour of life.
  The treacherous instrument is in thy
  hand,
  Unbated and envenom'd. The foul prac-
  tice*   359
  Hath turn'd itself on me. Lo, here I lie,
  Never to rise again. Thy mother's
  poison'd.
  I can no more. The king, the king's to
  blame!
HAMLET. The point envenom'd too? —
  Then, venom, to thy work!
  [*Stabs the* KING.]
ALL. Treason! treason!   365
KING. O, yet defend me, friends! I am but
  hurt.

348. **springe**: snare. 359. **practice**: stratagem.

HAMLET. Here, thou incestuous, murd'rous,
    damnèd Dane!
Drink off this potion!
    [*He forces the* KING *to drink from the
    poisoned cup.*]
                Is thy union* here?
Follow my mother!
    [*The* KING *dies.*]
LAERTES.   He is justly serv'd:
It is a poison temper'd by himself.   370
Exchange forgiveness with me, noble
    Hamlet.
Mine and my father's death come not
    upon thee,
Nor thine on me!
    [*Dies.*]
HAMLET. Heaven make thee free of it! I
    follow thee.
    [*Sinks down.*]
I am dead, Horatio. — Wretched queen,
    adieu! —   375
You that look pale and tremble at this
    chance,
That are but mutes or audience to this act,
Had I but time — as this fell sergeant,
    Death,
Is strict in his arrest — O, I could tell
    you —
But let it be. — Horatio, I am dead; 380
Thou livest. Report me and my cause
    aright
To the unsatisfied.
HORATIO.   Never believe it!
I am more an antique Roman* than a
    Dane.
Here's yet some liquor left.
    [*Lifts the poisoned cup.*]
HAMLET.   As thou'rt a man,
Give me the cup. — Let go! — By
    heaven, I'll have't!   385
O God, Horatio, what a wounded name,
Things standing thus unknown, shall live
    behind me!
If thou didst ever hold me in thy heart,

Absent thee from felicity awhile,
And in this harsh world draw thy breath
    in pain,   390
To tell my story.
    [*March afar off, and shot within.*]
              What warlike noise is this?
OSRIC. Young Fortinbras, with conquest
    come from Poland,
To the ambassadors of England gives
This warlike volley.
HAMLET.   O, I die, Horatio!
The potent poison quite o'ercrows my
    spirit.   395
I cannot live to hear the news from En-
    gland,
But I do prophesy the election lights
On Fortinbras: he has my dying voice.
So tell him — with the occurrents, more
    and less,
Which have solicited* — The rest is
    silence.   400
    [*Dies.*]
HORATIO. Now cracks a noble heart! Good
    night, sweet prince,
And flights of angels sing thee to thy
    rest!
    [*March within.*]
Why does the drum come hither?
    [*Enter* FORTINBRAS *with his army, the
    English Ambassadors, and others.*]
FORTINBRAS. Where is this sight?
HORATIO.   What is it ye would see?
If aught of woe or wonder, cease your
    search.   405
FORTINBRAS. This quarry cries on havoc.*
    O proud Death,
What feast is toward in thine eternal cell
That thou so many princes at a shot
So bloodily hast struck?
FIRST AMBASSADOR.   The sight is dismal;
And our affairs from England come too
    late.   410
The ears are senseless that should give us
    hearing,

---

368. **union:** a pun on (1) pearl and (2) marriage.
383. **Roman:** The Romans considered suicide a
noble act.

400. **solicited:** incited. 406. **This quarry cries
on havoc:** This heap of bodies proclaims general
slaughter.

To tell him his commandment is fulfill'd,
That Rosencrantz and Guildenstern are
   dead.
Where should we have our thanks?
HORATIO.   Not from his* mouth,
Had it the ability of life to thank you. 415
He never gave commandment for their
   death.
But since, so jump upon this bloody ques-
   tion,
You from the Polack wars, and you from
   England,
Are here arriv'd, give order that these
   bodies
High on a stage be placèd to the view; 420
And let me speak to the yet unknowing
   world
How these things came about. So shall
   you hear
Of carnal,* bloody, and unnatural acts,
Of accidental judgments,* casual slaugh-
   ters,*
Of deaths put on by cunning and forc'd
   cause,   425
And, in this upshot, purposes mistook
Fall'n on the inventors' heads.* All this
   can I
Truly deliver.
FORTINBRAS.   Let us haste to hear it,
And call the noblest to the audience.
For me, with sorrow I embrace my for-
   tune.   430
I have some rights of memory* in this
   kingdom,
Which now to claim my vantage doth
   invite me.
HORATIO. Of that I shall have also cause to
   speak,
And from his mouth whose voice will
   draw on more.*
But let this same be presently* per-
   form'd   435

414. **his:** *i.e.,* Claudius'. 423. **carnal:** murderous. 424. **judgments:** retributions. **casual slaugh-
ters:** accidental killings. 427. **inventors' heads:**
i.e., Claudius and Laertes. 431. **rights of memory:**
remembered rights. 434. **draw on more:** carry
more influence. 435. **presently:** at once.

Even while men's minds are wild, lest
   more mischance
On* plots and errors happen.
FORTINBRAS.   Let four captains
Bear Hamlet, like a soldier, to the stage;
For he was likely, had he been put on,*
To have prov'd most royally: and for his
   passage,   440
The soldiers' music and the rites of war
Speak loudly for him.
Take up the bodies. Such a sight as this
Becomes the field, but here shows much
   amiss. —
Go, bid the soldiers shoot.   445
   [*A dead march. Exeunt, bearing off
   the bodies; after which, a peal of
   ordnance is shot off within.*]

437. **On:** on top of. 439. **put on:** advanced to
the throne.

For Discussion

1. After the intensity of Act IV, Act V
opens comically. What is the effect of the
contrast in mood? Two gravediggers, shuffling
on, casually set about their chore. How would
you characterize the gravediggers? What
chore are they performing? What don't they
like about it? Hamlet, returned from his
voyage, engages the two in conversation, but
their banter and the prince's reflections about
death are interrupted. What is distinctive
about the funeral train that claims their attention? How does Hamlet learn the identity of
the person being buried? In the dramatic encounter between Laertes and Hamlet here, the
latter resorts to hyperbole at Scene i, lines 330 ff.
What drives him to that excess of diction?

2. Early in Scene ii we learn how Hamlet
escaped the fate that Claudius had planned for
him. How did he? What attitude toward the
doomed Rosencrantz and Guildenstern does
the prince express? How is that attitude to
be accounted for? Shakespeare's minor characters — porters, gravediggers, and the like —

are often astonishingly vivid. How would you characterize Osric? Is he a type or an individual? For what purpose does he address the prince?

3. Horatio has his doubts about the wisdom of Hamlet's dueling with Laertes. Why? Why does Hamlet accept the challenge? At the outset of the duel he apologizes to Laertes. For what? How does he account for the actions that have necessitated the apology? Notice the grim irony of Laertes' reply, especially at Scene ii, line 286. In the midst of the duel, the Queen mistakenly drinks poison. How does that mischance come about? How does Hamlet become wounded? In the last minutes of his life he learns of the King's treachery. Who tells him of it? Whom does Hamlet name as his successor, to restore order out of the chaos that has come to Elsinore? The final speech of the play, like the opening speech, touches upon identity. According to Fortinbras, what sort of man might Hamlet have become had he survived?

4. The structure of a play — like any structure — comes clear only when the entire work is considered. Traditionally, the climax of a Shakespearean play is said to occur around Act III, Scene iii. In *Macbeth*, that is the scene where Banquo's son escapes; in *Julius Caesar*, it is the scene where Antony manifestly has won the Roman populace to his cause. In Act III, Scene iii, of *Hamlet*, the prince passes up an opportunity to kill Claudius with impunity. Considering what follows in the play, why might that scene reasonably be regarded as the climax? Does Hamlet finally "avenge" his father's murder? Discuss.

The Play as a Whole

1. Ways to approach *Hamlet* are all but numberless, but one pertinent way to consider the play as a whole is through examining it in terms of the themes explored in this anthology. The question of identity is one such theme. Before his father's death, what sort of person was Hamlet? How do you know? How does Claudius regard him in the course of the play?

How does Fortinbras? How does the ghost of his father? How does Hamlet regard himself? Does he see himself clearly? On the basis of his words and actions, what dominant characteristics of the prince can you identify?

2. The question of what is true and what is false figures prominently in *Hamlet*, but perhaps nowhere is the question more crucial than as it applies to the ghost:

> The spirit that I have seen
> May be the devil — and the devil hath power
> T' assume a pleasing shape. . . . (II, ii, 700–702)

Suppose the ghost were not what it represented itself as being. Why is the question of truth important here? What would be the consequences if Hamlet were rashly to carry out its commands? To what extent does the question of truth govern Hamlet's actions?

3. The killer of Hamlet's father must in turn be killed by the son. Does such vengeance constitute justice? Do the crimes of murder and usurpation with which the play begins allow Hamlet any other course in seeking justice? What difficulties does revenge create in redressing wrongs?

4. "Rightly to be great," Hamlet says at one point, "Is not to stir without great argument, / But greatly to find quarrel in a straw / When honor's at the stake" (IV, iv, 53–56). State his definition of greatness in your own words. Can you suggest any problems that the definition might present? Hamlet refers to himself and Claudius as "mighty opposites" (V, ii, 62). What evidences of greatness do you find in the King? In Hamlet?

5. To what extent is Hamlet's will free? "The time is out of joint," he cries. "O cursèd spite / That ever I was born to set it right" (I, v, 189–190). How must the times be set aright? Why is Hamlet the only one who can rectify them? Later, before beginning the duel with Laertes, he tells Horatio, "We defy augury." What does his speech there (V, ii, 259 ff) reveal about his attitude toward fate?

6. Man's ambiguous place in nature is implicit in the frequently quoted speech that Hamlet utters to Rosencrantz and Guildenstern soon after their reunion with him

(II, ii, 332 ff). What two attitudes toward man in the universe are distinguished in that speech? What diction best reveals the two contrasting views? Earlier, in his first soliloquy, Hamlet saw the world as "an unweeded garden / That grows to seed; things rank and gross in nature / Possess it merely" (I, ii, 135–7). What view of the world and man's place in it is expressed in that image?

7. Hamlet's dilemma is in part that of a man enjoined to do good and evil at the same time. What aspects of good do you find in the action that the ghost commands him to perform? The evil aspects of such an act are, of course, all too obvious: Thou shalt not kill. Consider the character of Claudius. Is he unmitigatedly evil? Does he at any time feel remorse for what he has done? Is the evil act of Laertes toward Hamlet that ends the play in any way atoned for?

8. The powerful emotions expressed in this play flash like lightning between extremes of love and hate. Clearly Hamlet loved his father, and clearly he hates his uncle. What is his attitude toward Gertrude? Toward Ophelia? Do Gertrude and her new husband love each other, or do they marry simply for reasons of greed and ambition? Examine their words and behavior with each other to answer the question as accurately as possible. Old Polonius behaves ridiculously at times. How, then, do you account for the love that those who know him bear him? What evidences of that love do you find in the play? The relationship between Hamlet and Horatio is expressed most eloquently at Act III, Scene ii, lines 72 ff. What is that relationship?

For Composition

In Elizabethan times (as now too, for that matter) a jewel was often set against a foil to make it appear to best advantage; the foil would cause it to sparkle more brightly. In drama of the time, a *foil* was a character whose actions by contrast would set off the actions of someone else in parallel circumstances. Hamlet has two foils; his friend Horatio is one, but Laertes is the character who sets his own character off to most advantage.

1. **Comparison and Contrast.** Compare and contrast the characters of Hamlet and Laertes. What about their situations is similar? Is each moved by the claims of vengeance? What do you learn about Hamlet's character by comparing it with Laertes'?

2. **Exposition.** The exposition of a Shakespearean play is accomplished well before the end of the first act; from that point the play moves forward through complications to the climax and denouement. Examine the first act of *Hamlet,* and in a well-organized essay of four or five paragraphs describe the situation in Denmark at the time the play begins. Quote from the act only when quotation will add to the effectiveness of your explanation.

3. **Analysis.** In an essay of four or five paragraphs, analyze the language of Shakespeare as exemplified by any one of the famous soliloquies in *Hamlet.* You will find, of course, that the language is highly metaphorical. What functions do the metaphors serve? What effects do they create? How appropriate are they? How accurate are they?

4. **Argument.** After reconsidering Aristotle's definition of tragedy as presented on pages 388–389, write an essay conveying what might have been his opinion of *Hamlet.* What about the play would Aristotle have found impressive? What might have displeased him about it?

Words and Allusions

ALLUSIONS (page 53). *Hamlet* is the source of many allusions that are used so often they have become clichés. Among these are "Frailty, thy name is woman"; "in my mind's eye"; "sweets to the sweet"; "To be or not to be"; "Ay, there's the rub." Locate at least five other common phrases that allude to *Hamlet,* point out their meaning in the text, and explain how they are used today.

CHANGES IN LANGUAGE (page 188). Many words used by Shakespeare have different meanings today. What meanings did Shakespeare intend by the following words: *carefully* (I, i, 6), *admiration* (I, ii, 192), *humor* (II, ii, 12), *conceit* (II, ii, 652), *habit* (III, iv, 134), *quick* (V, i, 161), *fancy* (V, i, 234), *fond* (V, ii, 226)?

The Character of Hamlet

Every great actor aspires to play Hamlet, that character whose range of emotions is enormous, whose language is unfailingly marvelous, and whose presence onstage through a long dramatic evening is almost continuous. The character of Hamlet is indeed attractive, but it is also complex, and to observers of the play it has proved extremely puzzling. Is this simply the story of a man who cannot make up his mind? Why does he hesitate so long in pursuing vengeance?

One famous explanation for Hamlet's behavior was given by the German writer Goethe at the very end of the eighteenth century. The key to the prince's behavior Goethe found in his utterance at lines 189–190 of Act I, Scene v:

> The time is out of joint. O cursèd spite
> That ever I was born to set it right!

For Hamlet, Goethe says, is "polished by nature, courteous from the heart," and destined "to be the model of youth and the delight of the world." To such a nature the command to commit murder is insupportable; Shakespeare, Goethe felt, "sought to depict a great deed laid upon a soul unequal to the performance of it." The argument he clarifies by means of a famous analogy: "Here is an oak tree planted in a costly vase, which should have received into its bosom only lovely flowers; the roots spread out, the vase is shivered to pieces." And Hamlet's seemingly inexplicable behavior — part dilatory, part mad — becomes at last comprehensible.

Others, having read and considered *Hamlet* carefully, have come to conclusions about the prince's character not incompatible with Goethe's. One such evaluation was that of William Hazlitt, the English essayist, who wrote in 1817 that Hamlet's "is not a character marked by strength of passion or will, but by refinement of thought and feeling. . . . He is the prince of philosophical speculators. . . . His ruling passion is to think, not to act."

This way of accounting for the prince's tardiness as an avenger is related to but somewhat different from that of Hazlitt's contemporary — and perhaps the greatest of all the critics of Shakespeare — Samuel Taylor Coleridge. In Coleridge's view, Hamlet is essentially an intellectual; accordingly, "his thoughts and the images of his fancy are far more vivid than his actual perceptions. . . . Hence we see a great, an almost enormous, intellectual activity, and a proportionate aversion to real action consequent upon it. . . . This character Shakespeare places in circumstances under which it is obliged to act on the spur of the moment; Hamlet is brave and careless of death; but he vacillates from sensibility, and procrastinates from thought, and loses the power of action in the energy of resolve."

As penetrating as Coleridge's analysis is, it has by no means been universally accepted. The influential Victorian critic A. C. Bradley wittily reminds us that Hamlet "must have been quick and impetuous in action; for it is downright impossible that the man we see rushing after the Ghost, killing Polonius, dealing with the King's commission on the ship, boarding the pirate, leaping into the grave, executing his final vengeance, could *ever* have been shrinking or slow in an emergency. Imagine Coleridge doing any of these things!"

According to Bradley's detailed interpretation that follows that remark, Hamlet's behavior is largely attributable to a melancholy temperament, not to any reluctance to act. Melancholy in the Elizabethan sense — a kind of congenital condition, in this case aggravated by his mother's overhasty remarriage, the injunction to avenge his father's murder, and a sense of Ophelia's fickleness in declining to see him further. And the great twentieth-century critic George Lyman Kittredge agrees with Bradley's view of Hamlet as active as well as contemplative; only he goes on to remind us that until the scene of the play within a play, the prince can not be absolutely certain of the King's guilt, and after that scene he has only one opportunity to kill Claudius, at prayer. From then on, from immediately after Polonius' stabbing until the end of the play, the suspicious king keeps his antagonist under surveillance.

Yet astute as it is, Kittredge's is hardly the final word on Hamlet's character, either. Ernest Jones, for example, has examined the prince's behavior in the light of Freud's teachings — psychoanalyzed him, that is — and found that the "cause of Hamlet's vacillation lies in some special feature of the task which renders it peculiarly difficult or repugnant to him. . . . Hamlet at heart does not want to carry out the task." Why he does not, according to this explanation, has to do with subconscious rivalries with his father that date from earliest childhood — and with the guilt those rivalries have engendered.

Other penetrating interpretations have been put forward; so that the question naturally arises: Which of these various analyses is closest to the truth? As to that, each new generation of readers must decide for itself. To quote T. S. Eliot, writing in one of his essays on Shakespeare: "Whether Truth ultimately prevails is doubtful and has never been proved; but it is certain that nothing is more effective in driving out error than a new error." In other words, each of these interpretations may contain some truth and some misconception, but the value of them all is in part to remind us that any single one is inadequate to explain a character whom time has proved to be as complex as life itself.

1. What evidence do you find in the play to support the interpretations given in this essay? Which interpretation do you find most convincing?

2. What is your interpretation of Hamlet's behavior?

In Summary

1. In a well-known nineteenth-century essay, "On Going a Journey," William Hazlitt writes, "Oh! it is great to shake off the trammels of the world of public opinion — to lose our importunate, tormenting, everlasting personal identity and become the creature of the moment, clear of all ties. . . . " What does the comment mean? What attitudes toward one's identity does it suggest? In the selections you have read, which characters seem possessed of identities that are "importunate" and "tormenting"? Do the identities of any seem settled and confidently serene?

2. The question of identity is elusive; for instance, it changes as one grows older. What other aspects of a man's life, background, and surroundings affect his identity? Why does the quest for identity matter? Illustrate your answers by referring to selections you have read in this section.

3. The question of identity figures prominently in earlier sections of the anthology. In Mann's "Mario and the Magician" (page 530), for instance, understanding the identity of Cipolla is essential to understanding the story as a whole. What is ambiguous about his identity? In "A Rose for Emily" (page 630), Miss Emily Grierson's true identity is hidden within the dim mansion whose doors are closed to all her neighbors. But to them, what does her identity during her lifetime *appear* to be? Comment on the question of identity as it figures in at least two other selections in earlier sections of the anthology.

4. Distinguish between parallelism and antithesis, giving an example of each. What does the term *autobiography* denote? Verisimilitude refers to the illusion of factual truthfulness conveyed in a work of imagination. Mention specific ways in which verisimilitude may be achieved. What is a dactyl? How does it differ from an anapest? An iamb? A trochee?

5. **Creative Writing.** Tone, the attitude a speaker takes toward his subject, is conveyed in part by the details selected to convey that subject, in part by the diction chosen to express those details. Notice how diction and detail convey tone in the following passage from "Paul's Case" (page 643):

> The nearer he approached the house, the more absolutely unequal Paul felt to the sight of it all; his ugly sleeping chamber; the cold bath-room with the grimy zinc tub, the cracked mirror, the dripping spiggots; his father, at the top of the stairs, his hairy legs sticking out from his nightshirt, his feet thrust into carpet slippers.

Compare:

> The nearer she approached the house, the more the girl's heart began to flutter, until at last it soared with joy at the thought of being home: her own pink, cozy bedroom, the bathroom full of light, the gleaming big tub, the sparkling mirror, the silver faucets; her father, at the top of the stairs, beaming down at her, arms outstretched in greeting and welcome. . . .

Choose a single scene and describe it twice, allowing two different tones to emerge solely by means of contrasting details and diction. You may include people in the scene, use dialogue, and record action. Make the two treatments of approximately the same length — perhaps a page or two apiece — and revise to convey the tone effectively without resorting to any direct statement of attitude.

Reader's Choice

James Baldwin, *Go Tell It on the Mountain*.

The son of an evangelist preacher in Harlem rebels against the faith of his father and seeks to find his own identity in a world of contradictions.

Charles Dickens, *Great Expectations*.

A young man raised in humble circumstances receives an inheritance and, for a while, becomes confused about his identity.

Ralph Ellison, *Invisible Man*.

A young black man loses his trust in men, both black and white, who prefer to treat him as a symbol instead of as an individual human being.

William Faulkner, *Light in August*.

An angry man who looks white but senses his black ancestry rebels against a society that classifies men by race and origin.

Henry Fielding, *Tom Jones*.

In a long story filled with adventures and memorable characters, a foundling eventually discovers his true identity.

Bessie Head, *When Rain Clouds Gather*.

A young South African refugee seeking a better life finds purpose, love, poverty, suffering, and finally hope in this novel from Africa.

Homer, *The Odyssey*.

A hero of the Trojan War undergoes ten years of hardship and adventure before he is able to reclaim his proper role in his own kingdom.

James Joyce, *Portrait of the Artist as a Young Man*.

In this semi-autobiographical account, a young Dubliner asserts his identity as he moves from childhood, through adolescence, toward manhood.

Franz Kafka, *The Metamorphosis*.

Awakening one morning to find himself transformed into a huge insect, Gregor Samsa poses a problem of identity to himself and his horrified family.

Thomas Mann, *Death in Venice*.

An honored German author whose life has been governed by discipline and hard work discovers another self during a summer holiday.

Isaac Bashevis Singer, *The Slave*.

A Jewish peasant in seventeenth century Poland, seized in a Cossack raid and enslaved by a kindly but insensitive Christian master, strives to retain his faith and his moral values.

Thomas Wolfe, *Look Homeward, Angel*.

Eugene Gant, son of a hard-drinking father and an acquisitive mother, learns about life and himself in a small southern town.

About the Artists

Albright, Ivan (1897–   ). It was while working in an old wooden house in a shabby section of Chicago that the American painter Ivan Albright developed a style of his own. Albright finds his inspiration in dust-covered junk, symbolizing for him the melancholy of vanished life. His comment upon "That Which I Should Have Done I Did Not Do" (page 623), the painting of the decaying door hung with a funeral wreath, is "I just can't seem to paint nice things." Albright, now residing in Vermont, has been the recipient of coveted prizes, among them the J. Henry Schiedt Memorial Prize of 1956.

Blume, Peter (1906–   ). Since the age of eighteen, the Russian-born American artist Peter Blume has earned his living from his paintings. He came to America as a boy and first lived with twenty to thirty other refugees in his grandmother's apartment. Paying for his art education by designing jewelry, Blume gained early fame with his *South of Scranton*, receiving for this painting the Carnegie International Award in 1934. The social content of Blume's work is expressed symbolically in rich and elaborate allegory. He currently lives in Connecticut. (See page 568.)

Botticelli, Sandro (1445–1510). Living in Florence, Italy, at the time of the Medicis, Botticelli (pronounced bot′ə·chel′ē) began work as an apprentice to a goldsmith, then studied under the famous painter Fra Filippo Lippi. He won such renown for his *Adoration of the Magi* that Pope Sixtus IV engaged him to fresco the walls of the Sistine Chapel in the Vatican. A practical joker, Botticelli is said to have attached red paper hats, the headgear of the councillors of Florence, upon the angels surrounding a Madonna that one of his students had painted. Though thinking it strange, the purchaser bought the painting anyway. Botticelli's reputation rests upon his many decorative friezes in Italy's chapels and convents. (See page 616.)

Bronzino, Agnolo (1503–1575). Agnolo Allori, known as Bronzino (pronounced brōn·zē′nō), was an Italian poet and painter. As court portrait artist for Cosimo I of the Medici family, he painted three portraits of Cosimo's wife, Eleanora of Toledo (page 619). Other subjects of his portraits were Dante, Petrarch, Boccaccio, and various rulers of Europe. His style was in keeping with demands for elegance from an aristocratic clientele.

Bruegel, Pieter the Elder (1525/30?–1569). A Flemish peasant's son, Pieter Bruegel (pronounced brü′gəl; brė′gəl) the Elder popularized lay subjects at a time when painting was primarily religious art. Although emphasizing landscape and depicting folk customs and daily life of the peasantry, he found ready patronage among the intellectuals and court aristocrats of Europe. One often finds touches of humor in his works. His two sons, Pieter the Younger and Jan, were also painters. (See page 390.)

César (Baldaccini) (1921–   ). The sculptor who uses the name César (pronounced sā'zär') was born in Marseilles, France, of Italian parentage. He studied in Marseilles and later also in Paris, his present home. One of the creators of "pop art," César has exhibited his work in various countries, including the United States, Belgium, Italy, and Brazil. His crushed, compressed automobiles (page 167) belong to the New Realist School of Art and have been termed symbols of "acts of defiance."

Church, Frederic Edwin (1826–1900). Church began his career as a member of "The Hudson River School" of landscape painting, which flourished in the United States in the middle of the nineteenth century. These popular painters used idyllic Hudson River scenery, imported Italian ruins, and misty climatic effects. Seeking more distant subjects, Church roamed the world and came home to paint vast canvases of marvels of nature — Niagara Falls, the Andes, tropical forests, volcanoes in eruption, and icebergs. A tremendously popular artist, Church sold his paintings for extravagant prices. He was admired particularly for his skill in painting light and the phenomena of rainbow, mist, and sunset. (See page 452.)

Courbet, Gustave (1819–1877). Born in France near the Swiss border, Courbet (pronounced kür'bā') became a rebel both in art and politics. Influenced by the poet Baudelaire to paint "the heroism of modern life," Courbet attempted to paint objects more realistically than his contemporaries, and in so doing he attracted the wrath of the established art world of his day. His remarks about painting and politics were even more provocative, so that he often had difficulty in having his pictures exhibited. When the people of Paris rose against the French government in 1871, following the humiliating defeat of France in the Franco-Prussian War, Courbet became a popular hero for a few months. But when the government restored order, he was exiled to Switzerland, where he died six years later. (See page 693.)

Daumier, Honoré (1808–1879). Called "the Michelangelo of caricature," Daumier (pronounced dō'myā') divided his talents between social reform and higher spheres of art. Satirizing in comic journals the incompetence and corruption of France's public figures, he dared to caricature the king himself, which led to a brief imprisonment. He is known today for his fine paintings, among which his portrayals of Jesus and "Don Quixote and Sancho" (page 297) are outstanding, and also for his series of satirical lithographs. Unrecognized by his native France until a year before his death, Daumier, totally blind, could not see his own exhibition of art that gained him fame.

Da Verona, Cecchino (active 1447–1480). Da Verona (pronounced dä və·rō′nə) derived his name from his birthplace, Verona, a city in northern Italy on the Adige River. He is known chiefly for having painted *Virgin and Child, between Saints Vigilius and Sisinius,* which is on display in the cathedral at Tronto, a nearby city also on the Adige River. His art is related to the International Gothic style, a style characterized by a lack of technical perspective and by elongated, graceful figures, as well as small, isolated objects having no coherence. These characteristics are noticeable in *The Judgment of Paris* (page 397).

David, Jacques Louis (1748–1825). The French Revolution and the current fashion for imitating the Ancients were the two primary influences on the French painter David (pronounced dä·vēd′). This politically active artist was a member of the Revolutionary Convention that in 1793 voted for the French king's death. That membership led to the artist's exile and subsequent death in Belgium. *The Death of Socrates* (page 294) is one of his many works based on classical subjects, as was *The Oath of the Horatii,* which greatly aroused revolutionary feelings in France.

De Chirico, Giorgio (1888–   ). Born in Greece of Italian parentage, De Chirico (pronounced dā kē′rē·kō) now lives in Paris, where he enjoys a high reputation as an innovator and artist in various genres. In 1915 he formed the "Scuola Metafisica," which gave rise to Surrealism, but later he repudiated the technique of the school he had founded. *The Mystery and Melancholy of a Street* (page 39) exemplifies his youthful "romantic-sinister" interest. He later declared that he himself could not explain the incongruities in this picture. At the beginning of World War I when he was conscripted for military service, his contemporary Guillaume Apollinaire declared him to be "the most astonishing painter of the time."

Delacroix, Ferdinand Victor Eugène (1798–1863). The interests of Delacroix (pronounced də lä′krwä′) extended beyond his native France. His love of good literature inspired paintings such as *Hamlet and Horatio in the Graveyard* (page 696) and many others from the plays of Shakespeare. Historical events, especially the Greek resistance against Turkish invasions and the Crusader conquests, provided many other of his subjects. Later a visit to Africa furnished him with Near East themes, which were then popular. Delacroix is admired especially for his color harmonies.

Dürer, Albrecht (1471–1528). The greatest printmaker of his time, superb watercolor artist, refiner of the woodcut, and a proponent, through art, of Christian humanism — these are the characteristics of Albrecht Dürer (pronounced dü′rėr), of Nuremberg, then a free imperial city. Dürer was far ahead of his time; he set a standard for the art of the woodcut that transformed the technique all over Europe. Further, he devoted many years to art theory and invented a device that anticipated the principle of the photographic camera. There is a spiritual conviction throughout his art, won from his devotion to Martin Luther, Erasmus, and other humanists of the day, that shows in the austerity of style and in the subject matter of his religious works. (See page 169.)

Friedrich, Caspar David (1774–1840). A German landscape painter and engraver, Friedrich (pronounced frē′drik) in his time won the acclaim of artists in Europe, England, and America. He worked in Dresden where, at the age of fifty, he became professor of art at the city's university. His compelling imagination produced the famous *Wreck of the Hope,* depicting the end of an ill-fated expedition in the Arctic Ocean. Other notable works are *Two Men Contemplating the Moon* and *Rest in a Hayfield.* (See page 450.)

Gropper, William (1897–   ). Born in New York, Gropper (pronounced grop′ĕr) began his career as artist and illustrator for the *New York Tribune.* During the great depression of the 1930's, the Federal Art Project, in which artists were commissioned to paint murals in public buildings, provided him the opportunity to reveal his talent to the nation. Gropper's contributions now appear in New York, Detroit, and Washington, D.C. Recently he has written and illustrated books, including *American Folklore* and *The Little Tailor.* He lives in Croton-on-Hudson, New York. (See page 44.)

Gros, Antoine-Jean (1771–1835). An artist of the Napoleonic era, Gros (pronounced grō) learned drawing from his father, a French miniature-painter. Because Napoleon liked Gros's painting of his victory at Arcole in Northern Italy, he commissioned Gros to follow the army and record his career. The story goes that Napoleon, too impatient to pose, was made to sit still by his wife, who held him firmly in her lap. The defeat and exile of Napoleon cost Gros his reputation. Esteemed only for the work of his youthful days, he was found at the age of sixty-four drowned in the Seine. *The Battle of Eylau* (page 290) recalls the bloody engagement of 1807 in Germany between Napoleon's army and the combined forces of Russians and Prussians. The two sides lost respectively fifteen thousand and eighteen thousand men, a costly victory for the French.

Lorenzetti, Ambrogio (active 1319–1348). Of the two gifted Lorenzetti (pronounced lō′rən·zet′ē) brothers, Ambrogio was the younger and more distinguished artist. He was commissioned to paint numerous frescoes in church interiors, his most famous fresco being the *Allegory of Good Government* (page 170) in Siena, Italy, his birthplace. One of four huge panels, it combines Aristotle's political philosophy with Christian theology. Both brothers, Ambrogio and Pietro, are believed to have succumbed to the plague that beset Siena in 1348.

Masaccio (1401–1428). In his brief twenty-seven years, the Italian painter Tomaso Guidi — nicknamed Masaccio (pronounced mä·zät′chō), meaning *the careless one* — launched many innovations in the art of painting. Masaccio was born near Florence, the son of a notary. Three-dimensional space, laws of perspective, and accurate anatomical proportions received new attention under his influence. Unfortunately much of Masaccio's work is either destroyed or in poor condition. In existence are six famous frescoes on biblical subjects, including the *Expulsion from Paradise* (page 565), to be seen in a Florentine chapel. He did not complete the decoration. In 1428 he left for Rome and was reported dead soon afterwards.

Munch, Edvard (1863–1944). Norway's greatest artist, Munch (pronounced müngk) depicted feelings inspired by a troubled mind rather than impressions from external reality. From a family beset with death, anguish, and other griefs, Munch in his art reflects man's vulnerability to misfortune. *The Scream* (page 691) is typical of his work, an image of the terrifying unreasoned fear felt in a nightmare. It is reminiscent of his own description of his art — "I hear the scream in nature." His work includes landscapes, as well as frescoes in the Oslo University Festival Hall.

Picasso, Pablo (1881–1973). Inventive, controversial, prolific, the Spanish-born Picasso (pronounced pē·kä′sō) settled permanently in France in 1904. With George Braque he created cubism, a drastic break with conventional painting. He also used other styles, often simultaneously, to express his particular "truth," his own unique reactions to the external world. Besides his numerous paintings, Picasso produced sculpture, graphics, ceramics, even ballet costumes and scenery.

Raphael (1483–1520). Recognized as one of the greatest artists of all time, Raphael (pronounced raf′ā·el) (Raffaello Santi or Sanzio) did most of his work in Rome. When Michelangelo began painting the Sistine ceiling in the Vatican, Pope Julius invited Raphael from Florence to decorate a series of rooms in the Vatican Palace. *The School of Athens* (page 294) appears on the walls of what is believed to have been the Pope's library. The work is considered one of Raphael's finest, a perfect rendition of the classical spirit of the High Renaissance.

Rouault, Georges (1871–1958). The remarkably versatile Rouault (pronounced rü·ō′) mastered graphic arts, stained-glass design, and ceramics, but it is chiefly for his paintings that he is known. A native of France, in his youth he was in apprenticeship to a stained-glass maker, an experience which probably accounts for his luminous colors within a structure of black lines. Recently acclaimed are his religious paintings, reflecting the past — the cathedral art of the Middle Ages. Of his religious painting one critic has remarked: "From his earliest days, he painted the sacred subjects, until the ones he returned to again and again grew in force and monumentality beyond anything achieved in religious art for many years before him." (See page 567.)

Rousseau, Henri (1844–1910). The French artist Rousseau (pronounced rü′sō′), called "Le Douanier" from his profession of customs collector, began painting after retirement. He was a self-taught amateur whose "primitive" folk painting attracted the acclaim of Picasso and other artists. The naïveté and freshness that characterize his paintings have maintained popularity with painters today. (See page 446.)

Steen, Jan (1626–1679). Steen (pronounced stān), a master painter of Dutch subjects, supplemented his earnings by brewing and keeping a tavern, which perhaps explains the dramatic character of his scenes including that of *The World Upside Down* (page 394). His productions often tell stories that range from the stately actions of grave and wealthy citizens to tavern brawls. A good-humored observer of Dutch daily life, he is famous particularly for his paintings of children.

Turner, Joseph M. W. (1775–1851). Turner as a boy is said to have displayed his drawings in his father's store next to the wigs as marketable merchandise. He was a prolific artist, the creator of 282 paintings and over 19,000 drawings. Most famous are his landscapes (see page 448), which he often rearranged from nature to suit himself — moving mountains and adding waterfalls — and his sea pieces, which include the familiar *The Slave Ship* and *The Fighting Temeraire,* the latter commemorating a famous battleship. Turner left a huge fortune for, as he said, "the maintenance and support of male decayed artists, being born in England . . . and of lawful issue."

Van Steenwijck, Harmen (1612–c.1656). Little is known about the Dutch painter Van Steenwijck (pronounced vän stān′vīk), aside from his dates and his membership in the Guild of St. Luke at Delft, a city in southern Holland made famous for its manufacture of pottery. It is known that he visited the East Indies but was back home by 1655. The surname Steenwijck belongs to many of Holland's artists, Harmen's brother Peter among them. The creator of *Vanitas* (page 40) found still life his most congenial medium.

Vasarely, Victor (1908–   ). Born and educated in Hungary, Vasarely (pronounced vä·sär′lē) makes his home in Paris, where he first worked as a graphic designer and then cofounded an art gallery. An experimentalist in abstractions and in geometrical designs of linear and crisscross network, he has found artistic sources in pure physics and mathematics. (See page 393.) Vasarely's work encompasses a wide range, including the design of garden murals, and has won international recognition. One of his most recent awards was the First Prize at the Sao Biennale in 1965.

Watteau, Antoine (1684–1721). Today the paintings of Watteau (pronounced vä′tō′; wo·tō′) can be found in the finest galleries of the world. The life of this Flemish artist, however, was one of humble heritage, poverty, and illness, culminating in death from tuberculosis at the age of thirty-seven. Very briefly and late in life he enjoyed luxury provided by a financier-patron whose home he shared, which explains his canvases of a fashionable Parisian court. *A Pilgrimage to Cythera* (page 620) brought Watteau membership in the French Academy in 1712. A sense of the fleeting nature of happiness pervades this typical work and suggests the ephemeral quality of Watteau's life itself.

Glossary of Literary Terms

Allegory. A form of narrative, either prose or verse, in which the characters and often the setting represent moral qualities, general concepts, or other abstractions. In European literature, the medieval play *Everyman*, Edmund Spenser's poem *The Faerie Queene*, and John Bunyan's prose work *The Pilgrim's Progress* are all celebrated allegories. "Young Goodman Brown" (page 26) makes use of certain allegorical traits, both of character and of setting (the forest, for example, is both a literal and a moral wilderness). See PARABLE.

Alliteration. Repetition of consonants (generally initial consonants) in words that are close together. The following lines alliterate *s* and *h*:

> 'Tis evening on the moorland free,
>   The *s*tarlit wave is *s*till:
> *H*ome is the *s*ailor from the *s*ea,
>   The *h*unter from the *h*ill.
>   (Housman, "R. L. S.")

Allusion. Reference to a person or place with which the reader is presumed to be familiar:

> A little month! or ere those shoes were old
> With which she follow'd my poor father's body
> Like *Niobe*, all tears. . . .
>   (Shakespeare, *Hamlet*)

In this instance, the allusion, made to describe the mourning Gertrude, is to the legendary Niobe, emblem of grief, whose family the gods caused to be killed one by one as punishment for her arrogance.

Anapest. See METER.

Antithesis. A rhetorical device in which strongly contrasting meanings are set beside each other in phrases, sentences, or lines of verse that balance or are grammatically parallel. Prosperity and adversity are antithetical, and the following parallel statements about them exemplify antithesis:

> Prosperity is not without many fears and distastes; and adversity is not without comforts and hopes.
>   (Bacon, "Of Adversity")

Apostrophe. A rhetorical device in which the writer directly addresses an absent person, a place, or an abstraction.

> Hail to thee, blithe spirit!
> Bird thou never wert. . . .
> (Shelley, "To a Skylark")

> One lesson, Nature, let me learn of thee.
>   (Arnold, "Quiet Work")

Aside. A dramatic convention in which two people are understood to speak to each other without being heard by anyone else on stage, or in which one person in response to another's comment speaks briefly aloud without being heard by those around him. Claudius' speech at III, i, 49–54 of *Hamlet* (page 760) is an example.

Assonance. Repetition of vowel sounds in words close together. The following example repeats in the last two words of the line the vowel sound contained in "all":

> And *a*ll the summer through the w*a*ter s*au*nter.
>   (Auden, "Look, Stranger")

Auditory imagery. See IMAGERY.

Autobiography. See BIOGRAPHY.

Ballad. A brief poem that tells a story. Originally ballads were passed on from generation to generation by word of mouth, without being written down. Consequently, authors of most early ballads are not known; and many ballads, when they were finally transcribed, appeared in several versions. Because unlettered people generally composed them, sang them, and passed them on, most ballads use simple language and loose rhyme. Frequent repetition of words and lines makes them easy to learn and remember. Often the stories they tell are dramatic and violent — tales of murder or shipwreck or hopeless love or betrayal. Details of the story are left vague, so that an air of mystery combines with UNDERSTATEMENT to produce powerful feeling. "Edward" (page 599) is an example of a legitimate folk ballad, dating from the Middle Ages.

Later authors have employed techniques of the ballad on occasion, in order to invest their own work with ballad characteristics of universality, timelessness, and sincerity. What results is called a LITERARY BALLAD, to distinguish it from the anonymous folk ballad; García Lorca's poem on page 597 in many respects exemplifies the literary ballad.

Biography. Nonfiction that records the life of an individual. When written by the individual himself, the work is called AUTOBIOGRAPHY. Plato's *Apology* (page 245) is to some extent biographical (of Socrates' life), and James Baldwin's *Notes of a Native Son* (page 662) is to some extent autobiographical.

Blank verse. An unrhymed verse form in iambic meter, containing five metrical feet in each line:

> Of man's first disobedience, and the fruit
> Of that forbidden tree whose mortal taste
> Brought death into the World, and all our woe
> With loss of Eden, till one greater Man
> Restore us, and regain the blissful seat,
> Sing, Heavenly Muse. . . .
> (Milton, *Paradise Lost*)

Notice that each complete line has five

stressed syllables alternating with five unstressed syllables. The lines do not rhyme.

Caesura. A pause that falls naturally within a line of verse. In scansion, the caesura is designated by two diagonal lines:

> Once in a life, they tell us, // and once only,
> So great a thing as a great love may come —
> To crown us, // or to mark us with a scar
> No craft or custom shall obliterate.
> (Robinson, "Roman Bartholow")

Careful manipulation of the caesura helps a poet avoid monotomy of sound among verses of the same meter and line length.

Climax. The high point in the action of a play, long narrative poem, or story, marking the decisive moment of the PLOT. Before the climax, the action may develop in many ways; at the climax, alternatives are removed, and the narrative proceeds toward a single ending. The climax of "The Open Boat" occurs when the four men tumble from the boat into the sea (page 471); after that point there is no turning back, and given the characters at that moment, there are no alternatives different from the one that results. The climax of *Oedipus the King* occurs when the shepherd confesses to Oedipus that the infant he was supposed to have killed he gave to a man to take to a far country (page 377). Before then, alternatives are possible — most obviously, the king might break off the interrogation before his own identity is established beyond question. After that moment, however, the play must in broad terms resolve itself as in fact it does.

Complication. See STRUCTURE.

Connotation. Associated meanings that cluster around the literal meaning of a word. Every word has a literal, dictionary meaning, or DENOTATION. Scientific prose aims at precision by using only the denotations of words.

Most words, though, have connotations as well. In the following passage, connotations of the italicized words contribute to the impression of the speed and force of an express train:

> It is now she begins to *sing* — at first quite low
> Then *loud*, and at last with a *jazzy madness* —
> The sound of her *whistle screaming* at curves.
> (Spender, "The Express")

Dactyl. See METER.

Denotation. See CONNOTATION.

Denouement. See STRUCTURE.

Diction. See STYLE.

Dramatic monologue. See MONOLOGUE.

Dramatic poetry. See LYRIC.

Elegy. A meditative poem lamenting the death of a specific person. Milton's *Lycidas* and Shelley's *Adonais* (memoralizing the death of John Keats) are classic examples.

Epic. A long poem on a noble subject, narrated in an elevated style, and generally celebrating the feats of a hero representative of a race or nation. Traditionally, epics make use of such devices as invocations to the muses, APOSTROPHES, and extended formal similes, often called HOMERIC SIMILES. The Greek *Iliad* and the Anglo-Saxon *Beowulf* are legitimate epics, fashioned from legends of an heroic age; Milton's *Paradise Lost* (page 504) is a literary epic. The distinction is similar to that between folk BALLADS and LITERARY BALLADS.

Exposition. See STRUCTURE.

Fable. A short tale that illustrates some useful truth; often the characters of a fable are animals or even inanimate objects. See PARABLE.

Falling action. See STRUCTURE.

Figurative language. The opposite of literal language. Figurative language, which occurs frequently in literature, takes many forms, but it always calls on the reader to use his imagination to complete the author's meaning. To understand the figure "He's a ball of fire," we do not concentrate on the literal meaning of "ball of fire." Instead, we think of the figurative meanings — what the phrase connotes: fast motion, a consuming energy, an ability to transform things. Metaphors, similes, personifications, apostrophes, symbols, and hyperboles are some of the kinds of figurative language.

Foil. In Elizabethan drama, a less important character placed in a situation parallel to a more important one, in order that the latter may stand out in clearer relief through comparison and contrast. In *Hamlet* (page 726), the dead king and father, as Hamlet recalls him, may be regarded as the foil of Claudius, and in various ways Laertes, Horatio, and Fortinbras may all be seen as foils of Hamlet himself.

Foot. See METER.

Foreshadowing. Anticipation of what is to occur later in a narrative. As a structural device, foreshadowing adds to the coherence of a play or story. For example, the appearance of the blind Teiresias at the beginning of *Oedipus the King* (page 349) foreshadows Oedipus' own appearance blind at the end, and the second entrance, recalling the first, strengthens the structure of the play.

Form. See STYLE.

Free verse. Verse with an irregular rhythm. The meaning and emotion of the poem create a rise and fall of sound not fixed by any metrical pattern. Rhyme appears seldom in free verse, but other poetic devices (alliteration, parallelism, etc.) are often used. In addition to numerous other examples, the poems in this anthology by Yevtushenko (page 226), Kizer (page 427), and Jeffers (page 529) are in free verse.

Hexameter. See METER.

Homeric simile. See EPIC.

Hyperbole. A statement greatly exaggerated for purposes of emphasis or humor. "She was all ears" is hyperbole, as is "eyes as big as saucers." Blake, like many poets before and since, has made effective use of hyperbole:

> To see a world in a grain of sand
> And a heaven in a wild flower,
> Hold infinity in the palm of your hand
> And eternity in an hour. . . .
> (Blake, "Auguries of Innocence")

Iamb. See METER.

Imagery. Word pictures. Often the term is used to signify nothing more than literal descriptive passages in poetry. Keats's "The Eve of St. Agnes" is filled with images in that sense:

> St. Agnes' Eve — Ah, bitter chill it was!
> The owl, for all his feathers, was a-cold;
> The hare limped trembling through the
>   frozen grass,
> And silent was the flock in woolly
>   fold. . . .

The appeal of the image need not be limited to the visual sense. The following lines appeal notably to the sense of taste:

> Now no joy but lacks salt
> That is not dashed with pain
> And weariness and fault;
> I crave the stain
> Of tears, the aftermark
> Of almost too much love,
> The sweet of bitter bark
> And burning clove.
> (Frost, "To Earthward")

Imagery that appeals to the sense of hearing ("a knock on the door") is called AUDITORY; if it appeals to the sense of touch ("a raw throat"), it is called TACTILE; if it appeals to the sense of sight ("a tree in sunlight"), it is called VISUAL; if to the sense of smell ("ammonia in a bucket of water"), OLFACTORY; and if it creates in the mind a picture of movement — running, crouching, leaping — it is referred to as KINETIC imagery.

In addition, imagery may refer to figurative language, especially to metaphors and similes. The following image involves figurative as well as literal meanings:

> Cathedrals,
> Luxury liners laden with souls,
> Holding to the east their hulls of stone.
> (Auden, "On This Island")

The mind's eye sees a cathedral, but a cathedral viewed in a new light — as a beautiful ship bearing its cargo of souls eastward toward the Holy Land.

Irony. The effect of implying a meaning quite different from the apparent or surface meaning. VERBAL IRONY involves single words or phrases; an example occurs in the title of Thurber's story "The Greatest Man in the World" (page 219), where *greatest* suggests qualities quite different from those that "Pal" Smurch will be seen to exemplify. Verbal irony may be distinguished from IRONY OF SITUATION; an example of the latter occurs in "A Simple Heart" (page 266), where Félicité's humble situation in life leads ironically to the kind of culminating vision that would seem fittingly to conclude a life of the most glorious consequence — that of some heroine like Joan of Arc, granted at last a dazzling glimpse of the Holy Ghost. UNDERSTATEMENT is a form of irony. In "The Open Boat," it occurred to the correspondent just before leaping into the sea "that if he should drown it would be a shame" (page 470); to call such a disaster a "shame" is understatement. Similarly, PARADOX, a statement apparently false that proves to be true on examination, is another form of irony. In "Friendship," Emerson writes,

"Thou art to me a delicious torment," and the remark seems paradoxical: a friend should not be a torment — and yet in a sense (we realize on reflection and understand in the context of the essay) he should.

Irony of situation. See IRONY.

Kinetic imagery. See IMAGERY.

Literary ballad. See BALLAD.

Lyric. One of the three types of poetry. DRAMATIC POETRY appears in verse plays, such as *Hamlet* (page 726). NARRATIVE POETRY, such as *Paradise Lost* (page 504), tells a story. Lyric poetry, the most common type, includes all other verse forms (sonnet, ode, etc.). Lyrics were originally sung to the accompaniment of a lyre, from which the term is derived. Often lyrics are intensely personal; often they are brief and charged with emotion; and the effect they achieve is usually unified. To be sure, boundaries among the three types of poetry sometimes dissolve: a BALLAD, for example, narrates a story but at the same time seems lyrical, particularly since many ballads were first written to music. And the dialogue in which a ballad like "Edward" (page 599) is cast makes it seem dramatic as well.

Metaphor. An implied comparison between two dissimilar objects. Metaphors abound in everyday speech: "He's an old buzzard." "She has a sunny disposition." In each case, the meaning intended is not the literal one. Metaphors occur in the following lines:

A pity beyond all telling
Is hid in the heart of love.
(Yeats, "The
Pity of Love")

Love is compared to something with a vital center, or heart, and pity is compared to something that can be hidden.
A figure of speech that uses "like" or "as" to state a comparison is called a SIMILE:

Life, like a dome of many-colored glass,

Stains the white radiance of Eternity.
(Shelley, *Adonais*)

Both metaphor (implied comparison) and simile (stated comparison) involve relating something to something else, frequently an abstraction to something concrete in order that meaning may be expressed vividly. Metaphorical language includes PERSONIFICATION, SYMBOL, and APOSTROPHE, as well as simile and metaphor in the strict sense; in each instance, a comparison is involved — in personification, for example, between an inanimate object or idea and a living person.

Meter. The measurement of verse according to its pattern of stressed and unstressed syllables. A certain number of metrical FEET make up a line of verse. (TETRAMETER denotes a line containing four metrical feet; PENTAMETER five feet, and HEXAMETER six feet.) The most frequently encountered feet in English verse are:

1. IAMB. The first two syllables of the adjective i-*am*-bic reproduces the beat ($\smile$ $'$), an unstressed syllable followed by a stressed: a-*live*, con-*fer*, pre-*dict*. This is the most common metrical foot in English.

2. TROCHEE. The noun *tro*-chee reproduces the beat ($'$ $\smile$), a stressed syllable followed by an unstressed — the reverse of iambic: *foot*-ball, *run*-ning.

3. ANAPEST. The first three syllables of the adjective an-a-*pest*-ic reproduces the beat ($\smile$ $\smile$ $'$), two unstressed syllables followed by a stressed syllable: Hallow-*een*, in-ter-*rupt*.

4. DACTYL. From the Greek word for "finger," which has a long joint and two short ones; thus, a stressed syllable followed by two unstressed syllables ($'$ $\smile$ $\smile$) — the reverse of anapest: *ac*-ci-dent, *care*-ful-ly.

5. SPONDEE. Two or more stressed feet ($'$ $'$): quick-*step*, *heartache*. This foot occurs only occasionally in English, and as a variant among other metrical forms.

All five of these basic feet are illustrated in Coleridge's lines:

> Trochee trips from long to short;
> From long to long in solemn sort
> Slow Spondee stalks; strong foot! yet ill
>   able
> Ever to come up with Dactyl trisyllable.
> Iambics march from short to long; —
> With a leap and a bound the swift Ana-
>   pests throng.

Monologue. As a literary form, a narration entirely in the voice of a single speaker; "Haircut" (page 146) is a notable example. Browning utilized the form in poetry — a single voice speaking through a poem, as the Duke of Ferrara does in "My Last Duchess" (page 604). In such instances the form is called a DRAMATIC MONOLOGUE, because of the interaction of character between speaker and auditor that the verse implicitly reveals.

Motivation. The causes that account for a character's behavior. A man might be motivated to steal because he is in debt; a rash and impetuous type of man might be motivated to accept a dare that would involve risking his life. The question of what motivates Hamlet to delay his revenge is considered on pages 808–809; what motivates Paul to leave home in Willa Cather's story (page 643) is in general his sense of being a misfit in his father's world, and specifically his being forbidden to usher at or even enter Carnegie Hall again.

Narrative poetry. See LYRIC.

Octave. See SONNET.

Ode. A lyric poem characterized by dignity of style and expressive of noble feeling. Originally the form of the ode, in ancient Greek drama, was determined by the movement of a chorus chanting verses on a stage. In English literature a less rigidly controlled form developed in the seventeenth century. Keats' five great odes (including "Ode on a Grecian Urn," page 46) differ from earlier English odes in following a set stanza pattern; earlier, poets writing odes had allowed each stanza to determine its own line lengths, rhyme scheme, and number of lines.

Olfactory imagery. See IMAGERY.

Omniscient point of view. See POINT OF VIEW.

Onomatopoeia. A term that denotes words the sounds of which suggest their meaning; for example, *zoom*, *clank*, *roar*. A phrase or a whole sentence may be onomatopoetic. The following lines exemplify some of the contrasting effects onomatopoeia can achieve:

> As I gain the cove with pushing prow,
> And quench its speed i' the slushy
>   sand....
> A tap at the pane, the quick sharp scratch
> And blue spurt of a lighted match....
>   (Browning, "Meeting at Night")

Oxymoron. A figure of speech that juxtaposes words communicating opposing ideas: "sweet sorrow," "pleasing pains," "loving hate." The effect is paradoxical.

Parable. A short narrative that illustrates a moral or insight. The Gospels contain many parables, by means of which Jesus made his teachings vivid. Like FABLES, parables are brief stories that convey advice; but fables frequently use animals as characters, and their wisdom is less profound than that of parables. Compare, for example, the parable of the Good Samaritan (Luke 10: 30–37) with the fable of the goose that laid the golden eggs. ALLEGORIES are narratives that are designed to convey wisdom, but allegorical narratives are usually longer than either fables or parables, and the characters in allegories are usually personifications of abstractions — evil, virtue, universal man, etc.

Paradox. See IRONY.

Parallelism. Two or more balancing statements, with phrases, clauses, or paragraphs of similar length and grammatical structure.

The phrases in the following comment are parallel:

> Raphael paints wisdom; Handel sings it,
> Phidias carves it, Shakespeare writes it,
> Wren builds it, Columbus sails it, Luther
> preaches it, Washington arms it, Watt
> mechanizes it.
>
> (Emerson, "Civilization")

Often whole stanzas of poems are parallel, and the ideas that are balanced may be similar or contrasting. In the following example, two parallel ideas contrast:

> Every sweet has its sour; every evil its
> good.
>
> (Emerson, "Compensation")

See ANTITHESIS.

Personification. A special kind of metaphor in which abstractions or inanimate objects are given human characteristics. In the following example the abstract idea of time is personified as a thief, stealing youth away.

> How soon hath Time, the subtle thief of
> youth,
> Stolen on his wing my three and twenti-
> eth year!
>
> (Milton, Sonnet VII)

Death, too, has been personified as a thief, and in many other ways as well; for example, as a sheriff coming to arrest someone, as a judge passing sentence, as a reaper cutting down stalks, as a gentleman caller come to take someone for a carriage ride to eternity, as a footman holding someone's coat as he leaves a room. In each instance, the abstraction of death is made concrete, and attributes of the abstraction are stressed by the specific personification chosen.

Pentameter. See METER.

Personal point of view. See POINT OF VIEW.

Petrarchan sonnet. See SONNET.

Plot. Arrangement of the action in fiction or drama. Plot refers to what takes place in bare outline from the beginning to the end of the story.

Point of view. The position from which a story is told. To tell a story, an author may put himself figuratively into the body and mind of some character taking part in the action, For example, in "The Secret Sharer" (page 698), the author consistently assumes the point of view of the young novice ship captain; the entire story is related from that one consciousness. Because the action is revealed as seen and felt by some person taking part in it, this method of narration is called the PERSONAL POINT OF VIEW. Alternatively, an author may stand outside his story, knowing what each of his characters is doing and thinking at any moment. Tolstoy uses that all-knowing or OMNISCIENT POINT OF VIEW in "How Much Land Does a Man Need?" (page 303).

Quatrain. A stanza of four lines — the most common form in English poetry. "The Isle of Portland" (page 145) is written in quatrains.

Resolution. See STRUCTURE.

Rhyme. Repetition of the same stressed sound or sounds at the end of words. *Strange* rhymes with *change; token* rhymes with *broken.* Usually when rhyme is used in a poem, the end of one line will rhyme with the end of another line nearby. The pattern of rhyme, or RHYME SCHEME, is indicated by means of letters, a different letter being assigned to each rhyme sound newly introduced. Thus, the rhyme scheme of the following lines is *a b b a:*

> Death be not proud, though some have
> called thee
> Mighty and dreadful, for thou art not so,
> For those whom thou think'st thou dost
> overthrow
> Die not, poor death, nor yet canst thou
> kill me....
>
> (Donne, *Holy Sonnets: X*)

Rhyme scheme. See RHYME.

Rhythm. Melody of language — the flowing sound of words together, as distinguished from their meaning. Rhythm in this sense includes not only meter, but alliteration, onomatopoeia, and the harshness or softness of sounds within words and phrases.

Rhythms may be abrupt:

> Lion, fish and swan
> Act, and are gone
> Upon Time's toppling wave.
> (Auden, "Song: Fish
> in the Unruffled Lakes")

or gentle:

> When you are old and gray and full of
> sleep
> And nodding by the fire, take down this
> book,
> And slowly read, and dream of the soft
> look
> Your eyes had once, and of their shad-
> ows deep.
> (Yeats, "When You Are Old")

or explosive:

> Busy old fool! unruly Sun!
> Why dost thou thus,
> Through windows and through curtains,
> call on us?
> Must to thy motions lovers' seasons run?
> (Donne, "The Sun Rising")

or serene:

> It is a beauteous evening, calm and free,
> The holy time is quiet as a nun
> Breathless with adoration....
> (Wordsworth, Sonnet)

or powerful:

> Fierce-throated beauty!
> Roll through my chant with all thy law-
> less music, thy swinging lamps at
> night,
> Thy madly-whistled laughter, echoing,
> rumbling like an earthquake, rous-
> ing all....
> (Whitman, "To a Locomotive
> in Winter")

Rhythmic variations, in fact, are virtually endless. Meter is a fixed measure or beat; rhythm includes meter, plus all variations of sound that keep meter from becoming monotonous.

Rising action. See STRUCTURE.

Satire. Verse or prose that makes fun of popular institutions, customs, or beliefs. Generally satire is humorous; its tone may be gentle or scornful or bitter. Like a cartoon, it depends for its effect more on exaggeration than on accuracy. "Haircut" (page 146) contains elements of satire in its portrayal of small-town American life.

Scansion. The indication of foot divisions and accents in metrical verse. Unaccented syllables are usually indicated by the symbol ‿, accented syllables by ′. Thus, the opening lines of Keats' "On First Looking into Chapman's Homer" might be scanned:

> Much have/ I tra/veled in/ the
> realms/ of gold/
> And ma/ny good/ly states/ and
> king/doms seen/

Sestet. See SONNET.

Setting. The time and place of a story, play, or narrative poem. "Young Goodman Brown" (page 26) is set in Salem in the early seventeenth century; "Paul's Case" (page 641) is set in Pittsburgh and New York City near the beginning of the twentieth century.

Shakespearean sonnet. See SONNET.

Simile. See METAPHOR.

Soliloquy. In a play, a speech delivered by an actor alone on the stage. A soliloquy resembles a character's thoughts spoken aloud. Hamlet's speech at I, ii, 129–159 (page 733) is an example.

Sonnet. A lyric of fourteen lines, usually written in iambic meter, with five feet to each line. Two kinds of sonnets occur frequently in English verse. The SHAKESPEAREAN (English) SONNET is composed of three quatrains and a closing couplet, rhyming *a b a b c d c d e f e f g g*. An example appears on page 628. The PETRARCHAN (Italian) SONNET is divided into an OCTAVE (the first eight lines) rhyming usually *a b b a a b b a* and a SESTET (the final six lines) having any of various rhyme schemes. The content of the sestet often qualifies that of the octave.

Spondee. See METER.

Stanza. Lines of verse grouped systematically together. In conventional poetry, stanzas are usually parallel. In "The Isle of Portland" (page 145), for example, the first stanza ends at line 4. Each succeeding stanza is of equal length — four lines long — and each is written in the same meter and follows the same rhyme scheme as the preceding. The poems in this anthology illustrate some of the wide variations in stanza form that have been devised.

Stereotype. In fiction or drama, a character who lacks individuality, having no traits except the most obvious and expected of the group to which he belongs. Literally, a stereotype is a block used in printing; identical images can be made from the same block. In literature, the tough cop is a stereotype; so are the fluttery old maid and the sullen teenager. Because of their dullness, stereotyped characters almost invariably represent a fault in a story.

An author may, however, want to have a character exemplify a whole group. Such a character, being typical of that group, is called a TYPE. The gossipy barber in "Haircut" (page 146) is a type rather than a profound character study; so also is the peasant in "How Much Land Does a Man Need?" (page 303).

Structure. The arrangement of details and scenes that make up a literary work. Plays often conform to a structure that moves first through RISING ACTION, then after the climax through FALLING ACTION to the RESOLUTION, or conclusion. Early in most plays occurs the EXPOSITION of the situation when the curtain rises; into this situation a COMPLICATION is introduced, followed by other complications until the climax is reached. After the climax the play proceeds through the DENOUEMENT, in which the threads of the plot are unknotted and the crises are resolved. For the distinction between structure and FORM, see STYLE.

Style. An author's characteristic choice and arrangement of words. A style may be colloquial, formal, terse, wordy, rhetorical (like an orator's), subdued, colorful, poetic, or highly individual in any number of ways. The style of "Haircut" (page 146) is colloquial and slangy; Joyce's style in "Counterparts" (page 157) is concrete, with many qualifying adjectives and adverbs; "The Open Boat (page 456) is written in a style that makes abundant use of metaphor and verbal irony. DICTION refers to the choice of individual words. The arrangement of details and scenes make up the STRUCTURE of a literary work. All combine to influence the TONE of the work; all — diction, style, and structure — make up its FORM.

Subject. See THEME.

Symbol. An object that has a range of meaning beyond itself. Symbols have both literal and figurative meanings. The fork in Frost's "The Road Not Taken" (page 313) has, in addition to its literal meaning, a symbolic value as an irrevocable decision in life; so does the parrot in "A Simple Heart" come to have a symbolic meaning as the Holy Ghost (page 285). Often symbols, like connotations, are ambiguous, more a matter of intuition than logic.

Tactile imagery. See IMAGERY.

Terza rima. A three-line stanza form rhyming *a b a b c b c d c* etc. Dante's *Divine Comedy* (page 212) is written in the original in terza rima.

Tetrameter. See METER.

Theme. The generalized meaning of a literery work arising out of the specific SUBJECT that the work develops. The subject of "A Simple Heart" (page 266) is the life and death of a humble French servant named Félicité in the nineteenth century; the theme, on the other hand, deals with the ennobling quality of an unselfish and loving life that culminates finally in something approaching sainthood. One theme of "The Open Boat" (page 456) concerns the instructive value of a crucial, life-and-death experience that measures men's capacities to the utmost. Often themes are difficult to state briefly and precisely, and one work frequently expresses through its subject more than a single theme.

Tone. In a literary work, the attitude the author takes toward his subject. That attitude is revealed through choice of details, through diction and style, and through the emphasis and comments that are made. The contrasting tones in the following passages should be obvious:

> I wonder, by my troth, what thou and I
> Did till we loved? Were we not weaned
>   till then,
> But sucked on country pleasures, child-
>   ishly?
> Or snorted we in the Seven Sleepers'
>   den?
>   (Donne, "The Good-Morrow")

> Withal a meager man was Aaron Stark,
> Cursed and unkempt, shrewd, shriveled,
>   and morose.
> A miser was he, with a miser's nose,
> And eyes like little dollars in the dark.
> His thin, pinched mouth was nothing
>   but a mark. . . .
>   (Robinson, "Aaron Stark")

> Gr-r-r — there go, my heart's abhor-
>   ence!
> Water your damned flower-pots, do!
> If hate killed men, Brother Lawrence,
>   God's blood, would not mine kill you!
> What? your myrtle-bush wants trim-
>   ming?
> Oh, that rose has prior claims —
> Needs its leaden vase filled brimming?
> Hell dry you up with its flames!
>   (Browning, "Soliloquy of the
>   Spanish Cloister")

> An aged man is but a paltry thing,
> A tattered coat upon a stick, unless
> Soul clap its hands and sing, and louder
>   sing
> For every tatter in its mortal dress. . . .
>   (Yeats, "Sailing to Byzantium")

> White in the moon the long road lies,
> The moon stands blank above;
> White in the moon the long road lies
> That leads me from my love.
>   (Housman, "White in the Moon")

Like theme and style, tone is sometimes difficult to describe with a single word or phrase. Often it varies in the same literary work, as it does in *Hamlet* (page 726), to suit the moods of the characters and situations.

Trochee. See METER.

Type. See STEREOTYPE.

Understatement. See IRONY.

Verbal irony. See IRONY.

Verisimilitude. The effect of truthfulness in a work of fiction.

Verse. A line of poetry. Several verses grouped together in a pattern make up a stanza.

Visual imagery. See IMAGERY.

Dictionary

Most of the difficult words in *Themes in World Literature* are explained in footnotes. When a difficult word is not footnoted, it is probably in this dictionary; you will want to add it to your vocabulary when you look it up. If you look for a word and find it not listed, reread the sentence or paragraph in which it appeared. The word may not have been included here because the context gives clues to its meaning.

Guide words at the top of each page will help you locate the word you want. Use the key words at the foot of every page as a guide to pronunciation. When two pronunciations are given, both are used by people who speak correctly. The following abbreviations occur:

adj. adjective
adv. adverb
cap. capitalized
esp. especially

n. noun
pl. plural
prep. preposition
v. verb

A

a·bash (ə·bash′), *v.* To embarrass; shame; confuse.

a·bate (ə·bāt′), *v.* To lessen; reduce; decrease; put an end to.

ab·er·ra·tion (ab′ər·ā′shən), *n.* **1.** A wandering away from what is normal or true. **2.** A disorder of the mind.

a·bide (ə·bīd′), *v.* **1.** To remain. **2.** To last. **3.** To wait for. **4.** To put up with. — **abide by.** To live up to; accept the terms of.

ab·ject (ab′jekt, ab·jekt′), *adj.* **1.** Utterly wretched and hopeless; miserable. **2.** Contemptible. **3.** Very humiliating.

a·bom·i·na·ble (ə·bom′ə·nə·bəl), *adj.* **1.** Disgusting. **2.** Extremely bad.

ab·ra·sive (ə·brā′siv), *adj.* Having a rubbing, wearing, or irritating effect.

ab·stract (ab·strakt′), *v.* **1.** To take away. **2.** To remove secretly. **3.** (ab′strakt) To summarize; condense.

a·bys·mal (ə·biz′məl), *adj.* **1.** Immeasurable. **2.** Bottomless; of unbelievable depth.

a·byss (ə·bis′), *n.* **1.** A deep opening in the earth's surface. **2.** Any immeasurable depth.

ac·cen·tu·ate (ak·sen′chü·āt′), *v.* To emphasize; bring out; accent.

ac·cess (ak′ses), *n.* **1.** Approach; entrance. **2.** Ability or permission to approach or enter. **3.** A method or way of approach.

ac·qui·es·cence (ak′wē·es′əns), *n.* Quiet agreement or consent. — **ac·qui·es·cent,** *adj.*

ac·rid (ak′rid), *adj.* Sharp; harsh; biting.

ad·ja·cent (ə·jā′sənt), *adj.* Lying close to or next to.

ad·mo·ni·tion (ad′mə·nish′ən), *n.* Advice or gentle warning.

ad·u·la·tion (aj′ə·lā′shən), *n.* **1.** Excessive praise or flattery. **2.** Slavish worship.

ad·verse (ad·vėrs′, ad′vėrs′), *adj.* **1.** Opposing. **2.** Unfavorable; harmful. — **ad·ver·si·ty** (ad·vėr′sə·tē), *n.* Misfortune; suffering.

af·fa·ble (af′ə·bəl), *adj.* Friendly and courteous; easy to talk with.

af·fi·da·vit (af′ə·dā′vit), *n.* A sworn statement in writing.

af·front (ə·frunt′), *v.* **1.** To insult deliberately; offend. **2.** To defy. — *n.* An open insult.

ag·grieve (ə·grēv′), *v.* To offend; cause grief to; distress.

al·lege (ə·lej′), *v.* **1.** To assert, often without offering proof; declare. **2.** To give as a reason or excuse.

al·le·giance (ə·lē′jəns), *n.* **1.** Loyalty. **2.** Loyalty and duty due to one's ruler or country.

al·lude (ə·lüd′), *v.* To refer to indirectly; suggest indirectly.

al·lu·sion (ə·lü′zhən), *n.* An indirect reference; hint.

a·men·i·ty (ə·men′ə·tē), *n.* **1.** Pleasantness. **2.** *pl.* Attractive features, as of a place. **3.** *pl.* Courteous acts.

am·i·ty (am′ə·tē), *n.* Friendship; friendliness; peaceful relations.

an·arch·y (an′ər·kē), *n.* **1.** Absence of government. **2.** Political disorder. **3.** General disorder or confusion.

---

add, māke, fäther; edge, bē, hėr; it, tīme; hot, gō, ȯ = aw in draw; cut, fúll, rüle; boil; out; ə = the sound of the unaccented vowels in about, final, silent, pencil, contain, and circus; think, this; zh = s in pleasure; ⁿ = n in French *un*

a·nath·e·ma (ə·nath′ə·mə), *n.* **1.** A solemn curse. **2.** An accursed person or object. **3.** Anything greatly hated.

an·i·ma·tion (an′ə·mā′shən), *n.* **1.** Liveliness; zest. **2.** The act of giving life or lifelike movement to. — **an·i·mat·ed,** *adj.*

an·ni·hi·late (ə·nī′ə·lāt′), *v.* To destroy completely.

an·te·room (an′ti·rüm′), *n.* A room through which another room is entered.

an·ti·dote (an′ti·dōt′), *n.* **1.** A remedy that counteracts poison. **2.** Anything that works against an evil force. **3.** A preventative.

an·tip·a·thy (an·tip′ə·thē), *n.* **1.** Strong dislike. **2.** An object arousing strong dislike.

ap·o·plex·y (ap′ə·plek′sē), *n.* Sudden paralysis or loss of consciousness or feeling caused by the breaking of a blood vessel in the brain.

ap·pel·la·tion (ap′ə·lā′shən), *n.* A name or title, *esp.* a descriptive one.

ap·pur·te·nance (ə·pėr′tə·nəns), *n.* Something added to or belonging to a more important or larger thing.

ar·a·ble (ar′ə·bəl), *adj.* Suitable for plowing or farming.

ar·dent (är′dənt), *adj.* **1.** Passionate; fiery. **2.** Eager.

ar·du·ous (är′jü·wəs), *adj.* Very difficult; requiring hard work.

a·rid·i·ty (ə·rid′ə·tē), *n.* **1.** Dryness; barrenness. **2.** Lack of interest.

ar·rant (ar′ənt), *adj.* **1.** Downright; notorious. **2.** Thorough; genuine.

ar·ras (ar′əs), *n.* A tapestry wall-hanging.

as·pect (as′pekt), *n.* **1.** A position facing a particular direction. **2.** The appearance of something from a particular point of view. **3.** One's appearance.

as·per·i·ty (as·per′ə·tē), *n.* Severe harshness; roughness.

as·pi·ra·tion (as′pə·rā′shən), *n.* **1.** The act of breathing. **2.** A strong desire for something high or great; noble ambition.

as·sent (ə·sent′), *v.* To agree; consent.

as·suage (ə·swāj′), *v.* To quiet; calm; satisfy; ease; lessen.

a·thwart (ə·thwôrt′), *adv. & prep.* Across.

at·test (ə·test′), *v.* **1.** To declare true. **2.** To swear to. **3.** To give proof of. **4.** To bear witness to.

at·tri·tion (ə·trish′ən), *n.* **1.** A wearing away by rubbing. **2.** The act of weakening by constant abuse. **3.** Sorrow for one's sins.

au·dac·i·ty (ô·das′ə·tē), *n.* Boldness; impudence; daring.

au·gu·ry (ô′gyėr·ē), *n.* **1.** The art of foretelling the future by signs or omens. **2.** A sign; omen.

au·gust (ô·gust′), *adj.* Dignified; noble.

aus·pi·cious (ôs·pish′əs), *adj.* **1.** Favorable. **2.** Successful.

aus·tere (ôs·tēr′), *adj.* **1.** Stern; harsh; strict. **2.** Severely simple and unadorned. **3.** Grave; sober.

av·a·rice (av′ə·rəs), *n.* Greed.

a·vert (ə·vėrt′), *v.* **1.** To turn away or aside. **2.** To ward off; prevent.

a·vouch (ə·vouch′), *v.* **1.** To guarantee. **2.** To affirm.

az·ure (azh′ėr), *adj.* Sky-blue.

B

be·guile (bi·gīl′), *v.* **1.** To mislead by flattery or tricks; deceive. **2.** To charm; delight. **3.** To pass (time) pleasantly.

be·muse (bi·myüz′), *v.* To daze; confuse; preoccupy. — **be·mused,** *adj.*

be·nef·i·cent (bə·nef′ə·sənt), *adj.* Doing or producing good.

be·reave (bi·rēv′), *v.* **1.** To deprive of some cherished person or thing, *esp.* by death. **2.** To deprive.

be·seech (bi·sēch′), *v.* To beg urgently.

bev·el (bev′əl), *v.* **1.** To cut with a sloping edge. **2.** To slant.

biv·ou·ac (biv′ü·wak′, biv′wak), *n.* A temporary camp in the open, without shelter.

blas·pheme (blas·fēm′, blas′fēm), *v.* **1.** To curse. **2.** To speak profanely of or to God.

bla·tant (blā′tənt), *adj.* **1.** Disagreeably noisy. **2.** Very conspicuous. **3.** Gaudy; flashy; in bad taste; showy.

blithe (blīth, blīth), *adj.* Lighthearted; gay.

boon (bün), *n.* **1.** A favor; benefit. **2.** A blessing.

boo·ty (bü′tē), *n.* **1.** Goods taken from the enemy during war; loot. **2.** Any prize.

bour·geois (bür·zhwä′), *adj.* **1.** Referring to the middle class. **2.** Tending toward mediocrity; commonplace.

bran·dish (bran′dish), *v.* To wave threateningly.

bra·va·do (brə·väd′ō), *n.* Boastful pretense of bravery.

bra·zen (brā′zən), *adj.* **1.** Made of brass. **2.** Like brass in sound; loud; harsh. **3.** Bold; shameless.

breach (brēch), *n.* **1.** The breaking of waves, as on a shore. **2.** The breaking of any legal or moral bond; violation. **3.** A break in friendship. **4.** A gap made by breaking something.

bul·wark (bul′wərk), *n.* A defense or defense wall; protection.

bump·kin (bump′kin), *n.* A clumsy, stupid person from the country.

bump·tious (bump′shəs), *adj.* Irritatingly conceited. — **bump·tious·ness,** *n.*

bur·nish (bėr′nish), *v.* To shine; polish.

C

ca·dence (kā′dəns), *n.* **1.** Rhythm or beat. **2.** The rise and fall of sounds in rhythm. **3.** A fall of the voice in speaking.

cal·lous (kal′əs), *adj.* **1.** Hard and rough. **2.** Unfeeling; insensitive. — **cal·lous·ness,** *n.*

cal·um·ny (kal′əm·nē), *n.* Slander; malicious lies. — **ca·lum·ni·ous** (kə·lum′nē·əs), *adj.*

ca·price (kə·prēs′), *n.* A sudden whim or fancy.

car·nal (kär′nəl), *adj.* **1.** Of the flesh; not spiritual. **2.** Material; worldly. **3.** Sensual.

ca·rouse (kə·rouz′), *v.* To take part in a lively drinking party; drink deeply or freely.

cat·e·chism (kat′ə·kiz′m), *n.* **1.** A book of questions and answers used for teaching, *esp.* religion. **2.** A questioning or series of questions.

cen·sure (sen′shər), *n.* A blaming; condemning criticism.

ces·sa·tion (se·sā′shən), *n.* A stop.

chaff (chaf, chäf), *v.* To tease good-naturedly. — *n.* **1.** The husks of grain separated from the seed during threshing. **2.** Anything worthless. **3.** Light, teasing talk.

chasm (kaz′əm), *n.* **1.** A deep crack or opening in the earth's surface. **2.** Any gap or split; rift.

chas·ten (chās′ən), *v.* **1.** To correct by punishing; discipline. **2.** To subdue.

chas·tise (chas·tīz′), *v.* To punish, *esp.* bodily.

cir·cum·scribe (sér′kəm·skrīb′), *v.* **1.** To draw a circle around. **2.** To limit.

cir·cum·vent (sér′kəm·vent′), *v.,* To get the better of through the use of trickery.

cit·a·del (sit′ə·del′), *n.* A fortress; stronghold.

clam·ber (klam′bėr), *v.* To climb awkwardly or with difficulty, using both hands and feet.

clam·or·ous (klam′ər·əs), *adj.* **1.** Noisy. **2.** Demanding loudly or complainingly.

cleave (klēv), *v.* To split or divide.

cleave (klēv), *v.* **1.** To cling; stick closely to. **2.** To be faithful to.

clem·en·cy (klem′ən·sē), *n.* **1.** Kindness; an act of mercy. **2.** Mildness, as of the weather.

cli·en·tele (klī′ən·tel′), *n.* A group of clients, customers, or patrons.

co·erce (kō·ėrs′), *v.* **1.** To force. **2.** To restrain by force. — **co·er·cion,** *n.*

cog·ni·zance (kog′nə·zəns), *n.* **1.** An awareness; knowledge. **2.** Notice; observance.

col·lab·o·rate (kə·lab′ə·rāt′), *v.* **1.** To work together on a project. **2.** To cooperate with the enemy. — **col·lab·o·ra·tion,** *n.*

col·lat·er·al (kə·lat′ər·əl), *adj.* **1.** Parallel. **2.** Referring to security given until repayment of a loan. **3.** Having the same ancestors but from a different line. **4.** Accompanying. **5.** Of a similar nature, but less important.

com·mun·ion (kə·myün′yən), *n.* **1.** A sharing of thoughts, interests, or feelings. **2.** *cap.* The sacrament commemorating the last supper of Jesus Christ.

com·pa·tri·ot (kəm·pā′trē·ət), *n.* One living in or coming from the same country as another.

com·pli·ance (kom·plī′əns), *n.* **1.** A tendency to give in to the wishes of others. **2.** A yielding; consenting. — **com·pli·ant,** *adj.*

com·pos·ite (kom·poz′ət), *adj.* Made up of many parts or elements. — **com·pos·ite,** *n.*

com·po·sure (kom·pō′zhər), *n.* Calmness; self-possession.

com·pound (kom·pound′), *v.* **1.** To mix; combine. **2.** To compose; form. **3.** To compromise (a matter).

com·punc·tion (kəm·pungk′shən), *n.* Uneasiness or regret for wrongdoing; twinge of conscience.

con·cede (kən·sēd′), *v.* **1.** To admit as truth. **2.** To give in or agree to. **3.** To grant.

con·cen·tric (kən·sen′trik), *adj.* Having the same center.

con·cil·i·ate (kən·sil′ē·āt′), *v.* To win over; appease; pacify; gain the good will of. — **con·cil·i·a·to·ry** (kən·sil′ē·ə·tor′ē), *adj.*

con·jec·ture (kən·jek′chər), *v.* To guess. — *n.* **1.** A guess. **2.** Prediction based on incomplete evidence.

con·jure (kon′jėr), *v.* **1.** To summon or make appear by magic. **2.** To use magic. **3.** (kən·jür′) To implore solemnly.

con·gen·i·tal (kən·jen′ə·təl), *adj.* Existing as such from birth.

con·sort (kən·sòrt′), *v.* **1.** To associate. **2.** To suit; harmonize.

con·ster·na·tion (kon′stėr·nā′shən), *n.* Dismay; anxiety; amazed alarm.

con·strain (kən·strān′), *v.* **1.** To confine; hold by force. **2.** To force. — **con·strained,** *adj.*

con·straint (kən·strānt′), *n.* **1.** Confinement. **2.** Force. **3.** Forced, unnatural manner; embarrassment.

con·sum·mate (kon′sə·māt′), *v.* To complete; achieve.

con·sum·mate (kən·sum′ət), *adj.* Complete; perfect; of the highest degree. — **con·sum·ma·tion,** *n.*

con·tem·plate (kon′təm·plāt′), *v.* **1.** To gaze at closely. **2.** To consider long and carefully; think about; meditate. **3.** To intend; expect. — **con·tem·pla·tive** (kən·tem′plə·tiv), *adj.* Thoughtful; meditative.

con·tend (kən·tend′), *v.* **1.** To fight; to struggle. **2.** To argue; maintain. **3.** To compete.

con·trite (kən·trīt′), *adj.* Full of guilt or sorrow for a wrong committed; repentant. — **con·tri·tion,** *n.*

con·tu·me·ly (kon′tü·mə·lē), *n.* **1.** Humiliating treatment. **2.** An insult.

con·verse (kən·vėrs′, kon′vėrs), *adj.* Reversed in order or position; opposite; contrary.

con·viv·i·al (kən·viv′ē·əl), *adj.* **1.** Festive; jovial. **2.** Sociable; fond of eating and drinking.

con·vulse (kən·vuls′), *v.* **1.** To shake or twitch violently or uncontrollably. **2.** To cause to shake with laughter, anger, etc.

co·quette (kō·ket′), *n.* A female flirt. — **co·quet·tish,** *adj.*

cor·pu·lent (kòr′pyü·lənt), *adj.* Extremely fat.

cov·ert (kuv′ərt), *adj.* **1.** Hidden; secret. **2.** Sheltered. — *n.* **1.** A protected area. **2.** A

---

add, māke, fäther; edge, bē, hėr; it, tīme; hot, gō, ȯ = aw in draw; cut, fúll, rüle; boil; out; ə = the sound of the unaccented vowels in about, final, silent, pencil, contain, and circus; think, **th**is; zh = s in pleasure; **n** = n in French *un*

thicket or underbrush sheltering wildlife. **3.** A durable cloth woven from many-colored yarns.

coun·te·nance (koun'tə·nəns), *n.* **1.** Face. **2.** Facial expression; appearance.

cov·ey (kuv'ē), *n.* **1.** A small flock of birds. **2.** A group; bevy; company.

cow·er (kou'ər), *v.* To crouch or huddle from fear or cold; cringe.

cred·u·lous (krej'ü·ləs), *adj.* Tending to believe too quickly; easily deceived.

cu·rate (kyür'ət), *n.* A clergyman who assists the rector of a church.

D

dal·li·ance (dal'ē·əns), *n.* **1.** A playing, *esp.* at love; trifling. **2.** A toying; flirting. **3.** A loitering; wasting of time.

da·ta (dā'tə, dat'ə), *n. pl.* Facts; information about a particular subject.

daunt·less (dònt'ləs), *adj.* Unable to be frightened or discouraged; brave; fearless.

dearth (dėrth), *n.* A lack; scarcity.

de·bauch·er·y (di·bòch'ə·rē), *n.* Corruption; excessive giving in to one's sensual desires; intemperance.

de·cant·er (di·kant'ər), *n.* A decorative or ornamental glass bottle used for wine or liquors.

de·co·rum (di·kor'əm), *n.* **1.** Good taste or propriety in behavior or appearance. **2.** Orderliness.

deem (dēm), *v.* To think; believe.

def·er·ence (def'ər·əns), *n.* **1.** Polite respect. **2.** Courteous regard for the wishes or beliefs of another.

dell (del), *n.* A small, hidden valley.

de·lu·sive (di·lü'səv), *adj.* Deceiving; misleading.

de·mean (di·mēn'), *v.* To degrade; lower.

de·mean·or (di·mēn'ər), *n.* Behavior; conduct; outward manner.

de·mo·ni·ac (di·mō'ni·ak'), *adj.* **1.** Devilish; fiendish. **2.** Possessed or influenced by a demon. **3.** Frantic.

de·noue·ment (dā·nü'mäⁿ), *n.* **1.** The outcome of a plot, as in drama. **2.** A solution to a difficult situation.

de·prav·i·ty (di·prav'ə·tē), *n.* Corruption; evil; immorality.

de·rog·a·to·ry (di·rog'ə·tòr'ē), *adj.* Belittling; discrediting; expressing a low opinion.

de·scry (di·skrī'), *v.* **1.** To glimpse something far off. **2.** To detect.

des·ti·tute (des'tə·tüt'), *adj.* **1.** Extremely poor; lacking even the bare necessities. **2.** Lacking (with *of*).

de·ter (di·tėr'), *v.* To keep one from doing something through fear; discourage.

det·o·nate (det'ə·nāt'), *v.* To explode loudly and violently. — **det·o·na·tion,** *n.*

de·trac·tion (di·trak'shən), *n.* A taking away; lessening of reputation or high regard. — **de·trac·tor,** *n.*

de·vice (di·vīs'), *n.* **1.** A plan. **2.** A scheme or plot. **3.** A mechanism. **4.** An ornamental design, *esp.* on a coat of arms.

de·vi·ous (dē'vē·əs), *adj.* **1.** Rambling; not straightforward. **2.** Crooked; winding.

di·a·dem (dī'ə·dem'), *n.* A crown; jeweled headband.

di·dac·tic (dī·dak'tik), *adj.* Instructive; tending to lecture.

dif·fi·dent (dif'ə·dənt), *adj.* Awkwardly shy; lacking self-confidence.

dif·fuse (di·fyüz'), *v.* To spread out; scatter.

din (din), *v.* **1.** To strike with a loud noise. **2.** To repeat noisily or insistently. — **din,** *n.*

dire (dīr), *adj.* **1.** Terrible; horrible. **2.** Extreme. — **dire·ful,** *adj.*

dirge (dėrj), *n.* A song or poem of grief or mourning.

dis·cern (di·sėrn', di·zėrn'), *v.* **1.** To recognize clearly; see or distinguish; detect or discover with the eye or mind. **2.** To see the difference between.

dis·com·fit (dis·kum'fit), *v.* **1.** To frustrate; upset. **2.** To embarrass. — **dis·com·fi·ture,** *n.*

dis·cre·tion (dis·kresh'ən), *n.* **1.** The quality of being careful of one's behavior, or showing good judgment about what one says. **2.** The power to act, judge, or make decisions.

dis·crim·i·na·tion (dis·krim·i·nā'shən), *n.* **1.** The distinguishing between one thing and another; the recognizing of differences between things. **2.** The favoring of one person or thing over another; showing partiality.

dis·course (dis·kòrs'), *v.* To talk or write formally on a given subject. — **dis·course** (dis'kòrs), *n.*

dis·par·age (dis·par'ij), *v.* **1.** To discredit; speak slightingly of. **2.** To belittle; lessen in honor; lower.

dis·patch (dis·pach'), *n.* **1.** A sending off. **2.** The act of slaying. **3.** Speed, promptness. **4.** A message, *esp.* an important one. **5.** A story sent to a newspaper.

dis·pir·it (dis·pir'it), *v.* To depress; discourage; deject. — **dis·pir·it·ed,** *adj.*

dis·port (dis·pōrt'), *v.* To play; frolic; amuse oneself. — *n.* Sport; pastime; merriment.

dis·qui·et (dis·kwī'ət), *v.* To disturb; worry; make anxious or uneasy.

dis·rep·u·ta·ble (dis'rep'yə·tə·bəl), *adj.* **1.** Disgraceful. **2.** Not respectable.

dis·si·pat·ed (dis'ə·pāt'əd), *adj.* **1.** Scattered. **2.** Wasted; squandered. **3.** Indulging in foolish or harmful pleasures to excess.

dis·so·lute (dis'ə·lüt'), *adj.* Dissipated; immoral; evil.

dis·suade (dis·wād'), *v.* To talk out of; persuade otherwise; advise against.

dis·tend (dis·tend'), *v.* **1.** To swell; expand. **2.** To stretch out in all directions.

di·verge (də·vėrj', dī·vėrj'), *v.* **1.** To branch off. **2.** To differ.

di·vers (dī'vėrz), *adj.* Various.

di·vine (di·vīn'), *v.* **1.** To guess; detect by intuition. **2.** To prophesy; foretell.

dog·mat·ic (dog·mat'ik), *adj.* **1.** Having to do with established doctrines. **2.** Very positive with insufficient proof. **3.** Opinionated; arrogant in stated opinion.

dole·ful (dōl′fəl), *adj.* Full of grief; sorrowful; sad; dismal.

do·lor·ous (dol′ėr·əs, dō′lėr·əs), *adj.* 1. Sorrowful; mournful. 2. Painful; agonizing.

droll (drōl), *adj.* Oddly laughable; quaintly amusing; comical.

du·ly (dü′lē), *adv.* Properly; rightfully.

E

e·jac·u·la·tion (i·jak′yü·lā′shən), *n.* Throwing forth suddenly; uttering suddenly; exclamation.

e·lu·sive (i·lü′siv), *adj.* 1. Hard to grasp, evasive. 2. Puzzling; hard to understand. 3. Avoiding detection by skill, trickery, or speed.

em·a·nate (em′ə·nāt), *v.* To come out of; flow.

em·boss (im·bòs′), *v.* 1. To decorate with raised designs. 2. To raise in relief from a surface.

em·u·late (em′yü·lāt′), *v.* 1. To try to be as good or better than. 2. To compete successfully.

en·croach (in·krōch′), *v.* 1. To trespass; intrude. 2. To go beyond the proper or usual boundaries or limits.

en·mi·ty (en′mə·tē), *n.* Antagonism; the feeling existing between enemies; hostility; mutual hatred.

e·nig·ma (i·nig′mə), *n.* 1. A puzzle. 2. A puzzling or bewildering person or thing. — **e·nig·mat·ic** (en′ig·mat′ik), *adj.*

en·treat (in·trēt′), *v.* To beg; ask earnestly; implore.

e·nun·ci·ate (i·nun′sē·āt′), *v.* 1. To proclaim. 2. To pronounce. 3. To state.

en·vel·op (in·vel′əp), *v.* 1. To surround. 2. To cover completely; wrap up in.

en·vi·rons (in·vī′rənz), *n. pl.* 1. Suburbs or districts around a city. 2. Surroundings.

ep·i·thet (ep′ə·thet′), *n.* A descriptive word or group of words; phrase expressing a particular quality or characteristic attributed to a person or thing.

e·quiv·o·ca·tion (ē·kwiv′ə·kā′shən), *n.* 1. The use of expressions with two or more meanings for the purpose of misleading. 2. A suspicious, questionable, or uncertain statement.

e·the·re·al (e·thir′ē·əl), *adj.* 1. Light; airy; delicate. 2. Not of the earth; heavenly.

ev·a·nes·cent (ev′ə·nes′ənt), *adj.* Fleeting; quickly passing; tending to disappear quickly.

e·vince (i·vins′), *v.* To show clearly; display; reveal.

ex·as·per·ate (ig·zas′pə·rāt′), *v.* To irritate greatly; anger; annoy.

ex·e·crate (ek′si·krāt′), *v.* 1. To curse; swear. 2. To hate; detest.

ex·em·pla·ry (ig·zem′plə·rē′), *adj.* 1. Worthy of imitation; serving as an example or model. 2. serving as a warning.

ex·hil·a·rate (ig·zil′ə·rāt′), *v.* To stimulate; cheer; refresh.

ex·hort (ig·zòrt′), *v.* To urge strongly; warn.

ex·hor·ta·tion (eg′zòr·tā′shən), *n.* 1. Words of advice or warning. 2. The act of speaking such words.

ex·ploit (ik·sploit′), *v.* 1. To use; get the value out of. 2. To make unfair or unethical use of for one's own profit.

ex·pos·tu·late (ik·spos′chə·lāt′), *v.* To reason earnestly with someone, objecting to his actions.

F

fa·ce·tious (fə·sē′shəs), *adj.* Joking; intended to amuse, but often in poor taste or out of place; mischievously teasing.

fas·tid·i·ous (fas·tid′ē·əs), *adj.* 1. Scornful. 2. Very particular and dainty; fussy. 3. Oversensitive.

fe·lic·i·tous (fə·lis′ə·təs), *adj.* 1. Appropriate; suitably expressed. 2. Having a talent for appropriate expression.

fend (fend), *v.* To resist. — **fend for oneself.** To manage without help. — **fend off.** To ward off; repel.

fer·vid (fėr′vid), *adj.* 1. Very hot; burning. 2. Having intense feeling; passionate; very enthusiastic; fervent.

fes·ter (fes′tər), *v.* 1. To produce pus. 2. To decompose or rot. 3. To produce increasing irritation or resentment.

fes·toon (fes·tün′), *n.* 1. Wreath or garland of flowers, leaves, paper, etc. 2. Any carved or molded decoration of this sort. — *v.* To adorn with festoons.

feu·dal (fyü′dəl), *adj.* Referring to the social system in Europe during the Middle Ages by which people were allowed to live on land owned by lords in exchange for services to the lord.

fick·le (fik′əl), *adj.* Changeable; not firm.

fi·del·i·ty (fi·del′ə·tē, fī·del′ə·tē), *n.* 1. Faithfulness; loyalty. 2. Accuracy of reproduction.

fledg·ling (flej′ling), *n.* 1. A young bird that has just grown its flying feathers. 2. A young, inexperienced person.

flor·id (flòr′id, flor′əd), *adj.* 1. Brightly colored; reddish. 2. Richly ornamented; flowery; showy.

floun·der (floun′dər), *v.* 1. To struggle clumsily. 2. To speak or act clumsily or falteringly.

fluc·tu·ate (fluk′chü·āt′), *v.* To change continually and irregularly; rise and fall.

for·age (fòr′ij, for′ij), *v.* To search for food or supplies.

for·go (fòr·gō′), *v.* To give up; do without.

fort·night (fòrt′nīt, fòrt′nit), *n.* A period of two weeks; fourteen days.

foun·der (foun′dər), *v.* 1. To stumble; become lame. 2. To fill with water and sink.

fra·cas (frā′kəs), *n.* A noisy fight; uproar.

---

add, māke, fäther; edge, bē, hėr; it, tīme; hot, gō, ȯ = aw in draw; cut, fúll, rüle; boil; out; ə = the sound of the unaccented vowels in about, final, silent, pencil, contain, and circus; think, this; zh = s in pleasure; n = n in French *un*

fraud (frôd), *n.* **1.** Deceit. **2.** An intended dishonesty; a trick; hoax; something worthless or false passed off as valuable or genuine. **3.** A pretender.

fu·ne·re·al (fyü·nėr′ē·əl), *adj.* Fitting for a funeral; sad; dismal; gloomy.

G

ga·ble (gā′bəl), *n.* **1.** The triangular-shaped wall formed by the sloping sides of the roof of a house. **2.** In architecture, a triangular, decorative roof such as that over a door or window.

gall (gôl), *v.* **1.** To make sore by rubbing. **2.** To annoy; irritate.

gam·bol (gam′bəl), *v.* To jump and skip in play.

gape (gāp), *v.* **1.** To open wide one's mouth. **2.** To stare at with one's mouth open. **3.** To open widely.

gar·ish (gar′ish), *adj.* **1.** Too bright; glaring. **2.** Tastelessly showy.

gauche (gōsh), *adj.* **1.** Clumsy; inexperienced. **2.** Showing little or no knowledge of proper social behavior.

gaunt (gônt), *adj.* **1.** Very thin. **2.** Grim; forbidding.

gen·ial (jēn′yəl, jē′nē·əl), *adj.* Friendly; warm; kindly.

ger·mane (jėr·mān′), *adj.* Closely related to a subject; pertinent; relevant.

ges·tic·u·la·tion (jes·tik′yü·lā′shən), *n.* **1.** A wild or excited gesture or movement. **2.** The act of making such gestures.

gird (gėrd), *v.* **1.** To encircle; surround. **2.** To put or fasten on with a belt. **3.** To prepare.

goad (gōd), *v.* **1.** To prod; urge. **2.** To spur on by use of a pointed stick.

gran·di·ose (gran′dē·ōs′), *adj.* **1.** Showy. **2.** Impressive.

gra·tis (gra′tis, grā′tis), *adv. & adj.* Free of charge.

grav·i·ty (grav′ə·tē), *n.* **1.** Seriousness. **2.** Weight. **3.** The pull exerted toward the center of the earth.

griev·ous (grēv′əs), *adj.* **1.** Causing grief; deeply distressing. **2.** Showing grief. **3.** Atrocious; horrible.

gross (grōs), *adj.* **1.** Very wrong; shameful. **2.** Fat; thick. **3.** Coarse; vulgar. **4.** Glaring; obvious.

grov·el (gruv′əl), *v.* **1.** To crawl wretchedly. **2.** To lie face down on the ground, in fear or in the desire to please. **3.** To behave humbly and without self-respect.

H

hag·gard (hag′ərd), *adj.* Worn and thin from hardship; gaunt.

hale (hāl), *adj.* Healthy; strong.

hap·less (hap′lis), *adj.* Unlucky.

har·bin·ger (här′bin·jər), *n.* A forerunner; messenger sent ahead to announce something.

har·row (har′ō), *v.* **1.** To break up or level plowed land. **2.** To harm; hurt. **3.** To worry; annoy.

hear·ken (här′kən), *v.* To listen carefully.

heath (hēth), *n.* **1.** An area of open, uncultivated land, overgrown with low shrubs. **2.** The low shrubs found on such land.

hew (hyü), *v.* **1.** To cut or chop down. **2.** To make or shape by cutting.

hei·nous (hā′nəs), *adj.* Hateful; evil; cruel; outrageous.

hos·tel (hos′təl), *n.* **1.** An inn. **2.** An overnight lodge, *esp.* used by students or young people.

hu·mane (hyü·mān′), *adj.* Kind; concerned for the welfare of others.

I

i·dyll (ī′dəl), *n.* **1.** A short poem or prose work describing a simple rural scene. **2.** An event or scene appropriate for such a writing.

ig·no·min·i·ous (ig′nə·min′ē·əs), *adj.* **1.** Shameful; disgraceful. **2.** Humiliating.

im·mi·nent (im′i·nənt), *adj.* Likely to happen right away; near at hand.

im·mo·bile (i·mō′bəl), *adj.* **1.** Motionless. **2.** Unable to move or be moved. — **im·mo·bil·i·ty,** *n.*

im·mu·ta·ble (i·myü′tə·bəl), *adj.* Unchangeable.

im·part (im·pärt′), *v.* **1.** To give. **2.** To reveal; tell.

im·pec·ca·ble (im·pek′ə·bəl), *adj.* Free from error; faultless.

im·ped·i·ment (im·ped′i·mənt), *n.* **1.** Anything that hinders, delays, or obstructs progress; obstacle. **2.** A speech defect.

im·per·cep·ti·ble (im′pėr·sep′tə·bəl), *adj.* **1.** Not easily served or noticed. **2.** Very slight; hardly noticeable.

im·per·turb·a·ble (im′pėr·tėr′bə·bəl), *adj.* Calm; unable to be alarmed or upset.

im·pet·u·ous (im·pech′ü·əs), *adj.* **1.** Hasty in action; acting suddenly and with little thought. **2.** Violent; forceful.

im·pi·ous (im′pē·əs), *adj.* Irreverent; disrespectful of God; profane.

im·pla·ca·ble (im·plā′kə·bəl, im·plak′ə·bel), *adj.* Relentless; unable to be pacified or quieted.

im·pli·cate (im′pli·kāt′), *v.* **1.** To involve. **2.** To imply; suggest.

im·por·tu·nate (im·pȯr′chə·nit), *adj.* Persistent; asking or demanding repeatedly.

im·po·tent (im′pə·tənt), *adj.* Weak; powerless; helpless. — **im·po·tence,** *n.*

im·pro·pri·e·ty (im′prə·prī′ə·tē), *n.* An unfit act; something improper.

im·pu·dence (im′pyü·dəns), *n.* Disrespect; bold behavior or speech; insolence.

in·cense (in′sens), *n.* **1.** Certain gums and spices burned to produce a pleasant odor. **2.** The smoke or pleasant odor thus produced. **3.** Any pleasant fragrance.

in·ces·sant (in·ses′ənt), *adj.* Without stopping; constant; going on without interruption.

in·ci·sive (in·sī′siv), *adj.* Sharp; piercing; cutting.

in·ci·vil·i·ty (in′sə·vil′ə·tē), *n.* **1.** Rudeness. **2.** A rude or impolite deed.

in·con·gru·ous (in·kon′grü·əs), *adj.* Out of place; inappropriate; not suitable.

in·con·ti·nent (in·kon′tə·nənt), *adj.* Lacking self-control, *esp.* in the satisfaction of sensuous desires. — **in·con·ti·nence,** *n.*

in·cred′u·lous (in·krej′yu̇·ləs), *adj.* Doubting; unwilling or unable to believe. — **in·cre·du·li·ty** (in′krə·dü′lə·tē), *n.*

in·del·i·ble (in·del′ə·bəl), *adj.* **1.** Unable to be erased or removed. **2.** Making a mark not able to be erased.

in·dis·posed (in′dis·pōzd′), *adj.* **1.** Ill; mildly ill. **2.** Unwilling.

in·do·lent (in′də·lənt), *adj.* Lazy; idle; avoiding work.

in·ef·fec·tu·al (in′i·fek′chü·əl), *adj.* Useless; producing no effect or results.

in·er·tia (in·ėr′shə), *n.* **1.** The tendency of matter to remain motionless or continue in a set direction until moved by another force. **2.** Inability to move; inactivity. **3.** Tendency to remain motionless; sluggishness.

in·ex·o·ra·ble (in·ek′sėr·a·bəl), *adj.* Unyielding; unrelenting.

in·ex·pli·ca·ble (in·eks′pli·kə·bəl, in′ik·splik′ə·bəl), *adj.* Unexplainable.

in·fal·li·ble (in·fal′ə·bəl), *adj.* **1.** Incapable of being wrong. **2.** Not liable to fail or disappoint. — **in·fal·li·bil·i·ty,** *n.*

in·fer (in·fėr′), *v.* To come to a certain conclusion or opinion after considering known or assumed facts.

in·gen·u·ous (in·jen′ü·əs), *adj.* **1.** Frank; open; straightforward. **2.** Simple; naive.

in·or·di·nate (in·ȯr′də·nit), *adj.* Excessive; not limited.

in·qui·si·tion (in′kwə·zish′ən), *n.* A judicial investigation or questioning; an inquiry.

in·sen·si·ble (in·sen′sə·bəl), *adj.* **1.** Not capable of feeling; unconscious. **2.** Unaware. **3.** Indifferent. **4.** So small or gradual as to be hardly discernible.

in·sup·port·a·ble (in′sə·pȯr′tə·bəl), *adj.* Unbearable; not supportable.

in·tel·li·gence (in·tel′ə·jəns), *n.* **1.** The ability to learn and understand. **2.** The ability to cope with new or difficult situations or problems. **3.** Information; news. **4.** Secret service; persons obtaining information.

in·tel·li·gi·ble (in·tel′i·jə·bəl), *adj.* Understandable; clear.

in·tem·per·ate (in·tem′pėr·it), *adj.* **1.** Excessive; immoderate; extreme. **2.** Lacking self-control. **3.** Excessively giving in to appetite or desire, *esp.* that for drinking.

in·ter·lude (in′tėr·lüd′), *n.* Something that occupies the time between major events.

in·ter·mi·na·ble (in·tėr′mi·nə·bəl), *adj.* Endless.

in·ter·vene (in′tėr·vēn′), *v.* **1.** To come between. **2.** To happen between events. **3.** To come in to settle or prevent something.

in·ti·mate (in′tə·māt′), *v.* To hint; imply; suggest.

in·tri·cate (in′tri·kət), *adj.* Complicated; difficult to follow or understand.

in·tu·i·tive (in·tü′ə·tiv), *adj.* **1.** Knowing immediately without conscious reasoning; having insight. **2.** Characterized by intuition. **3.** Known or understood by intuition. — **in·tu·i·tive·ness,** *n.*

in·ure (in·yu̇r′), *v.* To harden or accustom to trouble, pain, etc.

in·vet·er·ate (in·vet′er·ət), *adj.* Habitual; firmly established in a particular habit.

ir·res·o·lute (i·rez′ə·lüt), *adj.* Undecided; not determined; hesitating.

ir·rev·er·ent (i·rev′er·ənt), *adj.* Disrespectful; showing no reverence, awe.

ir·rev·o·ca·ble (i·rev′ə·kə·bəl), *adj.* Unchangeable; not capable of being canceled or undone; final.

J

joc·u·lar·i·ty (jok′yü·lar′ə·tē), *n.* Fun; joking.

ju·di·cious (jü·dish′əs), *adj.* Wise; showing good judgment.

junc·ture (junk′chər), *n.* **1.** A joint; connection. **2.** A point of time, *esp.* a critical one; crisis.

L

lair (lār), *n.* **1.** The den or bed of a wild beast. **2.** A resting place; refuge.

lam·en·ta·tion (lam′en·tā′shən), *n.* **1.** A mourning cry or wailing. **2.** The act of grieving.

lan·guid (lang′gwəd), *adj.* **1.** Weak; spiritless. **2.** Listless; slow.

lax·i·ty (lak′sə·tē), *n.* **1.** Looseness. **2.** Negligence.

leth·ar·gy (leth′ər·jē), *n.* **1.** An abnormal drowsiness; dullness. **2.** Total indifference.

lib·er·tine (lib′er·tēn′), *n.* An immoral man.

li·cense (li′səns), *v.* To give formal permission; allow; permit.

lin·e·age (lin′ē·ij), *n.* **1.** Direct descent from an ancestor. **2.** Family; ancestry.

loath or **loth** (lōth), *adj.* Unwilling; reluctant.

lu·cid·i·ty (lü·sid′ə·tē), *n.* Clearness; the quality of being easily understood.

lu·di·crous (lüd′ə·krəs), *adj.* Utterly ridiculous.

lu·rid (lu̇r′id), *adj.* **1.** Glowing, as fire seen through smoke. **2.** Vivid in a shocking way.

M

mag·nan·i·mous (mag·nan′ə·məs), *adj.* **1.** High-minded; noble. **2.** Generous.

---

add, māke, fäther; edge, bē, hėr; it, tīme; hot, gō, ȯ = aw in draw; cut, fu̇ll; rüle; boil; out; ə = the sound of the unaccented vowels in about, final, silent, pencil, contain, and circus; think, ŧћis; zh = s in pleasure; ⁿ = n in French *un*

ma·lev·o·lent (mə·lev′ə·lənt), *adj.* Spiteful; wishing harm to others; malicious. — **ma·lev·o·lence**, *n.*

ma·li·cious (mə·lish′əs), *adj.* **1.** Spiteful; mean. **2.** Wishing harm to others.

man·date (man′dāt), *n.* **1.** A command. **2.** The will of the people as expressed to their elected officials. **3.** Authority given by an organization of nations to one of those nations to govern a particular territory or region.

man·i·fest (man′ə·fest′), *adj.* Apparent; evident; obvious; clear.

mar·tial (mär′shəl), *adj.* **1.** Of war; warlike. **2.** Military.

maze (māz), *n.* **1.** A confusing, intricate arrangement of paths or passages. **2.** Bewilderment; state of confusion.

med·i·tate (med′ə·tāt′), *v.* **1.** To think over; ponder; consider carefully. **2.** To plan. — **med·i·ta·tive**, *adj.*

med·ley (med′lē), *n.* **1.** A mixture of unlike things. **2.** A group of songs arranged for playing as one continuous piece.

me·te·or·o·log·i·cal (mē′tē·ər·ə·lòj′i·kəl), *adj.* **1.** Relating to the scientific study of weather, climate, atmosphere, etc. **2.** Relating to the atmosphere, weather, and other such phenomena.

mien (mēn), *n.* One's conduct; bearing; manner; appearance.

mi·gra·tion (mī·grā′shən), *n.* **1.** A resettling or moving to another region or country. **2.** A group (of people, animals, etc.) that is resettling or migrating.

min·is·ter (min′is·tər), *v.* To give aid; serve as a nurse; serve.

mis·de·mean·or (mis′də·mēn′ėr), *n.* **1.** A minor crime. **2.** A misdeed.

mit·i·gate (mit′ə·gāt′), *v.* To make less severe or painful.

mold·er (mōl′dėr), *v.* To crumble to dust.

mo·lest (mə·lest′), *v.* To injure; harm; annoy.

mol·li·fy (mol′ə·fī′), *v.* **1.** To soothe; calm. **2.** To make less severe.

mote (mōt), *n.* A speck or small particle.

mot·ley (mot′lē), *adj.* **1.** Having several colors. **2.** Consisting of various or mixed parts.

myr·i·ad (mir′ē·əd), *adj.* Countless. — *n.* A very great number.

N

neb·u·lous (neb′yü·ləs), *adj.* **1.** Cloudy; hazy. **2.** Vague.

net·tle (net′əl), *v.* To annoy.

nov·ice (nov′is), *n.* **1.** A beginner. **2.** A person who has entered a religious order but has not as yet taken final vows.

O

o·bes·i·ty (ō·bēs′ə·tē), *n.* Extreme fatness.

ob·lique (ō·blēk′), *adj.* **1.** Slanting. **2.** Not frank or straightforward.

ob·lit·er·ate (ə·blit′ə·rāt′), *v.* To blot out; destroy; wipe out.

ob·liv·i·on (ə·bliv′ē·ən), *n.* **1.** Unawareness. **2.** The condition of being entirely forgotten.

ob·se·quy (ob′si·kwē), *n.*, *usually pl.* A funeral or burial ceremony.

ob·strep·er·ous (əb·strep′ər·əs), *adj.* Unruly; uncontrollable; noisy.

oc·cult (ə·kult′, ok′ult), *adj.* **1.** Hidden. **2.** Secret; mysterious. **3.** Beyond the understanding of human beings. **4.** Concerning mystical studies or the supernatural.

o·di·ous (ō′dē·əs), *adj.* Disgusting; hateful.

of·fal (òf′əl), *n.* **1.** The intestines of a slaughtered animal. **2.** Garbage; rubbish.

of·fi·cious (ə·fish′əs), *adj.* **1.** Giving unasked for and unwanted advice or service. **2.** Interfering; prying.

om·nip·o·tent (om·nip′ə·tənt), *adj.* All-powerful; having unlimited power or rule. — **om·nip·o·tence**, *n.*

o·pal·es·cent (ō′pəl·es′ənt), *adj.* Having colors like an opal; reflecting light in many colors, as an opal.

o·paque (ō·pāk′), *adj.* **1.** Not transparent; not letting light through. **2.** Dark; dull.

op·por·tune (op′ər·tün′, op′ər·tyün′), *adj.* **1.** Timely; well-timed. **2.** Suitable; appropriate.

orb (òrb), *n.* **1.** A circle; globe; ball. **2.** Any spherical heavenly body, as the sun, moon, etc.

o·ri·son (or′i·zən), *n.*, *usually pl.* A prayer.

os·ten·si·ble (os·ten′sə·bəl), *adj.* Seeming; apparent; stated.

P

pall (pòl), *v.* **1.** To become dull, uninteresting. **2.** To have too much of something.

pal·lid (pal′əd), *adj.* Pale.

pal·lor (pal′ər), *n.* Extreme paleness.

pal·try (pòl′trē), *adj.* **1.** Worthless; trifling. **2.** Petty.

pan·to·mime (pan′tə·mīm′), *n.* **1.** A play using actions without words. **2.** Actions or gestures used in place of words.

pa·thos (pā′thos), *n.* A quality arousing pity or sympathy.

pa·vil·ion (pə·vil′yən), *n.* **1.** A large tent. **2.** An open-air building, *esp.* one used for exhibits.

ped·ant (ped′ənt), *n.* **1.** One who gives unnecessary stress to trivial points of learning. **2.** A narrow-minded teacher. — **pe·dan·tic**, *adj.*

pee·vish (pēv′ish), *adj.* **1.** Irritable; cross. **2.** Stubborn; contrary.

pent (pent), *adj.* Held or kept in.

per·chance (pər·chans′, pər·chäns′), *adv.* Perhaps; maybe.

per·emp·to·ry (pər·emp′tər·ē), *adj.* **1.** Final; decisive. **2.** Domineering. **3.** Demanding; unable to be argued with; haughty.

per·me·ate (pėr′mē·āt′), *v.* **1.** To spread through or throughout. **2.** To seep through.

per·pe·trate (pėr′pə·trāt′), *v.* To commit, as an error; do something wrong or evil.

per·son·i·fi·ca·tion (pər·sòn′ə·fə·kā′shən), *n.* **1.** A perfect or exact example. **2.** The act of treating or thinking of something as a person. **3.** Something imaginary used to represent an idea or thing. **4.** A figure of speech in which lifelike qualities and characteristics are attributed to inanimate objects.

per·turb (pər·térb′), *v.* To upset; alarm; trouble; disturb.

pe·ruse (pə·rüz′), *v.* **1.** To study carefully. **2.** To read. — **pe·rus·al**, *n.*

pet·ty (pet′ē), *adj.* **1.** Small-minded. **2.** Unimportant; trifling. **3.** Low in rank.

phos·pho·res·cence (fos′fə·res′əns), *n.* **1.** The state or condition of giving off light without heat. **2.** The light itself. — **phos·pho·res·cent**, *adj.*

phys·ic (fiz′ik), *n.* **1.** The art of healing. **2.** A medicine.

pil·lage (pil′əj), *v.* To rob, using violence; loot; plunder, *esp.* during war.

pith (pith), *n.* **1.** The soft, spongy center of certain plant stems. **2.** The important or essential part. **3.** Strength; vigor.

plau·si·ble (plò′zə·bəl), *adj.* **1.** Trustworthy. **2.** Seeming to be true; believable.

pol·lute (pə·lüt′), *v.* To make unclean; contaminate; dirty; taint.

pon·der·ous (pon′də·rəs), *adj.* **1.** Extremely heavy. **2.** Clumsy and dull.

por·ten·tous (pòr·ten′təs), *adj.* **1.** Being an omen of evil; threatening. **2.** Amazing; monstrous. **3.** Very serious.

po·tent (pō′tənt), *adj.* **1.** Powerful; strong. **2.** Effective. **3.** Convincing. — **po·ten·cy**, *n.*

pre·cept (prē′sept), *n.* A guiding rule for behavior.

pre·con·cep·tion (prē′kən·sep′shən), *n.* An opinion formed without any knowledge of or experience with something.

pre·ma·ture (prē′mə·tyür′, prē′mə·chür′), *adj.* Occurring or being done before the proper time; too early.

pre·or·dain (prē′ôr·dān′), *v.* To establish, order, or decide in advance.

pre·ten·sion (pri·ten′shən), *n.* **1.** A claim or an attempt to establish a claim. **2.** False importance; showiness; lack of integrity. — **pre·ten·tious**, *adj.*

pre·text (prē′tekst), *n.* A false reason given to conceal the true purpose.

pre·var·i·ca·tion (pri·var′ə·kā′shən), *n.* A lie; made-up story; evasion.

pri·mal (prī′məl), *adj.* **1.** Original; first. **2.** Most important; chief.

pro·cliv·i·ty (prō·kliv′ə·tē), *n.* An inclination; natural tendency.

pro·cure (prō·kyür′), *v.* **1.** To obtain; get. **2.** To cause or bring about.

pro·di·gious (pro·dij′əs), *adj.* **1.** Enormous; huge. **2.** Causing amazement.

pro·fess (prə·fes′), *v.* **1.** To state openly. **2.** To lay claim to something (an ability, knowledge, etc.) without really having it.

pro·jec·tile (prə·jek′təl), *n.* **1.** An object designed to be shot forward. **2.** Anything thrown forward. **3.** A rocket; guided missile.

pro·le·tar·i·an (prō′lə·târ′ē·ən), *adj.* Of the poorest, lowest class in a state or society. — *n.* Day-laborer; member of working class.

pro·sa·ic (prō·zā′ik), *adj.* Commonplace; dull; unexciting. — **pro·sa·ism** (prō′zā·iz′əm), *n.*

pro·tract (prō·trakt′), *v.* To draw out; prolong or lengthen in time.

prow·ess (prou′is), *n.* **1.** Bravery. **2.** Skill; ability.

pru·dent (prü′dənt), *adj.* **1.** Showing good sense in practical matters; wise. **2.** Cautious; careful.

punc·til·i·ous (pungk·til′ē·əs), *adj.* **1.** Paying great attention to the fine points of behavior and manners. **2.** Precise; conscientious.

pu·ni·tive (pyü′nə·tive), *adj.* Having to do with punishment or inflicting punishment.

Q

quag·mire (kwag′mīr′, kwäg′mīr′), *n.* Wet, soft ground; a bog; marsh.

quin·tes·sence (kwin·tes′əns), *n.* **1.** The purest or most essential part of anything. **2.** The most typical example of something.

R

ran·cid (ran′sid), *adj.* Having a strong, unpleasant taste or smell from decay or rotting.

ran·cor (rang′kėr), *n.* Bitterness; hatred.

rank (rangk), *adj.* **1.** Growing thickly, coarsely, vigorously. **2.** Having an unpleasant odor or taste.

rau·cous (rò′kəs), *adj.* Harsh; hoarse; shrill.

re·coil (ri·koil′), *v.* **1.** To spring back. **2.** To shrink back from.

rec·om·pense (rek′əm·pens′), *n.* **1.** Payment or return for a loss. **2.** A reward.

re·course (rē′kòrs, ri·kòrs′), *n.* **1.** A turning to for help. **2.** That to which one turns for help.

re·dou·ble (rē·dub′əl), *v.* **1.** To double; to increase. **2.** To double back.

re·fute (ri·fyüt′), *v.* To prove wrong. — **ref·u·ta·tion** (ref′yü·tā′shən), *n.*

re·it·er·ate (rē·it′ə·rāt′), *v.* To repeat one's words or actions; say or do over and over again.

re·lin·quish (ri·ling′kwish), *v.* To give up; let go.

ren·dez·vous (rän′də·vü), *n.* **1.** A meeting place. **2.** The meeting itself. **3.** An agreement to meet.

---

add, māke, fäther; edge, bē, hėr; it, tīme; hot, gō, ȯ = aw in draw; cut, fúll, rüle; boil; out; ə = the sound of the unaccented vowels in about, final, silent, pencil, contain, and circus; think, this; zh = s in pleasure; ⁿ = n in French *un*

re·past (ri·past′), *n.* A meal.

rep·er·to·ry (rep′ėr·tôr′ē), *n.* The poems, songs, etc., that one knows and is prepared to perform.

rep·u·ta·ble (rep′yü·tə·bəl), *adj.* Respectable; having a good reputation.

req·ui·site (rek′wə·zit), *adj.* Necessary, required; needed.

re·quite (ri·kwīt′), *v.* 1. To repay for; reward. 2. To retaliate; get even for.

re·sound (rē·zound′), *v.* 1. To echo; make a loud echoing sound. 2. To be proclaimed.

res·tive (res′tiv), *adj.* 1. Nervous; restless; impatient. 2. Unruly; hard to control.

re·tort (ri·tôrt), *n.* A sarcastic, sharp, or angry answer.

ret·ro·spec·tion (ret′rə·spek′shən), *n.* 1. The act of remembering the past. 2. A recollection of the past. — **ret·ro·spec·tive,** *adj.*

rhet·or·ic (ret′ə·rik), *n.* The art of speaking or writing well. — **rhe·tor·i·cal** (ri·tôr′i·kəl), *adj.*

ru·di·men·ta·ry (rü′də·men′tə·rē), *adj.* Relating to a beginning or an undeveloped stage.

rue·ful (rü′fəl), *adj.* Sorrowful; regretful.

ru·mi·nate (rü′mi·nāt′), *v.* 1. To revolve; turn over in the mind. 2. To ponder; meditate.

rus·set (rus′it), *n.* 1. A yellowish- or reddish-brown color. 2. A winter apple of this color. 3. A rough cloth of this color.

rus·tic (rus′tik), *adj.* 1. Rural. 2. Rough; simple; lacking refinement.

S

saf·fron (saf′rən), *n.* 1. A plant whose orange centers are used for dye and for seasoning. 2. The dried centers or stigmas themselves. 3. Orange yellow.

sage (sāj), *n.* 1. A wise man. 2. A philosopher.

sa·gac·i·ty (sə·gas′ə·tē), *n.* Quickness to understand; shrewdness.

sa·ti·ate (sā′shi·āt′), *v.* To gratify to excess so as to tire or disgust.

sat·yr (sat′ėr, sā′tėr), *n.* 1. In Greek mythology, a woodland deity represented as a man whose lower body and ears were those of a goat and who was given to sensual pleasure. 2. Any lustful man, given to such over-indulgence.

sa·vor·y (sā′vor·ē), *adj.* 1. Pleasant tasting or smelling. 2. Pleasant.

scathe·less (skāth′ləs), *adj.* Unharmed.

scru·ple (skrü′pəl), *n.* A feeling of doubt or uneasiness arising from one's conscience.

scul·lion (skul′yən), *n.* 1. A kitchen-servant. 2. A wretched person.

se·nile (sē′nīl), *adj.* 1. Relating to old age. 2. Mentally or physically weak due to age.

sen·su·al (sen′shü·əl), *adj.* 1. Relating to the body and its senses. 2. Pleasant to the senses. 3. Tending to overindulge the appetites of the body. — **sen·su·al·i·ty,** *n.*

sen·ti·ment (sen′tə·ment), *n.* 1. Emotion; tender feeling. 2. An opinion, view, or thought, *esp.* one influenced by such feeling.

sep·ul·chre (sep′əl·kər), *n.* A burial vault; tomb; grave.

ser·vil·i·ty (sėr·vil′ə·tē), *n.* 1. The quality of being slavelike. 2. Humble obedience.

sev·er (sev′ər), *v.* To cut off; separate; divide.

shear (shēr), *v.* 1. To cut, as with scissors. 2. To remove hair, wool, etc., by cutting or clipping. 3. To strip from or deprive of.

shorn (shôrn), *a past participle of* **shear.**

si·dle (sī′dəl), *v.* 1. To move sideways. 2. To move to the side, trying not to be seen.

sin·gu·lar (sing′gyü·lėr), *adj.* 1. Exceptional; outstanding; remarkable. 2. Unique. 3. Strange; unusual.

slack (slak), *adj.* 1. Slow; not energetic. 2. Not busy; inactive. 3. Loose; not firm. 4. Careless.

slake (slāk), *v.* 1. To decrease; make less intense; to quench, as thirst. 2. To slow. 3. To loosen.

slan·der (slan′dėr), *v.* To spread harmful rumors in order to ruin someone's reputation. — *n.* 1. The spreading of harmful rumors. 2. The rumors themselves.

slat·tern (slat′ėrn), *n.* An untidy, sloppy woman. — **slat·tern·ly,** *adj. & adv.*

sleight (slīt), *n.* 1. A trick. 2. Skill.

smite (smīt), *v.* 1. To hit hard. 2. To affect strongly and suddenly.

smote (smōt), *Past tense of* **smite.**

sol·ace (sol′is), *n.* Comfort; easing of grief; something that relieves.

so·lic·it (sə·lis′it), *v.* 1. To beg; ask earnestly. 2. To lure; tempt.

so·no·rous (sə·nōr′əs, son′ə·rəs), *adj.* Deep and rich in sound.

sov·er·eign (sov′rin), *adj.* 1. Chief; above all others. 2. First in rank or power. 3. Independent, as a state. 4. Excellent; effective. — *n.* A monarch; king.

spas·mod·ic (spaz·mod′ik), *adj.* Characterized by sudden, violent, and temporary activity; fitful.

spec·u·late (spek′yü·lāt′), *v.* 1. To think deeply; ponder. 2. To take part in a risky business venture with the hope of making a large profit. 3. To guess.

spe·cious (spē′shəs), *adj.* Appearing to be good, correct, or fair without really being so.

stac·ca·to (stə·kä′tō), *adj.* Short and clear-cut; disconnected; abrupt.

stal·wart (stôl′wərt), *adj.* Strong; brave; sturdy.

sta·tion·ar·y (stā′shən·er′ē), *adj.* Not moving; fixed in one place.

stealth (stelth), *n.* Secret movement; underhanded, sly action. — **stealth·y,** *adj.*

sti·fle (stī′fəl), *v.* 1. To suffocate. 2. To suppress or hold back.

strait (strāt), *n., often in pl.* 1. A narrow passage of water that joins two large bodies of water. 2. Difficulty; trouble; suffering.

stri·dent (strī′dənt), *adj.* Harsh-sounding; rasping; shrill.

strip·ling (strip′ling), *n.* A young boy.

suave (swäv), *adj.* Polished, as in manner; pleasingly polite or persuasive.

sub·jec·tion (səb·jek'shən), *n.* **1.** The act of subduing or bringing under control. **2.** The state of being under control.

sub·or·di·nate (sə·bôr'də·nāt'), *v.* **1.** To put in a lower or secondary position. **2.** To place under the authority of another. — (sə·bôr'də·nit), *adj.* **1.** Of less importance; lower rank. **2.** Under another's authority.

suc·cor (suk'ėr), *v.* To help in time of need. — *n.* Help; relief; aid.

suc·cumb (sə·kum'), *v.* **1.** To give in; yield. **2.** To die.

sump·tu·ous (sump'chü·əs), *adj.* **1.** Costly; luxurious. **2.** Splendid; superb.

sun·dry (sun'drē), *adj.* Various.

su·per·flu·ous (sü·pėr'flü·əs), *adj.* More than necessary; excessive.

sup·pli·cant (sup'lə·kənt), *adj.* Urgently begging; humbly asking.

sup·pli·ca·tion (sup'lə·kā'shən), *n.* **1.** Urgent begging; humble request. **2.** A prayer.

sur·mise (sėr·mīz'), *v.* To guess, often with little or no evidence.

syc·o·phant (sik'ə·fənt), *n.* One who seeks favors by flattering wealthy or important people. — **syc·o·phan·tic** (sik'ə·fan'tik), *adj.*

syl·van (sil'vən), *adj.* **1.** Relating to or characteristic of the woods or forest. **2.** Wooded.

syn·op·sis (si·nop'sis), *n.* Summary; condensation.

T

tab·er·na·cle (tab'ėr·nak'əl), *n.* **1.** A Jewish temple. **2.** A large church; place of worship. **3.** A temporary shelter; tent.

tac·i·turn (tas'ə·tėrn'), *adj.* Silent; not talkative.

tan·gi·ble (tan'jə·bəl), *adj.* **1.** Able to be felt or touched; solid. **2.** Real; actual; definite; capable of being understood.

tar·ry (tar'ē), *v.* **1.** To delay; linger. **2.** To stay for a while. **3.** To wait.

tem·pest (tem'pəst), *n.* **1.** A strong wind, especially one accompanied by snow, rain, or hail; storm. **2.** A violent disturbance.

teth·er (teth'ėr), *n.* A rope, chain, or leash used to fasten an animal.

throe (thrō), *n.* **1.** A stab of pain. **2.** *pl.* Agony; desperate struggle.

tor·tu·ous (tôr'chü·əs), *adj.* **1.** Twisting; winding; crooked. **2.** Roundabout.

tra·duce (trə·düs', trə·dyüs'), *v.* **1.** To slander; ruin the reputation of. **2.** To betray.

trans·fig·ure (trans·fig'yur), *v.* **1.** To change the appearance of; transform. **2.** To change spiritually; glorify; exalt; make bright.

trans·gress (trans·gres'), *v.* **1.** To sin (against); break (a law). **2.** To go beyond the limits.

trans·lu·cent (trans·lü'sənt), *adj.* **1.** Letting light pass through, but not transparent. **2.** Shining or glowing through.

trav·erse (trə·vėrs', trav'ėrs), *v.* To cross; pass over or through.

trem·u·lous (trem'yü·ləs), *adj.* **1.** Trembling; quivering. **2.** Timid.

tri·bu·nal (tri·byü'nəl, trī·byü'nəl), *n.* **1.** A court of law. **2.** A judge's seat. **3.** Anything that decides or judges.

tur·bid (tėr'bid), *adj.* **1.** Muddy; having the sediment disturbed, as the bottom of a river. **2.** Thick; dark; cloudy. **3.** Confused; not clear.

U

unc·tu·ous (ungk'chü·əs), *adj.* **1.** Greasy; oily. **2.** Pretending to be earnest or spiritual. **3.** Insincerely smooth.

un·daunt·ed (un·dônt'əd), *adj.* **1.** Fearless. **2.** Not discouraged.

un·in·tel·li·gi·ble (un·in·tel'ə·jə·bəl), *adj.* Not understandable; unclear.

un·pre·pos·sess·ing (un·prē'pə·zes'ing), *adj.* Unimpressing; unattractive.

un·wont·ed (un·wun'tid, un·wōn'tid), *adj.* **1.** Not used to; unaccustomed. **2.** Rare.

up·braid (up·brād'), *v.* To scold; find fault with.

ur·bane (ėr·bān'), *adj.* Smooth and polished in manner; suave; courteous.

us·age (yüs'ij), *n.* **1.** A custom; habit. **2.** A way of using or the using itself. **3.** The way in which a word is used to express something.

u·surp (yü·zėrp', yü·sėrp'), *v.* To take over by force; seize.

V

vain·glo·ri·ous (vān'glôr'ē·əs), *adj.* Extremely conceited or proud; boastful.

va·grant (vā'grənt), *adj.* **1.** Wandering from place to place. **2.** Irregular; not following a fixed pattern or course.

ve·he·mence (vē'ə·məns), *n.* **1.** Force; strong feeling; intensity. **2.** Eagerness. **3.** Anger.

ven·er·a·ble (ven'er·ə·bəl), *adj.* Worthy of respect or honor because of great age, dignity, or historical importance.

ven·er·ate (ven'ə·rāt'), *v.* To honor or respect greatly.

vent (vent), *v.* To let out; release. — *n.* **1.** An outlet; means of escape. **2.** A release. **3.** A narrow opening. **4.** A slit.

---

add, māke, fäther; edge, bē, hėr; it, tīme; hot, gō, ȯ = aw in draw; cut, fùll, rüle; boil; out; ə = the sound of the unaccented vowels in about, final, silent, pencil, contain, and circus; think, this; zh = s in pleasure; ⁿ = n in French *un*

ve·ran·da (və·ran′də), *n.* A porch, *esp.* a long, roofed porch along the side of a building.

ver·dant (vėr′dənt), *adj.* **1.** Green; covered with green vegetation. **2.** Inexperienced; immature; innocent.

ves·ti·bule (ves′tə·byül′), *n.* **1.** An entrance hall. **2.** An enclosed passage between cars of a train.

ves·tige (ves′tij), *n.* A trace; mark; sign, *esp.* of something no longer present or existing. — **ves·tig·i·al,** *adj.*

vi·al (vī′əl), *n.* A small glass container for liquids, *esp.* medicines.

vig·i·lant (vij′ə·lənt), *adj.* Watchful; alert.

vin·di·cate (vin′də·kāt′), *v.* **1.** To clear from guilt or blame; free from suspicion. **2.** To defend. **3.** To justify. — **vin·di·ca·tion,** *n.*

vin·dic·tive (vin·dik′tiv), *adj.* **1.** Vengeful; seeking revenge. **2.** Done or said in revenge.

vir·u·lent (vir′yù·lənt, vir′ù·lənt), *adj.* **1.** Poisonous; deadly. **2.** Full of hatred. **3.** Very infectious, as a disease.

vis·age (viz′ij), *n.* **1.** The face. **2.** One's look.

vi·vac·i·ty (vi·vas′ə·tē, vī·vas′ə·tē), *n.* Animation; liveliness; sprightliness. — **vi·va·cious** (vi·vā′shəs, vī·vā′shəs), *adj.*

vo·lup·tu·ous (və·lup′chü·əs), *adj.* Enjoying sensual pleasures.

vo·ra·cious (vò·rā′shəs), *adj.* **1.** Greedily hungry. **2.** Very eager; insatiable. — **vo·rac·i·ty** (vò·ras′-ə·tē), *n.*

vouch·safe (vouch′sāf), *v.* To do one the favor of granting; condescend or lower oneself to grant.

vul·gar (vul′gėr), *adj.* **1.** Relating to the common people; ordinary. **2.** Crude; unpolished in manner.

W

wane (wān), *v.* **1.** To near the end. **2.** To grow less.

wan·ton (wòn′tən, wan′tən), *adj.* **1.** Reckless. **2.** Immoral. **3.** Playful. — **wan·ton·ness,** *n.*

war·y (wār′ē), *adj.* Watchful and cautious of danger.

weal (wēl), *n.* Well-being; welfare; prosperity.

weal (wēl), *n.* A mark raised on the skin by a blow.

whee·dle (hwē′dəl), *v.* To coax; get by begging or flattering.

wield (wēld), *v.* **1.** To handle effectively (a tool, etc.). **2.** To exercise (power, etc.).

wi·ly (wī′lē), *adj.* Sly; crafty; cunning.

wil·ly-nil·ly (wil′ē-nil′ē), *adv.* **1.** Whether one wants to or not; willingly or not. **2.** Indecisively.

win·now (win′ō), *v.* **1.** To blow the chaff from threshed grain. **2.** To sift, or sort. **3.** To scatter.

wrack (rak), *v.* To wreck; destroy; render useless.

wont (wunt, wōnt), *adj.* Accustomed; in the habit of.

Index: *Types of Literature*

LITERATURE FROM THE BIBLE

PHILOSOPHY

POETRY

Index: *Authors, Artists, and Titles*

Titles of selections and works of art are in italics. Figures in italics after an author's or an artist's name designate pages on which biographical information appears.

Index: *Literary Skills and Word Study Programs*

Page numbers in boldface type indicate basic teaching. Numbers in lighter type indicate informal teaching, exercises, or follow-up activities. Linguistic materials are listed under the separate appropriate entries.

Irony, **37**, 132, 154, 228, 317, 386, 473, 674, 676, **821**; Socratic, **264**; of situation, **822**; verbal, **827**

Literal meanings, 684, 724
Lyric, 411, **822**

Metaphor, **156**, 240, 317, 423, 599, 627, **822**; extended, 53
Metaphorical language, 456, 778
Meter, 174, 175, 187, **314**, 325, 603, 627, **822**
Monologue, **154**, **823**
Mood, 24, 744, 805
Motivation, 154, **823**

Names, symbolic meaning in, **266**, **289**, 315
Narration and narrative, **74**, 211, 603
Narrative poetry, **823**
Narrator, 331, 560, 615

Octave, **823**
Ode, **46**, 386, **823**
Onomatopoeia, **428**, **823**
Oxymoron, **412**, **823**

Parable, 49, **481**, **823**
Paradox, **236**, 263, 265, **823**
Paragraph development, 227
Parallelism, **659**, **823**
Paraphrase, **175**, 629
Pathetic fallacy, **497**
Pentameter, **603**, **824**
Personification, **455**, 482, **824**
Plot, **444**, **824**
Poetry, Hebrew, **188**, 503
Point of view, **288**, 445, 636, **824**; omniscient, **288**, 657, **823**; personal, **288**, 324, **824**

Quatrain, **824**

Refrain, 599
Resolution, as part of dramatic structure: **131**, 386, **824**
Rhyme, **18**, 24, 187, 325, 676, **824**
Rhyme scheme, **234**, **824**
Rhythm, **825**

Rising action, **825**

Satire, **225**, **825**
Scansion, **314**, **825**
Sestet, **825**
Setting, **165**, 637, **825**
Simile, **156**, 473, 526, **825**
Slang, **154**
Soliloquy, 745, 759, 777, 792, 807, **825**
Sonnet, 228, 825; Petrarchan, **629**, **824**; Shakespearean, **629**, **825**
Spondee, **826**
Stanza, **826**
Stereotypes, **225**, **826**
Structure, **826**; dramatic, **131**, 806; of poem, **156**, 236; of story, 312
Style, **240**, 312, 413, 423, 473, **826**
Subject, **15**, **826**
Symbol, 497, **561**, 637, 684, **826**
Synonym, **14**, 22, 144, 387, 561

Terza rima, **211**, **827**
Tetrameter, **603**, **827**
Theme, **15**, 16, 36, 235, 314, 481, 661, 806, **827**
Tone, **423**, 426, 428, 605, 636, 670, 792, **827**
Topic sentence, **324**
Tragedy, **388**, **389**
Transitional expressions, as used in coherent writing: **419**
Trochee, **827**
Type, **225**, **827**

Understatement, **827**
Unity, **312**, 410

Verisimilitude, **684**, **827**
Verse, **827**

Words: ameliorative and pejorative meanings of, **725**; in context, **131**, 324, 423, 445, 474, 637; derivation of, **445**, 501, 587, 615; foreign, **324**; generalization of meaning, **596**; linguistic borrowings, **332**, 410; linguistic changes, **188**, 658, 807; related meanings of, **193**; roots of, **14**, **53**; specialization of meaning of, **23?** 725

Acknowledgments

Illustrations for this book were obtained from the following sources:

P. iv: left, Collection Haags Gemeentemuseum, The Hague; right, Museum of Art, Carnegie Institute, Pittsburgh; p. v: Loan from S. B. Slijper, Collection Haags Gemeentemuseum, The Hague. P. 4: Collection of C. V. S. Roosevelt, Washington, D.C.; p. 8: Courtesy of *Américas,* monthly magazine published by the Pan American Union; p. 11: F. Earl Williams, Black Star; p. 13: Courtesy of the American Museum of Natural History; p. 20: Radio Times Hulton; p. 25: John T. Urban; p. 28: Essex Institute, Salem, Mass.; p. 33: National Portrait Gallery, London; p. 35: Trustees of the British Museum; p. 47: Courtesy, Museum of Fine Arts, Boston, H. L. Pierce Fund; p. 57: Trustees of the British Museum; p. 58: Radio Times Hulton; p. 70: Georges Bloch, Zurich; p. 72: Spanish National Tourist Office, 589 Fifth Avenue, N.Y.; p. 76: Ewing Galloway; p. 78: Royal Norwegian Embassy Information Service, N.Y.; p. 127: The Museum of Modern Art.

P. 134: Ampliaciones y Reproducciones Mas, Barcelona; p. 138: top, Harrison Forman; bottom, Staatsbibliothek Bildarchiv, Berlin; p. 147: The Art Institute of Chicago; p. 148: Brown Brothers; p. 158: Constantine Curran, National Library of Ireland; p. 161: Henri Cartier-Bresson, Magnum; p. 178: Biblioteca Medicea-Laurenziana; p. 184: Courtesy, Museum of Fine Arts, Boston, Russell Collection; p. 192: Brown Brothers; p. 196: Staatsbibliothek Bildarchiv, Berlin; p. 197: Biblioteca Communale Imola; p. 203: *from La Divina Commedia — Inferno,* G. Biagioli.

P. 216: Alison Frantz; p. 220: Brown Brothers; p. 222: The Brooklyn Museum, J. B. Woodward Memorial Fund; p. 230: top, Prado Museum; bottom, Radio Times Hulton; p. 235: Albright-Knox Art Gallery, Buffalo, N.Y.; p. 237: Staatsbibliothek Bildarchiv, Berlin; p. 238: Radio Times Hulton; p. 244: Ansel Adams; p. 251: Alison Frantz; p. 260: Art Reference Bureau; p. 265: Culver Pictures, Inc.; p. 267: Courtesy of the Fogg Art Museum, Harvard University; p. 268: Staatsbibliothek Bildarchiv, Berlin; p. 272: Ray Wilson, V.I.P. Agency; p. 279: Louvre, Clichés Musées Nationaux.

P. 300: The Bettmann Archive, Inc.; p. 304: Radio Times Hulton; p. 310: Historical Pictures Service, Chicago; p. 319: Grey Villet; p. 320: Constance Stuart, Black Star; p. 322: Grey Villet; p. 329: Philip D. Gendreau; p. 336: Culver Pictures, Inc.; p. 338: Sovfoto; p. 343: Historical Pictures Service, Chicago; p. 350: Staatsbibliothek Bild-

archiv, Berlin; p. 353: Vatican Museum; p. 361: Alison Frantz; p. 380: Spillane Studio, Stratford, Ontario.

P. 400: Eliot Elisofon; p. 404: Peter Lessing; p. 405: A. E. Woolley, New Paltz, N.Y.: p. 407: A. E. Woolley, New Paltz, N.Y.; p. 416: The Corcoran Gallery of Art; p. 421: Courtesy of the Harvard College Library; p. 422: Brown Brothers; p. 425: Collection of the Newark Museum; p. 428: Courtesy of the Pennsylvania Academy of the Fine Arts; p. 432: Covell; p. 434: G. Ronald Austing from the National Audubon Society; p. 439: Karl H. Maslowski from the National Audubon Society; p. 457: State Historical Society of Wisconsin; p. 458: Manuscript Division, Syracuse University Library; p. 469: Addison Gallery of American Art, Phillips Academy, Andover, Mass.

P. 476: Victoria and Albert Museum; p. 480: Courtesy, E. B. White; p. 484: Radio Times Hulton; p. 485: Louvre, Clichés Musées Nationaux; p. 494: Liveright Publishers; p. 496: Japan National Tourist Organization, New York; p. 500: Radio Times Hulton; p. 505: The Detroit Institute of Arts; p. 506: Radio Times Hulton; p. 511: Mr. George Heard Hamilton, Williamstown, Mass.; p. 523: Courtesy, Museum of Fine Arts, Boston, M. and M. Karolik Collection; p. 532: Staatsbibliothek Bildarchiv, Berlin; p. 547: from *George Grosz,* ed. Walter Mehring.

P. 572: from *The Diary and Letters of Kaethe Kollwitz,* ed. Hans Kollwitz; p. 576: Alfred A. Knopf, Inc.; p. 586: Radio Times Hulton; p. 590: Radio Times Hulton; p. 591: Göteborgs Konstmuseum, Sweden; p. 595: Göteborgs Konstmuseum, Sweden; p. 598: Beatrice Glass, New York; p. 601: Staatsbibliothek, Munich; p. 607: Harrison Forman; p. 612: Harrison Forman; p. 632: Magnum; p. 634: Mrs. John W. Griggs, New York.

P. 640: Courtesy, Museum of Fine Arts, Boston, Bequest of William P. Babcock; p. 644: Brown Brothers; p. 646: Carnegie Library of Pittsburgh; p. 649: Carnegie Library of Pittsburgh; p. 663: UPI; p. 664: UPI; p. 667: Cultural Exchange Center, from *Prints by American Negro Artists* by T. V. Roelof-Lanner, PhD; p. 678: Schocken Books Inc.; p. 687: Courtesy of Kennedy Galleries, Inc., from the private collection of Mr. and Mrs. John B. Bunker; p. 700: Radio Times Hulton; p. 708: The Toledo Museum of Art, Toledo, Ohio. Gift of Edward Drummond Libbey, 1930; p. 728: Mansell Collection; p. 739: British Broadcasting Corporation; p. 772: British Broadcasting Corporation; p. 791: Tate Gallery.

A Guide for Writing About Literature

Houghton Mifflin

To the Student

When you study literary selections, you are often asked to interpret what you have read. When you put your interpretation in writing, the result is a literary essay. A literary essay may also be called a critical essay, an interpretive essay, a literary analysis, or a literary paper.

In the following pages, you will learn how to write a literary essay, applying what you already know about literature and about the writing process. The phases of the writing process outlined here will help you plan and write your literary essay, and the Continuing Assignments throughout these pages will guide you through that process.

1990 Impression

ISBN 0-395-48992-X

DEFGHIJ-RM-954321

The Nature of the Literary Essay

You may have heard someone say, "What a story or a poem means is just a matter of opinion. There is no right or wrong interpretation." It is true that no two readers react in exactly the same way to a piece of literature. It does not follow, however, that literature means whatever you want it to mean. You should base your interpretation on the ideas, characters, and details presented by the author. In addition, your literary essay should be written with a definite purpose and audience in mind.

Purpose and Audience

PURPOSE. When you write a literary essay, your purposes are to analyze, to interpret, and, possibly, to evaluate the work. A literary essay is different from a report that recounts an author's life, summarizes a plot, or discusses a literary period. In a literary essay, you demonstrate that you have formed some ideas about what you have read. In writing a literary essay, your purpose will be one or more of the following:

1. To explore the theme, or central meaning, of the work.
2. To show insight into the techniques that the author uses to create and develop meaning.
3. To make some judgment about the quality and the impact of the work.

AUDIENCE. When you write a literary essay, address an audience that includes anyone who might be interested in your view of the work that you discuss. Assume that most of your readers have read the work, but provide enough information to refresh their memories.

Tone, Point of View, and Tense

The literary essay observes certain conventions, or customs. The appropriate tone, point of view, and tense are illustrated in the following passage.

MODEL

> On the surface, Ogden Nash and Michel de Montaigne seem to have distinctly opposite feelings about lying. In his essay "On Liars," Montaigne asserts that lying is an "accursed vice." Nash, in his poem "Golly, How Truth Will Out," calls lying "one of the greatest abilities a person can have." In reality, the difference between these two writers exists not in their feelings about lying but in the style of their writing. Montaigne is serious and formal. Nash is irreverent and ironic.

TONE. The tone of any writing is the attitude that a writer conveys about the topic and the audience. Audience, purpose, and tone must work together. The tone of your literary essay should be serious, in keeping with your approach to the work that you are discussing. The tone of the preceding excerpt is rather formal, appropriate for a literary essay.

POINT OF VIEW. Use the third-person point of view in a literary essay. It is not correct to write in the first person, as in "I believe . . ." or "It is my opinion. . . ." The excerpt illustrates how using the third person keeps the focus of the essay on the author and the work. It also avoids the repetitious use of the pronoun *I*.

TENSE. Use the present tense when you refer to the characters, the actions, or the author's techniques or subject matter. For example, "Montaigne *is* serious and formal."

Begin to read a literary work of your choice or one that is assigned by your teacher. You will use this work as the basis of a literary essay of three to five pages.

Preparing to Write a Literary Essay

Getting ready to write a literary essay requires almost as much time and attention as the writing itself. First, you have to read much more carefully than when you read solely for pleasure. Then, as you choose a topic, you have to form your interpretation of it. Finally, you need to find specific incidents or statements from the work that support your interpretation.

Reading the Work Carefully

If you know in advance that you will be writing an essay about a literary work, keep the essay in mind as you read. If you are writing about a work that you have already read, reread it thoughtfully. As you read, ask yourself the following questions. If you need to review any of the concepts in the questions, consult your glossary of literary terms or a literary handbook.

QUESTIONS TO ASK ABOUT A LITERARY WORK

What is the theme or main idea? Is it stated or implied?
What is the tone of the work? What point of view is used?
What is distinctive about the author's style?

IF THE WORK IS FICTION OR DRAMA:
What is the main plot and who are the central characters?
What is the setting? Is there a certain atmosphere or mood?
What is the central conflict and how is it resolved? What is the climax?
Is it a tragedy, a comedy, a farce, or some other type of drama?
If it is a tragedy, what is the nature of the tragedy?
If it is a comedy, a farce, or a satire, what is ridiculed?

IF THE WORK IS A POEM:
Is there a persona (speaker) in the poem? What do you learn about the persona? Does he or she react to the situation?
What images does the poem contain? Are any of them symbols—that is, do they stand for something larger than themselves?
Is the poem in a particular form, such as an ode or a sonnet?
What patterns of sound—such as rhyme, alliteration, assonance, rhythm, or meter—are used? Does the sound help convey meaning?
How does figurative language—such as metaphors, similes, and personification—help to convey meaning?
Does the poem suggest anything beyond the literal situation?

IF THE WORK IS NONFICTION:
What is the subject of the work?
What evidence does the writer give to support the main idea?
Is the author's purpose to inform, to entertain, to persuade, or some combination?
Does the author use figurative language or images to convey ideas?

Choosing a Topic and an Approach

If your teacher does not assign a topic, take the time to choose your topic carefully. It should develop logically and naturally from your reactions to the work. You may want to choose one of the following approaches to a literary work.

1. **Interpreting the meaning of the work.** By providing evidence from the work, you can explain how the theme is developed. For example, you can show how James Thurber uses humor in "The Greatest Man in the World" to develop the theme that great deeds are not always done by great people.

2. **Analyzing a character.** You can show how a character is changed by his or her experiences—that is, how the character matures or develops. For example, you can explain how the young boy in Doris Lessing's "A Sunrise on the Veld" matures as a result of his experience.

3. **Analyzing a technique.** You can also investigate an aspect of the writer's craft, such as symbolism, imagery, poetic sound, characterization, or creation of setting. For example, you can examine the imagery used by Karl Shapiro in his poem "Auto Wreck."

4. **Comparing an element in two works.** Another approach is to compare the same element in two works. For example, you can discuss how William Faulkner, in his story "A Rose for Emily," and Robert Browning, in his poem "My Last Duchess," explore the relationship between love and hate. You can compare two characters in a single work or in two works.

Writing a Preliminary Thesis Statement

Writing a preliminary thesis statement—the statement of what you intend to prove in your essay—will help you to focus your attention as you search for evidence to support it. If you can find evidence to support your interpretation, the statement will become the main idea, and the final thesis statement, of your literary essay. If you cannot find sufficient evidence, you must be willing to revise or abandon that thesis statement.

A thesis statement should be precise and clear. The following are examples of suitable topics and preliminary thesis statements for literary essays.

TOPIC
The theme of "Young Goodman Brown," by Nathaniel Hawthorne
PRELIMINARY THESIS STATEMENT
One of the themes explored by Nathaniel Hawthorne in "Young Goodman Brown" is that hypocrisy, or secret sin, was the most destructive evil in Puritan society.

TOPIC
The use of poetic sound in "Dover Beach," by Matthew Arnold
PRELIMINARY THESIS STATEMENT
In the first stanza of "Dover Beach," Matthew Arnold uses poetic sound to set up the contrast between appearance and reality that is developed in the rest of the poem.

TOPIC
Character development in *An Enemy of the People*, by Henrik Ibsen
PRELIMINARY THESIS STATEMENT
In *An Enemy of the People*, the character of Dr. Stockman grows in awareness while remaining constant in attitude and outlook.

If you have not already done so, finish reading the work that you started for Continuing Assignment 1 on page A-4. Select a topic for a literary essay of three to five pages. Then write a preliminary thesis statement and save it for later use.

Taking Notes

Once you have written a preliminary thesis statement, you can begin to test your interpretation. Reread the work for details that can be used to support your preliminary thesis statement. For example, if your topic is the poet's use of sound in "Dover Beach," look carefully at the rhythm and the letter sounds in the words of the poem.

Gathering Evidence from the Work

Take notes on the details that you find. Perhaps the simplest and most efficient way to take notes is to use three-by-five-inch or four-by-six-inch note cards. Write only one piece of evidence on each card so that you can easily rearrange them for outlining. Each note card should include a subject heading at the top and, at the bottom, the number of the page on which the evidence appears in the work. When you take notes, record only the essential details of a passage. You need not write in complete sentences or connect one point with another, as the following example shows.

PASSAGE FROM *"YOUNG GOODMAN BROWN"*

"Too far! too far!" exclaimed the goodman, unconsciously resuming his walk. "My father never went into the woods on such an errand, nor his father before him. We have been a race of honest men and good Christians since the days of the martyrs; and shall I be the first of the name of Brown that ever took this path and kept—"

"Such company, thou wouldst say," observed the elder person, interpreting his pause. "Well said, Goodman Brown! I have been as well acquainted with your family as with ever a one among the Puritans; and that's no trifle to say. I helped your grandfather, the constable, when he lashed the Quaker woman so smartly through the streets of Salem; and it was I that brought your father a pitch-pine knot, kindled at my own hearth, to set fire to an Indian village, in King Philip's war. They were my good friends, both; and many a pleasant walk have we had along this path, and returned merrily after midnight. I would fain be friends with you for their sake."

NOTES ON PASSAGE

Devil knew Goodman Brown's grandfather and father
    Brown claims he comes from a family of honest men.
    Devil well acquainted with family
    Helped grandfather lash a Quaker woman
    Brought father a pitch-pine knot to set fire to Indian village
    Had many pleasant walks with them along same path
    pp. 27-28

In your notes you may include three special types of material: direct quotation, paraphrase, and summary.

DIRECT QUOTATION. If you find a particularly memorable statement or description that you think you might want to use in your paper, copy it exactly as it appears in the work and enclose it in quotation marks. The following example is also from "Young Goodman Brown."

Description of devil
"As nearly as could be discerned, the second traveler was about fifty years old, apparently in the same rank of life as Goodman Brown, and bearing a considerable resemblance to him, though perhaps more in expression than features. Still they might have been taken for father and son."
(p. 27)

PARAPHRASE. A **paraphase** is the expression of an author's idea in your own words. A paraphrase may be almost as long as the original passage, but it allows you to write in your own words in order to avoid too long or too frequent direct quotations. A paraphrase must be written in complete sentences. The quotation in the preceding example is paraphrased here.

Description of devil
He was about fifty years old and appeared to have the same position in society as Goodman Brown. They resembled each other, but more in facial expression than in features. They might have been thought to be father and son.
(p. 27)

SUMMARY. A **summary,** like a paraphrase, is the expression of the author's ideas in your own words. It, too, is written in complete sentences. However, in a summary, the author's narration and dialogue are condensed to essential details. In the following example, the passage from "Young Goodman Brown" is summarized in fourteen words.

PASSAGE FROM *"YOUNG GOODMAN BROWN"*

Thither came also the slender form of a veiled female, led between Goody Cloyse, that pious teacher of the catechism, and Martha Carrier, who had received the devil's promise to be queen of hell. A rampant hag was she.

SUMMARY
Faith's arrival at the meeting
A veiled woman was led in by pious Goody Cloyse and evil Martha Carrier.
p. 34

Using Secondary Sources

Secondary sources are books or essays written by scholars who specialize in interpreting literature. They can be helpful in giving you other views of the work that you will discuss. A secondary source, however, should not be regarded as a replacement for your own reading and interpretation of the work. In fact, many teachers prefer an interpretation to be based solely on a student's own reactions to a work. If you do use secondary sources, you can treat an idea or a quotation from the work as additional evidence to support your thesis statement.

When reading secondary sources, take notes just as you would for the work itself. At the top right of each note card, place the author's last name, so that you will know the work from which the information came. For each source, be sure to fill out a separate source card (like the one that follows) that lists the author, title, publisher, and place and date of publication. You will need this information when you prepare the Works Cited list at the end of your essay.

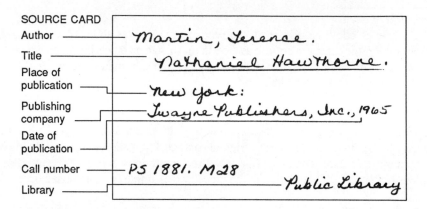

```
SOURCE CARD
Author  ──────┌─ Martin, Terence.
Title  ────────── Nathaniel Hawthorne.
Place of
publication ──┐
              └─ New York:
Publishing
company  ──────── Twayne Publishers, Inc., 1965
Date of      ──┘
publication
Call number ──── PS 1881. M28
Library ─────────────────────── Public Library
```

⬛▷ CONTINUING ASSIGNMENT 3 • *PREWRITING*

Reread the work that you will discuss in your essay. Take notes on evidence to support your preliminary thesis statement. Save them for later use.

Organizing Your Ideas

Revising the Preliminary Thesis Statement

After studying a literary work, you will often find that your first impression of it has changed to some degree. Before you begin to organize your notes, look critically at your preliminary thesis statement. Does your evidence support it? Is the statement clear and concise? Revise the preliminary thesis statement if necessary.

Outlining an Essay

The purpose of preparing an outline is to organize the ideas that you will present in your essay. The process of outlining and writing a literary essay will be illustrated later by a model essay that discusses one of the themes of Nathaniel Hawthorne's short story "Young Goodman Brown." This model is based largely on the original work, with minimal references to one secondary source. Literary essays often draw solely on the literary work under discussion and do not necessarily have to rely on any secondary sources. In the essay that begins on page A-12, the writer develops three main ideas that support a thesis statement about Hawthorne's concept of evil in Puritan society. The ideas are presented in the order of increasing importance, which is also the chronological order in which they appear in the story: (1) Hawthorne's description of the devil; (2) the devil's work; (3) the sins of the community.

These three points are the three main headings, indicated by Roman numerals, in a topic outline of the essay. In a topic outline, the points are not written as complete sentences. You may also use a sentence outline, in which each point is a complete sentence.

Supporting evidence for each main heading is listed under it as subheadings, indicated by capital letters. The introductory and concluding paragraphs are identified by Roman numerals.

Thesis Statement: One of the themes of Nathaniel Hawthorne's "Young Goodman Brown" is that hypocrisy was the real evil in Puritan society.

I. Introduction
II. Hawthorne's description of the devil
   A. Travels by supernatural means
   B. Wears "grave and decent attire"
   C. Resembles Goodman Brown
III. The devil's work
   A. Helped Brown's grandfather lash a Quaker woman
   B. Helped Brown's father set fire to an Indian village
IV. The sins of the community
   A. Spelled out in detail by the devil
   B. Language suggests secretiveness
   C. No distinction between churchgoers and professed sinners except hypocrisy of churchgoers
V. Conclusion

To prepare the outline of your essay, assemble your note cards and follow these steps.

STRATEGIES

1. Sort your note cards into several groups according to their subject headings. Each group will form one main heading of the outline.
2. Place the main-heading groups in a logical order. Use order of importance or chronological order (in this case, following the order of the work) or any other order that will enable you to present your evidence clearly.
3. Within the main-heading groups, choose the cards that will form the subheadings of the outline. Select only those cards that provide strong evidence for your points. Put the other cards aside.
4. Arrange the cards for the subheadings in a logical order. Your purpose is to make your discussion of each point easy to follow.
5. Write the main headings and subheadings in outline form. Place the thesis statement at the top of the outline. Add headings for the introduction and the conclusion.

▭▷ CONTINUING ASSIGNMENT 4 • *PREWRITING*

Look over your preliminary thesis statement and the notes that you took for Continuing Assignments 2 and 3 on pages A-6 and A-8. Revise your thesis statement if necessary. Then prepare an outline for your essay.

Writing the First Draft

Follow the outline as you write your first draft, making adjustments as you write. Your task is to work your evidence into the essay so that the sequence of ideas is logical and the writing is smooth. As you compose the essay, remember that your purpose is to interpret the literary work, not to explain your own philosophy to the reader. Therefore, make sure that all of your comments are directly related to the literary work and are supported by sufficient evidence.

The Parts of an Essay

THE TITLE.   Give your essay a specific title. The title should indicate the aspect of the work with which your essay deals: for example, "Symbols in Thomas Mann's 'Mario and the Magician'" or "The Theme of Ibsen's *An Enemy of the People*."

THE INTRODUCTORY PARAGRAPH.   Your introductory paragraph is an overview of the essay. You should include the author and the title of the work, any brief description of the work that will help the reader to understand your interpretation, and the thesis statement. At the same time, you should also attempt to interest the reader in what you have to say.

> **MODEL**
>
> Music is a universal language that can communicate emotions and ideas beyond the reach of words. In "Paul's Case," Willa Cather uses musical references to enrich her portrait of the central character. Paul hates the sordidness of his ordinary life and tries to escape from his ugly surroundings into the beautiful world of his fantasies. Through his work as an usher, he becomes familiar with several operas and classical compositions. Not only do the specific works that Cather mentions help the reader understand the character of Paul, but they also foreshadow his tragic end.

THE BODY PARAGRAPHS.   As you write the body paragraphs, consult your outline and incorporate the specific evidence from your note cards into the body of your essay. Be careful not to use too many quotations. Excessive use of quotations may suggest that you have not thought enough about ideas in the work to be able to put them into your own words. The body paragraphs should consist primarily of summarized and paraphrased evidence that is clearly related to your thesis statement.

THE CONCLUDING PARAGRAPH.   In the concluding paragraph, you close your essay by summarizing what you have shown. You also establish how and why the aspect of the work that you have discussed is important to the work as a whole. The following paragraph concludes an essay in which the writer examines Sophocles' portrayal of Oedipus in the light of Aristotle's definition of tragedy.

> **MODEL**
>
> True to Aristotle's definition of the tragic hero, Oedipus is neither completely virtuous nor entirely evil. He is a man whose pride and wrath do not serve him well but whose tragedy is ultimately not of his own making. It is this view of the flawed hero, who nonetheless does not deserve his tragic fate, that provides the cathartic experience for viewers of Oedipus the King.

Quotations

SHORT PROSE QUOTATIONS.   When you decide to quote a particularly significant passage from the work that you are interpreting, you should copy it in the essay exactly as it appears in the work. The correct way of incorporating the quotation in the essay depends on its length. Short quotations of no more than four lines are written or typed as part of the paragraph. They are enclosed by quotation marks and followed by the page reference, in parentheses, which identifies the location of the quoted passage in the original work. Notice that the final punctuation mark comes after the reference.

> The stranger that Goodman Brown meets is described by Hawthorne as wearing "grave and decent attire" (27).

In the preceding example, the author's name is used in the sentence and, therefore, only the page number is needed within the parentheses to identify the source of the quotation. Follow this method whenever possible. When it is not clear from the context of the sentence who is being quoted, however, you must include the author's last name within the parentheses: for example, (*Hawthorne 27*).

LONG PROSE QUOTATIONS.   Quotations of five or more lines are made easier to read by setting them off from the text: they are indented five spaces on both sides and single-spaced. For quotations that are set off in this manner, it is not necessary to use quotation marks. The following quotation from "Young Goodman Brown" is long enough to be set off from the text of an essay. In this kind of quotation, the page reference follows the final punctuation mark.

> The blue sky was still visible except directly overhead, where this black mass of cloud was sweeping swiftly northward. Aloft in the air, as if from the depths of the cloud, came a confused and doubtful sound of voices. Once [Goodman Brown] fancied that he could distinguish the accents of townspeople of his own, . . . many of whom he had met at the communion table, and had seen others rioting at the tavern. (31)

The preceding quotation illustrates the way in which a long quotation may be shortened by the use of ellipsis points (. . .) to indicate the omitted words. Use three points in the middle of a sentence, and use three points plus a period at the end of a sentence. When you shorten a quotation, you sometimes need to supply words that are not part of the original text but are needed for sense. As the preceding example shows, you enclose such words and phrases in brackets.

POETRY QUOTATIONS.   Quotations of up to three lines of poetry may be enclosed in quotation marks and run in with the text. The end of a line is indicated by a slash (/) with a space before and after it.

> "Let me not to the marriage of true minds / Admit impediments" is the beginning of Shakespeare's tribute to unconditional love.

When four or more lines of a poem are quoted, they are single-spaced and set off from the text just as a prose quotation is. No quotation marks are used.

Documentation

To **document** an essay is to supply information about the original works from which you copied the quotations in the essay. As you have seen, each quotation should be followed by a reference, in parentheses, to the page on which the quotation appears in that work. In an essay about a poem, use line numbers instead of page numbers; in an essay about a Shakespearean play, use the numbers of the act, scene, and line (such as III.i.56-65).

In addition to the references you include within your essay, you must provide complete information on the source quoted in the Works Cited section at the end of the essay. For a selection from an anthology, the following form is correct.

> Hawthorne, Nathaniel. "Young Goodman Brown." <u>Themes in World Literature</u>.
> Ed. George P. Elliott et al. Boston: Houghton Mifflin Company, 1989. 26-36.

The forms vary for other kinds of works, such as a collected edition of an author's works. For additional information about the Works Cited section, consult your composition textbook or a style manual. Your teacher may prefer that you use another way of citing the work from which your quotations come.

The preceding information applies to literary essays that are based entirely on the original work. If an essay also includes references to secondary sources (page A-7), you must give the same kind of information for each additional source you use. A complete entry for each secondary source should also be included in the Works Cited section. For additional information about documenting a paper that includes references to secondary sources, consult your composition textbook or a style manual. When you document any kind of literary essay, follow your teacher's instructions.

A Model Literary Essay

The literary essay about "Young Goodman Brown" is given on the following pages as a model for reference and study.

The Nature of Evil in Nathaniel Hawthorne's "Young Goodman Brown"

"Young Goodman Brown," by Nathaniel Hawthorne, is an examination of the nature of evil in Puritan society and of the effect of this evil on one human being. Nathaniel Hawthorne was not a Puritan, but his ancestors were, and he was fascinated by his heritage. As a result many of his greatest works, including "Young Goodman Brown," explore the Puritan preoccupation with and hypocrisy toward sin and guilt. Goodman Brown takes a mysterious journey into the forest with the devil and is never the same again. Whether his journey into the forest is interpreted as a dream of his or as an allegory, Hawthorne's message is clear: The real evil in Puritan society was hypocrisy, the secret sinning of the supposedly pious churchgoers. This theme is developed through Hawthorne's description of the devil, through the devil's own description of some of his deeds, and through the devil's enumeration of the secret sins of the community.

The devil in "Young Goodman Brown" resembles a very ordinary person. Hawthorne describes him as wearing "grave and decent attire" (27). In fact, in the following passage from the story, he is linked very closely with Goodman Brown:

(continued)

> As nearly as could be discerned, the second traveler was about fifty years old, apparently in the same rank of life as Goodman Brown, and bearing a considerable resemblance to him, though perhaps more in expression than features. Still they might have been taken for father and son. (27)

Since the devil represents evil, his outward appearance should give some indication of the nature of evil. Clearly, he has supernatural powers since he makes a fifteen-mile trip from Boston to Salem on foot in fifteen minutes. However, the devil's appearance gives no hint of his powers or his identity. In the description above, Hawthorne suggests that evil does not necessarily have a monstrous appearance but rather may appear in a very ordinary and innocent form. This is Hawthorne's first step in developing the theme that Puritan society, while outwardly pious, was in fact full of secret sinning.

A further development of this theme occurs when the devil reveals that he is well acquainted with many Puritan families, including Goodman Brown's own father and grandfather. In fact, he reveals that he helped Goodman Brown's grandfather whip a Quaker woman and that he provided Brown's father with a pitch-pine knot to set fire to an Indian village. The Puritans themselves would consider these activities part of their religious and moral obligation to punish the wicked. It is clear that to Hawthorne, however, acting violently against those who have done no harm is the devil's work. According to Hawthorne, for pious churchgoers to justify such violence in the name of religion is a false claim to virtue. In this way he again reinforces his theme that the great sin of the Puritans was hypocrisy.

Throughout his story, Hawthorne hints at the secret sins of Puritan society. In the climactic scene, he spells them out in the devil's own words:

> "This night it shall be granted you to know their secret deeds; how hoary-bearded elders of the church have whispered wanton words to the young maids of their household; how many a woman, eager for widows' weeds, has given her husband a drink at bedtime and let him sleep his last in her bosom; how beardless youths have made haste to inherit their fathers' wealth; and how fair damsels . . . have dug little graves in the garden, and bidden me, the sole guest, to an infant's funeral." (34)

This catalog of sins is full of examples of secretiveness. The elders "whispered" wanton words; the poisoners go to sleep with their victims as if all is normal; the devil is the only guest at the funerals of murdered infants. These secret sins are the result of a hypocritical society that talks openly and endlessly of religion and piety but acts in secret to fulfill base desires.

Hawthorne goes on to describe the scene in the forest where the pious churchgoers, who sin in secret, and the less respectable community members, who sin openly, are gathered together. In this scene Hawthorne provides further evidence that there is no difference between the two groups: "It was strange to see that the good shrank not from the wicked, nor were the sinners abashed by the saints" (32). In fact, they are so in harmony that the hymn they sing is a combination of solemn music and profane words. The pious

(continued)

churchgoers approve of the music and the sinners understand the profane words. Furthermore, when Faith is brought forward to be initiated into the group, she is led between the pious Goody Cloyse and the evil Martha Carrier. Thus, Hawthorne makes his point that there is no difference between the churchgoers and the sinners except the hypocrisy of the former. This revelation has an overpowering effect on Goodman Brown. As one critic says, "[Goodman Brown] has journeyed into the dreamworld of the forest, . . . and confronted a world steeped in guilt . . . that makes his return to the village a pilgrimage into hypocrisy" (Martin 84).

Many questions are left unanswered for the reader of "Young Goodman Brown." Is the journey into the forest merely a dream? Did Faith look up and resist the devil when her husband called to her? What exactly was the cause of Goodman Brown's final despair? These questions are open to each reader's interpretation. Hawthorne, however, makes his attitude toward Puritan society very clear. In his view it was characterized by hypocrisy and secret sinning, and anyone who confronted this fact, as Goodman Brown did, was doomed to live in despair.

Works Cited

Hawthorne, Nathaniel. "Young Goodman Brown." Themes in World Literature. Ed. George P. Elliott et al. Boston: Houghton Mifflin Company, 1989. 26-36.

Martin, Terence. Nathaniel Hawthorne. Boston: Twayne Publishers, 1983.

〖▯▷〗 CONTINUING ASSIGNMENT 5 • *WRITING*

Using the note cards and the outline that you prepared for Continuing Assignments 3 and 4 on pages A-8 and A-9, write the first draft of your literary essay.

Revising, Proofreading, and Publishing Your Essay

If possible, begin your revision a day or so after you have finished writing your first draft to be more objective. Revision is far more than proofreading. It is the reworking and polishing of the entire essay, both content and style. You may need to rewrite some passages and attach them to the appropriate portion of the first draft. For a thorough revision, use these guidelines.

STRATEGIES
1. Check the draft against the outline. Be sure that you covered all of the points in the right order. Add any sentences that seem needed.
2. Make sure that each piece of evidence supports your thesis statement. Eliminate any sentences that give unnecessary information.
3. Make sure ideas flow coherently. Rearrange them or use transitional words as needed.
4. Change wording where necessary to make your choice of words more precise or to make the sentence structure smoother.
5. Make sure that the tone of your essay is consistent. It should be serious and formal.
6. Make sure that you have used the third-person point of view consistently.
7. Make sure that you have used the present tense when you refer to the characters, the action, and the author's techniques or subject matter.

8. Proofread the essay. Correct errors in grammar, usage, spelling, and punctuation after you have revised your essay for content and style. Make sure that you copied quotations and page references accurately.

When you are satisfied that your essay is as good as you can make it, you have a final draft. Make a final copy of your essay, using the manuscript guidelines that follow here or any other guidelines that your teacher suggests. Proofread the finished paper carefully.

Manuscript Form

HANDWRITTEN MANUSCRIPTS. Use standard-size paper (8 1/2 x 10 inches or 8 1/2 by 11 inches) and write on one side only, using black or blue ink. Leave margins of 1 1/2 inches at the left side and 1 inch at the right side. You must make the left margin even. Write the title of your composition, centered, on the top line of your first page and then skip at least one line before beginning the first paragraph. Do not put quotation marks around the title. Indent the first line of every paragraph 1 inch.

TYPEWRITTEN MANUSCRIPTS. Use standard-size white typing paper (8 1/2 by 11 inches). Double-space, use only one side of the paper, and use a black typewriter ribbon. Leave margins of 1 1/2 inches at the left side and 1 inch at the right side. As in a handwritten manuscript, the left margin must be even. On all pages but the first, place the first line at least 1 inch below the top of the page and leave a margin of 1 inch at the bottom of all pages. Center the title about 2 inches below the top of the first page and do not put quotation marks around it. Begin the first paragraph four lines below the title and indent the first line of every paragraph five spaces.

LABELING AND NUMBERING PAGES. Write your name, the subject, and the date (in that order) in the upper-right corner of the first page. On every page except the first page, put the page number in the upper-right corner unless your teacher gives you other instructions. Use Arabic numerals. Attach the pages at the upper-left corner with a staple or a paper clip.

Publishing Your Literary Essay

When you have completed your literary essay, you may want to find some way of sharing your writing with others besides your teacher. Here are some possibilities:

1. Submit your essay to your school's literary magazine.
2. Talk with your teacher about posting essays on the class bulletin board.
3. Form a committee with others in your class to assemble an anthology of literary essays to be reproduced and distributed to the class.
4. Get together with a group of classmates who have written about the same work that you wrote about and take turns reading your essays aloud.

CONTINUING ASSIGNMENT 6 • *REVISING*

Revise the first draft that you prepared for Continuing Assignment 5 on page A-14. Then copy or type the finished paper and proofread it carefully. Submit your outline with the paper.

Checklist for Literary Essays

☑ 1. Did you limit your topic to an interpretation of one element of the work?

☑ 2. Did you write a "working" thesis statement to focus your attention as you searched for evidence to support your interpretation?

☑ 3. Did you take notes carefully as you read and gathered evidence from the work?

☑ 4. Did you revise your preliminary thesis statement, if necessary?

☑ 5. Did you prepare a logically organized outline that includes all the important points?

☑ 6. Did you write a title for your essay that indicates the aspect of the work that you are analyzing?

☑ 7. Did you include the author and title of the work and a clear thesis statement in your introductory paragraph?

☑ 8. Did you present your evidence clearly in the body of the essay?

☑ 9. Did you use the correct form for quotations and document them correctly?

☑ 10. Did you write a concluding paragraph that summarizes what you have shown in your essay?

☑ 11. Did you revise your essay to make it consistent, concise, coherent, and clear?

☑ 12. If you wrote an explication of a poem, did you explain the situation described; examine the poem's imagery, figurative language, and use of sound; and explain the total meaning of the poem?

☑ 13. Did you use correct grammar, usage, spelling, punctuation, and capitalization?

☑ 14. Did you prepare your finished copy according to your teacher's guidelines?

☑ 15. Did you carefully proofread your finished copy?

 Houghton Mifflin

2-26496